Marketing

Principles & Perspectives
Fourth Edition

Marketing

Principles & Perspectives
Fourth Edition

William O. Bearden
University of South Carolina

Thomas N. Ingram
Colorado State University

Raymond W. LaForge
University of Louisville

Boston   Burr Ridge, IL   Dubuque, IA   Madison, WI   New York
San Francisco   St. Louis   Bangkok   Bogotá   Caracas   Kuala Lumpur
Lisbon   London   Madrid   Mexico City   Milan   Montreal   New Delhi
Santiago   Seoul   Singapore   Sydney   Taipei   Toronto

The **McGraw·Hill** Companies

 Irwin

MARKETING: PRINCIPLES AND PERSPECTIVES
Published by McGraw-Hill/Irwin, a business unit of The McGraw-Hill Companies, Inc.,
1221 Avenue of the Americas, New York, NY, 10020. Copyright © 2004, 2001, 1998, 1995 by
The McGraw-Hill Companies, Inc. All rights reserved. No part of this publication may be
reproduced or distributed in any form or by any means, or stored in a database or retrieval
system, without the prior written consent of The McGraw-Hill Companies, Inc., including, but
not limited to, in any network or other electronic storage or transmission, or broadcast for
distance learning.
Some ancillaries, including electronic and print components, may not be
available to customers outside the United States.

This book is printed on acid-free paper.

domestic   1 2 3 4 5 6 7 8 9 0 DOW/DOW 0 9 8 7 6 5 4 3
international 1 2 3 4 5 6 7 8 9 0 DOW/DOW 0 9 8 7 6 5 4 3

ISBN 0-07-253909-7

Publisher: *John E. Biernat*
Associate sponsoring editor: *Barrett Koger*
Developmental editor: *Anna M. Chan*
Marketing manager: *Kim Kanakes*
Producer, media technology: *Todd Labak*
Project manager: *Catherine R. Schultz*
Senior production supervisor: *Michael R. McCormick*
Designer: *Matthew Baldwin*
Photo research coordinator: *Jeremy Cheshareck*
Photo researcher: *Mike Hruby*
Supplement producer: *Betty Hadala*
Senior digital content specialist: *Brian Nacik*
Cover design: *Jenny El-Shamy*
Typeface: *10.5/12 Sabon*
Compositor: *Carlisle Communications, Ltd.*
Printer: *R. R. Donnelley*

Library of Congress Cataloging-in-Publication Data

Bearden, William O., 1945-
    Marketing, principles & perspectives / William O. Bearden, Thomas N. Ingram,
Raymond W. LaForge.—4th ed.
      p. cm.—(McGraw-Hill/Irwin series in marketing)
    includes index.
    ISBN 0-07-253909-7
    1. Marketing—United States. I. Title: Marketing, principles and perspectives. II.
Ingram, Thomas N. III. LaForge, Raymond W. IV. Title. V. Series.
HF5415.1.B4155 2004
658.8—dc21   2002035590

INTERNATIONAL EDITION ISBN 0-07-121430-5
Copyright © 2004. Exclusive rights by The McGraw-Hill Companies, Inc. for manufacture and export.
This book cannot be re-exported from the country to which it is sold by McGraw-Hill.
The International Edition is not available in North America.

www.mhhe.com

To Patti, Anna, Wallace, and their families, and in honor of my parents.

Bill Bearden

To Jacque and Rocky.

Tom Ingram

To Susan, Alexandra, Kelly, and in memory of my mom and dad.

Buddy LaForge

Meet the Authors

William O. Bearden

(Ph.D., University of South Carolina) University of South Carolina

Bill Bearden is the Bank of America Professor of Business Administration at the University of South Carolina. He has focused his teaching and research interests in consumer behavior and marketing research. In addition, Bill teaches principles of marketing and marketing management. His teaching awards include Outstanding MBA Teacher, the College of Business Administration Alfred G. Smith Excellence in Teaching Award, and the University of South Carolina AMOCO Award for Excellence in Undergraduate Teaching.

He is currently a member of the Editorial Review Boards for the *Journal of Consumer Research,* the *Journal of Consumer Psychology,* the *Journal of Marketing,* the *Journal of Retailing,* the *Journal of Business Research,* and *Marketing Education Review.* His professional experience includes past president of the Southern Marketing Association and the Education Division of the American Marketing Association, and member of the American Marketing Association Board of Directors. Previously, he served as Co-Director of the USC Lilly Endowment Teaching Fellows Program, as an Associate Editor for the *Journal of Consumer Research* and currently coordinates the Ph.D. Program in Marketing at USC.

Bill lives in Columbia, South Carolina, with his wife Patti, while his two daughters, Anna and Wallace, live in Washington, D.C. and Columbia, S. Car., respectively. Bill and Patti are delighted to have a new granddaughter, Maggie.

Thomas N. Ingram

(Ph.D., Georgia State) Colorado State University

Tom Ingram is Professor of Marketing at Colorado State University, where he teaches principles of marketing, marketing management, and sales management courses. Before commencing his academic career, Tom worked in sales, product management, and sales management with Exxon and Mobil.

Tom has received numerous teaching and research awards, including being named the Marketing Educator of the Year by Sales and Marketing Executives International (SMEI). He is a recipient of the Mu Kappa Tau National Marketing Honor Society Recognition Award for Outstanding Scholarly Contributions to the Sales Discipline. Tom has served as the Editor of *Journal of Personal Selling and Sales Management,* Chairman of the SMEI Accreditation Institute, a member of the SMEI Board of Directors, and as Editor of the *Journal of Marketing Theory and Practice.*

Tom has published extensively in professional journals, including the *Journal of Marketing,* the *Journal of Marketing Research,* the *Journal of the Academy of Marketing Science,* and the *Journal of Personal Selling and Sales Management.* He is coauthor of *Sales Management: Analysis and Decision Making,* 4th ed. and *Professional Selling: A Trust-Based Approach.* He and his wife Jacque enjoy skiing, golf, and exploring the mountains of Colorado.

Raymond W. (Buddy) LaForge

(DBA, University of Tennessee) University of Louisville

Raymond W. (Buddy) LaForge is the Brown-Forman Professor of Marketing at the University of Louisville (*http://cbpa.louisville.edu/buddy/*). He founded the *Marketing Education Review* (*http://cbpa.louisville.edu/mer*), served as Editor for 8 years, and is currently Executive Editor. Buddy has coauthored *Marketing: Principles & Perspectives, Sales Management: Analysis and Decision Making, Professional Selling: A Trust-Based Approach, The Professional Selling Skills Workbook,* and co-edited *Emerging Trends in Sales Thought and Practice.* His research is published in many journals including the *Journal of Marketing,* the *Journal of Marketing Research,* the *Journal of the Academy of Marketing Science,* and the *Journal of Personal Selling and Sales Management.* Buddy has served on the Direct Selling Education Foundation Board of Directors and Executive Committee, Du Pont Corporate Marketing Faculty Advisory Team for the Sales Enhancement Process, Family Business Center Advisory Board

(*http://cbpa.louisville.edu/fbc*), as Vice President of Conferences and Research for the American Marketing Association Academic Council, and as Vice President/Marketing for the Academy of Business Education. He is developing The Sales Program at the University of Louisville and establishing The Sales Education Network (*http://cbpa.louisville.edu/salesnetwork*) linking sales faculty, students, and executives to improve sales education and practice. Buddy and his wife, Susan, and daughters, Alexandra and Kelly, enjoy golf and thoroughbred racing in Louisville, Kentucky.

Preface

The marketing world is changing rapidly. Global economic conditions, political situations, and competitive landscapes are in constant flux. Marketing approaches that worked yesterday may not work tomorrow. Increasingly, marketing success requires doing things differently. Students will face a marketing environment different from the one discussed in our classes today. Learning what was done in the past will not prepare them entirely for what they need to do tomorrow. Consequently, in the fourth edition of *Marketing: Principles & Perspectives,* we have presented the topics that remain relevant and important, while simultaneously emphasizing new thinking and approaches to marketing practice. Because students need to be prepared to operate in the complex and dynamic marketing world of the future, they need to develop the capacity to think and act like marketers in a difficult and uncertain environment. This requires the ability to assess complex and changing marketing situations, to determine the best marketing strategies for these situations, and to execute the strategies effectively.

Every idea presented in the text and expanded upon in the accompanying teaching resources is intended to help students develop the understanding and skills to become successful marketers. The text is designed to facilitate student learning from individual reading and study. The teaching resources provide useful tools for instructors to go beyond what is covered in the text. Together, the text and teaching resources represent an integrated package for preparing students for marketing in the future.

This package differs from currently available products in many important ways. The critical advantages include the integration of key marketing perspectives, the presentation of comments from practicing marketers, the implementation of an integrated marketing communications (IMC) approach, and an emphasis on decision making.

Key Features and Changes

In this version of our text, we have made a number of substantial changes, while at the same time revising some of the features from the third edition of *Marketing: Principles and Perspectives*. Each chapter has been revised to include the most current marketing thought and practice. New and updated examples, cases, and chapter openings have been incorporated into what we believe is a very up-to-date presentation.

The major features and changes include the following.

Prologue

The text begins with an exciting prologue that tells the marketing story of Yum! Brands, one of the most innovative marketers heading into the twenty-first century. The brief introduction provides a description of marketing practice at a well-known company of interest to students, which will get them enthused about the study of marketing. Two new Yum! Brands video segments, created specifically for this text, accompany the Prologue and Chapter 1; taken together, this in-depth examination of a leading-edge company creates an exciting introduction to the principles of marketing course.

Marketing Perspectives

In this edition, we continue to integrate seven perspectives that are critical to effective marketing practice; these are discussed within the text where appropriate. These key perspectives are as follows: global, relationship, ethics, customer value, productivity, technology, and entrepreneurship. They are integrated throughout the text by direct discussion, examples, photos, and ads. Student exercises, boxed inserts, and cases address these timely themes as well. Briefly, the perspectives can be summarized as follows:

Global—A global perspective includes searching for marketing opportunities around the world, competing effectively against international competitors, and working with multicultural suppliers, employees, channel partners, and customers.

Relationship—A relationship perspective consists of building partnerships with firms outside the organization, encouraging teamwork among different functions within the organization, and developing long-term customer relationships.

Ethics—The ethics perspective stresses the importance of incorporating moral and social responsibility issues, including ecological concerns, within marketing decision making.

Customer Value—A customer value perspective means constantly looking for ways to give customers "more for less," often by continually striving to improve product and service quality.

Productivity—The productivity perspective focuses attention on improving the management of marketing resources for optimum results.

Technology—The technology perspective encourages marketers to incorporate the latest technological advances to improve both marketing practice and the development of new products.

Entrepreneurship—The entrepreneurship perspective encourages marketers to emphasize creativity, innovation, and risk taking in their marketing efforts.

An Emphasis on Student Learning

We see important trends emerging in marketing education. For one thing, teaching is receiving more emphasis at most colleges and universities—but not teaching as traditionally viewed and practiced. It really does not matter what we teach, if students do not learn. And student learning is viewed differently, too. Learning is not just the recall of facts by passive students, but the understanding of concepts and the ability to apply them appropriately. Such learning requires the active participation of students.

The complete package for *Marketing: Principles & Perspectives, fourth edition*, is oriented toward student learning, and the text and the teaching resource materials are designed to complement each other toward that end. In keeping with our philosophy that students should be able to understand the text largely from their own reading and study, we write in a lively, interesting, informal manner to capture their attention and interest. Major concepts are presented clearly and simply in a way that students can understand. Encouraged by our reviewing panels, we did not include everything we know about every topic, but only what we believe students at this level need to know. We streamlined the discussion of concepts and then reinforced them with interesting examples and exciting visuals, and incorporated a number of learning tools to facilitate the learning process. The pedagogical features emphasize our student-focused learning approach:

HOME-PAGE CHAPTER OPENERS   Every chapter opens with an actual home page and discussion of how that site is being used to market the company or organization that created it. Companies represented include eBay, Pfizer, Disney, British Airways, and Dell Computer Corporation to name a few. The book's home page will include a hot link to all of the Web sites mentioned in the text, including these chapter openers.

THINKING CRITICALLY   Two critical thinking questions are included within each chapter to help emphasize the importance of effective decision making. Each question relates to one of the concepts within the chapter and is constructed to encourage the student to think critically about a complex issue. The decision-making scenarios presented here are drawn from both real and theoretical companies.

SPEAKING FROM EXPERIENCE   This edition also includes comments about marketing from business professionals. We highlight one such person in each chapter and include three of his or her comments on key issues discussed in that chapter. By inclusion of these "Speaking from Experience" remarks, practitioners help bring to life the text material and add additional depth of explanation. The marketers included represent a range of large and small companies from a variety of industries. Example companies include Bank of America, Consumer Metrics, The Pampered Chef, Brown-Forman, Doe-Anderson, Inc., Microsoft, and Du Pont. Interestingly, the positions represented by these marketers include both senior individuals and young professionals in the early years of their careers. Consequently, students should be better able to identify and understand the varied opportunities available in marketing and how important marketing can be to professionals in other functional areas of business.

USING THE WWW IN MARKETING   Internet exercises are found at the end of each chapter. These questions require the student to consider how the Internet can be used to address marketing concepts or decisions. In addition, you can visit our home page where additional marketing examples and up-to-the-minute information will be posted.

Other Student Features   All chapters in the fourth edition have been formatted so that each pedagogical feature contributes to student learning by supporting the text material, including the principles and concepts covered in the chapter.

STUDENT LEARNING OBJECTIVES   Every chapter begins with several learning guides to help students focus attention on major concepts in reading and studying the chapter. At the end of each chapter, the summary is organized around these introductory learning objectives.

BOXED INSERTS   Each chapter contains two boxed inserts designed to provide current examples of three important topics: **Building Customer Equity, Being Entrepreneurial,** and **Using Technology.**

EXHIBITS AND PHOTOS   The visual aspects of each chapter were designed to increase student learning. The exhibits, photos, and ads visually enhance and expand upon the chapter discussion.

UNDERSTANDING MARKETING TERMS AND CONCEPTS   The most important terms and concepts are in boldface and defined when first introduced. Each boldface term is listed at the end of each chapter with the page number where it is defined. A glossary of terms and definitions is also included at the back of the text.

THINKING ABOUT MARKETING   Ten review and discussion questions also are included at the end of each chapter. These questions reinforce the decision-making aspects of the text by including both critical thinking questions and recall of the most important material covered in the chapter.

APPLYING MARKETING SKILLS   Every chapter includes three application exercises. These exercises can be used as either homework assignments or as in-class discussion topics. The exercises provide varied and interesting ways for students to apply what they have read or are covering in class.

MAKING MARKETING DECISIONS   All chapters conclude with two cases representing well-known companies and current situations. At least one of each pair is global in orientation. Questions are included to encourage students to make decisions regarding the current activities of each company. A mix of both consumer and business-to-business cases, cases involving both multinational firms and small businesses, and cases reflecting both service and retail situations reflects the current diversity of the business world.

Organization

Marketing Principles and Perspectives, 4th Edition, is divided into eight parts. *Part One, Marketing in a Dynamic Environment,* defines and examines the scope of marketing. The first chapter, *An Overview of Contemporary Marketing,* presents an overview of marketing and the different philosophies that have guided marketing. An explanation of the marketing concept and the importance of satisfying customer needs, developing long-term profitable relationships with customers, and building customer equity are also discussed. Chapter 1 also describes the seven key marketing perspectives—global, relationship, ethics, productivity, customer value, technology, and entrepreneurship—that are integrated within the text and the many reasons why their consideration is needed for effective marketing practice. *Chapter 2, The Global Marketing Environment,* emphasizes the global marketplace and the external environments (e.g., social, economic, political, and competitive) that influence marketer decision making. *Chapter 3, Marketing's Strategic Role in the Organization,* describes the role of marketing at different levels within the organization and the importance of effective marketing strategy.

Part Two, Buying Behavior, contains two chapters that describe, first, the concepts and influences on consumer buying behavior and decision making, and second, business-to-business markets and organizational buying behavior. *Part Three, Marketing Research and Market Segmentation,* contains two chapters as well. In *Chapter 6, Marketing Research and Decision Support Systems,* an overview of the marketing research *process* and information systems is presented. *Chapter 7, Market Segmentation and Targeting,* includes the concepts of segmentation, targeting, positioning, and product differentiation.

The remaining four parts cover the marketing mix elements—product, price, distribution, and promotion or integrated marketing communications. In *Part Four, Product and Service Concepts and Strategies,* three chapters present basic product and service concepts (Chapter 8), new-product development (Chapter 9), and product and service strategies (Chapter 10). Marketing services are emphasized throughout this section of the book.

The next part of the text, *Part Five, Pricing Concepts and Strategies,* covers fundamental pricing concepts and customer evaluations of prices (Chapter 11) and price determination and the managerial strategies used to guide pricing decisions (Chapter 12).

The distribution aspects of the marketing mix are covered in *Part Six, Marketing Channels and Logistics.* In *Chapter 13, Marketing Channels,* the different types of direct and indirect channels are discussed. Retailing is covered in a separate chapter (Chapter 14), which includes the many new advances in retailing technology and methods. The place or distribution component of the text concludes with a chapter on wholesaling and logistics management (Chapter 15).

Part Seven, Integrated Marketing Communications, contains six chapters. First, an overview of promotion and integrated communications is presented in Chapter 16. This chapter describes the communications process and marketing communications planning. The major components of the promotions *mix* are then discussed in the remaining four chapters. First, up-to-date coverage of advertising and public relations is offered in Chapter 17. The objectives and methods of both consumer and trade sales promotions are described in Chapter 18. Personal selling and sales management, with particular emphasis given to relationship selling, are the focus of Chapter 19. A separate chapter on direct marketing is included in Part Seven; specifically, the newest direct marketing techniques are covered in Chapter 20, as well as the interactive aspects of marketing communications.

Appendix A presents an expanded marketing plan and a discussion of how to develop one. *Appendix B* describes many of the frequently used mathematical and financial tools used to make marketing decisions. A detailed glossary of terms and three indexes conclude the text. These indexes enumerate authors cited, companies and brands used as examples, and the subjects covered within the text.

Teaching Resources

INSTRUCTOR'S MANUAL   The instructor's manual comprises chapter outlines, lecture notes with supplemental lecture materials, answers to end-of-chapter questions, and ideas for individual and group student learning activities.

TEST BANK AND COMPUTEST   The test bank comprises more than 3,000 questions, including multiple choice, short answer, fill-in-the-blank, and critical-thinking essay questions.

VIDEO LIBRARY   This current, dynamic video library includes video segments, one for each chapter plus the prologue. The video segments, which run between 6 and 15 minutes, demonstrate the marketing concepts from the text and are tied to specific chapter concepts. Some of the companies featured include BMW, Lands' End, Southwest Airlines, and Specialized Bike to name just a few.

INSTRUCTOR CD-ROM   This exciting presentation CD-ROM allows the professor to customize a multimedia lecture with original material and material from our supplements package. It includes video clips, all of the electronic slides, art from the text, the computerized test bank, and the print supplements.

ELECTRONIC SLIDES   PowerPoint slides are rapidly becoming a staple in the presentation tools that instructors use. Three hundred slides, approximately 15 per chapter, are available to adopters of the text.

MEDIA RESOURCE GUIDE   This manual includes a summary of every segment within the video library, along with specific student learning objectives. Creative and thought-provoking application exercises are also included to further enhance the video experience.

HOME PAGE   The book's home page can be found at www.mhhe.com/bearden04. It contains Web Exploration Links (hotlinks to other Web sites) and Keeping Current (abstracts of issues in the news, referenced to a chapter in the book and accompanied by a list of discussion questions). For instructors, it will also offer updates of the examples and cases in the text, additional sources of marketing information, and downloads of key supplements.

Student Resources   The book's home page can be found at www.mhhe.com/bearden04. It contains Think Links, provocative Web links with accompanying questions, and StudentSpeak, a forum designed to encourage students to interact with one another.

Acknowledgments   Writing a text requires a team effort, and we have enjoyed a collaboration with the best teammates imaginable. Cooperative, knowledgeable, creative, candid, and always encouraging—these are but a few of the positive things we found in our teammates. We are especially appreciative of the countless number of people involved in this project who time after time put forth the extra effort necessary to accomplish our mutual goals.

- The professionals at McGraw-Hill/Irwin led the way on what we feel is a terrific revision. Thanks to many, many people at McGraw-Hill/Irwin, including Barrett Koger (sponsoring editor), Kimberly Kanakes (marketing), Catherine Schultz (production), Matt Baldwin (design), Jeremy Cheshareck and Mike Hruby (photo research), Melanie Becker (permissions), and Anna Chan (development editor).

- We would also like to thank several people who have been with us since the early days of this project. Eleanore Snow was our developmental editor on the first edition, and her early direction still serves as an inspiration to us. Rob Zwettler signed us to our first book contract years ago, and we truly appreciate his continuing support. Nina McGuffin and Lynn Mooney worked with us on previous editions—and sweated the deadlines as much as we did. Steve Patterson and Greg Patterson were instrumental in our decision to work with McGraw-Hill/Irwin on this book.

- We would also like to thank several individuals who have contributed significantly to the supplementary materials accompanying the text. Craig Hollinghead and Barbara R. Oates, both of Texas A&M, Kingsville, put together the comprehensive *Instructor's Manual*. An extensive set of objective test questions was developed by Ronald L. Weir of East Tennessee State University. The PowerPoint slides were developed by G. Bernard Levin of Virginia Intermont College.

- Our book has been improved by a long list of reviewers—both national and international—of three drafts of the manuscript. We were stimulated and encouraged by their comments and suggestions, and we incorporated many of their ideas into the text. Our thanks to our marketing colleagues listed below and to additional reviewers who prefer to remain anonymous. Because of length considerations we were not able to incorporate every good suggestion, but we considered all of them carefully and appreciate the reasoning behind them. We believe *Marketing: Principles & Perspectives* comes much closer to meeting your teaching needs and the learning needs of your students because of your efforts.

First, we would like to thank the following focus group participants and reviewers of the fourth edition:

Myra Jo Bates
Fort Hays State University

Stephen Batory
Bloomsburg University

James L. Brock
Susquehanna University

Joseph D. Brown
Ball State University

Mary Conway Dato-on
Northern Kentucky University

James T. Dixon, Sr.
Bowie State University

David J. Faulds
University of Louisville

Randy Frye
Saint Francis University

Dorothy Harpool
Wichita State University

Areti Jordan
University of Central Florida

Kathleen R. Krentler
San Diego State University

Marilyn Liebrenz-Himes
George Washington University

Ann Little
High Point University

Donna T. Mayo
Middle Tennessee State University

Chris Mbah
Cornerstone University

Terry Paul
Ohio State University

Dan Rajaratnam
Baylor University

Mohammed Rawwas
University of Northern Iowa

George A. Redmond
Agnes Scott College

Vicki D. Rostedt
University of Akron

William J. Sauer
Susquehanna University

Donald R. Schreiber
Baylor University

Richard L. Sharman
Montgomery College

Tom Smith
Texas Wesleyan University

John A. Sondey
South Dakota State University

Harlan E. Spotts
Western New England College

Scott J. Vittel
University of Mississippi

Irvin A. Zaenglein
Northern Michigan University

We would also like to thank the many survey respondents who helped to shape this new edition and thank again the reviewers of our previous editions:

Ronald J. Adams
University of North Florida

Nancy J. G. Adelson
North Seattle Community College

Arni Arnthorsson
College of St. Francis

Ramon Avila
Ball State University

Joe Ballenger
Stephen F. Austin University

Terri Feldman Barr
Thomas Moore College

Kenneth Bartkus
Utah State University

Stephanie Bibb
Chicago State University

Connie T. Boyd
University of Tennessee–Martin

John R. (Rusty) Brooks
Houston Baptist University

Phyllis Campbell
Bethel College

Paul Chao
University of Northern Iowa

Robert Collins
*University of Nevada at
Las Vegas*

Kent Cox
University of Houston-Central

Lyndon Dawson
Louisiana Tech University

Oscar DeShields
*California State
University–Northridge*

Ann M. Devine
Alverno College

Kathryn Dobie
*University of Wisconsin at
Eau Claire*

John Doering
Minot State University

Casey Donoho
Northern Arizona University

Michael Dore
University of Oregon

Robert Doukas
Westchester Community College

Michael Drafke
College of DuPage

Cemel Ekin
Providence College

Steven Engel
University of Colorado

Leisa Reinecke Flynn
Florida State University

Bob Franz
*Southwestern Louisiana State
University*

Barry Freeman
Bergen Community College

Ralph Gallay
Rider College

William G. Glynn
*University College Dublin,
Ireland*

Ronald E. Goldsmith
Florida State University

Pradeep Golpalakrishna
Pace University

Sandra K. Smith Gooding
Loyola College in Maryland

Bill Green
Sul Ross State University

Steve Grove
Clemson University

Robert F. Gwinner
Arizona State University

Fleming Hansen
*Copenhagen Business School,
Denmark*

James B. Hunt
*University of North Carolina at
Wilmington*

Eva M. Hyatt
Appalachian State University

David B. Jones
LaSalle University

David C. Jones
Otterbein College

Robert Key
University of Phoenix

Robert King
University of Hawaii at Hilo

Fredric Kropp
University of Oregon

Priscilla A. La Barbera
New York University

Irene Lange
*California State
University–Fullerton*

J. Ford Laumer, Jr.
Auburn University

Paul Londrigan
Mott Community College

Mike Luckett
University of Central Florida

Dale Lunsford
University of Tulsa

Mary Ann Machanic
University of Massachusetts

Ed McQuarrie
Santa Clara University

H. Lee Meadow
Northern Illinois University

Carla Meeske
University of Oregon

Carla Millar
*City University Business School,
London*

Michael S. Minor
*University of Texas–
Pan American*

Robert Morgan
University of Alabama

Linda Morris
University of Idaho

William F. Motz Jr.
Lansing Community College

Erik B. Ness
*Norwegian School of
Management, Oslo, Norway*

William Perttula
San Francisco State University

Linda Pettijohn
Southwest Missouri State

Marie A. Pietak
*Bucks County Community
College*

David Prensky
College of New Jersey

Milt Pressley
University of New Orleans

Andrea Prothero
*Cardiff Business School,
University of Wales*

Daniel Rajaratnam
Baylor University

Glen Reiken
East Tennessee State University

Rich Rexeisen
St. Thomas University

Glen Riecken
East Tennessee State University

Bob Robicheaux
University of Alabama

Carlos M. Rodriguez
Governors State University

Joel Saegert
*University of Texas at
San Antonio*

Nick Sarantakes
Austin Community College

Charlie Schwepker
Central Missouri State University

Don Self
*Auburn University at
Montgomery*

C. David Shepherd
*University of
Tennessee–Chattanooga*

Richard Sjolander
University of West Florida

Lois Smith
*University of Wisconsin–
Whitewater*

Jane Sojka
Ohio University

Carol Soroos
North Carolina State University

Michael J. Swenson
Brigham Young University

David Szymanski
Texas A&M University

Janice Taylor
Miami University

Ronald D. Taylor
Mississippi State University

Lou Turley
Western Kentucky University

Michael Tuttle
Northwood University

Sushila Umashanker
University of Arizona

David J. Urban
*Virginia Commonwealth
University*

Rockney G. Walters
Indiana University

Michael Welker
Franciscan University

Jim Wilkins
*Southwestern Louisiana
University*

Susan D. Williams
Jersey City State College

Ken Williamson
James Madison University

Kenneth Willig
LaSalle University

Robert Winsor
Loyola Marymount University

Terrence H. Witkowski
*California State University–Long
Beach*

Helen R. Woodruffe
University of Salford, England

Alyce Zahorsky
Golden Gate University

Sherilyn Zeigler
University of Hawaii–Manoa

**Bill Bearden
Tom Ingram
Buddy LaForge**

Guided Tour

The Cutting Edge of Marketing Education

The Fourth Edition of **Marketing: Principles and Perspectives** is your introduction to cutting edge coverage of marketing. Among other advantages, the new edition gives students a penetrating look at key issues and decisions facing marketers in a dynamic business environment. Featured topics include integrated marketing communications, sales promotion, direct marketing, customer relationship management, and supply chain management.

Marketing introduces basic topics such as marketing strategy, segmentation, and consumer behavior in such a way that you will not only learn about the important perspectives needed for effective marketing, but you will also benefit from this edition's interactive exercises and supplements. The remainder of material provides thorough and updated coverage of the firm's marketing mix—products, distribution, price, and marketing communications.

New Prologue

You will utilize information from a company simply named, YUM! This restaurant company features five brands and over 32,000 restaurants in over 100 countries. In the text's Prologue, you will be introduced to YUM!, and learn how that company utilizes all seven perspectives of marketing in order to initiate successful marketing in the U.S. and abroad.

Prologue: Yum! Brands

How many times in the last month have you eaten:

- Chicken at Kentucky Fried Chicken (KFC)?
- Mexican food at Taco Bell?
- Pizza at Pizza Hut?
- Seafood at Long John Silver's?
- Hamburgers, hotdogs, or root beer floats at A&W All-American Food?

Yum! Brands hopes you eat at these restaurants often, because it owns all of them! KFC, Taco Bell, and Pizza Hut were part of PepsiCo., Inc. In 1997, PepsiCo, Inc. decided to spin off its restaurants so it could focus more attention to its core beverage business. The new restaurant company was named Tricon Global Restaurants, Inc. to reflect the three restaurant icons or brands. Then, in May 2002 Tricon purchased Long John Silver's and A&W All-American Food from Yorkshire Global Restaurants. Since the company now consisted of five brands, its name was changed to Yum! Brands (www.yum.com).

According to Chairman and Chief Executive David Novak, the passion and mission of Yum! Brands "is to put a yum on our customers' faces all around the world." Many things are done to reinforce the "yum" focus. For example, company meetings often start with a YUM cheer, such as "Give me a Y, Give me a U, Give me an M." Stock options are called YUM-BUCKS, and the company newsletter is the Yum! Buzz.[1] Yum! Brands is the world's largest restaurant

xxxiii

Home Page Chapter Openers

Each chapter opens with a vignette highlighting how an exciting company applies marketing. That chapter opener includes the company's Web page to reinforce how the Internet is part of a successful marketing strategy.

www.3m.com

3M is a $15 billion company with more than 70,000 employees who create, manufacture, and sell 50,000 products in 200 countries around the world. The company has operations in more than 60 countries. Some of 3M's products, such as Scotch Magic Tape, are well-known brands purchased by individual consumers and organizations. Other products are components for automobiles, computers, and other products purchased only by business customers.

The real distinguishing characteristic of 3M is its continuous emphasis on innovation. One of the company's major objectives is to generate 30 percent of each year's sales from products that are less than four years old. This means that 3M must continually develop and introduce successful new products. Thus, one of the driving principles at 3M is "the promotion of entrepreneurship and insistence upon freedom in the workplace to pursue innovative ideas." Efforts are directed toward listening to commercial partners and consumers to identify problems to be solved and needs to be satisfied. Then, products are developed to solve these problems and satisfy these needs. The objective is to make people's lives better by providing new products with superior features, advantages, and

[...] 0th birthday in April 2002 [...] tury of Innovation." Despite

its success in new-product development, the company is involved in several changes. Jim McNerney was hired from General Electric as the first outsider to become chairman and CEO at 3M. He arrived during the tough economic times of 2001. Although 3M's performance held up better than that of many other manufacturers, the new CEO has targeted sales and profit growth of over 10 percent annually. Achieving these objectives will require some different approaches at 3M.

One is to make some large acquisitions. 3M has traditionally developed new products internally with only a few, small acquisitions. Another is to move into the services area and provide customers with services in addition to products. For example, 3M would not only sell fiber-optic components to phone companies but would also provide maintenance services. A final approach is to target areas for new-product development more specifically and to focus on launching new products more efficiently. This is a big change for 3M, as it has typically given business units and employees much freedom in creating ideas for new products. CEO McNerney realizes the challenge of bringing more financial discipline to the new-product development process but not stifling creativity at 3M: "If I end up killing that entrepreneurial spirit, I will have failed."

Speaking from Experience

"In recent years, the college market, especially in Principles of Marketing courses, has become very price sensitive. Professors and students are looking to get more for their money, in the form of student CDs, videos and DVDs, instructor resources, subscriptions, simulations, and Web content. While several books in the Principles market are hardcore, we offer this text in paperback and loose-leaf, with all the student and professor supplements a hardcover text package offers. The lower text price coupled with student and instructor resources offers a better value and increases demand for this text."

Kimberly Kanakes
Marketing Manager
McGraw-Hill/Irwin Higher
Education Group

Kimberly Kanakes earned a bachelor's degree in organizational communication with a minor in marketing. Her job consists of creating marketing plans and coordinating all internal and external communications for the promotion of marketing titles to two-year and four-year higher education institutions. She works closely with the editorial and production staff on book content, schedule, and production and partners with professors and the company's sales representatives analyzing text and supplement needs, territory sales, and trends in the marketing discipline.

Exhibit 12–3

Elastic and inelastic demand

A. Elastic demand

B. Inelastic demand

when buyers do not readily notice the higher price and are slow to change their buying habits or to search for lower prices, or when they think higher prices are justified by product improvements or inflation; and when the product or service represents a small portion of their household income.[6]

Where demand is price-elastic, marketers must carefully evaluate any proposed increases in price. Price changes may cause significant change in quantity demanded. Long-term elasticities may differ from short-term ones as customers become aware of changing prices and have time to search for alternative products or services.

Cross elasticity of demand relates the percentage change in quantity demanded for one product to percentage price changes for other products. For example, products are often part of a line of similar products; and changes in the price of one brand may affect the demand for other items in the product line. When products are close *substitutes*, such as cola beverages, a rise in the price of one will increase the demand for the other. For businesses, a sharp increase in prices of steel fasteners used in the construction of trucks would cause increased demand for less-expensive plastic or aluminum fasteners.

Alternatively, when products are *complements*, a price increase of one may decrease the demand for the other. For example, large price increases for personal computers would cause a decrease in the demand for printers. And price reductions of taco shells may increase sales of taco sauce.[7]

Some marketers believe that a primary objective is to create inelasticity for their products. This requires a thorough understanding

Being Entrepreneurial

Net serves up quotes

As the insurance industry moves to react to the Internet, Net upstarts, such as Quotesmith.com, are making online sales much easier than dealing with local insurance agents. The database for Quotesmith.com provides instant price quotes on auto, life, medical, and other forms of insurance from over 300 insurers. The site provides ready access to useful reference tools and comparative price information. Moreover, Quotesmith.com allows consumers to purchase from the company of their choice without having to deal with commissioned salespersons. The Internet company also offers two unique guarantees: (1) view the lowest rates on term life insurance or receive $500; and, (2) the quote will be accurate or receive $500. The company electronically collects consumer demand for coverages and can rapidly communicate such demand directly to insurance companies.

Speaking from Experience Boxes

Speaking from Experience boxes highlight the experiences of real business professional people talking about real marketing experiences, marketing in everyday life, and how marketing affects business functions within a company.

Thematic Boxes

Boxed inserts throughout the chapters present current examples of three necessary topics for successful marketing: *Building Customer Equity, Being Entrepreneurial,* and *Using Technology.*

Building Customer Equity

Subway's lean focus

Subway is now the largest chain in terms of number of stores and has a growth rate of roughly seven times the average of other restaurant chains. This growth helps build market share in that many consumers will not travel long distances if alternatives are available. More importantly, Subway has succeeded by pursuing a sound strategy to lure customers to their stores. Specifically, Subway's core concept and compelling value proposition have resonated with a large market: low-fat and full-taste menu items under various umbrella messages, such as "Eat fresh." This approach has focused the franchise system on low fat and improved quality. As such, Subway has substantially enhanced its position in the minds of consumers.

Being Entrepreneurial

Marketing opportunities to provide security

Douglas Electronics looks like a television repair shop in its redbrick building. In fact, the company started by repairing TVs. However, the company has continually changed to capitalize on marketing opportunities created by changes in customer needs and new technologies. It move from repairing TVs to VCRs, then began renting TVs to hospitals. It got into the security business because hospitals needed such security systems as infant protection systems. Two years ago, new technology led it into airport security systems. It installs systems that control access to an airport's jetways. Workers gain access using readable ID cards. If a door is violated, a camera snaps a picture that is given to airport security personnel. The company was growing the airport security business slowly until September 11. Now, business is booming and Douglas Electronics is looking for more ways to use the latest technology to meet the security needs of its airport customers.

Using Technology

Turning data into valuable marketing information

Business intelligence software (BI) is being used by many companies to increase marketing effectiveness and efficiency. The software analyzes price, sales, cost, and other data to produce reports that help companies make better marketing decisions. Consider the following examples:

- After September 11 Las Vegas hotels were empty. Harrah's used BI software to identify potential customers within driving distance. It sent special offers to these customers and filled its hotels within two weeks.
- Ace Hardware uses BI software to analyze price and sales data from its stores and those of competitors to help set its prices. Prices set in this manner have increased customer traffic at its stores and margins have grown from 32 percent to 39 percent.
- British Airways analyzed lost luggage complaints and found that it needed to increase minimum transfer times for luggage to connecting flights. It advised customers of these times and decreased complaints significantly.
- Coty analyzed sales data and found it was losing profits by focusing too much on makeup and not enough on toiletries, such as shampoo and shaving cream. It changed its strategy and profits increased.

Comprehensive Marketing Plan

An actual marketing plan for Acme Consulting is featured in the text's Appendix A. Acme Consulting is a global consulting firm specializing in marketing high-tech products to international markets. Acme provides a good example of a service (as discussed in Chapter 3) that fits within the text's discussion of both the global and technology environments (as discussed in Chapter 2).

Appendix A

Developing a Marketing Plan

A general strategic planning process is presented in Chapter 3. The basic stages include: examine the current situation, identify potential threats and opportunities, set objectives, and develop strategies. This appendix illustrates the types of information typically appearing in each section of a product marketing plan.

Business units within the firm have their own product marketing plans that focus on specific target markets and marketing mixes for each product. As explained in Chapter 3, product marketing plans typically include both strategic decisions (or what to do) and execution decisions (or how to do it). Marketing plans may be developed for a single brand, a product line, or a business unit that markets multiple product lines. For a product, a product line, or a business unit, the general strategic planning process includes the following stages: (1) examine the current situation; (2) identify potential threats and opportunities; (3) set objectives; and (4) develop strategies. These stages may overlap in that work is simultaneously underway regarding each stage. The plans themselves will also include projected financial outcomes and procedures for plan performance monitoring and control.

Overall, planning is a process directed toward making decisions with tomorrow in mind. As such, planning is a means of preparing for future decisions so that they can be made rapidly, economically, and with as little disruption to the business as possible.[1] Marketing plans may be for new products and services being introduced or for existing products or services. Regardless of the type of plan, all plans will be reviewed at least annually for needed revisions. Properly developed marketing plans can provide considerable benefits to firm performance. Plans:[2]

- Act as a road map to guide future decisions.
- Assist in management control and implementation of strategy.
- Assist in helping obtain resources for implementation.
- Stimulate thinking and encourage better use of resources.
- Help in the organization and assignment of responsibilities, tasks, and timing.
- Inform new employees of their roles in implementing existing plans and reaching objectives.
- Help generate awareness of strengths, weaknesses, opportunities, and threats.

Acme Consulting: Planning for High Technology Product Marketing Plan[3]
The following outline is consistent with the general planning procedure summarized above and depicted earlier in Exhibit 3–2. The format for marketing plans varies by industry and company. The

following plan is quite comprehensive and considers most important decisions. Frequently cited content issues and topics are enumerated (sometimes briefly) for each stage in this section.

Parts of the Marketing Plan
1. Executive summary
2. Situation analysis
3. Marketing strategy
4. Financials
5. Controls

Part 1.0 Executive Summary
Acme Consulting is a consulting company specializing in marketing of high-technology products in international markets. Its expertise is the marketing of personal computers and market research, all in international markets.

Part 2.0 Situation Analysis
Acme Consulting offers high-level expertise in international high-tech business development, channel development, distribution strategies, and marketing of high-tech products. It focuses on providing two kinds of international triangles:

- Providing United States clients with development for European and Latin American markets.
- Providing European clients with development for the United States and Latin American markets.

This year we intend to take on consulting work in related markets, specifically the rest of Latin America and the better markets in the Far East. We will also look for additional leverage by taking brokerage positions and representation positions to create percentage holdings in product results.

Part 2.1 Market Summary
Acme focuses on high-technology manufacturers of computer hardware and software, services, and networking, who want to sell into markets in the United States, Europe, and Latin America. These are mostly larger companies, and occasionally medium-sized companies.

Our most important customers are executives in larger corporations. They are marketing managers, general managers, and sales managers, sometimes charged with international focus and sometimes charged with market or even specific channel focus. They do not want to waste their time or risk their money looking for bargain information or questionable expertise. As they go into markets looking at new opportunities, they are very sensitive to risking their company's name and reputation.

Target Market Forecast

Potential Customers	Growth	2000	2001	2002	2003	2004	CAGR
US high tech	10%	5,000	5,500	6,050	6,655	7,321	10.00%
European high tech	15	1,000	1,150	1,323	1,521	1,749	15.00
Latin America	35	250	338	456	616	832	35.07
Other	2	10,000	10,200	10,404	10,612	10,824	2.00
Total	6.27	16,250	17,188	18,233	19,404	20,726	6.27

Contents in Brief

Contents

Part Four
Product and Service Concepts and Strategies

Part Six
Marketing Channels and Logistics
Chapter Thirteen

Chapter Fourteen

Where to Find . . .

Using Technology

Being Entrepreneurial

Building Customer Equity

End-of-Chapter Cases

Prologue: Yum! Brands

How many times in the last month have you eaten:

- Chicken at Kentucky Fried Chicken (KFC)?
- Mexican food at Taco Bell?
- Pizza at Pizza Hut?
- Seafood at Long John Silver's?
- Hamburgers, hotdogs, or root beer floats at A&W All-American Food?

Yum! Brands hopes you eat at these restaurants often, because it owns all of them! KFC, Taco Bell, and Pizza Hut were part of PepsiCo., Inc. In 1997, PepsiCo, Inc. decided to spin off its restaurants so it could focus more attention to its core beverage business. The new restaurant company was named Tricon Global Restaurants, Inc. to reflect the three restaurant icons or brands. Then, in May 2002 Tricon purchased Long John Silver's and A&W All-American Food from Yorkshire Global Restaurants. Since the company now consisted of five brands, its name was changed to Yum! Brands (www.yum.com).

According to Chairman and Chief Executive David Novak, the passion and mission of Yum! Brands "is to put a yum on our customers' faces all around the world." Many things are done to reinforce the "yum" focus. For example, company meetings often start with a YUM cheer, such as "Give me a Y, Give me a U, Give me an M." Stock options are called YUM-BUCKS, and the company newsletter is the Yum! Buzz.[1] Yum! Brands is the world's largest restaurant company with over 32,500 restaurants in more than 100 countries and territories generating systemwide sales in excess of $22 billion and employing around 750,000 associates worldwide.

Why has Yum! been so successful? There are many reasons. One is certainly the leadership provided by Chairman and Chief Executive David Novak. Effective marketing is another. We have studied leading marketing companies, such as Yum! Brands, and identified seven key perspectives that help these companies better identify and respond to market opportunities. Our objective is to discuss each perspective and to illustrate the importance of each to the success of Yum! Brands.

A Global Perspective

A **global perspective** means that marketers should consider the world as their potential marketplace. Customers, suppliers, competitors, partners, and employees can come from anywhere on the globe, no matter where a firm is located or where its product is marketed. Astute marketers take a global perspective in identifying growth opportunities and when developing and executing marketing strategies to capitalize on these opportunities.

Identifying Growth Opportunities

Many firms operate in mature domestic markets that provide only limited opportunities for future growth. These companies often cannot meet desired growth objectives unless attractive growth opportunities in international markets are identified.

Yum! Brands operates in the quick-serve restaurant (QSR) segment of the food service industry and competes against companies such as McDonald's, Subway, Burger King, Wendy's, Domino's Pizza, Dairy Queen, and many others. QSR growth in the United States is limited and competition is fierce. Because of this Yum! has two key growth strategies—international expansion and multibranding—combining two brands in one restaurant to provide greater choice and convenience for customers. Multibranding is a huge competitive advantage for Yum! Multibranding units generate higher sales than traditional stand-alone units. The company sees multibranding as a key way to unlock growth in the U.S. Yum! can potentially multibrand about 13,000 U.S. restaurants. Yum! is the world's largest multibrander with 1600 multibrand units. Since the formation of Tricon in 1997, the company has opened more than 5,100 restaurants with almost 3,200 of them abroad. More than one-third of Yum! restaurants are located internationally, and the firm plans to open around 1,000 international units annually. The geographic distribution of Yum! international restaurants is: 43 percent in Asia Pacific Rim, 21 percent the Americas (Canada, the Caribbean, Latin America, and South America), 25 percent Europe and South Africa, and 11 percent Greater China. Clearly, the future success of Yum! depends upon continued growth in international markets.

Successful Marketing Strategies

A global perspective is needed not only to identify potential market opportunities but to also guide firms in the development and implementation of marketing strategies to take advantage of these opportunities. Understanding the culture, language, customs, and other unique aspects of an international market is critical for marketing success.

Although Yum! looks for global opportunities, it develops marketing strategies to meet the needs of local markets. While its core products have universal appeal the company also develops products with local appeal. KFC, for example, offers tempura crispy

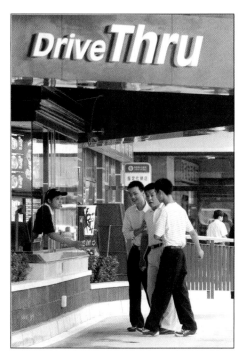

strips in Japan, gravy and potatoes in England, fresh rice with soy or sweet chili sauce in Thailand, and potato-and-onion croquettes in Holland, pastries in France, and it increases the spiciness of its chicken the farther inland in China. KFC has also been successful in marketing to children in China, where it has 700 restaurants and is the most recognized foreign brand. It offers special kids' meals and builds playgrounds inside each restaurant. It also developed "Chicky" as a friendly chicken character who interacts with children in KFC restaurants.[2] These examples illustrate how Yum! adapts its marketing strategies to reflect important differences in international markets.

A Relationship Perspective

The increasingly complex business environment drives companies and marketers to work together for mutual benefit. No longer can one individual or company have all of the knowledge, skills, or resources necessary for marketing success. Instead, networks of various relationships are necessary. A **relationship perspective** consists of building partnerships with organizations outside the company and encouraging teamwork among different functions within the firm to develop long-term customer relationships.

Customer Relationships

Marketing has traditionally been viewed as the sales-generating business function. Its importance is reflected in the adage "nothing happens until a sale is made." This sales orientation sometimes leads firms to focus too much on generating sales in the short run, with little consideration for customer retention or profitability over the long term. Fortunately, the short-term sales orientation is being replaced by more of an emphasis on developing, maintaining, and expanding long-term, profitable relationships with targeted customers.

The importance of customer relationships is expressed in both the vision and mission statements of Yum! Brands. The company is driven by a passion for satisfying

Our Mission Statement
We at Yum! Brands, Inc., pledge to conduct our business according to this set of truths, which we believe to be the foundation for building the best restaurant company in the world.
✓ **People Capability First** . . . *Satisfied customers and profitability follow.*
✓ **Respond to the Voice of the Customer** . . . *Not just listen.*
✓ **The Restaurant General Manager is Our #1 Leader** . . . *Not senior management.*
✓ **Run Each Restaurant As If It's Our Only One** . . . *Avoid the trap of the averages.*
✓ **Recognition Shows You Care** . . . *People leave when you don't.*
✓ **Great Operations and Marketing Innovation Drive Sales** . . . *No finger pointing.*
✓ **Operation Discipline Through Process and Standards** . . . *Consistency, "not program of the month."*
✓ **Franchisees Are Vital Assets** . . . *Operate as one system, not two.*
✓ **Quality in Everything We Do** . . . *Especially the food.*

customers every time they eat at a Yum! restaurant and doing it better than any other competitor. This is accomplished by offering customers food they crave and a unique eating experience that will make them smile and inspire their loyalty for life. The firm's mission statement presents the basic truths that must be implemented for the company to achieve its vision. Of particular importance is the emphasis on satisfying customers by listening to them and responding to their needs. This approach is the key to Yum!'s success in developing long-term profitable relationships with customers.

Organizational Partnerships

Few firms can themselves perform all of the necessary marketing activities productively and profitably; therefore, it is necessary to work with different organizations in various ways. Examples include relationships with marketing research firms to conduct marketing studies, advertising agencies to develop and execute integrated marketing communications programs, and wholesalers and retailers to distribute a firm's products. A company's success in establishing long-term customer relationships typically requires close working relationships with many different organizations.

Yum! Brands is involved in many different organizational partnerships. One example is how Pizza Hut and BBDO worked together to develop a television advertising campaign to introduce P'Zone®, a new sandwich-style product aimed at younger customers with the tag line "The pizza you eat like a sandwich!®"[3] Yum!'s most direct and enduring partnerships are with franchisees and joint-venture partners. Over 22,000 of Yum's! restaurants are owned and operated by franchise and license partners. This approach reduces Yum!'s capital requirements for restaurant expansion, but requires effective working partnerships to be successful. Yum! helps these partners in various ways and generates revenues in excess of $800 million annually from these arrangements. These and other organizational partnerships are critical for Yum! to achieve its growth objectives

Teamwork Relationships

The days when marketers operated in isolation from other business functions are over. Success in the contemporary business environment requires that all company members work as a team toward achieving common objectives. No single individual or function performs effectively as an independent entity. Cooperation and teamwork are critical to succeed in an increasingly complex and rapidly changing global business environment.

Yum! Brands is a people-oriented company and does many things to encourage employees to work together. Chairman and Chief Executive David Novak believes that it is important to focus on making employees happy and energizing them to work together as "customer maniacs" who make customers happy.

■ **worldwide code of conduct** ·

Yum! Brands is committed to providing safe and healthy work environments and to being an environmentally responsible corporate citizen. It is our policy to comply with all applicable environmental, safety and health laws and regulations.

We are dedicated to designing, constructing, maintaining and operating facilities that protect our people and physical resources. This includes providing and requiring the use of adequate protective equipment and measures and insisting that all work be done safely.

We believe that protecting the environment is an important part of good corporate citizenship. We are committed to minimizing the impact of our businesses on the environment with methods that are socially responsible, scientifically based and economically sound. We encourage conservation, recycling and energy use programs that promote clean air and water and reduce landfill waste.

The Yum! Brands Worldwide Code of Conduct means that Yum! Brands and its subsidiaries are committed to the following environmental principles:

- We conduct our business in an environmentally responsible way. We comply with all applicable laws and regulations and provide safe and healthy work environments. In the absence of specific laws and regulations we continue to operate responsibly.
- We strive to minimize the impact of our businesses on the environment. We seek methods that are socially responsible, scientifically based and economically sound.
- Using research and new technology, we work to improve our environmental performance through source reduction, recycling and innovative product packaging.
- We develop programs that promote clean air and water, conserve energy and reduce land fill wastes. Yum! Brands divisions are encouraged to both work together on programs that address environmental issues and to develop their own approaches when appropriate.
- We support programs that educate, train and motivate employees to conduct their activities on behalf of the corporation in an environmentally responsible manner. All employees should assume responsibility as environmental stewards.
- We cooperate with organizations and governments working to find solutions to environmental problems, and we support policies that aim to improve the environment by setting reasonable standards for future conduct.

These happy customers eat more often at Yum! restaurants, which increases company sales and profits. Employees are given the training to advance and have life-long careers. Much attention is given to recognizing the efforts and accomplishments of employees. Because employees are appreciated and valued, turnover is low and teamwork is high. These "customer maniac" teams drive the development of customer relationships.

An Ethics Perspective

Because marketers work at the interface between the company and its customers, partners, and other groups, ethical considerations are important and complex. An **ethics perspective** involves proactively addressing the morality of marketing decisions and practicing social responsibility to include ecological considerations.

Marketing Ethics

A company must project a high level of morality to establish trust between itself and its customers and other stakeholders. Trust provides the foundation for long-term customer relationships and organizational partnerships.

Yum! Brands is dedicated to meeting the needs of its customers, providing a safe and healthy work environment for employees, and being a responsible corporate citizen wherever it operates. Ensuring that everyone in such a large and diverse company understands and practices basic company values is very difficult. Yum! has developed a Worldwide Code of Conduct to communicate its core principles to employees and stakeholders. This code presents guidelines for specific operations and activities of the company's employees and units.

Ecological Orientation

Marketers practicing an ecological orientation consider the environmental impact of marketing decisions. This can result in making changes, such as using recyclable materials, in order to reduce the negative ecological effect of marketing activities. In addition, astute marketers are finding many profitable opportunities to appeal to the growing number of environmentally concerned consumers.

Yum! Brands Worldwide Code of Conduct addresses many areas of ecological responsibility. The company recycles packaging wherever possible. One success is that all Pizza Hut take-out/home delivery boxes are 100 percent recyclable. Energy has received considerable attention at Yum! with programs designed to reduce both ecological pollutants and energy usage. These and other efforts at Yum! make good business sense and have a positive impact on the environment.

Social Responsibility

Social responsibility refers to ensuring that marketing actions have a positive impact on society. This includes minimizing social costs, such as environmental damage, and taking specific actions that benefit society. Businesses are social institutions with a responsibility to contribute to societal welfare.

Yum! Brands prides itself on the many positive things it does in various communities. Several examples illustrate this social responsibility commitment. The Pizza Hut Book It!® Program motivates children in kindergarten through the sixth grade to read by rewarding them for their reading accomplishments. The Taco Bell TEEN-Supreme® Program is a strategic partnership with Boys & Girls Clubs of America. This partnership establishes centers for teen-oriented programs, a training academy for Boys & Girls Club professionals, and a special club to promote citizenship and leadership development for teens. KFC's Colonel's kids program helps provide extended-hour day care in a partnership with YMCAs. Yum! Brands is also the world's largest pioneer of prepared food to those in need. The company is fighting hunger by feeding families. These and many other programs and donations help Yum! contribute to communities around the world.

A Customer Value Perspective
Business buyers and consumers are continually trying to get more for less. Both groups assess what they get for what they have to give. "What they get" includes not only the basic features of the product but also other important factors related to the purchase, use, and disposal of the product. These might include the convenience of the purchase, training in product use, dependability of delivery, after-the-sale service, ease of disposing of the product, and other factors. "What they give" includes the monetary price of the product, but also time and effort to purchase the product, costs associated with using the product, and other factors. A **customer value perspective** means constantly looking for ways to give customers more for less.

Yum! Brands provides customer value in two fundamental ways. First, the company is a leader in multibranding by offering two or more brands at one restaurant location. Typically, these are combinations of KFC, Pizza Hut, Taco Bell, Long John Silver's and A&W All American Food. Customers can choose from a large variety of food options by traveling to only one location. Families with different food preferences find these multibranded restaurants especially valuable. Then, within each restaurant Yum! offers high-quality/value price options. Value meals also give customers a lower price for various combinations of menu items and drinks. Continuously providing customers with high quality, convenience, and value are important elements of Yum!'s success.

A Productivity Perspective

A **productivity perspective** is trying to get the most output for each marketing dollar spent. Productivity is typically defined in terms of output per unit input ratios. For marketers example outputs might be sales or market share. Inputs include the dollars spent on advertising, number of salespeople, or other marketing activity. Therefore, sales per advertising dollar or sales per salesperson are important productivity measures for marketers.

The multibranding strategy emphasized by Yum! Brands not only provides value to customers but also is a very productive use of marketing resources. Multibranding units benefit from national advertising. Since customers like the variety in multibranded restaurants, sales are much higher than for single-brand locations. Higher sales and profits have a positive impact on Yum!'s performance.

A Technology Perspective
Technology is advancing at a tremendous pace. New developments in artificial intelligence, biotechnology, optoelectronics, and many other areas are reported daily. The dizzying pace of technological change challenges marketers to embrace a **technological perspective** so they can translate new and emerging technologies into successful products and services, and use technology to improve marketing practice.

Yum! Brands uses new technology products to help market its brands. One example is when Taco Bell used Amazon.com CEO Jeff Bezos to hold its new chicken quesadilla product as if it were a handheld computer. Then, the chicken quesadilla was described in terms of its "gooey interface" and "ergonomic design for easy downloading" with the tag line "Think outside the bun."[4] Another example was the partnership with Microsoft to introduce its new video-game system, Xbox. Taco Bell supported the introduction with TV ads, in-store materials, window displays, tray liners, bags, and print ads. Taco Bell got product placements in some of the video games plus an association with a high-technology product.[5] Taco Bell and other Yum! brands all use Yum!'s Web site (www.yum.com) to market effectively to customers, franchisees, investors, employees, and other publics.

An Entrepreneurship Perspective
A dynamic business environment creates a need for firms to be flexible and responsive to marketplace demands. Slow and rigid bureaucracies need to be replaced by streamlined organizational structures and processes. Success often depends on being able to do some things differently from, sooner than, or better than competitors. This requires that marketers bring an entrepreneurial perspective to their work. An **entrepreneurial**

perspective has three basic dimensions: innovation, risk taking, and proactiveness. Marketers adopting an entrepreneurial perspective attempt to do things in new and unique ways, to make decisions in the face of uncertainty, and to be the first to try something different.

Yum! Brands has been proactive and innovative in introducing and expanding the multibranding concept. Different brand combinations are being tested. The number of possible combinations is much larger since the company now has five brands. Another example of entrepreneurship is Pizza Hut. It prides itself on a number of firsts such as the first Pan Pizza and the first Stuffed Crust Pizza. Rich Matteson, director of brand marketing and promotions, suggests that Pizza Hut puts "a big emphasis on being first to market with new ideas . . . it's the cornerstone of our value proposition for the customer. . . when a customer comes to a Pizza Hut, we want them to know they can always find something exciting and new."[6]

A final example of an entrepreneurship perspective is the joint venture Yum! Brands established with Hong Kong-based Favorite Restaurants Group to test and develop an Asian food restaurant concept called Yan Can. The first restaurant opened in San Francisco featuring fast casual dine-in and take-out menus developed by Martin Yan, the host of a television cooking show called "Yan Can Cook." This show is seen in more than 70 countries. Yan has developed signature sauces, such as Kung Pao, Black Bean, and Sweet and Sour, that are served with chicken, beef, shrimp, and vegetables. Yan Can started as a stand-alone restaurant, but could also have the potential to be integrated into the Yum! Brands multibranding strategy if it proves successful.[7]

Integrating the Perspectives

Although we have discussed each perspective separately, the perspectives are highly interrelated. For example, continuing developments in information and communication technologies make it easier for firms to productively engage in business globally and to develop relationships with customers, partnerships with other organizations, and teamwork within firms, even when employees are located in different areas. These new technologies also introduce new ethical issues that must be addressed if companies are going to be able to earn the trust necessary for successful relationships of all types. The rapid and continuous changes in the environment require firms to be entrepreneurial, especially in trying to provide customers with more value.

Many of these interrelationships are critical to the future success of Yum! Brands. Yum! must continue to be entrepreneurial if it is to keep ahead of competitors in creating value for and developing relationships with customers. The company must keep expanding globally through various types of partnerships based on an ethical foundation. Efforts must also be made to increase productivity often through the use of new technologies. Yum! is employing these marketing perspectives now and its future looks bright.

Chapter One

An Overview of Contemporary Marketing

After studying this chapter, you should be able to:

1 Discuss what marketing is and why it is important to organizations and individuals.

2 Distinguish between marketing as an organizational philosophy and a societal process.

3 Understand the components of a marketing strategy and the different activities involved in marketing products and services.

4 Be aware of the various types of marketing institutions and the different marketing positions available in these institutions.

5 Understand the basic elements and relationships in the contemporary marketing framework.

www.amazon.com

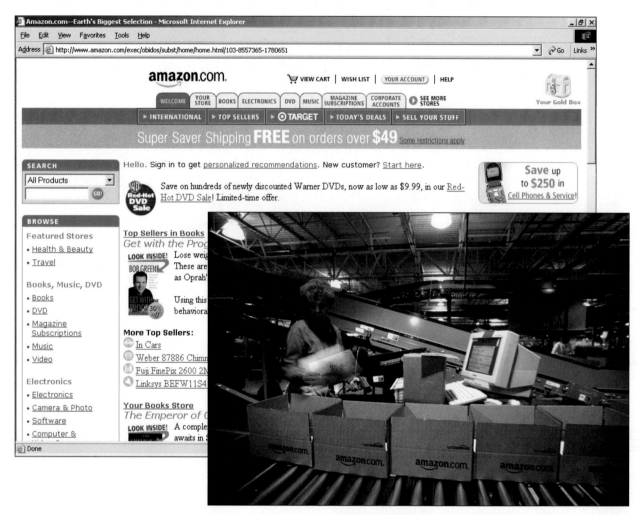

Amazon.com represents an interesting entrepreneurial story. Jeff Bezos started Amazon.com as a book retailer in 1995. The company's mission was to use the Internet to transform book buying into the fastest, easiest, and most enjoyable shopping experience available. Since Amazon.com did not have an inventory of books in a retail location, it could offer customers an enormous selection of books over its Web site. Customers could also shop and place orders 24 hours a day and seven days a week. The shopping experience was easy and fun, and various services were added to create value. This was the beginning, and growth has been phenomenal.

Sales have increased from about $150 million in 1997 to over $3 billion today. And, Amazon.com announced its first pro forma operating profit of $5.8 million for the fourth quarter of 2001. The company is doing several things to keep sales increasing and to become consistently profitable.

First, the company offers many different products and services through its stores on *www.amazon. com*. These include music CDs, videos, electronics, kitchen and houseware products, an auction service, a wedding gift registry, and many others.

Second, international sales have been increasing through international sites for the United Kingdom, Germany, Japan, and France.

Third, Amazon.com is using its logistics, customer service, and Web site operations expertise to provide services for other retailers. For example, it runs the Toys 'R' Us online site, and retailers such as Target now have an online store on its Web site. These services are important to the profitability of Amazon.com, because gross margins are much higher for providing these services than from the direct sale of products and services.

One of the major reasons for the success of Amazon.com is its growing number of satisfied and loyal customers. The number of customer accounts has grown from around 1.5 million to over 25 million. Amazon.com continues to add new customers and expand relationships with existing customers by offering a wide selection of products and by giving customers a personalized and satisfying shopping experience.

The Amazon.com story illustrates a basic principle of successful marketing: Identify market opportunities, and respond by developing and executing marketing strategies to take advantage of the opportunities better than competitors do. Jeff Bezos realized that the Internet had the potential to offer customers new and exciting shopping experiences. He started in book retailing, because Amazon.com could provide a better book selection, customized services, and lower prices than could typical book retailers. Finally, and most important, Amazon.com focuses on the customer; the company's key advantage is its large and growing base of loyal customers.

In a dynamic and turbulent business environment, marketers must continually revise their strategies to meet growth objectives. Amazon.com has done this by adding new product categories and new services. The firm now faces Internet competitors as well as traditional retail rivals. So it must continually look for ways to improve its existing operations and expand its offerings to increase the value provided to customers. Its rapidly growing customer base suggests that it is doing a good job in this area.

Amazon.com is actively involved in marketing. The most accepted definition of **marketing** is that adopted by the American Marketing Association:

Marketing is the process of planning and executing the conception, pricing, promotion, and distribution of ideas, goods, and services to create exchanges that satisfy individual and organizational goals.[1]

This definition views marketing as a process involving marketing exchanges, strategies, activities, positions, and institutions. Before discussing each of these areas in detail, we examine the importance of marketing and different views of marketing.

The Importance of Marketing

Marketing is usually associated with large business organizations. Most people are probably familiar with the marketing activities of consumer product firms such as Procter & Gamble, Sony, Nike, McDonald's, General Motors, and Sears. They also may be aware of marketing efforts by firms—such as Xerox, Monsanto, Caterpillar, Boeing, and DuPont—that market to other organizations.

Marketing also plays an important role for many different types of organizations, and the skills and knowledge possessed by effective marketers are valuable in many situations. Consider the following:

Marketing is important to many nonprofit organizations. The Humane Society uses advertising to promote animal protection.

- Washington's Arena Stage Theatre was America's first nonprofit theater. It had been very successful since being founded in 1950, but ticket sales and donations declined in the late 1990s and the theater was in financial trouble. The board of trustees developed a long-term marketing program to rebrand the theater and increase attendance and donations. Marketing research provided valuable information, which led to various marketing activities to include a new logo, direct mail, a new website, a newsletter for season ticket holders, redesigned brochures, and print ads. The marketing program has increased ticket sales by 28 percent and donations are up 48 percent.[2]

- The Marines Corps was having problems getting what the 173,000 marines wanted when they needed it. The Corps studied the marketing practices of companies like Wal-Mart Stores, UPS, Unilever Group, and Swissair. Based on these studies and working with consultants, new technology is being employed to improve all aspects of its supply chain. Inventory is being replaced with information to provide better "customer service" and lower costs. The Corps is also developing closer relationships with suppliers to facilitate access to hard-to-get items like tank parts.[3]

- There are about 500,000 Sikhs in the United States. The Sikhs, a religious and ethnic group originating in India, wear turbans and beards. After the terrorist attacks on September 11, some U.S. Sikhs became victims of hate crimes and one was killed. Sikh leaders contacted two marketing firms to help them educate the general public about Sikhism. A media relations strategy was developed to get a credible message to the widest audience. Stories were covered in the *New York Times, Miami Herald, Boston Globe,* and by CNN News, Associated Press, and Yahoo! News. An open letter from U.S. Sikhs to fellow Americans was run as an ad in local newspapers across the country. The high point was when President Bush invited Sikh leaders to the White House. This marketing campaign was successful, as many U.S. Sikhs reported being treated with more respect and kindness after it was executed.[4]

- There is a trend toward consolidation in many industries resulting in fewer, but much larger, firms. Mergers and acquisitions in the banking industry are an example. Interestingly, small community banks are using marketing to compete effectively against their large, national competitors. These banks are targeting markets that are being ignored by the large banks, such as small businesses, minorities, and rural areas, and providing superior customer service to these customers. Extended business hours, personal attention, free investment advice, and free coffee and baby-sitting services are examples. These marketing strategies have been very effective as small bank profits have increased 11.8 percent annually over the past five years, compared to 8.5 percent for the large banks.[5]

- There are many attractive jobs and career paths within the marketing profession. These are discussed later in this chapter and throughout the book. However, those with marketing backgrounds are prepared to be successful in many endeavors. Some of these opportunities are within the same company. For example, companies are selecting more CEOs from the marketing ranks, because these individuals have a strong customer focus and good communication skills. An example is GE, which replaced the legendary Jack Welch with Jeffrey Immelt, who held various marketing positions at GE for 20 years.[6] Other opportunities in marketing are to do new things. Examples include Ellen Shapiro moving from marketing video games to girls at Walt Disney to starting a toy invention company called Trixie Toys and George Gunn Jr. building on 30 years' experience in the advertising business to become CEO of a nonprofit organization.[7]

These examples illustrate the value of marketing to different types of organizations (nonprofit organizations, the military, religious and ethnic groups, and small firms) and to individual marketers (opportunities to advance within an organization or for different career options). Today, more organizations and individuals realize that marketing is critical for success.

Views of Marketing
Most of the emphasis in this book is on marketing as the process defined at the beginning of the chapter. Nevertheless, marketing can also be viewed as an organizational philosophy and as a societal process.

Marketing as an Organizational Philosophy

An organization typically has some type of philosophy that directs the efforts of everyone in it. The philosophy might be stated formally, as in a mission statement, or it might become established informally through the communications and actions of top management. An organizational philosophy indicates the types of activities the organization values. Three different philosophies deserve mention.

A **production philosophy** exists when an organization emphasizes the production function. An organization following such a philosophy values activities related to improving production efficiency or producing sophisticated products and services. Production drives the organization. Marketing plays a secondary role because the organization thinks the best-produced products can be easily marketed. High-technology companies often follow a production philosophy.

A **selling philosophy** predominates where the selling function is most valued. The assumption is that any product can be sold if enough selling effort is given to it. Marketing's job is to sell whatever the organization decides to produce. Although selling is one component of marketing, organizations driven by a selling philosophy emphasize selling efforts to the exclusion of other marketing activities.

A **marketing philosophy** suggests that the organization focuses on satisfying the needs of customers. This focus applies to people in the marketing function as well as to those in production, personnel, accounting, finance, and other functions. Production and selling are still important, but the organization is driven by satisfying customer needs. Applied Materials reinforces the importance of a marketing philosophy every payday. "Your payroll dollars are provided by Applied Materials customers" appears on the front of every employee's paycheck.[8]

MARKETING CONCEPT Marketing as an organizational philosophy has been based on the **marketing concept**. This concept consists of three interrelated principles:

1. An organization's basic purpose is to satisfy customer needs.
2. Satisfying customer needs requires integrated and coordinated efforts throughout the organization.
3. Organizations should focus on long-term success.

The marketing concept has been embraced by many firms since the 1950s.[9] In recent years, the term **market orientation** has been used to describe firms implementing the marketing concept. These firms are customer oriented and competitor oriented with the objective of satisfying customer needs better than competitors. However, the competitive business climate of the 2000s suggests that merely satisfying customers is not enough.

Satisfied customers often leave and purchase from competitors. For example, Xerox polls 480,000 customers per year regarding their level of satisfaction using a five-point scale from 5 (high) to 1 (low). Analysis of these data indicated that customers giving 5s were six times more likely to repurchase Xerox equipment than those giving 4s. Now, Xerox's objective is to have 100 percent of its customers being totally satisfied with Xerox products and services.[10] Xerox and other successful marketers are extending the focus beyond just customer satisfaction to customer loyalty.

BUILDING CUSTOMER EQUITY Companies are typically faced with focusing on short-term versus long-term sales and profit growth and emphasizing new customers versus existing customers. Too often, short-term considerations and new customer acquisitions take precedence over long-term performance and current customers. The concept of customer equity can help firms achieve a better balance in these areas.

Customer equity is the financial value of a firm's customer relationships. It consists of profits from first-time customers plus expected profits from future sales to these and other customers. Customer equity can be increased in three basic ways:

1. Decreasing the cost to acquire new customers.
2. Retaining more customers longer.
3. Increasing profits from retained customers by selling them more at higher margins and with lower marketing expenses.

Building customer equity integrates short-term and long-term orientations and addresses both new and existing customers. Short-term sales and profit growth comes from acquiring profitable new customers and expanding relationships with current customers. Long-term sales and profit growth is addressed by retaining new and existing customers longer and selling more profitable products at lower marketing expense to both groups. Customer equity is consistent with the marketing concept because it focuses on the customer and emphasizes integrated company efforts to achieve long-term success.[11]

Exhibit 1–1   *Customer equity relationships*

Organizational strategy & execution → Providing exceptional customer value → Achieving completely satisfied customers → Earning high customer loyalty → Increasing sales growth & profits → Building customer equity

The process for building customer equity is illustrated in Exhibit 1–1. It is based on three key relationships:

1. Earning high levels of customer loyalty leads to increased sales growth and higher profitability, and higher customer equity.

2. Completely satisfying and delighting customers is the best route for earning customer loyalty.

3. Providing exceptional value is needed to delight and completely satisfy customers.

The basic reasons for the close relationship between customer loyalty and sales, profits, and customer equity are presented in Exhibit 1–2. Loyal customers contribute to increased sales growth because they tend to buy more over time and are an excellent source of new business referrals. Getting new customers from referrals usually lowers customer acquisition costs significantly. Some companies calculate the **lifetime value of a loyal customer** as the revenue stream from repeat purchases and referrals. For example, the lifetime value of a loyal pizza eater can be $8,000, of a Cadillac owner, $332,000.[12]

Typically, loyal customers involve limited acquisition costs, low operating costs, and higher profit margins. The conventional wisdom is that it costs at least five times as much to serve a new customer as an existing one. Sometimes the efforts to get new customers may not even be profitable. For example, MBNA was spending 98 percent of its marketing dollars on getting new customers. It found that it cost about $50 to get a new credit card customer, these customers were not profitable until the second year, and many left before the second year. The company changed its strategy and focused on keeping existing customers. It increased the customer retention rate to 50 percent and became one of the most profitable banks in the country.[13]

The link between customer satisfaction and customer loyalty is especially interesting. One study of this link in the automobile, business personal computer, hospital, airlines, and local telephone service markets concluded that completely satisfied customers are much more loyal than merely satisfied customers. Another study in the banking industry found that completely satisfied customers were 42 percent more likely to be loyal than merely satisfied customers.[14] These results are consistent with the Xerox example presented earlier. There is increasing evidence of the close relationship between complete customer satisfaction and customer loyalty.

How can organizations completely satisfy their customers? The simple answer is by continuously providing customers with exceptional value. **Customer value** is de-

Exhibit 1–2   *Customer loyalty, sales, profits, and customer equity*

1. Keeping loyal customers requires no acquisition costs. Getting new customers often requires high acquisition costs.
2. The longer a firm keeps a customer, the more base profit earned from continuing purchases over time.
3. Loyal customers tend to buy more from a firm over time.
4. It usually costs less to deal with loyal customers than with new customers.
5. Loyal customers are typically an excellent source of referrals for new business.
6. Loyal customers are often willing to pay a price premium to receive desired value.

One way to promote customer loyalty is to reward customers for their loyalty. Friday's awards points to customers based on the amount spent. These points can be redeemed for free food at subsequent visits.

fined as what a customer *gets* (benefits from product use, related services) for what a customer *gives* (price paid, costs to acquire and use the product). Value is determined by the customer. For example, Southwest Airlines is the only major airline to be profitable for the past 20 years. One of the reasons for this success is that Southwest's customers value frequent departures, on-time service, friendly employees, and low fares. Southwest consistently provides customers exceptional value that translates into complete satisfaction, loyal customers, increased sales and profits and higher customer equity. Southwest does not assign seats, offer meals, or provide tickets as most other airlines do. Its customers do not value these services, so they are not offered.[15]

Organizations are faced with a difficult challenge in continually providing exceptional customer value, completely satisfying needs, and earning customer loyalty. Those successful in these endeavors are likely to achieve higher levels of sales growth and profitability and more customer equity than those that do not. Organizations increasingly have to be market-driven and customer-focused to compete effectively in the future. Some guidelines for executing a marketing philosophy that incorporates the marketing concept and a market orientation focused on building customer equity are presented in Exhibit 1–3. These guidelines are relevant for those in marketing and nonmarketing functions within an organization.

Marketing as a Societal Process

Marketing as a societal process can be defined as a process that facilitates the flow of goods and services from producers to consumers in a society. At this level, the emphasis is on issues such as:

- What institutions are involved in the societal marketing system?
- What activities do these institutions perform?
- How effective is the marketing system in satisfying consumer needs?
- How efficient is the marketing system in providing consumers with desired goods and services?

A society's marketing system is closely related to its political and economic systems. These close relationships are vividly illustrated by the tremendous changes that

---

Exhibit 1–3	*Executing a marketing philosophy*

1. Create customer focus throughout the business.
2. Listen to the customer.
3. Define and nurture your distinctive competence.
4. Define marketing as market intelligence.
5. Target customers precisely.
6. Manage for profitability, not sales volume.
7. Make customer value the guiding star.
8. Let the customer define quality.
9. Measure and manage customer expectations.
10. Build customer relationships and loyalty.
11. Define the business as a service business.
12. Commit to continuous improvement and innovation.
13. Manage culture along with strategy and structure.
14. Grow with partners and alliances.
15. Destroy marketing bureaucracy.

Speaking from Experience

David Power
President
Power Creative Inc.

"**Power Creative was regarded as just a supplier of advertising and marketing materials for many years. But in today's business world, with tight budgets and pressure to deliver higher margins, our customers view us as true business partners. Our objective is to improve the client's bottom line. Consistently delivering on this commitment has two major benefits. First, completely satisfied customers remain loyal. For example, we have worked with General Electric Appliances for many years. Second, loyal customers help us get new business. A recent example illustrates this. An individual we worked with at General Electric Appliances took a job as vice president and general manager of sales, marketing, and distribution for Lennox. He contacted us to develop programs to promote Lennox furnaces and air conditioners to housing contractors. We would never have been considered for this business without our previous successful relationship.**"

Power Creative provides integrated marketing communications services for the domestic and international operations of large blue-chip corporations. David received a BS in marketing from the University of Louisville in 1993 and joined Power Creative as an account executive, handling the RCA brand for Thomson Electronics. He has since been promoted to senior account executive, Vice President, and President of the company.

continue in Eastern Europe. Countries that operated under a communist political system with centrally planned economies did have some sort of marketing system, because products and services were provided to consumers. The marketing systems, however, were woefully ineffective and inefficient, largely because most "marketing" decisions were made centrally by government bureaucrats. With little consideration of customer needs, these officials decided what to produce, in what quantities, how products were to be made available to consumers, and at what prices.

Ineffective marketing systems contributed to the overthrow of the communist regimes in Eastern Europe, and these countries continue to struggle with developing democratic political systems and market-based economies. A market-based economy requires an effective and efficient marketing system that can identify and satisfy consumer needs for products and services. Although transforming political, economic, and marketing systems is painful and difficult in the short run, the changes promise to improve the standards of living in these countries in the long run.

However, the transformation process is often slow. For example, it took Russia over 10 years to be officially recognized as a market economy by the United States and European Union.[16] The benefits from a market economy may also not be distributed equally. More than half of China's population is rural and there is a wide disparity of income between rural and urban areas. For example, China's annual per capita income is about $847. However, it is around $3,000 in Beijing and $4,000 in Shanghai.[17] Consider the following family situations in China as illustrative:

Thinking Critically

- Compare the political, economic, and marketing systems of a developed country with those of a developing country.

- On the basis of these comparisons, what must be done to improve Afghanistan's political, economic, and marketing systems?

- Liu Fengtong used to be a welder at a coal plant a few miles away from Beijing. But he was laid off and now gives dance lessons to customers paying a 25¢ admission fee. Liu earns about $90 a month, about half of what he earned as a welder. This is the only work he can find to support his family.

- Frank Liu lives 700 miles away, in Shanghai. He heads a government agency that recruits foreign investors for the Waigaoqiao Free Trade Zone. He works in a wood-paneled office and wears expensive suits. His son attends an exclusive private school, and his family just bought a new apartment. Liu regularly meets with executives from Intel, Hewlett-Packard, and Dell and travels to the United States and other countries to develop business for the trade zone.[18]

These situations illustrate very different results from the move to a market economy and new marketing system. Over time, more people are likely to benefit from these changes, but market economies and marketing systems are not perfect. For example, a recent study of the contributions of the aggregate marketing system to U.S. society found both benefits and criticisms. Benefits included economic well-being, quality of life, and social/psychological benefits to individual workers and

The move to free-market economies and more open marketing systems offers tremendous opportunities for many firms. Many companies are marketing grocery products to consumers in Shanghai.

consumers. Criticisms included negative effects on societal values, unethical marketing practices, and ecological problems. This analysis did, however, conclude that the contributions from the U.S. aggregate marketing system outweighed the negative impacts.[19]

Important relationships exist between marketing at the organizational and societal levels. People moving from a planned to a market-based economic system must learn and implement basic marketing practices. The success of a society's marketing system depends on the ability of individuals in organizations to identify and respond to consumer needs effectively and efficiently. These individuals face the following problems, as expressed in a study of managers in several Eastern European countries:[20]

- Becoming more market-oriented and consumer-responsive.
- Improving product quality.
- Changing product design, assortment, finishing, and packaging.
- Increasing communications efforts such as personal selling and point-of-purchase sales.
- Increasing merchandising efforts.
- Using competitive pricing.
- Instituting promotional pricing and price discounts.

Marketing as a Process   Marketing as an organizational philosophy and a
societal process are related to the way marketing is performed by organizations and individuals. We are now ready to discuss the major aspects of marketing as a process.

Marketing Exchanges

Exchange is generally viewed as the core element of marketing.[21] Exchange has been defined as the "transfer of something tangible or intangible, actual or symbolic, between two or more social actors."[22] Thus, the basic purpose of marketing is to get individuals or organizations to transfer something of value (tangible or in-

Poland and Malaysia are two developing countries with improving marketing systems. Colgate-Palmolive is taking advantage of opportunities in these countries by marketing a variety of consumer products.

tangible, actual or symbolic) to each other. The most familiar type of exchange occurs when a customer exchanges money with a retail store for a product. Every time a customer pays a Papa John's pizza delivery person and receives a pizza, a marketing exchange takes place.

Marketing exchanges are not confined to transactions of money for products, as shown in Exhibit 1–4. Businesses engage in barter where they exchange their goods and services for the goods and services of another firm. Nonprofit organizations, colleges and universities, politicians, and many other "social actors" are also involved in exchanges. Volunteers and contributors to nonprofit organizations, for example, exchange their time and money for the satisfaction derived from helping a good cause. Or consider the tuition that students pay a university or college in exchange for the education they receive. Even politics involves exchanges, with people trading their votes for the promise of representation from a political candidate.

The major objective of marketing exchanges is to satisfy the needs of the individuals and organizations involved. For an exchange to take place, each party must

Exhibit 1–4   *Marketing exchanges*

The basic purpose of marketing is to facilitate exchanges. eBay facilitates exchanges through auctions on the Internet.

be willing to give up something to get something. What each party gets must be as satisfying as what it gives up. If someone decides to buy a delivered pizza from Papa John's, the pizza must be as important as the money exchanged to get it. Similarly, Papa John's must think the money it receives from the customer is as important as the delivered pizza it exchanges.

Creating exchanges that satisfy customer needs requires that marketing strategies be developed and marketing activities performed. The process involves people in various marketing positions who determine what is to be done (they plan) and then do it (they execute). Some people in marketing positions are employed by the firm that produces the product and some by other organizations that specialize in specific marketing activities.

Marketing Strategies

Marketing strategies consist of selecting a target market and developing a marketing mix to satisfy that market's needs. A **target market** is a defined group of consumers or organizations with whom a firm wants to create marketing exchanges. A **marketing mix** is the overall marketing offer to appeal to the target market. It consists of decisions in four basic areas: product (development of a product, service, or idea to exchange), pricing (what to charge for the exchange), integrated marketing communications (how to communicate with the target market about the possible exchange), and distribution (how to get the product, service, or idea to the target market to consummate the exchange). As is evident from Exhibit 1–5, many marketing decisions must be made within the product, pricing, communications, and distribution areas.

Exhibit 1–5	*Marketing mix decisions*

Product decisions
- Quality
- Design
- Branding
- Packaging
- Customer service
- New products
- Product life cycle strategies
- Product line strategies
- Product mix strategies

Integrated marketing communications decisions
- Objectives
- Communications mix
- Budget
- Messages
- Media
- Effectiveness

Marketing mix

Price decisions
- Objectives
- Strategies
- Methods
- Setting prices
- Price changes
- Discounting

Distribution decisions
- Type of channel
- Channel management
- Supply chain management
- Distribution intensity
- Logistics
- Transportation methods
- Service levels

Exhibit 1–6	*Marketing strategies*		
	Maybelline	**Mary Kay**	**Clinique**
Target market	Low end	Middle	High end
Product	Cosmetics	Cosmetics	Cosmetics
Price	Low	Moderate	High
Distribution	Mass merchandisers	Direct to consumers	Upscale department stores
Marketing communications	Advertising through mass media	Personal selling to consumers in home	Targeted advertising and personal selling to consumers in stores

The cosmetics industry is a good place to look for examples of different marketing strategies. Note in Exhibit 1–6 that Maybelline, Mary Kay, and Clinique all market a variety of cosmetic products to defined target markets. Brands differ, as do the prices charged, the methods of distribution, and the types of marketing communications. Each company effectively blends product, price, distribution, and integrated marketing communications decisions into a different marketing mix designed to serve its target market.

Marketing Activities

Regardless of an organization's specific marketing strategy, a number of different marketing activities must be performed to move products from producers to end users. Exhibit 1–7 illustrates these important activities schematically.

Buying and selling activities are required to finalize an exchange. The product assortments desired by buyers must be transported to appropriate locations and stored in inventory. The inventories must be financed and the risk associated with holding the inventory assortment assumed. Quality and quantity of product assortments must be standardized and graded. Finally, marketing information about buyers and competitors is needed to make marketing decisions.

Say you want to buy a DVD player. A number of producers of DVD players—Toshiba, Sharp, Panasonic, Sony—would like to sell you their brand. But it would be inefficient if you had to visit each producer to examine its product and then purchase directly from the factory. To facilitate the exchange process, the producers market their DVD players through various types of retailers, such as Circuit City.

So now you can go to Circuit City, try out different DVD-player brands, and easily purchase the one best suited to your needs. Circuit City has performed many of the marketing activities shown in Exhibit 1–7 that are required to complete an exchange between you and the producer of DVD players. Circuit City buys an as-

Exhibit 1–7	*Marketing activities*

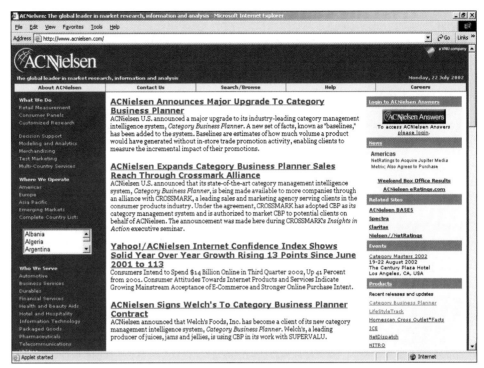

Marketing research firms specialize in performing marketing research activities to help firms make better decisions. ACNielsen is a global marketing research firm.

sortment of DVD-player brands, transports them to its retail outlets, and stores them there in inventory. It assumes the expense and risk of holding this inventory. It standardizes and grades the product quality and quantity. Because it wants to move the DVD players from inventory to end users, it advertises and promotes the brands it carries and the price at which it is willing to exchange each brand. Buyers come to the stores, talk with salespeople, and purchase desired brands.

This would be the typical approach for getting DVD players from producers to consumers. However, with the tremendous growth of the Internet, other options are available. You might go to the Web site of one of the DVD producers and obtain information about DVD players, locate dealers for its brand, and possibly make a purchase. Or, you could go to a shopping site, such as Amazon.com, and compare various DVD brands and purchase the one that best meets your needs.

One way or another, certain marketing activities must be performed for exchanges to occur between producers and end users. In some cases, marketing institutions, such as retailers like Circuit City, perform many of the marketing activities for producers. In others, most activities are performed by individuals within the producing firm. Sometimes consumers perform some of the required marketing activities.

Marketing Positions

There are a variety of marketing positions within most organizations. Examples are shown in Exhibit 1–8. Some of these positions, such as advertising manager, distribution manager, or sales manager, indicate specialization in one area of marketing. Others suggest working across marketing areas (marketing manager, product manager, marketing research manager). The reality is that most marketing positions require close working relationships among different marketing and business functions. For example, advertising, sales, product, marketing, production, and accounting managers typically work together to develop and execute marketing plans for specific products.

Exhibit 1–8	*Marketing positions*

Position/Alternative titles	Duties
Marketing manager Vice president of marketing, director of marketing	Directs all company's marketing activities, including planning, organizing, staffing, directing, controlling, evaluating performance
Product manager Brand manager	Develops goals, objectives, plans, strategies, marketing mixes for product line or brand
Advertising manager Advertising director, director of communications	Devises advertising policy and strategy, selects advertising agencies, develops promotional campaigns, selects media, allocates advertising expenditures
Distribution manager Logistics manager, traffic manager, transportation manager	Manages distribution system, including storage and transportation for all products, services
Purchasing manager Director of purchasing, director of procurement	Manages all purchasing activities, including buying product ingredients or components, supplies, equipment, needed materials
Marketing research manager Director of commercial research, director of market research	Develops research designs for specific problems; collects, analyzes, interprets data; presents results to top management
Public relations manager Director of public relations, director of communications, public affairs officer	Manages all communications with media and company stakeholders, to present favorable public image
Customer service manager Director of customer relations	Provides customer service, handles customer complaints
Sales manager Vice president of sales, director of sales, national sales manager, regional, district, or branch sales manager	Organizes, develops, directs, controls, evaluates salesforce

Marketing positions are most prevalent in business firms, although similar positions exist in nonprofit organizations, hospitals, government agencies, museums, accounting firms, and other organizations. For organizations that follow a marketing philosophy, many employees are involved in marketing activities even though they may not hold formal marketing positions.

David Power, President, Power Creative, talks about being involved in marketing throughout his career: "Successful organizations are becoming increasingly customer-focused and are investing in ways to develop one-to-one relationships. These companies rely on everyone in the enterprise, from CEO to product development engineer to receptionist, to contribute to customer relationships. This means that everyone in the organization is involved in some marketing activities. And, different positions perform different marketing activities. For example, as an account manager most of my job was to maintain and expand our relationship with one large account. Now, as president, I am involved in more strategic issues that span all of our customers. I still, however, call on prospects to get new business and on existing customers to keep their business."

Marketing Institutions

Some organizations specialize in specific marketing activities and become experts in performing them. Thus, a firm may work with several of these organizations to handle the required marketing activities.

We have already discussed the important role that retailers, such as Circuit City, play in making a variety of different products and brands available to consumers. Sometimes wholesalers also undertake specific marketing activities for producers and retailers. Wholesalers engage in exchanges with producers and subsequently exchange these products from their inventory to meet the needs of retailers. They might also perform specialized services for producers and retailers. Some of the leading wholesalers are McKesson Corporation (health care products), Fleming Co. (food), Produce Specialties (exotic fruits and vegetables), and United Stationers (office supplies).

Marketing research firms and advertising agencies also provide specialized services for client firms. Some firms emphasize specific types of marketing research, but the largest firms offer a full array of research services, including focus groups, concept tests, customer interviews, mail surveys, experiments, or other types of mar-

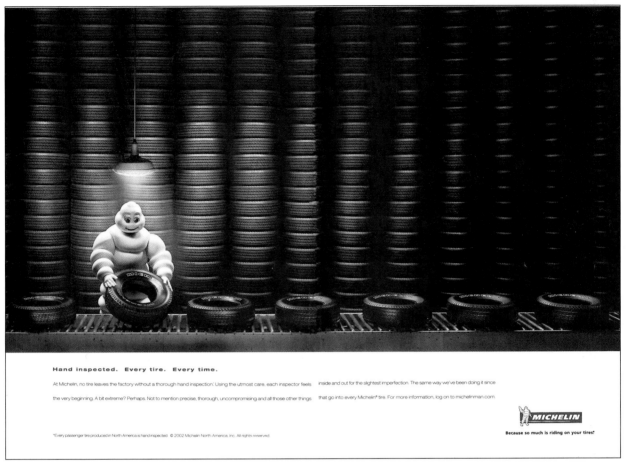

Hand inspected. Every tire. Every time.

At Michelin, no tire leaves the factory without a thorough hand inspection. Using the utmost care, each inspector feels inside and out for the slightest imperfection. The same way we've been doing it since the very beginning. A bit extreme? Perhaps. Not to mention precise, thorough, uncompromising and all those other things that go into every Michelin® tire. For more information, log on to michelinman.com.

MICHELIN

Because so much is riding on your tires!

The contemporary marketing framework provides a guide for developing effective marketing strategies. Michelin uses advertising as part of its marketing strategy for tires.

keting research. The largest marketing research firms include ACNielsen, IMS International, Information Resources, Inc., and the Arbitron Co.

Advertising agencies also provide various services to help firms develop and implement marketing communications campaigns. Again, some of these firms specialize in specific areas; others provide full services, often including marketing research. The leading advertising agencies include Young & Rubicam, Saatchi and Saatchi, BBDO Worldwide, DDB Needham Worldwide, and Ogilvy & Mather Worldwide.

A Contemporary Marketing Framework

The contemporary marketing framework that underlies the focus for this book is presented in Exhibit 1–9. The framework has three major elements: the marketing environment, key marketing perspectives, and marketing.

Marketing Environment

The larger circle represents the uncontrollable environment within which marketers must operate. The marketing environment is categorized further into social, economic, competitive, technological, legal/political, and institutional environments. Each of these categories is examined in detail in Chapter 2 *(The Global Marketing Environment)*.

Marketing is largely concerned with identifying market opportunities and responding to these opportunities by developing and executing effective marketing strategies. Market opportunities are typically the result of conditions or changes in the marketing environment.

Exhibit 1–9

A contemporary marketing framework

Thus, successful marketing requires constant assessment of the marketing environment to identify opportunities and to determine the best way to capitalize on them. The difficulty is that the marketing environment is complex, turbulent, and uncertain.

Key Marketing Perspectives

We have identified seven key marketing perspectives to guide marketers in responding effectively to opportunities offered by the marketing environment (see Exhibit 1–9). These perspectives provide links between marketing and the marketing environment. The seven key marketing perspectives are presented in Exhibit 1–10 and were discussed in the Prologue about Yum! Brands.

David Power, President, Power Creative, comments on the importance of these key marketing perspectives: "These key marketing perspectives are extremely important in my business. Our clients operate globally, so we must have a global perspective to meet their needs. Relationships with customers and teamwork within our company are critical to our success. We must continuously look for ways to create value for our customers and to ensure we do business ethically. Increasing our productivity and the productivity of our clients is a constant concern. Often, this requires being entrepreneurial, especially in using new technologies. We must be at the "cutting edge" in applying new technologies in innovative ways. This will continue to be a challenge as the use of the Internet in marketing and e-commerce grows."

Marketing

The inner circle represents marketing as an organizational philosophy and process. Most of this book expands on topics that fit within this circle: the marketing concept and customer equity, and marketing exchanges, strategies, activities, positions,

Exhibit 1–10   *Key marketing perspectives*

Marketing Perspective	Definition
GLOBAL	Viewing the world as the potential marketplace to include identifying and responding both to market opportunities around the world and to different cultural groups within each market.
RELATIONSHIP	Building partnerships with firms outside the organization and encouraging teamwork among different functions within the organization in order to develop long-term customer relationships.
ETHICS	Addressing the morality of marketing decisions and practicing social responsibility to include ecological considerations.
CUSTOMER VALUE	Constantly looking for ways to give customers more for less.
PRODUCTIVITY	Trying to get the best return for each marketing dollar spent.
TECHNOLOGY	Translating new and emerging technologies into successful products and services, and using technology to improve marketing practice.
ENTREPRENEURSHIP	Focusing on innovation, on risk taking, and on being proactive in marketing efforts.

and institutions. Special attention is given to the process of selecting target markets and creating marketing mixes for the development of effective marketing strategies.

After examining key aspects of the marketing environment in Chapter 2 (*The Global Marketing Environment*), we discuss the important strategic roles of marketing within an organization in Chapter 3 (*Marketing's Strategic Role in the Organization*).

Selecting target markets requires understanding buyer behavior. Chapter 4 (*Consumer Buying Behavior and Decision Making*) and Chapter 5 (*Business-to-Business Markets and Buying Behavior*) present buying behavior from the perspective of consumers and organizations. The process for obtaining information about buying behavior and other important information is covered in Chapter 6 (*Marketing Research and Decision Support Systems*). Chapter 7 (*Market Segmentation and Targeting*) shows how to use this information to segment markets and then target specific markets for the development of marketing mixes.

Each element of the marketing mix is then covered in detail. Chapter 8 (*Product and Service Concepts*), Chapter 9 (*Developing New Products and Services*), and Chapter 10 (*Product and Service Strategies*) address the important product strategy decisions to include developing new products and services and managing multiple products and services throughout their life cycles. Pricing decisions are discussed in Chapter 11 (*Pricing Concepts*) and Chapter 12 (*Price Determination and Pricing Strategies*). Important aspects of distributing products to customers are covered in Chapter 13 (*Marketing Channels*), Chapter 14 (*Retailing*), and Chapter 15 (*Wholesaling and Logistics Management*). Developing an effective integrated marketing communications strategy to achieve specific objectives is discussed in Chapter 16 (*An Overview of Marketing Communications*), Chapter 17 (*Advertising and Public Relations*), Chapter 18 (*Consumer and Trade Sales Promotion*), Chapter 19 (*Personal Selling and Sales Management*), and Chapter 20 (*Direct Marketing Communications*). An example that illustrates how all of these areas are interrelated and must be addressed to develop effective marketing strategies is presented in Appendix A (*Developing a Marketing Plan*).

Summary

1. **Discuss what marketing is and why it is important to organizations and individuals.** Marketing "is the process of planning and executing the conception, pricing, promotion, and distribution of ideas, goods, and services to create exchanges that satisfy individual and organizational goals." Marketing is important to all types of organizations because it focuses on satisfying the needs of customers. Individuals, such as politicians, also engage in marketing during campaigns for election and when developing and implementing policies. Marketing activities are performed by people in various positions at different organizations. Interacting with people is a major component of most marketing positions.

2. **Distinguish between marketing as an organizational philosophy and a societal process.** Marketing can be defined in different ways. As an organizational philosophy, marketing is an orientation where everyone in the organization is driven by the marketing concept to satisfy customer needs. At the societal level, marketing is the process that determines the flow of goods and services from producers to consumers in a society.

3. **Understand the components of a marketing strategy and the different activities involved in marketing products and services.** A marketing strategy consists of the selection of a target market and the development of a marketing mix to appeal to that target market. The marketing mix is an integration of product, price, communications, and distribution decisions to serve a target market better than competitors.

   Implementing marketing strategies to facilitate exchanges requires many activities, including buying, selling, transporting, storing, financing, risk taking, standardizing and grading, and obtaining marketing information.

4. **Be aware of the various types of marketing institutions and the different marketing positions available in these institutions.** The necessary marketing activities are performed by different institutions and various positions within these institutions. Although some producers can perform all required marketing activities, organizations specializing in specific marketing activities are often used. Typical marketing institutions are wholesalers, retailers, distributors, marketing research firms, and advertising agencies.

   Important marketing positions include marketing managers, product managers, advertising managers, purchasing managers, sales managers, marketing research managers, and individuals who report to these managers. Marketing activities are also performed by people in nonmarketing positions.

5. **Understand the basic elements and relationships in the contemporary marketing framework.** The contemporary marketing framework depicts the important relationship between marketing and the marketing environment. Seven key marketing perspectives are presented as orientations that drive marketing's interactions with the external environment.

Understanding Marketing Terms and Concepts

Thinking About Marketing

1. How can top management in an organization ensure that all employees are driven by a marketing philosophy?

2. What is an example of barter as a marketing exchange?

3. How would you describe the major target market and marketing mix for your college or university?

4. What are the marketing activities required to get toothpaste from a producer, such as Colgate-Palmolive, to a consumer, such as yourself?

5. What marketing activities do Internet auctions like ebay.com perform?

6. What are the relationships between marketing as a societal process and the economic and political systems in a country?

7. What do you think is the most innovative development in marketing practice during the past few years? Why?

8. What types of marketing positions interest you? Why?

9. Why is building customer equity important?

10. How can developing marketing knowledge and skills help you in your career?

Applying Marketing Skills

1. Pick a retail store at which you frequently shop. Identify and discuss the store's target market and the specific product, price, integrated marketing communications, and distribution decisions the management has made to develop a marketing mix.

2. Interview someone in a marketing position. Ask him or her about the activities involved in the position, about

any expected future changes in the position, and about career opportunities.

3. Identify a nonprofit organization in your community. Determine the role of marketing in this organization by reading promotional materials and talking with someone in the organization.

Using the www in Marketing

Activity One Go to Amazon.com's home page (http://www.amazon.com).

1. What are the latest products and services offered by Amazon.com?

2. What services does Amazon.com offer to help you select a DVD player that will best meet your needs?

3. Evaluate the selection and services offered by Amazon.com to help customers in purchasing books.

Activity Two Go to the Barnes & Noble home page (http://www.bn.com).

1. Compare and contrast the home pages of Amazon.com and Barnes & Noble.

2. Evaluate the selection and services offered by Barnes & Noble to help customers in purchasing books and compare with what Amazon.com offers.

3. What would you recommend Barnes & Noble do in order to provide more value to its book customers?

Making Marketing Decisions
Case 1-1 *Coca-Cola: Reviving a Marketing Giant*

Coca-Cola has been one of the world's great marketers. Under the tutelage of Roberto C. Goizueta, Coke built a strong market position around the world and achieved strong sales and earnings growth for 16 straight years. Its stock increased a whopping 3,500 percent during this period. Unfortunately, Mr. Goizueta died of cancer in 1997. M. Douglas Ivester, chief financial officer at the time, took over as CEO.

Mr. Ivester has faced a number of challenges during his tenure. Coke's international growth slowed considerably due largely to poor economic conditions and other problems in several international markets. For example, economic problems in Japan, Brazil, Russia, and Latin America have hurt sales.

The situation in the United States is also difficult. American consumers already drink more soft drinks than in any country in the world, except Mexico; therefore, domestic sales growth will have to come from increases in market share. But Coke's major competitor, Pepsi, is fighting for every piece of the market.

Although Coke's problems were not all Ivester's fault, the company's lackluster performance had reduced its stock price substantially and put Ivester under enormous pressure. On December 6, 1999, he stunned everyone by announcing his pending retirement in April 2000 and the appointment of Douglas N. Daft as the new CEO.

Daft had been in charge of Coke's Asia operations. Whereas Ivester had a financial background and spent

most of his career at Coke's headquarters in Atlanta, Daft is a marketing person with extensive experience around the world including the Middle East and China. Daft faced the same problems as Ivester. He tried to instill a more marketing-oriented philosophy throughout the company, increased marketing expenditures, and tried to improve relationships with bottlers. These efforts have not turned around Coke's situation as U.S. and international sales growth has been flat and earnings have declined for the past three years.

One new strategy is to focus more on health-conscious consumers who drink bottled water and sports drinks. The market for noncarbonated beverages is growing more than 60 percent faster than that for soft drinks. Coke owns Dasani water and Powerade energy drink. However, Pepsi has Aquafina water and Gatorade sports drink, which are market leaders. Americans now drink an average of only 10 cases of bottled water a year, so there is room for growth. There are also growth opportunities for noncarbonated beverages internationally, and Coke has a stronger position against Pepsi outside the United States. It will be interesting to see how the "cola wars" turn into the "noncarbonated drink wars."

Questions

1. Do you think Coke should focus on the U.S. or international noncarbonated drink market? Why?

2. Ivester employed a production-oriented philosophy during his tenure as CEO. What does Daft need to do to instill a marketing philosophy throughout Coke?

3. What would you recommend Coke do to increase its soft drink sales in the United States?

4. What would you recommend Coke do to increase its soft drink sales internationally?

Case 1-2 *Jollibee: Beating McDonald's in Burgers*

 McDonald's is clearly the most successful fast-food brand in the world, with annual sales around $30 billion. It dominates most markets by providing customers with consistent product quality and service—but not in the Philippines.

Jollibee Foods Corp. is a family-owned chain with about P6.1 billion annual sales. It has, however, captured about 52 percent of the Philippines market (compared with 16 percent for McDonald's). The company has twice as many stores in the Philippines as McDonald's does. How has Jollibee's been able to beat McDonald's in this market?

The major key to success is understanding and meeting the needs of the local market. Jollibee offers spicy burgers, fried chicken, and spaghetti and serves rice with all entrees. The food is similar to what "a Filipino mother would cook at home" and is designed "to suit the Filipino palate." And Jollibee charges prices from 5 to 10 percent lower than McDonald's. This combination of the right food at a lower price gives customers real value.

Jollibee also uses some marketing approaches that have been borrowed from McDonald's. It works hard to attract kids by targeting ads to children, providing in-store play activities, and offering signature characters and other licensed toys and products. The company locates restaurants in prime spots often surrounding a McDonald's outlet. And Jollibee maintains high standards for fast service and cleanliness.

The company is trying to duplicate its success in the Philippines in other international markets. It currently has restaurants in 10 countries—even in the United States. Although Jollibee has plans to expand internationally in Asia, the Middle East, and the United States, its major focus is to be the leading food service company in the Philippines.

The company now serves over one million Filipinos a day at its 400 restaurants. It has expanded into the pizza-pasta, French café-bakery, and oriental quick service restaurant market segments by acquiring Greenwich Pizza, Delifrance, and Chowking. The basic marketing strategy for all of its restaurants is based on a superior menu lineup, creative marketing programs, efficient manufacturing and logistics facilities, and cheerful and friendly service. The company is highly respected by the Filipino people. In fact, every time a new store is opened, especially overseas, Filipinos form long lines to support the store opening.

Questions

1. Why do you think McDonald's has not been more successful against Jollibee in the Philippines?

2. What would you recommend McDonald's do to increase its market share in the Philippines?

3. What is your evaluation of Jollibee's strategy to expand into Asian, Middle East, and U.S. markets?

4. What marketing strategy would you recommend to Jollibee for successful operations in the U.S. market? How do you think McDonald's will respond as Jollibee enters the U.S. market?

2

The Global Marketing Environment

After studying this chapter, you should be able to:

1 Understand the nature of the marketing environment and why it is important to marketers.

2 Describe the major components of the social environment and how trends in the social environment affect marketing.

3 Understand how the economic environment affects marketing.

4 See how the political/legal environment offers opportunities and threats to marketers.

5 Appreciate the importance of the technological environment to marketers.

6 Understand differences in the competitive environment.

7 Know how changes in the institutional environment affect marketers.

dell.com

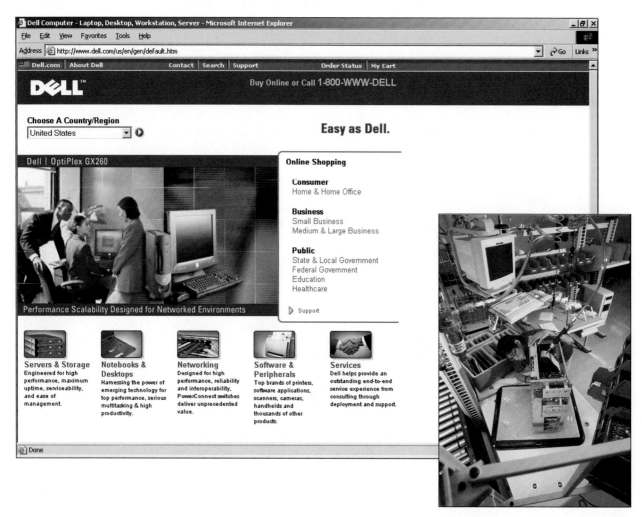

Michael Dell founded Dell Computer Corporation with $1,000 when he was a college student at the University of Texas at Austin in 1984. Today, Dell is the world's leading direct computer systems company with annual revenues in excess of $31 billion and over 34,000 employees.

Why has Dell been so successful? The major reason is that Michael Dell revolutionized the computer industry by introducing the direct model. Prior to Dell, most personal computers were sold through various middlemen—wholesalers and retailers—to the final customer. Dell did not think these middlemen added much value, so he developed a model to bypass them. The basic direct model aims "to deliver a superior customer experience through direct, comprehensive customer relationships, cooperative research and development with technology partners, computer systems custom-built to customer specifications, and service and support programs tailored to customer needs." So, if you go to the Dell Web site, you can select from various options to create the exact PC you desire. The computer will then be shipped directly to you. You can also check the Web site to follow your PC throughout the assembly process and keep track of it throughout the shipping process.

Dell now sells PCs and other computer products to business customers, government agencies, educational institutions, and consumers. The company is enhancing the direct model by applying the Internet to its entire business. Over $50 million is purchased from Dell's Web site each day. The company's Web site receives 775 million page requests per quarter at 80 country sites in 27 languages/dialects and 40 currencies. Dell also uses the Internet to interact with suppliers and to provide various customer services. For example, over 113,000 business and institutional customers are engaged in online business activities with Dell.

The poor economic conditions of the past few years have reduced PC purchases by individuals and organizations. Dell has responded to this situation by using its efficient business model to focus on the low-end server market. This has been a successful response. Even though industrywide server shipments dropped 2.3 percent in 2001, Dell's unit sales increased 27 percent with its market share increasing to 20 percent. Because Dell has much lower operating expenses than its major competitors, it can offer server customers low prices and still be profitable.

The Dell example illustrates how the marketing environment affects a firm's operations. The **marketing environment** consists of all factors external to an organization that can affect the organization's marketing activities. These factors are largely uncontrollable, although marketers can influence some of them. All marketers face the difficult task of identifying the important elements of the marketing environment for their organization, assessing current and likely future relationships between these factors, and developing effective strategies for a changing environment. This task has become increasingly difficult in recent years, as many elements of the marketing environment change rapidly and unpredictably. The objective of this chapter is to help you understand the important elements and relationships in the marketing environment.

The Marketing Environment

In the contemporary marketing framework diagrammed in Chapter One (Exhibit 1–9), the marketing environment appears in the outer circle. We now expand that framework by describing the major elements of the marketing environment. Exhibit 2–1 presents the addition of the social, economic, political/legal, technological, competitive, and institutional environments to the original diagram.

The best way to understand the marketing environment is to place yourself in the middle of the marketing circle. You are now a marketer for some organization and must make decisions about the marketing exchanges, strategies, activities, positions, and institutions employed by your organization. However, the decisions you *can* control depend on factors and trends in the marketing environment that you

Exbibit 2–1   *Expanding the contemporary marketing framework*

cannot control. Thus, your task as a marketer is largely to identify opportunities or threats in the marketing environment and then make marketing decisions that capitalize on the opportunities and minimize the threats.

Creation of Market Opportunities and Threats

The marketing environment creates opportunities or threats in two basic ways. First, changes in the marketing environment can directly affect specific markets. A **market** is a group of people or organizations with common needs to satisfy or problems to solve, with the money to spend to satisfy needs or solve problems, and with the authority to make expenditure decisions. Changes in the marketing environment can make markets larger or smaller or sometimes create new markets. Market opportunities typically arise when markets increase in size or new markets are created.

Take the Dell Computer situation. Increased layoffs, higher unemployment, and lower stock prices reduced the number of consumers and organizations willing to purchase PCs. Dell responded to this decrease in the size of the PC market by increasing its efforts in the low-end server market. Many organizations had to have more servers to increase their Internet capacity, even though economic conditions were not good. Dell offered the types of servers needed at a low price. These organizational customers found the low-priced servers very attractive, and Dell's server sales increased during a period when industry sales were decreasing.[1]

The second way the marketing environment produces opportunities or threats is through direct influences on specific marketing activities. Rapid advancements in Internet technology have provided Dell with opportunities to reach new markets and to serve customers more effectively and efficiently. Customers can now order customized computers, receive customer service, and get technical support 24 hours a day and seven days a week. Interacting with customers over the Internet is not only more convenient to customers, but is also less costly to Dell. So, utilization of the Internet gives customers a better experience and increases Dell's profitability. However, changes in the marketing environment also pose threats. Many companies, such as Gateway and IBM, are using a direct model and incorporating the Internet into marketing operations. This increases the competitive intensity within the industry.

The critical point of this discussion is that marketers need to understand the marketing environment to be able to make good decisions. Changes in the marketing environment may create opportunities or threats either by affecting markets or by

Using Technology

Turning data into valuable marketing information

Business intelligence software (BI) is being used by many companies to increase marketing effectiveness and efficiency. The software analyzes price, sales, cost, and other data to produce reports that help companies make better marketing decisions. Consider the following examples:

- After September 11 Las Vegas hotels were empty. Harrah's used BI software to identify potential customers within driving distance. It sent special offers to these customers and filled its hotels within two weeks.
- Ace Hardware uses BI software to analyze price and sales data from its stores and those of competitors to

help set its prices. Prices set in this manner have increased customer traffic at its stores and margins have grown from 32 percent to 39 percent.

- British Airways analyzed lost luggage complaints and found that it needed to increase minimum transfer times for luggage to connecting flights. It advised customers of these times and decreased complaints significantly.
- Coty analyzed sales data and found it was losing profits by focusing too much on makeup and not enough on toiletries, such as shampoo and shaving cream. It changed its strategy and profits increased.

directly influencing marketing activities. Interesting examples of using new technology to improve marketing efforts are presented in "Using Technology: Turning Data Into Valuable Marketing Information."

Identifying Market Opportunities and Threats

Many firms use **environmental scanning** to identify important trends and determine whether they represent present or future market opportunities or threats. As illustrated in Exhibit 2–2, this procedure consists of identifying relevant factors, determining expected trends, and assessing their potential impact on the organization's markets and marketing activities. This is simpler to say than do, because many of the potentially important environmental factors are interrelated and many of them change constantly.

Skandia, the $7 billion Swedish financial services giant, used an interesting approach to identify future growth opportunities. The company established a new unit, Skandia Future Center, and selected 30 diverse people from around the world to form five Future Teams. Each Future Team consisted of a mix of people from three generations (20-somethings to 60-somethings), who also represented a variety of functional roles, organizational experiences, and cultural backgrounds. The mission of each Future Team was to explore one of five major environmental forces (the European insurance market, demographics, technology, the world economy, and organizations and leadership) and develop a vision of the future for Skandia. The Future Teams presented their ideas to a group of 150 executives. The executives then formed 20 small groups to brainstorm responses to the ideas developed by the Future Teams. The process produced several innovative ways for Skandia to grow in the future.[2]

Marketers must continually monitor the marketing environment to identify trends in relevant areas and develop appropriate responses. Some aspects of the marketing environment are more controllable than others. For example, firms can have a direct impact on the legal/political environment through lobbying, campaign contributions, and various political activities. Many companies, therefore, are proactive in trying to influence the legal/political environment in a way that is advantageous for their business. In contrast, firms have little control over the demographic environment, so must typically react to current and expected demographic trends. The key is to understand what is happening and likely to happen in a firm's marketing environment and then determine the best proactive or reactive actions for the company to capitalize on opportunities and minimize threats.

| Exbibit 2–2 | *The environmental scanning approach* |

Social Environment

The **social environment** includes all factors and trends related to groups of people, including their number, characteristics, behavior, and growth projections. Since consumer markets have specific needs and problems, changes in the social environment can affect markets differently. Trends in the social environment might increase the size of some markets, decrease the size of others, or even help to create new markets. We discuss two important components of the social environment: the demographic environment and the cultural environment.

Demographic Environment

The **demographic environment** refers to the size, distribution, and growth rate of groups of people with different characteristics. The demographic characteristics of interest to marketers relate in some way to purchasing behavior, because people from different countries, cultures, age groups, or household arrangements often exhibit different purchasing behaviors. A global perspective requires that marketers be familiar with important demographic trends around the world as well as within the United States.

GLOBAL POPULATION SIZE AND GROWTH

Population size and growth rates provide one indication of potential market opportunities. The world population is now more than six billion, with almost 100 million people added each year during the 1990s. Thus, the world population grew about one billion during the decade of the 1990s. Approximately 95 percent of that growth took place in developing countries in Asia, Africa, and Latin America.[3] Population in the developed countries grew at a much slower rate. These trends are expected to continue with world population reaching 7.2 billion by 2015.

There is a tremendous disparity in population size and growth rates across countries, as shown in Exhibit 2–3. China currently has the largest population, followed by India, with the United States a distant third. The rapid growth of the Indian population is expected to make it the world's most populous nation. Other countries with large and growing populations are the developing nations of Indonesia, Brazil, Pakistan, Bangladesh, and Nigeria.

The market for many products and services is global. Gillette advertises razors to women in Germany.

Exbibit 2–3   *The most populous countries in 2025*

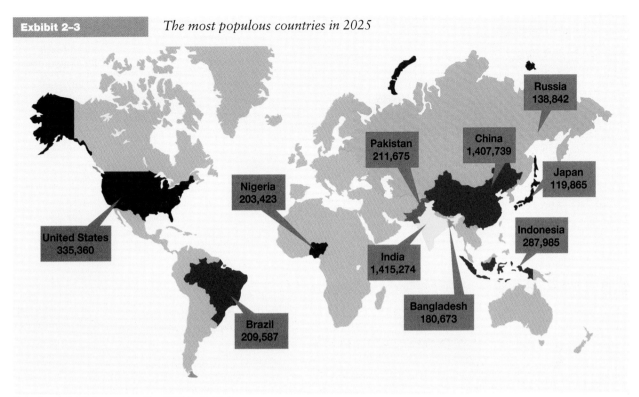

Note: Population in thousands—Year 2025 (estimated)

The world population situation can be summarized as follows. About every two seconds, nine babies are born and three people die, for a net increase of three people each second. This leads to a growth rate of 10,600 people per hour, 254,000 per day, 1.8 million per week, 7.7 million per month, and 93 million per year. Of this annual increase, developing countries will have 87 million new people, and developed countries, 6 million. Annual growth will increase to 98 million by the year 2020, with 98 percent occurring in developing countries.[4]

These world population statistics make it clear that marketers cannot rely on population growth in developed countries alone for general increases in market size. The largest growth markets, measured by population size, are in the developing countries. Yet, lower income levels in developing countries may limit the actual market size for many products. Thus, marketers will have to look hard to find attractive growth markets in developed and developing countries.

GLOBAL DEMOGRAPHIC CHARACTERISTICS AND TRENDS   Overall world and country population statistics are important, but most marketers target subgroups within these large populations. Trends in population subgroups are therefore typically the most useful to marketers.

An important trend in many countries is growth of the urban population. Current and projected populations for the world's largest cities are presented in Exhibit 2–4. In general, the largest cities and the highest city growth rates are in developing countries such as Mexico, Brazil, and India; however, growth in urban population is evident in many developed countries. For example, in 1900, the U.S. population was 39.6 percent urban and 60.4 percent rural; in 1990, the figures were 75.2 percent urban and 24.8 percent rural.[5] This means the largest and fastest-growing markets for many products are located in the urban areas of most countries.

Another interesting trend is the aging of the population in many countries. Current and projected median ages for selected countries are presented in Exhibit 2–5. The aging of the population is especially evident in Italy, Japan, Britain, and the United States. Notice, however, the relatively young populations in the developing countries, such as Nigeria, Mexico, Brazil, and China.

Exhibit 2-4	*The world's largest cities*

City	1995 (in thousands)	2015 (est.) (in thousands)
1. Tokyo, Japan	26,959	28,887
2. Mexico City, Mexico	16,562	19,190
3. São Paulo, Brazil	16,533	20,320
4. New York, U.S.	16,332	17,602
5. Mumbai (Bombay), India	15,138	26,218
6. Shanghai, China	13,584	17,969
7. Los Angeles, U.S.	12,410	14,217
8. Calcutta, India	11,923	17,305
9. Buenos Aires, Argentina	11,802	13,856
10. Seoul, South Korea	11,609	12,980

Exhibit 2-5	*Median age in selected countries*

Country	Median Ages Past & Projected	
	1990	2010
Italy	36.2	42.4
Japan	37.2	42.2
Britain	35.7	40.0
U.S.	32.9	37.4
Korea (North & South)	25.7	34.4
China	25.4	33.9
Brazil	22.9	29.2
Mexico	20.0	26.5
Nigeria	16.3	18.1

Age distribution trends in the United States are presented in more detail in Exhibit 2–6. The largest percentage of growth is occurring in the 45–64 and 65+ age brackets, with slight to moderate decreases in all younger age categories. These trends have important implications for marketers; older consumers have different needs and purchasing habits than do younger consumers. Marketers are responding to different age markets in a number of ways. For instance,

- Take Home Instead Senior Care is responding to the needs of those in their 70s and 80s. The company provides "nonmedical companionship" through services such as mail sorting, letter writing, meal preparation, incidental transportation, laundry, and helping clients remember to take medication. Business is booming.[6]

- Financial institutions have increased marketing efforts to attract mature Americans. Mutual fund giants T. Rowe Price and Vanguard offer software programs to help older consumers plan for retirement. Merrill Lynch hired a gerontologist to understand mature consumers better and to develop products to suit their goals.[7]

- ESPN developed the Alternative Sports Olympics to appeal to consumers aged 18 to 29. Also called The Extreme Games, the program features sports that attract the so-called Generation X (bungee jumping, street luging, sky surfing, and barefoot water-ski jumping) and are sponsored by companies trying to target those young consumers (Taco Bell, Mountain Dew, Nike, AT&T, and Pontiac). More than 130,000 spectators see the games live and millions watch on television.[8]

Exbibit 2–6   *Age distributon of U.S. population*

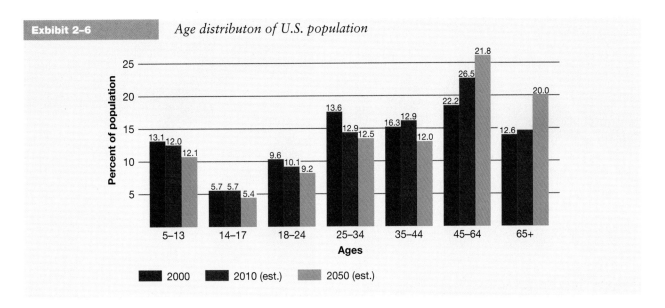

- Sega of America spends a great amount of time trying to understand teens. The company's advertising agency visits the homes of 150 teens and goes shopping with them at the malls. This information helps Sega introduce new video games successfully.[9]

Yet another relevant demographic trend is the declining number of household units consisting of the "typical" family: married couples with children living at home. Only 26 percent of U.S. households fall into this category, down from 45 percent in 1972. People living with nonrelatives is a fast-growing household type, up 62 percent since 1972.[10] In addition, about 23 million Americans live by themselves. This is an increase of 91 percent for women and 156 percent for men since 1980.[11] The needs and purchasing behaviors of different household arrangements represent important trends affecting marketers.

Cultural Environment

The **cultural environment** refers to factors and trends related to how people live and behave. Cultural factors, including the values, ideas, attitudes, beliefs, and activities of specific population subgroups, greatly affect consumers' purchasing behavior. Thus, marketers must understand important cultural characteristics and trends in different markets.

CULTURAL DIVERSITY   Cultural differences are important in both international and domestic markets. A cultural group's characteristics affect the types of products it desires and how it purchases and uses those products. Different cultural groups in international markets often require marketers to develop strategies specifically for them.

Campbell's Soup has had some successes and some failures in doing this. The successes include hearty vegetable and fat-free soups in Australia, duck-gizzard soup in Hong Kong, and the Godiva Chocolatier line in Japan. But the company has had some failures due to lack of understanding cultural differences in some markets. German consumers did not like Campbell's canned condensed soup. They prefer dry soups in envelopes. Polish consumers did not like Campbell's prepared soups, since they would rather cook soup at home.[12]

Much of the population growth in the United States is and will be accounted for by different cultural groups. The majority U.S. population grew about 3 percent between 1990 and 2000. Compare this with the 14 to 52 percent growth rates of different ethnic groups. A large portion of this population growth is accounted for by

There are 3 billion people in Asia. Half of them are under 25. Consider it a growing market.

You meet their needs. We meet yours. In the last two years alone, we've opened new offices in Bandung, Bangalore, Batam, Hanoi, Ho Chi Minh City, Kandy, Labuan and Qingdao. If it's in Asia, to us, it's just around the corner.   HongkongBank
The Hongkong and Shanghai Banking Corporation Limited
Member HSBC Group

Populations in developed countries are aging, while those in developing countries are much younger. These different demographic trends represent challenging marketing opportunities for many firms.

African-Americans, Asian-Americans, and Hispanics.[13] However, significant growth also came from other cultural groups: Arabs, Russians, Eastern Europeans, and Caribbeans.[14]

These different cultural groups retain many of their habits, attitudes, interests, and behaviors even though they are proud to be Americans. The United States is not a melting pot; it's a mosaic of unique people with a variety of cultures. Successful marketers understand the delicate balance between important cultural differences and similarities that unite different cultures.[15] For example, the Arab-American sector consists of a diverse group of people from 22 different countries, with the largest subgroups being Egyptians, Syrians, Lebanese, Palestinians, and Iraqis. Although these subgroups differ in various ways, there is also a cohesiveness among them due to their common Arab heritage.[16]

Another interesting trend is a blending of races and ethnic groups. It is estimated that by 2050, the percentage of the U.S. population that claims some combination of black, white, Hispanic, or Asian ancestry will triple to 21 percent. Singer Mariah Carey and TV news anchor Soledad O'Brien (black, white, and Hispanic) and golfer Tiger Woods (black, white, American Indian, and Asian) are prominent examples of this trend.[17]

This cultural complexity provides marketers with a continual challenge. Take the Hispanic market as an example. The Hispanic population in the United States is in excess of 31 million, with more than $300 billion in purchasing power. Effectively marketing to Hispanics requires much more than translating marketing communications into Spanish. The California Milk Processor Board (CMPB) found this out. It had used the theme "got milk?" to increase milk consumption by the mass market. When it tried to translate this theme to the Hispanic women's market, two interesting things were discovered. First, running out of milk is not funny to Hispanic women; it is an insult. Second, the translation of "got milk?" into Spanish means "are you lactating?" Based on these findings, the CMPB developed a multigenera-

More women are playing golf. This expanding market offers attractive opportunities for many firms.

tional, family-focused campaign about passing down milk-based recipes. Interestingly, Hispanic teens responded enthusiastically to the "got milk?" campaign.[18]

These examples in the Hispanic market illustrate the importance of understanding the diversity among and within different cultural markets for developing successful marketing strategies. There are typically opportunities to market products across some cultural groups and to also target specific cultural groups. Sometimes, products from one culture can appeal to consumers in another culture. Princess Asie Acansey of Ghana capitalized on such an opportunity when she formed Advanced Business Connections (ABC). She was disturbed about the imagery of Africa as typically presented in the United States and decided to do something about it. ABC infuses African culture into the American teddy bear. The teddy bears represent African royalty and follow African royal customs. The first teddy bear was the king's protocol officer, Kwesi-Bear, then King Tutu Bear, followed by Queen Abena. Most of ABC's marketing has been on the QVC home shopping network. The products have been well received beyond the African-American market in the United States, illustrating the potential from mixing different cultures.[19]

CHANGING ROLES   As more women enter the workforce and household compositions change, typical household roles are altered. No longer are financially supporting the household and developing a career solely the responsibility of men. No longer are household chores, child care, or grocery shopping solely the responsibility of women. In many households, roles have shifted and distinctions have become blurred. More men spend time on household and shopping chores, and many women are involved in career development and provide much or most of the financial resources for a household. Tremendous market opportunities exist for firms that can develop effective strategies for appealing to these changing roles.

Take golf as an example. Women now account for about 21 percent of the 25 million golfers in the United States. And this percentage is growing. Some of this growth is due to more women playing golf as part of their business or professional life. Others play the sport entirely for pleasure. In any case, women spend about $3 billion annually on golf equipment, clothing, travel, greens fees, and other related products. One study found that women are more likely to take golf lessons, are less price sensitive, and are more concerned about wearing fashionable clothing than are men golfers. This growing, upscale market of female golfers is attractive to marketers of golf products as well as marketers of other products.[20]

Busy people look for ways to make life easier. Lands' End provides a convenient way for men and women to shop for clothes.

EMPHASIS ON HEALTH AND FITNESS   Another cultural trend is an increased emphasis on health and fitness. The pursuit of a healthier lifestyle includes eating more nutritious foods, exercising regularly, participating in various sports activities, and focusing on wellness. This translates into potential market opportunities for firms that provide products and services geared toward improving health and fitness.

Consider how firms are taking advantage of this social trend in the beverage industry:

- Nutriceuticals combine exotic fruits with medicinal plants and herbs to promote various health benefits. For example, Mrs. Wiggle's Rocket juice offers Papaya Ginseng to boost energy; Nantucket Super Nectars markets Ginko

Mango to enhance mental acuity; and Fresh Samantha introduced Spirulina Fruit Blend to strengthen the immune system.[21]

- John Bello founded South Beach Beverage Company to market a line of herb-spiked teas and tonics. The drinks are intended "to uplift the mind, body, and spirit" and carry exotic names, such as Jing and Qi. Sales have been brisk.[22]

DESIRE FOR CONVENIENCE   Changes in household composition, increases in the number of working women, and a general shortage of time underlie an increased desire for convenience. Two-paycheck households often have more money than time. And they are willing to spend this money to avoid spending time doing undesirable chores, such as cooking, cleaning, or auto maintenance. Thus, many consumers buy products and services to minimize time devoted to such chores, opening new market opportunities for companies able to meet these needs.

Think of all the products and services that are focused on responding to the increased desire for convenience. Many stores are open for longer hours or even 24 hours; the increased use of drive-in windows for fast food, banking, and prescriptions; delivery services for dry cleaning, fast food, and groceries; and the increasing use of the Internet to shop, make purchases, pay bills, communicate with e-mail, and perform many other activities. The desire for convenience is likely to continue to increase in the future. This will create opportunities for marketers to offer their customers more convenient products and services.

CONSUMERISM   *Consumerism* is the movement to establish and protect the rights of buyers. Some say the consumerism movement will intensify as we move through the twenty-first century. Consumers are more educated, knowledgeable, and organized. They will demand better consumer information, quality, service, and dependability, and fair prices.[23] Giving consumers products that work, charging fair prices, being honest, and practicing social responsibility are the best ways to respond to consumerism.

One increasingly important consumer issue is environmentalism. As consumers worldwide become concerned with environmental issues, their purchasing behavior will change. Successful marketers can respond by developing environmentally safe products and communicating their environmental contributions.

Ogallala Down Co. is taking advantage of this trend. The company's philosophy is, "Healthy products for people and the environment." It markets down comforters and pillows that are hypoallergenic, warm, lightweight, breathable, and guaranteed for 10 years. Established in 1989, the company has enjoyed rapid sales growth in an industry long dominated by large firms. The American Marketing Association recognized the environmental achievements of Ogallala Down by presenting it with an Edison Environmental Award.[24]

POPULAR CULTURE   The final cultural trend we note is the popularization of the U.S. culture throughout much of the world. Movies, television shows, and commercials typically express a culture's values and attitudes, and U.S. food, fashion, and entertainment trends are becoming increasingly popular worldwide. Technological advances and globalization of the media allow the export of this popular culture, resulting in a variety of market opportunities.

China represents a good example of this trend. The Chinese market consists of 1.2 billion people and 305 million TV sets. Much of the TV programming contains U.S. popular culture. For example, Disney provides the

Consumers worldwide are becoming more concerned about the environment. Fordwerke appeals to these concerns by marketing a toy made from recycled auto parts. The headline reads: "I was a car."

Dragon Club Show on cable systems, and Viacom offers one to five hours daily of MTV on cable systems. The Chinese people seem to enjoy these shows. Peng Jinglong, a Beijing high school student, is a fan of the Cartoon Network's *Tom and Jerry* cartoons:

Chinese cartoons can't compare. American cartoons are more lighthearted and funnier. And the stories are better.[25]

Economic Environment

The **economic environment** includes factors and trends related to income levels and the production of goods and services. Whereas demographic and cultural trends generally affect the size and needs of various markets, economic trends affect the purchasing power of these markets. Thus, it is not enough for a population to be large or fast growing, as in many developing countries, to offer good market opportunities; the economy must provide sufficient purchasing power for consumers to satisfy their wants and needs.

Economic trends in different parts of the world can affect marketing activities in other parts of the world. For example, changes in interest rates in Europe affect the value of the dollar on world currency markets, which affects the price, and subsequently sales, of American exports and imports.

Market opportunities are a function of both economic size and growth. The **gross domestic product (GDP)** represents the total size of a country's economy measured in the amount of goods and services produced. Changes in GDP indicate trends in economic activity. However, changes in economic growth around the world mean that market opportunities are often shifting. For example, the Japanese economy experienced slow and erratic growth throughout most of the 1990s, and the Asian economic crisis of 1997, the Russian crisis of 1998, and the recent problems in Argentina reduced opportunities in these markets. Economic growth slowed throughout much of the world in 2001, but recovery began in late 2002. However, there were significant differences in both economic decline and recovery across countries. Korea and Japan are interesting examples. Korea experienced GDP growth of 8.8 percent in 2000, 1.7 percent in 2001, and about 3.3 percent in 2002. Compare this to the respective growth rates of 2.4 percent, −0.8 percent, and −0.7 percent for Japan. Similar analyses across other countries show differences in economic growth, but not to the extremes between Korea and Japan.[26]

The effect of economic growth on consumer purchasing power is illustrated by the economic downturn in the United States from early 2000 to late 2001. The drop in GDP, increase in unemployment, rise in consumer debt, and decline in the stock market produced a loss in wealth of 12.3 percent, or $4 trillion. The *Business Week* index of household prosperity combines worker income and household net worth. The index declined 2.8 percent from 2000 to 2001. It began to increase slowly in 2002, indicating that economic growth was translating into more purchasing power for consumers and more opportunities for marketers.[27]

Marketing opportunities can often be found by looking at economic differences within countries. For example, many developing countries have large populations relative to their economic strength; that is, the average consumer does not have much purchasing power. However, subgroups within these countries may have substantial purchasing power, or economic growth may offer substantial opportunities in the future. India, for example, has a large and growing population and a low but growing, percapita income. Within this relatively poor country, however, are about 250 million middle-class consumers. This is larger than the total U.S. market. Coca-Cola, Walt Disney, Kentucky Fried Chicken, Frito-Lay, and many other companies have started

Many developing countries have large and growing segments of middle-class consumers. Many companies are targeting the large group of middle-class consumers in India.

Indian operations to take advantage of this opportunity. Motorola estimates 40 to 50 million middle-class families there have the buying power to purchase a telephone or pager. It considers India one of the largest untapped markets in the world.[28]

Samuel Chi-Hung Lee, International Marketing Consultant, Benroth International, discusses the marketing opportunities available in China: "Many of the marketing opportunities available to companies in Hong Kong depend upon economic growth in China. China's entry into the World Trade Organization (WTO) has had a positive economic impact and created many business opportunities for Hong Kong. Many local and international companies have already moved to the northern Chinese cities of Beijing, Shanghai, and Guangzhou. As China prepares for hosting the 2008 Summer Olympics in Beijing many more opportunities will be available to Hong Kong and international companies. The Hong Kong and Chinese governments are also proposing the establishment of a Free Trade Zone in the Pearl River Delta in South China to increase economic activity in this area."

Political/Legal Environment

The **political/legal environment** encompasses factors and trends related to governmental activities and specific laws and regulations that affect marketing practice. The political/legal environment is closely tied to the social and economic environments. That is, pressures from the social environment, such as ecological or health concerns, or the economic environment, such as slow economic growth or high unemployment, typically motivate legislation intended to improve the particular situation. Regulatory agencies implement legislation by developing and enforcing regulations. Therefore, it is important for marketers to understand specific political processes, laws, and regulations, as well as important trends in each of these areas.

Global Political Trends

In today's world economy, international political events greatly affect marketing activities. Probably the most significant global political trend is the "war on terrorism" led by the United States and a coalition of many different countries around the world. These countries are responding to the September 11 terrorist attack on the United States, suicide bombings in Israel, terrorist activity in Kashmir and the Philippines, and other terrorist threats. The threat of terrorism and the "war on terrorism" have changed the way people live and companies do business in many parts of the world. For example, many consumers have reduced or changed their normal travel behavior. This has had a negative impact on all aspects of the travel industry, especially the airline industry. In contrast, the need for increased security has generated marketing opportunities for firms providing security products and services. An example of how one firm has changed its focus to take advantage of the security needs of airports is presented in "Being Entrepreneurial: Marketing Opportunities to Provide Security."

A second important political trend is movement toward free trade and away from protectionism. One approach is the development of trading blocs throughout the world. One of the most significant is the European Union (EU). It consists of 11 Eu-

Being Entrepreneurial

Marketing opportunities to provide security

Douglas Electronics looks like a television repair shop in its redbrick building. In fact, the company started by repairing TVs. However, the company has continually changed to capitalize on marketing opportunities created by changes in customer needs and new technologies. It moved from repairing TVs to VCRs, then began renting TVs to hospitals. It got into the security business because hospitals needed such security systems as infant protection systems. Two years ago, new technology led it into airport security sys-

tems. It installs systems that control access to an airport's jetways. Workers gain access using readable ID cards. If a door is violated, a camera snaps a picture that is given to airport security personnel. The company was growing the airport security business slowly until September 11. Now, business is booming and Douglas Electronics is looking for more ways to use the latest technology to meet the security needs of its airport customers.

ropean countries representing 290 million consumers and a combined GDP of $6.5 trillion. Another is the North American Free Trade Agreement (NAFTA). It consists of the United States, Mexico, and Canada and includes 360 million consumers and $6 trillion GDP.[29] The aim is to eliminate trade barriers and to promote easier access to the markets in each participating country. As this development continues, trading blocs have the potential to generate many opportunities for marketers.

The free trade trend goes beyond trading blocs and encompasses a global perspective. The best example of this perspective is the General Agreement on Tariffs and Trade, or GATT. This agreement was signed by 124 countries in 1994 to eliminate trade barriers worldwide. The World Trade Organization (WTO) was established as the watchdog organization, and a world court was set up in Geneva to arbitrate trade disputes. Although results have been mixed, the WTO is making slow but steady progress toward free trade around the world.[30] China was recently granted WTO membership, and Russia is likely to be admitted in the near future. New global trade talks in Qatar are also scheduled.

There are clear benefits to free trade. For example, a recent study showed that countries with the freest trade had the highest GDP growth from 1990 to 2000.[31] However, achieving free trade in the current environment is difficult for at least two reasons. First, there is often tremendous political pressure to protect specific industries. The United States is one of the major proponents of free trade, but it has established tariffs on imported steel and Canadian softwood lumber and has instituted new farm subsidies.[32] Second, free trade in a global economy requires the free movement of people, goods, and capital across borders. This is difficult to achieve given the need for more security in the "war on terrorism." There is likely to be continued tension among the desire for free trade, the political need for some protectionism, and the security requirements for combating terrorism.

Samuel Chi-Hung Lee, International Marketing Consultant, Benroth International, talks about the political environment in Hong Kong since July 1, 1997: "It has been five years since Hong Kong became a part of China. Certain government departments have been slow and inefficient, and failed to respond to the needs of the Hong Kong people. This has made it difficult for Hong Kong to transform itself economically and break free from its current economic problems. Hong Kong Special Administrative Region (HKSAR) Chief Executive Tung Chee Hwa is making changes to improve the government. The "Principal Officials Accountability System" will allow the chief executive to select a team of 14 key political leaders to guide the HKSAR government. This is a break from the old British system where these government officials came from the civil service ranks. The new approach should improve the government leadership team and make the HKSAR government more responsive and effective."

Legislation

Organizations must deal with laws at the international, federal, state, and local levels. U.S. laws directly affecting marketing typically fall into two categories: those promoting competition among firms and those protecting consumers and society. Exhibit 2–7 presents examples of each type.

Laws promoting competition focus on outlawing practices that give a few firms unfair competitive advantages over others. The specific impact of these laws depends on court rulings that may change over time or differ at the state and national levels. One of the highest profile cases in recent years is *United States* v. *Microsoft*. The government charged that Microsoft routinely used its monopoly power to crush competitors. The first round went to the government, when U.S. District Judge Thomas P. Jackson released his finding of facts in its favor. Microsoft appealed the verdict and has reached a tentative settlement with the Justice Department. However, several states are contesting this settlement, prolonging final resolution of the case.

Consumer protection laws generally indicate what firms must do to give consumers the information they need to make sound purchasing decisions or to ensure

| Exhibit 2–7 | *Key U.S. laws affecting marketing* |

A. Promoting Competition

Act	Purpose
• Sherman Act (1890)	Prohibits monopolistic practices
• Clayton Act (1914)	Prohibits anticompetitive activities
• Federal Trade Commission Act (1914)	Establishes regulatory agency to enforce laws against unfair competition
• Robinson–Patman Act (1936)	Prohibits price discrimination
• Lanham Trademark Act (1946)	Protects trademarks and brand names
• Magnusson–Moss Act (1975)	Regulates warranties
• United States–Canada Trade Act (1988)	Allows free trade between United States and Canada

B. Protecting Consumers & Society

Act	Purpose
• Food, Drug, and Cosmetics Act (1938)	Regulates food, drug, and cosmetic industries
• Fair Packaging and Labeling Act (1966)	Regulates packaging and labeling
• Consumer Credit Protection Act (1968)	Requires full disclosure of financial charges for loans
• Child Protection and Toy Safety Act (1969)	Prevents marketing of dangerous products to children
• Fair Credit Report Act (1970)	Regulates reporting and use of credit information
• Fair Debt Collections Practice Act (1970)	Regulates methods for collecting debts
• Child Protection Act (1990)	Regulates advertising on children's television programs
• Americans with Disabilities Act (1990)	Prohibits discrimination against consumers with disabilities

that the products they buy are safe. For example, the Fair Packaging and Labeling Act requires packages to be labeled honestly; the Child Protection Act regulates the amount of advertising that can appear on children's television programs.

The business press has been inundated with stories about companies such as Enron, WorldCom, Arthur Andersen, Qwest Communications, Tyco International, Global Crossing, and CEOs, such as Martha Stewart, Larry Ellison, Al Dunlap, Kenneth Lay, and Dennis Kozlowski. These stories report many examples of alleged misreporting of earnings, insider trading, tax evasion, securities fraud, obstruction of justice, and other questionable activities. Some of these activities result in unfair competition, others

The "war on terrorism" and corporate scandals will have a major impact on marketers and consumers for many years.

Exhibit 2–8   *Important U.S. regulatory agencies*

Agency	Responsibilities
• Federal Trade Commission (FTC)	Regulates business practices
• Consumer Product Safety Commission (CPSC)	Protects consumers from unsafe products
• Environmental Protection Agency (EPA)	Protects environment
• Food & Drug Administration (FDA)	Regulates food, drug, and cosmetic industries
• Interstate Commerce Commission (ICC)	Regulates interstate transportation industry
• Federal Communications Commission (FCC)	Regulates interstate communications industry

have an adverse effect on consumers. Appropriate government agencies are pursuing these cases under existing laws, but there is a high likelihood that new laws will be passed to improve corporate responsibility and to prosecute offenders more harshly.[33] Because of the global economy, this is a global problem. However, Germany, France, Italy, Finland, Sweden, Hong Kong, Japan, and other countries are implementing different approaches to increase corporate accountability and responsibility.[34]

Regulation and Regulatory Agencies

Most legislation in the United States is enforced through regulations developed by a variety of agencies, and marketers must often work with regulatory authorities at the federal, state, and local levels. Often, regulations are not the same at different governmental levels. For example, the Federal Trade Commission (FTC) enforces guidelines for how firms promote the environmental advantages of their products, but these guidelines do not supersede state laws or regulations. Now, 12 states regulate environmental claims in some way, with more states likely to follow in the future. Sorting through different regulations is a complex task for marketers.[35]

Several of the most important federal agencies are described in Exhibit 2–8. Some of these regulatory agencies cut across industries (FTC, CPSC, EPA); others focus on specific industries (FDA, ICC, FCC). The impact of these regulatory agencies is especially evident in the pharmaceutical industry. The FDA must approve a new drug before it is marketed and can place limitations on its use. For example, the FDA approved Warner-Lambert's anticonvulsant, Neurontin, but only as an add-on therapy for patients taking other epilepsy medications. This stipulation limits Warner-Lambert's marketing efforts for Neurontin.[36] FDA actions can also produce marketing opportunities. The approval of smoking-cessation nicotine drugs as over-the-counter products opened up a large market to marketers of nicotine gum and patches.[37]

One area receiving a great deal of regulatory attention is consumer privacy. This includes restricting the use of information consumers provide to companies, as well as protecting consumers from unwanted telemarketing and e-mail (SPAM) solicitations. The FTC under the Bush administration is taking a somewhat different approach than the Clinton administration by focusing more on enforcing existing regulations than developing new regulations. And, the FTC faces some difficult dilemmas. One example is the passage of the USA Patriot Act in October 2001. This law allows Internet Service Providers (ISPs) and other marketers who handle consumer information to give the government suspicious information, and the government can request specific information from these companies. Balancing the privacy desires of consumers with the information needs of the "war on terrorism" is a difficult task but an issue that will impact many marketers.[38]

Technological Environment

The **technological environment** includes factors and trends related to innovations that affect the development of new products or the marketing process. These technological trends can provide opportunities for new-product development, affect how marketing activities are performed, or both. For example, advances in information and communication technologies provide new products for firms to market, and the buyers of these products often

New technologies provide many opportunities to improve products and services. Advances in wireless technology are generating many new products and services.

use them to change the way they market their own products. Using these technological products can help marketers be more productive.

New technologies can spawn new industries, new businesses, or new products for existing business. Firms at the leading edge of technological developments are in a favorable position. Thus, marketers need to monitor the technological environment constantly to look for potential opportunities that will improve their positions.

Marketers also need to monitor the technological environment to minimize threats to their companies or industries. New technologies can, after all, *disrupt* entire industries as well as enhance them. For example, optical networks are affecting the telecommunications industry, diagnostic technologies are affecting the health care industry, systems-on-a-chip technologies are pressuring the microprocessor industry, and the Internet is having a significant impact on retailing, financial services, and education.[39]

Consider how the following new and emerging technologies offer potential marketing opportunities:

- Nanotechnology is the ability to manipulate individual atoms to create new materials. The technology has already been used to produce a number of interesting products: automotive sideboards that are stronger and lighter than existing ones, vinyl flooring that won't scuff, mattress covers that won't stain, transparent sunscreen, and tennis balls that last twice as long as normal. Products under development include faster semiconductor chips, implantable devices and biosensors for automatically delivering drug doses, hydrogen cells that can power cars, and tiny robots that could clean oceans and attack germs.[40]
- Developments in horticulture will result in new materials of unprecedented strength and flexibility, new sources of food and medicine, and new approaches for renewable energy. Although these developments are in the early stages, horticulture research has already produced from plants composite materials that are stronger than steel.[41]
- Ultrawideband (UWB) represents tiny pulses of radio signals that can zip through airwaves without interfering with cell-phone conversations or broadcasts. Potential applications include a fireman using a UWB "flashlight" to see through walls to locate victims, a camcorder fitted with a UWB chip that could beam home movies to a TV across the room, and a UWB anticollision device that regulates a car's speed, keeping it from getting too close to another car.[42]

Competitive Environment
The **competitive environment** consists of all the organizations that attempt to serve similar customers. Two types of competitors are of major concern: brand competitors and product competitors. **Brand competitors** provide the most direct competition, offering the same types of products as competing firms. For example, Nike is a brand competitor of Reebok, Adidas, and other firms that market different brands of the same types of sport shoes. These firms target the same markets and typically try to take customers away from one another.

Product competitors offer different types of products to satisfy the same general need. Domino's Pizza, McDonald's, and Kentucky Fried Chicken are product competitors. They attempt to satisfy a consumer need for fast food, but they offer somewhat different menus and services. Domino's, McDonald's, and KFC also have brand competitors, which market the same types of fast food to the same customers. Brand competitors of Domino's, for example, are Pizza Hut, Papa John's Pizza, and Little Caesar's Pizza.

The competitive environment for most firms is fierce and often global. Marketers must identify their relevant brand and product competitors in order to identify market opportunities and develop marketing strategies. One trend affecting many industries is the changing competitive landscape. Some product competitors have become brand competitors by expanding their product offerings.

Consider the financial services industry. Banks used to compete against banks, insurance companies against insurance companies, brokerage firms against brokerage firms. Now, many banks, insurance companies, and brokerage houses offer a range of financial services products that compete directly with one another. And new competitors are entering the market, especially through the Internet. It is now possible to do banking, buy and sell securities, and purchase many other financial service products on-line.

Keeping track of the number, types, and actions of competitors is becoming increasingly important, but much more complex and difficult. However, recent evidence suggests that it might be worth the effort. One study found that companies placing a premium on competitor information grew 200 percent faster than firms that did not. The three most crucial types of competitor information were changes in competitor pricing, new-product development, and changes in corporate strategy.[43]

Institutional Environment   The **institutional environment** consists of all

the organizations involved in marketing products and services. These include marketing research firms, advertising agencies, wholesalers, retailers, suppliers, and customers. Specific trends and characteristics of these institutions are discussed in detail in subsequent chapters.

Thinking Critically

The text discusses how competitive boundaries are being dissolved in the financial services industry. Consider the changes in the telecommunications industry to include local telephone service, long distance, cellular telephone service, and Internet access:

- Who are the major competitors in the local, long distance, cellular, and Internet access markets?

- What marketing strategies are these companies using?

- What competitive changes are taking place in the telecommunications industry?

- What changes do you predict for the future?

Many organizations are changing how they are structured and managed. These trends in the institutional environment include reengineering, restructuring, the virtual corporation, horizontal organizations, and empowerment. An organization's adoption of any of these concepts means that it is changing some elements of its structure and processes. These changes are likely to affect the amount and types of products the firm needs as well as the purchasing processes it uses. The potential marketing implications of organizational changes are illustrated by the restructuring efforts of many firms.

Many organizations are restructuring in various ways. Many companies now emphasize long-term relationships with selected suppliers instead of short-term transactions with a large number of suppliers. This trend means that the pool of potential customers for many marketers is becoming limited. Success in this type of environment requires that marketers focus on doing more business with fewer customers.

The downsizing of organizations is also commonplace. Sometimes entire departments are eliminated; in other cases, the number of employees within departments is reduced. The major purpose of downsizing is to lower costs and make the organization "leaner and meaner."

When an organization eliminates departments, it typically hires outside firms to replace them. This can offer market opportunities for accounting firms, advertising agencies, personnel firms, and other businesses that can perform the needed functions. When department personnel are reduced, fewer people are available to do the work. For example, many firms have downsized their purchasing departments, and purchasing managers at these companies are responsible for purchasing more products and services than in the past. Marketers can take advantage of this situation. Professional salespeople can work closely with these busy purchasing managers to help purchase quality products that add value to their businesses.

Consolidation throughout industries is another important trend. In the future, many industries will consist of a few large firms enjoying most of the market share, plus many small firms, each with limited market share. Some consolidation

Consolidation is a trend in many industries. The merger of Hewlett-Packard and Compaq is an example.

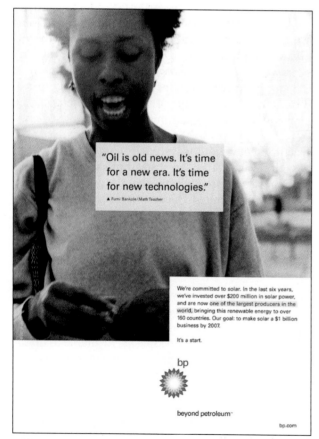

Many of the environmental trands are highly interrelated. BP capitalizes on the use of new technologies to meet consumer and government needs for a cleaner environment.

is occurring in most industries, but it is especially evident in the pharmaceutical, financial services, airline, and retail industries.

Consolidation has two important implications for marketers. First, organizations must develop marketing strategies to hold their own in a competitive environment consisting of a few large firms and many small firms. Second, they must develop effective marketing strategies to serve both very large and very small customers.

These and other institutional trends affect the way organizations operate. Marketers that serve organizational customers must examine these trends to identify market opportunities and develop effective marketing strategies. Moreover, these trends affect the competitive structure for all marketers and have important implications for the types of marketing strategies likely to be effective.

The Future

The only certainty about the future is that it will be uncertain and change will occur at an increasing rate. It will also be more complex. Businesses and consumers now must operate in an era of terrorism and lack of trust. Overlaying these factors on the typical interactions among the social, economic, political/legal, technological, competitive, and institutional environments produces a complex future for marketers. Those that identify the key trends among these factors and understand how these trends interact will be in the best position to take advantage of marketing opportunities and to minimize threats.

Summary

1. **Understand the nature of the marketing environment and why it is important to marketers.** The marketing environment consists of all factors external to an organization that can affect its marketing activities. Elements of the marketing environment are largely uncontrollable, although marketers have influence over some factors. Environmental factors can affect the size and growth rate of markets and can influence marketing activities. Thus, changes in the marketing environment offer opportunities and threats to marketers. Identifying and responding effectively to these opportunities and threats is a major challenge.

2. **Describe the major components of the social environment and how trends in the social environment affect marketing.** The social environment comprises all factors and trends related to groups of people, including their number, characteristics, behavior, and growth projections. Its major components are the demographic and cultural environments. The demographic environment refers to the size, distribution, and growth rate of people with different characteristics. The cultural environment refers to factors and trends related to how people live and behave. Demographic factors typically relate to the number of people in different markets, whereas cultural factors generally influence the needs of these markets.

3. **Understand how the economic environment affects marketing.** The economic environment includes factors and trends related to the production of goods and services and the relationships between this production and income levels. The economic environment affects the purchasing power of consumers, which is an important determinant of the size of a market.

4. **See how the political/legal environment offers opportunities and threats to marketers.** The political/legal environment, encompassing factors related to governmental activities and laws and regulations, directly affects marketing activities. Laws and regulations normally present constraints within which marketers must operate. These laws and regulations are closely related to current political trends. Some marketers, however, can identify market opportunities arising from these laws and regulations.

5. **Appreciate the importance of the technological environment to marketers.** The technological environment includes factors and trends related to innovations that affect the development of new products or improving marketing practice. Technological advances are happening so rapidly that marketers must constantly monitor the technological environment to keep abreast of latest developments.

6. **Understand differences in the competitive environment.** The competitive environment consists of all the organizations that attempt to serve the same customers. Brand competitors compete directly by offering the same type of product to the same market. Product competitors compete more indirectly by offering different types of products to satisfy the same basic need.

7. **Know how changes in the institutional environment affect marketers.** The institutional environment consists of all the organizations involved in marketing products and services. These include marketing research firms, advertising agencies, wholesalers, and retailers. As the characteristics of these and other institutions change, so will the marketing strategies necessary to serve different customers and to compete effectively in different industries.

Understanding Marketing Terms and Concepts

Thinking About Marketing

1. How do changes in the marketing environment generate opportunities and threats for marketers?

2. What are the major differences between the demographic and cultural environments?

3. Why are trends in the institutional environment important to marketers?

4. How does the Internet affect the competitive environment facing many firms?

5. Look at "Using Technology: Turning Data into Valuable Marketing Information." What are other examples of how marketers might use Business Intelligence software to improve marketing decisions?

6. How do political changes affect regulations and regulatory agencies?

7. What are the most important social trends facing marketers in the twenty-first century?

8. Refer to Being Entrepreneurial: Marketing Opportunities to Provide Security. Identify other opportunities for Douglas Electronics to meet the needs of airport customers.

9. How are the social and economic environments interrelated?

10. How can new technologies be used to help marketers scan and monitor the marketing environment?

Applying Marketing Skills

1. Identify several marketing environment trends that you think might affect enrollment at your college. Discuss whether each trend represents an opportunity or a threat. What strategy might your institution use to take advantage of the opportunity or minimize the threat?

2. Watch the complete evening news show on one of the major networks. Make a note of significant marketing environment trends examined during the newscast. After the news show is over, suggest the potential effect of each trend on marketing practice. Which trends represent opportunities? Which trends represent threats? Could any of the potential threats become opportunities if a marketer viewed it from an entrepreneurship perspective?

3. Contact a marketing executive at a local company and ask how he or she assesses changes in the marketing environment. Identify who in the company is involved in what types of environmental scanning. Ask the executive to identify the key trends affecting his or her company and what the firm is doing to respond appropriately to these trends.

Using the www in Marketing

Activity One Go to Dell's Web site (http://www.dell.com).

1. How does Dell's Web site add value to customers?

2. Using information on the Web site, describe and evaluate Dell's global marketing efforts.

3. What ideas do you have for improving Dell's Web site?

Activity Two As discussed in the chapter, laws and regulations typically are designed to promote competition among firms or to protect consumers and society. Some Web sites that present legal information are:

Federal Trade Commission (http://www.ftc.gov)
FedWorld Information Network (http://www.fedworld.gov)
Consumer Information Center (http://www.pueblo.gsa.gov)

United States Information Agency (http://www.usia.gov)
THOMAS: Legislative Information on the Internet
  (http://thomas.loc.gov)
National Archives and Records Administration
  (http://www.nara.gov)
Visit several of these sites and:

1. Select an example of legislation intended to promote competition among firms. Provide a brief synopsis of this legislation and indicate how the legislation affects marketing practice.

2. Select an example of legislation intended to protect consumers and society. Provide a brief synopsis of this legislation and discuss how the legislation affects marketing practice.

3. Which of these sites would you recommend that marketers monitor on a regular basis? Why?

Making Marketing Decisions

Case 2-1 Women's NBA: Women's Team Sports Taking Off

Women's individual sports, such as golf and tennis, have been successful for many years. The same cannot be said for team sports. Prior to 1997, at least three attempts had been made to establish women's professional basketball leagues. All had failed. So, why would anyone try again? Because the marketing environment changed.

Women's collegiate sports programs have expanded tremendously in recent years. This has produced a new generation of women athletes and fans. And the stunning success of women athletes at the 1996 Summer Olympic Games in Atlanta added to this interest. The result is the formation of four new women's professional leagues since the Olympics. One is the Women's National Basketball Association (WNBA).

The tip-off of the WNBA was in June 1997. The league initially consisted of eight teams operated by NBA teams in eight cities. The Western Conference included the Los Angeles Lakers, Phoenix Suns, Sacramento Kings, and

Utah Jazz. The Eastern Conference teams were the Charlotte Hornets, Cleveland Cavaliers, Houston Rockets, and New York Knicks. The season began after the NBA playoffs in June and concluded with a championship game on August 30.

The WNBA worked hard to make the new league a success. Sponsors were obtained and contracts to televise selected regular season and playoff games were secured. The league advertised during the NBA's regular season and playoff games. The results of these marketing efforts appear to have been successful.

The sixth WNBA season begins with preseason games in 2002. The league started with 8 teams, expanded to 12 in 1999, and now has 16 teams competing. The league drew its 10 millionth fan in 2001. Local, national, and international television coverage reached nearly 60 million fans in 23 different languages in 167 countries. Sponsors such as Nike, Sears, and Anheuser-Busch have extended their sponsorship deals and new sponsors, such as Gatorade, are being added.

The future looks good as well. The WNBA recently signed a six-year contract with ABC and ESPN to televise regular-season and playoff games beginning in 2003. A similar two-year deal was also signed with Oxygen Media. San Antonio is working hard to have a WNBA team competing in 2003. The league also has a popular Web site (www.wnba.com). The WNBA is considering more expansion in the future and continues to improve existing operations.

Questions

1. What trends in the marketing environment helped the WNBA be successful?

2. What trends in the marketing environment represent threats to the WNBA?

3. Why would companies like Nike, Sears, Anheuser-Busch, and Gatorade want to be sponsors of the WNBA?

4. What role does the WNBA Web site (www.wnba.com) play in the league's marketing strategy?

Case 2-2 *Kodak: Capitalizing on Marketing Opportunities*

Kodak had sales of over $13 billion in 2001, with about $2.6 billion being from the sales of film. However, film sales have been declining. The slow economy, the September 11 terrorist attacks, and the increasing acceptance of digital photography have led consumers to cut back sharply on the use of traditional film. This has reduced Kodak's profits by 54 percent from 2000 and reduced its stock price.

Kodak is responding by trying to penetrate the digital camera market. The company introduced five different products in its EasyShare digital camera line. These cameras make downloading images easy and have a longer battery life than other brands. These features address two of the major problems faced by digital camera users.

The EasyShare cameras have been successful since their introduction on April 23, 2001. A survey of 90 major retailers in December 2001 indicated that the Kodak cameras were the best-selling for 50 percent of the retailers, followed by Olympus, Fuji, and Sony. This success has increased Kodak's share of the digital camera market to 14 percent as it gains on market leader Sony with a 25 percent share.

Although Kodak is pleased with its results to date, digital camera sales represent only $500 million of its total $13 billion in sales. The digital camera market is expected to increase to 12 million units in 2003, but the average camera price is expected to decline from $462 to $270. So, gross margins will be lower and marketing expenses are likely to be higher as competition in the digital camera market heats up.

Because of this, Kodak is looking for more profitable opportunities. One opportunity is increased sales of photo-quality inkjet paper for consumers to print images at home. Only 15 to 20 percent of digital photos are printed now, but Kodak hopes this will increase, because it is easy to do with the EasyShare camera. Another opportunity is the company's Ofoto.com on-line photo-sharing and printing service. It currently has 2 million members and is one of the three photo-printing services featured in Microsoft's XP operating system. Both of these offer higher profit margins than digital cameras.

Questions

1. What trends in the marketing environment led Kodak to enter the digital camera market?

2. Why have the EasyShare cameras been so successful?

3. Which of the marketing opportunities being considered would you recommend Kodak emphasize? Why?

4. What other marketing opportunities can you identify that Kodak might pursue?

3

Marketing's Strategic Role in the Organization

After studying this chapter, you should be able to:

1 Discuss the three basic levels in an organization and the types of strategic plans developed at each level.

2 Understand the organizational strategic planning process and the role of marketing in this process.

3 Describe the key decisions in the development of corporate strategy.

4 Understand the different general business strategies and their relationship to business marketing, product marketing, and international marketing strategies.

5 Realize the importance of relationships and teamwork in executing strategic plans.

www.disney.com

Disney's long-run objective is to become the world's premier family entertainment company through the ongoing development of its powerful brand and character franchises. Relatedly, their business is "making people happy by turning fantasy into reality." Already, Disney has become a premier media company, with 114,000 employees and revenues of $25 billion in 2001, including 17 percent of their revenues coming from outside the United States and Canada.

The company has four business segments, each with recognizable lines. Their media networks include ABC, ESPN, the Disney channel, the ABC family channel, radio and TV channels, and the Toon network. Second, Disney produces and distributes motion pictures and TV animation. Their park and resort operations include the Florida, California, Paris, and Tokyo sites, plus a cruise line. In addition, significant revenues are realized through their extensive licensing of company characters and intellectual property. Each of these areas require a marketing strategy involving the identification of appropriate market segments and then design of a market mix offering for effectively appealing to these many and varied segments.

In spite of the obvious Disney brand strength and the company's extensive product line, recent economic events and questionable decisions make Disney an excellent example to follow as their marketing strategy evolves. ABC has encountered decreasing ratings in certain periods. Park and cruise line patronage has declined with uncertainty in the political environment. Fifty of their 500-plus stores were closed in 2001. Their Internet strategy has been disappointing to date. These problems reduced bottom-line results and stimulated cost-cutting endeavors as a result of poor financial performance. Questions are now being raised regarding the ability of the company and its CEO, Michael Eisner, to manage their extensive growth caused from the acquisition and start-up of such a large number of significant different business operations.

The complexity of the Disney conglomerate illustrates the importance of a well-designed corporate marketing strategy. The firm consists of unique business units, each offering an extensive array of products and services. Strategies and implementation of strategies must be developed and executed at the corporate, business-unit, and product levels. Overall, strategy and long-term planning are guided by the firm's vision as stated in their mission statement. At the business level, planning begins with an examination of the current situation, including technological changes and competitive effects. From this analysis, both threats and new business opportunities are identified. Decisions to pursue new opportunities are followed by the establishment of objectives, often stated in terms of market share, sales volume, or profitability. Subsequently, business and marketing strategies are developed to achieve those objectives. Effective execution of strategy in implementation must then occur for objectives to be realized. As such, strategies are made through a great deal of deliberation and rational evaluation of alternative strategies that should be guided by an overall vision of the organization. Here, analysis of the firm' strengths and weakness, as well as external threats and opportunities, is crucial to success. As strategies are subsequently implemented, creativity becomes a key aspect of the planning process.[1]

Many of the most familiar firms around the world are complex organizations that market many different products in many different business areas. Marketing efforts require planning and implementation across all the various business segments, business areas, incorporated companies, and profit centers. In today's environment, organizations must frequently cope with unexpected and anomalous events, referred to as crises, that create high levels of uncertainty and are potential threats to the viability of the company. The past decade has witnessed tremendous economic and political upheavals, including the outcomes of 9/11, the collapse of Enron and WorldCom, and the turmoil of some foreign currencies, such as the Brazilian real and the Mexican peso.[2]

As an example, Gateway cut back its international operations, reduced its work force, and eliminated some manufacturing and service operations in response to the September 11 attacks and a series of investment problems associated with their stock valuations.[3]

Often, a small company markets a few products to a well-defined market. Although this sort of marketing is not easy, the company directs all its efforts toward the initial products and market. If the firm succeeds and grows, competitors enter with similar products. Over time, the company's opportunities for marketing the same products to the same market decline. To continue growing, the firm must develop new strategies. Typically, it must either market different types of products to its current market, the same products to different markets, or new products to new markets. The relatively simple single-business, few-products firm becomes a complex multibusiness, multiproduct company.

Michael Porter, the famous Harvard Business School strategy professor, argues that long-term strategy is even more important in uncertain and turbulent times and/or environments. While change does occur more rapidly now, CEOs have too

Many corporations have individual business units. GE, a global company has multibusiness operations in many different markets and for a variety of products.

often downplayed the importance of marketing strategy. However, examples of successful firms, such as Intel, Wal-Mart, and Dell, provide evidence of the importance of a clear strategy and sense of purpose, which then provide firms with sustainable competitive advantage.[4]

The complexities facing Disney, Gateway, and other firms produce many of the key challenges for today's marketers. In this chapter, we examine the important role of marketing in the contemporary multibusiness, multiproduct firm. We classify organizations into corporate, business, and functional levels, and discuss strategic planning and strategic decision making at each level. Our focus is on the role of marketing. The chapter concludes with a discussion of teamwork in the execution of strategic plans.

Organizational Levels

The **corporate level** is the highest level in any organization. Corporate managers address issues concerning the overall organization, and their decisions and actions affect all other organizational levels. The **business level** consists of units within the overall organization that are generally managed as self-contained businesses. Often, the idea is to break a complex organization into smaller units to be operated like independent businesses. This is the level at which competition takes place; that is, business units typically compete against competitor business units, not corporate levels versus corporate levels.

The **functional level** includes all the various functional areas within a business unit. Most of the work of a business unit is performed in its different functions. A typical university provides a good illustration of different organizational levels. The president, vice presidents, and other central administration positions represent the corporate level. The different colleges within the university, such as the college of business or college of arts and sciences, can be considered business units. There are also different functions performed within each college. The typical functions are teaching, research, and administration carried out by faculty, staff, and administrators.

Organizational Strategic Planning

Strategic planning for multibusiness, multiproduct organizations typically occurs at each organizational level. Strategic plans at higher organizational levels provide direction for strategic plans at lower levels. In a sense, lower-level plans are developed to execute higher-level plans. Because of this relationship, strategic planning must be integrated and consistent throughout levels.

A study of U.S. and South African firms provides a general description of strategic planning.[5] These firms reported that the major benefits of strategic planning are improved performance relative to objectives and a better organizational focus and vision. Most of the firms prepare formal strategic plans at the corporate, business, and product levels, with different functional managers participating in the planning process. These include sales managers, product managers, marketing researchers, production managers, and financial managers. Many firms also incorporate customers into the process. Businesses and departments can be organized any number of ways—around products, brands, categories, geography, markets, or, as explained later, subsidiaries. P&G has a marketing unit just for Wal-Mart. However, and as research suggests, the best organizational structure is one that serves customers most effectively, irrespective of which channels buyers use to access the company.[6]

Types of Strategic Plans

The different types of strategic plans and important strategic decisions are illustrated in Exhibit 3–1. A **corporate strategic plan** provides guidance for strategic planning at all other organizational levels. Important corporate strategy decisions concern development of a corporate vision, formulation of corporate objectives, allocation of resources, determination of how to achieve desired growth, and estab-

Exhibit 3–1	*Organizational strategic plans*	
Organization Level	**Type of Strategic Plan**	**Key Strategic Decisions**
Corporate	Corporate strategic plan	• Corporate vision • Corporate objectives and resource allocation • Corporate growth strategies • Business-unit composition
Business	Business strategic plan	• Market scope • Competitive advantage
Marketing	Marketing strategic plan	• Target market approach • Marketing mix approach
	Product marketing plan	• Specific target market • Specific marketing mix • Execution action plan

lishment of business units. These decisions determine what type of company the firm is and wants to become.

A **business strategic plan** indicates how each business unit in the corporate family expects to compete effectively in the marketplace, given the vision, objectives, and growth strategies in the corporate strategic plan. Different businesses within the same organization are likely to have different objectives and business strategies. For example, the Hilton Hotels Corp. emphasizes growth of its gambling casino business by expanding throughout the United States and into foreign markets such as Egypt, Turkey, and Uruguay. Hilton is selling some downscale hotels to concentrate on ritzy resort hotels. These changes in corporate strategy influence the company's business strategies and are turning Hilton into more of a gaming than a hotel company.[7] Each business needs to make decisions concerning the scope of the market it serves and the types of competitive advantages to emphasize. Decisions in these areas contribute to a general business strategy.

Each business consists of different functions to be performed, and strategic plans may be developed for each major function. Thus, many organizations will have marketing, financial, R&D, manufacturing, and other functional strategic plans. A **marketing strategic plan** describes how marketing managers will execute the business strategic plan. It addresses the general target market and marketing mix approaches. Colgate, which competes effectively with P&G's Crest toothpaste, has benefited from its focused approach and evenly distributed sales worldwide. Colgate's marketing plan includes the maintenance of their "share of voice" in media spending and their strategy to "surround" consumers with samples targeted toward college students and other young adults.[8]

Each business unit has its own product marketing plans that focus on specific target markets and marketing mixes for each product. A **product marketing plan** typically includes both strategic decisions (what to do) and execution decisions (how to do it).

Pitney Bowes, originally founded as a producer of mailing equipment and postage meters, is now a multibusiness, multiproduct corporation. The Copier Systems Division, one of the company's new business units, develops and executes marketing and product plans to compete against Xerox, Canon, Minolta, and Konica. The division's basic business strategy is to target large Fortune 1000 companies and to differentiate its products from the competition on the basis of product quality and efficiency of distribution. Unlike many newcomers to an industry, Pitney Bowes does not claim to offer the lowest prices in the industry.[9]

Unilever has redesigned its strategy to focus upon 400 master brands from its complete portfolio of brands. Following rivals P&G and Colgate Palmolive, Wisk SKUs will be scaled down, while plans for the All detergent brand include doubled marketing budgets and the introduction of line extensions.[10]

The Strategic Role of Brand Loyalty

One of the primary objectives of marketing strategy is generation of market share and the development of a strong customer base. The determinants of market share are multifaceted. However, certain important concepts are recognized as critical. To begin, trust and liking for the firm's brands are the building blocks of success. Trust, in particular, is critical in the establishment of successful exchange relationships and is at the heart of "one-to-one" marketing. From brand trust and affect (liking) come purchase and attitudinal loyalty. That is, a customer base is possible that both purchases the brand(s) regularly but has an enduring positive attitude toward those brands. Strong and positive attitudinal loyalty inhibits competitor inroads as new brands enter the market and enables firms to charge higher prices.[11]

For most firms, **customer equity,** or the total of the discounted lifetime values of all the firm's customers, is certain to be the most important determinant of the long-term value of the firm. While customer equity is not the only determinant of firm value (e.g., assets, property, R&D capabilities), the firm's customers provide the long-term revenues and profits, and building customer equity should be the focal point for marketing strategy. As such, marketing strategy should involve the determination of the most critical drivers of customer equity for their brands, (e.g., quality, service, convenience).[12]

The Strategic Planning Process

Although individual organizations will differ in the way they approach strategic planning, a general process is illustrated in Exhibit 3–2. This process applies to strategic planning at every level. We present it as a step-by-step approach to make it easier to understand strategic planning. In the business world, most organizations are involved in different stages of the process simultaneously and do not necessarily follow such a step-by-step approach.

EXAMINE THE CURRENT SITUATION First, the managers evaluate the existing situation for the corporate, business, marketing, or product level. They typically analyze historical information to describe current strategies, assess recent performance, and evaluate the competitive situation. This background information provides a benchmark for the remainder of the strategic planning process. The planning process enables managers to maintain perspective even in rapidly changing times. For radically new products, the situation analysis pays attention to environmental change that comes from political, economic, social, and technological sources.[13]

IDENTIFY POTENTIAL THREATS AND OPPORTUNITIES Next, the focus changes from what has happened to what might happen. Managers identify key trends in the marketing environment, assess the possible impact of these trends on the current situation, and classify them as either threats or opportunities. Threats represent potential problems that might adversely affect the current situation; opportunities represent areas where performance might be improved. Thus, Specialized Bicycle Components must recognize trends in retailing and changing preferences among consumers. Managers typically rank potential threats and opportunities, ad-

| **Exhibit 3–2** | *General strategic planning process* |

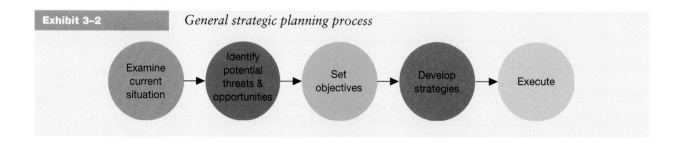

dressing the most important ones first in the next strategic planning stage. In the search for opportunities, problems sometimes generate opportunities. For example, the deregulation problems in the California electricity market caused a series of blackouts. In response to these problems, Capstone Turbine has marketed effectively microturbines, the size of refrigerators, to small businesses.[14]

SET OBJECTIVES   Managers must now establish specific objectives for the corporate, business, marketing, and product levels. Typical objectives involve sales, market share, and profitability. The specific objectives should be based on the analysis of the current situation and the marketing environment. As we discuss later, objectives at the different organizational levels must be consistent. For example, the sales objectives for all businesses must be set so that meeting them means meeting the corporate level sales objectives.

DEVELOP STRATEGIES   Finally, managers develop strategies for achieving the objectives. These strategies will indicate how the organization will minimize potential threats and capitalize on specific opportunities. The strategies developed at this stage represent what an organization plans to do to meet its objectives, given the current situation and expected changes in the marketing environment. A sample product marketing plan is presented in Appendix A at the end of the text.

EXECUTE   A clear strategy and well-crafted programs may still fail if execution and implementation efforts are misdirected or inadequate. Effective execution is enhanced when employees share common values and are properly trained and when sufficient resources and staff are provided to support implementation. It is important to note that both a sense of organizational-wide commitment to the adopted strategy and a sense of commitment by those managers responsible for implementation have been shown to be primary determinants of effective execution.[15] Recent research indicates that the effective implementation of marketing strategy is affected significantly by, again, widespread organizational commitment to the strategy, continuing dialogue between upper-level managers and second-level managers charged with implementation, and employee understanding regarding how individual strategies are consistent with the overall vision and orientation of the firm.[16]

The Role of Marketing

Marketing plays an important role in the strategic planning process for many organizations. Although some marketing positions are represented at the corporate level, most are at the functional level within the business units of an organization. As shown in Exhibit 3–3, however, marketing is involved in strategic planning at all organizational levels.

Strategic marketing describes marketing activities that affect corporate, business, and marketing strategic plans. Strategic marketing activities can be classified into three basic functions. First, marketers help orient everyone in the organization toward markets and customers. Thus, they are responsible for helping organizations execute a marketing philosophy throughout the strategic planning process.

Second, marketers help gather and analyze information required to examine the current situation, identify trends in the marketing environment, and assess the potential impact of these trends. This information and analysis provides input for corporate, business, and marketing strategic plans.

Third, marketers are involved in the development of corporate, business, and marketing strategic plans. Marketing's influence varies across organizations. For organizations driven by a marketing philosophy, marketing necessarily plays a key role in strategic decision making. The trend toward pushing strategic planning responsibility further down the organization is increasing marketing's clout in an organization's strategic planning process.[17]

Marketing management relates to specific product marketing strategies. It differs from strategic marketing in its basic orientation. Strategic marketing focuses on

Exhibit 3–3   *Role of marketing in strategic planning*

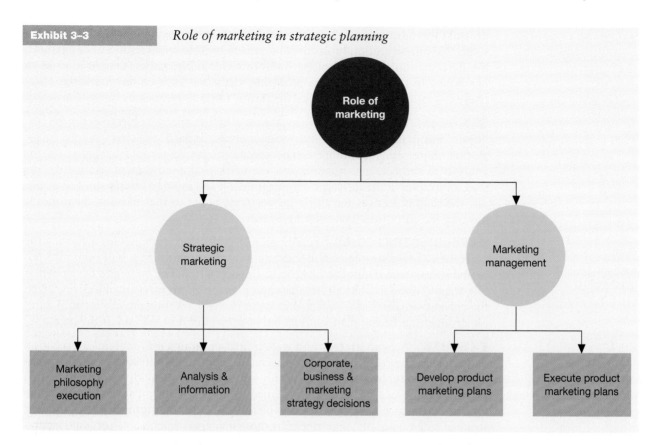

broad strategic decisions at the corporate and business levels. Marketing management is concerned, by contrast, with specific strategic decisions for individual products and the day-to-day activities needed to execute these strategies successfully. At the operating level, marketing managers focus on customers and the competition as well as on the four Ps of the marketing mix: price, product, promotion, and place (distribution).[18]

The strategic role of marketing and marketing management are now in a period of considerable change and evolution. These changes are due to a number of important environmental phenomena that are affecting the way many firms do business. To begin, many well-known companies work closely with dedicated partners on the supply side (often using single supply partners) and the distributor side of their business, expecting their distributors to play proactive roles in the development of services and marketing strategy. For example, on the supply side, the modern-day Nike does very little manufacturing of its own and focuses largely on marketing. In this vein, companies such as this are actually embedded in **business networks,** comprising strategic alliances among suppliers, distributors, and the marketing firm.[19]

Other influences on marketing include the connected-knowledge economy; globalized and consolidated industries; fragmented markets; and demanding customers and consumers. With these changes, new kinds of competitors will emerge, markets will continue to become homogenized across country boundaries, and mass markets will erode in the face of mass customization. Business customers and individual consumers expect diversity and have multiple means of obtaining products, as well as learning about company offerings. Some observers foresee a future in which the Web will enable automated purchasing, anonymous transactions, and the bypassing of most intermediaries.[20]

The role of marketing within the firm is in transition as well. For example, some scholarly observers have predicted that a cross-functional dispersion of marketing activities will occur as the firm becomes market oriented throughout. In a test of this premise, one study of managers across functions (i.e., marketing, human relations, operations, accounting, and finance) within their firms revealed that marketing as a separate function still contributes to a firm's financial performance, customer-relationship performance, and new-product performance beyond the performance attributable to the firm's general market orientation.[21] Therefore, an understanding of the strategic planning process is even more important in today's ever-changing marketplace.

Our discussion of organizational strategic planning provides an overview of different types of strategic plans, a general strategic planning process, and marketing's basic role in these areas. With this background, we are now ready to examine the major strategic decisions at the corporate, business, marketing, and product levels.

Marketing Strategy and the Internet

The failure of many dot com companies, after the promises of many marketing experts that the Internet would rewrite the rules of business, has raised many important questions regarding the lessons firms should learn from Internet business. Internet usage continues to grow globally, and many traditional firms have found viable applications of Web technology. These successes apply to both B2B and consumer-oriented firms. However, the basics of business success remain the same: customers, capabilities, and competitive advantage. Companies must be able to attract and retain profitable customers. Firms must also take advantage of their own unique strengths and capabilities. The maintenance of some distinctive competitive advantage, whether in terms of product and quality advantages, convenience and/or price/value, is a must. While online-only firms will certainly exist and succeed, most firms will employ Internet technology in efforts to offer complementary channels and/or to improve existing processes.

The question is not whether firms should employ the Internet. The objective is how to use the Internet profitably as part of their operations and marketing strategy. If marketing strategy is defined simply as the firm's identification of desirable market segments and the development of appropriate marketing mixes to appeal to these segments, then the important role of the Internet becomes obvious.[22]

Many businesses are using the Internet to interact with suppliers and large buyers. Internet selling direct to consumers is frequently employed as another channel of communication and interaction. The Internet also expands market coverage and opens up previously unreachable segments and markets. The Internet enables 24/7 convenience, as well as the opportunity to develop more personalized relationships with customers. As Michael Porter argues, the Internet can increase an industry's efficiency by expanding the overall size of the market by improving its position relative to traditional substitutes. Unfortunately, this expansion in market coverage also makes other firms, previously restricted by location, potential competitors.

One of the primary effects of the Internet has been the increased availability of information and the emphasis upon price. These changes have certainly made it more difficult for firms to be profitable. As such, the need to develop and maintain an effective marketing strategy consistent with the firm's capabilities and competitive advantages is even more important.[23]

Corporate Strategy Decisions
The key corporate strategy decision areas defined in Exhibit 3–1 are corporate vision, corporate objectives and resource allocation, corporate growth strategies, and business-unit composition.

Corporate Vision

A **corporate vision** represents the basic values of an organization. The vision specifies what the organization stands for, where it plans to go, and how it plans to get there. As indicated in Exhibit 3–4, a comprehensive vision should address the

Corporate vision components

- Markets
- Products and services
- Geographic domain
- Core competencies
- Organizational objectives
- Organizational philosophy
- Organizational self-concept
- Desired public image

organization's markets, principal products and services, geographic domain, core competencies, objectives, basic philosophy, self-concept, and desired public image.[24] Specialized Bicycle, for example, addressed these issues in its stated vision: "customer satisfaction, quality, innovativeness, teamwork, and profitability."

The ability to develop vision depends on the company's understanding of what should be enduring and what is subject to change. Companies that enjoy enduring success, such as Hewlett-Packard, 3M, Motorola, and Procter & Gamble, have core values and core purposes that remain fixed; but they endlessly adapt their strategies and practices to a changing world. A company's **core values** are the small set of guiding principles that represent the enduring tenets of an organization. The Disney Company's emphasis on imagination and wholesomeness reflect its essential core values. **Core purpose** reflects the company's reason for being or its idealistic motivation for doing work. Disney's core purpose is to entertain people; 3M's is "to solve problems innovatively" (see Exhibit 3–5).[25]

Sometimes organizations develop a formal mission statement to communicate the corporate vision to all interested parties. A mission statement can be an important element in the strategic planning process because it specifies the boundaries within which business units, marketing, and other functions must operate.

The mission statement for Ben & Jerry's is threefold: (1) to make and distribute the finest quality all-natural ice cream and related products; (2) to operate the Company on a sound financial basis of profitable growth, increasing value for our shareholders, and creating career opportunities and financial rewards for our employees; and (3) to operate the company in a way that actively recognizes the central role that business plays in the structure of society by initiating innovative ways to improve the quality of life of a broad community.[26] The statement emphasizes the importance of quality products, company performance and employee success, and the social responsibility aspects of business.

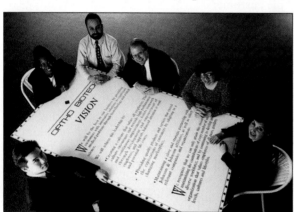

Mission statements provide direction for corporate leadership and help guide marketing strategy. At Ortho Biotech, a shared vision helps an increasingly diverse workforce make day-to-day decisions about what needs to be done.

Core purpose: A company's reason for being

3M: To solve problems innovatively.

Cargill: To improve the standard of living around the world.

Fannie Mae: To strengthen the social fabric by continually democratizing homeownership.

Hewlett-Packard: To make technical contributions for the advancement and welfare of humanity.

Lost Arrow Corporation: To be a role model and a tool for social change.

Pacific Theatres: To provide a place for people to flourish and to enhance the community.

Mary Kay Cosmetics: To give unlimited opportunity to women.

McKinsey & Company: To help leading corporations and governments to be more successful.

Merck: To preserve and improve human life.

Nike: To experience the emotion of competition, winning, and crushing competitors.

Sony: To experience the joy of advancing and applying technology for the benefit of the public.

Telecare Corporation: To help people with mental impairments realize their full potential.

Wal-Mart: To give ordinary folk the chance to buy the same things as rich people.

Speaking from Experience

"Computer technology has become pervasive in businesses and is fundamental to almost every business process. As a result, the information technology professionals inside businesses have an increasingly complex array of products and services they must elevate and manage. Recognizing this, we are changing the way we market products at Microsoft from focusing on the individual products to combining products into specific solution sets. We are moving from an organization focused on product marketing to teams focused on solution marketing. By doing this, we reduce the complexity of the IT managers' decision process and better meet the customer's needs."

Bobbie Oglesby
*Director of Windows Branding
and Communications*
Microsoft, Redmond, WA

Bobbie Oglesby holds a master's degree in marketing from the University of South Carolina. She was attracted to Microsoft because of the opportunity to shape how technology is developed and used. Advancements in technology, particularly the Internet, are opening up a new world of opportunities and challenges.

The vision statement for Whirlpool is similar but does not mention the role of business in society: "We create the world's best home appliances that make life a little easier and more enjoyable for all people. Our goal is a Whirlpool product in every home, everywhere. Created by: pride in our work and each other; passion for creating unmatched customer loyalty for our brands; and, performance results that excite and reward global investors."[27]

Marriott illustrates what some companies are doing. After management developed mission statements for the corporation and hotel division, each of the company's 250 hotels crafted its own mission statement. Staff members at each hotel spent three days participating in "visioning" exercises to develop the mission statements.[28]

Exhibit 3–6 lists questions that a firm's top managers should continually ask themselves in efforts to install a corporate vision for effectively competing in the future. The last two questions form the basis for recent views of successful competition; that is, the firm's comparative advantages and distinctive core competencies are the resources for competitive advantage. **Core competency** reflects a bundle of skills that are possessed by individuals across the organization. The core competency Federal Express possesses in package routing and delivery rests on the integration of bar technology, wireless communications, and network management. Boeing, the international manufacturer of airplanes, lists three core competencies on their Web site: (1) detailed customer knowledge and focus; (2) large-scale system integration; and (3) lean, efficient design and production systems.[29] Competitive advantage derived from these core competencies in turn yields superior financial performance. In summary, a successful corporate vision reflects the sequence from core competency to competitive advantage to financial performance.

| **Exhibit 3–6** | *Questions leading to an effective corporate vision* |

1. Which customers will you be serving in the future?
2. Through which channels will you reach customers in the future?
3. Who will be your competitors in the future?
4. Where will your margins come from in the future?
5. In what end-product markets will you participate in the future?
6. What will be the basis for your competitive advantage in the future?
7. What skills or capabilities will make you unique in the future?

Corporate Objectives and Resource Allocation

The second major corporate strategy decision area involves setting objectives for the entire organization and assigning objectives and resources to business units and products. Although the corporate vision provides general overall direction for the organization, corporate objectives specify the achievement of desired levels of performance during particular time periods. Corporate objectives are established for many areas, but the most visible tend to be financial objectives. Typical financial objectives concern sales growth, profits, profit growth, earnings per share, return on investment, and stock price. Some analysts argue that all actions of the firm should be oriented toward increasing the value of customer assets. Customer assets can be assessed in terms of measures of customer satisfaction and the strengths and weaknesses of customer relationships. Importantly, the value of customer assets including newly acquired customers affect the company's future ability to generate wealth.[30]

Sales and sales growth objectives are often of direct concern to marketers. Although sales-related objectives are set at the corporate level, actual sales are achieved by marketing individual products to individual customers. Therefore, corporate sales objectives influence marketing activities throughout the organization, as illustrated in Exhibit 3–7.

Suppose the corporate sales growth objective is to increase this year's sales by 10 percent over the previous year's total. To achieve the desired results, management must break down this objective into goals for each business unit and product. If all products and business units meet the assigned objectives, assuming generally equal sales across units, the organization will achieve the desired growth.

In Exhibit 3–7, 10 percent of the desired sales growth is assigned to Business 1, 8 percent to Business 2, and 12 percent to Business 3. The sales growth objectives for each business unit are then further assigned to the specific products marketed by each business. Again, the sales growth objectives are not equally divided across products, because the various products have different opportunities for increasing sales. But if each product achieves the desired sales increase, the business unit will meet its sales growth objective. And, if each business unit does so, the organization will meet its 10 percent objective.

This hierarchy of objectives represents the organization's sales growth plan. Now, corporate resources are allocated to the business units and business-unit resources are allocated to products. Business 1 receives more corporate resources than some other business units, and Product B receives more of the resources from Business 1 than the other two products it markets. The more sales growth required from a business unit or product, the more resources it typically needs to achieve the desired increases.

Corporate objectives and resource allocation affect marketers in two basic ways. First, marketers are involved in setting the objectives for different organizational levels. Although the amount of marketing participation varies across firms, setting realistic objectives requires the market information and analysis that marketers can provide. Assessments of trends in the size and growth

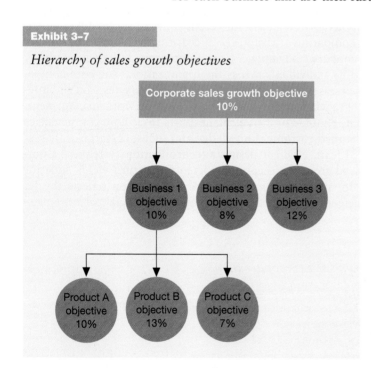

Exhibit 3–7

Hierarchy of sales growth objectives

rates of markets and the potential actions of competitors are inputs for setting objectives and allocating resources.

Second, corporate objectives and resource allocation decisions provide guidance for the development and implementation of business and marketing strategies. For example, the marketing managers for Products B and C in Business 1 have different objectives and receive different levels of resources to achieve them. Therefore, they are likely to develop and implement different marketing strategies for their products.

Although growth and new-customer generation are traditionally important, companies are increasingly framing objectives in terms of customer relationships and customer retention. Frequently cited corporate objectives based on relationships with customers are (1) retain most profitable customers, (2) increase sales volume from existing customers, and (3) protect core customers from competition. In fact, **customer relationship management (CRM)** has become a guiding premise of many companies. Briefly, CRM initiatives are designed to achieve a continuing dialogue with customers, across all contact and access points, with personalized treatment of the most valuable customers designed to increase customer retention and the effectiveness of marketing strategies. George Day of the Wharton School of Business summarizes the two important capabilities of successful market-oriented firms:

1. Market sensing capability—how well the organization is equipped to continuously sense changes in its markets and to anticipate the responses of their markets to changes in marketing actions.

2. Customer-linking capability—the skills and processes needed to achieve collaborative customer relationships so individual customer needs are quickly apparent to all functions.[31]

Corporate Growth Strategies

Corporate growth strategies describe the general approach for achieving corporate growth objectives. Exhibit 3–8 presents four general options.

A **market penetration strategy** represents a decision to achieve corporate growth objectives with existing products within existing markets. The organization needs to persuade current customers to purchase more of its product or to capture new customers. This typically necessitates an aggressive marketing strategy, which means increasing marketing communications, implementing sales promotion programs, lowering prices, or taking other actions intended to generate more business.

A **market expansion strategy** entails marketing existing products to new markets. The new markets might be different market segments in the same geographic area or the same target market in different geographic areas. Specialized Bicycle Components for example, has expanded into new markets by obtaining expanded distribution through new retail outlets.[32]

A **product expansion strategy** calls for marketing new products to the same market. The organization wants to generate more business from the existing customer base. Nike is not about to abandon athletic footwear, a business it dominates worldwide with more than $4 billion in revenues. However, footwear is a mature business, and Nike is embarking on an expansion strategy to transform itself into a global sports and fitness company.[33] As part of this expansion, Nike plans to offer 82 new stock keeping units (SKUs) in footwear for the committed golfer. These additions will be

Exhibit 3–8

Strategic options for corporate growth

	Products	
	Same	**New**
Markets — Same	**Market penetration**	**Product expansion**
Markets — New	**Market expansion**	**Diversification**

headlined by 50 Tiger Woods signature models. The expansion into golf products will be accompanied by "Nike Golf" operating as a separate company division with their own unique logo.[34]

One interesting perception in the field of new product introduction is that large, incumbent firms rarely introduce new product innovations. This (mis)perception is referred to as the "incumbent's curse." The belief among many academics and practitioners is that large firms are slow to react and typically only introduce modest incremental innovations. In contrast, however, a recent historical analysis revealed that most radical innovations for durables and office products introduced since World War II were generated by large incumbent firms.[35]

A **diversification strategy** requires the firm to expand into new products and new markets. This is the riskiest growth strategy, because the organization cannot build directly on its strengths in its current markets or with its current products. There are, however, varying degrees of diversification. **Unrelated diversification** means that the new products and markets have nothing in common with existing operations. **Related diversification** occurs when the new products and markets have something in common with existing operations. Blockbuster's move into music retailing has some relationship to video rentals since both are retailing operations in the electronic entertainment business.

DuPont pursues a "sustainable growth" strategy by striving to make more of the world's people their customers, but doing so by developing markets that promote and sustain economic prosperity, social equity, and environmental integrity. To pursue these lofty goals, DuPont's growth objectives are based upon the effective use of their scientific resources to enhance the environment. This emphasis has also led to new business opportunities. For example, their floor-covering business unit has shifted its focus from just selling carpet to carpet life cycle planning and removal of old carpet for recycling, as well as installation and maintenance.[36]

Bobbie Oglesby comments on new strategies with which to grow business:
"Microsoft is a strong believer and practitioner of strategic planning. Each year, Microsoft's chairman and president set key objectives for the company that ultimately drive all business and marketing plans for the year. In addition, we also create a three-year plan to ensure we are anticipating the right products and infrastructure for the future."

Business-Unit Composition

In pursuing its corporate growth strategy, an organization may operate in a number of different product and market areas. It does so through business units designed to implement specific business strategies. A **strategic business unit** (SBU) focuses on "a single product or brand, a line of products, or mix of related products that meets a common market need or a group of related needs, and the unit's management is responsible for all (or most) of the basic business functions."[37] A major structural issue for corporations is whether to group functions together or to operate semiautonomous business units. One benefit of separate business units is that they force profit and loss responsibility further down the organization and generate more entrepreneurial behavior.

SBUs are sometimes separate businesses from a legal standpoint. For example, Sears at one time consisted of Dean Witter Reynolds (investments), Coldwell Banker (real estate), Allstate Insurance, and the basic retailing business, Sears Merchandise Group. In other cases, corporate management establishes SBUs to facilitate planning and control operations. Additionally, they can change these SBU designations when conditions warrant. General Electric is composed of approximately 20 business units, including aircraft engines, appliances, NBC, and industrial systems. Within the appliance area, as many as 11 product lines have been marketed, including washers and dryers, refrigerators, and microwave ovens.

Changing a firm's business composition is not unusual these days. Corporate downsizing often causes a firm to exit from some business areas. Sears, for exam-

Thinking Critically

- Identify a set of strategic business units (SBUs), which you would consider vital for the effective management of _____. [a publishing house, an athletic footwear producer, or if you want to use a specific company, maybe Martha Stewart Enterprises]

- What factors influence market growth rates and market attractiveness for these SBUs?

- In an effort to evaluate the SBUs, identify three business strengths, weaknesses, or performance results that can be used to assess the business performance of each individual SBU.

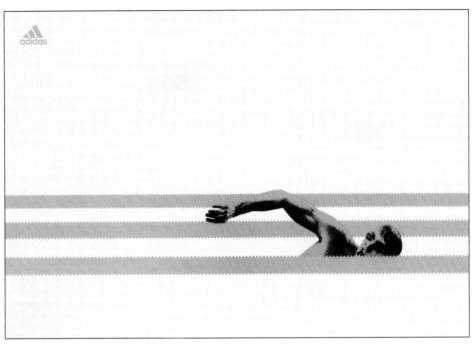

Adidas competes effectively with other companies by offering a mix of athletic apparel and related product lines.

ple, sold all or parts of its investment, real estate, and insurance businesses to concentrate on its retail business.[38] Whether the corporate decision is to increase or decrease the number of SBUs, once a given business composition is established, separate strategies are developed for each business unit. Ricoh has developed its copier industry portfolio by purchasing companies such as Lanier and Savin. The brand names for these units are then retained to capitalize on their strengths in particular market segments.[39]

Marketing strategy is the emphasis at the SBU level, where the focus is on market segmentation, targeting, and positioning (topics covered in detail in Chapter 7) in defining how the firm is to compete in its chosen businesses.[40] The configuration of a firm's business units can be evaluated in terms of market share and market growth using some variation of the Boston Consulting Group growth-share matrix. A very simple depiction of this matrix is shown in Exhibit 3–9.

An overriding decision for many companies is the determination of the firm's mix of strategic business units. Household products, specialty nonfood products, and dressings and sauces represent three of Clorox's strategic business units.

The matrix classifies the company's portfolio of SBUs into four categories: stars, cash cows, dogs, and question marks. Stars have a large share in growth markets. These products are profitable and require investment by the firm to support their continued performance. In contrast, cash cows have large market shares in slower-growth markets. These products generate significant cash relative to the expenses required to maintain share; hence, cash cows provide funds in support of other SBUs. Dogs, candidates for deletion or divestment, have modest market shares in low-growth markets. The remaining category, question marks, includes strategic business units that are problems. Ideally, these units with low market share but residence in high-growth markets should be supported and invested in to spur market share. If possible, the question marks should be shifted toward the star cell.

This view has proven useful over the years as a method for organizing and evaluating the mix of SBUs contained in company product/business portfolios. Consideration of strategy at the business-unit

Exhibit 3–9

Simple growth-share matrix

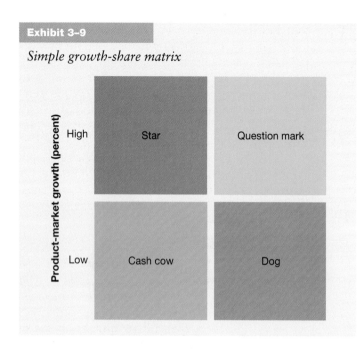

level enables management to stay in closer touch with customers, competitors, and costs and to maintain strategic focus. Further, this simplistic matrix based on market share and market growth has been expanded to include more complete definitions of market attractiveness (beyond market growth) and business strength (beyond market share).[41] Unfortunately, these business portfolios have been criticized for placing too much emphasis on market-share growth and entry into high-growth businesses to the neglect of managing current businesses well.[42]

More recent views of strategy formulation have evolved beyond discussion of star and question mark SBUs. New marketing strategic thinking emphasizes what can be, rather than what is. The emphasis is upon identifying opportunities for growth that do not naturally match the skills of existing business units. Companies have begun to redefine strategy generation and to search for creative ways to grow and compete effectively. Instead of figuring out how to position products and businesses within an industry, strategy should focus on challenging industry rules and creating tomorrow's industries, such as Wal-Mart did in retailing or as Charles Schwab did in the brokerage business.[43]

Companies now often organize around competency-based SBUs in efforts to establish *sustained competitive advantage,* that is, strategies not simultaneously being implemented by competitors and under conditions that make the duplication of such a strategy difficult. That is, the unique strengths and resources of the firm are used to guide business unit composition in lieu of current marketplace position and growth.[44]

Business Strategy Decisions

The basic objective of a business strategy is to determine how the business unit will compete successfully—that is, how the business unit's skills and resources can be translated into positional advantages in the marketplace. Management wants to craft a strategy difficult for competitors to copy so the business can sustain any advantages it has. For example, some retailers achieve sustainable advantages by selecting the best locations for their retail stores, effectively shutting out competitors from those areas. Other retailers try to gain advantages by offering the lowest prices. Price advantages are often difficult to sustain, however, because competitors can usually match them.

A business strategy consists of a general strategy as well as specific strategies for the different business functions such as marketing. The general strategy is based on two dimensions: market scope and competitive advantage.

Market Scope

Market scope refers to how broadly the business views its target market. At one extreme, a business unit can select a broad market scope and try to appeal to most consumers in the market. The business might consider all consumers part of one mass market; more likely, it will divide the total market into segments and target all or most of those. An example of a broad market scope strategy is the move by Nike beyond shoes into most every sports market. At the other extreme, a business unit can focus on only a small portion of the market. An example of a focused market

Wal-Mart competes globally on the basis of providing name brands at lower prices, made possible by low cost structure.

scope strategy for a large, known international firm is Honda's introduction of a limited number of new car models compared with the broad offerings of U.S. automobile manufacturers. In some situations, firms find that **deconglomeration** is beneficial. Deconglomeration refers to the divestiture behavior of a conglomerate firm and the transformation of its business portfolio to one composed of relatively fewer and related businesses. Research suggests that such a corporate strategy affects business strategies and make the firm more innovative, as well as competitor and customer oriented.[45]

Competitive Advantage

Competitive advantage refers to the way a business tries to get consumers to purchase its products over those offered by competitors. Two basic strategies are again possible. A business can try to compete by offering similar products and services as competitors, but at lower prices. Succeeding in a low-price strategy typically requires the business unit to have a lower cost structure than that of competitors. Wal-Mart is a good example of a business that prospers with a low-price strategy. It offers the same brands as many other retailers, but at lower prices. Wal-Mart can sustain this advantage and be profitable because it has a very low cost structure and constantly looks for ways to reduce costs. These capabilities lead to their competitive advantage. Wal-Mart's low cost structure comes from the firm's operations management skills and purchasing skills. Firms should seek to leverage those distinctive skills or competencies that provide them with a unique competitive advantage.[46]

A business may also compete through differentiation, that is, offering consumers something different from and better than competitors' products. If it is successful in achieving the desired differentiation, the business can typically charge higher prices than its competitors do. Neiman Marcus, for example, offers a unique product mix and exceptional service to differentiate itself from competition. Consumers are willing to pay higher prices to receive these benefits.

Building Customer Equity

Lands' End: Retention based on quality

Companies that focus on obtaining and keeping profitable customers, productive employees, and loyal investors generate consistently superior results. Lands' End, the second-largest clothing catalog retailer in the United States, is one such company. Lands' End maintains unusually high inventories to enhance its ability to fill customer orders. Every effort is made to retain customers, as repeat business is required to cover the costs of obtaining buyers. Michael J. Smith, new CEO for Lands' End, asserts that its customers will pay for great quality sold by employees who treat them well. Providing high-quality merchandise and excellent service are the two pillars that form the basis of Lands' End's efforts to retain customers and build customer loyalty. This basic strategy, coupled with deliberate innovation through international expan-

sion and specialized catalogs for certain segments has enable Lands' End to maintain its strong position in the marketplace.

Lands' End's strategy continues to evolve and improve as needed. Recent shifts from mass advertising to targeted magazine ads has improved their bottom line without hurting sales. Customers who use their instant-messaging capabilities spend 8 percent more than other customers. Custom-fitted products, such as jeans, are now easily purchased as buyers submit their own measurements. These developments have increased Internet sales by 35 percent from 2000 to 2001. One aspect of Lands' End's Internet strategy has been to not set up the Internet operations as a separate unit, so that employees do not feel the Web is cannibalizing sales.

Dell advertises Intel components as part of their alliance with another well-known company.

Bobbie Oglesby comments on competitive advantage: "Increasingly, competitive advantage in business is being powered by instant access to information. In addition, kids today carry pagers and phones so they are constantly connected to friends and family. Microsoft understands access to information will be one of the fundamental necessities in the twenty-first century. As a result, we've updated our corporate mission to state our vision of providing 'access to information anytime, anywhere, and on any device.' As a result, all our products are developed to be Internet-savvy, plus our corporate tag line 'Where Do You Want To Go Today' was developed to reflect this vision."

General Business Strategies

Combining the market scope and competitive advantage decisions produces the four general business strategies presented in Exhibit 3–10. The exhibit provides examples of each strategy for the airline industry.[47]

Most of the major airlines, such as American, United, and Delta, employ broad, differentiated strategies. These global carriers compete on many of the same routes, but try to differentiate themselves through service, frequent flier programs, and other benefits. These airlines must be price competitive, but their major strategic focus is to find ways to differentiate themselves on nonprice factors.

Although a strategy of broad scope and low price has been seen in the airline industry, several carriers have been unsuccessful in implementing it. Examples are People's Express, Braniff, and Eastern Airlines. These carriers all failed, largely because none could reduce its cost structure enough to be profitable at the low fares.

One airline that might succeed with this strategy is Southwest Airlines. Southwest began as a narrow-scope, low-price airline in 1971, and the company has posted profits for 29 consecutive years. The airline now serves 58 different cities and is expanding into several others. Thus, its market scope is broadening. Southwest may be able to do what most other airlines have not: make its no-frills approach work even with a broad market scope.[48]

As Southwest expands its market scope, many major carriers have announced plans to go after the short-haul market. Continental has already entered the short-haul business with CALite. USAir, Delta, and United have similar plans. The major carriers are trying to borrow from the strategies that have made Southwest successful.[49] Delta, for example, has partnered with Air France and Swissair in strategic alliances to expand its offerings. In addition, Delta Connection is affiliated with other southeastern airlines to cover short-haul travel, and it recently purchased Comair, enabling even greater accessibility throughout the eastern United States.[50]

Exhibit 3–10

General business strategies

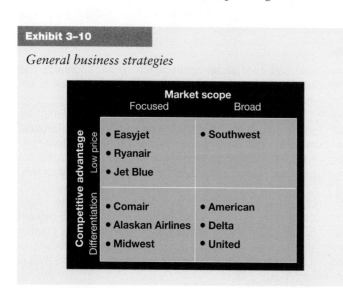

The *Rule of Three* states that naturally occurring competitive forces will create a consistent structure in many mature markets. These three major players often compete by offering a wide range of related products and services and serve most major market segments. Examples include ExxonMobil and ChevronTexaco in the petroleum industry and Gerber, Beech-Nut, and Heinz in the production of baby foods. Sheth and Sisodia argue that smaller players have to carve smaller niche markets that they can serve effectively.[51]

Marketing Strategy Decisions

Recall from Chapter 1 that a marketing strategy addresses the selection of a target market and the development of a marketing mix. The remaining chapters in this book discuss these areas in great detail. Our purpose here is to provide an overview of the two basic types of marketing strategies and to discuss international marketing strategy.

Marketing strategies are developed as functional strategies at the business-unit level and as operating strategies at the product level. The two strategies differ in specificity of decisions. Business strategy decisions are relatively general, intended to provide direction for all business-level marketing activities. Product strategy decisions are very specific, because they guide the actual execution of marketing activities for individual products. Exhibit 3–11 compares the decisions for the two types of marketing strategies.

Business Marketing Strategies

A business marketing strategy must be consistent with the general business strategy. For example, if the general business strategy includes a focused market scope, the target market strategy must concentrate on only a few market segments, perhaps only one. If the general business strategy is low price, the price strategy must be low price. Aside from these obvious constraints, several strategic options are typically available in each marketing strategy area.

Exhibit 3–11	*Business and product marketing strategies*	
Decision Area	**Business Marketing Strategy**	**Product Marketing Strategy**
Target market	Segmented or mass approach	Specific definition of target market to be served
Product	Number of different products	Specific features of each product
Price	General competitive price level	Specific price
Distribution	General distribution policy	Specific distributors
Marketing communications	General emphasis on marketing communications tools	Specific marketing communications program

Being Entrepreneurial

Abercrombie & Fitch: "Tween" the segments

Abercrombie and Fitch realizes that Joe College does not want to hang out with Joey Junior High. As such, A&F has made efforts to remain focused on its primary segment while expanding its appeal to younger market segments. That is, A&F wants to remain cool with college-age and young adults and not become diluted in its A&F positioning from attracting younger patrons. In efforts to appeal to multiple segments, A&F has begun a rollout of a lower-priced chain, Hollister, catering to 14-to-18-year-olds. This line of stores may also compete effectively with the value-oriented American Eagle. A third chain—"Abercrombie with a little 'a'"—is aimed at 7- to 14-year-old customers and has 100-plus stores. These entrepreneurial efforts will require creative strategy in efforts to effectively manage and coordinate different but complementary product lines and market mix configurations.

New technological features are emphasized in this ad promoting the ability of the Saturn Vue to handle any environment.

Thinking Critically

- What planning issues would the manufacturers of Saturn automobiles have to confront in deciding whether to use a standard-ized marketing strategy for promoting their cars in Europe?

- What effects would not using a stan-dardized strategy have on marketing costs?

- What possible marketing strate-gies might BMW implement in the United States as opposed to Europe?

Gillette has had to revamp its marketing strategy because of financial scrutiny from investors, increased internal and material costs, and growing competition. Strategy changes include the elimination of underperforming products, the intro-duction of new razors for female markets, and enhanced brand support for promising product lines. In conjunction with their ad agency, BBDO, Gillette spent $42 million on ads for their Mach 3 brand in 2001.[52]

Saturn focuses on the broad market but divides it into specific segments and de-velops strategies for each. It offers a relatively narrow product line with many op-tions available for each product. Pricing is based on value, and dealers typically do not negotiate. Distribution is selective, with only certain dealers chosen to market the Saturn vehicles. Marketing communications are balanced between advertising to inform consumers and get them into the dealers, and personal selling to sell the cars.

Product Marketing Strategies

Product marketing strategies require very specific decisions (see Exhibit 3–11). The target market is defined in detail, the product features and options specified, exact prices established, actual dealers identified, and a detailed communications pro-gram developed.

These decisions must be consistent with both the general business and the busi-ness marketing strategies. For example, Saturn's target market for each product fits within the market scope of the general business strategy. The unit decides on each product within the business product line, sets prices within the business product guidelines, uses appropriate dealers, and develops a communications strategy sim-ilar to the business communications strategy.

International Marketing Strategies

The development of effective global marketing strategies requires creative thinking. Modern marketing typically focuses on developed nations (or developed segments of nations), although most of the world market lies outside these segments. Selling washers to Japanese customers requires understanding how to market to individu-als with small homes. Global family networks offer opportunities for products to

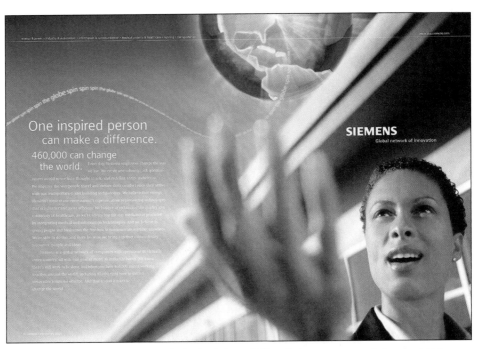

Siemens assumes a global view and adapts their marketing strategy across markets as needed.

be purchased for relatives and sent back home. Cellular telephones enable communications among customers previously deemed impossible because of inadequate telecommunications infrastructure.[53]

Marketers must address two key areas when developing international marketing strategies: selecting an entry strategy and deciding on a strategic orientation.

ENTRY STRATEGY   An **entry strategy** is the approach used to market products in an international market. The basic options include exporting, joint ventures, and direct investment. Each option has advantages and disadvantages in level of investment and amount of control.

Exporting is a method of selling products to buyers in international markets. The exporter might sell directly to international buyers or use intermediaries, such as exporting firms from the home country or importing firms in the foreign country. Exporting typically requires the lowest level of investment, but it offers limited control to the marketer. Carrier (commercial air conditioners), Caterpillar (construction equipment), and Chrysler (cars) are firms actively engaged in exporting.[54]

At the other extreme is **direct investment,** where the marketer invests in production, sales, distribution, or other operations in the foreign country. This normally requires the largest investment of resources, but it gives the marketer the most control over marketing operations. Wang Laboratories, for example, emphasizes direct investment by operating 175 sales and distribution offices worldwide.[55] United Kingdom's Cadbury Schweppes PLC purchased Industrias Dulciora SA to give Cadbury the second-largest market share in Spain's confectionery market.[56]

In between these extremes are various joint-venture approaches. **Joint ventures** include any arrangement between two or more organizations to market products in an international market. Options are licensing agreements, contract manufacturing deals, and equity investments in strategic partnerships. Investment requirements and marketing control are usually moderate, although this depends upon the details of each joint venture. Examples of joint-venture strategies include Apple Computer's licensing of its new PowerPC chip to Asian firms such as Taiwan's Acer; the joint venture for pesticides, named Qingdao Ciba Agro Ltd., between Switzerland's Ciba-Geigy AG and China's Qingdao Pesticides Factory; and the marketing partnership between Delta Airlines and Virgin Atlantic Airways to coordinate flights and give access to London's Heathrow Airport.[57]

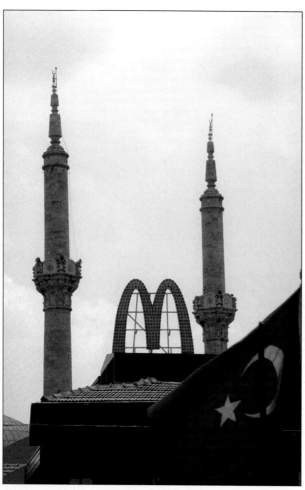

McDonald's is one firm that can utilize some of its promotional efforts in the spirit of a global standardized strategy. However, product variations across countries are common.

INTERNATIONAL STRATEGIC ORIENTATION

Firms operating in international markets can use two different orientations toward marketing strategy. With a **standardized marketing strategy,** a firm develops and implements the same product, price, distribution, and promotion programs in all international markets. With a **customized marketing strategy,** a firm develops and implements a different marketing mix for each target market country.[58] Most international marketing strategies lie somewhere between these extremes, leaning toward one or the other.

These different marketing mixes may involve changes to the communications mix, the product itself, or both. At the corporate level, a **global strategy** views the whole world as a global market. A **multinational strategy** recognizes national differences and views the collection of other countries as a portfolio of markets.

Coca-Cola, for example, uses a largely standardized marketing strategy, where the brand name, concentrate formula, positioning, and advertising are virtually the same worldwide, but the artificial sweetener and packaging differ across countries.[59] TGI Friday's restaurants are successful in the Far East using the same concepts as in the United States. The mix of American memorabilia and chatty, high-fiving waiters produces high sales per store. In fact, the TGI Friday's in Seoul generates double the sales volume of an average restaurant in the United States.[60]

Some marketing experts suggest the need for caution in the drive to create global brands. In truth, there are very few global brands if you consider the percentage of revenues brands realize from outside their domestic markets. Coca-Cola, Gillette, Pampers, Marlboro, Kellogg, and Nescafé derive 50 percent or more of their sales from outside the domestic market. In contrast, many well-known brands are not as global as we often think. For example, Campbell's soup receives only 6 percent of revenues from abroad. In many cases, local and regional brands offer opportunities for company expansion, as foreign markets resist for cultural reasons, particularly following 9/11.[61]

Nissan, in contrast, uses a more customized marketing strategy by tailoring cars to local needs and tastes. One success has been the Nissan Micra, designed specifically to negotiate the narrow streets in England.[62] Similarly, Campbell's Soup gets higher sales by adapting its products to local tastes. For example, sales accelerated when it introduced a cream of chile poblano soup to the Mexican market.[63]

Some companies are moving from customized to standardized marketing strategies. Appliance marketers traditionally customized products for each country. But Whirlpool, through extensive research, found that homemakers from Portugal to Finland have much in common. It now markets the same appliances with the same basic marketing strategy in 25 countries.[64]

The adaptation versus standardization decision is subject to a number of sometimes conflicting factors. Factors encouraging standardization include economy-of-scale advantages in production, marketing effort, and research and development. In addition, increasing economic integration in Europe and intensifying global competition also favor standardization. In many cases, however, demand and usage conditions differ sufficiently to warrant some modifications in marketing-mix offerings. The factors favoring adaptation in international strategy include differing use conditions, governmental and regulatory influences, differing consumer behavior patterns, and local competition. Adaptation is also consistent with the market orientation principles of the marketing concept. Accordingly, standardization may only hold for brands with universal name recognition and for products that require little knowledge for effective use, such as soft drinks and jeans.[65]

One study of 35 companies in Japan, Europe, and the United States that have successfully developed strong brands across countries revealed four common ideas about effective global branding:

1. Stimulate the sharing of insights and best practices across countries.

2. Support a common global brand-planning process.

3. Assign managerial responsibility for brands in order to create cross-country synergies and to fight local bias.

4. Execute brilliant brand-building strategies.[66]

Executing Strategic Plans

Developing strategic plans is one thing; executing them effectively is another. One route to effective execution of strategic plans is encouraging individuals within an organization to work together to achieve organizational objectives, reflecting the development of relationships within the organization. Two forms of teamwork are important: across the different functional areas and within the marketing function. In addition, comarketing alliances enable pursuit of strategic objectives under certain conditions.

Cross-Functional Teamwork

Traditionally, the different functions within an organization worked largely in isolation. Manufacturers manufactured, engineers engineered, marketers marketed, and accountants accounted. With little direct communication between these functions, their orientations were often more adversarial than cooperative, especially since each function has somewhat different objectives and operates from a different vantage point.

Exhibit 3–12 presents the different orientations between marketing and the other organizational functions. The potential difficulties in getting different functions to work together as a team are clear. Why should production care about marketing's interests when it is supposed to produce as much as possible as cheaply as possible? There was no reason for one function to care about another in this type of situation, and typically they did not.

The problem is that if an organization does not produce products that consumers will purchase, it does not matter how low production costs are. More and more organizations are realizing this and adopting a marketing philosophy, which means that everyone within the organization focuses on satisfying customer needs. And satisfying customer needs requires teamwork within an organization.

Many organizations have overcome differences in functional objectives and orientations by communicating the importance of teamwork. They reward the meeting of organizational goals such as customer satisfaction instead of merely functional goals such as low-cost production.

An interesting example of cross-functional teamwork is in the use of multifunctional teams to work with organizational customers. Companies such as Hewlett-Packard, DuPont, Polaroid, and CIGNA send multifunctional teams from marketing, manufacturing, engineering, and R&D to visit specific customers

Exhibit 3–12

Business function orientations

Function	Basic Orientation
Marketing	To attract and retain customers
Production	To produce products at lowest cost
Finance	To keep within budgets
Accounting	To standardize financial reports
Purchasing	To purchase products at lowest cost
R&D	To develop newest technologies
Engineering	To design product specifications

regularly. The objective is to promote teamwork among employees from different functional areas, to develop a customer focus in all functional areas, to collect useful marketing information about customers, and to improve customer relationships.

Nissan created nine cross-functional teams (CFTs) as a centerpiece of their complete reversal. CFTs represent a powerful vehicle for getting managers to see beyond functional and regional boundaries that define their direct responsibilities. As an example, the sales and marketing team consisted of the executive vice-presidents of overseas and domestics sales, plus managers of purchasing and sales and marketing. This group was then successful at deciding upon a single global ad agency, the reduction in Japanese distribution outlets, and the reduction of marketing costs by 20 percent.[67] One study of 141 cross-functional teams revealed that the success of cross-functional teams in generating innovation is a function of: the extent to which members identify with the team rather than with their own functional area; senior management concern and monitoring; social cohesion among the group members; and team attention to customer input.[68]

Marketing Teamwork

Even within marketing functions, teamwork is not universal. Different marketing functions often operate somewhat independently—advertising people perform advertising activities, salespeople sell products, brand managers manage their brands, and marketing researchers engage in marketing research. Many firms have little coordination among the different marketing functions. Today, however, the leading organizations are coordinating their marketing efforts and requiring close contact among the different marketing functions.

Many organizations have emphasized cross-functional teamwork to overcome barriers caused by pursuit of functional objectives, such as low-cost production, rather than long-term customer satisfaction. Hewlett-Packard combines new products with teamwork across functions to enhance market acceptance.

Many consumer product manufacturers, for example, foster close coordination among brand managers, salespeople and sales managers, and marketing researchers to execute tailored marketing programs for individual retail stores. Working as a team, they uncover information about the customers of each store. The sales and brand managers then work together to execute specific marketing programs for each store to improve sales and profits.

Kodak's reorganization illustrates the importance of marketing teamwork. In changing from a product-driven to a marketing-driven philosophy, the company established a group to integrate marketing functions that had been run separately, such as advertising, sales promotions, public relations, sales, and marketing research. The integrated group will work together in developing and executing all marketing plans.[69]

P&G uses a "business management team" approach to run each of its 11 product categories in efforts to encourage global brand success. The teams consist of four managers, headed by an executive vice-president, who have line authority for research and development, manufacturing, and marketing in each region. For example, the head of health and beauty aids in Europe also chairs the hair global category team. Because the teams are headed by top level executives, there are no organizational barriers to carry out decisions.[70]

Bobbie Oglesby comments on growth challenges: "The Internet is fundamentally changing how we market products at Microsoft. With our Web sites and e-mail alerts/newsletters, we are able to form direct relationships with customers. We are also able to provide much more personalized and customized information to meet their individual needs, making one-to-one marketing much more cost-effective than it was in the past."

Co-Marketing Alliances

Co-marketing alliances include contractual arrangements between companies offering complementary products in the marketplace. The alliance between Microsoft and IBM was instrumental in the growth of Microsoft. Such alliances are increasing in frequency and enable firms to gain specialized resources from previously competing organizations. The success of co-marketing alliances is dependent on the care exhibited in partner selection and the extent to which relationships are balanced in power and benefit to both partners. Like in relationships between suppliers, customers, and employees, trust and commitment to the relationship in a co-marketing alliance engender cooperation and profitable network performance.[71] IBM in just over one year forged 50 strategic partnerships with business software specialists and added $700 million sales revenues through sales of hardware, services, and database programs.[72]

Solution selling, in which products are marketed together as a means to construct a meal, has become quite popular. Interestingly, this approach has brought together previous competitors, such as Tyson and Pillsbury. Their coordinated effort to sell Sliced and Diced vegetables and chicken involved all aspects of partnering, from using national advertising to encouraging retailer support.[73]

Other alliances include Northwest Airlines and Visa, Kellogg's Pop-Tarts and Smuckers Jelly, and Krup's coffeemakers and Godiva chocolate. So, too, has Quaker Oats partnered with Nestlé in the development of granola bars with candy-bar appeal. Mattel and P&G are combining to share information and to promote their diaper brand, Pampers Playtime. And the co-branding of credit cards (e.g., Rich's and Visa) by retailers is also increasing; it enhances the visibility of the participating retailer. Determinants of the success of these alliances include prior attitudes toward the two brands and the perceived appropriateness of both brand fit and product fit. More-familiar and well-known brands are most effective at generating positive reactions to brand alliances. In particular, a branded component (e.g., Intel, NutraSweet) carries a certain equity and signals quality and performance more strongly than conventional attributes.[74] Research suggests that the results of horizontal alliances among competitors regarding joint new product development projects are often enhanced because of increased efficiency in information utilization due to common understanding of marketplace and product category phenomena.[75]

Summary

1. **Discuss the three basic levels in an organization and the types of strategic plans developed at each level.** Organizations can be defined at three basic levels. The corporate level is the highest and responsible for addressing issues concerning the overall organization. The business level is the basic level of competition in the marketplace. It consists of units within the organization that are operated like independent businesses. The functional level includes all the different functions within a business unit. Strategic plans are developed at each level. Corporate and business strategic plans provide guidelines for the development of marketing strategic plans and product marketing plans.

2. **Understand the organizational strategic planning process and the role of marketing in this process.** The general strategic planning process consists of examining the current situation, evaluating trends in the marketing environment to identify potential threats and opportunities, setting objectives based on this analysis, and developing strategies to achieve these objectives. Strategic marketing describes marketing activities at the corporate and business levels. Marketing management emphasizes the development and implementation of marketing strategies for individual products and services.

3. **Describe the key decisions in the development of corporate strategy.** The key corporate-level decisions include establishing a corporate vision, developing corporate objectives and allocating resources, determining a corporate growth strategy, and defining the business-unit composition. Corporate strategy decisions affect strategic planning at all lower organizational levels. And strategic plans at lower organizational levels are designed to execute the corporate strategy.

4. **Understand the different general business strategies and their relationship to business marketing, product marketing, and international marketing strategies.** General business strategies require decisions concerning market scope and competitive advantage. Market scope can range from focused to broad; competitive advantage might be based on pricing or differentiation. Combining the market scope and competitive advantage options produces four general business strategies. A firm's business marketing strategy must be consistent with its general business strategy. Decisions on market scope and competitive advantage directly affect business marketing strategies. Product marketing strategies must also be consistent with and serve to execute business marketing strategies. International marketing strategies require decisions about entry method and strategic orientation.

5. **Realize the importance of relationships and teamwork in executing strategic plans.** The complexity of today's business environment requires cooperation both across different business functional areas and within the marketing function itself. Cross-functional and marketing teamwork are necessary to execute strategic plans effectively.

Understanding Marketing Terms and Concepts

Thinking About Marketing

1. How does a firm's corporate vision affect its marketing operations?

2. How does marketing differ for a new, single-product venture and a large, multiproduct corporation?

3. What are the basic options for a corporate growth strategy?

4. Review the insert "Building Customer Equity." What factors determine the long-term value of the customers of Lands' End?

5. How do business marketing strategies and product marketing strategies differ?

6. What are the keys to effective execution of strategic plans?

7. Consider the various types of Abercrombie & Fitch stores. What are the dangers involved with having different types of stores targeted at different segments?

8. How does an understanding of the marketing environment, as discussed in Chapter 2, help in the development of strategic plans?

9. Why do firms change their business composition?

10. How do corporate objectives affect marketing operations?

Applying Marketing Skills

1. Read an annual report for any company. Using only the information in the report, describe the firm's corporate, business, and marketing strategies.

2. Pick a recent issue of *Business Week, Fortune,* or any other business publication. Review it to identify examples of corporate growth strategies used by different firms.

3. Interview a marketing executive at a local firm. Ask the executive what types of strategic plans the firm develops and what is included in each strategic plan. How does this approach coincide with the marketing plan presented in Appendix A?

4. Locate a current advertising campaign that exemplifies a co-marketing alliance. Postulate why these two companies decided to partner and what synergies (i.e., mutual benefits not available to either product on its own) the co-marketing alliance is trying to capture in the market.

Using the www in Marketing

Activity One Go to the home page of Disney.

1. What does the site say about core competencies and corporate vision?

2. How are the businesses organized within the larger corporation?

3. How does the site describe Disney's emphasis on the production of quality products and services?

Activity Two Find the Internet home page of a company that you admire and that offers multiple product lines.

1. What company did you choose? Why?

2. What strategic business units make up the company?

3. What is the overall mission for the firm? What marketing strategies are used to support that mission?

4. Describe the primary product benefits used as the focal point for the marketing strategy of one of the company's products.

Making Marketing Decisions

Case 3-1 SoBe: Marketing Outside the Box

PepsiCo now owns SoBe, a small but successful noncarbonated specialty beverage company (South Beach Beverage Company) built on out-of-the-box marketing thinking. This and other moves involving the acquisition of new beverage categories is a necessity as consumers demand new niche beverages and noncarbonated soft drinks. When big companies like Coke and Pepsi take over distribution of smaller brands, these giants become even more capable of demanding shelf space in stores. SoBe appeals to young consumers with appeals based upon fun, wellness, and value. Users receive nutrient value, as well as unexpected good taste. The healthy refreshment segment

is a huge growth market, and a shift seems to be occurring between carbonated and noncarbonated beverages. Alignment with Pepsi will help with distribution and increased availability.

SoBe's self-described approach is described as "guerrilla marketing"—grass roots marketing around fun events and sampling. One of their ad campaigns centers around two fans rapping about the beverage and touting the Lizard, Elixir, Power, and Tea lines. SoBe competes with Snapple and Arizona in the alternative or New Age beverage market. In some markets, it has surpassed Snapple. As one objective, Pepsi is trying to appeal to

Dr Pepper drinkers by offering a first SoBe carbonated beverage, Mr. Green.

New Age drinks are a loosely defined category growing more rapidly than traditional carbonated soft drinks. So far PepsiCo has not altered the company's marketing budget, letting SoBe keep its autonomy and attitude. It will be interesting to see if PepsiCo can really resist the temptation to meddle with a subsidiary whose CEO operates under the title "Lizard King." One interesting dilemma is the positioning of PepsiCo's Mountain Dew Amp energy drink versus SoBe's Adrenaline Rush drink. The goal is to maintain brand integrity and the great things SoBe represents while delivering it in a Pepsi distributor network.

Questions

1. What environmental and consumer factors have made the large beverage companies expand their product lines?

2. How does SoBe fit into the portfolio of PepsiCo's products in terms of market share and growth potential?

3. What is the basic marketing strategy for SoBe?

4. What are the advantages and disadvantages that will accrue to the managers of SoBe from being owned by a large company like SoBe?

Case 3-2 *Virgin Atlantic Airways: Flying toward U.S. Markets*

 Virgin is best known for its competition with the larger and more staid British Airways. Virgin has benefited greatly in Great Britain from its underdog role in competing for the lucrative transatlantic travel business. In the smaller and confined British environment, Virgin has gained wide recognition. The company aggressively promotes and prices air travel fees and services and has developed very strong brand recognition. Its corporate reputation, regardless of the business endeavor, is clear: innovation, value for the money, and an element of fun.

Virgin is now applying this philosophy in its efforts to break into the U.S. market. Questions remain, however, about its ability to succeed in the U.S. market where it will face both more competitors and an environment in which companies typically spend a lot more on marketing. One action taken by Virgin was the opening of a 75,000-square-foot megastore in New York's Times Square. The store is described as the world's largest record, movie, book, and multimedia store. Virgin's soft-drink brand, ranked in Great Britain above Pepsi, has been introduced in selected U.S. markets. Its airline does indeed possess considerable name recognition among business travelers in the United Kingdom. Recently, Virgin has begun aggressively promoting incentive vouchers that can be purchased and applied for whole or part payments on package holidays, flights, hotel accommodations, and car fares.

Virgin gets much credit for competing with British Airways, and its "cool" image has established a nice niche in the United Kingdom. The cola success has been due to

price; the airline success has been due to unique customer services and creative promotions and advertising. Yet, the hurdles confronted by Virgin in its efforts to successfully compete in the United States are formidable.

Significant changes are likely to impact the operation and marketing strategy for Virgin Atlantic. Sales of transatlantic flights have been affected by international events. These flights are the lifeline for both British Airways and Virgin Atlantic. Cost reduction efforts can improve the bottom line but detract from long-term customer service. Virgin is giving away $250 gift certificates from the Sharper Image to customers who sign up for their frequent-flier mileage program and purchase a round-trip ticket to London. Competition may become more intense as British Airways and American Airlines have been given antitrust exemption to coordinate pricing and schedules.

Questions

1. What major obstacles will Virgin face in the U.S. expansion that are not part of marketing within the United Kingdom?

2. What problems occur when products from the same corporate brand (Virgin) are differentiated on different bases (price versus service)?

3. Given 9/11, how will airlines change their marketing strategy?

Chapter Four 4

Consumer Buying Behavior and Decision Making

After studying this chapter, you should be able to:

1 Discuss the importance of consumer behavior.

2 Understand consumer decision making and some of the important influences on those decisions.

3 Distinguish between low-involvement and high-involvement consumer behavior.

4 Understand how attitudes influence consumer purchases.

5 Appreciate how the social environment affects consumer behavior.

6 Recognize many of the individual consumer differences that influence purchase decisions and behavior.

7 Recognize the outcomes of consumers' decisions to purchase or not to purchase and how they affect marketing success.

www usa visa com

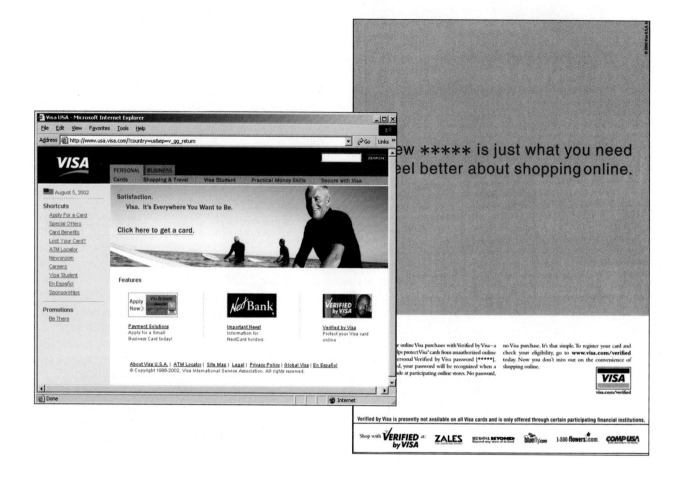

Alternatively reviled and adored, the credit card is an integral part of the American and global payment system. Visa credit cards are the world's most used form of "plastic" payment. According to the company's Web site, more than $1.8 trillion products and services are purchased annually using Visa credit cards, and Visa's worldwide market share is approximately 60 percent. Visa's cards are accepted at more than 21 million locations in over 300 countries. As such, Visa is a primary company in the minds and behavior of many consumers. The firm provides the ability to make purchases and ownership possible while offering consumers the ability to provide credit in support of their consumer behavior.

Visa's competition, in addition to American Express, Discover, and MasterCard, is cash and checks. Interestingly, the company's brand managers

view their objective as gaining greater control over consumer transactions. Currently, Visa outspends all others in terms of media expenditures ($319 million). Moreover, their quality rating and awareness levels exceed all other cards. While the Internet potential is enormous, Visa focuses its efforts upon traditional in-store purchases. In contrast, American Express and Discover are pressing their presence for use in Internet purchases.

Visa obtains revenues from fees associated with cards using the Visa logo and from charge activity. The company's income exceeds $1 billion annually. Rebecca Saeger, Executive VP for Brand Marketing, asserts that marketplace acceptance is a key driver of the brand's widespread preference among consumers. Visa's extensive marketing efforts are designed to reinforce that perception among credit users.

Visa's success is due to the company's ability to adapt to rapidly changing environments and evolving customer needs. Visa's adherence to the principles of the marketing concept has depended on the company's understanding of consumer decision making and the many internal and external factors that affect consumer choices. Marketers are increasingly emphasizing consumer loyalty and retention programs and have allocated marketing budget funds accordingly. These programs go by many names, including loyalty, frequency, retention, and relationship marketing. But all define the same basic concept: identify, segment, and retain profitable customers by communicating and rewarding desired behavior.[1]

In the development and execution of a marketing program, a company must consider consumer preferences, the motivations behind purchase decisions, and subsequent product use. Remember that the marketing concept is based on identification of consumer needs and customer satisfaction. Likewise, building customer loyalty and long-term profitability are not possible without a firm grasp of the company's current and future customers. The success of marketing strategy, including the identification of target segments and the design of marketing mix combinations, depends on knowing what motivates consumers and how they form preferences and make decisions. Even following the many dot com failures, online marketers, like traditional firms, must understand consumers. Attracting business and keeping consumers are now the greatest challenge. Understanding those consumers is critical.[2]

Consumer behavior is a complex topic and difficult to cover in a single chapter. In fact, consumer behavior is a separate course in many marketing programs. Additionally, the study of consumer behavior has historically been a multidisciplinary phenomenon. Researchers from psychology, anthropology, economics, and sociology, as well as marketing and consumer-behavior specialists, have all contributed greatly to our understanding of consumer preferences and decision making.

In this chapter, we try to describe many of the most important aspects of consumer behavior. Again, the study of consumer behavior is critical in helping to ensure adherence to the principles of the marketing concept and the development of effective marketing strategy. First, we offer a formal definition of consumer behavior and explain why the topic is so important. Then we use a model of consumer decision processes to explore consumer problem solving and decision making. Next, we describe important environmental, individual, and situational influences that affect consumer behavior. The chapter concludes with a discussion of the primary outcomes that can follow the purchase and use of products and services, as well as a number of ethical issues that involve individual consumer behavior.

The Nature of Consumer Behavior and Decision Making

Consumer behavior can be defined as the mental and emotional processes and the physical activities that people engage in when they select, purchase, use, and dispose of products or services to satisfy particular needs and desires. Identifying and understanding consumer needs and preferences and their determinants is critical in the pursuit of profitable business opportunities.

Today a number of factors make it all the more important to understand consumer markets and individual consumer behavior: the mere size of the consumer market, ongoing changes in consumer shopping habits and purchase decisions, the continuing emphasis on consumer-oriented marketing, and the design of effective marketing strategy.

Size of the Consumer Market

The U.S. consumer market consists of all individuals in the United States. In 2001, the consumption expenditures for this market were huge: $7.1 trillion out of a total gross domestic product of $10.2 trillion.[3] Demand of this magnitude is well worth understanding. Moreover, competition for consumer dollars will increase as

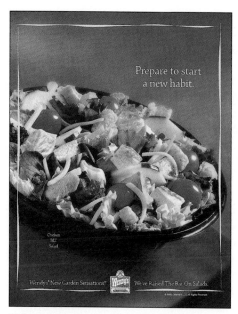

Shifts in consumer preferences for some markets have been driven by growing concerns about health and nutrition. Many food marketers have incorporated such preference shifts into the design of their menus.

populations in the United States and other countries age, resulting in declining expenditures for some products. Firms that understand consumer behavior will be best able to compete effectively.

Changes in the Consumer Market

Of equal importance are changes occurring in the consumer market. Some important growing markets are are detailed in Exhibit 4–1. They include consumers' concern for quality at reasonable and fair prices, for the effects of their purchases on the environment, and for health and diet.

Several fundamental demographic changes will affect the underpinnings of future consumer markets. These include the aging of the baby-boom generation, the increasing importance of children as consumers, differences between the haves and have-nots, and society's increasingly diverse population. Household budget expenditures will increase dramatically for health care and computers relative to declining dollars for furniture, food, and apparel.[4]

Other trends that have increased dramatically in the last five years and will continue to increase include the following: the growing importance of convenience such as bottled water; ready-to-eat consumption such as frozen pizza and refrigerated dinners and fresh salads; and the doubling of sales of health and self-care products. According to the Census Bureau, Hispanics make up the largest growing consumer segment, spending some $380 billion on products and services annually. Importantly, studies show that Hispanics are more loyal to the services, products, and companies that show a direct interest in them through electronic or print advertising.[5]

One of the largest transformations in households has been the changes that have occurred in gender roles and division of responsibilities between husbands and wives. The implications of this enormous change for the design of product and service offerings, as well as for the intended audience of advertising, are profound.

Nowhere are the complexities more obvious than in the food industry. The paradox here is that consumers may want low-fat, low-cholesterol salads for lunch and fish for dinner, but many also choose a hot fudge sundae for dessert. This means that some old-fashioned, middle-of-the-road products like ordinary ice cream are being squeezed by low-cal frozen yogurts on one side and extra-luscious, super-premium ice creams on the other.

Procter & Gamble continues to prosper and is growing worldwide. The primary impetus for the company's growth and profitability is its understanding of consumer demands for value. P&G's emphasis on volume growth, driven by innovation and lower prices, has been the primary contributor to higher earnings. The company's stated objective is to offer superior performance at competitive prices. It pursues this objective through price reductions on recognized brands, cost control throughout the organization, and the introduction of economy-priced products worldwide.[6]

Consumer-Oriented Marketing

To become more consumer-oriented and to build long-lasting relationships with their customers, companies need to understand what motivates buyers. This is an important aspect of the marketing concept. Ford Motor Company, for example, focuses on increased customer satisfaction and employee commitment. The company

- Is dedicated to being customer-driven.
- Makes carefully thought-out decisions about the customers to whom each product is to appeal.

Multicultural differences offer opportunities for marketers to capitalize on unique preferences among segments of consumers.

Exhibit 4–1	*Growing consumer markets*

1. Retail line-up changes—three new models: (1) "price-centric retailers"; (2) retailers organized by lifestyle (e.g., the Museum Company); and (3) "occasion-centric" retailers (e.g., gourmet cooking supply).
2. Outdoor living markets—garden, deck, patio, and pool design.
3. Consumer electronics—new digital conveniences.
4. Enhanced experience businesses—spas, travel with theme activities.
5. Anti-aging products and services—as boomers reach retirement.
6. Health as a national hobby—educated consumers are driving changes in health care.
7. High-end sports apparel and equipment—golf clubs, rackets, skis, skates, bikes, etc.
8. Safe packaging, pure contents, and "green" concerns—ecologically enhancing and safety concerns.

- Studies potential customers and what they most want.
- Develops detailed product attributes to fulfill customer wants; doesn't copy what someone else is doing.
- Follows up with customers to confirm that products and marketing programs meet objectives.[7]

Importantly, and as part of this customer orientation, firms are now focusing upon customer value and those customers whose long-term values are high. Research has shown that the value of a firm's customers—and by implication, the value of a firm—can almost double when the firm shifts from a low-retention, high-discount orientation to a high-retention, low-discount emphasis.[8]

To consistently deliver high-quality products and services, marketers must understand and respond to continually changing consumer needs and expectations.[9] And marketers with the best understanding and the least biased perceptions of consumer needs will be the most competitive.[10] This constant striving to understand and better serve consumers reflects the pursuit of total quality management (TQM) principles.

Design of Strategy

Last, an understanding of consumer behavior is required for the effective design and implementation of marketing strategy. Knowledge gained through experience and marketing research provides the basis for the development of brand images and market positioning strategies. The success of these efforts determines subsequent brand strength, or what is commonly called *brand equity,* the marketplace value of a brand. A strong, well-known consumer brand, such as Kodak, Gap, Coke, Nabisco, and others, can induce quick and favorable consumer reactions to the particular company's products and enable the successful introduction of new products using the same brand name. Understanding consumer behavior can assist marketers in their efforts at *service recovery*—winning back consumers who defect. Defection can be driven by complaints not handled, the competition offering a better value,

Building Customer Equity

Subway's lean focus

Subway is now the largest chain in terms of number of stores and has a growth rate of roughly seven times the average of other restaurant chains. This growth helps build market share in that many consumers will not travel long distances if alternatives are available. More importantly, Subway has succeeded by pursuing a sound strategy to lure customers to their stores. Specifically, Subway's core concept and compelling value proposition have resonated with a large market: low-fat and full-taste menu items under various umbrella messages, such as "Eat fresh." This approach has focused the franchise system on low fat and improved quality. As such, Subway has substantially enhanced its position in the minds of consumers.

"Most companies see consumer segmentation as the final phase to a research effort, when, in fact, it is the beginning of marketing effort to help the organization use the information. Too many times companies do not devote enough thought to training the organization on how they can utilize the results of consumer segmentation to develop new services, design more targeted communications, or consider repositioning alternatives."

Chet Zalesky
President
ConsumerMetrics, Inc.

ConsumerMetrics is an Atlanta marketing research firm that offers general research services, but specializes in analyzing complex issues and quantitative analyses. Chet

Zalesky earned his Master's of Science in Marketing degree from the University of South Carolina's Darla Moore School of Business.

or relocation. However, the primary reason for defection is benign neglect. Understanding consumer behavior enhances the marketer's ability to know the motivations and needs of consumers and their ability to communicate effectively with consumers.[11]

Understanding E-Customers

The profile of Internet buyers is certainly changing as consumers of all types are using the Web for making purchases. Researchers are monitoring consumer behavior on the Internet in efforts to understand what drives patronage and decision making, as well as the determinants of loyalty. One survey of 400,000 Internet customers revealed a number of findings. The 10 most important site attributes in order of ranking are: product representation, product prices, product selection, on-time delivery, ease of ordering, product information, level and quality of consumer support, product shipping and handling, posted privacy policy, and site navigation and appearance.[12]

Using the Claritas PRIZM segmentation scheme based on a combination of geographic and demographic characteristics, one research study revealed that Web users range from the Blue Blood Estates to the downscale country folk of Rustic Elders. The clusters with the greatest access to the Internet are still early-adopting, upscale consumers. However, many of the clusters with the greatest online activity and time spent online are working-class and lower income groups. And actually, the number of sites visited monthly by upscale consumers has declined.[13]

Consumers sometimes say one thing and do another. Webvan, an online grocery service, had 6.5 percent of the households in San Francisco order from the company in its first year and a half of operation. However, follow-up orders never achieved sufficient levels to justify the company's elaborate warehouse capabilities. Buying groceries online required more planning and effort than consumers initially anticipated.[14]

Consumer Decision Making

A general model of consumer decision making and influences on these decisions is presented in Exhibit 4–2. The consumer decision process, shown in the center of the model, assumes a conscious and logical decision-making process: from recognition of a need or problem to information search to evaluation of alternatives to purchase. This sequence can be affected by the social environment, individual differences, and situational factors. All have implications for the design and implementation of successful marketing strategy.

The Consumer Decision Process

A consumer's recognition of a *need* or *problem* may stem from an internal desire, the absence or failure of a product, or some external influence such as advertising. It can be as simple as getting thirsty and wanting a soda, or having to replace a used or outdated product or one that has lost its appeal. Advertising may also trigger the consumer's perception of a need or serve as a reminder.

Exhibit 4–2   *A general model of consumer decision making and influences*

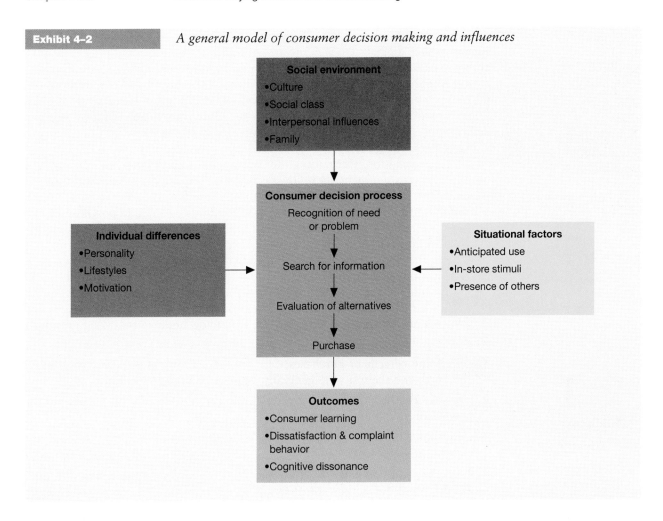

After recognizing a problem, the consumer engages in a search for information. An *internal search* involves a review of information stored in memory. Although readily available, internal information may be incomplete or inaccurate. An *external search* involves gathering information from marketing sources such as advertising or from nonmarketing sources such as friends or *Consumer Reports*. Nonmarketing sources of information may be particularly useful because they are likely unbiased. The degree of search can vary by the number of brands examined, the number of stores visited, the variety of attributes considered, the number of information sources consulted, and the time spent on searching. An understanding of consumer search behavior is important to defining a product's or brand's competition.

Consumer researchers have identified several interesting phenomena regarding search behavior and how search relates to knowledge acquisition by consumers. First, prior knowledge facilitates the learning of new knowledge and increases search efficiency. That is, more expert consumers are likely to search more, not less, than low-knowledge consumers. Experts know the questions to ask and can more easily understand the answers they receive. Relatedly, research suggests that marketers can benefit from teaching consumers the appropriate vocabulary associated with their product categories. This enhanced vocabulary enables consumers to learn more easily new product information and to form more stable brand preferences.[15]

The effects of online search and evaluation are already very evident and are profoundly affecting the manner in which consumers shop and the way in which firms compete. The Internet acts as a readily accessible source of external information and a facilitator of alternative evaluation. Psychologists and marketing experts have found that consumers who search on-line are impatient, in control, and quick to shift from Web site to Web site. Consumers in cyberspace are demanding more choices and more information. The most important attributes for encouraging consumers to shop a particular Web site are assurance of privacy, larger price discounts, ability to return products to a bricks-and-mortar store, and ability to speak with a customer representative. The shoppingbot phenomenon has also revised the decision-making process. A typical shoppingbot sequence might begin with a series of questions to narrow choices, then offer manufacturer-provided, detailed product descriptions, then end with links to retailers. In other instances, auction sites provide input regarding the possibility of bidding for decided-upon items.[16]

After searching for information, the consumer evaluates possibilities (products, brands). This *evaluation of alternatives* is based on the individual's beliefs about the products and their features or characteristics. These beliefs form the basis for the consumer's attitudes, which influence both intentions to buy and purchase behavior. Following purchase, outcomes such as feelings of satisfaction or dissatisfaction and the development of brand loyalty may occur.

Consumer behavior is a complex phenomenon, and many internal and external factors may influence an individual decision. Many decisions are motivated by specific needs and values; some involve a conscious and logical decision process; others are made with little or no thought. One in-store field study of 4,200 grocery and mass-merchandiser shoppers revealed the following findings regarding consumer decision making:

1. Fifty-nine percent of purchases were unplanned, 30 percent were specifically planned, and the rest were generally planned or brand switches.

2. In-store decision making is greater for larger households, for higher-income households, and for women.

3. Consumers are more likely to make an unplanned decision when the product is displayed at the end of an aisle.[17]

Two other concepts relate to consumer decision making. First, **conversion rates** are used to describe the percent of shoppers who are converted into buyers. Conversion rates vary widely depending upon the kind of store or department involved. In some parts of the grocery store, conversion rates are near 100 percent. In art galleries, the conversion rates are near zero. Conversion rates in e-commerce are lessened by the "abandoned basket" phenomena. Often consumers get far along the decision process and then walk away. Some reluctance is due to privacy and credit card information concerns. Other reasons are tied to uncertainty among consumers due to their limited ability to evaluate products with confidence. Second, **surrogate shoppers** are involved in a significant portion of consumer decisions. A surrogate shopper is defined as a commercial enterprise, consciously engaged and paid by the consumer or other interested partner on behalf of the consumer to make or facilitate consumer decisions. Familiar examples include financial advisers, travel agents, and wardrobe consultants. Surrogates may perform any or all of the activities involved in consumer decision making—from search to determination of the brand consideration set to choice.[18]

High- and Low-Involvement Decisions

Involvement represents the level of importance or interest generated by a product or a decision. It varies by the situation or the product decision at hand and is influenced by the person's needs or motives. Frequently, involvement is affected by how closely the purchase decision is linked to the consumer's self-concept and how personally relevant the product is to the consumer.

Involvement is an important concept because it affects the nature or complexity of the communications appropriate for promoting products and services. Relatedly, involvement influences the nature of information processing engaged in by consumers. **Consumer information processing** represents the cognitive processes by which consumers interpret and integrate information from the environment.[19]

High-involvement decisions are characterized by high levels of importance, thorough information processing, and substantial differences between alternatives.

Thinking Critically

Think of a purchase where you have gone through each of the four steps in the consumer decision process (see Exhibit 4–2).

- How did you become aware that a need existed for this product or service?

- Was this purchase a result of routinized response behavior, extensive problem solving, or limited problem solving? How might a company's marketing efforts differ under each of these problem-solving situations?

- What influence did your family have on the purchase?

- After purchasing the product or service did you experience any cognitive dissonance?

Thinking Critically

We all carry attitudes about people, objects, and behaviors. These attitudes can be both positive and negative in direction.

- Why would it be important for a company to understand the attitude consumers have toward its product? How might marketers use this information in marketing communications?

- What role do attitudes play in consumer satisfaction/ dissatisfaction?

The choice of a college to attend, the purchase of a home or vehicle, or the purchase of a bike for a sports enthusiast are all examples of high-involvement decisions. As such, high-involvement decisions are consistent with the logical and thoughtful sequence shown in the center of the consumer behavior model in Exhibit 4–2.

High involvement may be caused by a number of personal, product, and situational factors.[20] Again, importance of the purchase to one's self-concept increases involvement. If financial or performance risk is high, the decision is more likely to have high involvement. High involvement is also more likely when a gift is purchased or social pressures occur.

Low-involvement decisions occur when relatively little personal interest, relevance, or importance is associated with a purchase. These decisions involve much simpler decision processes, and little information processing, than the sequence described in Exhibit 4–2. For low-involvement decisions, consumers do not actively seek large amounts of information. Low-involvement purchases may include soft drinks, fast foods, toothpaste, and many snack foods. In these instances, repetitive purchase behavior may develop. Since these decisions involve little risk, trial purchases are often the consumer's major means of information search and product or brand evaluation.[21]

Types of Consumer Choices

Actually, the acquisition of goods and services is made up of many choices. At least six generic choices may be involved in consumer behavior: product, brand, shopping area, store type, store, and to an increasing degree, nonstore source (catalogs, PC and TV shopping).[22] The decision-making processes and the influences on those decisions discussed in this chapter apply to all six of these choices.

The choices consumers now face are enormous. Some experts believe that the choices are too many and that even dropping items (i.e., *SKUs* or stockkeeping units) within a product category can actually increase sales. Consumer product manufacturers introduced more than 31,000 new items in 2000. The typical grocer now stocks more than 40,000 items. The result is Kellogg Eggo waffles in 16 flavors, nine varieties of Kleenex tissue, and Glad garbage bags that have multiple varieties of ties.[23]

Consumers also must allocate their limited budgets across product categories. The average U.S. metropolitan household devotes half of its spending to housing, utilities, transportation, and food. Other categories allocated at least 5 percent annually are apparel, insurance, health care, and entertainment. As such, much consumer marketing funds are directed at these categories.[24]

Attitudes

Attitudes and attitude formation are related to the evaluation stage of the consumer decision process. **Consumer attitudes** are learned predispositions to respond favorably or unfavorably to a product or brand. Most of us take for granted our attitudes toward our favorite restaurant or soft drink. However, attitudes are instrumental in determining which alternative products and brands will be purchased and used. Attitudes have certain characteristics that make understanding them important to marketers trying to convince consumers to either buy their products for the first time or to remain loyal. First, attitudes have valence. That is, attitudes can be positive, negative, or neutral. Firms use creative messages and allocate huge amounts of funds to create or encourage positive attitudes. Second, attitudes that are strongly held and/or which are held with confidence are resistant to change. Therefore, the establishment of positive

Jeep employs unique visuals in their efforts to encourage consumer message processing and their distinctive brand positioning.

brand attitudes in the marketplace is a strategic objective for marketers. Last, attitudes can erode over time if not reinforced; hence, one role of advertising, as you will learn in Chapter 17, is to maintain awareness and to reinforce existing positive brand impressions and attitudes. It is particularly important to note that attitudes are a primary determinant of purchase behavior and their role in consumer behavior is a frequent area of inquiry for marketing researchers.

An understanding of consumer attitudes has very basic implications for marketing, for two reasons. Attitudes are based on beliefs consumers hold about the attributes or features (price, level of service, quality) of the products they are evaluating. In many instances, these attributes form the basis for the development of marketing strategies. And attitudes are primary causes of behavior, which makes them very relevant to marketers who want to understand why consumers buy—or do not buy—their products.

Consistent with one well-known psychological model, attitudes are often depicted as the combination of beliefs about the salient product attributes that consumers consider in evaluating alternative choices. The model and an example are presented in detail in the textbook's appendix. This theoretical view of consumer attitudes is rich in implications for developing effective marketing strategy. Briefly, attitudes are assumed to reflect the consumer's beliefs about product attributes (e.g., price, ability to clean, durability) and the weights or evaluation the individual has assigned to the different attributes. This multi-attribute view of consumer attitudes helps marketers assess which attributes are important to consumers, the strengths and weaknesses of brands based on those attributes, and areas in which the greatest improvement in attitudes might be realized.

Experiential Choices

So far, we have described consumer decision making as a logical process involving the conscious consideration of product information related to the attributes or the characteristics of the alternatives under consideration. The assumption is that consumers' long-term goals guide their preferences and that they make purchase decisions thoughtfully and logically. Routinized or habitual decision making is the only exception we have discussed to this point. However, consumers frequently make choices based on their emotions and feelings, adding an experiential perspective to the decision process. One such choice heuristic is termed **affect referral.** In such instances, consumers simply elicit from memory their overall evaluations of products and choose the alternative for which they have the most positive feelings. Affect referral explains why so many convenience items are purchased habitually. Another category of buying decisions that are made with little or no cognitive effort are **impulse purchases.** Impulse purchases are choices made on the spur of the moment, often without prior problem recognition, but associated with strong positive feelings.[25]

Consumers also often make irrational choices in which they act against their own better judgment and engage in behavior they would normally reject. These decisions are called *time-inconsistent choices* and, like impulse purchases, reflect consumer impatience and the urge to splurge. Psychologists have studied these choices as related to dieting and addiction for years. Yet all of us at one time or another have felt the urge to buy when better judgment suggests otherwise.[26]

Influence of the Social Environment   A number of external influences affect consumer behavior and purchase decision processes. The social environment directly affects sources of information consumers use in decision making and product evaluations. In many instances, personal sources, such as family and friends, may be more credible and influential to consumers than any other source of information.

The most important social influences are culture, subculture, social class, family, and interpersonal or reference group influences. These flows of influence within the social environment are summarized in Exhibit 4–3.

Exhibit 4–3   *Flows of influence within the social environment*

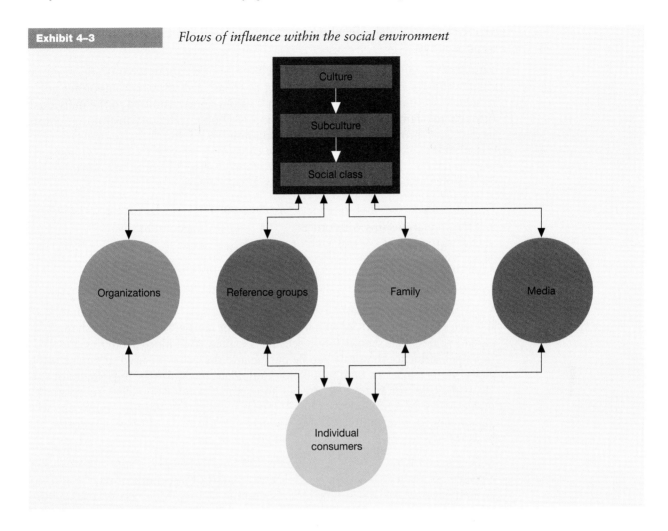

Cultural Influences

Culture refers to the values, ideas, attitudes, and symbols that people adopt to communicate, interpret, and interact as members of society. In fact, culture describes a society's way of life. Culture is learned and transmitted from one generation to the next. It includes abstract elements (values, attitudes, ideas, religion) and material elements (symbols, buildings, products, brands). The process of absorbing a culture is called **socialization.** It continues throughout one's life and produces many specific preferences for products and services, shopping patterns, and interactions with others. Applied to marketing and consumer behavior, it is referred to as *consumer socialization.*

In particular, the culture of a country has been shown to affect the appropriateness of different advertising strategies. Using the well-known categories of culture developed by an IBM executive, Geert Hofstede, one researcher discovered that in countries where people are not highly focused on social roles and group affiliation, such as Germany and Argentina, functional brand images are most effective. In countries where social roles are important, such as France and Belgium, images based on social and sensory messages are appropriate. Relatedly, cultures with low individualism (e.g., Asian countries) are also amenable to social appeals that emphasize group affiliation.[27] Cultural effects have been found also in terms of consumer product innovativeness. For example, consumers in more individualistic and masculine countries tend to be more innovative. Innovativeness decreased in countries scoring high in ethnocentrism, a more favorable attitude toward the past.[28]

The concept of culture has two primary implications for marketing: It determines the most basic values that influence consumer behavior patterns, and it can be used to distinguish subcultures that represent substantial market segments and opportunities.

VALUES   Values are shared beliefs or cultural norms about what is important or right. Values, such as the need to belong or to succeed, represent important goals to which consumers subscribe. A society's values are transmitted to the individual through the family, through organizations (schools, religious institutions, businesses), and through other people (the community, the social environment).

Cultural values directly influence how consumers view and use individual products, brands, and services. One typology of values used by consumer researchers is the List of Values (LOV).[29] It includes nine basic values:

- Self-respect
- Warm relationships with others
- Self-fulfillment
- Respect from others
- Excitement
- Security
- Sense of accomplishment
- Sense of belonging
- Fun and enjoyment in life

Another commercial method researching consumer values is the Values and Lifestyles program (VALS), which identifies eight market segments that share similar end values. This segmentation scheme is explained in more detail in Chapter 7.

Values influence the goals people pursue and the behavior used to pursue those goals. Many marketing communication campaigns recognize the importance of values as the basis for advertising themes and justification for purchase. For example, the desire for recognition and self-fulfillment is frequently used by companies selling self-improvement and exercise products. Or, the sense of belonging forms the basis for marketing many personal and gift products.

SUBCULTURES   The norms and values of specific groups or subcultures within a society are called **ethnic patterns.** Ethnic groups or subcultures may be formed around national, religious, racial, or geographic factors. Members of a subculture share similar values and patterns of behavior, making them attractive marketing targets for specific products and brands.

Unique subcultures often develop in geographic areas of a nation. The southwestern part of the United States is known for casual lifestyles, outdoor living, and active sports.[30] The Southeast is associated with a conservative lifestyle and friendly atmosphere. One system divides North America into "nine nations": the Foundry (industrial Northeast); Dixie; Ectopia (northern Pacific Rim); Mexamericana (southwestern area); the Breadbasket (Kansas, Nebraska, Iowa, etc.); Quebec (French-speaking Canada); the Empty Quarter (northwestern Canada); the Islands (tip of southern Florida, Caribbean Islands, some Latin American influence); and New England.[31] Each region contains many individuals who share similar values and lifestyles.

The black and Hispanic subcultures, while diverse themselves, are the largest ethnic subcultures. The black subculture is growing in size and spending power. Hispanics make up the second-fastest-growing subculture, behind the Asian subculture. Many Hispanics share a common language and a strong family orientation. Conservative Christian areas and Jewish centers also represent subcultures of influence.

Numerous demographic characteristics have been used to identify subcultures. Examples of these include:

Nationality—Hispanics, Italians.

Race—African-American, American Indian, Asian.

Region—New England, the South.

Cultural differences offer opportunities for marketers. Among the largest and fastest growing segment is the Hispanic market. *Latina,* a bilingual magazine for Hispanic women, is designed to appeal to those consumers who maintain ties with their heritage.

Age—elderly, teenager.

Religion—Catholic, Jewish, fundamentalist.

These subcultures include large numbers of consumers who share common values, behavior patterns, and beliefs that relate to consumer behavior. (Note that an individual can belong to more than one subculture.) The consumer socialization of individuals within those subcultures affects their purchase decisions.[32]

Demographic analysis can be used in other ways for understanding consumer phenomena. For example, the enduring characteristics of the generation from which consumers come remain important as individuals age. Marketers are increasingly using these shared generational experiences to reach and effectively appeal to consumer segments. For the Depression generation, that may mean stressing thrift; for the World War II generation, patriotism; boomers are often seen as independent types stretching society's bounds. The point is, as the young get older, their habits stick with them.[33]

Age, a commonly used segmentation variable, also can be used to understand subculture differences. The baby-boom, Generation X, and now Generation Y segments share common values much like other cultural subgroups. Even as Generation Y, or those individuals born between 1977 and 1994, reaches adulthood, many companies are positioning themselves to achieve a part of this complex and powerful market. Importantly, young consumers learn preferences and loyalties that continue for years. In addition, cohort experiences represent shared experiences that form values and life skills through which consumers interpret subsequent experiences. As such, age differences within a year certainly affect consumption and represent different market segments. Moreover, age generation or cohorts share common experiences and represent segments with common values over time.[34]

Social Class Influences

Social classes are relatively homogeneous divisions within a society that contain people with similar values, needs, lifestyles, and behavior. One approach for consumer analysis describes four social classes: upper, middle, working, and lower class, each of which can be further subdivided.[35] Identification with a social class is influenced most strongly by level of education and occupation. Social class is also affected by social skill, status aspirations, community participation, cultural level, and family history.[36] Social classes are relatively stable, but educational experiences and career moves enable individuals to shift from one class to another. Today, the middle class is declining in size. Economic conditions have limited upward mobility of the working class and caused many borderline families to fall into poverty.[37]

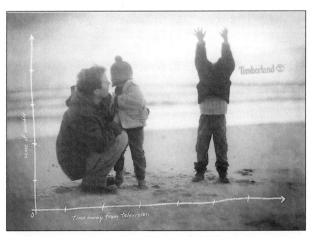

Timberland recognizes the importance of family influences in this brand advertisement.

One recent study asked individuals to classify themselves as lower, working, middle, or upper class. Forty-six and 47 percent categorized themselves as working and middle class, respectively. Occupation and education were again the primary reasons individuals gave for their assignments. Research suggests that the working class is becoming younger, more ethnically diverse, and more female. These changes offer opportunities for marketers in their desire to understand consumer behavior and to identify large segments of potential buyers.[38]

Social class influences the types of purchases consumers make and the activities they pursue. Who goes to wrestling matches and who goes to the opera? Who plays polo and who goes bowling? Exhibit 4–4 summarizes some of the differences among subclasses of the middle class. Although preferences do change

Exhibit 4–4		*Class distinctions: You are what you choose*		
		Lower Middle	**Middle**	**Upper Middle**
Car	1980s	Hyundai	Chevrolet Celebrity	Mercedes
	1990s	Geo	Chrysler minivan	Range Rover
Business shoe (men)	1980s	Sneakers	Wingtips	Cap toes
	1990s	Boots	Rockports	Loafers
Business shoe (women)	1980s	Spike-heel pumps	Mid-heel pumps	High-heel pumps
	1990s	High-heel pumps	Dressy flats	One-inch pumps
Alcoholic beverage	1980s	Domestic beer	White wine spritzer	Dom Perignon
	1990s	Domestic light beer	California Chardonnay	Cristal
Leisure pursuit	1980s	Watching sports	Going to movies	Golf
	1990s	Playing sports	Renting movies	Playing with computers
Hero	1980s	Roseanne Barr	Ronald Reagan	Michael Milken
	1990s	Kathie Lee Gifford	Janet Reno	Rush Limbaugh

within classes over time, more-significant differences in purchases and behaviors occur *between* classes.

Trickle-down theory offers another perspective on social class effects. "Top levels," who determine what is acceptable or hot, are less defined today by social class or money. Rather many trendsetters are young consumers, many of whom do not have high incomes. One resulting effect of this phenomenon is "cool-hunting," where market researchers observe covertly these trendsetters to learn of the latest styles before these styles reach the mainstream marketplace and culture.

Family Influences and the Family Life Cycle

Family influences play two important roles: in the socialization of people and in affecting individual purchase decisions. Families are the most influential factor on an individual's behavior, values, and attitudes. Patterns of behavior and values learned early in life are not easily changed. Lifestyles (athleticism, fondness for the outdoors) are usually learned from parents through **childhood consumer socialization**—the process by which young people acquire skills, knowledge, and attitudes relevant to their functioning as consumers in the marketplace.[39]

Individual family members also influence purchase decisions through their performance of different roles within the family. Members of a family or household may assume different roles—and roles may change, depending on the situation. In the choice of toys, for example, parents often determine the acceptable set of brands from which children may select. The parents make the decision to buy, yet the child makes the brand choice. In other cases, all family members may influence decisions to purchase large-ticket items such as homes and automobiles, and increasingly, men and teenagers are doing the grocery shopping; marketers target these shoppers with ads in the magazines they buy.

Developmental timetables are expectations or beliefs about what is normal for a child at a specific age. Socialization differences in terms of developmental timetables have been shown recently between Japanese and American parents. Specifically, Japanese mothers expect their children to develop consumer-related skills and understanding of advertising later than their U.S. counterparts. In addition, Japanese children are allowed less autonomy in their consumer behavior.[40]

Today, the role of children and teenagers within a family, and even as a market themselves, cannot be underestimated. A typical 10-year-old goes shopping two or three times per week with parents. Apparel spending is the fastest-growing category of expenditures, and preferences formed by the young influence brand recognition and success among other age groups. According to the 2000 Census, 41 million individuals aged 5–12 live in the United States alone. As the number of single-parent

Family buyer and user differences across purchase categories

	Purchase decision maker		
	One member	Some members	All members
One member	**1** Book	**2** Dad & Eric buy tennis racquet for Eric	**3** Birthday gift
Some members	**4** Mom buys breakfast cereal for kids	**5** Wine for dinner party	**6** Private school for children
All members	**7** Refrigerator	**8** Personal computer	**9** Everyone helps pick toppings on a pizza

(User is labeled vertically on the left side of the grid.)

households and working mothers has risen, the influence of children has increased as well. In total, $500 billion in household spending is affected annually, including $100 million spending direct expenditures.[41] A grid showing how family influences relate to different product decisions appears in Exhibit 4–5. It crosses the number of decision makers with the number of users, identifying nine categories of family influence, depending on who makes the purchase decision and who uses the item. Cereal, as shown in cell 4, might be consumed by multiple members of the family but selected by the primary grocery shopper.[42]

Television, the Internet, and other media are affecting teenagers globally. One consequence is a common culture of consumption among young people worldwide. For example, MTV networks are directly influencing the spending habits and brand preferences of young people everywhere. As in the United States and the United Kingdom, well-known brands like Levi's, Nike, and Timberland are preferred worldwide among teenagers and other young consumers.[43]

Family life cycle is also relevant to consumer behavior. It describes the sequence of steps a family goes through: from young, single adults, to the married couple whose children have left home, to, possibly, the retired survivor. The family life cycle suggests ways to develop marketing strategies and design products and services. Household consumption patterns vary dramatically across the family life cycle. Appliances and insurance are bought for the first time during the early stages, for instance. Luxury products, travel, and recreation are typical expenditures for middle-aged adults with no children at home. Companies tailor product variations for specific stages of the family life cycle, such as Campbell's soups or Chef-Boy-R-Dee pasta packaged in smaller sizes for households of single or older consumers.

Changing family life cycles also have implications for product needs and buying behavior. Dramatic increases in age associated with first marriages, women working outside the home, single parents, premarital births, single-person households, childless couples, divorces, remarriages, alternate forms of living arrangements, and lower fertility rates have produced striking changes in families and households.[44] Exhibit 4–6 shows the number of households comprising married couples with children at home and single-parent and single-person households. These numbers may decrease demand for large dining room tables, but they are good news for businesses that sell smaller tables, refrigerators, televisions, cleaning products, and other one-to-a-household items.[45]

Among the changes to the traditional family life cycle, the prevalence of dual-earner households and adult children living at home are phenomena well recognized

Household types

Total number of households	104,705,000
Young single households (under 40)	10%
Older single households (over 40)	21%
Single parent (under 40)	8%
Single parent (40 and over)	3%
Young couples (under 40, no kids)	5%
Empty nest (40 and over, no kids)	25%
Full nest I (under 40 w/kids including under 6)	11%
Full nest II (under 40 w/kids 6–17 only)	6%
Full nest III (40+ with kids including under 6) and (40+ w/kids 6–17)	11%

Anna
Kournikova's Choice

Tennis star Anna Kournikova chooses
the 18 k gold Constellation «Quadra»

Ω
OMEGA
www.omegawatches.com

The use of popular figures as product endorsers makes use of value-expressive interpersonal influences.

by marketers. Today, companies study dual-income households just as intently as they studied homemakers a quarter of a century ago. For example, college-educated households make large-ticket purchase decisions jointly. Less-educated dual-income couples often both work to just buy increasingly expensive necessities. Young adults are now waiting longer to leave the home. In most cases, the prolonged stay enables the young adult to spend wages on luxuries instead of paying rent.[46]

Interpersonal Influences

Marketers also recognize interpersonal influences beyond the family, including friends, co-workers, and others. These sources of influence are often referred to as **reference groups,** or those others look to for help and guidance. As shown in Exhibit 4–7, this influence affects brand and product decisions. They may be groups a person belongs to and ones she or he admires or wants to join.

INTERPERSONAL INFLUENCE PROCESSES   Three types of interpersonal processes—informational, utilitarian, and value-expressive—form the basis for interpersonal influences. **Informational influence** is based on the consumer's desire to make informed choices and reduce uncertainty. When we need to buy a complex product or face a new decision, we often seek information and advice from others we trust.

Utilitarian influence is reflected in compliance with the expectations, real or imagined, of others. These expectations are referred to as *norms*. Compliance to norms occurs in efforts to achieve rewards or avoid punishments. Rewards and punishments in day-to-day consumer behavior involve acceptance and peer approval and disapproval. These normative influences are particularly acute for young people. Sometimes these can be negative influences, such as peer pressure to use drugs, alcohol, or tobacco.

Value-expressive influence stems from a desire to enhance self-concept through identification with others. These influences are seen in the frequent use of popular spokespersons and attractive models in much consumer advertising. Celebrity endorsements from personalities such as actor Bill Cosby and Britney Spears are intended to encourage identification with these figures through brand purchases. In other instances, products or brands are purchased in support of one's real or desired image.

The latter two forms of influence are sometimes combined into a more general category labeled **normative influence.** Marketers attempt to use normative social influences by showing favorable consequences that can occur when their brands are used or unfavorable consequences that occur when not used. What many want, particularly young consumers, is to be acceptable

Peer influences among adolescents are important determinants of consumer behavior worldwide. Products are often purchased consistent with the need to identify with others and/or to express desired images.

to their peers. So what determines "cool" for teenagers is partly about individuality and partly about belonging. Companies like Levi Strauss spend millions generating associations with their products that reflect positive acceptance among peer groups.[47]

Social influence forms the basis of one principle of persuasion. Robert Cialdini, a noted social scientist, describes this premise as the "principle of social proof." As social actors, consumers rely heavily on the people around them for cues on how to think, feel, and act. For managers, testimonials from satisfied consumers work best when the satisfied consumer spokesperson and prospective buyers share similar characteristics and circumstances. Influence that operates horizontally is often effective, and firms can employ real and imagined peer influences when appropriate.[48]

Individual Differences
A vast number of individual differences can influence consumer behavior. Many people are swayed by various forms of word-of-mouth communications. Individual differences also stem from personality, lifestyles and psychographics, and motivation.

Word-of-Mouth Communications

Some people, traditionally labeled **opinion leaders,** influence consumer behavior through word-of-mouth communications. Opinion leaders were originally viewed as intermediaries between sources of information, such as advertising and other media, and the consumer. Their influence often stems from their involvement and interest or expertise in particular products. Marketers now recognize that communication flows both from and toward opinion leaders. In an application of the opinion leader concept, one research company focuses upon the 10 percent of Americans labeled "influentials." This segment of 20 million, by their inclination to use cutting-edge products, their income, their status, and their voice, exerts an inordinate amount of influence on the goods and services adopted by friends, coworkers, and acquaintances. Card issuer First USA has paid college tuition for students at Pepperdine University and the University of Southern California in return for their service as media and public relations spokespersons. The two students were selected based upon their academic and extracurricular activities and popularity, hence serving as paid opinion leaders.[49]

Market mavens are another type of information diffuser. These are consumers who know about many kinds of products, places to shop, and other facets of the market, and they like to share this information with other consumers.[50] Unlike opinion leaders, who know a lot about a few products, mavens know something about many products and enjoy discussing them. Market mavenism is a more general concept than opinion leadership in that mavens' influence results from the passing of information and expertise in the course of just making conversation. Mavens do not necessarily adopt new products or even use the products they are

Exhibit 4–7	*Reference-group influence on product and brand purchase decisions*	
Product / Brand	**Weak reference group influence** **(−)**	**Strong reference group influence** **(+)**
Strong reference group influence (+)	**Public necessities** *Influence:* Weak product & strong brand *Examples:* Wristwatch, automobile, business suit	**Public luxuries** *Influence:* Strong product & brand *Examples:* Golf clubs, snow skis, sailboat
Weak reference group influence (−)	**Private necessities** *Influence:* Weak product & brand *Examples:* Mattress, floor lamp, refrigerator	**Private luxuries** *Influence:* Strong product & weak brand *Examples:* Video game, pool table, CD player

knowledgeable about, but they influence other people's choices and diffuse information on new products.

Word-of-mouth communications from friends and family are among the most important influences on consumer behavior. Because of the credibility of word-of-mouth information, others we know can easily affect purchasing decisions, particularly by limiting the choices we consider. More than 40 percent of Americans seek the advice of family and friends when shopping for doctors, lawyers, and auto mechanics. Word-of-mouth information is also crucial to decisions about restaurants, entertainment, banking, and personal services.[51] A recent large-scale study of college students revealed that the influence of word of mouth (44 percent) is twice as influential in new-product purchases than either price (22 percent) or advertising (22 percent).[52] Family, friends, and business associates are the primary source of influence on the purchase of personal electronics and computers. P&G targeted "chatters" with direct-to-consumer samples and employed a Web site that encouraged visitors to tell friends about its Physique brand. Less than 15 percent of the brand launch costs were allocated to television advertising.[53]

Sometime in the last several decades the influence pattern has shifted from trickle-down from the fashion firms to trickle-up. Using an observational and in-depth interview form of market research, the objective now is chasing the elusive street cool, or "cool-hunting." Nike, for example, introduces new brands faster in efforts to react faster to new ideas from the street. The danger is that the better cool-hunters become at bringing the cutting edge to the mainstream, the more elusive the cutting edge becomes.[54]

Personality

Personality reflects a person's consistent response to his or her environment. It has been linked to differences in susceptibility to persuasion and social influence and thereby to purchase behavior. General personality traits related to consumer behavior include extroversion, self-esteem, dogmatism (closed-mindedness), and aggressiveness. For example, dogmatism might limit product trial or the adoption of product innovations for some consumers; aggressiveness may be related to the purchase of certain types of sporty cars and to consumer complaint behavior in reaction to unsatisfactory purchases. Self-esteem is thought to be inversely related to persuasibility—the more self-esteem, the less subject to persuasion—and has implications for the effectiveness of marketing communications.

The use of general personality measures to explain purchase behavior has been disappointing. Researchers need to develop marketing or consumer-related measures to determine the role of personality in the consumer decision process and explore whether findings can be generalized across product and service classes. Such consumer-related measures would help in identifying market segments and creating and sustaining effective promotional campaigns.

The notion of *self-concept* is one idea used to explain the products consumers buy and use. Self-concept is the overall perception and feeling that one has about herself or himself. Consumers buy products and brands that are consistent with or enhance their self-concept.[55]

Marketers try to create relationships between their products or services and consumers. Marketers can affect consumers' motivation to learn about, shop for, and buy the sponsored brand by influencing the degree to which people perceive a product to be related to their self-concept. This objective is clear in the many ads that emphasize image enhancement and personal improvement through use of the advertiser's brand of product or service.[56]

Different views of self-concept have been offered. Self-concept has been referred to as actual self-concept, ideal self-concept, and social self-concept, the latter often deemed the "looking glass" view of an individual's self-concept. The notion of ideal, or desired, self-concept reflects the image the individual would like to display to others. The social self-concept reflects the image the individual believes others hold. Consumers purchase, display, and use goods that reflect these views of themselves or that enhance self-concept through the consumption of products as symbols. Possessions play an important role in defining individual identities in today's contemporary Western economies.[57]

Lifestyles and Psychographics

An outgrowth from attempts to use personality measures to explain consumer behavior are the concepts of lifestyle and psychographics. *Lifestyle* describes a person's pattern of living as expressed in activities, interests, and opinions (AIO statements are discussed in more detail in Chapter 7). Lifestyle traits are more concrete than personality traits and more directly linked to the acquisition, use, and disposition of goods and services.[58]

Psychographics divide a market into lifestyle segments on the basis of consumer interests, values, opinions, personality characteristics, attitudes, and demographics.[59] Marketers use lifestyle and psychographic information to develop marketing communications and product strategies. For example, responses to questions about the frequency of outdoor activity, cultural arts viewing, and opinions on social issues can be related to product use and then used as the basis for advertising themes and other marketing communications.

Chet Zalesky notes: "The basis for segmentation will determine its usefulness throughout the organization. An attitudinal-based segmentation (lifestyles/psychographics) will be useful in advertising, communications, and positioning. On the other hand, a customer needs/benefits-based segmentation will identify unique product benefit segments that can be used to redesign current offerings, launch new offerings, or highlight the need for initiatives to change how the organization interacts with its customers."

Motivation

Motivation refers to a state or condition within a person that prompts goal-directed behavior. Motivation generally occurs with recognition of some need or problem and can affect information search, information processing, and purchase behavior.[60] For example, washing machine owners are not routinely motivated to evaluate washing machine ads. But if their Maytag fails, they will be motivated to evaluate washing machine brands. Motivation involves both energy and focus. Motives themselves may be obvious or hidden.

Researchers frequently cite the classification of motives proposed by Abraham Maslow.[61] In this approach, individuals evolve in their personal growth, with higher-level needs (esteem, self-actualization) becoming important only after lower-level needs (physiological, safety) are satisfied. Any unfulfilled needs are assumed to be "prepotent" and provide the most immediate motivation for behavior. Levels of needs in Maslow's hierarchy and examples of associated product purchases include:

Self-actualization needs—Art, books, recreation.

Esteem needs—Clothing, home furnishings.

Using Technology

Volvo: Online product introduction

Volvo became the first car manufacturer to introduce a new product using entirely the Internet. Volvo used America Online and its 24 million-plus subscribers to introduce the new S60 model, a luxury sports sedan. As an enticement to buyers, $2,100 of free options were offered only to AOL's subscribers. This arrangement led to positioning on the introductory Web page, plus banner ads were purchased on the auto and men's areas of the server's site. During the six-month campaign, 250,000 requests for information to Volvo were recorded and 45,000 viewers configured cars and asked for quotes.

Love and belonging needs—Mementos, gifts, photographs.

Safety needs—Burglar alarms, seat belts.

Physiological needs—Food, heat, shelter.

Motives that drive consumer behavior are affected by an individual's environment, including marketing communications and reference-group influences. The productivity of marketing communications is enhanced when marketers position products to satisfy consumers' needs and the motivations that generate them.

Situational Factors

In addition to the social environment and individual consumer characteristics, situational influences also affect consumer behavior.[62] Situational influences can involve purchases for anticipated situations, such as special occasions, and unanticipated occurrences, such as time pressures, unexpected expenses, and changed plans. In-store sales promotions and advertising can exert situational influences on consumers as they often make buying decisions while shopping. A common in-store situational factor is music, long considered an effective means for triggering moods. One study reveals that grocery-store sale volumes were significantly higher with slow rather than with fast music.[63]

Situational determinants of consumer behavior can be summarized as follows:

- Consumers purchase many goods for use in certain situations, and the anticipated use influences choice. Gift giving and social occasions are often important determinants of purchase behavior.

- Situational factors can be inhibitors as well as motivators. Inhibitors that constrain consumer behavior include time or budget constraints.

- The likely influence of situations varies with the product. Consumers buy clothing items, books, and many food products with anticipated uses in mind.

Situational store factors within the retail environment are also important. These store conditions include physical layout, atmospherics, location, the presence of others, the assistance of salespeople, and in-store stimuli. Merchandisers also try to capitalize on situational factors in developing their marketing plans. Gas stations have evolved into multiline convenience stores, for instance, and fast-food chains cater to situational needs with drive-through services.

Advertising often incorporates situational use into its message themes. For example, consider the well-known message "use Arm & Hammer Baking Soda as a refrigerator deodorant." This ad suggests the target brand (Arm & Hammer) as a reasonable choice for the target situation. In contrast, some ads compare the target brand with another product already associated with that situation ("Eat Orville Redenbacher Popcorn instead of potato chips as an afternoon snack"). Other ads compare the use of the target brand in a new situation with its use in a more familiar situation ("Special K breakfast cereal is as good at snack time as it is at breakfast").[64]

Consumer Behavior Outcomes

The study of consumer behavior does not end at purchase. Other phenomena or outcomes may and often do occur. These include consumer learning; consumer satisfaction, dissatisfaction, and complaint behavior; and cognitive dissonance.

CONSUMER LEARNING   When marketers set out to influence consumers, they typically try to impart knowledge through advertising, product labels, and personal selling—methods that are efficient and can be controlled by the marketer. Marketers hope consumers will attend to, comprehend, and then remember these messages. Yet, consumers also learn by experience. Experiential learning is highly interactive, and consumers often give it special status—experience is the best teacher.

Consumer learning happens when changes occur in knowledge or behavior patterns. Learning as knowledge gained is consistent with the decision process we have described.[65] Learning as behavior is also a critical outcome. Because successful marketing depends on repeat purchase behavior, providing positive reinforcement for the desired behavior is crucial.[66] Briefly, learning involves or is based on the combination of individual drives (needs), cues or stimuli in the environment, responses (consumer behavior), and reinforcement of those behaviors.

In addition to learning about brands and marketing organizations, knowledge is also gained by consumers over time regarding the tactics marketers use in persuading us. This **persuasion knowledge** helps consumers to understand why and how marketers are trying to persuade us and to adaptively respond to these attempts. Marian Friestad and Peter Wright, two consumer researchers, describe this learning as developing throughout one's life and resulting from our experiences as consumers with salespersons, family and friends, and advertising and from observing marketers and other persuasion agents.[67]

Consumer Satisfaction, Dissatisfaction, and Complaint Behavior

Consumer satisfaction, dissatisfaction, and complaint behavior are also important outcomes of consumer purchase-decision processes. *Satisfaction* and *dissatisfaction* describe the positive, neutral, or negative feelings that may occur after purchase; *consumer complaints* are overt expressions of dissatisfaction. Consumer satisfaction is central to the marketing concept and is a dominant cause of customer loyalty. Increased loyalty enhances revenues, lowers the costs of individual transactions, and decreases price sensitivity. Satisfaction also has benefits within the firm; costs associated with handling returns and warranty claims are reduced, as are those associated with managing complaints.[68]

Judgments of satisfaction and dissatisfaction are generally thought to result from comparisons between a person's expectations about a purchased product and the product's actual performance.[69] At first glance, service and satisfaction appear to be the same concept. Service is what the marketer provides and what the consumer gets. Satisfaction reflects the evaluation of the level of service provided.[70] Purchases that turn out worse than expected result in **negative disconfirmation** and negative feelings. Purchases that turn out better than expected (resulting in **positive disconfirmation**) are evaluated positively. The importance of consumer expectations in the determination of satisfaction cannot be understated. For marketers to be effective, the organization must understand how expectations are formed and the role that competitors have in establishing expectations for the firms in an industry. Moreover, it is critical that marketers monitor expectations and learn the extent to which expectations are static or change over time.[71]

A simple model of consumer satisfaction–dissatisfaction relationships is depicted in Exhibit 4–8. First, the consumer's prior experiences with products and brands establish expectations. Marketing communications, including advertising, and word-of-mouth communications also influence expectations. When you take your car to be serviced or repaired, what expectations do you have? Consumers thus develop expectations about what a product or service should be able to provide. Comparison between the buyer's expectations and the product or service performance levels results in the confirmation or disconfirmation of expectations and the outcomes of satisfaction or dissatisfaction. These positive or negative feelings serve then as input into the formation of future attitudes and expectations. Although disconfirmation is generally considered the most important determinant of satisfaction, expectations and performance directly influence satisfaction also. This is consistent with research showing that consumers with higher expectations experience higher levels of satisfaction and that performance, independent of positive or negative disconfirmation, exerts a direct effect on feelings of satisfaction.[72] Similarly, research

Exhibit 4–8	*A model of consumer satisfaction*

on cars shows that consumers with high product involvement tend to be more satisfied with their purchases than less-involved car owners.[73] Regardless, however, firms adopting a *customer value perspective* must employ marketing communications that convey realistic expectations.

Companies now regularly measure satisfaction and recognize it as an important determinant of customer retention. However, the measurement of satisfaction must consider not only what the customer did receive but what he or she could have received. That is, companies must study their competition as well. Overall quality has been shown to be a better predictor than satisfaction of customers' willingness to keep buying.[74] Practitioners now agree that only stellar performance makes a real difference in customer loyalty. The success of programs that measure satisfaction levels are dependent on benchmarking, either against competitor performance or performance goals established by management. Customer satisfaction measurement is useful for identifying areas in need of improvement to strengthen relationships with customers, as well as subsequent assessment of how efficiently and satisfactorily services and products are being provided.[75]

Recent research reveals a more complicated view of satisfaction than the traditional disconfirmation of expectations model. Based upon a series of in-depth interviews with consumers regarding their purchase of technological products, consumer researchers now recognize that satisfaction is often a more dynamic process in that:

1. Satisfaction judgments evolve and are changeable as products are used.

2. Satisfaction judgments have a social component determined by the satisfaction of others in the household.

3. Emotions are important and yield insights beyond simple comparison standards, such as expectations and performance.

4. Product satisfaction is also related, in some situations, to quality of life and life satisfaction.[76]

Besides influencing subsequent expectations, purchase behavior, and loyalty, dissatisfaction can result in several forms of consumer complaints: **voice responses** (seeking satisfaction directly from the seller), **private responses** (bad-mouthing to friends), and **third-party responses** (taking legal action, filing complaints with consumer affairs agencies).[77] Remember that word-of-mouth personal communications are very credible and influential.

Complaints are customer feedback about products, services, and company performance that marketers should never take lightly. Dissatisfied customers talk to

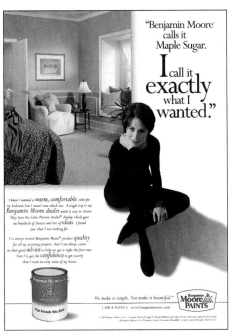

Moore Paints seems to provide some prior-to-purchase reassurance to inhibit cognitive dissonance.

more people than satisfied customers; often dissatisfied customers never make a complaint to the company.[78] Because new customers are harder to find, maintaining satisfaction among existing customers should be paramount.

To gain feedback, some companies even encourage their customers to complain. Companies that know what is bothering their customers have a better chance of correcting problems, retaining sales, and preventing further damage.[79] At Dell Computer Corporation, the mail-order PC marketer, staff, and managers meet every Friday morning to review customer complaints. The Dell vision is that every customer must be pleased, not merely satisfied.[80] In the same way, Coca-Cola wants to hear from its customers when they have a problem. According to its consumer affairs department, "Consumers who have a good experience with our company tell an average of five other people; but those who have a bad experience will tell twice as many people."[81]

Cognitive Dissonance

The final consumer behavior outcome we consider is **cognitive dissonance**, a form of postpurchase doubt about the appropriateness of a decision.[82] Cognitive dissonance may occur over major choices, such as college decisions and purchases of homes and expensive furniture, stereo systems, and appliances. Most students remember some uneasiness about whether they made the best choice of a college to attend. This uneasiness occurs because each alternative has attractive features. Cognitive dissonance is most likely to occur when the purchase is important, perceived risk is high, the purchase is visible, and the decision involves a long-term commitment.

Dissonance can affect postpurchase attitudes, change behavior, and cause additional information seeking. Strategies marketers can use to reduce postpurchase cognitive dissonance include regular programs of follow-up communications with buyers to discourage doubt and reinforce convictions about product strengths; solid service and maintenance plans to provide reassurance and increase postpurchase satisfaction; and warranty agreements arranged after purchase to protect buyers against problems that may occur.

Ethical and Social Issues   Some instances of consumer and business behavior raise ethical and social concerns.

Consumer Behavior

Unethical consumer behaviors include shoplifting and abuse of return policies. Shoplifting losses represent a tremendous cost to retailers and eventually to other consumers as retailers pass on the costs. Abuse of a company's return policies is also unethical; returns should be made only for reasonable problems.[83]

On the positive side, consumers are increasingly incorporating social concerns into their buying decisions. Environmentally concerned consumers show high awareness of label information and product content. Companies often market their products with messages and product information that recognize these environmental concerns.

Other consumer behaviors driven by ethical and social motivations are less personal and more political. For example, 1970s boycotts of infant formula products sold in Third World countries, suspended in the mid-1980s, have reemerged because consumers believe the manufacturer failed to live up to its promise of ethical practice. Minority and gay rights groups use their buying power to express

TEENAGE DRINKING IS DOWN BECAUSE PARENTS ARE DOING THEIR

HOMEWORK.

WE ALL MAKE A DIFFERENCE.

Budweiser

Both consumers and marketers have responsibilities to act ethically. Anheuser-Busch tries to inform parents about the best ways to communicate responsible behavior to young consumers.

opinions about political issues.[84] "Buy American" campaigns recognize the effects of individual consumer behavior on jobs and local economies. The motivation for many boycotts is simple. Sellers should abide by certain ethical standards. Products produced by child labor or workers severely taken advantage of is an issue that has drawn attention on occasion. Some argue that buyers have responsibilities to be informed about sellers' ethical behavior and to consider that behavior in deciding to make purchases.[85]

Business Behavior

Business behavior is evaluated in terms of two standards: corporate social responsibility and business ethics. For example, firms are expected to provide safe products for reasonable prices. Their actions are not expected to detract from the general well-being of consumers. Efforts to monitor waste and the effects of production on the environment stem from these firm responsibilities. Likewise, marketing practices should not offend individuals or specific groups. Hence, liquor and tobacco advertising has been moderated in recent years, and tobacco advertising has been banned from the networks. Many beer companies, such as Coors and Budweiser, now emphasize responsible use of their products. In the area of personal interaction between salesperson and consumer, the salesperson often feels pressure to make the sale, even if it means not being entirely straight with the potential buyer. Principles of both the marketing concept and the Golden Rule, however, underscore the ethical need and the advantages of consistently treating consumers honestly and fairly.[86]

Summary

1. **Discuss the importance of consumer behavior.** Marketers must understand consumer behavior to develop successful strategies and identify target market segments. Furthermore, awareness of emerging trends in the consumer marketplace is essential for quick recognition of and response to problems and opportunities with sound marketing strategies.

2. **Understand consumer decision making and some of the important influences on those decisions.** Consumer behavior describes the mental and physical activities that people engage in when they select, purchase, use, and dispose of products and services purchased to satisfy needs and desires. The traditional view of consumer decision making is sequential: recognition of problem, search for information (either internal or external), evaluation of alternatives, purchase, and postpurchase evaluation.

3. **Distinguish between low-involvement and high-involvement consumer behavior.** Involvement represents the level of importance or interest generated by a product or a decision. A person highly involved in a decision (the purchase is personally relevant) will likely go through the entire decision-making sequence, from problem recognition to postpurchase evaluation. High-involvement decisions are characterized by thorough information processing, significant personal relevance of the decision, and substantial differences between alternatives.

   Consumers with low involvement will probably not engage in an extensive information search. Low-involvement decisions have minimal personal relevance and are likely routine or habitual. Consequently, they require less mental or physical effort than extended or limited problem solving.

4. **Understand how attitudes influence consumer purchases.** Consumer attitudes, which are learned predispositions to respond favorably or unfavorably toward a product or service, are important primary causes of behavior. They are important for both explaining consumer behavior and designing marketing communications for changing consumer behavior. One useful view depicts attitudes toward purchase behavior as a combination of beliefs about the product's attributes and the relative evaluation of those attributes.

5. **Appreciate how the social environment affects consumer behavior.** Social influences on behavior must be understood prior to the development of sound marketing strategies. Social class and family influences affect consumer behavior and can be used to identify market segments.

   The culture in which consumers are raised is also critical in determining the values that matter to them; culture may be used to identify segments with unique needs (subcultures). A great deal of learning also comes from observing and interacting with others (informational interpersonal influence). Some behavior occurs with the expectations of others in mind (utilitarian influences) and some with how they will react to our own behavior (value-expressiveness). The latter two are normative social influences. Consumers are also influenced by the situations in which behavior occurs or is expected to occur.

6. **Recognize many of the individual consumer differences that influence purchase decisions and behavior.** Individual consumer differences affect consumer decision making and behavior. These include: personality differences; lifestyle differences, which are often measured as consumer activities, interests, and opinions; and differences in motivation.

7. **Recognize the outcomes of consumers' decisions to purchase or not to purchase and how they affect marketing success.** Some of the more important outcomes that occur after purchase are consumer learning, feelings of satisfaction or dissatisfaction, and cognitive dissonance. Learning may result from experience and knowledge gained through advertisements and marketing communications.

   Feelings of satisfaction and dissatisfaction occur when product performance exceeds or falls short of expectations. Dissatisfaction may lead to consumer complaints and loss of future business. Cognitive dissonance is postpurchase doubt about the appropriateness of a decision. It is most likely to occur when the purchase is important or involved, perceived risk is high, the purchase is visible, and the decision involves a long-term commitment.

Understanding Marketing Terms and Concepts

Thinking About Marketing

1. Describe the importance of understanding consumer behavior. How does this understanding relate to the identification of target markets?

2. Outline and discuss the steps involved in the consumer decision-making process. How might this sequence differ for routinized response behavior and limited problem solving?

3. What is meant by low-involvement consumer behavior?

4. Why are consumer attitudes important? What role do consumer beliefs about product attributes play in consumer decision making?

5. Outline the three types of interpersonal influence, and explain how each may affect purchase behavior.

6. Explain how understanding social class and the family life cycle can enhance marketing effectiveness.

7. How does culture affect consumer behavior, and what are the implications for marketers?

8. Discuss the ethical responsibilities that consumers have in the marketplace.

9. Contrast cognitive dissonance with consumer dissatisfaction. What determines feelings of satisfaction and dissatisfaction?

10. How can Web sites be used to generate loyalty, and what characteristics of Internet search and shopping behavior work against customer loyalty?

Applying Marketing Skills

1. Think about a recent clothing purchase. What was the motivation behind your purchase? Where would this need lie on Maslow's hierarchy of needs? What word-of-mouth sources did you check when making this purchase? How do you think these sources affected your decision to purchase the article of clothing? How important were your friends in making this decision? How did the visibility and necessity of this product affect the influence your friends had on your purchase?

2. Customer dissatisfaction can result when a consumer's expectation for the performance of a product or service exceeds the performance that they actually receive. Can you think of any instances where you have been dissatisfied with a purchase? What do you normally do when you experience a dissatisfying experience? Why is it important that companies try to prevent dissatisfaction from occurring in the first place? When dissatisfaction does occur, what can companies do to lessen the negative consequences?

3. Find examples of ads that exemplify the following consumer behavior concepts: safety needs, consumer satisfaction, family influences, and subcultures.

4. Compare a product's print advertisement in a popular magazine targeted toward the general population with the same product's advertisement in a Latino/Hispanic magazine or an African-American magazine. Do the ads emphasize the same product benefits? Are different cultural values used in the message themes for both ads? Do these differences reflect the firm's customer orientation or just opportunistic efforts to capitalize on ethnic identification?

Using the www in Marketing

Activity One Consider one of the following shopping comparison sites: www.bizrate.com, www.mysimon.com, or www.bottomdollar.com. These sources can be used in the selection of untold types of products.

1. How is the information organized and how do these sources affect the logical decision-making process around which this chapter was organized?

2. How do these sites make a profit or earn revenues?

3. Comment on the search and alternative information generated as it benefits the consumer, as opposed to information obtained from an in-store search designed to benefit the retailer?

Activity Two For the Disney home page, identify the following influences on consumer purchase behavior that Disney is trying to capitalize on:

a. Social influence

b. Family

c. Affect referral

d. Impulse purchase

Making Marketing Decisions

Case 4-1 Mercedes-Benz: Boosting Volume or Losing Esteem

Luxury car makers face a growing market *and* growing competition for younger buyers. Mercedes, Lexus, BMW, Volvo, and Saab all now offer entry-level sedans in the neighborhood of $30,000. Until now, Mercedes' position in the marketplace has been clear—high style, engineering, and quality at a premium price. No brand says upscale louder than Mercedes-Benz. In 2001, Mercedes-Benz posted its best year on record with sales of 206,639 units. The largest increase came from the entry-level CL-Class of new cars. The focus has shifted to younger owners who seek power and performance as much as leather and style, and a ride more in tune with the Autobahn than 18 holes of golf.

The new sports coupe cars are un-Mercedes-like in several ways. Two-door C230 hatchbacks are $4,000 below any other Mercedes. The shape is almost dragsterlike, and the interior does not include wood veneer. More emphasis is on performance and maneuverability than other attributes.

Unfortunately, these changes have not all been positive in their effects. Research in Europe and the United States reveal that the quality and satisfaction ratings for Mercedes have been dropping since 1999. J.D. Power recently lowered Mercedes' quality ranking from "good" to "fair." In addition, the quality ratings for competing cars have increased. What Mercedes has done is to offer smaller and cheaper cars than the market wants. As noted, worldwide sales have doubled since 1993. However, all these changes have hurt the overall brand reputation.

Questions

1. What role does quality play in the formation of attitudes?

2. How might Mercedes preclude any further dilution of its brand in the perceptions of consumers?

3. Comment upon the effects of increasing competition from Lexus and other brands on the search for information and decision making by consumers.

Case 4-2 The Gap, Inc.: Appealing to the Global Teenager

The list of "coolest" brands among U.S. teenagers includes Gap. Included in Gap Inc.'s set of over 2,400 stores are The Gap outlets, GapKids, Banana Republic, and Old Navy Clothing. Best known for casual and active clothing, Gap began in 1969 in San Francisco as a small store named after the "generation gap." During the 1970s, the company expanded its focus beyond sole emphasis on teenagers in efforts to appeal to a larger spectrum of consumers. Now the retail specialty chain has stores in 48 states, as well as in Canada, France, Puerto Rico, and the United Kingdom. In addition, the company is in the process of opening stores in Japan and exploring other ventures in Asia. Fourth-quarter 1998 sales rose to $3 billion, up 40 percent from the year before.

Japanese customers are not unlike American consumers in their desire for well-known brands for some products. However, cultural and value differences in Japan make competition more difficult. Retailers that are successful expanding across borders typically appeal to a common lifestyle that the company fully understands. Other recent trends are also influencing the purchase of casual clothing. In particular, demand for designer jeans is on the rise, jeans that often are priced at twice what a pair of Gap or Levi jeans cost. And a new array of colors and bright shades are now chic among consumers of all ages.

Gap traditionally had viewed its store windows as the primary means of advertising. As a result, the company's ad spending was below that of many competing retailers. Industry experts questioned the company's reluctance to use radio and television, media popular with the Gap's young target audience.

Gap has now gone global with its advertising as part of worldwide campaigns to battle Dockers for a portion of the growing khaki market. Their advertising has remained focused upon attractive models displaying their products, often in dance-oriented themes. This approach has been very successful, and it contrasts with the awkwardness of some of Levi's mixed-message advertising. In a very competitive retail environment, Gap, Inc., has been effective at maintaining a distinct identity for the firm's core brands—Gap, Banana Republic, and Old Navy.

Gap's sales growth and profitability performance have been disappointing in recent quarters. Experts agree that the stores remain stylish and the advertising has been strengthened. The themes are consistent and confident. The chain has a definite position in the minds of consumers. Unfortunately, marketing problems have detracted from the stores' ability to compete and draw consumers. Questions have arisen regarding merchandising, the assortment of clothes, and quality. Gap Inc. as an organization has a history of improving as needed. However, problems with both fashion and the balance sheet make Gap an interesting strategy case in terms of regenerating its position in the marketplace and in terms of consumer patronage preferences.

Questions

1. What role will the global teenager concept have in Gap's efforts to expand in Japan? Will the modest use of broadcast advertising influence consumer decision making enough to make the Japanese entries successful?

2. Once young consumers in an area learn about a new store's presence, is the decision to patronize the store an extended or limited problem-solving situation?

3. How will culture and subcultural factors affect Gap's performance in non-U.S. areas such as Japan?

4. What must Gap do to reposition itself favorably in the minds of consumers?

5

Business-to-Business Markets and Buying Behavior

After studying this chapter, you should be able to:

1 Define the nature of business-to-business buying behavior and markets.

2 Explain the differences between business-to-business buying and consumer purchase behavior.

3 Recognize the different types of buying decisions.

4 Define the different stages of the business buying process.

5 Describe the buying-center concept and the determinants of influence within the buying center.

6 Understand the nature of government, reseller, and other institutional markets.

www.heinz.com

H.J. Heinz is one of the world's leading marketers of food and condiments, in particular its high-quality ketchup and sauces. Its 50 companies operate in 200 countries, marketing the Heinz brand, along with other notables such as StarKist, Ore-Ida, BagelBites, and Classico. In 2001, Heinz announced an agreement with FreeMarkets, an Internet-based business-to-business electronic marketplace. Under the agreement Heinz would begin buying a significant amount of its packaging, ingredients, and operating products through online auctions conducted through FreeMarkets. The use of such an electronic marketplace is called e-sourcing. Since Heinz specifies its requirements in advance and supplier companies bid to fulfill those requirements, the online auctions are termed reverse auctions.

When choosing an electronic marketplace, Heinz searched for a provider that would meet strict criteria, including expertise in Heinz's industry, a global presence, good training for Heinz buyers, and well-defined processes supported by appropriate technology. In FreeMarkets, Heinz found a good match. According to Heinz CEO William R. Johnson, "In the past 18 months, we have formed a revolutionary business relationship with FreeMarkets that is transforming one of our most critical and traditional functions. Procurement has been a back-room process essentially unchanged since the days when Henry Heinz traveled from farm to farm to contract with growers for their crops. Today, it is an exciting new, global frontier for Heinz that is being transformed by modern technology and thinking."

In assessing the performance of the agreement with FreeMarkets, Heinz officials are quick to point out the cost savings, which average approximately 10 percent on $500 million in purchases. But they also identify some other benefits of e-sourcing with FreeMarkets. The time required to make purchases has improved, with it taking an average of 49 days to consummate transactions on new packaging requests, 41 days in the ingredients category, and 31 days for operating materials. Heinz also says that more visibility of buyers' decisions leads to better purchasing practices. Another benefit is FreeMarket's document standardization for multiple languages and multiple currencies. Totally sold on e-sourcing, Heinz expects to buy over a billion dollars of products a year through FreeMarkets by 2003.

Companies like Heinz spend enormous amounts on products and services for business operations, and then market products and services to other consumer or business buyers. As indicated in the Heinz example, these firms are making many changes to improve purchasing performance. Companies marketing to businesses and other organizations need to understand purchasing behavior to develop and execute marketing strategies successfully.

In this chapter, we define business-to-business buying, discuss its importance, identify emerging trends, examine important business purchasing concepts, describe government, reseller, and other institutional buying practices, and address relevant ethical considerations. As marketers, our objective is to understand what these buyers do and want, so we can market to them effectively.

The Nature of Business-to-Business Buying

Business-to-Business Buying Behavior Defined

Business-to-business buying behavior refers to decision making and other activities of organizations as buyers. It involves transactions between buying and selling organizations, and thus is often referred to as organizational buying. A primary element in business-to-business buying is the selection of **suppliers, sources, or vendors.** These are interchangeable terms for companies or individuals who sell products and services directly to buying organizations. In practice, industrial or manufacturing firms distinguish between two kinds of purchases: those involving production and operational products routinely needed in ongoing production or maintenance (raw materials, fasteners, bearings, paint) and those involving capital products (milling machines, power-generating devices, computers and telecommunications systems).

Organizations fall into four general categories: *business firms,* including manufacturers of tangible goods and firms that provide services such as health care, entertainment, and transportation; *government markets,* federal, state, and local; *reseller markets,* such as the many wholesalers and retailers; and other *institutional markets,* such as hospitals (profit and nonprofit), educational and religious institutions, and trade associations. Each of these categories includes organizations that purchase from other organizations. Increasingly, business buyers are involved in **supply-chain management,** or "the integration of business processes from end user through original suppliers that provides products, services, and information that add value for customers."[1] The basic concept is to cut across organizational and company boundaries to better serve the customer, thereby gaining a competitive advantage. Thus, purchasing personnel work with others inside and outside their companies as a key part of supply chain management. In doing so, purchasing personnel may be involved in information gathering and dissemination, negotiating, monitoring the system, evaluating suppliers, and other roles in addition to making purchases.

Supply chain management is distinguished from typical purchasing operations in several ways. In the former, there is a focus on end-to-end processes rather than on individual functional departments such as purchasing, manufacturing, and marketing. Supplier relations require more commitment from the involved parties, and information is more freely shared. In addition to goals for financial performance, targets are set for improved customer satisfaction, and measurement of progress toward these goals becomes more important.

The emphasis on supply-chain management has evolved into the broader term **supply management,** defined by the Institute of Supply Management as "the identification, acquisition, access, positioning, and management of resources the organization needs or potentially needs in the attainment of its strategic objectives."[2] According to this definition, supply management extends beyond physical and informational supply chains to include financial flows and working relationships between buyers and sellers. Properly conceived, supply management is aligned with the strategic priorities of the organization and takes an active role in identifying future needs of the organization.

Exhibit 5–1   *How business-to-business buying behavior differs from consumer buying*

1. Business-to-business buyers are fewer in number, larger, and more concentrated geographically than consumer buyers. This necessitates heavy emphasis on personal selling and trade advertising in business-to-business marketing.

2. Business purchase decisions often involve a more deliberate or thorough product evaluation and are subject to influence from multiple sources (purchasing, engineering) within a firm.

3. The demand for consumer products drives the purchases made by product manufacturers. Business purchase behavior is thus closely tied to economic fluctuations in the consumer market.

4. The demand for some products is related to the purchase of other products (joint demand). For example, if the demand for business personal computers declines, the demand for software applications and business computer printers may decline also.

5. Purchased industrial products are often complex, expensive, and bought in large quantity. Thus, many purchase decisions are based on detailed product specifications or choice criteria. Business markets also make greater use of leasing.

6. There is much more interdependence between business buyers and sellers. This underlies the need to build long-term buyer–seller relationships and leads to greater emphasis on after-sale service.

Some organizations approach buying tasks purely as a purchasing function. Others approach them as part of supply chain management function, and others incorporate them into the broad activity of supply management. Part of the challenge for business marketers is to determine the buying approaches and processes of specific customers, and to market to them accordingly.

Characteristics of Business-to-Business Buying Behavior

There are some similarities but many differences between consumer and organizational buying behavior and decision making. Principally, consumers buy for their own use and for household consumption. Business buyers purchase for further production (raw materials, components), for use in their firm's operations (office supplies, insurance), or for resale to other customers. Major distinguishing characteristics of business-to-business buying behavior are presented in Exhibit 5–1.

Demand for business-to-business products is often dependent on demand in consumer markets. This phenomenon is referred to as **derived demand**. For example, the demand for many products is derived from consumer demand for new automobiles. When demand for new autos goes up, the demand for products used to make them, such as steel, plastic, and textiles also goes up. The reverse is also true.

Evaluating Business-to-Business Markets

Marketers can evaluate the size and growth rates of consumer markets using demographic characteristics. Many information sources report population statistics by characteristics like age or income level for different geographical areas. These demographic characteristics are not useful for evaluating business markets.

The federal government has developed a numerical scheme called the **North American Industry Classification System (NAICS)** for categorizing businesses. As shown in Exhibit 5–2, NAICS uses the first two digits to identify

Exhibit 5–2

North American Industry Classification System

Examples of NAICS numbering system

- First two digits—economic sector
- Third digit—economic subsector
- Fourth digit—industry group
- Fifth digit—NAICS industry
- Sixth digit—country-specific industry

51	**Information**
513	**Broadcasting and telecommunications**
5133	**Telecommunications**
51332	**Wireless telecommunications carriers (except Satellite)**
513321	**Paging**
513322	**Cellular and other wireless telecommunications**

an economic sector such as the information sector. The third digit identifies an economic subsector (broadcasting and telecommunications), the fourth an industry group (telecommunications), the fifth an NAICS industry (wireless telecommunications carriers, except satellite), and the sixth a country-specific industry—in this case, the U.S. paging industry.

For each classification within NAICS, important economic data are available. This includes number of companies and employees, sales revenues, and percentage of sales occurring in large and small organizations. Such data are useful to marketers for estimating the size and growth rates of business markets. Mexico and Canada are also using the NAICS format, which allows comparisons for the entire North American market.

The Importance of Business-to-Business Buying

Business-to-business markets and purchasing behavior are important for two basic reasons. First, the size of business markets offers many opportunities for astute marketers. Second, many firms are trying to increase profits by improving purchasing practices.

Business purchasing far exceeds consumer purchasing in total dollars. Businesses are the prime buyers of raw materials, such as minerals and farm products that are further processed and resold in whole or as part of other products. Businesses and other organizations also purchase services from advertising agents, accountants, consultants, attorneys, airlines, railroads, and so on.

The purchasing budgets of companies such as General Electric, Du Pont, Wal-Mart, and Ford exceed the gross national product of many countries. It is easy to see that businesses represent potentially lucrative markets for the products and services of many suppliers.

Lowering the cost of purchased products can be an effective way to increase profits. Consider this simple example. Assume a firm has annual sales of $100 million and a net profit margin of 5 percent. If this firm wanted to increase profits by $1 million, it would have to increase sales by 20 percent ($20 million sales increase $\times$ .05 net profit margin = $1 million profit increase). This type of sales increase may be difficult to accomplish in the slow-growth markets facing many firms. But if the company reduced costs by $1 million through improved purchasing, it would achieve the profit growth objective. This may be more doable in many situations.

The reality is that most firms are trying to increase profits by both increasing sales and reducing costs. However, more and more firms realize the powerful impact that purchasing improvements can have on profits. As business buyers change purchasing practices, marketers need to be aware of the changes and adapt marketing efforts appropriately.

Trends in Business-to-Business Buying   The purchasing operations at many firms are undergoing substantial changes. Key results of an extensive study about the future of purchasing are shown in Exhibit 5–3. In this study, 160 purchasing executives were asked to identify important trends for purchasing through the year 2008. An examination of Exhibit 5–3 indicates that several key marketing perspectives are particularly relevant for business marketers who seek to effectively meet the needs of purchasers.

Productivity Improvement

Productivity improvement is emphasized throughout many companies. This affects purchasing in at least three major ways. First, firms find that it is often more productive to purchase products and services from other companies than to make the products or perform the services internally. This is called **outsourcing.** Second, corporate downsizing has often involved downsizing of the purchasing function. And third, purchasing is paying greater attention to reducing **cycle time,** or the total elapsed time to complete a business process.

| **Exhibit 5–3** | *Selected purchasing trends 1998–2008* |

1. Electronic commerce	7. Global-supplier development
2. Strategic cost management	8. Third-party purchasing
3. Strategic sourcing	9. Competitive bidding
4. Supply-chain partner selection and contribution	10. Strategic supplier alliances
5. Relationship management	11. Win–win negotiation strategy
6. Performance measurement	12. Complexity management

Outsourcing first became popular in the manufacturing sector, but has now spread to all sectors of the economy, including services and the government. With many companies pushing for productivity gains, outsourcing for specialized technology functions is on the rise. Companies such as IBM Global Services, Accenture, and Dataquest Inc. are key beneficiaries of the trend toward outsourcing, showing impressive sales growth while the world economy continues in a slow-growth mode.[3] Another growing market for outsourcing is corporate security. Firms seeking better security for their employees, facilities, and information systems often turn to external sources rather than trying to develop the expertise necessary to achieve a more secure environment.

Companies may push for further productivity gains by negotiating guaranteed contracts with outsourced partners. For example, Accenture guaranteed AT&T that it could run its sales and customer service information system for $2.6 billion over a five-year period. AT&T had figured that it cost $5 billion to do the job internally, so they are guaranteed a savings of $2.4 billion—regardless of the actual cost incurred by Accenture.[4] As indicated in Exhibit 5–4, several key questions should be addressed in determining if outsourcing would be appropriate.

A primary motivation to outsource is potential cost savings. According to some industry experts, the opportunity to save money through outsourcing is still important, but companies are also using outsourcing to better focus on core competencies and strategic priorities. According to Michael F. Corbett, a leading outsourcing consultant, "Outsourcing is not simply a by-product of the need to reduce costs. It is an integral part of an organization's strategy for excellence . . . it creates breakthrough thinking through a clearer focus on the organization's core competencies—those things it does best—combined with the unique capabilities of equally talented and focused partners. Seen this way, outsourcing becomes a powerful tool for organizational competitiveness."[5]

Another interesting aspect of outsourcing and its impact on organizational buying is that there is a growing trend toward outsourcing the purchasing and supply chain management functions in larger companies. According to the global managing partner for Accenture's supply-chain management consulting division, there is an increased use of outsourcing for these functions, enabling companies not only to save money but to enhance the effectiveness of these functions and thus competitiveness.[6]

| **Exhibit 5–4** | *Is outsourcing the solution?* |

Key questions to help determine if outsourcing is appropriate:

- Will outsourcing improve company profitability by lowering labor or procurement costs, reducing the level of capital expenditures, increasing revenues, or enabling economies of scale?
- Do potential suppliers provide a location or expertise that is hard to acquire?
- Can potential suppliers provide a safety margin to reduce supply surpluses and/or shortages?
- Is the function or activity under consideration a core competency for the firm? If not, outsourcing may be appropriate.
- Can the firm's financial risk be reduced through outsourcing?

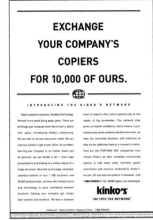

Business buyers often focus on improving productivity within their organizations. Kinko's has become a major corporation by fulfilling other companies' printing and copying requirements at significant cost savings for their customers.

Purchasing personnel are often involved in strategic planning, new-product development, and other diverse activities. Downsizing the purchasing function has been facilitated by technology, especially the automation of routine reordering from established suppliers. Beyond the gains made possible by technology, productivity improvements have been made by fewer people doing more work.

Use of Technology

Buyers are increasingly employing a technology to improve the productivity of purchasing operations. Reducing cycle time is an important purchasing trend (see Exhibit 5–3). Because time is money, buyers are interested in ways to reduce the purchasing, product-development, product-delivery, manufacturing, and inventory cycles. Reducing cycle times increases productivity by lowering the costs of doing business and can help increase sales. The use of new technologies often leads to shorter cycle times. For example, Toshiba Office Products Group and its resellers use Web sites to share order information, track sales, and conduct training. This has resulted in a 50 percent reduction in the time it takes to process orders handled by resellers in addition to reducing printing and mailing costs. By collaborating with suppliers and designers on the Web, General Motors has cut the cycle time for getting a new model into production to 18 months, down from 42 months in the mid-1990s. The same system has reduced the cycle time for completing a mock-up of a car from 12 weeks to 2. Such improvements in cycle time could provide GM with considerable benefits in the consumer market, as consumer preferences can shift quickly.[7]

Perhaps the most exciting technological development in recent years is the advent of electronic commerce in the purchasing function. In many industries, computer-to-computer systems link customers and suppliers, allowing automatic replenishment of inventory on a timely basis. Such systems include the shared networks of Wal-Mart and Procter & Gamble, Saturn and its automotive parts suppliers, and numerous hospitals and Allegiance (formerly Baxter). These company-to-company systems may link companies' private internal systems, which are called Intranets. When two or more companies' Intranets are linked, this forms an extranet. Increasingly, electronic data interchanges run over the Internet are also referred to as Extranets.

Some of the expected advances in organizational buying via the Internet have yet to fully develop. For example, electronic marketplace exchanges, usually referred to as **B2B exchanges,** were heralded as the next revolutionary development in organizational buying. In such an exchange, hundreds and even thousands of suppliers posted their goods and services for sale. The idea was that full disclosure of pricing and product information would ultimately develop a highly competitive marketplace in which organizational buyers would benefit from lower costs. Many of these exchanges were victims of the shakeout in e-commerce that occurred in the past few years. Industry researchers predict that only 200 to 300 B2B exchanges will be in business by 2004, as compared to approximately 1,500 in 2001. Among the casualties were MaritimeDirect, an electronic marketplace for the shipping industry, and Dell Marketplace, a small-business site sponsored by Dell Computer.[8] One problem with open-access exchanges is that some suppliers are reluctant to share sensitive information that might be available to competitors.

Of the exchanges that are succeeding, corporate auction site FreeMarkets Inc. and hospital supply exchange Neoforma Inc. are making progress with organizational buyers.[9] EBay is a profitable exchange company that serves both organizational and consumer buyers. **Private exchanges,** those that link invitation-only buyers and sellers, are now showing more promise than most of the open-access exchanges. Hewlett-Packard, IBM, and Ace Hardware are among the success stories in the private exchange arena. For more detail on how the Ace Hardware private exchange works, refer to "Using Technology: Ace Is the Place for Private Exchange."

Exhibit 5–5

Electronic commerce applications in purchasing

Business buyers frequently use the Internet for these activities:

- Requesting proposals and price quotes.
- Posting bids.
- Transmitting purchase orders.
- Using Electronic Data Interchanges.
- Ordering with electronic catalogs.
- Seeking suppliers.
- Tracking delivery schedules.
- Managing contracts.
- Managing inventory.
- Paying invoices/making payments.

Business buyers agree that security is the biggest obstacle to using the Internet in purchasing. But with virtually all business buyers reporting access to the Internet, electronic commerce in business markets is well established and growing rapidly. Exhibit 5–5 indicates how business buyers use the Internet.

A Relationship Perspective

The focus on supplier relationships by buyers is driving the emphasis on relationship marketing by sellers. Many of the purchasing trends reflect the emphasis on buyer–seller relationships (see Exhibit 5–3). These include supply-chain partner selection, relationship management, performance measurement, global-supplier development, strategic-supplier alliances, and win–win negotiation strategies. The goals of strong buyer–seller relationships, as shown in Exhibit 5–6, are to foster innovation and improve business efficiencies. By achieving these goals, customer satisfaction and profitability can be positively influenced. Over time, suppliers can earn loyalty from their buyers, as illustrated in "Building Customer Equity: Philmon Seafood Weathers a Tough Market."

Buyers are in a rather unique situation because they work directly with suppliers to purchase products for their firm (internal customers) that are used to produce products for external customers. Although it is important for buyers to meet the needs of their internal customers, ultimate success depends on contributing to the success of external customers. Buyers are spending more time with external customers to better understand how the products they purchase from suppliers affect the products purchased by external customers. This helps them make purchases that can both reduce costs and increase customer satisfaction.

Ethics is another important element of supplier relationships. Successful relationships must be based on trust. Buyers and sellers share a great deal of information and must trust that this information will remain confidential. Both parties must trust each is working for mutual benefit. Honest and open communication is necessary. Once developed, trust is a powerful asset in a supplier relationship. Once lost, it is very difficult—and maybe impossible—to reestablish.

A large number of suppliers to Daimler-Chrysler felt their trust of the automaker was diminished when Chrysler Group's CEO demanded that existing supply contracts be voided and new contracts issued with a 5 percent reduction in cost.[10] Facing a revolt among suppliers, Chrysler Group backed off and stated a willingness to renegotiate supply contracts. However, suppliers are wary, and Chrysler may

Using Technology

Ace is the place for private exchange

Ace Hardware, with 5,100 stores, wanted to reduce the costs of inventory management and collaborate with suppliers on a real-time basis. Using supply-chain software provided by Atlanta-based E3 Corp, Ace linked its computer systems in 14 distribution centers to those of nine key suppliers. Before the system was installed, Ace used faxes and some basic computerized ordering processes to supply its stores. It typically took a week to 10 days to process an order. Without a shared system, suppliers could not ac-

curately forecast how much inventory they should maintain for Ace. With the new real-time system, suppliers can monitor up-to-the-minute movement of products out of Ace stores. Better forecasting has resulted, which means the suppliers do not have to maintain excessive inventory to meet the needs of Ace. Suppliers report lower distribution costs, and Ace has increased its in-stock position, a benefit to the shopper.

Speaking from Experience

W. Wayne Whitworth
President
The Strategic Purchasing Group

"Technology is having and will continue to have a significant impact on both sales and purchasing professionals. Electronic commerce will move the transactional based, nonstrategic purchases to the Internet in a market place forum. From the seller's point of view, new skills will be required to service buyers on a more strategic level. Buyers, in turn, will be the visionary link within the supply chain bringing the full resources from strategic partners to manage total cost of ownership and supplier relationships."

W. Wayne Whitworth, C.P.M., is President of the Strategic Purchasing Group, a consulting firm specializing in purchasing and supply-chain management strategies. He is also Director of Purchasing for American Commercial Lines. His prior experience includes purchasing management positions with Brown-Forman Corporation and Dover Resources, Incorporated. He is a Certified Purchasing Manager (C.P.M.) and earned his BSBA degree from the University of Louisville and an MBA from Bellarmine College.

well have lost valuable goodwill it had developed over the years with its suppliers. One unidentified supplier said, "They're only interested in the bottom line. There's a sense they're going to nail suppliers."[11] In this case both Chrysler and its suppliers need each other in order to succeed. Only time will tell if diminished trust will cost Chrysler more than it saves in reduced prices, as suppliers may court other automakers with new product ideas before sharing the ideas with Chrysler.

Maytag provides a contrasting example of how a supplier can build better relationships by earning customer trust. Maytag's goal is to be the preferred appliance supplier to its customers by delivering a rapid, consistent flow of products to its regional distribution centers, which service its retail customers. To accomplish its goal, Maytag collaborates with its trading partners to optimize the flow of product and information. Maytag achieves its position as a trusted supplier through open communications with trading partners and a dedication to continuous improvement. According to Maytag vice-president John Nolan, "We never lose sight of the vision, we never stop improving things, but we improve at a rate that we can afford, that isn't too risky, and that allows us to learn as we go."[12]

| **Exhibit 5-6** | *Important features of strong buyer–seller relationships* |

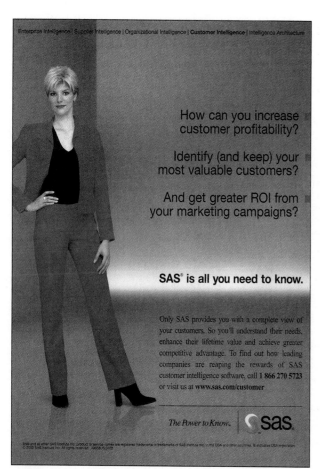

Business buyers often focus on improving productivity within their organizations. SAS appeals to such buyers, pointing out how their software can improve profitability and return on investment.

The final aspect of a *relationship perspective* is teamwork within the firm. Buyers are working more as teams with engineers and other functions in the selection of suppliers. In many respects, buyers orchestrate the purchasing process within their firms. They coordinate the flow of information between the seller and buyer and rely on people within and outside their firm for expertise in evaluating different products and suppliers.

Wayne Whitworth, President of the Strategic Purchasing Group and Director of Purchasing for American Commercial Lines, emphasizes the importance of relationships in purchasing: "The traditional role of purchasing will continue to change toward supplier management. This shift will place higher demands on interpersonal skills and the management of relationships with internal and external customers. The very nature of purchasing's new role will require a unique ability to develop collaborative partnerships with internal and external stakeholders to bring new products to market and to reduce total cost of ownership. Bringing multiple disciplines, functions, and cross-functional teams together to promote strategic organizational goals can only be accomplished by building relationships of trust, support and willingness to adapt to change."

Customer Value Considerations

One of the keys to successful supplier relationships is building customer value. Buyers are interested in suppliers that can add value to their business by continually increasing quality and lowering costs. Quality and cost considerations go beyond just the product being purchased to everything related to doing business together.

Siemens, an electronic business solutions provider to the health care industry, offers an example of how a supplier can distinguish its supplier status by moving from a product focus to a value-added orientation based on expertise, service, and continuous improvement of its offering. Siemens entered into a multiyear contract with Birmingham, Alabama–based HealthSouth Corp. to build the world's first digital hospital. Every patient will be monitored via wireless technology, which allows physicians and medical staff to oversee a patient's care remotely, yet respond to changes in the patient's status more quickly than with conventional systems. In this situation, Siemens has effectively achieved the status of business partner, far beyond the typical buyer-seller relationship in the medical and communications equipment industry.[13]

Building Customer Equity

Philmon Seafood weathers a tough market

James Philmon knows the importance of having good relationships with his customers. His Philmon Seafood, based in Suwanee, Florida, sells stone crab claws to Florida restaurants. Among his customers is the world renowned Joe's Stone Crab Restaurant in Miami Beach. In 2002, Florida restaurants were struggling through a sluggish sales period, and there was an oversupply of more expensive seafood products such as stone crab claws. Restaurants were serving fewer customers, cutting prices, and trying to reduce inventory costs. In this environment,

James Philmon is among the surviving seafood distributors due to the customer loyalty he has earned over the years. When business softened for Joe's Stone Crab Restaurant, CEO Stephen Sawitz cut the number of seafood suppliers from 20 to 6. Philmon was among the chosen six, with Mr. Sawitz citing Mr. Philmon's honesty, reliability, and thoroughness as deciding factors. Strong relationships with organizational buyers are always important. In downtimes, these relationships can mean survival for suppliers like Philmon Seafood.

Thinking Critically

Assume you are the buyer for liquid floor cleaner in the following situations. For each situation, specify what would be the most important purchase criteria that you would use to select a supplier.

- A buyer for a national chain of retail hardware stores.
- A buyer for a large manufacturing facility in Pittsburgh.
- A buyer for a janitorial-supplies wholesaler.

Environmental Impact

Many buyers examine the costs associated with product disposal and look for ways to recycle or reuse products. These types of programs are likely to be more important in the future, as buyers become more actively involved in the environmental area.

In an effort to make business practices more environmentally friendly and safe, 47 nations are working to implement ISO 14000 standards for environmental management. Many companies, most of which are certified under ISO 9000 standards (refer to Chapter 2), are now seeking certification under ISO 14000. For purchasers, there are several implications. First, purchasers should identify activities, products, and services that have an environmental impact. This includes recycling programs, emissions to air, discharges to water, use of raw materials, and storage and movement of hazardous materials and the impact of both on land and communities. Purchasers can work with suppliers to reduce excessive packaging, conserve natural resources, and minimize the dangers of products and processes that may harm the environment.

Herman Miller, a manufacturer of office equipment, has worked with suppliers to promote environmentally friendly purchasing practices. Wood is a critical raw material for Herman Miller. Nations with tropical wood forests are a main source of supply. These nations are often developing nations in which indiscriminate logging practices destroy entire forests and various species of wildlife and vegetation. Through its Design for the Environment (DfE) program, Miller promotes sustainability of threatened forests around the world and encourages its suppliers to use environmentally friendly materials and to clearly delineate low-impact disassembly and recycling procedures. The DfE program also has developed an environmental rating tool for new products, so that the impact on the environment is directly considered in purchasing decisions.[14]

Types of Buying Decisions

In Chapter 4, we classified consumer decisions on a continuum ranging from extensive problem solving (requiring development of criteria for a decision) to routinized response behavior (requiring only price and availability information). Business-to-business purchase decisions can be classed similarly: straight rebuy, modified rebuy, and new-task decisions.[15] These categories are described in a grid in Exhibit 5–7. Note that the classes are distinguished according to

Environmental issues are important to many business buyers. The Toyota recycling program keeps 400 million pounds of steel and scrap metal out of landfills around the world.

Exhibit 5–7	*The buying decision grid*		
Type of Buying Decision	**Newness of the Problem**	**Information Requirements**	**Consideration of New Alternatives**
New task	High	Maximum	Important
Modified rebuy	Medium	Moderate	Limited
Straight rebuy	Low	Minimal	None

the newness of the purchase decision, the information required, and the need to consider alternatives in the purchase, such as different suppliers.

New-Task Decisions

In **new-task decisions,** as shown in Exhibit 5–7, the buying problem is new and a great deal of information must be gathered. New-task decisions are relatively infrequent for a company, and the cost of making a wrong decision is high. Suppliers must convince the buyer their product will solve the buyer's problem; they cannot count on merely offering a price advantage to win the sale. New-task decisions are generally consistent with the sequence of activities in the buying process (discussed later).

When Wal-Mart contemplates a new-task buying decision, the purchase is considered from all angles. Both product and service suppliers must fill out an extensive questionnaire and submit detailed information about their offerings and their company's operating practices before they will be seriously considered as a supplier. Wal-Mart's supplier development group will analyze the company's financial standing, will determine if the supplier qualifies for its Minority & Women-Owned Business Development Program, and specify various technological, legal, and performance requirements to be met by all suppliers. In addition, the potential supplier's proposal must address a multitude of questions related to cost savings, service improvements, sources for future growth, identification of key competitors, target market characteristics, and positioning versus competitive products.[16] By requiring so much information of potential suppliers, Wal-Mart increases it chances of making sound new-task decisions.

Modified Rebuy Decisions

Modified rebuy decisions call for the evaluation of new alternatives for purchase decisions. A modified rebuy could involve considering either new suppliers for current purchase needs or new products offered by current suppliers. The amount of information required and the need to consider new alternatives are less than for new-task decisions but more than for straight rebuy decisions. More familiarity with the decision means less uncertainty and perceived risk than for new-task decisions.[17] Purchases of complex component parts from a new supplier are typical modified rebuy decisions. In these situations, the firm's buyer, often with some input from management, will make the decision.

Straight Rebuy Decisions

Straight rebuy decisions are the most common type. Products and services bought previously are simply repurchased. Delivery, performance, and price are the critical considerations in a straight rebuy. "Outsuppliers," or suppliers not currently being used, are at a considerable disadvantage in this case because "insup-

Insupplier salespeople provide ideas and programs to help their customers build their businesses. This Colgate-Palmolive salesperson provides advice on in-store displays and merchandising to a retailer in China.

Exhibit 5–8   *The business buying process*

pliers" have achieved their status by fulfilling purchase expectations over time. This being the case, the buyer is often reluctant to spend time evaluating other suppliers or risk changing suppliers. Purchase of office supplies, raw materials, lubricants, castings, and frequently used component parts involves straight rebuy decisions. Business buyers typically make these decisions.

The Buying Process

The buying process is presented in Exhibit 5–8. Like many consumer decisions, the decision sequence begins with problem or opportunity recognition. Problem recognition may be triggered by the depletion of supplies, worn-out equipment, or the need for improved technology. It may arise in various departments: operations, production, purchasing, engineering, or planning. New business opportunities may also generate the need for purchases. Once the firm recognizes a need to purchase, it determines the desired product characteristics and the quantity to buy. Then production, R&D, or engineering personnel determine specific details for each item. These "specs" are the needed levels of product characteristics.

Next, the firm searches for qualified sources or suppliers. Information about potential suppliers may be available from salespeople, exhibitions and trade shows, direct-mail advertising, press releases, trade news and trade advertising, word-of-mouth, and professional conferences. Suppliers are evaluated to ensure they can produce and deliver the product as needed and provide service after the purchase. Surveys indicate that buyers are also looking for more than a quality product and excellent service performance in their suppliers.[18] More buyers are expecting that suppliers will work closely with them to improve performance levels, contain costs, and develop new technologies. Buyers also prefer suppliers that will share data and resources to accomplish mutual goals, help improve the buyer's operations, and respond quickly to emergencies.[19] A formal procedure for evaluating suppliers is presented in Appendix B.

Wayne Whitworth, President of the Strategic Purchasing Group and Director of Purchasing for American Commercial Lines, considers several factors when choosing among potential suppliers: "There are a myriad of factors to consider when evaluating a potential or existing supplier. The most visible and quantifiable are those relating to price and quality. These attributes are readily identified and relatively easy to measure. The most difficult portion to quantify, however, is service since it entails a broad range of activities that are subjective in nature. When evaluating this component, I prefer to examine a supplier's cost contribution. Suppliers are rewarded based on cost savings contributions, innovations, new-product development activities and quantifiable measures that impact our total cost of ownership. The objective of this process is to remove subjective criteria from the evaluation process and recognize those suppliers that continually contribute value added, cost-effective products and services."

Once a decision has been reached, the firm makes the purchase. Typically, buyers negotiate the final purchase. Buyers try to get the best deal for their company and often negotiate for better payment terms, delivery schedules, or other benefits. After the purchase is finalized, buyers continually monitor the suppliers' performance.

The business buying process varies according to the type of buying decision. New-task decisions are the most complex and typically follow the process we discussed. Modified rebuy situations are less complex, but normally include most of the stages in the buying process. Straight rebuys are usually a reorder from a current supplier.

Thinking Critically

Assume you are the sales representative for a reputable company in the industrial-packaging business. You have just replaced another sales representative who recently resigned from the company. In making your initial sales calls, one of your customers tells you that he will never buy from your company again because he lost trust in the previous salesperson, who had lied to him.

- What can you do to rebuild trust with this customer?

The Buying Center

Sometimes one individual in a firm makes the buying decisions. Decisions made by a single individual occur most frequently for casual, routine, low priority, and simple modified repurchase decisions. In many instances, however, purchases are joint decisions of a buying center involving more than just a professional buyer. The **buying center,** a primary concept in business purchasing, includes more than the purchasing department or the purchasing function; it is made up of people throughout the organization at all levels. Moreover, the makeup of the buying center may vary as decisions change.

The number of people and departments represented and the levels of management involved are greater for new-task and complex modified rebuy decisions. The roles that people assume in influencing a purchase decision include initiator, decider, influencer, purchaser, gatekeeper, and user. These terms are largely self-explanatory, except for **gatekeepers,** those who control the flow of information and communication among the buying-center participants.

Vendors selling to industrial firms must recognize these multiple roles. The potential supplier may have to reach everyone involved in the decision process. That is, the seller must go beyond engineering and purchasing departments and talk to the gatekeeper, those who influence the decision, and the decision maker, for instance. IBM is a legendary example of how to do this well. IBM salespeople try to identify everyone involved in the purchase decision, the interrelationships among these individuals, the contribution of each, and the criteria each uses in making product or service evaluations.

Global firms face additional challenges, since international purchases can make buying decisions and processes even more complicated. Most firms prefer to use overseas purchasing offices, typically staffed with foreign nationals with both purchasing and technical training. Some companies hire import brokers to handle their international purchases.

Buying-center members, connected by both workflow and communication networks, receive information from several sources. These sources of information may be personal or impersonal, commercial or noncommercial. Commercial sources come from some *sponsor* that advocates purchase of a particular product or service. Noncommercial personal sources, such as professional contacts, are influential because they include actual users of the product. They also have more credibility because of their likely unbiased perspective.

Marketing efforts targeted toward businesses depend heavily on personal selling. However, commercial nonpersonal advertising through trade publications and other sales literature can stimulate customer leads, enhance a vendor's image, and generally support personal selling efforts. Once again, the Internet can be a valuable source of information for business buyers. In Asia, for example, the business-to-business segment is the fastest-growing area of e-commerce. With supply chains in Asia often extending from Taiwan to mainland China to the Philippines and the United States, the Internet is a tremendous resource for business buyers. As a result, marketers are rapidly seizing the opportunity to connect with purchasers by adding the Internet to their mix of communications tools for reaching business markets. In Asia, where face-to-face contact between buyers and sellers has been preferred for centuries, technology again comes to the forefront in business buying.[20]

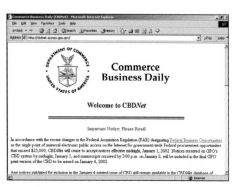

Online auction sites are becoming popular with government units that buy from the lowest bidder.

Government Markets

In the United States, the **government market** includes federal, state, and local government organizations that purchase goods and services for use in many activities. With total expenditures in the trillions of dollars, the government market is the largest in the world, with the United States federal government the largest customer in this market. The

Department of Defense, traditionally the federal government's biggest spender, now trails the Department of Health and Human Services in expenditures.[21] Waste in government purchasing is a perennial topic of discussion, but government buying practices have been reformed significantly in recent years. Taxpayers are less tolerant of frivolous purchases, and government buyers have responded.

The *Commerce Business Daily (CBD)* publishes notices of government procurement needs, contract awards, sales of government property, and other procurement information for the federal government. A new edition of the *CBD* is issued every business day. Each edition contains approximately 500 to 1,000 notices, and each notice appears only once. All federal procurement offices are required to announce in the *CBD* all contracts or subcontracts involving expenditures over $25,000.[22]

Competing for government business is a complex, time-consuming, and often frustrating endeavor. Government purchase decisions are subject to legislative direction and, in the case of the federal government, monitored by outside agencies such as the Office of Management and Budget (OMB). Most governments, whether national, state, or local, purchase through open bids or negotiated contracts. **Bids** are written proposals from qualified suppliers in response to published governmental requirements or specifications. The lowest bidder is typically selected. In some instances, small business suppliers get preferential treatment in bid evaluations. A negotiated contract is reached when a government unit works with a company to determine contract terms.

Reseller Markets

The **reseller market** is made up of firms that purchase goods and in turn sell them to others at a gain. This market includes wholesalers and retailers, totaling approximately 3.5 million companies with more than 20 million employees. Retailers and wholesalers are covered in detail in Chapters 14 and 15.

Retail businesses are everywhere. They make goods and services available to consumers at reasonable prices and in wide assortments. Most goods sold directly to consumers are first purchased by resellers. Wholesale firms tend to be more concentrated in trade centers surrounding larger population areas.

Retail establishments frequently use professional buyers to make their purchase choices. In many instances, say, for grocery chains, salespeople call on the buyers at central wholesale locations. Buyers at other retail firms, such as department stores, frequent trade shows where they place purchase orders directly with manufacturers.

Small retailers not part of large chain or franchise arrangements often band together to make purchases. Through buying-group memberships, these retailers get merchandise discounts or rebates they could not typically get on their own.

Food companies advertise to both consumer and reseller markets. Tyson advertises its chicken to resellers, offering restaurant operators easy-to-prepare recipes and menu suggestions.

Assortment and quantity decisions are the cornerstones of retailing and wholesaling success. Resellers must be able to purchase products with significant consumer demand or appeal. Their success also depends heavily on their ability to purchase products that they can resell at prices above their purchase price. Competitive pressures and growing consumer price sensitivity have greatly increased the need to make correct decisions.

Other Institutional Markets

Nonprofit organizations must also purchase goods and services to support their activities. These organizations include educational institutions, public and private hospitals, religious and charitable organizations, and trade associations. As buyers, they represent viable marketing opportunities, and many specialized firms meet needs in these unique market

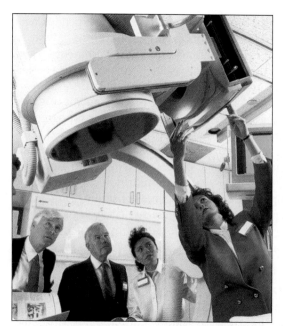

Business buyers sometimes visit supplier locations to become more knowledgeable about the products they purchase. Siemens Medical Systems, a supplier of medical equipment, has a fully operational demonstration facility in its New Jersey headquarters.

niches. For example, some architects specialize in church or school design and construction. Other companies specialize in supplies for public and private schools. And of course, institutional buyers have standard business needs too. Many firms produce and sell health care equipment and supplies. Concerns about communicable diseases have given rise to an entire industry of protective health equipment such as disposable gloves.

Ethical Issues

As discussed earlier in this chapter, ethics is a constant concern in business-to-business negotiations and transactions. Bribery is a particularly troublesome area. Bribery can take many forms: gifts from vendors to people involved in decision making, "money under the table," and promises for the future. Suppliers offer these financial inducements to increase their chances of being selected by firms. Another related practice that may occur in purchase interactions between organizations is **reciprocity**. Reciprocity is when firm A purchases from supplier B who in turn buys A's own products and services. Such practices are illegal if they restrict competition and must not be used in decisions to select suppliers unless the arrangements can be made legally.

The important values of fairness, honesty, and trust should influence all negotiations between business purchasers and their suppliers, including the selection of suppliers or vendors. Judgments of suppliers should be made impartially and fairly. Unfair trade promises should not be extracted from companies that are in dire need of business or at some other disadvantage. This is the inverse of price discrimination, when firms unethically and illegally charge different prices to different customers for similar products and services. Purchasers should not unfairly require different suppliers to charge different prices for similar goods and services.[23]

For firms pursuing global markets, the possibility of encountering ethical dilemmas is multiplied many times. Practices in some countries differ dramatically from domestic expectations. In Japan, South Korea, and Taiwan, for example, failure to accept a business gift can imply insensitivity and disrespect. Many international companies have therefore had to develop well-defined policies that address the issue of receiving favors and gifts from overseas suppliers.

Summary

1. **Define the nature of business-to-business buying behavior and markets.** Business-to-business buying behavior refers to the process through which organizations make purchase decisions involving other organizations as suppliers. Increasingly, business buyers are concerned with supply-chain management, which integrates business processes from end users through original suppliers, providing products, services, and information that add value for customers. The four broad business markets are business firms, including manufacturers and service providers; federal, state, and local governments; wholesale and retail firms that buy products and then resell them; and institutional firms, including hospitals, educational institutions, and trade associations.

2. **Explain the differences between business-to-business buying and consumer purchase behavior.** Business buyers differ from consumer buyers in important ways. Overall, industrial and business buyers are more geographically concentrated, purchases are larger, decisions are subject to multiple influences and often approached more analytically, and demand is derived from consumer markets and trends in those markets. Organizational buying decisions typically rely on a number of choice criteria, including quality and reliability of performance, price, inventory service, reputation of supplier, and the ability to provide technical and service support.

3. **Recognize the different types of buying decisions.** Business-to-business purchase decisions can be classified into one of three categories, differentiated by complexity: new-task decisions, where the choice criteria must be determined and substantial information gathered; modified rebuys, where new sources of supply may be evaluated for situations previously encountered or the decisions are only moderately complex; and straight rebuys, where products and services bought previously are repurchased from known vendors.

4. **Define the different stages of the business buying process.** The most complex purchase decisions involve this sequence: (1) Recognize the problem or opportunity; (2) determine desired product characteristics and quantity; (3) describe desired product specifications; (4) locate and qualify suppliers; (5) evaluate and select suppliers; and (6) evaluate performance.

5. **Describe the buying-center concept and the determinants of influence within the buying center.** The buying center for an organization is responsible for selecting suppliers and arranging purchase terms. It is made up of people involved in routine and nonroutine purchase decisions. They may come from different departments (purchasing, engineering, production) and levels within the organization and may play one or more roles: initiator, decider, influencer, purchaser, gatekeeper, or user. Buying-center members vary in their influence on decisions, and a number of factors affect the relative power they hold in business-to-business purchases.

6. **Understand the nature of government, reseller, and other institutional markets.** The primary organizational markets include the government market, resellers, and other institutional firms. The federal government is the largest single purchaser. State and local governments make many purchases as well. Resellers are wholesale and retail firms that purchase goods to resell to other organizations or directly to consumers at higher prices.

Understanding Marketing Terms and Concepts

Thinking About Marketing

1. What are the distinguishing characteristics of business-to-business buying behavior?

2. What is the North American Industry Classification System? How can it be used to assist in marketing to business buyers?

3. Describe some of the current trends in business-to-business buying behavior.

4. Refer to "Using Technology: Ace Is the Place for Private Exchange." What are some key benefits of using the Internet to facilitate purchasing and supply-chain management?

5. Refer to "Earning Customer Loyalty: Philmon Seafood Weathers a Tough Market." Comment on this statement: Buyer–seller relationships are not just about eco-

nomics; trust is just as important. Agree or disagree and give your reasoning.

6. What are the different types of buying decisions, and how do the information requirements vary across the decisions?

7. What is the general sequence of activities in new-task purchase decisions?

8. What is the buying center? Who are some of its typical members?

9. Contrast personal and impersonal sources of information. How might credibility differ across sources of information that are available to organizational buyers?

10. What is reciprocity? Why might it be illegal?

Applying Marketing Skills

1. Assume you must purchase new personal computers for your medium-sized company. What decision criteria would be involved, and how might the decision be reached?

2. Assume your manufacturing company has made the decision to begin importing critical component parts from country X. It is common practice for companies in that country to offer their customers personal gifts and small amounts of cash for their business. These parts, which are critical to your company's success, can be purchased abroad in country X at a much lower price and at a quality

that matches that of current U.S. suppliers' products. What policies should be established for guiding the behavior and decision making of your company's purchasing personnel?

3. Describe the way the buying needs of a small retail clothier (the business owner and four employees) might differ from the needs of a manufacturer of industrial forklifts. The manufacturer makes purchases through its buying center. Discuss the likely differences in the decision processes involved for the two businesses.

Using the www in Marketing

Activity One Compare the online purchasing sites for OfficeMax (www.officemax.com) and Staples (www.staples.com). Assume you are a buyer for office supplies for a large national manufacturer in the United States and that you want to purchase the majority of your office supplies from one vendor. In making your assessment, compare these attributes: ease of navigation, product availability, customer support, and ease of ordering. Rate each site on each attribute, and make an overall assessment of the strengths and weaknesses of each site.

Activity Two Online auctions have become part of business buying. Go to www.ebay.com to investigate an online auction site. Click on the business and industrial category. How useful do you think online auctions could be for business buyers? Based on what

you see at www.ebay.com, does it seem that some business buyers might benefit more from online auctions than would others? If so, for which product categories would online auctions seem most promising for business buyers?

Activity Three Dell Computers uses its Internet site to appeal to different categories of business and government buyers. Go to www.dell.com and compare the information available to federal government buyers with the information available to medium and large businesses (those with over 400 employees). What specific information does Dell offer potential buyers in these two categories? Is it adequate? Are there significant differences in the available information for buyers in the two categories?

Making Marketing Decisions
Case 5-1 Harley Davidson's Customer-Centered Supply Chain

Harley Davidson is best known for its high-quality motorcycles, but the company is also getting a lot of press about its customer-centered supply chain. By listening to its customers, and getting its suppliers to also listen to customers, Harley has built a strong foundation for its supply chain. In the process, Harley reinforces customer loyalty in a customer base already fiercely loyal to the leading American manufacturer of motorcycles.

In selecting suppliers for its supply chain, Harley expects that all suppliers will practice open communications and participate in important Harley processes such as market research and product development. Suppliers must be dedicated to reducing supply chain costs, provide 24-hour, seven-day accessibility, integrate effectively into the Harley Davidson organization, and align with Harley's strategic direction. In upgrading its supply chain to ultimately meet dealer and consumer needs more effectively, Harley has reduced its supplier base by 80 percent, down from 4,000 to 800. Of these 800, Harley has strategic partnerships with its 125 most crucial suppliers. It has greatly reduced its material costs, product development cycle time, and defective parts percentage. All of these improvements have paid off with a huge reduction in waste and assembly-line slowdowns.

It all starts with the customer, and Harley hits the road to learn from its ultimate buyers. Among the most important venues for listening to the customer are semiannual biker rallies in Florida and South Dakota. Bikers from all over the United States attend these rallies, where Harley sets up booths, display areas, and test rides. Key suppliers join Harley at these rallies to gather customer input through surveys, interviews, and less-formal one-on-one conversations with riders. This connection of customers with Harley personnel and suppliers helps ensure that consistent information is passed back from customers to the critical parties in the supply chain.

In addition to the rallies, Harley hosts dealer shows, also attended by supplier representatives. Harley can learn about dealer concerns at these shows, and key suppliers can provide information about technical concerns. All dealer information, as is the case with ultimate consumers at rallies, is documented and entered into the supply-chain database for appropriate follow-up. Eventually, Harley compares notes with suppliers, and joint decisions are made that better meet the needs of all parties.

The level of detail in this information-gathering process is impressive. For example, Harley riders are sticklers for detail when it comes to paint and chrome. Harley and its suppliers ask for customer input on bike colors and just how much chrome it needs in order to give the bikes that unmistakable Harley look.

By implementing a customer-centered supply chain, Harley enjoys many benefits. It helps attract world-class suppliers such as Delphi Automotive Delco Electronics Systems, which supplies speedometers, tachometers, cruise control, and other electrical devices. The efficient supply chain also makes it easier for dealers to be competitive against rival retailers. Harley also supports its dealers through its online RoadStore.

RoadStore provides consumers with information about Harley products and also allows shoppers to buy online through authorized Harley dealers. Harley also supports its dealers with advertising, merchandising consultation, and in-store programs. One of its most successful 2002 programs is its Rider's Edge New Rider's Course, held in conjunction with 44 of its 630 U.S. dealers. New riders receive 25 hours of riding time and classroom instruction. Participating dealers are delighted with the program, which has given them exposure and sales opportunities with a new customer base—females under the age of 35. With its supply chain running at near-optimal levels and the dual focus of its supply chain on dealers and riders, Harley is poised to continue is impressive sales growth. For one thing, dealers and customers are less likely to have to wait for that new Harley, as one result of the supply-chain improvements is a better match between supply and demand.

Questions

1. How can Harley Davidson marketing and sales personnel interact with its purchasing personnel to further strengthen the supply chain and improve customer loyalty?

2. What is the role of technology in Harley's supply chain? What additional uses of technology can you identify that might be useful to Harley's focus on the dealer and the ultimate customer?

3. Some of Harley's suppliers also supply key Harley competitors. How can Harley be sure these suppliers will not share competitive information with its competitors? How important is trust between suppliers and business buyers?

Case 5-2 *Big Three Automakers Pressure Suppliers*

The relationships between the Big Three automakers (Ford, General Motors, and Daimler-Chrysler) and their suppliers offer some interesting contrasts. On one hand, automakers and suppliers are heavily involved in collaboration on product development and quality improvement. This collaboration is widely viewed as necessary in order to satisfy changing consumer tastes and compete effectively against other automakers, chiefly Toyota, Honda, Nissan, and to a lesser degree, companies from Germany, Korea, and occasionally other countries.

On the other hand, Detroit automakers have sometimes been adversarial in their relationships with suppliers. The tension between automakers and their suppliers made headline news in the business world throughout the 1990s. General Motors was portrayed as the chief protagonist during this period, led by controversial purchasing chief J. Ignacio Lopez de Arriotura. Lopez approached purchasing as a win–lose proposition, and his goal was for GM to beat their suppliers at the game of constantly trying to buy at lower prices. While a storm of negative publicity surrounded GM's purchasing practices under Lopez, he was able to wring tremendous cost savings out of GM suppliers, and other automotive purchasing groups took notice. None of the major manufacturers could afford to be at a cost disadvantage to the others, a reality that became even more meaningful in the slow economic times of 2000–2002.

Daimler-Chrysler, badly pinched from a profitability point of view, began implementing some of the same tactics GM had used with suppliers. As part of a huge cost-cutting initiative, the company asked suppliers to tear up existing supply contracts and sign new contracts with a 5 percent reduction in costs. Many key suppliers balked, and some privately complained of Daimler-Chrysler's heavy-handed approach to solving their profitability problem. Some went beyond that, saying that they would not give Daimler-Chrysler the first look at new technologies and ideas for new designs.

Another development that irked many major suppliers was the Big Three's move to public exchanges, or electronic marketplaces. Here, the automakers could use public exposure to keep competitive suppliers' prices down, and suppliers did not like parading their offerings for all, including their own competitors, to see. General Motors struck first with its TradeXchange. Ford followed with its own exchange. Now the Big Three have collaborated with a co-owned site called Covisint. Their hope is to have all the key suppliers active on Covisint, something that many suppliers are not happy with.

In the power struggle to exercise control in the automotive supply market, the Big Three obviously have a lot of economic clout. Ford and General Motors have the two largest purchasing budgets of U.S. corporations, and Daimler-Chrysler's budget is significant as well. But there are thousands of automotive suppliers, and they too have a lot of collective clout. Some of the suppliers are large in their own right. Delphi, a key supplier, has the 17th largest purchasing budget in the United States, well ahead of corporate giants such as Dell Computer, International Paper, and Lockheed Martin. Johnson Controls, another key supplier, has the 38th largest purchasing budget in the United States, ahead of large companies such as Bristol-Meyers, Sprint, and Conoco.

Large suppliers like Delphi and Johnson Controls are called Tier 1 suppliers in the automotive industry. They sell directly to the automobile companies. Tier 2 suppliers are smaller than Tier 1 suppliers, and usually sell to Tier 1 suppliers. They may sell directly to the automakers, but most of the time they sell to Tier 1 suppliers. Tier 3 suppliers sell to Tier 1 and Tier 2 suppliers, but rarely do they sell directly to the automakers. Tier 1 suppliers are gaining power in the marketplace as they buy up Tier 2 and Tier 3 suppliers. For the automakers' Covisint site to work, a large percentage of Tier 1, 2, and 3 suppliers must participate. Many Tier 2 and Tier 3 suppliers are small businesses and are fearful that price cuts will put them out of business. Should this happen, the financially healthy supplier would buy them out, or simply expand its own business to meet demand. Analysts say that suppliers are gaining clout, as the cost-cutting demands of the automakers ultimately create consolidation on the supply side. Already, the number of North American suppliers in the past decade has dropped from 30,000 to 8,000, a 75 percent reduction.

Questions

1. Can the Big Three's emphasis on lower costs have any detrimental effects on their ultimate ability to deliver what the consumer wants?

2. Do you see any ethical issues in the way the Big Three conduct their purchasing practices?

3. What can suppliers do to negotiate mutually beneficial contracts with the Big Three automakers? From the suppliers' point of view, what are the pros and cons of participating in Covisint?

Chapter Six

Marketing Research and Decision Support Systems

After studying this chapter, you should be able to:

1 Understand the purpose and functions of marketing research.

2 Be familiar with the stages of the marketing research process.

3 Discuss different types of research designs, data collection methods, and sources of secondary and primary marketing research data.

4 Understand many of the major issues involved with survey design and sampling.

5 Appreciate the role of marketing research within decision support systems.

www.nfow.com

NFO is one of the world's leading providers of research-based marketing information, providing in-depth knowledge and understanding of consumers and brands through research. NFO offers a full array of both custom and syndicated products and services. The company offers access to the industry's largest online and off-line panel data resources. Recently, NFO has joined forces with Interpublic Group, one of the world's largest ad agencies and communications companies. NFO brings to Interpublic expertise in brand tracking and predictive modeling to help design marketing budgets.

Forty percent of NFO's resources are derived from Internet-based market intelligence activity. On-line research offers advantages in terms of cost and speed of doing research. Its proprietary panel includes more than 700,000 households. Six hundred thousand of these households are in North America. NFO serves more than 3,000 clients, including nearly 60 of the largest 100 companies of the *Fortune* 500 list. NFO offers services designed to understand what drives customers to stay or move to the competition, the nature of customer relationships in terms of satisfaction and loyalty, and the nature of customer segments in terms of their attitudes toward client companies. NFO has 13,000 employees organized across three regions—North America, Europe, and the Middle East and Asia.

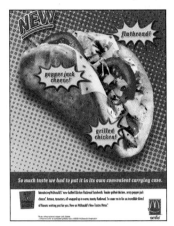

Marketing research is used in planning to identify the needs of product users and in problem solving to evaluate the types of products to offer.

Marketing research companies like Information Resources, Inc., and A. C. Nielsen are among the largest providers of marketing research data and offer a wide variety of services. Smaller research firms often specialize in industry types or individual services, such as measurement of customer retention and customer satisfaction. IRI makes a large portion of its revenues from the sale of product-movement tracking data derived from large surveys of grocery stores and drug stores; whereas, other research firms provide for their clients individually designed studies that address particular situations or problems. IRI's research enables its customers to monitor sales and promotional activities across product categories, to understand the effects of promotions on consumer activity, and to identify problems and opportunities in distribution.

The overall objective of marketing research is to reduce risk in decision making by helping management understand its uncertain and changing marketplace and the consumers and competitors that make up its markets. The marketing research process involves the collection, interpretation, and use of data to make decisions. Such understanding makes a firm better able to provide products and services that meet customer expectations and needs. Marketing research enhances communication between a firm and its markets with the aim of improving managerial decision making. The aim of research is not to confirm that decisions already made are correct, but to identify alternative choices and to support the decision-making process.[1]

What Is Marketing Research?

In its definition of **marketing research,** the American Marketing Association recognizes the complexity of the process and the different activities that may be performed.

Marketing research links the consumer, the customer, and the public through information used to:

- Identify and define marketing opportunities.
- Generate, refine, and evaluate marketing actions.
- Monitor marketing performance.
- Improve understanding of marketing as a process.

Marketing research:

- Specifies the information required to address these issues.
- Designs the methods for collecting information.
- Manages and implements the data collection process.
- Analyzes the results.
- Communicates the findings and implications.[2]

This definition emphasizes the generation of information that assists in managerial decision making. We adapted the second half of the definition as an outline for discussing the stages of the marketing research process in this chapter.

Marketing research is useful in planning, problem solving, and control, as shown in Exhibit 6–1. Marketers use marketing research to provide guidance in decision making. This enables them to spend their resources more effectively. Researchers must understand the research process, the marketing process, and the industries in which the firm operates.[3] Take the research team for Stouffers, a national organization that manages private restaurants and clubs, for example. Stouffers researchers must understand the growth and image objectives of the organization, besides identifying new market opportunities and conducting customer satisfaction surveys. Only by knowing the club business can meaningful research be conducted to support the Stouffers organization. Pizza Hut now links its unit managers'

Speaking from Experience

Terry Vavra
President
Marketing Metrics, Inc.

"Make no mistake about it, marketing researchers are sometimes criticized for their orientation to objectivity, especially by individuals in positions where personal creativity is viewed as paramount (e.g., brand managers, creative directors). But the tide is turning. Today, fewer and fewer upper-level managers will commit company resources based on only one person's intuition. They increasingly demand supportive evidence available only from properly designed research."

Terry Vavra has a B.S. degree in marketing from the University of California, Los Angeles, and a Ph.D. degree in marketing from the University of Illinois. Marketing Metrics, Inc., founded in 1983, is a marketing research firm that specializes in customer retention and global marketing strategy. Vavra discusses the growing importance of research.

bonuses to the results of customer satisfaction surveys. Questions address satisfaction with service, food quality, and other issues.

Answers to important and interesting questions are possible through the use of marketing research. Should McDonald's focus upon a more clear market position as opposed to ever-changing menu explorations? The company now faces the need to reawaken its brand diluted by movement away from their initial emphasis on performance and firm management. Could Webvan, the online grocer, have avoided its problems with the consideration of marketing research in lieu of focusing exclusively upon developing complex inventory and distribution systems?

Exhibit 6–1	*Kinds of questions marketing research can help answer*

I. Planning

  A. What kinds of people buy our products? Where do they live? How much do they earn? How many of them are there?

  B Are the markets for our products increasing or decreasing? Are there promising markets that we have not yet reached?

  C. Are the channels of distribution for our products changing? Are new types of marketing institutions likely to evolve?

II. Problem Solving

  A. Product

    1. Which of various product designs is likely to be the most successful?

    2. What kind of packaging should we use?

  B. Price

    1. What price should we charge for our products?

    2. As production costs decline, should we lower our prices or try to develop higher quality products?

  C. Place

    1. Where, and by whom, should our products be sold?

    2. What kinds of incentives should we offer the trade to push our products?

  D. Promotion

    1. How much should we spend on promotion? How should it be allocated to products and to geographic areas?

    2. What combination of media—newspapers, radio, television, magazines—should we use?

III. Control

  A. What is our market share overall? In each geographic area? By each customer type?

  B. Are customers satisfied with our products? How is our record for service? Are there many returns?

  C. How does the public perceive our company? What is our reputation with the trade?

In the Webvan instance, it is amazing that its substantial investment was made with almost no research into whether consumers would want its service.[4]

Marketing research is often used to evaluate the characteristics and potential of markets prior to making decisions about product introductions and new-market entry. Research is helpful in evaluating new-product concepts and advertising campaigns under consideration. It is also used to monitor market performance and competitive reaction. Nielsen Inc., one of the oldest and largest marketing research firms, provides data to packaged-goods manufacturers like Coca-Cola and Nabisco about their product sales. Research is also used to identify and solve problems. Municipalities, for example, frequently conduct marketing research to identify citizens' needs and methods for attracting shoppers to the area.

Most important, marketing research should support the firm's overall market orientation. Research links marketers to markets through information and scientific study. It is used to explore opportunities and problems, monitor performance, refine marketing strategy, and improve understanding of marketing efforts and markets themselves. As such, research enhances a firm's closeness with its customers and enables the marketer to anticipate latent unfulfilled needs and wants.[5]

Marketing Research in the New Millennium

Significant environmental phenomena will affect the marketing research industry in the next decade and beyond. First, the traditional time line of four to six weeks for the typical research project will no longer be acceptable in many cases. However, researchers will still need to balance time pressures with quality. Second, gatekeeper technology, such as caller ID and privacy-related services, will limit researcher access to consumers. And, discussed later, pending federal and state legislation may restrict the data collection process as well. Marketing research is also becoming more a part of the marketing strategy development process. This shift to more of an advisory role represents less emphasis on the more traditional marketing research roles of testing and evaluation.[6]

Interactivity, e-commerce, and the Internet are certainly affecting the practice of marketing, and likewise are affecting the conduct of marketing research. New consumer information is pouring in at incredible speed from scanners, loyalty program tapes, syndicated data services, and the Internet. Marketing researchers within firms and researchers within the marketing research industry itself are going to be required to adapt to this technological wave of change. The problem is no longer how to get information; the problem today is how will data be managed. As examples, the research departments at the Campbell's Soup Company and Procter & Gamble have been renamed "Information Management" and "Consumer Market and Knowledge," respectively.

At GM, the company now has a database of 12 million credit card holders, giving access to the buying habits of their customers. Blockbuster has a database of 36 million households. The information is used to determine movie choices and to cross-promote its affiliates such as Discovery Zone for children. Analyses of these databases also reaffirm Pareto's Law. For example, 13 percent of Diet Coke drinkers represent 83 percent of the product's volume; for Taster's Choice, 4 percent of their customers generated 73 percent of their sales. These databases and information at the customer level will be instrumental in enabling companies to build long-term relationships with their core and loyal segments.[7]

The marketing research industry itself is in transition. Consolidation among companies has resulted in market dominance by the top 25 firms. Companies like A. C. Nielsen, IMS, IRI, and Kantar hold significant industry market share. And, these companies are truly global in their customer base and offerings. It is important to note the evolution of firms from market and opinion research firms to suppliers of information, consulting, and data exchange. These changes have made easy entry into the industry much harder. Previously, small firms could easily exist and succeed, even with minimal capital investment.[8]

The Marketing Research Process

Exhibit 6–2 presents the stages of the **marketing research process.** The sequence begins with an understanding of the problem and ends with analysis and interpretation.[9] The overall objective should be to generate useful, timely, and cost-effective information. That is, the resulting reduced risk and improved decision making should justify the research costs involved. Even a small study involving 500 local telephone interviews can cost more than $10,000 when researcher time and other costs are considered. Consequently, the cost–benefit trade-off of doing research is always an issue for a firm.

Alternative research approaches and methods should not be considered competing but viewed as both substitutes and complements. In fact, in many instances, firms should consider the use of multiple methods in the spirit of "research triangulation." New insights can be gained from research employing different methods (e.g., focus groups, telephone surveys). Moreover, confidence is enhanced in the validity of findings if results converge from studies conducted using alternative methods. Also, small-scale qualitative information is used as a precursor to subsequent more formal and standardized questioning. For example, a series of small-sample in-depth interviews could be conducted to generate basic understanding of research issues and relationships. Subsequently, large-scale sample surveys could be employed to generate data that enable tests of statistical significance and the identification of quantifiable findings.[10]

Problem Definition

Problem definition is depicted in Exhibit 6–2 as the first step in any marketing research project and is critical to its success. Problems in a business are often defined as differences between the way things should be and the way they are. Both researchers and management (the users of the research) need to understand the research problem clearly.

It should be noted that a substantial amount of research is ongoing and is used for general control and planning purposes. For example, the many companies that use data on in-store sales and product movement provided by IRI or A. C. Nielsen engage in research continuously in their efforts to monitor competitive activity in the marketplace. Thus, often in the problem definition stage of the research process, a problem is not formally identified. Instead, ongoing research may lead to identification of a problem, such as declining sales, low turnover, declining brand appeal, or the emergence of competitive offerings.

The problem definition stage is often difficult because the expectations and desires of managers and researchers frequently differ. Researchers generally take an exploratory perspective, whereas managers may prefer research that confirms their expectations and provides few surprises. For best results, all parties involved must take a constructive stance in defining the research problem. They must focus on the real problem and not the symptoms; anticipate how the information will be used; and avoid prescribing a specific study until the problem is fully understood and defined.

Exbibit 6–2   *The marketing research process*

Research Designs

Marketing research designs are general strategies or plans of action for addressing the research problem and the data collection and analysis process. The problem definition stage is likely to suggest approaches for determining which marketing research design to use. Research generally has three purposes: exploration, description, and explanation.[11] They result in three general types of research designs: exploratory, descriptive, and causal. Common methods and example studies for each of these designs are shown in Exhibit 6–3.

EXPLORATORY DESIGNS **Exploratory research** is typically carried out to satisfy the researcher's desire for better understanding, or to develop preliminary background and suggest issues for a more detailed follow-up study.

As shown in Exhibit 6–3, exploratory research can be conducted using literature reviews, case analyses, interviews, and focus groups.[12] Better understanding of a problem might begin with a review of prior research. A researcher working for a bank would not begin a study of the bank's image, for example, without some review of the banking literature on what determines a bank's image. In-depth interviews with individuals who already have some knowledge of the problem may shed some light on the issue.

Interviewing techniques that generate narrative descriptions of consumers' roles in life can be useful in the generation of new innovation ideas. One approach focuses on the conflicts and confusions that consumers report from in-depth interviews regarding their important life "orienting values." Example orienting values include "being professional" or "being cutting edge." Narrative descriptions about pursuit of these defining objectives collected in exploratory interviews and the conflicts that arise in consumers' lives from pursuit of the values represent potential sources of new product ideas.[13]

DESCRIPTIVE DESIGNS **Descriptive research** is normally directed by one or more formal research questions or hypotheses. Typically, a survey or questionnaire is administered to a sample from a population of interest to the firm, such as female household heads or purchasing agents in an industry. Examples include consumer surveys to estimate market potential, segmentation research to identify demographic consumer segments, attitude and opinion surveys, and product usage surveys.

Descriptive studies may be cross-sectional or longitudinal, depending on the timing of the observation. For example, a survey of customers administered at a given time to assess perceived satisfaction with service is a *cross-sectional study*. Consumers who participate in panel studies of purchase behavior over a period of time are involved in *longitudinal research*.

Exhibit 6–3	*Three general research designs*	
Type	**Common Methods**	**Example Studies**
Exploratory designs	Literature reviews Case analyses Interviews with knowledgeable persons In-depth interviews, focus groups	Evaluation of new-product concepts, environmental-trend analysis, identification of product attribute importance
Descriptive designs	Cross-sectional surveys Panel studies Product movement surveys Store audits Telephone, mail, personal interviews	Market potential, image studies, competitive-positioning analysis, market characteristic examinations, customer-satisfaction studies
Causal designs	Experimental designs (lab and field studies) Market tests	Evaluation of alternative marketing mix combinations (varying price levels, changing promotional appeals, reallocation of salesforce efforts)

NOT ALL OUR GUESTS ARRIVE IN RANGE ROVERS.

At South Seas Plantation, some of our guests actually sail oceans to visit us. But no matter what method of transportation you choose, you'll be welcomed by a Resort and Yacht Harbour that *Motorboating and Sailing* magazine named among the dozen most spectacular cruising grounds in North America.

Located at the end of a private channel at Intracoastal Mile Marker 39, with a 6 ft. low tide depth, our full-service marina can easily accommodate craft up to 110 feet and offers more than 3,600 feet of berthing space. Amenities include fuel, electricity, water, complimentary pumpout facilities, telephone, ice, and cable TV. And the Ship's Store is stocked with supplies, marine charts, groceries, and packaged goods.

So next trip, set your course for South Seas Plantation. Because no matter how you arrive, we promise you'll leave with more wind in your sails. For more information, call your travel agent or 1-800-237-3102.

South Seas Plantation
Captiva Island, Florida

Focus groups are commonly used to explore new concepts and to obtain consumer reactions to ad campaigns under development. South Seas Plantation used focus groups of guests and resort prospects to help make decisions about themes, logos, TV spots, and brochures.

CAUSAL DESIGNS Exploratory and descriptive studies can help answer certain questions, but identification of cause-and-effect relationships requires **causal research.** Causal designs call for *experiments*, in which researchers manipulate independent variables and then observe or measure the dependent variable or variables of interest.

Suppose a direct marketing company wants to see the effect on sales of increasing its 50¢ coupon to $1. To test this, the company matches two markets, using key variables such as product sales, consumer demographics, and market size. In one market, consumers receive the $1 coupon; in the other market, they receive the 50¢ coupon. At the end of the experiment, the company compares sales in the two markets and learns that the $1 coupon generates more sales. When it incorporates the cost/profitability of each coupon value into the analysis, however, the company finds the $1 coupon results in a loss, while the 50¢ coupon is profitable. This analysis convinces the company to continue its 50¢ coupon promotion.

Data Types

Marketing research methods and data can be categorized in various ways. One description of research categories described total U.S. spending for marketing, advertising, and opinion research in 2001 at nearly $6.2 billion. By segment methods, this spending was broken down as follows: qualitative research—18.2 percent; syndicated research—41.8 percent; and, survey research—40.0 percent. The use of syndicated research increased almost 10 percent from the previous year.[14]

Marketing research information can also be categorized as either primary data or secondary data. Interrelationships among the different types of data and the various data collection methods are summarized in Exhibit 6–4.

PRIMARY DATA   **Primary data** are collected specifically for a particular research problem. This is the type of information most frequently associated with marketing research, such as survey data from a sample of customers about satisfaction with services. Polls on the standing of political candidates prior to elections are another example. Primary data have the advantage of currency and relevance for a specific research problem. Their primary disadvantage is cost.

SECONDARY DATA   **Secondary data** are those already collected for some other purpose and are available from a variety of sources. As a rule, researchers should

Exhibit 6–4	*Data collection methods and examples*

Sources of Information

Primary Data	Secondary Data
SURVEYS	**INTERNAL DATA**
• Mail	• Company records
• Telephone	• Data from marketing design support systems
INTERVIEWS	**EXTERNAL DATA**
• Mail intercepts	Proprietary
• Personal interviews	• Custom research
	• Sydicated services
FOCUS GROUPS OBSERVATION	Nonproprietary
• Personal	• Published reports
• Mechanical	• Census data
	• Periodicals

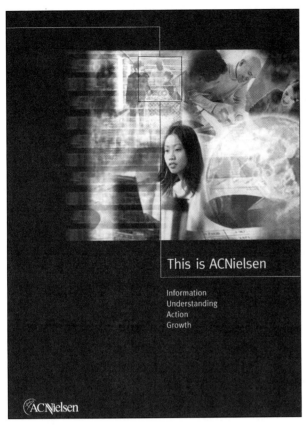

This is ACNielsen

Information
Understanding
Action
Growth

ACNielsen

Large research firms provide proprietary, secondary research data for use by other firms in analyzing consumer purchase patterns and brand switching. A. C. Nielsen's Homescan panel of 40,000 households tracks consumer purchases at the household level across all types of store outlets.

consult secondary data before collecting primary data. Corporate libraries and outside vendors (firms that specialize in providing research data) provide secondary data. Some public and private universities offer secondary research services. Japanese firms have long recognized the value of secondary data within their firms and regularly use it to compare product movement.[15]

Internal secondary data are collected within a firm and include accounting records, salesforce reports, or customer feedback reports. *External secondary data* may be nonproprietary or proprietary. *Nonproprietary* secondary data are available in libraries and other public sources. For example, information from *Sales & Marketing Management*'s "Survey of Buying Power" about population, income, and age groups can help managers estimate market potentials and identify likely market segments.

Obviously, the fastest growing source of secondary data is the Internet. The Internet represents the infrastructure (the machinery, computers, lines, and equipment) that supports what has become known as the World Wide Web or the "the Web." Individuals and firms with personal computers, a modem, and software access or browser can generate information from both Web sites and home pages around the Web. Information sources include product and company data, business and article reviews, as well as data from companies such as Dow Jones and Dun & Bradstreet.[16]

Terry Vavra talks about the use of available secondary sources of information: "Declining response rates to consumer marketing research is probably the biggest problem marketing research faces. We depend on information collected from individual consumers and businesspeople; failure to respond increases costs and decreases the accuracy of findings. Some would claim that newer technologies (like Internet interviewing) are the answer, but the modality of the interview is a different issue. Industry response rates are becoming unacceptable across all modalities. There are two answers to the problem of declining survey response rates: better discipline (on the part of interviewing practices) and reinforcing the benefits of participation to those who agree. When our firm pretested electronic toll collection for the states of New Jersey and New York, we experienced a response rate of 55 percent (for a combination telephone-mail-telephone design). This high rate was attributable to the relevance of the topic to the commuters we contacted and to the disciplined protocol we used. In our ongoing customer satisfaction work, we don't ask questions the sponsoring organization already knows (model owned, when and where purchased, etc.)—this information is extracted from databases and we're passionate about providing responding customers with acknowledgment and feedback."

Online computer databases using CD technology are often free or available in libraries for minimal fees. Many companies now purchase demographic and geographic census data on CD-ROM for use in selecting store sites, mapping sales territories, and segmenting markets.[17]

Primary data are collected for a specific product or situation. In-home surveys, a means of collecting primary data, can provide detailed explanations regarding actual product use.

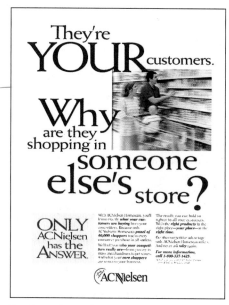

Purchase data collected on samples of consumers can identify what consumers are buying, who are new adopters, and which firms represent the competition.

Syndicated secondary data are provided by commercial marketing research firms that sell their services to other firms. Commercial firms can establish *diary panels* of representative households that record product and brand purchases. These data can help companies evaluate market share and purchase patterns. **Scanner data** obtained from Universal Product Code (UPC) information read in grocery stores provide timely information on actual purchase behavior. Scanner information is forecast to eventually enable companies to model their decisions and to allow management to allocate advertising and promotional dollars across actions to achieve optimum marketplace performance.[18]

Advances like these enable retailers to monitor product movement and to assess the effectiveness of advertising and in-store promotions. Several firms, including Nielsen and Information Resources, Inc., developed proprietary systems that combine information on product purchasing behavior with TV viewing behavior to produce **single-source data.**[19]

Computer technology is used in novel ways to combine U.S. census data with internal customer data. For example, *geographic information systems (GIS)* provide digitized maps that can be displayed on color computer terminals.[20] There is a huge difference between a stack of printed customer names and addresses and a color-coded map showing where the customers are located. GIS systems save marketing researchers hours of tedious plotting. GIS maps were used in the Clinton/Gore presidential campaign to improve volunteer and media efforts.[21]

Geographic displays have significant potential for marketing research use in the next decade. The Bureau of Census now sells street maps with economic and population data detailed to city blocks on compact discs. Programmers can mesh customer data with these spatial databases, allowing display of three-dimensional plots of customers. Chemical Bank uses GIS to ensure the bank acts in a socially responsible manner and lends money fairly in poor neighborhoods.[22]

Data Collection Methods

Some of the more popular methods of primary data collection include focus groups, telephone surveys, mail surveys, personal interviews, mall intercepts, and Internet surveys. Their principal advantages and disadvantages are summarized in Exhibit 6–5.

FOCUS GROUPS   The most common exploratory procedure is the **focus group.** Focus groups usually comprise 8 to 12 individuals led by a moderator in a focused, in-depth discussion on a specific topic. Usually lasting no more than two hours, the sessions are designed to obtain participant feedback on a particular subject. Focus groups of consumers are well suited for examining new-product concepts and advertising themes, investigating the criteria underlying purchase decisions, and generating information for developing consumer questionnaires.[23]

Using Technology

Cyber shopping and conjoint analysis

Conjoint analysis is a frequently applied research technique that involves soliciting consumers' opinions about various stimuli, often product configurations. Consumer preferences (often rank-order data) for various combinations of products are decomposed such that feature or attribute preferences are obtained. Researchers can identify the relative contribution of price, service, size, warranty level, and other attributes, to determine which are most important to product references. Lands' End has made novel use of this approach via a simple questionnaire included on their Web site. For example, six pairs of outfits are shown to the shopper, who chooses a preferred outfit from among each pair. Through conjoint analysis of these choices and the answers to a few other questions, the site sorts through 80,000 apparel options and presents the most suitable ones to the consumer.

Exhibit 6–5		*Advantages and disadvantages of frequently used data collection methods*
Method	**Advantages**	**Disadvantages**
Focus groups	• Depth of information collected • Flexibility in use • Relatively low cost • Data collected quickly	• Requires expert moderator • Questions of group size and acquaintanceships of participants • Potential for bias from moderator • Small sample size
Telephone surveys	• Centralized control of data collection • More cost-effective than personal interviews • Data collected quickly	• Resistance in collecting income, financial data • Limited depth of response • Disproportionate coverage of low-income segments • Abuse of phone by solicitors • Perceived intrusiveness
Mail surveys	• Cost-effective per completed response • Broad geographic dispersion • Ease of administration • Data collected quickly	• Refusal and contact problems with certain segments • Limited depth of response • Difficult to estimate nonresponse biases • Resistance and bias in collecting income, financial data • Lack of control following mailing
Personal (in-depth) interviews	• More depth of response than telephone interviews • Generate substantial number of ideas compared with group methods	• Easy to transmit biasing cues • Not-at-homes • Broad coverage often infeasible • Cost per contact high • Data collection time may be excessive
Mall intercepts	• Flexibility in collecting data, answering questions, probing respondents • Data collected quickly • Excellent for concept tests, copy evaluations, other visuals • Fairly high response rates	• Limited time • Sample composition or representativeness is suspect • Costs depend on incidence rates • Interviewer supervision difficult
Internet surveys	• Inexpensive, quickly executed • Visual stimuli can be evaluated • Real-time data processing possible • Can be answered at convenience of respondent	• Responses must be checked for duplication, bogus responses • Respondent self-selection bias • Limited ability to qualify respondents and confirm responses • Difficulty in generating sample frames for probability sampling
Projective techniques	• Useful in word association tests of new brand names • Less threatening to respondents for sensitive topics • Can identify important motives underlying choices	• Require trained interviewers • Cost per interview high
Observation	• Can collect sensitive data • Accuracy of measuring overt behaviors • Different perspective than survey self-reports • Useful in studies of cross-cultural differences	• Appropriate only for frequently occurring behaviors • Unable to assess opinions of attitudes causing behaviors • May be expensive in data-collection-time costs

The guidelines for using focus groups often vary by the research problem or situation of the firm. For example, groups of executives who may hold strong opinions or teenage consumers who can be shy argue for mini–focus groups of four to six participants. Also, focus groups need not necessarily be homogeneous demographically. The rule of thumb is that subjects should be comfortable with one another and that some diversity is beneficial. In many cases, budgets do not afford the luxury of separate focus groups, which can run as high as $20,000, for each demographic group in each market.[24]

Interestingly, focus groups have become so common that at least 10 episodes of TV sitcoms have employed focus groups as part of their plot. Unfortunately, these depictions are misleading. Multiple groups are typically required before large decisions are made. Participants must be screened for appropriateness, and unbiased

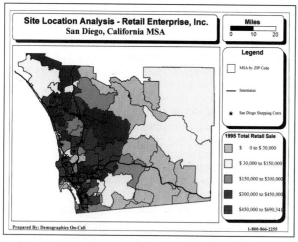

Geographic information systems provide digitalized maps of customer markets that are easily color coded to display differences in area effective buying income or other characteristics. These systems have been used effectively in making retail site selection decisions.

and competent moderators are a necessity. Further, groups should not become dominated by a single or few strong participant personalities.[25]

P&G uses research to make most new product decisions; $150 million is spent on 4,000 to 5,000 studies per year. Focus groups comprise a large portion of this activity. Outside firms specializing in focus group research are often employed to recruit and screen participants. As part of these studies, residents of Cincinnati, the home of Procter & Gamble, are a frequent source of study subjects, testing products from Pampers to cleaning products.[26]

Focus groups, along with some research information obtained from in-depth interviews and the observation research methods described later, provide **qualitative data.** Qualitative data are characterized by the depth of responses obtained and richness of description. The open-ended nature of the responses, coupled with typically smaller samples, makes predictions and generalizations tentative or difficult. However, qualitative information from focus groups, for example, is particularly useful in exploratory studies where problem understanding and initial insights are needed.

In contrast, descriptive surveys using large-sample telephone surveys or sales-tracking data from store panels such as IRI yield **quantitative data.** These data, collected using structured response formats, can be easily analyzed and projected to larger populations. For example, quantitative information from political polls can be used to predict voter opinion. Or, marketing surveys can be used to identify the content and rank order of reasons underlying customer satisfaction.

TELEPHONE SURVEYS Telephone interviews are relatively cost-effective; a large number of them over a wide geographical area can be conducted quickly and efficiently. Many firms use telephone interviews as their primary means of conducting survey research.

Telephone interviews also enable centralized control and supervision of data collection. *Random digit dialing* and *plus-one dialing* methods have become increasingly popular in the telephone interview process. In one popular version of random-digit dialing, four random digits are added to three-digit telephone exchanges. In plus-one dialing, a telephone number is randomly selected from the local directory, and a digit or digits added to it. This enables the inclusion of unlisted numbers in the sample and increases the likelihood of sampling a working number.

Problems with the use of telephone interviews limit their effectiveness. Questionable ethical practices, such as the use of marketing research as a sales ploy, hurt

Being Entrepreneurial

Online marketing research

Questions remain regarding the representativeness of online samples and the actual cost efficiency of online research. The cost of maintaining online panels is high, and the novelty of the Internet has dissipated, making it more difficult to get the attention of respondents. However, online data collection does offer the potential for significant growth. ITracks has a software for conducting online focus groups. Respondents with broadband capabilities can easily view pictorials and videos. As such, new product research is facilitated. Burke has done substantial research on how consumers respond to scales online versus traditional telephone surveys. With the dot com failures, questions have arisen within the research firms themselves. Knowledgeable industry experts advise that successful integration of online research into the traditional mix of research alternatives requires risk taking by upper management. Moreover, research employees charged with implementation warrant reassurances and possibly different reward systems until costs are stabilized.

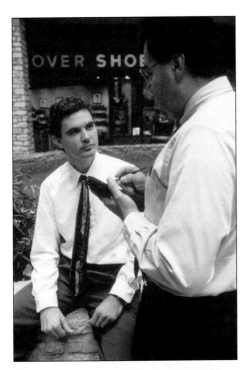

Personal interviews enable the collection of in-depth information in one-on-one situations. Such interviews can be conducted in-house or in-store. For in-store situations, researchers may actually observe behaviors and choices as evaluations and decisions are made.

the research industry. Both the European Society for Opinion and Marketing Research (ESOMAR) and Council of American Survey Research Organizations (CASRO) have called for self-regulation among companies doing telephone interviews to stem the growing backlash against researchers.[27] Many states are contemplating legislation to restrict telephone survey research. In addition, the breadth and depth of information that can be obtained from telephone interviews are limited.[28]

MAIL SURVEYS   Mail surveys can obtain broad geographical market coverage, are generally less expensive per completed survey than other methods, and can be used to collect data rather quickly. Surveys can address a range of issues in a single questionnaire. Studies based on mail questionnaires, and to lesser degrees those using telephone and personal interviews, suffer from nonresponse. Inaccurate mailing lists, questions about who exactly answers the survey, and the inability to handle respondent questions are additional shortcomings of mail surveys.

Although mail questionnaires are relatively inexpensive, conducting a mail survey can involve investments that may be prohibitive for smaller firms. Costs can be reduced by a number of means. For example, Plymart Company, a large southeastern building supply company, chose a university professor over an independent marketing research contractor to design and administer a survey of customer perceptions. The results persuaded management to add framing supplies, which increased sales by 22 percent. For less than $5,000, the company received $100,000 worth of information.[29]

PERSONAL INTERVIEWS   Personal interviews involve one-on-one interactions between a consumer, customer, or respondent and the researcher or some field interviewer paid to conduct the interviews. Personal interviews have relatively high response rates. In addition, they are conducive to the collection of substantial in-depth information and provide visual stimuli such as products and advertisements. Some researchers believe personal interviews are even more flexible than focus groups in that questioning adjustments can be made between interviews if necessary.[30] In addition, shy respondents can have their say, and sensitive topics can be more easily covered than in focus groups.

Disadvantages of personal interviews include the time and travel costs, concerns of personal safety of the interviewer, and inability to cover a wide geographical area. Although personal interview response rates average 70 percent, participation varies widely over types of neighborhoods. People living in metropolitan areas tend to be the least responsive.[31]

Thinking Critically

How do questions regarding the representativeness of online respondents affect the kinds of research problems for which online data is most appropriate? Does post hoc sample analysis in terms of demographic description alleviate concerns about sample representativeness?

MALL INTERCEPTS   The shortcomings of personal interviews have led to increased use of **mall intercept interviews.** In a mall intercept, consumers are approached and interviewed while on shopping trips. One-on-one interaction provides the chance to show visual cues, while overcoming many of the time, travel, and safety concerns associated with door-to-door personal interviewing. Research has shown mall intercept interviewing to provide findings and quality of responses similar to telephone and mail survey collection methods.[32]

Technological advances have enhanced the productivity of mall intercept research. MarketWare Corporation solicits participants for their "virtually real shopping" simulation: "strolling" through store aisles via computer screen. Research can be conducted on any number of variables simultaneously, such as price, package information, and shelf location.[33]

INTERNET SURVEYS   The Internet is fast becoming a popular means of conducting survey research, as are modified focus group discussions. With technology

Some Internet panels use incentives to encourage respondent participation. Questions still arise regarding the representativeness of Internet samples due, in part, to self-selection biases.

changing rapidly, the future of Internet-based research is both promising and hard to predict. The primary methods of online research are (1) online surveys in which respondents participate on-site following some solicitation or agreement to visit that site and (2) e-mail surveys.[34] However, and as shown in Exhibit 6–5, Internet-based survey research has its advantages and disadvantages like other methods of conducting surveys. On the positive side, research can be done faster, easier, and more cheaply than surveys conducted by mail, in the mall, or over the phone. The surveys are less intrusive and more convenient for respondents, and the potential exists to present visual cues, unlike traditional telephone interviews.

Concerns have been raised regarding privacy and validity. Regarding the latter, the primary concern for now is that Internet surveys provide largely self-selected, convenience samples. Sample frames are more difficult to define than for telephone and mail surveys. Relatedly, most Internet surveys are volunteer-based, as participants can select which studies interest them. Hence, care must be taken to ensure that Internet surveys are not just 1-800 or 1-900 polls.[35]

PROJECTIVE TECHNIQUES AND OBSERVATION Marketing researchers sometimes use projective techniques and observation for data collection. **Projective techniques,** such as word association or sentence completion, allow a researcher to elicit feelings that normally go unexpressed. They may be particularly useful in eliciting honest opinions about sensitive subjects. They can be used effectively in focus groups, mall intercepts, and personal interviews. In one application, consumers are asked to react to different forms of an advertisement or pictures without any brand or product information included in the mock-up. Reactions are reassessed when brand names are added.[36]

Observation research monitors customer behavior by a researcher or by video camera. Much can be learned by unobtrusively observing how customers use a firm's or its competitor's products. In some instances, observation may provide more accurate information than might survey data.[37] Observation research is also useful when traditional survey methods may not reveal the process by which goods and services are bought and used.

In another form of observation research, mystery shoppers evaluate the consistency and quality of services offered. Banks frequently use this practice to evaluate the service quality provided by their tellers and service personnel. Field observation requires patience, discipline, and enthusiasm on the part of the observer. However, in-store observations coupled with a few open-ended questions can yield insights into the role of price, the importance of ingredients, the effects of packages, and so on. In all cases, the researcher or field worker is there when the consumer or buyer behavior happens.[38]

Ethnographic research attempts to record how consumers actually use products, brands, and services in day-to-day activity. This form of direct observation, called *ethnography,* is based on techniques borrowed from sociology and anthropology. For example, a researcher may actually enter a consumer's home, observe consumption behavior, and record pantry and even garbage content, which can result in the collection of realistic data and richer descriptions of consumer behavior.[39]

One form of ethnographic research employs the use of pictures. Consumers are recruited to select pictures that convey their deeper feelings about a concept. This research, designed by Professor Jerry Zaltman of Harvard, is designed to help companies learn what consumers really want and to enhance the marketer's ability to develop campaigns that resonate with consumers on an emotional level. Selected individuals are asked to bring to the research site pictures that serve as metaphors for the deeper thoughts consumers have regarding a concept. This technique has been used successfully to assist Pittsburgh in promoting the arts and Kraft in designing foods for after work.[40]

The richness of explanation and unique perspectives possible from ethnographic research observation have helped some of the largest marketing firms. For example, Procter & Gamble placed cameras in 80 households in the U.K., Italy, Germany, and China to record their daily habits. Best Western paid 25 over-55 couples to tape themselves in cross-country trips. After observing how 64 households balanced complicated schedules, 3Com designed an extremely compact electronic home organizer.[41]

Data Collection Instruments

The collection of marketing research information typically involves construction of a data collection instrument called a *survey* or *questionnaire*. Once a survey has been drafted, the instrument should be pretested on a representative sample and revised accordingly. The final instrument should consist of unambiguous, concise, and unbiased questions that respondents will be able and willing to answer.

Data collection instruments vary in structure. The degree of structure is influenced both by the research design (exploratory versus descriptive) and the method of data collection (focus group versus mail survey). Questions may take an open-ended, multiple choice, or scaled response format. Examples of questions and response formats are shown in Exhibit 6–6.

Errors in question design include at least five types:

- *Double-barreled wording:* "How would you rate the handling ability and gas economy of your new Taurus?" very good, good, fair, poor, very poor.

- *Loaded wording:* "Given the growing rate of product recalls, how likely would you be to complain about problems with a new car purchase?" likely, unlikely.

- *Ambiguous wording:* "Have you purchased a home appliance within the last six months?" yes, no.

- *Inappropriate vocabulary:* "Do you feel the current discount rate is too high?" yes, no.

- *Missing alternatives:* "Which of the following includes your age?" 25 and under, 26 to 49, and over 50.[42]

Exhibit 6–6	*Types of questions used in survey research*

Scaled

Likert agree-disagree

I favor the increased use of nuclear power. (Circle one)

Strongly agree   Agree   Neither agree nor disagree   Disagree   Strongly disagree

Semantic differential

For me, tennis is . . .

Important _____ : _____ : _____ : _____ : _____ : Unimportant

Multichotomous (multiple choice)

Which of the following is the primary reason you selected our bank for your personal checking account?

_____ Location   _____ Service

_____ Interest rates _____ Other _____ (Please specify)

_____ Reputation_____

Categorical

Which of the following categories includes your total income for 199x? (Please check)

_____ $30,000 and under

_____ $30,001–$35,000

_____ $35,001–$50,000

_____ $50,001–$65,000

_____ Over $65,000

Open-ended

What suggestions can you make to improve our service? _____

"Margaret, I want to know the real you...subject to a sampling error plus or minus three percentage points, of course."

Sampling and nonsampling errors may affect marketing research results. When even carefully selected probability samples do not exactly mirror the population, sampling error occurs. Nonsampling errors are due to such factors as interviewer bias, nonresponse bias, and improperly worded questions.

The emphasis on brand equity, marketing return on investment (ROI), and the long-term value of customers has increased both the importance of marketing research and the range/complexity of the types of variables and questions that market research now often addresses. A complete listing of all types of required measures is beyond the scope of this text and course. However, an ongoing program of research to assess marketing effort ROI would include measures of brand awareness, brand image, and customer satisfaction from current and potential customers. Measures related to transactions would include revenues per sale, transaction profitability, and costs per sale. Presale data would include initial response rates and leads generated from marketing communication programs. Ongoing measures would include customer retention rates and over time purchase data.[43]

Sample Design

The decisions and sequences involved in sampling are presented in Exhibit 6–7. The particular purpose of any research greatly influences the nature of the sampling process; of course, the population or group to be studied is determined by the issue of interest. If a wholesale bakery experiences declining product sales at the store level, it would want to sample individual purchasers and users of bakery products. Researchers might decide to sample household heads who regularly purchase bakery products.

Sampling saves money and time in that a smaller subgroup (or sample) is assumed to represent a larger population. Inferences from sample responses are then made to the population. The quality of these projections depends largely on how representative the sample is.

In B2B research situations, it will often be necessary to survey multiple informants within the organization. For example, senior executives are appropriate for strategic vision issues, while boundary personnel who interact directly with the firm's customers may answer questions tied to daily operations. In one study for a health care product marketer, researchers surveyed both hospital physicians and administrators. Compiling appropriate sample lists of customers is surprisingly difficult in doing marketing research for business-to-business firms.[44]

PROBABILITY SAMPLING In **probability sampling**, each person or unit in the population has a known, nonzero chance of being selected by some objective procedure. Probability samples are desirable, because the use of an objective, unbiased selection technique enhances the representativeness of the sample. There are several probability sampling approaches. In *simple random sampling*, each unit has an

Exhibit 6–7 *Sampling decisions and data collection issues*

Basic research question → Probability versus nonprobability sampling → Specification of sampling frame → Sample size → Data collection: Sampling, follow-up & verification

Time, cost & precision constraints

equal chance of being selected, such as the use of a random number table to select phone numbers. *Stratified sampling* occurs when the population is divided into mutually exclusive groups, such as consumers with different income levels, and random samples are taken from each group. *Cluster sampling* consists of organizing units into smaller groups or clusters, such as similar neighborhoods or census tracks, then selecting clusters randomly and including each house in the selected clusters in the sample.

NONPROBABILITY SAMPLING   In **nonprobability sampling,** the selection of a sample is based on the judgment of the researcher or field worker. When funds or time are limited, or when only preliminary insight into a problem is needed, nonprobability samples may be appropriate. Nonprobability samples include convenience samples: for instance, the use of student samples in academic research; quota samples, in which a sample is selected to conform to some known distribution such as half female or 30 percent minority; and judgment samples, in which sample members are selected because researchers believe they bring some unique perspective to the research problem.

SAMPLING FRAME   Once the type of sample and the target population have been determined, the **sampling frame** is specified. The sampling frame is the outline or working description of the population used in sample selection. A frequently used sampling frame is the telephone book. For business-to-business marketing research, customer or firm lists might serve as the sampling frame. Today, firms often purchase sample lists from companies that specialize in providing them. Care must be exercised in selecting a sampling frame (say, a telephone listing) to minimize the exclusion of relevant population members. Telephone directories do not include unlisted households and households without telephones.

SAMPLE SIZE   The desired **sample size** is based on a combination of factors: the anticipated response rate, the variability in the data, cost and time considerations, and the desired level of precision.

In practice, a sample size is often some even number (say, 500 or 1,000) large enough to give the user confidence in the results, on which he or she will base decisions. As a rule, researchers may benefit by taking smaller samples selected by more rigorous but possibly more expensive probability sampling procedures. That is, research users will be more confident in the representativeness of samples selected by some unbiased selection process.

RESPONSE RATES   A disturbing trend in the past quarter century has been the slow but steady decline in sample cooperation. A recent study by the Council for Marketing and Opinion Research (CMOR) estimated that 45 percent of consumers refused to participate in a survey in 2001. This estimate does not include the use of caller IDs and answering machines to avoid telephone surveys—factors that would have made the annual refusal rate estimate much higher.[45] The causes of this trend include an increase in percentage of working women, the increase of telemarketing, and the growth of screening devices. High-quality samples will be possible only with greater cost and effort. The changes required to generate higher response rates will include increased compensation to respondents and interviewers, more contact attempts to locate respondents, and greater use of mixed modes of survey administration, including e-mail and Internet research.

The primary concern with nonresponse is the realization that nonrespondents differ from respondents in terms of their opinions about the issues being studied and in terms of their demographic composition. Hence, it is necessary to contact a subset of nonrespondents so that findings can be adjusted. In addition, the computation of response rates is required and should be included in marketing research reports and summaries. For example, the response for a telephone survey can be computed as follows:

$$\text{Response rate} = \frac{\text{Number of complete from those contacted}}{\text{Number of complete + number of refusals + number of terminations}}[46]$$

Fieldwork

Fieldwork is the process of contacting respondents, conducting interviews, and completing surveys. In the case of mail surveys, field workers must prepare mailing labels, develop introductory and follow-up letters, and carry out the mailings. Telephone surveys, personal interviews, and mall intercepts require the recruitment and training of interviewers to collect the data from the designated sample.

In many instances, the data collection process, and perhaps data analysis, will be subcontracted out to a supplier or field service firm. That is, the actual interviews may be performed by a company that specializes in collecting marketing research data. Under these circumstances, the subcontractor supervises the data collection process and verifies the quality of the information collected. This should include verifying that the interviews were indeed conducted and that the responses to certain key questions are valid or correct.

Terry Vavra underscores the pitfalls of failing to monitor data collection fieldwork: "Although many research projects are well conceived and designed, all too frequently they fail where 'the rubber meets the road'—the fieldwork component. Much fieldwork is subcontracted to specialty fieldwork companies (e.g., telephone interviewing firms). As researchers look for cost efficiencies in conducting their fieldwork, they often rely on poorly trained and inadequately supervised field staffs. As you become involved in marketing research, monitor very carefully how your data are collected from respondents. Fieldwork is often the weakest link in the research process chain."

Analysis and Interpretation

There are a variety of techniques for analyzing marketing research data, ranging in complexity from straightforward frequency distributions, means, and percentages to complex multivariate statistical tests. Statistical analyses typically look at group differences (males versus females, users versus nonusers) or the strength of association between marketing variables (advertising and sales, prices and sales). The most frequently used statistical tests include those of mean differences (*t*-tests, analyses of variance) and correlation tests (chi-square cross-classification tests, Pearson correlations, regression).

The types of analysis to be performed on the data should be anticipated at the design stage so the appropriate data collection forms are developed. As a rule, managers prefer simple understandable presentations of findings. Reports should focus on the original problem and objectives of the research.

Changing Technology

Technology has both positive and negative effects on the conduct of marketing research. As mentioned previously, scanner data and the ability to collect single-source data from households are dramatically affecting the research industry. On the positive side, the availability of computer-assisted telephone (CAT) interviewing has enhanced sampling, data entry, and data processing. Interviewers can read questions from a computer screen and record answers directly on the computer. This process results in instantaneously updating data. Moreover, WATS services have lowered the cost of telephone surveying. Yet technology has some negative effects on the use of telephone interviews too. Answering machines and voice-mail responses inhibit both consumer and business-to-business telephone research.[47] Call waiting also hampers the conduct of telephone surveys and is another factor contributing to the decline of telephone response rates. Sadly, the large increase in telephone sales calls and the difficulty of distinguishing between sales calls and survey research are the primary determinants of declining response rates.[48]

Technology is affecting other aspects of marketing research as well. For example, videoconferencing capabilities enable clients from a distance to monitor focus groups and provide the opportunity to involve more participants in observation.

The savings from videoconferencing result because clients do not have to travel to locations to view focus group sessions. Breakthroughs in technology have also increased the potential for using faxes in survey research. Early research on survey effects suggests that fax surveys could make the administration of short questionnaires less expensive and faster than mail surveys. Likewise, e-mail offers the potential for increasing survey efficiency. Last, freestanding touch-screen computers at retail kiosks are now programmed to administer complicated surveys, show full-color images and video clips, and play stereo clips. With little need for instruction, in-store patrons freely use the interactive kiosks without reservation.[49]

International Considerations

Rote application of U.S. research practices to other countries is not likely to be appropriate. Firms operating globally must understand that cultural and economic differences between countries add a layer of complexity. One researcher identified eight common errors in conducting an international research project:[50]

1. *Selecting a domestic research company to do international research*—It is best to choose a company with experience in conducting global research.

2. *Rigidly standardizing methods across countries*—In certain countries, postal problems present unique difficulties; and in many countries, communications systems are inadequate for telephone interviews.

3. *Interviewing in English around the world*—Depth of responses is greatest when the local language is used.

4. *Implementing inappropriate sampling techniques*—Probability sampling designs are difficult to implement in many foreign countries.

5. *Failing to communicate effectively with local research companies*—Everything should be put in writing and all deadlines should be specified exactly to avoid delays.

6. *Lack of consideration given to language*—For some research studies, measurement instruments should be "back translated" to ensure equivalence in meaning.

Conducting research across cultures can be difficult. International marketing researchers encounter such added problems as language differences, product use differences, and technological differences that limit data collection alternatives. Zespri used marketing research to investigate cultural differences prior to positioning their new flavoring product in Singapore.

7. *Misinterpreting data across countries*—Cultural and ethnic differences can affect response, the meaning of concepts, and even responses to measurement scales. For example, Asians may use the midpoints of scales, whereas the English tend to understate responses.

8. *Failing to understand preferences of foreign researchers regarding the effective conduct of qualitative research*—For example, Europeans expect focus group moderators to have training in psychology; Asian mixed-sex group discussions do not yield useful information.

Conducting research using Japanese participants in particular requires some adjustment of American and European methods. Moderators or interviewers must repeatedly reassure Japanese respondents that negative statements are acceptable. Open-ended questions, lacking some illustration, will not elicit adequate responses from Japanese consumers. Nonverbal responses, such as body movement and facial expressions, often yield more information than will verbal answers.[51] Responses to scale items can vary across cultures as well. Three respondents, all equally likely to buy a product from a market test, may give different responses based upon their interpretation of rating scales. Interpreting these meanings in global research can become even more difficult. For example, in a study of Brazilian and Japanese consumers, a "5" from a seven-point scale corresponded to 75 percent probability of purchase. For the Japanese data, a score of about 3.8 corresponded to a 75 percent probability of purchase.[52]

Marketing research in the 15 nations comprising the European Union will remain challenging. While the Euro currency will enhance the market's buying power and make price differences across countries transparent, unique differences in terms of country economic cycles, enduring cultural differences, and variations in marketing retail and distribution channels will affect the researcher's ability to collect information throughout Europe. In addition, two anticipated demographic shifts in the EU will affect marketing practice and the conduct of marketing research. As in the United States, two demographic segments will dominate—Generation Y and the large segment of older but more active consumers.[53]

Evaluating Marketing Research

A research proposal is often developed prior to conducting a research study. These proposals outline the purpose of the research, the activities of the project, the costs and time constraints, and the likely implications or outcomes. The most important questions to ask in evaluating a research design prior to conducting research are presented in Exhibit 6–8.

Once a research project has been completed, the validity and reliability of the procedures used should be evaluated. **Validity** of questions on a survey refers to the extent to which the measures truly assess the concepts being studied. Consider the item, "I like BMW sedans." Results showing significant agreement with this statement would not be a valid measure of consumer opinions about purchase attitudes; rather, they would indicate an overall liking for the brand. **Reliability** reflects the consistency of responses or the extent to which measurement results are reproducible. A related validity issue, and important in determining the value of

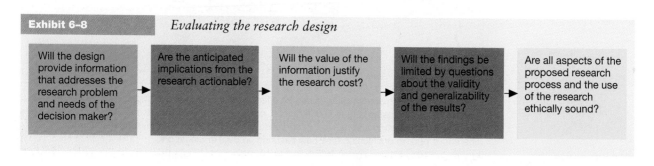

Exhibit 6–8   *Evaluating the research design*

| Will the design provide information that addresses the research problem and needs of the decision maker? | Are the anticipated implications from the research actionable? | Will the value of the information justify the research cost? | Will the findings be limited by questions about the validity and generalizability of the results? | Are all aspects of the proposed research process and the use of the research ethically sound? |

many research projects, is the concept of external validity. *External validity* reflects the extent to which the results from a research study can be generalized to other contexts, situations, and populations.[54]

Ethical Issues in Marketing Research

Research ethics are increasingly debated. The American Marketing Association (AMA), the Advertising Research Foundation (ARF), and the Council of American Survey Research Organizations (CASRO) are collaborating on a code of ethics. Self-regulation among firms conducting research is increasingly being called for in efforts to improve the practice of marketing research. If these efforts are not successful, respondent cooperation will continue to erode.[55]

Questionable tactics in marketing research that are frequently criticized include excessive interviewing, lack of consideration and abuse of respondents, and delivering sales pitches under the guise of marketing research.[56] The latter is particularly important for the research industry, as two-thirds of Americans consider survey research and telemarketing to be the same thing.[57] Legislation that now addresses only unsolicited commercial telephone calls could easily be extended to cover survey research.[58] Legislation already exists in most European Community nations that restricts the research industry by protecting privacy rights of consumers.

Ethical considerations are involved in researchers' relationships with all parties in the process, including respondents, the general public, and clients. First, marketers have the responsibility to treat respondents fairly by being candid about the nature and purposes of the research, by not using research as a sales ploy, and by not violating the confidentiality of respondents' answers. Researchers' obligations to the general public include being unintrusive, being considerate, and protecting the rights of privacy.

At the same time, researchers have a responsibility to gather accurate and reliable data for their clients.[59] Researchers should not manipulate findings to present a more favorable image of themselves or the firm. The significance of results should not be overstated. Questionable research practices, such as incomplete reporting of results, misleading reporting, and nonobjective research, can bring the integrity of the entire research process into question. For example, a cigarette ad once claimed that "an amazing 60 percent" of a sample said Triumph cigarettes tasted "as good as or better than Merit." Although this statement was technically correct, the results also indicated that 64 percent said Merit tasted as good as or better than Triumph, which was not reported to the public.[60]

Another issue is the subsequent use of data and the confidentiality of information collected for a client by a firm specializing in marketing research. Data collected for one client should not be made available to other clients.

Advertising on television programs shown in public schools has been criticized as being exploitative of children and as being excessively commercial. Similar issues are arising regarding the conduct of marketing research. Increasingly, schools are partnering with research firms in programs that allow those firms access to students for research purposes in exchange for funds to support school needs. As an example, Noggin cable television in Montclair, New York, recently paid $7,100 to support the purchase of school word processors for the right to use students once per week during school time in 30-minute focus groups. The ethics of these and other programs are certainly an issue.[61]

Marketing Decision Support Systems (MDSS)

Glaxo Inc., a pharmaceutical maker in Research Triangle Park, North Carolina, spends about $2 million a year on its sales and marketing decision support system for hardware, software, user training, and personnel. Donald Rao, manager of market analysis and decision support at Glaxo, claimed a return on investment of 1,000 percent since the system's development in 1987. The system provides detailed data on physician locations within sales territories, which allows managers to fine-tune marketing plans and product-sample allocations. In addition, it allows substantial savings in managerial time.[62]

Like Glaxo, many firms view all marketing data and information as part of a larger entity called a **marketing decision support system (MDSS)**. All activities and computerized elements used to process information relevant to marketing decisions are components. These systems are now commonplace in many *Fortune 500* business-to-business giants in industries such as airlines, banking, insurance, and pharmaceuticals.

A schematic overview of an MDSS is shown in Exhibit 6–9. Such systems represent a comprehensive perspective allowing a combination of different sources of information from different departments. MDSS are useful for both manufacturing and service companies.

Marketing decision support systems are generally designed to:[63]

- Support but not supplant management decision making.

- Apply to semistructured decisions of middle and upper management, such as pricing, promotion, and location decisions.

- Provide interaction between and among people and systems.

- Center on a segment of related decisions (the allocation of marketing effort and resources).

- Be user-friendly.

An MDSS is designed to enhance managerial decision making and firm performance by providing relevant and timely internal and external information. Input comes from many sources: the economic environment, social trends and changing consumer tastes, and the legal environment. Data from consumers, customers, and competitors are relevant. Prior experiences and decisions are also fed back into the system. Even permanent links with customers are now included in some MDSS systems. For example, a system linking Levi Strauss and Milliken, a textile manufacturer, significantly reduced costs for both companies and enabled Levi Strauss to respond to fashion changes and bring new products to market more quickly.[64]

External marketing research data may come from syndicated sources or various nonproprietary sources of secondary data. Syndicated market databases are useful for comparison with internal sales data to gauge market penetration. Internal data normally come from the marketing research department's own input, accounting records, and salesforce reports.

Computer technology now enables a variety of outputs from an MDSS. Output might include forecasts of sales, comparison of sales relative to forecasts, analysis of competitor performance, estimation of market potentials, evaluation of advertising effectiveness, and monitoring of consumer expectations and satisfaction. Some researchers predict that in the coming decades, a growing proportion of marketing decisions will be automated by ever-more-powerful combinations of data, models, and computers. As such, some aspects of marketing decision support sys-

Exhibit 6–9 *Marketing decision support system*

Marketplace
Social environment
Economic environment
Political/legal environment
Technological environment
Competitive environment
Institutional environment

Decision support system
Internal
Secondary data
Marketing research department
Marketing intelligence
External
Syndicated data
Nonproprietary secondary data
External marketing research

Managerial decision making and firm behavior

tems will involve marketing decision *automation.* These changes will occur as firms increase their marketing activities into smaller units (i.e., individual stores, customers, and transactions). The resulting amount of data and numerous decision-making points can be more effectively handled by automated systems.[65]

Database Marketing

A significant technological innovation is **database marketing,** the collection and use of individual customer-specific information to make marketing more efficient. The term *database* refers to customer/prospect information stored in a computer with software to process the information. Computer technology provides the ability to pull apart and recombine information in ways previously impossible. Knowing which customers are predisposed to which products allows a firm to tailor marketing efforts to individual customers.

Database marketing can be instrumental in the success of companies' direct-marketing efforts. In many cases, customers respond to such efforts by making orders and inquiries via toll-free phone numbers. Companies use marketing research principles in developing customer databases and analyzing the information obtained from customer responses to direct-marketing efforts, such as tele-marketing and direct mail. This information can enable a company to tailor individual messages at the customer level. Database marketing extends the traditional customer address list by including purchase records, demographics, psychographics, and information on media use. Note, however, that consumer advocates and government officials are increasingly raising ethical concerns about individual privacy as a result of the use of such data.

One extension of the use of information at the customer level has been the evolution of **customer relationship management,** commonly referred to by marketers as **CRM.** The shift in emphasis to customer relationship management from a transaction orientation has been one of the significant developments in the practice of marketing. Linking research and CRM systems can be very beneficial to the marketer. To merge CRM and marketing research, organizations must create unified systems that hold information on customer characteristics and historical transaction data, as well as data that reflects consumer preference ratings, perceptions, and behavioral intentions. Use of this detailed customer information enables marketers to better understand the customer and to target effectively better defined segments and even individual customers with tailored offers.[66]

One important aspect of data-based marketing is the ability to evaluate return on investment (ROI) of marketing expenditures. By merging descriptive attitudinal data with behavioral purchase records, direct marketers can both target mailings and craft messages to their most profitable customers. The behavioral data can be used to estimate incremental purchases from a targeted campaign with certain estimated costs. Moreover, such information, as expected return on investment, can be used to argue for additional resources and support for marketing effort within the firm.[67]

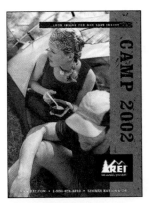

Database marketing involves the collection and use of individual customer-specific information. Catalog companies now analyze individual customer purchase patterns to tailor their direct marketing efforts.

With better targeting of prospects for products and promotions, data-based marketing clearly contributes to increased efficiency. When practiced properly, data-based marketing yields double-digit response rates, compared with 2 to 4 percent for "junk mail." For example, Hilton Hotels offers targeted promotions to senior citizens in its Senior Honors program, prompting almost half of the members to take previously unplanned trips that included stays at the Hilton.[68]

Last, the development and use of databases comprising information on individual customers raises ethical concerns regarding privacy. First, marketers must thus continue to work at self-regulation regarding privacy protection. Second, it should be noted that firms that build their databases from within, as opposed to purchasing lists from other sources, are able to maintain the privacy of their customers. Third, customer permission and notification should be regularly sought. And fourth, firms should take into consideration that customers generally want firms to reduce the volume of catalog and advertising mail while simultaneously increasing the relevance of that information.[69]

Summary

1. **Understand the purpose and functions of marketing research.** The function of marketing research is to generate information that assists the firm's managers in making decisions. Marketing research helps managers respond to the ever-changing environment in which businesses operate. It is useful in problem solving, planning for the future, and controlling or monitoring ongoing performance. Marketing research links the marketer, the customer, and the public through information used to identify and define marketing opportunities; generate, refine, and evaluate marketing actions; monitor marketing performance; and improve understanding of marketing as a process.

2. **Be familiar with the stages of the marketing research process.** There are six stages of the marketing research process, through which primary data are generated to address a specific marketing problem or issue. In the first stage, problem definition, both the researcher and the user develop a clear conception of the problem that the research is intended to address.

   The second stage is specification of the appropriate research design, which is then used in the third stage, determination of the types of data to be collected and the methods of collection.

   In the fourth stage, researchers develop a data collection form, often a survey or questionnaire. In the fifth stage researchers design the sample, specifying the fieldwork required to collect the data. Finally, the data collected are analyzed, summarized, and presented to the users or firm management.

3. **Discuss different types of research designs, data collection methods, and sources of secondary and primary marketing research data.** Exploratory research designs are used to obtain general familiarity with a topic or problem. Focus groups, literature reviews, case analyses, interviews with knowledgeable individuals, and convenience sampling are examples of exploratory research.

   Descriptive designs are typically guided by some specific research question or hypothesis. Cross-sectional designs involve surveys administered at a given time. Longitudinal designs examine research questions over time through repeated measures of a common sample. Causal designs involve experiments, in which researchers manipulate independent variables of interest, such as price or advertising.

   Marketing data can be primary or secondary. Secondary data may be either internal, coming from within the firm, or external. External secondary data may be either nonproprietary (noncommercial) or proprietary.

4. **Understand many of the major issues involved with survey design and sampling.** Each survey method has its advantages and disadvantages. The different survey methods include telephone interviews, mail questionnaires, personal interviews, and mall intercepts. Researchers must carefully construct items or questions in a survey to ensure that the data collected are reliable (yield consistent responses) and valid (reflect the concepts being studied).

   Researchers can use probability or nonprobability samples, depending on the objectives, characteristics, and budget of the research. Probability samples are selected by some objective, unbiased process. Simple random samples are the most typical example.

   To assemble a nonprobability sample, the judgment of the researcher enters into the selection. Examples of nonprobability samples are convenience samples and quota samples. The researcher must decide on the population to be sampled, the sample size, and the sampling frame.

5. **Appreciate the role of marketing research within decision support systems.** Within the firm, the marketing decision support system (MDSS) consists of all activities and the hardware and software regularly used to process and provide marketing information relevant to marketing decisions. The firm may also employ outside agencies to provide marketing input.

Understanding Marketing Terms and Concepts

Thinking About Marketing

1. How might a clothes manufacturer employ focus groups in their search for what is "cool"? Would observation be a better approach?

2. What is the purpose of marketing research? What are the primary stages of the marketing research process?

3. Explain differences among exploratory, descriptive, and causal designs, and give examples of each.

4. Differentiate these pairs of concepts:
   a. Cross-sectional versus longitudinal designs.
   b. Secondary versus primary data.
   c. Field market tests versus simulated market tests.

5. Describe the primary advantages and disadvantages of mail surveys, telephone interviews, personal interviews, and mall intercepts. What advantages are offered by virtual shopping technology over simulated test markets?

6. What are the different types of probability and nonprobability samples? Give examples of each.

7. What is the difference between projective techniques and observation research? What is ethnographic observation?

8. What factors determine sample size? What is involved in fieldwork?

9. What is an MDSS? Describe its primary advantages.

10. Identify three ethical issues in marketing research. Cite some concerns faced by firms conducting marketing research.

Applying Marketing Skills

1. Develop a sampling plan to conduct a telephone survey of residents in the county where your university is located. Assume you want to investigate opinions about the construction of a nuclear power plant in a nearby county. Who should be interviewed? How will the sample be drawn?

2. A manufacturer of roller blades is interested in assessing the satisfaction of its retailer customers. What are the advantages and disadvantages of the alternative data collection methods in gathering customer satisfaction data for the firm?

3. Suppose you were considering selling a new personal data assistant (PDA) that was designed specifically for university students. To ensure that you are successful, it would be necessary to determine the student makeup of the university, whether the students would be willing to buy the PDA, and how best to inform the students about the product. What types of marketing information would you need to consult? Where would you obtain this information? What information would be available only through primary data collection, and how would you collect it?

4. Research Incorporated, a regional marketing research firm that does tailored primary research projects in California, has been contacted by ABC Company for what appears to be a very profitable research project involving the demand for catalog shopping services. Research Incorporated recently completed a similar project for XYZ Company, a competitor of ABC. Both ABC and XYZ are large retail discount chains with over 50 stores in the Southwest. Should Research Incorporated accept the project? Should the information obtained for XYZ be given or sold to ABC?

Using the www in Marketing

Activity One   This chapter is organized around a description of the marketing research process. Consider this explanation as you access the IMS Health site.

1. The IMS Health firm is one of the world's largest research firms. What can be learned about information on the Internet as a source of secondary data?

2. What services does IMS offer regarding data for its prescription drugs?

Activity Two   Consider the Web site NFO Inc., the company whose home page opened the chapter.

1. What services and products are offered by the company?

2. Do their information services represent primary or secondary data?

3. What kinds of companies could make the best use of the information this company provides?

Making Marketing Decisions

Case 6-1 *Bayer: Aleve and the Road to Recovery*

Bayer inherited the poorly performing Aleve pain reliever from Procter & Gamble in 1996. The brand had never achieved more than a 6 percent market share. In 1997, the Bayer team hired CLT Research Associates to conduct 800 in-home interviews, a random sample of men and women ages 18 to 75, who had used a nonprescription pain reliever in the last year. CLT discovered that 24 percent of the sample were "pain busters"—consumers who are heavy users of pain relievers. Additional research was conducted to identify the various statements about Aleve that could be used to convince this segment to buy Aleve. Bayer managers also analyzed data from Medioscope—a syndicated source for OTC drug data—Nielsen Panel data, and Simmons, as well as information from focus groups.

Subsequently, BBDO designed Aleve's "Dramatic Difference" campaign that was successful in substantially raising sales and brand aided and unaided recall. New campaigns emphasize the need for only two dosages all day long. Empowering consumers to rid themselves of pain seems to have been just the medicine Aleve needed.

Questions

1. How do different types of research complement each other in diagnosing brand problems?

2. What types of research are needed to monitor Aleve's performance in today's marketplace? What role does repeat purchase play in the brand's success?

3. Describe the performance of Aleve relative to competing products for 2003.

Case 6-2 *Avon Products: Questions Abroad*

 Avon is currently the largest direct seller of cosmetics, with annual sales of approximately $6.0 billion. Avon sells to women in 143 countries through 3.5 million independent sales representatives. About two-thirds of its business is outside the United States. Sales have been weak in the United States, and they've been volatile in international markets due to currency fluctuations and other problems.

Sales and profit results around the world are mixed. Profits were up in Brazil, Mexico, Venezuela, and Central America, but down in Chile and Argentina. In the Pacific region, sales and profits were up strongly. There was substantial improvement in China, where Avon was forced to cease operations temporarily last year due to China's ban on direct selling. Sales in Europe were down overall, but up when currency exchanges were excluded. Profits were up everywhere in Europe, except in Russia, which is still plagued by economic turmoil. Avon recently opened for business in Singapore, South Korea, Morocco.

When Andrea Jung was recently named CEO, Avon became the second-largest U.S. company to be run by a woman. Jung started as an Avon consultant in 1993 and became president and COO in 1998. Her vision is to "make Avon the most relevant beauty brand for women in the world."

Further expansion into global markets would require careful planning and decision making. While the demand for quality products in previously untapped markets was evident and there was a ready available source of willing salespersons, uncertainties about markets and buyer behavior in countries such as China, Vietnam, Romania, and Ukraine suggested the need for marketing research.

Avon promotes predominantly using female salespersons in their widely known direct personal-selling strategy. In addition, orders can be made from catalogs, e-mail, and faxes. Support for Avon's image is enhanced worldwide through the company's cause-related marketing (CRM) program. Avon focuses on different issues in different countries: breast cancer in the United States, Canada, Mexico, and Spain; care for senior citizens in Japan; AIDS in Thailand; and support for mothers in Germany. These programs demonstrate the firm's social responsibility via charitable contributions by Avon from revenues produced through sale of its products.

Distribution changes are affecting the very core of this conservative company. First, Avon announced that it is negotiating to sell a new line of cosmetics through JC Penny and Sears. The effects of this new distribution channel on the direct North American sales force is unknown. Moreover, the effects of Internet sales on the direct sales force worldwide are also as yet undetermined. As part of this new alternative, Avon targets teens, who are more attached to the Internet.

Questions

1. What information could be collected to assist Avon in deciding which countries to emphasize?

2. How can marketing research be used to investigate cultural differences affecting the use of cosmetics? What secondary data sources might be helpful in estimating market potentials for East European countries?

3. What kind of research could be used effectively to monitor the morale and satisfaction of Avon's global direct sales force?

4. Can marketing research determine the likely effects of crude distribution and retail systems in lesser developed markets? If so, how?

Chapter Seven

7

Market Segmentation and Targeting

After studying this chapter, you should be able to:

1 Define and explain market segmentation, target markets, and product differentiation and positioning.

2 Understand the criteria used for evaluating the likely success of a segmentation strategy.

3 Know the role of market segmentation in the development of marketing strategies and programs.

4 Describe the issues involved in product and brand positioning.

5 Understand the alternative bases for segmenting consumer and business-to-business markets.

6 Evaluate alternative approaches for pursuing segmentation strategies.

www.sric-bi.com

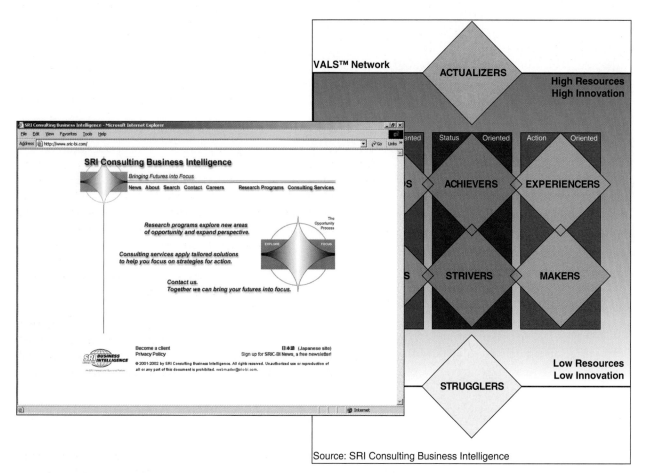

SRI Consulting Business Intelligence offers VALS (Values and Lifestyles) as a segmentation program to companies. VALS uses demographic characteristics such as age, income, education, and gender, in combination with psychological attitudes about one's self to provide a richer description of U.S. consumers. VALS groups American consumers into one of eight segments based on how they respond to the VALS questionnaire. The main dimensions of the typology are self-orientation and resources. This questionnaire is integrated in large national surveys of products, services, and media to discover the preferences by VALS type. Clients also use the VALS questionnaire in their custom research. The eight segments of adult consumers have different attitudes and exhibit distinctive decision-making patterns.

As described on their Web site, typical applications of VALS include new-product development, identification of target-market advertising design, media planning, and public relations. For example, a beverage company used VALS to identify its target market and to create an image and communications strategy for appealing to that market. One analysis examined geographic differences. The results revealed that Southeasterners score highest in the two most physically active groups: the young, rebellious excitement-seeking "experiencers" and the "makers," who are people with construction skills and who value self-sufficiency. According to SRI researchers, this suggests that marketers in the Southeast must consider both "How does the product make me feel?" as well as "What does the product do for me?"

VALS can also be used as a tool for understanding new-product acceptance and innovation. For example, "experiencers" are quick to pick up on new products that provide an outlet for social interaction, fun, and excitement. "Believers," on the other hand, tend to stick with products and brands that they know, so it is not usually wise to target this group with a brand-new product. Also, SRI now offers consulting to clients who want to advertise on the Internet by helping them understand the attitudes and preferences of online service and Internet users. The VALS Web site allows visitors to take the VALS questionnaire and to see which consumer type they are most like. Interestingly, the results indicate that the largest segment of Web users falls into the upscale, well-educated "actualizer" VALS type.

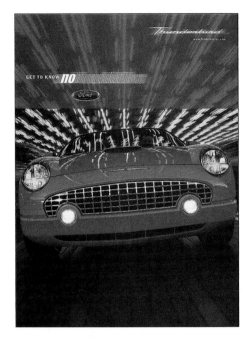

Market segmentation involves the identification of market segments that will respond differently to varying marketing mix combinations. Ford offers products and communications designed to appeal to car-buyer segments formed on the basis of desired end benefits.

The VALS typology offers firms that employ the approach a unique understanding of differences in consumer segments identified using a combination of survey responses to questions about individual lifestyles, values, and demographics. A firm's researchers can use the variables to group consumers into eight market segments and then examine those segments for differences in product preferences and desires. Market segmentation allows a company to treat distinct consumer groups differently, thus enhancing its competitive advantage. That is, the company can effectively vary product offerings and marketing communications to capitalize on segment differences.

Market segmentation is among the most popular and important topics in the entire field of marketing. Market segmentation is consistent with the marketing concept and enhances a firm's ability to understand its core customers or who its core customers will be in the future. As such, segmentation helps the marketer identify important consumption patterns. Furthermore, market segmentation strategies are necessary both for consumer goods and services marketers and for firms operating in business-to-business markets. Segmentation starts with the notion that a company is not able to be all things to all customers. Customers must be treated differently based upon the firm's knowing what a customer wants and its ability to profitability deliver those needs.[1]

In this chapter, we explore the concept of market segmentation and how firms develop their market segmentation strategies. We define target markets and product differentiation and positioning, and we discuss the stages involved in developing a segmentation strategy.

Market Segmentation, Target Markets, and Product Differentiation

Mass markets and widespread brand loyalty, once taken for granted in business, have given way today to market segments of widely varying tastes, needs, and sensitivity to competing products. The emergence of these fragmented markets, new economic demands, changing technology, and intense international competition have altered the ways firms must compete.

In this section, we distinguish between market segmentation, target markets, and product differentiation. Throughout the section and the chapter, issues related to market segments, target segments, and targeting are discussed. Although similar terms, these reflect different concepts. Briefly, market segments are groups of prospective customers who share similar needs and wants. No firm can operate in every market and satisfy every need, nor can firms operate effectively within very broadly defined markets. Thus, target segments represent those groups the firm selects to focus on with separate marketing mixes. Targeting then involves selecting which market segments to emphasize and designing efforts to appeal to the unique differences and motivations that define those selected segments.

Market Segmentation

Firms often pursue a market segmentation approach to meet today's market realities. As discussed in Chapter 1, a market is a group of consumers or organizations with which a firm desires to create marketing exchanges. **Market segmentation** divides a market into subsets of prospective customers who behave in the same way, have similar wants, or have similar characteristics that relate to purchase behavior. The overall market for a product consists of segments of customers who vary in their responses to different marketing mix offerings. Market segmentation attempts to explain differences among groups of consumers who share similar characteristics and to turn these differences into an advantage.[2] As such, marketing effectiveness is enhanced by an understanding of who the firm's best customers are, what's on their minds, where and how they can be reached, and what they are buying.

A segmentation strategy can be pursued through variations in some or all aspects (product, marketing communications, price, distribution) of the marketing mix elements. For example, many widely purchased products such as soft drinks, computers, and clothing involve variation in both product and marketing communications to reach market segments and increase sales. In other instances, a single product may be marketed to different segments using different marketing communication campaigns. For example, a pharmaceutical manufacturer may promote the same new drug product to physicians, pharmacists, and hospitals using a different communication program for each. Sheraton's loyalty programs, costing up to $50 million annually, are based upon the data-based segmentation scheme comprising business travelers and leisure guests.[3]

A number of factors are making understanding market segmentation more important:

- Slower rates of market growth, coupled with increased foreign competition, have fostered more competition, increasing the need to identify target markets with unique needs.

- Social and economic forces, including expanding media, increased educational levels, and general world awareness, have produced customers with more varied and sophisticated needs, tastes, and lifestyles.

- Technological advances make it possible for marketers to devise marketing programs that focus efficiently on precisely defined segments of the market.[4]

- Marketers now find that minority buyers do not necessarily adopt the social and economic habits of the mainstream. As one market researcher observed, America is no longer a melting pot, but more of a mosaic or "salad bowl."[5]

- Roughly 4 in 10 residents in the United States identify with some segment or niche group that does not reflect the white, heterosexual consumer that historically defined the marketing mainstream.[6]

Market segmentation is appropriate not just for firms marketing tangible products; nonprofit and service organizations also find it useful. For example, realizing that it had many different types of donors and volunteers, the Arthritis Foundation looked for an effective way to reach the right person, at the right time, with the proper request amount, and with the right message. To address the diversity in possible donors and volunteers, the foundation identified 12 categories of individual households defined by location, housing type, and income. The foundation found the segment labeled "urban gentry" (upper-income city dwellers) four times more likely than any other group to contribute both money and time.[7]

International marketing may be based on the cultivation of **intermarket segments,** which are well-defined, similar clusters of customers across national boundaries. This view of segmentation allows firms to develop marketing programs and offerings for each identified segment on a global basis.[8] Reliance on a single standardized global strategy can cause a firm to miss important target markets or to position products inappropriately. Similarly, customizing marketing strategy only to individual countries may result in a firm's losing either potential economies of scale or opportunities for exploiting product ideas on a wider scale.[9]

Some consumer-product businesses, such as McDonald's, Coca-Cola, and Colgate-Palmolive, use globally standardized products and marketing themes for some of their products. For most consumer products and brands, however, international marketing benefits from segmentation principles. In these instances, customized strategies may be developed for different countries or groups of countries. One recent study of soap and toothpaste preferences, for example, revealed four segments across consumers in the United States, Mexico, the Netherlands, Turkey, Thailand, and Saudi Arabia. The largest segment comprised substantial numbers of consumers from

Speaking from Experience

"Sodexho-Marriott Services provides on-site foodservice to over 4,000 clients across the United States and Canada, so understanding and reacting to customer differences are critical. Our clients view on-site foodservice as an important contributor to overall employee/student/patient satisfaction and, in some cases, even their productivity. Segmentation of on-site foodservice customers is an important tool for achieving that understanding and helping our clients reach their goals."

Meredith Heckman earned her Bachelor of Science degree in Marketing from the University of Tennessee and now works for

Sodexho-Marriott Services in Gaithersburg, Maryland. She was previously employed by American Express and Burke Research, Inc.

Meredith Heckman
Senior Director, Marketing Research,
Sodexho-Marriott Services

Saudi Arabia, Mexico, and the Netherlands. These people all shared preferences for selected product benefits.

Many international marketers believe that teenagers represent the first truly global segment. Teens worldwide show remarkably similar attitudes and preferences. For instance, common clothing preferences are baggy jeans, T-shirts, and Doc Martens. An interest in MTV is also prevalent. There are similarities in the way teens look and the consumption patterns they exhibit. The emergence of this common ground will make marketing to this global segment more efficient. However, companies must still acknowledge subtle differences in culture and national preferences, particularly in the advertising messages used to promote nonlocal brands.

India has a very heterogeneous population, but the mere size of the market is attractive to consumer goods marketers. With a population exceeding one billion, the potential demand is obvious. Consumer goods marketers like Pizza Hut, Kentucky Fried Chicken, Honda, and General Motors have simplified their strategies by focusing on the middle-class segment of the 250 million well-educated, Westernized residents of the largest cities.[10]

Evian multinational campaign recognizes the existence of segments across country lines. The ads are included in women's magazines in Switzerland, Japan, France, Spain, Singapore, Italy, Austria, Hong Kong, Germany, the United Kingdom, and the United States.

Target Markets

Market segmentation lets a firm tailor or develop products and strategies to appeal to the preferences and unique needs of specific groups of customers. These groups are typically referred to as target markets: groups of consumers or organizations with whom a firm wants to create marketing exchanges.[11] Examples include the elderly, the Hispanic, or the college-student markets, each of which can be targeted for specific products and reached through specific marketing programs. **Targeting** involves selecting which segments in a market are appropriate to focus on and designing the means of reaching them. Appealing to an entire market is often too costly. Moreover, a focus on certain markets can increase the efficiency and effectiveness of marketing efforts. However, a firm should target only those markets it can effectively reach and serve. Further, finely defined segments with their own marketing-mix strategies should be justified only on a return-on-investment evaluation.

As we shall see later in this chapter, segmentation may be appropriate for businesses of all sizes, not just for large firms with many products. Many small- and medium-sized companies find it better to concentrate on gaining a large share of one segment or a few, rather than small shares of all possible segments in a product market. For example, Liberty Bank of Philadelphia generates a profitable business from a market segment overlooked by many of its competitors: small businesses.

Product Differentiation

Related to market segmentation is **product differentiation.** Product differentiation exists when a firm's offerings differ or are perceived to differ from those of competing firms on any attribute, including price. A product differentiation strategy positions a product within the market. Marketers attempt to position a product or service in customers' minds—to convince customers the product has unique and desirable characteristics. By developing these perceptions, marketers seek to establish a competitive advantage relative to competing firms that offer similar products or brands.

In the mid-1980s, for example, brands in the frozen entrée market were differentiated on convenience, and consumers traded taste for that convenience. Stouffer's changed that balance by introducing a line of entrées positioned on taste but offered at a premium price. By focusing on a key benefit previously missing from other frozen dinners, Stouffer's expanded the market and became the category leader. Product differentiation and positioning are explained in more detail later in this chapter.

From Mass Marketing to Mass Customization

Among the most notable changes in this century has been the shift from mass marketing to **mass customization.** Companies like Dell Computers have proven that complex manufactured products can be made to order. Now, companies throughout the world have embraced mass customization in an attempt to satisfy the diverse needs of their customers and to provide unique value. The concept is made possible by advances in manufacturing and information technology that enable firms to provide product variety and customization through flexibility and quick responsiveness.

Various approaches have been used, and these approaches can range in the extent to which interactions with customers occur. "Collaborative customizers" conduct direct dialogue with customers to determine their needs and to identify the precise offering that is required to satisfy those needs. Other firms only package the offering individually in what is termed "cosmetic customization." The National Bicycle Company of Japan serves both ends of the mass market to mass customization continuum by operating two separate manufacturing facilities. The mass-production facility caters to their large market segment and is organized around traditional production facility efficiency. The mass-custom bicycle plant is directly linked to retail outlets where customers can choose from among eight million possible variations.[12]

One summary of the possibilities describes the alternatives as follows. At the least-specific level, mass marketing involves the company offering a standard product to markets worldwide, such as Diet Coke. Companies that practice target marketing focus upon niches in the market. Godiva Chocolate is directed at a more focused market comprising consumers with specific tastes. Sometimes companies focus upon market cells, many more in number and varied in description than typical larger target markets. These cells are derived from company databases through the process of **data mining,** which uses sophisticated analytical and statistical procedures to discover interesting patterns within company data sets. Data mining enabled Capital One to market 7,000 different MasterCard and Visa variations.

In developing mass customization strategies, firms face a number of challenges. These potential problems include obtaining information from customers, identifying the tangible and intangible factors that are important to each customer, dealing with higher customer expectations, limiting the complexity of options to a reasonable number, and pricing customized offerings.[13]

When Is Market Segmentation Appropriate?

Market segmentation can be useful for both new ventures and mature brands. In the case of new products, marketers target segments likely to respond positively to the introduction. Products that have been on the market for a while face an increasing number of competitive offerings, making it more difficult for any mass marketer to dominate in its product categories. Some frequently used approaches include developing brand-line extensions, repositioning the product for additional uses, or identifying the needs of a particular segment, or segments, and developing marketing strategies for each.[14]

The frozen entrée category again provides an example of a combined approach. Once Stouffer's successfully introduced its line of frozen entrées, the competitors came running. Stouffer's built on its success by extending its product line, tapping another key segment in the marketplace: the weight-conscious consumer. Stouffer's Lean Cuisine frozen entrées offered this segment low-calorie, tasty meals and the convenience of quick preparation. The frozen entrée category continues to be one of the most competitive in the grocery store, but Stouffer's maintains dominance through its target marketing approach.

A market segmentation strategy is not always appropriate, however. Advertising and marketing research practitioners suggest segmentation may not be useful when the overall market is so small that marketing to a portion of it is not profitable, or when the brand is dominant in the market and draws its appeal from all segments.[15] Segmentation strategies fail most often when firms target consumers on the basis of simple demographics, or in the case of B2B marketing, "firmographics," yet the segments do not buy different products or respond differently to alternative marketing communications. Segmentation built around income differences, for example, can easily result in a direct mail list. The problem is that simple demographics may not correlate well with customer behavior.[16]

Criteria for Effective Segmentation

Successful execution of a market segmentation strategy depends on the presence of several characteristics in the overall market and its various segments. In determining strategies to pursue, marketers should judge potential segments against five criteria: measurability, accessibility, substantialness, durability, and differential responsiveness.

Hispanic-Americans represent a substantial and responsive demographic segment. Telefutura makes effective use of market segmentation by targeting this growing and lucrative consumer segment.

MEASURABILITY **Measurability** reflects the degree to which the size and purchasing power of segments can be assessed. Measurability is enhanced if segments are defined by concrete variables enabling easily obtainable data. Demographic characteristics, such as income and age, are examples. Firms can use such data to reach segments and to estimate the size and potential of target markets. Marketers recognize that the age of the populations of advanced Western economies is changing. Data from the European Commission indicates that around 30 percent of the population in many countries is over age 65. Estimates of the percent over 65 in 2050 are Italy and Spain—70 percent, Germany—57 percent, France—53 percent, and Britain—49 percent.[17]

ACCESSIBILITY **Accessibility** describes the degree to which a firm can reach intended target segments efficiently. That is, the selected market segments must be reachable with unique marketing communications and distribution strategies. The Hispanic market is an example of a growing segment that can be reached by specific media (newspapers, radio, television). More than 14 percent of U.S. residents aged five and over speak a language other than English at home. Hence, the total market for non-English programs could reach a figure of more than 40 million residents by the end of 2000. The growth of cable and satellite television programs for targeted audiences give advertisers the opportunity to access in-language television audiences.[18] In another example, previously successful albums now available on CDs, such as Led Zeppelin albums, are marketed to middle-aged consumers by ads on the cable channels ESPN and Arts and Entertainment.[19] Accessibility relates to the communication channels used by buyers. To understand customer communication characteristics, sometimes referred to "infographics," marketers should consider three questions: where do customers go for information; how do they like to communicate; and, how do they prefer to buy?[20]

SUBSTANTIALNESS **Substantialness** refers to the degree to which identified target segments are large enough or have sufficient sales and profit potential to warrant unique or separate marketing programs. The growing Hispanic population is

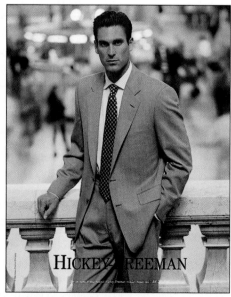

Market segments are often defined in terms of price sensitivity. Hartmarx Corporation offers multiple product lines to various price-sensitive segments. These offerings include Hart Schaffner & Marx and Hickey-Freeman, the latter of which appeals to the more price-conscious segment.

a sizable market that merits specifically designed products, advertising campaigns, and even distribution approaches. The 2000 census shows that Asian Americans are the fastest growing racial group. (The census considers Hispanics as a population group comprising multiple races.) Regarding segmentation and buying power, Asians have the highest education level and household income, own the most expensive homes on average, and are among the most tech-savvy.[21]

DURABILITY   **Durability** has to do with stability of segments—whether distinctions between segments will diminish or disappear as the product category or the markets themselves mature.[22] The development of differentiated products, communication campaigns, or distribution strategies often involves considerable financial and time commitments. Segments selected for targeting should offer reasonably enduring business opportunities. The Hispanic market meets this criterion, as it is a significant and, perhaps more important, a growing segment of the population. Current population trends indicate the Hispanic population will be a key segment for marketers for many years to come. Another is the aging U.S. population. As of the end of 2000, there were expected to be 59 million people over 55 years of age. This segment is ripe for targeting products and services oriented toward health and conservation of income.[23]

DIFFERENTIAL RESPONSIVENESS   **Differential responsiveness** refers to the extent to which market segments exhibit different responses to different marketing mixes.[24] If segments do not respond differently to varying marketing communications or product offerings, there is little need to segment. People interested in price will respond differently to low prices from people who seek high quality and assume price and quality are related.

Hartmarx Corporation provides a good example of the way a manufacturer segments target markets by price sensitivity. Hartmarx, a national producer and marketer of men's and women's fashions, developed brands and strategies to fill unique market voids.[25] Once Hartmarx acknowledges that different groups of consumers are sensitive to different price levels, it designs marketing strategies to differentiate variations in product (quality), communications (types of ads), and distribution (types of retail outlets). For example, the company targets Hart Schaffner & Marx to the upscale segment. Jaymar dress slacks and Sansabelt slacks are sold to the moderate segment. Kuppenheimer Men's Clothiers and Allyn St. George are included in the popular value offerings. Each brand name provides a product designed for different price-sensitive segments. Exhibit 7–1 is an example of how a retailer might segment men's clothing by price range.

Satisfying the Segmentation Criteria

By satisfying these various criteria, a company can choose market segments that can be described in managerially useful terms (measurability); that can utilize its communication and distribution channels (accessibility); that are sufficient in profit potential (substantialness); that will persist for some reasonable period (durability); and that vary in their reactions to different marketing efforts (differential responsiveness).

The Hispanic market provides a good example of combining segmentation criteria to evaluate a market. Although there are subsegments within it, the overall Hispanic market possesses unique cultural characteristics that make it an attractive

Exhibit 7–1	*Hypothetical retail market segments and price points*						
Retail market segments	**Business Clothing**			**Furnishings**		**Casual Wear**	
	Suits	**Jackets**	**Dress slacks**	**Dress shirts**	**Neckties**	**Sport shirts**	**Casual slacks**
Upscale	$600 & over	$475 & over	$150 & over	$55 & over	$45 & over	$47.50 & over	$95 & over
Upscale moderate	$450–$600	$350–$475	$100–$150	$39.50–$55	$37.50–$45	$37.50–$47.50	$65–$95
Moderate	$375–$450	$250–$350	$75–$100	$30–$39.50	$25–$37.50	$32.50–$37.50	$45–$65
Value conscious	Under $375	Under $250	Under $75	Under $30	Under $25	Under $32.50	Under $45

target segment. The unique language and cultural characteristics of this market clearly make the segment *measurable* and *responsive* to appeals designed directly for it. Hispanic-Americans accounted for over one-fourth of the population by the end of 2000; the market thus represents both a *substantial* and *durable* opportunity. The market is also *accessible*—both broadcast (radio, television) and print (newspapers, magazines) media reach the Hispanic community efficiently with specialized ads.

Marketing to Hispanic consumers has international implications as well. Wal-Mart, Sears, McDonald's, Ford, General Motors, and PepsiCo target Mexico for expanded export and local operations. McDonald's earmarked $500 million to open 250 new restaurants in Mexico, and relaxed trade restrictions have opened opportunities for Ford and GM to export luxury automobile models.[26] By 2010, one in five teens will be Hispanic. While all young consumers are hard to reach with their ever-growing assortment of media channels, Hispanic youth are even more difficult to target. Unlike their non-Hispanic counterparts, many Hispanic youth are bilingual and have access to another set of media. Previously, Spanish-language media was sufficient for marketing to Hispanic adults.[27]

In fact, ethnic commonalities make marketing in native languages to subcultures within countries worldwide, particularly in the United States, worthwhile. For example, the purchasing power of Arab, Asian, Hispanic, Russian, Eastern European, African, and Caribbean immigrants in the United States is now over $400 billion. Cultural differences exist within countries, and businesses that market to other countries should recognize segment differences. Like India, China has a very large population, and firms look at China as having a 1.3 billion-plus population. However, the most important market for a lot of products is the 200 million to 250 million middle-class, urban residents in the major cities along China's east coast.[28]

Stages in Developing Market Segmentation Strategies

Stages required in the development of a market segmentation strategy are summarized in Exhibit 7–2. The organization's core business determines the product or service market in which it operates, be it the restaurant industry, computer software, lawnmowers, cleaning services for office buildings, or whatever. Given its overall product or service market, a firm identifies the distinguishing characteristics, or **bases of segmentation,** for the segments within that market. After describing these segments, the firm evaluates them for potential and likely success, then selects the key segment or segments to target. Finally, the firm develops marketing mix strategies, including various product and service forms, and price and distribution strategies and communication appeals for each segment.[29]

Bases for Segmentation

Logical bases to define market segments have to do with characteristics of the firm's customers or their behaviors. Exhibit 7–3 describes some of these bases for both consumer and business-to-business marketing situations.[30] The Levi Strauss strat-

| **Exhibit 7–2** | *Developing a market segmentation strategy* |

1	2	3	4	5	6
Define overall product market in which company operates.	Identify distinguishing characteristics of segments or bases for segmentation.	Describe segments.	Evaluate approaches for potential & likely success.	Select target markets.	Determine desired positioning and then develop marketing mix to achieve desired position

| **Exhibit 7–3** | *Frequently used consumer and business-to-business segmentation bases* |

Consumer Marketing

USER-RELATED

Demographics: age, gender, race, income, education, family size, family life cycle stage

Social class: lower, middle, upper

Culture: religion, nationality, subculture

Geographic: region, state, metropolitan location and size, urban versus rural

Lifestyles and psychographics: quiet family person, traditionalist attitudes, progressive, conservative

BEHAVIORAL

Benefits: desired product attributes

Usage: users versus nonusers, light versus heavy

Price or promotional sensitivity: high versus low

Brand loyalty: loyal versus nonloyal

Buying situation: kind of store, gift giving (kind of shopping)

Economic: profitability and potential

Business-to-business

USER-RELATED

Customer size: annual sales

Geographic location: Northeast versus West Coast

Organizational structure: centralized versus decentralized

Stage of buying process: decision at hand versus initial stages of decision making

Attitude toward vendor: current purchaser versus new account

Buying decision criterion: price versus quality

Type of product: installations, supplies, services, raw materials, component parts

Type of organization: manufacturing, government, public utility

BEHAVIORAL

End use: resale versus production component

Usage: users versus nonusers, light versus heavy

Product/service application: insurance versus banking

Economic: profitability and potential

egy uses some of the most easily identified consumer segmentation bases, including age, race, and gender. Brand-loyalty segments and the heavy-user segment are among the most important and now are the focus of many customer retention efforts. For business-to-business marketing, computer companies provide an example. They frequently organize their selling efforts around different industries, such as banking, insurance, and educational institutions.

DEMOGRAPHICS   For consumer marketing, demographic segments are particularly significant. Some products are targeted for teenagers and others for the elderly; others are designed for young couples just beginning a family. Vacation decisions are uniquely related to family life cycle characteristics, with children having significant

Being Entrepreneurial

Nokia on target

As the market for mobile telephones becomes mature and many consumers and business customers have adopted them, segment opportunities for the entrepreneurial thinker still exist. For example, Nokia has targeted the very wealthy with luxury products, which include casings of gold, platinum, and expensive leather and a ringing tune that sounds like an orchestra. A special "concierge" button on the phone links users to a service that can book tickets to plays or reserve a restaurant table. In terms of satisfying the criteria for effective segmentation, this small niche market is substantial in buying power, enduring, can be reached through specific campaigns, and responds to such exclusive offerings.

input even at young ages. Marketing researchers often rely heavily on occupation and education to form social-class segments.

The demographic makeup of the typical American household continues to change. Married couples are now barely the majority. Households are growing more slowly and getting older. College-educated people earn a lot more than less-educated consumers, and sadly, the gap between these two groups is growing wider. More and more jobs are being found in service industries, and the population shift to western and southern states continues.[31]

These trends and demographic phenomena are important to marketers' understanding of segment characteristics. For example, age differences are often used individually or with other demographic variables, such as gender, income, and education, to describe market segments. Five generations are often used to categorize age differences:

- *The millennial generation*—Born between 1977 and 1994, this large new generation numbers 70 million.
- *Generation X*—Born between 1965 and 1976, this well-educated, media-savvy generation now makes up the young adult population of the United States.
- *Baby-boom generation*—Born between 1946 and 1964, this is the largest single generation of Americans and remains a focus of marketers.
- *Swing generation*—Born between 1933 and 1945, this small generation of Americans now holds top positions in business and government.
- *World War II generation*—Born before 1933, the oldest consumers are the most affluent in history.
- *Generation Y*—the 71 million children of baby boomers now coming of age.[32]

AARP offers a variety of products for the growing and lucrative segment of consumers over fifty.

Three of these age groups are particularly important in terms of marketing: teens, Xers, and boomers; and similarities among these groups offer unique insights into differences in consumer behavior. Of note, teens spend over $65 billion each year of their own money and influence considerably more in aggregate expenditures by either spending their family's money or determining how their parents make decisions.

Xers are more likely than boomers to seek a balance between leisure and work activities as young adults. They care deeply about buying "cool" brands that match their own image needs and often serve as trendsetters for the population at large. In addition, following their college years, young adults now more often live at home as their careers are formed; hence, they have considerable discretionary income. This group actually consists of three significant and overlapping submarkets: college and graduate students, up-and-coming professionals, and married couples. Firms who have been successful in reaching this group typically use the Internet as part of a larger campaign, particularly TV advertising. However, care must be exercised in the design of these campaigns, since Generation X consumers are often cynical about advertising.[33]

With boomers continuing to age, the marketing opportunities associated with an aging population are profound. Previous generations retired and lived off fixed incomes. Boomers are expected to

Thinking Critically

- What media might be effective for reaching the most profitable consumer customers for large banks?

- What bases would be appropriate for use in the development of a segmentation of business-to-business marketers? Evaluate this scheme using the five criteria for effective segmentation.

continue working in the marketplace and to place a positive spin on aging. Consequently, products and services that appeal to older consumers with younger, positive self-images will be effective. Moreover, major life events like diet changes, divorce, and retirement open fertile ground for marketers.[34]

The presence and surprisingly the absence of children in families have become noticed by marketers in their efforts to identify potentially profitable market segments. The generation comprising the children of baby boomers, more than 79 million strong, will have purchasing power beyond their parents. Almost 30 million are already in their teens and spend an estimated $150 billion annually, and influence another $300 billion in spending by their parents. In contrast, families who have made the conscious decision to not have children represent a lucrative and neglected market segment as well. According to *American Demographics*, childless couples spend more per person in almost every consumer category than their married-with-children counterparts. Their unique buying power and growing size warrant marketer attention in certain segmentation situations.[35]

GEOGRAPHICS   Geographic differences are sometimes important in the development of marketing strategies. For example, cellular-phone marketers use geographic analyses to evaluate their distribution effectiveness. In addition, gaps in geographic coverage can also signal effective area campaigns by cellular-phone competitors that must be countered.[36]

One method of categorizing geographic differences uses census data to identify metropolitan areas. There are three types: **metropolitan statistical areas** (MSAs), **primary metropolitan statistical areas** (PMSAs), and **consolidated metropolitan statistical areas** (CMSAs). MSAs must have a city with a population of at least 50,000 or be an "urbanized area" with 50,000 people that is part of a county of at least 100,000 residents. The largest designation is CMSA. These are the approximately 20 largest markets in the United States that contain at least two PMSAs. PMSAs are major urban areas, often located within a CMSA, that have at least one million inhabitants. New York, Los Angeles, and Chicago are among the largest CMSAs. Populated areas within these markets, such as Marietta near Atlanta and Ventura near Los Angeles, represent PMSAs.

The combination of geographic information and demographic characteristics is called **geodemographics.** Much published geodemographic data are available that firms can use in evaluating the size of potential market segments. Products are often directed toward geographic markets, particularly when tastes differ between regions. Further, it is important for marketers to know which areas are the fastest growing and represent the greatest future opportunities.

Meridith Heckman notes: "Our approach uses a mix of off-the-shelf geodemographic clustering and proprietary psychographic/benefits segmentation approaches. This mix gives us segments which are identifiable, marketable, effective, and relevant. The end result is a method that can be applied in any of our foodservice categories to identify and serve the interests of tightly defined and lucrative 'target segments.' "

Firms use geodemographic data systems to integrate geographic information with census data. The fundamental premise in such geodemographic systems is that households in neighborhoods share similar lifestyles ("birds of a feather flock together") and that such neighborhoods repeat themselves, allowing similar neighborhoods to be classified into market segments.[37] Using a geographic information system (popularly labeled GIS), the lifestyle cluster system groups households into one of 40 residential types. Marketers can append lifestyle codes to customer records to expand their customer profiles and to enhance the study of the relationship of lifestyles to purchasing patterns.[38] Southwestern Bell Corporation (SBC) uses geodemographic analysis to develop marketing strategies for its European cable operations in the United Kingdom. The company uses the data to identify neighborhoods susceptible to sales through direct marketing campaigns and to screen bad-debt areas.[39]

Geographic clusters reflect segmentation targets that enable marketers to more efficiently employ their resources. Consider your own neighborhood. The cars and homes are probably of similar value. The mailboxes contain many of the same magazines, the cabinets the same products. The households have similar incomes and educations, as well as attitudes and product preferences.[40]

Cultural differences between countries have been used to identify segments comprising countries assumed to share similar values. Hofstede's classification scheme proposes five cultural dimensions for classifying countries: individualism versus collectivism, power distance, uncertainty avoidance, masculinity, and long-term orientation. For example, Austria, Germany, Switzerland, Italy, Great Britain, and Ireland form one segment that is medium high on individualism and high on masculinity. These cultural characteristics suggest preferences for high-performance products and a "successful achiever" theme in advertising. Similar comparisons have been made in terms of individualism–collectivism for Japanese versus U.S. consumers.[41]

PSYCHOGRAPHICS AND LIFESTYLES   Psychographic or **lifestyle research** attempts to segment customers according to their activities, interests, and opinions.[42] Such research uses survey responses to items concerning individual *activities, interests,* and *opinions*—called **AIO statements**—to develop in-depth profiles of consumer groups or segments. By tapping into a consumer's preferences and learning where her/his passions lie, firms increase the receptivity of their messages. If marketers can adopt the proper focus and promote benefits that sustain or become a part of the customer's lifestyle, then selling products and services is enhanced.[43] Examples of AIO statements are:

- "A person can save a lot of money by shopping around for bargains" *(price conscious).*
- "An important part of my life is dressing smartly" *(fashion conscious).*
- "I would rather spend a quiet evening at home than go to a party" *(homebody).*
- "I am uncomfortable when my house is not completely clean" *(compulsive housekeeper).*[44]

Psychographic research has been used successfully in a variety of segmentation applications. As an example, one study of women over 65 combined psychographic research with an analysis of segments identified by media preferences. This study of the growing over-65 market described the following media consumption patterns:

- *The engaged*—High levels of newspaper readership and high viewing levels of television news programming.

- *The autonomous*—Moderate levels of newspaper readership, and low use of media in general.
- *The receptive*—High viewing levels of television comedy programs and moderate levels of newspaper readership.[45]

A follow-up study using responses to a series of AIO agree–disagree statements provided a richer description of lifestyles within these segments. For example, women in the engaged segment were heavier users of cosmetics, considered cooking and baking extremely important, and were quite negative toward large companies and business practices.

Psychographic analyses have also been used to identify the defining events that will shape the 70 million-plus Generation Ys. The most noteworthy of the events included Columbine, Oklahoma City, the Clinton impeachment trial, and the Lewinsky scandal. The MTV style of programming affects marketing and advertising messages. Shorter attention spans and information overload are the outcome of the current media environment faced by this developing and large segment of consumers. Relative to their Gen X predecessors, 18- to 24-year-olds are active channel surfers, interactive with technology, possess more positive attitudes toward their ability to make money, and like to spend.[46]

A popular application of the lifestyle and psychographic approach to segmentation is the **Values and Lifestyles Program** of SRI Interna-

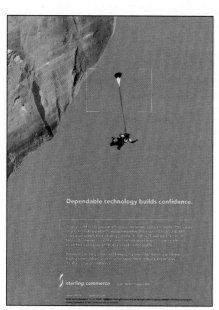

Sterling Commerce targets business customers and stresses desired end benefits sought by B2B market segments.

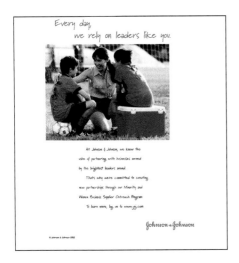

Business-to-business situations can benefit from segmentation practices. For example, Johnson and Johnson targets minority businesses in efforts to build relationships.

tional. VALS segments consumers into eight groups: actualizers, fulfilleds, believers, achievers, strivers, experiencers, makers, and strugglers. Firms can use this system to effectively develop advertising and promotional campaigns, including the selection of media and the design of message content. As shown in Exhibit 7–4, the groups are arranged along two dimensions: self-orientation and resources. Self-orientation refers to the attitudes and activities people use to maintain their social self-image and self-esteem. Resources include attributes such as education, income, age, energy, self-confidence, and even health.[47] For example, the actualizers, the smallest segment at 8 percent of the U.S. population, have the highest incomes and self-esteem. The remaining seven segments each represent from 11 to 16 percent of the population.[48]

BENEFIT SEGMENTATION Many firms segment markets according to the particular attributes or benefits that consumers want.[49] **Benefit segmentation** enhances the design and marketing of a product to meet expressed consumer needs for quality, service, or unique features. In fact, benefit segmentation is most consistent with assumption of demand variation between segments. For example, Apple targeted a segment that wanted easy-to-use computers, consumers put off by what they saw as complications in operating other PCs. Defining this niche and simplifying the process of learning built Apple into a major factor in this market.

Benefit segmentation is consistent with the provision of *customer value* and the marketing concept—that is, to be customer-oriented and to provide consumer benefits to generate long-term customer satisfaction. The belief underlying benefit segmentation is that true segments are best described in terms of the causal factors or basic reasons for purchase.[50]

Benefit segmentation works in marketing services as well as products. Through its novel promotional messages, Andersen Consulting markets itself as a provider of much-needed benefits to many companies—information systems that do not threaten the firm's employees and that make computer technology a real contributor to the firm's performance. Users of the Internet have been segmented into those seeking adventure and exploration, information, entertainment, and on-line purchase of products and services. These segments of Internet users are labeled (1) adventurers (37 percent); (2) fact collectors (28 percent); (3) entertainment seekers (12 percent); and (4) social shoppers (9 percent).[51]

ECONOMIC SEGMENTATION Firms are increasingly segmenting their customers based upon the profit potential associated with individual accounts. Such economic-based segmentation occurs in both consumer marketing situations and business-to-business competitive markets.

Exhibit 7–4

VALS2: Eight values and lifestyles segments from SRI International

VALS™ Network

Actualizers

High resources
High innovation

Principle Oriented   Status   Oriented   Action   Oriented

Fulfilleds   Achievers   Experiencers

Believers   Strivers   Makers

Low resources
Low innovation

Strugglers

As shown in Exhibit 7–3, economic considerations are a behavioral-based segmentation characteristic. For example, banks often segment their customers into A, B, and C categories based upon profitability data generated through information on customer accounts and their previous account activity. The low revenue/low profit customers will receive minimum service, and in the case of banks, may be charged higher fees. In contrast, high revenue/high profit customers are targeted with personal communications, while direct mail is used for moderate revenue/moderate profit accounts. Factors such as cost of retention, potential for expansion, and customer contributions to profits are instrumental in determining these segment identifications.[52] Data from the University of Michigan's Business School and its American Customer Satisfaction Index has documented a steady decline in service satisfaction for airlines, banks, stores, hotels, personal computer companies, and telephone services. One reason for these declines is the uneven way in which customer segments are treated. Financial institutions prefer day traders and heavy card users who pay substantial interest charges. At Charles Schwab, their Signature clients, who process $100,000 in assets or trade at least monthly, never have to wait more than 15 seconds to get a call answered.[53]

The most frequently used B2B segmentation variables are firm demographics, purchasing approaches (buying center approaches), and purchase characteristics (specific applications, product urgency, order size). An economic value approach bases segmentation upon how the firm's customers deliver value to their customers. Federal Express, for example, segments its customers based upon their needs for parcel security and on-time arrival. In addition, it is important to focus upon those segments for which the marketer can provide superior value relative to their competitors. A value-based segmentation approach, based upon the differentiation or competitive strengths of the firm, enables the firm to realize premium prices and frequent repeat business.[54]

INTERNATIONAL SEGMENTATION   Segmentation is an important part of international marketing as well. Firms can employ one—or some combination—of three approaches. First, companies may use a single standardized strategy in all international marketing. Second, customized strategies may be developed for different countries or groups of countries. In these cases, the countries represent different segments. Third, and as explained earlier, intermarket segments, comprising similar clusters of consumers across national boundaries, may be identified. Variables that are typically used to form country segments include income and GNP per capita, telephones and TV sets per capita, percent of population in agriculture, and political stability. For example, a company considering the sale of durable electronic products (VCRs and CD players) identified two important segments formed by combining countries: (1) Holland, Japan, Sweden, and the United Kingdom; and (2) Austria, Belgium, Denmark, Finland, France, Norway, and Switzerland. Those segments were found to share similar patterns of new-product adoption and, hence, were addressed with similar marketing efforts.[55] The growing spending power of European teens, individuals who harbor national loyalties often ignored by American marketers, represent a growing market segment. The challenge for brands, whether they are American or European, is to communicate brand attributes in messages consistent with the cultural languages of the European teen segment being pursued.[56]

Combining Bases of Market Segmentation

Exhibit 7–5 diagrams one way a firm might combine consumer characteristics to decide on a market segmentation strategy. Here a two-stage process begins with research designed to identify the heavy users of a product or service. If the heavy-user segment has unique or consistent demographic characteristics, such as income or education, the firm's decisions about how to reach that segment are easier; that is, which magazines or television programs can be used efficiently. Similarly, identifying certain lifestyle characteristics of the heavy-user segment gives the firm additional insight about which product configuration or advertising theme is likely to be successful.

Exhibit 7–6 gives another approach for combining different variables to describe segments of teenage consumers. Nissan's 2002 campaign for its upgraded Maxima targets married men in their late 30s who make $125,000 plus and love driving a more powerful automobile. This demographic segment was marketed to

Exhibit 7–5   *A two-stage segmentation example*

Exhibit 7–6   *Teen Segmentation Bases*

Teen Segment	Key Definers	Activities and Purchases
Thrills and chills	Fun Friends Irreverence Sensation	Eating out Going to bars Attending concerts Fast food Acne medication Perfume/cologne Body rings Hair dye Tobacco Alcohol
Resigned	Friends Fun Family Low expectations	Drinking Smoking Heavy metal music Fast food Low-ticket clothes Hair dye Tobacco Alcohol
World savers	Environment Humanism Fun Friends	Attending plays Camping/hiking School clubs Going to bars Doing something creative
Quiet achievers	Success Anonymity Anti-individualism Social optimism	Studying Listening to music Visiting museums CDs Stereo equipment
Bootstrappers	Achievement Individualism Optimism Determination Power	Studying Housework Spending time with family Visiting relatives Attending religious services Premium brands Luxury goods
Upholders	Family Custom Tradition Respect for individuals	Reading books Spending time with family Visiting relatives Playing/watching sports

by advertising on cable channels such A&E, Discovery, and the History Channel. Print ads were placed in *Smithsonian, Fortune,* and *Forbes.*[57]

Basically then, firms identify and combine distinguishing buyer segment bases to:

- Help them design product or service offerings to market to targeted consumer segments.

- Help them choose media vehicles.

- Help them develop marketing themes for use in communicating to a particular segment or segments.

Segmentation Strategies

Strategies for engaging in segmentation are often categorized as undifferentiated, differentiated, or concentrated. These approaches provide firms alternative methods for enhancing the execution of their marketing programs. These strategies range from appeals based upon "mass marketing" to strategy focused on predetermined target markets. From our earlier discussion, other more-specific segmentation approaches target large numbers of market cells, or involve customer-based marketing, in which mass customization is used to combine basic product modules in different ways for each customer, or customized marketing is used in which products are developed from scratch for each individual customer. Exhibit 7–7 is a schematic view of the three approaches.

UNDIFFERENTIATED STRATEGY A company adopts an **undifferentiated strategy** when it markets a single product using a single communication and distribution mix for the mass market. Neither the product nor the promotional theme is varied or differentiated. Undifferentiated approaches are most often used early in the life of a product category. Initial product introductions, such as the early introduction of the automobile, often use a single mass-marketing approach. The undifferentiated strategy offers some advantages because of economies of scale but opens the firm to competition. Today, even water is marketed in brands to different segments. Truly undifferentiated strategies are largely a theoretical impracticability, or at least, a phenomenon that occurs infrequently.

DIFFERENTIATED STRATEGY At the other end of the scale is the **differentiated strategy,** under which a firm uses different strategies for most or a large number of different segments. In some cases, a unique product and communications campaign may be developed for each segment. In other instances, a common product may be marketed to different segments with varying communication strategies. Of note, a differentiated strategy does not simply mean a change in product, although it may. Frequently, variations in multiple aspects of the marketing mix are involved. The Hartmarx and Levi Strauss approaches, with their multiple product versions and advertising campaigns, are examples of complex segmentation schemes. Differentiated strategies are often the choice of companies such as soft-drink manufacturers and life insurance firms, which offer many product versions to meet different preferences. McDonald's, for example, embodies segmentation principles in its offerings. Happy Meals and playgrounds are offered for children, while nutritional information on trays and commercials

Exhibit 7–7

Three alternative market segmentation strategies

Undifferentiated strategy

Company marketing mix → Market

Differentiated strategy

Marketing mix 1 → Segment 1
Marketing mix 2 → Segment 2
Marketing mix 3 → Segment 3

Concentrated strategy

Segment 1
Company marketing mix → Segment 2
Segment 3

showing parent/child interactions are targeted toward adults. Likewise, traditional burgers are offered along with healthier salads and sandwiches. Although a differentiated strategy is often useful for increasing sales and profits, continual adjustments to segmentation programs may prove expensive.

CONCENTRATED STRATEGY A firm pursues a **concentrated strategy** when it seeks a large share of just a few profitable segments, perhaps only one, of the total market. With such a strategy, a company concentrates more on serving segments innovatively and creatively than on pricing.[58] American Express, for example, has traditionally sought upscale instead of middle-income customers. Thus, the company concentrates its advertising resources in pursuit of a large share of the higher-income consumer market.

COUNTERSEGMENTATION STRATEGY **Countersegmentation** is an alternative strategy to traditional segmentation approaches. It involves combining market segments and assumes an increasing consumer willingness to accept fewer product and service variations for lower prices. Countersegmentation is seen in the move toward generic brands and retail superstores and warehouse stores and reflects segmentation by demand for low price. Sam's outlets and Toys "R" Us appeal to a broad range of consumers and do not emphasize finely focused target segments. Countersegmentation is seen also at IBM and Chrysler, which have streamlined their product lines by combining operations and eliminating some brands.

FACTORS INFLUENCING SEGMENTATION STRATEGY A number of market, product, and competitive factors may influence a firm's choice of segmentation strategy. They include size and type of the market and a variety of competitive factors.

If consumers are not particularly sensitive to product differences, an undifferentiated strategy may be appropriate. But if the firm sells to an overall product market with many different segments, a differentiated or concentrated approach is the better choice. Two product-related factors are also relevant: stage in the product life cycle, and the degree to which the product may be varied or modified. If the product is new, a concentrated segmentation strategy may be best—that is, offering only one product version or a few at most. If the firm's interest is to develop primary demand, an undifferentiated strategy may be appropriate. In the later stages of a product's life, large firms tend to pursue a differentiated segmentation strategy.

For example, consumer product giant Procter & Gamble pursues a differentiated strategy in the laundry detergent category. P&G markets powdered laundry detergents such as Cheer and Tide to different segments of the product market. The company constantly differentiates its products within and across brands to address the segments vital to its success. Potential growth segments are prime candidates for differentiated products. When the liquid detergent segment was growing, P&G introduced a liquid version of Tide; later, the company addressed another potential growth segment with Concentrated Tide.

Competitive factors are particularly important in a firm's market segmentation strategy. If its major competitors pursue an undifferentiated approach, a firm may decide to engage in a differentiated or concentrated approach. If a firm has many competitors, its best strategy may be to concentrate on developing strong brand loyalty and buyer preferences in one target segment or perhaps a few. Finally, a firm's size and financial position can influence the choice of strategy. Smaller firms with relatively limited resources often find it necessary to pursue a concentrated segmentation strategy.

A firm adopting an undifferentiated approach or pursuing only the largest segments may well invite substantial competition. This is the **majority fallacy:** although large "majority" segments may appear to offer a firm potential gains, pursuing only them may involve confronting overwhelming competition. In this case, it is better for a firm to pursue a concentrated strategy, focusing on one segment, or a few, to obtain larger shares of markets in which it can compete effectively.

Targeting Market Segments and Positioning Products

Once a firm has chosen its overall market segmentation strategy, it then must select specific segments and position products for effective appeal to those segments. Factors that affect the choice of a segmentation strategy also influence which specific segments should be targeted.

Estimating Segment Potentials

To estimate market potential and likely sales, the firm should distinguish between firm and industry potentials and between forecasts of the best possible results and expected results. As Exhibit 7–8 shows, **market potential** is the maximum amount of industry sales possible for a product or service for a specific period. The **market forecast** for that same period is a function of the amount of marketing effort (expenditures) put forth by all companies competing in that market. Total market potential then represents an upper limit on total sales. **Sales potential** is the maximum amount of sales a specific firm can obtain for a specified time period.

To produce a sales forecast, a company should screen out market segments that represent insufficient potential sales and analyze further the remaining segments. Company forecasts must consider competitive activity and the availability of channels of distribution and marketing media. What brands are already in the market? What are the strengths and weaknesses of the competition? What distribution outlets and supporting channels of distribution are available? What is the cost of access to the appropriate media? One set of steps firms can use to estimate potential for a segment is:

1. Set time period of interest.
2. Define product level.
3. Specify segment characteristics or bases.
4. Identify geographic market boundaries.
5. Make assumptions about marketing environment (uncontrollable factors such as competitive activity).
6. Make assumptions about company's own marketing efforts and programs (controllable factors).
7. Make estimates of market potential, industry sales, and company sales.[59]

Exhibit 7–9 sets out data on market potential for pizza across four age groups. Population information of this sort is obtainable from U.S. census or state records. The product purchase percentage data can be obtained from an annual "Survey of Buying Power" in *Sales & Marketing Management*. The use of these data are explained in Appendix B.

Developing Forecasts

Forecasts represent the amount the company expects to sell in a market over a specific time period. The period will vary by company and use of the forecast. Forecasts are used to evaluate opportunities, budget marketing efforts, control expenditures, and assess subsequent sales performance. High forecasts can lead to excessive investment and expenditures, whereas low forecasts can result in lost opportunities.

Exhibit 7–8		

Firm and market potentials and forecasts

	Best possible results	Expected results for given strategy
Industry level	Market potential	Market forecast
Firm level	Sales potential	Sales forecast

| Exhibit 7–9 | | | *Estimating market potential for frozen pizza for Arizona and Colorado (in thousands)* | | |

Age Group	Percent Purchasing Frozen Pizza	Population		Potential Pizza Sales	
		Arizona	**Colorado**	**Arizona**	**Colorado**
18–24	10.4	384	341	39.94	35.46
25–34	25.8	634	607	163.57	156.61
35–44	24.3	568	622	138.02	151.15
45–54	14.5	381	384	55.25	55.68
				396.78	398.90

There are a number of methods for forecasting sales, some of which are explained below. These methods can be grouped into *qualitative* procedures, which employ judgmental opinion and insight, and *quantitative* methods, which use historical data to make trend extensions or numerical estimates of forecasted sales. The primary qualitative forecasting methods are a survey of buyers' intentions, expert opinion, and a composite of salesforce estimates. The primary quantitative methods are trend analysis, market tests, and statistical demand analysis.

A **survey of buyers' intentions** is useful in certain situations. Under this method, forecasts are based on surveys of what consumers or organizational buyers say they will do. First, the buyers must have well-formed intentions and be willing to follow those intentions. In addition, they must be willing to disclose their intentions accurately. These conditions are most often satisfied for durable consumer goods and for large purchases in business-to-business marketing.

Expert opinion represents another qualitative or judgmental approach to forecasting. Using this approach, analysts ask executives within the company or other experts to provide forecasts based on their own judgments or experiences. This can be a quick and perhaps inexpensive method; however, the forecast accuracy depends on the knowledge of the executives or experts involved and their ability to provide realistic estimates.

A **composite of salesforce estimates** provides another means of forecasting sales. Under this method, sales representatives give forecasts for their individual territories, which can then be combined across territories. Sales reps have unique exposure to the competition and market trends. Plus, these estimates can be obtained cheaply and regularly. However, reps may give low forecasts in efforts to keep their own sales quotas low.

Trend analysis, a quantitative forecasting approach, often referred to as *time-series analysis,* examines historical sales data for predictable patterns. If the environment is reasonably stable, extrapolating past sales data can provide a quick and efficient means of making forecasts. Often the firm will identify trend, cyclical (economic cycles), and seasonal effects in its past sales pattern. Exponential smoothing is a frequently used form of trend analysis in which the most recent sales data are weighted the heaviest in determining each new forecast. The major problem with time-series or trend analysis is that the firm is assuming that what happened in the past will continue in the future, making no attempt to determine what caused the sales.

When the firm is uncertain about its subjective judgment or the ability of past data to forecast the future, a market test may be necessary. Market tests are particularly useful for evaluating the likely success of new-product introductions. **Market tests** involve marketing the product in test locations using the planned communications, pricing, and distribution strategies. Forecasts for other areas can then be obtained from sales in the test markets.

Statistical demand analysis involves developing forecasts from the factors thought to be most important in determining sales. Under this method, sales are forecasted from equations in which price, advertising and sales promotion, distribution, competitive, and economic factors serve as independent variables. Regression analysis is the most frequently used estimation procedure. Statistical demand analysis is advantageous in that it forces the firm to consider the causal factors that determine sales. Also, the relative importance of the independent factors can be evaluated. Although computers have made demand analysis readily available to forecasters, the usefulness of the method depends on appropriate application. Some sophistication in data analysis procedures is clearly a prerequisite to their use.

Forecasting is not a rigorous science, in spite of the availability of some very sophisticated methods. When using any of the methods described above, forecasters should be careful to avoid several common errors. These errors include the failure to carefully examine any assumptions made, such as anticipated social and technological changes; excessive optimism that inhibits consideration of the downside risks involved; failure to specify the time frame involved and the intended purpose of the forecast; and the failure to blend both quantitative and qualitative methods such that mechanical extrapolation is combined with reasoned judgment.[60]

Targeting Market Segments

To select target segments, the firm must consider a combination of factors, including the segment's potential sales volume and profits, competition currently selling to the segments, and the firm's abilities and objectives.

Although large segments with a substantial number of buyers seem to promise high potential sales volume and profits, smaller segments served by a unique marketing mix may also provide lucrative business opportunities. Specialty stores in large malls serve many of these segments. For example, General Nutrition Center targets health-conscious people, and Lady Foot Locker, women sports enthusiasts.

The large markets may also attract the greatest number of competing firms (the majority fallacy). In general, a firm will have to assess market potential in light of competitive issues. If the firm has a competitive advantage that cannot be easily copied, it may attempt to approach the larger market segments.

The selection of target markets has a lot to do with the firm's objectives and distinctive competence. A firm specializing in innovative technological products, for example, may compete on total value, rather than on price alone, focusing on one segment or a few segments where high-quality, innovative products appeal.

Targeting also requires designing advertising and promotional mixes to reach the intended segments. Resources are wasted if the advertising results in duplication of audience or reaches nontarget market consumers. Accurate identification of the marketing segments appropriate for a particular product is critical if firms are to target those segments efficiently.

Technology brings new precision to both the selection of specific target segments and the ability to reach them. When Buick's analysis of the large station wagon segment revealed that upscale suburbs, particularly in the Midwest and Northeast, were potentially lucrative markets, it targeted consumers with ads in magazines sent to the relevant zip codes. Targeted ads promoting the Roadmaster station wagon ran in issues going to 4,940 of the more than 40,000 U.S. zip codes. That was 20 percent of U.S. households, but those households represented 50 percent of the buyers of large wagons.[61]

The benefits of targeting are prevalent in the marketplace—the grocery, clothing, and shoe industries included. For example, the use of in-store scanners and grocery card loyalty programs are enabling grocery retailers to more precisely target their consumers. In an application of economic segmentation, Sav-O's Piggly Wiggly stores are focusing on the top 50 percent of their customers, who represent 90 percent of their business. These customers are targeted with special promotions and advertisements designed to increase their transaction numbers per store visit. Moreover, data on the preferences of these desirable consumers are useful in determining shelf-space allocations among competing brands. Targeting specifically toward baby boomers has also enabled New Balance to compete successfully with Nike in the very competitive athletic-shoe market.[62]

S3 - Inner Suburbs

The four clusters of the S3 Social Group comprise the middle income suburbs of major metropolitan areas, straddling the United States average. Otherwise, the clusters are markedly different. Two clusters have more college-educated, white-collar workers; two have more high school-educated blue-collar workers; two are young; one is old; one is mixed; but all show distinct, variant patterns of employment, lifestyle, and regional concentration.

23 Upstarts and Seniors   Middle-Income Empty Nesters

Cluster 23 shows that young people and seniors are very similar if they are employable, single, and childless. *Upstarts and Seniors* have average educations and incomes in business, finance, retail, health and public service. Preferring condos and apartments, they live in the Sunbelt and the West.

Middle (28)   Age Groups: 25-54, 65+   Predominantly White

24 New Beginnings   *Young Mobile City Singles*

Concentrated in the boomtowns of the Southeast, the Southwest, and the Pacific coast, *New Beginnings* is a magnet for many young, well-educated minorities who are making fresh starts. Some are divorced, and many are single parents. They live in multi-unit rentals and work in a variety of low-level, white-collar jobs.

Middle (29)   Age Groups: 18-44   Ethnically Diverse

25 Mobility Blues   *Young Blue-Collar/Service Families*

These blue-collar counterparts of *New Beginnings* are young, ethnically mixed, and very mobile. Many are Hispanics and have large families with children. These breadwinners work in transportation, industry, public service, and the military.

Middle (41)   Age Groups: Under 18, 25-34   Ethnically Diverse, High Hispanic

26 Gray Collars   *Aging Couples in Inner Suburbs*

The highly skilled blue-collar workers of Cluster 26 weathered the economic downturn of America's industrial areas and now enjoy a resurgence of employment. Their kids grew up and left, but the Gray Collars stayed in the Great Lakes "Rust Belt."

Middle (42)   Age Groups: 65+   Ethnically Diverse

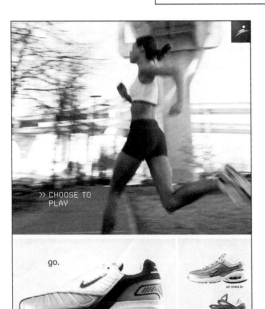

Segmentation schemes involve identifying groups defined in terms of geodemographics and in terms of desired end benefits, as in this Nike advertisement.

Meridith Heckman stresses the importance of the knowledge gained from segmentation: "By using customer segmentation to understand the unique requirements among foodservice patrons—whether they are in a school, college/university, office/factory, or health care facility—we are able to offer the optimal mix of menus, service, food promotions, merchandising, atmosphere, etc. Depending on the needs of customers at an account (needs that may exist within a few key segments or go across all segments), we can tailor our total package to address specific taste preferences, nutritional concerns, price sensitivities, and values/personal interests."

Positioning

Once segments have been selected and targeted, the firm must position its products and services in the minds of its customers. **Positioning** a product or service involves designing a marketing program, including the product mix, that is consistent with how the company wants its products or services to be perceived. The strategy a firm adopts is driven then by the desired positioning. Positioning aims to influence or adjust customer perceptions of

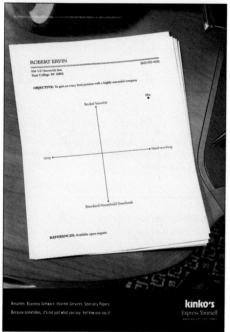

These Kinko's advertisements depict a humorous perceptual map which makes the important point that even students must 'position' themselves in the marketplace.

a product or brand. An effective position lets a brand occupy a preferred and unique position in the customers' minds while being consistent with the firm's overall marketing strategy.[63] As such, positioning involves the selection of target segments and the formulation of product attributes that make up the brand. Recently, Snackwell's successfully halted dramatically falling sales volume by repositioning itself. This repositioning included product reformulation, an increased marketing budget, and a drastic shift in advertising redirected toward the brand's new core audience—women. Nabisco is also building its relationship with its primary target market by creating a Web site directed at women and an ongoing direct-mail campaign augmented by women-targeted promotions.[64]

Positioning a new brand requires distinguishing it from other brands. Customers must perceive it as sharing important attributes with other brands in the product category but as being superior on differentiating attributes.[65] **Repositioning,** called for when a firm wants to shift consumer opinions about an existing brand, requires development of new marketing programs.

Product attributes, price, and image enhancements are major components in positioning. **Perceptual maps,** spatial representations of consumer perceptions of products or brands, are often used to evaluate brand positions in a market. Exhibit 7–10 is a perceptual map for the softdrink market. Brands are positioned on the map according to consumer perceptions of price and brand expressiveness. Note that over time, a brand's market position can shift.

Perceptual maps often show positions for competitors' brands. They also convey to a company how much it must change consumer perceptions in order to achieve parity with or differentiation from competitors. By combining segmentation and positioning research, a company can learn which segments are attractive and how consumers in specific segments perceive the company's products relative to competing products and brands.[66]

Micromarketing

The ultimate in target marketing is **micromarketing,** which frequently combines census and demographic data to identify clusters of households that share similar consumption patterns. The PRIZM market segmentation system is one example. Demographic descriptions of county, zip code, and census tract locations combined with information about area values, preferences, and purchasing habits enable companies to pinpoint likely or desired customers. Firms use micromarketing to increase the productivity of their marketing expenditures. Micromarketing enhances the effectiveness of marketing efforts by enabling marketers to:

Building Customer Equity

"Priceless" MasterCard

MasterCard, one of the world's most recognized and respected brands, is constantly striving to increase customer loyalty as well as the value of their customers. The company's customers include 20,000 financial institutions serving consumers in 210 countries. As part of their objective to serve consumers, principles of market segmentation are employed. These principles are recognized in extensions of their award-winning ad campaign aired worldwide entitled "Priceless." For example, the company recognized that only one-third of the $440 billion U.S. market has credit cards. In recognition of this attractive credit opportunity, MasterCard launched a major campaign using a variation of the "Priceless" theme coupled with education intended to assist U.S. Hispanic newcomers to employ credit responsibly. The question remains is whether editing a mainstream campaign for a niche market will be effective.

Exhibit 7–10   *Perceptual map of "fifteen" soda beverages*

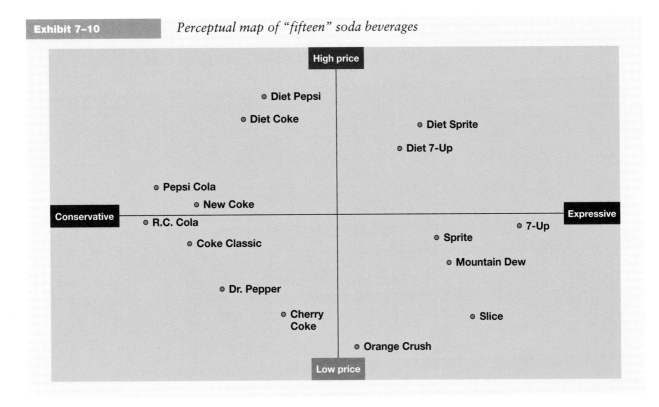

- Identify potential markets for direct selling through mail and telemarketing campaigns.
- Profile their customers by matching them to demographic and lifestyle clusters.
- Learn which areas offer the greatest potential in site selection for new stores or offices.
- Tailor their advertising themes and plan their media.[67]

Market Segmentation and Ethics

Targeting selected market segments can provide substantial benefits to both marketers and consumers: the marketer gains sales and the consumers receive the particular products and services they most want and value. Yet, segmentation practices can be so effective that they are fraught with opportunities for exploitation. Marketers must consider the ethical issues associated with some segmentation and targeting practices.

Advertising to Children

Advertising to children, a large and influential market segment, can stimulate demand for expensive and unnecessary products. Such advertising has been criticized for developing unrealistic expectations and demands for some youthful consumers who can least afford unnecessary expenditures. Demand for expensive athletic shoes or certain kinds of jackets or jewelry is easily fostered. Further, very young children sometimes have difficulty differentiating between program content and commercial messages.

Reaching children, whose influence and discretionary-funds growth exceeds inflation, is big business. However, some of the member countries of the European Union believe that overtly selling to children via television advertising is unethical. As an example, the British Independent Television Commission states that ads targeting children must not:

- Take advantage of their natural credulity.
- Lead them to believe they will be inferior if they do not have the advertised product.

- Harm them.
- Force them to pester their parents.

The same concerns hold in the United States for young consumers. The results from congressional legislation and government restrictions will place tight reins on the ability of firms to collect information from children via the Internet. In particular, the Children's Online Privacy Protection rules are in response to parental concerns and Federal Trade Commission study regarding the susceptibility of children to marketing tactics, predominantly those associated with interactive communications available on the Internet.[68]

Harmful Products

Marketing harmful products, such as cigarettes and alcohol, to young people raises important ethical issues. Some brands of cigarettes, such as Virginia Slims, are positioned to attract young women. Models in cigarette and beer ads are youthful, active, and attractive individuals. Messages for these products often emphasize the social acceptability of smoking and drinking, minimizing the impact of package warnings regarding the negative effects of their use.

Privacy Issues

As marketers are increasingly able to target precise consumer segments, concerns about privacy arise. Consumer purchase histories, credit histories, and telephone numbers can be combined for use in developing and targeting direct marketing campaigns. Care must be exercised in the use of this information.

Product Proliferation

Over 30 food products are introduced every day, or 25,000-plus per year in packaged goods, including food, beverages, health and beauty aids, household products, and pet products. Is this ever-increasing proliferation needed? The continuing segmentation of markets and products to serve those products seems endless. Consumers are often bewildered by the number of choice alternatives.[69]

Some researchers and practitioners are now arguing for a plan labeled the "Efficient Consumer Response." One pillar of this grocery-industry recommendation is **efficient assortment.** While product issues are addressed in the three chapters that follow, keep in mind that the practice of developing finer and finer product distinctions designed in part to appeal to more-specific market segments has been questioned from both the perspective of improving consumer decision making and retailer performance. In fact, a number of studies have shown that the number of brands and brand sizes (i.e., stock-keeping units) can be reduced without affecting sales or consumers' perceptions of variety. In addition to simplifying decisions for consumers, cutbacks in category SKUs allow the retailer to reduce the occurrence of out-of-stocks, to cut back on stacking frequency, and to lower warehouse costs. For example, one summary of industry research reported a study in which the number of alternatives of cat-box filler was reduced from 26 to 16. There were no effects on category sales, but savings in logistics costs increased operating profit 87 percent.[70]

Summary

1. **Define and explain market segmentation, target markets, and product differentiation and positioning.** Market segmentation is used when consumer groups (segments) share needs or preferences that differ from other segments. Market segmentation strategies attempt to take advantage of these differences and to meet each segment's demands. The segments served by firms are often called *target markets.*

    Product differentiation exists when customers perceive that a firm's product offerings differ from those of competing firms on any physical or nonphysical attribute. Positioning a product within a market is the process of exercising a differentiation strategy to convince consumers that the product has unique desirable characteristics.

2. **Understand the criteria used for evaluating the likely success of a segmentation strategy.** Five criteria are relevant in the design of a market segmentation strategy. Measurability refers to the extent to which the size and purchasing power of segments can be defined. Accessibility is the degree to which firms can efficiently reach intended target segments. Substantialness addresses the size of the target segment and its potential sales and profits. Durability refers to a persistence—the extent to which segments will persist over time as good business opportunities. Differential responsiveness is the degree to which market segments differ in their response to varying marketing mix combinations.

3. **Know the role of market segmentation in the development of marketing strategies and programs.** Market segmentation can be useful for both new and mature products or services. New products can be targeted to segments promising opportunities for introduction and growth. Mature brands can be repositioned, extended, or marketed to appeal to specific segments. An appropriate market segmentation strategy can help marketers focus on growth and expansion opportunities in an increasingly competitive marketplace.

4. **Describe the issues involved in product and brand positioning.** After determining the segmentation strategy, the marketer must take care in selecting the appropriate segments and positioning the firm's brands for those segments. Positioning refers to consumers' perceptions of the particular product or brand in relation to its competitors. Overall, the firm must identify the existing competitive products and brands within a market. It then must assess which attributes determine product preferences for the brands in that market. An examination of the fit between existing preferences and beliefs, ideal preferences, and brand capabilities will assist the firm either in positioning a new brand or in repositioning an already available brand.

5. **Understand the alternative bases for segmenting consumer and business-to-business markets.** Variables used to develop segmentation schemes may be either user- or behavior-based, and they may apply in either consumer or business-to-business marketing situations. User-related characteristics include demographic and psychographic variables for consumers, and customer size and geographic location for business-to-business applications. Behavior-related characteristics include benefits desired and extent of usage for consumers, and product application for business-to-business markets.

6. **Evaluate alternative approaches for pursuing segmentation strategies.** Segmentation strategies are of three types: undifferentiated, differentiated, and concentrated. An undifferentiated strategy involves the use of only one combination of marketing mix variables to meet the demands of the entire market. This strategy is appropriate if consumers are insensitive to product variations, if the competition is light, or if the product itself cannot be easily varied.

    A differentiated strategy involves the use of different marketing mix combinations to meet all or many of the segments constituting a market. A concentrated strategy aims to achieve a large share in just one or a few segments.

    In practice, many firms evolve from using an undifferentiated or concentrated strategy to adopting a differentiated approach, either as the firm can produce variations of the product or as the product develops beyond its introductory stage. An alternative approach, countersegmentation, combines market segments to provide consumers lower-priced products with fewer product variations.

Understanding Marketing Terms and Concepts

Thinking About Marketing

1. What is market segmentation, and how does it differ from product differentiation?

2. How might a marketer attempt to differentiate a product from competing products?

3. What are the criteria for segmenting a market, and what is meant by each one? Contrast differential responsiveness with segment accessibility.

4. Describe the different bases for segmentation. In doing so, explain the differences between user-related and behavior-related characteristics. How does PRIZM, described in Case 7–1, make use of these bases?

5. What bases might be used to define segments for these products: cassette recorders, hand calculators, personal computers, and public universities?

6. What is benefit segmentation? How does demographic segmentation differ from psychographic segmentation?

7. Define the different segmentation strategies. Compare and contrast each strategy with the others, and explain the conditions under which each may be appropriate.

8. What implications does the majority fallacy hypothesis have for the pursuit of a concentrated segmentation strategy?

9. How might Fingerhut use its databases to strengthen its marketing efforts?

10. Why is the practice of market segmentation and targeting now more important than ever?

Applying Marketing Skills

1. Compare the audiences of *Time* and *Rolling Stone* magazines. How does advertising in these magazines relate to market segmentation?

2. A large U.S. manufacturer of heavy-duty carpet for use in office buildings is considering expanding its marketing efforts to include European countries. The company has segmented its marketing efforts geographically and by company size. What market segmentation decisions does the company face as it expands its efforts to include both Eastern and Western European countries?

3. Air Canada (Canada's national airline) has recently introduced a new level of service (Tango), which is a full-fledged airline catering to more economy-minded passengers seeking no-frills service (an alternative to its service-based core brand). It also operates Air Canada Jazz (short haul routes) and Air Canada Jetz (charter service for groups such as sports teams and corporate clients). How likely can one company effectively appeal to a mass market and a more narrowly defined market at the same time?

Using the www in Marketing

Activity One
This chapter's opening discussed the VALS Web site (http://www.sric-bi.com). Select the Values and Lifestyles Program, and then at the bottom of the page click on "Find your own VALS-type now."

1. What demographic descriptors are used to define the VALS segments?
2. Comment on the number and nature of the agree–disagree attitude statements? Do your responses reflect stable or temporary opinions about yourself? Were you surprised by your own VALS categorization? How do your own values and lifestyles compare with others?
3. What other information must companies have before this segmentation scheme is useful in a practical sense?

Activity Two
Many e-commerce companies are now using heavy advertising to market their online services. Consider the Barnes and Noble site: http://www.barnesandnoble.com.

1. What aspects of this site are designed to develop a "loyal" segment?
2. How does Barnes and Noble compete with Amazon.com?
3. What behavioral segmentation characteristics of online book buyers would be helpful in the design of marketing strategy?

Making Marketing Decisions
Case 7-1 PRIZM by Claritas: You Are Where You Live

For the past two decades, the Alexandria, Virginia–based company Claritas Inc.'s geodemographic segmentation product, PRIZM (potential rating index by zip market), has been one of the most highly used tools to identify consumers. PRIZM is a micromarketing tool that categorizes consumers into lifestyle segments. The basic notion behind PRIZM is that "birds of a feather flock together"; that is, people who live together often purchase the same types of items. The original designer of the PRIZM database, Jonathan Robbin, categorized U.S. Census Bureau data in zip codes and analyzed each for social rank, mobility, ethnicity, family life cycle, and housing. These data are supplemented by market research surveys and other statistics obtained from the A. C. Nielsen Co. and 1,600 municipal and regional agencies. Currently, PRIZM also segments consumers by block tracts and zip-plus-four. The newest version of the PRIZM software consists of 62 consumer segments. This growing number of consumer segments is an indication of the increasing economic and ethnic complexity within consumer markets.

The 62 clusters are organized into 15 standard social groups, indicated by the degree of urbanization, from the rural countryside to urban high-rises. The 15 groups cover the range of affluence, from "rural-landed gentry" to "urban cores." Survey Sampling, Inc., adds PRIZM codes to their random telephone samples to add lifestyle information such as interests, hobbies, education, and spending patterns. By identifying the neighborhood types where existing customers are located, accurate predictions can be made where prospective customers are located. This information can then be used in designing direct-mail campaigns, media planning, site analysis, and product positioning.

Users of PRIZM include restaurant chains, banks, and stores in search of the best locations for new outlets. For example, Premier Bank in Baton Rouge, Louisiana, merges PRIZM with its internal database to find neighborhoods with households that match the traits of its best customers. Additionally, direct marketers develop target mailings based on information provided by PRIZM. Finally, advertising agencies explore the PRIZM database for insights concerning consumers. As an example, Hyundai, the Korean auto manufacturer, uses PRIZM to target American consumers. It identified several promising clusters including "Kids and Cul-de-Sacs"—upscale suburban families (median household income $68,900) and "Bohemian Mix"—professional aged 25 to 44 (median incomes of $38,500). Rather than blanket cites, Hyundai selects zip areas and sends test-drive incentives. The marketing effort increased sales and reduced by 50 percent the cost per vehicle sold.

Having successfully developed the original PRIZM software, Claritas Inc. has recently introduced a segmentation system that can accurately profile a market's workday population as well as illustrate the difference between the area's daytime and nighttime demographics. This segmentation product, Workplace PRIZM, provides marketers with valuable information concerning the daytime demographics of an area. Therefore, companies can evaluate whether their products and services are needed for the daytime population.

The development of the Workplace PRIZM software was based on the original PRIZM residential tracts. Workplace PRIZM weights the original tracts by the percentage of residents commuting to specific employment tracts. These newly developed workday tracts are often quite different than the original population tracts.

Overall, the PRIZM system is based on the theory that by knowing the location, education level, traits, and habits of each cluster in a community, retailers and shopping-center marketers can market to specific clusters. Therefore, the use of PRIZM software as a consumer segmentation tool should provide marketers with valuable information concerning consumers.

Questions

1. Why is PRIZM software an effective marketing tool?

2. How does the PRIZM approach satisfy the criteria for effective segmentation?

3. How might cultural changes involving the Hispanic and Asian populations affect the effectiveness of PRIZM?

4. What are the advantages of the newly developed Workplace PRIZM software?

Case 7-2 *Marriott International: "Suite Deals"*

Marriott International is a worldwide operator and franchiser of hotels and senior living communities. Marriott has subsidiaries in 59 countries and regions. The lodging business includes over 2,100 operated or franchised properties. Marriott, which operates nine chains of hotels and suites, focuses its hotel marketing efforts on two groups: middle-class families and business travelers. Unlike other hotel competitors, Marriott uses separate brand names on their different lines. Examples of their product mix, approximate prices, and the intended target market for each are as follows:

Fairfield Inn—$45–$65; the economizing business and leisure markets.

SpringHill Suites—$75–$95; members of business and leisure markets looking for more space, amenities.

Courtyard—$75–$105; the "road warrior."

Residence Inn—$85–$110; travelers seeking residential-style hotel.

Marriott Hotels/Resorts—$90–$235; members of the discerning business and leisure markets.

Ritz-Carlton—$175–$300; senior executives and others looking for luxury.

Recently, Marriott restructured its management to ensure more-effective coordination of their complex operations. Specifically, three business categories were established, each headed by a senior VP: full service (e.g., Marriott Hotels), extended stay (e.g., Residence Inns), and select services (e.g., Courtyard, SpringHill). This organization allows shared resources for such activities as strategic development, market analyses, and the Rewards loyalty program. Category teams structured around these three groupings should enhance decision making and implementation of marketing changes and strategies.

The SpringHill introduction is one of Marriott's most recent product-line additions.

Questions

1. What are benefits and drawbacks from such a diverse offering of hotel chains?

2. What segments remain untapped?

3. To what extent does price sensitivity affect choice of alternatives within the line of hotels and suites?

4. What are the bases that could be used to segment the market for all types of hotel patrons?

8

Product and Service Concepts

After studying this chapter, you should be able to:

1 Understand the differences between goods and services.

2 Differentiate between consumer and business products, and discuss the different types of each.

3 Recognize that marketers need to appreciate the perspective of the consumer.

4 Define and discuss the importance of product quality, product design, branding, packaging, and customer service.

5 Explain how the different product components need to be integrated to meet the needs of customers.

www.fritolay.com

Frito-Lay is worldwide marketer of snack foods. The history of Frito-Lay is especially interesting. Elmer Doolin started The Frito Company in 1932 based on the new product Frito Corn Chips. Herman W. Lay founded the H. W. Lay & Company in 1938 to market potato chips. In 1945, The Frito Company granted H. W. Lay & Company an exclusive franchise to manufacture and distribute Frito Corn Chips in the Southeast. The two companies developed a close affiliation and merged in 1961 to form Frito-Lay, Inc. In 1965, Frito-Lay, Inc., and the Pepsi-Cola Company merged into PepsiCo. Frito-Lay remains a separate operating division of PepsiCo, producing almost 60 percent of the parent company's profits.

Today, Frito-Lay has sales in excess of $9.6 billion a year. The company has more than 100 product lines with many well-known brands such as Lay's, Ruffles, Doritos, Tostitos, Fritos, Rold Gold, and Sun Chips. Nine of Frito-Lay's brands are among the 10 best-selling snack food brands in major U.S. supermarkets. Lay's and Ruffles potato chips and Doritos tortilla chips are the leaders in the potato chip and salty snack food categories. Doritos, Chee-tos, Lay's, 3D's, and Ruffles are global brands.

Frito-Lay continually adapts to changes in the marketing environment. One example is the introduction of its "Lay's Tastes of America" promotion. It is introducing Lay's Potato Chips in flavors that celebrate regional tastes across the United States, such as San Antonio Salsa, New Orleans Cajun Gumbo, Coney Island Hot Dog, and Wisconsin Cheddar. Another example is offering Go Snacks. These are snack foods in mini shapes and special packaging to fit the need for convenience in the active, fast-paced, go-anywhere lifestyles of today's consumers. Doritos Mini 3D's, Chee-tos Asteroids, and Fritos Hoops were introduced in small, sturdy canisters that fit perfectly into a car's cupholder. Additional Go Snacks will be added in the future.

Frito-Lay is noted for the quality of products it provides to consumers and the exceptional service it gives to retail customers. The company's basic business philosophy is: "Make the best product possible; sell it at a fair profit; and make service a fundamental part of doing business." This philosophy guided The Frito Company and H. W. Lay & Company from the beginning and continues to drive Frito-Lay today.

The Frito-Lay example illustrates the importance of product and service concepts to a company's success. Frito-Lay meets the needs of different customer segments by offering many different brands in different shapes, flavors, and packages. Product quality and customer service have been emphasized throughout the company's history. We examine these key product and service concepts by defining different types of products and then discussing the critical components of a product: quality, design, branding, packaging, and customer service.

What Is a Product?

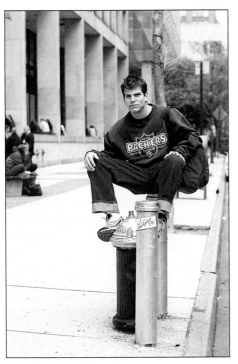

Consumers purchase products to receive benefits. This sweatshirt provides the benefits of warm and stylish clothing to the customer.

The term **product** is defined as an idea, a physical entity (a good), a service, or any combination of the three that is an element of exchange to satisfy individual or business objectives.[1] From a marketing viewpoint, the key element of this definition is "to satisfy individual or business objectives." Individuals and businesses purchase products to solve problems or satisfy needs. That is, products provide benefits. Successful marketers focus on the benefits products supply to customers.

Let's examine the term *product* from a consumer's viewpoint. Say a consumer bought some product—maybe purchased a notebook for a course, or bought lunch at a local restaurant, or perhaps picked up some dry cleaning. Why did the consumer make each purchase? The major reason is the consumer wanted the benefits offered by the purchased product. The notebook, the lunch, and the dry cleaning provided benefits—in the ability to take notes in class, to satisfy hunger, and/or to have clean clothing. The specific features of each product (the type of notebook, specific restaurant and meal, characteristics of the dry cleaner) are important only insofar as they are translated into the specific benefits the consumer wants.

While reading these three chapters in Part Four, it is critical to think about products from a customer's viewpoint. Customers purchase products for their benefits, and astute marketers emphasize product benefits in their marketing efforts. For example, focusing on customer benefits is the basic marketing philosophy of Hewlett-Packard: "Many companies build a product and look for a market. We listen to our customers, research their needs, and build products that provide solutions for their problems."[2]

Types of Products

Marketers often classify products into specific categories. We focus on the categories of goods and services, and consumer and business products. We then discuss different types of consumer and business products.

Goods and Services

Goods are usually defined as physical products such as cars, golf clubs, soft drinks, or other concrete entities. **Services,** in contrast, are normally defined as nonphysical products such as a haircut, a football game, or a doctor's diagnosis.

Products, however, do not necessarily fall into one category or the other. Almost all products incorporate some characteristics of both goods and services. "Using Technology: Integrating Goods and Services" illustrates a successful example of combining goods and services.

A useful way to view goods and services is on a continuum, as presented in Exhibit 8–1. Where a product lies on this continuum affects how it should be marketed, because goods and services possess several unique characteristics. The more a product lies toward the services end of the continuum, the more it is intangible, perishable, inseparable, and variable in quality. The more a product lies toward the goods end, the more it is tangible, storable, separable from the producer, and standardized in quality.

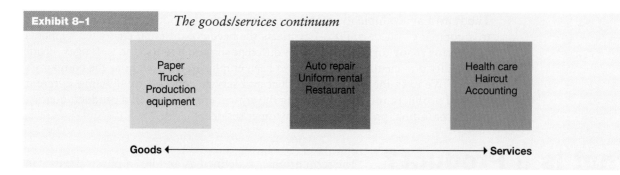

Exhibit 8–1   *The goods/services continuum*

Paper
Truck
Production
equipment

Auto repair
Uniform rental
Restaurant

Health care
Haircut
Accounting

Goods ←————————————————————————→ Services

The purchase of a soft drink such as Pepsi-Cola in a restaurant can illustrate these differences. The soft drink is a good. It is tangible; it can be touched when it is served from the can. The restaurant can stockpile cases of Pepsi-Cola to serve when needed. The companies manufacturing and distributing the Pepsi are separated from the customer when the product is consumed. Finally, the quality of the Pepsi is expected to be the same from can to can, because the manufacturing process is standardized.

The service provided by the restaurant, however, is different. The activity of serving the Pepsi is not tangible; it cannot be touched. The restaurant cannot store the service provided by a waiter; if there are no customers, the potential service of a waiter is wasted. The waiter's service cannot be separated from the restaurant, and it is performed in the presence of the customer. Consumers consider the waiter and the restaurant to be the same. And finally, the service provided by the same waiter to different customers, or by different waiters, is likely to vary in quality.

GOODS AND SERVICES STRATEGIES   Although the tangibility, perishability, separability, and variability characteristics differentiate many products and services, new technological developments are blurring some of these differences. Some services have characteristics similar to those of goods. For example, online databases are services, but the information provided is tangible, it can be stored until a customer needs it, the provider of the service is separated from the user, and there is little service variability.

In addition, the service content of many goods is a key component of the value received by customers. Take computers as an example. The hardware is clearly a good, but much of the value provided to customers is through the services accompanying the good, such as customizing a system to meet the specific needs of a customer. These services might include installation, software modifications, training, and ongoing support.

Using Technology

Integrating goods and services

Copart is in the auto-salvage business and has a 30 percent share of the market for wrecked vehicles. The business works this way. Insurers consider a wrecked vehicle to be a total loss and pay the car owner. Copart auctions the wrecks to auto dismantlers, rebuilders, or used-car dealers. The insurer gets the proceeds minus a fee or percentage that is paid to Copart. In this situation, wrecked vehicles are the goods being sold and Copart is providing various services to insurance companies.

One of the reasons for Copart's success has been its use of the Internet to provide additional services to insurance

companies and wrecked vehicle buyers. Insurers can track the sales of their wrecked vehicles from a real-time, online database. Copart has also added online bidding to its physical bidding process. Online bidding has increased sales dramatically. Even the physical auctions typically include one or more online bids. The auctions now incorporate more bidders and more bids. These Internet services have made it possible to sell wrecked vehicles quicker and at higher prices than in the past. The insurance companies like this and so does Copart, with sales up 31 percent and profits up 40 percent in the past year.

Exhibit 8–2	*Characteristics and strategies for services*	
Service Characteristic	**Service Strategy**	**Examples**
Intangible	Associate the service with something tangible.	General Motors' Mr. Goodwrench; models of buildings prepared by architects.
Perishable	Manage demand to utilize supply.	Reduced prices for afternoon movies; lower rates for off-season accommodations at tourist attractions.
Inseparable	Capitalize on advantages of person providing the service.	Motivating service providers through compensation and recognition programs; continual training of all customer contact personnel.
Variable	Standardize service delivery as much as possible.	Use of technologies, such as automated teller machines, to provide service; implementation of quality-improvement programs.

As suggested earlier, it is important to think about products from a customer's viewpoint. Customers are making purchases to satisfy needs or solve problems. Increasingly, this often requires marketers to offer products that represent a mix of goods and services. It is still important, however, to understand the typical differences between goods and services and how these characteristics lead to different strategies for the goods and service components of a product offering. We discuss these differences below and present specific strategies for services in Exhibit 8–2.

TANGIBILITY   One of the most interesting differences between goods and services relates to tangibility. Because goods are tangible, marketing strategies typically emphasize the intangible benefits derived from consuming the product. For example, many ads for Coke convey an intangible excitement associated with drinking the product. On the other hand, because services are intangible, marketers often try to associate them with something tangible. This approach is evident in the insurance industry: Consider the "good hands" of Allstate, the "rock" of Prudential, the "cavalry" of Kemper, and the "good neighbor" of State Farm.

PERISHABILITY   Perishability also has an important effect on the marketing of services. Services cannot normally be stored, so marketers of services use different strategies to manage demand. For example, higher prices are charged when demand is expected to be high, but prices are lowered when demand is expected to be low.

Airlines offer a good example of this type of strategy. Passengers flying to the same destination often pay very different fares, depending on flight schedule and time of booking. During holiday periods, fewer discounted tickets are available. Various types of discounted tickets are offered at other times to fill planes that would otherwise fly with empty seats not purchased at regular fares. The earlier customers make reservations and pay for tickets, the lower the fare. Low fares also go to those on standby, that is, customers willing to wait for an available seat after all reserved passengers are boarded. Airlines use standby to generate revenue for seats that have not been purchased in advance and would otherwise go to waste.

SEPARABILITY   Goods like tennis racquets, tuxedos, or tomatoes can be produced, stored, and then sold to customers. Services, on the other hand, are typically produced and consumed simultaneously. For example, a dentist produces dental service at the same time the patient consumes it. The customer, then, tends to see the person and the

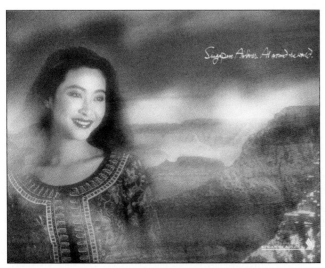

The production and consumption of services are often inseparable. Singapore Airlines emphasizes the importance of its flight attendants in delivering services to customers.

business providing the service as one and the same. Thus, bank tellers are the bank, nurses or billing personnel are the hospital, and salespeople are the firm.

The close relationships between the production and consumption of services and between the person and the business providing the service have significant implications. Whether a business provides goods or services, it must be concerned with the management of service employees. Every employee who has contact with customers is part of the firm's service offering. Therefore, effective management and training of employees who see customers is critical for providing quality services. Training of executive-level managers is not enough; service employees at all levels need the appropriate attention if they are to "be" the company.

VARIABILITY   The difficulty of standardizing services, especially when they are delivered by people, has important implications for marketers. Even well-trained and professional service providers have bad days. Therefore, there will always be some variability in service quality. Even so, leading firms analyze their service processes and develop standards and procedures to minimize variability to the extent they can.

Consumer and Business Products

Another important distinction is between consumer and business products. This categorization is based on the way a product is used, and not on the specific characteristics of the product. **Consumer products** are those purchased by consumers for their own personal use. **Business products** are those purchased by a firm or organization for its own use. Thus, the same product could be classified differently depending on the purchase and use. For example, if Elena buys a pencil to use at home, it is considered a consumer product. If Elena's employer purchases the same pencil for her to use at work, it is considered a business product.

We have seen that the buying behaviors of consumers and businesses differ in important ways. These differences motivate different strategies, depending on whether a product is marketed to consumers or businesses. Take Singing Machine as an example. The company began by trying to market $2,000 karaoke machines to nightclubs. After limited success, it switched its focus to home-karaoke machines. These machines are connected to TV sets and play special compact discs that allow users to read lyrics on the screen. A marketing tie-in with MTV, distribution through retailers like Best Buy and Target, and a price under $300 have made the product a success. Sales grew 83 percent annually for three years, reaching $59 million in 2001.[3] The move from a business to a consumer product made a major difference for Singing Machine. There are also different types of consumer products and business products, as Exhibit 8–3 demonstrates.

TYPES OF CONSUMER PRODUCTS   There are millions of consumer products, and they can be classified in a number of ways. One especially useful approach is to classify products according to how consumers shop. Such an approach is valuable because it suggests that specific marketing strategies are relevant for a particular consumer-product category. Relevant shopping behavior by category is described in Exhibit 8–4. Of course, the same product can be classified differently by different buyers.

Convenience products are items consumers do not want to spend much time shopping for. Buyers of convenience products typically want to make a quick purchase at the most convenient location. Although they may prefer a specific brand, they will buy something else if that brand is not available. Convenience products are normally low-priced, often-purchased goods. They might range from staples (toothpaste, bread, or mustard), to products bought on impulse (chewing gum, magazines, or candy bars) or in an emergency (umbrellas, antifreeze, or snow shovels).

A key to marketing convenience products is to obtain extensive distribution. Marketers should make such products available at all convenient locations so con-

Exhibit 8–3   *Consumer and business products*

sumers will be able to find the brand they want and not have to switch to another. Widespread distribution is especially important for products bought on impulse, because consumers purchase them only when they see them during their shopping trip. Distribution is also important for products bought in emergencies.

Soft drinks are convenience products for most consumers. Although consumers might prefer Coke over Pepsi or vice versa, they tend to switch to the other if the preferred brand is not available. Coke and Pepsi marketing strategies are designed to ensure that their brands are readily available. Thus, the brands are marketed through all types of retail outlets, restaurants, vending machines, and now at the checkout counters in many grocery stores.

Shopping products, in contrast, are items consumers are willing to spend time shopping for. When consumers perceive all the product alternatives as similar, they often shop around for the best price. A family might shop at several electronics stores, for example, to get the best deal on a television. For other shopping products, consumers might see alternatives as differing in important ways and shop for the one that best meets their needs. A family might shop at Honda, Toyota, and Ford dealerships to determine which minivan suits them, as well as to obtain the best price.

Consumers are willing to spend time shopping if the purchase is important to them, particularly if the product is expensive. For marketers, the key strategic implication is to facilitate the shopping process. Typically, a shopping product needs to be readily available, but not as widely available as a convenience product. Distribution outlets for a shopping product should provide extensive information to help consumers in the purchase decision. This may be accomplished with knowledgeable salespeople and informative communications and promotional materials. Salespeople and printed brochures for car models at dealerships illustrate typical marketing approaches for shopping products. Locating several car dealers in the same general area also would help to facilitate the shopping process.

Exhibit 8–4

Types of consumer products

	Prefer Specific Brand	Willing to Shop
Convenience	May	No
Shopping	No	Yes
Specialty	Yes	Yes

The Internet has, however, changed the purchasing process for shopping goods. Consumers do not have to physically visit retail stores to get information about shopping goods. They can now "click" to many different sites to get needed information and then decide to make the purchase online or at a retail store. Consumers still spend time on shopping good purchases, but the Internet makes it possible for them to get more and better purchasing information in a convenient manner.

Specialty products are different yet, in that consumers both want to purchase a specific brand and are willing to look to find it. They are neither willing to switch brands, as they are for convenience products, nor shop to evaluate product alternatives, as for shopping products. They want one brand, and they will travel to buy it.

Marketers might limit distribution of specialty products to exclusive outlets and can typically charge high prices. Such marketing efforts should focus on maintaining the loyalty of customers and the image of the product. Certainly, most marketers would enjoy selling a brand considered a specialty product. These are rare circumstances, however, for few consumers are committed to only one brand in many product categories.

TYPES OF BUSINESS PRODUCTS Classifying business products is difficult because a vast number of different products are used by for-profit firms, nonprofit organizations, and government agencies. Our categorization groups products according to the way they are used in the operation of a business (see Exhibit 8–3).

Capital products are expensive items used in business operations but do not become part of any type of finished product. Because they are used over long periods of time, their cost is normally depreciated or spread over some useful life rather than expensed completely in the year of purchase. Capital products range from physical facilities such as manufacturing plants, office buildings, and major equipment, to accessory equipment such as desks, copy machines, fax machines, or forklifts.

The purchasing process for capital products may be long and involve many individuals. Marketers of capital products emphasize personal selling as the major communication tool. Prices are often negotiated, and sometimes businesses decide to rent or lease capital products rather than buy them outright.

Production products become part of some finished product. Raw materials, such as coal, oil, or farm products, are the basic type of production product. Component materials and component parts are also production products. Component materials are products that require further processing to be included in the finished product. Examples are steel, paper, and textiles. Component parts are fabricated for the finished product. They may require some minor processing or be used as is in the finished product. Thermostats and disk drives are examples.

The purchasing process for production products is extensive but typically less involved than for capital products. Businesses want to receive quality production products when they are needed, otherwise the production process may be interrupted. Marketers of production products therefore must emphasize both product quality and reliability in meeting delivery schedules. A buyer does not necessarily select the supplier with the lowest initial price. Increasingly, the long-run cost of doing business with suppliers is more important to firms than the short-run price of the product.

Operational products are used in a firm's activities but do not become part of any type of finished product. Maintenance, repair, and operating supplies are considered operational products. These include lightbulbs, cleaning materials, repair parts, and office supplies. Also included are services such as accounting, engineering, and advertising that are purchased from outside vendors rather than provided from within the business.

Capital products are expensive items used in business operations. Komatsu markets construction equipment to business customers.

The purchasing process for many operational products is the least extensive for any business product. After an initial purchase, and assuming the business is satisfied, subsequent purchases may be straight rebuys; that is, the buyer merely places an additional order with the same supplier. Thus, it is important for a seller to get the initial order and to ensure that the buyer is satisfied with all aspects of the purchase. If this happens, it is almost impossible for a competitor to get its foot in the door.

Product Components

We have said that consumers purchase products to satisfy needs. Another way to say this is that people really want a "bundle" of benefits when they purchase a product, and different consumers are likely to want different benefits from the same type of product. For example, some consumers purchase Rollerblade skates for fun, others as a way to increase health and fitness, and others because of the excitement involved with in-line roller skating.

To provide the benefits consumers want, marketers need to integrate the components that make up a product effectively. These consist of the product and customer service features illustrated in Exhibit 8–5. Product features include quality, design, branding, and packaging. Customer service encompasses various purchase and usage services. Different blends of product features and customer service provide different benefit bundles.

Credit cards offer a good example. Although all credit cards provide a basic benefit (credit), they offer different mixes of benefits to appeal to specific consumers. Credit cards differ in annual fees, rewards for use of the card, payment terms, design of the card, brand name, and services provided. All these components interact to produce the product, or the benefits, consumers purchase. For example, American Express launched a new credit card, the Blue card. In addition to offering typical credit card features and benefits, the Blue card offers users access to the American Express Online Wallet. This new feature provides customers with the benefit of faster and more-secure online purchases. Consumers concerned about Internet security are likely to value the benefit bundle offered by the Blue card.[4]

Some firms are practicing **mass customization** by offering each customer a customized bundle of benefits. New information and communications technologies are making this possible. For example, many Internet sites allow each individual user to select specific types of information to be continuously downloaded and displayed on the user's screen. Each customer can select the stock prices to be reported, the cities for weather forecasts, the types of sports information desired, and other specific types of information to be communicated. Another example is the marketing by Levi's of custom-fitted jeans to women. As technology develops, more opportunities to increase customer value through mass customization will become available.

Exhibit 8–5

Products components

Product components

Product features
- Quality
- Design
- Branding
- Packaging

Customer service
- Purchase services
- Usage services

Quality

As a product component, product quality represents how well a product does what it is supposed to do as defined by the customer. Rational, a German manufacturer of computer-controlled ovens that combine convection and steam heat, recognizes the importance of defining product quality from the customer's viewpoint. Everywhere in the plant, signs say, "Gut genug? Der Kunde entscheidet" ("Good enough? The customer will decide").[5]

Improving product quality as consumers define it can be an effective way to increase product sales. For example, most consumers probably consider a quality turtleneck to be one that looks good, fits well,

Speaking from Experience

Doris K. Christopher
President and Founder
The Pampered Chef

"Satisfying the needs of customers is the key to our success. The philosophy of direct selling is based on one-on-one interacton with customers. Through this direct interaction, customers provide feedback directly to the company regarding product quality, design, and service. At the Pampered Chef we believe that our products should earn the right to be in your kitchen. We say 'This is a good product, now how can we make it better?' We've made our mark by listening to our customers, improving our products, and offering them at competitive prices."

Doris started The Pampered Chef as a direct seller of high-quality kitchen tools in her suburban-Chicago basement in 1980. Company sales now exceed $700 million with over 67,000 Kitchen Consultants working in the United States, Canada, Germany and the United Kingdom. Doris has served as the Chairperson of the Direct Selling Association, was named a regional winner of Ernst & Young's National Entrepreneur of the Year Award, and wrote *Come to the Table: A Celebration of Family Life.* She earned a B.S. in Home Economics from the University of Illinois at Urbana-Champaign.

Thinking Critically

You have decided to open a pizza restaurant that would provide customers with the highest-quality pizzas.

- What are the characteristics of a quality pizza as defined by most customers?

- How do you evaluate the quality of the pizzas offered by the existing pizza restaurants (Pizza Hut, Godfather's, Papa John's, etc.)?

- What do you plan to do to make your pizzas higher quality than what competitors offer?

and lasts a long time. JCPenney found that its turtlenecks were of lower quality than those offered by competitors like The Gap, Lands' End, and L.L. Bean. Penney's turtlenecks lost their fit and did not last very long, because they shrank and puckered at the seams upon washing. To improve the product's quality, the Penney company stiffened its specifications for fabric, fit, and construction, and added Spandex to the neck and cuffs. By introducing higher-quality turtlenecks and reducing the price to provide more value, the company saw sales triple in a year.[6]

Consumers define quality of turtlenecks in terms of looks, fit, and durability. In other markets, consumers define quality differently. In the prestige fountain pen market, for example, consumers consider utility along with glamour and distinction. Cross, Waterman, Montblanc, and Parker compete in this market. All these products offer similar utility, but each provides prestige differently. One maker may emphasize glamour, citing the famous people who use its pens; another may emphasize distinction, pointing to the historical documents signed with its pens. Consumers have responded to these pitches about quality by using as many as eight different pens during a year, with specific pens to match wardrobes or to sign different sorts of documents.[7]

Sometimes, seemingly minor differences between products lead consumers to perceive significant differences in quality. Avonex and Betaseron, for example, are competing multiple-sclerosis drugs. The drugs are nearly identical, but Avonex is injected only once a week compared with every other day for Betaseron. The fewer injections for Avonex make the drug more convenient to use and reduce the number of purple blotches produced at the site of each injection. Many consumers perceive this usage difference to represent a substantial improvement in quality even though the drugs are similar otherwise. This quality difference has made Avonex the market leader.[8]

Marketers, however, cannot always be sure consumers have accurate perceptions of the quality of their products. This has been an especially difficult problem for the U.S. automobile industry. Objective assessments of quality by trade observers or groups such as J. D. Power and *Consumer Reports* have consistently shown improvements in the quality of American cars. For example, *Consumer Reports* found that the average number of problems per 100 new vehicles built by General Motors, Ford, and Chrysler dropped from 105 in 1980 to 23 in 2002.[9] Yet, many consumers are not aware of these quality improvements. They typically base purchase decisions on personal perceptions of quality, not necessarily objective evaluations, and these perceptions have lagged reality.

Quality is what consumers consider it to be. Marketers should ensure that their products provide the desired level of quality, work to constantly improve this qual-

Product quality is defined by customers. Callaway emphasizes the quality of its drivers.

ity, and convey to consumers an accurate picture of the quality. These are difficult tasks, but they are essential for success in today's competitive marketplace.

Design

Product design includes the styling, aesthetics, and function of a product. How a product is designed affects how it works, how it feels, how easy it is to assemble and fix, and how easy it is to recycle.

Product design decisions can be pivotal in a product's success. Consider one example: the introduction by Reebok and Nike of basketball sneakers with inflatable air cushions for better ankle support. The Nike shoe required the wearer to carry a separate hand pump to inflate the shoe. The Reebok shoe design included a pump tucked neatly into the shoe's tongue. Reebok's Pump was successful; Nike had to drop its shoe from the market.[10]

Much of the current focus on product design is to improve the performance of a product and to reduce the cost of producing it. Boeing did this when it designed the fighter jet for the twenty-first century. The design was very innovative with an unusual modular wing, a front-mounted engine, and stealth capabilities. This design improved jet fighter performance, but it also significantly reduced production costs.[11]

Another emphasis in product design is to add more features but make it easier for customers to use the product. Whirlpool is trying to do this with kitchen appliances. One approach is to make the control panels for all appliances have a common look, feel, and function. Once customers learn how to use one Whirlpool appliance, it will be easy for them to use other Whirlpool appliances. Another approach is to simplify the control panels. Current microwave ovens have 75 separate functions. The plan is to increase the number of functions to 250 but to present them to users in layers so that users are presented the functions in small groups. Preliminary tests show that customers are able to access the 250 functions in less time and with 30 percent fewer errors.[12]

Product design is becoming increasingly important for all types of products, even low-cost ones. For example, Century Cuddle Tub & Huggy Bath is a baby bathtub. The company knew that it is difficult to bathe a newborn, since one hand has to hold the baby's head and the other the washcloth. So it designed a baby bathtub that consists of a simple hammock in the tub with a headrest to hold the baby's head securely. This leaves the parent's hands free to do the washing. The cost of the product is $19.99. M&M even polled consumers to determine the newest color for M&Ms. Purple won. As suggested by William Stumpf, a judge for the Industrial Design Excellence Awards, "Good design is now across all product lines, from computers to appliances."[13]

Product design is an important product component for both goods and services.

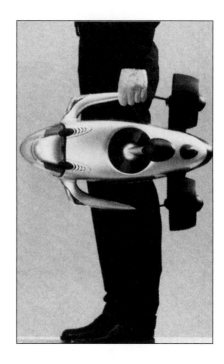

Branding

It is critical that a firm identifies its products to distinguish them from similar products offered by competitors. This is the **branding** process. Several key terms need defining for this discussion:

- **Brand**—A name, term, sign, symbol, design, or combination that a firm uses to identify its products and differentiate them from those of competitors.
- **Brand name**—The element of a brand that can be vocalized, such as IBM, Tide, Snickers, or Diet Coke.
- **Brand mark**—The element of a brand that cannot be vocalized, such as the MGM lion, the Buick symbol, or the Nike Swoosh.
- **Trademark**—A brand or part of a brand that is registered with the U.S. Patent and Trademark Office. This registration gives the owner exclusive rights to use the brand and may even preclude other firms from using brand names or marks that are similar.

The global marketplace and new technologies are adding to the complexity of protecting brand names and brand marks. For example, World Wrestling Federation Entertainment Inc. had been using wwf.com as its Internet address and "WWF" as its logo. However, the World Wildlife Fund had been using the "WWF" initials in its marketing materials and Internet address for many years. The "WWF" initials were generally understood to represent the World Wildlife Fund in many countries around the world. An initial court and an appeals court in the United Kingdom found this to be the case and ordered the World Wrestling Federation to remove the "WWF" from its Internet address and logo outside the United States.[14]

IMPORTANCE OF BRANDING   Branding is important to both consumers and marketers. From a consumer's viewpoint, branding facilitates buying. If there were no brands, consumers would have to evaluate the nonbranded products available every time they went shopping. They could never be sure they were purchasing the specific desired products and would have difficulty evaluating the quality of some. When selecting from among branded products, consumers can purchase specific ones and be reasonably certain of their quality. For example, one study found that 67 percent of consumers felt more confident buying familiar brands.[15]

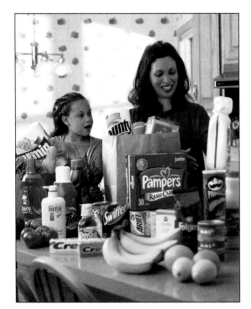

Building strong brands and protecting brand names and brand marks is critical for many firms. P&G presents many of its successful brands in this picture.

Branding also provides psychological benefits to consumers. Some buyers derive satisfaction from owning brands with images of prestige. These brands convey status. Examples are Rolex watches, Mercedes-Benz automobiles, and Waterford crystal.

From a marketer's viewpoint, branding has considerable value. A brand can be used to represent the benefits of a product to include those associated with specific product features and those relevant to the product purchase and use experience. This can make it easier to differentiate a company's product from competing offerings. Branding also facilitates and focuses a firm's marketing efforts.

BUILDING BRANDS Because brands are important to consumers and marketers, many firms focus considerable attention to building brands. The basic brand-building process is depicted in Exhibit 8–6.

To build a strong brand, marketers need to first determine the brand identity. A **brand identity** is the brand concept from the brand owner's viewpoint. It should be relatively simple and clearly understood by everyone in the company. All marketing communications should be designed to support and reinforce this brand identity. Examples of effective brand identities are profit-with-a-principle (Body Shop); thicker, creamier, and pricier than any other ice cream on the market (Häagen-Dazs); and low-cost watch of excellent Swiss quality with a stylish, fun, youthful, provocative, and joyful brand personality (Swatch).[16]

The second step in brand building typically focuses on generating brand awareness. **Brand awareness** is achieved when target consumers know about a brand and call it to mind when thinking about the product category. For example, Procter & Gamble has achieved brand awareness with Tide, which many consumers automatically recall when thinking about buying laundry detergent.

Brand awareness must then be translated into a **brand image,** or the impression that consumers have about a brand. Marketers should ensure that consumers have accurate ideas of the brand's advantages and positive impressions of it. P&G is successful if consumers perceive that Tide gets clothes cleaner than do competitive brands. Consumers' image of a brand should match the brand identity established by the company.

The generation of brand awareness and development of brand image culminates in a brand promise to potential customers. A **brand promise** represents the benefits customers should expect from purchasing and using a brand. So, customers should expect cleaner clothes if Tide is purchased. Advertising and other marketing communication tools are typically used to make consumers aware of the brand promise. If consumers desire the expected benefits, they are likely to purchase the brand.

If consumers receive the expected benefits offered by the brand promise, their **brand experience** has been good and they are likely to purchase the brand on a regular basis. For example, if customers get cleaner clothes from using Tide, some will normally purchase Tide when shopping for laundry detergent. Such buyers exhibit **brand loyalty.** The most brand-loyal customers will select Tide on almost every purchase opportunity.

The more brand-loyal customers for a brand and the more brand loyal these customers are, the higher the **brand equity,** or the value the brand has in the marketplace. Brand equity has a financial dimension, especially important in any merger or acquisition transaction. The financial value of P&G's Tide would be significant in any discussion of an acquisition price, for instance.

Exhibit 8–6	*Brand-building process*

Brand Identity → Brand awareness → Brand image → Brand promise → Brand experience → Brand loyalty → Brand equity

Brand equity also affects marketing efforts. The same marketing strategy and level of expenditures used for different brands are likely to have different results, depending on brand equity. Typically, marketing efforts built on an established positive brand awareness, image, and loyalty—or high brand equity—are more successful. Exhibit 8–7 presents examples of the world's most valuable brands.

Building strong brands is extremely important to many companies. The typical approach is to focus efforts on media advertising to generate brand awareness, to develop a desired brand image, and to get consumers to purchase the brand. This is important, but only part of the brand-building process. Research indicates that strong brands are built on the favorable experiences consumers have with a firm's products and services. Effective advertising can only drive consumers to an Internet site or retail store or to try a product or service. Brand loyalty and brand equity depend on the experiences consumers have once at the Internet site, retail store, or when the product or service is purchased and used.

T. Rowe Price is a mutual fund company that has focused on consistent financial performance for investors. The declining stock market in recent years led many mutual fund companies to increase advertising to stimulate growth. Not T. Rowe Price. The company actually cut its ad budget by 27 percent. Instead, it continued to focus on achieving consistent financial performance and providing customers with valuable information and services. A quarterly newsletter presents articles about different financial management topics that customers like, as circulation is up 30 percent in the past two years. The company also has an advisory services team that conducts personal telephone interviews with clients rather than have them complete and submit forms, as most competitors do. This attention to consistent financial performance and personalized customer service resulted in T. Rowe Price being at the top of a recent brand loyalty study of mutual fund companies.[17]

Doris Christopher, President and Founder, The Pampered Chef, discusses the brand-building process: "Building brands is important for many firms. In the direct-selling industry, to build a brand means to build a trusting relationship with customers. Customers will continue to buy products from companies with whom they have good experiences. The Pampered Chef believes in building brands through fulfilling promises. We make a promise to our customers that with every product we sell they will get the best quality product at the best price, with service that exceeds their expectations.

TYPES OF BRANDS   Marketers must decide early on whether to brand a product, and if so, which type of brand to use. **Generics** are products that are typically not branded. They are normally labeled instead by their generic name and may be of lower quality and cost less than branded competitors. Usually, plain black-and-white labels identify the product by its generic name, such as peas, aluminum foil, or tomato soup.

Exhibit 8–7	*The World's 10 Most Valuable Brands*	
RANK	**BRAND**	**2002 BRAND VALUE ($billions)**
1	COCA-COLA	69.6
2	MICROSOFT	64.1
3	IBM	51.2
4	GE	41.3
5	INTEL	30.9
6	NOKIA	30.0
7	DISNEY	29.3
8	McDONALD'S	26.4
9	MARLBORO	24.2
10	MERCEDES	21.0

In the pharmaceutical industry, generic products can have brand names and must meet the quality standards set by the Food and Drug Administration. Many doctors specify generic drugs in an effort to reduce the patient's costs. Indeed, pharmaceutical companies that once marketed only branded products are hopping on the generic bandwagon. Merck, for example, has established its West Point Pharma division to market generic pharmaceuticals for brands no longer protected by patents. It will continue to market its branded products through other divisions.

If a firm decides to brand its products, it can choose one of two types of brands. The first and most familiar type is a **manufacturer brand.** Sometimes referred to as a **national brand** or **regional brand,** it is sponsored by the manufacturer of the product. The manufacturer is responsible for the product's quality and marketing. Many firms, such as P&G, IBM, Gillette, and Xerox, use manufacturer brands for their products.

The other type is a **distributor brand.** Also called **store brand, private brand,** or **private label,** it is sponsored by a distributor such as a wholesaler or retailer. Although the manufacturer's name may be indicated somewhere on the label, the distributor is responsible for the product's quality and marketing. Familiar store brands are Craftsman tools (Sears) and President's Choice grocery products (Loblaw). Many distributors are introducing their own brands. The lower marketing costs for private-label brands make it possible for distributors to maintain high profit margins while charging lower prices than for manufacturer brands.

Intense competition today between manufacturer and distributor brands has been termed the *battle of the brands.* Initially, the mass-marketing power of large manufacturers gave them the edge in this battle. Recently, however, large retailers with tremendous amounts of consumer purchasing information have improved their position substantially.

The competition for market share involves the value provided to consumers. They typically perceive manufacturer brands as of higher quality than distributor brands. Yet, the quality and cost differences vary considerably. When consumers perceive large quality differences, manufacturer brands may provide the most value and are purchased. When consumers perceive small quality differences, then distributor brands may provide the best value and are purchased.

Federated Department Stores is one company that is trying to push private brands throughout its network of department stores. These private brands help to differentiate its stores from competitors and contribute to improved profitability. Instead of the typical 50 percent markup on manufacturer brands, Federated can

Thinking Critically

The increasing attention given to private brands by many retailers is causing problems for manufacturer brands.

- What strategies would you recommend manufacturers employ in order to strengthen their brands and combat the increasing penetration of private brands?

- What strategies should retailers use to offer the best mix of manufacturer and private brands?

Private labels provide retailers the opportunity to charge low prices and earn high profit margins. Sam's Choice and Great Value are distributor brands of Wal-Mart.

take as much as an 80 percent markup on private labels and still give customers lower prices. Current private brands for Federated include Charter Club, Alfani, Arnold Palmer, Club Room, I.N.C., M.T., Studio, The Cellar, and Tools of the Trade.[18]

The battle between manufacturer and distributor brands is likely to intensify in the foreseeable future. Private-label sales are increasing more than those of manufacturer brands in many product categories.

CHOOSING A BRAND NAME   Choosing an effective brand name is an important decision for both manufacturer and distributor brands. The brand name communicates a great deal, which can facilitate brand awareness and brand image. In general, an effective brand name suggests something about the product's benefits; is easy to pronounce, recognize, and remember; is distinctive in some way; and can be translated into other languages.

Ideally, a brand name should help to communicate to consumers the major benefits of the firm's product. If this is achieved, the brand name helps to link brand awareness with brand image. As consumers become aware of the brand name, they begin to associate it with specific product benefits. Sometimes this association can make it difficult for companies to change strategies. Take the banking industry as an example. Many banks are trying to expand into different financial service areas, such as investment management and insurance. A problem is that many consumers perceive banks to be very conservative and not innovative, friendly, or aggressive. Thus, many banks either avoid using the word *bank* in their name or play down the *bank* part of their name. Examples include Chase Manhattan and Wells Fargo.[19]

A brand name that is easy to pronounce, recognize, and remember helps in establishing brand awareness. The name should also be distinctive. Brand names that meet these criteria are Mustang, Kodak, and Crest. Sometimes a brand name can be effective and not really mean anything in real words. Manfred Gotta develops brand names using "artificial nomenclature." Names he has created for companies include Vitek (fitness products), Tornac (umbrellas), Dogstix (dog snacks), and Ernty (baby food). For cars, his specialty, he has come up with the Opel Calibra, Mazda Xedos, and Volkswagen Corrado. None of these brand names is a real word, but each communicates an image and is distinctive and easy to pronounce, recognize, and remember.[20]

A brand name should be translatable into different languages for global business. Many a firm has been embarrassed when introducing a brand name into a different language; others have been able to capitalize on effective brand names. For example, brands that translate well into Russian include Sony, Adidas, and Ford. As P&G introduces brands in Russia, it alters its usual names somewhat. Oil of Olay becomes Oil of Ulay, Tide becomes Ariel, and Pert Plus is Vidal Sassoon Wash & Go.[21]

An alternative to developing a brand name is licensing an existing name or logo. **Licensing** typically consists of the right to use a trademark in exchange for paying royalties on the sale of the licensed product. For example, Coors licensed the name of its upscale beer Irish Red from a long-defunct brewery.[22] A familiar use of licensing is putting a university's name or seal on different products. Sales of licensed university products are around $2.5 billion a year. Notre Dame and the University of Michigan are at the top in sales of licensed products.[23]

Co-branding combines two brand names on the same product. Duracell and Procell illustrate co-branding for a battery.

Another approach is **co-branding,** where two brand names are used on a product. The objective is to capitalize on the brand equity in each brand as a way to appeal to defined target markets more effectively. Co-branding has become commonplace in the credit card industry. For example, the Visa brand name is often combined with another brand name to focus on specific markets. The other brand might be another company trying to generate sales for its products, such as Ford, Traveler's Advantage, or Churchill Downs, or a nonprofit organization trying to generate revenue, such as your university or its alumni association. Another example of co-branding is the inclusion of "Intel Inside" on specific personal computer brands. Although there are similarities in many co-branding relationships, the details of each situation are typically negotiated and formalized into a contractual arrangement.

Packaging

Packaging is an important component for many products. A *package* is the container or wrapper for a product. It typically includes a *label,* a printed description of the product on the package. Packaging is important to both consumers and distributors of a product. A product's package might perform a number of different functions, including protecting the product until consumed, storing the product until consumed, facilitating consumption of the product, promoting the product, and facilitating disposal of the product.

Because many retailers are self-service sellers, a product's package must communicate the brand's image and help to sell the product. Distinctive packages help capture the attention of consumers as they view competitive products. Both package and label also provide important information that consumers use in evaluating competing brands.

Black & Decker markets Quantum tools to the do-it-yourself market and DeWalt tools to the professional market. The Quantum package is green to appeal to the dominantly masculine market and has a photograph of the product and the Black & Decker name prominently displayed on the package, because the Black & Decker name had credibility in the nonprofessional market. Packaging for the DeWalt products features a neon yellow background and black type and has no references to Black & Decker, since professionals do not associate the Black & Decker name with professional tools. The different packages have helped to increase sales of both brands by appealing to the targeted market segments.[24]

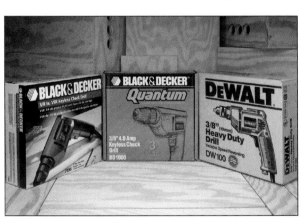

Packaging is an important component of many products. Black & Decker uses different packages for its different brands.

Innovations in packaging offer ways to differentiate brands that consumers might otherwise perceive as very similar. Whereas once all toothpaste brands were packaged in tubes, they now come in pumps, squeeze containers, and stand-up tubes. This new packaging accounts for almost 20 percent of toothpaste sales.[25] It is normally hard to sustain an advantage with new packages, however, because competitors are quick to imitate successful innovations.

An ecological concern is critical to packaging success in the current environment. Many consumers complain about packages that use too much material or material that is difficult to dispose of. Compact discs were introduced with excessive packaging, and many people remember the flap over McDonald's Styrofoam containers. Today, the CD industry uses a new standardized package that is much smaller than the original versions, and McDonald's now packages all its hamburgers in paper wrappers. L'eggs has replaced its plastic egg with a recyclable cardboard box; Kodak has eliminated its cardboard box. And P&G markets superconcentrated liquid detergents. There are many opportunities for marketers to develop innovative packages that help sell a brand, improve its function, and have environmental advantages.

Customer Service

The final product component is **customer service**, which describes the assistance provided to help a customer with the purchase or use of a product. Customer service applies to both goods and services. For example, a consumer purchasing phone lines from Bell South for a new home is buying the basic service of being able to communicate by phone from specified locations within the home. These are the basic features of the phone service. However, customer service concerns all the contacts the customer has with Bell South employees. This includes the person taking the order and the employee installing the phone line. For instance, customers might evaluate the service according to how well the service options were explained, whether the installer arrived on time, and whether the work was completed as promised.[26]

For many products, especially business goods, customer service differentiates competitors. One study found that the best customer service was provided by Nordstrom, Home Depot, American Express, Saturn, Lands' End, and Starbucks. These companies differentiate themselves from competitors by providing better customer service regardless of whether marketing goods or services.[27]

Providing exceptional customer service can give a firm a marketing advantage. Since competitors can quickly copy changes in basic product components, the key to success in many industries is beating the competition in customer service. An innovative customer service can sometimes provide exceptional and unique value to customers as indicated in "Building Customer Equity: Giving Customers What They Want."

Few things can help a firm more than giving customers exceptional service, even under trying conditions. An example will illustrate. The warehouse manager of Miller Business Systems received an order for 20 desks, 20 executive chairs, 40 side chairs, and 20 file cabinets that the customer wanted delivered and set up later in the afternoon. But there were no trucks or employees available to make the delivery. On hearing about the problem, the president had the warehouse manager rent a truck, and the two delivered and installed everything that afternoon as requested. It was an unusual situation, but what to do was clear: "If you promise a customer, deliver."[28]

Important elements of customer service during the purchasing process include providing information about product alternatives, training in product use, and credit and financing services. Exceptional customer service prior to a purchase can produce competitive advantages. Consider the case of Curry Hardware in Boston. This small hardware store is located next to a huge Home Depot store that offers much lower prices. Curry thrives in this situation because it has lots of salespeople available to answer customers' "how to fix it" questions. Customers are willing to pay more to receive this valuable service.[29]

Building Customer Equity

Giving customers what they want

Avis has achieved the highest level of brand loyalty in the rental car industry. Hertz, the market leader, spends about $53 million annually on advertising and provides good customer service. Avis spends only around $9 million a year on advertising but gives customers exactly what they want. Its objective is to manage the entire rental car experience in a way that delights customers. Delighting customers increases customer equity.

Each year Avis determines the set of factors that car renters care about the most. This year the factors are price, convenience, safety, and customer service. The company then breaks the entire car rental process into more than 100 incremental steps and then looks for ways to infuse the important factors into these steps. One example from this process is the Avis Preferred service program. This was the first in the industry, and it reduces the time it takes a customer to pick up a car at an airport by 5 to 10 minutes. Customers love it, as more than one million have signed up. Avis advertises 'We Try Harder,' and it does!

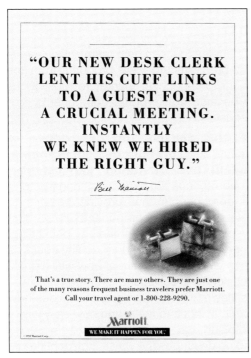

"OUR NEW DESK CLERK
LENT HIS CUFF LINKS
TO A GUEST FOR
A CRUCIAL MEETING.
INSTANTLY
WE KNEW WE HIRED
THE RIGHT GUY."

Bill Marriott

That's a true story. There are many others. They are just one
of the many reasons frequent business travelers prefer Marriott.
Call your travel agent or 1-800-228-9290.

Marriott
WE MAKE IT HAPPEN FOR YOU.

Providing exceptional customer service is one way to gain competitive advantage. Marriott celebrates how one employee did something exceptional to help a hotel guest.

Important elements of customer service after the purchase include fast and reliable delivery, quick installation, accessible technical information and advice, repair services, and warranties. Sometimes just showing concern for customers after the sale can do wonders. An interesting example is Yolanda Eijgenstein, head of Wie Mailt Wat? (Who's Mailing What?) in Rotterdam. Her company collects, categorizes, and reports on every piece of direct mail in the Netherlands. Clients are mostly banks and consumer-product companies. After reports are sent to clients, she calls to see how they like the service. Most are astonished that she has called, and many place additional orders.[30]

Doris Christopher, President and Founder, The Pampered Chef, emphasizes the importance of providing customers with excellent service: "Selling a product is only the first step in building a relationship with customers. Many times when a customer takes home a product they are unsure how to use it. At The Pampered Chef we make sure this does not happen. At our Kitchen Shows, the customer has the opportunity to try the product before he or she buys it. We also ensure that once the customer gets the product home, they know how it will meet their needs in the kitchen. With each product we provide easy-to-read instructions detailing how to properly care for and use it, along with recipes that utilize the product. Our Kitchen Consultants also offer ongoing customer service and support after the sale."

The critical task facing marketers is to combine quality, design, branding, packaging, and customer service components into an effective product offering. A product must meet the needs of the target market and also have advantages over competitors on important product components. Moreover, businesses must constantly be ready to alter product components to adapt to a dynamic marketing environment.

Summary

1. **Understand the differences between goods and services.** Products can be viewed as a continuum, with goods at one end and services at the other. Goods are physical products; services are nonphysical products. Goods are more tangible, perishable, separable, and standardized than services. Most products represent a mixture of goods and services.

2. **Differentiate between consumer and business products, and discuss the different types of each.** Consumer products are those purchased by consumers for their personal use. Business products are those purchased by a firm for its own use.

   Different types of consumer products include convenience, shopping, and specialty products, which differ in the amount of shopping consumers are willing to undertake. Consumers are not willing to shop for convenience products, will shop to make the best purchase for shopping products, and will shop to purchase a specific product for specialty products.

   Business products include capital, production, and operational products. Capital products are expensive goods that do not become part of a company's finished product. Production goods become part of a finished product; operational goods are used in a company's operations but do not become part of a finished product.

3. **Recognize that marketers need to appreciate the perspective of the consumer.** People purchase products to satisfy needs or solve problems. They perceive products as bundles of benefits that can help them satisfy needs or solve problems. To view products from the customer's perspective, marketers must focus on the benefits that product components provide to customers.

4. **Define and discuss the importance of product quality, product design, branding, packaging, and customer service.** Marketers need to look at products as consisting of various components that provide benefits to consumers. The major components are product quality, product design, branding, packaging, and customer service. Product quality could be described as an assessment of how well a product does what it is supposed to do from the customer's viewpoint. Product design includes how the product looks and feels, and how easy it is to assemble and use.

   Branding describes the way a firm identifies its products from those offered by competitors. Packaging addresses the container or wrapper for a product and any labeling that might be provided. Customer service refers to any activity intended to facilitate the purchasing or use of a product.

5. **Explain how the different product components need to be integrated to meet the needs of customers.** Marketers must integrate all product components to offer the bundle of benefits desired by customers. Marketers can achieve competitive advantages by skillfully mixing the different product components into an effective, complete product offering.

Understanding Marketing Terms and Concepts

Thinking About Marketing

1. What are the basic differences between goods and services?

2. Why is it important to differentiate between consumer and business products and among different types of each?

3. Refer to "Using Technology: Integrating Goods and Services." How does Copart represent a blend of goods and services?

4. Refer to "Building Customer Equity: Giving Customers What They Want." What are other things Avis can do to build customer equity?

5. Why is brand equity important?

6. Explain what product quality is. Why might it be important to your classmates?

7. Explain how firms can develop competitive advantages through customer service.

8. How does a global perspective affect product component decisions?

9. Why is it important to incorporate environmental issues into packaging decisions?

10. How are customer value and customer service related?

Applying Marketing Skills

1. Go to a large chain supermarket. Select any one specific product and identify the manufacturer brands, distributor brands, and generics that this store stocks. List each specific brand under each type and compare the product components for each. Summarize your findings to report the results.

2. Assume you have developed a new type of microwave popcorn that tastes as good as competitive products but takes only half the time to prepare. Develop a manufacturer brand name for this product. Compare the name you have chosen with brand names for other microwave popcorn brands. Discuss why you think your brand name will be effective.

3. Look through the ads in the local newspaper. Identify all the examples of customer service you find. Summarize your findings into a list of the ways marketers are using customer service to differentiate their products.

Using the www in Marketing

Activity One   Go to Frito-Lay's home page (http://www.fritolay.com).

1. For most consumers, are Frito-Lay's products convenience, shopping, or specialty products? Citing evidence from the Web site, is Frito-Lay's marketing strategy consistent with your classification?

2. How would you evaluate the brand names of Frito-Lay products? Which are the best? Why?

3. How does this Web site help Frito-Lay provide added value to customers and retailers?

Activity Two   The most obvious examples of product design are for physical goods such as cars and home appliances. However, product design is also important for services. View the following Web sites:

Yahoo! (http://www.yahoo.com)
MSN (http://www.msn.com)
AOL (http://aol.com)

1. How does product design apply to these services?

2. Compare the design of each of these sites.

3. What recommendations do you have to improve the design of each site?

Making Marketing Decisions
Case 8-1 *IBM: Integrating Goods and Services*

IBM has traditionally been involved in marketing goods such as computers and servers. It recently began offering various services such as consulting. One new idea is to use new technology to integrate services into some of its products.

Computer networks can be temperamental, as all computer users know. Mechanical failures, software glitches, and traffic bottlenecks are normal problems. The typical solution in many organizations is to contact the technical services department to get the problem fixed. But the cost of maintaining an adequate technical services department is high and growing. And many of the tasks performed by the technical people are tedious and labor intensive. Examples include updating software, changing settings, formatting drives, and many others.

IBM is trying to improve this approach by developing hardware and software systems that can take care of themselves. This is called autonomic computing.

Robert Morris, director of IBM's Almaden Research Center, explains: "Systems will self-manage and self-repair, learning from mistakes, always aware of what can help them get things done." IBM's newest servers already use autonomic systems to configure themselves on networks and to order replacement parts when needed. Research is under way to expand the use of autonomic computing in many different ways.

All of this sounds well and good, but what happens if something goes wrong. One of the causes of the 1987 stock market crash was that automated stock-trading programs continued to sell shares even as the market continued to fall. Other potential catastrophes are possible. IBM recognizes this and plans to build self-checks and safety protocols into the systems.

One of the potential benefits to organizations using autonomic computing systems is that fewer people will be needed to keep complex computer systems running. This could reduce the cost of technical service departments dramatically. But if technical service workers think they will lose their jobs, will they embrace the autonomic systems and help get them established in an organization?

IBM calls its autonomic computing services effort Project eLiza. As its research develops more applications, the potential to make it easier and less expensive for organizations to keep complex computer network systems running smoothly increases. The addition of autonomic computing services to IBM hardware should make the products more valuable to customers.

Questions

1. What is your assessment of the value of the autonomic computing services being developed by IBM? What problems need to be addressed? How?

2. What markets would you recommend that IBM target initially? Why?

3. What key quality elements should IBM emphasize in marketing the autonomic computing services?

4. Should products that include the autonomic computing services be branded? Why or why not? If so, what brand name would you suggest? Why?

Case 8-2 *Columbia Sportswear: Designing Quality Products*

Gertrude Boyle, known as Gert, had helped her husband operate Columbia Sportswear Company in its early years. For example, she sewed the company's first fishing vest at her kitchen table. It included many pockets, because customers wanted more places to store flies, pliers, and fishing line. Unfortunately, her husband died of a heart attack in 1970. She tried to sell the company but could not get a good price. So, with the help of her son, Timothy Boyle, she decided to run the company.

Gert and Timothy began by listening to customers and innovating. Quad jackets for hunters were one success. These jackets represented an innovative design that featured a weatherproof outer shell and an insulated inner jacket that could be worn together or separately. A similarly designed Bugaboo ski jacket was another success. This approach led to high-quality outdoor sportswear at lower prices than the major competitors, Patagonia and North Face.

Columbia also used an innovative advertising approach to communicate to customers. The humorous ads are called "Mother Gert" ads and include Gert and Timothy in various situations. Usually, "Mother Gert" is portrayed as a tyrant who makes sure that the company's products live up to her tough quality standards. Her favorite line is: "Old age and treachery will overcome youth and skill."

High-quality, well-designed clothing at reasonable prices, effective ads, and rapid expansion of the outdoor-sportswear market helped Columbia increase sales

23 percent annually from 1999 to 2001. Profits rose 43 percent a year over this period. The company went public in 1998, with its stock price doubling in the following four years.

It may be difficult to continue this type of growth. A warm winter and depressed economy in the United States have slowed growth to 2 to 4 percent. This is not expected to increase in the near future, so the firm is looking for new growth approaches. One is to lessen the company's reliance on weather-related clothing. Footwear and sportswear are being considered. Another option is to expand into overseas markets, with Europe a first choice.

Gert is now 78 years old, but she has no intention of retiring. She has built one of the world's largest outdoor apparel companies during the past 32 years. She and Timothy will, however, have to develop a strategy to continue growth in the future.

Questions

1. What are the key product components of the company's products?

2. Why is design such an important element of outdoor sportswear?

3. Would you recommend expansion into footwear or sportswear? Why or why not?

4. Would you recommend international expansion? Why or why not?

Chapter Nine

9

Developing New Products and Services

After studying this chapter, you should be able to:

1 Recognize the different types of new products.

2 Discuss the different sources of new products.

3 Understand the stages in the new-product
development process.

4 Describe the way marketing research is used in the
new-product development process.

5 Appreciate the keys to new-product success.

www.3m.com

3M is a $15 billion company with more than 70,000 employees who create, manufacture, and sell 50,000 products in 200 countries around the world. The company has operations in more than 60 countries. Some of 3M's products, such as Scotch Magic Tape, are well-known brands purchased by individual consumers and organizations. Other products are components for automobiles, computers, and other products purchased only by business customers.

The real distinguishing characteristic of 3M is its continuous emphasis on innovation. One of the company's major objectives is to generate 30 percent of each year's sales from products that are less than four years old. This means that 3M must continually develop and introduce successful new products. Thus, one of the driving principles at 3M is "the promotion of entrepreneurship and insistence upon freedom in the workplace to pursue innovative ideas." Efforts are directed toward listening to commercial partners and consumers to identify problems to be solved and needs to be satisfied. Then, products are developed to solve these problems and satisfy these needs. The objective is to make people's lives better by providing new products with superior features, advantages, and benefits.

3M celebrated its 100th birthday in April 2002 using the theme "A Century of Innovation." Despite its success in new-product development, the company is involved in several changes. Jim McNerney was hired from General Electric as the first outsider to become chairman and CEO at 3M. He arrived during the tough economic times of 2001. Although 3M's performance held up better than that of many other manufacturers, the new CEO has targeted sales and profit growth of over 10 percent annually. Achieving these objectives will require some different approaches at 3M.

One is to make some large acquisitions. 3M has traditionally developed new products internally with only a few, small acquisitions. Another is to move into the services area and provide customers with services in addition to products. For example, 3M would not only sell fiber-optic components to phone companies but would also provide maintenance services. A final approach is to target areas for new-product development more specifically and to focus on launching new products more efficiently. This is a big change for 3M, as it has typically given business units and employees much freedom in creating ideas for new products. CEO McNerney realizes the challenge of bringing more financial discipline to the new-product development process but not stifling creativity at 3M: "If I end up killing that entrepreneurial spirit, I will have failed."

3M provides an especially interesting example of the importance of new-product development. If the company generates 30 percent of sales from products less than four years old, then over $4 billion of its $15 billion total sales come from relatively new products. To meet this objective year after year, 3M must continuously churn out new products and effectively market many of them. New products are clearly the key to 3M's growth and success.

In this chapter we examine new-product development. We begin by discussing the types and sources of new products. Then, we discuss the various stages of the new-product development process. Finally, we suggest several keys for successful new-product development.

New-Product Overview

Developing successful new products drives sales and profit growth for many companies. One study found that companies leading their industries in profitability and sales growth gain 49 percent of their revenues from products developed in the most recent five years. Companies at the bottom in sales and profit growth achieve only 11 percent of sales from new products.[1]

New-product development is a key element of success for many firms. Crest Whitestrips is a new teeth whitening product from P&G.

Another study of 2,000 companies predicted that new products would account for 37 percent of total sales in the future, up from the then-current level of 28 percent.[2] This seems reasonable since companies often set specific goals for new products. We have already mentioned 3M's new-product goals. Rubbermaid is an additional example. Rubbermaid wants to enter a new-product category every 12 to 18 months and expects to get 33 percent of sales from products introduced within the past five years.[3]

Companies also use new products to try to gain market share from competitors. Take the fast-food industry. Total industry sales are slowly declining. Major industry players, such as McDonald's, Burger King, and Wendy's, are engaged in fierce competition to grow in this declining industry. The introduction of new products is critical. For example, Burger King did not introduce a new product between December 1998 and March 2001. During that time it lost 17 percent of its customers. It recently introduced the Chicken Whopper and has sold over 50 million. This is its most successful new product ever. Other new product successes in the fast-food industry include: Sonic's pancake-on-a-stick, Wendy's Garden Sensation salads, KFC's Popcorn Chicken, McDonald's Grilled Chicken Flatbread sandwich, and Arby's Market Fresh line of sandwiches. There have been some notable failures as well, such as the $200 million McDonald's lost on the Arch Deluxe.[4]

Despite the importance of developing new products, a large percentage of them fail. One study of 11,000 new products launched by 77 manufacturing, service, and consumer products companies reported that only 56 percent of these products were still on the market five years later.[5] Other studies have suggested the failure rate is even higher, maybe up to 80 percent. Whatever the exact figure, new-product failures are costly. The failures of Ford's Edsel, DuPont's Corfam, Polaroid's Polarvision, RCA's Videodisc, Cadillac's Allante, and IBM's PCjr cost each company millions.

These and other costly failures motivate companies to improve their new-product development process. The aim is to decrease the percentage of new-product failures, reduce the cost of development, and shorten the time required to get new products to market. These objectives drive most of the changes companies are making in the new-product development process. Herman Miller, for example, incorporated customers, cross-functional teams, and computer software to develop new office furniture that satisfies customer needs. This approach shortened the new-product development cycle by 50 percent, lowered costs substantially, and led to an 11 percent sales increase in a sluggish market.[6] A study of consumer product manufacturers found that most

Speaking from Experience

L.A. Mitchell
Account Executive for Large
Business Accounts
Lucent Technologies

"Getting new products to market quickly is critical to success in today's business environment. If you can't be the first to market, you run the risk of your competitor being several jumps ahead by the time you introduce a new me-too product. Small, innovative companies with first-to-market products often find themselves acquired by larger companies who are willing to pay high premiums for the advantages of early market entry. The challenge Lucent faces in the communication industry is in being able to take advantage of technological advancements while not forcing your customer to continuously replace costly infrastructure. The difficulty lies in anticipating technological advances and being able to integrate them into existing products. Lucent is no longer just in the business of producing telephones. Today, we must compete in unfamiliar industries such as cable, the Internet, and wireless data transmission."

L.A. Mitchell is Account Executive for Large Business Accounts at Lucent Technologies. She has worked on developing sales forecasts for new and existing products, developed marketing plans for various sales teams, and currently assists local phone companies in marketing communications features to large business accounts. L.A. earned her M.S. in marketing from Colorado State University.

---

are shortening product development time to meet the needs of retailers. Study results indicated that 36 percent had one- to three-month development cycles, 36 percent had three- to six-month cycles, and 28 percent took six months to a year for new-product development.[7]

Types of New Products

At first glance, defining a new product would seem to be easy. Yet, the term *new* can be defined from different vantage points and in a number of ways. The first issue is, new to whom? The first time a customer uses a product, it is a new product to him or her, even if it has been available and used by others for a long time. In this case, though the product newness affects the customer's purchasing behavior and the firm's marketing strategies, it does not have a major impact on an organization's new-product development process.

What does directly affect this process is how new the product is to the organization. And even from an organizational perspective, there are degrees of newness. Exhibit 9–1 presents several categories of new products, organized by how new they are to the company developing and marketing the product.

New-to-the-world products are the only ones that are new to both consumers and organizations. These products have never been offered before to any group of consumers; and if successful, they spawn a completely new industry. Obvious examples are the introduction of the first car leading to today's automobile industry, the first airplane and the aircraft and airline industries, and the first microcomputer and the personal computer industry.

The other types of new products in Exhibit 9–1 describe products new to the marketing firm but not new to some other firms or to consumers. From the firm's point of view, the product could be a new-category entry, an addition to an existing product line, an improvement to an existing product, or a new use of an existing product.

A large percentage of new products introduced each year are in the less innovative categories, particularly in many consumer product areas. One study found that of the 15,866 health, beauty, household, food, and pet products introduced, nearly 70 percent were different varieties, formulations, sizes, or packages of exist-

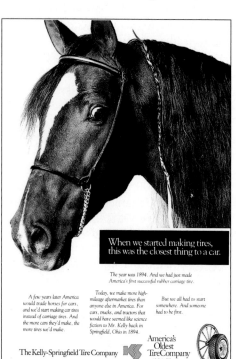

New-to-the-world products create new industries. The Kelly-Springfield Tire Company was established when the automobile was introduced to replace travel by horse with travel by car.

Exhibit 9–1	*Types of new products*

- **New-to-the-world products:** Product inventions, such as Polaroid instant camera, the first car, rayon, the laser printer, in-line skates.
- **New-category entries:** Products new to the firm, but not to the world, such as P&G's first shampoo, Hallmark gift items, AT&T's Universal Card.
- **Additions to product lines:** Line extensions or flankers on the firm's current markets, such as Tide Liquid detergent, Chrysler K cars.
- **Product improvements:** Current products made better; virtually every product on the market today has been improved, often many times.
- **Repositionings:** Products retargeted for a new use or application, such as Kellogg's Frosted Flakes cereal (now targeted to adults), and pork repositioned by National Pork Producers in recent years from being similar to beef to being the "other white meat."

ing brands; only 5.7 percent of new products in these categories represented breakthroughs in technology, formulation, packaging, or even positioning.[8]

Some companies are involved in all of the new-product categories. Sony, for example, introduces around 1,000 new products each year, about 4 every business day. About 800 of these are improved versions of existing products. Typically, improvements consist of new features, better performance, or a lower price. The other 200 Sony products are aimed at creating new markets. They may not all be completely new to the world, but they are very innovative. Recent examples include Data Discman, PalmTop, and Mini Disc.[9]

Moving down the list of product types from new-to-the-world products to repositionings, the product is less new to the firm. This means that its development and introduction is less risky too, because the firm is building on areas of experience. Lower risk also typically makes the new-product development process shorter and less rigorous.

An interesting trend for lowering risk is to capitalize on nostalgia by reintroducing products that were popular in the 1950s through the 1980s. These are typically brands that were successful in the past, but have faded away. The challenge is to build on positive brand associations from the past, but to adapt to the needs of current customers. Examples include Triumph and Indian motorcycles, the Nissan Z and Ford Thunderbird, Tang powdered orange drink, Doan's backache pills, Lavoris mouthwash, Breck shampoo, and Care Bears.

Remember that in our discussion of the new-product development process we use the general term *product* to refer to both goods and services as well as to consumer and business products. The stages in the new-product development process generally apply to all types of products. Examples throughout the chapter include goods, services, and consumer and business products.

Sources of New Products
Firms can obtain new products in a number of ways, with the two extremes being through external sourcing or through internal development. **External sourcing** is any approach by which a firm receives either ownership of another organization's products or the right to market the products of another organization. In such a case, products are new to the firm but not to consumers.

A number of alternative arrangements describe external sourcing. In an acquisition, the buying firm purchases another firm to obtain ownership of all the latter's products. The buying firm owns these products and may either merge them into its existing operations or allow the acquired firm to continue current operations. Newell Rubbermaid represents a good example of this approach. The Newell Co. started as a drapery hardware manufacturer. Since the 1960s, the company has acquired 75 consumer product companies. During the 1990s, the company made 18 major acquisitions adding $2 billion in sales. The most noteworthy was the acquisition of Rubbermaid completed in March 1999. This acquisition led the company to change its name to Newell Rubbermaid. Newell Rubbermaid generates sales in

NTT/VERIO

Collaborative ventures are an increasingly important approach for developing new products, NTT and Verio have formed a collaborative venture to meet the Internet needs of their customers.

excess of $6 billion annually by manufacturing and marketing consumer products through mass retailers and home centers. Its acquisitions over the years have added many new products into the corporate family, such as Rubbermaid plastic products, Anchor Hocking glassware, Levelor blinds, and Rolodex files.[10]

Sometimes a firm purchases only specific brands from another firm. This approach is often used to enter international markets. For example, Colgate-Palmolive purchased all of S. C. Johnson's liquid hand-and-body soap brands in Europe and the South Pacific. Sales of these brands were about $75 million. The purchase was viewed as a quick means for Colgate-Palmolive to add new products for the European and South Pacific markets.[11]

Other arrangements can be classified as some type of **collaborative venture.** Collaborative ventures allow two or more firms to share in the rights to market specified products. Often-used collaborative arrangements include strategic partnerships, strategic alliances, joint ventures, and licensing agreements. Although the specifics may vary considerably, in every case there is some agreement that allows a firm to market products new to it.

The French pharmaceutical company Sanofi SA has used this approach very successfully. Sanofi has about 30 new drugs under development, with each costing up to $400 million. It cannot afford to spend this amount of money on product development. So its strategy is to find partners that will share in the development costs of a product for a license to sell the product when, and if, it is approved. These collaborative ventures allow Sanofi and partners to share the risks and rewards of new-product development.[12]

Internal development means that a firm develops new products itself. The firm may work with other firms for some parts of the process; it might subcontract product design, engineering, or test marketing to other firms. Or it might work in partnership with another firm throughout the entire process. The key point is that in internal development the firm is directly involved in the development of a new product, even though it may not accomplish every step by itself. An interesting approach for new product development is presented in "Being Entrepreneurial: Innovation Principles."

Internal development is riskier than acquiring new products from external sources. A firm developing new products assumes all or most of the costs and risks involved. When acquiring through external sources, a firm purchases or receives the rights to sell products that have a history in the market. External sourcing requires a firm to identify products of other firms, make the necessary agreements to obtain the desired products, and market them. Many firms use both external sourcing and internal development for new products.

Being Entrepreneurial

Innovation principles

Seagate Technology is a leading disk-drive manufacturer. After having some setbacks, it has recovered and is beating competitors to the market with new products. The Seagate management team developed five key principles to guide the new-product development process:

1. Get new ideas from your customers' customers
2. Force your research team to think five years ahead
3. Fix your supply chain to get new products to market faster

4. Build teams that cut across old lines of command and business functions
5. Set some prices lower, so new markets can grow.

These principles have helped Seagate introduce new products for new markets successfully. For example, it has begun to develop disk drives for six different segments of the consumer mass market, such as Microsoft's Xbox videogame console.

Exhibit 9-2   *New-product development process*

Idea generation → Idea screening → Concept development & testing → Business analysis → Prototype development → Test marketing → Commercialization

Reducing new-product development time can produce a competitive advantage for many firms. Companies use various approaches to test new products.

New-Product Development Process

The new-product development process can be conceived as consisting of the seven stages presented in Exhibit 9–2.[13] The process is presented as a logical series of steps for discussion purposes. In reality, the lines between each step are often blurred as companies are involved in different stages at the same time; sometimes they even eliminate specific stages. Also, the specific process for any one product will vary by company, industry, and type of new product.

Two issues related to the new-product development process deserve some discussion. First, as a firm moves from one step in the process to the next, costs increase substantially. A major objective is to weed out potential failures as early as possible without eliminating products that might be successful. This is a difficult balancing act, but one that cannot be avoided. Rigorous analysis to evaluate products at each stage and to determine which warrant further attention can help firms be both productive and successful in developing new products. Because of this, each stage requires a "go" or "no-go" decision. And since approximately 46 percent of new-product development costs are wasted on products that ultimately fail, firms must make such decisions as early as possible.[14]

The second issue of note is that the traditional approach to new-product development has been a functional, linear process as shown in Exhibit 9–3. Typically each functional area works on specific stages of a process in isolation. When one step is concluded, the results go to the following functional area for the next step. For example, R&D might conceive a product idea and give it to the design function, which would design the product. Design passes it to engineering, which develops engineering specifications and gives it to manufacturing to produce. Manufacturing produces the product and gives it to marketing to sell. Although this type of approach has resulted in some successes, the process can be very slow and costly.

Many firms have improved the new-product development process by adopting a multifunctional, simultaneous approach as shown in Exhibit 9–3. This approach requires all relevant functions to work together during all stages, with several steps typically performed simultaneously. Some firms benefit from including suppliers, distributors, customers, and other interest groups.

3M has formalized this approach through its Pacing Plus initiative. This initiative is intended to accelerate the development of high-impact new products and bring them to market faster. Criteria for qualifying for the Pacing Plus program are new-product development projects that change the basis for competition in new or existing markets, offer large sales and profit potential, receive priority access to 3M resources, operate in an accelerated time frame, and employ the best available commercialization processes. About 25 Pacing Plus programs are underway for products ranging from microflex circuits for electronic products to films that increase the brightness of notebook computer screens.[15]

Voyant Technologies developed an interesting teamwork approach. The company established the position of new-product officer to coordinate the

Exhibit 9–3

New-product development approaches

Traditional approach

R&D → Design → Engineering

Manufacturing → Marketing → Sales

Simultaneous approach

R&D

Design

Engineering

Manufacturing

Marketing

Sales

efforts of engineers and product managers. Joint meetings with engineers and product managers intermingled led to more cooperation throughout the new-product development process. This teamwork approach produced three new products, improved time to market by 40 percent, and reduced R&D development costs by 20 percent.[16]

Idea Generation

Idea generation is the initial stage of the new-product-development process. A new product begins as someone's idea. Firms typically generate a large number of ideas relative to the number of successful products introduced. One study reported that 13 new-product ideas were needed for every successful new product.[17]

Ideas for new products can come from different methods and sources. Analyzing the products offered by competitors can generate ideas for new products or improvements in existing products. Typically, these ideas are ways to differentiate a firm's new product from competitive offerings. Ford used this approach in designing the Mercury Mystique. The company evaluated the characteristics of the Honda Accord, Pontiac Grand Am, Mazda 626, Nissan Altima, and Mitsubishi Galant. As a result of this analysis, the Mystique is larger, roomier, and much easier to maintain than competing cars. Its engine needs a tune-up only every 100,000 miles.[18]

By watching customers use existing products, firms can generate ideas for new products. Employees at John Deere visit dealers and farmers to observe their products in use and to talk about potential problems. These visits often produce ideas for improved products for farmers or better ways to service John Deere dealers.[19] Karen Bertiger wanted to place a cellular call from the Bahamas to her home in Arizona, but she could not get through. She asked Bary Bertiger, her husband and vice president of the satellite systems group for Motorola, why the cellular phone won't work everywhere. Because of his wife's question, he came up with the idea to create a satellite-based wireless-telephone system that would allow anyone to call anybody from anywhere in the world.[20]

In addition, technological developments can be a useful source of new-product ideas. Firms think about ways they might transform emerging technologies into successful new products. Even the government is getting into the act. Government agencies of all types are introducing a growing number of electronic services. It is the beginning of the e-government era. The state of Georgia offers citizens the opportunity to purchase hunting, fishing, and boating licenses over the Internet. College students can apply for financial aid from an Education Department student aid Web site. The National Science Foundation is currently conducting a study of the feasibility of "cybervoting." These new electronic services provide convenience to citizens while also reducing the cost of government. For example, Maryland saved $1.6 million when 250,000 professionals renewed their annual licenses online.[21]

Employees often suggest ideas for new products, and some firms reward them for doing so. Since salespeople have the most direct contact with customers, some companies motivate them through rewards for reporting new-product ideas to their managers.[22] Creative group methods, such as brainstorming, to stimulate thinking about new-product ideas are also useful. Sharing information and ideas can also be valuable, especially across international markets. For example, Pillsbury invites executives to training sessions to swap ideas. One success from this approach was the dulce de leche flavor for its Häagen-Dazs ice cream. This supersweet, butterscotch-like flavor was developed and introduced at the only Häagen-Dazs store in Buenos Aires. It immediately became the store's best seller. When this idea was presented at a training session, Häagen-Dazs executives from the United States and Europe decided to introduce the new flavor in their markets. It has been a terrific success in both markets.[23]

L. A. Mitchell, Account Executive for Large Business Accounts, Lucent Technologies, discusses sources for new product ideas: "New-product ideas can come from just about anywhere. Lucent has entire organizations whose sole function is to continually explore and develop new-product ideas. These organizations frequently employ focus groups, surveys, and other marketing research techniques to generate new ideas. Some of the best ideas come from needing to solve a significant customer problem. For example, the increase in automobile accidents due to people talking on cell phones while driving has generated many ideas for new products and features. Some of these include products that allow cell phones to be used "hands free" and new features that make it possible to dial a number by simply speaking the name of the person or business you wish to call."

Idea Screening

Since the idea-generation stage is relatively inexpensive, the major objective is to create a large pool of ideas for potential new products. The purpose of **idea screening** is to evaluate the idea pool and reduce it to a smaller and more attractive set of potential new products. The ideas should be screened for consistency with company vision and strategic objectives, potential market acceptance, fit with the firm's capabilities, and possible long-term contribution to profit. A major objective is to eliminate as early as possible ideas that have little chance of resulting in successful new products. Ideas that remain after screening move to the next stage in the new-product development process.

Mattel launched Project Platypus to bring together 15–20 employees from engineering, design, marketing, and copywriting to invent original new toys. The employees leave their jobs for three months and move out of Mattel headquarters to a nearby building with open-plan offices. Group sessions are designed to generate creative ideas and then to refine them into specific new products. The first output from this process was Ello, a construction and activity toy for girls. Mattel hopes Project Platypus will produce 2–3 viable product ideas each year.

A popular idea-screening approach is to use a checklist. The basic procedure is to identify the factors that are important to a firm and to evaluate each new-product idea against each factor. Adding the individual factor scores for each idea produces an overall idea-screening score. The higher this score, the better the new-product idea. Sometimes firms have a cutoff score; they drop ideas scoring below the cutoff and retain those scoring above for further development. Or companies might rank the idea-screening scores from highest to lowest and focus efforts on the ideas with the highest scores.

Exhibit 9–4 presents an example of a checklist used by 3M. 3M decided that customer need, competition, technology, marketing, manufacturing, price versus competition, and performance versus competition are important factors. The company rates ideas against each factor on a scale ranging from zero to five. The individual factor ratings are then summed to produce a total score. As shown in the exhibit, the idea is evaluated very high on each factor, for a total score of 30. On the basis of this score, a go decision is likely. If the score had been very low, say 15, the new-product idea would not have been developed any further.

Exhibit 9–4 *3M's idea-screening checklist*

| | Scale | | | | | | | |
Factor	**0**	**1**	**2**	**3**	**4**	**5**		**Rating**
CUSTOMER NEED		Nice		Definite utility		Critical		*5*
COMPETITION		Many		Limited		None		*4*
TECHNOLOGY		None in 3M		Within 3M		Within ISD*		*4*
MARKETING		None in 3M		Tape Group		ISD		*5*
MANUFACTURING		None in 3M		Equipment modification		Existing equipment		*4*
PRICE VERSUS COMPETITION		Competitive advantage		Neutral		Strong 3M		*3*
PERFORMANCE VERSUS COMPETITION		Strong competitive		Neutral		Strong 3M		*5*
Industrial Specialties Division.						Total		*30*

Concept Development and Testing

Concept development is the process of shaping and refining the idea into a more complete product concept. In the generation and screening stages, the product idea is typically very general, perhaps a soft drink with added nutrients for health-conscious consumers or a direct-mail service for marketing textbooks to students. The evaluation of product ideas to this point is generally done by people within the firm, with little if any assessment by potential customers.

The major objective of concept development and testing is to formalize product concepts and have them evaluated by potential customers. Formalizing the product concept means describing the basic product idea in detail. This usually entails describing all of the product's components, including its projected price. If possible, a picture of the product should be included with the concept description. Exhibit 9–5 presents a product concept for a new healthful soft drink.

Concept tests are then used to get potential customers to evaluate the product concept. Sometimes multiple variations of the basic product concept are provided, so consumers can indicate which they like best. In other cases (see Exhibit 9–5), consumers are asked to respond to various questions about only one product concept. Besides assessing the concept provided to them, consumers are usually given an opportunity to suggest improvements. Concept tests are most often conducted as personal interviews, but they can be performed through mail surveys.

If the concept tests indicate a low level of consumer acceptance and low likelihood of purchase, the firm makes a no-go decision. If the tests indicate a high level of consumer acceptance and high probability of purchase, the firm makes a go decision. The results of the tests may also provide ideas for revising the concept to better meet the needs of consumers.

Business Analysis

Ideas that survive concept development and testing are subjected to detailed business analysis. The **business analysis** stage of the new-development process calls for preparing initial marketing plans for the product. This requires developing a tentative marketing strategy and estimating expected sales, costs, and profitability for the product. A product idea reaching this point has passed general company screening criteria and been accepted by consumers. The purpose of the business analysis is to determine if it makes business sense to introduce the product.

Exhibit 9–5   *Product concept test*

NEW HEALTHFUL SOFT DRINK

This new drink is as refreshing and thirst-quenching as a normal soft drink, but much more healthful. It contains only natural ingredients. Three 12-ounce cans contain the normal vitamin and mineral daily requirements for an average adult. The drink will be available in several fruit flavors, will be clear in appearance, and will be packaged in recyclable aluminum cans. The cost of a 12-ounce can will be 69¢.

1. How likely are you to buy this product?
   Definitely would buy   _____
   Probably would buy   _____
   Might or might not buy   _____
   Probably would not buy _____
   Definitely would not buy _____

2. What do you like the most about this product?

3. How could this product be improved?

The firm must assess whether it can market the new product profitably. This requires estimating costs, which is difficult but easier than forecasting sales. Several types of sales estimates may be necessary. For infrequently purchased products, such as appliances, production equipment, or personal computers, the firm must estimate initial sales and long-term replacement sales. For frequently purchased products, like toothpaste, business supplies, or cookies, it must forecast both first-time sales and repeat sales over time.

The firm must attempt to predict sales over several purchasing cycles, because the ultimate success of a new product depends on consumers' trying the product and then repurchasing it. Pillsbury's experience with Oven Lovin' Cookie Dough shows what can happen. Within months of introduction, the product was available in 90 percent of supermarkets and sales were growing. In less than two years, however, sales crumbled. After using the product, consumers did not think it was much different from the dough they were using previously, so they switched back to their old product.[24]

Because it is so difficult to estimate new-product sales and costs, the real value of the business analysis is in identifying products that are not likely to succeed commercially. Consumers might like the product, and it might meet the firm's general criteria, but the market might be too small or the marketing costs too high for the new product to have a reasonable chance of long-term profitability. If this is the case, the firm makes a no-go decision. Although a no-go decision at this point has some costs, it can save the firm the very high costs associated with the remainder of the new-product development process. A go decision means that the new product offers the potential profitability to warrant continued development.

Chrysler provides an example of a no-go decision. The company put together a formidable team to develop a luxury car code-named LX. The LX would be a rear-wheel drive luxury car with a new 32-valve V-8 engine of over 300 horsepower. The car would be fast, but it would handle well and be able to compete with BMW, Mercedes, Jaguar, Lexus, Infiniti, and Cadillac. Everyone was excited about the project as Chrysler moved closer to actually producing the car. However, after analyzing the market, management concluded that increased competition would reduce margins to a level where the product would not generate sufficient profits. Although everyone involved wanted to produce the car, management made a no-go decision because of the limited profit potential.[25]

Prototype Development

Prototype development means converting the concept into an actual product. The objective is to use the information obtained from the concept tests to design an actual product that can be further tested. New-product costs begin to escalate at this stage because developing a prototype normally requires a considerable investment. Product ideas that make it to this stage should have a high probability of succeeding. Firms are doing a better job of weeding out poor product ideas earlier in the development process, as evidenced by a decrease in the number of new products that make it to the prototype stage from about 50 percent to 20 percent.[26]

Firms need to focus on two areas during prototype development. The first is to design the product to satisfy the needs expressed by consumers in the concept tests. One approach is through **quality function deployment (QFD),** a procedure that links specific consumer requirements with specific product characteristics. A simplified QFD matrix for a new copier product to be marketed to business users is presented in Exhibit 9–6. In this example, each product characteristic is designed to provide at least one benefit desired by customers. This approach directly links product features to customer requirements.

The second area is to build quality into the product. In the past, a product would be designed and then given to manufacturing to produce. Sometimes it would be difficult and costly to produce to the design specifications. Now, many firms include people from product design, engineering, and manufacturing in designing the prototype. Manufacturing considerations are incorporated directly into product design. This approach ensures not only that the prototype will satisfy customer needs on paper, but that it can be produced to the desired quality level. An interesting example of developing prototypes is presented in "Using Technology: Robotic Pets."

Test Marketing

Once a product prototype is developed, it can be tested. **Test marketing** involves testing the product prototype and marketing strategy in simulated or actual market situations. Test marketing can be both expensive and risky. Full-scale test marketing can cost over $1 million and last up to 18 months. Competitive reactions have taught even savvy marketers like Procter & Gamble to be cautious in their testing. Several years ago, P&G was testing a ready-to-spread frosting brand. Taking note of the test, General Mills rushed to introduce its own Betty Crocker brand, which now dominates the market.[27] The two primary methods for testing are simulated test marketing and standard test marketing.

Simulated test marketing refers to evaluating a new product in situations contrived to be similar to how consumers would purchase and use it. A typical simulated test involves intercepting shoppers at a high-traffic location in a mall.

Using Technology

Robotic pets

Sony's Digital Creatures Laboratory introduced the world's most sophisticated entertainment robot. The new product is a robotic dog that can bark for attention, sit up, lie down, scratch its face, wag its tail, play ball, change eye color, and learn as it grows. It is named AIBO, which is a Japanese word for "companion" and short for Artificial Intelligence Robot. The price for AIBO was $2,000. Sony hopes this is the first in a line of robotic dogs, cats, monkeys, and other creatures.

But, getting AIBO to market was a real challenge. The product development team built six prototypes over five years before coming up with one that had the desired quality. It took five prototypes before they were able to get one that could walk. The seventh prototype required tremendous work to "debug" software glitches and to finalize the desired appearance of the robotic dog.

The AIBO was launched based on the seventh prototype. It has been successful with a second-generation version of the product introduced with upgraded features and higher speeds and at a lower price of about $1,300. Club AIBO has also been established to facilitate communication among customers and with Sony.

Exhibit 9–6	*Product function deployment matrix*

NEW COPIER PRODUCT Product characteristics						
Customer requirements	Multiple-size paper tray	Touch controls	Energy-efficient	Slip-in toner cartridges	Long-term warranty	High speed
Fast copies						X
Versatile	X					
Durable		X	X		X	
Low maintenance		X	X	X		
Easy to operate	X	X		X		X
Low operating cost			X			

X = Specific product characteristics designed to meet specific customer requirements

Surveyors ask them about their use of various products and expose them to a concept or commercial for a new product. Respondents then participate in a shopping exercise during which they can purchase the new product. After the exercise, they are asked about their purchases. They are then contacted at a later date about their use of and intentions to repurchase the product.[28]

In **standard test marketing,** a firm tests a new product and its marketing strategy in actual market situations. The size and number of test markets depend on the need for reliable information, the costs associated with test marketing, and the potential reactions from competitors. Selected test markets should be representative of the characteristics of the target market for the new product. A typical approach is to execute the marketing strategy for the new product in the selected test markets and to carefully track results. Sometimes firms vary elements of the marketing mix in different test markets to identify the most effective marketing strategy.

Ameritech uses an interesting approach to test marketing. It goes to small towns in its region and has the citizens test new products and services. For example, the company enlisted more than 100 people in Woodstock, Illinois, to evaluate its Clearpath digital cellular service. The feedback from these test-market towns has provided useful information for improving Ameritech's new products prior to launch. Interestingly, people from these towns who have actually participated in the test-marketing programs are often used in Ameritech's "Human Factors" advertising campaign. These ads show the people using the new products in sometimes humorous ways. The underlying logic behind the test marketing and advertising is that "if technology doesn't work for people, it doesn't work."[29]

Test marketing represents the final exam for a new product. If the new product passes this exam, a go decision will lead to the commercialization stage. If the new product fails this exam, a no-go decision will lead

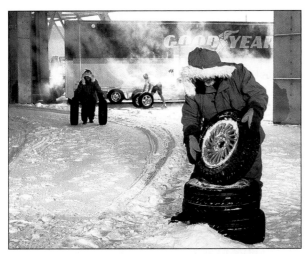

Test marketing products is one way to gauge consumer response prior to launching a product. Goodyear uses test marketing to evaluate new tire products.

Exhibit 9–7	*Consumer adoption process*

Consumer adoption stage	Marketing strategy objective
Awareness	Communicate the availability of the new product.
Interest	Communicate benefits of new product to gain consumer interest.
Evaluation	Emphasize the advantages of new product over alternatives currently on the market.
Trial	Motivate consumers to try the new product.
Adoption	Make sure consumers are satisfied with use of the new product.

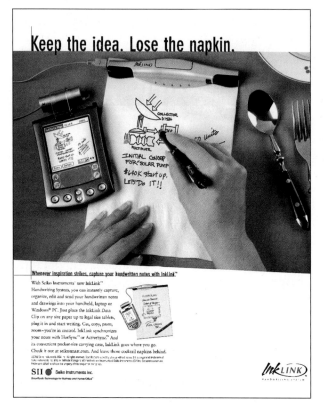

Innovative approaches are often used to introduce new products. Seiko emphasizes the value of its new InkLink handwriting system.

to dropping the new product or going back to the drawing board to make significant changes. Even though test marketing is expensive, it is typically much less costly than commercializing the product. So a firm is much better off stopping an unsuccessful product at this stage than during the commercialization stage.

Commercialization

During the **commercialization** stage, the firm introduces the product on a full-scale basis. The level of investment and risk is generally the highest at this stage. Investments in production, distribution, and marketing support can be extremely high. However, the firm can reduce some of this risk by performing the other stages of the new-product development process appropriately. Successful commercialization requires understanding consumer adoption, timing decisions, and coordinating efforts.

CONSUMER ADOPTION The **adoption process** describes the steps consumers follow in deciding whether or not to use a new product. The stages in the adoption process are presented in Exhibit 9–7. Marketing strategies must be designed to move consumers through these stages to achieve the adoption of new products.

Research suggests two important considerations about the adoption process. First, consumers differ in their rates of adoption. There is usually a small group of consumers who are the most willing to adopt new products. Typically called **innovators,** they normally represent the first 2.5 percent of the adopters. Identifying the innovators and targeting marketing efforts to this group are keys to successful commercialization of a new product.

Second, the characteristics of a new product affect its rate of adoption. The more complex the product, the slower the rate. For example, it takes 5 to 15 years before new electronic technologies (e.g., VCRs, cable TVs, PCs, and cell phones) catch on among consumers and penetrate a large portion of the market.[30] The rate of adoption is facilitated, however, when the new product is compatible with existing products, has clear and readily observable advantages over those products, and can be tried on a limited basis. Marketing strategies should capitalize on the characteristics that facilitate adoption and minimize the characteristics that slow adoption.

L. A. Mitchell, Account Executive for Large Business Accounts, Lucent Technologies, talks about facilitating the adoption of new products: "Even good new products can become old products very quickly if the customer has difficulty in accepting the new product. High-tech products traditionally have very high initial costs. For these new products, Lucent targets customers in very competitive industries where product differentiation is critical to a company's success. It is here that we will most likely find early adopters willing to take on new products. In order to capture the early adopter market, we need to present a product that can integrate quickly into the customer's product offering and demonstrates a quick return on investment or a significant competitive advantage."

TIMING   In most cases a firm can introduce a new product on its own timetable. A threat of competitive entry, however, can pressure a firm to launch the product quickly. The first entry in a market can often establish a long-term advantage. One study found that for technology-based companies, the profitability of new products is related more to getting to the market on time than to staying within the product development budget.[31]

Late entry can be advantageous if competitors have entered the market and developed interest and demand for the new product. Later entrants may be able to reduce the costs of market entry, avoid some of the mistakes made by the early entrants, or introduce better products. Compaq did this with its subnotebook computer. After many competitors were in the market, Compaq introduced a subnotebook similar to what was available but priced $1,000 below the competition. This entry appealed effectively to the home market.[32]

COORDINATION   As the new-product development stages have progressed, a marketing strategy for commercialization has evolved. A firm needs to coordinate all functions to implement this strategy effectively. Production, distribution, and all other marketing and company efforts must ensure that sufficient product is produced and available to satisfy the demand generated from the commercialization strategy.

One study found that new-product launches were more likely to be successful when the firm had a structured commercialization process that was understood by everyone involved and when there was frequent communication within and across department and divisional boundaries. It is also important that the product launch be given priority status with objectives set and specific responsibilities for all tasks assigned. Once the product is introduced, tracking results and providing feedback are critical.[33]

One of the worst things that can happen is to get consumers interested in a new product and then not have it available when they are ready to purchase. For example, photography retailers were promoting the Advanced Photo System with the line, "The dawn of a new era in photography is here!" Developed by five of the world's largest photo manufacturers, the system was supposed to solve many picture-taking problems. Small, light cameras would be available in various designs. The cameras would take three different sizes of pictures on the same roll of film, and many picture-taking errors could be corrected during photofinishing. Consumers were ready to purchase, but the cameras were not available. Six months after introduction, few retailers had the products because of production problems and demand miscalculations. The net result was frustrated retailers and consumers and, in the words of one executive, "the worst product launch in the history of the photographic industry."[34]

Adoption of new products is facilitated if the new product has clear advantages over existing products. Memorex emphasizes the storage capacity of its recordable DVDs.

Keys to New-Product Sucess

Studies of new-product introductions identify a number of reasons for failures and successes. Many executives are not satisfied with the speed of new-product development in their companies and have difficulty in planning and budgeting for new projects. Front-end planning is critical to improving the new-product development process.[35] A synthesis of these studies provides the keys for new-product success, as presented in Exhibit 9–8.[36]

Exhibit 9–8   *Keys to new-product success*

- Number-one factor: unique, superior, differentiated product that delivers unique benefits and superior value to customer.
- Market-driven and customer-focused new-product process.
- More predevelopment work before development gets under way.
- Sharp and early product definition.
- Right organizational structure.

- New-product success is predictable: Use profile of winner to sharpen project-selection decisions.
- New-product success is controllable: Emphasize completeness, consistency, quality of execution.
- Speed is everything! But not at the expense of quality of execution.
- Companies that follow multistage, disciplined new-product game plans fare much better.

Many of these keys to new-product success are consistent with the perspectives emphasized throughout this book. New-product development should be market-driven and customer-focused, aimed at developing superior products that offer consumers unique benefits and exceptional value. The predevelopment efforts, such as idea screening, concept development and testing, and business analysis, appear to be critical to new-product success. In fact, establishment of a disciplined and rigorous new-product development process, effectively executed at each step of the process, is an important determinant of success.

Organizational Approaches

The use of cross-functional teams working simultaneously on different steps helps shorten the new-product development process and increases chances for success. Three organizational arrangements have been found to work well. A **balanced matrix organization** calls for a project manager to oversee the project and to share responsibility and authority with functional managers. Decision making and approval are a joint process.

A **project matrix organization** assigns a project manager to take primary responsibility and authority for the process. Functional managers then assign personnel as needed to perform various activities throughout the process.

In a **project team organization,** a project manager heads a core group of people selected from various functional areas. Managers from the different functional areas are not formally involved in the process.

Teamwork across functional areas is essential for new-product success. The emphasis throughout the process should be on producing products that offer the quality and value desired by consumers. In many cases, this means constant awareness of how new technologies may be used to solve customer problems. Although many of the keys to success seem obvious, the majority of new products still fail. The reason for many of these failures may be that firms did some of the obvious things wrong or failed to do them at all.

Marketing-Research Support

Marketing research can make important contributions to the new-product development process. Concept tests and test marketing were discussed earlier in this chapter, and other marketing research approaches were cov-

Teamwork is often required to make the new-product development process successful. Thermos used a cross-functional team to develop a new electric grill that won four design awards.

Marketing-research support for new products

Prelaunch	**Rollout**
• Focus groups • Name & package evaluation • Market definition studies • Product tests • Target segment • Copy tests identification • Simulated test • Concept tests markets • Test markets	• Awareness, • Product refinement attitude studies tests • Usage studies • New advertising • Tracking studies strategy tests

ered in Chapter 6. Exhibit 9–9 highlights some of the types of marketing research that might be used throughout the new-product development process.

Prelaunch activities refer to marketing-research studies prior to commercialization. These types of studies typically introduce consumer input into the decisions made at each stage of the new-product development process. *Rollout studies* are performed after the product has been introduced in the commercialization stage. These studies assess consumer response to the new product and its marketing strategy.

The successful introduction of Banana Nut Crunch illustrates the important role that marketing research can play. The cereal maker, C. W. Post, wanted to develop a banana-flavored cereal. Bananas are America's favorite cereal fruit and consumers had responded favorably to the banana-flavored cereal concept. The initial cereal included dried banana pieces, but this flopped in product tests. Then, the idea to make the cereal like banana-nut bread was generated. Consumers responded positively to this new concept. Prototypes were produced and tested in several hundred households. Again, the response was positive. Banana Nut Crunch was then introduced, and tracking studies indicated strong initial and repurchase demand. Today, the cereal is a strong success and one of Post's hottest brands. Information provided by consumers through various marketing-research approaches produced the key information to make the product introduction successful.[37]

Successful New Products

Although many new products are failures, there are always many interesting successes. Let's conclude our discussion of new-product development by looking at several products selected as "The Best Products for 2001":[38]

- Harmony is a new low-fat cereal from General Mills. It comes fortified with calcium, folic acid, and iron with toasted wheat, rice flakes, and vanilla-almond oat clusters.

- The Samsung 1300 from Sprint PCS combines the functions of a cell phone with those of a palm organizer into one product.

- Microsoft's Xbox incorporates a cutting-edge graphics, hard-disk, and DVD player into a video game player.

- Credit Watch monitors your credit report daily and e-mails you if there has been any unauthorized activity.

- Hitachi's DZ-MV100A camcorder records onto a DVD that can be edited on the camcorder or on a TV screen.

- Apple's iPod digital music player can download 1,000 songs and play nonstop for more than 10 hours.

- Listerine's PocketPaks contain 24 stamp-sized starch-based strips that contain mouthwash that can be used in place of chewing gum to freshen breath.

Summary

1. **Recognize the different types of new products.** Products differ in how new they are to customers or to the firm introducing them. From a firm's perspective, new products can be classified as new-to-the-world products, new-category entries, additions to product lines, product improvements, or repositionings.

2. **Discuss the different sources of new products.** New products can come from external sources or be developed internally. External sourcing includes acquisitions or various types of collaborative arrangements allowing a firm the right to market the products of another firm. Internal development is when a firm is directly involved in the development of new products. The firm might work with other firms on some new-product activities, but it is actively involved in the process.

3. **Understand the stages in the new-product development process.** The new-product development process consists of the interrelated stages of idea generation, idea screening, concept development, business analysis, prototype development, test marketing, and commercialization. As a firm moves through this process,

costs rise substantially. A prime objective is to eliminate potential product failures as early as possible and to spend time and resources on the ideas with the largest chances for success.

4. **Describe the way marketing research is used in the new-product development process.** Marketing research goes on throughout the new-product development process. Specific types of marketing research are valuable in the prelaunch stages. These studies help to assess market acceptance of the product and the likely success of particular marketing alternatives. Different marketing research approaches are used to monitor and evaluate results during the commercialization stage.

5. **Appreciate the keys to new-product success.** A synthesis of new-product research suggests the nine keys to new-product success presented in Exhibit 9–8. In general, the keys to success are market orientation, customer focus, effective execution of a rigorous new-product development process, adoption of a multifunctional new-product organizational approach, and development of products that deliver the benefits and value desired by consumers.

Understanding Marketing Terms and Concepts

Thinking About Marketing

1. How does the new-product development process differ for different types of products?

2. What are the advantages and disadvantages of using external sources for new products?

3. Look at "Using Technology: Robotic Pets." Suggest five new-product ideas using robots that are not pets.

4. Should all new products be test marketed? Why or why not?

5. What should be included in a business analysis for a new product?

6. Reread "Being Entrepreneurial: Innovation Principles." What are the three mistakes you think companies often make in developing and marketing new products?

7. Describe the use of marketing research throughout the new-product development process.

8. What factors should be considered during the idea-screening stage of the new-product development process?

9. How is the development of new services likely to differ from the development of new goods?

10. How is the development of consumer products likely to differ from the development of business products?

Applying Marketing Skills

1. Assume that students are complaining about how hard it is to get information about scheduled school events. Being entrepreneurially oriented, you would like to develop a product to solve this problem. Go through the idea-generation, idea-screening, and concept-development stages of the new-product development process. Bring one or more new-product concepts to class for testing.

2. Contact a local firm in your area that is active in new-product development. Interview people at the firm, and find out as much as possible about the company's new-product development process.

3. Identify a recent new product that you think has been very successful. Select a product that allows you to obtain information from both published sources and company officials. Evaluate how well the firm introducing this product followed the keys to new-product success presented in Exhibit 9–8.

Using the www in Marketing

Activity One   Go to the 3M Web site (http://www.3m.com).

1. Select one of the inventors in the "Our Pioneers" section. Describe the invention and how it led to new 3M products.

2. Based on information available from the Web site, why do you think 3M has been so successful in developing new products?

3. What are 3M's plans for new product development in the future?

Activity Two   One example of a truly innovative product can be found at http://www.sleddogs.com.

1. Describe this product.

2. Why is this product so innovative?

3. What are the keys to marketing this innovative product successfully? How does understanding adoption and diffusion help you in developing a successful strategy for introducing a new, innovative product such as this?

Making Marketing Decisions

Case 9-1 *Eclipse Aviation: Developing an Innovative Jet*

Eclipse Aviation was founded by former Microsoft executive Vern Rayburn. The company is trying to develop a twin-engine jet that could revolutionize the aviation industry. The jet would resemble a luxury sedan and be equipped with the latest flight controls and safety features. It could fly almost 450 miles per hour at altitudes up to 41,000 feet but would be small and maneuverable enough to land at almost every small airport. The cost of operating the jet would be about 40 percent of what it costs to operate today's cheapest jet. And, the price of the Eclipse 500 would be about $850,000!

The company has been working on the jet for four years. The design has passed computer-simulated tests, so a prototype has been built. It will have to undergo a year of rigorous certification tests by the government. If it fails any of them, design changes would have to be made and the tests retaken. The Eclipse design team includes about 180 engineers to get the design right.

Even if the design tests go well, new government regulations regarding security for private jets will also have to be addressed. Eclipse plans to train all Eclipse 500 pilots rather than have it done by flight training schools. This would give the company more control and help to minimize any safety or security problems.

The company hopes to have the jet in service in early 2004, but many things could go wrong and delay or kill the project. Even with all of this risk and uncertainty, the company has raised over $220 million from private investors such as Bill Gates, and it expects to get the additional $100 million needed soon. Customers have put down nonrefundable deposits for over 500 orders. This has generated $38 million and would fill the company's production capacity through the fourth quarter of 2006.

Why so much interest in the Eclipse 500 jet? If the jet delivers as promised, it has "dynamite potential" and "could change the industry," according to an aerospace analyst at Morgan Stanley. First, private pilots currently flying piston-engine planes could move up to the level of executive travel. Second, the low purchase price and low operating expenses could open up a new market for private jet service. More individuals and companies would be able to purchase jets outright or become involved in some type of fractional ownership program of the Eclipse 500 than are able to for available private jets.

The most intriguing opportunity is for the Eclipse 500 to be used as an air taxi for average travelers. A traveler would call an air taxi service to make a reservation. An Eclipse 500 would then pick up as many as six passengers at the local municipal airport and deliver them to any other municipal airport. And, the cost for this service would be similar to a commercial airline coach seat!

Questions

1. How has Eclipse Aviation followed the new-product development process?

2. Would you recommend that the company focus on upgrading existing private jet travelers or getting new private jet travelers? Why?

3. How would marketing strategies differ for existing versus new private jet travelers?

4. What is your assessment of the air taxi concept? How would you recommend this new approach be marketed?

Case 9-2 *Ford: Revamping Sales with New Products*

Ford Motor Company lost $5.5 billion in 2001. William C. Ford, Jr., great-grandson of founder Henry Ford, was named chief executive to turn the troubled company around. The Ford Division accounts for about 80 percent of the company's U.S. volume and most of its profit in the past. Chief Executive Ford promises a "product-led renaissance" to get the Ford "blue oval shining again."

The recent situation has not been good. In 2001 industry sales were down 3 percent, but Ford's dropped 10 percent. Market share has slipped from 19 percent to 17.5 percent, and further erosion is possible. Ford's once lucrative sport-utility vehicles and pickup trucks face aggressive competition that has hurt sales and profit margins. Over a dozen Ford models, from the subcompact Focus to the giant Excursion SUV, have posted sales declines. And, the only new products introduced in the past year were the new Expedition SUV and a diesel-equipped pickup.

One of the reasons for the lack of new-product introductions is that the profits of the 1990s were invested in e-commerce ventures, luxury-car brands, and even junkyards. Little attention was given to the core mass-market cars and trucks, and the competition took advantage of this situation. For example, General Motors, Toyota, and Dodge all introduced new pickups that took business from Ford's F-series. Ford did not have a new pickup to fight back with until 2003. Since it has not had new products to market, Ford has focused on rebates, cut-rate financing, and targeted price adjustments to sell its existing products.

New products are on the way, however. One bold move is to replace its top-selling Taurus with a variety of new midsized sedans, car-based SUVs, and sport wagons. The Taurus was the best-selling car in the U.S. from 1992 to 1996, but the Honda Accord and Toyota Camry have overtaken it. Current plans are to introduce an F-150 pickup truck, hybrid Escape compact SUV, Mustang sports car, Windstar minivan, and GT40 muscle car in 2003. These products will all emphasize improved quality. In 2004, a Five Hundred sedan and CrossTrainer car SUV will be launched. Both of these products are positioned as upscale Taurus alternatives. A smaller midsize sedan and Focus subcompact are planned for 2005, and a midsize SUV, midsize "multi-activity vehicle," and Super Duty pickup truck are expected in 2006.

If all goes well, Ford will have a stream of new products to compete more successfully in the future. However, replacing the large volume from the Taurus will be difficult. Each of the new products focuses on a particular market segment, so many of the new products will have to sell well to achieve the volume once held by Taurus. Ford intends to push its most profitable models and to encourage customers to add high margin options.

Questions

1. Why has Ford introduced so few new products in the past year?

2. What is your assessment of dropping the once successful Taurus? Should Ford have tried to revive it? Why or why not?

3. What do you think are the keys to the success of the "product-led" renaissance at Ford?

4. What type of new car product (not mentioned in the case) would you recommend Ford develop? Why?

10

Product and Service Strategies

After studying this chapter, you should be able to:

1 Understand the different characteristics of a product mix.

2 Recognize the stages and characteristics of the product life cycle.

3 Identify appropriate marketing strategies for products in different life cycle stages.

4 Describe the limitations of the product life cycle concept.

5 Discuss different product-mix and product-line strategies.

www.starbucks.com

The first Starbucks coffee shop was at Pike Place Market in Seattle in 1971. The concept was successful, and 165 Starbucks locations were opened in 1992, when the company went public. The chain now has more than 2,800 retail locations in the United States and Canada and over 300 in Europe and Asia. The Starbucks strategy is to create a unique experience based on mellow ambience, premium coffee beans, and coffee beverages.

Future growth will come from several areas. There are many international opportunities, and Starbucks hopes to have 1,000 international locations within the next five years; Japanese outlets are doing well, and the company recently entered China and the Middle East. There are also growth opportunities in the United States, where gourmet-coffee sales have increased by 46 percent during the past two years. Starbucks has less than 6 percent of the coffee market allowing plenty of room for growth. Starbucks is also expanding its in-store product line with more coffee choices and has added tea by purchasing Tazo, a premium tea company. Further, there is an effort to expand market share in the office-coffee service market and to open licensed stores on university campuses and in grocery stores.

Starbucks is beginning to offer wireless Internet access in some stores and is using its own Web site to complement store sales. For example, freshly brewed coffee is the best seller in stores and cannot be purchased on the Web. Web sales are more for merchandise like espresso machines, which sell for as much as $399. Selling merchandise on the Web eliminates the need for as much inventory in the stores.

The Starbucks Card is another successful example of integrating Starbuck stores and its Web site. Customers can order a card and make deposits on the Web or in stores. Then, they can use the cards to make Web or store purchases. More than 4 million cards are currently being used. The cards are so popular that some companies use them in their employee reward and incentive programs.

A recent new product is a bottled espresso drink called DoubleShot. The company formed the North American Coffee Partnership with Pepsi as a strategic partnership to market bottled Frappuccino coffee drink and DoubleShot. This partnership builds on Starbuck's strength in specialty coffee and Pepsi's extensive distribution system. The first joint national advertising campaign was recently launched.

The future looks bright for Starbucks to add more retail stores, expand its product mix, and leverage its Web site to build customer equity around the world.

Most companies market many different products. Pfizer Consumer Healthcare shows some of the many products in its product mix.

The experiences Starbucks has had illustrate the challenge of marketing multiple products and services, where success depends upon developing and implementing effective strategies for specific products, individual product lines, as well as the entire product mix. The task becomes even more difficult for companies such as Starbucks because product strategies for their stores must be integrated with those for electronic commerce. But, this is the task faced by more and more firms.

Even small, entrepreneurial firms based on a single product normally add new products to achieve growth objectives. One reason for this is that once a new product passes the commercialization stage and is introduced into the market, it typically goes through some type of life cycle. At the later stages of this life cycle, sales and profits decrease significantly. Thus, firms introduce new versions of existing products to extend this life cycle or new products in other areas to meet company growth objectives and take advantage of market opportunities. Smart companies employ effective product and service strategies to direct this growth.

In this chapter we introduce the product mix concept and discuss strategies for individual products, product lines, and the overall product mix. We emphasize the role of the product life cycle as a basis for strategy development.

Product Mix

A **product mix** is the total assortment of products and services marketed by a firm. Every product mix consists of at least one product line, often more. A **product line** is a group of individual products that are closely related in some way. An **individual product** is any brand or variant of a brand in a product line. Thus, a product mix is a combination of product lines, which are combinations of individual products.

A product mix, relevant product lines, and individual products can be defined at different levels. In Chapter 3, we discussed organizational strategic planning at the corporate, business, and marketing levels. At the corporate level, the product mix would be defined as all products marketed by the entire corporate entity, with each business unit typically representing one or more product lines. Each business unit,

Speaking from Experience

John V. O. Kennard
Senior Vice President
Executive Director of
Global Brand Development
*Brown-Forman Beverages
Worldwide*

"Developing strategies for multiple products within a company presents challenges and trade-offs. Companies are often trying to boost the growth of well-established brands. At the same time, they focus budget and energy on creating product line extensions and new product lines. If done correctly, multiple product strategies can be the key to increasing total sales and profits. Successful product line strategies satisfy customer needs and enhance brand equity. Expanding the product line also helps increase shelf space for the company's products. Shelf space gains are extremely important in the battle for market share."

John V. O. (Jack) Kennard is Senior Vice President, Executive Director of Global Brand Development, Brown-Forman Beverages Worldwide. He directs strategy and global marketing for the company's leading spirits brands: Jack Daniel's family of brands and Southern Comfort. His responsibilities include global growth and customer equity building,

brand strategy, positioning, target audience selection, advertising, packaging, product development, and pricing. Jack previously held marketing positions for Kraft/General Foods and R.J.R./Del Monte, and earned his B.A. in English Literature and M.B.A. from the University of Virginia.

Exhibit 10–1   *Product mix characteristics*

Kodak Camera Product Mix			
Consumer Cameras	**Digital Cameras**	**Industrial Cameras**	**Motion Analysis Products**
•KODAK ADVANTIX 2000 AUTO Camera •KODAK ADVANTIX 2100 AUTO Camera •KODAK ADVANTIX 3100AF Camera •KODAK ADVANTIX 3200AF Camera •KODAK ADVANTIX 3600ix Camera •KODAK ADVANTIX 3700ix Camera •KODAK ADVANTIX 4100ix Zoom Camera •KODAK ADVANTIX 5600 MRX Text-Date Camera •KODAK ADVANTIX Cameras •KODAK CAMEO Auto Focus Camera •KODAK CAMEO cameras •KODAK CAMEO Focus Free Camera •KODAK CAMEO Motor 110 Camera •KODAK CAMEO Motor EX Camera •KODAK CAMEO Zoom Plus Camera •KODAK FIESTA 35 Camera •KODAK FUN SAVER 35 Camera •KODAK FUN SAVER 35 Camera with Flash •KODAK FUN SAVER 35 Camera with Flash Wedding Edition •KODAK FUN SAVER ADVANTIX Single-Use Flash Camera ...and 15 others	•KODAK DC25 Digital Camera •KODAK DIGITAL SCIENCE 420 Color Infrared Camera •KODAK DIGITAL SCIENCE 420 GPS Camera •KODAK DIGITAL SCIENCE DC20 Camera •KODAK DIGITAL SCIENCE DC40 Camera •KODAK DIGITAL SCIENCE DC50 Zoom Camera •KODAK DIGITAL SCIENCE Professional DCS 410 Camera •KODAK DIGITAL SCIENCE Professional EOS-DCS 3 Digital Camera •KODAK Megapixel Image Technology Camera System •KODAK Professional DCS 420 Digital Camera •KODAK Professional DCS 460 Digital Camera •KODAK Professional DCS 465 Digital Camera Back •KODAK Professional DCS IR Digital Cameras •KODAK Professional EOS-DCS 1 Digital Camera •KODAK Professional EOS-DCS 5 Digital Camera	•KODAK MEGAPLUS Camera, Model 1.4 •KODAK MEGAPLUS Camera, Model 1.6 •KODAK MEGAPLUS Camera, Model 4.2	•KODAK EKTAPRO EM Motion Analyzer, Model 1012 •KODAK EKTAPRO EMP Motion Analyzer •KODAK EKTAPRO HS Motion Analyzer, Model 4540 •KODAK EKTAPRO Hi-Spec Motion Analyzer •KODAK EKTAPRO Intensified Imager, Model SI •KODAK EKTAPRO Intensified Imager, Model UVX •KODAK EKTAPRO Intensified Imager, Model VSG •KODAK EKTAPRO Motion Analysis Workstation

Product Line Length (vertical label, left side)

Product Mix Width

however, also has its own relevant product lines made up of related products. For example, General Electric is organized into eleven core-product business units. The appliance business unit consists of the following product lines: refrigerators and freezers, gas cooking, washers and dryers, room air conditioners, venting systems, electric cooking, dishwashers, compacters and disposers, microwaves, water systems, and small appliances and electronics. The gas cooking product line is made up of various free-standing ranges, single wall ovens, slide-in ranges, and cooktops.[1]

Any product mix can be defined in terms of width, length, and consistency. Exhibit 10–1 illustrates these characteristics for the camera product mix at Kodak a few years ago. **Product mix width** refers to the number of product lines in the product mix. The more product lines, the wider the product mix. The camera product mix is relatively narrow, because it consists of only four product lines: consumer cameras, digital cameras, industrial cameras, and motion analysis products.

Product line length refers to the number of products in a product line. In the Kodak example, the consumer cameras product line is the longest, with 35 products.

Exhibit 10-2   *Product and service strategies*

The industrial cameras product line is the shortest, with only three products. It is also sometimes useful to talk about the average product-line length across a firm's product mix. For Kodak cameras, the average product-line length is 15.25, since there are 61 products organized into four product lines.

Product mix consistency refers to the relatedness of the different product lines in a product mix. The product mix throughout Kodak is very consistent, because all of the products are related to imaging. So even if we expanded our focus to the corporate or business-unit level, the product mix would still be relatively consistent. The products would not all be cameras, but they would be associated with imaging.

Firms marketing multiple products and services must devise strategies for individual products, specific product lines, and the overall product mix. Key strategies at each level are presented in Exhibit 10–2. Although we discuss each level separately, the strategies are interrelated. Effective firms integrate product and service strategies across these levels. "Being Entrepreneurial: Developing an Effective Product Mix" provides an interesting example in the footwear industry.

Individual Product Strategies
An important factor in the development of marketing strategies for individual products is the product life cycle. The **product life cycle (PLC)**, like the biological life cycle, describes the advancement of products through identifiable stages of their existence. The stages are introduction,

Being Entrepreneurial

Developing an effective product mix

After being pushed aside by L.A. Gear, Robert and Michael Greenberg have created a footwear company that is number three in the United States behind Nike and Reebok. The typical footwear company has a product mix of 100 to 200 selections within a specific type of shoe class, such as athletic shoes. Skechers USA produces over 1,500 selections for all kinds of shoe buyers and many different types of shoes. For example, its product mix includes athletic shoes, clunky boots, basic brown shoes, trendy platforms, steel-toed sneakers, fuzzy slippers, and others. These shoes are sold to men, women, teens, and kids through retailers like Athlete's Foot, JCPenney, Sears, and its own Skechers USA stores. Even though overall footwear sales have been sluggish, Skechers' sales rose 42 percent in the past year.

One reason for its success is that it pays special attention to young women, because they tend to buy shoes for all members of a family when shopping for themselves. It also aims its styles at teens and young adults, and responds to changing needs quickly. For example, when clunky shoe styles lost popularity, the company immediately launched a "sexy and frivolous" line called Skechers by Michelle K targeted to trend-conscious women in the 18–34 age bracket. Skechers has also been able to keep prices lower than competitors. These entrepreneurial strategies have produced annual sales of almost $1 billion and many opportunities for a bright future for Skechers.

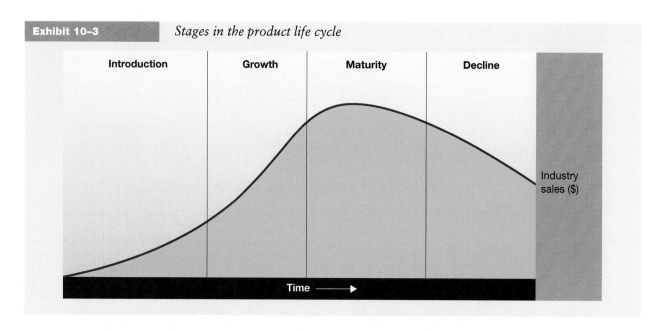

Exhibit 10–3   *Stages in the product life cycle*

growth, maturity, and decline, as shown in Exhibit 10–3. The product life cycle concept applies best to new product forms; it does not work as well to describe stages for general product classes or for the specific life of individual brands.[2] Thus, marketers at AT&T would find the product life cycle concept of most value for product forms such as portable telephones, cellular telephones, or video telephones. The concept is less useful in analysis of the basic product class of telephones or of specific AT&T brands of telephones.

The product life cycle concept is based on four premises:

- Products have a limited life.
- Product sales pass through distinct stages, each with different marketing implications.
- Profits from a product vary at different stages in the life cycle.
- Products require different strategies at different life cycle stages.[3]

Before discussing relevant stages, characteristics, and marketing strategies, we should examine the diffusion process as a basis for the product life cycle concept.

Diffusion Process

When a new product form, such as the cellular telephone or the compact disc, is first introduced to the market, consumers go through a process in determining whether or not to adopt it. We discussed this process and factors that facilitate adoption in Chapter 9. Research suggests that different groups of consumers adopt innovations at different rates. Some consumers adopt a new product when it is first introduced; others wait until the innovation has been on the market for some time. These different adoption rates mean that it typically takes time for an innovative new product form to diffuse throughout a market. The **diffusion process** describes the adoption of an innovation over time.

The general diffusion process is presented in Exhibit 10–4. The process is depicted as a bell-shaped curve with five different adoption groups. As discussed in Chapter 9, **innovators** are the first to adopt a new product; they represent about 2.5 percent of a market. The diffusion process then moves to the **early adopters** (13.5%), **early majority** (34%), **late majority** (34%), and finally the **laggards** (16%). The types of consumers in each group differ depending on the type of innovation. However, as shown in Exhibit 10–4, consumers within each category have several common characteristics.

Exhibit 10-4	*Diffusion process*

Innovators: 2.5% Venturesome, higher educated, use multiple information sources	**Early adopters: 13.5%** Leaders in social setting, slightly above-average education	**Early majority: 34%** Deliberate, many informal social contacts	**Late majority: 34%** Skeptical, below-average social status	**Laggards: 16%** Fear of debt, neighbors & friends are information sources

The different categories of adopters in the diffusion process are one reason new products go through life cycles. As an innovative product diffuses through these adopter categories, competitors enter the market and marketing strategies change. The interaction of the diffusion process and firm competition means that marketers face a different situation at each stage of the product life cycle (see Exhibit 10–5).

PLC Stages and Characteristics

The **introduction stage** starts with the launch of a newly developed product into the marketplace. Thus, the introduction stage of the product life cycle extends the commercialization stage of the new-product development process discussed in Chapter 9. Sales growth in the introduction stage is often slow because innovators typically represent a small portion of the market. Profits are low or nonexistent because of heavy expenses incurred in product development and intensive marketing to launch the product. There are no direct competitors for the first market entry, but competitors will likely enter over time.

Ideally, a new product would remain in the introduction stage for only a short time. However, some products never get out of this stage or remain in it for much longer than desired. A case in point is the introduction of handheld computing products. Apple's Newton MessagePad was among the first entries in this market. Adoption was much slower than expected because consumers did not perceive sufficient value from the initial product. Apple responded by introducing new models, the Newton MessagePad 110, and 2100, with many new features. However, consumers did not value these new features either, and sales of handheld computing products languished. The situation changed when 3Com Corporation introduced its Palm Pilot 1000 and Palm Pilot 5000 handheld products. These products were

Exhibit 10-5	*PLC stages and characteristics*

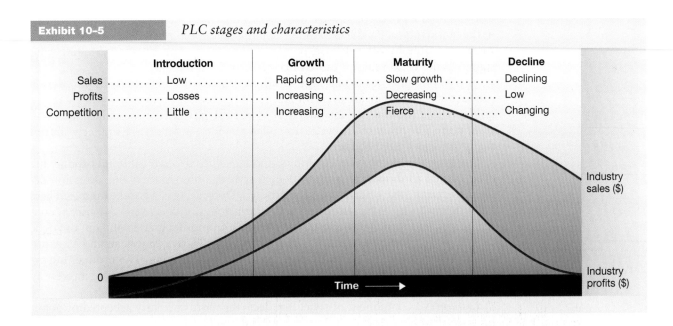

simple, easy to use, extremely portable, and able to be automatically synchronized with the data on a personal computer. Consumers saw real value in these products, and sales took off.[4]

The second phase in the product life cycle is the **growth stage.** During this time, sales and profits increase rapidly. Innovators, early adopters, and the early majority buy the product. Recognizing the potential for profits, additional competitors enter the market with different product versions. The number of competitors and the rate at which they enter affect how long the growth stage will last. It will be shorter the faster competitors enter the market and the more aggressive their marketing strategies. Handheld computing products are now in the growth stage. Palm, Handspring, Compaq, Sony, and other companies all have one or more handheld computer products. All of the products have some basic features, but each marketer is trying to differentiate its brand in some way. The lower level products, like the Palm 101, have come down in price, but those with the latest technology, like the Compaq iPac, are still relatively expensive. Sprint PCS, Nokia, and other companies are also trying to integrate the important features of handheld computers into cellular phones, so that users would only have to carry one piece of equipment to meet their computing and communication needs.[5]

When the marketing efforts of all competitors begin to get adoptions from the late majority, the **maturity stage** begins. Profits peak, then begin to decline, reflecting intensified competition, especially on price. Competition becomes even more fierce during the latter part of the maturity stage, when laggards adopt the product. The market gets saturated such that increased sales come more from taking business away from competitors than from getting business from new adopter categories. Most companies market products in the maturity stage of the product life cycle.

When falling sales persist past the short run, a product enters the **decline stage.** Profits decline and competition is changing. A product can reach this stage for a variety of reasons. One, most consumers who could buy the product may have done so. Another reason may be a shift in consumers' tastes, which is common in the clothing industry. Sales can also decline because of technological advances. The rotary telephone, for example, has largely been replaced by touch-tone phones that make it easier and quicker to place a call. Compact discs and digital audiotape formats hastened the decline of long-playing records. Digital imaging could have the same effect on film photography.

PLC Length and Shape

The length of a product life cycle depends on how well the product meets the needs of the marketplace. Products such as the basic household refrigerator have endured for a long time by offering consumers a good value. For less than $1,000, consumers can buy 20 years or more of convenient food storage.

In many industries, technology is advancing rapidly, which tends to shorten product life cycles. The life cycle for laptop computers was only a few years, as technology paved the way for introduction of equally powerful but smaller notebook computers. The product life cycles for styles, fashions, and fads are similarly shorter than for many other products.

Life cycle curves for styles, fashions, and fads differ from traditional product life cycle curves, as shown in Exhibit 10–6. A *style* is a unique form of expression defined by certain characteristics of the product. Decorating is a good example. There are different styles of furniture and home furnishings, such as early American, contemporary, and French provincial, and one style or another goes in and out of vogue over time. The Southwestern style, characterized by Native American and Mexican design and influence, is currently popular in home decorating. The product life cycle curve for a style fluctuates, reflecting periods of renewed and waning interest by consumers.

Fashion is a component of style. It reflects the more currently accepted or popular style. Fashions tend to follow the typical product life cycle curve. A few con-

Exhibit 10–6   *PLC for styles, fashions, and fads*

sumers interested in differentiating themselves from the norm start a trend. Soon, more consumers follow the lead of these innovators in the desire to copy the latest fashion. The mass market adopts the popular fashion as the norm, and eventually the fashion goes into decline as the cycle starts all over with another new and different fashion. This is especially evident in the apparel industry. Ask Levi Strauss. Levi's sales slid from over $7.1 billion in 1996 to about $4.2 billion in 2001 with its men's and women's market share down from 18.7 percent to 12.1 percent. The reason. Young consumers perceive Levi's jeans to be for the middle-aged. These consumers want more fashionable jeans like those from Seven and Blue Asphalt. Levi's is trying to meet these fashion needs by introducing jeans with flared legs, jeans with low waists, and dark denim jeans with bright stitching and large pockets.[6]

However, sometimes fashions return to popularity. For example, designer jeans were very popular in the late 1970s and early 1980s. The tight, blue, straight-legged, denim jeans with designer labels then went out of fashion. But they came back, although with a lot more flair. Designers added rhinestone buttons, groovy new hues and prints, and laminate trims, and blended other fabrics with the denim. Apparel companies Pepe Jeans, Versace, Tommy Hilfiger, and Ralph Lauren all took advantage of the fashionable return to designer jeans.[7]

Finally, *fads* are a subcategory of fashion. Fads have dramatic product life cycles. They capture attention and grow quickly, but last only a short time and attract a limited number of consumers. Fads do not last long because of their limited benefits. They merely satisfy the need to be different and interesting. Some examples of fads are Cabbage Patch dolls, high-power water pistols, and games such as Trivial Pursuit. The life cycle of a fad is thus a very steep curve over a short period.

Sometimes it is difficult to determine if a sharp gain in sales is a fad or whether sales growth will continue. Harley-Davidson faced this situation when its large motorcycles gained popularity and stretched production capability. Management was contemplating a large expenditure to increase production but was concerned that the sales spike was due to a short-lived fad. Further analysis indicated this was not the case, Harley-Davidson increased production capacity, and sales have continued to grow.

Shortening lengths of product life cycles and their different shapes increase the complexity of marketing decisions. Firms respond to these trends by developing marketing strategies to take advantage of each life cycle stage. Some marketing strategies for each stage in a typical life cycle (Exhibit 10–5) are presented in Exhibit 10–7.

Introduction Strategies

The overall objective in the introduction stage is to increase awareness and stimulate trial of the new product. If there are no competitors, marketing efforts focus on generating **primary demand,** or demand for the new product form. As competitive brands are introduced, the focus shifts to generating **secondary demand,** or demand for the firm's specific brand.

Exhibit 10–7		*PLC marketing strategies*	
Stage	**Objective**	**Marketing strategy**
Introduction	Awareness and trial	Communicate general product benefits to consumers and channel members.
Growth	Usage of firm's brand	Specific brand marketing communications, lower prices and expanding distribution
Maturity	Maintain market share and extend life cycle	Sales promotion, lower prices, expanding distribution, new uses, and new versions of product
Decline	Decide what to do with product	Maintain, harvest, or divest

Two different pricing strategies are possible. Firms often set high introductory prices for new products to quickly recover the costs associated with development and introduction. Examples of this type of strategy are seen frequently in high-tech products. Most technologically advanced products start out at a high price that innovators are willing to pay. VCRs, home computers, and cellular phones, for example, were all introduced at a high price. Firms modified their pricing strategies as these products moved through the life cycle, making them much more affordable to the mass market.

Another strategy is to set a low introductory price. This approach is intended to generate faster market penetration. Because of the low price, it will take longer for a firm to recover new-product development costs. However, the low-price strategy can lead to a larger market share and long-term profits. P&G normally introduces new products at a high price and then cuts the price as competitors move into the market. However, it changed its approach for the extremely successful launch of the Crest SpinBrush electric toothbrush. It used a low introductory price of $5 to gain market share quickly and make it less attractive for competitors to enter the market. The results of this strategy were spectacular. The Crest SpinBrush is the best selling toothbrush in the U.S. with global sales in excess of $200 million annually.[8]

Distribution in the introduction stage is typically limited. Marketing efforts must be targeted to channel members as well as final customers. Marketers use different communication tools to persuade resellers to stock the product and to get consumers to try it.

Marketing strategies during the growth stage typically focus on the competitive advantages of a firm's brand. Panasonic emphasizes the durability of its notebook computers.

Growth Strategies

When a product enters the growth stage, the firm's basic objective is to build consumer preference for its brand. Because of the favorable characteristics of the growth stage, many competitors are likely to enter the market. These competitors usually challenge existing brands by offering improved versions of the product. Early fax machines, for example, were in the growth stage when they were challenged by plain-paper versions.

Increased competition often results in the lowering of prices, especially toward the end of the growth stage. In addition, marketers usually expand distribution to make it easier for consumers to purchase the product. Communication efforts emphasize the competitive advantages of each firm's brand.

Maturity Strategies

The overall objectives at the maturity stage are to defend market share and extend the product life cycle. With the diffusion process nearing completion, opportunities to get new adopters are limited. Marketing efforts focus more on taking customers away from competitors than bringing new adopters into the market. But this is difficult and costly. Several strategies might be used during the maturity stage.

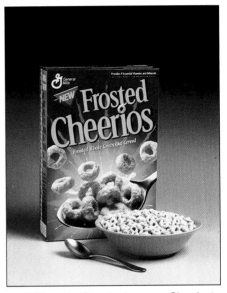

Introducing new and improved versions of a product is one strategy for extending a product's life cycle. Cheerios began as Cheerioats in 1941 and has been improved many times to extend its life cycle to over 50 years.

Thinking Critically

Select a product that you use and think is in the maturity stage of its life cycle:

- Propose three different strategies to extend the life cycle for this product.
- Which of these strategies would you recommend to the marketer of this product? Why?

One popular strategy is to offer incentives to consumers for purchasing the firm's brand. These include lowering the brand's price relative to that of competitors or using sales promotions, such as coupons or rebates, to reduce the brand's price. Although incentives can produce more sales from existing customers and take sales from competitors, their cost reduces a firm's profit margins.

Another approach is to get consumers to use the product in different ways. This strategy can lead to more purchases from existing customers or might extend the product life cycle by bringing new consumers into the market. For example, Arm & Hammer successfully expanded the uses of its baking soda product. Originally used in cooking, baking soda is now used as a deodorizer in refrigerators, in carpet cleaning, in toothpaste, in antiperspirants, and most recently in wintergreen-flavored gum. Eagle Brand Sweetened Condensed Milk has followed a similar strategy. It has been used for more than a century in Mom's Thanksgiving pumpkin pies. The brand is now being marketed to busy moms for use in all types of recipes, such as no-bake bars, shareable crumble treats, and an after-school beverage.[9]

A final approach is to extend the life cycle by continually introducing new and improved versions of the product. Since these new versions are not new product forms, they do not start a new product life cycle. They do, however, help prevent the product from moving into the decline stage. Procter & Gamble uses this strategy often. For example, P&G has improved Tide detergent many times during its long history.

Hasbro uses an interesting approach to extend the life of some of its toys for toddlers. It has developed a process to make the toys 99.9 percent germ-free. The plastic in the toys is embedded with Microban, a germ-killing chemical. The chemical is nontoxic and will not wash off because it is incorporated chemically into the plastic. Hasbro will add the germ-free concept to all of its Playskool toys beginning with the Roll and Rattle Ball and Busy Band Walker.[10]

The sales, profit, and competitive characteristics of the maturity stage produce a difficult situation for marketers. Marketing strategies used in the introductory and growth stages are not normally successful in the maturity stage. Firms often try many different strategies to maintain market share and extend the product life cycle.

Decline Strategies

When a product reaches the decline stage, marketers must make tough decisions on what to do with their brand. Sales and profits are decreasing and competition is strong. However, the picture can change depending on what competitors do. If many competitors decide to leave the market, sales and profit opportunities increase. If most competitors stay in the market, opportunities are limited. Thus, the appropriate strategy depends a great deal on the actions of competitors.

Three basic strategic choices are available: maintaining, harvesting, or deleting the product. Maintaining refers to keeping a product going without reducing marketing support, hoping that competitors will eventually leave the market. Some people, for example, still prefer (or can only afford) black-and-white televisions. Similarly, rotary or dial telephones persist in some areas of the country for reasons of technology.

A harvesting strategy focuses on reducing the costs associated with a product in the decline stage as much as possible. Advertising, salesforce time, and research and development budgets are limited. The objective is to wring out as much profit as possible during the decline stage.

Finally, deleting refers to dropping a product altogether. A firm might withdraw the product from the market, ending its life cycle, or might be able to sell it to another firm. Deleting products is difficult for many firms, but it may be the best strategy. The resources expended on a product in the decline stage may produce only minimal returns. Productivity can normally be increased by allocating these resources to products that will produce higher returns.

Limitations of the PLC

The product life cycle is meant to be a tool to help analyze the characteristics of products and design marketing strategies. The concept, however, has limitations. Marketers should be aware of these before jumping to conclusions based solely on the product life cycle.

First, remember that the life cycle concept applies best to product forms rather than to classes of products or specific brands. If marketers look only at the brand and not the overall product form, they may not see the whole picture. Brand sales can fluctuate for reasons unrelated to the product life cycle.

Second, the life cycle concept may lead marketers to think that a product has a predetermined life, which may produce problems in interpreting sales and profits. A dip in sales, for example, may be taken to mean that a product is entering the decline stage. Managers could prematurely drop the product when the dip represents only a temporary blip in the marketplace. Many products have survived for decades without decline because they were managed correctly. Ivory Soap (introduced in 1879) and Morton's Salt remain stalwart competitors. In other cases, declining products can experience a jump in sales with some new development in the environment, as was the case with cereals. When medical research seemed to show that oat consumption reduces cholesterol, sales of Quaker Oats soared.

The final and most important limitation of the product life cycle is that it is merely a descriptive way of looking at the behavior of a product. There is no way the life cycle can predict the behavior of a product. That is, the product life cycle has limited relevance for forecasting future performance. Rather, marketing strategies help move a product along the life cycle. It is an interesting paradox that the strategies marketers adopt are both a cause and result of the product's life cycle.

Product-Line Strategies   Individual products that are related in some way

form product lines. Firms must integrate strategies for individual products within the strategy for a product line. The basic strategic alternatives are to increase or decrease the length of a product line.

Increasing the Product Line

Most firms have growth objectives, so they tend to adopt strategies that add products to a product line. Since few firms have product lines that cover all market segments, they focus on where to add products. Sometimes additions to product lines

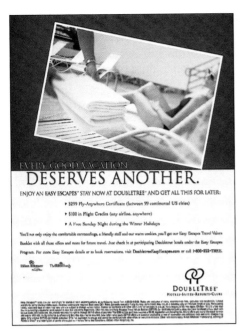

A downward-stretch strategy adds products to the lower-cost end of the product line. Doubletree appeals to customers who value a lower price and fewer amenities than upper-end Hilton customers.

are needed to keep customers coming back. An example of this strategy is presented in "Building Customer Equity: Keeping Customers Coming to Thorton's."

A **downward-stretch strategy** is an attempt to add products to the lower end of the product line. Luxury car makers are introducing lower-priced cars to get new customers. For example, Mercedes C-Class cars cost around $30,000. Compare this to other Mercedes cars that sell for $100,000 or more. The strategy is designed to get consumers to try a luxury car at the low-end and then to sell them higher-priced luxury cars in the future.

An **upward-stretch strategy** is just the opposite: Products are added at the higher end of a product line. This has been a favorite approach for Japanese companies in the U.S. market. All the Japanese car marketers initially entered the U.S. market at the low-priced end. As companies achieved success with these products, they gradually added higher-priced products. Now, most Japanese companies market products at all levels, even at the luxury end of the market with products such as Lexus and Infiniti.

An interesting example of an upward-stretch strategy is the Boeing Business jet service offered by Deutsche Lufthansa. Instead of just offering a few business class seats on a 247-passenger plane, Lufthansa has introduced private business class service for all 48 seats on the plane flying from Newark, New Jersey to Dusseldorf, Germany. No crowds, good food, and personal Sony watchman movie players. All for $5,900. The flights are about 60 percent full and already profitable.[11]

A **two-way-stretch strategy** entails adding products at both the high and low ends of the product line. Firms that have focused on the mass market might use this strategy to appeal to both price-conscious and luxury-seeking consumers. Marriott has used this strategy for its hotel product line, adding Marriott Marquis at the high end and Courtyard and Fairfield Inn at the low end. Marriott's product line now cuts across most segments of the lodging industry.

A **line-filling strategy** involves adding products in different places within a product line. A firm might use this strategy to fill gaps in its product line that are not at the high or low end. Candy marketers have used this approach with varying degrees of success. Hershey Chocolate successfully added Hershey's Hugs to its Hershey's Kisses product line. But it experienced disappointing results when it added Crunchy Peanut Butter Cups to the Reese's product line.[12] Honda has always trailed import rival Toyota in U.S. sales, even though its Accord is very successful. One reason is

Building Customer Equity

Keeping customers coming to Thorton's

Thorton's operates convenience stores in Kentucky, Indiana, Illinois, Ohio, and Connecticut. The typical convenience store strategy has been to focus on gasoline sales but sell customers a few high-margin, fill-in items after they fill their gas tanks. Gasoline is still important in terms of sales volume and revenue. However, because of the volatility of gasoline prices, increased price competition from Wal-Mart and Kroger, and possible gas shortages, Thorton's is implementing a strategy to expand its product mix and build customer equity.

The objective is to have half of its profits come from food and grocery items by 2007. It plans to achieve this objective by getting customers to make their two or three grocery store fill-in purchases at Thornton's instead of the grocery store. Stores are being redesigned with carpeting, hardwood floors, and shelves filled with paper products, cleaning supplies, pet foods, and other popular grocery items. Products being emphasized include pasta, ice cream, fruits, vegetables, and health and beauty aids. These are the types of products consumers typically purchase in a $30 trip through the fast-lane checkout at a grocery store. The Thorton image is moving from just a convenience store to more of a corner market for its customers. It seems to be working as one store manager said: "We sell 100 bananas a day here and we've never sold bananas before."

What if Gatorade made water?

Lightly flavored. Vitamin charged. **Propel. The fitness water.**

A line-filling strategy adds products throughout a product line. Gatorade is adding Propel fitness water to its product line.

that Honda does not have pickup trucks to compete with Toyota's Tacoma or Tundra or the pickups offered by General Motors and Ford. The company realizes its growth in the United States is limited unless it adds pickups within its product mix.

A key concern in adding products to a product line is evaluating whether a new product will add new sales or take sales away from current products in the line. **Cannibalization** occurs when a new product takes sales away from existing products. A great deal of cannibalization shifts sales from one product to the new product, with little overall gain for the firm.

Strategies for adding products to a product line are typically most successful when cannibalization is low. For example, Yoo-Hoo has been around for 70 years and is the number-one chocolate beverage in the United States. The company wanted to increase sales, so it added new flavors to its product line. Called Yoo-Hoo Mix-ups, they are blends of the basic chocolate drink with other flavors such as coconut, mint, banana, and strawberry. An initial concern was that sales of Mix-ups would merely replace those of the original chocolate beverage. However, early focus groups and initial sales indicate that cannibalization will be minimal and the Mix-ups will increase total sales for the company.[13]

Jack Kennard, Senior Vice President, Executive Director of Global Brand Development, Brown-Forman Beverages Worldwide talks about increasing a product line: "Effective strategies for increasing a product line should enhance product image and satisfy different customer needs. Brown-Forman has used upward-stretch strategies to increase sales and enhance product image. For example, our best selling brand is Jack Daniel's Tennessee Whiskey. We successfully introduced Gentleman Jack Tennessee Whiskey as a premium quality addition to the original line. Then, Jack Daniel's Single Barrel Tennessee Whiskey was released as a new super-premium product. Cannibalization has been zero, as these new product "family members" met different customer needs, boosted volume and profit, and enhanced brand image both within the United States and internationally."

Decreasing the Product Line

Firms must consider deleting products when they are not successful, when they have reached the decline stage of the life cycle, or when the costs of marketing long product lines are high. Such **product line contraction** is normally painful but often necessary to improve performance. For example, because of intense price competition and decreasing consumer demand, ConAgra deleted breaded fish patties and breakfast sandwiches from its Healthy Choice product line.[14]

The more products a company sells in a product line, the higher its marketing expenses tend to be. Deleting products reduces expenses and can lead to improved profitability. For example, Borden reported disappointing financial results for several quarters. In examining strategies to turn performance around, the company realized it had 2,800 products in its snack-food product line, compared with 445 for industry leader Frito-Lay. The revised strategy was to discard marginal products and eliminate product items so that the remaining products could be better supported.[15]

Product-line strategies are extremely important, and they are the result of complex and difficult decisions. The products in a product line represent a firm's offerings to its customers. As customer needs change or competitors introduce new products, a firm must be able to respond. One proper response might be to add products to a product line; another response, to delete some.

Product-Mix Strategies

The product mix consists of all product lines and individual products marketed by a firm. Strategies at all levels must be consistent for maximum effectiveness.

Strategic Alternatives

The basic product mix strategic alternatives are to add new product lines or to delete existing ones. Many firms achieve growth objectives by expanding the product mix through the addition of new product lines. Successes are most likely to occur when a new product line has some similarity to existing product lines. For example, Fidelity Investments is an established mutual funds marketer. When its business plateaued at 6.2 million accounts, Fidelity decided to expand its focus from mutual fund investment to serving all of a customer's financial needs. It added several new financial service product lines, from credit cards to insurance.[16]

Some similarities between product lines may not seem obvious at first glance. For example, Circuit City has added used cars to its product mix. How are used cars similar to Circuit City's established consumer electronics and major-appliance product lines? President and chief executive officer Richard L. Sharp commented: "We believe that automobile retailing offers opportunities to capitalize on Circuit City's strengths in customer service and big-ticket retailing."[17]

Although expanding into new product lines might seem to be an easy growth strategy, many firms find such success elusive. Adding new product lines can be risky. The more different a new product line is from existing lines, the more risk involved. This is especially true for firms that move into products outside their areas of expertise. The popular business press presents almost daily examples of firms that have downsized by dropping unrelated product lines. For example, Ford Motor Credit is getting out of online brokerages, mortgages, and commercial lending to focus on financing sales of Ford vehicles and dealer loans.[18] Bank of America is dropping auto leasing and high-risk mortgages to emphasize product lines with less risk and more profit potential.[19]

There are, however, many success stories of firms moving into new product and service areas. Texas Instruments, for example, has performed well with a product mix consisting of semiconductors, defense electronics, printers, notebook computers, productivity software, and consumer electronics products. And the company is capitalizing on recent technological advances to position itself to move into different areas of the emerging information super highway.[20]

Jack Kennard, Senior Vice President, Executive Director of Global Brand Development, Brown-Forman Beverages Worldwide emphasizes the value of adding new product lines: "Adding new product lines can provide an ongoing source of novelty, create excitement, and help capture new customers. Jack Daniel's Country Cocktails is one example. This new product line helped Brown-Forman enter the premium low-alcohol beverage market. Jack Daniel's Country Cocktails expanded the Jack Daniel's brand into new consumer markets, particularly females. By attracting new customers, Brown-Forman increased sales and enhanced the Jack Daniel's brand."

Branding Strategies

Our discussion of branding in Chapter 8 focuses on branding decisions for a single product. As firms expand product mixes and extend product lines, brand decisions become more complicated. Companies marketing multiple products and services need a strategy to guide branding decisions. The basic options are presented in Exhibit 10–8.

One option is to use an **individual brand name strategy;** that is, the firm establishes specific brand names for each individual product in a product line. This approach allows a firm to choose what seems like an effective brand name for a particular product. The drawback is that because individual brand names are unrelated, products stand alone. Brand equity from one brand cannot benefit another. Procter & Gamble is probably the most famous user of individual brand names. P&G's objective is for

Many companies market a diverse product mix. Adidas emphasizes a product mix to meet different customer needs.

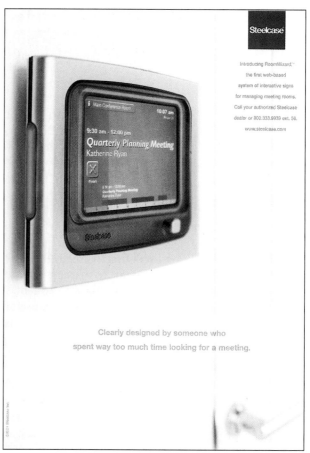

Sometimes firms add product lines in new business areas. Steelcase added Web-based interactive signs to its office furniture product mix.

Exhibit 10-8   *Branding strategies*

all products to compete on their merits, so each product has its own brand name. For instance, P&G's detergent products have well-known individual brand names such as Tide, Cheer, Bold, Dash, and Oxydol.

The other basic option is to adopt a **family brand name strategy;** in this case, all brand names are associated with some type of family brand name. One approach is to brand all product items in the product mix with the company name, as Heinz and General Electric do. Another choice is to use different family brands for different product lines, with all items in a given product line bearing that same family brand name. Sears does this by using the Craftsman brand for tools, the Kenmore brand for appliances, and the Die Hard brand for batteries. A final alternative is to use both a family and an individual brand name for each product—for example, Kellogg's Rice Krispies and Kellogg's Raisin Bran.

Family brand name strategies can help firms increase product lines or add product lines. New products that build on the brand equity of an established brand are called *brand extensions*. Research indicates that the positive associations consumers have with a brand can be transferred to new products in the same category (increasing product lines) as well as to new products in different product lines (adding product lines). If successful, these extensions build additional brand equity.[21] Milky Way has used a family brand name strategy successfully in adding products to its candy-bar line and establishing an ice-cream product line.[22] There is some risk to using a family brand name strategy, however, because unsuccessful new products could weaken the brand equity of the established brand.

Ethical Issues in Product and Service Strategies

Marketers should ensure that products are safe and not harmful, consumers receive relevant product information, there are meaningful differences among products in a product line, and if something goes wrong, there is a mechanism for redress.[23] It is important to continuously assess performance and safety issues from the new-product development process through production and marketing. Any identified problems should be corrected as soon as possible. Failure to do so can lead to dissatisfied customers, product recalls, and expensive lawsuits.[24]

Product recalls mean the marketer must allow customers to return the product to get the performance or safety defect corrected. This can be very expensive and harmful to a company's image. Companies can limit expenses and harmful effects by establishing a procedure to recall the product voluntarily. Without an established procedure, the process is likely to be inefficient and costly. If marketers do not proactively recall the product, they can be coerced to do so by various government agencies. For example, the National Highway Traffic Safety Commission forced Chrysler's three recalls of its Neon car, and the Consumer Product Safety Commission recalled several brands of crayons containing hazardous lead levels.[25]

Potential harmful effects from products is a difficult issue. Should firms market products that consumers want but that are harmful to them? Some observers argue consumers should be allowed to decide through their purchasing practices; others think companies should not market products with harmful effects. The current battle over the marketing of cigarettes is an example of this issue. Another example is movie-theater popcorn. Most movie theaters prepare popcorn with coconut oil, which raises blood cholesterol more than any other fat or oil. Movie theaters could change to a more healthful way of preparing their popcorn, but consumers like the smell and taste of coconut oil-popped popcorn better. This issue will continue to receive attention because it is being pushed by the Center for Science in the Public Interest.[26]

The issue of harmful effects goes beyond individual consumers to society at large. Products that are not harmful to consumers may create environmental problems for society as a whole, such as emissions from automobiles, nonbiodegradable packaging, and polluting chemicals. Marketers should act in a socially responsible manner by addressing the potential environmental problems associated with product use and disposal.

Product counterfeiting is an increasing problem for many products. A U.S. Customs agent drives a steamroller over 17,000 counterfeit designer watches smuggled into the country. These watches were worth $620,000.

An increasingly important ethical and legal issue from a global perspective is product counterfeiting. *Product counterfeiting* occurs when a company copies another firm's trademark, copyright, or patent. Although this sometimes happens with U.S. firms, product counterfeiting by foreign companies is a major problem. The U.S. International Trade Commission estimated that counterfeit products by foreign companies cost U.S. firms between $6 and $8 billion a year in sales.[27]

The problem is especially difficult in China. Chinese stores carry products that look like Colgate toothpaste, Del Monte canned food, or Kellogg's Corn Flakes. But the toothpaste isn't Cologate, the canned food is made by a company called Jia Long, and the cereal is Kongalu Corn Strips. The damage from product counterfeiting in China is estimated to be $800 million a year. Microsoft argued that Chinese software pirates cost it $30 million annually, and this cost is growing. The developing legal system in China makes it difficult to stop these infringements on property rights.[28] China's entry into the World Trade Organization (WTO) was supposed to make counterfeiting harder and prosecuting easier. However, the wording of the Agreement on Trade-Related Aspects of Intellectual Property (TRIPs) is ambiguous and not much has been accomplished to stop counterfeiters in China.[29]

To ensure they are operating in an ethical manner, marketers need to answer the following questions appropriately:[30]

- Is the product safe when used as intended?
- Is the product safe when misused in a way that is foreseeable?
- Have any competitors' patents or copyrights been violated?
- Is the product compatible with the physical environment?
- Is the product environmentally compatible when disposed of?
- Do any organizational stakeholders object to the product?

Conclusions

As this chapter clearly shows, product and service strategies are extremely important. These decisions must be integrated at different levels of the organization, and they provide direction for the other areas of the marketing mix. Pricing, distribution, and marketing-communications decisions are all influenced by the product and service strategies of a firm.

Summary

1. **Understand the different characteristics of a product mix.** A product mix is the assortment of products marketed by a firm. It consists of individual products organized into product lines. The basic characteristics of a product mix are its width, length, and consistency. Product mix width refers to the number of different product lines in the mix; product line length to the number of different products in a product line; product mix consistency to how related the product lines are.

2. **Recognize the stages and characteristics of the product life cycle.** Products go through a life cycle similar to a biological life cycle. The basic stages of the product life cycle are introduction, growth, maturity, and decline. Sales and profits change over the life cycle as competitors enter the industry and markets become saturated.

3. **Identify appropriate marketing strategies for products in different life cycle stages.** Marketing strategies differ for products as they move through different life cycle stages. In the introduction stage, the firm emphasizes generating consumer awareness and stimulating trial of the product. During the growth stage, it focuses on building consumer brand preference to secure a strong market position. The maturity stage calls for a variety of strategies to maintain market share and extend the life cycle. During the decline stage, the firm must consider options to maintain, harvest, or drop the product.

4. **Describe the limitations of the product life cycle concept.** The product life cycle concept applies mainly to product forms rather than to product classes or specific brands. If, because of the concept, a marketer thinks a product has a predetermined life, it could adopt a marketing strategy that limits the product's life. The product life cycle concept is descriptive, not predictive.

5. **Discuss different product-mix and product-line strategies.** The basic product-mix strategic alternatives are to add to or drop product lines from the mix. The similarity between product lines and the use of a firm's strengths are key considerations in making these strategic decisions. Branding strategies are also important as firms add products to a product mix.

   The basic product-line strategies are to increase or decrease the length of a line. Downward-stretch, upward-stretch, two-way-stretch, and line-filling strategies can be used to increase product line length. Product line contraction will decrease product line length.

Understanding Marketing Terms and Concepts

Thinking About Marketing

1. What are the major differences between the growth and maturity stages of the product life cycle?

2. What are the alternative marketing strategies firms might use for products in the maturity stage?

3. What are the major differences between style, fashion, and fad?

4. How do shortened product life cycles affect marketers?

5. Look at "Being Entrepreneurial: Develop an Effective Product Mix." Why has Skechers been so successful?

6. How would you define the product mix for any firm?

7. Reread "Building Customer Equity: Keeping Customers coming to Thorton's." What else might Thorton's do to increase customer equity?

8. Why is product line contraction so difficult?

9. What is meant by the term *cannibalization*?

10. What are the risks associated with adding new product lines that differ greatly from a firm's existing product lines?

Applying Marketing Skills

1. Go to a local supermarket, drug store, or discount store. Walk through the packaged-goods aisles, consider promotional and packaging information, and identify at least five examples of marketing strategies for mature products. Evaluate each marketing strategy example.

2. Obtain the annual report for any firm. Draw a chart that illustrates the product mix for this firm. Evaluate the firm's product mix.

3. Assume you have just invented a new-to-the-world product. Describe the product, and develop the marketing strategies you would use in the introduction and growth stages of the product life cycle.

Using the www in Marketing

Activity One   Go to the Starbucks Web site (http://www.starbucks.com)

1. Discuss the product mix offered by Starbucks.

2. How does Starbucks use this Web site to expand relationships with customers?

3. What recommendations can you offer to improve the Starbucks Web site?

Activity Two   Fender Musical Instruments is one of the largest and most famous guitar manufacturers in the world. The Guitar Center retail chain is the largest reseller of Fender products. Go to the following Web sites:
Fender (http://www.fender.com)
Guitar Center (http://www.guitarcenter.com)

1. Describe the product mixes offered by each company.

2. Describe the product lines offered by each company.

3. Discuss the reasons for the similarities and differences in the product mixes and product lines offered by the two companies.

Making Marketing Decisions

Case 10-1 *American Express: Expanding Electronically*

American Express has developed a trusted brand name in its 140-year history. The company is a giant in the financial services and travel industries with over 24 million customers. Several new products and product lines are being introduced to make American Express a giant on the Web. It wants to provide customers with a seamless web of financial planning, banking, travel, and shopping services.

One service is an addition to the American Express credit card product line. The Blue card is being introduced with very low interest rates: zero interest for six months, followed by fixed rates of 9.99 percent to 15.99 percent with no annual fee. It includes a "digital wallet," which stores all of a customer's key shopping information—for example, addresses and credit card numbers—on a secure American Express site. The Blue card has a built-in computer chip; the card can be plugged into a special reader attached to the customer's computer to verify the shopper's identity and unlock the "digital wallet." Once this is done, American Express zaps the information to the electronic merchant and the purchase is completed. This approach is easier than filling out forms with each digital retailer and provides the security desired by many customers.

American Express also has a new product line called Membership B@nking. This is an online bank providing many financial services. In order to attract customers, the bank is currently paying top rates for one-year certificates of deposit. It hopes to move many of its existing customers to electronic banking and expand relationships with them by selling them credit cards, insurance, and financial planning services.

The company's final new product line is AmEx Brokerage. American Express tried to enter the online brokerage market with Financial Direct but was unsuccessful. This second attempt is more promising: AmEx Brokerage will provide stock trades, with neither commissions nor money-management fees, to customers who keep at least $100,000 on deposit. These customers can also tap into research used by the company's mutual-fund managers and use new online financial planning tools. The expectation is that brokerage customers will translate into more business for the firm's financial planners and advisors.

American Express is trying to leverage its brand name into the online world. It is, however, using a low-price strategy to attract customers. This is a different pricing strategy for the firm and raises questions as to how profitable these new online products will be.

Questions

1. How do the new online products and product lines change the American Express product mix?

2. What is your evaluation of the strategy for AmEx Brokerage? Do you think the firm will be successful in its second online brokerage attempt? Why or why not?

3. How important is the American Express brand name to the success of the firm's electronic strategy?

4. What is your evaluation of the low-price strategy for these online products in the short run and in the long term?

Case 10-2 Hewlett-Packard and Compaq: The Right Product Mix

After a long and hard fight, the merger between Hewlett-Packard (HP) and Compaq was finally approved. Many meetings have been conducted to make sure the merger works. However, a number of issues are unresolved, and whether the merged company will be able to achieve its objectives is still unclear. One of the toughest issues is determining the right product mix. There is clear overlap in some product lines, so dropping some product lines will certainly eliminate costs, but it will also reduce sales and might hurt some customer relationships. The new company needs to achieve expected profits by limiting sales declines and meeting cost-reduction projections.

The first step was to compare competing HP and Compaq products side-by-side and kill the weaker one. This resulted in eliminating a number of products and product lines, notably HP's branded servers, business PCs, and its Jornada handheld computer, and Compaq's Tru64 Unix operating system. The companies started with 85,000 products, and this process reduced the total number to 62,000. Costly duplication still remains, so more work will have to be done to identify products to be eliminated.

One surprising decision was to continue selling both HP and Compaq PCs in stores. The combined brands represent 60 percent retail market share. Keeping both brands will give the merged company more retail shelf space. This should help keep competitors off the shelves and lead to increased sales. In addition, the brands are targeted at different market segments. Compaq is focused on consumers who want to set up home offices and connect wirelessly to the Internet. HP PCs, in contrast, are positioned as home entertainment devices and as digital imaging machines for photography enthusiasts. The critical question is if this strategy will lead to more PC sales and more sales of add-ons, such as printers and digital cameras that have high profit margins.

This decision is complicated by the sluggish PC market. Total PC sales declined in 2002 and are expected to only grow slowly in the immediate future. Also, the retail strategy used by HP and Compaq is costly. During the current PC slowdown, HP and Compaq PC inventories reached six weeks as compared to four days at Dell. The new company will have to figure out a way to make the direct model work better as a merged company than it did for each company separately.

There are some bright spots. Both the printer and services businesses are growing and profitable. These may be the bookends of the new product mix. What products and product lines should be between these bookends is the question to be answered.

Questions

1. What are the critical product mix decisions for the HP and Compaq merger?

2. What process would you suggest for determining which products to eliminate?

3. Do you think both the HP and Compaq PC brands should be kept? Why or why not?

4. What new products might be appropriate for the merged company?

Pricing Concepts

After studying this chapter, you should be able to:

1 Realize the importance of price and understand its role in the marketing mix.

2 Understand the characteristics of the different pricing objectives that companies can adopt.

3 Identify many of the influences on marketers' pricing decisions.

4 Explain how consumers form perceptions of quality and value.

5 Understand price/quality relationships and internal and external reference prices.

www.edmunds.com

Headquartered in Santa Monica, California, Edmunds.com is the Internet's pioneer and leader in providing free unbiased automotive information. Users are offered automotive pricing data, automobile and other vehicle reviews, and rebate and incentive information. Edmunds.com was ranked #1 in The Wall Street Journal's Survey of Car-Shopping Web sites. Edmunds.com, which spends millions of dollars on outdoor, print, and radio ads to promote itself as an unbiased source of vehicle pricing and reviews, makes its money from referrals to marketing partners. Edmund's True Market Value system lets customers find the right prices per region for a vehicle, and then helps them decide how and where to buy it. Dealers, hesitant at first, now praise Edmunds as the most accurate site.

Edmunds.com is now planning for global expansion. As part of this expansion, Edmunds.com has partnered with UK-based Autologic, a market leader in automotive logistics and outsourcing. Like the original U.S. site, pricing and financial information will provide consumers the increased opportunity to make informed choices and save money.

Pricing information offered by Internet Web sites like Edmunds.com has forced major manufacturers, such as Ford and General Motors, to reconsider their traditional price advertising, which historically has been based upon "manufacturer suggested retail prices." However, expanded price information on the Internet now allows consumers to negotiate based upon wholesale prices gathered free on the Web. In reaction to pressure to provide more information to their consumers, Ford has already run a pilot program in Arizona in which consumers are able to click from Ford's Web site to dealer information that includes price points closer to the invoice price Ford charges the dealer. The ability of consumers to gather price information from sites like Edmunds.com will increase their ability to judge offered prices and to make purchase decisions with more confidence.

Edmunds.com has begun to let outside advertisers promote on their Web site. These additions enable less reliance on banner advertising, which is meeting with increasing disfavor, and facilitates interactions between advertisers and consumers close to purchase. For instance, if a consumer clicks on the Lexus page, she or he will see a vertical banner ad alongside a complete list of the luxury-car models. If the viewer clicks on the banner, a short ad presentation using slide-show technology will appear. This additional advertising presents information regarding pricing, financing, and product features.

Many factors influence price, which in turn influences sales and profits. Companies can charge premium prices because they offer high-quality products that consumers value. The premium prices enable distributors of the products to maintain sizable margins (the difference between price and cost of goods sold) and gain healthy profits. Perceptions of value at the consumer level allow higher prices, which can be used to maintain high quality in production and gain enthusiastic support by distributors and retailers.

Determining prices for complex product lines is an important task. Prices set too high will discourage sales; prices set too low may result in unprofitable business and a revenue stream that does not cover costs and expenses. Buyers in business-to-business markets, as well as individual consumers, often evaluate other factors, but price remains a primary choice determinant. And the interaction of prices with promotional activities often affects the firm's image.

In this chapter, we discuss the role of price and the major influences on pricing decisions. We explore the various pricing objectives governing marketers' decisions. Finally we discuss how advertised prices affect consumer perceptions of value and decision making.

The Role of Price

Price is the amount of money a buyer pays to a seller in exchange for products and services. It reflects the economic sacrifice a buyer must make to acquire something. This is the traditional economic concept of price, called the **objective price.** Where barter and exchanges pass for currency, prices may be nonmonetary. Much trade between developed and less-developed countries involves barter. This practice, called *countertrade* by economists, holds particular promise as a means of helping Eastern European economies. For instance, Germany has traded Mercedes-Benz trucks to Ecuador for bananas, and Russia has traded passenger aircraft to China for some consumer goods. An additional method of payment is equity. This method was frequently used in the technology sector in 2000, when the customers were small businesses buying hardware. West End Resources, a New-York–based consultant to small businesses, regularly receives payment part in cash and part in customer equity.[1]

Prices frequently have other labels. The price of a university or college education is called *tuition.* The prices charged by professionals such as doctors and lawyers are referred to as *fees.* Loans are paid for by *interest payments;* charges for meter violations and overdue books are paid as *fines;* apartment charges are called *rents.* Other terms used to describe prices include *premiums, taxes,* and *wages.* In nonprofit situations, *donations* and *time* represent prices to support charities and political candidates. In all cases, however, these terms reflect prices associated with the receipt of something of value.

Speaking from Experience

Mack Turner
Managing Director
Bank of America

"Banks have learned that a key to influencing price elasticity is the management of the perceived importance of the bank to the customer. In corporate and investment banking, firms strive to be perceived as their customer's top bank. This is frequently referred to as 'relationship banking.' The customer looks to the relationship bank not only for products (services) but for advice and guidance. The value of the relationship and proactive attention is seen by the customer as justification for a higher price."

Turner joined Bank of America in 1981 after completing his MBA at the University of South Carolina. Previously, he managed marketing research and the bank's service quality and incentive plan management divisions. Turner stresses the importance of relationships and the value of services. If the banker does a good job understanding the customer's business strategy and truly finds creative solutions to his or her clients' business needs, he or she will be rewarded with additional business and less price sensitivity. Research has consistently shown that customers do have relationships with banks and within that small set of relationship banks they have "lead" banks. The lead bank receives the majority of the revenue the customer awards his or her banks.

Telephones and telephone services have become quite price competitive and frequent dealing is used to attract price sensitive customers.

List prices, set before any discounts or reductions, may differ from the actual market price or price paid. Price discounts, allowances, and rebates may make the market price different from the list price. Also a product's price may differ for particular uses or segments. In pharmaceuticals, for example, a drug might have a prescription price, a hospital price, and a Medicare price.[2] *Partitioned prices* involve services for which different prices are listed separately, and customers of all types need to examine their bills carefully. For example, package carriers, such as FedEx and UPS, include a growing list of fees that do not fall under normal delivery pricing.[3]

Basic Price Mix versus Price Promotion Mix

A recent view of the marketing mix (price, product, marketing communications, distribution) makes a distinction between the firm's basic price mix and the price promotion mix,[4] described in Exhibit 11–1. The **basic price mix** includes those components that define the size and means of payment exchanged for goods or services. Examples include the list price, usual terms of payment, and terms of credit. The **price promotion mix** includes supplemental components of price, which aim at encouraging purchase behavior by strengthening the basic price mix during relatively short periods of time. These include sale prices, end-of-season sales, coupons, temporary discounts, and favorable terms of payment and credit. For business-to-business marketers, a number of factors may reduce the invoice price to a final transaction price. The most common include prompt payment discounts, volume buying incentives, and cooperative advertising incentives.[5]

Price promotions are designed to attract nonusers of products and services, as well as product users of competing brands. Price promotions may also be intended to increase the quantity amount and/or frequency of consumption among current brand users. Marketers must be careful, however, that price promotions do not detract from perceptions of quality, which eventually lowers overall perceived value and intentions to buy. Some argue that consumers who buy only because of the promotion will cease to buy once the price reduction is retracted. For these reasons, nonmonetary promotions such as premiums and extra quantity may be as effective in generating loyal behavior in the long term.

Often retail-grocery and discount-store prices are described as being either EDLP ("everyday low price") or HiLo ("high-low"). The latter strategy involves offering temporary but deep discounts in a small group of product categories. EDLP as-

Exhibit 11–1   *The basic price and price promotion mixes*

	The mix	Components	Examples
	Basic price mix	Fixed prices and terms of exchange	List price, usual terms of payment, terms of credit
	Price promotion mix	Additional price reductions in various forms for short periods to tempt people to buy	Exceptionally favorable price, end-of-season sales, exceptionally favorable terms

Thinking Critically

- Manufacturers may charge different prices for the same product in different markets. The pharmaceutical industry has come under criticism for charging high prices for certain drugs, such as AIDS medicines, in the United States, while providing the same medicines at substantially reduced prices in less developed countries. Is this practice justifiable from a consumer and a business perspective?

- Introduction of the euro has been predicted to improve transparency and create pressures for uniform pricing. Will the euro necessarily lead companies to adopt a single pricing structure across the European marketplace? What factors might contribute to price differentials in the euro zone?

sumes constant low prices across a wide assortment of product categories. In practice, retailers do not adopt a single position, but customize their pricing strategies and tactics to market conditions, to categories, and to brands. In fact, price strategies can vary on at least four dimensions. *Price consistency* reflects the EDLP/HiLo continuum. *Price promotion intensity* represents the frequency, depth, and duration of price discounts. *Price/promotion coordination* represents the extent to which price discounts occur with supporting in-store displays and/or newspaper feature advertising. Last, the brand price level relative to the cost of other brands in a category is important. For example, higher-priced national brands are often effectively price discounted.[6]

The Importance of Price and Pricing Decisions

Price is the one aspect of the marketing mix that is most easily changed. Setting a price does not require the investment involved with advertising or developing products or establishing distribution channels. Price changes are certainly more easily implemented than distribution and product changes. Consequently, the fastest and most effective way for a company to realize its maximum profit is to get its pricing right.[7]

Price also affects customer demand. **Price elasticity of demand,** or the responsiveness of demand to changes in price, is more than 10 times higher than advertising elasticity. That is, a certain percentage change in price can lead to 10 to 20 times stronger effects on sales than the same percentage change in advertising expenditures.[8] For these reasons pricing decisions are among the most important decisions that marketers regularly confront.

Price promotions or price reductions have become so common in some consumer product categories that sale prices represent the norm. Price reductions provide many benefits to consumers, manufacturers, wholesalers, and retailers. The primary benefits are listed in Exhibit 11–2.

Both the importance and difficulty of pricing decisions have increased in recent years. These changes have arisen because of several environmental phenomena.[9]

- Introduction of look-alike products increases sensitivity to small price differences.

- Internet access to price and competitive information have made price comparisons easier and have increased pressures on prices.

- Demand for services, which are labor-intensive, hard to price, and sensitive to inflation, has increased.

- Increased foreign competition has placed added pressure on firms' pricing decisions.

- Changes within the legal environment and economic uncertainty have made pricing decisions more complex.

Exhibit 11–2	*Benefits of price promotions*

- Stimulate retailer sales and store traffic.
- Enable manufacturers to adjust to variations in supply and demand without changing list prices.
- Enable regional businesses to compete against brands with large advertising budgets.
- Reduce retailer's risk in stocking new brands by encouraging consumer trial and clearing retail inventories of obsolete or unsold merchandise.
- Satisfy trade agreements between retailers and manufacturers.
- Stimulate demand for both promoted products and complementary (nonpromoted) products.
- Give consumers the satisfaction of being smart shoppers who are taking advantage of price specials.

- Shifts in the relative power within distribution channels from manufacturers to retailers, who are more price-oriented, also has increased the importance of price decisions.

- A bottom-line emphasis places more pressure on performance. Price reductions boost short-term earnings more effectively than does advertising.

- Technology that has reduced the time from new-product idea generation to production also shortens the average life span of products.

The downward price pressure from a business slowdown requires careful pricing execution. Lowering prices may help cover fixed costs and enhance short-term performance. Managerial pricing decisions should attempt to stabilize prices and limit industry price erosion in economic downturns and to maintain price margins for select customers and markets. Companies with low-cost structure, such as Dell, Southwest Airlines, and Wal-Mart, may be able to cut costs, lower prices, and build market share in weak economic situations. However, for many firms, pricing decisions during an economic downturn should not necessarily involve distinctively cutting prices. Instead of sales goals, firms often set profit contribution goals for individual products, market segments, and individual customers.[10]

The general limits on prices are depicted graphically in Exhibit 11–3. Prices are limited on the high side by what the market will accept and by competitive prices. On the low side, prices must cover costs plus some return on investment. Corporate objectives generally increase pressure toward higher prices to cover overhead and fixed costs and generate an adequate return or profit level. The exhibit depicts the limited latitude that managers may actually have in setting prices.

Exhibit 11–3

Limits to price setting

Price ceiling (demand limits)

Competitive factors

Final pricing discretion

Corporate objectives

Price floor (direct variable costs)

Internet Pricing Effects

Interactive shopping on the Internet continues to improve consumer customer access to price and quality information. And, across-store and across-source comparisons are facilitated. These phenomena hold for individual consumers and business-to-business buyers. Questions remain, however, as to whether price sensitivity will increase from this easier access to information or whether easier access to other information that differentiates products will offset these pressures toward price sensitivity.[11]

For goods that are common across stores or business-to-business sellers, price sensitivity will undoubtedly increase. Prices for many products sold on the Internet are being pulled downward by cost-conscious consumers who cross-comparison shop. Auctioneers, such as eBay.com and icollector.com, offer competitive prices for even hard-to-locate items and are particularly well suited to marketing smaller items that can be scanned for viewing and easily shipped.[12] During the dot com period of rapid growth, online retailers used giveaway prices to attract consumers. Unfortunately, these buyers were the types of consumers firms needed to avoid. Also regarding the effects of the Internet on prices, the prevalence of fixed prices may diminish due to the Internet in that the public arena, in which consumers decide to buy based upon the manufacturer's suggested price, is less used. Auctions, in which supply and demand set prices, reach new customers and free selling efforts to focus upon brand benefits. However, the drawbacks of online auctions include the growing realization that some customers will resent paying more than someone else for the same item and that auctionlike mechanisms focus on price comparisons that may erode brand loyalty.[13]

For sellers, savings come from lower real-estate and rental costs and reduced outlays for advertising, inventory, and transportation. However, price is not the only avenue to success for marketing on the Internet. Customer satisfaction and customer service are paramount. Customers lured online with low prices, no search costs, and easy ordering are demanding service like traditional customers. Increasingly, companies are making available service reps, offering the ability to track orders, and responding more quickly to e-mail. Recently, Compaq Computer Corporation had to offer $250 gift certificates to appease customers who were dissatisfied with their Internet shopping service.

Of particular importance, marketers who begin to sell online face problems in balancing their online efforts with their traditional outlets. This balance has been particularly difficult for computer companies like Dell and Gateway that sell to both individual consumers and businesses. Dell sells direct to consumers and uses the Internet to sell and support corporate buyers. Online sellers must consider the effects of both their Internet efforts and the prices they are charging on their own dealers and outlets.[14]

Global Pricing Considerations

Pricing in international markets is particularly difficult. Firms pursuing global opportunities find that prices for the same item can be extraordinarily different across countries, even within countries; prices seem to be driven by different dynamics in each situation. The changes caused by the introduction of the *euro* currency in Europe are currently evolving. With the introduction of the euro, consumers should be able to more easily compare prices, which should lead to some lower prices for some goods. Clothing items are still often bought regionally, while mass-produced autos—Volkswagen, Fiat, Renault, and Peugeot—should be negatively affected by greater transparency in price differences. On the practical side, currency changes have made operations initially more difficult for retailers, banks, and vending machine companies.[15]

International pricing is also made difficult by exchange-rate differences and the need to present prices in foreign currency values. The **exchange rate** is the price of one country's currency in terms of another country's currency. Changes in exchange rates can affect the prices consumers in different countries have to pay for imported goods. Also, prices of goods are often driven up by taxes, tariffs, and transportation costs. *Protective tariffs* are taxes levied on imported products to raise the prices of those products in efforts to keep local prices competitive.

With the transition in Europe to the euro monetary system, marketers will encounter a market system that rivals that of the United States. The use of a single currency will force marketers to restructure their pricing decisions. This adoption of a single currency will weaken what has been a powerful marketing tool—price differentiation by country. Once the single currency is completely operative, price differences between countries that are now hidden by currency differences will be apparent and will force companies to differentiate their products in other ways.[16]

Pricing Objectives

Pricing decisions are made to achieve certain objectives consistent with a firm's overall mission and marketing strategy. Five objectives commonly guide pricing decisions: ensuring market survival; enhancing sales growth; maximizing company profits; deterring competition from entering a company's niche or market position; and establishing or maintaining a particular product-quality image.[17]

Firms may pursue a combination of these objectives. The objective at Texas Instruments in pricing calculators is to achieve a cost advantage by virtue of growth in sales and dominant market share.[18] For Texas Instruments, large market share translates into competitive advantage through economies of scale from high-volume production and marketing operations. Kmart emphasizes low prices in efforts to generate sales growth and volume. Such objectives provide long-term direction to a company's pricing and promotion decisions.

Market Survival

In some instances, a firm must set prices to ensure its short-term survival. That is, the firm adjusts prices so it can stay in business. Excess production capacity, for example, may require a firm to lower prices so it can keep plants open and maintain operations. In some instances, a firm may adjust prices upward if increased revenues are required.

Recently, the cruise industry's top two carriers, Carnival Cruise Line and Royal Caribbean Cruise Line, for example, broke all reservation records. To fill their rooms, however, they had to resort to deep price discounts. Increasing price consciousness and worries about the economy had led consumers to postpone trips, to trade down to less-expensive accommodations, and to demand lower prices.[19]

Frequent end-of-season deals by retailers represent efforts to move inventory and thereby recoup cash for investment in continuing operations and for purchasing new merchandise. Similarly, manufacturers may reduce prices as new products are introduced in place of existing models. In some cases, even very successful companies like Procter & Gamble have lowered prices to lessen erosion in sales.[20] Pricing for survival is a short-term objective, however. At some point, profitability and return on investment must be satisfactory to ensure long-term success.

Banks in recent years have seen their market share erode significantly and have begun to price aggressively. In efforts to combat this erosion of interest income, banks have resorted to charging extra fees for some services, such as ATM machines and credit cards. These fee increases represent higher prices to consumers. However, many feel these charges are unethical and reflect unnecessary gouging of customers in efforts to earn extraordinary profits.[21]

Sales Growth

Often companies set prices to stimulate sales growth, realizing that price and sales volume are inversely related such that lower prices will normally increase volume. The benefits from higher volume are based on the assumption that increased sales lower unit production costs, increase total revenues, and enhance profits at lower unit prices. **Penetration pricing** is often the strategy used to accomplish this objective. Firms set penetration prices low to encourage initial product trial and generate sales growth, often as part of market entry strategies. The assumption is that the market is sensitive to price differences and that low prices will drive up sales. In this case, short-term profits are sacrificed for future growth. Penetration pricing is also useful for deterring new competitors and reducing short-term costs through high-volume production runs. For international market entry, particularly for unknown companies or companies entering developing countries, a penetration approach is often useful. Penetration pricing can be effective for limited periods of time and in the right competitive situation. However, firms can overuse this approach and end up creating a market situation where everyone is forced to lower prices continually, driving some competitors from the market but limiting the return on investment for all firms in a market.[22]

Often firms set a high list price but then use a low introductory offer to generate initial sales. This approach is advantageous in that the high list price can signal product quality; otherwise, some buyers may question the quality if a low introductory price is used alone.[23]

Market share describes the firm's portion, or percentage, of the total market or total industry sales. Price setting to maximize market share is similar to price setting in pursuit of sales growth. Greater market share increases a firm's market power, which enables it to extract more-favorable channel arrangements (price and distribution advantages with suppliers) and, in turn, to maintain higher margins.[24]

Banks compete on the basis of different changes and fees associated with their line of services.

Mack Turner discusses the short-term effects of price reductions and the attraction of new business: "When interest rates are high, many banks offer high promotional rates in hopes of attracting new customers. However, some of these offers only attract short-term investors that quickly leave the bank for even more attractive deals elsewhere. Relatedly, some banks give away free checking hoping the new customers will purchase other loans and credit cards. Yet, banks that follow this strategy but do not have specific sales strategies in place to cross-sell additional services to these new customers frequently find this tactic to be unprofitable."

Market share and firm profitability are often related. As in the case of Texas Instruments, greater market share leads to economies of scale. Economies of scale produce competitive advantages because of increased experience and efficiency; that is, companies learn to produce more efficiently with experience, and per-unit costs decline as volume increases.

Even companies with high market shares can be affected by price competition. Gerber, for example, held 72 percent of the $1.1 billion baby-food market. When it raised prices by 5.5 percent, however, competitors Beech-Nut and Heinz began discounting their prices. Monthly sales for Gerber fell quickly by 16 percent.[25] Similarly, price competition between Kellogg's, the number-one marketer of cereals, and Post has forced Kellogg's to reduce prices on some of its most popular brands, like Rice Krispies and Fruit Loops, to fight declining market share.[26]

An increase in market share is a reasonable pricing objective, but not when competitors have lower unit costs. In such instances, it may be impossible to build market share by lowering prices. Similarly, it is foolish for a company to use pricing strategies to increase market share when customers are not price sensitive.[27] In this case, a firm may be better served by targeting particular market segments in which new products have a competitive advantage other than price.

For many companies, the immediate emphasis will be growth in volume, irrespective of market share. This may occur when there are many firms in a market and all have low share. In addition, growth in sales may be derived from generating new customers or getting current customers to buy more per occasion or to buy more frequently, beyond increased growth from attracting competitors' customers.

Exhibit 11–4   *Optimal pricing decisions*

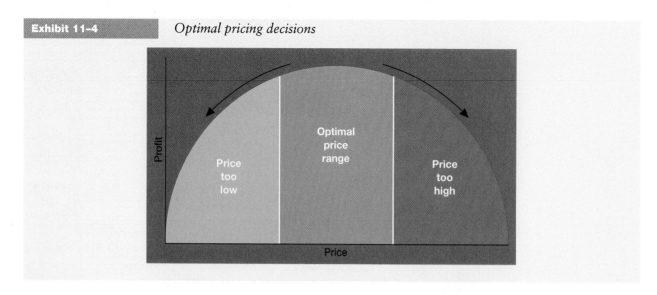

Profitability

Maximization of profits is a frequently stated objective for many companies. Yet, this objective is difficult to implement. Profit maximization requires complete understanding of cost and demand relationships; and estimates of cost and demand for different price alternatives are difficult to obtain. As Exhibit 11–4 demonstrates, if prices are set too low, marketers' profits are insufficient; if set too high, no one will buy. Clearly, however, adequate profits are required, and companies are sensitive to changes in profits over time as indications of performance.

Increased prices can affect profitability three to four times more than increases in sales volume at constant prices. One consumer-durable-products company increased operating profits by nearly 30 percent with only a 2.5 percent increase in average prices. An industrial-equipment manufacturer boosted operating profits by 35 percent by raising prices only 3 percent.[28]

Price skimming is a strategy often associated with profit maximization. It includes setting prices high initially to appeal to consumers who are not price sensitive. In sequential skimming, the firm subsequently lowers prices to appeal to the next most lucrative segments.[29] This strategy allows companies to maximize profits across segments. Besides improving short-term profitability, price skimming lessens demand on production capacity, recoups R&D expenditures, and obtains profits before competitors enter the market. Moreover, consumers may associate product prestige and quality with the high introductory prices prevalent in a skimming approach. Du Pont and IBM are well known for using high introductory prices and skimming practices in marketing new products.[30]

Profitability is often related to **return on investment (ROI)**. ROI is the ratio of income before taxes to total operating assets associated with the product, such as plant and equipment and inventory. As for profitability objectives, the evaluation of the effects of alternative prices on ROI requires realistic estimates of cost and demand for a product or service at different prices. Firms attempting to obtain a desired ROI must take a longer-term, visionary view.

Competitive Pricing

Prices may also be set in reaction to competition. As in penetration pricing, a firm may keep prices low to inhibit competition from entering. Or it may set prices close to those of lower-priced competitors to avoid losing sales. **Price competition** occurs most often when the competing brands are very similar, or when differences between brands are not apparent to prospective buyers.

Prices charged for products must cover the entire bundle of product attributes. These prices also apply to complex offerings such as financial services.

ITT Sheraton's simplified pricing system, modeled on the airlines' pricing approach, has been criticized by competitors as "rate cutting." The Sheraton pricing structure involves one room rate for business travelers, another for 14-day advance reservations, and a third for weekend rates. Sheraton also lowered its standard price. Not surprisingly, Hilton and Hyatt spokespeople warned that price competition would hurt the industry.[31]

Price competition may result in price wars, with prices spiraling downward in succeeding rounds of price cuts. They may lead to such low prices that all competitors operate at a loss in the short run. Price wars are frequent in the airline and computer software industries. Recent price wars over software in Europe may reduce the sizable margins U.S. companies once obtained for their products, margins once justified by the costs of translation.

In **nonprice competition,** the firm attempts to develop buyer interest in benefits such as quality, specific product features, or service. For this to work, customers must view the distinguishing attributes as desirable. Finally, focusing on unserved target markets in which competition is minimal may allow a firm to charge higher prices. For example, Charles Schwab uses its technological communications advantages to offer low competitive prices for financial services.

Competitive strategies have been described as being arrayed on a continuum labeled the **competitive strategy-positioning continuum.** This continuum is anchored by "low-cost leadership" on one end and "differentiation" on the other. For example, one furniture store may emphasize low costs of overhead and operation, a "no frills" warehouse positioning. Alternatively, a competing store may emphasize a more luxurious atmosphere with extensive decorations that appeals to more sophisticated customers. This latter store is more likely to compete on attributes other than price, while the former retail outlet attempts to attract consumers largely by low prices.[32]

Quality and Image Enhancement

Firms often keep prices at a premium to maintain an image of product-quality leadership. **Prestige pricing** is based on the premise that some buyers associate

Scanner technology: Concerns about price accuracy

Scanner technology has become an integral part of the consumer environment. The benefits to retailers are well documented: decreased labor costs, improved inventory control, and enhanced information about buying patterns. In addition, customers benefit from less waiting due to faster checkout processing. These benefits and improvements in technology will undoubtedly yield further development of scanner technology. For example, Kmart, Home Depot, and grocery chains have introduced a self-scanning system where customers charge themselves for their own shopping. Self-check systems improve service when staffs are small and reduce labor costs. Scanner technology also provides benefits to retailers by making available inventory reports to show vendors exactly what is moving and what is not. As such, the retailer is better able to negotiate orders for products that are actually selling. The acquisition of scanner data also facilitates the analysis of historical data

by region, which yields insight into the effects of demographics on product category movement.

Concerns remain, however, regarding the effects on consumer welfare stemming from errors in prices charged to consumers at the cash register. Opinions vary widely, and retailers are often uneasy about discussing the accuracy of scanner systems. However, the cumulative effects of inaccurate pricing are an important issue that directly affects customer satisfaction. In California, Kmart was ordered to institute a program to correct inaccurate shelf prices; the program involved $3 discounts on items scanned higher than the advertised price. One study of 15 grocery stores found that errors in prices systematically favored the retailer for purchases of advertised specials and items on end-of-aisle displays. Also in California, a three-week undercover investigation found 60 percent of retailers failing to accurately charge posted prices.

price with quality and avoid products or services for which they perceive prices as too low. The American Express Gold Card and Lexus are examples of products that have images of exclusivity generated through premium prices. Professionals such as lawyers, doctors, and consultants often charge high fees for similar reasons. In these instances, low prices might imply lower-quality service or expertise; the reputations of these service providers allow the higher prices to be charged. The prestige associated with high-price/high-quality products and services is particularly important in gift-giving situations.

Economic events affect the purchase of luxury goods for all classes, not just the very upscale. During the boom cycle of the 1990s, the percentage of Americans buying image products, including $50,000 autos and $50 socks, was quite high. As the economy weakened, pressures became even more acute on companies that market luxury goods. Firms from car manufacturers to jewelers are marketing their luxury goods to broader audiences using mass-marketing campaigns. As the spread of small luxury BMWs and Mercedes suggest, previously upscale image brands are now readily available. Questions remain regarding the long-term effects of these new lower-priced entries on quality image perceptions.[33]

When the costs of malfunction are high, business buyers often purchase the highest-quality product available, regardless of price. They believe the risk of nonperformance—say, shutting down an entire production line or process—outweighs the risk of paying too much. Likewise, critical component parts that form the core of manufactured goods, such as electronic circuit boards, are likely to carry high prices.

Influences on Pricing Decisions: The Five Cs of Pricing

To ensure that pricing decisions are effective and consistent with the firm's objectives, marketers should consider the **five Cs of pricing** shown in Exhibit 11–5: costs, customers, channels of distribution, competition, and compatibility.[34] These five elements represent the critical influences on pricing decisions.

Costs

Costs associated with producing, distributing, and promoting a product or service are instrumental in establishing the minimum price or floor for pricing decisions. Prices must cover, at least over the long term, the investment and support behind the product, as well as provide enough income and profit to the company. In some instances, costs must be reduced to maintain price competitiveness. This phenomenon is evident in the airline industry. Low-cost providers such as Southwest Airlines have forced full-service airlines, such as American, United, and Delta, to control costs in efforts to maintain competitive prices. These cost reductions have been forced by consumers who are willing to accept fewer extras in service for lower fares.[35]

| Exhibit 11–5 | *Influences on pricing decisions* |

Exhibit 11-6   *Product prices as the mix of costs and profit*

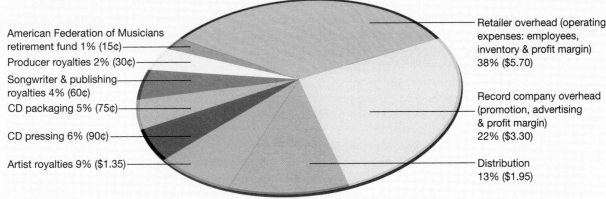

Retailers pay record companies $7 to $11 & more for the CDs they sell for $11 to $17. Who gets that money depends on contracts & market forces: big-name artists may get 20% or more royalties; when a CD goes gold (500,00 copies) or platinum (1 million), marketing costs drop & the record company's profits rise. Here's how the take on a typical $15 CD—one that's gone gold—is split:

American Federation of Musicians retirement fund 1% (15¢)

Producer royalties 2% (30¢)

Songwriter & publishing royalties 4% (60¢)

CD packaging 5% (75¢)

CD pressing 6% (90¢)

Artist royalties 9% ($1.35)

Retailer overhead (operating expenses: employees, inventory & profit margin) 38% ($5.70)

Record company overhead (promotion, advertising & profit margin) 22% ($3.30)

Distribution 13% ($1.95)

Exhibit 11–6 details the various costs that must be covered by a $15 price for a CD. The largest of these costs are marketing related: retailer overhead, including operating expenses and profit margin, is 38 percent of the total price; record company overhead, including promotion, advertising, and profit, is 22 percent; and distribution is 13 percent. For this product, nonproduction costs far exceed the other sources of costs that must be covered by price.

Timex also bases its pricing and production decisions on cost considerations. Timex used to make most of its parts itself. Today, the company outsources its components (buys the parts from other manufacturers) so it can make production changes quickly. It is able to use its position as a dominant buyer of watch components to keep costs competitive and get faster payback on watches with shorter life cycles.[36] Old Navy maintains low prices by keeping the design of its products simple and by making use of less-costly fabrics. Through clever packaging and color design, Old Navy successfully offers products, unlikely to go out of style, at cut-rate prices. Procter & Gamble has reduced costs by standardizing product formulas and packaging, reducing reliance on consumer promotion, as well as trade promotions, and limiting costly new-product launches. Intel Corporation has instituted a cost-reduction program aimed at limiting costs of materials through purchasing from their suppliers. Their emphasis is on the entire supply chain and on programs that regularly identify low-cost alternatives that maximize value to Intel.[37]

Pricing strategies, product image, and distribution exclusivity must be coordinated. For example, higher priced and upscale products are associated with a unique image and limited distribution.

Customers

Customer expectations and willingness to pay are important influences on pricing decisions. Buyer reactions are primary determinants of demand. In some instances, customers may be willing to trade off increased prices for more benefits or enhanced product features.

The customer interest in value has not gone unnoticed. Many firms now emphasize value by offering lower prices and higher quality. Penney's returned to its original position as a moderately priced merchant. General Motors has seen substantial customer approval of its value-pricing approach that reduces the prices of its cars, including those models with attractive options.[38]

Service companies occasionally use **value-in-use pricing** to factor customer input directly into pricing decisions. They base prices on customer estimates of the costs if the service could not be obtained. Such firms are responding to consumer perceptions of value. Computer repair services, for example, might be based on some percentage of the savings to the company from limiting computer downtime. This approach, while requiring some market research, satisfies customer needs and requirements for service at the price the customer defines as reasonable value.[39]

Target costing, a concept developed in Japan, combines both cost and customer input into price decisions. The process results in a market-driven cost estimation procedure to determine for a product what the manufacturing costs must be to achieve (1) the profit margin the company desires, (2) the features sought by customers, and (3) the prices that will be attractive to potential buyers. The result is the development of a product geared toward the needs of buyers at prices they are willing to pay.[40]

The effects of technology on prices paid by individual consumers are still evolving. Amazon was caught pricing the same DVD differently for different customers on the same day. Their behavior caused a substantial uproar that alarmed pricing managers. Faster computers, more sophisticated analyses, and large amounts of data that retailers are collecting allow grocers, drugstores, mortgage lenders, and computer makers, plus other merchants, to charge consumers "special prices." Of course, airlines have perfected the practice of pricing the same seat and trip differently for business travelers versus vacation travelers who book tickets in advance. Grocers post one price but charge another to their card holders and another to customers redeeming coupons.[41]

Consumers vary in their reactions to price. For example, one study found that more-educated consumers and consumers with less income constraints were less price sensitive. In addition, the effects of price promotions on consumers are often described as being asymmetric. First, reactions to price reductions vary by brand type, with price reductions for premium brands drawing consumers from segments who regularly buy competing brands and consumers who usually buy moderate or private-label brands. Price reductions for lower-priced brands are less effective at generating incremental sales. Second, and as will be explained in Chapter 12, consumers react more strongly to price increases than decreases. Hence, consumer effects on price increases should be carefully considered.[42]

Channels of Distribution

Prices charged by manufacturers to their distribution partners should be set such that members of the channel of distribution can profit as well. Distributors and retailers must be able to establish sufficient margins to profit from their purchase and resale of manufacturer's goods.

Prices must be set so that other members of the channel of distribution earn adequate returns on sales of the firm's products. Marketers must consider the margins that others in the channel can make. If channel intermediaries cannot realize a sufficient margin, they will not market the products adequately. Moreover, the product's image must be consistent with the channels of distribution. For a product that attracts buyers with a low price, the goal would be low-cost distribution. For a product that attracts buyers with its superior attributes despite a high price, distribution must complement those attributes.[43] Blockbuster changed its relationship with suppliers by agreeing to give movie studios a share of rental fees in return for lower up-front prices on tapes. These arrangements in the channel of distribution increased the availability of hit movies, making customers happy, as well as increasing profits for both Blockbuster and its suppliers.[44]

Marketers give special sales promotion allowances and support to channel members to encourage purchase. These trade sales promotions now represent the largest of all marketing communications expenditures. Channel arrangements also involve restrictions on resale price, although manufacturers cannot require independent wholesalers and retailers to charge certain prices. Price guarantees stating that prices are the lowest available are also often given to retailers and wholesalers to encourage their patronage.

Competition

Prices charged by competing firms and the reaction of competitors to price changes also influence pricing decisions. Haggar cotton pants and Levi's Dockers are but one example of products that actively compete on price. As a rule, pricing decisions should not be made simply to make the next sale or to meet some short-term pricing objective. Companies that price successfully in competitive markets know that the goal is not just winning sales; they want to maintain those sales in the future.

American products are experiencing increasing competition in Eastern Europe as shoppers become hesitant about higher-priced brands from Western companies. For example, given the still-small average monthly salary in Poland (about $300), consumers are returning to cheaper homegrown merchandise. In response, Western companies are introducing low-cost, low-priced alternatives to compete with the cheaper Polish products. For example, Germany's Benckiser compensated for its expensive laundry detergent, Lanza, by introducing a much cheaper brand, Dosia. This strategy enabled the German firm to still compete with lower-priced Polish products without damaging the reputation of its higher-priced Lanza brand.[45]

Competitive effects on prices are complex and can vary due to technological influences, the market position of the brands involved, and regulatory changes affecting some industries. For example, competitive pressures from the Internet and the ability of consumers to make price comparisons across outlets are helping pull prices downward. One study noted that, even after accounting for shipping costs, prices for prescription drugs and apparel were over 20 percent less than those in traditional retail outlets.[46]

For many consumer packaged goods, competition among products of different quality is asymmetric. Price promotions by higher-quality brands draw disproportionately more market share from lower-quality brands. Firms in previously regulated industries, such as utilities, are finding much more intense competition and must manage pricing decisions carefully.[47]

Compatibility

Finally, the price of a product must be compatible with the overall objectives of the firm. Again, a firm's long-term image considerations will influence the prices it establishes. High brand equity enables a firm to launch brand extensions, to extract better arrangements from distributors and retailers, and to charge higher prices.[48] Dial soap, after 40 years, is still the category leader; Chips Ahoy, a 25-year-old brand, is still the leading chocolate chip cookie. These brands have strong brand equity and hence high prices and excellent margins. In both cases, the prices charged are compatible with the overall marketing strategy for the brand.

In pricing a product, a firm must also consider the prices of other products within its product line. The price of one product or brand should not cannibalize sales, that is, shift sales from other brands within the same line of products. If a top-of-the-line model in a line of running shoes is priced at $150, a low-end model targeted to the novice runner should be priced so as not to steal sales from the higher-end model. Likewise, Boeing prices its line of commercial airlines so that low-end models do not detract from the larger, top-of-the-line airplanes.

Thinking Critically

- Manufacturers may use penetration pricing as a way to lure new customers to try a new product with low financial risk. Once established, the companies may raise their prices over the long term. Given that those consumers most likely to switch to the new product at a low price are those consumers assumed to be most price sensitive, what can companies do to retain these customers when they subsequently raise prices?

Ethical and Legal Restraints on Pricing   Marketers

must consider more than the influences of the five Cs in price decisions. Pricing practices must also conform to laws and regulations and ethical expectations of customers and society in general. A variety of legislation affects the pricing decisions of firms. The objectives of this legislation are largely twofold: to protect competition among companies within markets and to protect the rights of consumers. The most important of these laws, summarized in chronological order of enactment in Exhibit 11–7, influence the ethical aspects of pricing decisions.

The Sherman Act (1890) inhibited price fixing and restraint of trade among competitors. Pricing practices designed to drive competitors from the market and conspiracy among competitors are limited by the case law established following this legislation. The act represents one of the government's first attempts to establish antitrust policies. A recent case involved allegations that 55 private educational institutions engaged in price-fixing agreements that resulted in overly high student fees. The Sherman Act was also used by the American Football League in its suit against the National Football League.

The Federal Trade Commission Act (1914) established the FTC as the administrative organization for monitoring unfair and anticompetitive business practices. The FTC is charged with limiting deceptive pricing and advertising practices.

The Clayton Act (1914) restricted price discrimination and purchase agreements between buyers and sellers and strengthened the antitrust limits on mergers and competitor arrangements of the Sherman Act. The act also limited requirements that a purchaser of one product must buy other products from the seller.

The Robinson-Patman Act (1936) placed more stringent restrictions on **price discrimination** practices—selling the same product to different customers at different prices. Price discrimination can inhibit competition, particularly among resellers. It is legal to charge final consumers different prices (senior citizen discounts, student rates), because this does not impair competition. A manufacturer, however, may violate the law by charging different prices to different retailers. Quantity discounts are not an issue so long as all buyers can take advantage of uniform discount policies.

All price discrimination is not illegal, however. Under certain conditions, price discrimination may be permissible if the buyers are not competitors; the prices charged do not limit competition; the price differentials reflect differences in costs of serving the different customers; and the price differences occur because of efforts to meet competitor prices.

Acceptable price discrimination may reflect price differences based on time, place, customer, and product distinctions. For example, different prices are charged for telephone use and movies depending on the time of the day. Place differences account for differences in prices at hotels and entertainment events. Even individual customers may be charged different prices based on negotiations or differences in need.

Exhibit 11–7	*Significant U.S. legislation influencing price decisions*

- **Sherman Act, 1890:** Establishes illegality of restraint of trade and price fixing. First antitrust policy instituted by U.S. government. Predatory pricing to drive competitors from market is also restricted.
- **Federal Trade Commission Act, 1914:** Establishes Federal Trade Commission, which is charged with limiting unfair and anticompetitive practices of business.
- **Clayton Act, 1914:** Restricts price discrimination and purchase agreements between buyers and sellers; strengthens antitrust limits on mergers.
- **Robinson-Patman Act, 1936:** Limits the ability of firms to sell the same product at different prices to different customers. Price differentials can lessen or harm competition, particularly among resellers.
- **Wheeler-Lea Act, 1938:** Allows the Federal Trade Commission to investigate deceptive practices and to regulate advertising. Also ensures that pricing practices do not deceive customers.
- **Consumer Goods Pricing Act, 1975:** Eliminates some control over retail pricing by wholesalers and manufacturers and allows retailers to establish final retail prices in most instances. Places limits on resale-price-maintenance agreements among manufacturers, wholesalers, and retailers.

Charges of price discrimination do occur in the marketplace. For example, many pharmacists charge that they pay more for prescription drugs than managed care providers who command discounts for large purchase quantities. In past years, drug manufacturers have pledged to limit price increases to inflation rates or less. However, recent price increases in prescription drugs have risen above those rates as health care reform pressures subsided. Now many pharmacists claim that they are unfairly burdened and at a competitive disadvantage to hospitals and HMOs that pay lower prices for drugs.[49] The popularity of free music sites on the Internet and the ability to pirate CDs has prompted music labels and retailers to make CD prices more affordable and to more quickly discount existing CDs.[50]

Dumping—selling a product in a foreign country at a price lower than its price in the domestic country, and lower than its marginal cost of production—is a form of price discrimination. Most governments have antidumping regulations that protect their own industries against unfair foreign pricing practices. Typically, appeals for government assistance are based on the argument that offending firms are practicing **predatory dumping**—pricing intended to drive rivals out of business. A successful predator firm raises prices once the rival is driven from the market. One famous case involved Sony Corporation of Japan. Sony was selling TV sets for $180 in the United States, while charging $333 in Japan for the same Japanese-made product. Threats of increased tariffs on Japanese TVs eventually forced increases in the prices of those exported to the United States.

The Wheeler-Lea Act (1938) expanded the FTC's role to monitor deceptive and misleading pricing and advertising practices. More recently, the Consumer Goods Pricing Act (1975) supported the right of retailers to determine final prices. The effect of the legislation is to limit the ability of manufacturers to control prices in their channels of distribution.

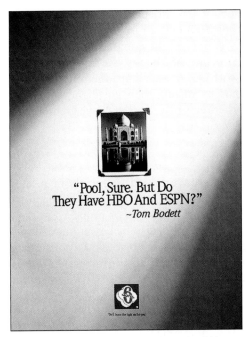

"Pool, Sure. But Do They Have HBO And ESPN?"
~Tom Bodett

Even ads that do not promote prices should be consistent with the overall pricing strategy of the firm. This nonprice communication subtly reinforces the low price positioning of Motel 6.

Implications for Pricing Decisions

Primary implications of legislation and case law for pricing include the following:

- Horizontal price fixing among companies at the same level of a distribution channel is illegal.

- In most cases, retailers are free to establish their own final selling prices. Prices charged by manufacturer- or wholesaler-owned retailers may still be restricted by the owner.

- Some states have enacted minimum price laws that prevent retailers from selling merchandise for less than cost.

- Prices must not be presented in a way that deceives customers.

Building Customer Equity

Drug companies facing increasing generic pressures

Firms are constantly engaged in either introducing new products or reacting to new entries in their markets. For example, drug companies face increasing competition as patents expire on a variety of blockbuster medications, restricting their ability to sustain success and growth. The advent of generic products, which compete directly upon price, is affecting the prescription drug industry. It appears that branded drug companies will continue to invest heavily in traditional media and direct-to-consumer advertising while also experimenting with other means of promoting including more effective use of the Internet and tie-ins with other promotions. Generic pressures will undoubtedly lower consumer prices overall, but branded products will strive to maintain their customer base by fighting generic entries and lowering their profit margins.

- Discrimination that reflects extremely low prices to eliminate competition, or that does not reflect cost differentials, may be illegal.
- In industries with a few large firms, it is generally acceptable for the pricing behavior of smaller firms to parallel that of larger firms.

International Agreements and Organizations

The prices charged for products and services are also affected by a number of international agreements or organizations. Among the more important agreements are the General Agreement on Tariffs and Trade (GATT); the Organization of Petroleum Exporting Countries (OPEC); the European Union (EU); and the North American Free Trade Agreement (NAFTA). All have wide-ranging effects on the prices charged in global markets.

For example, OPEC is a loose federation of many of the oil-producing countries. This cooperative arrangement is designed to influence market prices and short-term profits for crude oil. The cartel has been affected by acts of cheating on production among its own members as well as nonmembers' independent pricing actions. OPEC's effectiveness at controlling prices has been uneven in recent years.

Coffee cartels in South America actually enhanced the competitive positions of high-priced marketers of coffee—companies like Starbucks. Restrictions placed upon production of coffee, similar to those of OPEC on oil production, have hurt lower- and moderate-priced national brands by raising their costs and squeezing their already low margins. Starbucks and other high-priced sellers have greater margins to absorb the rising costs.

Customer Price Evaluations
We have talked so far about pricing from the perspective of the marketer or the seller. But how does the buyer judge prices? What determines a customer's evaluation of a product or brand?

The key to learning how prices influence purchase decisions lies in understanding how buyers perceive prices.[51] This **perceived monetary price** is the consumer's reaction that the price is high or low, fair or unfair. Further, consumers do not always remember prices, even within the store, and often encode or process them in personally meaningful ways.[52]

Judgments of Perceived Value

Perceived value describes the buyer's overall assessment of a product's utility based on what is received and what is given. It represents a trade-off between the "give" and the "get" components of a purchase transaction and plays a critical role in purchase decisions.[53] Some observers describe perceived value as "quality per dollar."[54]

The give is mainly the product's price. Increasingly, consumers base brand decisions on their notions of a "reasonable price" and compare prices regularly.[55] Exhibit 11–8 summarizes the effects of price on buyer judgments of value. Perceived value ultimately determines willingness to buy. Perceived value in turn is determined by a combination of the perceived benefits, or quality received, and the monetary sacrifice made; higher benefits enhance value; higher monetary sacrifice detracts from it. These offsetting effects reflect the trade-off of the give and get components inherent in consumer perceptions of value.

The power of consumer perceptions of value has not gone unnoticed by marketers. Well-known consumer companies whose stated primary emphasis is on consumer value include McDonald's, Wal-Mart, Sara Lee, Toyota, and Taco Bell. Business-to-business marketers now focusing on value through lower prices and enhanced quality include Emerson Electric, Electronic Data Systems (EDS), and 3M.

Relationships among price, perceived value, and willingness to buy

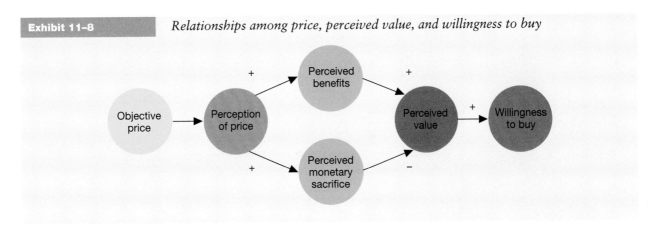

The determinants of value for services are even more critical to understand. As one noted expert in services marketing emphasizes, the lack of differentiation among many competing services encourages managers to overuse price as a marketing tool; the mistake is thus made that price and value are equivalent. In truth, value represents the benefits received for burdens endured. These burdens not only include price, but also slow service, busy telephone lines, and rude boundary employees who interact directly with the customers of service providers.[56]

Price/Quality Relationships

Consumers trade off prices paid for benefits received, or product or service quality. The **price/quality relationship** describes the extent to which the consumer associates the product's price with higher quality. Higher prices do not always signal higher quality, however. Evidence suggests that, if there is a positive relationship, it is not very strong.[57] Sometimes uninformed consumers mistakenly use price to make quality judgments. When price and quality are not related, buying a higher-priced brand is a poor decision.

One study of *Consumer Reports* ratings revealed some interesting findings regarding the existence of actual price/quality relationships.[58] In tests across brands within nine product classes, prices and objective quality ratings were found to be positively related, negatively related, and not related, depending upon the products investigated. For example, positive relationships between price and quality existed for bicycles, washing machines, and frozen pizza. Negative relationships were observed for stereo speakers, blenders, and spray cleaners. Thus, consistently assuming higher prices mean higher quality does not always result in wise decisions.

Consumer Use of Price Information

The effect of prices on consumers varies across people and situations.[59] Uncertainty about prices and quality can make purchase decisions difficult. The importance of quality and a buyer's previous experience determine the role of price in consumer evaluations. Ideally, consumers should use a **best-value strategy,** picking the lowest-cost brand available with the desired level of quality. In a **price-seeking strategy,** some consumers make a price/quality assumption and choose the highest-priced brand to maximize expected quality. Other consumers follow a **price-aversion strategy,** buying the lowest-priced brand simply to minimize risks of having spent more than necessary.

Mack Turner comments on pricing strategy: "With e-commerce achieving critical mass, the consumer—both the retail and corporate consumer—has the tool to gain broad knowledge of product offerings, deep knowledge of product benefits, and the ability to act on that knowledge immediately. From a pricing point of view, e-commerce creates the potential of a 24-hour-by-7-day auction. The customer can quickly visit multiple online stores, shop prices and availability, and

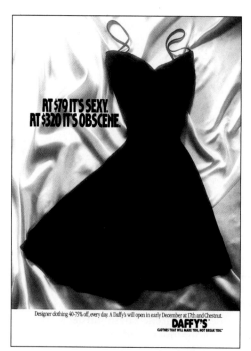

AT $79 IT'S SEXY.
AT $320 IT'S OBSCENE.

Designer clothing 40-75% off, every day. A Daffy's will open in early December at 17th and Chestnut.

DAFFY'S
CLOTHES THAT WILL MAKE YOU, NOT BREAK YOU.

Consumer expectations about market prices affect decisions to buy. Prices noticeably above and below expectations can lead to unfavorable reactions to product offerings.

select the lowest price. New channels for borrowing have been created in which several e-commerce lenders compete head-on for the borrower's business. E-commerce retailers will have to aggressively manage their product availability, distribution, and after-sale service. Service providers, such as banks, will have to provide more-current and complete online research and information, as well as excellent execution and after-sale support."

Recognition that consumers use different purchase approaches can influence the firm's marketing strategies. If product quality is not obvious to the consumer but has high importance (imported wines, for example), firms often use a *price signaling strategy:* They set prices higher to imply higher quality. Where quality information is more readily available and the importance of quality is high (appliances, perhaps), firms often pursue a value-based strategy and use informative advertising. In this case, the firm keeps prices competitive and focuses marketing communications on the benefits and quality of the product. Firms market generic brands and brands that compete largely on low price in recognition that some consumers are price-averse. Interestingly, low prices or heavy advertising expenditures can signal high quality in some instances. When quality is not observable and can only be assessed through consumption (i.e., experience goods), "wasteful" expenditures by the firm via low introductory prices or an expensive ad campaign may signal high quality for products dependent on repeat business.[60]

How Are Price Judgments Made?

How do people judge whether prices are too low, too high, or fair? Consumers compare product prices with internal and, in some cases, external reference prices. **External reference prices** include those charged by other retailers or comparison prices that a retailer provides to enhance perceptions of the published price.

Internal reference prices are comparison standards that consumers remember and use to make their judgments. There are several internal reference prices. One is the expected price, a primary determinant of whether a buyer perceives a price as fair and reasonable. Another is the **reservation price,** an economic term for the highest price a person is willing to pay. Expectation of future prices is also a key internal reference, as the forward-looking consumer evaluates the costs and benefits of buying now versus buying at some future time.[61] Other internal reference prices include "the price last paid, the average retail price, and the price I would like to pay."[62] Consumers sometimes infer motives for prices, particularly unexpected high prices, and these motives affect perceptions of price fairness. When high prices are assumed to reflect marketer "greed," fair-price perceptions generate negative inferences to the seller. As such, fair price is an important internal reference price in certain circumstances.[63]

A model of consumer evaluations of prices is presented in Exhibit 11–9.[64] It assumes that consumers have price information through past experiences with purchases of the same product or similar products.[65] Most people may be uncertain about specific prices but have some general expectations about market prices and a range of acceptable prices. They evaluate how the price of a product fits these expectations. They may interpret prices judged as too low as indicating suspect product quality; prices judged as too high are dismissed as out of the question or associated with a different product category.

Individual price evaluations may be influenced by external factors such as budget constraints, time pressure, anticipated use situations, or the cost of further search for lower-priced items. Consumers are generally less willing to pay higher prices for brands they perceive to have frequent price promotions.[66]

Exhibit 11–9   *Consumer evaluations of prices*

Exhibit 11–10   *A model of comparison reference price effects*

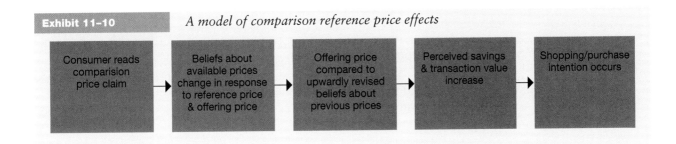

Advertised Comparison Prices

Advertisers often provide comparison prices (external reference prices) to persuade shoppers to buy. Comparison prices generally take one of three forms: prices previously charged by the retailer, prices charged by other retailers in the area, or manufacturer-suggested prices. Exhibit 11–10 summarizes the effect of comparison prices.[67] Comparison pricing increases the perceived **transaction value** of the purchase (the perceived merits of the deal) by raising the shopper's internal price standard, which makes the advertised price appear more attractive.[68] Increased transaction value then enhances overall acquisition value, which increases the likelihood of purchase. Such price-induced incentives are particularly effective for positioning products that are relatively undifferentiated from those of competitors. These transaction value-enhancing strategies are prevalent for jewelry, luggage, and some electronic products. In fact, retailers such as Best Buy and Circuit City often present sale prices coupled with either "previously offered prices" or manufacturers' suggested prices.[69]

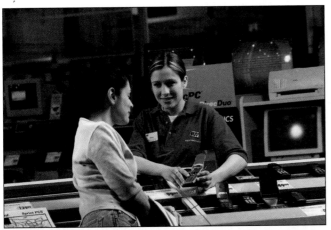

Comparison prices are used to "frame" offerings as a good deal or high value. Many electronics retailers present both MSRP and sale prices.

Summary

1. **Realize the importance of price and understand its role in the marketing mix.** For every good or service sold, the determination of price is critically important to the level of demand and the profits earned. A price set too high will discourage demand; a price set too low will result in less revenue; both lead to lower total profits. Determining an optimal price is becoming more difficult with changing marketplace trends, including faster technological progress, the proliferation of new products, increased demand for services, and growing global competition.

   Relationships between the determined price and the other marketing mix variables affect sales of the product and others the company offers. Price is only one aspect of the firm's marketing mix; other aspects, such as product and distribution, must be considered in pricing decisions. Further, price offers the selling firm a basis for competing whenever other differences among competing brands are not apparent to buyers.

2. **Understand the characteristics of the different pricing objectives that companies can adopt.** Common objectives that guide company pricing decisions include ensuring market survival, enhancing sales growth, increasing market share, maximizing profits, realizing a certain return on investment, deterring competition, and establishing or maintaining a particular quality image. Firms often pursue profitability objectives by a price-skimming strategy and growth and competitive deterrence by a penetration-pricing strategy. Prestige pricing is consistent with quality and image-enhancement objectives.

3. **Identify many of the influences on marketers' pricing decisions.** Pricing decisions are influenced by the five Cs of pricing: costs, customers, channels of distribution, competition, and compatibility. Costs determine the minimum level of prices. Prices must at least cover costs in the long term, or insufficient profits and income result. Customer expectations, as well as perceptions of value and fairness, determine price acceptability.

   Price determination must also take into account other members of the channel of distribution. Intermediaries in the channel must be able to earn sufficient margins. Competitive factors also influence prices. When products are similar and price differences are important to consumers, prices will tend to move toward the going price.

   Pricing decisions must also be compatible with the overall marketing and communications objectives of the firm. Finally, national and international laws and agreements also influence price decisions.

4. **Explain how consumers form perceptions of quality and value.** Potential buyers, including individuals and business buyers, form perceptions of value that influence their willingness to buy (purchase behavior). Perceived value is the overall assessment of the utility of a product, depending on what is received and what is given or paid. Price influences perceived value in terms of perceived benefits and perceived monetary sacrifice. Consumers vary in their reactions to price, but they typically adopt one of three strategies: a best-value strategy, a price-seeking strategy, or a price-aversion strategy.

5. **Understand price/quality relationships and internal and external reference prices.** Consumers frequently infer quality from prices. This reaction describes the price/quality relationship. These opinions, regardless of their accuracy, influence the buyer's decision; customers are more likely to pay a higher price if they believe a product to be of higher quality.

   Many consumers compare advertised prices with expected prices, a frequently used internal reference price. If prices are above expectations, perceived value of a product declines; lower-than-expected prices may cause perceived value to rise. Companies often provide external reference prices by pairing an offered price with a higher comparison price designed to make the lower price more attractive. These comparison prices may be previously charged prices, manufacturer-suggested prices, or competitive prices.

Understanding Marketing Terms and Concepts

Thinking About Marketing

1. What is the meaning of price? Contrast the basic price mix with the price promotion mix.

2. Why are pricing decisions so important? What are the effects of setting prices too low? Too high?

3. What environmental conditions make pricing decisions so difficult? How might these effects influence estimation of costs and revenues?

4. How do these pricing objectives differ: quality enhancement versus market survival? Sales growth versus profitability?

5. Describe briefly how information on the Internet affects price sensitivity? How might these effects differ for well-known versus less-familiar brands?

6. How does Charles Schwab compete with other brokerage houses such as Merrill Lynch? What influences Schwab's pricing strategy?

7. What are some of the primary legal restrictions on marketers' pricing decisions?

8. Contrast external reference prices with internal reference prices. Give several examples of each. How do reference prices affect consumer reactions to prices?

9. Define consumer perceived value and explain what determines it. How do price and perceived quality affect perceptions of value? Explain the relationship between price and quality.

10. Explain these purchase strategies that consumers use to evaluate prices: best value, price seeking, price aversion.

Applying Marketing Skills

1. Interview a small retailer. Ask how prices are determined and how products put on sale are selected. Does support from the manufacturer influence the initial price of goods? What role does consumer demand play?

2. Find in your local newspaper reference-price advertisements from two different retailers. What are the original prices and the sale prices? What are the percent reductions? With whom or with what is the sale price compared? What wording is used to make the reference-price claim?

3. Interview a close friend or relative. Ask the question: "What comes to mind when you consider the purchase of

a personal computer?" At what point does the person mention price? To what extent does the order of the attributes mentioned reflect their importance in determining the purchase?

4. How are frequent price fluctuations (e.g., sales promotions, discounts, couponing, or inflation) likely to affect consumers' reference prices? If it is assumed that frequent price promotions lower consumers' reference prices and create some resistance to returning to higher "normal" prices, is an EDLP strategy superior to a price promotion strategy?

Using the www in Marketing

Activity One
As you know, more and more consumers are using the Internet to shop and gather information. This phenomenon is particularly prevalent in the sports industry. Consider the price information for two brands of tennis rackets. Wilson and Prince offer a variety of models:

1. How is the price information presented? Can consumers make easy price comparisons within lines?

2. Why are the dealer companies unable to present discounted-price information for the most recent models?

3. Why have price discounters for sports equipment been so successful? Is it ethical for consumers to shop at local retail stores—and even borrow equipment from the store for trial use—but then purchase from a price discounter using a magazine advertisement or the Internet?

Activity Two   Assume that you are shopping for a Tommy Hilfiger casual shirt for a younger brother in high school.

1. How might price comparisons differ between shopping on the Internet versus a trip to the mall?

2. Describe the differences in price between those presented on the Tommy Hilfiger site versus in-store prices. How do the total prices charged compare (i.e., including shipping costs)?

3. What role does price play in the overall strategy of Tommy Hilfiger?

Making Marketing Decisions

Case 11-1 *Warner Brothers: Pricing DVDs*

DVDs are big business in terms of sales and luring customers for large retailers such as Target and Wal-Mart. In contrast, rental income is the key to success for Blockbuster and other rental chains. As such, the movie studios are faced with complex pricing issues and the effects of pricing on relationships with their largest customers. One solution would be to create initial time periods for which DVDs are available only as rentals, an option opposed strongly by large retailers. According *The Wall Street Journal,* Wal-Mart and Target want to aggressively promote DVDs to both drive up their own sales and also to take shopping trips from category-specific retailers like Best Buy.

Warner Home Video held the initial strongest position with the biggest DVD hit of 2001: "We are expecting big things from Harry Potter." Sales of the movie were strong in both the United States and Europe. The initial price was $26.98. Columbia TriStar Home Video and Warner have led the enactment of large-scale price declines, with many catalog offerings ranging from $14.95 to $19.95. Warner's low-priced strategy has helped it dominate the DVD market to this point. Until now, Disney and others have held their prices higher than Warner and sales have been strong. Retailers sometimes drop prices below wholesale to draw customers.

Other environmental phenomena are affecting the growth and prices of DVDs. As examples, European consumers have complained that digital video disks were significantly more expensive in Europe than in the United States, and the European Commission has investigated. Warner's packaging improvements have made grocery sales more lucrative. The package changes inhibit shrinkage from theft and allow greater allocated in-store shelf space for DVD display.

Questions

1. What are the pressures forcing the prices of DVDs to decline?

2. What is the nature of price elasticity for new DVDs? How does movie popularity affect single DVD demand responsiveness?

3. What role does price play in the distribution of Warner's DVDs?

Case 11-2 *Priceline.com: Price Search and Competition*

 Priceline.com has pioneered a unique type of e-commerce known as a "demand collection system" that enables consumers to use the Internet to save money on a wide range of products and services, while enabling sellers to generate incremental revenue. Priceline.com has generated substantial success in the sales of airline tickets and hotel rooms. The firm now offers the ability to buy cars, long-distance telephone services, and grocery products for home delivery, while other purchase opportunities are available or under development. Home loans can even be arranged using priceline.com.

Priceline.com makes money on the spread between what a customer is willing to pay and the price offered by the vendor. Priceline.com collects information regarding the numbers of customers, their product and service preferences, and the amount they are willing to pay. Partnerships between priceline.com and other companies provide the opportunity to generate incremental demand for the partnering firms, without disturbing partner-firm normal pricing structures. Consumers must guarantee their offer by credit card, must agree to keep their offer open for a certain period of time, and must be flexible regarding brand selection.

Competition for priceline.com on the Internet in terms of price services and auctions is evolving at a very fast rate, and online haggling is now among the hottest phenomena in e-commerce. As examples, Amazon.com has begun an auction service and America Online now offers eBay as one of its features. Potentially, cyberauctions could push aside normal sticker prices and begin an era of dynamic pricing. The no-cost aspects of using the Internet make price bargaining an easy means of shopping.

The financial situation for Priceline has become perilous as their stock price has fallen drastically. New advertising, without William Shatner, is more consumer-oriented and aimed at spurring higher revenues. The company is now more focused upon name-your-own prices for hotels, airlines, rental cars, home finance, and new cars. The company remains, however, essentially an online travel agency for leisure travelers. After failures in gasoline and grocery offerings, the company now recognizes that consumers desire convenience and fast service as much as cost savings. Currently Priceline is faced with a troublesome future. It has lost customer loyalty, and a new competitor, Hotwire, has signed deals with eight major airlines.

Questions

1. What effects will priceline.com have on brand integrity for the companies with which it is involved? Will sites like priceline.com undermine brand loyalty?

2. What other industries represent potential opportunities for priceline.com?

3. What effects, if any, will Internet offerings like priceline.com have on both consumer search behavior and sensitivity to prices?

4. As competive alternatives expand on the Internet, what will priceline.com have to do to maintain its competitive advantage?

Chapter Twelve

12

Price Determination and Pricing Strategies

After studying this chapter, you should be able to:

1 Discuss the interrelationships among price, demand, demand elasticity, and revenue.

2 Understand methods for determining price.

3 Recognize the different pricing strategies and the conditions that best suit the choice of a strategy.

4 Recognize the importance of adapting prices under shifting economic and competitive situations.

5 Understand the ethical considerations involved in setting and communicating prices.

www.eBay.com

eBay continues to be among the most consistently profitable Internet companies used by 50 million consumers worldwide. The site offers online trading opportunities in which consumers can bid on products and in which sellers can auction items for sale. Of particular importance, and unlike traditional exchange relationships in the marketplace, buyers have significant input into the determination of prices. Through eBay, 170 million times in 2002, users exchanged some $9.3 billion worth of goods in 18,000 categories that cover virtually the entire universe of human artifacts.

As one of the few dot com companies to have made a profit from the beginning, the site tries to establish a sense of community by drawing together people with similar perspectives and interests. eBay enables consumers to pursue their individuality and offers sellers financial opportunities. eBay enables one-to-one transactions across divisions caused by geography and class. Trust among individuals is critical to the success of relationships, and fraud on the site has been remarkably infrequent. eBay offers free insurance in case transactions go bad, as well as escrow accounts that, for a fee, hold funds until deals are complete. Trust is engendered by the site's feedback forum, in which auction winners are encouraged to describe their experiences and transactions. Sellers on eBay with positive comments are subsequently sought out by others and command better prices.

Meg Whitman, eBay's CEO, now has a firm understanding of what technology means to her company and is determined to develop the kind of e-commerce system previously believed impossible. Continued development of eBay should enable the company to continue to prosper, as growth projections suggest significant potential market demand.

During Whitman's tenure, revenues have grown from $47 million in 1998 to over $1 billion in 2002, and the company has posted profits every quarter. However, satisfying the 1 million daily visitors and 30 million eBay member buyers and sellers is an ongoing endeavor. ebay's international operations include presence in 17 markets worldwide, with a strong brand in Europe following the merger with iBazar located in Paris. Retailers are now opening sites on eBay to move goods that previously were not selling in brick-and-mortar operations. ebay is a unique outcome of the Internet, as outside of the Web, the company could not operate. Without buying, selling, or stocking any inventory whatsoever, eBay has managed to not only survive but actually grow throughout the fall of many dot.coms.

Internet influences on consumer prices and the prices charged for products have been profound. In this example, the eBay situation underscores the importance of price when products can be reasonably evaluated and when consumers have some idea of their needs and the kinds of products and services that can satisfy those needs. The example illustrates only one approach to pricing, however. In this chapter, we examine the processes companies use to select a specific pricing strategy. Additionally, we discuss some theoretical and practical issues affecting the determination of prices. Some of these issues involve ethical considerations. Price determination and evaluation of appropriate pricing strategies are a continual managerial challenge.

As many now believe, electronic commerce is leading to fundamental changes in the way companies relate to their customers and, in the case of auctions, the way consumers relate to one another. The effects are being felt as much as anywhere in the area of pricing. For example, comparing insurance rates from hundreds of companies would take hundreds of calls. Now, price comparisons are possible with the click of a mouse. Allstate has already reduced its labor force and begun selling on the Internet. Sites such as eCoverage and Quotesmith.com make comparisons readily available.

This chapter describes many procedures and strategies for use in setting and changing prices. Developing pricing capabilities allows firms to respond more effectively to competitor actions and to match prices more closely to what consumers are willing to pay. Such pricing capabilities become an important source of competitive advantage.[1]

Price Determination: An Overview

The step-by-step procedure diagrammed in Exhibit 12–1 presents a logical approach for setting prices.[2] Execution of this process requires an understanding of the concepts described in Chapter 11. First, the firm must set pricing objectives consistent with its overall marketing

---

Exhibit 12–1   *The price-setting decision process*

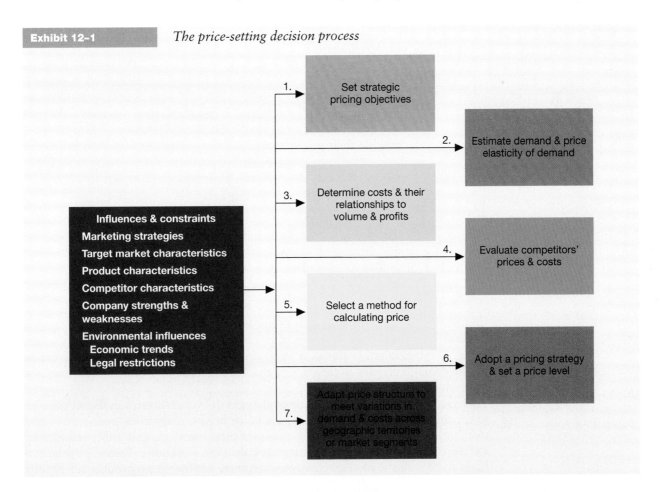

and strategic efforts and with the product's image and quality. Common pricing objectives are to maximize profits or sales growth. Second, the firm must consider market demand and the responsiveness of demand to different prices. What will the level of sales be at different prices? How do sales change as prices vary?

Next, the firm determines the costs to manufacture products or provide services and the relationship of costs to volume. The company evaluates competitor prices and costs. If prices are set well above market prices, consumers will not purchase. If prices are too low, revenues and profits may be lost. Then the firm may use one of various methods for determining prices, including markup pricing, break-even analysis, and target-return pricing methods.

Finally, the firm must set specific prices, often using one of the common pricing strategies. After setting prices, the firm monitors and adjusts them to adapt to differences in demand and costs across market segments or to meet competitive reactions.

As Exhibit 12–1 shows, the stages in this pricing process are subject to several influences and constraints. These include product characteristics, company strengths and weaknesses, and legal constraints. Moreover, both costs and demand are difficult to estimate. Sometimes, price determination involves setting a price first, then revising in response to market performance.

Price and Demand

Demand curve representing relationship between price and quantity demanded

Demand Curves

The relationship between price and demand is expressed in the traditional market **demand curve** labeled D in Exhibit 12–2. Under normal conditions, customers buy more as prices drop; they buy less when prices rise. If price is set artificially low, excess demand will occur, as the $325 typical price for a 2002 Super Bowl ticket that failed to balance supply and demand. Moreover, artificially low prices may result in secondary markets, such as online auctions.[3] Price is only one determinant of demand, however. Others include household income, tastes and preferences, population growth, and prices of related products. For many business-to-business situations, demand is driven by general economic conditions and consumer demand, as well as by the preferences and needs of the firm's buyers. New software technologies are greatly enhancing retailers' ability to merchandise their products through the analysis of historical price sales data, as well as consumers' responses to the determinants of demand, such as price, inventory levels, promotion, and seasonality.[4]

Price Elasticity of Demand

Price elasticity of demand is a basic business concept. The relationship between price and quantity demanded varies; as one increases, the other decreases. Price elasticity of demand is computed as:

$$\text{Price elasticity of demand} = \frac{\text{Percent change in quantity demanded}}{\text{Percent change in price}}$$

Computational procedures and an example are shown in Appendix B.

Elastic demand exists when small price changes result in large changes in demand. When demand is elastic, a small decrease in price increases total revenues. Elastic demand prevails in the motor vehicles, engineering products, furniture, and professional services industries.

Inelastic demand exists when price changes do not result in significant changes in demand. Inelastic demand often occurs for books, magazines, newspapers, and clothing, as well as in the banking and insurance, beverage, and utility industries.[5] Exhibit 12–3 depicts elastic and inelastic demand situations. Overall, demand is likely to be inelastic to price changes when there are few or no product substitutes;

Speaking from Experience

Kimberly Kanakes
Marketing Manager
*McGraw-Hill/Irwin Higher
Education Group*

"In recent years, the college market, especially in Principles of Marketing courses, has become very price sensitive. Professors and students are looking to get more for their money, in the form of student CDs, videos and DVDs, instructor resources, subscriptions, simulations, and Web content. While several books in the Principles market are hardcover, we offer this text in paperback and loose-leaf, with all the student and professor supplements a hardcover text package offers. The lower text price coupled with student and instructor resources offers a better value and increases demand for this text."

Kimberly Kanakes earned a bachelor's degree in organizational communication with a minor in marketing. Her job consists of creating marketing plans and coordinating all internal and external communications for the promotion of marketing titles to two-year and four-year higher education institutions. She works closely with the editorial and production staff on book content, schedule, and production and partners with professors and the company's sales representatives analyzing text and supplement needs, territory sales, and trends in the marketing discipline.

Exhibit 12–3

Elastic and inelastic demand

when buyers do not readily notice the higher price and are slow to change their buying habits or to search for lower prices, or when they think higher prices are justified by product improvements or inflation; and when the product or service represents a small portion of their household income.[6]

Where demand is price-elastic, marketers must carefully evaluate any proposed increases in price. Price changes may cause significant change in quantity demanded. Long-term elasticities may differ from short-term ones as customers become aware of changing prices and have time to search for alternative products or services.

Cross elasticity of demand relates the percentage change in quantity demanded for one product to percentage price changes for other products. For example, products are often part of a line of similar products; and changes in the price of one brand may affect the demand for other items in the product line. When products are close *substitutes*, such as cola beverages, a rise in the price of one will increase the demand for the other. For businesses, a sharp increase in prices of steel fasteners used in the construction of trucks would cause increased demand for less-expensive plastic or aluminum fasteners.

Alternatively, when products are *complements*, a price increase of one may decrease the demand for the other. For example, large price increases for personal computers would cause a decrease in the demand for printers. And price reductions of taco shells may increase sales of taco sauce.[7]

Some marketers believe that a primary objective is to create inelasticity for their products. This requires a thorough understanding

Being Entrepreneurial

Net serves up quotes

As the insurance industry moves to react to the Internet, Net upstarts, such as Quotesmith.com, are making online sales much easier than dealing with local insurance agents. The database for Quotesmith.com provides instant price quotes on auto, life, medical, and other forms of insurance from over 300 insurers. The site provides ready access to useful reference tools and comparative price information. Moreover, Quotesmith.com allows consumers to purchase from the company of their choice without having to deal with commissioned salespersons. The Internet company also offers two unique guarantees: (1) view the lowest rates on term life insurance or receive $500; and, (2) the quote will be accurate or receive $500. The company electronically collects consumer demand for coverages and can rapidly communicate such demand directly to insurance companies.

of demand, allowing the firm to offer brands with attributes that customers find irresistible regardless of price. That is, brands are designed to offer benefits that entice consumers to pay prices high enough to be profitable to the firm. Relatedly, efforts to retain customers through loyalty programs and specialized services are designed to inhibit shifts in demand resulting from changing prices of the firm's products or competing products.

Costs, Volume, and Profits

Price plays a critical role in competition among firms for some industries. Here, Norwegian Cruise Line promotes price to attract travelers.

We have seen the trade-offs between prices and quantity demanded. Yet price determination must also consider the costs incurred in the production and sale of goods. **Fixed costs** (FC) such as plant and large equipment investments, interest paid on loans, and the costs of production facilities, cannot be changed in the short run and do not vary with the quantity produced. These costs would occur even if the quantity produced were zero. Many advertising costs are viewed as fixed costs, at least over a predetermined period.[8]

Variable costs (VC) such as wages and raw materials change with the level of output. Marketing variable costs include packaging and promotional costs tied to each unit produced.

Total costs (TC) are the sum of variable costs (VC) and fixed costs (FC). Variable costs are made up of the variable cost per unit times the number or quantity of units manufactured (Q):

$$TC = (VC \times Q) + FC$$

Marginal costs (MC) are incurred in producing one additional unit of output. They typically decline early over some level of production because of economies of scale, but eventually begin to increase as the firm approaches capacity and returns diminish.

Marginal revenue (MR) is the additional revenue the firm will receive if one more unit of product is sold. This amount typically represents the price of the product. **Total revenue** (TR) is total sales, or price times the quantity sold:

$$\text{Total revenue} = \text{Price} \times \text{Quantity}$$

To determine the price that maximizes profits, the firm combines cost information with demand or revenue information. Simply viewed:

$$\text{Profits} = \text{Total revenue } (TR) - \text{Total costs } (TC)$$

This difference is greatest at the point where profits are maximized, where the firm's marginal revenue (MR) equals marginal cost (MC). When marginal revenue exceeds marginal cost, additional profits can be made by producing and selling more product. An example of these computations is presented in Appendix B.

Kimberly Kanakes, McGraw-Hill/Irwin Marketing Manager, had this to say about pricing strategies:

"When determining the price of our textbooks, we must consider the costs associated with producing the product and the supplements that support the book. Our fixed costs include the EDP (Editing, Design, Production) and Editorial plant (marketing research, grants, product development honoraria)— all the costs associated with developing a book

Low-priced autos can use warranties and other information to provide assurances about quality.

before it's printed. These costs are considered "fixed," because they do not vary with the number of copies printed or sold. Our variables include PPB (paper, printing, and binding) and author royalties. We calculate our total costs and refer to our initial pricing strategy. We price our texts competitively, or we may try to use price as a competitive advantage. We experiment with tentative pricing by using a break-even analysis—we calculate the number of units we need to sell in the first year to cover our investment."

Price Determination Methods

A firm may choose from several methods of determining price. It may subjectively determine a price based on what management feels is appropriate at the time. Or it may use a combination of methods or procedures. It is important to note that firms should stress both demand and cost considerations in determining prices. Following initial price setting, firms can adjust prices according to trial-and-error experiences and fluctuations in demand. Some basic approaches are markup pricing, break-even analysis, target-return pricing, and price sensitivity measurement.

Markup Pricing

Retailers typically use some form of **markup pricing,** where markup is the difference between the cost of an item and the retail price, expressed as a percentage. A product's price is determined by adding a set percentage to the cost of the product. These percentages are often standardized across product categories. Formally:

$$\text{Price} = \text{Unit cost} + \text{Markup, or}$$
$$\text{Price} = \text{Unit cost}/(1 - k)$$

where k = desired percent markup.

Assume, for example, that a retailer purchases a popular branded tennis racket at $80 and adds $40 to the cost, for a retail price of $120.

$$\text{Markup as a percentage of selling price} = \frac{\text{Markup}}{\text{Selling price}}$$
$$= \frac{\$40}{\$120} = 33\%$$

$$\text{Markup as a percentage of cost} = \frac{\text{Markup}}{\text{Cost}}$$
$$= \frac{\$40}{\$80} = 50\%$$

In some cases, the retailer may wish to know the markup charged for a product given the price and the original cost. This markup percentage can be computed simply as:

$$\text{Markup (\%)} = [(\text{Price} - \text{Unit cost})/\text{Price}] \times 100\%$$

Using Technology

Pricing discrimination

Revenue management systems, also called yield management systems, are already in use by airlines, which use them constantly to adjust prices and the number of seats allocated to different fares. Hotels now employ these systems to discriminate among different classes of patrons. Varying prices across days and length-of-stay restrictions are commonplace. Now, experts predict massive expansion in price discrimination practices as computing technology and data processing capabilities increase. Staples sends out catalogs with different prices to the same customers, knowing that the price-sensitive customers will know which one to buy from. Like some practices already in place, Bill Gates predicts Web sites will soon recognize customers and charge them based upon their history of buying. For example, the "clickstream" navigated by a consumer on Amazon.com can be employed to target that person as being price sensitive and consequently lower prices may be offered. Yield management allows airlines and many other industries, including media companies and even universities, to get the most dollars possible out of perishable products. However, as the science of yield management has gotten more sophisticated, pricing options and fares have become much more complex.

Other procedures and examples for determining retail prices and markups are summarized in Appendix B.

Break-Even Analysis

Exhibit 12–4

Break-even analysis

BEP
Quantity (units)

Break-even analysis is a useful guide for pricing decisions. It involves calculating the number of units that must be sold at a certain price for the firm to cover costs and, hence, break even. The approach is shown graphically in Exhibit 12–4. The *break-even point* (BEP) is determined by the intersection of the total revenue line ($TR = P \times Q$) and the total cost line ($TC = FC + VC \times Q$). The area between the two lines and to the right of the intersection represents profits. To make a profit, the quantity sold must exceed the BEP.

The slope of the total revenue line is determined by the price charged. A higher price would make the total revenue line steeper, and the BEP would be lower. Lower costs would also reduce the BEP.

Washburn Guitars provides an excellent example of the relationships between total revenues, total costs, contribution margin, and break-even quantity. The instruments Washburn sells to first-time buyers are mass-produced items; thus they have much lower variable costs in terms of labor and materials per unit than the guitars designed individually for rock stars. In addition, the lower prices appeal to the more price-sensitive entry-level buyer. Consequently, lower variable costs per unit enable Washburn to price its mass-produced items competitively and to sell beyond needed break-even quantity levels at modest market prices.

The BEP in units is

$$Q(BEP) = FC/(P - VC)$$

where P = unit price and $Q(BEP)$ = break-even quantity. The quantity ($P - VC$) is typically referred to as the product's **contribution margin.**

Consider a case of plastic medical gloves priced at $7.25 and entailing $2.25 in variable costs. At total fixed costs of $200,000, the required break-even quantity would be 40,000 units. That is,

$$40,000 = \$200,000/(\$7.25 - \$2.25)$$

If the price were raised to $12.25, and assuming sufficient demand existed, the BEP would drop to 20,000 units.

BEP can also be expressed in dollars:

$$Q(BEP\$) = FC/(1 - VC/P)$$

Using the previous medical gloves example, the BEP in dollars would be:

$$\$289,855 = \$200,000/(1 - \$2.25/\$7.25)$$

Break-even analysis is useful for evaluating the effects of various price and cost structures on needed demand levels. And by adding a desired profit amount to the fixed-cost portion of the equation, a firm can calculate the number of units that must be sold at a certain price to achieve a certain profit level.

Break-even analysis can be expanded to consider different price and quantity combinations. This modified break-even analysis (described in Appendix B) recognizes that the BEP can vary depending on the price chosen. Profits do not necessarily increase as quantity increases, as lower prices may be needed to generate the increased demand.

Break-even analysis is useful for evaluating how alternative cost and price combinations affect the quantity required to break even.

- The break-even point can be lowered by raising the price. However, what if similar products in the marketplace are offered at prices below the higher price under consideration?

- Likewise, the break-even point can be lowered by reducing variable costs. However what if reducing variable costs hurts product quality?

Target-Return Pricing

Target-return pricing is a cost-oriented approach that sets prices to achieve some desired rate of return. Cost and profit estimates are based on some expected volume or sales level. The price is determined using the equation:

$$\text{Price} = \text{Unit cost} + \frac{(\text{Desired return} \times \text{Invested capital})}{\text{Expected unit sales}}$$

Assume a national manufacturer of office supplies sells a computer-paper organizer. Average variable costs for the product are $8; total assets employed in the business are $4,500,000. The firm desires a 15 percent return and expects to sell 200,000 units. Therefore, the target-return price is:

$$\text{Price} = \text{Unit cost} + \frac{\text{Desired return} \times \text{Invested capital}}{\text{Unit sales}}$$

$$= \$8 + (0.15 \times \$4,500,000)/200,000 = \$11.38$$

The firm would price the product at $11.38. Again, the success of the approach assumes the supplier can reach the expected sales volume of 200,000 units.

Target-return pricing forecasts a fair or needed rate of return. However, the effects of other variables in the marketing mix and competitive factors are not considered directly; and target-return pricing, like break-even analysis, is best used in combination with consideration of other determinants of demand.

Some Japanese firms use an approach to pricing that recognizes the effects of price on demand and the role of costs in determining demand. As Exhibit 12–5 shows, the Japanese specify a target cost based on the price they believe the market is most likely to accept. Designers and engineers then meet target costs. This approach emphasizes the product's ability to achieve market acceptance by considering more directly the interface between the prices buyers are likely to accept and the costs necessary to produce products at those prices. As such, the Japanese recognize the effects of both demand and cost considerations in determining their prices. Nissan, Sharp, and Toyota use this approach.

Some U.S. and European companies design a new product first, and then calculate the cost. If the cost is too high, the product must be redesigned or the company must settle for a lower profit level.[9] Generally, the Japanese worry less than American and European manufacturers about cost accounting. They work backward from a price and make sure the product can be produced with the quality demanded at that price.

A related concept is **target-cost pricing** in which new products are developed based upon what the market wants and the price it will accept. Briefly, a six-step process is involved:

1. Define the market segments that will be targeted for the sale of the new product.

2. The design of the new product should be based upon an analysis of competitive advantages and disadvantages.

3. The positioning of the new product should be viewed within the context of the company's overall strategy.

4. The product design and pricing should be fine-tuned based upon customers' preferences, perceived value of individual features, and willingness to pay.

5. Market simulations are used to estimate price-responses for various combinations of specific features using marketing research techniques such as conjoint analysis.

6. Target costs are then estimated as the difference between the optimal price given demand effects from the desired target margin (e.g., 20 percent).[10]

Income-Based Pricing

One important and often-used pricing approach involves the determination of price based upon the income to be generated by the product under consideration. **Income-based pricing** is frequently used for pricing real estate property, marketable

Exhibit 12–5

The role of cost in Japanese pricing

JAPAN

▼

Marketing research

▼

Product characteristics

▼

Planned selling price
less desired profit

▼

Target Cost

▼

Design   Engineering   Supplier pricing

Target costs for each component force marketers, designers, & engineers from all departments & suppliers to struggle & negotiate trade-offs.

▼

Manufacturing

▼

Continuous cost reduction

securities, and businesses. For example, consider a business that is for sale that has annual net income (i.e., income after salaries and so forth are paid) of $600,000. The typical return on investment for similar companies in this industry is 18 percent. A beginning purchase price would be $3.33 million ($600,000/.18). This selling price for the business might be adjusted for unique competitive strengths or the likelihood of improved revenue streams in the future.[11]

Prices and Customer Value

Effective value creation is based upon thorough understanding of target customers, including an exploration of how value is created. Determining price is a critical aspect of this valuation creation. Prices set too high result in limited trial, while prices set too low result in poor positioning and missed opportunities.

One approach for setting realistic consumer prices is the *BDM,* named for the three researchers who developed the technique. BDM enables the estimation of how much consumers are willing-to-pay (WTP) at the point of purchase under marketing mix conditions the marketer desires. Briefly, and as summarized in Exhibit 12–6, the process operates as follows. Target consumers are told that they have a chance to buy the product without spending more money on the purchase than they want. They are told that the price has not been set and will be determined randomly. Respondents are asked to offer a price for the product, which should equal the highest price they are willing to pay. A price is then drawn randomly from a distribution of prices. If the drawn price is less than or equal to their offer, they are required to buy the product at the drawn price. If the drawn price exceeds their offer, they are not allowed to buy the product. This process has been shown to result in a fair estimate of consumers' WTP, since understating one's true WTP reduces the chance of buying at a gain and overstating WTP increases the chance of buying at a loss.[12]

Value in use (VIU) analysis is a useful approach for determining the economic value that a product has relative to an existing competitive offering. This approach is useful for assisting in the determination of what price to charge and in the determination of the arguments suppliers can use to justify higher prices. An example is shown in Exhibit 12–7. In this case, the analysis reveals the new product has seven times the value of an existing product and that a price for the new product well

---

Exhibit 12–6   *Flow chart of BDM procedure*

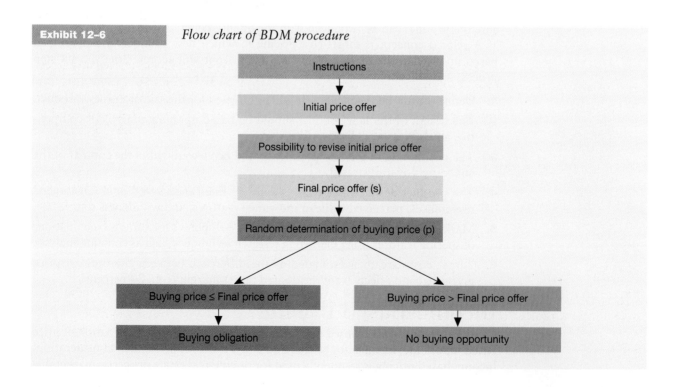

Exhibit 12–7	*Value in use (VIU) pricing*

Example

A chemical plant uses 200 O-rings to seal valves carrying corrosive materials. Those O-rings cost $5.00 each and must be changed during regular maintenance every two months. Suppose the equipment must be shut down each time the O-rings are changed and the cost of a shutdown is $5,000.

A new product has 2 $\times$ the corrosive resisting power of the incumbent O-rings. What is the VIU of the new product?

Incumbent product   New product

$200 \times 6 \times \$5 + \$5,000 \times 6 = 200 \times 3 \times VIU + \$5,000 \times 3$

Equipment cost	Shutdown cost	Equipment cost	Shutdown cost

$(\$6,000) + (\$30,000) = \boxed{(600 \times VIU) \atop \text{Solve for VIU}} + (\$15,000)$

$\boxed{VIU = \$35}$ The VIU is seven times that of the incumbent product!

above the $5 being charged already would be appropriate. If the product cost $10 and the price were set at $25, the purchasing company would be $10 better off (i.e., $25 versus $35 VIU) if the switch were made to the new product.[13]

Pricing Strategies

Setting prices to achieve the firm's objectives requires the selection of a specific pricing strategy or a combination of strategies.[14] The eleven pricing strategies shown in Exhibit 12–8 fall into four categories: differential pricing, where the same brand is sold to consumers under different prices; competitive pricing, where prices are set to take advantage of competitive market conditions; product-line pricing, where related brands are sold at prices to take advantage of interdependencies among brands; and psychological pricing, where prices are based on consideration of consumer perceptions or expectations.

The appropriateness of a particular pricing strategy depends on several circumstances: the variability of demand (the presence of different market segments), the competitive situation, the characteristics of consumers in the market, and the expectations or perceptions of consumers.

Several commonsense assumptions about buyers underlie all pricing strategies. First, some buyers have search costs in taking time and effort to obtain information about which firms sell what products and at what prices. Second, some buyers have low reservation prices, the highest prices they are willing to pay. That is, some price-sensitive buyers do not need a product enough to pay the high price others pay.

Differential Pricing

Differential pricing involves selling the same product to different buyers under a variety of prices. This is price discrimination, or the practice of charging different buyers different prices for the same quantity and quality of products or services.[15]

Exhibit 12–8	*Example pricing strategies*

Differential pricing	Competitive pricing	Product-line pricing	Psychological pricing
Second-market discounting	Penetration pricing	Bundling	Odd-even pricing
Periodic discounting	Price signaling	Premium pricing	Customary pricing
	Going-rate pricing	Partitional pricing	One-sided claims

Prices are often varied across segments. Reduced prices for senior consumers are a frequently and effectively used form of price discrimination.

Differential pricing works because the market is heterogeneous, or more simply, differences in reactions to price exist among consumers or consumer segments in the market.

The ability to engage in differential pricing has been facilitated greatly by the ever-growing number of online auction sites, such as priceline.com, and shopbots that search the Web for low prices. If a business sells a product or service that rapidly depreciates in value, such as computers, or that becomes worthless in a moment, such as airline seats, then online auctions with their ability to differentiate prices are viable sales channels. Moreover, one additional benefit from consigning products to online auction houses is that the auction site sells to end consumers and sellers avoid the perception of undercutting their own prices.[16]

SECOND-MARKET DISCOUNTING   The most common form of differential pricing, **second-market discounting,** occurs when different prices are charged in different market segments. (Recall that this practice may be legal in retail, but illegal in wholesale if it harms competition.) Second-market discounting is useful when the firm has excess capacity and different market segments exist. Generic brands and some foreign markets often provide opportunities for second-market discounting. For example, if a firm can sell its product cost-effectively in a foreign market, it may be profitable to export even at a price below local prices. The exporting firm must have excess production capacity (so no new fixed costs are required), and the markets must be sufficiently separated so that transaction costs prevent interaction between markets.

Second-market discounting also occurs when the company sells a portion of its output as generic brands at lower prices to price-sensitive segments. Other examples include differences in student and senior citizen discounts for entertainment ticket prices.

For price discrimination to be successful, some rather restrictive conditions must be satisfied:

- The market must have segments that respond differently to price variations.
- Members of the market paying the lower price must not be able to resell the product to the people paying the higher price.
- Competitors should not be able to undercut the prices charged to the higher-price segment.
- The cost of segmenting and policing the market should not exceed the extra revenue derived from charging the higher prices.
- The practice should not cause consumer resentment.
- The form of price discrimination used should be legal.[17]

PERIODIC DISCOUNTING   In some cases, it is advantageous for a firm to offer periodic or occasional discounts. **Periodic discounting** enables a firm to take advantage of the presence of consumer segments that differ in price sensitivity. This approach includes **price skimming,** where an initial high price is determined for new products to skim the market. Price skimming allows product development costs to be recovered when introductory sales are growing. People willing to pay the high price purchase first, and then the firm lowers prices as sales slow to attract the next-highest level of price-sensitive buyer. Du Pont, a well-known innovator of industrial products, frequently uses a price-skimming strategy.

Competitive Pricing

Competitive pricing strategies, based on the firm's position in relation to its competition, include penetration pricing, limit pricing, price signaling, and going-rate pricing.

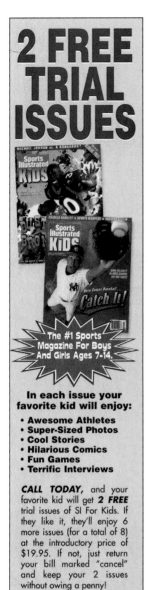

2 FREE TRIAL ISSUES

The #1 Sports Magazine For Boys And Girls Ages 7-14.

In each issue your favorite kid will enjoy:

- Awesome Athletes
- Super-Sized Photos
- Cool Stories
- Hilarious Comics
- Fun Games
- Terrific Interviews

CALL TODAY, and your favorite kid will get **2 FREE** trial issues of SI For Kids. If they like it, they'll enjoy 6 more issues (for a total of 8) at the introductory price of $19.95. If not, just return your bill marked "cancel" and keep your 2 issues without owing a penny!

1-800 424-9999

Rebates and trial products are used with introductory low prices to stimulate initial product sales and to build sales volume.

Penetration pricing calls for a low initial price to generate sales volume and take advantage of economies of scale (larger production runs at lower unit costs). It is often used when the marketer wants to maximize sales growth or market share. Penetration pricing may be particularly beneficial when there are a significant number of price-sensitive consumers in the market (demand is price-elastic) or the firm fears early entry of a competitor if prices are set high and margins appear attractive. **Limit pricing,** another term for low penetration pricing, also entails setting prices low to discourage new competition. In situations in which competitive reaction is unlikely, firms may engage in price skimming, described earlier.

Price signaling puts high prices on low-quality products. This approach, while clearly not beneficial to buyers, may reflect unethical behavior; but firms can pursue it successfully if several conditions are satisfied. First, there must be a segment of buyers whose experience is consistent with a price/quality relationship, who believe firms spend more to provide higher quality, or who trust the market and assume a positive relationship between price and quality exists.[18] Second, information on the level of quality should be hard for buyers to obtain.[19] *Consumer Reports* regularly reports examples of successful brands that have high prices and suspect quality.

Going-rate pricing reflects the tendency of firms to price at or near industry averages. This approach is frequently used when products compete on the basis of attributes or benefits other than price. Going-rate pricing has the additional advantage of lessening the threat of aggressive price wars, which may be unprofitable to all competitors.

Competitive pricing strategies also determine the positioning of many retail organizations. Value retailers, like Family Dollar and Dollar General, are becoming the newest high-growth concept. These low-overhead, low-price general merchandisers compete with the "big three"—Wal-Mart, Kmart, and Target—by offering lower prices to the growing segment of households earning $25,000 or less. Both Family Dollar and Dollar General target lower-income and fixed-income families, often in neglected geographical markets.[20]

Product-Line Pricing

Firms often offer a line of multiple versions of the same product, such as Radio Shack stereo speakers priced from $59.99 to $149.99. Low- and high-end prices may influence buyer perceptions of quality and set standards for comparing items within the product line.

Low-end prices frequently influence doubtful or price-conscious buyers to purchase and are often used as traffic builders. The high-end price has considerable influence on the quality image of the entire product line. Marketers must be sensitive to price changes in the product line. A price change in one product can detract from sales of other products in the line, because they are often substitutes for one another.[21]

BUNDLING   Increasingly, companies are realizing the value of combining separate products into bundles. **Bundling** is marketing two or more products or services in a single "package." The practice is seen frequently in the marketing of ski packages, hotel services, restaurant meals, and stereo and computer systems. Bundling also occurs in the purchase of health care equipment by hospitals. in these cases, the bundle price is typically less than if each item in the package is bought separately.

Bundling terms are used interchangeably and can cause some confusion. Two marketing scholars, Stefan Stemersch and Gerard Tellis, have recently provided a summary of term definitions that are both simple and consistent with legal interpretations:

1. *Bundling*—sale of two or more separate products (and/or services) in one package (e.g., opera tickets).
2. *Price bundling*—the sale of two or more separate products as a package at a discount, without any integration of the products (e.g., variety pack of cereals).

Product-line pricing decisions pose a common dilemma for marketers. Price ranges associated with items in a line affect the perceived levels of quality for the line, while individual prices must be set so that sales are increased for the line without negatively affecting the sales of items within the line.

3. *Product bundling*—the integration and sale of two or more separate products at any price (e.g., sound systems).

4. *Pure bundling*—a strategy in which a firm sells only the bundle and not (all) the products separately (e.g., IBM's bundling of tabulating machines and cards).

5. *Mixed bundling*—a strategy in which a firm sells both the bundle and (all) the products separately (e.g., Telecom bundles).[22]

Monsanto has maintained its market position for the herbicide Roundup by dropping its price before patent expiration but tying the purchase of Roundup to the firm's patented and genetically modified seeds. This combination may make Monsanto the world's most profitable agriculture company, commanding 80-plus percent of its two primary agricultural-related markets.[23]

In addition to often selling at lower prices than if unbundled, bundling reduces the costs to consumers from searching and the cost to sellers from individual transactions. New computers come bundled with software, the shopping for which most consumers desire to avoid. Bundling has other benefits to the seller as well: Price bundling can increase frequency of purchase and profitability. This conclusion is based upon recent findings that suggest consumers allocate lower cost to each bundled unit following purchase.

PREMIUM PRICING When a firm offers several alternative models, it often uses a premium-pricing strategy. **Premium pricing** sets higher (premium) prices on more deluxe product versions. The various models are designed to appeal to different price-sensitive segments or to segments wanting different combinations of features. Typically the firm (the manufacturer or the retailer) makes most of its profits on the expensive models and less on lower-priced models in a product line. Premium pricing occurs often for beer, clothing, appliances, and automobiles. Hewlett-Packard successfully competed with IBM for corporate data-center business by aggressively promoting its top-line models in its HP9000 series.[24]

PARTITIONED PRICING   Many firms divide the prices they charge into parts, in lieu of charging a single price. These "part" prices are often termed the *base price* and the *surcharge*. This practice is called **partitioned pricing.** Examples include catalog or Internet prices for items on sale, plus the shipping and handling charges associated with delivery. A Sony telephone from a mail catalog for $69.95, plus $12.95 for shipping and handling, is one specific combination used in a well-designed study of partitioned prices. Recent research suggests that this practice is common in the marketplace because consumers do not process the base price and surcharges completely and accurately, and as such, the total cost remembered is less and therefore demand is increased.[25]

Psychological Pricing

Psychological pricing recognizes that buyer perceptions and beliefs affect their price evaluations. Prestige or premium pricing and comparing competitors' prices with a firm's lower sale prices deal with the psychological aspects of consumer reactions to prices. Odd–even pricing and customary pricing are other applications of psychological pricing.

ODD–EVEN PRICING   **Odd–even pricing** presents prices at values just below an even amount, a common practice. Instead of pricing contact lenses at $200, for example, the price is set at $199.95. The marketer intends for consumers to associate the price with the $100 to $200 range, assuming that demand for the contacts will be less at $200 than at $199.95. In addition, the precision associated with the $199.95 price implies a bargain.

Odd–even pricing, or just-below pricing as it is sometimes called, may be beneficial for other reasons as well. First, evidence suggests that when low price is important to the consumer, the just-below price is more effective at getting consumers' attention. Second, just-below prices may have memory effects; that is, the left-most digits of a price represent the greater amounts of money and are therefore the most important. Some studies have revealed that people recall the just-below endings as underestimates from memory. Odd prices created from round-number prices have been shown to be the most effective. For example, a price such as $199.95 would likely lead to a substantially lower average recalled price than $249.95.[26]

CUSTOMARY PRICING   In the past, consumers associated a **customary price** with a product, but frequent price promotions and price increases have made this practice less prevalent today. The classic example of customary price is the much-dated 5-cent candy bar; today's customary price might be 50 cents. Customary-price beliefs represent consumers' strongly held expectations. Pricing strategies that set customary prices typically modify the quality, feature, or service of a product without adjusting the price.

"Package shrink" has become a common strategy for increasing margins in recent years for coffee, candy bars, diapers, and more recently, some snacks. For example, Frito-Lay passed along silent price hikes to its customers by shrinking Lay's regular 13.25-ounce bags to 12.25 ounces. New versions of Ivory and Joy, hand-washing dish detergents offered by P&G, come in smaller bottles at the same price. However, the taller containers are designed to look bigger and pour faster, adding up to an effective 12 percent price increase.[27]

ONE-SIDED PRICE CLAIMS   Concerns arise regarding the implications of one-sided price claims in which superiority in price for one attribute or offering is made. However, what happens when the prices of firms' other offerings are actually higher? One study of prices for mail delivery services found that consumers overgeneralize one-sided price claims to the prices for other but omitted services. Specifically, a significant number of subjects in a recent study erroneously concluded that a well-known mail carrier had the lowest overall prices just because the firm promoted its low price for guaranteed morning delivery, when in fact its prices were higher for package pickup and delivery by 5 P.M. the next day. These issues are important to those concerned with consumer welfare to the extent that such practices lead to deception and inaccurate decision making.[28]

B2B Pricing Strategies

One view of industrial and B2B pricing strategies organizes the various pricing practices used by firms marketing to other firms into four major categories: (1) new-product pricing situations, (2) competitive pricing situations, (3) product line pricing situations, and (4) cost-based pricing situations. This organization is shown in Exhibit 12–9. The specific strategies within each category overlap with many of the strategies and definitions associated with consumer goods pricing. For example, new-product pricing approaches include price skimming, penetration pricing, and experience curve pricing. The definitions of these pricing strategies are given in Exhibit 12–6, along with related strategy terms.

Exhibit 12–9	*Industrial pricing strategies*	
Strategy	**Description**	**Related Strategies**
New Product Pricing Situation		
Price Skimming	We set the initial price high and then systematically reduce it over time. Customers expect prices to eventually fall.	Premium Pricing, Value-in-Use Pricing
Penetration Pricing	We initially set the price low to accelerate product adoption.	
Experience Curve Pricing	We set the price low to build volume and reduce costs through accumulated experience.	Learning Curve Pricing
Competitive Pricing Situation		
Leader Pricing	We initiate a price change and expect the other firms to follow.	Umbrella Pricing, Cooperative Pricing, Signaling
Parity Pricing	We match the price set by the overall market or the price leader.	Neutral Pricing, Follower Pricing
Low-Price Supplier	We always strive to have the low price in the market.	Parallel Pricing, Adaptive Pricing, Opportunistic Pricing
Product Line Pricing Situation		
Complementary Product Pricing	We price the core product low when complementary items such as accessories, supplies, spare parts, services, etc. can be priced with a higher premium.	Razor-and-Blade Pricing
Price Bundling	We offer this product as part of a bundle of several products, usually at a total price that gives our customers an attractive savings over the sum of individual prices.	System Pricing
Customer Value Pricing	We price one version of our product at very competitive levels, offering fewer features than are available on other versions.	Economy Pricing
Cost-based Pricing Situation		
Cost-Plus Pricing	We establish the price of the product at a point that gives us a specified percentage profit margin over our costs.	Contribution Pricing, Rate-of-Return Pricing, Target Return Pricing, Contingency Pricing, Markup Pricing

A sample of 270 industrial firms revealed that cost-plus pricing was the most frequently employed pricing strategy. However, most firms employ multiple strategies, depending upon the situation. For example, price skimming was used most often in markets with a great deal of product differentiation and when firms were at a cost disadvantage due to limited economies of scale. Cost-based pricing is used in those situations in which demand is very difficult to estimate. Customer value pricing involves the offer of a stripped-down version of a current product to appeal to more price-sensitive segments and to take advantage of new distribution channels.[29]

Adapting Prices

Determining a pricing strategy and setting prices are only the beginning. Prices change as competition occurs and as the firm's marketing and production expertise improve. The firm must react to competitive price changes as well, constantly considering how often and how much to change prices. Price discounts and geographical pricing decisions also require marketers to adapt their prices.

Price Decreases and Increases

Over the last few years, many companies have tried unsuccessfully to raise their prices, losing volume as customers (consumers or businesses) shifted to lower-priced competitors or found substitute products. In many instances, raised prices were forced lower again in efforts to recoup lost market share.[30] Sometimes, lowering price improves profits through higher sales. When market share is declining or excess production capacity exists, the firm may lower prices. This may stimulate demand and allow greater use of production or plant investments. Depressed economic conditions may also necessitate price reductions. The lack of pricing power and discretion, and in many cases pressures to cut prices, is affecting business across manufacturing and services. One reason the economy is weak and corporate profits are minimal is the pricing pressures that face companies in 2002 and 2003. In addition, weak corporate earnings limit subsequent investment, which causes economic growth.[31]

Price reductions, however, are risky. Competitive retaliation to price decreases is particularly important. Firms may encounter three traps in reducing prices:[32]

- **Low-quality trap**—Buyers may question the quality of low-priced products.
- **Fragile market share trap**—Price-sensitive buyers may switch to the next lower-priced product that comes along.
- **Shallow pockets trap**—Higher-priced competitors that reduce prices also may have longer staying power due to higher margins.

Price decreases may be implemented in several ways, with direct reductions from the original price most common. Firms may also reduce prices by offering quantity discounts or rebates. Bundling additional products or services with the basic product, while maintaining the current price, is another tactic.

Price promotions by manufacturers affect the strategies engaged in by resellers of grocery and other packaged goods. In fact, many grocery retailers and wholesalers are dependent upon the purchase of products at reduced manufacturer prices. In these instances, reseller firms become dependent upon forward buying, a practice in which large quantities of products are bought on sale, enabling the wholesalers and retailers to subsequently have larger margins when the products are then sold to consumers. These practices lead then to consumers' spending heavily for products that are on sale. For example, almost 71 percent of total supermarket sales for carbonated beverages in one 52-week period occurred when the products were being price promoted.[33]

Price increases are also common. A primary reason is inflationary pressure; increases in the costs of inputs and production force prices upward. In Central and South America, price increases from inflationary pressures are common, often requiring high increases over very short time periods. Also, when demand is great, firms often raise prices. Moreover, they may do so indirectly by reducing or eliminating quantity discounts, cash discounts for prompt payment, and trade allowances. Services once included with a product may be unbundled so the buyer actually receives less for the same price. In effect, these tactics enable firms to adjust real prices upward without raising list prices.

Both price increases and decreases must be noticeable to affect purchase decisions. For example, a reduction from $5.75 to $5.45 may not influence demand, while a reduction to $5.15 might be meaningful. Buyers have **price thresholds** for products, and they notice when prices go under or above those limits. Thresholds depend on the average price of the product. A 10-cent reduction on a $10 product, for example, differs from the same reduction on a 50-cent product.

Ranges of acceptable prices also exist. The **acceptable price range** includes prices buyers are willing to pay. Airwalks, for example, demonstrates the role of price as part of a product's marketing mix. With its low-cost structure, due largely to outsourced foreign manufacturing and corresponding low price, the Airwalks shoe offers an acceptable and generally low price range to a segment of young consumers. Buyers may react negatively when prices move outside the acceptable range, above or below. Prices raised too high may exceed buyer budgets or be judged as unfair. Marketers that gouge buyers by charging excessively high prices are often publicly criticized. Prices reduced below the acceptable range generate concerns about product or service quality, the low-quality trap.[34]

Buyers, both consumer buyers and organizational buyers, often resist price increases and are particularly hesitant to pay prices perceived as unfair. Price changes that result in undue profits for the firm are perceived as unfair, while price increases that just maintain firm profit levels are judged as fair. This notion is referred to as the "principle of dual entitlement." Relatedly, there is growing irritation among many business travelers with increasing airline fares and rules that guarantee that executive travelers are charged the highest prices.[35]

Reacting to Competitive Price Changes

Competitive pressures affect pricing decisions of retailers and companies that sell to other businesses. Price competition among retail marketers is particularly acute with the advent of Wal-Mart, grocery superstores, and club warehouses. Recently, Target ads accused Wal-Mart of using misleading pricing tactics. Price comparisons by large retailers are likely to intensify as Wal-Mart, Kmart, Target, and others run out of territories to conquer.[36]

John Deere, the farm equipment company, took advantage of a recent merger among competitors that created GNH Global. Deere offered owners of the competing firms' equipment large price reductions, reduced interest, and cash to trade in their equipment for Deere products. Deere then slashed prices on the trade-ins, affecting sales of new CNH products and generating concerns among buyers about the subsequent trade-in value of the newly formed company's offerings.[37]

Brand managers should react to competitive price changes case by case. If price decreases among competitors do not increase total market demand, then price competition can hurt all competitors. The firm must try to determine the purpose of its competitive price change, its likely duration, and the reaction of other competitors in the market.

If buyers make decisions on nonprice characteristics, a reactive price decrease to meet the competition may not be necessary. Competitors instead might try to compete on service, quality, and features. When competition is based largely on price, however, a price decrease to match the competition may be required.

Examples of competitive price reactions are easy to find even among the most well-known companies. Pressures to reduce prices have been particularly strong in the computer software market, where competitors have undercut rivals by as much as six times. IBM reacted to the success of Toshiba and Compaq in the PC notebook market by aggressively promoting the capabilities of its line and offering competitive prices. In a similar move, Apple reduced its base price by more than $1,000 to stimulate sales of notebook computers.[38] Hertz cut its car-rental rates to match competition from Alamo Rent-A-Car and Budget. Hershey Foods was forced to match price reductions by M&M Mars.[39]

Price reductions are often implemented to give the impression of low costs and to enhance the firm's ability to compete. However, and as has occurred in the telecommunication and airline industries, price reductions can result in unprofitable price wars. Kmart's unsuccessful attempt at EDLP pricing resulted in price reductions by Wal-Mart. In these instances, competitive actions based upon price and countermeasures are typically retaliatory price cuts. However, there are nonprice strategic alternatives that may preclude the beginning of a price war. For example, firms may offer to match all competitor prices, promote everyday low prices, and emphasize their cost advantages in marketing communications. Marketers may also increase product quality and differentiation by adding features and building awareness of unique benefits. Advertising can also emphasize the performance risk associated with low-priced alternatives.[40]

GENERALIZATIONS ABOUT PRICE CHANGES   Considerable research has been conducted regarding the effects of price changes. These studies have involved experiments in which price levels were systematically varied and analyses of scanner data were collected in-store. A review of these studies yielded the following conclusions:

- Temporary retail price reductions substantially increase store traffic and sales.

- Large-market-share brands are hurt less by price changes from smaller competitors.

- Frequent price dealing lowers consumers' reference prices, which may hurt brand equity.

- Price changes for high-quality brands affect weaker brands and private-label brands disproportionately.[41]

Kimberly Kanakes, McGraw-Hill/Irwin Marketing Manager, talks about competitive packaging: "One way we strategically compete against other publishers and the used-book companies is with value packages. For example, we can package a study guide, newspaper or magazine subscription, or a CD-ROM so students get better value when they purchase a new book as opposed to a used book. The combination package price of the new text and supplement is often lower than the price of purchasing a used text and the supplement individually. It's a win-win situation for both the student and the publisher: the student gets a new book with a value-added package and the publisher sells more books."

Marketing policy and practice that continually allocate large percentages of budgets to price-related promotions serve only to reduce baseline revenues from higher-margin and unpromoted sales. As such, many brand managers worry that funds are being taken away from image advertising designed to nurture brands for the long haul and that constant price-promotion activity will only damage brand equity that enables firms to charge more-profitable premium prices.[42]

Price discounts and trade allowances are used by manufacturers to encourage retailers to carry their products. In this General Mills trade ad to retail buyers, the message emphasizes advertising support and price discounts to retailers.

Price Discounts and Allowances

The actual price a customer pays may differ from the market or list price, perhaps because of discounts from the original price. Discounts, which take many forms, occur in consumer and reseller transactions. They include cash discounts, trade promotion allowances, and quantity discounts.

Marketers often offer *cash discounts* for prompt payment by retailers. For example, terms of payment may be "3/10, net 30," indicating that the full amount of purchase is due in 30 days with a 3 percent discount available if the customer pays the bill in 10 days.

Trade sales promotion allowances are concessions a manufacturer pays or allocates to wholesalers or retailers to promote its products. The manufacturer or wholesaler may reduce prices on certain items so retailers can offer sale prices. Or the manufacturer may give additional marketing communications incentives to help the retailer pay for advertising. In fact, much of the newspaper advertising for grocery stores is actually supported by manufacturers' cooperative advertising payments.

Marketers give *quantity discounts* when the customer buys large quantities of a product. For example, full price might be charged for 500 or fewer reams of computer paper. For purchasing 501 to 1,000 reams, the customer receives a 3 percent discount per ream. For purchases over 1,000 reams, a 5 percent reduction off list price would be offered. A cumulative quantity discount entitles the purchaser to a larger discount as the sum of purchases within a specified time period, usually a year, exceeds a certain amount. Noncumulative quantity discounts apply to onetime purchases and are based on the size of the order.

Geographical Pricing

Companies with geographically dispersed customers sometimes adjust prices because of costs resulting from distance. Shipping costs may be substantial and detract from profit if they are not included in the price. Marketers use geographical pricing approaches to address these issues.

One of the more commonly used methods is **FOB origin pricing.** FOB stands for free on board, meaning the goods are placed on a carrier (truck, train, barge) and shipped to the customer. FOB pricing requires customers to pay the unit cost of the goods plus shipping costs, which differ with location or market. An opposite strategy is to charge the same price and transportation cost to all customers. Using a **uniform delivered price,** the company charges each customer an average freight amount. A principal advantage of this method is ease of administration.

Zone pricing is an approach between FOB pricing and uniform delivered pricing. Customers within an area (say, the Northeast) are charged a common price. More-distant zones or areas are charged higher freight amounts.

Freight absorption pricing is another form of geographical pricing. Here the seller absorbs freight costs—offers free or reduced costs of delivery—to attract more business. This practice occurs when competition among sellers is heavy.

Competitive Bidding and Negotiated Pricing

In the United States, retail prices for most consumer goods normally are not negotiable. However, outside the United States, price negotiations for consumer goods occur regularly. Likewise, almost all business-to-business purchases are negotiated to some extent. In fact, many organizational buyers now view every aspect of their purchase transactions as negotiable. Negotiated pricing is the norm in marketing to the federal government, the largest purchaser of goods and services.

Sealed-bid pricing is unique in that the buyer determines the pricing approach and the eventual price. The buyer encourages sellers to submit sealed bids, or prices, for providing their products or services;[43] the sellers set prices on the basis of cost considerations and expectations about what competitors will bid.

Sealed-bid pricing may be difficult for the seller. First, the seller must determine the costs involved in providing the product or service. The seller must then set a price according to the prices it expects competing firms to submit. The price must cover costs, provide a reasonable return, and be low enough to be selected by the purchaser. Overall, the bidding company must be able to evaluate the chances of

Exhibit 12–10	*Alternative bid prices and expected values (in $000)*			
Submitted price (bid)	**Costs**	**Contribution to profit**	**Probability of selection**	**Expected value**
$250	$170	$ 80	.75	$60.00
275	170	105	.70	73.50
300	170	130	.65	84.50
325	170	155	.50	77.50
350	170	180	.45	81.00

Note: Expected value = (Contribution to profit) × (Probability of selection).

winning a particular contract at different prices, determine the profit potential under various bidding outcomes, and identify projects for which the expense of preparing and submitting a bid is economically justified.[44]

An example bidding situation is shown in Exhibit 12–10. This framework allows the seller to evaluate alternative bids in terms of the costs of the project, the contribution of each alternative to profits, and the probability of winning the job at each bid price. As the price or submitted bid increases, the probability of winning decreases.

Negotiated pricing is common for large investments, such as building or other installations, and for consulting arrangements, many professional services, or governmental work. Negotiation between vendor and supplier replaces evaluation of multiple bids. If these are long-term arrangements, or agreements likely to involve future negotiations, concern for developing and maintaining relationships is critical. In some smaller deals, sales reps may negotiate prices and margins for the company in the field on a transaction-by-transaction basis. Field salespeople can help identify situations when price quotes need to be more competitive to avoid losing profitable business.[45]

Reverse auctions, in which sellers bid instead of buyers and prices fall instead of rise, enable buyers to negotiate lower prices from multiple suppliers. That is, the competition is from the buyers' side. In one B2B example for plastic automobile parts, with 25 suppliers bidding, the starting price was $745,000, the most recently paid price. After 20-plus minutes into the auction, the bidding was concluded at $518,000, a 31 percent saving for the customer.[46]

Pricing Services

The unique charateristics of services—intangible, perishable, inseparable, and nonstandardized—make their pricing difficult. Price determination is influenced by the nature of the service involved. For professional services, such as those provided by attorneys and accountants, prices vary according to the complexity of the service and the amount of work or services provided. However, pricing decisions for services, as for tangible products, should consider expenses or costs involved with service delivery, price expectations of customers, management objectives of a reasonable return, and pricing for similar services by competitors.[47] Generally, the larger the share of the market held by a service provider, the higher the price it can charge relative to competition.

One difficulty in pricing services is the need to manage off-peak periods of demand. Movies, airlines, and car-rental firms, for example, price services to shift demand to periods of excess capacity. The perishable nature of these services makes creative pricing and demand management an important aspect of service pricing. That

Pricing services and utilities can be difficult. As deregulation spreads, utility companies will face increasing pressures to price competitively.

is, once a movie starts, an airline flight takes off, or a rental car remains unused over a weekend, the potential income from these unpurchased intangibles is lost.

In some industries, pricing of services is extremely competitive. The airline industry has wide differences in prices across markets, time periods, and competitors. The entry of competitive firms can influence prices dramatically. Recently, Morris Air, one of a handful of low-cost, low-fare airlines, forced Delta Airlines to cut its fares up to 80 percent and to offer double miles to frequent fliers in efforts to retain customers. Morris normally flies only short routes under 500 miles and offers no hot meals. Morris's discounted fares are more flexible than Delta's and those of other large airlines. In addition, prices are kept low by flying only Boeing 737s, which saves money on parts inventory and maintenance demands.[48]

Bundling of services into a single package and price is a common strategy. Hotels (lodging, meals), banks (large deposits yield free travelers' checks), physicians (exams, diagnostic tests), and airlines (travel, rental cars), for example, provide services for a single bundle price.[49] Bundling increases demand by providing increased savings and convenience to the consumer.

Ethical Issues and Deceptive Practices

Ethical problems associated with business pricing are not uncommon and are often the focus of much public scrutiny. A recent congressional investigation into the pricing practices of a national hospital company revealed significant bill padding. Patients were charged $44 for saline solutions (salt water) costing 81 cents and $103 for crutches costing $8.[50] Pharmaceutical companies have been cited for overpricing life-saving drugs, as in the case of AIDS vaccines.[51] Claims of price gouging have also been leveled against major airlines for their pricing during peak travel times or in geographic areas where a major carrier dominates. Following Hurricane Andrew, Florida's attorney general subpoenaed top plywood manufacturers for records justifying soaring prices. Evidence of profiteering and consumer gouging was found among sellers of batteries, chain saws, and flashlights. Similar accusations arose after the 1994 Los Angeles earthquake. In contrast, Home Depot, a national retailer of home building supplies, sold its products at cost immediately following Andrew.[52] Undoubtedly, Home Depot's positive response earned the company much goodwill.

FTC Guidelines and Deceptive Pricing

Many advertised prices include comparison prices. These can enhance the attractiveness of the offer by making the price reduction appear lower than merely stating it alone. Comparison price advertising typically pairs the sale price with prices formerly charged by the retailer, competing retailer prices, or manufacturer-suggested prices.

Comparison price advertising is effective, and it provides useful information to buyers. Unfortunately, the ease with which claims can be made and their influence on buyers increase the likelihood of deceptive pricing practices. Federal Trade Commission (FTC) guidelines provide specific procedures for avoiding deceptive price advertising. The most common practices addressed by the guidelines include:[53]

- **Comparisons with former prices**—Prices claimed as former prices charged by the retailer ("Regularly $XX, Now Only $YY") must have been offered to the public on a regular basis for a "reasonable" period of time. Although sales are not required at the higher price, the former price must have been a genuine offer for some period.

- **Comparisons with other retailer prices**—When prices are said to be lower than those being charged by other retailers for the same merchandise in the advertiser's trade area, the advertised higher prices must be based on fact.

- **Comparisons with prices suggested by manufacturers or other nonretail distributors**—If prices are said to be reductions from the manufacturer's list price or suggested retail price, these comparison prices must correspond to the prices at which a substantial proportion of the product's sales are made.

Several years ago May Department Stores in Denver was cited by the attorney general of Colorado for "engaging in continuous and repeated patterns of deceptive price advertising and sales practices." Examples included houseware products "on sale" at the same sale prices for two years and luggage advertised as discounted from "regular" prices that never were May's prevailing prices and that were double the luggage prices for the same items charged by other local retailers.[54]

The context under which consumers make decisions can affect the ethics of marketing practices as well. For example, in cases where individuals are suffering from extreme grief, such as following the death of a loved one, decisions regarding funeral arrangements are difficult. Retailing experts have learned that presenting only corners of caskets in a product line arrangement, instead of using large showrooms displaying numbers of whole caskets, makes decisions easier for the buyer. However, the practice raises the average price paid from $200 to $400, as consumers avoid lower-end models. The ethics and fairness of this product-line pricing strategy certainly warrant evaluation.[55]

Bait and Switch

Grocery stores and department stores advertise some brands at cost or near cost to attract consumers. These marketers hope that low-priced items or *loss leaders* will generate traffic and sales of other items in the store. A **bait and switch** occurs when the retailer advertises but does not actually offer a reasonable amount of the promoted product. If the product is not, or was not, actually available, consumers may trade up and buy a more expensive version of the advertised loss leader. This bait-and-switch practice is illegal and unethical.

Predatory Pricing

In some instances, companies charge very low prices to drive competition from the market. Any losses incurred can be recouped later by charging higher monopoly prices once competition has been discouraged. This practice is called **predatory pricing.** A company that claims predatory pricing by a competitor must demonstrate that the low-priced firm, typically a larger firm, charges prices below its average total costs, with the *intent* to harm competitors.

Predatory pricing is difficult to prove in the courts, for juries are skeptical of these claims.[56] The company that sues must show not only that a rival firm prices below cost but also that it does so intending to raise prices later. Wal-Mart was once accused of predatory pricing by pharmacy chains because of its aggressive drug pricing practices. The Justice Department charged American Airlines of illegally forcing smaller competitors out of its Dallas hub. After the smaller carriers left, prices to consumers were raised. Predatory pricing has also been discussed in the government's case against Microsoft, which often gives away software to build market share.[57]

Unit Pricing

The number of products, brands, and package sizes in the marketplace presents a bewildering array of choices. The potential to be misled or at least confused is likewise great. Many states have passed **unit pricing** legislation to help consumers process in-store price information. Unit pricing presents price information on a per-unit weight or volume basis to facilitate price comparisons across brands and across package sizes within brands. Unit pricing is intended to help low-income consumers and price-vigilant shoppers.[58] Although not an ethical issue per se, unit pricing is designed to improve consumer decision making and to reduce the potential for being misled or misinformed by the vast amount of in-store information.

Summary

1. **Discuss the interrelationships among price, demand, demand elasticity, and revenue.** Marketplace conditions influence prices. The higher the price of most goods or services, the lower the demand. These relationships are depicted in the familiar economic demand curve. The extent to which demand changes as price changes is the price elasticity of demand. Inelastic demand exists when a seller increases price and sees little decrease in sales. Demand is elastic when small changes in price cause large changes in the quantity demanded.

   The profit-maximizing price level is the point where total revenues minus total costs is highest. This point occurs at the price where marginal revenue equals marginal cost. This expression of profit maximization does not consider factors such as the seller's ability to influence demand through promotional activities.

2. **Understand methods for determining price.** Cost-oriented methods for determining price include markup pricing, where the price is set as a certain percentage increase above its cost; break-even analysis, which calculates the number of units required to be sold to cover costs at a certain price; and target-return pricing, where the price is set to provide some specific desired rate of return on investment. A competition orientation to determining price suggests firms charge prices similar to competitors' prices.

3. **Recognize the different pricing strategies and the conditions that best suit the choice of a strategy.** Four broad categories of pricing strategies are differential pricing, competitive pricing, product-line pricing, and psychological pricing.

   When differences exist across consumer segments, differential pricing is effective. Examples include second-market discounting, where different prices are charged to different segments, and periodic discounting.

   Competitive pricing includes penetration pricing, where a firm sets an initial low price to stimulate demand or deter competition, and price signaling, or offering a high price for a low-quality brand in hopes consumers will infer high quality.

   Product-line strategies are important for firms that sell a variety of brands of the same product, as the price set for one of the brands often affects sales of the entire product line. Some firms use bundling strategies, where separate products or services in a line are sold as a single bundle. Premium pricing, when the firm charges higher prices for deluxe brands within a product line, is most successful when market segments want different combinations of features. Psychological pricing includes the practice of odd–even pricing and customary pricing.

4. **Recognize the importance of adapting prices under shifting economic and competitive situations.** Prices are reduced under several circumstances: declining market share, changing customer preferences, or lower competitive prices. If competitors can easily detect price reductions and are willing to retaliate, price reductions are risky. Lowering prices may also affect consumer perceptions of quality, may work only until an even lower-priced product is available, and may be difficult to maintain in the presence of larger and stronger competitors.

   When products compete on attributes other than price (service, features), price changes in face of competitive price shifts may not be required. In homogeneous markets, however, where products are similar and compete largely on price, price reductions by competitors will probably have to be matched. Inflation or excessive demand sometimes leads to price increases.

   For a price change to affect demand, the increase or decrease must exceed some minimal threshold so as to be noticeable. Buyers also have a range of acceptable prices. Prices reduced below the lowest acceptable price may generate perceptions of inferior quality; prices above the highest acceptable price will be rejected.

5. **Understand the ethical considerations involved in setting and communicating prices.** Ethical considerations are an issue in pricing decisions. Prices must not potentially mislead or take advantage of customers. The FTC offers guidelines that govern advertised price specials and comparison pricing. The most common aspects of comparison pricing governed by the FTC include comparisons with former prices, comparisons with other retail prices, and comparisons with prices suggested by manufacturers or distributors.

   Another unethical practice involves predatory pricing: pricing below average cost until competitors are forced out of the market. After driving out competitors, the firm raises its prices. Unit pricing is required in some states to provide information on prices on a per-unit or volume basis to enhance consumer decision making.

Understanding Marketing Terms and Concepts

Thinking About Marketing

1. Define price elasticity, and explain its relationship to demand.

2. Briefly explain the steps that should be considered in determination of a price.

3. Why are pricing decisions so important, and why are these decisions becoming more difficult?

4. Why may pricing decisions involving international marketing be so problematic?

5. Contrast break-even analysis pricing with markup pricing. What are the shortcomings of each approach?

6. How might the pricing strategies for a line of low-calorie Chinese grocery items vary over time?

7. Contrast penetration pricing with price skimming.

8. Identify two examples of both pure price bundling and product bundling.

9. Consider the pricing of services. What will determine the prices charged by firms that provide accounting services to small businesses?

10. How does the Federal Trade Commission view reference claims for advertisements involving (a) former price comparisons and (b) comparisons with competing retailers?

Applying Marketing Skills

1. Identify a new-brand entry in two different product categories. How do its prices compare to competing brands in each category? What factors might account for differences between prices within the categories?

2. Are the following practices ethical? Explain.

   a. John Doe is a retailer of brand X fountain pens, which cost him $5 each. His usual markup is 50 percent over cost, or $7.50. Doe first offers the pens for $10, realizing he will be able to sell very few if any. This offer lasts for only a few days. He then reduces the price to $7.50 and promotes as follows: "Terrific bargain: X Pens, Were $10, Now Only $7.50!"

   b. Retailer Doe advertises brand X pens as having "Retail Value $15, My Price $7.50," when only a few distant suburban outlets charge $15.

3. Explain why long-distance telephone suppliers charge different prices at different times of the day.

Using the www in Marketing

Activity One   The eBay Web site discussed in the introduction of this chapter has been influential in affecting how consumers search for low prices. Consider the following questions as they relate to price search using eBay:

1. What activities are required for an individual consumer to offer products for sale on eBay?

2. What are the characteristics of products that are most consistent with selling on sites such as eBay?

3. What advantages does eBay offer traditional retailers?

4. For what kinds of pricing situations are online auctions likely to be most effective?

Activity Two
Identify and describe the pricing strategies for the following products. Explain why these pricing objectives are appropriate for the respective environments in which the organization operates:

1. Florida Power and Light http://www.fpl.com
2. Boeing http://www.boeing.com
3. L'Eggs http://www.pantyhose.com
4. Goodyear http://www.goodyear.com

Making Marketing Decisions
Case 12–1 *P&G's Price-Promotion Approach*

The world's largest advertiser, Procter & Gamble, helped originate EDLP, or everyday low pricing, in efforts to enhance brand loyalty, cut costs, and end the wide fluctuations caused by price promotions. More recently, the strategy has been introduced into Europe by P&G for the same reasons. So far, EDLP has been used for certain products in Italy, the United Kingdom, and Germany. However, the success of this approach in international markets, such as Europe, remains to be determined.

Deep price discounts in European retailer markets, particularly in the United Kingdom and Germany, are commonplace. According to consumer surveys of customer preferences and purchases, 44 percent of German customers said they take home the cheapest brand they can buy. Fifty-three percent of UK consumers said retailers' private labels are just as good as manufacturer brands. This suggests that retailers would prefer high-low pricing strategies, where brands are offered on temporary discounts. Again, these price cuts would be largely supported by trade allowances from manufacturers to the retailers. Yet in spite of these conditions, P&G has moved ahead with its introduction of EDLP pricing into European markets.

One interesting aspect of the pricing strategies used in Europe is that price cuts are being made without increases in media spending. That is, firms are seeking more efficiently targeted media, in addition to cutting prices and reducing sales promotion expenditures. The switch to EDLP, which is being funded in the United Kingdom from reductions in advertising and promotional budgets, is an attempt to halt the aggressive growth of retailers' own-label brands. In addition, firms are announcing price cuts first to the news media prior to discussions with retailers, which places increased pressure on retailers to support the EDLP pricing strategy.

Procter & Gamble's move from high-low pricing to everyday low pricing (or value pricing) was first met with considerable resistance by the grocery industry. By now, the P&G position is established. The objective is to establish the value of product to the retailer or wholesaler and then to charge prices consistent with that value "every day." Prices are set so that the cost of goods sold to the retailer would be the same under either plan, adjusting for the differential costs under the high-low plan and the additional costs of inventory required when goods are purchased in quantity under the high-low plan. Beliefs among managers regarding consumer behavior are also important. Coupons are expensive, particularly when values are doubled, and many managers believe coupon and other price-reduction campaigns only serve to make consumers perennial bargain hunters.

The initial move to limit price promotions in Europe caused a slight decrease in sales and some friction with retailers. EDLP defenders at Procter & Gamble respond that retail multi-buying practices lower turnover and argue that value pricing has become successful in the United States after some initial year sales declines.

P&G's global support of Tide includes a relentless stream of new and improved products, with total new-product research and development expenditures of $2 billion. The only way to compete against Tide is a better idea—P&G will match price and advertising competitive attempts. Unilever, the maker of Wisk, Tide's major competitor, has introduced in Europe a compressed detergent tablet and has already gained 6 percent market share. In other developments in Europe, P&G lost 16 percent share in the UK on average across 24 product categories. Competitors did, to some extent, follow P&G in raising net prices and reducing coupons, but competitors increased price promotions against P&G and did not increase advertising.

Questions

1. What risks does Procter & Gamble face in this global pricing decision?

2. What factors make pricing decisions for foreign markets so difficult?

3. Why do retailers prefer that manufacturers offer deep price discounts in efforts to get them to stock certain products? How does EDLP in the United States or elsewhere affect retailer markups as part of the distribution chain?

4. Why are private-label brands, or own-labels as they are called in Europe, so price competitive?

5. Some argue that price elasticities are up to 10 times greater than advertising elasticities. Comment on the effectiveness of EDLP versus Kilo pricing strategies.

Case 12-2 Starbucks: Brewing High-Priced Beverages

 Starbucks is opening stores at a rapid pace and is now serving over 15 million customers per week. If master plans succeed, there will be 10,000 Starbucks stores worldwide by 2005. Its largest U.S. competitor, Diedrich Coffee, Inc., based in Irvine, California, has only 380 stores. The strategy in New York is interesting and somewhat mixed. The strategy of serving as a "third place" appears to have worked in the city in which the first place is a cramped apartment and the second place is a cubicle. The coffee shops provide a place for doing homework, holding business meetings, and socializing or reading the newspaper. However, attempts to sell lunch and housewares have not been as well received.

The marketing mix for Starbucks includes minimal advertising, but the brand has remarkable recognition fueled significantly by word of mouth. One restaurant consultant asserts that "the stores are the marketing for Starbucks." Prices are high, and the premium coffee outlets are supported by distribution through their ever-expanding network of stores and in-grocery store sales. Starbucks concentrates its efforts on key neighborhoods, even at the expense of possibly hurting existing stores. The success of the high-priced beverage sold so easily by Starbucks has led some small restaurant chains to offer profitably high-priced sandwiches instead of burgers and fries. Some of these premium sandwich chains, like Cosi, Panera, and Briazz, have names designed to convey European sophistication.

Criticism predicted that the Starbucks venture into Japan would fail in a country strong on tea consumption. Japan now has 300 successful stores, and 30 percent of the business is takeout. Will the strategy is Europe be successful? The Starbucks model, with long on-site consumption or paper-cup takeout, is foreign to European patterns of coffee drinking. The experience in Vienna has been profitable so far. The company expects more resistance in Italy and France, but anticipates that younger consumers will endorse the Starbucks concept.

Questions

1. What role does price play in the purchase of Starbucks coffee? Is the demand elastic or inelastic? Why?

2. How does the price menu detract or enhance the image of Starbucks?

3. What is the competition that Starbucks faces?

4. How does the role of price in the United States compare with the role of price in European markets?

Chapter Thirteen

Marketing Channels

After studying this chapter, you should be able to:

1 Explain the functions and key activities of marketing channels.

2 Discuss the role of intermediaries in marketing channels.

3 Distinguish between direct and indirect marketing channels.

4 Illustrate how some firms use multiple channels successfully.

5 See how marketing-channel decisions are related to other key marketing decision variables.

6 Understand how power, conflict, and cooperation affect the operation of a marketing channel.

7 Give examples of ethical and legal issues encountered in the operations of marketing channels.

www.apple.com

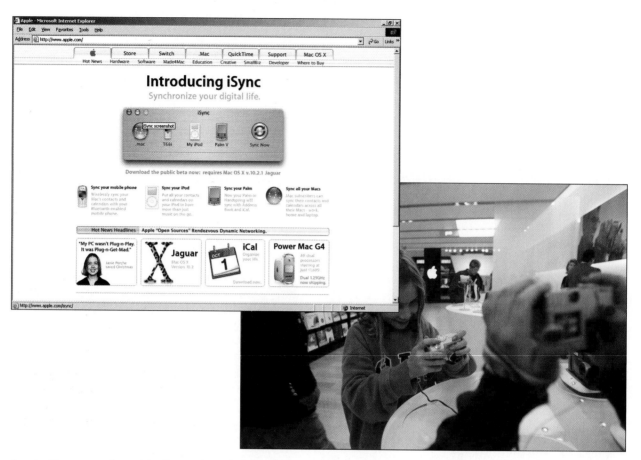

Apple Computer, based in Cupertino, California, is a worldwide company noted for its innovative personal computers. Since its inception in the 1970s, the company has reached its customers in a variety of ways. Apple has sold through computer resellers, a particularly important means of reaching the educational market, where Apple is among industry leaders. The company has also reached its market through computer stores, at one time naming CompUSA as its exclusive retail outlet. Later it worked with Circuit City and The Wiz to generate more visibility and sales through retailers. Apple has also sold its products via authorized Internet and catalog marketers.

In 2001, Apple announced a bold move to open its own stores to support its goal of increasing sales and profits. By mid-2002, thirty Apple stores were in business across the United States. In opening its own stores, Apple was the second major computer manufacturer to do so, following Gateway. Gateway opened its first store in 1996 and now has more than 400 stand-alone stores and 800 stores-within-a-store located in retailers such as Office Max.

In opening its own stores, Apple says that it does not want to compete with retailers who also sell Apple products. Chairman Steve Jobs says that no other retailer can do as good a job demonstrating the full range of capabilities of Apple products as the company-owned stores. In the company-owned stores, Apple can demonstrate networking, Internet usage, unique software applications, and how computers can work with digital cameras, portable music players, and personal digital assistants (PDAs).

Though Apple claims it wants to showcase its products more than compete in the retail market, it does have profitability expectations for its stores that it expects to meet in 2002. Apple's traditional distributors, catalog sellers, and retailers are nervous about the establishment of company-owned stores. Apple does not want to hurt sales through existing outlets, but the company needed more growth than was occurring with traditional means of reaching the market. Most industry analysts feel that Apple had to do something to get more exposure for its brand; otherwise it might remain a niche player with less than 5 percent of the total personal computer market.

While the company-owned stores have been making the headlines, Apple has also been strengthening its company Web site, where it makes exclusive offers on several versions of its products. Apple, a company known for innovative products and creative advertising, is showing that it can bring a fresh approach to how it manages its marketing channels.

Consumer and business-to-business marketing channels

The Apple profile introduces several issues of interest in this chapter. First, the right product produced at the right time must be matched with the right means of distributing it to the marketplace. Second, the right means of distribution often changes over time. Third, understanding buyer needs is crucial for success.

In this chapter, we explore the **marketing channel,** or channel of distribution, defined as a combination of organizations and individuals (channel members) who perform the required activities to link producers of products to users of those products to accomplish marketing objectives.[1] In thinking about marketing channels, keep in mind that products can be goods, services, or ideas. Producers could be manufacturers, service organizations, or idea-generating groups or companies. Some alternative consumer and business-to-business channels are shown in Exhibit 13–1.

Different types of marketing channels require the services of **intermediaries,** often referred to as *middlemen,* who are directly involved in the purchase or sale of products as they flow from the originator to the user. Intermediaries include retailers, which sell to ultimate consumers, and wholesalers, which sell to retailers, other wholesalers, government buyers, manufacturers, and other business customers. Retailers and wholesalers are discussed in detail in subsequent chapters.

We introduce various types of marketing channels in this chapter. Some companies, such as Burger King, reach their customers through franchising. As illustrated in the opening example, personal computer manufacturers use a variety of channels, including electronics stores, computer specialty stores, printed catalogs, membership clubs, and office-supply stores. Apple and Gateway have added their own retail stores, and many sell directly to customers over the Internet or with their own salespeople. Decisions on marketing channels are prime elements in a firm's overall marketing strategy and a factor in pricing, product, and marketing-communications considerations.

Importance of Marketing Channels
Since marketing channels determine how and where customers buy, the establishment of and any subsequent change in channels is indeed critical. Other marketing variables can be manipulated frequently, and changes are often easy to make. Marketers can raise and lower prices, vary advertising media and messages, and add and delete products from their market offerings without revolutionizing the way they do business.

Making major changes in marketing channels is not so easy. Marketing channels are harder to change because other parties, such as retailers and wholesalers, may play important roles in the channel. For example, several manufacturers receive a sizable portion of their sales volume from Wal-Mart. Home appliance manufacturer National Presto Industries gets more than 40 percent of its sales volume from

Wal-Mart, and a sizable percentage from Target.[2] Koss Headphones receives 75 percent of its sales volume from five major discounters, including Wal-Mart and Target.[3] Where would these companies make up the lost volume if they decided not to sell through Wal-Mart and Target. It would require a marketing miracle for these companies to sell as much merchandise without giant discounters.

Marketers are sometimes bound to their channels when significant sunk costs are involved. For example, the franchise system of McDonald's and company-owned outlets such as Exxon's convenience stores represent huge dollar investments. Such investments are made only after much forethought, and abandoning them is the last resort. For these reasons, marketing channels take on more of a sense of permanence—change is certainly an option, but one that is not so likely to be frequently exercised as with other marketing variables.

Functions of Marketing Channels

By performing five critical functions, marketing channels play an important role in accomplishing the key marketing activities discussed in Chapter 1 (Exhibit 1–7). These functions, shown in Exhibit 13–2, include the management of marketing communications, inventory, physical distribution, market feedback, and financial risk. It is important to note that none of these functions can be eliminated, but they can be shifted from one channel member to another.

Marketing Communications

Channel members are frequently involved in marketing communications activities, which include advertising and public relations, sales promotion, personal selling, and direct marketing communications. Home Depot, for example, a leading retailer of home improvement products, aggressively advertises and provides a trained sales staff to assist customers. Home Depot also uses in-store displays to demonstrate the mechanics of various home improvement projects such as building decks or installing ceiling fans. TAG Heur, a luxury watchmaker, often uses its print advertising to support dealers by pointing out that the only way to be assured of buying an authentic TAG Heur watch is to buy from an authorized dealer. The ads warn consumers that a watch bought from unauthorized dealers may be counterfeit, damaged, tampered with, or contain inferior parts. The ads also provide a Web site for locating authorized dealers.

| **Exhibit 13–2** | *Key functions performed in marketing channels* |

Marketing communications
- Advertising the product
- Providing point-of-purchase displays
- Providing a salesforce that offers information & service to customers

Inventory management
- Ordering an appropriate assortment of merchandise
- Maintaining adequate stock to meet customer demand
- Storing merchandise in an appropriate facility

Physical distribution
- Delivering products
- Coordinating delivery schedules to meet customer expectations
- Arranging for the return of defective merchandise

Market feedback
- Serving on manufacturer advisory boards
- Informing other channel members of competitive activity
- Participating in test market evaluations

Financial risk
- Offering credit
- Managing risks related to product loss or deterioration
- Managing risks related to product safety & liability

Inventory Management

Marketing channel members sometimes provide inventory management functions. For example, auto parts wholesalers must stock thousands of products, many of which sell for under a dollar each, to be a competitive supplier to the independent repair shop market. In contrast, a Corvette-only parts wholesaler may stock fewer products but offer virtually every part available for repairing Corvettes of all vintages.

Physical Distribution

The actual movement of products and other physical distribution activities are important elements in a marketing channel. For example, it is not unusual for suppliers of raw materials and components to a high-volume, fast-paced manufacturing plant to be given windows of only a few minutes to make deliveries. The coordination of delivery times is thus a major issue in meeting customer expectations, and suppliers who cannot meet such operating demands will lose business.

Marketing Information

Buyer–seller relationships are enhanced when channel members provide valuable information to other channel members, leading to better performance in the channel. One company that provides useful information to intermediaries is Building Materials Distributors (BMD), an international distributor of building materials and construction tools. BMD supports home improvement retailers, one of its key customer groups, with its product knowledge and expertise in retailing and an extensive line of services designed to help retailers improve sales and profitability. Product literature, assistance with desktop publishing, merchandising plans, market research, product catalogs, in-store training, and trade-show assistance are among the tools offered by BMD to support its retail customers.[4]

Financial Risk

The last function performed in marketing channels relates to ownership of the products passing through the channel. With ownership, or taking title, come various forms of risk. Perishable products may deteriorate; thefts may occur; or nature may deal out a flood, fire, or some other disaster.

Another risk involves accounts receivable: Who gets stuck if the customer doesn't pay the bill? For example, Kmart's suppliers took a big risk when it continued to ship to the discounter after Kmart declared bankruptcy. Major vendors such as Martha Stewart were relatively safe; that is, Martha Stewart would be paid if any vendor were paid. Some vendors were not guaranteed payment under the bankruptcy proceedings, however, and did not receive payment. Colgate, for example, wrote off $15 million in bad debt when it could not collect from Kmart.[5] Others waited long periods only to receive reduced payments.

The assumption of risk is part of the quest to make a profit. It is an essential part of the job for members of any marketing channel.

Contributions of Intermediaries
It can be fashionable to rail about the perverse influence of channel intermediaries, or middlemen. Wholesalers and retailers in the grocery industry are sometimes portrayed as antiheroes, for example, whereas farmers may be seen as economic victims.

Those who take these views typically feel that intermediaries reap unfair profits. It is true that short-term imbalances in the economic system may allow opportunistic retailers and wholesalers to capture largely unearned windfall profits. For example, hotels may inflate prices for rooms, food, and beverages to maximize profits from a captive market, say, fans attending the Super Bowl.

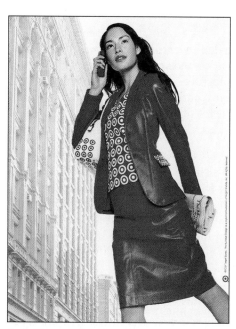

A retail intermediary, Target performs a wide range of functions, including advertising, selling, managing inventory, delivering merchandise, providing feedback to suppliers, and assuming financial risk.

In the long run, however, intermediaries must justify their existence on economic and societal terms to survive. An intermediary must be able to perform some marketing channel activity better than any other channel member. For example, Spiegel, Inc., a major intermediary for apparel and home furnishings manufacturers, has a catalog division and more than 560 Spiegel, Eddie Bauer, and Newport News stores in the United States. Spiegel provides a wide range of marketing channel activities to boost sales in its stores, including sales and advertising support, store displays, inventory ordering and storage, delivery, and consumer credit. Manufacturers such as Sony, RCA, Calvin Klein, and Reebok benefit from the channel activities of Spiegel and other retailers. Without retail intermediaries, these manufacturers would have to build their own stores or sell directly to consumers through catalogs or some other means. If they could market more effectively and efficiently without Spiegel, good business sense says they would do so. Obviously, Spiegel is performing some of the marketing channel functions better than the manufacturers could.

Justifying their existence is painfully necessary for intermediaries in the highly competitive grocery products industry. Large supermarket chains continue to move away from independent wholesalers to their own distribution networks in an effort to control costs and improve product availability. Even Fleming, one of the world's largest grocery wholesalers, has struggled in recent years. Fleming's traditional customer base, small independent grocers, is losing business to the large chains. At the same time, large manufacturers such as Procter & Gamble have cut back on discounts and promotional allowances. Since wholesalers such as Fleming traditionally kept a sizable portion of these moneys, profit margins are under even more pressure. Fleming and other wholesalers will have to be more efficient to survive. Fleming has shown improved performance in recent years, growing internationally and through acquisition of other firms. In addition, it has gained expertise in supply-chain management and now targets all sorts of food retailers, including chains and discounters who have become a more important element in grocery retailing.[6] Once again, Fleming's place in the channel is becoming more important—the company is justifying its existence by performing some functions better than other channel members.

In the vast majority of cases, intermediaries are not profiteering parasites; they are simply businesses trying to compete by adding value to the market offering. Given far-flung global markets, intense competition, and specialized support services, intermediaries are likely to remain integral in most marketing channels.

Speaking from Experience

**Hanoch Eiron,
Channels Manager**

*Software Engineering Systems Division
Hewlett-Packard*

"Manufacturers are constantly trying to improve the productivity of their channels. One way to do this is to use indirect channels rather than a direct sales orgaization. While direct channels are often necessary for specialized products, they are expensive—as much as 30 cents for each dollar of revenue generated. If manufacturers can decrease the level of specialization necessary to sell their products, indirect channels can boost productivity."

As Channels Manager in a software division of Hewlett-Packard, Hanoch is responsible for improving selling efficiencies and developing new sales channels. Prior to joining HP, Mr. Eiron was General Manager with Franz, Inc., a California software manufacturer. He earned an MBA from U.C. Berkeley and an undergraduate degree from Tel-Aviv University, Israel.

Types of Marketing Channels

The major alternatives available for structuring a marketing channel include direct and indirect channels, single and multiple marketing channels, and vertical marketing systems.

Channel management sometimes requires that existing channels be modified. Avon has begun selling through retail stores in the United States to supplement its traditional direct marketing channel.

Direct and Indirect Marketing Channels

A marketing channel may be direct or indirect. A **direct channel** describes movement of the product from the producer to the user without intermediaries. An **indirect channel** requires intermediaries between the originator and the user to perform some functions related to buying or selling the product to make it available to the final user. A given company might employ both direct and indirect channels.

DIRECT CHANNELS Direct channels frequently occur in the marketing of medical and professional services, where the use of an intermediary is often impractical. Direct channels are also frequently used in business-to-business markets, where production equipment, components, and subassembly manufacturers sell directly to finished product manufacturers. Exhibit 13–3 gives some examples of direct marketing channels. Increasingly, consumer goods manufacturers are adding direct channels via the Internet for at least some of their products to reach ultimate consumers. For example, Mattel, Polaroid, and Levi Strauss have active Web sites where consumers can bypass traditional retailers and buy directly from the company.

Some of the more spectacular marketing success stories come out of companies using direct channels of distribution. Dell Computer Corporation, sells its products directly to customers. Dell has earned many industry-wide awards for product quality and customer satisfaction, including a designation as one of *Fortune*'s "most admired" companies. Using a customer-focused approach, Dell sells more than $31 billion worth of computers, software, and accessories worldwide, the majority of which go to demanding, large business customers. The first company to offer customers direct, toll-free technical phone support and next-day on-site support, Dell management believes its close relationships with customers are the key to its success.

Direct channels can also be used to market services. Banking, employment services, home mortgages, and insurance providers are well represented on the Internet, with small companies sharing the spotlight with companies such as Bank of America, which offers online banking.

Cummins Engine Company successfully uses direct channels in business-to-business markets. Cummins's salespeople must be knowledgeable about maintenance costs, engine operating costs, and other technical data to effectively sell directly to truck manufacturers such as Chrysler, Navistar, Kenworth, and Volvo-GM.

INDIRECT CHANNELS Despite the increasing popularity of direct channels, most consumer purchases (homes, automobiles, groceries, appliances, clothing) are still made in an indirect marketing channel, where there is some intermediary between the producer and the end user. Indirect channels are also important in some business-to-business settings.

Exhibit 13-3   *Companies using direct marketing channels*

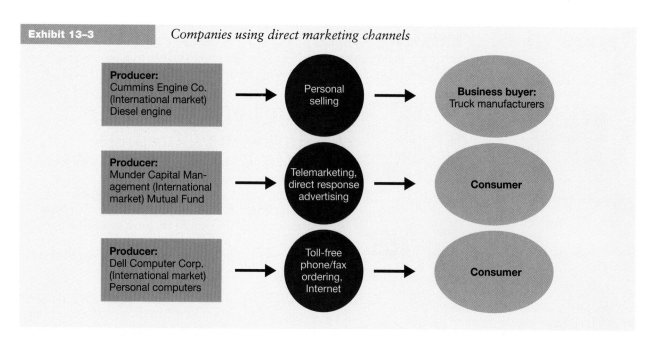

Exhibit 13-4   *Examples of indirect channels*

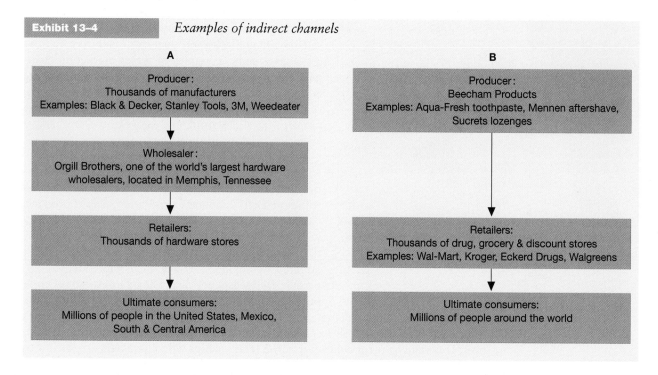

Two examples of indirect marketing channels are shown in Exhibit 13–4. Orgill Brothers, one of the world's largest hardware wholesalers, is an important intermediary for thousands of manufacturers that want to reach small- and medium-sized retail hardware stores. It would not be economically feasible for most manufacturers to provide the sales support to individual hardware stores that Orgill Brothers provides. Example B is Beecham Products, which uses indirect channels to sell to ultimate consumers through retail intermediaries.

Single and Multiple Marketing Channels

Some companies use a **single-channel strategy** to reach their customers; others rely on a **multiple-channels strategy.** Some companies with multiple products or brands may use a single-channel strategy in one situation and a multiple-channels strategy

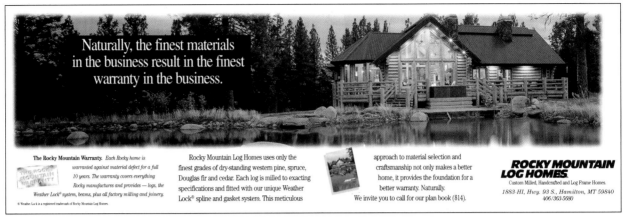

The Rocky Mountain Warranty. *Each Rocky home is warranted against material defect for a full 10 years. The warranty covers everything Rocky manufactures and provides — logs, the Weather Lock® system, beams, plus all factory milling and joinery.*
© Weather Lock is a registered trademark of Rocky Mountain Log Homes.

Rocky Mountain Log Homes uses only the finest grades of dry-standing western pine, spruce, Douglas fir and cedar. Each log is milled to exacting specifications and fitted with our unique Weather Lock® spline and gasket system. This meticulous

approach to material selection and craftsmanship not only makes a better home, it provides the foundation for a better warranty. Naturally. We invite you to call for our plan book ($14).

ROCKY MOUNTAIN LOG HOMES.
Custom Milled, Handcrafted and Log Frame Homes.
1883-HI, Hwy. 93 S., Hamilton, MT 59840
406/363-5680

Most consumers buy houses in an indirect marketing channel with the assistance of a real estate agent. Others may buy in a direct channel from producers such as Rocky Mountain Log Homes.

in another. A single-channel strategy involves the use of only one means of reaching customers. For example, Nexxus shampoo is distributed exclusively through hair care professionals. Prell shampoo, widely available at discount, drug, and grocery stores, is a product distributed through multiple channels. Liz Claiborne uses a multiple-channels strategy to reach different market segments. Its Elisabeth stores serve large-size customers, while Claiborne outlet stores market unsold inventory from past seasons. Liz Claiborne merchandise is also widely distributed in department and specialty stores.

As markets become increasingly fragmented, more firms use a multiple-channels strategy to appeal to as many potential buyers as possible. The basic idea is to allow customers to buy the way they want to and where they want to.

Hanoch Eiron, Channels Manager in a software division of Hewlett–Packard, discusses why the popularity of multiple channels is increasing: "The move to multiple channels in many industries is driven by market fragmentation and buyer preferences. For example, in the computer industry, there are significant markets for home computers and business computers. Within these two broad categories, individual buyers have different preferences. Some like to buy in a retail store, some on the Internet or toll-free phone system, some from a local dealer, some directly from the manufacturer sales specialist. A manufacturer that uses only a single channel will most likely miss sale opportunities. Multiple channels let customers buy like they want to."

Vertical Marketing Systems

Emphasis on buyer–seller relationships has contributed to the growth of vertical marketing systems. These systems are centrally coordinated, highly integrated operations that work together to serve the ultimate consumer. The word *vertical* refers to the flow of the product from the producer to the customer. This flow is usually thought of as "down the channel" or "downstream," meaning that the product flows down from the producer to the customer.

Vertical marketing systems are now used in a sizable majority of the total sales of consumer goods. Exhibit 13–5 gives examples of the three basic types of vertical marketing systems: corporate, contractual, and administered channel systems.[7]

CORPORATE CHANNEL SYSTEMS Vertical coordination in a corporate channel system is achieved through ownership of

---

Exhibit 13–5

Types of vertical marketing systems

Channel systems

Corporate
Forward integration:
  Polo, Laura Ashley, Gulf States Paper Corp.
Backward integration:
  Winn-Dixie grocery chain
Description
One channel member owns one or more other channel members

Contractual
Wholesaler-sponsored voluntary groups:
  Ace Hardware, Western Auto
Retailer-sponsored cooperative groups:
  Affiliated Grocers, Cotter & Company (True Value Hardware)
Franchise systems:
  McDonald's, Holiday Inns, Personnel Pool of America
Description
Channel members operate according to contractual agreement

Administered
Abbott Labs, General Electric, Rolex
Description
Channel members operate according to agreed-upon plan

two or more channel members on different levels of distribution. A corporate channel system in which one channel member owns one or more of its buyers downstream is called **forward integration.** Some of the companies that have used forward integration to open their own stores are Polo, Esprit, and Laura Ashley.

Business-to-business marketers also use forward integration. For example, Gulf States Paper Corporation, a manufacturer of assorted food-service products such as paper plates, bowls, and serving trays, owns a chain of wholesale paper distributors in the southeastern United States.

Other companies attempt to improve the efficiency and effectiveness of their marketing channels through ownership of one or more of their suppliers, not their buyers. This practice is called **backward integration.** The Winn-Dixie grocery store chain, for example, acquired its own cattle farms, coffee plantations, and ice cream manufacturing facilities for better control of the price and availability of key food products.

The global integration of marketing channels allows companies to take advantage of the strengths of various countries or regions of the world to maximize marketing efforts. For example, a company might manufacture its products in low-wage countries and use forward integration to establish retail distribution in more lucrative markets. This has been the channel strategy used by S. C. Fang Brothers, a Hong Kong textile manufacturing firm with a global sales base of more than $450 million. Fang Brothers was successful making T-shirts for The Gap and blouses for Calvin Klein, but it saw another retail opportunity. The company seized that opportunity in the late 1980s when it opened Episode stores in the United States. Fang Brothers opened 26 retail stores in the United States and then sold its successful retail operation to Mother Works, Inc., in 1986.[8]

CONTRACTUAL CHANNEL SYSTEMS Contractual systems may allow some channel members to gain clout in the marketplace and compete effectively with large corporate systems. Coordination between independent firms is achieved through contractual agreements rather than through ownership of channel members upstream or downstream. In this way, contractual channel members try to improve their buying power, gain economies of scale, and realize greater efficiencies through the standardization of operating procedures. The three primary types of contractual channels are wholesaler-sponsored voluntary groups, retailer-owned cooperative groups, and franchise systems.

Wholesaler-sponsored voluntary groups consist of independent retailers that operate under the name of a sponsoring wholesaler. Examples of wholesaler-sponsored voluntary groups are Ace Hardware and Western Auto. The wholesaler (Ace Hardware) buys in quantity, makes deliveries to the individual stores, and offers a variety of services that benefit its retailers. These services may include merchandising, advertising, and pricing support based on quantities purchased. Ace Hardware retailers buy most of their merchandise from the group wholesaler and pool their funds for advertising.

Retailer-owned cooperative groups operate like wholesaler-sponsored voluntary groups, but the retailers actually own the wholesaler. Affiliated Grocers and Cotter & Company's True Value are two well-known examples of this type of system.

The third type of contractual channel system is the **franchise system.** One party, the **franchisor,** grants another party, the **franchisee,** the right to distribute and sell specified goods and services. The franchisee agrees to operate according to marketing guidelines set forth by the franchisor under a recognized trademark or trade name.

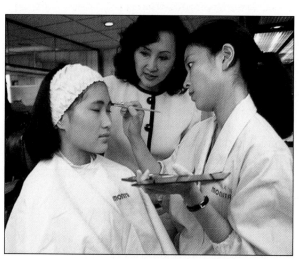

Cheng Ming Ming used forward integration to sell her own brands of beauty products through an international chain of beauty schools and salons that extends from Southeast Asia and China to the United States.

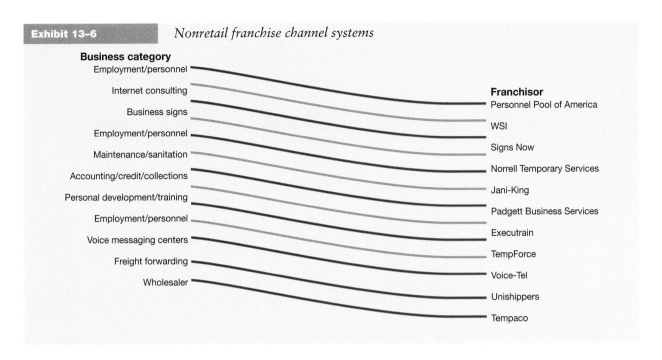

Exhibit 13–6   *Nonretail franchise channel systems*

Business category

Business category	Franchisor
Employment/personnel	Personnel Pool of America
Internet consulting	WSI
Business signs	Signs Now
Employment/personnel	Norrell Temporary Services
Maintenance/sanitation	Jani-King
Accounting/credit/collections	Padgett Business Services
Personal development/training	Executrain
Employment/personnel	TempForce
Voice messaging centers	Voice-Tel
Freight forwarding	Unishippers
Wholesaler	Tempaco

Franchise systems have been responsible for the growth of some of the most recognizable names in the business world, such as McDonald's and Holiday Inn. Nonretail franchise operations are also prominent, with companies such as Snelling & Snelling and AccounTemps in the personnel placement business and the Coca-Cola bottlers at the wholesale level. Exhibit 13–6 lists some other examples of nonretail franchise organizations. Retail franchising is discussed in more detail in Chapter 14.

ADMINISTERED CHANNEL SYSTEMS   A system designed to control a line or classification of merchandise is called an **administered channel system.** Here, channel members agree on a comprehensive noncontractual plan, and no channel member owns another. The parties in an administered system may work very closely to reduce joint operating costs for advertising, data processing, inventory control, order entry, or delivery schedules.

One example of an administered channel system is Agco Corporation's dealer network, which numbers 7,750 around the world. Agco has distribution rights to several leading brands of farm tractors, including Massey Ferguson, Agco Allis, and Fieldstar, and supports its dealers with business planning, training, cash incentives, and constant communication. A key component of this administered system is Dealer Central, a telemarketing operation in Agco's Georgia headquarters. Dealers can call in for technical advice and product and parts availability when Agco's territory managers are not readily available. Agco's administered channel system has been instrumental in growing existing business through dealers. It also helps bring in new products that open new markets for dealers, such as its agreement with Caterpillar to market the Challenger tractor line.[9] For another example of a successful administered channel, see "Building Customer Equity: IBM Serves Its Channel."

In the retail sector, successful administered marketing channels include General Electric and Rolex. Both companies have reputations for quality products backed by highly effective marketing plans and activities. As a result, retailers are usually quite receptive to suggestions made by General Electric and Rolex for pricing and display practices.

Managing Marketing Channels   The management of marketing
channels requires decision making and action in the six areas shown in Exhibit 13–7. First, the firm formulates its marketing objectives and strategy. Only then

| Exhibit 13–7 | *Managing marketing channels* |

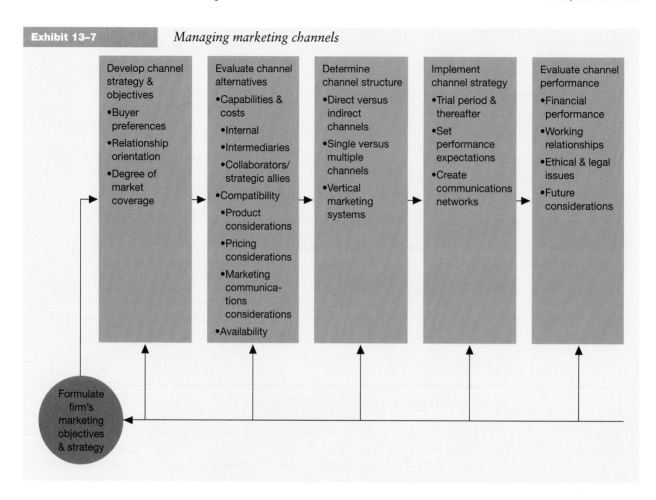

can managers develop marketing-channel strategies and objectives. Various channel alternatives are then evaluated to determine capabilities, costs, compatibility with other marketing variables, and their availability to the firm. Next, the firm establishes its channel structure and implements the channel strategy. Finally, the firm must constantly evaluate channel performance, which may lead to adjustment in one or more of the other five management areas shown in the exhibit.

Building Customer Equity

IBM serves its channel

IBM is second in market share to BEA Systems in the Java applications server market, but it is number one in the hearts of its resellers. In a poll conducted by *Crn,* a technology industry trade magazine, IBM topped BEA, Sun/iPlanet, and Oracle to win the Channel Champion 2002 award. IBM finished in first place in seven of nine categories, gaining its highest score in the technical support category.

IBM stood out from its competition in the area of channel support, which is intended to help channel partners make profitable sales. All competitors scored high in technical support, with IBM finishing just ahead of Sun and BEA. IBM pulled away from the pack in other areas, scor-

ing well ahead of its competitors in training and certification, marketing support, and sales support.

Ann Szerlip, vice president of global alliances at Divine, a Chicago-based systems integrator, said that it took a lot of time and effort to build a strong relationship with IBM but that the effort was paying off. She noted that selling alongside IBM representatives was working particularly well.

In the highly competitive applications server market, a team approach with channel partners is increasingly effective. When it comes to building equity with channel partners, helping them achieve sales growth and profitability is ultimately the best strategy.

Formulate Marketing Objectives and Strategy

Marketing channels often represent a significant dollar investment, and established channels can be difficult to change without risking lost sales volume. As a result, it is imperative that a firm develop marketing-channel objectives and strategy only after formulating its overall marketing objectives and strategy.

Lexus by Toyota has become one of the biggest success stories in the luxury car market by positioning the exclusivity of the brand. The Lexus marketing strategy called for extending the marketing channel beyond existing Toyota dealers to a relatively small number of selected Lexus dealerships. With less competition between dealers, maintaining higher prices to support the exclusive image is not as problematic as when a geographic market is flooded with competing dealers. Higher prices mean higher profit margins, which makes it possible for dealers to provide exceptional service to its customers, an objective that is also compatible with the overall marketing strategy. By ensuring that other marketing-mix variables were compatible with the chosen marketing channel, and that the entire mix was compatible with the exclusive image of the product, Lexus has become a huge success.[10]

Develop Channel Objectives and Strategy

Channel objectives should be specifically stated, measurable, and consistent with the firm's marketing objectives. Objectives are often stated in terms of sales volume, profitability, market share, costs, number of wholesale or retail outlets, or geographic expansion. **Channel strategy** then is an expression of a general action plan and guidelines for allocating resources to achieve the channel objectives.

The development of channel strategy involves decisions in three key areas: buyer preferences, relationship orientation, and the degree of market coverage.

BUYER PREFERENCES   Buyer preferences are important in determining channel strategy. Understanding the logic behind letting customers buy the way they want to is a hallmark of both established marketing leaders and entrepreneurs who beat the odds by breaking into long-established markets. Sellers of thousands of products, most notably books, recorded music, computers, and financial investments have found that millions of consumers worldwide prefer to buy online. Sellers of these products who did not fully appreciate buyer preferences are now playing catch-up.

Ignoring buyer preferences is contrary to any sort of rational marketing thinking. Nonetheless, industry leaders sometimes have to be prodded into action only after more opportunistic marketers have tapped the market via a new channel. For example, Dell, then Gateway, developed the direct-to-customer market for computers. Reluctantly, IBM, Compaq, and others followed years later. E*Trade pioneered online brokerages, a move resisted by Merrill Lynch and other traditional brokerage houses. Amazon.com built the market for online book purchasing, while small independent stores and large chains such as Barnes and Noble were slow to react. If a company does not pay attention to the channels preferred by the customer, the risk of competition from new entries into the market is indeed a real threat.

RELATIONSHIP ORIENTATION   Most successful organizations try to establish strong relationships with others in their channel—not only because it is profitable in the long run, but also because they believe that to do otherwise would be risky. Recall from Chapter 5 that a relationship orientation between buyers and sellers is a major trend, and that negotiations between parties often seek an outcome whereby both can win. This is the case with antivirus vendor McAffee, a unit of Network Associates. Network Associates had been criticized by some of its resellers for selling directly to end users rather than through the reseller channel. Network Associates revamped its channels program, pledging to sell only through resellers

IT TAKES MORE THAN GOOD INTENTIONS TO WIN THIS AWARD THREE TIMES.

At FORD, we take the business of expanding opportunities for minority-owned companies very seriously. As a result, we've earned the NMSDC/NMBEIC Corporation of the Year Award three times. But the real secret of our success is the network of suppliers who, through their professionalism and quality of service, have made doing business with them very good business for us. Thank you.

Ford Motor Company

www.fordmsd.com

The benefits of a relationship perspective can extend beyond economic advantage to the promotion of socially desirable results. Ford Motor Company has been recognized for its efforts to develop business relationships with minority-owned suppliers.

except on large sales, where a direct sale better serves the end user. The company also set up 10 technical training centers to provide training for resellers and set up a channel partner advisory board to enhance the working relationship between Network Associates and its resellers."[11]

Hanoch Eiron, Channels Manager in a software division of Hewlett–Packard, comments on the importance of manufacturers working with others in the channel: "Good working relationships with channel intermediaries is absolutely essential for success. Manufacturers should view their wholesalers and retailers as extensions of their companies, and use a team approach to maximizing channel performance. This is sometimes difficult, as these intermediaries sell competing manufacturers' brands. It is necessary that a manufacturer's objectives are compatible with those of the intermediary, and that there is a strong commitment to work together toward common objectives."

DEGREE OF MARKET COVERAGE Market coverage has to do with the number of outlets used to market a product. Market coverage commonly takes one of three forms: intensive, selective, or exclusive distribution. With **intensive distribution,** the product or service is distributed through every available outlet. For example, PepsiCo has long used intensive distribution with its soft drinks, selling through all sorts of retail stores, vending machines, restaurants, and concessionaires. Pepsi is now competing aggressively with coke to intensify its sales to restaurants, theaters, sports arenas, and schools in the fountain-sales category.

Selective distribution involves selling a product in only some of the available outlets. This is commonly used when after-the-sale service is necessary, as with home appliances. Maytag, for example, sells appliances via selective distribution, and the company is even more selective in designating certain dealers as authorized service centers. In a metropolitan area of a million residents, Maytag products might be sold through a dozen retail stores, only two or three of which are designated as authorized service centers.

Exclusive distribution occurs when only one outlet is used in a geographic marketplace. In contrast to home electronics producers like Sony who use intensive distribution, high-end audiophile equipment manufacturers typically use exclusive distribution. Such manufacturers include Marantz, McIntosh, NAD, and Manley Labs.

The Internet offers a convenient way to use exclusive distribution for selected products on a limited time basis. IBM and Procter & Gamble have used the Internet in this fashion, and music artists often offer concert tickets and recorded music on an Internet-only basis for limited time periods. Consumer goods companies also use exclusive distribution to offer retailers different version of products, so that each competing retailer has exclusive rights to a particular model or brand. For example, Stride Rite offers its Kid Smart and Baby Smart brands exclusively to Target Corporation.[12]

Evaluate Channel Alternatives

As shown in Exhibit 13–7, the evaluation of channel alternatives requires analysis in three related channel areas: capabilities and costs, channel compatibility with other marketing variables, and availability.

Thinking Critically

Rebecca Wetzel has just been appointed to a newly created position, manager of retail dealer development for HomeRight, a major home appliance company. She is responsible for providing training for retail salespeople and advice to dealers in the areas of merchandising, store promotions, and advertising. In the past, the HomeRight salesforce had provided these support activities to the retail dealers. In her first few weeks on the job, Rebecca visited several dealers in different markets and found that the retail support provided by the salesforce had been inconsistent—good in some cases, bad in others.

- What should Rebecca do within her own company to begin building a solid retail support program?
- To maximize dealer support and increase sales, what suggestions can you make to Rebecca for getting input from HomeRight dealers?

CHANNEL CAPABILITIES AND COSTS Marketers must determine exactly who will perform the various channel activities and at what cost. Establishing marketing channels can be expensive and difficult to reverse, so firms should carefully assess the costs and capabilities of each channel alternative.

The evaluation of channel alternatives often begins with an assessment of how the firm's internal resources might be used to accomplish channel activities. This naturally leads to subsequent examination of how intermediaries could fit in, if at all.

In the travel market, airlines and rental car companies have been through this evaluation in recent years, resulting in widespread elimination of commissions for travel agents. With travel information so widely available through airline and rental car Web sites, the need for travel agents for booking routine trips has been greatly reduced. Customers who wish to use travel agents typically pay an additional fee rather than the carrier paying a commission to compensate the travel agent.[13]

The analysis of channel capabilities and costs sometimes leads companies to join together to jointly market a product. For example, PepsiCo distributes Starbucks Frappuccino to grocery stores, and Dreyer's Ice Cream distributes Starbucks coffee ice cream. In a similar arrangement, Coca-Cola Company distributes the French-based Groupe Danone SA's Evian mineral water in the United States.[14]

In the wake of the shakeout among Internet retailers, channel partnerships among Web-based marketers have become commonplace. Some Internet marketers have found it more efficient and effective to partner with Internet marketing specialists rather than approach the online channel on their own. Amazon.com, through its international Amazon.comAssociates program, now serves as a link for 600,000 vendors who sell a huge assortment of goods ranging from toys and games to tools and hardware. Toys "R" Us is among those who have decided to partner with Amazon instead of servicing the online segment alone.[15]

CHANNEL COMPATIBILITY Channel alternatives need to be compatible with other marketing variables affecting a firm's offering, including product, pricing, and marketing communications factors. For example, product perishability, consumer sensitivity to purchase price, and the nature of point-of-sale promotion could affect the compatibility of a particular marketing channel. Research suggests that channel variables such as amount and kind of shelf space and feature displays may interact with both price and perceived quality to affect purchase intentions or sales volume. In one study, store brands were rated much higher in attractive supermarkets than in less attractive stores. Two-thirds of shoppers who tasted store-brand jelly in a high-image store rated it very good or excellent. Only 38 percent rated it just as positively in an older, less appealing store.[16]

PRODUCT CONSIDERATIONS A product-related consideration is the product's desired image. Consider the case of OshKosh B'Gosh Inc. Oshkosh, a maker of children's clothing, traditionally relied on expensive department stores and specialty stores for retail distribution, in keeping with its high-quality image. When OshKosh expanded into Sears and JC Penney stores, the company was concerned that such a move would affect its image and, subsequently, sales in upscale department stores where image is important.

OshKosh hoped to avoid problems with the upscale department stores by offering them exclusive, higher-profit items such as a novelty denim line. OshKosh was trying to minimize a possible product/channel incompatibility by differentiating its product offerings to two different types of retail customers.

PRICING CONSIDERATIONS Which marketing channels are appropriate can also depend on pricing strategies and tactics. The recorded music industry is facing a tough dilemma in matching the price of its number one seller, the compact disc, to its channels. Traditionally, recorded music has been sold through music stores, general discounters such as Wal-Mart, and home electronics and entertainment

Some companies join forces to move products through marketing channels. Coca-Cola distributes Evian mineral water, a product from France, in the United States.

stores such as Best Buy. The problem is that list prices for CDs are getting too high for the average consumer, who increasingly is downloading digital versions of songs, borrowing copies and reproducing them at home, or simply cutting back on purchases. Most music industry analysts believe that music companies must offer lower priced formats and tap less expensive channels, such as electronic distribution, to avoid a continuing downward sales spiral with the upcoming younger generation.[17]

MARKETING COMMUNICATIONS CONSIDERATIONS
Compatibility with marketing communications plans and strategies also determines the suitability of various marketing channels. Sony, in an attempt to showcase its full product line better, supplements its independent dealer network with its own Sony Gallery and Song Style stores in Chicago, New York, and San Francisco. Reebok now sells directly to colleges and high schools while continuing to sell through its traditional retail channel. Reebok took this action to address a lack of representation among American basketball players, a market dominated by Nike.

AVAILABILITY   Another important issue in the evaluation of various channel alternatives is whether the channel is available under reasonable conditions. Quite often, new companies may have a hard time establishing an appropriate marketing channel. The right channel may simply be unavailable, or the desired channel is too expensive.

For large, powerful sellers, channel availability is less of a problem. Indeed, a firm with the financial wherewithal can simply purchase a channel of distribution. Such is the case with the CarMax chain of used and new car dealerships. Backed by Circuit City, CarMax essentially bought its 38-location dealer network, creating a new channel that is now successful enough to operate on its own without continued financial support from Circuit City.[18]

To protect its high-quality image after expanding sales to Sears and JC Penney, Oshkosh offered upscale department stores exclusive, profitable merchandise.

Determine Channel Structure
The fourth phase of managing marketing channels shown in Exhibit 13–7 is to determine channel structure. The major decisions here concern whether to use direct or indirect channels, a single channel or multiple channels, or one of the many forms of vertical marketing systems. Firms often mix direct and indirect channels, and many firms use multiple channels, especially to reach new markets.

Implement Channel Strategy
The first four phases of managing marketing channels concentrate on planning the appropriate channel strategy and structure. The task now is to implement channel strategy. The full-scale implementation of a new channel strategy is often preceded by a trial period. Other important implementation tasks include setting performance expectations and creating communications networks.

RUN A TRIAL PERIOD   The results of a trial period may indicate that a change is warranted, or just the opposite—that an existing strategy should stay in effect. Trial periods helped convince marketers at General Mills that additional channels would be beneficial for its Chex cereals, Yoplait yogurt, Betty Crocker baking mixes, and Fruit Roll-Ups. New channels include convenience stores, gas stations, and mass discounters such as Target and Wal-Mart.[19] In other cases, most notably some companies who extended their channels to the Internet, trial periods convince the company to stick with existing channels. For example, Reebok stopped selling its athletic shoes online after a four-month trial, when backlash from existing retailers outweighed the benefits of selling online.[20]

SET PERFORMANCE EXPECTATIONS As marketing-channel members have become more interdependent, the setting of performance expectations has evolved into more of a joint decision process, rather than one party's dictating standards to another. Procter & Gamble, one of the world's most powerful and effective marketing organizations, has learned the advantages of jointly setting performance standards with its wholesale and retail accounts. More than a hundred P&G key-customer marketing teams see reaching agreement on performance standards with their customers as an important part of their mission.[21]

Lack of agreement on performance standards could indicate that some other channel arrangement might be appropriate. If a channel is set up without advance agreement on performance standards, evaluation of channel performance becomes much more difficult.

CREATE COMMUNICATIONS NETWORKS Another crucial aspect of channel strategy implementation is to establish communications networks among channel members. Sophisticated computer and communications technologies have greatly enhanced the capabilities of channel members to share important information on a timely basis, maintain goodwill, and solve problems in the mutual interest of channel members. For an example of how a computerized network facilitates communications among channel members and ultimate consumers, see "Using Technology: Bridgestone/Firestone's Database Saves the Day."

The importance of ensuring adequate communications in the marketing channel is seen in the case of the National Franchise Council, an organization supported by the 15 largest franchise companies and overseen by the Federal Trade Commission. The council sponsors a traveling reform school, giving remedial training to franchise companies that have miscommunicated with franchise owners and potential owners. Among the companies learning how to better communicate with their channel partners are Atlanta-based Aaron Rents Inc., Noble Roman's Pizza of Minneapolis, and AlphaGraphics, headquartered in Tucson, Arizona.[22]

Evaluate Channel Performance

The evaluation of channel performance, the last area in Exhibit 13–7, can necessitate changes in any of the other decision areas. Evaluating marketing channels requires attention to four key areas: financial performance, working relationships with other channel members, ethical and legal issues, and future plans.

Using Technology

Bridgestone/Firestone's database saves the day

When Bridgestone/Firestone faced the massive tire recall for Ford Explorer customers in 2001, its centralized database for its 2,200 company-owned stores helped the company survive the potentially disastrous situation. Having consolidated all of its customer records in one database, Bridgestone/Firestone was able to locate buyers of the recallable tires and keep them informed throughout the recall process.

The company also identified customers for focus groups, where it gained a better understanding of their attitudes and how they might affect brand and store loyalty. The focus groups indicated that brand and store loyalty was not likely to be affected as long as the recall was handled fairly and expeditiously.

The recall took a year, and it appears that the company maintained good relationships with most of its previous customers. In general, customers thought that Bridgestone/Firestone did a good job handling the recall. Customers liked the systematic way in which they were kept informed. They also liked the personal communications added by store personnel that supported the database-generated messages from the Bridgestone/Firestones corporate headquarters. As is so often true, Bridgestone/ Firestone shows that clear, timely communications can go a long way toward supporting all functions in a marketing channel.

FINANCIAL EVALUATION   For the short run, channel members may be willing to operate at low levels of financial performance. Over time, however, financial results must be positive to sustain relationships in the channel.

An interesting example here involves Procter & Gamble. After years of offering significant discounts and costly promotions to retailers in the grocery trade, P&G concluded its marketing channel was too expensive. One step the company took was to drastically reduce discounts and other trade promotions. This angered some of P&G's retailer customers, but some analysts think the company was deliberately shifting some of its distribution from grocery stores to discount stores, where the everyday-low-price policy is more welcome.

EVALUATE WORKING RELATIONSHIPS   Three related concepts—power, conflict, and cooperation—are important in evaluation of working relationships among channel members. A firm may gain power in a variety of ways and use it to enhance its position in the marketing channel. Conflict among channel members is natural and sometimes constructive, but it can become destructive if it rages out of control. As power is wielded and conflicts ensue, channel members often find cooperation is essential if they are to flourish and survive.

CHANNEL POWER   Channel members may gain **channel power** in many ways.[23] For example, a giant retailer like Home Depot offers vendors the opportunity to sell their products in more than 1,400 stores in the United States. In effect, Home Depot is in a position to use **reward power** when it agrees to buy from a vendor—the reward being widespread distribution and the high probability of large sales volumes. Other examples of reward power might be a manufacturer's granting exclusive distribution rights to a wholesaler, offering special credit terms to deserving customers, or extending lenient returned-goods policies.

Another form of power is **legitimate power,** which lies in ownership or contractual agreements. Holiday Inn has a certain amount of legitimate power over its franchisees through contractual agreements, for example, and Polo controls one of its channels by ownership of its own retail stores.

Power developed through the accumulation of expertise and knowledge is called **expert power.** Large retailers have gained a tremendous amount of expert power using point-of-sale scanners to gauge product movements, price sensitivities, and trade promotion effectiveness. In fact, retailers can know more about how manufacturers'

Some companies have achieved the status of channel leaders because of their expertise in marketing. Foot Locker is a channel leader in the athletic footwear market.

products are doing in the marketplace than do the manufacturers. This expertise gives large retailers more power to negotiate favorably with their suppliers.

Power based on the desire of one channel member to be associated with another channel member is called **referent power.** For example, a jewelry store may wish to be selected as an exclusive dealer for Rolex watches. The store's desire would put Rolex in a powerful position with such a retailer.

Another form of power sometimes seen in channel relationships is **coercive power.** A manufacturer that threatens to cut off a distributor's credit unless the distributor pays its bills more promptly exemplifies coercive power. The use of coercive power can become abusive and even illegal. For instance, a distributor's coercing a manufacturer into dropping a competing distributor might be ruled a conspiracy in restraint of trade, a violation of federal antitrust legislation. Another example involves Coca-Cola and its bottlers in Mexico, where the antitrust commission found they had abused their market power. Coke was ordered to suspend certain marketing and sales practices, including illegally preventing small independent retailers from selling rival products.[24]

All channel members must develop some sort of power to survive. Some may build enough power to act as a **channel leader,** that is, a channel member with enough power to control others in the channel. Current channel leaders include Wal-Mart, Kroger, General Electric, and Foot Locker. Foot Locker has 3,600 stores with plans to open another 1,000 in the coming years. Foot Locker uses its size to advantage, negotiating to get the hottest products from Nike and Reebok earlier and at lower costs than its competitors.[25] Large, successful organizations can gain buying power and selling power by controlling economic assets and resources, but smaller companies can also build power, especially by developing knowledge and expertise to gain expert power. Before they became a huge company, Foot Locker built its power base by becoming adept at mixing athletic shoes with clothing, something it does better than its competitors.

CHANNEL CONFLICT   It is inevitable that channel members experience conflict with one another. **Channel conflict** may result from poor communications, a struggle over power in the channel, or incompatible objectives. For example, some AT&T Wireless distributors are upset, claiming that AT&T is selling customers direct instead of allowing them to buy from distributors. Bob Norton, vice-president of Select, a large Massachusetts distributor, says, "We've abandoned AT&T. I'm sufficiently disgusted with what the big wireline carriers have been doing to the channel."[26] AT&T blames poor-performing distributors, saying that not all add value to the sales process. Exhibit 13–8 provides several examples of routine channel conflict.

Channel conflict is commonplace in a competitive market where profitability is a requirement for survival, pointing up the importance of cooperation in resolving conflict to avoid senseless disagreements that can drain channel members' resources.

Exhibit 13–8		*Examples of channel conflict*	
Who is upset?	**With whom?**	**Why?**	**Consequences**
Tommy Hilfiger	Wal-Mart	Wal-Mart's sale of imitation HIlfiger clothing	Wal-Mart is fined and ordered (by federal court) to cease
Bayer	Rite Aid drugstores	Unauthorized deductions from invoices	Reduce profits for Bayer
Auto dealers	General Motors	Use of dealer money for national advertising	Lawsuit against GM
Music distributors	Music retailers	Sale of used CDs cuts sales of new CDs, deprives artists of royalties	Sony, Warner Music, and others halted co-op advertising allowances to retailers that sell used CDs

Exhibit 13–9	*Examples of ethical and legal problems in marketing channels*

Situation	Ethical/Legal Problem
Large retailer threatens to stop buying unless supplier grants unreasonably low prices.	Unfair use of coercive power (unethical)
Powerful producer of consumer goods dictates how its products will be displayed without regard for space constraints in smaller stores.	Unfair use of coercive power (unethical).
Large wholesaler demands supplier replace its male sales rep with a female because the purchasing agent does not like to deal with men.	Unfair use of coercive power (unethical, potentially illegal).
Desperate to sign up new franchises, franchisor's sales rep downplays financial risk of owning franchise.	Deceptive communications (unethical, potentially illegal).
Wholesaler requests supplier stop selling to competing wholesaler; supplier grants request.	Excessive cooperation among channel members (illegal).
Two manufacturing companies agree not to sell to a particular wholesaler in an effort to damage the wholesaler's business.	Excessive cooperation among channel members (illegal).
Salesperson agrees to give retailer a lower price than competing retailers, based solely on friendship.	Excessive cooperation among channel members (illegal).

CHANNEL COOPERATION Channel cooperation can help to reduce the amount of conflict and to resolve conflicts once they do occur.

The incentive to cooperate with other channel members is clearly strongest if all parties agree on their functional roles, and if agreement on performance standards has been reached prior to or early in the business relationship. When channel members do not agree on these matters, conflicts may be settled according to where the power lies. But conflicts settled only by the exercise of power often resurface, especially if the loser in the prior conflict gains an edge in the power dimension. As we suggest frequently in this book, more and more companies are embracing cooperation and building relationships as a superior way to ensure lasting market strength.

ETHICAL AND LEGAL ISSUES The management of marketing channels calls attention to a number of ethical and legal issues, some of which are illustrated in Exhibit 13–9. Certainly, some channel conflicts have ethical and legal implications. And, strange as it might sound, cooperation taken to the extreme may also present problems, especially if agreements between channel members violate the key laws affecting marketing discussed in Chapter 2.

Because of the range of marketing activities that occur within any marketing channel, the potentially relevant legal issues for channels are numerous. Laws pertaining to pricing, product liability, and truth in advertising are a few examples of thousands of international, federal, state, and local regulations that might pertain to a given channel situation. Our discussion here focuses on the legal environment as it affects channel structure and selected buyer–seller interactions.

Producers may want to set up channel arrangements to ensure their products are given substantial market support by either wholesalers or retailers. One producer might wish to set up **exclusive territories,** so that no other reseller in a given geographic area sells a particular brand of a product. Another might enact **exclusive dealing agreements,** which would restrict a reseller from carrying a competing product line.

Another possibility is **tying contracts,** which require a reseller to buy products besides the one it really wants to buy. For example, a copier manufacturer may also require a customer to buy ink cartridges on the grounds that the printer can reach acceptable performance standards only if the specified cartridge is used.

Exclusive territories, exclusive dealing agreements, and tying contracts are legally acceptable unless they have anticompetitive effects or tend to create monopolies. A substantial reduction in competition through such arrangements is a violation of federal or state antitrust laws.

FUTURE CONSIDERATIONS   The final requirement in the evaluation of channel performance is to cast an eye to the future. Essentially, the firm should ask itself one key question: How well can this channel be expected to perform in the future? The answers can have far-reaching implications, as marketers make necessary changes in pursuit of their long-term goals.

Sometimes customers drive changes in channels, as we have seen with e-commerce in both consumer and business markets. In other cases, working relationships between channel members or a company's financial situation may suggest that a change is in order. For example, candymaker Hershey Foods was not satisfied with the return on some of its brands. Hershey was getting 35 percent of its sales from its top three brands, while key competitor Mars was getting 67 percent of its sales from its top three brands. This led Hershey to reevaluate all aspects of its marketing, and eventually the company began marketing aggressively through convenience stores, previously a minor channel.[27]

Changing marketing channels is a major undertaking, and companies do not change if they are convinced the tried-and-true channel will get the job done. In the current environment characterized by changing consumer preferences, intense competition, and information-technology innovation, expect more companies to alter their channels.

Summary

1. **Explain the functions and key activities of marketing channels.** A marketing channel, sometimes referred to as a *channel of distribution,* is a combination of organizations that perform the activities required to link producers to users to accomplish particular marketing objectives.

   The primary goal of a marketing channel is to allow companies to reach their customers with the right product at the right time, to meet customer expectations, and to stimulate profitable sales volume. The key functions of marketing channels are marketing communications, inventory management, physical distribution, market feedback, and the assumption of financial risk.

2. **Discuss the role of intermediaries in marketing channels.** Intermediaries, often called *middlemen,* provide key marketing channel functions. To survive in the economic system, an intermediary must perform its particular functions more efficiently than any other channel member.

3. **Distinguish between direct and indirect marketing channels.** Direct marketing channels use no intermediaries to move products from producers to end users. Indirect marketing channels use at least one intermediary before the product reaches its final destination. Despite the dramatic growth of direct marketing channels, most products reach ultimate consumers through indirect marketing channels.

4. **Illustrate how some firms use multiple channels successfully.** As markets become increasingly specialized and companies seek to globalize their marketing efforts, the use of multiple channels is growing. Several examples of companies using multiple channels were presented in the chapter.

5. **See how marketing-channel decisions are related to other key marketing decision variables.** Marketing-channel strategies and objectives must be based on a firm's overall marketing strategies and objectives. After a channel strategy has been developed, different channel alternatives can be evaluated for capabilities, costs, and availability. Channel alternatives can also be evaluated for compatibility with product, pricing, and marketing communications variables.

6. **Understand how power, conflict, and cooperation affect the operation of a marketing channel.** Channel members develop power based on such factors as economic strength or market knowledge. In some instances, this power may be abused, leading to conflict between channel members.

   Conflict can also result from poor communications or incompatible goals among channel members. It is becoming increasingly necessary that channel members cooperate to resolve conflict and pursue mutually beneficial goals.

7. **Give examples of ethical and legal issues encountered in the operations of marketing channels.** The unfair use of power can raise ethical concerns. For example, a large buyer might try to force a small supplier to grant unreasonably low prices as a condition for continuing to be a supplier.

   If taken to the extreme, cooperation between channel members can be a violation of the law, as competition may be unfairly constrained. Certain arrangements between channel members may violate antitrust laws if they reduce competition. Exclusive territories, exclusive dealing agreements, and tying contracts are examples of potentially illegal channel arrangements.

Understanding Marketing Terms and Concepts

Thinking About Marketing

1. What are the key activities performed in a marketing channel?

2. How do indirect marketing channels differ from direct marketing channels? How do intermediaries contribute to marketing channels?

3. Explain the concepts of forward and backward integration.

4. How do franchisees and franchisors work together in a franchise system?

5. Review "Building Customer Equity: IBM Serves Its Channel." Citing specific points in the boxed insert to support your answer, what type or types of power did GE use to support its dealers?

6. Describe the varying degrees of market coverage—intensive distribution, exclusive distribution, and selective distribution—and give examples of each.

7. Channels must be compatible with the other elements of the marketing mix. Give examples that reflect compatibility between channels and product, pricing, and marketing communications considerations.

8. How might channel members build their power bases relative to other members of the channel?

9. Review "Using Technology: Bridgestone/Firestone's Database Saves the Day." What steps would have been necessary to successfully recall the defective tires if the company had not previously developed a centralized database?

10. How can poor communication, abuse of power, and too much cooperation in marketing channels create ethical and legal problems?

Applying Marketing Skills

1. Discuss the advantages and disadvantages to the consumer of buying these products in alternative channels as opposed to grocery stores:

Product	Alternative channel
Citrus fruit	Farmers' market
Rib-eye steaks	Specialty meat market
Milk	Home delivery
Popcorn	Movie theater
Bottled soft drink	Vending machine

2. Assume you own the concession rights for the New York Yankees' home baseball games. What factors should you consider and what specific information would you need in deciding whether to buy soft-drink cups from a local distributor, who buys the cups from a Taiwanese manufacturer, or directly from the manufacturer?

3. Beth Norman is a sales rep for a leading manufacturer of commercial air-conditioning systems. She currently sells to three distributors in Dallas, who in turn sell exclusively to building contractors. One of Beth's distributors, Maverick Supply Company, has produced disappointing sales results for Beth during the past six months. Upon investigation, Beth discovered that Maverick bought heavily from one of her chief competitors. How might Beth use the five power bases discussed in this chapter to regain her lost position with Maverick?

Using the www in Marketing

Activity One As explained in the chapter opener, Apple Computer uses multiple channels to sell computers around the world. Access the Apple Web site at *www.apple.com* and respond to the following questions:

1. Can you find examples of channel cooperation on the Apple site? To answer this question, you should explore the links that refer to resellers and consultants.

2. How can Apple minimize the friction it caused with existing retailers by opening its own retail stores?

3. Compare two of Apple's online retailers. Are there differences in how the two retailers market the Apple products? Which is a better approach?

Activity Two Visit the Rite Aid Web site at www.riteaid.com. As a major drugstore chain, Rite Aid depends on hundreds of suppliers. From the site map, locate the Our Company link, then explore the supplier-related links such as How to Become a Supplier and EDI/EC. Now answer the following questions.

1. What evidence can you find that Rite Aid might be a channel leader? Which types of channel power (reward, legitimate, expert, referent, and coercive) does Rite Aid use in dealing with its suppliers?

2. What criteria does Rite Aid use in selecting suppliers? How do these criteria relate to improving value for Rite Aid's retail customers?

3. How important is it for Rite Aid's suppliers to be technologically competent in terms of managing the flow of products to Rite Aid?

Making Marketing Decisions

Case 13-1 *Will CarMax Revolutionize Used-Car Channels?*

Consumer dissatisfaction is the driving force behind a revolution in the automobile industry. Consumers enjoy having a new automobile, but they hate the buying experience. This is especially true in the used-car market, where sales practices are so bad that jokes and even movies ridicule dealers. Enter CarMax, a creation of electronics giant Circuit City.

In direct contrast to most used-car dealers, CarMax offers a huge inventory, a pleasant showroom, a food court, a children's play area, low-pressure salespeople, and no-haggle pricing. Customers can use computer kiosks to search for the right vehicle, and CarMax backs its vehicles with a five-day, 500-mile money-back guarantee.

CarMax has attracted a lot of attention, some of which translates into competitive activity. Local used-car dealers have responded by improving service and taking advantage of CarMax's no-haggle policy to undercut prices. Republic Industries, the parent company of AutoNation, a CarMax competitor, bought ADT, Ltd., the second-largest auto auction company in the United States. This gives AutoNation a direct link to the supply of late-model used cars, which are increasingly hard to find. Through one of its investors, AutoNation also has access to cars from Greater Auto Auctions, the fourth-largest auction company in the United States.

Increasingly, consumers are turning to the Internet for both new- and used-car purchases. While state franchise laws make it practically impossible for dealers to sell directly to consumers, the major manufacturers are setting up Web sites to facilitate sales through their dealers. Third-party online car companies, including Autobytel.com Inc. and Microsoft's CarPoint have become a much larger factor in the market.

Used-car sellers are also feeling the competitive pressure from new-car dealers. Generous lease deals are attracting some customers who might typically buy used cars. These lease deals also keep a huge number of late-model autos in the market, which helps keep prices down.

CarMax was one of the first companies to see the opportunity for a new marketing channel in the used-car market. The company realized that consumers had gotten used to better shopping experiences—on the Internet and through other venues—for most products and services that exist in superstores, shopping malls, and catalogs. In recent years, mass-market distribution for everything from home electronics to vacation packages had brought prices down. Consumers are more demanding that prices be as low as possible, but they expect great selection and service. In short, they have discovered that they can get what they want at a reasonable price, with retailers such as department store Nordstrom's and online bookseller Amazon.com becoming the new standard. Auto industry analysts believe that these same consumers will shape the future of used-car marketing channels.

By mid-2002, CarMax had performed well enough to gain its independence from Circuit City. It had grown to 51 locations with over $3 billion in sales per year, returning an annual profit of approximately $90 million. Analysts predict more CarMax outlets in the future, and they expect the company to become even more price competitive with other dealers. CarMax managed to avoid the industry slump following the events of September 11, 2001. Prior to September 11, CarMax had predicted a glut of used cars on the market and had reduced inventory levels, something many used car dealers failed to do. Poised for more growth, CarMax executives like to point out that 97 percent of the company's customers say they would recommend its stores to friends.

Questions

1. What marketplace conditions led to the emergence of CarMax?

2. What are the biggest threats facing CarMax as it attempts to become the preferred outlet for used automobiles? How can the company address these threats?

3. How can independent, local used-car dealers respond to CarMax and other used-car chains?

Case 13-2 *Caterpillar's Channels Span the Globe*

 Caterpillar is well positioned to further strengthen its reputation as a worldwide leader in the construction and mining equipment industry. The company has more than held its own against Japanese rivals Hitachi and Komatsu in recent years. Sales volume is strong, despite

the fact that most of Cat's sales are in sectors where the economy is in recession—Asia, Latin America, and the Middle East. Cat's salesforce has been recognized as one of the best in the world by *Sales & Marketing Management* magazine, primarily for its success in building close relationships with its 220 dealers in 200 countries. This is consistent with Caterpillar's Code of Worldwide Business Conduct, which identifies close, long-lasting relationships with dealers as a key priority.

Having parts and service readily available is important to Caterpillar customers, and the dealers play an important role in adding value after the sale. The typical Caterpillar dealer stocks 40,000 to 50,000 parts and has a huge investment in warehouses, fleets of trucks, service bays, highly trained technicians, and service equipment. Many provide around-the-clock service.

Caterpillar supports its dealers in several ways. Caterpillar rejects the notion of selling directly to end users with three exceptions: newly opened markets of formerly socialist countries, original equipment manufacturers, and the U.S. government. Even in these cases, dealers provide most of the after-sales service and support.

Caterpillar also supports its dealers by providing financing on equipment purchased, and offering programs on inventory control, equipment management, and maintenance programs. Additional support is available to dealers in quality management and continuous improvement, training on a wide variety of topics, and localized marketing programs.

Cat is also encouraging its dealers to open Cat-branded rental stores and reduce the amount of inventory held at the dealer level. Though both of these moves will hurt Cat's short-run profits, it will strengthen the dealers' competitiveness. In the long run, Cat should benefit from these tactics. Caterpillar dealers operate more than 1,800 branch locations and in excess of 600 Cat Rental Stores. Cat features a worldwide dealer locator service on its Web site and introduces visitors to rental stores via Web storefronts.

Another important element in the management of Caterpillar's marketing channel is a comprehensive communications program. According to Mr. Fites, "We communicate fully, frequently, and honestly. There are no secrets between our dealers and us." To communicate effectively, it is imperative that mutual trust exists between Caterpillar and its dealers. Trust is essential because of the sensitive nature of some of the information

that is exchanged, including financial data and strategic plans. Technology plays an important role in communications, as dealer employees have real-time access to continually updated databases of service information, sales forecasts, and customer satisfaction surveys.

Communications are further enhanced by personal visits and other routine contacts between people at dealerships and all levels of Caterpillar. Top Caterpillar executives meet annually with key dealers at regional conferences to discuss sales goals for each product line and the activities necessary to achieve the goals.

Caterpillar management is candid in pointing out that relationships with dealers are not perfect. For example, problems arise over pricing policies and dealer service-territory boundaries. When conflicts do arise, the chances of a mutually agreeable resolution are high, as Caterpillar and its dealers respect one another. By making its dealers its partners, Caterpillar has strengthened its position as a world leader in its industry and has positioned itself well for future success. Cat's dealer network is twice the size of that of its four major competitors, and it continues to widen the market share gap with Komatsu, its chief competitor. In a tough time for capital investment, Cat and its dealer network are setting the pace in heavy equipment.

Questions

1. What are the advantages to Caterpillar of using its dealer network rather than selling directly to equipment users?

2. Caterpillar sells directly to end users in just three cases: newly opened markets in formerly socialist countries, original-equipment manufacturers, and the U.S. government. Why would Caterpillar sell direct in these situations? Since some dealers might resent Caterpillar's selling direct in these situations, how might Caterpillar minimize any conflict that might arise?

3. How does Caterpillar contribute to its partnership with dealers? How do the dealers contribute?

Chapter Fourteen

14

Retailing

After studying this chapter, you should be able to:

1 Understand the economic importance of retailing and its role in the marketing channel.

2 Cite evidence of the globalization of retailing.

3 Discuss some of the advances in retailing technology.

4 Explain the reasons behind the growth of nonstore retailing.

5 Describe key factors in the retail marketing environment, and understand how they relate to retail strategy.

6 Cite important ethical and legal issues facing retailers.

www.williams-sonomainc.com

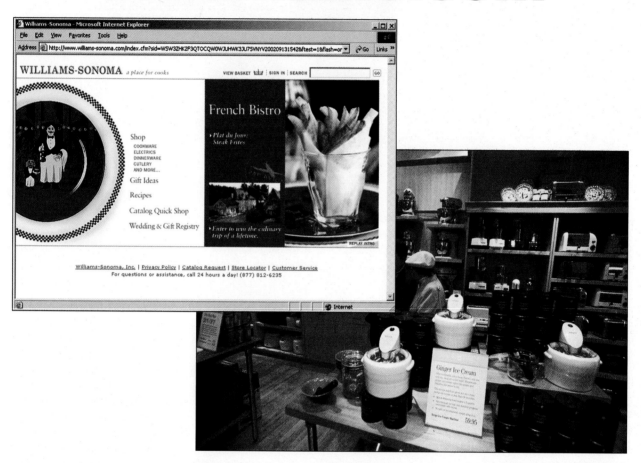

Williams-Sonoma, Inc., is one of the leading home specialty retailers in the world. Founded in San Francisco in 1956, it has evolved into a multichannel retailer, reaching its customers by catalog, via the Internet, and with its own stores. In addition to the company name, its brands include Pottery Barn, Pottery Barn Kids, Chambers, holdeverything, and its most recent market entry, West Elm, a furniture catalog. West Elm is positioned as a lower priced alternative to Pottery Barn.

Throughout its history, Williams-Sonoma has shown a keen understanding of consumer trends and how to translate that knowledge into viable retail markets. Its Williams-Sonoma stores were years ahead of other retailers in spotting the trend toward gourmet cooking and entertaining at home. Its cookware, glassware, specialty cookbooks, and decorative kitchen accessories virtually created a market later expanded by celebrity chefs and designers such as Martha Stewart. Now that Americans are spending more time at home, Williams-Sonoma is a preferred retailer for a huge market. Williams-Sonoma was also among the first

to spot the trend toward retro home furnishings. Its Pottery Barn chain has done extremely well in head-to-head competition with Restoration Hardware in its sale of vintage-style furniture and decorating accessories.

Now that Pottery Barn is a mature brand, the company is pushing for more sales through Pottery Barn Kids and other newer brands, including holdeverything and West Elm. While Pottery Barn Kids is distinct from Pottery Barn, some analysts think that West Elm may present more of a challenge for Williams-Sonoma. These analysts point out that the West Elm/Pottery Barn relationship may turn out like Old Navy and its parent, The Gap. Old Navy offers similar products, perhaps of lower quality than The Gap. Instead of growing its own customer base, however, Old Navy gained a lot of customers at The Gap's expense, thereby hurting overall company profitability. It is too early to tell if West Elm will have a similar effect on Pottery Barn. In retailing, it is hard to stay ahead of a changing consumer market, but one thing is certain: Williams-Sonoma has done it a lot better than most retailers for almost half a century.

Retailing, an important part of many marketing channels, includes all the activities involved in selling products and services to the ultimate, or final, consumer. This chapter explains the importance of retailing in the U.S. economy, discusses the functions retailers perform within the channel, and illustrates different types of retailers. Several trends in retailing are discussed: globalization, advances in technology, the focus on customer service, and nonstore retailing. We explore factors in the retail environment—both controllable and uncontrollable—that a firm must constantly monitor and coordinate to ensure a successful retail strategy. Finally, we examine some important ethical and legal issues in retailing.

The Role of Retailing

The role of retailing is to supply products and services directly to the final consumer. Retailers are differentiated from wholesalers according to the primary source of sales. **Retail sales** are sales to final consumers; **wholesale sales** are those to other businesses that in turn resell the product or service, or use it in running their own businesses. To be classified as a retailer, a firm's retail sales must equal or exceed 50 percent of its total revenues. Firms with less than 50 percent retail sales are classified as wholesalers. Wal-Mart was reminded of the distinction when its Sam's Wholesale Club was forced to change its name to Sam's Club in states in which its retail sales exceeded the 50 percent benchmark. Ultimately, the word *wholesale* was dropped from all Sam's Club store names.

Economic Importance

Retailing is a major force in the economy. Approximately 3 million retailers in operation in the United States employ 14 million people, about 10 percent of the total U.S. labor force. Retailers generate an astonishing $2.5 trillion in annual revenues. This translates into a $9,100 retail expenditure for every man, woman, and child in the United States.[1] Leading retailers are shown in Exhibit 14–1.

Retailing also includes a diverse range of **service retailers.** Service retailers include dry cleaners, photo developers, shoe repair shops, banks, fitness clubs, movie theaters, game arcades, rental businesses (automobiles, furniture, appliances, videos), tourist attractions, hotels and restaurants, automotive repair shops, and some providers of health care services. Spending for services has fueled increasing consumer-spending growth rates, exceeding expenditures on products for quite some time.

Retailers' Uniqueness in the Channel

Retailers differ from other marketing channel members in that they handle smaller but more frequent customer transactions; they also provide assortments of products. A pleasant shopping environment is also more important in most

Exhibit 14–1	*Leading retailers*		
Company	**Sales ($ millions)**	**Profits ($ millions)**	**Employees**
1. Wal-Mart	219,812	6,671	1,383,000
2. Home Depot	53,553	3,044	256,300
3. Kroger	50,098	1,043	288,000
4. Sears Roebuck	41,078	735	310,000
5. Target	39,888	1,368	223,550
6. Albertson's	37,931	501	220,000
7. Kmart	36,910	(95)	240,525
8. Safeway	34,301	1,254	193,000
9. JC Penney	32,004	98	270,000
10. Walgreen's	24,623	886	106,000

forms of retailing than at other levels in the channel. Creation of a pleasant shopping atmosphere entails additional expense, which contributes to higher prices.

SELL SMALLER QUANTITIES MORE FREQUENTLY Retailers offer products in the sizes suitable and convenient for household consumption. Besides buying smaller sizes, most consumers buy products frequently because they lack sufficient storage space and funds to maintain large inventories of products. The average convenience store transaction is for only a few dollars, for example, but the average convenience store handles thousands of transactions per week.

PROVIDE ASSORTMENTS Retailers assemble assortments of products and services to sell. If retailers did not do so, shoppers would have to go to the bakery for bread, the butcher shop for meat, the dairy for milk, and the hardware store for lightbulbs; and a simple shopping trip could take hours to complete. By providing assortments, retailers offer the convenience of one-stop shopping for a variety of products and services. The typical supermarket carries over 15,000 different items made by more than 500 different manufacturers.

An assortment of items seen by the customer as reasonable substitutes for each other is defined as a **category**. Discount retailers that offer a complete assortment and thus dominate a category from the customer's perspective are called **category killers.** These include Toys "Я" Us, Home Depot, and Circuit City. Since category killers dominate a category of merchandise, they can negotiate excellent prices from suppliers and be assured of dependable sources of supply.

Today's retailing environment finds numerous retailers experimenting with the assortments they offer, attempting to get the right combination to entice consumers. Target and Kohl's, for example, have moved into designer apparel, attempting to lure shoppers away from department and apparel stores. Target has added Mossimo clothing, while Kohl's moved into the designer niche with Nine West and Liz Clai-

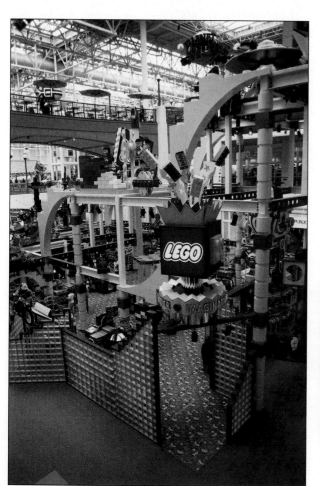

borne. Target and Kohl's are exploiting consumers' lack of excitement with department store assortments, as many of these traditional stores are focusing on selling their own private labels along with the lines of leading designers such as Polo and Tommy Hilfiger.[2] In the durable goods category, Wal-Mart and Home Depot now sell major home appliances, while Circuit City has dropped them from their assortment. Wal-Mart is further expanding its assortment by selling automobiles at select locations.[3]

EMPHASIZE ATMOSPHERICS Atmospherics refers to a retailer's combination of architecture, layout, color scheme, sound and temperature monitor-

Atmospherics are an important part of retailing. The Mall of America near Minneapolis uses a variety of dramatic atmospheric factors to attract and stimulate consumers.

ing, special events, prices, displays, and other factors that attract and stimulate consumers. Retailers spend millions of dollars to create the retail atmospheres that enhance their respective images and the products and services they offer for sale. NikeTown, Planet Hollywood, F. A. O. Schwartz, and Express are pioneers in the use of atmospherics in retailing. As NikeTown and Planet Hollywood have learned, however, changing the atmosphere is important to keep customers coming back. Declining numbers of customers at Planet Hollywood suggest that no matter how interesting consumers find the environment on the first visit, they may treat it like a museum—"Great! I really enjoyed it and may come back someday. Now where are we going?"

In response to an increasingly hard-to-impress consumer, retailers are seeking active involvement of shoppers, that is, they are trying to give the shopper a memorable experience, or "shoppertainment." For example, Toys "Я" Us has a huge showplace store in New York's Times Square that features a 60-foot indoor Ferris wheel and a larger-than-life robotic dinosaur that overlooks its *Jurassic Park* display. Barbie has a 2,000-square-foot playhouse in the store, and other areas are designed to maximize shoppers' enjoyment while in the store.[4] Galyan's, and REI, both sporting goods chains, create interesting atmospheres with rock climbing walls near the front of some of their stores. For many retailers, there is no doubt that the consumer has become an important role player in creating the right atmospherics and shopping experience.

The best-known retail operation to gain headlines for its atmospherics is Mall of America, located in suburban Minneapolis. The Mall of America has a two-story miniature golf course, a 300-foot walk-through aquarium, Knott's Camp Snoopy (an amusement park with more than 20 attractions), and a Lego Imagination Center, complete with dinosaurs 20 feet tall. These features create an exciting atmosphere for shoppers who roam the 4.2-million-square-foot facility (2.5 million square feet of retail shopping space). Mall of America draws more than 42 million people per year, more than Walt Disney World and the Grand Canyon combined.[5]

Atmospherics, though expensive to create, can generate considerable benefits for retailers. Atmospherics can boost the number of consumers who visit a retail location. Indeed, some retailers are trying to make their stores a "destination" for shoppers, a place a shopper will make a special effort to reach. Atmospherics can also boost the average time a shopper spends at the location and the average amount spent on each shopping trip. Atmospherics often allows retailers to charge higher prices. Compare the atmosphere of a discount store to that of a full-line traditional department store or an exclusive specialty shop, for example.

Types of Retailers

Retailers can be classified according to the type of merchandise and services sold, location, various strategic differences, and method of ownership. Here we examine different ownership categories to provide an overview of several types of retailers.

Some significant retail enterprises, such as military exchange stores and public utility appliance stores, operate outside the realm of private enterprise. Within the private sector, there are several major retail ownership categories, including independent retailers, chains, franchising, leased departments, and cooperatives.

Independent Retailers

Independent retailers own and operate only one retail outlet. Independent retailers account for more than three-fourths of all retail establishments, a testament

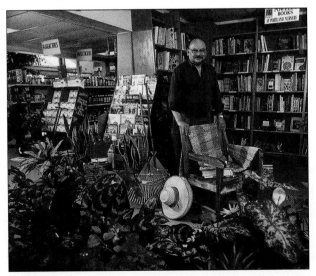

Powell's City of Books, an independent retailer in Portland, Oregon, competes effectively against large chains by offering a broad range of titles, including used books.

Many leading franchisors are expanding their international operations. A 7-Eleven subsidiary operates this popular franchise in Japan.

to Americans' desires to own and operate their own businesses and a relative lack of barriers to entry. There are no formal education requirements, no specific training requirements, and few legal requirements to owning a retail business. This ease of entry likely accounts for the unpreparedness and the high failure rate experienced by new retailers.

Chains

A **retail chain** owns and operates multiple retail outlets. Examples are Nordstrom, Mervyn's, Musicland, Pappagallo, The Gap, and JCPenney. By far, chain stores sell more merchandise than any other category of retailers. Their major advantage is the ability to service large, widespread target markets by selling a large assortment of products and services. For an illustration of how a successful chain operates, see "Building Customer Equity: Hot Topic Draws Teens."

Franchising

Retail franchising is a form of chain ownership in which a franchisee pays the franchisor (parent company) fees or royalties and agrees to run the franchise by prescribed norms, in exchange for use of the franchisor's name. Well-known franchisors include McDonald's, Holiday Inn, Avis, Mrs. Fields', and Jiffy Lube. According to the International Franchise Association, about 3,000 franchise companies operate in the United States. Franchising operations employ 8.5 million workers at approximately 558,000 separate establishments. Franchises generate approximately a trillion dollars per year in sales.[6]

Franchising is also a major retailing force outside the United States. McDonald's decided to go international in 1967, and now has almost 12,000 units in 113 countries outside the United States.[7] The largest market for franchising outside the United States is Europe, with franchising popular in France, Germany, and the United Kingdom. Japan is the most active franchising market in the Asia-Pacific region; there is a significant amount of franchising in Australia, Hong Kong, Singapore, Indonesia, Malaysia, and India; and franchising is also well-established in Canada and Mexico.[8]

Building Customer Equity

Hot topic draws teens

Hot Topic and its teenage customers have a love-hate relationship. Teens love the merchandise in Hot Topic stores, but they claim to hate the malls where the stores are located. The merchandise is 180 degrees away from what teenagers would find at Abercrombie & Fitch, with blue hair dye and black gothic platform boots as featured items, not tank tops and cargo pants. While other teen-oriented retailers such as The Gap and American Eagle have struggled recently, Hot Topic's 346 stores are showing steady sales increases, and the chain plans to add 85 new stores within a year.

The secret to Hot Topic's success is that it constantly researches the market and gives its customers what they want. Constant research is necessary because the desires of the alternative fashion teen market can change overnight. Hot Topic's favorite research method is to have employees attend rock concerts and rave dance parties to see what the bands and wannabes are wearing. The company also polls teens on what bands they are listening to. This research results in the top-selling category for the chain, the rock band T-shirt. T-shirts featuring the pioneers of punk rock such as the Ramones and Black Flag are hot sellers, along with those of emerging bands like the Strokes.

Hot Topic has built a loyal shopper base by listening to its customers' wishes and building a product assortment around those wishes. Even if these teens hate the mall, they still flock to Hot Topic stores.

While many successful international franchised retailers are U.S.-based, there is an increasing number of expansion-minded franchisors outside the United States who view the world as their market. For example, Canada's Tim Horton's bakery/coffee restaurants, Taiwan's Kumon Math and Reading Centers, and Australian-based Cash Converters—a second-hand-store operator—are all highly rated by *Entrepreneur* magazine as leading international franchised retailers.[9]

The arrangements between franchisors and franchisees illustrate the benefits of a relationship perspective. In return for fees or royalties, the franchisee may receive management training, participation in cooperative buying and advertising, and assistance in selecting an appropriate location. The franchisor benefits in turn from a constant stream of income, fast payment for goods and services, and strict control over franchised operations that encourages consistency among outlets.

Franchising systems are popular because they offer the franchisee a proven business and the franchisors the ability to establish a national presence with the funds provided by the sale of franchises. Although risk is a factor in any business, franchising has a better track record than most start-ups. Approximately half of new U.S. businesses fail during the first five years, whereas almost 90 percent of franchises survive.[10]

Exhibit 14–2 presents some of the best-known franchise operations. These franchise companies were selected by *Entrepreneur* magazine based on financial strength and stability, size, growth rate, years in business and in franchising, and start-up costs.

Leased Departments

Leased departments are sections in a retail store that the owner rents to a second party. Typically, department stores rent their jewelry, shoe, hairstyling, and cosmetic departments. For example, Fox Photo leases space in Kroger grocery stores; travel agencies and hair salons often lease space in department stores; and cosmetics such as Estée Lauder and Clinique are sold through leased space in department stores.

As with franchising agreements, a leased-department arrangement benefits both lessor (the department store) and lessee. The lessor receives rental fees, can reduce inventory investment and subsequent risk, gains expertise in a specialized area, and enjoys the benefits derived from the store traffic generated by the leased department. Lessees benefit by operating in an established location with the assurance of store traffic and advertising.

Cooperatives

Responding to competitive pressures exerted by the buying power of chain stores, independent retailers sometimes band together to form **retail cooperatives.** Although each store remains independently owned, the retail cooperative generally

Exhibit 14–2	*Leading international retail franchise companies*

1. McDonald's
2. Great Wraps
3. Subway
4. Kentucky Fried Chicken
5. Kumon Math & Reading Centers
6. Meineke Discount Muffler Shops
7. TCBY Treats
8. Thrifty Car Rental
9. Blimpies Subs & Salads
10. Mail Boxes Etc.
11. Rocky Mountain Chocolate Factory
12. Arthur Treacher's Fish & Chips
13. Dollar Discount Stores
14. CD Warehouse
15. Charley's Steakery
16. Budget Rent-A-Car
17. Glamour Shots
18. GNC Franchising
19. Church's Chicken
20. RAMCO Transmission

Global retailing can be quite sophisticated, as is the case with this superstore in Poland, which offers a wide variety of food and nonfood items. In contrast, retailing can be quite simple, as is the case for this Chinese consumer who is buying Head & Shoulders shampoo in a small sidewalk store.

adopts a common name and storefront. The stores participate in joint purchasing, shipping, and advertising, which allows cost savings normally enjoyed by chain outlets. Retail cooperatives include Sentry Hardware, Associated Grocers, and Ace Hardware.

Trends in Retailing

We have seen dramatic examples of change in retailing, such as the decline, then reemergence, of Sears as a retail power. Kmart is operating in bankruptcy, and hundreds of Internet-based retailers have come and gone since the turn of the century. Wal-Mart has increased its dominance as a general-line discount store and become a major player in the grocery sector. Among the most noteworthy retail sectors when it comes to dealing with change is the department store sector. Penney's was struggling just a few years ago with its private labels such as Arizona jeans losing out to designer labels such as Polo and Hilfiger in the more upscale department stores and to less expensive clothing at Target and Wal-Mart. But now Penney's has gained momentum with improvements in cost-cutting, store layout and checkout upgrades, and finding the right combination of private label and national labels such as Levi, Mudd, and l.e.i.[11]

Meanwhile, other department stores have evidently failed to connect with shoppers. Kohl's, a hybrid discounter/department store, is performing well, but most others are stalled, with no major plans for expansion. Consumers say department stores are boring, with too much of the same merchandise featured at competing stores.[12] For struggling retail sectors like the department store sector, as well as growing sectors such as discount stores and upscale automobile dealers, future success is likely to hinge on how well they seize upon important trends in retailing. Notable current trends in the retailing environment include global retailing, the increasing use of technology, a renewed emphasis on customer service, and the rapid expansion of nonstore retailing.

Global Retailing

With domestic markets becoming saturated and sales growth slowing, many retailers are exhibiting a global perspective. U.S.-based retailers have long been the leaders in global expansion, with, for example, McDonald's, Kentucky Fried Chicken, Radio Shack, and Wal-Mart being among the more progressive companies and L. L. Bean, Eddie Bauer, and The Gap expanding in Japan with great success.

Self-checkout counters speed up the checkout process for customers while giving store managers greater flexibility with staffing. Consumers like the increased privacy of their purchases and control over how to bag their purchases.

Retailers from other countries are becoming more active in global retailing. In recent years, retailers based outside the United States have become more aggressive in global marketing. A fine example is Europe's largest retailer, France's Carrefour. Carrefour, through company-owned stores and those generated by franchisees and partners, operates 9,300 stores in 30 countries. Poised to fight Wal-Mart around the world, Carrefour has been a pioneer in store design, softening the look of its gigantic stores with wood floors and softer lighting. Carrefour is known for selling groceries, clothing, and other merchandise under one roof. This format, which combines a discount store with an oversized supermarket, is called a **hypermarket.** The format, now becoming popular in America, was begun in France. Carrefour operates approximately 700 hypermarkets around the world. Many of its stores also offer a myriad of services, such as watch-repair services, cell-phone service, and travel services. Although Carrefour is not expected to challenge Wal-Mart in terms of sales volume, the company has already proven to be a formidable competitor against Wal-Mart in several markets, including those of Brazil and Argentina. In addition to the markets in these two countries, Carrefour is the leading retailer in France, Taiwan, Spain, Portugal, Greece, and Belgium.[13]

Technological Advances

Retailers have embraced the technological perspective, and advances in retail technology have developed at a phenomenal pace. A familiar example is the scanner linked to computerized inventory systems that greatly improve a retailer's efficiency level. Scanners speed the checkout process, reduce computational errors, and instantaneously input the transaction into the inventory system. This allows retailers to precisely track sales on a per-item basis, minimize out-of-stock problems, and judge the effectiveness of various pricing and marketing communications tactics. Other technological advances that directly influence customers include automated cash registers that can issue temporary charge cards and gift certificates, provide customer information, and process customer payments, as well as passenger computer terminals and the aircraft satellite systems that make in-flight shopping possible.

Using Technology

Are talking chips the next big thing?

Leading retailers and their key suppliers are excited about the potential impact of "talking chips." These computer chips, called ePCs, come with a built-in antenna and are about the size of a postage stamp. The antenna allows communication through a wireless network, thus the term "talking chip." Wal-Mart, Procter & Gamble, and Gillette are among those testing the chips, and the consensus is that these talking chips will someday be applied to practically everything sold in retail stores. Products with the chips can communicate with retailer and supplier computers, home computers, cell phones, e-mail, and home appliances.

Shoppers could benefit from ePCs by checking their home inventory from their personal computer before heading out to shop. A frozen dinner could transmit cooking instructions to a microwave, or a music fan could browse her CD collection to see which ones were in the car, on the boat, or in the house. In the medicine cabinet, prescription drugs could talk to each other and warn the consumer if any dangerous interactions might occur.

Retailers and their suppliers could use ePCs to keep track of product movement throughout the entire supply chain. Restocking fast-moving items would be made easier. Checkouts could become as simple as the consumer passing by a scanner, which reads the product code and charges the customer to a predesignated credit card. Though the testing is highly secret, industry rumors say Wal-Mart and Pepsi-Cola have found that ePCs work better than expected. Widespread use is predicted by 2005. With benefits for the shopper, the retailer, and key suppliers, ePCs may indeed be the next big thing.

Speaking from Experience

Kelly Seibels
Owner
Seibels

"We try to provide excellent customer service for both new and returning customers by focusing on four key principles. First, we hire conscientious employees who clearly understand the importance of giving good service. Second, we model our customer service according to how we would like to be treated if we were customers. In cases involving home delivery, we follow up after the delivery to ensure that we have met or exceeded all customer expectations. Finally, we constantly search for suppliers who will work with us to not only meet our expectations, but also to help us provide our retail customers with excellent service."

Kelly Seibels is the owner of Seibels, a specialty retailer based in Homewood, Alabama. Seibels sells home furnishings and accessories to the camp and cottage market through its retail store, a print catalog, and an online catalog. Before founding Seibels, Kelly worked as a professional writer. He earned a B.A. degree in English from the University of Alabama.

Thinking Critically

- If everyone agrees that customer service is important to retail success, why is good service still an exception to the rule?
- What can retailers do to ensure good service?

Wireless computer technology is finding many applications in retailing: Electronics Boutique uses wireless registers to check customers out during peak times; The Gap uses wireless technology to check product availability in the stockroom and in surrounding stores; ski resorts are using wireless scanners so that skiers can go directly to the lift rather than stand in a separate line to buy a lift ticket. Retailers have long tried to find ways to reduce the amount of time customers must wait in line to pay, and wireless technology is helping to achieve this objective.

Retailers are also using wireless technology to contribute to shopper's enjoyment in other ways. In Seattle and San Francisco, coffee shops offer Wireless Fidelity networking, commonly referred to as Wi-Fi, so customers can surf the Web while having a cup of latte. The idea is that if customers enjoy the experience, they will stay longer and spend more. Analysts predict there will be some 12,000 wireless networks in restaurants by 2004, another 2,000 in leading malls, and 5,800 Wi-Fis in hotels.[14]

Technology, most notably the Internet, has also affected nonstore retailing, to be discussed shortly. For an example of how technology can affect retailers and its shoppers, see "Using Technology: Are Talking Chips the Next Big Thing?"

Customer Service in Retailing

Customer service refers to the activities that increase the quality and value customers receive when they shop and purchase merchandise. Retailers rush to give lip service to the importance of customer service, but many still fall woefully short of providing it. Today's consumers are tougher, more informed, and so sensitive to poor service they often walk away and never come back to a store rather than point out the service problem to the retailer. Worse yet, the average consumer with a service problem tells several other people about the problem.

Different types of retailers offer a variety of customer services to correspond with the image they need to project. Exhibit 14–3 compares some department store services with those offered by the typical discount store.

Store loyalty is the major reward of customer service, a benefit that builds on itself, as customers well served are customers retained. One company that has built a solid business based on customer service is The Container Store, a Dallas-based chain of 28 stores with $250 million in annual sales. The Container Store sells shelving systems, boxes, buckets, bolts, jars, trunks, baskets, hangers, drawer dividers, and more to help customers get organized in their garages, home offices, closets, hobby rooms, and kitchens. The retail philosophy of The Container Store is to equip its sales personnel to solve customer problems and to work together as a team to get the job done. Container Store personnel receive 235 hours of training in their first year, and 162 hours in each following year. The average training time in retailing is just 10 hours a year. By emphasizing customer service, The Container

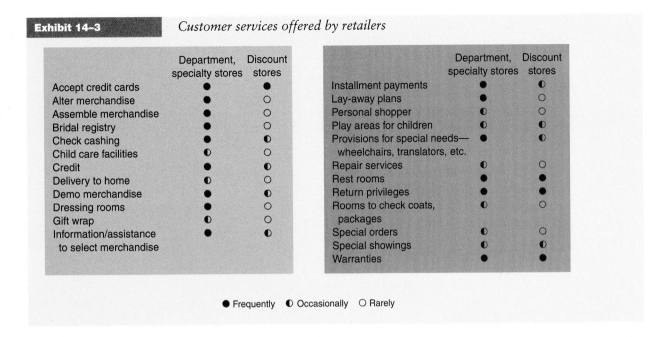

Exhibit 14–3			*Customer services offered by retailers*		
	Department, specialty stores	Discount stores		Department, specialty stores	Discount stores
Accept credit cards	●	●	Installment payments	●	◐
Alter merchandise	●	○	Lay-away plans	●	○
Assemble merchandise	●	○	Personal shopper	◐	○
Bridal registry	●	○	Play areas for children	◐	◐
Check cashing	●	◐	Provisions for special needs— wheelchairs, translators, etc.	●	◐
Child care facilities	◐	○	Repair services	◐	○
Credit	●	◐	Rest rooms	●	●
Delivery to home	◐	○	Return privileges	●	●
Demo merchandise	●	◐	Rooms to check coats, packages	◐	○
Dressing rooms	●	○	Special orders	◐	○
Gift wrap	◐	○	Special showings	◐	◐
Information/assistance to select merchandise	●	◐	Warranties	●	●

● Frequently   ◐ Occasionally   ○ Rarely

Store has been growing in excess of 20 percent annually, a rate that most retailers will never experience.[15]

Retailers can provide good service without necessarily providing personal service. Automated teller machines, credit card—processing gas pumps, and point-of-sale audiovisual materials in home improvement stores are examples of how technology can assist in providing customer service.

Nonstore Retailing

Traditional retailing is generally thought of as the selling of products and services in stores or some other physical structure. In contrast, **nonstore retailing** refers to sales outside a physical structure. Although stores account for almost 90 percent of all retail sales, the growth rate of nonstore retailing has far surpassed that of store-based retailing in the past few years.

Nonstore retailing offers consumers the convenience of selecting and purchasing merchandise according to their own schedules. Merchandise is delivered directly to consumers or shipped to convenient vending locations, methods that particularly appeal to consumers with few store choices, busy people who care little for shopping, those who are bored or dissatisfied with store shopping, and consumers with limitations on movement, such as some nondrivers or disabled people. There are disadvantages of nonstore retailing. Customers cannot try on merchandise, test it out, or have it altered before delivery. In addition, some nonstore retailers offer limited assortments.

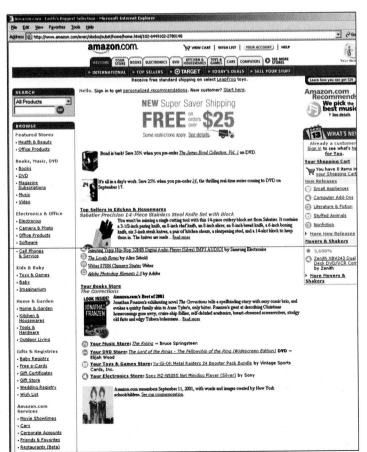

Consumers can buy almost anything via nonstore retailing. Amazon.com, which began as an online bookseller, now offers thousands of products ranging from home electronics to baby toys.

The three most common forms of nonstore retailing are direct retailing, direct selling, and vending machine sales. Direct retailing is discussed in more detail in Chapter 19.

DIRECT RETAILING   **Direct retailing** is the portion of direct marketing in which ultimate consumers, not business customers, do the buying. **Direct marketing** can be defined as "the distribution of goods, services, information, or promotional benefits to targeted consumers through interactive communication while tracking response, sales, interests, or desires through a computer database."[16] The consumer is exposed to the merchandise through a nonpersonal medium (catalogs, TV shopping programs, interactive electronic networks), and then purchases the merchandise by computer, mail, or telephone. Familiar direct retailers include Amazon.com, Etoyz, Cdnow, L. L. Bean, Spiegel, Fingerhut, Lands' End, and Lillian Vernon. More recently, TV home shopping has become a legitimate form of retailing and major retailers Spiegel, Nordstrom, Bloomingdale's, and The Sharper Image are involved in TV home-shopping programs.

Direct retailing sales growth has been steadily outpacing growth for total retail sales for several years. It is estimated that direct retailing will top $1.3 trillion in sales in 2005, up almost 50 percent from direct retail sales in 2000.[17] More than half of the U.S. adult population buys from at least one direct retailer each year, with clothing being the most popular item. Direct mail, including catalogs, remains the most popular direct retailing method, followed by telephone, newspaper, and television.

Without question, the most attention-getting sector of direct retailing in recent years is that conducted over the Internet. While retail sales over the Internet, often referred to as **e-retailing,** presently account for less than 4 percent of total retail sales, its growth rate indicates that it is becoming an important form of direct retailing. In a period of slow growth rates for retailing in general, e-retailing is growing rapidly. In 2002, retail sales were expected to grow approximately 4 percent, while e-retailing was expected to grow 40 percent to $72 billion.[18] For some product categories, e-retailing has already become an important form of retailing. In computer hardware and software, e-retailing generates approximately 23 percent of all sales and about 13 percent of all book sales. Other popular categories include travel, flowers, event tickets, recorded music and video products, and consumer electronics.

The e-retailing industry has been extremely competitive in recent years, with numerous business failures in the sector. Notables include EToys, Fogdog.com, MotherNature.com, Pets.com, PlanetRX., and Value America. Nonetheless, e-retailing has a bright future, as indicated by several industry developments and shopper behaviors. First, retail shoppers like having online buying as an alternative. Approximately a third of all retail shoppers buy in all three of these retail channels: store, catalog, and online.[19] A very high percentage of online shoppers also shop in retail stores, and a similar percentage use the Web to research products they are buying. Thus, retailers who ignore e-retailing run a big risk of missing out on a significant portion of the market.[20] Second, major retailers now dominate the e-retailing industry. In the early days of e-retailing, Internet-only companies such as Amazon.com and CDNOW were key players, but the bulk of business is now accounted for by multichannel retailers. Established retailers like Barnes & Noble, Best Buy, and L. L. Bean are among these multichannel marketers driving the growth of e-retailing.[21] Third, the e-retailing industry is now profitable. Profits from successful companies have overcome the losses of marginal performers, and the overall outlook is that e-retailing can be profitable.[22] The previously mentioned high growth rate also bodes well for the future of e-retailing.

Retailers may use **portals,** or virtual shopping malls, to generate more traffic for their individual store Web sites. For example, Yahoo! Shopping links thousands of large and small retailers in its portal. Companies such as Eddie Bauer, Brooks Brothers, Old Navy, and OfficeMax pay a monthly hosting fee of $49.95 plus a dime per

Several direct-selling companies are expanding their efforts in international markets. One of the leaders, Avon, is enjoying spectacular growth in Taiwan.

month for the average number of products featured. In addition, merchants pay Yahoo! transaction fees ranging from a half a percentage point up to three and a half percentage points on every dollar in sales depending on which Yahoo! networks the merchant participates in.[23]

E-retailing offers several advantages compared with shopping in a store. Consumers can order from stores around the world 24 hours a day from home or from any location with Internet access. There is no waiting in line to check out, nor the hassle of transporting purchases home. On the other hand, there is not the instant gratification that comes with a store purchase, and some consumers are worried about credit card security when buying online. Others find navigation around e-retail Web sites to be cumbersome and slow. On balance, a growing number of consumers enjoy shopping online, and growth will likely be dramatic in the coming years.

DIRECT SELLING   **Direct selling** involves the sale of a consumer product or service, person-to-person, away from a fixed retail location.[24] In approximately 80 percent of all direct selling transactions, the salesperson interacts with the customer or group of customers in a face-to-face encounter. The most popular setting for face-to-face direct selling is the home, with such encounters also taking place in the workplace, exhibition halls, theme parks, fairs, and shopping malls. Person-to-person direct selling is also conducted over the phone and the Internet. There are 11 million direct sellers in the United States, almost all of whom are part-time independent contractors. Three-quarters are females who primarily sell products in the home/family care, personal care, services, wellness, and leisure/educational categories.[25] Mary Kay, Avon, Cutco Cutlery, and Tupperware are familiar examples of companies that use direct selling.

VENDING MACHINE SALES   Vending machines allow customers to purchase and receive merchandise from a machine. Estimates of industry size range from $19 billion to $28 billion annually, with offerings of predominantly beverages, food, and candy.[26] Vending machines are frequently located at work sites, hospitals, schools, tourist destinations, and travel facilities.

Developing Retailing Strategy
The scope of retail products and services and the demands of consumers combine to produce a constantly changing business environment. A successful retailer must effectively manipulate the factors it can control to survive in a largely uncontrollable environment. A few uncontrollable and controllable factors of interest to retailers are listed in Exhibit 14–4.

Uncontrollable Factors
A number of constantly changing factors in the retail environment are beyond the retailer's control. To survive, retailers must constantly monitor and adapt to changing, uncontrollable factors in the marketing environment such as legal restrictions, discussed later in the chapter, and advances in technology. The important uncontrollable factors we describe here are consumers, competition, economic conditions, and seasonality.

Exhibit 14-4   *Understanding retail strategy: Important controllable and uncontrollable factors*

CONSUMERS Consumer demographics and lifestyles undergo constant changes, which retailers must recognize to satisfy the needs of their customers. For example, home improvement retailers have seized upon a shifting demographic among home buyers to fuel sales growth. Single women are the second largest category of home buyers behind couples. Increasingly, women are taking on a major shopping role in the home improvement category. Both Lowe's and Home Depot estimate that half of all purchases are made by women and that women influence many additional buying decisions. For the growing female market, Home Depot has added some women-only clinics in its stores to supplement the clinics open to both men and women. Despite some thought that such clinics might be politically incorrect, the chain reports increased sales as a direct result of the clinics. Lowe's does not offer gender-specific clinics but does acknowledge that it has attempted to make its stores more female-friendly through improved merchandising and sales practices.[27]

Kelly Seibels, owner of Seibels, comments on the importance of adapting to consumer trends, specifically the fact that consumers are busier than ever: "We know that people are generally rushed when they are shopping, and we try to offer a relaxing, inviting shopping experience that will encourage shoppers to spend enough time in our store to get the feeling of being at home in their camp or cottage. Rather than departmentalize by product types, we group lifestyle settings complete with accessories to help shoppers visualize just how unique and comfortable our furnishings can be. Barney, my chocolate Lab, is always around the store, and he adds to the relaxed setting which customers find enjoyable. There is no question that people are busier than ever, and that success in retail depends on offering a shopping environment in the store and, in our case, in our print catalog and on our Web site, that encourages shoppers to slow down and shop."

COMPETITION Whether from new entries into the marketplace or from existing marketers, retail competition is fierce. One indicator of competition intensity is retail bankruptcies. Kmart, the largest retailer in history to declare bankruptcy, joins a long list of retail bankruptcies in recent years. Other well-known retailers filing for bankruptcy were Service Merchandise, Montgomery Ward, Filene's Basement, Caldor, Bradlee's, Levitz Furniture, and catalog retailer J. Peterman. And small independent retailers, especially bookstores, have been hit especially hard by competition. Independent booksellers saw their market share drop by 50 percent in the past decade. Some independents tried to form regional chains to compete with the larger national chains, but none of these regional chains survived. Competitive pressure from large chains such as Borders and Barnes & Noble, warehouse clubs, and online booksellers such as Amazon.com is intensifying even further, and the outlook for independent bookstores is grim.

Although the major chains have hurt smaller chains and independents, they, too, are feeling the effects of increased competition. Retailers expanded aggressively in the latter 1990s, and now find that many markets are overbuilt; that is, there are more retail stores than needed to meet consumer demand. As a result, Staples, Toys "Я" Us, OfficeMax, and Pep Boys are but a few of many national chains to close stores.[28] Of course there are success stories amidst the reports of failing chain retailers. Wal-Mart and Target are doing well in the discount sector, Best Buy continues to perform well in consumer electronics, and both Home Depot and Lowe's are succeeding in the home improvement area. Dillard's department stores and Kohl's, a discount/department store hybrid, have also posted impressive results recently.[29] With overall store retailing sales growth averaging 4 percent annually, success for these successful companies usually comes at the expense of their competitors.

To survive, retailers try to improve the productivity of their operations, attract new customers, and get existing customers to buy more. This sometimes requires redefining the business, as has occurred with Radio Shack. Radio Shack was having a hard time getting brand-name products into its stores. Management was also unhappy with the lower operating margins on the sale of electronics equipment caused by price competition from Best Buy and other discounters. Noting that manufacturers were not satisfied with their lack of dedicated selling space in larger retail stores, Radio Shack felt that manufacturers would respond to a well-trained sales staff, something not found in the discount stores. Radio Shack refurbished its stores and partnered with Compaq, RCA, Verison, and Sprint to better diversify its product sales mix. As a result, audio and video equipment have been displaced by telephones and electronic parts, accessories, and batteries as the top sellers.[30] Another key element of Radio Shack's redefinition of its retailing strategy is to become a leading access point to the Internet via Microsoft's Internet service. The Radio Shack experience serves as a reminder that retailers must sometimes undergo substantial changes in order to remain competitive.

In a broad sense, there are two major types of competition: intratype and intertype. **Intratype competition** describes competition among retailers that use the same type of business format. McDonald's, Wendy's, and Burger King are intratype competitors, for example; they are all fast-food restaurants. **Intertype competition** prevails among retailers using different types of business to sell the same products and services. The intertype competitors of McDonald's would include all other food retailers, ranging from vending machines to fine restaurants. Retail businesses that appreciate both types of competition tend to be better prepared to face challenges and avoid the pitfalls of marketing myopia—that is, too narrowly defining the scope of their business.

ECONOMIC CONDITIONS   Economic conditions are another factor beyond the retailer's control. The robust growth in retail sales at the turn of the century has softened, especially since the events of September 11, 2001. Travel-related retail sales have been hit particularly hard, with decreases in automobile sales and gasoline showing declines in 2002 compared to 2001. As expected, a decline in travel hurts all sorts of retailers, including restaurants, hotels, rental car companies, and resort operators. In these circumstances, retailers can expect more price competition in numerous sectors of the economy as consumers delay or cancel intended purchases. For example, until conditions improve, automobile dealers will periodically use heavy discounting to bring consumers into their showrooms, or face the possibility of building up costly excess inventory.[31]

The state of the economy also significantly affects retail growth strategy. In some cases, even successful retailers scale back on their expansion plans. Best Buy, for example, is experimenting with smaller stores during the down cycle in the economy.[32] If successful, the electronics chain may once again increase the rate at which it opens new stores. Kohl's is taking advantage of relatively cheap financing to aggressively expand while some of its competitors cut back expansion plans.[33]

SEASONALITY   **Seasonality** refers to demand fluctuations related to the time of the year, which may be moderated or exacerbated by unpredictable changes in weather and in consumer preferences. Retailers specializing in clothing, sporting equipment, amusement parks, fresh food, hotels, and car rentals are particularly affected by seasonality. A retailer may minimize the effects of seasonality by adjusting some controllable variables within its retail strategy mix. For example, some retailers initiate special promotions to encourage consumers to buy during the off-season. Other retailers, like sporting goods stores, alter their product mix by focusing on different products for different seasons. Ski resorts have redefined their businesses to become year-round attractions, adding summer festivals, mountain biking, water slides, golf, and other activities to their product assortment.

Controllable Factors

The four categories of controllable factors we discuss are location, the goods and services the retailer offers, the prices the retailer charges for products and services, and the marketing communications consumers receive.

LOCATION   The old saying—and experts confirm it—is that the three most important factors in retailing are location, location, and location. To most retailers, location *is* the most crucial factor and the least flexible element of retail strategy. A retailer can modify prices, products and services, and marketing communications relatively easily, but a poor location is difficult for even the best merchant to overcome. Moving is complicated by lease agreements, the transfer of inventory from one location to another, and perhaps even the sale of the building if the retailer owns it.

Retail locations can be found in practically every nook and cranny of the world, ranging from street vendors and mall kiosk operators up to familiar superstore operators. With the growth of nonstore retailing, cyberspace is an increasingly important location. Mixed-use spaces that include retail, office, and housing are becoming more popular in urban and suburban locations. Themed shopping areas such as River Walk in New Orleans and Ghirardelli Square in San Francisco are popular tourist destinations. These newer developments in retail location strategy are exciting, but four retail location alternatives remain most important in terms of total sales generated: the central business district (CBD); strip centers; shopping malls; and freestanding locations.

The **central business district (CBD),** commonly known as downtown areas, remain an important part of the retail scene in the United States and many major cities around the world. These districts are designed to meet the day-to-day shopping

Retailers, especially those operating in large urban areas, are concerned that shoppers may shop less frequently or only shop during certain hours of the day because they are fearful of crime. This shopping mall in Miami uses additional security measures to ensure shopper safety.

Exhibit 14–5   *Selected criteria to consider when evaluating retail locations*

Location Issues	CBD	Strip Center	Shopping Mall	Freestanding
Large size draws people to area	+	–	+	–
People working/living in area provide source of customers	+	+	–	–
Source of entertainment/recreation	?	–	+	–
Protection against weather	–	–	+	–
Security	–	–	+	–
Long, uniform hours of operation	–	+	+	+
Planned shopping area/balanced tenant mix	–	–	+	–
Parking	–	+	?	+
Occupancy costs (e.g., rent)	?	+	–	+
Pedestrian traffic	+	–	+	–
Landlord control	+	+	–	+
Strong competition	+	+	–	+
Tax incentives	?	?	?	?

needs of the surrounding neighborhood. **Strip centers** feature parking in front of all stores and are not enclosed under one roof. This form of retail location may be found in small neighborhoods within a community, may draw from the entire community, or even have more of a regional draw depending on size and mix of retailers that locate in the strip. **Shopping malls,** unlike strip centers, are designed more for pedestrian flow under an enclosed roof. **Freestanding sites** are not adjoined to other retail structures but are often located adjacent to other retail locations. For example, Home Depot, Circuit City, Best Buy, Sam's Club, and P. F. Chang's restaurants often utilize freestanding locations near large strip centers or shopping malls. Freestanding locations are also popular at exits along interstate highways and busy city streets where car dealers may congregate. In recent years, the popularity of shopping malls has waned somewhat, and there has been a resurgence in the popularity of strip centers. Another popular strategy for retail developers has been to combine a mall with surrounding strip centers and freestanding locations, as has been done with great success at Flatirons Crossing near Denver. The advantages and disadvantages of the major types of retail locations are shown in Exhibit 14–5.

GOODS AND SERVICES   Another controllable factor in the retail strategy is the goods and services offered for sale. Retailers must decide on the number of product lines to carry, referred to as width or variety. They must also decide on the assortment of each product line, called length or depth. These decisions require several considerations. Major product considerations include compatibility (how well the product fits in with existing inventory), attributes (such as bulk, required service, selling levels), and profitability. Market considerations include stage in the product life cycle, market appropriateness (a product's appeal to the store's current target market), and competitive conditions. Finally, supply considerations such as product availability and supplier reliability need to be explored.

Retailers must be alert to the effects of changes in their product mix and open to a redefinition of competitors. For example, the practice of adding unrelated product categories to existing product lines is referred to as **scrambled merchandising.** In the not-too-distant past, grocery stores predominantly sold food items. Today, consumers can buy motor oil or rent movies at grocery stores. Scrambled merchandising allows grocery stores to obtain higher profit margins than the traditional 1 to 2 percent made on food items. Consumers, in turn, enjoy the extra convenience of one-stop shopping provided by a wide array of merchandise; in effect, they have received improved quality and value in their overall shopping experience.

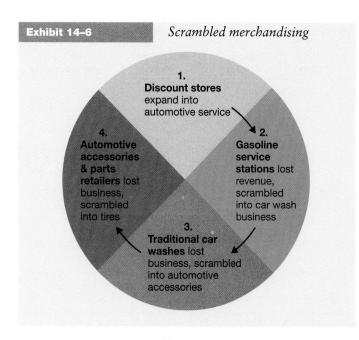

Exhibit 14-6   *Scrambled merchandising*

1.
Discount stores expand into automotive service

2.
Gasoline service stations lost revenue, scrambled into car wash business

3.
Traditional car washes lost business, scrambled into automotive accessories

4.
Automotive accessories & parts retailers lost business, scrambled into tires

Scrambled merchandising has had a chain-reaction effect something like that shown in Exhibit 14–6. When discount stores aggressively expanded into automotive service, traditional gasoline service stations lost revenue and scrambled into the car wash business. Traditional car-wash operations then expanded their sale of automotive accessories, causing lost volume for traditional automotive accessory and parts retailers. These retailers responded by scrambling into tires to supplement their lost sales on accessories.

Amazon.com provides an example of scrambled merchandising in e-retailing. Originally a bookseller, Amazon expanded into music and videos, then followed with a wide range of products, including electronics, computers, sports equipment, tools, software, and other offerings on its way to becoming the world's largest online retailer, serving customers in 220 countries. Amazon is making these products available through its zShops concept, where independent vendors pay a small monthly fee to link with Amazon. As Amazon scrambles its merchandise to the extreme, it excludes only items it considers to be unethical or illegal, including stolen and counterfeit goods, promotional media, unauthorized and unlicensed merchandise, and recopied media.[34]

PRICING   Retailers also control the final prices they charge consumers for their products and services. Retail prices are ultimately based on the store's target market, the desired store image, and the congruence between price and other elements of the retail mix (location, quality of products and services, marketing communications). Although price-conscious consumers may appear to dominate in many markets, successful retailers are found at all price ranges, from high to low.

Everyday-low-pricing (EDLP) strategies, pioneered by Wal-Mart, are now used by many retailers. With EDLP, retailers demand low prices from their suppliers, minimize costly advertising and promotions, and keep their retail prices consistently low to lure consumers. Now, many retailers are adopting "low-price leader" or "value pricing" programs. These programs feature low competitive prices across the board and a continual mix of special offers to keep consumers coming back.

MARKETING COMMUNICATIONS   Decisions about the mix of marketing communications are also controllable. These decisions specify how the retailer allocates resources among personal selling, advertising, public relations, direct marketing, and sales promotion. Retailers such as The Limited emphasize personal in-store selling and do very little advertising; convenience stores promote sales by placing signs in their windows; others promote "a sale a week."

Marketing communications influence **store image,** the picture shoppers conjure up of a store's identity. This image is a composite of shoppers' perceptions of the store's location, goods, and services sold, and atmospherics. Essentially, store image is a reflection of consumers' feelings about a store. It affects consumer perceptions of the quality of products and services offered, prices, and the store's fashionability.

Types of Strategy Mix

Retailers differentiate themselves from one another according to the **strategy mix** they pursue. The elements of the retail strategy mix are the controllable variables

Giant Food Incorporated uses extensive advertising as part of its marketing communications program. It also gains favorable publicity from outdoor advertising, as seen at Baltimore Oriole's Park at Camden Yards.

Exhibit 14–7		*Examples of retail strategy mixes*			
Type of Retailer	**Location**	**Merchandise**	**Prices**	**Atmosphere and Services**	**Marketing Communications**
Convenience store	Neighborhood	Medium width and low depth of assortment; average quality	Average to above average	Average	Moderate
Superstore	Community shopping center or isolated site	Full assortment of supermarket items, plus health and beauty aids and general merchandise	Competitive	Average	Heavy use of newspapers and flyers; self-service
Warehouse store	Secondary site, often in industrial area	Moderate width and low depth; emphasis on national brands purchased at discounts	Very low	Low	Little or none
Specialty store	Business district or shopping center	Very narrow width of assortment; extensive depth of assortment; average to good quality	Competitive to above average	Average to excellent	Heavy use of displays; extensive salesforce
Department store	Business district, shopping center, or isolated store	Extensive width and depth of assortment; average to good quality	Average to above average	Good to excellent	Heavy use of ads; catalogs; direct mail; personal selling
Full-line discount store	Business district, shopping center, or isolated store	Extensive width and depth of assortment; average to good quality	Competitive	Slightly below average to average	Heavy use of newspapers; price-oriented; moderate salesforce
Factory outlet	Out-of-the-way site or discount mall	Moderate width, but very poor depth of assortment; some irregular merchandise; low continuity	Very low	Very low	Little; self-service

we have discussed: location, products and services, pricing, and marketing communications. Exhibit 14–7 describes a range of retailers and their strategy mixes. Although a multitude of combinations exist, specialty stores, department stores, and convenience stores are the more obvious examples of retailers that combine the strategy mix variables in different ways to achieve their desired positions in the marketplace.

SPECIALTY STORES   Specialty stores sell a narrow variety of products but offer a deep assortment of product choices. Typical examples of specialty stores are The Limited, Radio Shack, and The Sharper Image.

Because many specialty stores are not large enough to generate sufficient customer traffic on their own, most are commonly located in shopping clusters (malls, shopping centers) where their product selections complement goods provided by neighboring retailers. The marketing communications mix of a specialty store generally includes personal selling along with advertising that emphasizes the uniqueness of offerings and the depth of assortment. Specialty stores are also known for their medium to high prices.

Hot Topic is a specialty clothing and accessories chain that caters to the teen market. By thoroughly understanding its customers, Hot Topic competes quite effectively against other more established retail chains.

DEPARTMENT STORES   Department stores are characterized by a wide variety of merchandise and extensive depth of assortment, and they offer customers one-stop convenience for multiple shopping needs. Operations are typically organized around sales departments such as apparel, home furnishings, cosmetics, and housewares. Employees also work within centralized functional departments such as buying, merchandising, and advertising. Some of the more well-known department stores are Bloomingdale's, Dillard's, and Macy's.

Department stores generally occupy **anchor positions** in shopping centers, shopping malls, or downtown areas; that is, they are strategically placed at different ends of the shopping cluster. Because department stores generate a lot of customer traffic, this placement creates a traffic flow throughout the entire shopping facility.

Marketing communications for department stores focus on product selection and quality; services offered such as alterations, gift wrapping, and credit; shopping atmosphere; and store image. Department stores are heavy users of newspaper advertising, catalogs, direct mail, and personal selling. As do specialty stores, department stores commonly charge at or above competitive prices.

CONVENIENCE STORES   Convenience stores have developed their own unique marketing mix. They carry a modest variety and shallow assortment of products. Prices are high, which consumers tolerate because of the ease of shopping offered by such retailers. Convenience stores often occupy **interceptor locations** between residential areas and the closest supermarket. Marketing communications are predominantly limited to the store's sign and banners displayed in the front windows.

Two convenience stores, Circle K and 7-Eleven, have been in bankruptcy, and the entire industry faces a predicted decline in new-store growth over the next decade. The industry's problems can be traced to three main sources. First, the industry is overbuilt, with the proliferation of convenience stores constructed by major oil companies such as Shell, Texaco, and BP. Second, as drugstores and supermarkets extend their hours of operation, convenience stores have increasing difficulty differentiating themselves on convenience. Moreover, increases in the minimum wage, store rents, and other general expenses have dramatically increased operating costs. Even though sales through convenience stores are increasing, profit margins are declining.[35] Profit margins on merchandise are increasing, but this increase is more than offset by declining profit margins on motor fuel. Convenience stores have had difficulty passing on wholesale-price increases for motor fuel to the ultimate consumer.

To survive, many convenience stores have repositioned themselves as quick-service eateries specializing in "one-handed" food—items you can eat with one hand while driving with the other, such as hot dogs, corn dogs, pizza, burritos, and egg rolls. Compared to past sales patterns, convenience stores are increasing their sales of general merchandise, including items such as scooters and electronics, coffee, publications, and health and beauty items. These shifting patterns indicate that convenience stores may be moving slightly away from meeting shoppers' fill-in needs to becoming more of a general retailer that has some characteristics of general stores, drugstores, newsstands, and health food stores.[36]

MARGIN AND TURNOVER STRATEGY MIXES   Besides type of store, another distinction between retailers is gross margin and inventory turnover. **Gross margin** refers to sales revenue less the retailer's cost of goods sold. A retailer with higher margins makes more from each dollar of sales. **Inventory turnover** refers to how quickly merchandise is sold; it describes the number of times the retailer sells its average inventory during the year. Margin and turnover concepts are illustrated in Appendix A at the end of the text.

There are three strategic combinations of gross margin and inventory turnover among successful retailers. Jewelry stores exemplify a high-margin/low-turnover strategy. They realize high profits per sale but make fewer sales. Such retailers are also noted for their attention to personal service and attractive atmospheres that help support the merchandise.

Grocery stores use a low-margin/high-turnover strategy. They typically have a net profit margin of 1 to 2 percent but turn merchandise over very quickly. The third option is high-margin/high-turnover, demonstrated by convenience stores.

Kelly Seibels, owner of Seibels, points out that teamwork can be an important part of a successful retail strategy: "At Seibels, all employees are equal partners in serving the customer. We all have different areas of particular expertise, so the right person can step up and help when the situation calls for it. We keep files on all of our customers' purchase history, including pending order for delivery. All employees have instant access to these files, so no matter who is on the floor, they can follow up on customer inquiries in short order. By working together to serve the customer, Seibels enjoys a high level of customer satisfaction, which brings loyal shoppers back to us time after time."

Ethical and Legal Issues in Retailing
Retailers engage in highly visible activities, and their marketing communications are similarly visible and thus subject to a fair amount of scrutiny. Ethical or legal violations that retailers have been accused of include deceptive advertising, dishonest sales practices, charging unreasonably high prices to disadvantaged consumers, selling potentially harmful products without adequate control, and selling prohibited products to underage consumers.

Additional factors pose special concerns for retailers: consumer fraud, supplier labor practices, shoplifting, slotting allowances, the use of personal customer information, and ecological considerations.

Consumer Fraud
Retailers that adopted the customer-is-always-right concept are having second thoughts when it comes to liberal return policies. Known in the industry as return churn or boomerang buying, return fraud is a growing problem for retailers. Fraudulent returns cost retailers more than a billion dollars annually. L. L. Bean notices more requests for returns in the spring, when yard sales pick up and old boots and camping equipment are bought cheap and then returned with a request for a full refund. And some customers take merchandise off the shelf, then proceed to customer service for a refund, claiming that the receipt has been lost. Others use retailers as

free rental centers for big-screen TV sets, snow blowers, and formal apparel. Retailers are fighting back, cutting down on the time during which returns are accepted and being more insistent that the customer has a receipt. Among those cracking down on returns are Target, Home Depot, Best Buy, The Gap, and JCPenney. Some retailers remain lax in their return policy, saying that most consumers are honest and that strict policies would punish the majority because of the actions of a small minority. Among those taking this stance are Circuit City, Crate & Barrel, Williams-Sonoma, Radio Shack, and Nordstrom.[37] Fraudulent consumers drive up the cost of retailing, which ultimately translates into higher prices for honest consumers.

Supplier Labor Practices

Many retailers, including Wal-Mart, JCPenney, Talbots, and Macy's, have been part of a controversy involving the working conditions in their supplier manufacturing facilities. Referred to as sweatshops, these facilities are located primarily in low-wage countries in Asia, Latin America, and Eastern Europe. Sweatshop workers, many of whom are underage, are subjected to adverse working conditions and extremely low wages.

A storm of bad publicity began in the mid-1990s and continues today, with retailers, manufacturers, and celebrity spokespersons receiving unwanted exposure. Since then, many retailers have strengthened existing policies and adopted new procedures to address the sweatshop issue. The U.S. Department of Labor has commended several retailers for their active role in eliminating sweatshops, including Express, Nordstrom, The Limited, Patagonia, Nicole Miller, Lane Bryant, and Liz Claiborne. Nonetheless, the issue is far from resolved, and college students are among the most outspoken critics of retail-supplier labor practices. Campus protests across the country frequently highlight student dissatisfaction with sweatshop operations. More than 300 leading retailers have signed the National Retail Federation's Statement on Supplier's Legal Compliance, which pledges that retailers will not buy from vendors who violate labor laws of the United States and other countries. Even so, antisweatshop groups feel that enforcement is insufficient and that retailers should do more to pressure their suppliers in the area of humane labor practices. The issues surrounding sweatshop-produced merchandise are likely to remain key ethical issues for retailers well into the future.

Retail Theft

Retailers lose approximately $10 billion a year to shoplifting by customers and an additional $15 billion to employee theft.[38] Nationwide, the incidence of shoplifting has increased sharply in recent years. Experts claim the primary contributors to increased shoplifting are fewer clerks per store and new floor layout arrangements that divide stores into separate boutiques. This type of layout creates barriers between departments, which makes it easier for shoplifters to conceal their activities. Specialty clothing stores, drugstores, convenience stores, and department stores are hit hardest by shoplifting. Items most frequently stolen are fashion accessories, costume jewelry, fine jewelry, recorded music, health and beauty aids, sporting goods, radios, and television sets.

Manufacturers are taking steps to reduce shoplifting in retail stores. Johnson & Johnson, Eastman Kodak, and Procter & Gamble are developing security-alarm tags for products ranging from film and cameras to Pampers and Tylenol. These three companies have formed the Consumer Products Manufacturers' Consortium to develop the tags and institute a global standard for the tags that can be used by all retailers and manufacturers.[39] The consortium hopes to have the participation of most retailers by 2003. If successful, the system could have a major impact on shoplifting in drug and grocery stores, where currently only 30 percent of all products are protected by security tags. Some methods for deterring shoplifting are detailed in Exhibit 14–8.

Exhibit 14–8   *Shoplifting deterrents*

- Use electronic tags on vulnerable merchandise
- Install surveillance cameras in plain view
- Install convex mirrors to observe corners and aisles
- Use locked cases for expensive and frequently stolen goods
- Closely supervise the selling floor
- Instruct personnel to make eye contact with customers
- Make it easy for employees to contact security
- Publicize that shoplifters will be prosecuted
- Monitor entrances and exits from the store
- Lower displays that could limit visibility of the sales floor
- Monitor fitting areas

Slotting Allowances

Another retailing issue that has legal or ethical implications is the use of slotting allowances. **Slotting allowances** are fees manufacturers pay to retailers or wholesalers to obtain shelf or warehouse space for their products. In other words, retailers and wholesalers receive money from manufacturers in exchange for allocation of shelf space.

Slotting allowances, a common practice in grocery retailing, are controversial. They were first instituted to keep manufacturers from introducing not-so-new brands or bogus product-line extensions. Colorado State University professor Joseph P. Cannon notes that "the reason slotting fees came about was the number of new products, making it more difficult to evaluate them. Test marketing fell by the wayside because of the [importance of] speed to market and also because if you test your product, your competitors can see it before you go national."[40] Even though test marketing is less popular than in the past, slotting fees are more established than ever. Large manufacturers resist paying these questionable fees, but large wholesalers and retailers insist slotting fees be paid as a condition of doing business. In effect, slotting allowances place manufacturers in direct opposition to their customers: wholesalers and retailers.

Overall, slotting allowances are predominantly associated with negative consequences. They may increase conflict between channel members and reduce competitiveness at some levels. Large channel members can demand slotting allowances that increase their profit margins, while the smaller members must fend for themselves.

Slotting allowances may also reduce customer service by forcing fewer brand choices, higher retail prices, and less prepurchase information. This could ultimately threaten the quality of product provided to the consumer. The costs of slotting allowances incurred by vendors is typically a well-guarded secret. Neither vendors nor retailers are required to disclose slotting allowance payments. In a quirky one-year exception to the rule, the U.S. Financial Accounting Standards Board required that companies restate their 2001 accounts by subtracting slotting allowances from their sales revenue. The amounts paid by food and beverage companies to gain shelf space was astounding. For example, Campbell Soup, Kellogg, Coca-Cola, PepsiCo, and Kraft averaged about 13 percent of sales in slotting allowances. Kraft, for example, spent $4.6 billion on slotting allowances. Such large numbers and the secrecy of the practice has attracted government attention, so it is plausible that we may know more about the scope and impact of slotting allowances as time passes. A prime concern of regulators is the overall impact on competition, and thus consumer prices. Small manufacturers claim that slotting allowances may drive them out of business, thus creating a less competitive marketplace.[41]

Use of Customer Information

Advances in database technology provide retailers greater access to and storage of consumer information and purchase histories. For example, when a customer calls

Spiegel to check a catalog order, the service rep has instant access, via an order number, to the customer's previous sales and service transactions. This information can be used to sell other products and service warranties and to process orders more efficiently.

Are retailers free to use such information for any purpose, or is the customer's right to privacy being violated? Although this question is the subject of much debate, public sentiment favors the protection of consumer privacy. Some of the major videotape rental firms no longer maintain records of customers' past rentals. Other companies that fear adverse publicity will quite likely take a right-to-privacy stance.

Ecological Considerations

Retailers have begun to pay more attention to how their operations affect the environment. Wal-Mart, for example, has created Environmental Demonstration Stores in Kansas, Oklahoma, and California. These stores feature recycled construction materials, solar energy, and ozone-friendly air-conditioning systems. Local Wal-Mart stores have a "Green Coordinator," a specially trained associate who coordinates efforts to make the store environmentally responsible.[42] Home Depot also shows its awareness of ecological issues by refusing to sell wood from environmentally endangered areas. Home Depot sells more lumber than any other company in the world, and its move was influential in getting other retailers to be more supportive of environmental issues.[43]

Another indication that retailers are becoming more concerned with environmental issues is a move to ban smoking in shopping malls. Since the Environmental Protection Agency released a report on the dangers of secondhand smoke, shopping centers across the country have not waited for legal prompting; instead, they have taken the initiative to ban smoking.

Like all marketing institutions, retailers are finding that following an ethical perspective can be good for business. They are also acutely aware that questionable ethical practices can lead to consumer protest, tarnished images, and lost sales. Consumers must also take some responsibility for correcting some of the ethical problems in retailing. Shoplifting and consumer fraud hurt retailer profits. They also hurt honest consumers in the form of higher prices and inconvenient security measures.

Summary

1. **Understand the economic importance of retailing and its role in the marketing channel.** The role of retailing in the marketing channel is to provide products and services to the ultimate, or final consumer. Retailing is an important economic activity in that (1) there are approximately 3 million retailers in the United States; (2) nearly 14 million people, 10 percent of the U.S. labor force, are employed in retail or retail-related activities; and (3) retailers generate approximately $2.5 trillion in sales. Retailers differ from other channel members in that they sell smaller quantities more frequently, offer assortments of products, and emphasize atmospherics in their selling.

2. **Cite evidence of the globalization of retailing.** McDonald's, Wal-Mart, The Gap, Radio Shack, France's Carrefour, and L. L. Bean are but a few companies expanding retail operations around the globe. Markets in countries with highly developed economies such as the United States are somewhat saturated, thus retailers are increasingly eager to expand to less-competitive markets.

3. **Discuss some of the advances in retailing technology.** Retailing has benefited from various technologies in recent years. Automated cash registers, electronic kiosks, Universal Product Code scanners, and wireless networks are some examples of technology put to good use in retailing. The explosive growth in nonstore retailing is fueled in part by computer and communications technology.

4. **Explain the reasons behind the growth of nonstore retailing.** Busy people like to shop at their preferred times in the convenience of their own homes. Successful catalog retailing has encouraged consumers to try other forms of nonstore retailing such as TV shopping and online shopping. The growth of nonstore retailing is

probably also the result of consumer boredom and dissatisfaction with some traditional retail stores.

5. **Describe key factors in the retail marketing environment, and understand how they relate to retail strategy.** Controllable factors include location, products and services, pricing, and marketing communications. Uncontrollable factors are consumers, competition, economic conditions, and seasonality. To be successful, retailers must effectively manipulate the controllable factors to manage the environment created by always-changing uncontrollable factors.

6. **Cite important ethical and legal issues facing retailers.** Routine legal restrictions govern practically every aspect of retailing. Contemporary ethical and legal issues of special concern are consumer fraud, supplier labor practices, retail theft, the use of slotting allowances, the use of customer information, and ecological considerations. Consumer fraud in the form of unwarranted return of merchandise costs retailers more than a billion dollars a year, which ultimately is passed on to consumers. Some progressive retailers began monitoring the labor practices of their suppliers after sweatshop practices made the headlines, resulting in negative publicity for retailers, suppliers, and celebrity spokespersons. Employee, consumer, and supplier theft are costly to retailers, resulting in higher prices for consumers. Slotting allowances are fees manufacturers pay to retailers or wholesalers to obtain shelf or warehouse space for their products. It's an ethically questionable practice and may be illegal. Other concerns are the retailer's use of customer information versus the individual's right to privacy, and the ecological impact of retail operations.

Understanding Marketing Terms and Concepts

Thinking About Marketing

1. What evidence can you cite supporting the economic importance of retailing?

2. How do retailers differ from other members in the channel of distribution?

3. How can retailers improve customer service by using technology?

4. Review "Building Customer Equity: Hot Topic Draws Teens." Realizing that consumer tastes can change quickly, how can fashion retailers get timely ideas for new fashions?

5. Review "Using Technology: "Are Talking Chips the Next Big Thing?" How does this concept create value for consumers? For retailers and their suppliers?

6. What uncontrollable factors affect the retail environment? What can retailers do to minimize the impact of these factors on sales?

7. What types of locations are possible alternatives for retailers? Briefly define each type of location.

8. List and describe the three types of nonstore retailing. What are the advantages and disadvantages of nonstore retail operations?

9. Discuss the benefits of retail franchising from both the franchisor's and franchisee's point of view.

10. Discuss some of the key ethical and legal issues in retailing.

Applying Marketing Skills

1. Retailers that sell secondhand merchandise, such as flea markets or Salvation Army stores, have been doing relatively well in recent years. Can you explain their success in terms of economic conditions and consumer preferences discussed in this chapter?

2. Tune in to a television shopping program once a week for a month, and analyze the products sold and the sales methods used. In particular, assess the following issues:
- What is the primary pricing strategy?
- What role do celebrities play in the programming?
- Can you generalize about the size and colors offered in apparel sales?
- Is it important to have merchandise with easy-to-demonstrate features?

3. For each of the following types of retail operations, suggest complementary products, either goods or services, that could logically be added to the merchandise mix:
- A small coffee shop that features light desserts, pastries, espresso, cappuccino, and gourmet coffees.
- A small independent bookstore located near a retirement community.
- A large parking garage adjacent to a downtown office building.
- A hairstyling salon.
- A pet supplies store.

Using the www in Marketing

Activity One
L. L. Bean is a successful retailer in both store and nonstore formats. One reason for L. L. Bean's success is excellent customer service. Visit the Web site at http://www.llbean.com and identify customer services not typically available from retail stores (refer to Exhibit 14–3 for services typically offered by retail stores). How do these services build stronger customer relationships?

Activity Two
Compare online retailers at Yahoo!com, www.yahoo.com. From the home page, select the "shopping" link. Select any two of the retailers listed and answer these questions:

1. How would you describe the target market for each retailer? This will require some speculation on your part, but describe the likely demographic and lifestyle characteristics of the intended target markets for each retailer.

2. Which of the two retailers has done the best job in appealing to its target market with its online offerings? Please support your answer.

Making Marketing Decisions
Case 14-1 Chico's Sales Are Booming

The women's retail apparel market is an interesting scene these days, that is, if you like mysteries. One of the big mysteries in women's apparel is why more retailers are not paying attention to the desires of the important segment in the market. Baby boomer women, those aged from the mid-30s to the mid-50s, comprise 43 percent of the U.S. population, and they account for 40 percent of sales. Retailers, however, are focused on GenX and GenY shoppers in their early teens to their mid-20s who contribute only 17 percent of the women's apparel dollars. As a result, middle-aged women have gone beyond complaining about ill-fitting clothes in styles they do not like—they have slowed down their purchases. Retailers have begun to notice and say they are adjusting their product assortments. But they will have a long way to go to catch Chico's, a Florida-based chain of 320 stores, most of which are located in upscale malls. Chico's sells clothing, shoes, and fashion accessories, targeting mid-to higher income women aged 30 to 60.

Chico's was named after the bilingual parrot of a friend of the founders, Marvin and Helene Gralnick. The Gralnick's moved to Florida from Mexico and opened their first store in Sannibel Island, Florida, in 1983. Since then, their success has been built on understanding the female baby boomer market and giving them an alternative between the extremes of young, sometimes too casual for the office attire and the more tailored look as typified by Talbot's.

Middle-aged women have grown tired of trying to fit into fashions designed for a younger demographic. Shoppers openly complain at The Gap, Banana Republic, Old Navy, Urban Outfitters, and even department stores such as Macy's. Many are dismayed when they have to increase their sizes, even though they have not gained weight in recent years. Store buyers say that middle-aged women are generally in much better shape than previous generations, and that they are not heavier. Yet, today's fashions often make them feel as if they are. Chico's offers a simplified sizing scheme ranging from 0 to 3, where 0 is equivalent to sizes 4–6; 1 equals 8–10; 2 is 12–16; and 3 equals 16–18. The clothes are generously cut and comfortable. Granted, not all women like the roomier styles. But Chico's is on target with most women in the boomer demographic. Sales have grown at a double-digit rate annually since 1997. In 2002, sales and profits are increasing at a remarkable rate. Sales are up 30 percent over 2001 figures, and profits are up more than 50 percent. This comes at a time when apparel sales to the boomer demographic are down 7 percent across the United States.

With results like these, Chico's can expect increased competition. Nordstrom is finding success with Cambio, a German manufacturer that offers more fashions such as mid-rise jeans for middle-aged customers. The Gap is swinging back toward more traditional clothing, and Neiman Marcus is signaling its designers to get more in tune with the boomer market. Eileen Fisher and J. Jill are courting the same market targeted by Chico's and will turn up the competitive heat. Another new competitor is the private label show, where women meet in friends' home, sort of like a Tupperware party, to shop for lesser-known, more conservative labels.

Chico's management is confident that they can handle the competition, and the chain continues to expand aggressively. Chico's executives think they have figured out how to give women a comfortable fit without making them look foolish. The large number of women in their target market and a healthy $85,000 average annual household income gives Chico's the opportunity to offer more upscale merchandise than some of the mass retailers they compete with. To hedge their bets, Chico's also sells via the Internet and through its catalog. Combined sales in these two channels are growing steadily, and Chico's reports that both the Web site and the catalog are also driving more traffic into their stores. Never a company to advertise in its early days, Chico's has now been running a national TV advertising campaign in major markets the past five years. Same-store sales are up when supported by advertising, and Chico's could be expected to continue with its advertising. A loyalty program called Passport rewards customers who spend $500 with a lifetime 5 percent discount. Among the first to see the opportunity in serving the most lucrative niche in the women's apparel industry, Chico's will be a tough act to beat.

Questions

1. Why have so few retailers successfully targeted and met the needs of the middle-aged women's apparel market?

2. How does Chico's sizing method add customer value?

3. How can Chico's stay ahead of the pack in serving its market?

Case 14-2 Home Depot and Lowe's Go Head-to-Head

Recent market conditions have been favorable for home improvement retailers. Mortgage rates for new homes have been favorably low the past few years, keeping the market for new houses strong despite a slow economy. The resale home market has been strong as well, as some consumers find more value for their dollar in resales. As Americans spend more time at home, a trend called cocooning, the remodeling market has also been strong. Even the weather has been cooperating, with milder winters extending the busy season for home improvement retailers. Industry leaders Home Depot and Lowe's have benefited from these favorable conditions and are now more than ever locked in a head-to-head battle to lead this retail sector.

Based on size, Home Depot is winning the battle. The company has grown from four stores in Atlanta in 1979 to almost 1,400 in four countries in 2002. It is the nation's second largest retailer behind Wal-Mart, having passed Sears several years ago. Lowe's, by comparison, has 785 stores. Home Depot sells almost twice as much merchandise as Lowe's, with an expected 2002 revenue of $62 billion. Home Depot earns about 5.5 percent of sales in profits while Lowe's earnings are about 4.5 percent of sales. In recent years, however, Lowe's earnings growth has bettered that of Home Depot. Investors currently favor Lowe's, as its stock price rose 31 percent by mid-2002 compared to mid-2001, while Home Depot's shares dropped 19 percent in the same time period.

Both Lowe's and Home Depot recognize the importance of the female shopper in the home improvement market. Half of Lowe's clientele is female, and the chain is attracting more and more nonprofessional home improvement shoppers. Bolstered by higher margin items such as Laura Ashley paints and high-end bathroom fixtures, Lowe's has recently shown steady increases in its gross margins.

Home Depot, known for its customer service despite the huge size of its stores, was showing some signs in 2001 that its aggressive drive to open new stores was beginning to catch up with the company. It is hard to maintain good service when the emphasis is on opening new stores. New CEO Bob Nardelli argues that customer service is not overlooked at Home Depot. He ordered stores to restock at night so forklifts in the aisles would not detract from shopping during the day. Salespeople now spend 70 percent of their time with customers, where in the past they spent only 30 percent of their time with customers. Nardelli put Home Depot on a cost-cutting program and reengineered basic processes such as accounting, purchasing, and logistics. In effect, he overhauled the company's supply chain, tightening up inventory controls and customer return policies.

Home Depot, like Lowe's, also recognizes the importance of the female customer. Both chains are cleaning up their stores to reduce the clutter and warehouse feel. Better signage directs shoppers to the various departments, and better lighting improves the ambience of the stores. Lowe's is sticking with its singular format, while Home Depot is adding the Expo Design Center, an upscale design concept that will add up to 100 stores by 2004. Home Depot is also instituting a program called At-Home Service to set up and install everything it sells to tap into the convenience-seeking portion of the home improvement market. Among its other innovations is Pro Set, a center within the store to cater to professional contractors. Pro Set will be staffed by licensed plumbers, electricians, and other building professionals. By the end of 2002, there will be between 900 and 1,000 Pro Sets in Home Depot Stores.

Both Lowe's and Home Depot plan to add new stores as they fight for market share. Interestingly, Home Depot is downsizing many of its new stores so that they can fit into densely populated areas. At the same time, Lowe's is moving away from its focus on small towns into Home Depot's backyard, opening larger stores in metro areas. In terms of their emphasis on the female consumer and in their plans for expansion, it certainly appears that Home Depot and Lowe's are going head-to-head in a fierce competitive battle.

Questions

1. Critics claim that Home Depot is doing too much too fast with its new Home Design Expo chain, the in-store Pro Set concept, and its continuation of expanding through new stores. Is this a better strategy than Lowe's emphasis on a single store format?

2. How can Home Depot and Lowe's go beyond what they have done to attract the female shopper without losing ground with male shoppers?

3. How would the marketing strategy differ for the Pro Set shopper as compared to that for the nonprofessional home improvement shopper at Home Depot?

Chapter Fifteen

Wholesaling and Logistics Management

After studying this chapter, you should be able to:

1 Understand wholesaling and describe the three basic categories of wholesalers.

2 Identify and discuss the roles of different types of full-service and limited-function wholesalers.

3 Explain differences among the functions of agents, brokers, and commission merchants.

4 Understand the differences between manufacturers' sales branches and offices.

5 Appreciate how slow growth rates and globalization will affect wholesaling in the future.

6 Define logistics management and explain its key role in marketing.

7 Understand logistics activities, including warehousing, materials handling, inventory control, order processing, and transporting.

8 Discuss how some of the key ethical and legal issues affect logistics.

www.grainger.com

W. W. Grainger, Inc., was founded in 1927 to meet the needs of customers who required products faster than manufacturers could deliver. Today, Grainger is a leading business-to-business wholesaler, providing over 500,000 supply products and 5 million repair parts to more than 1.5 million commercial, industrial, contractor, and institutional customers around the world. Grainger represents some of the top suppliers in the world, including companies such as Fuji, Champion, Nutone, Briggs & Stratton, General Electric, and John Deere. The company's vision statement provides direction for its business: "To be a primary source through the breadth of our offering and a focus on the lowest total cost solution for each of our customers."

Grainger serves its customers from 400 branches with 15,000 employees, 1,900 of whom are customer sales representatives. A satellite network links all of the branches and nine distribution centers. Grainger truly covers the market, with 70 percent of all U.S. businesses located within 20 minutes of a Grainger branch.

A key part of Grainger's marketing communications effort is its catalog, which lists 220,000 products. Now available on CD-ROM, Grainger's catalog reaches 2.6 million customers annually. E-commerce is also important to Grainger; online sales exceed $330 million. The company also has an online auction site and another site featuring six different companies offering thousands of products not stocked by Grainger. Only Cisco Systems, IBM, and Dell Computer Corporation sell more over the Internet.

Grainger clearly listens to its customers. The company uses surveys and focus groups to get feedback about product availability and service quality. Grainger's "No Excuses" policy empowers its employees to solve problems and ensure customer satisfaction. It has earned the trust of its customers, being named a preferred, distinguished, or select supplier for organizations such as Abbott Laboratories, Campbell Soup Company, 3M, Motorola, Tyson Foods, and Yale University.

Respect for the environment is another noteworthy aspect of Grainger's approach to business. Its catalog is printed with soy-based, nonpetroleum ink, and the color section and index are printed on recycled paper. Grainger also works with its paper suppliers to replenish natural resources; two trees are planted for every one that must be cut to print the catalog. The catalog also features many energy-saving products, identified with the "Energy Right" symbol.

The world of wholesaling, in contrast to retailing, does not often feature glamorous products. Nor are wholesaling companies part of our daily lives. Rather, it is from behind the scenes that Grainger and other leading wholesalers build value for their customers and keep the wheels of commerce rolling.

Ingram Micro is the largest global wholesaler of technology products, offering 280,000 products from 1,700 technology manufacturers.

In this chapter we discuss two key areas related to the marketing channel and the other marketing mix elements: wholesaling and logistics management. Briefly, **wholesalers** are intermediaries in the marketing channel that sell to customers other than individual or household consumers. **Logistics management** is the planning, implementation, and movement of goods, services, and related information from point of origin to point of consumption. Increasingly, logistics management involves supply-chain management and the broader term supply management, discussed in Chapter 5.

Wholesalers are often involved in all five key functions of the marketing channel: marketing communications, inventory management, physical distribution, provision of market feedback, and assumption of financial risk. Logistics management also has some relevance to those functions, but it normally relates more specifically to inventory management and physical distribution activities. Logistics is an important function for wholesalers, especially if they handle the products they are reselling.

Wholesaling

Wholesaling is an important aspect of the marketing channel strategy for many firms. It refers to the marketing activities associated with selling products to purchasers that resell the products, use them to make another product, or use them to conduct business activities. Wholesaling does not include transactions with household and individual consumers, nor does it include the small purchases businesses occasionally make from retail stores. Essentially, wholesalers sell to manufacturers and industrial customers, retailers, government agencies, other wholesalers, and institutional customers such as schools and hospitals.

We mentioned in Chapter 13 that all intermediaries in a marketing channel, including wholesalers, must justify their existence by performing at least one function better than any other channel member. For wholesalers, this often means adding value to goods and services as they pass through the channel. For example, Computer Associates, a leading software company, uses **value-added resellers (VARs)** to sell to small- and medium-sized business customers. Many of these customers do not have their own computer departments to design, implement, and maintain management information systems, so they need VARs to do it for them. Computer Associates VARs add value in many ways, including showing customers how to integrate existing systems with new technology, training customer employees, and providing technical support.

Types of Wholesalers

According to the U.S. Department of Commerce, the three basic categories of wholesalers are merchant wholesalers; agents, brokers, and commission merchants; and manufacturers' sales branches and offices. Exhibit 15–1 shows the three categories and the main types of wholesalers within each. Independent wholesalers that take title to the products they sell are called **merchant wholesalers.** Wholesalers in the second category, agents, brokers, and commission merchants, do not take title to the products bought or sold. They are sometimes referred to as *functional middlemen.* Those in the third category, manufacturers' sales branches and offices, are owned by producers or manufacturing firms.

Speaking from Experience

"We have to add value to the products we buy from manufacturers in order to justify our position in the channel. How? By being the absolute product specialist in our custom polyethylene packaging niche—the go-to-guy for our customers, by providing the largest line of custom products available in the marketplace (perhaps 20–30 times what any one single manufacturer could provide), and by buying with such clout that we are competitive even when we have to compete with other manufacturers, and by servicing our customers better than our competition."

Don Becker
Owner
Becker Marketing Services

Before founding his packaging wholesaling company, Don Becker worked in sales, product management and sales management with Procter & Gamble and Mobil Corporation. He is a graduate of Drury College in Springfield, Missouri. Don is well aware of the need for wholesalers to constantly justify their position in the marketing channel.

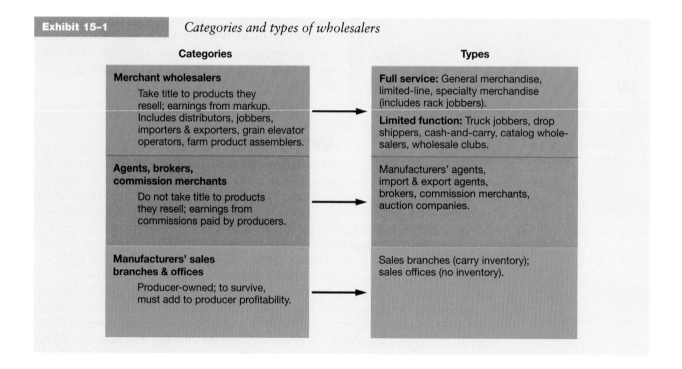

Exhibit 15–1   *Categories and types of wholesalers*

Categories	Types
Merchant wholesalers Take title to products they resell; earnings from markup. Includes distributors, jobbers, importers & exporters, grain elevator operators, farm product assemblers.	**Full service:** General merchandise, limited-line, specialty merchandise (includes rack jobbers). **Limited function:** Truck jobbers, drop shippers, cash-and-carry, catalog wholesalers, wholesale clubs.
Agents, brokers, commission merchants Do not take title to products they resell; earnings from commissions paid by producers.	Manufacturers' agents, import & export agents, brokers, commission merchants, auction companies.
Manufacturers' sales branches & offices Producer-owned; to survive, must add to producer profitability.	Sales branches (carry inventory); sales offices (no inventory).

MERCHANT WHOLESALERS According to the *Census of the Wholesale Trade,* published by the Department of Commerce, there are more than 375,000 merchant wholesalers based in the United States, accounting for 83 percent of the wholesale establishments in the country.[1] Merchant wholesalers, often called *distributors,* are categorized as either full-service wholesalers or limited-function wholesalers.

FULL-SERVICE WHOLESALERS **Full-service wholesalers** by definition perform a wide range of services for their customers and the parties from which they purchase. These wholesalers might perform all key activities in an entire marketing channel (as in Exhibit 15–2), whereas limited-function wholesalers are likely to specialize in only a few activities.

Full-service wholesalers include general merchandise, limited-line, and specialty-line wholesalers. For a better idea of services available from full-service wholesalers, see Exhibit 15–3. **General merchandise wholesalers** carry a wide variety of products and provide extensive services for their customers. A typical example is Alabama

Exhibit 15–2			*Functions performed by wholesalers*		
Type of Wholesaler	**Marketing Communications***	**Inventory Mgmt. and Storage**	**Physical Distribution**	**Market Feedback/ Advisory Board**	**Financial Risk/ Offer Credit†**
Full-service merchant wholesalers	Yes	Yes	Yes	Yes	Yes
Truck jobbers	Yes	Yes	Yes	Sometimes	Sometimes
Drop shippers	No	No	Yes	Yes	Yes
Cash and carry	No	Yes	No	Sometimes	No
Catalog wholesalers	Yes	Yes	Yes	Sometimes	Sometimes
Wholesale clubs	Sometimes	Yes	No	Sometimes	No
Mfrs.' agents	Sometimes	Sometimes	Sometimes	Yes	No
Auction companies	Yes	Sometimes	No	No	No
Import and export agents	Sometimes	Sometimes	Sometimes	Yes	No
Brokers	No	No	No	Yes	No
Commission merchants	Yes	Yes	Sometimes	Yes	Sometimes
Mfrs.' sales branches	Sometimes	Yes	Yes	Yes	Yes
Mfrs.' sales offices	Sometimes	No	No	Yes	Yes

Note: Refer to Exhibit 13–1 for multiple examples of each functional area.

*By definition, all wholesalers are involved in at least one form of marketing communications (selling).

†All wholesalers not classified as agents, brokers, or commission merchants incur financial risk when they assume ownership, or take title, to the products they subsequently resell. This exhibit refers to the financial risk taken by wholesalers that offer credit to their customers.

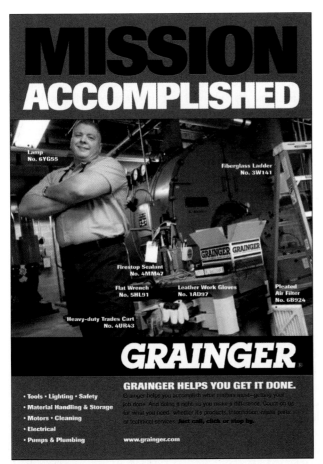

W. W. Grainger, featured in the chapter opener, uses the latest technology in its use of an electronic catalog that generates more than $330 million in annual sales.

Paper Company, which serves retail, industrial, and business customers throughout Alabama from its Birmingham warehouse. Its diverse product line, in excess of 5,000 items, includes consumer electronics, fishing and hunting merchandise, industrial adhesives and packaging materials, office supplies, and home improvement items. As a full-service wholesaler, Alabama Paper performs many marketing channel functions and provides services for its customers and their suppliers.

Limited-line wholesalers do not stock as many products as general merchandise wholesalers, but they offer more depth in their product offering. Among merchant wholesalers, **specialty-line wholesalers** carry the most narrow product assortment—usually a single product line or part of one. To justify their existence, specialty-line wholesalers must be experts on the products they sell.

Rack jobbers, a category of specialty-line wholesalers, sell to retail stores. They set up and maintain attractive store displays and stock them with goods sold on consignment (the retailer pays for the goods only when sold). Rack jobbers are also called *service merchandisers,* a term that better captures the service-oriented aspects of their roles. Retailers depend on rack jobbers particularly in the provision of health and beauty aids, hosiery, and books and magazines. Some rack jobbers might be considered limited-function wholesalers if they carry very small inventories or fail to provide other services listed in Exhibit 15–2.

Exhibit 15-3	*Services provided by full-service wholesalers/distributors*	
Distributor Services	**To Manufacturer**	**To Retailer**
Sensible buying	• Market feedback improves production planning, reducing costs of raw materials, components.	• Distributor buying clout passed on through low prices. • Dealing with only one or two wholesalers cuts purchasing costs, leads to one-stop shopping.
Distribution flow	• Reduces storage needs, moves products faster, cuts inventory costs. • Products stored closer to retailer for faster delivery; may cut need for costly distribution centers.	• Weekly deliveries reduce need for product storage, increase selling space. • Faster turnover increases profits.
Timely delivery	• Large orders, retail delivery fleets & coordinated back-haul programs reduce transportation costs, keeping product prices competitive.	• Regular deliveries permit better planning, cut receiving costs. • Fast restocking of high-demand products for immediate display.
Traffic-building promotion	• Centralized co-op programs maximize ad dollar at local level. • Increases consumer awareness, establishes products, builds market share.	• Direct-mail circulars, ads, etc., build retail traffic, increase store capabilities, save administrative effort. • Co-op programs save time, money.
Marketing	• Reduces selling costs, frees executive time as distribs serve many retail accounts; products receive wider representation.	• Retail sales training, merchandising, display, layout improve with distributor aid. • Computer systems provide price stickers, program margin requirements, optimize profits. • Hundreds of mfrs' products in one retail location.

LIMITED-FUNCTION WHOLESALERS   Exhibit 15–1 shows five primary types of **limited-function wholesalers:** truck jobbers, drop shippers, cash-and-carry wholesalers, catalog wholesalers, and wholesale clubs. As Exhibit 15–2 shows, these wholesalers do not offer the comprehensive services of full-service wholesalers.

Costco Wholesale Corporation is an international operator of Wholesale clubs with stores in North America, Asia, and the United Kingdom. Its clubs are larger than the average discount store and sell a variety of perishable and packaged food, clothing, automotive supplies, electronics, and other products.

Producers of fast-moving or perishable goods that require frequent replenishment often use **truck jobbers.** These limited-service wholesalers deliver within a particular geographic area to ensure freshness of certain goods (bakery, meat, dairy). Marketers often choose truck jobbers, with their quick delivery and frequent store visits, to wholesale miscellaneous high-margin items such as candy, chewing gum, cigarettes, novelty items, and inexpensive toys sold in retail stores. Retailers hate to be out of these items, for consumers will usually buy them at the next-most-convenient store instead.

Drop shippers arrange for shipments directly from the factory to the customer. Although they do not physically handle the product, drop shippers do take title and all associated risks while the product is in transit. They also provide the necessary sales support. Drop shippers operate in a wide variety of industries, including industrial packaging, lumber, chemicals, and petroleum and heating products.

As the term implies, **cash-and-carry wholesalers** do not deliver the products they sell, nor do they extend credit. Small retailers and other businesses whose limited sales make them unprofitable customers for larger wholesalers are the primary customers for cash-and-

Exhibit 15–3	*Services provided by full-service wholesalers/distributors (concluded)*	
Distributor Manages Assets	**Manufacturer Benefits**	**Retailer Benefits**
Product inventory	• Storage and delivery costs reduced to minimum. • Feedback on item movement improves production planning and use of assets.	• Turnover improved, promotional impact maximized, cash flow/return on investment increased. • In stock, good prices, superior service.
Physical plant	• Majority of plant used for production, not storage. • Need for regional redistribution facilities reduced or eliminated.	• More productive use of square footage ensured by lower inventory requirements, distributor printouts on product movement and margin management. • Market impact from merchandising assistance, in-store displays, signing, customer traffic flow.
Cash flow and credit	• Receivables minimized, credit risks reduced. • Administrative workload reduced.	• Cash flow accelerated through more-frequent small purchases, less cash tied up in inventory. • Best credit terms, extended dating, less paperwork.
People	• Can concentrate on manufacturing and marketing; distributors take product to market. • Concentrating on distributor customers enhances strong relationships with fewer customers.	• Selling techniques, product knowledge enhanced through distributor training, sales aids. • One-on-one contact with distributor management to seize market opportunities.

carry wholesalers. For example, cash-and-carry wholesalers are common in coastal towns, serving restaurant and grocery customers who make daily trips to the wholesaler to purchase fresh seafood.

Catalog wholesalers serve both major population centers and remote geographic locations and offer an alternative to cash-and-carry wholesalers. Most catalog wholesalers use delivery services such as UPS and require prepayment by check, money order, or credit card. Catalog wholesalers such as BrownCor International have established a large customer base by offering a wide range of competitively priced products, including office furniture, equipment and supplies, directional signs, packaging materials, and shelf and storage systems. These products can be conveniently ordered using toll-free telephone or fax systems.

Wholesale clubs are a growing phenomenon. These enterprises, which also serve retail customers under the same roof, are especially popular with small-business customers, civic and social organizations, and church groups. Wholesale club members pay an annual fee that entitles them to make tax-free purchases at lower-than-retail prices. As leaders such as Costco, BJ's Wholesale Club, and Sam's Club enjoy steady expansion, wholesale clubs are making major inroads into markets once dominated by older forms of wholesaling, such as office supply and institutional food wholesalers. They are also taking business away from certain types of retailers, such as supermarkets and tire dealers.

AGENTS, BROKERS, AND COMMISSION MERCHANTS Almost 48,000 agent, broker, and commission merchant organizations operate at the wholesale level, making up approximately 11 percent of all wholesale establishments. As Exhibit 15–1 indicates, these wholesalers do not take title to the products they resell. They perform a limited number of marketing channel activities, emphasizing sales or purchases (see Exhibit 15–2). Since these wholesalers perform so few marketing channel functions, they must be very knowledgeable and build strong relationships with their customers and suppliers to generate income through commissions.

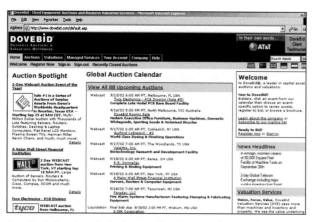

Agent wholesalers, including auction houses, do not take title to the products they sell. DoveBid is an online auction house specializing in busines-to-business auctions.

AGENTS **Manufacturers' agents,** also called manufacturers' representatives or reps, constitute the largest group in this wholesale merchant category. There are more than 29,000 manufacturers' agents in the country, all of which sell related but noncompeting product lines for manufacturers. For example, Ruddell and Associates, a San Francisco firm, sells Christmas ornaments, greeting cards, candles, books, calendars, and novelty items to gift stores, all furnished by different manufacturers. Manufacturers' agents frequently work by contract with the companies they represent; they usually have exclusive rights to represent each manufacturer within a specified geographic area.

Another type of agent is the auction company, of which there are approximately 1,300 in the United States. Auction companies, also called **auction houses,** sell merchandise at a given time and place to the highest bidder. They typically promote the sale of the merchandise through advertising that specifies the time, date, and location of the auction, along with a description of the merchandise to be sold and the auction rules.

Auction houses are a popular way to sell livestock, tobacco, used automobiles, and art and antiques. Famous art auctioneers are Sotheby's, Phillips, and Christie's, where works by noted artists sometimes fetch millions of dollars. Both the London-based Christie's and the New York–based Sotheby's are expanding into new international markets and searching for ways to further use the Internet for live auctions. An **online auction company** uses a computer network, typically the Internet to bring buyers and sellers together. Online auction companies typically charge a nominal listing fee and collect a 5 percent commission on goods sold.

The explosive growth of online auction sites is having a significant impact on wholesaling. Previously, online auction sites were dominated by person-to-person and business-to-person transactions. However, the business-to-business sector, including wholesaling, is showing signs of rapid growth. The leading online auction company, eBay, offers thousands of products at wholesale in large quantities. Books, computers, clothing, jewelry, tools, office supplies, toys, and electronics are just a few of the categories available at wholesale on eBay. To better service large-volume transactions, eBay has partnered with Accenture, a leading consulting and technology services organization, to provide sellers with value-added services, including sales strategy development, enhanced customer service, and improved logistical support.[2] eBay has also teamed up with Sotheby's to auction fine art online, a move that will allow Sotheby's to streamline its operation and reach a larger online market.[3]

Online auction houses have established a strong presence in the sale of surplus equipment and other capital assets. DoveBid, a leading auction company in this sector, has handled the disposition of surplus goods for major corporations around the world, including Bank of America, IBM, Motorola, General Electric, and Xerox.[4] Both buyers and sellers like the large market reach of online auctions, and buyers especially like the idea of getting a bargain through the auction process. For sellers, the prospect of getting a fair market price for no longer needed or wanted merchandise is appealing. Further, online auctions are frequently a faster alternative for buyers compared to researching the market and finding a vendor. With technology constantly improving and easy access becoming more commonplace, expect online auctions to continue to grow in popularity.

Two other types of agents, import and export, specialize in international trade. **Import agents**—approximately 600 in the United States—find products in foreign countries to sell in their home countries. For example, cut flowers, available at lower cost outside the United States, are flown into the country daily. On a typical day, import agents arrange air cargo shipments from the Netherlands and South

America to bring tulips, carnations, and roses to the United States. In many countries, it is extremely difficult (or even illegal) to try to sell products from another country without going through an import agent or similar intermediary.

On the other hand, **export agents** locate and develop markets abroad for products manufactured in their home countries. Basically, they function as manufacturers' agents in the home country and are paid commissions by the companies they represent. There are more than 1,200 export agents in the United States. Export agents offer several advantages for companies seeking new markets, especially smaller companies. They offer exporters an opportunity to increase market exposure and sales volume with very little financial investment or risk.

BROKERS   Brokers are intermediaries that bring buyers and sellers together. They are paid a commission by either the buyer or the seller, depending on which party they represent in a given transaction. Unlike manufacturers' agents, brokers do not enter into contracts for extended periods with the parties they represent. Instead, they work on a transaction-by-transaction basis. There are approximately 8,600 wholesale broker firms in the United States, many of them in food and agricultural businesses.

COMMISSION MERCHANTS   Commission merchants provide a wider range of services than agents or brokers, often engaging in inventory management, physical distribution, and promotional activities, and offering credit and market feedback to the companies they represent. More than 6,700 commission merchants operate in the United States, primarily working to sell agricultural products for farmers.

MANUFACTURERS' SALES BRANCHES AND OFFICES   More than 29,000 manufacturer-owned wholesalers operate in the United States. Approximately 58 percent of these, or 17,000, are **manufacturers' sales branches,** which maintain inventory and perform a wide range of functions for the parent company. Manufacturers' sales branches handle delivery and act as an extension of the manufacturer to provide credit, market feedback, and promotional assistance.

Manufacturers' sales offices are the other significant type of producer-owned wholesaler, with more than 12,000 outlets in the United States. Sales offices do not maintain inventory, but they perform a limited range of functions, including assisting with sales and service, providing market feedback, and handling billing and collection of products sold.

Developments in Wholesaling

Three developments in wholesaling deserve special attention: the continuing struggle to grow, the globalization of wholesaling, and the increasing emphasis on developing relationships with others in the marketing channel.

WHOLESALERS FACE SLOW GROWTH   Wholesalers play an important role in the world economy, but growth is difficult to achieve. As power retailers such as Kroger, Office Depot, and Wal-Mart take over a larger share of the retail market, there has been an associated increase in retailers' buying directly from manufacturers, thus eliminating wholesalers.

Wholesalers' positions in markets served by retailers could grow even more precarious. Industry observers see power in the channel continuing to shift toward retailers. As shown in Exhibit 15–4, chains, wholesalers, and manufacturers generally agree that power is shifting in the grocery industry. Wholesalers are split on which way the power is shifting—23 percent say toward retailers, 48 percent say manufacturers. The point is that wholesalers are caught in a crossfire between retailers and manufacturers, with both sectors eager to improve their own profitability.

Other circumstances have threatened wholesalers, including a move to reduce overall health care costs. This puts pressure on a wide variety of wholesalers to reduce their costs; in addition, sales growth is decreasing as hospitals and other health

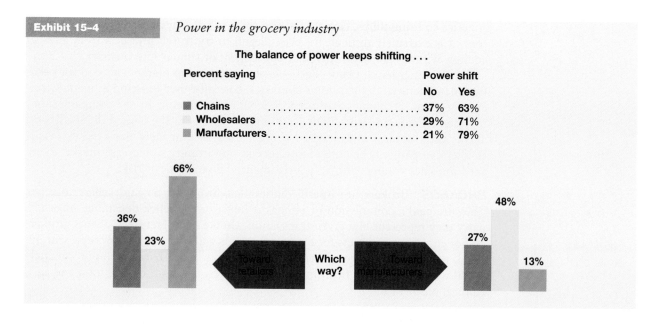

Exhibit 15-4   *Power in the grocery industry*

The balance of power keeps shifting . . .

Percent saying		Power shift	
		No	Yes
■ Chains	....	37%	63%
■ Wholesalers	....	29%	71%
■ Manufacturers	....	21%	79%

66%

36%

23%

◄ Toward retailers

Which way?

Toward manufacturers ►

48%

27%

13%

Thinking Critically

Brothers Office Supply is a traditional office-supply company, operating in a midwestern college town of 100,000. In addition to office supplies, Brothers sells high-quality office furniture. The company also sells calculators and electronic organizers, but it does not sell computers. Brothers' primary target market has been small- and medium-sized companies. Business was good until Sam's Club opened a store nearby last year. Rumor has it that Office Depot will open within the coming year.

• How can Brothers Office Supply compete with these lower-priced competitors?

care facilities are trying to reduce their usage of supplies and delaying major purchases, more so than in the past. Travel agents have also felt the pressure, with airlines and rental car companies cutting their commissions. Further, traditional wholesalers are facing more competition from transportation and distribution companies that are expanding the scope of their operations by offering services traditionally performed by wholesalers.

Wholesalers have taken several steps to combat tough market conditions. Some have grown through acquisition of other wholesalers, and others have expanded into retailing. Supervalu, the largest food and grocery wholesaler, has done both with its acquisition of another large wholesaler, Wetterau, and by operating its own stores under various names, including Cub Foods, bigg's, Farm Fresh, Scott's, and Shop'n Save. Many others, including Fleming, are expanding into international markets and focusing on building customer value through stronger relationships with customers and suppliers.

GLOBALIZATION OF WHOLESALING   In response to tougher conditions in domestic markets, many American wholesalers have moved into international markets. Office Depot, which serves both retail and wholesale customers, has aggressively expanded its wholesale operations in international markets. It acquired Viking Office Products, a catalog and Internet wholesaler, to gain more coverage in seven European countries, Japan, and Australia. Office Depot is further expanding its international reach through its Business Services Division. In a dozen European countries it has established its own salesforce to develop new business on a contract basis with large corporate accounts.[5] The Business Services Division can work more on an individual basis with major customers, offering them customized pricing and tailored logistics programs rather than the standard offerings available in the store, on the Internet, or from a catalog.

As U.S. wholesalers become more prominent in international trade, they are following a pattern of development shown in Exhibit 15–5. This pattern suggests that international wholesalers play an important role in servicing the needs of a country with a simple economy. As the country's economy reaches the advanced stage, however, the role of conventional wholesalers becomes less important. Finally, when the country becomes part of a global economy, international wholesalers reemerge as an important element in the economic system. The United States, along with its primary trading partners, is part of a growing global economy, a factor that may help wholesalers maintain or expand their base of business.

| Exhibit 15–5 | *Cyclical wholesaling patterns by stages of economic development* |

Stages of Economic Development	Wholesaling Patterns
Simple economy	Dominance of international wholesalers (channels controlled by all-purpose wholesale merchants)
Expanding economy	Emergence of interregional wholesalers (regional specialization)
Maturing economy	Growth of specialized wholesalers (product-line and functional specialization)
Advanced economy	Decline of conventional wholesalers and regrouping by wholesalers (channels controlled by large-scale retailers and manufacturers)
Global economy	Reemergence of international wholesalers

RELATIONSHIPS IN WHOLESALING   Many wholesalers are turning to partnerships with suppliers and customers to strengthen their market positions. Exemplifying the partnership approach is the highly successful Ingram Micro Inc., a large wholesale distributor of computer products. Ingram has designed storefront Web sites for the value-added resellers in its national distribution network that buy through Ingram. These Web sites feature the VARs' own brand. Customers who access the VAR sites see Ingram's enormous inventory, wide range of services, and 24-hour delivery system. To the customer, the full scope of the local VAR's offering, as supplemented by Ingram, is readily apparent. The local VAR gets the credibility of a major corporation without the high overhead.[6]

Manufacturers are also finding that partnering with wholesalers can pay off. Square D, the North American division of electrical industry leader Schneider Electric, generates 85 percent of its sales revenue through 2,000 North American wholesalers. Square D partners with its wholesalers, which are typically small and lacking big budgets, to provide training. The self-paced training program includes CD-ROMs, videos, and workbooks to teach sales skills and product knowledge to distributor personnel. The program is a huge success, with 96 percent of the participating wholesalers indicating that the training has had a positive impact on business. This pays off with increased sales for Square D, a company that sees its dealers as a competitive edge.[7]

Don Becker, owner of Becker Marketing Services, Inc., fully understands the importance of strong relationships with suppliers and customers: "It's only natural that there will be some friction and conflict in a marketing channel. As a wholesaler, my company is often caught in the middle, with the supplier pushing me in one direction and the customer pulling me in another. Our people have been able to establish strong relationships with most of our customers and suppliers. When it looks like we're heading for a major disagreement, I remind customers and suppliers that we are in this together, and that everybody has to benefit. Sometimes, I'll sacrifice, sometimes the customer compromises, and sometimes the supplier has to pitch in something extra—all for the good of the long-term relationship."

Logistics Management

Logistics management, as defined at the beginning of the chapter, deals with the movement of goods, services, and related information from point of origin to point of consumption. The importance of logistics management has increased in today's environment, marked by the use of speed as a competitive edge (to deliver customers' orders, for example), development of exciting new computer technologies, and increased realization that overall operating costs are extremely sensitive to the various costs of handling and holding inventory.

In progressive companies, logistics management has moved far beyond shipping and receiving to become a differentiating factor in marketing strategy. Logistics is instrumental in meeting such challenges as increasing responsiveness to customers,

Logistics management relies on a variety of methods for moving products and materials, including cargo planes and oceangoing supertankers. In some cases, simple means of transportation are used, such as with these UPS motorcycles in Brussels and this dogsled for newspaper delivery in North Dakota.

maintaining market position, stemming price erosion, and maintaining competitiveness in domestic and international markets. Consumers and business buyers are increasingly saying "I want it now!" More and more marketers are providing quality products at competitive prices. But that is not enough unless the product is available at the right time in the right place. As electronic commerce becomes more prevalent, marketers face the challenge of developing new logistics systems to deal directly with customers rather than always relying on wholesalers and traditional retail stores for distribution. Technology is a key element in meeting this challenge, as illustrated in "Using Technology: TaylorMade-adidas Turns on Tech."

Importance of Logistics to Marketing

The drive to enhance customer satisfaction while simultaneously improving productivity and profitability has put logistics in the spotlight in the marketing efforts of many successful firms. Amazon.com, for example, completed its long journey to profitability by revamping its logistics system. Through better sales forecasting, Amazon cut its inventory levels by 18 percent, thus cutting carrying costs. The company also revamped its storage system, reducing the number of items that were stored in wrong locations. This helped the company ship 35 percent more units than in the previous year without increasing the number of warehouse workers. This resulted in a 22 percent cut in the cost of filling orders, even as sales grew by 15 percent. Amazon's other key move in the logistics area was to consolidate shipments into full trucks driven to specific cities, thereby bypassing the cost of routing shipments through regional postal-sorting facilities. This move saved Amazon additional millions of dollars that transferred directly to the bottom line, putting the company in the black for the first time.[8]

The logistics system should be as economical as possible while achieving an acceptable level of customer satisfaction. To keep customers satisfied, a logistics system should be easy to use and dependable and offer timely information. These attributes are detailed in Exhibit 15–6.

Key Activities in Logistics

Logistics includes five key functions: warehousing, materials handling, inventory control, order processing, and transporting raw materials and finished products from origin to destination. In the best logistics systems, these areas are carefully coordinated to gain customer satisfaction at an affordable cost.

WAREHOUSING   Companies can choose private or public warehouses or distribution centers. *Private warehouses* are operated by the company using the ware-

| **Exhibit 15-6** | *Customer expectations of suppliers' logistics systems* |

- Timely pickups for outgoing orders
- On-time delivery
- Prompt settlement of claims for damaged or lost merchandise
- Accurate invoicing
- Interactive Web site for tracking and customer service
- Well-trained drivers and customer support staff
- Process for analyzing and correcting service failures
- Centralized, accessible customer service
- Good communication with customers
- Responsiveness from all supplier departments

house. *Public warehouses* are for-hire facilities available to any business requiring storage or handling of goods. Public warehouses charge fees for storage and handling (receiving and moving goods out of storage).[9]

Distribution centers are superwarehouses that serve a large geographic area. These automated warehouses do more than store products; they receive, process, and ship customer orders. Technological advances have allowed companies to save money and provide better service through distribution centers. Among the many companies using distribution centers are manufacturers such as Nike, Komatsu Dresser (heavy equipment), and Troll Associates (children's books), and retailers such as 50-Off Stores, Athlete's Foot, Williams-Sonoma, Wal-Mart, McCrory Stores, and General Motors.

With the increased volume of online buying, many companies are utilizing distribution centers that specialize in e-commerce. Warehouses designed for e-commerce differ than those designed for distributing consumer goods to retail stores. E-commerce warehouses are designed to pick and ship individual items to customers in a wide geographic area, whereas traditional warehousing for retail stores typically distributes large quantities of a given item in palletized truckload or railcar shipments. The demise of many e-retailers in the early part of this decade opened up a lot of available warehousing capacity, but prospective users had to consider whether the storage, stock picking, and conveyor systems would be compatible with their needs. In some cases, the fit matched, and companies were able to add warehousing at bargain prices. Such was the case with KB Toy Stores, which acquired a 440,000-square-foot distribution center from the bankrupt eToys.com. KB uses the center to supplement its distribution system for its online division.[10]

Using Technology

TaylorMade-adidas turns on tech

TaylorMade-adidas Golf is one of the key players in the highly competitive golf club industry. The industry is characterized by a steady stream of new technologies and innovations as golfers perpetually strive to hit the ball longer and straighter. In this industry, it is important to clear out the old inventory and have the new models readily available. Otherwise, the retailer and the ultimate consumer may choose a competing brand.

TaylorMade-adidas chose a software application from i2 that allowed it to link suppliers, distributors, and retailers to TaylorMade's production and marketing operations. Managing inventory depends in large part on accurate sales forecasting. With the support of i2, TaylorMade was able to improve forecasting accuracy, thus reducing back orders to distributors and retailers. The company was also able to transport raw materials to production facilities with greater efficiency, double the rate of its inventory turnover, reduce markdowns and write-offs, and increase positive communication with its retailers and distributors. By having a better handle on inventory planning, order fulfillment, and shipping, TaylorMade expects to generate $50 million in cost savings and added value over a three-year period for members of its supply chain. The end consumer will benefit as well, with full information, including an interactive Web site, to assist the customer in three purchase venues: online, on the phone, or in a retail store.

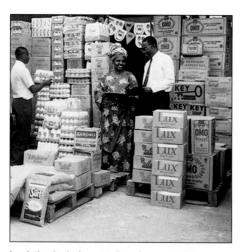

Logistics includes warehousing, materials handling, inventory control, order processing, and transporting products to customers. This Unilever facility conducts all of the major logistical functions for retail customers in Nigeria.

MATERIALS HANDLING   Materials-handling activities include receiving, identifying, sorting, and storing products, and retrieving the goods for shipment. The use of technology is extremely important in this area of logistics. Bar coding is among the most noteworthy of the technological advances in materials handling, particularly in distribution centers. **Bar coding,** which allows a product to be identified by its computer-coded bar pattern, is used in a variety of logistics functions. Big Dog Logistics uses bar coding as an integral part of its systems for servicing a wide range of clients, including publishing companies, pharmaceutical companies, retailers, and transportation companies. Bar codes facilitate warehousing, sorting, and shipping functions in a mobile network of cell phones, personal data appliances such as the Palm Pilot, and two-way radios. The bar codes allow accurate tracking of shipments and inventory assessment as products move through the supply chain.[11]

A radio frequency identification (RFID) may eventually replace bar codes. Introduced in Chapter 14 (refer to Using Technology: Are Talking Chips the Next Big Thing?), RFID allows the printing of radio antennas that can be affixed to products in place of a bar code. The advantage is that an entire container of diverse items could be scanned instantly at a distance, rather than up close and one item at a time, as is the case with bar codes. The application of RFID to warehousing, order processing, and shipping seems inevitable now that costs for producing the radio tags are declining. Wal-Mart and Home Depot are among the most enthusiastic backers of RFID, with Wal-Mart already using the technology to track Coca-Cola, Bounty paper towels, and Gillette's Mach 3 razors through Sam's Club.[12]

INVENTORY CONTROL   Another key area of logistics is inventory control, which attempts to ensure adequate inventory to meet customer needs without incurring additional costs for carrying excess stock. Two such inventory control systems are in place in many industries: just-in-time and quick-response systems. Rarely used before 1990, these systems are now commonplace.

Just-in-time (JIT) inventory control systems apply primarily to the materials-handling side of logistics. These systems deliver raw materials, subassemblies, and component parts to manufacturers shortly before the scheduled manufacturing run that will consume the incoming shipment, thus the JIT label. Automobile manufacturers are among the most enthusiastic users of JIT systems, and suppliers often locate manufacturing or distribution facilities near automobile plants to provide prompt service at a reasonable cost.

Don Becker, owner of Becker Marketing Services, Inc., comments on the JIT process: "In the years I have had my own company, as a middleman (broker) selling to other middlemen (stocking wholesale distributors), it has been very important for us to select and sell our products to wholesale distributors that believe in buying in large quantities (of custom produced product), and providing JIT to their customers, the end users. By JIT, I mean the end user customer calling for an order and the wholesale distributor delivering the order in one hour, if necessary. By our linking ourselves to the right distributor, we have been able to build a large business satisfying hundreds of end user customers."

Quick-response (QR) inventory control systems are used by companies that provide retailers with finished goods. Quick-response systems are based on frequent but small orders, since inventory is restocked according to what has just been sold—yesterday, or even today in some systems. By melding strategy and technology, retailers such as Wal-Mart, Kmart, and Dillard's have matched up with vendors like Procter & Gamble, Gitano, and baby-clothes manufacturer Warren Featherstone to improve both responsiveness to the marketplace and productivity. Exhibit 15–7 describes the key steps required to implement a QR system.

Exhibit 15-7	*Key activities in quick-response systems*

- Retailers track sales and inventory for each item (stock-keeping unit).
- Automatic replenishment systems monitor stock to support smaller, more frequent shipments.
- Retailers assume responsibility for inventory carrying costs.
- Vendors commit to high level of service, stressing shipping accuracy and on-time delivery.
- Retailers share data with vendors to help plan production and commit to specific volume of purchases.
- Vendors mark shipping containers to speed delivery through distribution center to stores.

Thinking Critically

Jean Robbins is a sales representative for Cribben Paper and Plastics Supply Company, a wholesaler to the garment manufacturing industry. One of Jean's customers is a large Arrow shirt manufacturing plant. The plant buys preprinted bags in which the shirts will be displayed and sold in retail stores. Cribben maintains a stock of the shirts in its warehouse and ships to Arrow on a JIT basis. Recently, the plant manager has threatened to buy directly from the bag manufacturer in truckload quantities, approximately 1,000 cases, or a month's supply. He claims he can get the bags at a 20 percent discount by buying direct.

- What should Jean do to keep her business with Arrow?

Participants in quick-response systems must join together in a logistics partnership. A true partnership is necessary because buyers and sellers share sensitive information and must maintain constant communication. In fact, QR systems require so much information exchange that they take massive investments to implement. Bar coding and point-of-retail-sale scanning devices are needed. **Shipping container marking (SCM)** systems must be installed so tracking information can be fed into a computerized information system. This system is referred to as an **electronic data interchange (EDI)**.

EDIs are becoming increasingly popular for firms operating in global markets. For example, Xicor, Inc., a California-based computer circuit manufacturer with about 60 percent of its sales outside the United States, developed an EDI system to better meet the needs of its customers, including IBM, Samsung, Motorola, and Alcatel. Around the world, Xicor uses independent salespeople and distributors who need real-time information about product availability and shipping status. Xicor's EDI system bypasses regional and local offices in favor of a centralized location for all data utilized in the system. The system allows trading partners, salespeople, and end-user customers to coordinate production and shipping, saving Xicor time and money and virtually eliminating the possibility of inventory management mistakes.[13]

As EDI becomes more popular, progressive companies are trying to move beyond linked systems to those that can run on the Internet. Cost savings can be substantial, and access is available with a PC and an Internet connection. Home Depot, Office Depot, and Barnes & Noble are among those making extensive use of Web-based EDI. Barnes & Noble, for example, uses Web-based EDI for about 1,200 of its 30,000 suppliers. Those using the Web-based version of EDI tend to be Barnes & Noble's largest suppliers, while smaller publishers use traditional EDI.[14] The growth of Web-based EDI is promising, yet traditional EDI with direct communication between companies' computers is expected to remain a significant means of conducting business for years to come.[15]

With a true partnership agreement, technology such as electronic data interchanges, and other resources such as personnel and training, QR systems offer the potential benefits shown in Exhibit 15–8.

Although JIT and QR systems offer impressive advantages, they can present drawbacks as well. Heightened security on shipments, particularly those coming from foreign countries, has slowed shipments and jeopardized production schedules of manufacturers that use JIT. Most major U.S. automakers have been affected, causing them to scale back production and even close plants. Ford, for example, closed five factories and cut production 13 percent in response to slower shipments from Mexico, Japan, and Europe. With no extra inventory on hand for key parts, Ford had little choice but to close plants once the delays set in.[16] Ford's ordeal serves as a reminder that marketers are never completely insulated from inventory control problems, whatever the technological advances. Cautious marketers may shun quick-response systems in favor of carrying extra inventory, at a cost.

| **Exhibit 15–8** | *Potential benefits of quick-response inventory control* |

- Reduced negotiating costs for both buyer and seller.
- Increased responsiveness to marketplace needs.
- Stability of supply to the buyer and demand to the seller.
- Smoothing of production runs (fewer peaks and valleys).
- Decreased investment in inventory and storage space.
- Fewer out-of-stock occurrences.
- Higher levels of customer satisfaction.

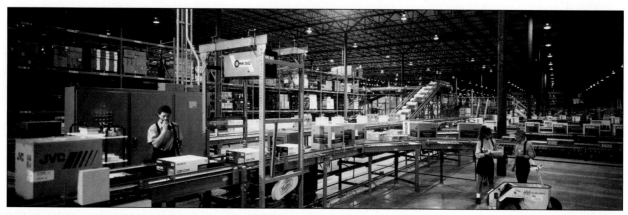

This distribution center in St. Louis, Missouri, features bar-code scanners for routing orders through an automated system that selects the items to be shipped, prints the customer invoice and sends the products to the shipping docks.

ORDER PROCESSING   Order-processing activities are critical to ensure that customers get what they order, when they want it, properly billed, and with appropriate service to support its use or installation. Accuracy and timeliness are key goals of order-entry processes. QR and JIT systems automatically handle order-processing activities. In other situations, order processing includes order entry, order handling, and scheduling for delivery. The term *order* here refers either to a customer's purchase order or to an order transmitted by a salesperson. Order handling entails procedures such as communicating the order to the shipping department or warehouse, clearing the order for shipping, or scheduling it for production. Eventually, the order is selected from stock, packaged, and scheduled for delivery. The order documentation becomes part of the customer's file of transactions with the seller. See Appendix B for mathematical calculations related to the determination of order quantities.

TRANSPORTING   The final logistics activity we consider in this chapter is transporting, which starts with selecting modes of transportation for delivery of products or materials. Shippers have five basic ways to move products and materials from one point to another—rail, truck, air, pipeline, and water transport—and each has its advantages and disadvantages. Logistics managers must assess each mode for costs, reliability, capacity, ability to deliver to customer receiving facilities, transit time, and special handling requirements such as refrigeration and temperature control, safety controls, and the capacity to deliver undamaged goods.

RAILROADS   Railroads carry approximately 40 percent of all U.S. freight, most of which is heavyweight, bulk cargoes. Railcars are the major shipping mode for coal, grain, chemicals, metallic

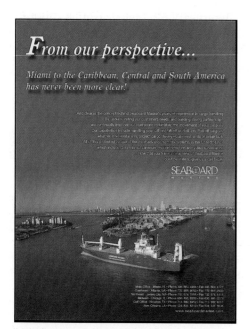

Creating and continuously enhancing customer value is a key focus of logistics companies. In this ad, Seaboard Marine stresses its understanding of customer needs, including providing enhanced security for all shipments.

ores, stone, sand, and gravel. Two-thirds of the automobiles manufactured in the United States move at least part of the way to dealerships on railroads.[17]

Rail transport is fairly reliable but subject to interruption due to periodic labor disputes. These interruptions are usually short, and the federal government has often intervened to prevent massive shutdowns of rail service.

In recent years, the railroad industry has undergone a major consolidation, with several mergers between large rail companies. Since this wave of mergers began in the late 1990s, shippers have complained about shipping delays and poor customer service from railroad companies. Some industry analysts predict that the mergers will not be good for shippers, as the rail companies may approach monopoly status and thus not feel a need to improve service. This remains to be seen, and some industry analysts predict that service will begin to improve now that the major wave of mergers has swept through the industry.[18]

TRUCKS Trucks can deliver almost anywhere, particularly important for customers that lack a rail siding. Their fairly fast transit time makes trucks extremely effective and efficient for delivery to destinations within 500 miles. Although generally reliable, trucks can be negatively affected by inclement weather. Trucking has also been hampered at times by labor strikes, more so than have railroads.

Technology, especially in mobile communications and tracking equipment, plays an important role for successful trucking companies such as Roadway Express, J. B. Hunt, and M. S. Carriers. The human factor is important too. From a marketing point of view, the top priority for most trucking firms is recruiting, training, and retaining drivers. Considering the role that logistics can play in increasing customer satisfaction and profitability, trucking firms should emphasize hiring dependable drivers who can enhance customer relationships. With the increasing need for home delivery from e-retailers, and the expectation that the world economy will grow at least moderately in coming years, there is little doubt that a shortage of qualified truck drivers will continue to be a major concern for trucking firms. The results of a poll conducted by the Gallup Organization for the American Trucking Association suggests that trucking companies should look to hire more females, as the traditional source of truck drivers, males in their twenties, will grow more slowly than job openings through 2005.[19]

Trucking companies face more competition, primarily from railroads, on long-haul trips than on short-haul trips. For an example of how one entrepreneur has carved a niche in the short-haul business, see "Being Entrepreneurial: Heartland Express Does Details."

Being Entrepreneurial

Heartland Express does details

Russell Gerdin, CEO of trucking company Heartland Express, is a fanatic about the rather dull details of the trucking business. He studies mileage, revenue per mile, and deadhead trips, those where the trucks are rolling without any cargo on board. Mr. Gerdin immerses himself in detailed data so that he can keep the company focused on what it does best—making short-haul delivery trips of 500 miles or less. Shunning the long-haul business, Mr. Gerdin refuses to bid on longer trips, even for Sears, its top customer. According to Mr. Gerdin, "They can get somebody to do it cheaper. But they can't get the short-haul freight done any cheaper."

To offer the most competitive rates in the short-haul market, Heartland Express focuses relentlessly on its operating costs. It has the lowest costs-to-revenues ratio in the industry, slightly edging out key competitor Knight Transportation, but having a substantially lower operating cost than all other competitors. With costs averaging 82.5 percent of revenues, Heartland executives must make every run for each of its 2,000 trucks as efficient as possible to maintain its healthy profit margins. At the same time, Heartland must meet or exceed customer expectations in this highly competitive market. By tending to the details, the company has succeeded at doing both. It is twice as profitable as most trucking firms, and Sears selected Heartland from its 10,000 vendors for its highest quality award, the first time a transportation company had won the award. Georgia Pacific also named Heartland its carrier of the year.

AIR FREIGHT   Air freight is tops in speed but highest in transportation cost. Sometimes air freight is an integral part of a company's operations, as with catalog businesses or firms marketing perishable items from faraway destinations, such as Maine lobster delivered to seafood restaurants in California. The air freight business is experiencing little growth, with the average air freight volume of FedEx and UPS, the dominant air shippers, dropping for more than a year. Interestingly, FedEx and UPS are partly responsible for their own decline in air shipping, as both companies have made significant upgrades to their ground shipping alternatives. With improved delivery from their trucks, FedEx and UPS are finding that many customers simply do not see the value in paying more for air shipments. Another factor working against air shippers is increased airport security, especially if shipments are going into the cargo hold of a commercial flight. As global trade increases, air shipping will benefit. For domestic deliveries, however, overnight shipping, the key service offered by FedEx, UPS, and Airborne, is not expected to return to its days as a growth business.[20]

PIPELINES   Pipelines, such as the Alaska Pipeline, transport chemicals, gases, liquefied fossil fuels, and petroleum products. They offer fairly low-cost, reliable transportation to a limited number of destinations. Although the operation of a pipeline uses little energy, pipeline construction arouses environmental concerns about the land under which the line must travel.

WATER   Water transport is a good, low-cost alternative for large quantities of bulky products that must be shipped long distances. This includes bulk shipments of agricultural products, automobiles to and from foreign countries, and petroleum from distant oil-producing nations.

In the United States, water transport is available primarily in the eastern part of the country. The Mississippi River carries a large proportion of the country's water transport, and other rivers serve Cincinnati and Chicago. Rivers are also shipping routes for large amounts of cargo along the Gulf Coast between New Orleans and Houston, and between the Pacific Ocean and Portland, Oregon.

In the Great Lakes region, freighters carry huge shipments of raw materials—such as iron ore to Detroit—to service the automobile manufacturing industry. Other destinations served via the Great Lakes include Milwaukee, Buffalo, Chicago, and Toronto. The St. Lawrence Seaway, stretching from Lake Ontario to Montreal, can handle both barge traffic and oceangoing vessels. This project was jointly financed by the United States and Canada, with Canada providing approximately three-fourths of the necessary funds.

INTERMODAL   Although one mode of transportation may get the job done for a given shipper, **intermodal shipping** is often the choice. This involves the use of two or more modes of transportation. Loaded trailers, for example, may travel piggyback on railcars or in "stack trains."

Large retailers, including Home Depot, JCPenney, Gart Sporting Goods, and Target, receive goods that are shipped by intermodal means. This method is particularly well suited for shipments that originate in distant locations. For example, U.S. retailers receiving goods from Asia might best be served by a combination of water, rail, and truck delivery to move the product from point of origin to in-store locations.

The outlook for intermodal shipping is fairly positive, as the right combination of transportation modes can optimize costs versus speed and other service considerations. The increased size of the Panama Canal will also contribute to the growth in intermodal shipping, as will increased growth in international trade.[21]

Both the relationship and global perspectives are illustrated with YFM Direct, a strategic alliance between Yellow Freight System and Royal Mass Group of The Netherlands. YFM provides truck delivery of trans-Atlantic shipments throughout North America and Western Europe.

Ethical and Legal Issues in Logistics

The legal environment for logistics is shaped by thousands of local, state, national, and international laws, tax codes, and tariff regulations that govern the movement of materials and products. The Interstate Commerce Commission, Federal Maritime Commission, and Department of Transportation are the major U.S. regulatory agencies.

The **deregulation** of transportation industries that began in the 1970s sought to promote free competition among carriers. Over the past three decades, many marginal transportation providers that engaged in unethical and/or inefficient practices have disappeared from the scene. Generally speaking, deregulation helped to reward companies that strive for high levels of customer satisfaction, facilitated the move to expand internationally, and encouraged the development of solid business relationships based on both economics and trust between parties.

An emphasis on ethical considerations remains an important aspect of logistics management. This is readily apparent with safety issues. Recent events have led to more vigilance over products as they move through the supply chain, and there is an important need for cooperation between government agencies, shippers, receivers, and law enforcement agencies to minimize the risk to employees and the general public. Both shippers and receivers must be patient while enduring delays due to more inspections of cargo. For example, a Nike spokesperson says, "We're a partner in the voyage and there is a cost associated with implementing cargo security screening."[22] Companies can benefit from cooperating with government agencies and law enforcement personnel to meet security regulations. Some, such as Liz Claiborne, have earned a "low risk" designation from U.S. Customs, meaning that their shipments are subjected to minimal delay on the way into the United States. There are only 150 such companies in the United States.[23] In addition to the concerns of what may happen to cargo while in transit, other safety issues include the use of oversized truck trains, trucking rigs pulling two 28-foot trailers, and working conditions for operators. In the trucking and water transportation industries, operator fatigue has been a long-standing safety issue. As the trucking industry grows faster than the highway infrastructure, traffic congestion is a growing concern for safety and air-quality reasons. Such issues raise ethical and legal questions.

Shippers have a responsibility to protect their employees and the general public from unsafe practices and materials. It is obvious that some materials such as explosives or corrosive chemicals would require special handling; but other less-obvious products might also pose dangers. Ignorance or negligence can be costly, as in the deadly 1996 Value Jet airlines crash, which was caused by improper shipping of oxygen tanks.

As logistics managers and wholesalers face the future, they must surely see the exciting prospect of playing an ever-increasing critical role in marketing. Change and adaptation will be necessary for survival of individual firms, and the management of information will play a key role for survivors. But wholesalers and logistics managers have tremendous technology at their disposal and can remain strong links in the chain that ultimately delivers customer satisfaction, profitability, and success.

Summary

1. Understand wholesaling and describe the three basic categories of wholesalers. An important part of marketing, wholesaling refers to the activities associated with selling products to purchasers that resell the products, use them to make another product, or use them to conduct business activities.

The three basic categories of wholesalers are merchant wholesalers; agents, brokers, and commission merchants; and manufacturers' sales branches and offices. Some of these wholesalers provide a wide range of services, while others offer a narrow range of specialized services.

2. Identify and discuss the roles of different types of full-service and limited-function wholesalers. There are three main types of full-service wholesalers: general merchandise, limited-line, and specialty-line wholesalers. Of these, general merchandise wholesalers carry the broadest assortment of products and provide extensive services to their customers. These services may involve promotional assistance, inventory management and storage, physical distribution, market feedback, assumption of financial risk, and offering of credit.

The two others carry progressively smaller and more-specialized assortments and provide different levels of service. Limited-function wholesalers include truck jobbers, drop shippers, cash-and-carry wholesalers, catalog wholesalers, and wholesale clubs. Of these, catalog wholesalers and wholesale clubs showed the most growth in recent years.

3. Explain differences among the functions of agents, brokers, and commission merchants. Agents, brokers, and commission merchants concentrate on making sales or purchases. They do not take title to the products they resell. These types of wholesalers must be quite knowledgeable in order to develop strong relationships with their customers and suppliers. They are paid a commission, a percentage of the value of each completed sale or purchase.

4. Understand the differences between manufacturers' sales branches and offices. Manufacturers' sales branches maintain inventory, handle delivery, and act as an extension of the manufacturer for a wide variety of services. Manufacturers' sales offices offer a narrower range of services, primarily because they do not maintain inventory.

5. Appreciate how slow growth rates and globalization will affect wholesaling in the future. Slow growth rates in most developed economies are putting a significant amount of pressure on wholesalers, which often face declining profit margins. As large retail chains gain more power and increase direct purchases from manufacturers, wholesalers can expect tough operating conditions to continue.

To cope with slow growth, wholesalers often enter into relationships with manufacturers, customers, and in some cases, other wholesalers. Global markets offer more potential of growth for some wholesalers. As trade between nations becomes easier, wholesalers will have opportunities that have been difficult to realize in the past. Further, as developing economies grow, wholesalers that have the capability to conduct business outside the domestic marketplace can benefit by supplying them.

6. Define logistics management and explain its key role in marketing. Logistics management describes the planning, implementing, and controlling of the movement of goods, services, and related information from point of origin to point of consumption. In recent years, logistics management has grown more important in overall marketing strategies, because customer satisfaction is greatly affected by factors such as responsiveness to special shipping requirements and condition of delivered merchandise.

7. Understand logistics activities, including warehousing, materials handling, inventory control, order processing, and transporting. Some firms use independently owned public warehouses; others operate their own private warehouses or distribution centers. Materials-handling activities include receiving, identifying, sorting, storing, and retrieving goods for shipment. Inventory control is used to meet customer stock requirements without incurring excessive costs of carrying inventory. Just-in-time and quick-response systems are examples of inventory control programs used in a wide variety of industries.

Order processing, triggered by the customer's purchase order, includes order entry, order handling, and delivery scheduling. The final part of logistics is transporting, which requires decisions about how to ship the product. Shippers may choose among rail, truck, air, pipeline, and water transport, or some combination of these modes.

8. **Discuss how some of the key ethical and legal issues affect logistics.** The deregulation of the freight delivery industry over the past three decades has generally produced positive results. Shippers are more competitive post-deregulation, and there is more emphasis on customer satisfaction, partnerships between shippers and clients, and ethical business behavior. Safety issues are more important than ever in the shipping industry. Protection of in-transit cargo, working conditions for vehicle operators, and the use of oversized trucking trains are among the safety issues with ethical and legal implications.

Understanding Marketing Terms and Concepts

Thinking About Marketing

1. What is wholesaling? What are the three basic categories of wholesalers?

2. Which category of wholesalers does not take title to products they resell? What types of wholesalers fall into this category?

3. How do manufacturers' agents differ from manufacturers' branch offices?

4. In the grocery industry, are wholesalers becoming more or less powerful in the marketing channel?

5. Why has logistics management become more important in marketing during recent years?

6. Review "Using Technology: TaylorMade-adidas Turns on Tech." How can the technologies described in this insert improve customer satisfaction?

7. What are the key activities in logistics management?

8. What are the benefits of a quick-response inventory control system?

9. What are the five basic ways to move products and materials from one point to another? What are the key factors to be considered when choosing among these modes of transport?

10. Review "Being Entrepreneurial: Heartland Express Does Details." What are the likely areas of Heartland's emphasis on maintaining the lowest cost among short-haul shippers?

Applying Marketing Skills

1. Assume you are the traffic manager for a large manufacturer of consumer goods. Your company is designing a quick-response delivery system for several large retail accounts. The system includes railcar delivery to distribution centers, direct-to-store truck delivery in a few isolated locations, and emergency service by air freight. What can you do to get feedback from your customers to aid in the design and implementation of the system?

2. During the midwestern flood of 2001, grain shippers that normally use barges for transport had to resort to other modes of transportation. Which other modes would be logical for shipping grain? How would massive flooding affect these modes?

3. An established rock group is thinking about firing its agent of five years. The agent gets 10 percent of all concert revenues and 1 percent of all other band-related profits, including those from merchandising agreements, commercial work, and paid TV appearances. The band members basically feel the agent is not really earning his seven-figure annual income. How would you advise the band? What factors should be considered before hiring another agent or, alternatively, eliminating the agent in favor of a less-expensive salaried manager? [*Hint: this exercise pertains to the wholesaling portion of the chapter.*]

Using the www in Marketing

Activity One

Grainger, described in the chapter opener, is a leading business-to-business wholesaler. Review the Grainger Web site at http://www.grainger.com and answer these questions.

1. In which category of wholesalers does Grainger fit? Within the chosen category, which type is Grainger (refer to Exhibit 15–1).

2. What services does Grainger offer its international customers? Do these services add value to the tangible products sold by Grainger?

Activity Two

Many countries are signing on the Internet to facilitate trade with other countries. Check the Trade Commission of Mexico Web site at http://www.mexico-trade.com. This site lists selected Mexican exporters classified by industry sector. There is also a comprehensive resource guide covering Mexico's economic, legal, and political systems.

1. Select three exporters that you think would be promising for national distribution in the United States, and give your reasoning. To complete this portion of the exercise, click on the "services" link, then "online services," then the "trade leads" link.

2. Write a brief report on what exporters to Mexico should know about Mexico's economic, legal, and political systems. To complete this report, you can explore several links under the "Information Center" link. These include "Information on NAFTA" and "Legal Resources/Information on Mexico and Latin America." Under the "Quick Reference/Index" link, you will find other useful links, including "Mexico Investment Guide."

Making Marketing Decisions

Case 15-1 *Gallo: Distributor Support a Key to Success*

E & J Gallo Winery, based in Modesto, California, is a world sales leader in a wide variety of categories. In the United States, Gallo sells about 25 percent of all wine, accounting for $19 billion per year. Among its most important corporate priorities is to expand and strengthen its distribution network, comprising 600 distributors who sell Gallo's 3,000 products to 300,000 retail accounts in 120 countries.

To support its wholesale distribution network, Gallo coordinates its marketing, sales, supply-chain management, and information systems activities. Gallo's supply-chain management is responsible for synchronizing the receipt of raw materials, glass manufacturing, wine processing, and logistics management of its regional distribution centers. By managing the supply chain from the flow of raw materials at their points of origin all the way to the retailer or distributor, Gallo gives its distributors the quick, dependable delivery with minimal back orders that drive maximum sales in the field. Tight controls minimize the opportunities that competitors may have from Gallo out-of-stock occurrences at the retail level.

Gallo's marketing personnel provide distributors with consumer research, media planning and advertising support, and videos to support distributor training and promotional activities. Marketing personnel work with Gallo's information systems personnel to keep distributors up-to-date on changes in the marketplace, and detailed shopping information that can be used to tailor promotions for individual retail stores. For example, when Gallo introduced Turning Leaf wines in a 1.5-liter bottle, having specific retailer-level information helped distributors decide which stores would be best for point-of-purchase displays and other in-store promotions. The information system, called the Sales Management Information System (SMIS), is updated monthly, an important activity, since competitive activity varies widely and an estimated 6,000 retail stores open, close, or change ownership every month.

Prior to implementing SMIS, Gallo lacked a complete view of what was happening once its product entered the distributor's stock. Losing sight of shipments once they got to the distributor made it difficult to plan, execute, and measure the success of various retailer-aimed marketing efforts. Now, distributors give Gallo high marks for supplying them with relevant information. Impressed with how much Gallo knows about its retail customers, distributor customer satisfaction with Gallo is on the increase.

Gallo's salespeople work directly with their distributors to build sales volume and market share. They are responsible for distributor support in shelf, cold box, and special display merchandising, facilitating advertising and promotion, keeping the distributor competitive in the pricing area, assisting in restaurant merchandising, and making sales calls with distributor salespeople.

Throughout its 70-year history, Gallo has depended on its wholesale distribution network to reach its market. Through market research and analysis on systematic basis, along with on-site support from Gallo salespeople and marketing campaigns designed for local retailers, Gallo continues to pursue its stated corporate priority of strengthening its wholesaler network.

Questions

1. Getting the product "on the shelf" is only half the task when selling through retailers and wholesalers. Explain how Gallo helps distributors and retailers get the product "off the shelf."

2. Why does Gallo choose to sell through wholesalers rather than directly to retailers? In other words, what value do Gallo's distributors provide to both Gallo and to the retail customers?

3. Other than making money from one another's efforts, how can Gallo and its distributors work together to build long-term beneficial relationships between the two parties?

Case 15-2 *Columbia Sportswear: A Logistics Leader*

Founded in 1938, Columbia Sportswear is one of the world's largest marketers of outdoor clothing and skiwear. The chairman of the board, 78-year-old Gert Boyle, is often featured in Columbia's off-beat, humorous TV ads. These ads typically show Ms. Boyle putting her son and company president through outdoor ordeals to test the durability of Columbia's products. Headquartered in Portland, Oregon, Columbia owns and operates sales offices in North America, Europe, and Asia. Columbia also owns and operates retail stores in the United States, Japan, and Australia.

When Columbia's retail customer base reached 10,000 retailers around the globe, its distribution system was in need of an overhaul. The market for outdoor clothing was attracting new competitors, some of whom are among the leading marketers of brand-name clothing. Both Polo and Tommy Hilfiger had expanded their lines beyond dress and casual dress clothing to include parkas, windbreakers, and fleece products. Large retail chains were also gaining marketplace clout and demanding fast, accurate delivery from their suppliers. In response, Columbia enhanced and expanded its distribution center in Portland's Rivergate Industrial District; the purpose of the $34 million center is simple enough—to store incoming products from subcontractors in Asia until they are repackaged and shipped to customers in the United States.

At 650,000 square feet, the new facility, which opened in 1999, is more than double the size of the previous distribution center. It is so large that personnel use adult-sized tricycles to get around. Highly automated, the center employs 400 at peak times. Approximately six truckloads of merchandise are shipped out every hour of the 18-hour work day. According to Columbia president Tim Boyle, "More and more retailers are asking suppliers to fulfill customized orders, which takes more time, space, and resources. We are committed to offering these value-added services to our customers, and the Rivergate expansion will help us achieve that goal, while giving us the ability to lower our per-unit processing costs over time."

The new facility features five miles of conveyor belts that bring products to the order processing area, rather than employees' having to go to the product storage areas for retrieval. The facility utilizes the Rapid Unit Replenishment System, which allows storage of partial cases of products in a mechanized carousel. Partial cases can be retrieved quickly and forwarded to the packing area when less-than-a-case orders are filled. This can improve order efficiency and accuracy by up to 30 percent. The control system allows tracking of all processes and products throughout the distribution center, and computers and radio technologies allow the center to operate in a paperless environment.

With its new system in place, Columbia can now receive and process 1,500 cartons per hour, versus 5,000 per day with the old system. The company can now fulfill approximately 450 simultaneous orders, more than double the capacity with the previous system. Improvements in shipping now allow Columbia to ship 2,200 cartons per hour. These improvements have led to improved customer satisfaction and contributed to impressive sales growth. The director of distribution at Columbia comments: "Part of our growth can be tied to the fact that we provide excellent customer services. The combination of our highly trained, motivated, and dedicated people and our state-of-the-art facility will allow us to continue to provide our customers with the high level of service they have come to expect."

In the planning stages, Columbia considered outsourcing its distribution function to logistics specialists. By keeping the distribution center in-house, Columbia is able to provide specialized service for retail accounts. Some retailers want price tags added, and some want product shipped on hangers ready for display on retail racks. By owning its own facility, Columbia can control the process and provide customized services—a definite advantage in a highly competitive market.

Questions

1. What are the advantages of Columbia's automated system for retailers? For Columbia?

2. In this situation, Columbia spent $34 million for its new distribution center. What factors should be considered to determine whether or not the system is a good investment?

3. As technology evolves, what factors should Columbia consider before changing its current system?

16

An Overview of Marketing Communications

After studying this chapter, you should be able to:

1 Discuss the objectives of marketing communications.

2 Understand the marketing communications mix and its role.

3 Explain the key elements of the marketing communications process.

4 Discuss the seven steps in the marketing communications planning process.

5 Demonstrate awareness of some of the key ethical and legal issues related to marketing communications.

www.miniusa.com

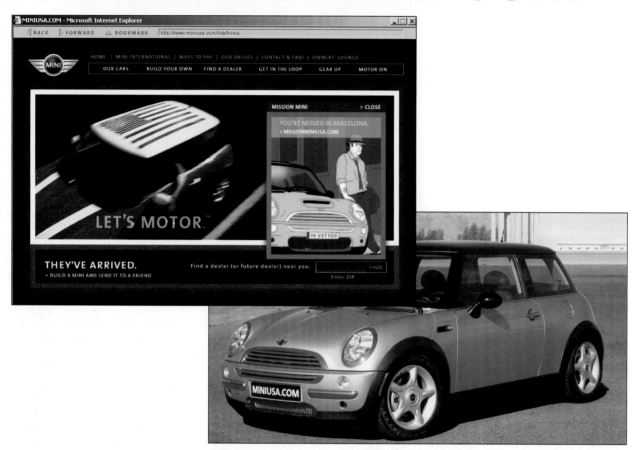

BMW is known worldwide as a producer of high-quality automobiles and for its marketing prowess. Its coveted brand image has been carefully nurtured by paying close attention to product quality, traditional advertising, and a highly professional sales and service operation. In 2002 BMW reintroduced the Mini Cooper, a reincarnation of a car last sold in the United States in 1967. Rather than follow the conventional BMW marketing communications model, however, the company took a fresh approach that contributed to the Mini Cooper's new success.

The integrated marketing communications campaign was meant to be quirky and fun to match the personality of the car. Nine months in advance of product availability, MiniUSA, working with its ad agency, began an advance campaign to build awareness and stimulate demand for the Cooper. A key element of the campaign was the car's Web site at www.minusa.com. Here, consumers could learn about the car, configure a model, price it out, and arrange the purchase. They could also take a humorous quiz to see if they were "ready for motoring" to tie in with Mini's campaign theme, "Let's motor." Visitors could also sign up for a monthly newsletter and buy Mini merchandise.

Mini's research indicated that potential buyers would be risk takers, nonconformists, and adventure seekers. Instead of fancy television ads and splashy magazine ads, Mini's plan was built around alternative forms of communication. In addition to the Web site, a Mini was mounted on top of a Ford Excursion SUV for a tour of 21 major cities. Minis were shown in major league sports stadiums, in the spectator section, not on the sidelines, where its fuel economy was touted with the slogan "Sip, not guzzle."

A month before the Mini was introduced, billboard ads appeared. Later, history-making ads appeared in seven magazines, including *Maxim, The New Yorker, Rolling Stone,* and four auto magazines. The ads ran along the edges of editorial pages with the tagline: "Nothing corners like a Mini. Let's motor."

Mini's unconventional communications campaign was a big hit. Before the car was introduced, there were almost a half a million visitors to the Web site. Fifty-five thousand Web visitors signed up for regular e-mails, and over 40 percent of those e-mails are opened. Several thousand Coopers were sold in advance, giving the company a running start on its annual sales goal of 20,000 units. The Mini is now easily meeting its sales goals. A good product backed by a great marketing communications campaign turned heads in the business world, just as the Mini does motoring down the road.

Marketing communications, sometimes referred to as *promotion,* involve marketer-initiated techniques directed to target audiences in an attempt to influence attitudes and behaviors. The Mini Cooper example mentions several forms of marketing communications, reminding us that different techniques are appropriate in different situations. It also illustrates the importance of careful planning prior to implementing a major marketing communications effort. As is increasingly the case in contemporary marketing, Mini Cooper used the Web in conjunction with traditional media, public relations, and salespeople to get its message to target audiences. This example also reinforces the importance of the relationship perspective with Mini Cooper's collaboration with dealers and its advertising agency in the development of the comprehensive communications program. Further, it is important to note that a solid marketing communications program may be in place for a significant amount of time before the payoff of increased sales is realized. MiniUSA's marketing communications program is off to a great start and no doubt had a major impact on the successful reintroduction of the Mini Cooper.

Marketers may use one or all of several marketing communications methods. There are five major categories: advertising, public relations, sales promotion, personal selling, and direct marketing communications. Together they constitute the **marketing communications mix,** often referred to as the *promotional mix.*

This chapter explores these five major categories, as well as the major objectives of marketing communications and the way the communications process works and is implemented. We discuss how the marketing environment, including ethical and legal concerns, can influence the marketing communications effort.

The Role of Marketing Communications

The ultimate goal of marketing communications is to reach some audience to affect its behavior. There may be intermediate steps on the path to that goal, such as developing favorable consumer attitudes. Exhibit 16–1 lays out the three major objectives of marketing communications: to inform, to persuade, or to remind the marketer's audience.

Informing

Informing present or potential customers about a product is an important marketing communications function. Any time a new product is launched and promoted, marketing communications serve to inform audience members (the target market) about it. For example, Volkswagen used an extensive ad campaign in Germany when it introduced the Phaeton, its first luxury car. This was quite a challenge, as Volkswagen has a long-standing reputation as the "people's car," and the Phaeton is meant to compete with Mercedes and BMW. Volkswagen used television and magazine ads along with direct mail to introduce the Phaeton. Singer Bob Dylan, who does not appear in ads in the United States, was featured in the print ads. While industry analysts think the introduction of the Phaeton is a risky move, the marketing communications campaign is doing its job at building awareness, stimulating sales, and upgrading Volkswagen's overall image.[1]

Marketing communications also serve an important role when new companies are founded and are seeking to build brand awareness. San Diego–based Leap Wireless broke into the highly competitive cell phone market

Exhibit 16–1

The marketing communications mix

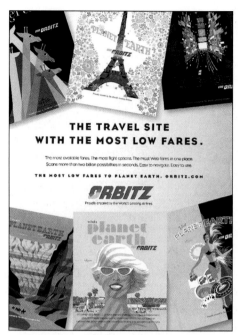

One major objective of marketing communications is to inform both customers and potential customers. Procter & Gamble used this ad to announce the availability of Crest toothpaste with built-in Scope mouthwash.

Marketing communications are also used to remind consumers and reinforce positive perceptions. This ad reminds consumers that Orbitz offers low fares on its Internet travel site.

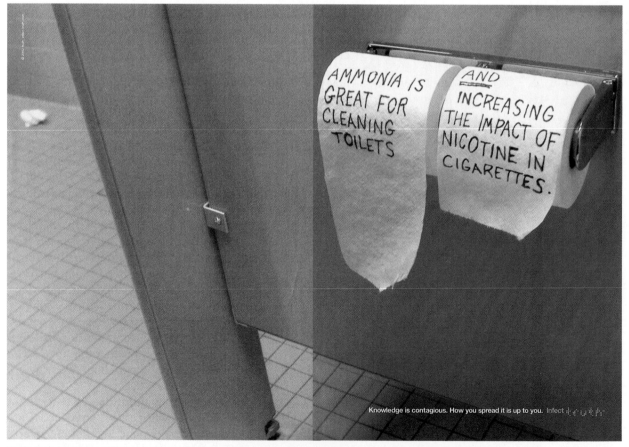

Marketing communications can be used to persuade others to take action. This ad encourages people to stop smoking by pointing out cigarettes contain ammonia.

Dorothy Brazil Clark
Director, Market Research and
Strategic Planning
Ralston Purina

"Competitive leadership has never been more challenging than in today's marketplace. Those who succeed in leading their respective fields will win the battle by directly linking the message (the objective), medium (all marketing communications components) and the target (minds of the intended consumers who must be receptive to the message), all at a cost compatible with bottom line objectives."

Dorothy Brazil Clark, Director, Market Research and Strategic Planning, at Ralston Purina in St. Louis is well aware of the need to maintain close relationships with customers at a reasonable cost. Her previous experience includes business development and sales with Norden Laboratories, a subsidiary of SmithKline Beecham. Dorothy earned her B.A. degree from the University of Iowa and an MBA from the University of Missouri.

with its Cricket Comfortable Wireless service thanks to a clever integrated campaign featuring advertising, public relations, personal selling, and sponsorship of high-profile events. In its first major market, Denver, Cricket became a presence with its overstuffed, yet comfortable, bright green couch serving as a promotional tool to draw traffic. In some cases, couches were given away in consumer contests held at Denver Broncos games and concerts at the nearby Red Rocks outdoor amphitheater. Cricket was aiming for virtually 100 percent brand awareness within 90 days, which it achieved. In a one-year period, Cricket's subscriber base increased tenfold, to 1.1 million.[2]

Informing the public can be an important objective, even for goods, services or ideas that have been around for a while. For example, the French government ran an antismoking campaign designed to create awareness about the dangers of smoking. Rather than warning about health risks, the ads warned the public about a mass-produced product (without specifying cigarettes) that contained traces of ammonia, acetone, cyanidic acid, and mercury. The ads urged consumers to call a toll-free hotline for more information. The response to the ad was phenomenal, with half a million worried consumers calling the hotline. Though controversial, the French government felt the ads succeeded in building awareness about the potential dangers of smoking.[3]

Persuading

Marketing communications may concentrate on persuading customers to purchase a firm's market offering. For instance, airline company JetBlue used advertising to stimulate air travel during an industry slump. JetBlue had always used humor in its advertising prior to the events of September 11, 2001, but like many other advertisers, it ceased using humor in its ads after disastrous occurrences shook the confidence of air travelers. Eventually, JetBlue returned to television ads, but their humor took a different approach. Travelers gave their reasons for flying, such as to visit family, get away from family, to take off, or to come back. One ad playfully made fun of the way airlines greet their customers, while others poked fun at competitors that do not offer DirectTV on their flights. In a time when customers were reluctant to fly, JetBlue's ads were persuasive and helped rebuild their passenger volume.[4]

Persuasive advertising is also used by nonprofit and government organizations. For example, the Office of National Drug Control Policy, with its Partnership for a Drug-Free America, frequently uses persuasive advertising aimed directly at young people, encouraging them to call a toll-free number or visit a partnership Web site for advice if they have no one at home to talk with about drugs. The same organization runs ads directed at parents who need guidance in how to talk with their children about drugs.[5]

Reminding

When consumers are aware of a firm's brand and have positive attitudes toward it, a reminding objective may be appropriate. Although consumers may be sold on the product, they are still vulnerable to competitors' appeals. Marketing communications can remind consumers of a product's benefits and reassure them they are making the right choice. CDnow uses **permission marketing** to remind its online customers of new audio and video releases and special promotions. Permission marketing occurs when the customer grants the marketer permission to send regular updates of interest to the consumer. E-mail is typically used for permission marketing, but regular mail or a fax could also be employed for this purpose.

Personal selling is another way to remind buyers of the value of continuing the relationship and making repeat purchases. Among the best at using personal selling for all three objectives of marketing communications, including reminding, are Dell Computer, Charles Schwab, Cisco Sytems, Northwestern Mutual, and General Mills.

The Marketing Communications Mix
To inform, persuade, and remind targeted consumers effectively, marketers rely on one or more of the five major elements of the marketing communications mix. We discuss these briefly here and in more detail in subsequent chapters.

Advertising

Advertising is nonpersonal, paid for by an identified sponsor, and disseminated through mass channels of communication to promote the adoption of goods, services, persons, or ideas. Marketers use media such as television, radio, outdoor signage, magazines, newspapers, and the Internet to advertise. Its ability to reach a mass audience often makes advertising an efficient method for communicating with a large target market.

Traditionally, advertising has been the most recognized form of marketing communications largely because of its high visibility. We cannot escape the advertising that surrounds us in our daily lives. This high visibility is achieved through enormous expenditures. For example, General Motors, Procter & Gamble, and Phillip Morris spend in the neighborhood of $5 billion each on advertising on an annual basis. The 100th largest advertiser in the United States, Dillard's department stores, spends almost $300 million annually. The U.S. government is a major advertiser, ranking in the country's top 25 with expenditures of almost a billion dollars a year, more than L'Oréal, IBM, Target, Microsoft, or Nissan.[6]

The global advertising industry has been rather stagnant lately, with declining expenditures in 2001 and 2002. However, prospects look better for 2003, and modest increases are expected. One analyst notes that, in general, advertising expenditures outpace the economy in good times and lag behind in downtimes.[7] When economic times are less than favorable, as they have been in recent years, advertisers seem to try even harder to improve the creative aspects of their work. Some of the best examples of creative advertising are displayed in France each year at the Cannes International Advertising Festival. For more on Cannes, see "Being Entrepreneurial: Nike Gives a Lesson."

Public Relations

The **public relations** function seeks to positively influence feelings, opinions, and beliefs about a company and its market offering to variety of publics, or stakeholders. Employees, customers, stockholders, community members, and the government are examples of various publics for many firms.

This ad illustrates the combination of sales promotion and advertising. The sales promotion message (instant prizes) is part of a magazine ad for Gillette Mach3 razors.

A key aspect of public relations is publicity. **Publicity** refers to non-paid-for communications about the company or product that appear in some media form, often the news media. Since the firm cannot completely control the message being disseminated, publicity may generate more believable messages than paid-for communications such as advertising. Many firms hire outside agencies to handle their public relations and publicity requirements.

Sales Promotion

Sales promotion includes communications activities that provide extra value or incentives to ultimate consumers, wholesalers, retailers, or other organizational customers and that can stimulate immediate sales.[8] Sales promotion attempts to stimulate product interest, trial, or purchase. Coupons, samples, premiums, point-of-purchase displays, sweepstakes, contests, rebates, and trade show exhibits are all examples of sales promotion.

Consumer sales promotion is directed at ultimate users of the product or service; *trade sales promotion* is directed at retailers, wholesalers, or other business buyers. Marketers spend comparable amounts of money for consumer and trade sales promotion. While comprehensive estimates of consumer and trade sales promotion expenditures are not available, trade sources estimate that the two forms of sales promotion, when combined, account for more expenditures than the total spent on advertising.[9] One reason that it is difficult to get a good estimate on trade promotions is that trade promotions are not readily observable outside a given industry. For example, slotting allowances (discussed in Chapter 14) are not clearly identified as an expense item in most cases. Nonetheless, we can safely conclude that expenditures on both consumer and trade promotions are significant, particularly for consumer goods.

Dorothy Brazil Clark, Director, Market Research and Strategic Planning at Ralston Purina, points out the need to understand marketing communications an an integrated process focused on targeted consumers: "The requisite for good marketing communications in a world that demands end-to-end service is a total understanding of both communicator and the organizations involved as well as the place each occupies during all phases of the process. Successful management of the communication process then demands complete mastery of the process and its components, synchronization between existing components and a dismantling of the 'mass market' concept in favor of one emphasizing a family of segmented consumer groups."

Marketers typically use sales promotion in conjunction with other marketing communications elements. For example, sales promotion programs such as sweepstakes or contests may use advertising to spread the word to mass consumer markets. Marketers also frequently link sales promotion with many forms of direct

Being Entrepreneurial

Nike gives a lesson

Can big companies be entrepreneurial? Nike makes a convincing case, displaying a creative, innovative, risk-taking approach to its advertising that must make founder Phil Knight proud. Over the years, Nike has used its swoosh and "Just do it" tagline to craft some of the world's most memorable ads. Sensing that both the swoosh and the tagline were wearing a bit thin, the company took a calculated risk to alter its brand image with a new campaign.

The just-do-it theme was seen by some as being a bit harsh and perhaps a bit serious as it extolled the virtues of getting out of the house and into active athletics. Not everyone aspires to be a fitness buff, and Nike really did not have much of a message for these consumers. The just-do-it ads made athletics look like hard work, with training regimens associated with professional athletes. To move to a

more fun, playful theme, Nike created the "tag" campaign, which involves an entire city, Toronto, playing a game of tag. There is no athlete role model, just a Nike-wearing man walking down the street with his coffee, minding his own business—that is, until he is tagged "it." He then chases hundreds of people into the subway, left with only one late-arriving passenger as his quarry. The entire ad evokes a feeling of "let's have some fun," perfectly capturing the mood of people around the world who long for a bit more fun in their lives. It was awarded the highest honor for a filmed ad at the annual International Festival of Advertising at Cannes. Creativity, innovation, and risk taking taken together define entrepreneurship. Nike proves that entrepreneurship is not the sole province of small companies.

Professional salespeople play an important role in the marketing communications effort for complex products. Shown is a marketing representative for Health Images, Inc., who educates physicians on the use of MRI (magnetic resonance imaging) equipment.

marketing, especially direct mail, or include it as part of a trade show (product giveaways, merchandise imprinted with ad messages or logos).

Unlike some other forms of marketing communications, sales promotion is usually intended to produce immediate results. This probably explains why marketers have increasingly turned to sales promotion to improve sales volume and market share in a wide variety of highly competitive markets.

Personal Selling

Personal selling involves interpersonal communications between a seller and a buyer to satisfy buyer needs to the mutual benefit of both parties. The personal nature of this method distinguishes it from nonpersonal forms of marketing communication. Personal selling allows immediate feedback, enabling a message to be tailored to fit the buyer's individual needs. Its dynamic nature and flexibility make personal selling an excellent communications medium for establishing and nurturing customer relationships.

Personal selling is an important element of marketing communications when the product is complex. The sale of medical equipment to hospitals and physicians would be practically impossible without well-informed salespeople who can provide the necessary details to prospective buyers.

Direct Marketing Communications

Direct marketing communications is a process of communicating directly with target customers to encourage response by telephone, mail, electronic means, or personal visit. Popular methods of direct marketing communications include direct mail, telemarketing, direct-response broadcast advertising, online computer shopping services, cable television shopping networks, infomercials, and in some instances, outdoor advertising.

Direct marketing communications are used by all types of marketers, including retailers, wholesalers, manufacturers, and service providers. A fast-growing segment of the marketing communications field, direct marketing often uses precise means of identifying members of a target audience and compiling customer/prospect databases with postal addresses, telephone numbers, account numbers, e-mail addresses or fax numbers to allow access to the buyers.

Integrated Marketing Communications

Today's highly competitive business environment puts considerable pressure on marketing communications to reach and spur busy, value-conscious consumers to buy. As a result, marketers are increasingly turning to **integrated marketing communications (IMC)**, which is the strategic integration of multiple means of communicating with target markets to form a comprehensive, consistent message. According to an expert in the field, this involves using new media along with more established forms of marketing communications: " . . . My cry is to integrate, not isolate. Yes, we need to explore and develop the new media and new approaches, but we need to do that within the context of what exists and what is likely to evolve. We need to integrate the new media with the old, melding e-commerce and across-the-counter commerce."[10]

In one sense, marketing communications are integrated horizontally, or across various methods of communications. For example, the advertising message must be consistent with the personal selling message. But a campaign can also be integrated vertically, extending from the marketer down through the marketing channel. For example, salespeople are often dispatched to retailers to arrange for adequate inventory levels and to assist in setting up in-store displays.

Another aspect of integrated marketing communications is that it considers any contact with a brand, product, or company to be part of marketing communications. As a result of integrated marketing communications, consumers could see a product in a movie, a commercial message or brand name on a T-shirt, and a company name prominently displayed on a hot-air balloon. Television viewers often see branded products become part of the show, as was the case with Reebok on *Survivor*. Pro golfers and tennis players frequently become live billboards, with logos on their clothing featuring everything from consulting companies to airlines. A variation on this theme has been to insert a plug for one product into the ad for another product. For example, when Toyota introduced the Matrixx, a passenger in the vehicle was spotted playing a video game on a Sony Vaio. Tobasco sauce appears in ads for other products, usually to suggest that the other products are "hot."[11] Some companies, such as Quicksilver clothing company, use video games as a vehicle to market their products. Quicksilver had previously promoted its products by supplying extreme athletes with complimentary clothing.[12]

These sorts of marketing communications are sometimes called **stealth marketing,** because their intent is not as blatant as some forms of marketing communications such as advertising. Such efforts are actually publicity generators and thus part of the marketing communications mix as we define it. These activities are increasing as marketers try to find new ways to reach audiences that may have become jaded by too much advertising, sales promotion, and other traditional methods of communicating with a target audience. It will be interesting to see how long it takes for consumers to tire of marketing communications in these alternative venues. On popular beaches, Hawaiian Tropic's swimsuit-wearing employees supply free sunscreen, and Panama Jack logos adorn concession stands, rental equipment, and lifeguard clothing. Planes circle overhead with promotional messages, and beach vehicles are often loaned from manufacturers to earn the "official vehicle" designation. Ads are now appearing routinely in parking garages, restrooms, and department store windows (Häagen-Dazs has used Macy's for this); *GQ* magazine has opened a cocktail lounge in California to promote its look; and Puma displayed its soccer shoes under glass on the tables of sushi restaurants in 15 cities around the world.[13] With ads and other marketing communications becoming omnipresent, marketers will eventually have an even harder time getting consumers' attention.

Sponsorship programs, an investment in causes and events to support overall corporate objectives and marketing objectives,[14] may be an important part of an integrated marketing communications strategy. Sponsors may back a single event, such as the Olympics or the World Cup, or multiple events, as State Farm Insurance does with golf tournaments on the LPGA tour. Organizations may also sponsor places, such as sports stadiums. For example, Invesco is paying $60 million over 20 years to sponsor the Denver Broncos NFL playing field, while American Airlines is paying $195 million over 30 years for the American Airlines center in Dallas. Even areas in and around stadiums are up for sponsorship. In Miami's NFL stadium, the parking lot is divided into sponsored zones, each bearing the name of a Toyota model, including Camry, Tundra, and Sequoia. Sponsorship of places has spread to school gyms, convention centers, hospitals, performing arts centers, museums, and other places where people congregate.[15]

Expenditures on sponsorships are growing faster than those for advertising and sales promotion.[16] They offer a good opportunity to match with particular lifestyles, to gain exposure beyond traditional avenues, and in some cases, to be associated with worthwhile causes. Sponsorships also allow small organizations to compete locally against larger rivals that have extensive communications budgets.

Most sponsorships have multiple objectives for the marketer and utilize multiple means of communicating with target audiences. For example, Jack In The Box's Seattle region sponsored western Washington's Puyallup Fair to generate awareness

Sponsorship programs can be an important element of integrated marketing communications. In this ad, the United States Postal Service promotes the New York Cycling Championship while simultaneously promoting its sponsored team with top cyclist Lance Armstrong.

Credibility is critical in marketing communications. Tennis stars Serena and Venus Williams are highly credible presenters attesting to the healthy benefits of drinking milk.

and trial of new fast-food menu items, build sales through sales promotion, expand its use of broadcast advertising, and give its employees more experience with various marketing techniques.[17]

Coca-Cola and Procter & Gamble are masters at integrating their marketing communications efforts. Both are well known for consumer advertising. Their sales promotion efforts, in the form of coupons, sweepstakes, and contests are also familiar to millions of consumers. The average consumer, however, does not see their highly trained salespeople who call on wholesalers and retailers. Both P&G and Coke have used direct marketing effectively. Like many others, Coca-Cola and P&G also manage sophisticated public relations and publicity efforts to support their marketing communications campaigns. Coke underscored its commitment to sponsorship as a major piece of its integrated marketing communications strategy by paying $500 million to become the sponsor for the National Collegiate Athletics Association for the 2003–2014 period. Under the agreement Coke will have beverage marketing and media rights to NCAA championship events and will support the events through advertising, sales promotion, and other marketing initiatives.[18]

The Marketing Communications Process

Communication is the process of establishing shared meaning, exchanging ideas, or passing information between a source and a receiver. Exhibit 16–2 shows how the marketing communications process works. Note that the intended target for any basic communication is the **receiver.** This could be a purchasing agent listening to a sales presentation, a consumer reading a magazine ad, or another of the various publics served by the marketer, such as stockholders or government officials.

Sources of Marketing Communications

The marketer is the **source,** or message sender of marketing communications. Two types of sources normally play a role in marketing communications, the message sponsor and the message presenter. The **message sponsor** is typically the organiza-

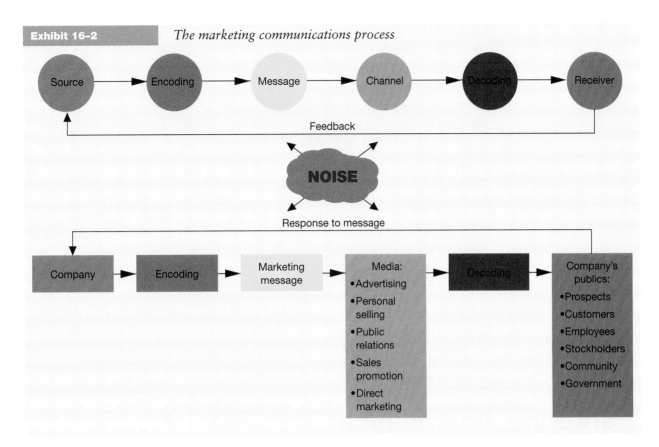

Exhibit 16–2   *The marketing communications process*

tion attempting to market its goods, services, or ideas. The **message presenter,** perhaps a salesperson, actor, or television personality, actually delivers the message. For instance, Nike is a message sponsor, whereas Tiger Woods is one of Nike's message presenters.

Communications Messages

The source sends a message through a channel to a receiver. The **marketing communications message** represents what the company is trying to convey about its products. A **message channel** is the means by which the message is conveyed. In advertising, message channels are often referred to as *media,* a reference to advertising vehicles such as newspapers, television, magazines, outdoor, and radio. Mail, telephones, audio- and videocassettes, salespeople, and computer networks and disks are also examples of message channels.

Encoding and Decoding

The source does the **encoding** by choosing the words, pictures, and other symbols used to transmit the intended message. **Decoding** is the process by which the receiver deciphers the meaning of the words, pictures, and other symbols used in the message. When the message is not decoded as the source intended, a lack of communication results. For example, a consumer may find the copy in a magazine ad too technical and thus not understand the message.

Feedback

Feedback is the part of the receiver's response that is communicated to the sender. Depending on the nature of the communication, the sender can assess feedback to judge the effectiveness of the communication. Personal selling and many forms of sales promotion offer relatively quick feedback. Feedback is not so immediate for mass advertising and public relations, and only subsequent sales figures or marketing research will indicate the effectiveness of the message.

Noise

Noise is any distraction or distortion during the communication process that prevents the message from being effectively communicated. Competing messages and interruptions, such as a telephone call during a salesperson's sales presentation, constitute noise. Noise can even come from within the message itself, sometimes at quite an expense. For example, consumer feedback indicated excessive noise in AT&T Wireless ads built around asking viewers "What's an mLife?" Consumers were confused by the ads and rarely paid close enough attention to learn that mLife stood for a mobile life that one could obtain with AT&T's wireless phone service. Only 4 percent of consumers in the ad's targeted audience liked the ads and thought they were effective. Many others thought the ads were really for Metropolitan Life, an insurance company, which sued AT&T over the ads. Later, Metropolitan settled the suit, and some analysts suggested they did so because AT&T was in effect giving the insurance company a lot of free advertising. The ads were puzzling, because AT&T made consumers work doubly hard to get their message. First, consumers had to stop thinking the ads were for an insurance company. Then, if they were still paying attention, they had a hard time figuring out if AT&T's cell phones could do anything that others could not.[19] The obvious lesson here is that noise should be eliminated or at least minimized, lest the communications task become more difficult.

Marketing Communications Planning

There are seven key tasks in **marketing communications planning:** marketing plan review; situation analysis; communications process analysis; budget development; program development; integration and implementation of the plan; and monitoring, evaluating, and controlling the marketing communications program. These are diagrammed in Exhibit 16–3.

Marketing Plan Review

Marketing communications planning draws heavily on the firm's overall marketing strategy and marketing objectives. A review of the marketing plan is thus a logical place to start the process of marketing communications planning. The marketing plan often contains detailed information that is useful for marketing communications planning.

Situation Analysis

An analysis of the marketing communications situation considers how internal factors, such as the firm's capabilities and constraints, and other marketing mix variables will affect marketing communications. The situation analysis is also concerned with the marketing environment now and in the future. For example, competitive, economic, and social factors affect marketing communications. The political and legal environments, discussed later in this chapter, are also addressed in the situation analysis.

Exhibit 16–3   *Key tasks in marketing communications planning*

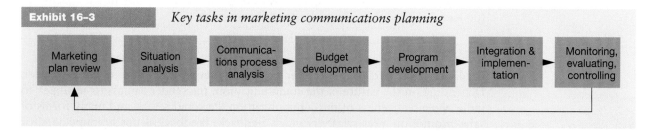

THE COMPETITIVE ENVIRONMENT Marketing communications are often used to foil the actions of competitors. For example, competitive strategy affected marketing communications in the long-distance telephone market, with major providers increasing their national television advertising in an attempt to hold and build market share. Sports celebrities Terry Bradshaw and Mike Piazza joined country singer Toby Keith in an intensive campaign for 10-10-220. Michael Jordan and actor Verne Troyer (Mini-Me from the Austin Powers movies) pitched 1-800-Collect. At the same time, comedian Carrott Top was featured in a long-running campaign for 1-800-Call-ATT.[20] Never had the long-distance market seen so much national advertising running simultaneously, but then again, competition in the long-distance market had never been so intense.

THE ECONOMIC ENVIRONMENT Budgets for marketing communications often decline in hard economic times, yet savvy marketers resist large reductions in their communications spending. They know that brand awareness, image, and equity are hard to achieve, and drastic reductions in communications budgets can endanger hard-won marketplace victories. Even though the world economy has been lackluster in recent years, overall marketing communications expenditures have dropped less than 5 percent. Most companies, rather than cutting their budgets significantly, have been searching for the most productive means of communicating with customers. This has meant that an increased portion of the communications budget is being spent on highly measurable communications activities or in new vehicles. For example, a lot of companies integrated the Web into their communications mix in recent years, while others increased the proportion of direct mail, e-mail campaigns, sponsorships, and various forms of stealth marketing. At the same time, expenditures have decreased for newspaper and other print advertising. Cable television, with its highly targeted audiences, is typically gaining ground at the expense of the traditional major networks such as ABC, NBC, and CBS.

To properly budget marketing communications, companies should decide if expenditures are an investment in the future of their brands or if expenditures represent an expense for which an immediate return is expected. In reality, most companies view their communications expenditures as part investment and part current expense. When economic times are tough, there is an undeniable pressure to make every dollar spent pay off—often in the short run. But the best marketers know that some money has to be dedicated to preserving what has already been achieved and for building brands of the future. Immediate payoff is not likely the best indicator of communications success in these cases.

The economic environment may cause firms to reconsider which components of the marketing communications mix to emphasize. One significant change in the economic environment is that electronic commerce has become a much more important part of the U.S. economy in recent years. As a result, major marketing organizations such as Procter & Gamble, Walt Disney, Philip Morris, AT&T, and Johnson & Johnson will increase their proportion of spending on Internet advertising. A survey of 1,800 corporate executives indicates that in the three-year period of 2000–2003, a higher percentage of marketing communications budgets will be dedicated to Internet advertising, direct mail advertising, and sales promotion.

Marketers recognize that women are buying products traditionally bought by men and vice versa. This ad uses a humorous approach to encourage male patronage of a florist shop.

THE SOCIAL ENVIRONMENT Communications messages often reflect social trends. For instance, many marketers communicate supposed environmental benefits of their products. Although shoppers indicate that they are concerned about the environmental impact of the products they purchase, companies have typically had difficulty translating this concern into a competitive advantage in the marketplace. It seems that the desire for convenience is actually a much stronger social trend, with plastic disposables replacing glass containers for baby food, water, and food-service items. Another social trend of note is that personal wellness and safety is a prime concern. Seventh Generation, a brand of natural household products, changed its slogan from "Products for a healthy planet" to "Safer for you and the environment."[21]

Perhaps the most important social trend is the changing composition of the population in many countries of the world. As discussed in Chapters 2 and 7, multiculturalism in the United States is a far more important trend than in the past because of the emergence of some ethnic groups as prime markets for a wide range of products. It is estimated that U.S. marketers spend more than $2 billion annually to target the Latino market, $1.5 billion on the African-American market, and $250 million on Asian-American initiatives.[22] Further, it is estimated that diverse markets will grow faster and outspend the so-called mainstream market by the year 2020.[23]

The concept of multicultural marketing communications and specific campaigns targeting one or more ethnic or alternative lifestyle groups is becoming far more commonplace than just a few years ago. Gateway, H&R Block, and Lincoln-Mercury have all successfully launched multicultural campaigns. These three companies, along with many others, realize that they must successfully communicate with emerging markets of importance in order to succeed. At Gateway, the term *growth* is largely synonymous with multicultural markets, and the company has appointed a director of growth markets to head up multicultural marketing communications.[24]

Dorothy Brazil Clark, Director of Market Research and Strategic Planning at Ralston Purina, is mindful of the importance of approaching diverse markets with appropriately tailored marketing communications: "Those aspiring to be market leaders must successfully forge new communication pathways focused on and mirroring the diversity and pluralism reflected in the collective social, economic, political, and technological impact on both domestic and international environments. These customized pathways can serve as the integrating forces that connect the organization with its intended audiences."

MARKETING MIX CONSIDERATIONS   Compatibility of product, price, and channel characteristics with marketing communications is essential. The physical characteristics of a product or product package (color, size, shape, texture, ingredients) and its brand name communicate a lot to consumers. For instance, the bright colors on the Cheer detergent package imply it is powerful enough to get clothes bright and clean without fading them. Brand names such as Arrid Extra Dry, Finesse, Ivory, Total, Huggies, Sheer Energy, and Angel Soft convey certain messages about the products.

The product's price also conveys a message. Consumers often use price as an indicator of product quality. The $18,900 price tag on a Rolex President watch indicates more than the cost of the watch; it also conveys a message of quality and prestige. Although both Rolex and Timex watches keep good time, each conveys a different message with its pricing strategy, and each has built an image consistent with its price.

The chosen marketing channel also communicates to the consumer. For instance, Wal-Mart and Neiman-Marcus each conveys a different message. Wal-Mart stands for everyday low prices—products that are very expensive and of the finest quality are typically not found there. Consumers generally assume items sold at Neiman-Marcus are of high quality because of the store's well-established image. The prices of products at Neiman-Marcus help convey that message.

Communications Process Analysis

In this step, marketers analyze the various elements of the basic communications model shown in Exhibit 16–3. Objectives for marketing communications are also set in this part of the planning process.

APPLYING THE BASIC COMMUNICATIONS MODEL   Marketers try to understand the decoding processes of potential receivers of marketing communications in order to create effective messages and select appropriate message channels.

Exhibit 16–4   *Examples of marketing communications objectives*

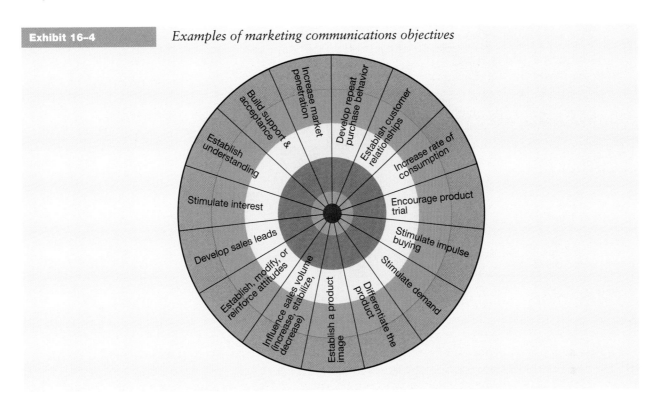

For example, will the consumer need detailed information from a well-trained salesperson to make a favorable decision? Or can simple point-of-sale displays achieve the desired results?

SETTING MARKETING COMMUNICATIONS OBJECTIVES   Exhibit 16–4 lists several general marketing communications objectives. Like all business objectives, a marketing communications objective should be stated as specifically as possible to help gauge the effectiveness of marketing communications efforts. It is also necessary to set objectives for each marketing communications effort, assuming separate programs are developed for individual products, product lines, geographic areas, customer groups, or different time periods. For example, greeting-card marketer Hallmark might run separate sales promotion programs to correspond with major occasions such as Christmas, Mother's Day, and Halloween.

Budget Development

Determining the optimal amount to spend on marketing communications involves considerable subjective judgment. Further, it is hard to measure precise results achieved by most forms of marketing communications. For example, some corporations spend more than $150,000 per year on rent, food, and drink for skyboxes at National Football League stadiums. Selected customers are invited to the games, at which they are hosted by company representatives. Although the companies use this form of entertainment to enhance customer relationships, it is virtually impossible to calculate the precise results of these expenditures. Likewise, it is difficult to tie concrete dollar results to most advertising and public relations expenditures.

INFLUENCES ON BUDGETING   The budget depends on the size of the company, its financial resources, the type of business, the market dispersion, the industry growth rate, and the firm's position in the marketplace. As shown in Exhibit 16–5, marketing communications expenditures also vary by industry.

The marketing communications budgets for business marketers are generally quite different than budgets for consumer products and service companies. For example, business marketers spend a majority of their marketing communications

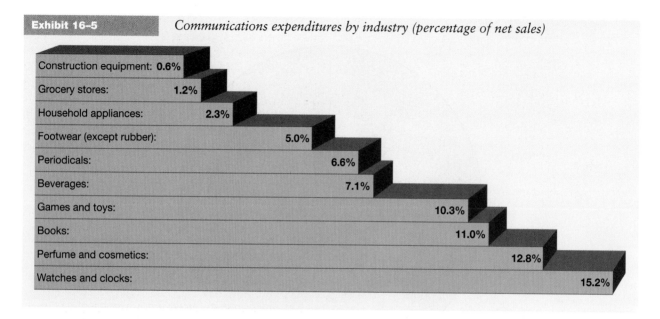

Exhibit 16–5   *Communications expenditures by industry (percentage of net sales)*

Construction equipment: 0.6%
Grocery stores: 1.2%
Household appliances: 2.3%
Footwear (except rubber): 5.0%
Periodicals: 6.6%
Beverages: 7.1%
Games and toys: 10.3%
Books: 11.0%
Perfume and cosmetics: 12.8%
Watches and clocks: 15.2%

dollars on personal selling, whereas consumer marketers spend more on other forms of communications, with various forms of advertising leading the way.

BUDGETING METHODS   Firms typically use any of four methods to determine the marketing communications budget: **percentage of sales, competitive parity, all-you-can-afford,** and **objective-task.**

PERCENTAGE OF SALES   Using the preceding year (or even a longer period) as a basis, a company can set its marketing communications budget as a percentage of sales. A drawback is that the assumed causal sequence of effects is reversed; that is, expenditures for marketing communications should partially determine sales levels, rather than past sales levels determining marketing communications expenditures.

Firms can also budget according to percentage of forecasted sales. When doing so, they often use industry standards such as those shown in Exhibit 16–5 as guidelines for determining a percentage. Percentage-of-sales approaches ensure some stability in planning, but they fail to consider competitive and economic pressures.

COMPETITIVE PARITY   Some firms set marketing communications budgets to equal the percentage allocated by other companies in the industry. This approach at least acknowledges competitive actions. The disadvantage is it assumes that the competition is correct, that marketing communications dollars are spent with equal effectiveness across companies, and that other firms have similar objectives and resources. These assumptions may be dangerous oversimplifications of actual conditions.

ALL-YOU-CAN-AFFORD   Sometimes firms spend what they can afford, or some amount left over after covering other costs. Such a budgeting technique fails to consider a firm's objectives and to commit expenditures necessary to achieve them. This is a questionable approach for the firm struggling to make a profit, because reduction of marketing communications expenditures may prevent any improvement and actually speed a downturn.

OBJECTIVE-TASK   More detailed than the other budgeting methods, this approach sets the budget at the level necessary to achieve stipulated marketing communications objectives. The objective-task method forces identification of tasks that must be achieved to meet established objectives and provides a way to evaluate results. It has the advantage of requiring management to spell out its assumptions about the relationships among dollars spent, exposure levels, product trial, and continuing consumer purchases.

Ironman® chronograph gives him:

A styling watch.

An accurate stopwatch.

A cozy night-light.

Leftover money to buy other stuff.

Paul's >

TIMEX It takes a licking and keeps on ticking®

Paul's dress Ironman® chronograph with Indiglo® night-light is about $70. For retailers, U.S. call 1-800-367-8463 or Canada 1-800-263-0981. See more at timex.com

This ad illustrates how both explicit and implicit marketing communications can be part of the same message. Just like the watch, this Ironman competitor can "take a licking and keep on ticking."

Research indicates that marketing managers rely heavily on historical data—for example, last year's sales results—in allocating dollars to various marketing communications tools. This may be an acceptable practice in stable business environments; in many marketing environments, however, there is significant variation from year to year in consumer tastes, economic conditions, and competitive activity. When managers are operating in such unstable environments, they will likely be more successful if they rely more on objective-task, or zero-based, budgeting.[25]

Marketing Communications Program Development

Developing a marketing communications program involves developing general marketing communications strategies and allocating budgets to specific programs. A firm must decide the proper uses of explicit and implicit communications. And it must decide whether to adopt a push strategy, a pull strategy, or a combination strategy.

EXPLICIT AND IMPLICIT COMMUNICATIONS

Marketing communications may be either explicit or implicit. **Explicit communications** convey a distinct, clearly stated message through personal selling, advertising, public relations, sales promotion, direct marketing, or some combination of these methods. **Implicit communications** are what the message connotes about the product itself, its price, or the places it is sold. Candymaker Mars, for example, wanted to appear more local in various European markets rather than as a U.S. brand. Departing from its regular advertising strategy, the company paid far more attention to local detail than ever before in a major campaign featuring 10 television ads and 20 print ads. In the United Kingdom, the theme for the ads was "Pleasure You Can't Measure," in Germany it became "It is Mars—das hat was" ("that's it"), and in France the theme was "Mars—Quede bonheur" ("Mars—What happiness"). In England, the ads were associated with World Cup soccer; in France, the month of August, the popular time for vacations; and in other countries, adaptations were made specifically for each country. For Mars, the campaign marked a departure from featuring the physical attributes of the brand toward more of an emotional appeal. The implicit part of the communication was that Mars, an old established brand in Europe, was now more a part of local tastes and traditions.[26]

PUSH, PULL, AND COMBINATION STRATEGIES   A **push strategy** involves convincing intermediary channel members to "push" the product through the channel to the ultimate consumer. The company directs its marketing communications efforts toward promoting and selling the product to a reseller, which then does the same to another reseller or to the ultimate consumer. Personal selling is a primary tool in this method. Sales promotion and advertising directed at channel members may also be used. For example, manufacturers may provide sales incentives to retailers or place ads in retailer-oriented trade magazines.

A **pull strategy** attempts to get consumers to "pull" the product from the manufacturing company through the marketing channel. The company concentrates its marketing communications efforts on the consumer; that is, it hopes to stimulate interest and demand for the product at the end-user level. If consumers want and ask for the product, resellers are more likely to carry and distribute it. A firm with a new and unproven product might find a pull strategy useful if distributors are reluctant to carry the product. The firm then uses advertising and sales promotion tools such as coupons to get many consumers to go to the retail store and request the product, thus pulling it through the channel.

Many firms practice a **combination strategy,** aiming marketing communications at both resellers and ultimate consumers. Nabisco, for example, uses personal selling and trade promotions to sell its products to grocery retailers. At the same time, it makes extensive use of advertising and sales promotion directed at ultimate consumers. Strict reliance on either a push or a pull strategy does not take full advantage of the power of marketing communications. A firm with limited resources, however, may not be able to follow both strategies and may emphasize one over the other.

Integration and Implementation

Implementation is setting the marketing communications plan into action. Depending on which tools the firm uses, it creates ads, purchases media time and space, and begins its sales promotion programs. If appropriate, the firm's personal selling, public relations, and direct marketing components also direct their efforts toward achieving the marketing communications objectives. The key aspect of implementation is coordination.

Monitoring, Evaluating, and Controlling

Firms can use a variety of methods to monitor, evaluate, and control marketing communications. For example, a firm might monitor sales promotion by the number of coupons redeemed or measure the effectiveness of a new personal selling strategy by looking at the number of new accounts opened by the salesforce. After an advertising campaign, a firm might run tests to see if consumers noticed the ad. Researchers could ask how many of those who noticed the ad linked the company name to it or actually read it. They might also ask consumers about their attitude toward the company and the product both before and after a marketing communications program to see what effect, if any, the program had.

Marketers often rely on surveys and tests to evaluate marketing communications. Sometimes they look at sales results and attribute fluctuations in sales volume to the marketing communications, while largely ignoring the effects of other factors. Unfortunately, this narrow view prevails in many business settings.

Even though it may be difficult to measure the absolute effectiveness of most marketing communications, marketers have certainly not given up on the task. Quite the opposite is true, in fact, as marketers are increasingly under pressure to justify money spent on communications. In some cases, the effectiveness of marketing communications cannot be accurately assessed until a significant amount of time has passed. For example, a five-year antidrug campaign by the U.S. government was declared a failure when ads apparently had little effect on actual or intended drug use. In seeking a continuation of the $180 million annual budget for the program, the U.S drug czar pledged that all ads would be tested for effectiveness before they were released, compared to only a third that were tested during the previous campaign. In this case, pretesting could have saved a lot of money, and the effectiveness of the ads could have been assessed without waiting five years to declare the program a failure.[27]

The effectiveness of marketing communications designed to elicit a straightforward consumer response in a fairly short time period are easier to measure than those having to do with lifestyle or attitude modification. For example, British Airways ran ads in *The New York Times* Web edition to lure new members for its frequent-flyer program. The cost of the online campaign was $300,000, and it ex-

Money isn't everything.

It takes people, too. For example the people who initiated the Shell Youth Training Academy in South Central Los Angeles. This school helps inner-city high school students develop academic and social skills by providing them with both classroom training and paid, on-the-job experience. It's been so successful, Shell has started a second academy in Chicago.

Shell volunteers are frequently found helping repair, paint and fix up buildings that provide services to both young and old, like the Martin Luther King, Jr. Community Center in Houston. Shell employees

refurbished classrooms and the senior center, and established a state-of-the-art playground for the children of the neighborhood.

And whenever there's a need for disaster relief, Shell people go above and beyond to help their neighbors through earthquakes, hurricanes and floods with relief stations that provide essentials during tough times.

These are just a few of the hundreds of community projects across the nation where Shell employees are donating so much more than money.

Marketing communications can be used to communicate a corporation's role in socially responsible activities, which may also encourage other people to make contributions that will benefit society. This ad explains how Shell employees volunteer their time to worthwhile causes and projects.

ceeded its goal by 40 percent, signing up 12,000 new members. The cost of acquiring a new customer was $25, or three-fourths of the average acquisition costs in previous on-line campaigns. Additional revenue will more than pay for the costs of the campaign.[28] Results like these are what all marketers aspire to. With Web sites becoming a more important part of marketing communications, there is a strong interest in how to measure the effectiveness of these sites. For more information, see "Building Customer Equity: Creating Friendly Web Sites."

Ethical and Legal Considerations

Exhibit 16–6 notes the ways the five areas of marketing communications may be subject to criticism from an ethical and legal viewpoint. Much to the dismay of upright professional marketers, ethical problems and legal violations in marketing communications continue. The good news is that an *ethical perspective* is also evident in marketing communications. In fact, marketing communications are frequently used to encourage responsible behavior such as contributing to charitable causes, practicing safe driving, and supporting community action programs. Marketing communications are also used to inform buyers about legal issues with reminders like "buckle up, it's the law," or "you must be 21 years old to purchase this product."

An example of marketing communications contributing to society is the Target stores' "Take Charge of Education" program, whereby a percentage of sales is returned to participating schools in local communities. Target generates a considerable amount of favorable publicity with this program, and promotes the program on its Web site, with in-store signage, and in some of its advertising. The program has returned more than $56 million to deserving schools, students, and teachers.[29] Such programs remind us that marketing communications are essential not only to profit-seeking marketers but also to groups that support the improvement of our society. In some instance, the two constituencies overlap.

Building Customer Equity

Creating friendly Web sites

To ensure that their Web sites are accomplishing their marketing communications objectives, Avis, McDonald's, Staples, and Holiday Inn are among the companies using outside specialists to evaluate their effectiveness. These companies use focus groups, surveys, and online observation to uncover how customers use the Web sites and how this interaction effects brand image and feelings toward the company. More than 15 large companies specialize in this sort of research. Results of their work can help marketers establish long-term customer relationships and bring new users to the Web sites.

The costs of Web site usability research can range from $25,000 to several million dollars. The experience of TD

Bank Financial Group in Toronto is fairly typical. Research showed that customers could not easily find needed information on the TD site and that the look and feel of the site was not consistent from one section to the next. Corrections were made, and positive results followed.

An industry group has also developed self-assessment tools for evaluating Web sites. The Interactive Advertising Bureau in New York encourages the use of five guidelines: ad impressions, clicks, page impressions, total visits, and unique visits. By better understanding what customers want from Web sites and how a specific Web site measures up, marketers can add value, increase customer equity, and make the site pay off.

Exhibit 16–6	*Ethical and legal concerns in marketing communications*
Marketing Communications Element	**Ethical/Legal Concerns**
Advertising	• Using deceptive advertising • Reinforcing unfavorable ethnic/racial/sex stereotypes • Encouraging materialism & excessive consumption
Public relations	• Lack of sincerity (paying lip service to worthwhile causes) • Using economic power unfairly to gain favorable publicity • Orchestrating news events to give false appearance of widespread support for corporate position
Sales promotion	• Offering misleading consumer promotions • Paying slotting allowances to gain retail shelf space • Using unauthorized mailing lists to reach consumers
Personal selling	• Using high-pressure selling • Failing to disclose product limitations/safety concerns • Misrepresenting product benefits
Direct marketing communications	• Invading privacy by telemarketing • Using consumer database information without authorization of consumers • Creating economic waste with unwanted direct mail

Legal—but Ethical?

Some marketing communications may be technically legal but raise significant ethical questions. For example, after four decades of self-imposed restrictions, the liquor industry now advertises on cable and local television stations. Critics, citing problems arising from excessive consumption of alcohol, are outraged. Citing lost market share to beer and wine manufacturers, liquor companies argue that they are legally entitled to use advertising to promote their businesses. In 2002, it appeared that liquor advertising would begin on national television when NBC signed a lucrative deal with British-based Diageo, marketer of Smirnoff and other leading brands. NBC had the legal right to accept the advertising but bowed out after a backlash of public opinion and signals from the U.S. government that stricter regulation might be forthcoming if liquor ads appeared on national television. Many feel that NBC's last-minute refusal to run the ads may not last and that if NBC or any other major network accepts liquor advertising, all major networks will accept liquor ads.[30]

Another apparently legal but ethically questionable practice is the extensive promotion of higher-cost drugs when health care costs are spiraling out of control. The Federal Trade Commission is considering a probe into prescription drug pricing, as complaints have arisen that pharmaceutical firms have been marketing directly to patients who are using drugs for which patents are about to expire. Such drugs would then face intense price competition from generic drugs. There are also questions about the drug firms' use of heavy promotional allowances to pharmacies in return for pharmacies' agreements to push proprietary instead of generic drugs.[31]

Critics of legalized gambling have tried to attack the industry by supporting restrictions on advertising of state lotteries and other gambling activities. The American Advertising Federation opposes restrictions on advertising for gambling or any legal producer service, claiming that restrictions on truthful, nondeceptive advertising could lead to the curtailment of advertising other products, services, and activities.[32]

Deception in Marketing Communications

Exhibit 16–6 indicates that many problems relate to deception of consumers. Although this may happen in any area of the promotion mix, deceptive advertising is a prime concern. **Deceptive advertising,** communications intended to mislead consumers by making false claims or failing to disclose important information, is a major focus of the Federal Trade Commission (FTC), the government agency responsible for overseeing American business practices.

Deceptive advertising often involves false pricing offers, apparently to appeal to consumers' desire to get something for nothing. Office Depot, for example, ran ads promising free personal computers but failed to mention the mandatory three-year sign-up for Internet service at a cost of $800. Gateway, Hewlett-Packard, Sharp Electronics, and Microsoft are among others that the FTC found used deceptive advertising by not disclosing the full cost of advertised products.[33] The FTC also prohibits misrepresentation regarding product quality and availability. It found Keith's Wholesale and Bargains and Deals Wholesale (both owned by the same parent company) guilty of selling fraudulent merchandise in the form of counterfeit Oakley, Foster Grant, and Ray-Ban sunglasses. The advertised product was not shipped, and in some cases, even the counterfeit products were not shipped.[34] Visits to the Better Business Bureau Web site at www.bbb.org and the FTC site at www.ftc.gov can be educational for those who wish to learn more about deceptive advertising. These sites offer tips for consumers on how to avoid scams and guidelines for ethical and legal marketing communications.[35]

Another area of concern is substantiation of claims made in marketing communications. For example, the FTC found that Novartis Corporations could not substantiate its claim that its Doan's Pills were more effective than other pain relievers for back pain. Doan challenged the FTC ruling in court, but the FTC position was supported. As a result, Doan's was ordered to include clarifying messages in its packaging and advertising correcting the unsubstantiated claim. Over a five-year period, Doan's must spend $8 million to correct the false impression it had made with previous ads and packaging.[36]

Additional Regulatory Concerns

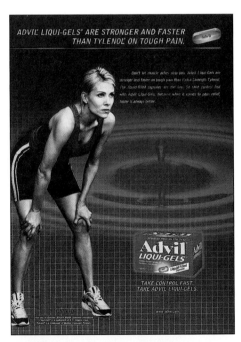

Marketers who use comparative advertising must be able to substantiate their claims. In this instance, Whitehall Laboratories uses comparative advertising to claim that Advil is gentler on the stomach than aspirin and that it works better on headache pain than Extra Strength Tylenol.

Additional FTC guidelines can affect marketing communications. The FTC requires that any claims made about product performance be capable of verification. Although the FTC provides for **comparative advertising** (which compares one product with other products), it also requires that comparative claims be supported. If Pontiac wants to claim that its Bonneville costs thousands of dollars less than, but performs as well as Lexus or BMW, it must make the basis for comparison clear to the consumer.

Product endorsers must be qualified to make judgments and must actually use the product being endorsed. Moreover, any demonstrations used in advertisements must be accurate representations and not images that are misleading.

Packaging and labeling practices of food and drug marketers are heavily scrutinized by consumers and regulatory agencies. At the national level, the Food and Drug Administration (FDA) keeps a watchful eye on health-related messages. In 1991, the FDA's regulatory power was extended by legislation that required manufacturers to disclose dietary and nutritional information on product labels about the amounts of fat, sugar, cholesterol, additives, and certain other elements in the product. The National Advertising Association Review Board (NARB) is also active in monitoring health and nutritional claims. In one case, the NARB found that Kellogg's had not substantiated implied claims that K-Sentials cereals provide a unique blend of vitamins and minerals or that all K-Sentials cereals contained additional calcium. Kellogg's agreed to modify their packaging and television, print, and Web advertising to correct the problems.[37]

Effects of Globalization

The increasing globalization of marketing often requires adjustment of the communications mix from country to country to avoid legal and ethical problems. From country to country, differences in language, culture, legal and ethical norms, and availability of various media are usually significant: Telemarketing laws, for example, in some European countries are far more stringent than are those in the United States. The use of humor and sex in marketing communications across countries and cultures can be a high-risk tactic due to the potential of misunderstandings' occurring. Sales promotion techniques that involve contests and giveaways are regulated quite differently in various countries. And of particular importance, effective advertising messages in one country may be offensive to residents of other countries, and what constitutes acceptable personal selling behavior also varies significantly across countries and cultures; for example, in many Latin and Far Eastern countries, establishing a personal relationship prior to developing a business relationship is crucial.

Recall that the global perspective also includes a recognition of multiculturalism within a given market or country. In a growing number of countries around the world, including the United States, marketing communications are addressing multicultural aspects of the market. Marketers must take special precautions not to perpetuate unfavorable stereotypes of ethnic and racial groups; often, these precautions include hiring ad agencies, research firms, and other specialists to guide their marketing communications efforts. Even so, consumers may be offended, which reinforces the importance of paying careful attention to cultural differences in marketing communications.

Summary

1. **Discuss the objectives of marketing communications.** The primary objective of marketing communications is to reach an audience to affect its behavior. In general, the three major objectives of marketing communications are to inform, to persuade, and to remind. The emphasis placed on one of the five primary communications methods to achieve these objectives depends on the company's marketing and communications strategy.

2. **Understand the marketing communications mix and its role.** Marketing communications allow marketers to reach current and potential customers. Advertising, public relations, sales promotion, personal selling, and direct marketing are the primary categories of marketing communications. Each of these tools has its unique advantages, providing a variety of techniques for reaching consumers. It is important that marketing communications be consistent with a firm's overall corporate and marketing strategy. Marketing communications must be coordinated with product, price, and channel factors to reach the desired target audience effectively.

3. **Explain the key elements of the marketing communications process.** Communication occurs when there is shared meaning between source and receiver. Communication is considered effective to the extent that the source gets a desired response from the receiver. From a marketing communications perspective, a firm as the source sends a marketing communications message through any of several message channels to its target audience, the receiver. The firm encodes the message by putting it into words, pictures, or symbols that best convey the message. Target audience members then decode the message by determining the meaning of the words, pictures, and symbols. Sometimes the intended message is not received if there is noise in the communications process.

4. **Discuss the seven steps in the marketing communications planning process.** The key tasks of marketing communications planning include marketing plan review, situation analysis, communications process analysis, budget development, program development, integration and implementation of the plan, and monitoring, evaluating, and controlling the marketing communications process.

5. **Demonstrate awareness of some of the key ethical and legal issues related to marketing communications.** All areas of marketing communications have come under criticism for unethical and illegal activities. Some of the more frequently publicized problems include deceptive advertising, inability to substantiate comparative claims, unfair reinforcement of ethnic, racial, and sex stereotypes, and encouragement of materialistic values.

Understanding Marketing Terms and Concepts

Thinking About Marketing

1. Briefly define marketing communications and describe the elements of the marketing communications mix.

2. What is sponsorship? What are some of its advantages and disadvantages? Give an example of sponsorship, and comment on its effectiveness.

3. What is the goal of marketing communications? Name three major objectives of marketing communications. For each objective, give an example of how an actual firm uses marketing communications to reach it.

4. Refer to "Being Entrepreneurial: Nike Gives a Lesson." What are the risks for the marketer of a mature brand when the advertising theme is changed?

5. What factors could cause a marketing communications message to be decoded differently from the way the source intended?

6. Briefly describe the steps in marketing communications planning.

7. How can other aspects of the marketing mix affect the marketing communications mix?

8. What influences the amount of money a company might spend on marketing communications?

9. Refer to "Building Customer Equity: Creating Friendly Web Sites." In addition to the five areas for assessing Web sites (ad impressions, clicks, page impressions, total visits, and unique visits) suggested by the Interactive Advertising Bureau, can you suggest other criteria for assessing the marketing effectiveness of Web sites?

10. Give several examples of ethical or legal issues related to marketing communications.

Applying Marketing Skills

1. Select a major marketer of consumer goods that has advertised on national television within the past month. Try to identify approaches other than television advertising that have been part of this company's recent marketing communications mix.

2. Identify several specific examples of marketing communications that you feel are either ethically or legally questionable. What elements in each communication cause the problem? How could each communication be improved to remove any doubt about its ethical or legal acceptability?

3. Choose a product you are familiar with, and illustrate how product, pricing, and marketing-channel factors influence the marketing communications activities for the product.

Using the www in Marketing

Activity One
The MiniUSA Web site at www.miniusa.com offers an opportunity to learn more about the marketing of the Mini Cooper automobile in the United States. Explore the Web site and answer the following questions:

1. What evidence can you find that BMW uses a customer-oriented approach to marketing the Mini Cooper?

2. How could Mini Cooper salespeople use the information from the Web site to facilitate the sales process?

3. Assess the "Our Values" section of the Web site. How could the values statements (including diversity) influence the marketing of the Mini Cooper?

Activity Two
Part of being a professional is keeping up with your field. In today's environment, this increasingly means staying abreast of international developments. Trade publications are useful for this purpose. For example, *Advertising Age* is one of the most widely read trade sources for all forms of marketing communications. Access the Web site http://www.adage.com and click on menu items of interest. Be sure to investigate the Ad Age Global menu.

1. What developments are occurring outside the United States that you find noteworthy?

2. Check the Ad Age Data Center to see if there is information related to international advertising and marketing.

Making Marketing Decisions
Case 16-1 *Liquor Companies Eye National TV Networks*

Major liquor companies have been rethinking the industry's self-imposed ban on television advertising. Since the mid-1990s, Seagram's and other major distillers have dabbled with cable television advertising, a move that raised the eyebrows of consumer watchdogs and government regulators. In 2002, it appeared that the major liquor companies were ready to expand their advertising efforts to the national television networks. NBC had signaled a willingness to accept liquor ads and began running a spot featuring the Smirnoff brand that urged the use of designated drivers. NBC intended to run such public-service ads for four months, then begin mainstream ads emphasizing liquor, not safety. The network backed off when the public and political backlash grew too strong. Many industry analysts think it only a matter of time before liquor companies advertise on national TV, because the liquor industry is losing market share to wine and beer purveyors.

The controversial aspects of liquor ads on TV revolve primarily around social questions. Opponents argue that drinking alcohol leads to increased social costs as a result of alcoholism, more automobile accidents, acts of violence, and employee absenteeism, and that alcohol, when consumed in excessive amounts, contributes to physical and mental disorders. Particularly troublesome to critics is that they feel that liquor companies target young, and in some cases, underage consumers.

Although Seagram and other liquor companies deny targeting young consumers, there is a fair amount of evidence to the contrary. Certainly print advertising by liquor companies includes blatant appeals to consumers under 21 years of age, a group that accounts for 30 percent of the United States population. *Spin, Rolling Stone,* and *Allure* magazines, all popular venues for liquor ads, have a third to almost half of their readers in the under-21 category, an age group that most agree should not be targeted for liquor ads.

There are some risks to liquor companies if they persist with television advertising. The federal government has increased its scrutiny of liquor marketing. The FTC reviewed ad content and media placement of eight major advertisers of beer, liquor, and wine. The FTC recommended improvements in self-regulatory codes and

will undoubtedly investigate further the age profiles of television programs and print media where alcoholic beverages are advertised. Since there is bipartisan political support against advertising liquor on television, an increase may bring counter measures such as increased taxes on alcohol, point-of-sale restraints, and restrictions on ad content. It appears that these are risks that the liquor companies are willing to take.

Questions

1. The U.S. government may enact regulations to prohibit liquor advertisements on television. How would liquor companies argue against such regulation?

2. Should liquor companies withhold advertising on television in an attempt to be more socially responsible?

3. How could liquor companies convince the public and government officials that their ads are not targeted toward consumers under the age of 21?

Case 16-2 Vans and Nike Go Toe-to-Toe

Vans, a Southern California Company, is the largest and oldest company in the skate-shoe business. Not known for being particularly innovative, the company has succeeded by relying heavily on its checkerboard-print slip-on with "grippy" soles and a constant dedication to promoting the sport of skateboarding. Vans sells more than $350 million a year in the skate-shoe market, while its chief competitors such as Quicksilver, DC Shoes USA, and Volcom rarely exceed $100 million in annual sales.

Nike, through its purchase of Savier, a Portland, Oregon, skate-shoe company, represents a significant new competitive threat for Vans. Further, Nike has purchased Hurley's, an Orange County, California, clothing competitor of Vans. Hurley's does not yet make shoes, but industry observers expect Nike will use Hurley's to broaden its push into the fast-growing skateboarding market.

Nike tried unsuccessfully in the 1990s to break into the skate-shoe market. Its reputation as a corporate giant did not sit well with independent-minded teens and preteens, the prime demographic in the skateboarding market. Historically, Nike has been viewed as a supporter of team sports and conformity by skateboarders, while skateboard retailers see the company as arrogant and unwilling to support the industry in the committed fashion demonstrated by Vans throughout its 38-year history.

Some of these perceptions are changing. For one thing, Vans has gotten to be quite a corporate entity itself. Its products are distributed well beyond the skateboard specialty shops, where image is of paramount importance. Vans can be found in Foot Locker and other mainstream retail stores. Vans also has a music label, produces sports television shows for two networks, and has produced a movie called *Dogtown,* which it hopes will become a skateboarding cult classic just as *Endless Summer* was for surfing. *Dogtown* will be backed by a $5 million marketing communications campaign from Sony Pictures, and Vans is selling *Dogtown*-licensed merchandise in conjunction with the film's release. Working with Sony Pictures and selling to Foot Locker may seem just as "corporate" to members of the young target market as some of Nike's mainstream moves.

Meanwhile, Nike is keeping its ownership of Savier as quiet as possible. The emphasis has been on how Savier shoes fit, and Nike is going toe-to-toe with Vans in a fight for market share. One of its prime marketing communications tools is the "Trade'Em Up" tour, which features a van (a coincidence?) that visits skateboard parks in an attempt to get Vans wearers to trade up to a pair of Saviers. Kids like the comfort of the Saviers, and they now seem less concerned about Nike's association with the company. There are 1,000 skateboard parks in the United States, with 200 of them built since early 2001. Nike first concentrated on 47 parks in California, since California skateboarders tend to be the trendsetters. The tour then moved on across the country into key markets. Feedback and sales have been good, with durability joining comfort as key product attributes that skateboarders like.

Vans marketing personnel are worried about Nike's presence in the market, noting that Nike does not give up easily when faced with a marketing challenge. The antiestablishment sentiment that dogged Nike in the past does not seem as strident now, and Vans must face the fact that they too are part of the same establishment that Nike belongs to. Nike is redoubling its efforts to reach suburban white males, and the skateboard market may be a profitable avenue for doing just that. Industry analysts think that skateboarding is becoming a mainstream sport, and that sports like little league baseball may be considered alternative in a few years. Traditionally, Nike has built its brand image on advertising using celebrity sports figures. A survey of preteen boys found that retired skateboarder Tony Hawk has more status than Michael Jordan. The sneaker market, following a big surge in the late 1990s for basketball shoes, has essentially leveled off. Nike, ever the hungry giant, may make it rough for Vans in the coming years. But no one expects Vans to give up easily either.

Questions

1. What directions can you suggest for Vans as it plans its marketing communications strategy in the near future. How much attention should be paid specifically to the Savier/Nike threat?

2. How should Nike proceed with its marketing communications in the near future to reach the skateboarding market? Can you make specific "do" or "don't" recommendations for reaching a preteen and teen male market?

3. How could both companies use multiple marketing communications tools (advertising, public relations, personal selling, sales promotion, and direct marketing) in an integrated marketing communications program?

Chapter Seventeen

Advertising and Public Relations

After studying this chapter, you should be able to:

1 Understand the characteristics, functions, and types of advertising.

2 Realize how people process advertising information and how it affects buyer behavior.

3 Discuss approaches to developing advertising campaigns.

4 Describe different advertising objectives and the message strategies used to achieve them.

5 Understand the decisions involved in selecting media and scheduling advertising.

6 Explain how marketers assess advertising effectiveness.

7 Appreciate the roles of public relations and publicity in marketing.

www.british-airways.com

After several turbulent years, British Airways is shrinking its capacity by going to smaller planes and fewer routes. The efforts are designed to increase profitability by recasting British Airlines as the preferred choice for business and corporate travelers. As long as the airline dominates British airports, it will be able to charge premium prices for a large portion of transatlantic travel. In addition, the firm is determined to return to its tradition of innovation. These changes include seats that can turn into beds and face the rear of the plane and that are connected with multichannel entertainment centers. New television advertisements concentrate on customer service and benefits. The challenge is to maintain the airline's premium positioning in the marketplace while still being concerned with the sale of unsold seats through Internet auctions and price-search avenues. This is a difficult task, as the airline's primary target audience is busy, watches little TV, and is overexposed to advertising.

British Airways has used its advertising in a variety of efforts. For example, the company's "Future and Shape" strategy includes a marketing blitz to combat

its damaging reputation as an expensive airline. BA, which has seen its market share eroded by budget carriers, invests heavily in tactical advertising to promote competitive fares to Europe. Recent plans also include heavy use of public relations to introduce their lower fares and to fight against budget airlines such as easyJet. The company realizes the need to compete more on price. One aspect of this effort is the attempt to get more customers to buy tickets on-line. The company has not fared well lately, but hopes to improve its profits by reducing costs and appealing still to premium business travelers on transatlantic flights, which provide most of the company's profitable routes.

Information about all aspects of BA's marketing mix can be obtained from the firm's site (http://www.british-airways.com). For example, the site provides in-depth descriptions of the types of planes the airline uses, the services offered, special ticket prices to certain locations, and the locations that can be reached. Details about the company's use of media and press releases are available from the site's media and public relations archives.

The British Airways marketing program is a good example of how marketers use different advertising media and communications approaches to reach their desired target segments. To handle its Internet presence, BA has selected an advertising agency that specializes in designing interactive Web sites. The airline promotes its services through both traditional advertising and other marketing communications, such as public relations and sales promotions, along with the interactive aspects of its Web site.

In this chapter, we explore issues associated with advertising, the most visible marketing activity. We discuss the related topic of public relations as well.

The Nature of Advertising

Advertising Defined

Advertising is the activity consumers most associate with the term *marketing*. **Advertising** is defined as a marketing communications element that is persuasive, non-personal, paid for by an identified sponsor, and disseminated through mass channels of communication to promote the adoption of goods, services, persons, or ideas.[1]

Effective advertising can present information about new or existing products, demonstrate meaningful uses of the product, and establish or refresh the brand's image.[2] It can reach a diverse or wide audience with repeated communications and gives a company the opportunity to dramatize its products and services in a colorful way.

Advertising stimulates demand, helps build brand success, develops and shapes buyer behavior, and gives the seller a measure of certainty about the level of sales. In addition, it informs buyers about product characteristics and availability and makes markets more competitive.[3]

In many markets, first-time purchasers are rare. Here advertising is critically important in affecting brand shares by inducing switching or retaining customers who otherwise might switch. Brand switching is generated from advertising through building brand awareness or altering consumer beliefs about brands.[4]

Advertising performs other functions as well. Some advertising supports personal selling efforts. For example, many companies advertise to increase consumer awareness of products, making later personal selling efforts easier. Such advertising, if executed effectively, generates sales leads and communicates product advantages to prospective buyers.

Advertising and the Marketing Concept

It is important to remember that advertising is expensive and must be targeted effectively to achieve a firm's objectives. Firms do not have unlimited budgets; thus, the allocation of these funds must be made with a clear view of target markets and, hence, the audience for the organization's advertising. Further, conceiving product offerings on the basis of consumer needs and benefits is not sufficient without some form of communication, frequently advertising. That is, communication (advertising) *and* desired product attributes are both integral aspects of the marketing concept.

Mass media and advertising are playing a critical role in the creation of global consumption symbols. The direct influence of MTV and similar channels is evidenced by teens who watch these channels being more likely to display the signs of global teen culture and a global culture of consumption. Recent scholars have proposed that advertising can be used to position brands by a strategy referred to as *global consumer culture positioning*. This approach, not entirely the same concept as standardization discussed in Chapter 7 on market segmentation, can be contrasted with strategies in which the brand is associated with local cultures (i.e., Budweiser's small-town American culture in its U.S. advertising) and foreign consumer culture positioning in which

Exhibit 17–1	*Total national advertising spending by type of medium*

Medium	Expenditures ($ millions)
Network TV	$ 18,417
Newspapers	18,817
Spot TV*	17,107
Magazines	16,697
Cable TV networks	9,506
Syndicated TV	2,804
National newspapers	3,785
National spot radio	2,672
Outdoor	2,391
Sunday magazine	1,110
Network radio	871
Internet	4,333
Yellow pages	13,228
Total measured media	111,739
Unmeasured spending estimates	131,941
Total U.S. advertising	243,680

*Spot TV refers to purchased time on selected television stations affiliated with one of the major networks.

the brand is positioned with a specific foreign culture (e.g., Singapore Airline's use of the "Singapore Girl in Its Global Media Advertising").[5]

The Advertising Industry

Advertising is a huge industry, with annual global expenditures close to $300 billion worldwide. General Motors, Procter & Gamble, and Daimler-Chrysler each spend more than $1 billion on media advertising.[6] Exhibit 17–1 presents the amount advertisers spend in the United States on each medium.

Two of the fastest growing media are magazines and cable TV networks. In fact, their growth has caused average nightly audience shares of the major networks (ABC, NBC, CBS) to drop to under 50 percent; hence network advertising revenues have dropped by more than 10 percent.[7]

Ad Agencies

Many advertisers hire **advertising agencies** to create ad campaigns and to purchase media time and space. Exhibit 17–2 lists the world's top five advertising organizations as measured by gross income. All of them employ many people in organizations worldwide, and two have their central offices in London or Tokyo.

Ad agencies employ creative people who develop unique advertising messages and media specialists who provide media planning and scheduling. Creative strategies and a proven track record clearly are good reasons to hire an ad agency. To limit costs and save on commissions, however, some large companies such as Benetton have in-house advertising functions to handle everything from creative design to media decisions. Other companies, such as Procter & Gamble, now buy their own media space and time instead of relying entirely on ad agencies. Other companies, such as IBM, Bayer, 3M, and Campbell Soup, have pared down the number of agencies used globally. This consolidation further enhances the "single voice" aspects of integrated marketing communications.

The choice of a competent ad agency is especially important for firms targeting new global markets. One U.S. soap manufacturer, for example, simply dubbed its commercials—showing people singing in the shower—into Polish TV ads. Poles laughed heartily at the advertiser's naiveté: There are very few showers in Polish homes, and because hot water is so limited, no Pole would take a leisurely shower.

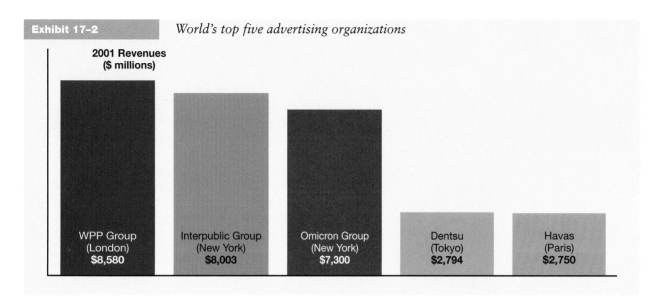

Exhibit 17–2   *World's top five advertising organizations*

2001 Revenues
($ millions)

| WPP Group (London) $8,580 | Interpublic Group (New York) $8,003 | Omicron Group (New York) $7,300 | Dentsu (Tokyo) $2,794 | Havas (Paris) $2,750 |

Marketers can avoid such gaffes by establishing close partnerships with a capable advertising agency.[8] Coca-Cola has shifted its $1.6 billion worldwide account to the Leo Burnett and the McCann-Erickson agencies.

Historically, agencies have been able to charge a 15 percent commission of their gross billings for time and space purchased for their clients. More recently, accountability and economic pressures have led to alternative compensation plans. First, many firms now charge rates below 15 percent. Second, some agencies use a labor-based system based on the number of hours worked. Third, in some instances, advertisers pay their agencies under an incentive program based on the extent to which the advertiser's objectives are met. Driver's Mart, which owns a network of used-car dealerships and spends $40 million on advertising, pays its agency a commission for every car sold.[9] The U.S. Army also has shifted to a pay-for-performance plan in which its advertising agency will be paid based upon recruitment success.

P&G has also decided to pay its agencies according to increases and decreases in sales, instead of paying labor-based fees or commissions based on media spending. The sheer size of the company's ad budget has resulted in significant attention to this shift toward pay for performance. In contrast, advertising executives worry about the other factors that affect sales and factors that are not under ad agency control. For instance, if an agency does great work, but the company fails to run the ads frequently enough, should the agency suffer? Conversely, if a company designs a great product that would sell without a lot of advertising, should the ad agency benefit?[10]

Advertising agencies and the advertising industry have been negatively affected by recent events. Revenues were reduced following the post-dot-com advertising crash and the 9/11 terrorist attacks. Advertising effectiveness is constrained by the increasing number of sensory media to which consumers are now exposed and new technologies like TiVo in which commercial messages can be bypassed. A number of other factors can lead to an agency getting fired: a general cost-saving initiative or change in leadership at the client; merger fallout; ineffective work; and a depressed industry in which the client operates.[11]

Industry in Transition

Today, marketers increasingly question each advertising expenditure. Targeting mass markets with advertising alone no longer makes sense for many companies. Simply buying airtime during a specific TV program or buying a certain page in a specific magazine is not enough to reach targeted audiences. Advertisers often must

Ariel recognizes cultural influences in its advertising that promotes stain remover capability.

use multimedia campaigns, combining television, print ads, videos, billboards, trade shows, direct mail, and activities such as event sponsorship into an *integrated marketing communications program*.[12]

Globalization of marketing efforts is another example of changing times. In many instances, both product and advertising must meet local market needs and fit in with cultural practices. Religious-dominant areas such as Saudi Arabia and Iran, areas with multiple cultural influences such as Japan and Korea, and more-homogeneous areas such as Sweden and Australia each require different advertising communications.[13] For example, Kraft advertised its processed cheese slices using a common theme (milk content) but different advertising styles and presentations to match the consumer preferences and uniqueness in Canada, the United Kingdom, Australia, and Spain.[14]

Japanese advertisers favor "soft selling" and often use indirect messages. The typical Western emphasis on product merit and use of spokespeople directly stating brand advantages are missing in much Japanese advertising.[15] And surprisingly, given the Japanese attraction to Western culture, the appearance of American images and settings has increased only modestly in Japanese advertising. Foreign advertisers in Japan should recognize these differences.

Technological changes keep the advertising industry in transition as well. The extension of cable TV, the widespread penetration of VCRs, the introduction of TiVo and remote-control capability all suggest some loss of effectiveness of TV commercials. Remote-control use, in particular, has given rise to **commercial zapping,** or changing the channels during commercials.[16] One study revealed that ads aired during competing sports events encountered audience losses up to 50 percent. Zapping is heaviest during news and late-night programming.[17] In addition, younger viewers and members of higher-income households are more likely to get up and do something else during TV commercial breaks.[18] Prerecorded shows that allow skipping forward through ads and these other technological advances have advertisers and media executives very concerned. Television as a free service enjoyed by consumers depends upon effective exposure to advertising. Otherwise, advertisers will not purchase the time and the economics of advertising as a means of supporting television will not work.[19]

What then does this transition mean for advertising? The future looks brightest for media that reach target audiences more efficiently than broad-based ones like network TV. The winners are expected to be radio stations, specialized cable networks, new kinds of in-store advertising, and weekly newspapers, all of which appeal to specific rather than to broad audiences.[20]

Internet Advertising

Online advertising is predicted to reach $15.9 million by 2007. The evolution of the Internet as a meaningful channel of commercial communications is profoundly affecting the way firms do business. For example, advertising designed to establish consumer brand images will no longer focus only upon the 30-second commercial complemented by some print advertising. Advertisers and agencies alike are now required to consider all contacts with consumers in efforts to develop strong brands and brands that can be effective across borders. Advertisers on the Web have already begun to move beyond simple measurement of impressions.

Three factors hit the online industry in 2001 and 2002—failing dot coms that were heavy Internet advertisers, low clickthrough rates for most banner ads, and a general recession for all types of media. Other concerns include ads that obscure site editorial content, ads that promise one thing and deliver another, and multiple ads on a page competing for attention. In response to poor performance, new ad-

Speaking from Experience

Jim Ensign
Senior Vice President
Doe-Anderson, Inc.

"We approach our clients' marketing communications challenges from a 'media neutral' basis. That is, we are never predisposed to believe that the best way to accomplish the goal is advertising. We go through a rigorous analysis of the challenge, the consumer, the competition, and the client's capabilities, and develop integrated programs that will best accomplish the goal—this may include no or little advertising, or may rely *heavily* on advertising."

Doe-Anderson, Inc., is an integrated marketing communications company, providing advertising, public relations, direct marketing, promotion, and interactive media counseling and services for national and international clients. Companies such as Valvoline, Sony Music and Entertainment, Allied Domecq Distilled Spirits, and National City Corporation use Doe-Anderson's integrated approach to develop marketing programs for their brands. Jim is the director of the advertising media planning and placement department and is also director of Doe-Anderson's Interactive Group, which develops Internet marketing programs and Web sites.

Jim earned a BS degree in business administration from Miami University in 1984 and held management positions at both Foote, Cone & Belding and Bayer, Bess, Vanderwarker in Chicago before joining Doe-Anderson, Inc., in Louisville, Kentucky, in 1992.

vertising formats have been introduced that include oblong ads on the side of a page and rectangle boxes much larger than banners, as well as mini-windows that open independently and will not disappear until closed by the viewer. Advergames, such as Dodge Speedway, represent a new genre of computer games that market everything from dandruff shampoo to movies. In fact, consumer advertisers are adopting online advertising programs used by B2B marketers, such as creating extranets and building microsites with their marketing partners.

While the growth of online advertising for Yahoo and AOL is expected to remain modest, many well-known brands, like Pepsi, Volvo, Frito-Lay, and others, have begun to view online advertising as an interactive supplement to their traditional advertising. Online advertising is more than clickthrough rates. Branding advantages are important as well. The manner in which online advertising should be evaluated depends upon the situation. If the firm is Lands' End or L. L. Bean, clickthrough

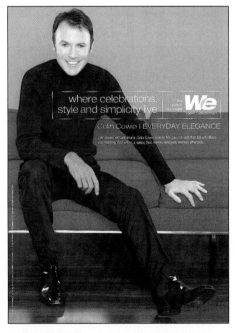

The increasing number of specialized cable channels enables marketers to more effectively reach target markets with unique characteristics and specific interests.

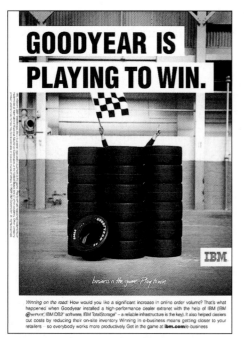

IBM promotes one of their successful technology enhancements in this B2B print advertisement.

conversion is important. If the firm is focused upon branding, the awareness, recall, and attitudes are important. The New York–based Interactive Advertising Bureau has proposed a series of guidelines that are designed to improve the accuracy of Internet audience measurement.[21]

Classifications of Advertising

Advertising can be classified by target audience, geographic area, medium, and purpose, as shown in Exhibit 17–3.[22] The special types discussed here are corporate image advertising, corporate advocacy advertising, public service advertising, classified advertising, direct-response advertising, business-to-business advertising, and cooperative advertising.

Corporate image advertising, directed toward the general public or investors and stockholders, promotes an organization's image and role in the community as a corporate citizen, independent of any product or service. **Corporate advocacy advertising** announces a stand on some issue related to the firm's operation, often one threatening the company's well-being. For example, Exxon addressed environmental issues in advocacy advertising following its Alaska oil spill.

Public service advertising is donated by the advertising industry to promote activities for some social good. For example, the World Wildlife Fund presents environmental public service advertisements. Frequently, marketers donate advertising time to drug and alcohol abuse prevention efforts, such as the "Just Say No" program and Mothers Against Drunk Driving (MADD).

Exhibit 17–3	*Classifications of advertising*		
By target audience	**By geographic area**	**By medium**	**By purpose**
Consumer advertising: Aimed at people who buy the product for their own or someone else's personal use.	**Local (retail) advertising:** Advertising by businesses whose customers come from only one city or local trading area.	**Print advertising:** Newspaper, magazine.	**Product advertising:** Intended to promote goods and services.
Business advertising: Aimed at people who buy or specify goods and services for use in business:	**Regional advertising:** Advertising for products sold in one area or region, but not the whole country.	**Broadcast (electronic) advertising:** Radio, TV.	**Nonproduct (corporate or institutional) advertising:** Intended to promote firm's mission or philosophy rather than a product.
• **Industrial:** Aimed at people who buy or influence the purchase of industrial products.	**National advertising:** Advertising aimed at customers in several regions of the country.	**Out-of-home advertising:** Outdoor, transit.	**Commercial advertising:** Intended to promote goods, services, or ideas with the expectancy of making a profit.
• **Trade:** Aimed at wholesalers and retailers who buy for resale to their customers.	**International advertising:** Advertising directed at foreign markets.	**Direct-mail advertising:** Advertising sent through the mail.	**Noncommercial advertising:** Sponsored by or for a charitable institution, civic group, or religious or political organization.
• **Professional:** Aimed at people licensed to practice under a code of ethics or set of professional standards.			**Action advertising:** Intended to bring about immediate action on the part of the reader.
• **Agricultural (farm):** Aimed at people in the farming or agricultural business.			**Awareness advertising:** Intended to build the image of a product or familiarity with the product's name and package.

The Ad Council has been instrumental in supporting public service advertising for over 60 years as a means for generating positive social change. The issues addressed include supporting higher education, advancing diversity, encouraging volunteerism, and promoting health and safety issues.[23]

Direct-response advertising (discussed in more detail in Chapter 20) is intended to elicit immediate action, often a purchase. Direct-response ads on TV typically request immediate calls to telephone numbers shown on the TV screen. Direct-response ads also appear in magazines and direct mail. **Classified advertising,** mainly in newspapers, typically promotes transactions for a single item or service.

Firms use **business-to-business advertising** to promote their products or services directly to other firms. The largest B-to-B advertising buyers are Verizon, Microsoft, IBM, and Sprint. Most business advertising involves print ads in trade periodicals or direct mail sent to targeted buyers. In trade or business-to-business advertising, just as in consumer advertising, product benefits must be highlighted and a solution offered to prospects' problems. A significant portion of business-to-business advertising should also be devoted to building and nurturing the brand images for the company as well as promoting/developing/enriching its key products and services."[24] Some business marketers, such as Ricoh Copiers, IBM, and Federal Express, advertise on TV in time slots likely to reach sophisticated adult audiences. Like business-to-consumer advertisers, B2B advertisers must coordinate trade magazine advertising, trade-show activity, and online database efforts in an integrated marketing communications program. B2B trade advertising must also have a strong visual to attract attention and a clear selling proposition. Too often advertising of all types, including B2B appeals, are so clever that the message is not processed.[25]

Cooperative advertising entails manufacturers contributing to a local dealer or retailer's advertising expense. The amount is based on the quantity of product the retailer purchases. The local marketer typically runs manufacturer-developed advertising that includes the outlet's name and logo.

Consumer Ad Processing
How then does advertising actually influence consumers? In this section, we explain how consumers process advertisements and how ads affect consumer attitudes and decisions.

Hierarchy of Effects
Advertising's influence on consumers is often explained by using the **hierarchy of effects,** or information-processing, model. This sequence of effects—exposure, attention, comprehension, acceptance, retention—is shown in Exhibit 17–4. Of course, every consumer does not consciously, or even subconsciously, go through a sequence of steps for all ads. Yet each stage of this hierarchy represents a specific goal for advertisers to pursue.

A marketer achieves *message exposure* by placing ads in appropriate media, such as magazines, TV programs, or newspapers, which gives the consumer the opportunity to process the message. According to the "mere exposure" hypothesis, positive evaluation of a brand can occur simply from repeated exposure to an advertisement.

Consumer *attention* is the next step. The ad must stimulate the consumer to direct mental effort toward it. The primary attention-getting properties of an ad are its physical characteristics. For print ads, these include size, number of colors, and brightness. Motion, attention-getting models, and novelty also help grab attention.[26]

Exhibit 17–4   *Advertising hierarchy of effects*

Message exposure → Attention → Comprehension → Acceptance → Retention

Attention does not necessarily mean the consumer will process a message further. *Message comprehension,* the next stage, means the consumer understands the ad's meaning. Comprehension includes categorization of the stimulus or advertised brand based upon prior information stored in memory. Elaboration of the information included in the ad furthers comprehension. Comprehension is enhanced to the extent the individual is motivated at the time of exposure and has some prior product category knowledge. Ad information that appears first (primacy effects) or last (recency effects) is often most comprehended.

Then, *message acceptance* must occur for the consumer to develop favorable attitudes about the advertised product or service and its subsequent purchase. Message acceptance includes both cognitive thoughts or responses related to the information in the ad as well as feelings, or affective responses, that occur because of the advertisement.

Message retention occurs when the consumer stores ad information in long-term memory, which is critical for affecting later purchase decisions and behavior.

A related view of how advertising works, and one developed recently by two advertising scholars from the London Business School, can be summarized partially as follows. First, advertising from the target brand and competing brands serves as input to the consumer. Strategic variables, including the scheduling of media, message content, and repetition, are components of this input. The individual's motivation and ability (consumer involvement) filter this input. Initial consumer responses include thoughts and thinking (e.g., cognition) and feelings and "affect" (e.g., attitudes). These consumer outcomes then lead to choice behavior, consumption, loyalty, and habit formation.[27]

Selective perception can occur at any stage. Exposure varies when consumers change channels during commercial breaks on television. *Selective attention* occurs when consumers notice certain ads but not others. Advertisers and advertising creative personnel expend considerable effort in developing ads that generate attention. Color, sexual images, attractive celebrity endorsers, and humor are frequently employed to garner attention.

Selective comprehension involves consumer interpretation of information provided in ads. Persuasion researchers have documented the tendency of individuals to perceive incoming information consistent with their own opinions and preferences. For example, an ad that disparages a consumer's favorite brand may be seen as biased or untruthful and its claims not accepted. *Selective retention* relates to what parts of the advertised information consumers actually remember. Given the low-involvement nature of ad encounters, messages are often kept simple and advertisers frequently use mnemonics, such as symbols, rhymes, and unique images, that assist the learning and remembering of brand information.

Influences on Ad Processing

Buyers' needs influence their processing of advertising messages. For example, a firm with a pressing need for waste removal would pay more attention to ads for this service than to aesthetic ads from a plant service to beautify the corporate office.

In addition, the buyer's motivation, ability, and opportunity to process brand information come into play. These concepts serve as important filters between advertising input (e.g., message content, media scheduling, and repetition) and the consumer. Consumer responses include thoughts or cognitions, affective feelings, and experiences.[28] First, *motivation* is related to the concept of consumer involvement, or the personal relevance or importance of the marketing communications message. Motivation is the desire to process the information. When motivation is low, potential customers pay little attention and remember minimal information, if any. *Ability* implies the buyer knows enough about the product category to understand the advertised message.[29] *Opportunity* is the extent to which distractions or limited exposure time affect the buyer's attention to brand information in an ad.

The opportunity for processing any single brand advertisement is diminished to the extent that the ad is surrounded by ads for competing brands. Consequently, advertisers attempt to avoid competitors' ads when buying advertising time and space. Competitive interference effects are particularly likely to occur for new brands. Since consumers' stored memory is limited, it is much more difficult for them to remember product information from ads for new brands in heavily advertised product categories. In contrast, well-known brands are less affected by competitive brand advertising; hence, they have important advantages in maintaining market share in the face of competing new brands.[30]

Product involvement may also affect the extent to which advertising is processed. Highly involved consumers are more likely to process the information in advertising and to notice differences in product attributes as advertised. In addition, extended problem solving is more likely; hence, complex advertisements may be more effective, since thoughtful processing of information is common in high-involvement situations.[31]

One well-known theory of persuasion, the **elaboration likelihood model,** includes individual motivation and ability to elaborate information in advertisements as determinants of two different "routes" to persuasion. Specifically, when consumer motivation and ability are high, persuasive message arguments are more thoroughly processed and the strength of the arguments influences persuasion in what is termed the "central route" to persuasion. However, when motivation and ability are low, peripheral cues become important in enhancing persuasion. In these cases, aspects of advertisements such as pictures and the use of celebrity and/or attractive models are important. In these latter cases, persuasion occurs through what is labeled the "peripheral route" to persuasion.[32]

Developing an Advertising Campaign

An ad campaign requires an analysis of the marketing situation, the target market involved, and the firm's overall communication objectives. As Exhibit 17–5 shows, once the firm has selected its target market, it must determine advertising objectives, determine the advertising budget, design the creative strategy, select and schedule media, and evaluate advertising effectiveness.

Selecting Target Markets

The development of an effective advertising campaign is dependent upon the selection of target markets that the company can effectively serve. As explained in both Chapter 3 and Chapter 7, the selection of which target markets to serve is based

| Exhibit 17–5 | *Advertising development and evaluation* |

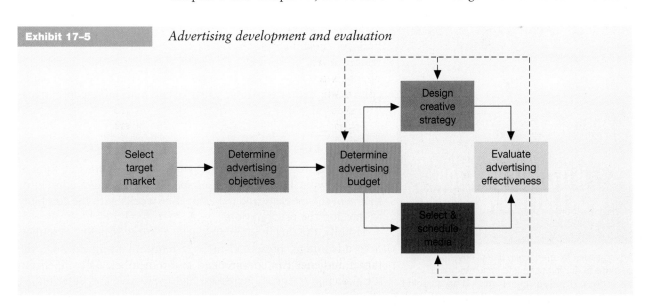

upon a number of factors related to the marketplace and the advertiser. The most important of these determining factors include the firm's core competencies, its overall vision, and the potential of the intended targets in terms of long-term sales and profits. For the placement of advertising during TV programs, the shows are selected for their ability to deliver exposure to intended target markets. Segments that advertisers are trying to reach are traditionally identified by age, income, gender, education, and ethnicity. The youth are often the focus for their ability to establish what is trendy, while the older baby boomers offer attractive markets because of their substantial disposable incomes.

Determining Advertising Objectives

Advertising objectives should be realistic, precise, measurable, and consistent with the firm's overall marketing and communications objectives. One objective might be to increase brand awareness from 10 to 35 percent of all consumers within a particular market—say, cereal eaters between the ages of 18 and 55. Another might be to increase sales or market share, say, to achieve a sales growth of 2 percent in the next quarter. Setting objectives enhances the firm's ability to evaluate the effectiveness of its advertising expenditures.

The dot coms are spending extraordinary amounts of money on media advertising to build brand positioning and market share. For example, Hotjobs.com spent $12 million of $16 million raised from venture capitalists to start operations on broadcast and outdoor media. In some cases, advertising objectives may be tied to other variables, such as market awareness, that are indirectly tied to sales objectives. In the face of low share for some of its products, Minolta used advertising to increase awareness of its entire line of products. Likewise, IBM recently spent $75 million on a global print campaign developed by Ogilvy & Mather just to improve the awareness of its technology services and consulting.[33]

Determining Advertising Budget

The size of the advertising budget depends on the size of the company, its financial resources, the industry growth rate, market dispersion, and the firm's position in the marketplace. Smaller firms usually spend less; dominant firms may spend a disproportionately large amount to maintain market share and discourage competition. And a growing industry may warrant higher advertising budgets to build awareness, sales, and market share.

As explained in Chapter 16, budgets are often based on percentage of sales, competitive parity, all the firm can afford, or allocation by objectives, the recommended approach. Advertising budgets are more important in today's business environment, which more and more views marketing communications as a profit center. Advertising generates income, but expenses must be controlled, and advertising, as well as all marketing communications, should show a net profit.[34]

Designing Creative Strategy

Creative strategy combines the "what is said" with the "how it is said." Typically, the advertiser specifies the general content or theme of the message and the ad agency works with the company to develop the presentation.

Usually, the theme is the product's primary benefit or competitive advantage, presented in an attention-getting message the target audience can comprehend and remember. As competition for audience attention increases, highly creative and entertaining commercials become commonplace.[35]

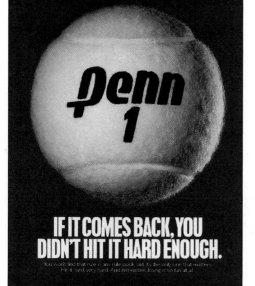

Advertisements often make use of novel pictorial displays to get attention and generate brand awareness. These ads are effective at encouraging information processing after initial exposure.

Increasingly, advertisers are recognizing the influence of cultural diversity on advertising. As noted earlier, this is particularly true for international advertising, where standardization of advertising across national lines is on the decline. In addition, national advertisers often use specialized campaigns to target minority and other groups.

On occasion, failures in creative execution occur. Chrysler botched the introduction of its Intrepid by the use of very high-tech advertisements that only briefly showed the car at the end of the commercial. Sometimes questionable advertising is unintentionally humorous. For example, one sleep aid promoted the cautionary message "may cause drowsiness," while one snack brand advertised its contest as "You could be a winner! No purchase necessary. Details inside."[36] Levi's has returned to emphasizing its authentic heritage, instead of chasing after street fashion and transient "cool."[37]

MESSAGE STRATEGY ALTERNATIVES   Advertising messages can make objective or subjective claims. **Objective claims** describe product features or performance in measurable terms, such as "Chevy mid-sized vans are available with V-6 or V-8 engines." Objective claims often promote the benefits customers receive from the price paid. For example, Reebok advertises the custom fit from its pump technology. AT&T advertises service reliability for its monthly charges.

Subjective claims are not measurable, often stress image enhancement, and may include *puffery,* which is simply some level of acceptable exaggeration, such as Budweiser's "the King of beers" or Del Monte's "super natural" advertising phrases.[38]

Some advertising for brands with high awareness and high penetration is designed to increase usage by current customers. This type of advertising is termed **expansion advertising** and is intended to encourage "substitution in use." Advertising messages such as "use A-1 to grill burgers" or "consume Special K as an afternoon snack" have been found effective for encouraging expanded usage.[39]

Another strategy used by advertisers emphasizes the product's relative competitive value in the marketplace. Such value-based advertising is now prevalent in many consumer goods categories. The danger in heavy reliance on advertising messages that focus predominantly on value or price claims is that these strategies increase consumer sensitivity to price and make price differences more salient to buyers.[40]

Jim Ensign, Senior Vice President, Doe-Anderson, Inc., discusses the characteristics of effective advertising: "The advertising messages we create for our clients must accomplish at least two things to be successful. First, the messages must be *relevant* to the consumer. Advertising will never make a person interested in a product or a service if it does not appeal to or address a preexisting need or desire. Second, the message must be presented in an unexpected manner or environment. In the United States, adults are exposed to over 5,000 "promotional" messages every day. To break through the clutter, the message must stand out in an appealing way."

Message strategies frequently attempt to convey a distinct product image or quality appeal. Timex ads, for example, consistently focus on product quality; Lexus ads appeal to buyers' self-images. Some messages appeal to the hedonistic, or pleasure-seeking, side of consumers.

Comparative advertising relates a sponsored brand to a competitive brand on at least one product attribute. Objective attribute comparisons seem to be most effective at enhancing consumer attitudes about the sponsoring brand. Well-known comparisons include MCI against AT&T; Subaru against Volvo; Toshiba computers against Compaq; Maxwell House coffee against Folgers; American Express credit cards against Visa; Pizza Hut versus Domino's; and Weight Watchers diet meals against Lean Cuisine.[41] Gillette's Duracell brand has raised its market share relative to Energizer from the use of a series of indirect comparative ads.[42] In some countries, like Greece and Argentina, comparative advertising is restricted to brand X comparisons. In Japan, comparative advertising is not used at all.

Thinking Critically

Typically it is branded product manufacturers that undertake heavy advertising and promotion to increase awareness about not only a specific brand but also an entire product category. Generic or store brands may also reap the benefits of increased category awareness without having incurred substantial advertising costs, and are therefore able to offer the same product at a lower price. What can brand advertisers do to limit this "free-rider" effect?

Typically, the advertiser claims superiority of its product on the most important features being compared. By not claiming superiority on a less important attribute, the advertiser implies admission of a slight shortcoming, which may actually enhance the credibility of the other claims. An advertiser may also enhance a lesser-known product by comparing it with a well-known product. Comparative claims may represent either direct comparative advertising or indirect comparative advertising. In direct comparative advertisements, the advertised brand is compared overtly with a named competitor or competitors. Indirect claims involve no mention of competing brand names but assert generally that the advertised brand is superior or better.

Message strategies with *emotional appeals* attempt to evoke feelings, moods, and memories. Diet Pepsi and Dr Pepper commercials, for example, associate warm feelings with their brands. Marketers of insurance, tires, and automobiles may use *fear appeals* related to safety. The "baby in a tire" theme, produced by DDB Needham Advertising Agency of New York for Michelin Tires, recognizes the value of such advertising. The Club, an auto-theft device, stresses fear in its advertisements. And deodorant, shampoo, and toothpaste ads frequently play on the consumer's desire to be liked or to avoid disapproval.

A *celebrity endorsement* may be an element of the creative message strategy. Well-known spokespersons, such as Mike Piazza, Shaquille O'Neal, Britney Spears, and Tiger Woods, can enhance the persuasive impact of a message. The Williams sisters' endorsement deals have made them the most highly paid females, promoting such brands as Reebok, Avon, and Nortel Networks.[43]

The milk-mustache appeals have been very effective at encouraging attitude change among consumers toward the use of milk and its nutritional benefits. These ads have included models, actors, and athletes as celebrity endorsers. This strategy is not without some risk, however, as evidenced by problems encountered by former frequent endorsers Michael Jackson, Madonna, Burt Reynolds, and O. J. Simpson.

Humor appeals can increase consumer attention and recall. The Energizer Bunny campaign created by TBWA Chiat Day agency has been rated as the most effective by consumers.[44] The most traditional of Super Bowl advertisers, Anheuser-Busch, relies heavily upon humor and has been particularly successful when animals are used in its ads to generate humorous situations. In fact, the company's ads, including the 2000 entry in which a dog gleefully chases a Budweiser truck until crashing into a parked service van, have won two recent Super Bowl Ad Meter competitions.[45]

Building Customer Equity

Leo Burnett's repeat business

More than anything else, Leo Burnett, the global, Chicago-based advertising agency, is dedicated to keeping its clients from leaving the agency. Leo Burnett's customer retention rate is among the highest in the advertising industry. As part of this commitment, clients and employees are treated as the firm's most important assets. The agency's success is based on creating value that ties the clients to the agency—value generated from the development of creative ad campaigns that are effective at achieving client objectives.

Creativity is a sensitivity to human nature and an ability to communicate it, and the best creative advertising comes from an understanding of what people are thinking and feeling. It is this understanding of client customers—that is, a thorough commitment to the principles of the marketing concept—that enables Leo Burnett to earn client loyalty and, hence, maintain the agency's own customer base.

Burnett is now subsumed as one of the brands under Bcom3, which has been acquired by Publicis Groupe, a large international conglomerate. These changes, along with the alliance involving Dentsu, the Japanese ad giant, are indicative of the reconfigured advertising agency industry. As a former private enterprise begins the process of answering stockholders, Leo Burnett must move forward without losing what made it so successful: a tight-knit and familial culture with a devotion to work and satisfying customers. The firm's recent billings and revenues have been flat at $3.1 billion and $350 million, respectively. Concerns have arisen because of questions associated with the U.S. Army account and the loss of Celebrex, as well as Pepto-Bismol and some of Coca-Cola's Minute-Maid business.

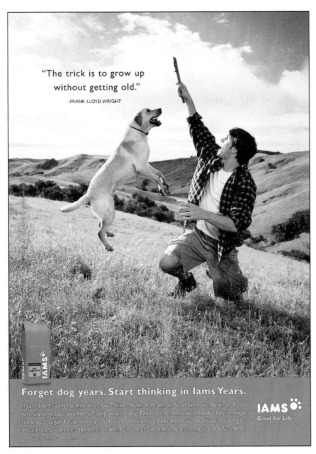

Emotional appeals that evoke feelings of warmth and caring are an effective means of instilling positive brand attitudes.

Fear appeals are often used to encourage support for programs related to violence, drug use, and other social issues.

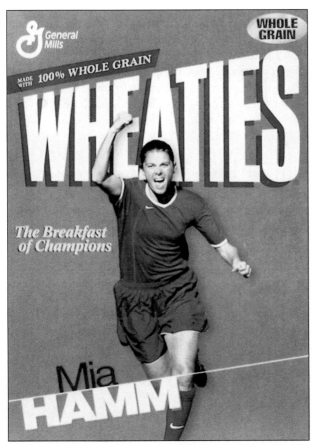

Celebrity endorsers are a frequent means of getting attention and generating positive attitudes toward sponsored brands.

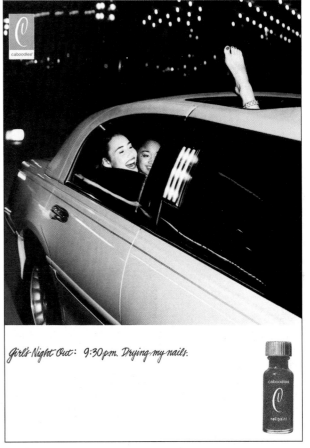

Homor also generates interest and attitude change as an advertising message strategy.

Celebrities are often selected for advertisements because of their perceived expertise. The Nuprin–Steve Young pairing promoting solutions for aches and pains from athletic competition is one example. In other instances, celebrity endorsements are intended to help consumers identify with the product. For example, ads that include professional athletes appeal to young people who dream of successful sports careers themselves.

Regardless of the punch celebrity endorsements or humor can have, however, the message still must reflect some competitive advantage, unique product benefit, and value.[46]

One strategy alternative that is controversial in terms of both the ethical issues involved and practical effectiveness is **subliminal advertising.** Although initially related to ad messages presented at a rate or level below thresholds of conscious awareness, this practice today most often involves the embedding of hidden symbols, such as sexual images or brand information, in advertisements. A number of books have been written on the dangers of subliminal advertising, but evidence supporting its practical effectiveness is virtually nonexistent. Most important, the very fact that such messages are embedded or concealed make the subliminal information extremely weak relative to more vivid stimuli.[47]

A growing phenomenon is the **advertorial,** a special advertising section with some nonadvertising content included in magazines. Advertorials are typically sold as special deals to advertisers that would not normally advertise in the magazine. An example is the "Guide to Entertainment" presented in *The New Yorker,* paid for by Chrysler. Advertorials offer advertisers a way to stand out in a cluttered media environment.[48] Television's counterpart is the **infomercial,** a 30-minute ad that resembles a talk show or news program. This form of direct marketing is now frequently seen on both network and cable TV.

A new form of advertising, **product placement advertising,** combines the efforts of marketers with moviemakers. Noteworthy examples include Apple in *Forest Gump* and Dr Pepper in *101 Dalmations.* Cingular Wireless was placed in the megahit *Spiderman.* Recently, however, marketers have been reluctant to participate in Hollywood deals due to increasing prices and questionable increases in sales.[49] Both obtained considerable product exposure within a unique medium. A related phenomenon is the use of joint advertising efforts to promote movies and products. Milk producers used *The Phantom* for a milk-mustache ad. PepsiCo and *Star Wars* have been featured in joint advertising, much like the long-term agreement between McDonald's and Disney.[50]

Selecting and Scheduling Media

Media planning involves decisions on *media class* (television, magazines) and *media vehicles* (specific television programs, specific magazines). Marketers must then decide on *media schedules* (frequency, timing of ads).

MEDIA CLASSES   There are seven classes of advertising media: television, magazines, newspapers, radio, outdoor, transit, and direct mail. There are advantages and disadvantages of these, and the effectiveness of each approach depends on its unique capabilities.

Television, magazines, and radio are useful in building brand awareness. TV, in particular, can reach mass markets. And with the advent of cable and specialized networks, TV can target specific markets at a relatively cheap cost per individual exposure. Television commercials, however, are expensive in total. The most expensive buys for the 2001–2002 season, for example, were for 30-second slots during *Survivor: Africa* ($445,000), *ER* ($425,000) & *Friends* ($353,000); keep in mind, too, that these figures include only airtime, not production costs. Moreover, since TV ads typically last 15 to 30 seconds and are surrounded by other messages, consumers can easily tune them out.

Magazines can present complex and factual information. Messages can be read leisurely, have a long life, have pass-along exposure, and can be targeted to specific audiences. One study that compared magazine and TV ratings found that the top 25 women's magazines command larger audiences among women age 18 to 49 than the top female-targeted TV shows.[51] But magazine ads are subject to interference from competing ads and take a substantial time to develop and introduce. The largest spenders on magazine advertising are Philip Morris, General Motors, and Procter & Gamble. The magazines that produce the most advertising revenue are *People, US Weekly, Time,* and *Sports Illustrated.*

Newspaper advertising is excellent for local retail sales promotions. It can be developed quickly and can effectively target particular locations. But newspapers contain many ads and do not typically generate much audience involvement. The production quality of newspaper advertising is fairly low, though newspaper inserts do enable higher quality. For retailers, however, newspaper advertising is an effective communications medium.

Radio advertising can be quite cost-effective, the commercials can be targeted to specific audiences, and repetition of messages is possible. However, radio messages are subject to channel zapping and of course have no visual impact. Further, radio messages have a short life and typically generate only minimal involvement.

Outdoor advertising consists mainly of billboards constructed on leased property and rented to advertising companies. Billboards reach large numbers of consumers effectively and inexpensively. Billboard advertising is useful in supporting TV and radio campaigns and is particularly effective for building awareness of new brands. The average American now spends more time driving than eating meals, and two-thirds of that time is spent driving alone. U.S. outdoor advertising includes more than 400,000 billboards, plus billboard-sized ads placed on 37,000 buses. The costs for billboards are based upon traffic counts and the average number of daily impressions.[52] However, billboards present only limited message content, the span of exposure is brief, and messages must be viewed at a distance.

Jim Ensign, Senior Vice President, Doe-Anderson, Inc., comments on the use of the Internet and advertising: "The Internet, specifically the World Wide Web, is being integrated into all of our clients' marketing communications programs. In fact, a number of our clients are 'dot coms,' conducting their business primarily on the Web. We are rarely using the Web as only an 'advertising' medium. We are using it as an incredible tool to provide alternative sales channels, customer service, public relations, and direct marketing."

Transit advertisements—signs and messages on or in public buses and trains—are billboards on wheels. Transit ads inside vehicles are low in cost and provide frequent and lengthy exposure to riders. But message space is limited and typically reaches a restricted audience. The vehicle environment may detract from the prestige of the advertiser or message, and crowded conditions during rush hours may limit the opportunity to process the messages.

Direct mail, among the fastest-growing means of advertising today, has several significant advantages. It can reach narrow markets and enable the advertiser to elaborate on ad claims. Direct mail is also important in support of business-to-business marketing communications programs and is available to small and large companies. When coupled with toll-free numbers or return envelopes, direct mail can generate direct-response sales. But the frequency of direct-mail advertising can limit its effectiveness. Many consumers perceive such ads as junk mail and don't pay much attention to them. The success of direct-mail campaigns depends on the quality of the mailing lists used to target customers. In addition, printing, mailing, and development costs can make direct-mail marketing expensive.

MEDIA VEHICLES Once the marketer has selected the media class, it must choose the specific advertising vehicles (specific magazines, radio or TV shows). The selection depends on the cost-effectiveness of a particular outlet for reaching desired market audiences. Factors include audience size and composition and the cost of running the ad. Advertisers seek to find audiences that contain high proportions of target customers. It is in making these decisions that demographics (i.e., characteristics of audiences) are often so important. Firms such as Simmons Research Bureau

"Drive":30
1.) Title card: "I Can Be Better" With Tiger Woods. Brought to you by the new Air Zoom TW.
Anncr. (VO): I can be better with Tiger Woods, Brought to you by the new Air Zoom TW.

2.) (Cut to Tiger)
Tiger: Today's topic . . . tee height.

3.) (Cut to close-up of golf ball on tee)
Tiger (VO): I like to tee off my ball just above the club head.

4.) (Cut to Tiger watching to see where his golf ball lands)
SFX: Sprinkler comes on.

5.) (He keeps watching . . .)
SFX: Lawn mower.
(. . . and watching)

6.) Tiger: Experiment and you'll find the tee height that's right for you.
Title card: Nike and Tiger Woods logo.

TV story boards are used to display the sequence and content of advertisements. Here, a humorous theme is employed using Tiger Woods as the spokesperson for Nike.

can help here. For example, an advertiser can request data exposure or magazine readership for women with incomes over $30,000 who regularly purchase tennis equipment. Similar sources for TV and newspaper audiences are provided by Arbitron, A. C. Nielsen, and MediaMark.

A common method to evaluate vehicles within a specific medium is by **cost per thousand (CPM)**. For magazines, the formula is:

$$CPM = [(\text{magazine page cost} \times 1,000)/\text{circulation}].$$

Using data for 2000 from www.mediastart.com, assume *Sports Illustrated* charges an insertion cost of $215,000 for a full-page, four-color advertisement and has a paid circulation of 3,150,000. The CPM for *SI* would be:

$$[(\$215,000 \times 1,000)/3,150,000] = \$68.25$$

Thinking Critically

The objectives of many consumer ads for individual brands seen on national network and cable programs are to build brand recognition, attitudes, and sales. Hence, the effectiveness of these ads will eventually be considered in light of brand performance (i.e., sales, market share).

- What criteria or outcomes might be used to evaluate the effectiveness of corporate image campaigns? Of corporate advocacy advertising?
- How might a business-to-business company evaluate its own trade advertising when personal selling is the business's primary means of promotion?

Marketers can calculate this value for other magazines in that class and make comparisons for the decision. Rate and circulation statistics can be obtained from *Standard Rate & Data Services: Consumer Magazines*. Although this is a useful decision tool, CPM figures cannot be used to make comparisons across media and do not account for the quality of the audience, pass-along readership, the appropriateness of the media vehicle for the product category, or the nature of the editorial content.

An alternative to the CPM concept is CPM-TM, or the cost per thousand to reach a desired target market segment. Consider again the *SI* example and assume that Cadillac, a frequent sponsor of golf events, wishes to reach men with incomes over $50,000. This group makes up 40 percent of *Sports Illustrated* readership. The effective circulation then is only 1,260,000, and the CPM-TM increases to $170.63. This figure reflects more closely the cost-efficiency of reaching an important target segment for Cadillac.

MEDIA SCHEDULES   The most basic concepts in media scheduling are reach and frequency. **Reach** refers to the number of different people or households exposed to an ad or campaign over a specified time period (usually four weeks). **Frequency** refers to the number of times a person or household is exposed to a communications vehicle. Advertisers must address the basic question: Emphasize reach or frequency? When advertising is for a new brand, reach may be the paramount objective. Messages presenting detailed information or vying with heavily advertised competitors need greater frequency or repetition.

Increased repetition relative to competing brands has been shown effective at increasing top-of-mind awareness and brand preference. Advertising works cumulatively and messages are stronger when repeated. As such, advertising expenditures and brand equity are related in many mature product categories, such as cereal, soft drinks, and beer. Since advertising is often directed at consumers with existing knowledge and preferences, increased repetition helps maintain the ready accessibility of brand associations in the minds of consumers.[53] In addition, research has shown that higher levels of repetition for even incongruent or surprising brand extensions enhance new product brand attitudes when the message focuses on primary product benefits.[54]

One rule of thumb has been that three exposures are required for impact; that is, three exposures on average per individual are thought necessary to generate adequate message processing. More recently, practitioners have begun to realize that for large, well-known consumer brands, two repetitions within a purchase cycle may be sufficient. In truth, there are a large number of variables that affect advertising frequency, including how old the brand is and how well-known it is among its target audiences.[55] In summary, new or unfamiliar brands may require more ad frequency to break through the clutter of competing ads in the marketplace. Complex ads, including emotional appeals, may be able to benefit from higher exposure. All advertisements are subject to wearout, and new campaigns warrant consideration.[56]

For TV advertising, several conclusions regarding media schedules and the amount of advertising were recently offered in a summary of a large number of tests of the effectiveness of split-cable advertising. Specifically:

1. Brands in categories in a growth mode are more likely to benefit from increased TV advertising.
2. Increased advertising added to either the front end or back end of a media plan is more likely to result in higher sales than is increased advertising distributed throughout the plan.
3. Increased spending is generally only effective when coupled with changes in creative executions.
4. Increased spending for new brands or line extensions is more effective than similar increases for established brands.[57]

Interestingly, the findings from a series of additional split-cable studies conducted by Frito-Lay confirmed these conclusions. Moreover, their results showed a significant increase in sales within the first three months for the effective campaigns (i.e., those campaigns resulting in significant increases in sales compared with comparison control areas in which the campaigns were not run).[58]

Evaluating Advertising Effectiveness

The evaluation of advertising typically includes pretesting or copytesting, posttesting, and sales effectiveness research. Given today's bottom-line emphasis, firms are making the evaluation of advertising effectiveness a much more important task. Often the objective has been to maximize efficiency of advertising budget expenditures in terms of prices paid for media exposure. Ultimately, however, the marketer's effectiveness is judged by sales, profits, and return on investment. Likewise, the contributions of advertising and media are increasingly being asked to judge their effectiveness using similar criteria.[59]

PRETESTING   In general, **pretesting** proposed print and broadcast ads is done by evaluating consumer reactions through direct questioning and focus groups. Marketers evaluate the ads for overall likability, consumer recall of information, message communication, and their effects on purchase intentions and brand attitudes.

Research Systems Corporation (RSC) evaluates advertising for marketers and ad agencies.[60] From 500 to 600 randomly chosen consumers view TV pilot programs and a number of commercials, including the ones being evaluated. Before the screening, participants are shown various consumer products and are asked to indicate which they would like to receive. After the screening, a second questionnaire is administered. A persuasion score is computed for each commercial, which indicates the differences in percentages of consumers selecting the advertised product before and after the screening. Respondents are also called 48 hours later to explore estimates of recall. These viewer reactions are used to predict sales effectiveness of the ads.

POSTTESTING   Marketers use **posttesting** through recall and attitude tests and inquiry evaluations to assess the effectiveness of an ad campaign. In **unaided recall tests** for print ads, respondents are questioned with no prompting about ads included in magazines. In **aided recall tests,** subjects are given lists of ads and asked which they remembered and read. An **inquiry evaluation** comes from the number of consumers responding to requests in an ad, such as using coupons or asking for samples or more product information.

Starch Message Report Services provides awareness and readership data about ads carried in consumer and business magazines. Burke Market Research administers a day-after-recall program (DAR) for TV commercials. DAR is the percentage of individuals in an audience who recall something specific about the ad being posttested. High levels of recall do not necessarily result in increased sales, however.

Using Technology

In-store TV

If you are interested in various aspects of television advertising and new network branding operations, then consider the aisles of Wal-Mart. Eight feet above every fifth aisle are monitors designed to get consumers to buy more. The system is operated by PRN, Premium Retail Networks. With more than 90 million shoppers per week in U.S. Wal-Mart and Supercenter locations, plus Sam's Club stores, the 10 to 12 monitors per store offer exposure to information and entertainment programming, as well as cost-efficient paid advertising by marketers such as Unilever, P&G, and Sony. Advertising rates are competitive for the number of viewers reached depending upon frequency and time of day. Nielsen provides the appropriate advertising measurement results. PRN also creates customized programming for other retailers such as Sears and Best Buy.

SALES EFFECTIVENESS EVALUATIONS   **Sales effectiveness evaluations** are the most stringent tests of advertising efficiency. They assess whether the advertising resulted in increased sales. Given the many factors that affect sales and the number of competing messages, sales effectiveness evaluations are difficult, and marketers and ad agencies can differ on measures of results. Increasingly, however, evaluations of advertising effectiveness based on brand awareness will no longer be sufficient. Advertising evaluations instead will be based on its contributions to sales growth.

Some newer programs combine awareness and sales data to evaluate advertising effectiveness. For example, ASI Monitor combines three data sets: (1) traditional ad awareness and attitude telephone surveys, (2) Nielsen household panel purchase data, and (3) Nielsen Monitor Plus data that include gross rating point (GRP) measures. The GRP measures incorporate both reach and frequency information. This tracking program allows advertisers to determine if advertising messages are getting through to consumers as schedules are run over time and the effects of that advertising on sales.[61]

Recognizing the need to provide quality advertising that improves company performance, DDB Needham rebates a substantial portion of its fee if sales for an advertised product do not improve. If ad campaigns are successful, DDB Needham receives a bonus in addition to its fee.[62] A. C. Nielsen has been a leader in studying the effects of advertising on sales. In one Nielsen study using matched samples of 4,000 households, results showed that for 9 of 10 packaged goods investigated, households exposed to magazine ads were more likely to purchase the advertised product than were those who had not seen the magazine ads. A. C. Nielsen is also developing measurement procedures for assessing the global effectiveness of Internet ads and audiences via a service called Nielsen/NetRatings.[63]

An understanding of the effectiveness of direct TV advertising on purchase behavior is emerging as advertisers study the results of their practices as part of direct-response television messages. For example, the effects of 1-800 direct-response advertising mostly disappear within eight hours. Response to daytime advertising is highest in the hour in which the ad is run. It is important to note that the sales effects differ substantially by station and creative design.[64]

Ethical and Legal Issues in Advertising

Advertising provides many useful functions for buyers, advertisers, and society. For buyers, benefits include comparative information about the availability and the characteristics of products and brands. For advertisers, advertising builds long-term brand recognition, introduces new products, and enhances corporate images. For society, advertising increases economic efficiency by enabling products to be sold in mass markets at lower unit costs and to be distributed over wide geographic areas.

Advertising does have its critics, however, and abuses do occur. In some instances, advertising malpractice has received considerable notoriety. Several years ago, Volvo Cars of North America altered cars in its "monster truck crushing" ads, for example. Other ethical issues related to advertising are more subtle. We discuss them below.

Is Advertising Manipulative?

Some critics charge that advertising stimulates needs and wants by creating unrealistic ideals about appearance and social identity. And indeed, students of marketing agree that advertising is intended to influence buyer behavior. Are ads that are designed to emphasize the idea that happiness and well-being are dependent upon physical attractiveness ethical? Hair-loss remedies and surgical "lift" procedures are frequently advertised with their messages and themes tied to enhanced self-esteem.[65] But if it's so easy to manipulate people into buying, why do so many products fail? It would seem more likely that instead of being manipulated by advertising, the reverse is true, and buyers exercise control over the marketplace by the choices they make with their discretionary income.

Is Advertising Deceptive or Misleading?

The Federal Trade Commission (FTC), which monitors marketplace abuses, prohibits advertising messages that deceive consumers by presenting false claims, by omitting relevant information, or by giving misleading impressions that result in faulty decisions.

In some instances the FTC requires **corrective advertising** to remedy misleading impressions or information in an ad. The offending advertiser or marketer must develop and pay for advertising that counters the misperceptions. Corrective advertising is required most often when there have been outright misrepresentations of fact, rather than presentation of half-truths.

In one of the earliest cases, Warner-Lambert was required in 1975 to spend $10 million in advertising to correct misleading claims about the ability of Listerine mouthwash to combat colds. Volvo was instructed to run corrective ads in local newspapers, *USA Today,* and *The Wall Street Journal* to explain its withdrawal of ads misrepresenting the effect of the "monster truck crushing" demonstration discussed above.[66] The FTC required Volkswagen (and Audi) to run a series of full-page national magazine ads to inform consumers about product performance problems. The magazine advertising was required to reach a nonduplicated audience of at least 75 million adults. The FTC has also become very involved with the deception that can occur from "implied claims" included in the advertising of dietary-supplement products. H&R Block was ordered to stop advertising "rapid refunds" of taxes. The court found that H&R Block concealed that their clients were actually receiving high-interest loans just to get their refunds a few days early.[67] The FTC forced Wonder Bread to not use unsubstantiated ads claiming that the bread can improve brain power and memory.[68]

How Does Advertising Affect Children?

The youth market offers tremendous potential to business, and much advertising is directed toward children. Advertisers know young consumers influence parental decisions and exert significant buying power themselves. Concerns about advertising to children center largely on three important issues:

- Children's ability to understand advertising's intent to persuade.
- The nutritional value of food and candy products marketed to children.
- The influence of advertising on children's demands to parents for advertised products.

On the other hand, some opponents of limits on advertising to children argue that:

- Parents are better able than the FTC to help children interpret information and make decisions.
- Children know that fruits and vegetables are more nutritious than sugared foods.
- Banning TV advertising to children limits free speech.[69]

In response to criticisms about questionable program content that carries advertising designed to appeal to children, Procter & Gamble and other major advertisers, such as IBM, GM, Sears, and Johnson & Johnson, are paying the Time-Warner WB network to develop and air shows with less sex and violence. Many parents are opposed to exclusive marketing deals, signed by such companies as Coca-Cola and PepsiCo, that pay schools for the right to sell their products in the classroom. Schools obtain money, supplies, and programming in exchange for the right to beam ads to students on classroom TVs.[70] Concerns about advertising and marketing to children relate to the Internet as well. In fact, online marketer deception has increased calls for legislation to protect both children's privacy as well as the future of e-commerce.[71]

Is Advertising Intrusive?

Many people are irritated by unwelcome advertising messages that threaten their right to privacy. Most observers agree the marketplace is cluttered with advertising messages and that any one ad has limited ability to influence consumers. Yet recognition of this limitation only reinforces pressures to increase ad repetition.

Related questions have to do with methods of ad communications delivery. Is it ethical for infomercials to package commercial messages as regular programming? What about the practice of allowing TV advertisers into school classrooms? Intrusiveness concerns about technology also extend to junk faxes and "spam advertising." Specifically, the same laws that require telemarketers to maintain "do-not-call" lists—the Telephone Consumer Protection Act—also prohibit marketers from sending unsolicited advertisements to facsimile machines. Recipients of faxed coupons from a Hooters restaurant won a $12 million judgment in a class action lawsuit. Complaints can be filed with the Federal Communications Commission, the recipient's state attorney general, or the sender's state attorney general.[72] Several state legislatures have passed laws and federal legislation has been drafted governing unsolicited e-mail, or "spam advertising."[73]

Cause-Related Advertising

An extension of corporate advocacy advertising is the concept of **cause-related marketing (CRM)**, or social advertising. Cause-related marketing is the increasingly common phenomenon of companies' aligning themselves with causes, such as AIDS research, drug-abuse prevention, gay rights, racial harmony, and conservation. The real objectives of these campaigns vary from solely economic (i.e., the cause affiliation is entirely strategic) to solely social where there is extraordinary commitment to the cause. One well-known example is the campaign of Benetton shock ads that combine both economic and social objectives. The ads, which highlight issues such as AIDS, the Bosnia conflict, and the plight of refugees, are designed to both get attention and position Benetton as a cutting-edge social marketer. Sears stopped selling Benetton clothes for a period in 2000, in reaction to Benetton's campaign tied to capital punishment. For these programs to work, the objectives for the campaign should be long term, the cause should fit the company, and the employees should believe the issues are important.[74] While most cause-related marketing is designed to enhance corporate image perceptions, P&G is tying CRM to individual brands, such as Ariel and Daz, in efforts to build trust among consumers by linking individual brands to environmental causes. Also, this example tied to P&G in Europe, where New Covent Garden Soup linked with a homeless charity to raise funds through sales of its soup to help refurbishment of their kitchens.[75]

Advertising Harmful Products

The use of advertising to market harmful products, such as cigarettes and alcohol, is frequently criticized. Regulations, both legislated and self-imposed, exist, but critics often argue for further restrictions on such advertising. In markets without restrictions, tobacco advertisers frequently connect smoking with glamour, excitement, and the great outdoors.

The Joe Camel campaign was quite successful in raising brand recognition, particularly among children and adolescents. In response to much criticism of the ads, however, Camel recently agreed to discontinue the use of the well-recognized cartoon character. Substantial opposition has arisen also to previously announced plans to advertise liquor products on TV.[76]

Public Relations

Public relations (PR) is often used as a complement to support advertising, personal selling, and sales promotions for disseminating marketing communications. Public relations has evolved from a discretionary part of the marketing mix to a critical component of most company communications programs, serving to enhance other aspects of the marketing mix, as well as working on media relations and public opinion.[77] PR communications are not overtly sponsored in the typical advertising sense and are a useful support to other forms of marketing communications. PR is an attempt to improve a company's relationship with its publics. Public relations may focus on customers, employees, stockholders, community members, news media, or the government. Most large corporations operate central PR departments to carry out coordinated public relations programs, and smaller companies with limited resources must also deal with PR issues. AT&T and other companies support scientific studies to reduce fears about links between the use of cellular phones and cancer.[78] Public relations was used effectively in multicultural communications to help the half million U.S. Sikhs, a religious and ethnic group with origins in India, following the September 11, 2001, terrorist attacks. These PR efforts were designed to tell Americans that this peaceful group is not affiliated with terrorism.[79]

As advertising becomes less effective, companies of all sizes try to build public awareness and loyalty by supporting customer interests. The general public increasingly demands that companies behave responsibly toward society as a whole and that they have obligations to more than their customers and stockholders. Profit maximization and social responsibility need not be incompatible, however. Today, companies show greater concern for employee welfare, minority advancement, community improvement, environmental protection, and other causes. A PR department plays a critical role in planning, coordinating, and promoting these visionary activities for an organization.[80] Some companies have effectively embodied public relations principles into their overall marketing communications program. For example, Members Only fashion company funded over $100 million worth of social consciousness–raising advertising about drug abuse and voter registration. More recent advertising promotes care for the homeless.

Public Relations Functions

Most frequently, PR functions support a firm's products and services. Often, however, public relations activity addresses corporate image and social responsibility. Exxon Corporation's varied program to maintain and improve its corporate image is a good example. Its PR activity ranges from an ongoing campaign about environmental damage from the Alaskan oil spill targeted toward the scientific community to charitable support of the Special Olympics.[81] The remarkable turnaround of Sears during 1995 and 1996 is attributed in part to its effective use of PR communications in rebuilding relationships with the financial community and the media.

Public relations functions include press relations; product promotions; internal and external corporate communications; lobbying to promote, defeat, or circumvent legislation and regulations; advising management about public issues and company positions and image; and overall, responding to a variety of occurrences in the marketplace.[82] Driven by the Internet, the thrust of public relations firms is moving more from influencing the press to influencing companies. PR firms and PR departments within companies are acquiring new skills as they work with dot com companies to build business strategies and to establish marketplace presence and positioning. These dot com companies often start with PR work, even before advertising, in efforts to generate word-of-mouth communications. Gaining positive exposure among investors and analysts is crucial to young high-tech companies' survival.[83] Public relations can be **proactive** or **reactive,** as shown in Exhibit 17–6. For reactive PR efforts, crisis managers need to move faster and use communica-

Exhibit 17–6	*Proactive and reactive marketing public relations*

Proactive marketing PR	**Reactive marketing PR**
• Product release announcements, statements by firm's spokespeople, even sponsorship, articles in business press.	• Firm's response to negative events and damaging publicity.
• Corporate image enhancement and development of goodwill; corporate advocacy advertising supports certain position on given social issue.	• Negative information comes from news media, consumer advocacy groups, government agencies; usually related to product defects or problematic company practices.
• Cause-related marketing in which firm contributes specified amount to designated cause when customers buy firm's products.	• Success depends on firm's ability to align its interests with the public's interests so both are served.

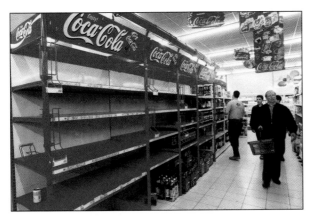

Public relations can support the communications efforts for all types of organizations. Large firms, such as Coca-Cola, should have the proactive plans in place to use if negative events occur.

tions vehicles such as Web sites and chat rooms that reach consumers in real time. Consumers have become more accustomed to bad news, and the time available for effective firm reaction is diminishing due to the frequency of corporate misdeeds and poor management, investigative 24-hour TV shows, and a proliferation of class action lawsuits.[84]

Publicity

Publicity, the generation of information by a company to the news media, has a narrower focus than public relations. The primary publicity techniques are news releases, press conferences, and feature articles, often presented in the business press.

One advantage of publicity is its relatively high credibility, because the messages are not paid for by a commercial sponsor. Information about a company presumably must be newsworthy to be published by an objective source. However, publicity messages may be revised by the media, then released at times most convenient to the broadcaster or publisher. Unfortunately, some publicity may be negative news stories beyond the firm's control, as when product tamperings occurred for Tylenol and Diet Pepsi. A firm's PR department must be prepared to react constructively and without delay when unfortunate events occur.

One very effective publicity stunt was the April Fools' joke by Taco Bell. The company announced in full-page ads in six major city newspapers and *USA Today* that it had purchased the Liberty Bell. At the end of the day, Taco Bell made a retraction and offered to give $50,000 to help restore the Liberty Bell. Even those most initially irate at the apparent inappropriate corporate sponsorship were amused. More important to Taco Bell, the company received at least 400 TV mentions, including network evening news coverage. This represented millions of dollars in exposure for $300,000 in media costs.[85]

As companies such as Intel and Polaris Software, which saw flaws in their products exposed to the world via the Internet, have learned, negative publicity can spread extremely fast via the new technology. Ameritech Corp., Quaker Oats Co., and Allstate Corp. have gone so far as to monitor Internet discussion groups or chat rooms in efforts to learn of negative comments about their products and services.[86]

Proactive PR requires that the firm formulates a crisis plan for communications in the event of an emergency. Such a plan should try to determine what unfortunate events might occur and specify who will speak for the company and who will be the audience. In times of emergency, one primary audience likely will be the news media. In instances of product recall, an important audience will be retailers.[87]

Summary

1. **Understand the characteristics, functions, and types of advertising.** Advertising, like other promotional elements, plays an important role in the total marketing communications program. Advertising is impersonal, paid for by an identified sponsor, and disseminated through mass channels of communication to promote the adoption of goods, services, persons, or ideas.

   Advertising can serve a number of functions, including heightening consumer awareness, disseminating information about a product's attributes or social value, shaping product images or emotional responses, persuading buyers to purchase, or reminding consumers about products, brands, or firms.

   Advertisements can be classified according to the target audience, geographic area, medium, and purpose. Corporate image advertising promotes an organization's image and role in the community as a corporate citizen. Other types are corporate advocacy, public service, classified, direct-response, business-to-business, and cooperative advertising.

2. **Realize how people process advertising information and how it affects buyer behavior.** Advertisements rely on successive stages of processing by a targeted individual: exposure (presenting the information to a receiver), attention (the conscious direction of a receiver's mental effort toward the advertising stimulus), comprehension (the degree to which the receiver correctly understands the intended message), acceptance (the degree to which the receiver accepts or yields to the message), and retention (the extent to which the receiver can recall or recognize the message at a later time).

   The relationships between these stages, and therefore the effectiveness of the advertising itself, may be affected by consumer needs as well as consumer motivations, opportunities, and abilities to process the information.

3. **Discuss approaches to developing advertising campaigns.** The steps in developing an ad campaign are (1) determining advertising objectives, (2) determining advertising budget, (3) designing appropriate creative strategies, (4) selecting and scheduling media, and (5) evaluating ad effectiveness.

4. **Describe different advertising objectives and the message strategies used to achieve them.** Advertising objectives should be consistent with the organization's overall marketing objectives and be realistic, precise, and measurable. Advertising objectives may be to inform, to persuade, or to remind.

   Many different message strategies can be used to achieve the advertising objective. One strategy is to compare the advertised brand to another. Celebrity endorsements, humor, and fear appeals are other tactics used to enhance the persuasive impact of advertisements.

5. **Understand the decisions involved in selecting media and scheduling advertising.** Decisions on media class involve choosing the most appropriate media channels, such as television, magazines, or radio. This choice depends on both the size and characteristics of the firm's target markets and the characteristics of the message itself.

   Decisions on media vehicles refer to the selection of the specific outlets within the chosen media class. These decisions usually depend on factors such as cost and the size and characteristics of the audience. Reach and frequency are important considerations in making these decisions.

6. **Explain how marketers assess advertising effectiveness.** Effectiveness evaluations involve some combination of pretesting, posttesting, and sales response research. Pretesting usually involves evaluating consumer reactions to proposed advertisements. Posttesting is used to measure the effectiveness of the chosen strategy during or after the ad campaign. Posttesting may include aided or unaided recall measurements, attitude evaluations, and sales impact effects.

7. **Appreciate the roles of public relations and publicity in marketing.** Public relations functions include the dissemination of press releases, product promotion efforts, and corporate communications, as well as lobbying and advising corporate executives about public issues affecting the firm. Publicity refers to the dissemination of nonpaid communication in news outlets and represents only a part of the larger activity of public relations.

   Marketing-oriented public relations can be proactive or reactive. Proactive marketing public relations refers to the initiation of positive public relations; it may take the form of corporate image advertising, advocacy advertising, or cause-related marketing. Reactive marketing public relations refers to defending an organization from negative and potentially damaging information, including negative events and adverse publicity.

Understanding Marketing Terms and Concepts

Thinking About Marketing

1. What different functions can advertising perform?

2. What are advertising agencies, and what services do they provide?

3. Explain why advertising expenditures have declined during recent years.

4. Define the following: business-to-business advertising; corporate image advertising; corporate advocacy advertising; direct-response advertising; and corrective advertising.

5. What steps are involved in a consumer's processing of advertisements? Why is understanding this sequence of these stages important to advertisers?

6. What can advertisers do to increase exposure, attention, and retention? How does audience involvement influence these processes?

7. Identify the steps involved in the development of an advertising campaign.

8. What are media class decisions, and how do they differ from media vehicle decisions?

9. Contrast pretesting with posttesting in the evaluation of advertising effectiveness. Explain the problem with using sales results as a measure of advertising effectiveness.

10. Explain the differences between advertising and public relations.

Applying Marketing Skills

1. Collect two examples each of: (a) corporate image advertising; (b) corporate advocacy advertising; (c) public service advertising; (d) comparative advertising; (e) classified advertising; (f) direct-response advertising; and (g) business-to-business advertising.

2. Consider the differences across magazine, radio, television, and outdoor advertising. Describe how each works to get consumers' attention and ensure retention.

3. Assume the 2002 average issue circulation for *People* magazine is 3,350,000. The cost for a one-page ad in a regular issue is $128,500. Estimate the CPM for that magazine. Compare it with similar data for *Time:* page

cost, $202,000; circulation, 4,000,000. What might you advise a potential advertiser of personal computers? Of cosmetics?

4. Critics contend that advertising induces consumers to buy products that they don't really need. For example, direct-to-consumer (DTC) advertising of prescription drugs has been shown to increase patient demand for pharmaceuticals that are often not medically necessary (e.g., for hair growth, weight loss, wrinkle removal). Is DTC advertising creating better-informed consumers or an overmedicated population?

Using the www in Marketing

Activity One   Consider the current Web site of British Airways, the company whose home page introduced the chapter.

1. How would you characterize the company's image based upon the Web site? Using examples, what

elements of British Airways' communication mix are mentioned?

2. Examine the site of one of British Airways' competitors. How do the advertising strategies differ?

Activity Two   The Federal Trade Commission is the regulatory body that governs advertising at the federal level and rules on a case-by-case basis regarding deceptive advertising. Consider the information available on the Internet regarding the ongoing activities of the FTC:

1. What guidelines are available that define or describe what constitutes deceptive advertising?

2. Refer to a recent cease-and-desist order in which a company was prevented from further deceptive practices. In this case, what circumstances led the FTC to find the company's advertising deceptive?

3. What guidelines are offered regarding advertising substantiation (i.e., test results or data that support ad claims)? Consider the May Department Stores (of Denver) case. What was deceptive about their price advertising?

4. Telemarketing critics refer to this practice as a nuisance and intrusive. Some states have already passed legislation, and federal legislation is being considered, to regulate unsolicited telemarketing calls. If government regulation is warranted for telemarketing, is it also warranted for other types of advertising that may be considered intrusive—such as Internet ads, television commercials, and radio spots?

Making Marketing Decisions
Case 17-1 Spirits: An Advertising Elixir?

Historically, beer and wine products have relied heavily upon television advertising. Eighty-three percent of the almost one billion advertising dollars in beer advertising was allocated to television in 2001. Now, a series of low-alcohol alternative beverages, such as Miller's Skyy Blue, Smirnoff Ice, and Anheuser-Busch's Bacardi Silver, are being promoted on TV. Since 1997, more than 400 TV stations and cable systems representing 76 percent of U.S. subscribers have accepted some liquor ads, according to the Distilled Spirits Council, a lobbying group.

Recently, NBC announced, and then recanted its decision, that it would become the first broadcast television network to accept hard-liquor commercials in more than 50 years. The initial decision was made amid a depressed advertising environment, with all media outlets desperate for more advertising. The networks have resisted voluntarily the urge to allow liquor firms access as a much needed revenue stream for fear of public backlash.

Restrictions have been discussed. For example, NBC devised policies would allow advertising for liquor only after nine, no one in the ad spots could be under 30, and 85 percent of audiences must comprise adults over age 21. The concern is that liquor ads will encourage underage drinking. The issue is—how much underage alcohol consumption (said to be 11 million Americans under 21) is ad induced or just youth behavior? MADD and other advocacy groups hope that legislation will prevent further spread of alcohol advertising and that the U.S. Congress will fund additional antialcohol campaigns.

Questions

1. How will the effects on young consumers be minimized?

2. What are the pros and cons associated with the implementation of network broadcast alcohol ads?

3. Why is it fair for beer and wine industries to rely so heavily on television, but not traditional liquor brands?

Case 17-2 Toyota: Advertising Drives to Success in Europe

 More and more international companies are moving away from global standardized advertising—that is, presenting the same advertising campaign in every country in which the company conducts business. A standardized strategy often fails to provide the most effective advertising for a given geographical area, because each area has its own distinctive political, legal, and cultural characteristics. The use of advertising suited to the particular characteristics of a country may be more effective.

Toyota has always taken an unstandardized approach, tailoring its advertising on a country-by-country basis. It lets the local marketers handle all the aspects of advertising for their particular area on the theory that they know the market best. Toyota simply supplies the local advertisers with the necessary raw materials (information pertinent for promoting Toyota vehicles) to develop effective advertisements for their area. This system has been effective for Toyota, which enjoys a significant market share in countries in North America, Asia, and Europe.

Eased trade conditions within Europe could allow Toyota to reevaluate just how integrated (if at all) it wants to make its advertising. Today, Toyota uses an integrative European approach to its advertising for only one brand, the Lexus luxury automobile, which has met with some success. The company might also find it profitable to reduce the number of advertising agencies it works with in Europe. Becoming more standardized in its advertising could offer Toyota certain economies of scale.

Additional growth will occur in Europe as barriers limiting imports from Japan fall away. Under export restraint conditions so far, Japanese car dealers have been forced to promote largely their most expensive brands. Now dealers are learning how to sell higher volumes of lower-margin models. Two other phenomena are occurring in the advertising and marketing strategy for Toyota in Europe. First, Toyota Europe has contracted with Saatchi & Saatchi Advertising to handle strategic brand issues for all of Europe. This change suggests a move toward a consolidation of advertising support for Toyota in Europe. Second, the number of dealers receiving new cars has been reduced substantially, with the affected smaller dealers serving as partners providing only service and the taking of new orders. With these changes, the time could be right for Toyota to implement a more standardized advertising program across Europe.

Toyota, a Japanese firm, faces a number of unexpected global obstacles. Concerns in Japan have given recognition that Toyota's American strategy has become the company's lifeline. The United Kingdom offers Toyota a particular global challenge. Having long suffered from a reliable but dowdy image, Corolla, the best-selling car in the world, has performed poorly in the UK. The objective for Saatchi & Saatchi is very much one of changing consumers' perceptions of the car. As part of their European campaign, Toyota has engaged in the UK's largest railway poster campaign in an effort to reach busy commuters with advertising promoting Corolla. In addition, Toyota is sponsoring programming on satellite channels to reach a younger demographic segment. The "pride" campaign depicts people who do not own a Corolla, but would like to give the impression that they do.

Questions

1. Enumerate and explain the advantages and disadvantages to Toyota of using an integrative, standardized approach versus maintaining its current approach to advertising in Europe.

2. What would you recommend Toyota do regarding its advertising in the UK? Elsewhere in Europe?

3. Explain the impact that differing cultural values, legal considerations, and economic considerations have on international advertising.

4. Why is Toyota more successful in the United States than Japan, assuming that this situation holds?

18

Consumer and Trade Sales Promotion

After studying this chapter, you should be able to:

1 Explain the role and significance of sales promotion in the marketing communications mix.

2 Understand why sales promotion expenditures account for a significant portion of many firms' marketing communications budgets.

3 Discuss the objectives and techniques of consumer sales promotion.

4 Discuss the objectives and techniques of trade sales promotion.

5 Explain the limitations of sales promotion.

6 Realize how deceptive and fraudulent sales promotion victimizes both consumers and marketers.

www.valpak.com

Val-Pak, a subsidiary of Cox Target Media, is the oldest and largest local cooperative direct-mail company. Founded in 1969 in St. Petersburg, Florida, by an unemployed autoworker, Val-Pak now serves a customer base of 130,000 businesses through 220 field offices. Val-Pak mails 15 billion coupons annually in its familiar blue envelopes to 50 million consumers and small businesses. Its customer-advertisers share the cost of the mailing.

Val-Pak is also the leading distributor of online coupons. By accessing Val-Pak's Web site, consumers can download free coupons from a broad range of product and service categories, which are redeemable at local businesses across the United States and Canada. To further its online coupon-distribution business, Val-Pak has partnered with Yahoo!, a major Internet access company with 218 million users each month. Consumers can get Val-Pak coupons directly from Yahoo! or from the Val-Pak site. Popular brands promoted online include Goodyear, Fantastic Sam's, Subway, and Jiffy Lube. Val-Pak has also partnered with Pricegrabber.com, Dealcatcher.com, Rebatecatcher.com, and Startsampling.com to offer consumers additional services, including comparison shopping, online deal searching, rebate locators, and free samples through the Valpak.com Web site.

While becoming a leader in sales promotion, Val-Pak has also been a good corporate citizen. Through its Canadian operation, the company donated its expertise in printing and brochure production to benefit the Canadian Cancer Society, helping to raise $112,000 over a two-year period. Val-Pak's Tampa, Florida, office teamed up with the Tampa Bay Devil Rays, the U.S. Postal Service, Time Warner Communications, and local TV and radio stations to donate sports equipment to local youth athletic organizations. Such programs are part of Val-Pak's ongoing commitment to social responsibility. Val-Pak also rates highly with its franchised branch offices. *Entrepreneur* magazine has named it the top direct-mail franchisor in the United States, based on factors such as growth, financial strength, percentage of franchisees maintained, and financial support provided to franchisees.

Although primarily viewed as a direct-mail company, Val-Pak utilizes all forms of marketing combinations to grow its business. As a franchise organization, Val-Pak depends on franchise salespeople to continue to sell the customers on direct-mail sales promotion and advertising. The company also benefits from public relations efforts, with support for events such as the Canadian Cancer Society fundraiser generating favorable publicity. With growth expected in alternative media and direct marketing, and the continued important role of sales promotion, Val-Pak is well positioned for the future.

As the Val-Pak example illustrates, sales promotion is designed to boost sales. **Sales promotion** consists of media and nonmedia marketing communications employed for a predetermined, limited time to stimulate trial, increase consumer demand, or improve product availability.[1] Common sales promotion tools are coupons, samples, displays, contests, and sweepstakes. Sales promotion may be directed at ultimate consumers, retailers, or wholesalers. **Consumer sales promotion** is directed at consumers, and **trade sales promotion** is directed at resellers.

This chapter examines the growing role of sales promotion in marketing communications. The objectives, techniques, and limitations of consumer and trade sales promotion are explored. The chapter also looks at ethical and legal issues related to sales promotion.

The Role of Sales Promotion

Sales promotion is used to reach a variety of markets and buyers. This Samsung promotion emphasizes free services for a limited time period to both business customers and ultimate consumers.

A unique characteristic of sales promotion is that it offers an incentive for action. A consumer might receive a rebate for making a purchase, for instance, or a retailer may be offered an allowance for purchasing a specific quantity of a product within a specified time period. In contrast to many forms of advertising, sales promotion is oriented toward achieving short-term results. Sales promotion activities rarely stand alone, however; they are typically combined with other forms of marketing communications to create an integrated program.

Effective sales promotion, like all forms of marketing communications, should result from adequate planning as discussed in Chapter 16. Since sales promotion seeks results in the near future, it is possible to set specific, measurable objectives and to accurately monitor results. It should also be understood, however, that since sales promotion often works in conjunction with other communications, coordination of messages and timing is crucial for success. Exhibit 18–1 presents the primary considerations in sales-promotion planning.

The Significance of Sales Promotion

As discussed in Chapter 16, the expenditures for most forms of marketing communications have not increased significantly in the early years of the 21st century. Expenditures for sales promotion have remained fairly stable, suggesting that marketers see sales promotion as an important marketing communications tool in both strong and weak economic times. Given an ongoing need to stimulate sales for most product categories, expenditures for sales promotion are expected to remain at significant levels in the coming years.

Sales Promotion Expenditures

The combined expenditures on consumer and trade sales promotion are estimated to exceed the expenditures on advertising. What has motivated the significant expenditures on sales promotion in recent years? Changes in the marketing environment—consumer attitudes, demographic shifts, and lifestyle changes—are favorable for sales promotion, as are emerging technology and changes in retailing. Also, marketers are under pressure to perform well in the short term and are increasingly accountable for achieving measurable results.

CONSUMER FACTORS With the U.S. population growing at less than 1 percent annually, most mature products see only modest growth in per capita consumption. The natural result is increased competition for market share. Sales promotion techniques, particularly price breaks, are therefore key.

Exhibit 18–1   *The 10 commandments of creative sales promotion*

1. **Set specific objectives.** Undisciplined, undirected creative work is a waste of time and resources.
2. **Know how basic promotion techniques work.** A sweepstakes shouldn't be used to encourage multiple purchases or a refund to get new customers. A price-off deal can't reverse a brand's downward sales trend.
3. **Use simple, attention-getting copy.** Most promotions are built around a simple idea: "save 75 cents." Emphasize the idea, and don't try to be cute.
4. **Use contemporary, easy-to-track graphics.** Don't expect to fit 500 words and 20 illustrations into a quarter-page, freestanding insert.
5. **Clearly communicate the concept.** Words and graphics must work together to get the message across.
6. **Reinforce the brand's advertising message.** Tie promotions to the brand's ad campaign.
7. **Support the brand's positioning and image.** This is especially important for image-sensitive brands and categories, like family-oriented Kraft.
8. **Coordinate promotional efforts with other marketing plans.** Be sure to coordinate schedules and plans. A consumer promotion should occur simultaneously with a trade promotion; a free-sample promotion should be timed in conjunction with the introduction of a new line.
9. **Know the media you work through.** Determine which media will work best. Should samples be distributed in stores, door-to-door, or through direct mail? Does the promotion need newspaper or magazine support?
10. **Involve the trade.** Build relationships with key resellers.

Today's busy consumer cares less about shopping. If two spouses work outside the home, shopping time is limited. This makes consumers inevitably more responsive to sales promotion deals that encourage multiple purchases and to in-store displays.

Another factor in favor of sales promotion is simply that consumers like it. Shoppers get a lot of satisfaction from getting a good deal, and they are accustomed to special sales, rebates, and other forms of sales promotion. One comprehensive study found that consumers derive six unique benefits from sales promotions. First, monetary savings can be realized with some promotions. Second, consumers may be able to buy higher quality products as a result of some promotions. Next, promotions can be a convenience to shoppers by helping them find the product they are looking for or reminding them of the product they wish to buy. For some consumers, promotions offer consumers the opportunity to express or enhance their self-concept and personal values, such as being a responsible buyer. A fifth benefit is that promotions can fulfill consumers' needs for stimulation and variety as they explore products and services featured in new promotions. Finally, consumers find some forms of promotions, such as sweepstakes and games, to be fun and entertaining.[2] With such a wide range of consumer benefits, it is understandable that businesses will engage in consumer and trade promotion to build consumer traffic, sales, and satisfaction. In today's competitive environment, promotions are often the necessary stimuli simply to maintain, much less increase, consumer purchases.

IMPACT OF TECHNOLOGY   There is ample evidence of technology as a stimulus for the growth of sales promotion. Computerized scanning devices let retailers know what is and what is not selling every day. They also provide quick input on which brands are most profitable. In the case of trade sales, portable computers in the hands of field salespeople let vendors track product movement practically instantaneously. As a result, both retailers and manufacturers can measure the effectiveness of various sales promotion programs very quickly. Manufacturers can thus adjust or eliminate unproductive programs, freeing up investment for more productive ones. Practically all major consumer-goods manufacturers, including PepsiCo, H.J. Heinz, and Procter & Gamble use scanner-tracked promotional programs.

INCREASED RETAIL POWER   Huge retailers such as Wal-Mart and Kroger wield tremendous clout by virtue of their immense purchasing power. Sales promotions directed at both retailers and consumers make the manufacturer's product more appealing.

As retailers gain more power, they have tried to increase sales of their own private-label products. Although retailers can tout their private labels while limiting in-store promotions for national brands, they cannot do much about sales-promotion efforts such as couponing. No doubt the struggle of national brand marketers against private labels has contributed to the growth of sales promotion.

The private-label trend is also occurring in European markets, where a lingering recession has compelled consumers to seek more value for their money. Private-label products are increasing in France, Switzerland, and Italy. To combat private-label sales, multinationals such as Unilever and Nestlé are promoting both their traditional brands and "Eurobrands," products designed for the entire European market.

Consumer Sales Promotion
Consumer sales promotion, with techniques such as coupons and rebates, helps pull a product through the channel of distribution. Both small and large companies can effectively use it with either new or existing products. Sometimes sales promotion may increase interest in mature or mundane products by imparting a sense of urgency to buy before the promotion ends.

Sales promotion can play an important role in stimulating consumers to try the product. In this ad, the offer of a free protein bar will stimulate consumer trials of the product.

Objectives of Consumer Promotions

Sales promotion may accomplish a variety of objectives, all related to affecting present or prospective consumers' behavior. As Exhibit 18–2 shows, objectives may be to stimulate trial; increase consumer inventory and consumption; encourage repurchase; neutralize competitive promotions; increase the sales of complementary products; stimulate impulse purchasing; and allow for flexible pricing.

STIMULATE TRIAL   Marketers commonly use sales promotion to stimulate product trial—to get consumers to try a product. This is particularly so for newly introduced or improved products. The decision to buy a new product entails risk, which may prompt buyer resistance. Sales promotion techniques that reduce consumer cost, such as coupons, rebates, or samples, help alleviate this risk. When Bristol-Myers Squibb wanted to encourage trial of its cholesterol-reducing medication Pravachol, it offered a free 30-day trial supply. In the minds of most people, no cost means no risk.

INCREASE CONSUMER INVENTORY AND CONSUMPTION Sales promotion sometimes encourages consumers to increase their inventory or consumption of a product by enticing them to buy

Exhibit 18–2	*Objectives of consumer sales promotion*

- Stimulate trial.
- Increase consumer inventory and consumption.
- Encourage repurchase.
- Neutralize competitors.
- Increase sales of complementary products.
- Stimulate impulse purchasing.
- Allow flexible pricing.

Sales promotion can help to stimulate impulse buying in retail stores. This ad from Duraflame encourages retailers to use the company's special display to stimulate impulse buying.

more than they would in the absence of a special incentive. The idea is that people tend to consume greater quantities of a product if it is on hand. For instance, a buy-one-get-one-free special on potato chips may stimulate consumers to buy more than normal. Because chips can get stale if not eaten within a certain time, and since they are around the house, people are likely to eat more than they normally would. Also, the more inventory of a given brand that consumers have, the less interest they have in stocking up on a competitor's brand.

ENCOURAGE REPURCHASE   Sales promotion offers a variety of ways to help establish repeat-purchase patterns, on which the product's survival ultimately depends. Vail Resorts, operators of Vail, Keystone, and Breckenridge resorts in Colorado, uses a program whereby skiers and snowboarders earn points toward free lift tickets, meals, and clothing when they make purchases. BMG Music Club awards bonus points redeemable for free CDs when members make a regular-price purchase. Office supply wholesalers offer free merchandise and other rewards based on total purchases, and most airlines offer frequent-flier programs designed to stimulate repurchase. Other examples of repeat-purchase promotions are the special price incentives magazines use to gain subscription renewals and the on-the-package coupons for future discounts that companies such as Domino's and Pizza Hut feature.

NEUTRALIZE COMPETITIVE PROMOTIONS   Sometimes marketers use sales promotions to combat competitive promotions. Consider the perennial battle between Coca-Cola and Pepsi-Cola, for example. Both firms constantly use promotions to attract consumers. As a result, the two firms often compete on price. Promotions to neutralize other retailers are also commonplace in the fast-food and cellular telephone markets.

INCREASE SALES OF COMPLEMENTARY PRODUCTS   Using sales promotion to attract buyers to one product can increase sales of a complementary product. A rebate Gillette offered for its Mach 3 razor, for example, allowed consumers to get the product for practically nothing. Gillette hoped to cash in on sales of its Mach 3 razor blades, a complementary product the consumer must buy on a recurring basis. The promotion worked as planned, and Mach 3 is now a leading brand.

Speaking from Experience

Kevin Marie Nuss
Vice President of Marketing
Churchill Downs

"Consumer sales promotions can be used to achieve several objectives. We use some promotions to encourage casual race fans to come to Churchill Downs. These promotions are intended to generate new customers by providing other activities for customers in addition to horse racing. For example, the Kentucky Microbrew and Barbecue Festival is a promotion during which customers can sample different microbrewery and barbecue products from Kentucky in the Churchill Downs Infield during the race day. Other promotions are directed to increase frequency of attendance. This year we gave away Churchill Downs T-shirts on Mother's Day. Customers wearing these T-shirts receive free admission to Churchill Downs during the remainder of the meet."

Kevin Marie Nuss is Vice President of Marketing for Churchill Downs, the home of the Kentucky Derby. Her responsibilities include advertising, promotions, group sales, sponsorships, licensing, and merchandising for the Churchill Downs and Sports Spectrum facilities. She earned a B.A. in English from the University of Louisville. Kevin comments on the different objectives for consumer sales promotions.

STIMULATE IMPULSE PURCHASING   Many people do not take the time to develop shopping lists. This tends to increase impulse purchasing. As the term implies, an impulse purchase is unplanned. It satisfies a strong desire to acquire a product quickly, without a lot of forethought. Retailers use special feature displays to generate impulse purchases.

ALLOW PRICE FLEXIBILITY   Sales promotion facilitates tailored price changes, which allow marketers to pursue opportunities as they arise. Suppose a manufacturer has set relatively high list prices, intending to appeal to the least price-sensitive segment of the market. Later the manufacturer can appeal to price-sensitive segments of the market through sales promotions. Automobile manufacturers follow this strategy despite the advent of no-haggle pricing.

Consumer Sales Promotion Techniques

Most people recognize the familiar consumer sales promotion techniques and have probably participated in some. Exhibit 18–3 lists some popular ones.

PRICE DEALS   A **price deal** is a temporary reduction in the price of a product. Marketers may use price deals to introduce a new or improved brand, to convince current users to purchase more, or to encourage new users to try an established brand. There are two primary types of price deals: cents-off deals and price-pack deals. **Cents-off deals** offer a brand at less than the regular price. Sometimes the manufacturer's package itself specifies a price reduction in dollars or cents or by a certain percentage, say 25 percent off. Such deals are often promoted in the store in some manner and may also be advertised.

Price-pack deals offer consumers something extra through the packaging itself. Perhaps they can buy a package of Martha White brownie mix that is 20 percent bigger than usual or a box of Double-Chex with 40 percent more cereal for the price of the normal size.

Marketers would be smart not to overuse price deals, however. If a brand is frequently offered on a price deal, consumers come to expect it. They hold off purchasing the product until the company offers another deal. Frequent deals on the same product eventually erode its normal retail selling price and may diminish its brand value.

Price deals are also commonplace with nonpackaged goods such as consumer durables and services. They are also used extensively by online retailers in an attempt to attract customers and build market share. For example, Overstocks.com lists daily bargains in numerous categories, including books, electronics, apparel, jewelry, and sporting goods. It also features a "Recent Markdowns" section and a "Clearance Center" section where shoppers can buy even further discounted products.[3] Better-informed consumers know when a price deal is really a deal, and comparing prices is becoming easier thanks to comparison-shopping sites on the Web. For price-sensitive consumers, a deal featuring some form of discount is indeed a popular sales promotion tactic. Research, however, suggests that monetary-based promotions can have detrimental effects on market share when used to promote

Exhibit 18–3	*Consumer sales promotion techniques*

- Price deals
- Coupons
- Rebates
- Cross-promotions
- Contests, sweepstakes, games
- Premiums
- Sampling
- Advertising specialties

certain brands with high customer equity against low-priced brands. The use of monetary promotions with high-equity brands that offer consumer benefits related to self-esteem, fun, and stimulation may not be as effective as nonmonetary promotions that offer gifts, prizes, or a fun experience for the consumer.[4]

COUPONS   A **coupon** is typically a printed certificate giving the bearer a stated price reduction or special value on a specific product, generally for a specific period of time. Coupons allow the manufacturer to reduce the product's price at any time. They are particularly useful in encouraging new-product trials.

Couponing is the most popular consumer sales promotion tool in the U.S. packaged-goods industry; it is also a significant factor in Canada, Italy, and the United Kingdom. The most popular product categories for coupon use are household cleaners, medications, condiments, paper products, and prepared foods. While popular, coupons have lost some ground in recent years. For example, in 2000, a third of brand marketers cited coupons as one of the three most important marketing tactics. By February 2002, that figure had dropped to only 13.6 percent.[5] Retailers, never fond of manufacturers' coupons, have increased their handling fees, especially for coupons that cannot be scanned. On the other hand, some manufacturers, including market leader Procter & Gamble, have reduced couponing expenditures, primarily because they feel it is a wasteful means of promoting their products.

The number of coupons distributed and redeemed has been on the decline since the early 1990s, yet more than 80 percent of consumers continue to use coupons. Less than 2 percent of the several hundred billion coupons distributed annually are redeemed.[6] Analysts point out that couponing has been negatively affected by manufacturers' use of shorter expiration periods on coupons and their attempts to get consumers to make multiple purchases to take advantage of coupons. Electronic promotions have also contributed to a decline in the use of coupons. Nonetheless, coupons are expected to be a primary consumer-sales-promotion tool well into the future. One reason for this is that some major companies have introduced couponing into their sales promotions. For example, Fashion Bug, a moderately priced clothing and accessories chain, joined traditional coupon users by offering a $10 coupon. Bed Bath & Beyond and Linens 'n Things also added coupons for up to 20 percent off the sales price to their promotional mix.[7] These promotions are noteworthy, not only because these are three large retailers, but also because these retailers are not selling the typical products supported by coupons. They are seeking value-conscious consumers to build sales, and coupons remain an important avenue to reach these customers.

Coupons may be distributed in several ways. The most popular method is through the **freestanding insert (FSI),** a preprinted coupon (sometimes contained in an ad) placed into a separate publication, such as a newspaper. FSIs represent more than 80 percent of the coupons distributed in the United States annually. In-store handouts deliver about 5 percent of all coupons; coupons in or on the package also make up approximately 5 percent. The remainder of coupons are distributed by direct mail, magazine, newspaper, and miscellaneous methods such as distribution at special events and via the Internet.

One technique to distribute in-store coupons, **on-shelf couponing,** uses a dispenser mounted near the manufacturer's particular product. Retailers also use in-store **checkout dispensers.** Catalina Marketing, the leading dispenser company, operates checkout dispensers in supermarkets around the world. Although coupons dispensed through Catalina are more expensive to manufacturers than those in newspapers, consumers redeem in-store coupons at a much higher rate.

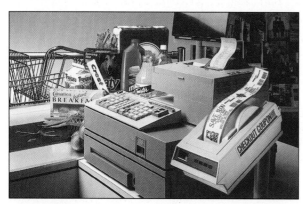

Issuing coupons to consumers during checkout at the grocery store is growing in popularity. Catalina Marketing's Checkout Direct dispenser compiles customer profiles using check-cashing-card data and issues coupons to match predicted future purchases.

Rebates are a popular consumer sales promotion tool. In this case, FISKARS uses a rebate as part of a seasonal sales promotion program.

Using checkout scanner data about the consumer's purchases, the Catalina system dispenses coupons for similar products or beyond-the-store promotions. For example, a consumer who buys baby food might receive a coupon for Sears Portrait Studios.

Online couponing, the distribution of coupons on the Internet, is a growing phenomenon. Catalina is also in this business, as are companies such as Val-Pak and other entrepreneurial ventures.

REBATES   A **rebate** is a cash reimbursement to a buyer for purchasing a product. The consumer typically must mail a rebate form, the purchase receipt, and some proof of purchase (often the universal product code) to the manufacturer within a certain time frame. Although consumers often purchase as a direct result of a rebate offer, many forget to send for the reimbursement or run out of time. Incentives such as coupons are easier to use, and rebates may not offer consumers the instant gratification that makes other incentives attractive.

Rebates serve several functions. They act as an economic appeal to attract customers, particularly price-conscious buyers. They have a deadline, thus consumers are encouraged to act by a certain time. They also offer a good way to reduce the perceived risk in trying a new brand, as a lower price represents less risk to most consumers.

Rebates also encourage increased consumption. The Quaker Oats Company, for instance, may offer a rebate on the purchase of two or more packages of instant oatmeal when the typical purchase is for only one package. Offering a rebate also allows the manufacturer to maintain a brand's original price while enjoying the benefits of a temporary price reduction. Manufacturers are also assured that the savings goes directly to the consumer, rather than to the retailer. This is an advantage to the manufacturer that wishes to build brand loyalty with the ultimate consumer.

Some manufacturers are extending the use of rebates to Internet sites that specialize in promoting products with rebates. For example, RebateCatcher.com features rebates on brand-name merchandise from companies such as Nike, Motorola, Olympus, Panasonic, Canon, and Sony.[8] Promising products free to consumers after rebates has produced some questionable business practices and misleading sales promotion. CyberRebate.com declared bankruptcy, leaving many consumers awaiting approximately $80 million in unpaid rebates. Some "free-after-rebate" sites, including CyberRebate.com, offered nonrebate merchandise for sale, often at higher-than-market prices.[9] Consumers should be skeptical of deals that sound too good to be true and engage in comparison shopping for significant purchases.

Kevin Marie Nuss, Vice President of Marketing, Churchill Downs, discusses the value of cross-promotions: "Cross-promotions can be beneficial to all participating companies. We partner with different companies in a variety of cross-promotions. One example is a cross-promotion with a local dry cleaners and pizza restaurant. These partners sold reduced-price admission to our Festival in the Field promotion. This increased their business and gave our event exposure in their advertising efforts. Both partners sold all of their tickets, so we knew we would have a big crowd for the event. Another example is with Tricon Global Restaurants. Tricon sponsors the Junior Jockey Club for children. Participating families receive coupons for Taco Bell, KFC, and Pizza Hut products. This cross-promotion increases the attendance at Churchill Downs and also increases business at Tricon's different restaurants."

CROSS-PROMOTIONS   A **cross-promotion,** sometimes called a *tie-in,* is the collaboration of two or more firms in a sales promotion. Cross-promotions enhance the communications effort of all the participating firms. For example, Loews Cineplex teamed up with General Mills to run a "picture perfect" campaign to promote Pop Secret popcorn and Loews' summer movie schedule. Consumers could redeem cut-outs from Pop Secret's packaging for free popcorn or soda at the movies,

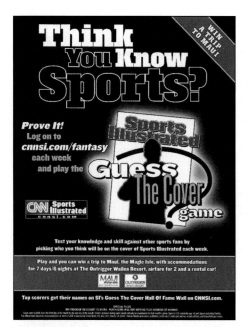

Sports Illustrated uses a Web-based contest to test the knowledge of sports fans. Such contests are fun for consumers and can help build an emotional attachment to the brand.

and moviegoers had a chance to enter a movie-trivia contest with more than 50,000 prizes.[10] Cross-promotions have been particularly popular with online retailers who link with well-known brand marketers to get more exposure for their own name. Amazon.com for example, has run cross-promotions with Target, Toys "R" Us, and Hamilton Beach.

Cross-promotions offer several advantages. Relationships forged between strong brands reinforce the image of each. The image of a new product, or one with low market share, may be enhanced through association with a leading brand. Also, the resources pooled in a cross-promotion enable larger incentives to be offered and generate more fanfare in introducing the promotion to consumers. For more on cross-promotions, see "Building Customer Equity: Xbox Wins with Cross Promotion."

CONTESTS, SWEEPSTAKES, AND GAMES A **contest** offers prizes based on the skill of contestants. Participants must use a skill or some ability to address a specified problem to qualify for a prize. Kodak has used photo contests successfully for decades, and contests are popular in association with major sporting events such as the Olympics and the Super Bowl. Internet-based contests, sweepstakes, and games are becoming more popular. For example, Autobytel.com, an Internet automotive sales site, ran a "Match & Win" instant winner game that required consumers to match their "car key" (distributed both online and off-line) with the key featured on the Autobytel site. Prizes included a new car, computers, free pizza, and movie certificates. Results exceeded expectations, as 3 million new consumers accessed the Autobytel Web site. Response rates to follow-up e-mail promotions ranged from 5 to 45 percent, topping industry standards. Autobytel registered 200,000 new users of its service as a direct result of its online game promotion.[11]

A **sweepstakes** offers prizes based on a chance drawing of participants' names. Sweepstakes have strong appeal because they are easier to enter and take less time than contests and games. Kraft Foods promoted its Balance Bar product with a sweepstakes offering a trip to a mountain resort in Colorado and Balance Bar clothing to winners. Activities at the resort over a four-day period included horseback riding, kayaking, mountain climbing, and night navigation. With simplified registration available in stores and on the Web, the sweepstakes proved to be effective in reaching a highly targeted market of outdoor adventure-oriented men and women.[12] By law, purchase cannot be a requirement to enter a sweepstakes.

Building Customer Equity

Xbox wins with cross promotion

Microsoft Corporation teamed up with Taco Bell and SoBe, a beverage company, to promote the release of Xbox, a home video gaming system. The objectives of the promotion were to stimulate trial, increase brand awareness, and encourage purchase. To accomplish these objectives, Microsoft conducted a 48-hour, nonstop gaming marathon in New York and Los Angeles with free food and beverages from Taco Bell and SoBe. More than 50 gaming kiosks were set up, 16 dedicated to competitive play, with winners receiving trips, Xbox merchandise, and additional prizes from Taco Bell, SoBe, and Ford. Live music was furnished by

Bush and Seven-Dust, with DJs from Korn and Limp Bizkit also appearing at the marathon.

An online postcard to more than 200,000 Xbox fans and 20 Xbox Web sites generated interest in the marathon, and consumers lined up to take part 10 hours before the event began. All indications were that the Xbox cross-promotion, in combination with a radio advertising campaign, achieved its objectives. By bringing existing fans of Xbox something new and exciting while introducing the system to new consumers, Microsoft demonstrated how customer equity can be built via sales promotion.

Games are similar to sweepstakes, but they cover a longer period. They encourage consumers to continue playing in order to win. The William Wrigley Company used a game to build brand awareness and increase the number of consumers registered at its online site for Juicy Fruit gum. The game format was that of a scavenger hunt, where targeted consumers aged 6 to 24 searched for Juicy Fruit icons on 13 Web sites popular with young consumers. By clicking on the icons, they could win instant prizes such as trips to New York to view the taping of MTV's *Total Request Live* show, video games, and a year's supply of Juicy Fruit. The promotion increased brand awareness and doubled the number of consumers registered on the Juicy Fruit Web site.[13]

Contests, sweepstakes, and games can create interest and motivate consumption by encouraging consumer involvement. They are often used in integrated marketing communications programs along with in-store displays (part of trade promotion) and advertising. The future for these types of promotions is promising. Consumers seem to enjoy the friendly competition, and technology is lending a hand. Contests and games frequently appear on the Internet, where marketers are trying to get consumers to spend more time, thus increasing involvement and interest in the product or service. Automobile and truck manufacturers have been active in this area, including Jeep and Ford. Jeep used an Internet-based photo contest in which consumers submitted photos to address the contest theme, "What the Jeep Brand Means to You." The grand prize was modest, a Jeep boombox, yet the contest drew 250 entries and gave Jeep valuable insights into brand image among some of its most enthusiastic owners. Jeep also has used the Internet to conduct virtual off-road driving contests leading to a final competition at its annual Camp Jeep, held in mountainous venues around the country.[14]

PREMIUMS   An item given free or at a bargain price to encourage the consumer to buy is called a **premium.** Prepaid phone cards, for example, are often used as premiums. These cards, one of the most popular premiums in recent years, are imprinted with the company or brand logo, thus reminding the consumer of the sponsor every time the card is used. In addition, callers will often hear a short promotional message when they dial the free access number to use the card. Other popular premiums include consumer electronics, gift certificates, especially if they are redeemable online, and items that exploit consumers' love of animals. For example, Hallmark uses its Kiss-Kiss Bears, a premium that can be purchased at a bargain price with another purchase, to help spur non–greeting card sales. Kimberly-Clark gave away 5 million stuffed animals as premiums, and Frito-Lay gives away toys based on its Chester Cheetah mascot in Subway restaurants. The Chicago Cubs used a variation on the bobble-head doll fad to give away rubber duckies that look like their players.[15]

Premiums are intended to improve the product's image, gain goodwill, broaden the customer base, and produce quick sales. Premiums that require saving in-pack coupons, proofs of purchase to be redeemed, or multiple purchases to complete a set can create consumer loyalty. For instance, McDonald's offers young female consumers especially attractive premiums compared to premiums targeted to young boys. This is because young men grow up to become the most loyal of McDonald's customers, whereas many young women lose interest in eating at McDonald's. In one promotion, Matchbox toy cars with a retail value of $1.29 were the premium included in a Happy Meal oriented toward boys, while the female-oriented premium was a miniature Madame Alexander doll, worth several times the value of the Matchbox car. According to McDonald's personnel, the more expensive female-oriented premiums are succeeding in building more enduring brand loyalty in the female segment.[16] In the promotions to both boys and girls, McDonald's increased consumer loyalty by offering a series of toy cars and dolls.

Research comparing the effectiveness of premiums with that of price discounts suggests that marketers might want to experiment with premiums, especially if their competitors are heavy users of price promotions. For example, a free spatula worth

Thinking Critically

Assume you are a brand manager for a specialty manufacturer with only one product, a high-priced toothpaste with extraordinary whitening power. The product has been highly successful in Europe, and now you are planning national distribution in the United States. If you could only use one consumer-sales promotion technique of those shown in Exhibit 18–3, which one would you use? Support your reasoning.

$3.99 at retail generated more consumer interest than a $2 price discount on pizza; and an offer of $2,500 worth of camping gear had a higher impact on consumer interest in buying a $28,500 utility vehicle than did a $2,000 discount on the vehicle. Since these premiums can be acquired by marketers at wholesale prices, the return on investment in these promotions can be highly attractive. Further, there is less danger of eroding brand image, which sometimes occurs with price-based promotions.[17]

SAMPLING　A **sample** is a small size of a product made available to prospective purchasers, usually free of charge. Marketers use samples to demonstrate a product's value or use and encourage future purchase. Sampling reduces the consumer's perception of risk by allowing product trial before purchase of a full-size version.

Marketers find sampling particularly useful for new brands with features that are difficult to describe adequately through advertising. Samples also draw heightened attention to a brand. For instance, Procter & Gamble promoted its well-established Secret antiperspirant with a sampling program in malls in six cities under the banner of the Teen Esteem Tour. Each mall site featured a rock-climbing wall, an inspirational message wall, DJs, and pop singer Christina Milian. In each of the six cities, sampling teams worked five days in the mall and in other venues, including movie theaters, concerts, restaurants, and sporting events.[18] For Procter & Gamble and many other companies, sampling is a versatile promotion tool that can be used for many purposes, from introducing a new product to reinforcing already established customer relationships.

Although usually mailed to prospective customers, samples may be distributed door-to-door; at trade shows, movies, and special events; or in-store. They sometimes accompany the purchase of a related product, such as a free sample of laundry detergent with the purchase of a washing machine.

Sampling can be expensive; thus marketers must determine the most cost-effective manner of distribution. This depends on the target audience and the size of the sample. Although larger samples cost more, the sample should be big enough for consumers to make an adequate evaluation. Some companies have found unusual ways to get their samples into consumers' hands. In Brazil, most home cooking stoves run on small tanks of compressed gas that are delivered door-to-door. The delivery personnel know their customers personally and have built trust-based relationships over the years. Sara Lee, Johnson floor wax, Procter & Gamble, and Unilever detergents, and Nestlé are among the brands that have used the home-gas delivery system to distribute samples. Ultragaz, a subsidiary of Royal Dutch/Shell Group, charges five cents for each sample distributed, which marketers consider a very reasonable fee compared to other methods of sampling.[19]

ADVERTISING SPECIALTIES　An **advertising specialty,** also called promotional product, is an item of useful or interesting merchandise given away free of charge and typically carrying an imprinted name or message. These items are typically low in cost, although some can be expensive. According to the Promotional Products Association, the most popular advertising specialty products categories are clothing, writing instruments, desk accessories, calendars, bags, and glassware.[20]

Specialty advertising has several common uses. It can reinforce other advertising media to strengthen a message. It can also produce or foster high levels of brand recognition when the item has a relatively long life. A unique specialty advertising item can attract interest among target audience members and perhaps stimulate action. In addition, a useful specialty item can create a positive attitude toward the provider. Poor-quality merchandise, however, may detract from the marketer's image. For an illustration of how advertising specialties can be used to promote a social cause, see "Being Entrepreneurial: Success of *Accidental Magic* No Accident."

Trade Sales Promotion
Trade sales promotion at the wholesale and retail level helps push products through the marketing channel. Unlike consumer sales promotion, trade promotion is not easily observed by ultimate consumers. Al-

though consumer sales promotions are very visible, in fact they are dwarfed by the magnitude of trade sales promotion. Marketers spend approximately twice as much money on trade promotion.

Exhibit 18–4

Objectives of trade sales promotion

- Gain/maintain distribution.
- Influence resellers to promote product.
- Influence resellers to offer price discount.
- Increase reseller inventory.
- Defend against competitors.
- Avoid reduction of normal prices.

Objectives of Trade Promotions

Sales promotions aimed at the trade have many and varied objectives. As listed in Exhibit 18–4, common trade promotion objectives are to gain or maintain distribution; influence resellers to promote a product; influence resellers to offer a price discount; increase reseller inventory; defend a brand against competitors; and avoid reduction of normal prices.[21] Trade promotions may be conducted by manufacturers, service providers, or wholesalers, all directing their efforts toward other channel members, most notably retailers.

GAIN OR MAINTAIN DISTRIBUTION   Sales promotion influences resellers to carry a product. Manufacturers selling directly to retailers may strike special introductory deals to get established with the retailer. Later, sales promotion may help maintain distribution in the face of competition or a flat sales period. Such is the case in the soft-drink market, in which Coke and Pepsi use sales promotion on a regular basis. Other incentives, such as providing free in-store displays, may encourage retailers to purchase by reducing their perceived risk. A trade show is another example of sales promotion that may provide a way to introduce the product to potential distributors and gain their business.

INFLUENCE RESELLERS TO PROMOTE THE PRODUCT   Getting a product into a reseller's inventory is not always enough to realize sales objectives. In other words, it's not enough to get the product on the shelf; it may take sales promotion to move it off the shelf. Ways manufacturers can influence retailers to promote a product include offering incentives to the retail salesforce, splitting advertising costs with the retailer, furnishing free display materials, or various other techniques. Quaker State, for example, could encourage service station attendants to promote the sale of motor oil by paying them 25 cents per can sold during a contest period. At the end of the contest, the attendant with the most sales would receive two free tickets to a NASCAR race. The basic idea is for additional sales volume to offset expenses involved in running the promotion or for sales to clear the dealers' inventory to make way for more profitable sales in the future.

INFLUENCE RESELLERS TO OFFER A PRICE DISCOUNT   Sometimes the manufacturer gives wholesalers and retailers allowances or discounts so that its product will be offered at a reduced price. The manufacturer hopes the lower price will lead to increased sales. This often occurs with end-of-season merchandise. For

Being Entrepreneurial

Success of *Accidental Magic* no accident

Roy H. Williams is president of Williams Marketing, Inc., an ad agency that teaches creative thinking, strategic planning, and human persuasion to its clients. Mr. Williams, also an author, applied some of his entrepreneurial thinking to the publication and marketing of one of his books on creative writing. The proceeds for the book were donated to needy citizens in Guatemala.

To promote the book, entitled *Accidental Magic,* Williams used promotional products in a special mailing to hundreds of media contacts, university professors, busi-

ness associates, and other people he knew who shared an interest in Guatemala. To spur interest in the country, Mr. Williams included a small handmade product from Guatemala in each mailing. One item was a cloth bracelet with the message "We Guatemalans invite you to wear a goodwill bracelet as a token of our friendship."

Roy Williams showed the creativity of a true entrepreneur with his promotional products mailing. Not only did *Accidental Magic* become a successful book, but good sales promotion helped raise money for deserving people.

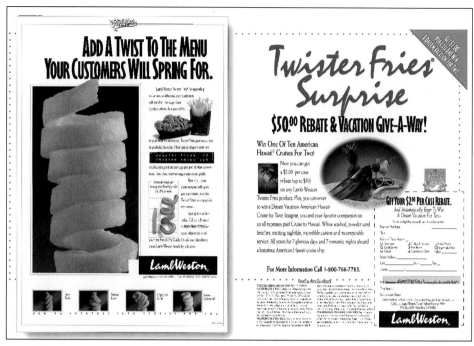

Lamb Weston used a rebate and the chance to win a dream vacation—a Hawaii cruise for two—as extra incentives for restaurant operators to try Twister Fries. This promotion was designed to simultaneously maintain and build distribution through Lamb Weston distributors.

example, fishing equipment manufacturer Zebco might offer sporting goods stores a clearance price on factory-premarked rods and reels and a special display barrel with promotional signs indicating "Rod & Reel Riot! $12.99 While They Last!"

INCREASE RESELLER INVENTORY   Suppliers do not want channel members to run out of stock. A product being out of stock results in more than lost sales; it creates dissatisfaction among customers seeking to make a purchase. Sometimes a manufacturer may want to shift products to wholesalers or retailers because of the costs involved in holding inventory. The other channel members, of course, are well aware of the cost and risks of holding excess inventory, and the supplier may grant them special deals in exchange for doing so. Such an approach is commonplace in the greeting card industry, in which suppliers offer retailers special pricing and deferred payment in exchange for their booking orders well in advance.

DEFEND AGAINST COMPETITORS   Just as at the consumer level, sales promotion can stave off competitors at the trade level. An incentive may prompt channel members to choose one firm's brand over a competing one.

Kevin Marie Nuss, Vice President of Marketing, Churchill Downs, talks about the use of trade sales promotions: "Many companies use their sponsorship of the Kentucky Derby as basis for various trade sales promotions. Companies, such as Pepsi-Cola, establish contests for their retailers. The winning retailers are provided tickets to the Kentucky Derby and entertained at the Marquee Village at Churchill Downs. The equine division of Bayer takes a different approach. The company set up a tent at the Churchill Downs backstretch stable area for the two weeks before the Kentucky Derby. The tent contained displays and information about Bayer equine pharmaceutical products. This mini-trade show was visited by many veterinarians and horsemen during the two-week period."

AVOID PRICE REDUCTIONS   Rather than reduce the price of a product permanently, marketers may use some form of trade promotion to offer channel members a temporary price reduction. If there is a momentary oversupply of product on the market, for example, a manufacturer might elect to maintain sales volume by offering a "1 free with 10" program of short duration. In effect, the customer gets a discount in the form of free goods, but the manufacturer avoids a permanent price reduction.

Trade Sales Promotion Techniques

Trade sales promotion techniques can be applied independently or in combinations. And firms often link trade sales promotion with consumer sales promotion and other elements of the communications mix. Some frequently used trade sales promotion techniques are shown in Exhibit 18–5.

TRADE ALLOWANCES   **Trade allowances** are short-term special allowances, discounts, or deals granted to resellers as an incentive to stock, feature, or in some way participate in the cooperative promotion of a product. There are several kinds of allowances, including slotting allowances, which we discussed in Chapter 14. Another type, the *buying allowance,* is payment of a specified amount of money to a reseller for purchasing a certain amount of a product during a particular period. The payment may be by check or as a credit against an invoice. A manufacturer usually offers a buying allowance to increase the size of the reseller's order.

A *display allowance* is money or a product provided to a retailer for featuring the manufacturer's brand in an agreed-upon in-store display. An *advertising allowance* is money paid a reseller for including the manufacturer's product, along with other products, in the reseller's advertising efforts. Somewhat similar to this, *cooperative advertising* occurs when the manufacturer helps finance the reseller's advertising efforts featuring only the manufacturer's product. For example, Pioneer may help a local electronics store pay for a newspaper ad featuring Pioneer products.

DEALER LOADERS   A **dealer loader** is a premium given to a reseller to encourage development of a special display or product offering. Loader techniques help ensure proper stock and display of the item, of particular interest to many manufacturers at certain seasons or holidays.

There are two common types of loaders. A *buying loader* is a gift, such as a free trip, for buying, displaying, and selling a certain amount of a product within a specified time. A *display loader* allows the reseller to keep some or all of the display when the promotion ends. A tennis racket manufacturer, for example, might allow qualifying retailers to keep an expensive, custom-produced lighted display featuring action photos of top players to help promote sales.

TRADE CONTESTS   A **trade contest** typically associates prizes with sales of the sponsor's product. As do consumer contests, trade contests generate interest, which makes them useful for motivating resellers. Effective trade contests should be held periodically rather than all the time—otherwise, they lose some of their motivating potential. Effective contests can boost short-term sales and improve relations between manufacturer and reseller. Dinosaur Adventure, an educational software company, used a trade contest to increase sales and build better relationships with 1,500 dealers. As part of the promotion, dealers competed for a $2,000 prize for the best in-store display for a software package called the Gargantuan Dinosaur Adventure. When the two-month-long promotion began, the software package was the 25th best-selling educational software title. At the conclusion of the promotion, the package had become the number one selling title.[22]

POINT-OF-PURCHASE DISPLAYS   **Point-of-purchase displays** are generally used at the retail level to call customer attention to a featured product. Point-of-purchase displays are popular in grocery, drug, and discount stores and in the restaurant, food service, and tavern industry. Typically provided free or at low cost by the manufacturer to the reseller,

Point-of-purchase displays call attention to featured products. Duracell uses this eye-catching display to boost sales for several different sizes of batteries.

point-of-purchase displays attract consumers while they shop, encouraging purchase of the particular product. With much of retailing self-service today, point-of-purchase displays support the retail sales effort by highlighting the product and offering information. Given that consumers make many purchase decisions in the store rather than before entering it, these displays can be important selling tools.

A disadvantage of displays is that manufacturers must assemble and place them. Retailers are busy, and they are deluged with point-of-purchase materials, many of which never make it to the sales floor. Displays often become unused throwaways, an unnecessary waste in marketing communications. Displays come in many varieties, including special racks, display cartons, banners, signs, price cards, video and computer monitors, mechanical dispensers, and robots. The names given to several popular point-of-purchase displays by retailers are shown in Exhibit 18–6, along with their descriptions.

TRADE SHOWS   A **trade show** is a periodic, semipublic event sponsored by trade, professional, and industrial associations at which suppliers rent booths to display products and provide information to potential buyers. Trade shows are big business in the United States, Europe, the Middle East, Africa, Asia, and Latin America. In many of these markets, trade shows are a more influential part of the marketing process than in the United States.

Marketers can use trade shows to accomplish any number of objectives, including demonstrating products, acquiring new-prospect leads, making sales, providing information, comparing competing brands, introducing new products, enhancing the corporate image, and strengthening relationships with existing customers.

Some shows are simply too large for customers to effectively visit each exhibit. Many companies use preshow mailings or phone calls to boost exhibit traffic. Companion promotional products are also effective for generating traffic and creating a memorable exhibit. For example, The Learning Channel, part of the Discovery Network, distributed archeological brushes to cable TV executives in their hotel rooms at a major trade show along with a message to "Turn on TLC's Hidden Treasures on Channel 2" and entry forms for The Learning Channel's contest. The hotel's television channel 2 gave instructions on how to get answers for the contest. Trade show attendees then brought the brush and entry forms to the Learning Channel booth, where they could "dig" for buried treasure such as trips, donations to local libraries, and Learning Channel promotional products. The promotion-within-a-promotion increased booth traffic, received coverage in trade media, and helped generate new subscriptions from cable operators to The Learning Channel.[23]

Passing out T-shirts or other specialty advertising items carrying the company's name and logo or constructing an unusual and eye-catching display can also generate booth traffic. It is important for companies to have well-trained salespeople available at a trade show. In addition, follow-up after the show is critical.

Major trade shows are held in large cities; thus lodging and associated expenses for company personnel can be expensive. To hold travel expenses to a minimum, many companies prefer regional trade shows. Even in Chicago, home to several major international trade shows, most conventioneers are attending smaller events, with 1,000 or fewer participants, and most are traveling less than 400 miles to attend.

Trade shows allow marketers to accomplish several objectives as they gain exposure with interested prospects and strengthen relationships with existing customers. This photo is from the annual Comdex trade show, one of the world's largest, which brings computer-industry buyers and sellers together.

TRAINING PROGRAMS   Some manufacturers sponsor or pay for training programs for customer employees. Armstrong Tile, for example, a manufacturer of

Exhibit 18–6	*Types of point-of-purchase displays*

Sign Language

AISLE INTERRUPTER	Cardboard sign that juts into the middle of the aisle.
DANGLER	Sign hanging down from a shelf that sways when shoppers pass.
DUMP BIN	Box-shaped display holding products loosely dumped inside.
GLORIFIER	Small plastic "stage" that elevates one product above the rest.
WOBBLER	A jiggling sign.
LIPSTICK BOARD	Plastic surface on which messages are written with crayons.
NECKER	Coupon hanging on a bottle neck.
Y.E.S. UNIT	"Your Extra Salesperson," a fact sheet that pulls down like a shade.

Trade sales promotion sometimes includes reseller training. In this photo, Hewlett-Packard dealers receive training at the company's facility in Mexico City.

floor tile, provides sales training to teach some of its key dealer personnel how to sell or use its products.

Marketers may also provide training on a number of other topics, including retail and wholesale management procedures, safety issues, or current technical developments in an industrial field. Training programs are expensive, and results are often hard to measure. To be effective, training should be continual, or at least periodically reinforced, thus adding to the expense. Even though it is expensive, training can build productive relationships with customers.

PUSH MONEY   **Push money,** also called **spiffs** (for special promotional products incentive funds), is what a manufacturer pays to retail salespeople to encourage them to promote its products over competitive brands. This payment may be in the form of money, merchandise, or other incentives with monetary value such as a gift certificate.[24] Push money may also be used to encourage the retail sale of specific products in the manufacturer's line. This extra incentive helps to get the manufacturer's brand special representation or favored treatment. The disadvantage is that the retail salesperson's extra enthusiasm for the manufacturer's product may wane once the spiff is eliminated, especially if another manufacturer offers a new spiff.

Limitations of Sales Promotion   Although sales promotion can
accomplish a variety of objectives, there are certain things it cannot do. Sales promotion can help boost sales, but it typically cannot reverse a genuine declining sales trend. If sales are slipping, marketers should evaluate and perhaps change the product's marketing strategy. Attempting to use sales promotion as a quick fix may temporarily postpone worsening of the problem, but it cannot eliminate it.

In a similar vein, marketers cannot reasonably expect sales promotion to convert rejection of an inferior product into acceptance. Consumers judge a product on whether it satisfies their needs. Products that do not meet consumer needs naturally fade from the market over the course of time.

Beyond its inability to improve a brand's image, sales promotion may even weaken the brand image. As a sales promotion develops a life of its own, perceived product differentiation can be blurred; consumers may come to see the deal as more important than any other real or perceived brand difference. In essence, buyers reach a point at which they fail to see any differences among brands, and the marketer has unwittingly created short-run price-oriented behavior. In the soft-drink market, for instance, many consumers see Coca-Cola and Pepsi-Cola as interchangeable and decide which of the two they will purchase primarily on the basis of price (which is the better deal?).

Sales promotion, far more than other marketing activity, has also been blamed for encouraging competitive retaliation. Promotions can be developed quickly, and one company can respond to a competitor's sales promotion with its own. Quick response may stave off the potential of sales lost to the competitor's promotion. Although a promotion battle benefits consumers, two firms that compete head-to-head often both lose profits. Other forms of marketing communications are less likely to evoke such quick retaliatory efforts.

Sales promotion can result in manufacturers' gaining short-term volume but sacrificing profit. Special incentives and deals promote **forward buying,** both among distributors and consumers. That is, people buy more than they need at the deal price. They purchase enough to carry them to the next deal, when once again they can stock up at low prices. Thus, the manufacturer may sell more at the expense of less profit.

To overcome this problem, manufacturers are increasingly using **pay-for-performance trade promotions,** through which retailers are rewarded for making sales to consumers rather than making purchases from manufacturers. Scanner data can be used to measure results, and the incentive to overload warehouses to take advantage of lower prices during deal periods is reduced.

Ethical and Legal Issues in Sales Promotion

The American Marketing Association Code of Ethics stipulates the "avoidance of sales promotion that uses deception or manipulation." Sales promotion provides an environment ripe for exploitation, and many of the ethical and legal problems in marketing communications are related to questionable promotions. Deception and fraud are the primary issues. Global marketing poses added ethical concerns because of requirements specific to different cultures. Deceptive sales promotion costs consumers millions of dollars annually, not to mention the time spent pursuing worthless "free" offers of unethical businesses. The use of push money is drawing increasing attention, as consumers often depend on salespeoples' recommendations in making purchasing decisions. Obviously, push money can bias these recommendations. In some industries, including music for radio air play and pharmaceuticals, promotional dollars are adding significantly to the cost of gaining distribution to the point where the ethics of the practice is the subject of hot debate.[25]

A popular consumer sales promotion tool, the sweepstakes, is often used deceptively. As a result, a variety of regulatory agencies, including the U.S. Postal Service and the Federal Trade Commission, actively police sweepstakes. In addition, all 50 states have various combinations of gambling, lottery, and consumer protection laws that regulate sweepstakes. At least nine states regulate the use of simulated checks, and separate restrictions exist for sweepstakes promoting tobacco, liquor, milk, and time-share lodging.

The increased scrutiny of sweepstakes by lawmakers has somewhat simplified consumers' participation in sweepstakes but makes it more difficult to use as a promotional tool. One industry executive says, "I'm doing a project now that, if I didn't know it was a sweepstakes, I would swear that I was building an airplane."[26] With consumer privacy a key issue, regulators will likely be more interested in how marketers use and store data that is collected through sweepstakes, contests, and games. With a history of deceptive practices, sweepstakes users can expect little tolerance for deception with future sweepstakes.

Caution is the best policy when designing a sweepstakes program. In fact, the same could be said for any sales promotion—to ensure that manufacturers, wholesalers, and retailers steer clear of unethical or illegal activity. Basically, marketers must tell consumers the truth and clearly spell out the action necessary to enter the sweepstakes. In addition, marketers must take responsibility for the fair and equitable treatment of buyers and nonbuyers during a promotion, taking care not to make it significantly more difficult for nonbuyers to enter. Finally, a legitimate sweepstakes program entails honest distribution of prizes, which may require the services of a sweepstakes management company to avoid insider rigging.

Fraud

Another significant problem involves coupon and rebate fraud, with manufacturers the intended victims. Exhibit 18–7 points out some of the ways cheaters can profit from coupons and mail-in offers. Industry analysts say that unethical retailers are responsible for a majority of fraudulent coupon claims.

Manufacturers have resorted to high-tech methods to combat coupon fraud. To circumvent coupon counterfeiting, special inks produce the word *void* on coupons exposed to the light used in copier machines. New checkout scanner technology now polices misredemption at the store level. Even low-tech methods, such as shortening the redemption period, are used.

The most widespread effect of fraud and deceptive sales promotions is that, in the long run, consumers pay more for products than they would otherwise. Consumers also pay through taxes for the considerable government regulation needed to combat fraud and deception.

Diverting

Consumers are not the only victims of unethical and illegal sales promotion. Manufacturers can also be the targets of fraud. A controversial, yet commonplace, activity is **diverting** (also called *arbitraging*), or secretly purchasing a product where it is less expensive, usually as a result of a trade promotion, and reselling in areas where prices are higher.

Diverters use up-to-the-minute computerized information to find out where the deals are, purchase merchandise for shipment to a buyer authorized by the manufacturer to receive the deal, then divert all or part of the shipment to an unauthorized location while the goods are in transit. Diverters include both intermediaries and chain stores. Intermediaries are fairly tight-lipped about diverting, and some even maintain secret operations in the offices of legitimate wholesalers and supermarket chains.

Diverting can distort supply and demand and cause marketing strategies to backfire on manufacturers. Industry analysts believe diverting is inevitable so long as manufacturers offer the same products at different prices in different geographic markets. Some manufacturers, most notably Procter & Gamble, have instituted a one-price nationwide policy to reduce diverting.

| **Exhibit 18-7** | *Examples of coupon and rebate fraud* |

The Fake Storefront

A scam artist rents space cheap, sets up a store, then starts sending in coupons to manufacturers for payment. Pretty soon the store's shelves are bare, but the "owner" is still sending in coupons obtained illegally.

Stuffing the Ballot Box

A retailer legitimately obtains cash from clearinghouses and manufacturers for coupons handed in by shoppers, but boosts the take illegally by sending in extra coupons purchased at steep discounts from various sources, such as unscrupulous printers.

Playing the Middleman

An ambitious operator makes money supplying other operators—collecting coupons by the pound and selling them to retailers, buying and selling proofs of purchase, or counterfeiting coupons and proofs of purchase.

The Redemption Scam

Manufacturers offer big cash rebates on large items to shoppers who mail in forms, together with proofs of purchase-receipts, labels, or box tops. A con artist uses the rebate forms and proofs of purchase, real or counterfeit, to illicitly collect refunds without buying products.

Global Concerns

The *global perspective* requires marketers to make an extra effort to become familiar with local laws and customs. In Spain, for example, it is legal to require the purchase of the product for entry in sales promotion contests, whereas such a requirement is illegal in most other European countries. Further, according to an expert on sales promotion in Spain, the Spanish people are generally keen on gambling and participate heavily in promotional games of chance. Logically, sales promotion in Spain is extremely popular, more so than in other European countries with stricter regulations. As a result, it is impossible to design a sales-promotion campaign for the entire European market—marketers must adapt programs to the appropriate legal framework.

In Canada, a variety of laws affects sales promotion. For example, if entry into a contest requires that the consumer send in a UPC label, entrants are also allowed to submit a handwritten facsimile of the label. In Quebec, language laws require that most marketing communications be in French. Also, most contests must be structured to require that entrants answer a skill-testing question to be eligible for a prize.

These examples from Spain and Canada are reminders that marketing activities should be conducted to meet varying applicable local requirements, often a composite of national, state (or province), and local laws. As most sales promotion tools involve mass distribution of written documents, extreme caution should be used to ensure compliance with relevant laws.

Summary

1. Explain the role and significance of sales promotion in the marketing communications mix. Sales promotion is one way firms may communicate with intended target audiences. Sales promotion uses media and nonmedia marketing communications for a predetermined, limited time at either consumer, retailer, or wholesaler level to stimulate trial, increase consumer demand, or improve product availability. Sales promotion is unique in that it offers an extra incentive for action. Its importance is evidenced by the considerable amount of money firms invest in it.

2. Understand why sales promotion expenditures account for a significant portion of many firms' marketing communications budgets. Expenditures in sales promotion have been fueled by changes in consumer demographics, lifestyles and attitudes, technological advances, a shift of power to retailers, a focus of firms on the short term, and an increasing emphasis on accountability for results.

Many shoppers today are busy and price-conscious, making sales promotion attractive. Scanning technology allows both retailers and manufacturers an opportunity to gauge the effectiveness of promotions quickly and accurately, thus reinforcing the use of sales promotion. Retailers have gained considerable power in the marketing channel in recent years, and manufacturers are virtually required to engage in sales promotion to increase or maintain distribution. Since sales promotion is generally short term, it fits with the time horizon most favored today in business. Finally, the results of sales promotion are easier to assess than the results of advertising, prompting its use in an era of accountability.

3. Discuss the objectives and techniques of consumer sales promotion. Consumer sales promotion attempts to stimulate trial, increase consumer inventory and consumption, encourage repurchase, neutralize competitive promotions, increase the sales of complementary products, stimulate impulse purchasing, and allow for flexible pricing policies. Consumer sales promotion techniques include price deals, coupons, rebates, cross-promotions, contests, sweepstakes, games, premiums, sampling, and advertising specialties.

4. Discuss the objectives and techniques of trade sales promotion. Trade sales promotion can help gain or maintain distribution, influence retailers to promote a product or to offer a price discount, increase reseller inventory, defend against competitors, and avoid price reductions. Popular trade sales promotion techniques involve trade allowances, dealer loaders, trade contests, point-of-purchase displays, trade shows, training programs, and push money.

5. Explain the limitations of sales promotion. Sales promotion cannot permanently reverse a genuine decline in sales, nor can it work to capture enduring acceptance of an inferior product. Overused sales promotion may actually weaken a brand image rather than strengthen it. Because it is short term and often highly visible, sales promotion can spur retaliation from competitors, which tends to diminish its effectiveness. In addition, consumers and resellers may engage in forward buying to take advantage of sales promotions, possibly causing the manufacturer to gain volume at the expense of declining profitability.

6. Realize how deceptive and fraudulent sales promotion victimizes both consumers and marketers. Deceptive sales promotion costs consumers millions of dollars annually. Moreover, manufacturers pay consumers and resellers hundreds of millions a year for fraudulently submitted rebates and coupons. The average consumer eventually pays a higher price for products to cover the cost of fraud in sales promotion. In addition, taxpayers have a heavier burden due to the increased costs of regulation at the federal, state, and local levels.

Understanding Marketing Terms and Concepts

Thinking About Marketing

1. What factors have contributed to significant expenditures in sales promotion?

2. What are the objectives of consumer sales promotion?

3. Define and briefly discuss these consumer sales promotion techniques: price deals, coupons, rebates, cross-promotions, contests, sweepstakes, games, premiums, sampling, and advertising specialties.

4. How do the objectives of trade sales promotion differ from those of consumer sales promotion?

5. Define and briefly discuss these trade sales promotion techniques: trade allowances, dealer loaders, trade contests, point-of-purchase displays, trade shows, training programs, and push money.

6. How would these parties be affected if consumer and trade sales promotions on grocery products were banned by law? (*a*) consumers; (*b*) retailers; (*c*) manufacturers with their own brands.

7. Discuss the issue of deception in sales promotion, and give examples of deceptive sales promotion.

8. Discuss the problem of coupon and rebate fraud, and identify several ways unscrupulous operators could exploit manufacturers through fraud.

9. Refer to "Building Customer Equity: Xbox Wins with Cross Promotion." What factors should a company consider before joining with another company to promote its brand?

10. Refer to "Being Entrepreneurial: Success of *Accidental Magic* No Accident." Promotional products are useful in getting the customer's attention. Are they useful for building a longer-term relationship?

Applying Marketing Skills

1. Consult the Sunday edition of a local newspaper. Identify examples of as many consumer trade promotion techniques as possible. You may find examples of price deals, coupons, rebates, cross-promotions, contests, sweepstakes, games, premiums, and even sampling. Select one example from each category of consumer sales promotion techniques that you have identified, and try to determine the main objective of the promotion: stimulating trial, increasing consumer inventory and consumption, encouraging repurchase, neutralizing competitive promotions, or increasing the sale of complementary products.

2. Look again at the Sunday newspaper. Collect a minimum of 10 coupons or other sales-promotion materials intended to stimulate trial of a new product. You may need to review the paper for a couple of weeks to collect 10 examples. Now, visit local retailers to determine whether the new products are in stock. If the product is in stock, note any other point-of-purchase materials that encourage a purchase. If the product is not in stock, see if you can find out why.

3. Assume you are the owner of a small independent bookstore in a large metropolitan area. You face heavy competition from Amazon.com and large national chains such as Walden Books and Barnes & Noble. Your clientele is more upscale, educated, and intellectual than that of your competition. You are attempting to develop a sales-promotion program to encourage your clientele to become loyal customers. Explain how you would choose one or more consumer sales promotion techniques to accomplish this objective.

Using the www in Marketing

Activity One
As mentioned in the chapter opener, Val-Pak is best known for mailing coupons to consumers. Access the company's Web site at http://www.valpak.com, then answer these questions:

1. Coupons are available on the Val-Pak Web site. What are the advantages and disadvantages of distributing coupons online as compared with traditional methods such as distributing them in the newspaper, via direct mail, or in a store?

2. Other than coupons, do you see any evidence that Val-Pak uses sales promotion at its Web site? If not, how could Val-Pak use sales promotion to build awareness and usage of its services?

Activity Two
Specialty advertising products are often used in sales promotion. One Web site that can be useful in planning sales promotions is PromoMart, developed on behalf of the Advertising Specialty Institute.

1. Access the PromoMart site at http://www.promomart. com. Click on the "Promotional Ideas," icon, then the "Idea Stores" icon, to learn about successful campaigns that use specialty advertising items.

2. Select three ideas that you think are good examples of sales promotion, and explain why you chose them.

Making Marketing Decisions
Case 18-1 Women on Their Way by Wyndham

Headquartered in Dallas, Texas, Wyndham International, Inc., is one of the world's largest hotel operators. Wyndham owns, leases, manages, and franchises properties in the United States, Caribbean, Europe, and Canada. The company has 28,000 employees. Wyndham serves both business and leisure travelers and has become particularly well-known for catering to female business travelers, a fast-growing segment of the business travel market.

Wyndham began intensifying its efforts to develop the female business traveler market in 1995, when it held its first annual "Women on Their Way Contest." Contest entrants were asked to describe how they would improve business travel for women. Over the years, many suggestions from customers have been implemented at Wyndham properties. Women indicated they would like to have a comfortable, private place for conversation, not the hotel bar or lobby. Wyndham responded with its signature library in its Garden Hotel properties, a location convenient to the lobby and bar, but distinctly separate from these facilities. Guest suggestions led to an option of receiving prenotification by phone before room-service delivery, a safety and courtesy measure.

Over the years, the theme for the annual contest has changed. In 2002, the contest asked entrants to give advice on how to conquer life's challenges and enjoy its wonderful moments, both personally and professionally. Such information is a valuable input into an ongoing relationship marketing program between Wyndham and its female customers. As part of the relationship marketing program, Women on Their Way members (membership also open to males) receive an e-mail newsletter featuring travel news and special promotional offers.

In addition to its annual contest, Wyndham uses other sales-promotion tools to provide incentives and add value for its customers. Price deals such as two nights for one and special weekend rates help Wyndham boost sales volume, and cross-promotions with major airlines are also popular.

When Wyndham registers a guest for the Women on Their Way program, the company learns how often the person travels, how much travel is business or leisure, whether children accompany the guest, and with which airlines the guest flies. Prospective members also indicate if they are members of the National Association of Business Owners or the National Association of Female Executives.

There are signs that Wyndham's Women on Their Way program is helping position the company as a specialist in meeting the needs of traveling women. The program has been featured on international television via Cable News Network (CNN). Overall bookings are up for the Wyndham chain, though it is hard to tie booking results directly to the program. It is also difficult to tie specific results of the program to increased sales volume, because Wyndham has grown rapidly since it began the program in 1995, causing an overall increase in bookings. Inquiries to Wyndham's Web site are increasing, and feedback from guests and the female executive advisory board continues to be positive. Wyndham books 59 percent more women travelers than its competitors while spending only a million dollars annually on women-specific marketing. Cary Broussard, vice president of the Women on Their Way program, says, "We value the opinions of women business travelers who have the expertise necessary to make acute assessments of our room service program. Their feedback helps us to improve the experience not just for other women travelers, but for all of our customers."

Questions

1. Explain how Wyndham uses a sales promotion tool, the annual contest, to better define and meet the needs of its female guests.

2. Wyndham often engages in cross-promotions with airlines and other travel-related companies. What other cross-promotion opportunities do you see for Wyndham?

3. What other sales-promotion objectives and tools could you recommend for Wyndham?

4. The results of sales promotion should be measurable. What can Wyndham do to better measure the sales-promotion aspects of its Women on Their Way program?

Case 18-2 GlaxoSmith-Kline's Sales Promotion in India

GlaxoSmith-Kline (GSK) is a leading worldwide pharmaceutical company based in the United Kingdom. GSK puts a lot of emphasis on research and development of new pharmaceuticals, and it also invests heavily in the marketing area. Of GSK's 100,000 employees, 40,000 are in sales and marketing. The company has the largest global salesforce in the pharmaceutical industry.

The practice of using special incentives to encourage physicians to prescribe specific branded drugs, not generics or competitors' brands, has been part of the pharmaceutical industry for decades. So has the practice of offering incentives to pharmacists to honor these prescriptions rather than switching to a generic or competitive brand when the patient fills the prescription. Recently, the practice has become more controversial for two primary reasons. First, the overall cost of health care has risen around the world. Some believe that promotional costs incurred by pharmaceutical companies ultimately result in higher costs to consumers. In some cases, higher costs mean lack of access to consumers with low incomes or those not insured. The second reason that pharmaceutical promotional spending has become more controversial is that some companies have expanded the use of incentives, raising ethical questions about the practice.

A case in point is how GSK and other companies promote their pharmaceutical products in India. Pharmacy owner Ranjit Ranawat surprised his wife by bringing home a new 29-inch television set he received for ordering 600 vials of Fortum, an antibiotic, and 100 boxes of Ceftum, a drug for urinary-tract and respiratory infections. Mr. Ranawat ordered these products from GSK in quantities approximately 10 times his normal quantity in order to receive the television set. Such incentives have become commonplace in India, where many consumers are too poor to see a doctor and rely on medical advice from the pharmacist. There are approximately a half a million pharmacists in India, and they have quite a bit of clout in determining which drugs will be best-sellers.

The widespread use of special incentives to pharmacists in India is troubling to health care professionals for several reasons. First, special incentives based on high-volume purchases require that the pharmacist push the product hard when it may not be appropriate for all patients. Second, by giving extra profits to the pharmacist instead of dropping the retail price, consumers are paying more for needed drugs. Third, about one-half of the highly promoted drugs are antibiotics, which experts say are overused and abused in India.

GKS and other drug companies defend the use of promotional incentives, saying they are not intended to increase total industry sales but to persuade pharmacists to substitute their drugs when prescriptions are written for a competitive drug. According to GKS's director of pharmaceuticals, for every two GKS prescriptions that are written, only one is actually filled because druggists make a switch. GKS thus justifies the use of incentives as simply defending its market share.

The role of sales incentives in India in the future is unclear. Current law allows easy duplication of patented drugs, which means there are thousands of drug manufacturers there. With so many companies, self-regulation of the industry would be difficult, as some competitors would undoubtedly rely on incentives to build their business. India's patent law is due for an overhaul in 2005, but the results of the new law remain to be seen. Pharmacists are powerful, and it is customary for their trade associations to demand special allowances. Some pharmacists claim they need the additional profit that promotional incentives bring since some of their customers are poor and do not pay their bills. When pharmaceutical companies have resisted paying promotional incentives, some pharmacies immediately reduced the amount of their purchase orders.

The international pharmaceutical industry is interested in what happens in India, but offers little advice. For example, the Pharmaceutical Research and Manufacturers of America (PRMA), a major trade group, notes a "disturbing" trend toward shifting the responsibility for prescribing drugs away from doctors toward other health care professionals, including pharmacists. While noting that price controls do not work, the PRMA does not take an explicit stand on incentives granted to pharmacists.

It is not clear what GKS and other industry leaders will do with their promotional allowances in the future. For now, none have spoken out against the practice. GKS says its expenditures on promotional allowances in India represent less than 1 percent of sales. At such a small percentage, there is little incentive to reduce the allowances from a cost-cutting perspective.

Questions

1. Is the payment of promotional allowances to pharmacists in India justified from an economic point of view? From a societal point of view?

2. What other types of sales promotion could GKS engage in that would not be so controversial?

3. Are industry leaders such as GKS under any obligation to set the standards for ethical sales promotion practices?

Personal Selling and Sales Management

After studying this chapter, you should be able to:

1 Understand the role and importance of personal selling in the marketing communications mix.

2 See how the key steps in personal selling depend on a relationship perspective.

3 Identify the similarities and differences in the job responsibilities of salespeople and sales managers.

4 Describe the key activities in sales management.

5 Appreciate important ethical issues faced by salespeople and sales managers.

www.pfizer.com

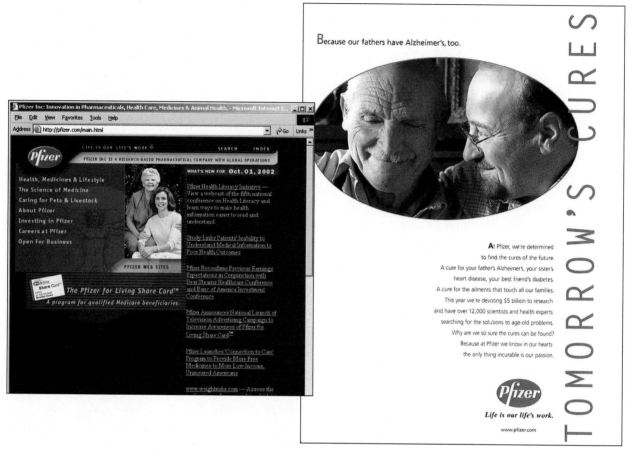

Started in 1849, Pfizer has grown to be a worldwide pharmaceutical company. Much of this success has come under the leadership of CEO William Steere. Steere started as a Pfizer sales representative in San Francisco 40 years ago. He was then promoted to district sales manager and, after 12 other promotions, was named CEO in 1991. During his tenure as CEO, Pfizer has advanced from 13th in worldwide prescription drug sales to 2nd.

Pfizer's success is due to many factors. Steere divested unrelated businesses so the company could focus largely on pharmaceuticals. Pfizer also spends heavily on research and development, the efforts of which have produced a number of new drugs that have been successful in the marketplace.

Developing new drugs is one thing; making them successful in the marketplace is another. This is largely the role of Pfizer's award-winning salesforce. The Pfizer salesforce is the largest in the industry, with 5,400 sales representatives in the United States and more than 17,000 worldwide. A survey of U.S. physicians ranked Pfizer's salesforce first overall in terms of their disease-and-product knowledge, credibility, and service. This was the fifth straight year Pfizer was ranked first, which is a record for the pharmaceutical industry.

The basic role of Pfizer salespeople is to provide physicians with reliable information about drugs so that they can confidently prescribe them to their patients. As described by CEO Steere: "The sales representatives are the ultimate technology transfer between our laboratories and the practicing physician. Doctors get a lot of information from our representatives, ranging from technical information on new products to new information on older drugs." The Pfizer salesforce is so good that other pharmaceutical companies have partnered with Pfizer to bring new products to market. For example, Pfizer salespeople helped launch Warner-Lambert's cholesterol-lowering drug, Lipitor, and G. D. Searle's arthritis drug, Celebrex.

Steere retired as CEO in January 2001, but not before he directed the acquisition of Warner-Lambert. Hank McKinnell took over as CEO and shortly thereafter announced the $60 billion acquisition of Pharmacia. If this deal goes through as expected, Pfizer will be the leading pharmaceutical company in the world, with annual sales in excess of $48 billion. It will have 12 products with annual revenues in excess of $1 billion and a pipeline full of potential new drug products.

The Pfizer example highlights the important role that personal selling can play in a firm's marketing strategy. Continuously introducing new drugs is critical to success in the pharmaceutical industry and requires both a concerted R&D effort and a strong marketing effort. Although Pfizer does advertise to physicians and consumers and informs them about diseases and new drug products, the Pfizer salesforce is critical to the success of new-product launches. Pfizer salespeople develop close relationships with physicians, and physicians rely on them as an important source of information about new drug products. It is also interesting to note that the company's previous CEO—William Steere—started his career as a Pfizer salesperson and that his first promotion was to district sales manager.

Personal selling is another element of the marketing communications mix, the face-to-face interaction between a seller and a buyer for the purpose of satisfying buyer needs to the benefit of both. This chapter describes the roles of professional salespeople and illustrates various types of sales jobs. We look at the key personal selling activities, especially the way salespeople work with customers to establish mutually beneficial relationships.

The remainder of the chapter deals with sales management. In simple terms, **sales management** provides leadership and supervision of an organization's personal selling function. Besides managing sales personnel, sales managers develop and implement sales strategy. As in other areas of marketing, personal selling and sales management roles are being redefined to meet the challenges of today's competitive, customer-driven marketplace.

We also discuss ethical issues in personal selling and sales management. Salespeople are among the most visible representatives of an organization's marketing effort, and they operate under considerable pressure to generate sales revenue. Because of these factors, it is extremely important for salespeople and sales managers to be aware of their ethical and legal responsibilities.

The Multiple Roles of Salespeople

Salespeople fulfill multiple roles that contribute to the overall success of a business. We look at these roles in two ways: as contributions to the marketing effort, and as functional roles (the different types of personal selling jobs).

Contributions of Personal Selling to Marketing

Personal selling contributes to a firm's marketing efforts by producing sales revenue, meeting buyer expectations, and providing marketplace information. The key to successful marketing lies in understanding customer requirements and then matching a firm's offerings to those requirements. Because salespeople are often the most direct link between a firm and its customers, they can heavily influence whether or not the firm succeeds.

PRODUCING SALES REVENUE   Salespeople make perhaps their most important contribution to the marketing function as revenue producers. Businesses scrambling for survival in a highly competitive world have become more profit-oriented in recent years. To produce an adequate bottom-line profit, it is imperative to achieve a suitable top-line, or sales revenue, figure. And salespeople are on the front line, supported of course by marketing research, product development, distribution, and other areas of the business. Sales personnel, along with management, are the prime bearers of the burden of contributing to profit by producing revenue.

Personal selling is an important element of a firm's marketing strategy. A sales representative helps a retail store manager improve the display of clothing.

Speaking from Experience

"We have come to realize at Du Pont that sales is not just an individual effort by salespeople. Anyone involved at the customer interface or in support of the customer plays a key role in overall sales success. The actions of a customer service representative, a technical representative, a truck driver, or a CEO can make or break the sale. Processes and systems need to be made customer-friendly to give our customer team efficient and effective support. Roles need to be clear, and redundancy eliminated. At Du Pont, we realize that our competitive advantage comes from our organizational capacity and capability. The combined capability of people is hard to duplicate, and the people of Du Pont are our strength."

Gerald J. Bauer
Sales Competency Leader and
Field Marketing Manager (ret.)
Du Pont Company

Gerald Bauer recently retired from Du Pont where he held a variety of positions, including sales, sales management, product management, industry management, customer service management, purchasing management, and sales training. He continues to work for Du Pont as a consultant and trainer. Jerry earned a BBA and MBA in marketing from the University of Toledo.

MEETING BUYER EXPECTATIONS   To succeed in a competitive marketplace, salespeople must—at a minimum—meet buyer expectations. Salespeople are at the heart of building customer relationships. There is no question that the competitive environment has given buyers more clout in dealing with salespeople. According to the Institute for Supply Management, buyers are less likely to tolerate salespeople who waste their time with poorly prepared sales presentations or who will not address their concerns.[1] Dennis Ferguson, a buyer for California-based Rayley's supermarkets, advises salespeople: "I'm busier than ever. Don't tell me what I already know. Tell me why and how your product . . . will disappear off the shelf."[2]

Exhibit 19–1 presents a number of dos and don'ts for salespeople. As suggested by the exhibit, many buyers today take a no-nonsense attitude when dealing with salespeople. They expect straightforward, honest communication. In short, they expect salespeople to live up to high professional standards.

PROVIDING MARKETPLACE INFORMATION   Because personal selling involves face-to-face interaction with buyers, salespeople can get immediate feedback from customers. Just as marketplace feedback can help in a firm's development of future products and promotional programs, direct customer feedback adds value to the personal selling function. Feedback to the company can include information on competition and analysis of existing and potential customers and markets, which is useful in sales forecasting.

New technologies can help salespeople perform their job roles more productively. The use of laptop computers turns a car into a virtual office for a salesperson.

Job Roles of Salespeople

Although all personal selling involves face-to-face interactions with customers, there are distinct differences in the nature of these interactions. Salespeople's contributions to the overall company effort may be made in a variety of job roles. Exhibit 19–2 classifies personal selling jobs into two major categories: business-to-business and direct-to-consumer.

BUSINESS-TO-BUSINESS SALES   Business-to-business selling involves the sale of products and services that are resold by the customer, used as part of the customer's manufacturing process, or used to facilitate the operation of the customer's business. Business selling involves three major types of salespeople: sales support, new business, and existing business.

Exhibit 19–1	*What buyers expect from salespeople*

Dos	**Don'ts**
• Know your product and its competition better than the buyer does.	• Use industry buzzwords without knowing what you're talking about.
• Be a tough, but open, negotiator.	• Portray your company as quality-conscious if it's not.
• Have the backing of your company to make strategic partnerships.	• Focus exclusively on short-term sales goals.
• Understand the customer's future plans and offer ideas about how your company can help further them.	• Talk about strategic alliances without having the support of your company.
• Be willing to change your processes and products.	• Say, "We want your business, and we'll make it up later."
• Offer something unique—a technological change, a new way of delivering, or a large price concession.	• Try to persuade purchasers to buy something that doesn't meet their needs.
• Get to know all the people interested in the product, from purchasing managers to engineers.	• Simply talk pricing.
• Keep on top of potential product problems.	• Give a canned presentation.
• Be able to explain how your company plans to improve the quality and reliability of its products.	• Come without ideas.
	• Know nothing about the competition.
	• Fly by the seat of your pants.
	• Offer product today that you're not likely to have tomorrow.
	• Roll over dead in negotiations.

Exhibit 19–2	*Types of personal selling jobs*

Business-to-Business	
Sales support:	Promote the product or provide technical service. Includes missionaries and detailers.
New business:	Focus on sales growth by selling new products or new customers. Some salespeople are trade-show specialists, and some work in the field (out of the office).
Existing business:	Maintain and enhance relationships with an established customer base. Includes salespeople who follow an established route, writing up routine orders.
Direct-to-Consumer	
	Represent the seller in transactions with ultimate consumers. Includes retail salespeople and representatives of direct selling firms and most real estate and financial services.

Sales support salespeople are not directly involved in concluding customer purchases. Rather, they support the personal selling function by promoting a product or providing technical support. Sales support salespeople may work in coordination with other salespeople who actually solicit customer purchases, and their activities can be modified to meet the needs of individual customers.

One primary type of sales support job is that of the *missionary*. Missionary salespeople, like religious missionaries, work at the grassroots level to spread the "gospel," that is, help promote their company's products. In this instance, the grassroots level means with product users or with a channel intermediary such as a retail store. Broker organizations often use sales support personnel to visit individual grocery stores, assisting in merchandising and providing point-of-purchase sales information, thereby providing support to build sales volume for the broker's products. Textbook salespeople, such as those from McGraw-Hill/Irwin, are a type of missionary salespeople.

In the pharmaceutical industry, highly specialized missionaries, or *detailers*, work for most major drug firms. Detailers call on medical professionals and provide them with technical information and product samples to encourage doctors to write prescriptions for the company's drugs. Pfizer salespeople represent a good example of detailers.

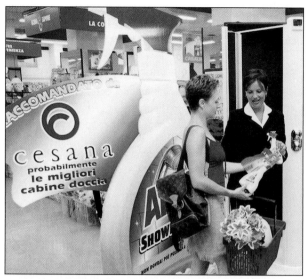

Retail salespeople sell to individual consumers. A salesperson uses giant displays, a contest, and a demonstration to sell Ajax Shower Power to an Italian customer.

Technical support salespeople are an important element of the sales support function. They have expertise in areas such as design and installation of complex equipment and may provide specialized training to customer employees. Technical support salespeople are especially effective in sales teams formed to address customer needs. For example, the shipping and weighing division of Pitney Bowes sells sophisticated computerized systems that weigh, rate, and track packages for customers like FedEx and UPS. The Pitney Bowes sales team includes a sales rep and two sales support personnel—a shipping expert and a sales engineer.[3]

Members of the salesforce who concentrate on selling new products or selling to new customers are called **new-business salespeople.** These people are extremely important to companies focusing on sales growth. Suppose a newly established franchising firm depends on the sale of new franchises to achieve its growth objectives. Salespeople representing the franchising company may then travel the country in search of new franchisees.

Many salespeople are assigned to work with established customers to produce a steady stream of sales revenue. **Existing-business salespeople,** sometimes called *order takers,* include wholesaler reps who follow an established route, writing up fairly routine orders from their customers.

Business-to-business salespeople often represent some combination of the sales support, new-business, and existing-business roles. For example, salespeople from General Mills serve all three functions. They seek new business when new grocery retailers enter the market or when General Mills introduces a new product; they work with existing grocery chains and co-ops to maximize sales of existing and new products; and they provide sales support as they visit individual grocery stores to maximize the General Mills presence at the point of sale.

DIRECT-TO-CONSUMER SALES   **Direct-to-consumer salespeople** sell to individuals who personally use the products and services. This category includes over 4.5 million retail salespeople and over a million others who sell residential real estate and financial securities to ultimate consumers. Several additional million direct-to-consumer salespeople represent firms such as Avon, Mary Kay, Tupperware, Creative Memories, Amway, and other direct-selling companies.

The Sales Process: A Relationship Approach

Whatever their role, salespeople try to maximize their effectiveness in the **sales process,** which involves initiating, developing, and enhancing long-term, mutually satisfying relationships with customers. This view of selling—called **relationship selling**—is a departure from the old approach that focused more on a salesperson's ability to make a compelling, and often manipulative, sales presentation than on customer needs. Exhibit 19–3 describes its components.

Exhibiting Trust-Building Attributes

To succeed in relationship selling, salespeople must have certain attributes. Although specific attributes vary depending on the sales context, the ability to build trust is basic. Research has shown that five attributes help to build relationships with customers. Salespeople must be customer-oriented, honest, dependable, competent, and likable.[4] Teresa McBride, head of a consulting firm that is the nation's

| Exhibit 19–3 | *The sales process: A relationship approach* |

Salesperson attributes
• Customer-oriented
• Honest
• Dependable
• Competent
• Likable

Selling strategy
• Sales territory
• Each customer
• Each sales call

Initiating customer relationships
•Prospecting
•Precall planning
•Approaching the customer

Developing customer relationships
•Sales presentation delivery
•Gaining customer commitment

Enhancing customer relationships

Salespeople should develop selling strategies for each customer and for each sales call. Successfully executing these strategies often requires salespeople to perform a variety of activities.

fastest-growing Hispanic-owned business, said the smartest sales policy is one based on honesty. By following a trust-based sales strategy, the 31-year-old McBride doubled sales revenue to *Fortune 500* clients in a single year.[5]

Developing a Selling Strategy

It is not enough for salespeople to exhibit the right attributes; they must also develop a selling strategy, an overall plan for a course of action. As part of integrated marketing communications programs, selling strategies should be developed at three levels: sales territory, customer, and individual sales call.

A sales territory, usually defined geographically, consists of specific customers and prospects assigned to a specific salesperson. Salespeople need an overall territory strategy regarding the amount of time to spend working with current customers versus trying to generate new customers. Lisa Paolozzi uses a specific territory strategy to sell successfully for FIND/SVP, a market research and consulting company. She spends Mondays and Tuesdays cold-calling prospects and making appointments with existing customers. The rest of the week she makes sales calls to customers and prospects. This approach allows her to plan effective coverage of the customers and prospects in her territory as well as manage her time better.[6] Salespeople should also have a territory strategy focusing on specific customer needs they can satisfy. The territory strategy of an advertising sales rep for *Sports Illustrated,* for example, might be to provide high-quality, cost-effective print advertising to those who wish to reach an active, upscale audience.

Selling strategy should next be developed for each customer within a given sales territory. The *Sports Illustrated* salesperson might focus on the manufacturer of Prince tennis racquets and develop an advertising plan to coincide with tennis Grand Slam events: the Australian Open, the French Open, Wimbledon, and the U.S. Open. The salesperson might develop entirely different sales strategies for other sporting goods manufacturers, depending on the needs of the customer.

Finally, each sales call, or every meeting with the customer, should be guided by a strategy compatible with customer needs. By developing a specific plan of action for each sales call, the salesperson capitalizes on a major advantage of personal selling as a marketing communications tool. The *Sports Illustrated* salesperson, for example,

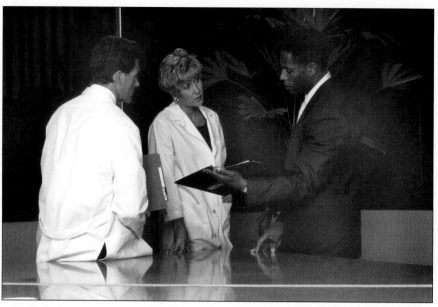

Salespeople play an important role in the pharmaceutical industry. Different strategies are used for different customers.

would probably have to meet with Prince executives individually and in groups, along with ad agency personnel several times to gain a commitment for the Grand Slam advertising program and to customize the program to the specific needs of the customer.

Initiating Customer Relationships

Exhibit 19–3 breaks initiating customer relationships into three primary activities: prospecting, precall planning, and approaching the customer. These activities, like the other parts of the sales process, are highly interrelated. They are not necessarily separately distinguishable actions.

PROSPECTING   **Prospecting** is defined as the seller's search for and identification of qualified buyers. Potential prospects come from a variety of sources, including existing customers, personal contacts, directories, computerized databases, trade publications, and trade shows. Prospects may respond to advertising by placing a telephone call or writing for more information. Such responses, called *inquiries,* are often assigned to salespeople for follow-up.

One interesting prospecting approach is to use educational seminars. Gartner, a research and consulting firm, uses its 400-person salesforce to invite clients and prospects to over 300 seminars each year. Each seminar addresses a specific content area. Participants are charged to attend the seminars, but this fee is refunded if an attendee purchases Gartner services within 30 days of an event. These educational seminars have helped Gartner get new customers and also to sell additional services to existing clients.[7]

A qualified buyer must be reasonably accessible to the seller, able to afford the purchase, and at least willing to consider making it. To define qualified prospects, salespeople or companies may establish additional criteria involving elements such as geographical proximity, marketplace function (sales only to wholesalers, for example), or minimum sales-volume levels.

PRECALL PLANNING   In **precall planning,** the salesperson focuses on learning more about the customer's situation. Salespeople might visit the prospect's place of business to learn more about their needs. BellSouth, a major telecommunications company headquartered in Atlanta, instructs its salespeople to follow up a qualifying call with an information-gathering meeting with the prospect. After the proper information is gathered, the BellSouth account rep plans a sales presentation to be delivered at a later date.

A sales rep must consider a multitude of factors in planning a specific sales presentation. A good idea is to formulate a measurable *sales call objective* to guide the planning process. This should specify the desired customer action resulting from the call; for instance, "the customer will place an order of 400 units for immediate shipment."

Planning involves selecting a format for the sales presentation. In most cases, a two-way dialog between the buyer and the seller may be facilitated by an *organized sales presentation,* a mental or written outline developed by the salesperson. The outline should be flexible enough to allow **adaptive selling;** that is, the salesperson must be able to adjust her or his behavior to respond appropriately to the situation and to address the issues that are most important to the customer.[8]

A format at the other extreme from adaptive selling is a *canned sales presentation.* In effect, this is a fully scripted presentation that the sales rep memorizes; it could even be an automated presentation using audiovisual media. Although generally ineffective in business-to-business personal selling, canned presentations have worked well in consumer settings such as the sale of encyclopedias to families. Although they may be complete and logical, the relative inflexibility of canned presentations limits their usefulness.

Word processing supported by graphics facilitates another presentation format, the *written sales proposal.* Long used in major sales, written sales proposals can now easily be tailored to individual customers with diverse needs. Sales proposals are usually accompanied by face-to-face meetings between the buying and selling parties to define product specifications and negotiate details.

During precall planning, salespeople also decide how to use sales tools such as brochures, audiovisual support material, and computer technology. As an example, Dun's Marketing Services, a subsidiary of Dun & Bradstreet, greatly improved the effectiveness of its sales presentations by using a computer to demonstrate how its BusinessLine product works.

Precall planning requires a salesperson to think about communicating to customers how various product or service features translate into explicit benefits. A **feature** is merely a statement of fact about some aspect of a product or service. A **benefit** describes what the feature can do for the customer. For example, one feature of a Mitsubishi portable fax machine is a built-in speakerphone. The benefit of the speakerphone is that it allows hands-free conversation. Effective salespeople communicate more about benefits than features, focusing on those of particular interest to each customer.

APPROACHING THE CUSTOMER   The final phase of initiating the relationship is approaching the customer. This involves arranging the sales call, usually by making an appointment, and extends into the first sales call when introductions are made and the salesperson attempts to develop the basis for further sales activity. Common courtesy and business etiquette can help make a good initial impression. Improper behavior, on the other hand, can diminish the salesperson's opportunity to proceed in the sales process. Examples of behaviors to avoid are shown in Exhibit 19–4.

Developing Customer Relationships

After successfully approaching the customer, the salesperson can begin to develop the customer relationship. To do this, he or she must deliver an effective sales presentation or, more likely, multiple sales presentations. The relationship is established when the customer makes a commitment to take an action such as making a purchase.

SALES PRESENTATION DELIVERY   To make a successful sales presentation, the salesperson must achieve **source credibility**—that is, the customer must perceive its needs being satisfied by the combination of the salesperson, the product

| Exhibit 19–4 | *Approaching the customer: Violations of ethics and etiquette* |

A survey of 250 secretaries, administrative assistants, and other "gatekeepers" responsible for scheduling appointments for visiting salespeople revealed these violations of sales etiquette and sales ethics:

- Arriving unannounced to make a sales call.
- Pretending to know the decision maker.
- Treating secretaries disrespectfully.
- Being reluctant to state the purpose of the proposed visit.
- Arriving late for appointments.
- Being overly persistent in attempts to get an appointment.
- Wasting time with unnecessary conversation.
- Failing to cancel appointments that cannot be met.

| Exhibit 19–5 | *Questioning and listening in sales* |

- Remember that you cannot possibly suggest solutions for your clients if you have not listened to what they have said.
- When you are a good listener, you run less chance of dominating the conversation and losing the client's attention.
- You will always learn something valuable from listening. In building customer relationships, this learning process never stops.
- Listening provides feedback on how your sales presentation is going. React to what the prospect is telling you. Clarify the prospect's message when necessary.
- Plan and organize your presentation so you know which questions to ask. Make your questions clear and concise to avoid confusing the client.
- During the presentation, take notes to ensure appropriate follow-up activities or to plan for the next call.

or service, and the salesperson's company. The salesperson's personal characteristics such as dress, appearance, and manner may be important in achieving source credibility.

Certain sales approaches can also help achieve source credibility. Prospect-oriented questioning and active listening, as illustrated in Exhibit 19–5, is very important.[9] The salesperson should be careful not to overstate any claims about the product or service and should be prepared to substantiate any that are made. Using third-party evidence such as letters from satisfied customers, called *testimonials,* can enhance source credibility. Finally, pointing out guarantees and warranties that reduce the buyer's risk can assist in establishing source credibility.

Jerry Bauer, Sales Competency Leader and Field Marketing Manager, Du Pont Company, (ret.) talks about the importance of questioning and listening during a sales presentation: "Many people think that the key to a successful sales presentation is for a salesperson to be a good talker. At Du Pont, we think the key to sales success is to be a good listener. We emphasize this point in our sales training by saying that salespeople should talk about 20 percent of the time and listen 80 percent of the time. This might be a little stretch, but it encourages salespeople to focus on the listening aspect of the job. A parallel skill is the ability to ask good questions. Questioning and listening skills are a focal point of our sales training at Du Pont."

During the sales presentation, the sales rep should expect to resolve buyer concerns before the customer makes a commitment to buy. Buyer concerns, called *objections,* come in many forms ("Your price is too high"; "I don't like the color"; "I am happy with my current supplier") and must be dealt with successfully to make a sale. Objections are a form of *sales resistance,* which also includes unspoken customer concerns. To the extent possible, the salesperson should anticipate these concerns and formulate appropriate customer-oriented responses prior to the sales

Exhibit 19–6   *Dealing with unreasonable customer concerns and objections*

> **When a customer lodges a completely unjustified objection, one that is knowingly untrue or unreasonable, salespeople can follow these guidelines for responding.**

- Allow customers to retain their dignity. State your position politely.

- Do not argue with a customer. Winning an argument can have detrimental effects on the relationship.

- Appeal to the customer's sense of fair play. Tell the customer you want to do what is right, and try to reach agreement on a course of action to be taken.

- Stand firm, so long as your position is based on facts.

- Do not use company policy as a reason for your position. This tends to invite criticism of the policy.

- If absolutely necessary, be prepared to say no to an unreasonable demand. Agreeing to an unreasonable demand can open the door for more of the same, which will ultimately endanger or ruin the relationship.

presentation. Salespeople must understand that questions and concerns are part of the buyer's attempt to make a sound purchase decision; addressing these concerns is an integral element in the sales process.

Many buyer concerns arise when a sales rep has not taken enough time to qualify a buyer and thus calls on a marginal prospect, perhaps one who cannot afford the product or will derive only limited benefits from a purchase. Under any set of circumstances, salespeople should treat buyer questions with patience and respect. Exhibit 19–6 details some ideas on how to deal with customers' unreasonable concerns and objections.

GAINING CUSTOMER COMMITMENT   In most cases, a buyer can choose from among a number of potential sellers; hence, sales reps are responsible for gaining customer commitment. This remains true even when the seller is the only available alternative, for a customer may elect to make no purchase at all.

A successful relationship between buyer and seller requires a firm commitment from both parties. Essentially, customer commitment involves an economic transaction between the buyer and the seller (customer buys when salesperson closes a sale), or an agreement between the two parties that moves them toward such a transaction. Some customer commitments take the form of a purchase order. Other examples are agreeing to continue sales negotiations, signing a long-term distribution contract, or accepting the seller's suggestion to maintain specified inventory levels to meet local demand.

To gain a commitment, a professional salesperson must be willing to spend the time necessary to give the customer all the pertinent information. Further, professional salespeople understand that when buyers do not want to make a commitment, it is because they see a commitment as simply not in their best interest at that time.

Relationship-oriented salespeople must walk a fine line between being persuasive and being overly persistent or pushy in an attempt to gain commitment. Buyers do not like being pressured into making decisions they feel are premature, and salespeople must realize that decisions made under pressure are likely to create postpurchase doubts. This can jeopardize the relationship and even lead to its termination.

Enhancing Customer Relationships

The final phase of the sales process shown in Exhibit 19–3 is enhancing customer relationships. The purpose of this step is to ensure that customer expectations are met or exceeded, so that an ongoing, mutually satisfying relationship between the buyer and seller may continue. This stage involves postsale follow-up activities such as entering and expediting customer orders, providing training for the customer's employees, assisting in merchandising and installation activities, and solving customer problems.

Salespeople can enhance the relationship by continuing to provide timely information, alerting the customer to forthcoming product improvements, monitoring customer satisfaction and making improvements as necessary, showing the customer additional ways to use the product, and acting as a consultant to the prospect's business. It is not unusual for salespeople to become confidants of customers, offering opinions when asked on a wide range of topics, some of which are unrelated to the sales offering.

Salespeople should seek feedback from customers, rather than wait for problems to surface. Asking questions such as "How are we doing as your supplier?" is important, as well as follow-up action to continually build value for the customer. Salespeople must never take existing customers' business for granted. The added value to customers can be reinforced through periodic business reviews, where salespeople and perhaps their management meet with customers to analyze sales and profit performance and identify areas for future emphasis. The importance of enhancing customer relationships is illustrated in "Building Customer Equity: Getting Customer Feedback."

Sales Management Activities

Sales managers must move their salesforces toward the ideal. Typically, successful sales managers were successful salespeople before being promoted. They usually continue some form of personal selling after becoming managers, perhaps selling to their own set of customers, accompanying salespeople on sales calls, or serving as a member of a selling team. Exhibit 19–7 presents management activities, including developing a sales strategy, designing the sales organization, developing and directing the salesforce, and evaluating effectiveness and performance.

These activities require more of sales managers than is expected of salespeople. Whereas salespeople concentrate mainly on relationships with customers, sales managers must work well with customers, salespeople, and many other people in the company to do a good job.

Exhibit 19–7	*Key sales management activities*

Develop a sales strategy → Designing the sales organization → Developing the salesforce → Directing the salesforce → Determining salesforce effectiveness & performance

Building Customer Equity

Getting customer feedback

The hospitality industry was hit hard by the September 11 terrorist attacks. Although The Ritz Carlton has annual sales revenues of about $1.5 billion, its revenue per available room dropped 30 percent after the attacks. The company responded by putting executives on the road to meet with 400 customers in one week. The executives asked customers how The Ritz Carlton salespeople were doing. Customers indicated that they needed more flexibility in canceling or rebooking orders. Current contracts were too rigid in the uncertain business climate.

Management took this feedback and made contracts more flexible. The value proposition to customers was also enhanced by including upgrades, food and beverage costs, and reception space. Salespeople received training about these changes and reemphasized the company's basic sales process, called LEAP (listen, empathize, ask, produce). Time was spent identifying roadblocks customers might present and developing appropriate responses. This response to customer feedback has helped the company increase business with existing customers and get new customers, especially for new properties such as the hotel in lower Manhattan that overlooks Ground Zero.

Developing a Sales Strategy

The starting point for sales management is developing a sales strategy to execute the firm's marketing strategy. A marketing strategy emphasizes the development of a marketing mix to appeal to defined target markets. A sales strategy focuses on how to sell to specific customers within those target markets.[10] Two key elements of a sales strategy are a relationship strategy and a sales channel strategy.

DEVELOPING A RELATIONSHIP STRATEGY   Although there is a clear trend toward relationships, especially in business-to-business selling, different types of relationships are possible. Buyers have different needs and desire to purchase in different ways for different products. Therefore, it is important that the selling firm develop specific **relationship strategies** for specific customer groups. Most firms will need to develop relationship strategies for three to five different customer groups. Exhibit 19–8 presents four basic relationship strategies.

The relationship strategies range from a transaction relationship to a collaborative relationship, with a solutions relationship and partnership relationship in between. As a company moves from transaction to collaborative relationships, the focus changes from just selling products to adding more value, the time frame of the relationship becomes longer, the products become more customized, and the number of customers becomes fewer. Also, the cost to serve customers becomes higher and there is a greater need for commitment between the buying and selling organization.

DEVELOPING A SALES CHANNEL STRATEGY   A **sales channel strategy** addresses how the company initiates and maintains contact with customers. It may involve the use of a company field salesforce, telemarketing, independent sales reps, distributors, the Internet, and/or trade shows.[11] Such a strategy should ensure that customers receive the necessary attention from the salesforce. A sales channel strategy must be both effective (get the job done) and efficient (at a reasonable cost).

The key strategic decision is to balance the customer's preference with the cost to serve the customer. In general, lower-cost methods are used in transaction relationships and the highest-cost methods in collaborative relationships. For example, allowing customers to purchase directly from the Internet can be a cost-effective way to serve customers in a transaction relationship. At the other extreme, many companies such as IBM use expensive multifunctional global account teams to serve collaborative relationship customers. Different approaches are typically used for the intermediate solutions and partnership relationship strategies. Thus, relationship and sales channel strategies are closely related.

The traditional sales strategy is to have a field salesperson perform all selling activities to all customers. This can be an effective approach, but is typically very costly. Therefore, many sales organizations are looking for ways to replace expensive field selling with

Team selling is being used by more firms to better meet the needs of large and important customers. Some firms employ multifunctional sales teams as part of their sales channel strategy.

Exhibit 19–8	*Relationship selling strategies*			
	Transaction Relationship	**Solutions Relationship**	**Partnership Relationship**	**Collaborative Relationship**
Goal	Sell products	⟶		Add Value
Time frame	Short	⟶		Long
Offering	Standardized	⟶		Customized
Number of customers	Many	⟶		Few
Cost to serve	Low	⟶		High
Commitment	Low	⟶		High

Thinking Critically

Select a familiar product that is sold through personal selling by a field sales-force:

• What other sales channels might be used in conjunction with personal selling by a field salesforce?

• What are the advantages and disadvantages of each sales channel?

• What are the key challenges facing sales managers when multiple sales channels are used?

less costly sales channels such as telemarketing or the Internet. The potential benefits from this approach are clear. Let's assume the cost of a personal sales call is $250 and the cost of a telephone sales call is $25; each time a personal sales call is replaced by a telephone sales call, the company saves $225. The savings are even greater if the personal sales call is replaced by an electronic interaction over the Internet.

For small customers and many transaction relationships, field selling can be totally replaced by using telemarketing, the Internet, or other sales channels. In other cases, field selling might be integrated with telephone selling or the Internet. For example, prospecting might be performed over the phone or the Internet. Once good prospects are identified, a salesperson makes personal sales calls to establish solutions, partnership, or collaborative relationships. Then, various service and re-ordering activities are performed over the telephone or the Internet. A couple of examples illustrate how companies are doing this:

• Applied Industrial Technologies distributes 1.5 million different industrial products through 380 branch offices with 900 field salespeople and 1,400 inside sales-people. Annual sales are over $1.5 billion. The field salespeople work with customers to determine their needs in order to negotiate pricing agreements. Each customer is then provided a private Extranet that can be used to purchase products, check on the status of orders, and get various types of information. Customers can also order or receive information over the phone from the inside salespeople. This approach allows customers to select the sales channel they want for each interaction. And, as customers interact more over the telephone and—especially—the Internet, Applied's costs to serve these customers goes down.[12]

• Xerox is integrating the Internet into a complicated sales channel strategy that includes retail stores, distributors, and field salespeople. Smaller transaction-type customers typically purchase supplies and smaller systems from retail stores. These customers can now purchase on-line from the Xerox Web site. If they have questions, the site provides toll-free numbers to reach Xerox service people. Field salespeople establish different types of relationships with larger customers; however, once the relationship is established, much of the customer service functions are being performed electronically through private Extranets developed for each customer.[13]

These examples are representative of the types of sales channel strategies being implemented by many companies. The trend is to use different sales channels for different types of customer relationships and to replace more-expensive with less-expensive sales channels whenever possible.

Although these trends apply to most customers, many companies use various types of **team selling** for their very best customers. These sales teams are typically multifunctional and can include people from different management levels. Normally used in partnership or collaborative relationships with key customers, these approaches are often called *national account, major account,* or *global account* programs. Team selling is an expensive sales channel, but can produce significant sales and profit growth in some situations. The approach used at Kele & Associates, a manufacturer of building automation peripherals, is illustrative. The company developed a national account program. Sales teams consisting of members from marketing, sales, accounting, and information technology plan and execute customized strategies to serve the company's best customers. The sales team analyzes each customer's business to identify ways Kele can add more value to the relationship. The strategy has been successful in growing business with these customers.[14]

Designing the Sales Organization

To implement a successful selling strategy, the company must design an appropriate sales organization and adjust it according to subsequent strategic changes. Some key questions to address in designing the sales organization include:

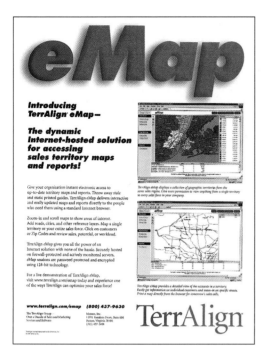

Sales managers can use new technologies to help make better sales organization design decisions. Mapping software, such as TerrAlign is useful in designing effective sales territories.

- Should the salesforce be generalists (salespeople who sell the entire product line) or specialists (only sell specific products or only sell to specific customers)?
- If specialists are used, should they be product specialists, market or customer specialists, or functional (new-business or existing-business) specialists?
- Should tight control be maintained with a centralized salesforce, or should sales activities and decision making be moved closer to the customer with a decentralized salesforce?
- How much total selling effort is needed to provide adequate sales coverage? How large should the salesforce be?
- How should specific customers and geographic areas be assigned to salespeople to form sales territories?
- How should *salesforce turnover* (the proportion of salespeople who leave their jobs) be factored into sales organization design decisions?

All these decisions are complex, and they may be addressed with any number of analytical tools. Computer algorithms and sophisticated decision models can give some quantitative input. Dictaphone, for example, used a computerized mapping program to realign sales territories when its poorly designed territories caused high salesforce turnover. The reconfiguration reduced salesforce turnover and improved morale and productivity.[15]

Also, companies often use different approaches to address similar situations. For example, Microsoft is responding to the slowdown in corporate technology spending by adding 450 salespeople to develop teams that will focus on securing multiyear software contracts from big customers in 12 industries.[16] Carbis, in contrast, decided to reduce its salesforce by 25 percent as a response to reduced capital equipment purchases by oil refineries and chemical companies. The remaining salespeople only spend their time with customers interested in buying immediately.[17]

Developing the Salesforce

There are three main activities in developing the salesforce: recruiting, selecting, and training salespeople.

RECRUITING AND SELECTING   *Recruiting* is the process of finding prospective job candidates; *selecting* involves choosing the candidates to be hired. Recruiting and selecting salespeople are challenging tasks. According to one survey, over 30 percent of 645 firms reported "some difficulty" or "great difficulty" in recruiting salespeople. There simply are not enough well-educated and skilled workers. For example, for its salesforce, pharmaceutical firm G. D. Searle recruits registered nurses and pharmacists, of which there are severe shortages in the United States.[18] Approximately 60 percent of all sales reps in the pharmaceutical industry are pharmacy school graduates, but the difficulty of recruiting pharmacists may cause some firms to seek candidates with nonpharmaceutical backgrounds.[19]

Another problem is lack of time to recruit qualified salespeople. In one survey, sales executives said that because of a lack of time, they sometimes rely on "warm body" recruiting—hiring under pressure to fill a vacancy.[20]

Observers predict that to meet the challenges in recruiting and selecting salespeople, companies will hire more part-time and older salespeople and increase efforts to diversify their salesforces ethnically and culturally. The number of women entering sales is also expected to continue to grow.

TRAINING   There are two categories of sales training: initial and continual. Newly hired salespeople receive *initial training,* which typically focuses on product

Sales training is conducted in a variety of ways. A salesperson from a suit manufacturer trains a retail sales staff so they can deliver greater value to customers.

knowledge and sales techniques. *Continual training* for all salespeople is becoming more standard as firms attempt to stay current and competitive in an ever-changing environment. "Using Technology: e-Training" presents examples of how new technologies can improve sales training.

Sales training is key for companies interested in continual improvement. At Union Pacific, for example, salespeople go through 21 courses over a five-year period to learn to deliver total quality management, including the improvement of customer relationships. The first year focuses on product knowledge and selling skills. The second year concentrates on working effectively in teams. In the third year, salespeople learn how to be team leaders. Then training moves to advanced stages of total quality management. According to Fred Henderson, vice president of sales and marketing, "We had to create a company strategy that was focused on the true requirements of the customer and the marketplace, and then build a training strategy to take it there."[21]

A study of 300 sales executives found that almost 80 percent considered sales training to be very valuable to both new and current salespeople. The topics covered most in sales training programs were product knowledge (88 percent), sales skills (79 percent), computer skills (61 percent), and communication skills (52 percent). Most sales training was performed by in-house trainers using classroom instruction (77 percent), workbooks/manuals (54 percent), public seminars (46 percent), role plays (44 percent), CD-ROM (39 percent), audiocassettes (34 percent), and the Internet (32 percent). Over 40 percent of the sales executives indicated they were considering using some type of online sales training in the near future.[22]

Directing the Salesforce

Directing salespeople to meet goals and objectives consumes much of the typical sales manager's time. These activities include motivation, supervision, and leadership of the salesforce.

MOTIVATION   Salesforce motivation involves maximizing the effort salespeople direct toward specific objectives and helping them persist in the face of adversity. Most sales companies offer a variety of financial and nonfinancial rewards in their salesforce motivation programs.

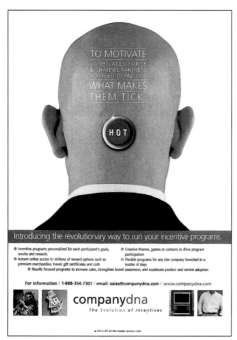

Many sales organizations offer salespeople a variety of different rewards as incentives. Companydna offers unique incentive programs to sales organizations.

Money remains the most sought-after reward among salespeople, with the opportunity for promotion into management also highly desired.[23] Most companies pay salespeople a combination of salary and incentives. Incentive pay could include commissions, bonuses, or both. About three-fourths of U.S. firms use a combination pay plan; less than 15 percent pay a straight salary; and some 10 percent pay by straight commission.[24] Salesperson compensation has been increasing in recent years. A study of 2,644 sales and marketing executives indicated total compensation (salary plus bonus plus commission) levels for salespeople in 2001 were: $139,459 for top performers, $77,179 for mid-level salespeople, and $51,992 for low-level sales representatives.[25]

Incentive pay can have dramatic effects on salesforce motivation. Creative Works, a Northbrook, Illinois, school supply company, established an additional 2 percent bonus on top of the existing 5 percent commission for the addition of new customers. The company also introduced a one-dollar-per-case bonus on the opening order of any new products sold to new or existing accounts. In one year, sales jumped from $700,000 to $3 million and the customer base grew from 80 to 200.[26]

Most companies also use sales contests and formal recognition programs to motivate their salesforces. Such programs may offer exotic travel, merchandise, or high-visibility award ceremonies in addition to money as an incentive.

SUPERVISION AND LEADERSHIP   Supervision of a salesforce deals with direction of day-to-day operations. Computerized **sales automation systems** are one way to assist sales managers in routine supervisory chores such as processing salespeople's call reports, itineraries, and expense reports.

Leadership activities, on the other hand, use more subtle communication to influence salespeople to achieve the company's overall objectives. One leadership function is *coaching,* or providing guidance and feedback on a regular basis to direct salespeople's activities. Another important leadership activity is conducting sales meetings that unite a salesforce in an effort to meet common goals.

Many companies use mentoring programs to help develop salespeople. For example, Sealed Air Corporation selects top sales performers to coach new and underperforming salespeople for three-year periods. The mentors spend as much as 20 percent of their time working directly with mentees to help them improve in desired areas. One useful approach is to coach a mentee salesperson throughout the entire sales call process with a difficult customer. Serving as a mentor also helps prepare top salespeople for sales management positions. Over 90 percent of Sealed Air's management has participated in the mentoring program.[27]

Using Technology

e-training

Many companies are conducting sales training online. Large companies might develop their own online learning platforms, but smaller companies are likely to work with vendors in the e-learning market. Consider these two examples:

- Fisher Scientific sells more than 600,000 separate items to science labs and hospitals. It uses e-learning to shorten the time lag in training its 400-person salesforce about new products. The online training consists of read-only and interactive content with tests to en-

sure the salespeople have the needed product knowledge.

- David Weekly Homes integrates online and traditional classroom sessions to improve the selling skills of its 300 salespeople. The training focuses on the company's highly structured selling process. Salespeople earn a certificate upon completing the training.

Both of these companies report that the online training was effective and less costly than taking salespeople out of the field for traditional training programs.

The supervision and leadership of salespeople is very much a human endeavor, despite the help of technology. Sales managers routinely deal with human relations problems such as drug and alcohol abuse, sexual harassment, employee job stress, expense-account fraud, and any number of other people problems. Salespeople are no different from any other group of employees when it comes to problem areas.

Jerry Bauer, Sales Competency Leader and Field Marketing Manager, Du Pont Company, (ret.) discusses the importance of leadership within the sales function:

"With a constant eye on achieving profitable growth, we are having to change the way we manage our salesforces at Du Pont. Downsizing has led to larger spans of control and more self-managed teams. Mentoring and networking are becoming more and more important. We are looking for leaders who can provide a compelling vision. We want sales leaders who can build self-esteem, emotional involvement, and the knowledge, skills, and abilities of their team, and also instill a sense of excitement. You might say we are moving from 'sales management' to 'strategic leadership.' "

Evaluating Performance and Effectiveness

Sales managers must establish standards by which performance and effectiveness are measured, evaluate performance and effectiveness against these standards, and then take appropriate follow-up action. *Salesperson performance* refers to how well individual salespeople meet job expectations. An evaluation of *salesforce effectiveness* is in fact an assessment of the entire sales organization. Factors within and outside the sales organization, such as product quality or competitors, can also influence salesforce effectiveness.

SETTING STANDARDS   Standards by which performance and effectiveness are assessed usually relate to quantitative outcomes, or *quotas,* such as total sales volume, gross margin, market share, number of new accounts added, and accounts retained. These quotas typically are based on a forecast developed at least in part by the sales manager.

Sales managers must also get the job done within a specified budget. Given the high costs of personal selling, achieving objectives within budget constraints is a constant challenge. For example, the median cost per sales call exceeds $200, despite increased efforts to trim sales costs. Travel-related costs, such as lodging and meals, continue to climb, along with salespeople's pay levels.[28]

It is becoming increasingly difficult to raise selling price only because of increasing sales costs. Thus, to maintain favorable sales-expense-to-sales-revenue ratios, most salespeople are asked to sell more each year, whether economic conditions are favorable or not.

EVALUATING PERFORMANCE   To evaluate individual salesperson performance, sales managers may take a behavior-based perspective, an outcome-based perspective, or a combination of the two. A *behavior-based perspective* defines the sales behaviors expected, such as how many sales calls to make or which sales presentation tactics to use. The salesperson is then evaluated on how well he or she executes the behaviors. An *outcome-based perspective* focuses on the results of sales behavior, such as total sales volume. As relationship selling spreads, the behavior-based perspective to evaluate salesperson performance is gaining more acceptance than the outcome-based approach.

ANALYZING EFFECTIVENESS   Managers may analyze sales, costs, profitability, and productivity to evaluate the effectiveness of the sales organization. They compare figures of one year with those of the previous year to gauge progress. Managers also compare their own salesforce effectiveness with that of competitors, if possible. For example, in the packaged-grocery business, market share data by brand are readily available, and comparisons with key competitors are commonplace.

| Exhibit 19–9 | *Example of a salesforce effectiveness evaluation* |

	District 1	District 2	District 3	District 4
Sales	$10,000,000	$12,000,000	$10,000,000	$12,000,000
Selling expenses	$ 1,000,000	$ 1,200,000	$ 1,500,000	$ 1,500,000
Sales calls	5,000	4,500	4,500	6,000
Proposals	100	105	120	120
Number of salespeople	10	15	10	15
Sales per salesperson	$ 1,000,000	$ 800,000	$ 1,000,000	$ 800,000
Expenses per salesperson	$ 100,000	$ 80,000	$ 150,000	$ 100,000
Calls per salesperson	500	300	450	400

A simple example of salesforce productivity analysis is shown in Exhibit 19–9. Note that District 2 is tied for the lead with District 4 in total sales volume. Also, the sales per salesperson and expenses per salesperson figures in District 2 compare favorably with the other districts. Yet the number of sales calls made per salesperson is low. This may explain why expenses are low, but it may also suggest that salespeople in District 2 may not be providing adequate contact with their customers.

Numbers, then, do not tell the whole story; analysis of the numbers can, however, suggest areas worth further investigation by the sales manager. By combining quantitative analysis with personal observation, information from customers, and review with salespeople, sales managers can evaluate the effectiveness of their salesforces.

Ethical and Legal Issues in Personal Selling

Because personal selling activities are highly visible, ethical and legal issues are extremely important for salespeople and sales managers. In building trust-based customer relationships, ethical behavior is even more critical. Major professional groups such as Sales and Marketing Executives International, the American Marketing Association, and the Direct Selling Association have adopted strict codes of ethics for salespeople, as have many companies. An example is shown in Exhibit 19–10.

Sales managers must take responsibility for the proper behavior of their salespeople, and they must also lead by example. They must know the laws related to buyer–seller interactions, the gathering of competitive information, and the management of personnel.

To be on the safe side, salespeople should be honest in their dealings with customers and be informed of relevant laws governing their business situation. All salespeople are subject to some form of contract law, which regulates transactions. Purchase orders are binding contracts, as are oral commitments made by a salesperson. An extensive review of 50 years of legal cases revealed that salespeople can, by inappropriate oral statements, create undesirable legal obligations for their firms. Problems include creation of unintended warranties, understatement of warning messages, disparagement of competitors' offerings without substantiation, misrepresentation of company offerings, and illegal interference with business relationships.[29]

Exhibit 19–11 presents some specific sales behaviors deemed unethical by buyers. Salespeople interested in developing lasting relationships with their customers should refrain from those behaviors, for research suggests that buyers will go out of their way to avoid doing business with salespeople they see as unethical.[30]

Exhibit 19–10	*Code of ethics for professional salespeople*

As a Certified Professional Salesperson, I pledge to the following people and organizations:

The Customer. In all customer relationships, I pledge to:

Maintain honesty and integrity in my relationships with customers and prospective customers.

Accurately represent my product or service in order to place the customer or prospective customer in a position to make a decision consistent with the principle of mutuality of benefit and profit to the buyer and seller.

Keep abreast of all pertinent information that would assist my customers in achieving their goals as they relate to my product(s) or service(s).

The Company. In relationships with my employer, co-workers, and other parties whom I represent, I will:

Use their resources that are at my disposal for legitimate business purposes only.

Respect and protect proprietary and confidential information entrusted to me by my company.

The Competition. Regarding those with whom I compete in the marketplace, I promise:

To obtain competitive information only through legal and ethical methods.

To portray my competitors and their products and services only in a manner that is honest, that is truthful, and that reflects accurate information that can or has been substantiated.

Exhibit 19–11	*Unethical sales behaviors*

Research indicates sales behaviors that are unethical in the eyes of customers:

- Exaggerates the features and benefits of his/her products/services.
- Lies about availability to make a sale.
- Lies about the competition to make a sale.
- Sells products/services people don't need.
- Is interested only in own interests, not the clients'.
- Gives answers when doesn't really know the answers.
- Falsifies product testimonials.
- Passes the blame for something he/she did onto someone else.

- Poses as a market researcher when conducting telephone sales.
- Misrepresents guarantees/warranties.
- Makes oral promises that are not legally binding.
- Does not offer information about an upcoming sale that will include merchandise the customer is planning to buy.
- Accepts favors from customers so the seller will feel obliged to bend the rules/policies of the seller's company.
- Sells dangerous or hazardous products.

There are also numerous ethical and legal issues relevant to relationships between sales managers and salespeople. For example, the Civil Rights Act of 1964 prohibits discrimination based on age, race, color, religion, sex, or national origin. The act has implications for recruiting and selecting salespeople and evaluating and rewarding their performance. The Americans with Disabilities Act of 1992 also affects recruiting and other sales management functions, as do guidelines for minimizing sexual harassment issued by the Equal Employment Opportunity Commission.

This is only a brief discussion of the ethical and legal consequences of marketers' actions. Given the pressure on the sales function to generate revenue, it is particularly important for sales managers to know and adhere to the laws of the marketplace and the workplace. They should be models, provide adequate training, and monitor, reinforce, and direct sales personnel. In developing trust-based relationships with customers, marketers should follow these guidelines not just because of laws or because it's the right thing to do—but because it is also a sound business practice.

Personal Selling and Sales Management in the Future

The changes in the business environment are having an important effect on personal selling and sales management. Salespeople and sales managers will have to have different skills to be successful in the future. Two studies by MOHR Development suggest the competencies needed by salespeople and sales managers in the future.[31] Salesperson competencies involve the ability to:

1. Align customers' strategic objectives with your company's so both gain.
2. Go beyond product needs to assess business potential and add value to the relationship.
3. Understand the financial impact of the decisions made by your company and the client's organization.
4. Organize company resources to build customer-focused relationships.
5. Develop consultative problem solving and a willingness to change.
6. Establish a vision of a committed customer/supplier relationship.
7. Utilize self-appraisal and continuous learning by requesting feedback from customers, colleagues, and managers.

Sales manager competencies involve the ability to:

1. Provide strategic vision.
2. Organize company resources by leveraging relationships.
3. Influence company strategy.
4. Coach effectively.
5. Diagnose performance.
6. Select high-potential salespeople.
7. Leverage technology.
8. Demonstrate personal selling effectiveness.

These competencies indicate what it will take to be successful in the future. Notice the focus on developing relationships with customers by salespeople and developing relationships with salespeople by sales managers. Both salespeople and sales managers must possess communication and "people" skills as well as understand the strategic and financial aspects of business. And, the need to understand and be able to use technology effectively will be extremely important.

Summary

1. **Understand the role and importance of personal selling in the marketing communications mix.** Personal selling is a valuable part of the promotion mix and the overall marketing effort of many companies. Salespeople fulfill the extremely important role of generating revenue. In today's competitive environment, paying close attention to customer needs and expectations is necessary, and personal selling can help in this endeavor. Salespeople provide crucial marketplace information to their companies, which may further improve the marketing effort.

2. **See how the key steps in personal selling depend on a relationship perspective.** The sales process involves three steps: initiating, developing, and enhancing customer relationships. To initiate customer relationships, salespeople must first locate qualified potential customers through prospecting. They must then plan the initial sales call and the way to approach the customer.

   In developing customer relationships, salespeople must be able to deliver effective sales presentations. During a sales call, it is extremely important that the salesperson use questioning and listening skills to attend to all of the customer's requirements and to gain a commitment from the customer.

   To enhance relationships with customers, salespeople must be customer-oriented and continue to meet or exceed customer expectations. Relationship selling also requires that salespeople formulate and implement different strategies for different customers and that they minimize wasted time in each sales call.

   To be successful in relationship selling, salespeople gain the trust of their customers. To build trust, salespeople should be customer-oriented, honest, dependable, competent, and likable.

3. **Identify the similarities and differences in the job responsibilities of salespeople and sales managers.** Along with their other job duties, sales managers are usually involved in personal selling to some degree. Using an athletic team analogy, the salespeople are the players, and the sales manager is the coach. The sales manager must do everything necessary to field a competitive sales team year after year, including developing the team strategy. Salespeople concentrate on taking care of their customers; sales managers must work not only with customers, but also with others in the company to ensure success.

4. **Describe the key activities in sales management.** The key job activities of sales managers are developing a sales strategy, designing the sales organization, developing the salesforce, directing the salesforce, and evaluating performance and effectiveness. Sales managers must recruit and select salespeople and provide them with sufficient resources to be effective. Most sales managers play an active role in training their salespeople. They must also help motivate salespeople to reach their full potential and evaluate their performance. Sales managers must accomplish all these activities in a rapidly changing environment, which means they may need to adapt sales strategies to remain competitive.

5. **Appreciate important ethical issues faced by salespeople and sales managers.** Salespeople can develop trust with their customers by avoiding a range of unethical sales behaviors. Examples are lying, selling customers products they do not need, withholding information, and selling dangerous products.

   Sales managers lead by example. They must not abuse the power of their positions in dealing with their employees. Sales managers must also be prepared to deal with human relations issues such as drug abuse, sexual harassment, and employee job stress. Ignoring such issues would be less than ethical.

Understanding Marketing Terms and Concepts

Thinking About Marketing

1. Discuss the three major roles salespeople play in the overall marketing effort.

2. How are the roles of sales support salespeople different from those of new-business salespeople?

3. Give several examples of different types of direct-to-consumer salespeople.

4. To practice relationship selling, salespeople must be able to cultivate the trust of their customers. What attributes should salespeople have to cultivate the trust of their customers?

5. The first step in the sales process is to initiate customer relationships. Discuss the three primary activities during this initial step.

6. Review "Building Customer Equity: Getting Customer Feedback." What happens to a company if customers are dissatisfied with its products or services?

7. How important is ethical behavior by salespeople in dealing with customers? Think about trust-building salesperson attributes, and consult Exhibits 19–3 and 19–10 before completing your answer.

8. Consult "Using Technology: e-Training" What other technologies could be used to improve sales training?

9. Describe the key responsibilities of sales managers in each of the five activity areas shown in Exhibit 19–7.

10. How are the recruitment and selection of salespeople related to designing the salesforce?

Applying Marketing Skills

1. Review the unethical sales behaviors in Exhibit 19–11. Can you recall from your own experiences as a consumer examples of any of those behaviors? In those instances, did you eventually come to trust the salesperson? Did you make purchases? What kind of sales behavior could you suggest for salespeople who wish to earn the trust of their customers?

2. When a commitment is not readily forthcoming from a prospect, some salespeople might use a "buy now" method to get the sale, which gives the buyer a good reason to make an immediate purchase. For example, the salesperson might suggest that the buyer can avoid a planned price increase by placing an immediate order. If no such price increase is actually planned, has the salesperson acted unethically? What if the buyer has been promising to place an order for months, but never has, and now seems to be stalling?

3. Visit a retail store with the aim of getting some details about a product you plan to buy at some future date. Evaluate the listening skills of the salesperson you encounter. Is the salesperson a good listener or not? How was the salesperson's credibility affected by his or her listening skills?

Using the www in Marketing

Activity One   Visit the Pfizer Web site
(http://www.pfizer.com):

1. What are the requirements to become a sales representative for Pfizer?

2. Has the strategic merger between Pfizer and Warner-Lambert taken place? If so, what changes are being made? If not, why was the merger not completed?

3. How is Pfizer involved in e-commerce? Who can purchase what products from this site?

Activity Two   Review the Web site
www.salesforce.com. You can register for free and get detailed information or browse the site to get basic information.

1. What sales tools are available to help salespeople develop relationships with customers?

2. How could sales managers use this site to help them in training salespeople?

3. How could this site be improved?

Making Marketing Decisions

Case 19-1 *Saturn: Taking a STEP to Equip Its Salesforce*

In the late 1980s, the American automobile industry was struggling. Consumers were unhappy with product quality, pricing, advertising, and inane industry sales practices. Foreign automakers were continuing to build market share at the expense of domestic manufacturers. In this environment, General Motors departed from tradition and offered a "different kind of car from a different kind of company." The Saturn success story had begun.

By 1993, Saturn had become a force to be reckoned with. Sales were soaring, and GM was eager to transplant Saturn's winning ways to other divisions. Industry analysts cited several reasons for Saturn's rise to prominence: no-haggle pricing, customer-oriented selling, elimination of confusing rebates, and basically, a good car for a reasonable price.

Many competitors followed Saturn's lead with a one-price, no-haggle selling strategy. American automobile manufacturers also improved product quality, and many dealers adopted one-price policies similar to Saturn's. In the face of intensified competition, Saturn's salesforce has helped to sustain the company's edge in the marketplace. A key element in equipping the salesforce is the Saturn Training and Education Partnership, or STEP, a comprehensive program designed to develop job skills.

The STEP program reinforces five key values Saturn wants to instill in all facets of its operations: customer enthusiasm, excellence, teamwork, trust and respect, and constant improvement.

To reinforce these values in sales training, Saturn established the objectives for STEP long before its first dealership opened. Sales managers refined the program with salespeople from dealers who were interested in becoming Saturn dealers, and then with salespeople who had been hired to staff the still-unopened Saturn outlets.

The STEP program requires salespeople to abandon the conventional way of selling cars, which often involves high-pressure manipulative sales techniques. Instead, Saturn's sales philosophy casts the salesperson in a consultative role to build customer enthusiasm, with six key elements: listening to the customer; creating an environment of mutual trust; exceeding customer expectations; creating a "win-win" culture; following up to ensure that customer expectations are met; and constantly improving customer perceptions of quality.

The sales training consists of self-study modules and seminars. The self-study portion, which takes about 11 hours to complete, features learning activities based on short reading assignments and video vignettes. The short assignments can easily be completed one at a time, allowing training to be interspersed with other job activities.

Saturn measures the effectiveness of its training in three ways. For each module, trainees provide a written evaluation of materials, methods, and trainers. Each module is followed by a written test. Sixty days later, trainees are evaluated in a performance check that requires demonstration of the skills developed in training. All indicators point to a successful sales training program.

Questions

1. What is your assessment of the Saturn STEP program?

2. Would previous sales experience be an asset to a Saturn job candidate? If so, what kind of experience?

3. How would Saturn's recruiting, selection, motivation, and evaluation of sales performance likely differ from that of a high-volume, conventional automobile dealer's sales operation?

4. How does the Saturn Web site (http:www.saturncars.com) supplement the efforts of Saturn salespeople?

Case 19-2 *Edward Jones: Building Customer Relationships*

Edward Jones operates the country's largest network of brokerage offices, over 8,000. John W. Bachmann has been managing partner for the past 22 years and is responsible for much of the company's growth. He has done it very differently than other brokerage firms.

Brokers at Edward Jones sell an array of financial products to include mutual funds, life insurance and annuities, credit cards, and home loans. They receive 40 percent of all commissions, and this is made clear to all clients. There are no outlandish salaries or bonuses.

The company only does a little investment banking, so there is little chance for conflicts of interest between the investment banking and brokerage operations. Research analysts are not allowed to own stock in the companies they cover. This removes another potential conflict of interest. Edward Jones does not offer online trading and does not emphasize margin trading. Most brokerages have emphasized both of these in recent years. There are also no call centers to market financial products aggressively to customers.

Since Edward Jones does not do many of the things most brokerage companies do, it has benefited greatly from the insider trading, accounting problems, fraud, and conflicts of interest reported in the business press. At one point it was getting around 1,000 Merrill Lynch clients a month, even though it was not going after them.

Bachmann has helped build a company based on strong relationships with employees and customers. The company started in rural and small towns, but has moved successfully into most of the major metropolitan areas in the United States, as well as into Canada and Great Britain. The business is built on careful planning based on setting clear objectives at the top, then creating a supportive environment where brokers can grow and be successful.

The approach to customers is similar. The company has been criticized for being very conservative. It did not, for example, recommend the initial public offerings of dot com companies. Although this may have cost some clients, it seems to have been a good approach, given the ultimate failure of many dot com companies. According to Bachmann: "The market we serve values relationships. We do not want to encourage you to gamble."

Questions

1. Why do you think Edward Jones has been so successful?

2. What could competitors do to take business from Edward Jones?

3. Do you think Edward Jones should offer online trading? Why or why not?

4. What changes would you suggest to increase the growth of Edward Jones in the future?

20

Direct Marketing Communications

After studying this chapter, you should be able to:

1. Understand the objectives of direct marketing communications, and describe its distinguishing characteristics.

2. Discuss the factors driving the growth in direct marketing communications.

3. Understand traditional direct marketing communications techniques such as direct mail, broadcast and print media, and telemarketing.

4. Recall examples of the use of technology such as electronic media in direct marketing communications.

5. Understand some of the ethical and legal issues facing marketers who use direct marketing communications.

coldwatercreek.com

In 1984, Coldwater Creek was a home business that consisted of taking orders on one telephone and shipping merchandise from a combination storage room/closet. Today it is a multichannel retailer with annual sales in excess of $450 million. In addition to its spacious headquarters campus in Sandpoint, Coldwater Creek now has a distribution center in West Virginia, a telemarketing center in Coeur d'Alene, Idaho, and a growing number of retail stores across the United States. By 2006, Coldwater Creek expects to have a total of 80 stores nationwide.

Coldwater mails more than 160 million catalogs per year under three names: North Country, Spirit of the West, and Natural Elements. Its offerings include women's apparel, jewelry, gift items, home accessories, and furniture. The target audience is the same for all three catalogs and the Coldwater Web site: professional women 35–55 years of age, well-educated, with more discretionary income than time available for shopping.

The Coldwater Creek formula for success is to be driven by the customer. To ensure that customers receive outstanding service and enjoy a pleasant buying experience, the firm relies on technology, strong relationships with vendors, and direct marketing communications. Fast, courteous service coupled with unusual, high-quality merchandise produces satisfied and loyal customers. The company is a multiyear winner of the Customer Relationship Management Grand Prix Award for superior customer service via the telephone, Internet, and e-mail.

Selecting the right customers, determining their needs, and working hard to satisfy those needs are critical to Coldwater Creek's success. At the heart of the Coldwater operation is a sophisticated computer system that keeps up with the details of the business. While the business details are handled by computer, customers only talk to people and are never put on hold. Coldwater Creek has used this blend of high-tech, high-touch to become a leading direct marketing company.

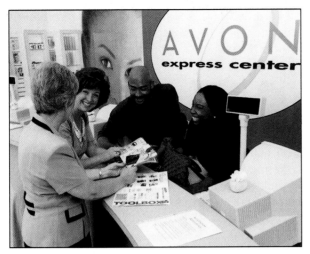

Avon is best known for direct selling through several hundred thousand sales representatives. The company also uses a variety of direct marketing communications methods, including direct-response magazine ads and telemarketing as part of its worldwide integrated marketing communications effort.

In Chapter 16, we saw that most marketers use more than one way to communicate with their target markets. These multiple means of reaching target markets are sometimes developed into integrated marketing communications (IMC) programs. At the heart of many of these programs lies direct marketing communications. This chapter discusses the role and characteristics of direct marketing communications and examines the reasons for its growth. Direct marketing communications (DMC) methods are discussed, including a variety of interactive methods such as mail, video, telephone, salesperson, and computer. The chapter concludes with a discussion of ethical and legal issues in direct marketing communications.

Role of Direct Marketing Communications

Direct marketing communications have two primary objectives. The first is to establish relationships by soliciting a direct and immediate response from prospects or customers. Customer response could be a purchase, a request for additional information from the marketer, or a reply that furnishes data related to the customer's desires and interests. The second, and increasingly important, objective of DMC is to maintain and enhance customer relationships, whether those relationships have been established by direct marketing communications or by some other means.

Direct marketing communications techniques are used to reach both individual consumers and businesses. For example, in the United States, direct marketing generates almost 900 billion dollars in annual sales in business-to-business markets and more than a trillion dollars in sales to ultimate consumers.[1] In business-to-business markets, direct marketing is extensively used for business services, chemicals and allied products, real estate, and wholesaling. The most important tools in business-to-business direct marketing from a sales volume perspective are telephone marketing and direct mail, which account for almost 70 percent of all sales.[2] Newspaper, television, radio, and **interactive marketing** also are used in business-to-business direct marketing. Interactive marketing, also referred to as online direct marketing, is that portion of electronic business, such as marketing on the Internet, that meets the definition of direct marketing communications given in Chapter 16: communicating directly with target customers to encourage response. It is important to note that not all electronic marketing involves online direct marketing.

Popular products bought by consumers via direct marketing include software, computers, recorded music, books, personal gift items, home decorating products, and clothing. In consumer markets, the largest sales generators are telephone marketing, direct mail, newspaper, and television.[3] Interactive marketing is still relatively small from a sales-volume point of view but is growing at approximately 7 percent per year—roughly the growth rate for most other forms of direct marketing to ultimate consumers.

Direct marketing can be an important ingredient in integrated communications strategies. For example, General Motors used direct marketing communications along with personal selling, advertising, and public relations to promote its GMC Suburban, Yukon, and Yukon Denali sport utility vehicles. The direct portion of the integrated campaign was so successful that GM plans to include direct marketing communications in future integrated campaigns for some of its other brands.[4]

In the business-to-business area, Hewlett-Packard uses direct marketing in conjunction with other forms of marketing communications such as mass-media advertising, personal selling, sales promotion (trade shows), and public relations to sell computers. Sales by telephone make up an especially important part of Hewlett-Packard's direct marketing efforts.

Characteristics of Direct Marketing Communications

Several characteristics distinguish direct marketing from other marketing communications methods. First, direct marketing targets a carefully selected audience, as opposed to a mass audience. Second, it typically involves two-way communication; direct responses from customers make it interactive. Finally, direct-response results are quite measurable—marketers can determine what works and what does not.

Customer Databases

A key element of direct marketing communications is the use of a list or database of current or potential customers. **Lists** of names and addresses may also provide telephone numbers and data on demographics, lifestyles, brand and media preferences, and consumption patterns. Business-to-business lists may also indicate company characteristics such as annual sales, key decision makers, credit and purchasing history, and current suppliers. Lists can be developed from customer-transaction records, newspapers, trade show registration, or other sources that identify specific groups of customers or prospects. Rather than compiling its own lists, a company can purchase (in some cases), rent, reproduce, or use a list on a one-time basis.

Lists, often in the form of sophisticated computerized databases, allow direct marketers to focus on a precisely defined target market, as opposed to using mass-market appeals. **Database marketing,** or the use of computer database technologies to design, create, and manage customer lists, has become commonplace.[5] For an illustration of how databases aid in marketing communications, see Exhibit 20–1.

Customer databases can be quite large. For example, list provider Focus USA offers a database of 7 million small businesses containing e-mail addresses, fax numbers, company type, number of employees, and annual sales information.[6] Consumer databases are often larger than business-customer databases. MKTG Services offers a database of 13 million consumers who have relocated their residences within the past 30 days. Marketers of a wide variety of products and services ranging from gardening supplies to financial services use this list to reach this market.[7]

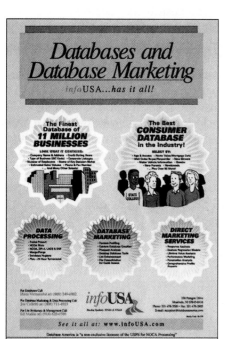

Marketers are increasingly taking advantage of technological advances in their direct marketing programs. Metromail fits nicely with this movement by providing computerized databases and related services to facilitate direct marketing.

Companies use database information to deliver marketing communications tailored to the unique needs of a target audience. Ladies clothing retailer J. Crew uses its database to personalize appeals to individual consumers, especially those who visit the company's Web site but do not make a purchase online, from a catalog, or in one of the company's 170 retail stores. According to a J. Crew executive, the company understands the preferences of current buyers and personalizes its marketing appeals accordingly. By tracking nonbuyers' interactions online, the company plans to improve its rate of converting these customers to active buyers.[8] Industry experts consistently point out that personalizing appeals to individual consumers in a database can generate significantly better results for marketers. For more on how databases are used in direct marketing communications, see "Using Technology: Before You Go."

Exhibit 20–1   *Customer databases aid communications planning, integration, and execution*

Promotional history

Records of marketing, promotions & other activities supplied by marketing department & selling channels (direct mail, sales reps, telemarketing)

The customer database

Customer data

Marketing department
- Inputs results of promotions and other activities
- Receives detailed customer/ prospect data to formulate future marketing plans

Direct mail

Telemarketing: Inbound/Outbound

Field sales

Consumers

Small accounts

Large accounts

Immediate-Response Orientation

Direct marketing communications often have deadlines for action and offer special incentives for taking immediate action. An example would be a direct-mail piece from a bank saying, "Call now for superlow 7 percent mortgages. Free property survey. Offer expires June 1." Other marketing communications methods are not typically oriented toward gaining an immediate response from prospects and customers. Publicity, for example, and many forms of advertising are aimed more at achieving results over a period of time. Personal selling seeks a response, but salespeople typically cultivate customers for some time.

Using Technology

Before you go

Direct marketing communications are often used to initiate a transaction, and thus a relationship, with the customer. New technology is now allowing the marketer to insert direct communications as an added dimension to an ongoing interactive dialog, such as when the customer is visiting an online retailer.

One of the most common problems facing online retailers is that of the abandoned shopping cart. In this situation, the customer has browsed the online site and selected merchandise for purchase. But before the transaction is completed, the customer terminates the visit and aban-

dons the shopping cart. Jupiter Media Metrix estimates that two-thirds of online shoppers routinely abandon shopping carts. To entice shoppers who try to leave the site before completing their purchase, FlowersUSA.com and JustFlowers.com use direct communications, a pop-up ad, to offer price discounts if the purchase is completed immediately. Discounts average $5. For FlowersUSA.com, this has meant reducing its abandoned shopping carts by 15 percent and increasing its annual sales by 5 percent. Advancing technology is an important enabler of effective direct marketing communications.

Don Condit
President
Condit Communications

"The ability to measure results precisely is always a key advantage of direct marketing communications, particularly when compared to space advertising. For business-to-business clients in intensely competitive markets, another huge advantage is the ability to act covertly. To assess the scope and intent of our campaigns, competitors must rely on reports from field salespeople, a method that can be slow and inaccurate."

Don Condit, President of Condit Communications in Fort Collins, Colorado, specializes in business-to-business marketing communications. Before founding his own company, Don worked with Poppe Tyson Advertising in New York for 10 years as a senior copywriter and as an account supervisor. Don's work has won him honors, including the American Marketing Association's coveted Gold Effie, for having the year's most successful marketing program. Don, a graduate of Hamilton College in New York, comments above on the advantages of direct marketing communications.

Measurable Action Objectives

Although all marketing communications should try to achieve measurable results, their objectives are generally not as action-specific as those of direct marketing. For instance, an advertising campaign for a new brand may have the goal of achieving brand awareness among 65 percent of its target audience. In DMC, however, marketers usually set much more specific action objectives, such as a purchase or a request for information. Achievement of such objectives can then be measured by calculating the number of purchases or requests for information that result from the campaign.

Action objectives allow the marketer to test several different forms of a direct marketing communication. The marketer can then adjust the message and the medium to achieve optimum results. For example, *Reader's Digest* magazine traditionally relied on a direct mail sweepstakes to acquire new subscribers. The effectiveness of sweepstakes began faltering in the late 1990s due to competition, consumer boredom with sweepstakes, and more interest among consumers in participation in state lotteries. *Reader's Digest* engaged in extensive testing, what one executive called "10 years of testing in 10 months." By testing the appeal of different formats and offers, *Reader's Digest* found the right combination and will not use sweepstakes as part of its direct mail campaigns in the foreseeable future.[9]

Growth of Direct Marketing Communications

Direct marketing communications have become a larger part of the total marketing communications picture in recent years. From 2000 to 2005, direct marketing is forecast to increase in efficiency with annual sales growing steadily at more than 9 percent.[10]

Total direct marketing expenditures will reach an estimated $270 billion by 2005, split fairly evenly between business and consumer markets. Expenditures on direct marketing are growing at a healthy rate, with the 2000–2005 growth rate expected to be 7.1 percent.[11] In the remainder of this section, we will examine the global growth of DMC and some of the catalysts behind the growth.

Global Direct Marketing Communications

Direct marketing communications are becoming more important in global marketing efforts. This has been true for U.S.-based marketers who have faced a fairly saturated domestic market for several years. It is becoming more commonplace for direct marketers outside the United States to expand their operations, including entry into the U.S. market. Even though the U.S. market may be crowded in some product categories, unique international offerings have a good chance of success in

Expansion into global markets is one reason for the growth of direct marketing communications. For more than three decades, Johnson & Hayward, Inc., has been involved in direct marketing communications on a global basis.

Thinking Critically

Courtney Knowlton, marketing manager for a popular women's magazine, is preparing a direct mail campaign to attract new subscribers. She is interested in getting the highest possible rate (the ratio of positive responders to the total number of pieces mailed). She has carefully prepared high-quality copy and removed the names of current subscribers from her mailing list. What additional suggestions can you give Courtney to maximize a positive response rate?

the United States. For example, the British Tourist Authority used a direct mail campaign to target 750,000 senior citizens in the United States, drawing 8,000 direct responses and more than 28,000 Web site hits. The 4 percent response rate was more than double the objective for the campaign and more than paid for itself with increased tourism to the United Kingdom.[12]

Asia has been a particularly attractive region for direct marketing efforts. Neiman Marcus, Patagonia, Eddie Bauer, J. Crew, and Victoria's Secret have been highly successful with their catalogs in Japan, Singapore, and Hong Kong. The forecasted growth in direct marketing expenditures in Asia and the Pacific Rim outpaces the expected 7 percent annual growth rate in the United States during the 2000–2005 period by significant margins. Taiwan, South Korea, Hong Kong, Malaysia, and the Philippines are forecasting annual growth rates of 15 percent or higher. Australia and Thailand expect direct marketing to grow at approximately 10 percent per year through 2005. Only Japan shows moderate direct marketing expenditures growth in the region, with a forecasted 5 percent per year.[13]

The European nations' annual growth in direct marketing expenditures exceeds that of the United States, led by Ireland at 19 percent. Germany, Italy, the Netherlands, Austria, Spain, and France are growing at approximately 10 percent annually. Latin America is also a growth area. Even Argentina, with its bruised economy, will almost match the United States in annual growth of direct marketing expenditures.[14]

One factor that could slow direct marketing in Europe is the European Union's strict consumer privacy rules, which went into effect in 1998. These rules, discussed in more detail in the section discussing invasion of privacy near the end of the chapter, require marketers to get permission in advance for any use of customer financial information in direct marketing campaigns. For example, building a database that includes customer income levels is forbidden without explicit advance consent of all customers in the database. To date, the European Union has not strictly enforced the rules for non-European companies. Should strict enforcement begin, the costs of direct marketing in Europe will increase dramatically.[15]

Growth Catalysts

The increase in customized products, fragmented markets, and product price sensitivity; shrinking audiences for network television and newspapers; and emphasis on immediate sales all contribute to the expansion of direct marketing communications. Marketers are now forced to identify their target markets more specifically in order to reach them more effectively.

Other forces also contribute to the growth of direct marketing communications. Changes in lifestyles create a need for convenient, time-saving, and dependable ways to shop. Two-worker families have more discretionary income but less time. These conditions make shopping at home, at one's leisure, very appealing. The ease of communication between buyer and seller, combined with the increased use of credit cards and acceptable products, makes direct purchasing an attractive alternative for many consumers.

A major reason for the growth in direct marketing communications has been advancing technology, which allows more precise construction and manipulation of customer databases. **Predictive modeling** on a database allows the marketer to reach a desired target more effectively, thus avoiding waste and enhancing profits. Sophisticated computerized statistical techniques known as *neural networks* can calculate weights for customer characteristics such as age, income, education, or time on the job. Using artificial intelligence, neural networks "learn" which targets are more likely to respond by examining data examples and calculating the relationships between predictor characteristics and known results.

Direct Marketing Communications Techniques

Direct marketing communications include direct mail and some forms of broadcast advertising, such as infomercials and direct-response television and radio advertising. Direct-response advertising appears in newspapers and magazines as well. Other techniques include telemarketing and supplementary electronic media.

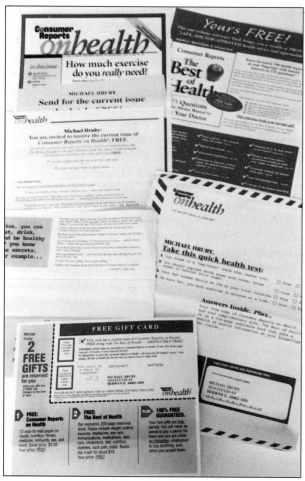

Direct mail can be a simple one-piece flyer or a more sophisticated multiple-piece mailer. In this case, Consumer Reports uses a multi-piece mailer to sell subscriptions for its magazine.

Direct Mail

Direct mail includes any form of advertising addressed to prospects through public or private delivery services. It can range in complexity from a simple flyer to a package including a letter, multipage brochure, video, and response card. The direct-mail response rate per thousand people reached is generally higher than for any other advertising medium, which may explain why both small companies and industry giants such as IBM, General Motors, Lockheed, and American Express use direct mail. Advantages and disadvantages of direct mail are summarized in Exhibit 20–2.

Direct mail has considerable flexibility in its self-contained message and the form used to convey it. A message could be written on a postcard or conveyed by videocassette. Moreover, direct mail can appeal to a narrow audience and be designed to suit a prospect's specific needs. Midwest Corvette Specialties, for example, can reach Corvette owners through its parts magazine. Working from a list of Corvette owners, the company avoids advertising to consumers who have no interest in its products. Direct mail can also be used effectively by small businesses, as illustrated in "Being Entrepreneurial: Angel's Books Hits the Target."

Don Condit, President of Condit Communications, offers these thoughts on what makes effective direct mail: "In direct mail we often search for gimmicks to make a piece of mail resemble a personal letter written for one reader. But the best device of all is copy that truly speaks to each reader personally—about relevant issues with a voice that is direct, honest, and disarming. By splitting copy, we can tailor each piece of mail for each audience segment and achieve the most important direct-mail success of all—readership."

Exhibit 20–2	*Advantages and disadvantages of direct mail*

Advantages	Disadvantages
• Self-contained message	• High cost per exposure
• Flexibility in message content and form of delivery	• Potential delivery delays
• Thorough coverage of target market	• Lack of support from other media
• Fewer distractions from other media	• "Junk mail" easy to ignore
• A large number of consumers like to make mail-order purchases	• Seen as wasteful, harmful to environment

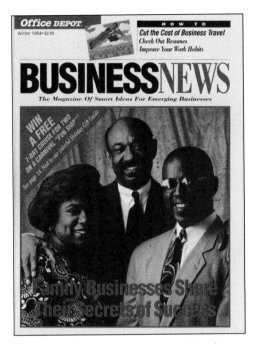

Office Depot's house organ *Business News* is a full-color, 40-page magazine of how-to's and free advice mailed to more than a million businesspeople.

The marketer can achieve nearly 100 percent coverage of the intended target market with direct mail, with fewer distractions than in some other media. For example, television or radio commercials are broadcast along with other ads and the regular programming. And magazine ads are juxtaposed with articles and other ads. A direct-mail piece, however, is typically viewed with less competition.

Perhaps the biggest advantage of direct mail is its potential effectiveness. Purchasing from a catalog or other mailed solicitations is a routine practice in many countries, including the United States and Great Britain. Purchases resulting from direct mail are more frequent among higher-income consumers, prompting upscale businesses not known for using direct mail to do so. For example, upscale retailer Neiman Marcus has used a special Christmas catalog for years, and Nordstrom has increased its catalog mailings to the upscale female shopper. Other prominent upscale direct mail marketers include Robert Redford's Sundance, The Sharper Image, Herrington, and clothing retailer The Territory Ahead.

Direct mail does have its flaws, however. It has one of the highest costs per thousand of any form of advertising. And it suffers potential delivery delays; it may take up to six weeks for bulk mail to reach its destination. In addition, consumers can easily ignore it, tossing the junk mail without ever being exposed to its message. While popular in many countries, it is not yet a significant method of marketing in some countries. For example, catalog and other direct mail appeals are not particularly effective in South Africa, Australia, and Brazil.[16] And finally, consumers increasingly view direct mail as wasteful and harmful to the environment.

TYPES OF DIRECT MAIL   Direct mail comes in many formats, as shown in Exhibit 20–3. The most common form of direct mail is the *sales letter,* which typically includes the recipient's name and may be mailed with brochures, price lists, and reply cards and envelopes. *Postcards* generally offer discounts, announce sales, or generate customer traffic. Postcards may be combined with a larger piece, such as a magazine cover or product information sheet. The idea is to cut through mailbox clutter with the larger piece, yet have an economical, easy way for the consumer to respond. This combination—called Double Postcard Plus, or DPC+—gives marketers a chance to deliver descriptive messages and compelling graphics not possible with an unaccompanied postcard. Even though costs are higher, more favorable response rates make it feasible in some situations.

Being Entrepreneurial

Angel's books hits the target

Before the age of 30, Nicole Williams demonstrated that she knew the basics of direct marketing communications. Select a target audience, reach them with compelling, yet inexpensive messages, and establish a database to fuel repeat business. Her Houston-based online bookstore, www.angelsbookstore.com, targets the African-American market with books by and about people of African descent.

To reach her target market, Ms. Williams first used a postcard mailing to five thousand subscribers to *Essence* magazine, a monthly publication geared toward African-American women. She scored a 60 percent response, a high number for such mailings. Later she added a toll-free number and a printed catalog for those who preferred not to buy from her Web site. The response to both methods was favorable, and she now mails the catalog four times a year. Ms. Williams continued to build her business with monthly mailings to a thousand potential new customers. These mailings produced a phenomenal 50 percent response by phone or to her Web site. To retain customers, she relies on a monthly e-mail newsletter and specific e-mails to keep customers coming back. Direct marketing is working well for Angel Books, which has become a profitable company at a time when many online retailers have failed.

Exhibit 20–3	*Types of direct mail*

Sales letter: typically includes recipient's name; may be mailed with brochures, price lists, reply cards, and envelopes.

Postcards: generally used to offer discounts, announce sales, or generate customer traffic.

Catalogs: describe and often picture the product sold.

Video catalogs: serve same purpose as print catalog, but are on videocassettes.

Promotional videocassettes and audiocassettes: used to send product information to selected audiences.

Promotional interactive computer disks: allow the recipient to select information of interest.

Leaflets and flyers: typically single pages that can be folded and included with sales letters.

Statement stuffers: ads included in other mail such as bank or credit card statements or shipped with catalog orders.

Catalog sales are on the increase. Consumers like the convenience, simplicity, and reliability of catalog buying.

Some companies produce publications referred to as *house organs* for mailing to particular audiences. These may be newsletters, consumer magazines, stockholder reports, or dealer publications. Increasingly popular are electronic house organs in the form of e-mail newsletters. For example, House of Blues, the nightclub chain, offers subscribers a free weekly electronic newsletter updating performance schedules and other information for live music fans.

By 2005, sales from printed *catalogs* will reach $155 billion.[17] Lands' End, Eddie Bauer, Patagonia, and JCPenney produce well-known catalogs. Catalogs offer a comfortable, convenient alternative to in-store shopping. Consumers enjoy browsing through the pages and using the simple, reliable means such as the mail, telephone, or fax to place orders. Most catalog retailers have well-trained staffs and efficient delivery systems, which further enhances the shopping experience. Catalogs also play a major role in business-to-business direct marketing, particularly in the office supply and furnishings category.

Catalogs, pioneered by general merchandise retailers such as Sears, are more likely to appeal to a niche market today. In the home furnishings market, successful niche catalogers include L. L. Bean Home, Linen Source, Restoration Hardware, Pottery Barn, and Hold Everything.

Promotional videocassettes, DVDs, and *CD-ROMs* filled with product information are becoming popular direct-mail pieces. CD-ROMs offer several advantages, including more storage space and smaller size, which minimizes postage costs. DVDs offer the additional advantage of playability on both computers and mass-market DVD players. BMW inserted DVDs in a mail campaign to *Vanity Fair* readers to promote its 3-series automobiles. Trying to reach a younger audience than BMW's traditional buyer, the DVDs featured films starring actor Clive Owen and pop singer Madonna as they drove BMWs to complete their daring missions. In this case, the DVD medium was compatible with the younger target market, and BMW achieved its brand awareness and sales objectives.[18]

Leaflets or *flyers* are typically single pages printed on one or both sides of standard-sized paper (8 1/2 by 11 inches) and folded. *Statement stuffers* are ads included in other mail such as bank or credit card statements.

BUSINESS-TO-BUSINESS DIRECT MAIL   All the forms of direct mail discussed above are frequently used in business-to-business marketing. With the increasing costs of sales calls, marketers use direct mail to generate sales leads, solicit sales, and provide after-sale support and service information. For example, Net Ledger, Inc., a provider of Oracle's Small Business Suite software, uses a continual direct marketing effort to reach a half million small businesses. Over time, 10 per-

Exhibit 20-4

To maximize business-to-business direct mail:

- Target all decision makers from the senior level on down.
- Reach decision makers as early as possible in the sales cycle.
- Deliver messages tailored to the purchase responsibility of each job at each stage of the buying process.
- Communicate at the proper technical level for different people who share the buying decision.
- Recognize that CEOs will probably not have much involvement unless the purchase is large enough to warrant their attention.
- Know the length and stages in the sales cycle, and plan accordingly.
- Develop direct messages based on the buyer's needs, objectives, and strategies.
- Be sure that responses to direct communications are promptly followed up.
- When referring customers to your own Web site, ensure that your direct message is compatible with the image and content of your site.

cent of the businesses in the database have been converted to customers, at which point they get direct mail and e-mail communications to strengthen their relationships with Net Ledger. The continual direct marketing program has proved far more effective than Net Ledger's previous direct effort, which consisted of one-shot mailings.[19] For an indication of what makes a successful business-to-business direct mail piece, see Exhibit 20–4.

Broadcast Media

Although used mostly for mass advertising, television and radio are also used for direct marketing communications. Infomercials and direct-response advertising on TV and radio are popular DMC formats.

INFOMERCIALS **Infomercials** are extended (usually 30-minute) commercials cast in a television-show format. Mixing information and entertainment, they strive to look more like a regular TV program than a commercial. Infomercials have become well established on cable television, generating well over a billion dollars a year in sales. Popular product categories for infomercials include health and fitness equipment, cosmetics, small kitchen appliances, and hair and personal care items. Familiar infomercial offerings include Ab Rocker, Total Gym, Torso Gym, George Foreman Indoor/Outdoor Grill, California Tanning System, Ronco appliances, and Tae Bo fitness techniques.

The infomercial format provides an opportunity to stand out in a cluttered environment. A 30-second commercial is more likely to get lost in the shuffle than a 30-minute one. In addition, an infomercial's length makes it possible to explain an advertised product more fully. For instance, Adams Golf introduced its unconventional "Tight Lies" golf club with infomercials. Legendary golf commentator Jack Whitaker and professional golfers Bill Rogers and Hank Haney explained and demonstrated how the club's bottom weighting made hitting the ball easier than it is with traditional fairway woods. The original Tight Lies club was named the International Network of Golf's "Breakthrough Product of the Year," and the company went on to sell millions of units. Adams has since relied on infomercials for other product introductions with great success.

By featuring a direct-response telephone number, an infomercial guarantees a quick means for measuring results. Moreover, information obtained from those ordering can be used to develop a database.

Infomercials also have certain disadvantages. For one thing, airing is confined largely to cable TV and late-night programming on major networks, perhaps making it difficult to reach the target market with the desired message. Although potentially cost-effective, average production costs for infomercials are high. Thus, production costs added to airtime costs make infomercials more expensive than most direct marketing communications methods.

Finally, infomercials have a poor image. Many suffer from exaggerated claims, low-quality production standards, and unprofessional presentation. Moreover, there is some concern that they are deceptive by appearing in the guise of programs. Infomercials for some products have drawn fire from the public, such as Eli Lilly's infomercial for its antidepressant, Prozac. While people recognize that depression is a serious problem and that public discussion might eventually lead to better treatments, they were upset at the overt sales pitch for the drug via an infomercial.[20] Problems such as these may be overcome as the format develops and attracts more credible sponsors. In recent years, major companies such as Pennzoil, Ford Motor Company's Mercury division, and Internet job site Monster.com have used infomercials, which indicates that these extended direct appeals are gaining in credibility.[21]

DIRECT-RESPONSE TELEVISION ADVERTISING Direct-response television advertising includes an 800 or 900 telephone number and an address for placing orders in a typical 30-, 60-, or 90-second commercial. Unlike typical mass advertising, direct-response ads attempt to get an immediate answer from the consumer. Music is often featured in direct-response television ads with major advertisers such as Time Life Music (*AM Gold* and *Ultra Mix*) and Millennium Partners (*Swing is King*). Other major products advertised for direct response on television include Intuit's Quicken financial software, Mead Johnson's Boost Vanilla Shake, Glaxo Wellcome's Flonase, Sears's tools, and E*Trade's electronic stock-trading site. Print media, most notably magazines and newspapers, also used direct response TV ads to reach new subscribers. For example, *Time* magazine and *Sports Illustrated* frequently use the method. The *Chicago Tribune* combines direct response TV ads with direct mail to generate new subscriptions and maintain renewals.[22]

Although sometimes aired on network television, direct-response commercials are more widely broadcast on cable TV. Cable TV allows effective targeting of audiences through special-interest programming. Bass Pro Shops, a Springfield, Missouri, catalog retailer, for example, uses direct-response advertising on popular cable-TV fishing programs. As with infomercials, this form of DMC enables database building and immediate assessment of results.

DIRECT-RESPONSE RADIO ADVERTISING Direct-response radio advertising also offers the ability for immediate feedback through a telephone number or address provided with the commercial. In addition, it can be directed toward a very targeted audience and is relatively inexpensive compared with other forms of direct marketing communications. Radio, however, is not a particularly dynamic medium. Radio audiences tend to be too preoccupied with other things to focus on an address or a telephone number. Certainly a listener hearing a radio commercial while driving cannot easily record an address.

Busy Body uses telemarketing as part of its communications mix. A toll-free number for inbound telemarketing is featured in print ads and on the company's Web site. Inbound telemarketing gives customers an alternative to purchasing in Busy Body stores or on the Web.

Print Media

Although not so tightly targeted as other direct marketing communications media, newspapers and magazines can also provide an opportunity for direct response. Consumers can respond to ads carrying an address, order form, coupon, or telephone number. The response can be either to purchase or to request additional information. One way to use direct-response print advertising is with a freestanding insert (FSI), discussed in Chapter 18.

Magazines may include other forms of direct marketing communications. Some marketers insert reply cards into magazines. **Reader-response cards** are sometimes used in conjunction with ads to allow consumers to request additional information. Readers wanting more information on a product would circle a number on the card corresponding to the product's ad in the magazine and send the card to the magazine's publisher. Another magazine insert is the floppy disk. *Forbes* magazine, for example, included a disk that contained information from such advertisers as American Express, Chevrolet, Embassy Suites, and Merrill Lynch, among others. America Online has used disk inserts extensively to attract new subscribers.

Telemarketing

Telemarketing is an interactive direct marketing communications approach that uses telephone calls to initiate, develop, and enhance relationships with customers. On a cost-per-contact basis, telemarketing is less expensive than personal selling, but much more expensive than mass advertising and direct mail. However, its high return often justifies the added expense. According to the Direct Marketing Association, telemarketing sales will exceed $935 billion by the year 2005.[23] In terms of expenditures and sales generated, telemarketing is the leading direct marketing communications technique.

Outbound telemarketing, sometimes called *teleselling,* occurs when the marketer actively solicits customers or prospects. Inbound telemarketing occurs when a customer calls the marketer to obtain information or place an order. Either case offers the advantage of two-way conversation, allowing the respondent to ask questions and give answers and the marketer to tailor a message to the individual needs of the prospect.

Very popular in business-to-business marketing, telemarketing can be effective in expanding international marketing operations. Gateway, the direct supplier of computers, established a telemarketing center in Dublin, Ireland, as a first step toward entry into European markets. Holiday Inn and Radisson have established telemarketing operations in Australia to handle the entire Asia Pacific region, and Apple serves Europe with telemarketing centers in France, the United Kingdom, and Germany.

Technology has made telemarketing very productive. **Predictive dialing systems** save telemarketers as much as 20 minutes an hour by passing over answering machines, busy signals, and no answers. Predictive dialers automatically dial a designated amount of numbers per minute. Completed calls are immediately passed on to a live telemarketer, who simultaneously receives customer information on a computer terminal.

Unfortunately, telemarketing does not have a good image. Consumers view telemarketers as uninvited nuisances. In one survey, 77 percent of the respondents said telemarketers were rude and pushy, while only 18 percent said they were reasonable and effective.[24] Other common complaints are that telemarketing is an invasion of privacy, uses misleading tactics, and is a waste of time. Consumer organizations routinely warn consumers to be wary of telemarketing. Some go beyond warnings, urging consumers to take the offensive against telemarketing. For example, Junkbusters offers an antitelemarketing script at its Web site (www.junkbusters.com) under the question, "Telemarketers always use a script: why shouldn't you?" Junkbuster's script is recommended as "what to say when they call if you don't want junk calls."[25]

The public's irritation with telemarketers and unethical practices by some telemarketers has prompted the Federal Trade Commission (FTC) to consider a national "do not call" list that would prohibit telemarketing calls to consumers who register with the FTC. There are already such laws in 15 states, with 11 more states having announced that do-not-call laws are forthcoming.[26] It is uncertain what the FTC will decide, but the message to telemarketers is increasingly clear: to be accepted as a legitimate marketer, don't bother calling those who do not wish to be contacted. From a commonsense perspective, telemarketers should focus on interested prospects, a practice encouraged by the Direct Marketing Association (DMA).

Thinking Critically

Blake Stanley, Director of Promotions for a book retailer, is contemplating running a contest for consumers on his company's Web site. Winners would receive free books and merchandise. Currently, Blake's company enjoys sales from around the globe on its Web site. Since this is the first time that Blake has considered running a contest, he is wondering if any precautions are appropriate. What advice can you share with Blake?

The DMA maintains its own do-not-call list and asks its members to abide by it. However, there is no penalty for calling those on the list. Telemarketing can be a mutually beneficial tool for businesses and consumers. In many cases, particularly in business-to-business settings, it is a productive marketing method and a preferred way to stay in touch from the customer's point of view.

Unfortunately for legitimate companies, consumers do have to exercise caution when dealing with telemarketers. The National Consumers League identifies the top telemarketing fraud schemes in Exhibit 20–5. Telemarketers, then, should provide short, compelling messages, as most people will not spend more than a few minutes on the phone for an uninvited sales call.

Electronic Media

Several other electronic forms of direct marketing communications are available besides broadcast media. Although not used as often as other methods, interactive computer services, kiosks, and fax machines are growing in popularity.

INTERACTIVE COMPUTER SERVICES   As illustrated throughout this book, **interactive computer networks** are increasingly used for direct marketing communications. Traditional networks work via modem over telephone lines. Wireless Internet services, which utilize communications satellites, are also available, and simple Web-access appliances, not full-blown computers, are becoming a factor in this form of direct marketing communications.

As the rapid growth of electronic commerce continues, it is logical to expect more direct marketing communications via the Internet. This is because a key ingredient of DMC, the use of customer databases, is facilitated by electronic commerce. That is, once consumers buy electronically, they become part of that seller's customer database and may be receptive to direct communications. The obvious low cost of transmitting electronic messages when compared with other forms of direct marketing communications and the global reach of this medium provide strong incentives for marketers to use this communications tool.

Some cautionary notes are worth considering. First, although the total number of Internet users is large and growing, not all are relevant for direct marketers. Further, online users are very particular about unsolicited advertising that arrives by e-mail, called *spam*. Consumers receiving spam often react angrily, boycotting the spammer and "flaming" the offender. Flaming involves negative responses to the advertiser, such as deluging them with thousands of reply messages or sending e-mail "bombs" containing huge files that tie up computers for hours.

Exhibit 20–5	*National Consumers League's top 10 telemarketing frauds list*

1. *Work-at-home schemes*—Kits sold with false promises of profits.
2. *Prizes/sweepstakes*—Phony prize awards requiring payment of fees first.
3. *Credit card offers*—Phony promises of credit cards requiring payment of fees in advance.
4. *Advance fee loans*—Empty promises of loans requiring payment of fees in advance.
5. *Magazine sales*—Fake sales or renewals for magazine subscriptions that are never received.
6. *Telephone slamming*—Consumers' phone service is switched without their knowledge or consent.
7. *Buyers clubs*—Consumers' credit card and bank accounts may be charged with unauthorized purchases.
8. *Credit card loss protection*—Unnecessary insurance sold using scare tactics or misrepresentations.
9. *Nigerian money offers*—Consumers are lured into revealing their bank account number against which fraudulent checks are written.
10. *Telephone pay-per-call services*—Some 900 number and other "pay-per-call" services are not worth the price of the call.

Another area of concern is that the Internet is suffering from congestion. Users complain that it takes too long to navigate the vast array of sites, and this could diminish the viability of computer networks as a communications vehicle. One additional concern is that computer vandals or "hackers" may interfere with a Web site's operation, even closing it down. Hackers have succeeded in closing down some of the most popular Web sites for several hours, including Amazon.com, Yahoo!, Microsoft, and eBay. The FBI has warned marketers that their Web sites are only as secure as the other Web sites they link to; thus well-protected sites can still be vandalized through less-protected linking sites.

Despite the uncertainties, direct marketing communications via interactive computer networks is growing rapidly. It is an ideal medium for computer-equipped consumers who want to stay in touch with retailers and service providers. Companies encourage this link by publicizing their Web addresses in ads and on product packaging.

Don Condit, President of Condit Communications, comments on the growth of the Internet in marketing communications: "The value of promotion over the Internet will grow more slowly for clients selling expensive capital equipment than it will for others. For each client, the rate of growth will also vary from one target audience to another. Pharmaceutical process engineers, for example, are already accustomed to using the Internet to find new equipment choices and alternate vendors, while engineers in the food-processing industry will not rely on the Internet for years to come."

INTERACTIVE COMPUTER KIOSKS   Another electronic marketing medium is the **interactive computer kiosk.** These kiosks typically use touch-screen technology that allows the consumer to access specific information of interest. Some interactive computer kiosks include catalogs (video or paper) featuring items not stocked in the retail store, with a direct toll-free number for placing orders. Cities frequented by tourists sometimes use kiosks to help sightseers find their way around. These kiosks are often used as direct marketing communications vehicles for restaurants, hotels, and other services and attractions of interest to travelers. Catalog retailers are also using computer kiosks to gain additional exposure and sales from mall and airport shoppers. With consumers becoming increasingly comfortable with computer technology, the use of kiosks is increasing. Best Buy, Office Depot, and Staples use kiosks to allow direct purchases of computers and other items from company Web sites. IBM uses kiosks to communicate directly with job seekers at career fairs, and some pharmaceutical companies are using kiosks in doctor's offices to promote their drugs.

FAX MACHINES   Fax machines allow customers to transmit written documents via telephone. However, their use as a direct marketing communications tool has been restricted primarily to business-to-business customers. Direct marketers routinely use fax machines to receive customer orders. Newer technology called **fax-on-demand systems** allows instant response to 800-number requests for information using a fax. In these systems, a fax machine receives the request for information and immediately faxes the information back to the requester. For example, the Internal Revenue Service operates the largest fax-on-demand service in the world, handling 7,000 calls per hour during peak periods. Callers request tax forms through a voice-activated menu and the forms are immediately faxed to the taxpayer.[27]

One problem with using fax machines in business-to-business marketing communications is that most businesses do not want to tie up their incoming fax lines with unsolicited information. It is now a fairly common practice to send unsolicited marketing communications after normal business hours, a practice made easy by the delayed-dialing capabilities of most fax machines. Some states, including Texas, Oregon, and Florida, prohibit the transmission of unsolicited fax communications.

Many business-to-business marketers, including accounting firms and equipment manufacturers, depend on disseminating information as a means of attracting clients. Some of these marketers find an advantage in transmitting information in written, rather than audio or video form. Many prospective customers would rather read a customized report than listen to one, since it is easier to access important parts of the written report. Prices, product availability, shipping schedules, and other marketing mix variables can change frequently, and the fax is extremely accommodating when such changes occur. Many fax documents are never in hard copy form, but exist in computer files that can be changed with the flick of a key stroke just before dissemination. Now that the same function can be accomplished with e-mail, direct marketing communications via fax is declining in importance.

Ethical and Legal Issues in Direct Marketing Communications

In this section, we discuss three key areas of ethical and legal concern in direct marketing communications: invasion of privacy, deceptive practices, and waste of natural resources.

Invasion of Privacy

As consumer databases become more sophisticated, there is growing concern about invasion of privacy. According to a survey conducted by Harris Interactive, consumers do not trust companies to protect their private information, and a majority feel that an independent third party should verify a company's privacy policies.[28] In the same survey, more than 80 percent of all respondents felt that is highly important that companies have adequate security procedures to protect personal data, and make sure that personal information is used or shared only according to stated privacy policies.

Consumers are concerned with a loss of control over how their personal information is used by companies and that they do not wish to receive more advertising messages as a result of divulging their personal information. Some are also concerned that detailed profiling of individual consumer behaviors could lead to discrimination by marketers. For example, if a company learns that a consumer shops a lot but does not buy much, the company can leave him or her on hold on help lines and not offer the consumer special deals.

The privacy of teens and younger children is a particularly sensitive issue. Consumer groups point out that online services may surpass television in influencing younger consumers' lives in the future and believe that some marketers manipulate children. For example, companies offer prizes for personal information—such as e-mail addresses and birthdays—that will be used in direct marketing communications. Critics believe that marketers should fully disclose how such information will be used and get parental consent if information will be identifiable by individuals rather than aggregated into group data.[29]

U.S. marketers are leery of legislative attempts to regulate potential threats to consumer privacy. Consumers in other countries, however, are accustomed to strict privacy statutes. European Union (EU) countries guarantee European citizens absolute control over their private information. If a company wants a consumer's personal information, they must get the individual's permission and explain how the information will be used. The European Union is pressuring marketers from other countries to follow the strict laws adopted by the European Union. According to EU law, no company can transmit personal data about EU citizens to countries whose privacy laws are not as strict as those in the European Union. EU law also prohibits data tags, or "cookies," that track customer preferences on the Web and does not allow marketers to use databases obtained from another marketer to solicit business.[30]

To ward off potential legislative action, some direct marketing companies are taking actions to avoid invading consumers' privacy. Fewer firms make their in-house lists available for rental to other companies. McDonald's, Fisher-Price, and

Exhibit 20–6	*Telemarketing sales rule*

All businesses conducting outbound telemarketing must comply with the Telemarketing Sales Rule after passage of the Telemarketing and Consumer Fraud and Abuse Prevention Act of 1994. Major provisions of the rule include:

- Telemarketers must disclose costs associated with the purchase, limitations, restrictions, and refund/cancellation policies.
- Abusive acts are prohibited, including profane language and calling people who have indicated that they do not wish to be contacted.
- A "do not call" list must be maintained by the company using telemarketing. Telemarketers are restricted from making calls before 8:00 A.M. and after 9:00 P.M. local time.
- Companies must maintain records on transactions for a period of 24 months.
- The Telemarketing Sales rule is enforced by both the Federal Trade Commission and by a state's Attorney General, who can impose penalties of $10,000 per violation per day.

Citicorp, for example, no longer rent their customer lists. Many firms allow consumers to choose whether or not they are included on lists made available to other firms. Others ask consumers how often they would like to receive mail solicitations.

Deceptive Practices

Attempts at telemarketing legislation have increased at least in part to address numerous telemarketing abuses (see Exhibit 20–6). Consumers exhibit high levels of trust in sellers when they order and pay for a product sight unseen. Direct-response marketers rely on this trust. Yet, certain direct-marketing activities have damaged that trust.

After 30 years, marketers have finally convinced consumers that 800-number telephone calls are toll-free. But some marketers ask 800-number callers to punch codes into their telephones that, unbeknownst to them, convert the call to a billable 900 number. Another abuse comes from sweepstakes marketers that promote 900-number calls for prizes worth much less than the cost of the call.

Automatic number identification and **caller ID intrusion** systems pose additional ethical and legal problems. These systems let incoming telephone numbers of respondents to an ad or a promotion be identified at the onset of the call without the caller's consent or knowledge. Not only is this a possible invasion of privacy, but it also presents an opportunity to capture and sell unlisted numbers.

Internet fraud is another area of concern in direct marketing communications. Many of the scams in telemarketing (see Exhibit 20–5) are also promoted via e-mail. Nigerian money offers, work-at-home schemes, and bogus credit card offers are frequently transmitted by e-mail. In addition, e-mail is frequently used to offer fraudulent business opportunities and franchises.[31]

Wasteful Practices

People are concerned about the environmental consequences of marketing decisions, thus increasing attention on use of natural resources. In the direct-mail industry, consumer complaints and regulatory interest concerning junk mail have motivated discussion about excessive contributions to landfills, impact on timber production and harvesting, and the economic waste associated with rising paper costs.

It is commonly known that consumers do not want to receive all their unsolicited mail. Two alternatives are easily available to marketers that want to cut down on waste by minimizing undeliverable and unwanted direct-mail pieces. First, a marketer can increase the accuracy of a mailing list by running it through the U.S. Postal Service's national file on changes of address. By using this service, mailers could cut down on undeliverable pieces and perhaps qualify for lower postage rates in the process.

In addition, direct marketers could better inform consumers of their right to remove their names from mailing lists. The Direct Marketing Association coordinates a "preference" program that allows consumers to stop mail and telephone solicitation if they so choose. There may be some way marketers can make consumers more aware of this program, which would eventually lead to less unwanted mail and more efficient direct marketing communications.

Another element of waste in direct marketing communications is the time lost at home and in the workplace dealing with unsolicited messages. The widespread occurrence of spam has irked consumers and had an unknown but significant downward effect on workplace productivity. One survey indicates that more than two-thirds of online users say that they get too many e-mail offers and promotions, while only 5 percent say they often buy merchandise offered by e-mail.[32] The excessive use of unsolicited e-mail has spurred legislators and regulators to clamp down. The FTC has trained 1,700 individual representatives of state, local, and federal law-enforcement agencies in cases where spam contains deceptive content, as is often the case.[33] The U.S. Congress is contemplating antispam laws, though free-speech advocates are fighting restrictions on commercial expression, arguing that controls would threaten the right to free speech. To repeat a familiar refrain, most legitimate marketers are far more interested in targeting consumers who can benefit from their offerings, then communicating with them in a straightforward manner.

Cutting out waste in DMC requires that consumers join with concerned companies to bring about the desired changes. This is true of most ethical and legal problems facing marketing. Whether we are talking about invasion of privacy, deceptive practices, waste of natural resources, or any other significant ethical or legal issue in marketing, the consumer must take an active role in effecting favorable change.

Summary

1. **Understand the objectives of direct marketing communications, and describe its distinguishing characteristics.** Direct marketing communications are directed at target audiences using one or more media. One objective of direct marketing communications is to elicit a response by telephone, mail, or personal visit from a prospect or customer. Another objective, to maintain and enhance customer relationships, is growing in importance.

   Direct marketing is distinguished from other marketing communications methods in several ways. First, it uses customer databases, or lists, to target an audience precisely. Next, it is oriented more toward an immediate response than are most other forms of marketing communications. Finally, its objectives are specific consumer actions, so results are highly measurable.

2. **Discuss the factors driving the growth in direct marketing communications.** Increasingly fragmented markets make the narrowly focused methods of direct marketing quite attractive. Changes in lifestyles have created a need for convenient, time-saving, and dependable ways to shop. Perhaps one of the biggest motivators of growth in direct marketing communications has been the emergence of database marketing, which gives marketers a more in-depth understanding of productive target customers.

3. **Understand traditional direct marketing communications techniques such as direct mail, broadcast and print media, and telemarketing.** Direct mail comes in a variety of forms, from postcards to video catalogs. Print and broadcast media are used for direct-response advertising, and the infomercial has become a significant means of communicating directly with the target market. Inbound and outbound telemarketing have become extremely popular, even though outbound telemarketing is a nuisance to many consumers. Each of these methods has unique capabilities and limitations, one reason marketers typically use multiple methods to reach a given audience.

4. **Recall examples of the use of technology such as electronic media in direct marketing communications.** Interactive computer services, interactive computer kiosks, and fax on demand are three examples of relatively new technology now widely used in direct marketing communications. These tools offer immediate information to consumers and business-to-business buyers, and sometimes allow the customer to do business with the seller after normal business hours.

5. **Understand some of the ethical and legal issues facing marketers who use direct marketing communications.** As database lists become more sophisticated, there is increased concern about invasion of privacy. Abuse of consumers' privacy is likely to lead to legislation to curb it. Telemarketing has come under the heaviest attacks, as unethical marketers use deceptive methods in dealing with consumers. Actions can and should be taken to avoid unwarranted or abusive intrusion. Junk mail and unsolicited e-mail have been accused of wasting natural resources and customers' time. Concerned marketers, consumers, and associations such as the Direct Marketing Association must work together to curb these problems. Otherwise, it is certain that some consumers will be victimized and that legislation will be enacted to address the issues.

Understanding Marketing Terms and Concepts

Thinking About Marketing

1. Define direct marketing communications and describe their distinguishing characteristics.

2. What is database marketing? How has it contributed to the growth of direct marketing communications?

3. Refer to "Using Technology: Before You Go." Are there any disadvantages to offering last-minute incentives to buyers to prevent the abandonment of online shopping carts?

4. Describe advantages and disadvantages of direct mail.

5. Refer to "Being Entrepreneurial: Angel's Books Hits the Target." How can a customer database be used to generate future sales?

6. What is an infomercial? What types of products do you think would benefit most from using this type of advertising and why?

7. What is an interactive computer service? How does it differ from an interactive computer kiosk?

8. Database marketing has come under attack from those who believe it is an invasion of privacy. Should marketers be concerned about this? What can be done to deal with consumers' concerns? Explain.

9. Review the Telephone Sales Rule in Exhibit 20–6. Is it necessary to have federal government intervention to regulate telemarketing?

10. What can direct marketers do to cut down on the waste generated by their communications methods?

Applying Marketing Skills

1. Working in groups of three to five students, analyze two current infomercials to see if they meet the standards of conduct as set forth by the National Infomercial Marketing Association:

   a. A "paid advertisement" disclosure must appear at the beginning and end of each infomercial and at each ordering opportunity.

   b. The name of the sponsor must be disclosed.

   c. There can be no misrepresentations as to format, no false claims or deception through omission, and no indecent or offensive material.

   To what extent do the members of the group agree on the last point? Summarize your opinions for class discussion.

2. Assume you are the chair of an alumni fund-raising committee for your college or university. The committee is charged with the task of contacting approximately 30,000 alumni to solicit donations for a new library. The goal is to raise $1 million from the alumni within the next 18 months. The first order of business is to determine what form of communication is to be used in the campaign. The alumni are scattered across the United States, and approximately 10 percent live in a variety of foreign countries. Which

means of reaching these alumni would you recommend the committee consider? Briefly explain your reasoning.

   a. Direct mail

   b. Telemarketing

   c. Personal selling

   d. Direct-response television advertising

   e. E-mail

   f. Fax solicitation

3. Which types of direct marketing communications would you choose for each task?

   a. Informing your customers of an upcoming sale in your retail store.

   b. Introducing yourself and your company to new prospects in your sales territory.

   c. Inviting current customers to visit your booth at a trade show next month.

   d. Demonstrating a new software program offered by your company.

   e. Familiarizing European construction managers with your latest piece of earth-moving equipment.

   f. Bringing your 1,200 dealers up-to-date on a variety of happenings in your company.

Using the www in Marketing

Activity One   Visit the Coldwater Creek Web site (http://www.coldwatercreek.com).

1. How does this Web site fit with Coldwater Creek's other direct marketing communications efforts?

2. Identify examples of how Coldwater Creek implements an ethics perspective.

3. What Web site improvements can you recommend to Coldwater Creek?

Activity Two   Trade associations often use the Internet to provide valuable information to consumers and managers. The Direct Marketing Association maintains a comprehensive Web site at http://www.the-dma.org. What evidence can you find that the Direct Marketing Association promotes an ethical perspective in the practice of direct marketing?

Making Marketing Decisions

Case 20-1 *Cisco Hits the Target with e-mail*

Cisco Systems built its reputation as the world's leading provider of computer networking products that help other companies use the Internet and corporate intranets.

Always focused on the bottom line, Cicso used its own Web site at www.cisco.com to slash customer service costs, moving most of its customer service support online. With strategic partners such as Microsoft, Oracle, IBM, EDS, and Hewlett-Packard, the company has been recognized as belonging to an elite group of technology companies for almost two decades.

Now Cisco is making industry headlines through its use of direct marketing communications. Complex equipment requires personal selling to complete the sales cycle, but Cisco is using direct marketing to supplement the selling efforts of its own salesforce and that of its field partners. For several years, the company has used computer networks to provide direct communications with salespeople and customers. Recently, Cisco made a strong move into the contemporary version of direct mail by mounting massive e-mail campaigns.

Early e-mail campaigns proved to be highly effective and profitable. One campaign generated a 55 percent response rate, $2.2 million in additional sales, and a return on investment of 1,200 percent. A later campaign targeted CEOs, technical staffers, and managers of large corporations such as AT&T, Wells Fargo, and Deutsche Bank. In one part of this campaign, 40,000 technical staffers, all of whom had opted in or given their permission to receive information about optical data products, were offered a technical book as a premium. In return, prospects furnished information that Cisco used to determine if they were viable leads for the salesforce. Another part of this campaign was a three-part traditional hard-copy mailer sent to CEOs and nontechnical managers, because research indicated that these people preferred traditional approaches over e-mail. While this campaign turned up some viable sales leads, Cisco's management was somewhat concerned about the quality of those leads. There was some thought that the technical book offered as a premium might have produced some less-than-sincere leads. Even so, the company indicated that it was pleased with the overall results of the campaign, with conversion-to-customer ratios in an acceptable range.

In a follow-up e-mail campaign, Cisco e-mailed 124,000 current customers in an attempt to move the customers into a higher-ticket networking system. According to clickthroughs on its Web site, the mailing drew a 35 percent response rate. The cost savings with e-mail versus postal mail was approximately 50 percent.

In addition to responses to its e-mail initiative, Cisco received a large number of leads from ads it ran on Hoover's Online, Bloomberg.com, CFO.com, and direct response ads it placed in such publications as *The New York Times, Fortune,* and *The Wall Street Journal.* The leads were turned over to Cisco's field salesforce. Before the salesforce received the leads, a public relations firm further qualified the leads, determining when the companies planned to buy and how much they were willing to spend.

Cisco views its direct marketing efforts as a necessary element in stimulating demand for its products. Due to the complexity of the products, networking customers do not always know exactly what they need to buy. To speed up the sales cycle, direct marketing communications in the form of e-mail are becoming a more important strategy for Cisco.

Cisco CEO John Chambers came up through the sales ranks with IBM before joining Cisco. He has always been an advocate of superior customer service and building customer value through technology. In this instance, Cisco is once again demonstrating that it can use technology, even a fairly simple one like e-mail, to reduce its costs and reach customers with a timely message. Customers win too, as keeping up their technology network infrastructure is crucial for success.

Questions

1. Other than supplying sales leads, how does Cisco's e-mail direct marketing communications supplement the efforts of its salesforce?

2. Other than e-mail marketing, what other forms of direct marketing communications could be effective for Cisco?

3. What are some ways that Cisco can measure the effectiveness of its e-mail marketing? Would these methods be any different for direct-response print or Internet ads?

Case 20–2 Musicland Builds Relationships with DMC

Musicland, a wholly owned subsidiary of Best Buy Company, Inc., operates 1,300 music, video, and software stores in the United States, Puerto Rico, and the Virgin Islands under the names Suncoast Motion Picture, Media Play, Sam Goody, and On Cue. Musicland makes extensive use of direct marketing communications (DMC) in its customer loyalty program, which is designed to encourage repurchase and give regular customers additional value. At one point, however, this program, called Replay, began experiencing serious problems, causing large numbers of customer defections. Inbound telemarketing representatives were overwhelmed with

customer complaints. Record-keeping was poor, preventing qualified customers from receiving rebate checks when they made major purchases in a timely manner. As membership in Replay dropped, store managers became reluctant to promote the program. Musicland's loyalty program was quite simply having the opposite-than-hoped-for effect.

Musicland improved its loyalty program with the help of database marketing specialists from Minnesota-based Group 3 Marketing. The basic idea of Replay remained the same: that it is a consumer club offering its members discounts and other promotions, reviews, information about new releases, and related information. In return, members pay $7.99 a year to belong. To improve the program, the frequency of direct mail contact with members increased and the content of the mailings became far more customized.

Now bimonthly newsletters and four to five postcards are sent out monthly. The newsletters generate in-store or online responses of 16 to 18 percent, while the postcards typically generate a 5 to 7 percent response. The newsletters are more customized than the postcards, with message content dependent upon customer information from the database. In most cases, content is tailored to music and film preferences, birthdays, proximity to retail stores, and recent purchases. Postcards usually focus on new-product releases.

Basic demographic data is captured when members join Replay, and purchase information is gathered when the membership card is swiped in the store. This data is transferred electronically every day to Group 3 Marketing; online purchases are automatically recorded into the database.

One page of each newsletter is predominantly tailored to the individual Replay member. Personalized information includes accumulated point balances, gift-certificate rewards status, and product information that matches the member's interests. Other customized material is included in free-standing inserts.

Each Musicland store receives a report on the purchasing activity of its 50 top-spending customers. When these customers make purchases, their names appear on the electronic cash register screens. This allows store personnel to greet the key customers by name and to eventually recognize them as they enter the store. In some cases, this leads to personalized in-store service deserving of a top customer.

Musicland uses the Replay database to send e-mail promotions and special offers to members, but only after the member has signed up for these notices. When they sign up online, members have an option to receive their newsletters online. This option will save Musicland a significant amount of money in the years to come, as more and more consumers will opt for online direct marketing communications.

Store managers give their enthusiastic support to Replay, and promotional signage for Replay is prominent in the stores. Musicland is looking to expand the online aspect of the program. With 1.6 million paying members, a meaningful database, a user-friendly interface, and highly customized direct marketing communications, the future looks good for Replay.

Questions

1. How could Musicland use the information from its database to enhance in-store promotions and personal selling?

2. How could Musicland use its database to improve market segmentation and target marketing?

3. What methods could you recommend to assess the effectiveness of the various direct marketing communications vehicles used in Musicland's Replay program?

Appendix A

Developing a Marketing Plan

A general strategic planning process is presented in Chapter 3. The basic stages include: examine the current situation, identify potential threats and opportunities, set objectives, and develop strategies. This appendix illustrates the types of information typically appearing in each section of a product marketing plan.

Business units within the firm have their own product marketing plans that focus on specific target markets and marketing mixes for each product. As explained in Chapter 3, product marketing plans typically include both strategic decisions (or what to do) and execution decisions (or how to do it). Marketing plans may be developed for a single brand, a product line, or a business unit that markets multiple product lines. For a product, a product line, or a business unit, the general strategic planning process includes the following stages: (1) examine the current situation; (2) identify potential threats and opportunities; (3) set objectives; and (4) develop strategies. These stages may overlap in that work is simultaneously underway regarding each stage. The plans themselves will also include projected financial outcomes and procedures for plan performance monitoring and control.

Overall, planning is a process directed toward making decisions with tomorrow in mind. As such, planning is a means of preparing for future decisions so that they can be made rapidly, economically, and with as little disruption to the business as possible.[1] Marketing plans may be for new products and services being introduced or for existing products or services. Regardless of the type of plan, all plans will be reviewed at least annually for needed revisions. Properly developed marketing plans can provide considerable benefits to firm performance. Plans:[2]

- Act as a road map to guide future decisions.
- Assist in management control and implementation of strategy.
- Assist in helping obtain resources for implementation.
- Stimulate thinking and encourage better use of resources.
- Help in the organization and assignment of responsibilities, tasks, and timing.
- Inform new employees of their roles in implementing existing plans and reaching objectives.
- Help generate awareness of strengths, weaknesses, opportunities, and threats.

Acme Consulting: Planning for High Technology Product Marketing Plan[3]

The following outline is consistent with the general planning procedure summarized above and depicted earlier in Exhibit 3–2. The format for marketing plans varies by industry and company. The following plan is quite comprehensive and considers most important decisions. Frequently cited content issues and topics are enumerated (sometimes briefly) for each stage in this section.

Parts of the Marketing Plan

1. Executive summary
2. Situation analysis
3. Marketing strategy
4. Financials
5. Controls

Part 1.0 Executive Summary

Acme Consulting is a consulting company specializing in marketing of high-technology products in international markets. Its expertise is the marketing of personal computers and market research, all in international markets.

Part 2.0 Situation Analysis

Acme Consulting offers high-level expertise in international high-tech business development, channel development, distribution strategies, and marketing of high-tech products. It focuses on providing two kinds of international triangles:

- Providing United States clients with development for European and Latin American markets.

- Providing European clients with development for the United States and Latin American markets.

This year we intend to take on consulting work in related markets, specifically the rest of Latin America and the better markets in the Far East. We will also look for additional leverage by taking brokerage positions and representation positions to create percentage holdings in product results.

Part 2.1 Market Summary

Acme focuses on high-technology manufacturers of computer hardware and software, services, and networking, who want to sell into markets in the United States, Europe, and Latin America. These are mostly larger companies, and occasionally medium-sized companies.

Our most important customers are executives in larger corporations. They are marketing managers, general managers, and sales managers, sometimes charged with international focus and sometimes charged with market or even specific channel focus. They do not want to waste their time or risk their money looking for bargain information or questionable expertise. As they go into markets looking at new opportunities, they are very sensitive to risking their company's name and reputation.

Target Market Forecast

Potential Customers	Growth	2000	2001	2002	2003	2004	CAGR
US high tech	10%	5,000	5,500	6,050	6,655	7,321	10.00%
European high tech	15	1,000	1,150	1,323	1,521	1,749	15.00
Latin America	35	250	338	456	616	832	35.07
Other	2	10,000	10,200	10,404	10,612	10,824	2.00
Total	6.27	16,250	17,188	18,233	19,404	20,726	6.27

Target markets

- US high tech
- European high tech
- Latin America
- Other

2.1.1 Market Demographics

Large manufacturer corporations: Our most important market segment is a large manufacturer of high-technology products, such as Apple, Hewlett-Packard, IBM, Microsoft, Siemens, or Olivetti. These companies will be calling on Acme for development functions that are better spun off than managed in-house, for market research, and for market forums.

Medium-sized growth companies: Particularly in software, multimedia, and some related high-growth fields, Acme will offer an attractive development alternative to the company that is management constrained and unable to address opportunities in new markets and new market segments.

2.1.2 Market Needs

When a company, like those that are our clients, wants to open a new market, there is a temporary need for very high-powered expertise. They need to establish distribution, evaluate distributors' merits and problems, and select and open new channels.

Our clients come to us for scalable, temporary expertise. They understand that our kind of expertise would be very difficult and expensive to get from full-time, permanent employees. Furthermore, their needs are temporary: The crunch is at the time of opening the new market and setting up the channel; later on it is not as important.

From their point of view as managers, our clients come to us at least in part because we reduce their sense of risk in the management and politics of new market introductions. If things go wrong, they have experts to blame. If things go right, they get the credit. There's the old saying that "nobody ever got fired for choosing IBM," meaning choosing a highly respected visible source for computers. We are that kind of low-risk option for opening new markets.

2.1.3 Market Trends

We stand to benefit from some specific market trends:

- *There is a major trend towards internationalization.* The Internet has brought a larger world into direct communication with manufacturers. Europe has created a major new unified market, this time for real. Latin America is healthy and growing. Asia, despite recent setbacks, is still a very good market. Our potential client base, the manufacturers, wants to expand into new markets.

- *Communications technology is a new industry explosion.* Also because of the Internet, growth in communications technology items is explosive. Modems, network cards, communications software, routers, cables, connectors, all of these are growing at 35 percent per year and up. Margins aren't great in the more standard hardware categories, but growth is enormous.

- *Contracting, consulting, and ad-hoc management teams are a trend.* Even the larger businesses are turning more frequently to temporary expertise instead of permanent fixed cost employees. This is the latest new application of the buzz-word "scalable." Acme Consulting is an especially attractive alternative to our clients, because of the economic advantages of variable vs. fixed costs, and the growing liabilities and overhead of taking on long-term employees.

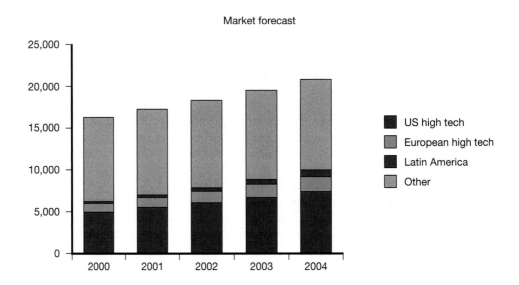

Market forecast

2.1.4 Market Growth

The U.S. Association of Marketing Consultants reports a 30 percent growth in average revenues for consultants focusing on marketing of high-tech products. We are a subset of this market, possibly due for even higher growth than the mainstream. The local electronics industry association in California reports a trend towards additional consulting solutions, as manufacturers turn to variable cost solutions.

We talked to industry associations in Japan and several in Europe. Overall, the growth in interest for moving into new markets is phenomenal. Tahahashi Sato, director of the local association in Tokyo, told us "we don't have statistics, but the growth in new international marketing projects has to be greater than 100 percent per year." Jens Lundeson, of the Association in Europe, said "We see growth in this kind of project at 40 percent or better per year."

Part 2.2 SWOT Analysis

The SWOT analysis covers strengths, weaknesses, opportunities, and threats. Strengths and weaknesses are generally internal attributes, which we can address by changing our business. Opportunities and threats are generally external.

Overall, the mix is exciting. We live in an age of growth, change, and business revolution. The Internet offers us opportunities and threats. We need to make our dealing with it one of our biggest strengths, to minimize our weaknesses.

2.2.1 Strengths

1. *True expertise.* All of our principals know this area very well. Our experience and expertise is better than anybody we know of in this particular niche area.

2. *Dominance of communications technologies from a user's point of view.* We have an excellent Web site, secure File Transfer Protocol (FTP) facilities with password protection for sending and receiving documents from clients, major bandwidth, and an automatic link to training allies to help clients come up to speed with the facilities we offer. We can even hold Internet meetings with shared interface and visuals.

3. *Manageable size.* We don't have to support a large overhead, and our clients know that we deliver what we promise ourselves. Our competition, the larger consulting houses, tend to build on the structure of the major partners doing the selling, and younger associates with far less experience actually delivering the consulting.

4. *Contacts.* Years of industry experience mean a lot of word-of-mouth marketing, contacts, and networking.

2.2.2 Weaknesses

1. *Marketing.* As a group, we are good at the direct sales involved in making a close, but we don't have the resources required to do much general marketing. We will depend on word of mouth first as our main form of generating leads.

2. *Staff.* Without the overhead of staff, we can't leverage on people to develop documents and presentations, research in detail, and fill in the blanks. We are short on support for telephones, fax, and e-mail.

3. *Brand.* Sometimes a Booz Allen or McKinsey is a safer buy for the executives, in the sense of "nobody ever got fired for hiring IBM." We are a new entity, we can be perceived as an innovative—and therefore risky—choice.

2.2.3 Opportunities

1. *Internet growth.* Companies are being dragged into worldwide marketing, like it or not. Growth rates are very high, opportunities are obvious.

2. *International market growth.* Europe and Latin America are booming. Asia has suffered a bit but is recovering. Manufacturers are anxious to take their new technologies across borders.

3. *Growing red tape involved with hiring full-time employees, especially internationally, and especially at the executive level.*

2.2.4 Threats

1. *The Internet is a threat as well as an opportunity.* Our expertise is about crossing borders, managing multiple markets, and the problems we solve are being reduced in importance by the growing availability of information. Specific example: software companies used to charge huge premiums for software available in the different smaller markets, but their potential customers are now much more likely to see available prices elsewhere and buy over the Internet.

2. *The larger, branded competition is recognizing our niche.* They are beginning to compete in our area, recognize our niche. We are no longer alone.

3. *New competitors are developing in new markets.* Particularly as the European market grows, competitors developing in that area become more significant.

Part 2.3 Competition

The key element in purchase decisions made at the Acme client level is trust in the professional reputation and reliability of the consulting firm.

THE COMPETITION COMES IN SEVERAL FORMS:

1. The most significant competition is no consulting at all, companies choosing to do business development, channel development, and market research in-house. Their own managers do this on their own, as part of their regular business functions. Our key advantage in competition with in-house development is that managers are already overloaded with responsibilities; they don't have time for additional responsibilities in new market development or new channel development. Also, Acme can approach alliances, vendors, and channels on a confidential basis, gathering information and making initial contacts in ways that the corporate managers can't.

2. The high-level prestige management consulting firms are: XXXXX, XXXXXXXXXXXX, XXXXX-XXXXX, (names omitted to protect confidentiality), etc. These are essentially generalists who take their name-brand management consulting into specialty areas. Their other very important weakness is the management structure that has the partners selling new jobs, and inexperienced associates delivering the work. We compete against them as experts in our specific fields, and with the guarantee that our clients will have the top-level people doing the actual work.

3. The third general kind of competitor is the international market research company: XXXXXXXXX, XXXXXX, XXXX-XXXXX, (names omitted to protect confidentiality), etc. These companies are formidable competitors for published market research and market forums but cannot provide the kind of high-level consulting that Acme will provide.

4. The fourth kind of competition is the market-specific smaller house. For example: Nomura Research in Japan and Select S.A. de C.V. in Mexico (now affiliated with IDC).

5. Sales representation, brokering, and deal catalysts are an ad-hoc business form that will be defined in detail by the specific nature of each individual case.

Part 2.4 Services

Acme offers expertise in channel distribution, channel development, and market development, sold and packaged in various ways that allow clients to choose their preferred relationship: these include retainer consulting relationships, project-based consulting, relationship and alliance brokering, sales representation and market representation, project-based market research, published market research, and information forum events.

1. *Retainer consulting.* We represent a client company as an extension of its business development and market development functions. This begins with complete understanding of the client company's situation, objectives, and constraints. We then represent the client company quietly and confidentially, sifting through new market developments and new opportunities as is appropriate to the client, and representing the client in initial talks with possible allies, vendors, and channels.

2. *Project consulting.* Proposed and billed on a per-project and per-milestone basis, project consulting offers a client company a way to harness our specific qualities and use our expertise to solve specific problems, develop and/or implement plans, and develop specific information.

3. *Market research.* Group studies are available to selected clients at $5,000 per unit. A group study is a packaged and published complete study of a specific market, channel, or topic. Examples might be studies of developing consumer channels in Japan or Mexico, or implications of changing margins in software.

2.5 Keys to Success

1. Excellence in fulfilling the promise—completely confidential, reliable, and trustworthy expertise and information.

2. Developing visibility to generate new business leads.

3. Leveraging from a single pool of expertise into multiple revenue generation opportunities: retainer consulting, project consulting, market research, and market research published reports.

2.6 Critical Issues

The most critical issue is repeat business. We can't build this company on a faulty foundation; we have to have a core group of satisfied clients who come back to us on a regular basis. We can't afford to spend the capital it would take to generate new clients constantly. The repeat business costs about a tenth as much in sales and marketing as the new client.

Repeat business is built on the correct strategic mix of excellence in delivery, clear communication of promise and scope, and follow-through.

Most of our competitors build on a structure that has the partners selling the jobs and new hires, bright young people without a lot of experience, delivering. We can't afford to follow that lead. We can use a staff to leverage some of the footwork and analysis work, but ultimately our work must be our own.

2.7 Historical Results

To analyze our historical data, we've made a projection based on what might have been, had the partners been involved in a separate company. It is a composite of the combined consulting of the three main partners.

What we see in the table is that we're taking up a very small portion of the overall consulting dollar spent in this market. There is a lot of room to grow. We have always been profitable, but we expect to do much better than we have after we combine our forces.

Historical Data

Variable	1997	1998	1999
Industry revenue	$10,000,000.00	$15,000,000.00	$20,000,000.00
Company market share	0%	0%	0%
Company revenue	$10,000	$37,500	$84,000
Industry variable costs	$2,500,000.00	$3,750,000.00	$5,000,000.00
Company variable costs	$2,500.00	$9,375.00	$21,000.00
Industry gross contribution margin	$7,500,000.00	$11,250,000.00	$15,000,000.00
Company gross contribution margin	$7,500.00	$28,125.00	$63,000.00
Marketing expenses	$1,750.00	$3,500.00	$5,750.00
Company net contribution margin	$5,750.00	$24,625.00	$57,250.00

2.8 Macroenvironment

New technology has become the driving force of our market. The Internet is changing high-tech marketing overnight. While the manufacturers used to deal with distributors in smaller national markets, nowadays the distributors are terribly concerned about our pricing and marketing over the Internet.

On one hand, the manufacturers need loyal local allies, good distribution, and value added. On the other hand, they can't pretend to offer protected markets. The Internet changes the game.

Another major factor is the growth expected in Europe and Latin America. While Asian markets are hanging back a bit with the lingering effect of recent economic problems, the Latin American markets are growing smartly as a result of decreasing protectionism, and the European markets are enjoying the new Eurodollar boom.

3.0 Marketing Strategy

Strategy is focus. Our strategy involves focusing on a specific area of expertise in which we are as strong a group as in any company anywhere in the world. We are true experts in the introduction of new technology products, especially through channels of distribution.

Acme will focus on three geographical markets: the United States, Europe, and Latin America, and in limited product segments: personal computers, software, networks, telecommunications, personal organizers, and technology integration products.

The target customer is usually a manager in a larger corporation, and occasionally an owner or president of a medium-sized corporation in a high-growth period.

3.1 Mission

Acme Consulting offers high-tech manufacturers a reliable, high-quality alternative to in-house resources for business development, market development, and channel development on an international scale. A true alternative to in-house resources, we offer a very high level of practical experience, know-how, contacts, and confidentiality. Clients must know that working with Acme is a more professional, less risky way to develop new areas even than working completely in-house with their own people. Acme must also be able to maintain financial balance, charging a high value for its services, and delivering an even higher value to its clients. We focus on development in the European and Latin American markets, or for European clients in the United States market.

3.2 Marketing Objectives

1. *We need to establish ourselves as experts.* This means being quoted in major trade press, speaking at industry events, and gaining recognition. Our measurable and specific objective is to be introduced in three major events as established experts in the field of international market entry.

2. *We need brand-name reference clients.* By the end of this year, we need three major brand names we can cite as clients. We need to be able to reference by name and contact phone number.

3. *We need at least one client in each of three main regions.* United States and Europe for sure, and also either Latin America or Asia. We can't be who we claim to be without being truly multicontinental.

3.3 Financial Objectives

1. Sales of $350,000 in 1995 and $1 million by 1997.
2. Gross margin higher than 80 percent.
3. Net income more than 10 percent of sales by the third year.

3.4 Target Markets

As indicated by the previous Table 2.1, Target Market Forecast, we must focus on a few thousand well-chosen potential customers in the United States, Europe, and Latin America. These few thousand high-tech manufacturing companies are the key customers for Acme.

3.5 Positioning

For high-technology companies who are looking to enter new international markets, Acme Consulting offers a unique team of experienced managers with proven expertise, on a temporary contract basis. Unlike in-house expertise, Acme Consulting is a temporary variable cost. Unlike most management consultants, Acme Consulting is specialized on a very focused expertise that is hard to duplicate.

3.6 Services Offered

The service itself is a key component to our marketing mix. Our service should be our best advertisement. In this case even more so than with many other similar businesses, because our specialization on channels for international product marketing means we develop contacts with people who can be our recommenders.

We need to fulfill the promise we make: we take a product across national boundaries into new markets, explore channels, guide our client through the maze, and establish the relationships the client needs. This is a very focused deliverable. We aren't just doing international marketing or marketing consulting; we're getting products into channels.

The service itself is a key to our markets.

3.6.1 Price

We need to make sure that our services are adequately priced. Our positioning, as well as our finances, demands high pricing. When a job is exactly our expertise, we should expect to price high.

Ultimately, our client will end up spending less on us than on the branded major consultants, because they will wrap the consulting around a lot of additional research and their standard packaging that doubles or triples cost. We'll focus in on the exact target and charge more per day and less for the total job.

We should expect to be much more expensive than the second-tier generalists.

3.6.2 Promotion

For promotion, we follow the mainstream thinking about high-end consulting. There are three main components of promotion:

1. Getting recognized and quoted as experts. Our public relations expense is intended to position us as the experts the business press calls on for information on international channel marketing. We need to be quoted in *Business Week, Fortune,* and *The Wall Street Journal,* as well as *Wired, Red Herring, Upside,* and the like. Along the same lines, we need to get the speaking engagements at the major trade shows and events.
2. Word of mouth and reference sites. This goes back to our core value, the importance of fulfilling the promise.
3. The Internet. We need to dominate the Internet, search terms, placement in searchers, etc.

3.6.3 Service

Service in this topic refers to our client service—not what we sell as a service company, but the service we deliver as an add-on to the basic service we sell. Confusing? Perhaps, but let's look at client service for a consulting service:

1. First, service begins with how we communicate with the client, during and after the consulting job. This is where most of our competitors fall down. Far too often the consultants disappear from the client in what feels like hiding while doing the work. We're going to use the Web site in password-protected draft

mode so that our clients are always in touch with us. They can log into the Web site and see our drafts. We'll give them real service, instead of just sales.

2. We also need to give much better service to clients after the job: better accessibility to our work once done. Studies should be available to management: contacts, recommended channels, information that they own and they can use, when they need it, and when they want it.

3.7 Marketing Research

We need to cover two main elements of market research:

1. *Manufacturers*. We need to know the market of manufacturers in all three target continents, including market trends and developments related to manufacturers of personal computers, peripherals, connectivity and Internet, and software.

2. *Channel marketing*. We need to know the trends in channel competition, emergence of new channels, economics, major competitors, new technologies, and major players in all three continents.

At this stage of our development, our research is mainly secondary research generated by keeping up with the media, including trade press and the Internet. We should quickly establish a strong filing system so that we can use the information that appears in secondary sources and catalog and organize it for effective use later on.

4.0 Financials

Our plan calls for sales of nearly $600,000 this year growing to $1.8 million by 2004, on marketing expenses of slightly more than $200,000, which is about 35 percent of sales. By the last year in the plan, our marketing expenses of $480,000 will be only 25 percent of sales.

The plan assumes two important trends:

First, a steady decline in cost of sales and growth in gross margin percentage as we build more of our resources, as full-time personnel and fixed costs instead of contractors and outside consultants. That means that as we grow we take on more risk—if the plan is implemented. Step by step we'll have to watch the growth of sales relationships that imply the advisability of taking on more people as partners and employees, instead of as contractors.

Second, a decline in marketing expenses as a percent of sales. The 35 percent figure we project for the first year is quite high, unacceptably high except that we are building a reputation and marketing without the leverage of past marketing, starting from zero. By the fifth year of the plan, we should be spending 25 percent of sales on marketing. This is a better figure.

4.1 Break-even Analysis

For consultants, we have an unusually high variable cost of 30 percent of sales. This makes sense for us at this point, because turning to experts on a per-job basis, as long as these are the people we know and trust, reduces the risk of fixed costs.

This break-even is a reflection of our first year, in which we are building our fulfillment based on variable-cost people instead of fixed-cost people. The risk profile should look very different by the last year.

Break-even Analysis:

Monthly units break-even	21,429
Monthly sales break-even	$21,429

Assumptions:

Average per-unit revenue	$1.00
Average per-unit variable cost	$0.30
Estimated monthly fixed cost	$15,000

Break-even analysis

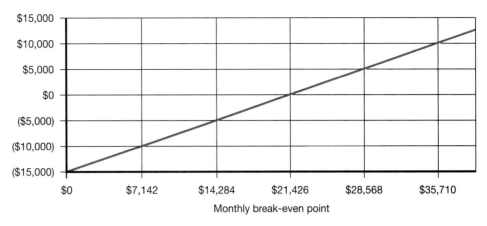

Break-even point = where line intersects with 0

4.2 Sales Forecast

Our sales for this start-up period grow from $10,000 per month at the beginning—retainer business from our founding partner, with existing clients—to $90,000 next fall. The sales forecast is aggressive, assuming financing for our marketing expense and bringing on partners and staff as planned.

We intend to continue to increase billings throughout the forecast period, reaching annual totals increasing from less than $600,000 in the first year to $1.825 million in the fifth.

Sales Forecast

Sales	2000	2001	2002	2003	2004
Retainer consulting	$200,000	$350,000	$ 425,000	$ 500,000	$ 550,000
Project consulting	270,000	325,000	350,000	400,000	450,000
Market research	122,000	150,000	200,000	250,000	300,000
Strategic reports	0	50,000	125,000	250,000	375,000
Other	0	25,000	50,000	100,000	150,000
Total sales	592,000	900,000	1,150,000	1,500,000	1,825,000

Direct Cost of Sales	2000	2001	2002	2003	2004
Retainer consulting	$ 30,000	$ 20,000	$ 15,000	$ 10,000	$ 10,000
Project consulting	45,000	20,000	15,000	10,000	10,000
Market research	84,000	86,000	88,000	90,000	92,000
Strategic reports	0	20,000	25,000	32,500	40,000
Other	0	10,000	10,000	10,000	10,000
Subtotal cost of sales	159,000	156,000	153,000	152,500	162,000

Monthly sales forecast

Notes

1. Subhash C. Jain, *Marketing Planning Strategy,* 4th ed. (Cincinnati, OH: South-Western Publishing Company, 1993), p. 5.

2. William A. Cohen, *The Marketing Plan* (New York, NY: John Wiley and Sons, 1995), p. 2.

3. The marketing plan outline included in this appendix is available from Marketing Plan Pro: Palo Alto Software (http://www.mplans.com/spm/ or http://www.paloalto.com).

Appendix B

Applications of Mathematical and Financial Tools to Marketing Decisions

Marketing decisions are often enhanced by the use of mathematical and financial analyses. These computations are helpful in setting prices, evaluating financial aspects of the firm, evaluating suppliers, determining inventory order quantities, and estimating segment potentials. Analysis of the firm's income statement is crucial for control and performance evaluation. This appendix describes and presents example calculations for some of the most frequently used mathematical and financial tools.

Supplier Selection

Business buyers frequently use weighted indexes to evaluate suppliers. As explained in Chapter 5, buyers base decisions regarding selection of suppliers or vendors on the criteria they consider most important. Exhibit B–1 shows a simplified weighted index approach for evaluating two suppliers, A and B. This example is from the experiences of General Electric and its purchases of electrical wiring devices.

In this example, five criteria are used to evaluate two suppliers: quality performance, delivery performance, technical capability, quoted price, and service factors. Price and delivery performance are weighted most heavily. These weights reflect a consensus of managerial judgment and past experiences with purchases of this type of product. Each supplier is evaluated on a 1-to-10 scale for each attribute, with 10 being the best possible rating. The scores are multiplied by an importance weight

Exhibit B–1	Simplified weighted decision matrix				
		Supplier A		**Supplier B**	
Evaluation Criteria	**Importance Weight**	**Score**	**Total**	**Score**	**Total**
Quality performance	16%	9.6	154	9.3	149
Delivery performance	22	8.1	178	7.6	167
Technical capability	8	10.0	80	8.0	64
Quoted price	44	7.5	330	9.3	409
Service factors	10	6.4	64	8.8	88
Overall total	**100%**	—	**806**	—	**877**

for each criterion. The "total" columns are summed to produce a score for each supplier. In this case, supplier B, with an overall total score of 877, is selected as the preferred vendor.

Estimating Segment Potentials

The "Survey of Buying Power" published annually by *Sales & Marketing Management* magazine, enables the computation of the *buying power index (BPI)* for individual geographic market segments. Frequently used to evaluate market segment potentials, the BPI is a measure of a particular market's ability to buy. The index converts three basic elements—population, effective buying income (EBI), and retail sales—into a measure of a market's ability to purchase, expressed as a percentage of the total U.S. potential. The three elements are weighted as follows: 0.2, population; 0.3, U.S. retail sales potential; and 0.5, EBI, or effective buying income. The latter weight reflects the importance of income to buying potential. The BPI for a market can be computed as:

$$BPI = (0.5)(EBI) + (0.3) \text{ (Retail sales \%)} + (0.2) \text{ (Population \%)}$$

The computations in Exhibit B–2 provide an example. Specifically, a skiing equipment company in West Virginia is considering expanding its sales operations into one of two neighboring states, Pennsylvania or Kentucky. The company offers premier equipment that it sells at premium prices. Their equipment is targeted toward young adults, aged 25 to 45 years old, with an EBI of at least $35,000.

The figures in Exhibit B–2 suggest that Pennsylvania offers the greatest potential as a market. However, other factors, such as the cost of living, competition, and the legal environment, may differ between these two states as well. Consequently, BPI comparisons should be used in conjunction with other information.

Exhibit B–2	*Evaluating geographic target segments*		
	Pennsylvania	**Kentucky**	**United States**
Households aged 25–45	1,805,780	590,118	41,231,931
Households EBI > $35,000	2,046,065	483,254	42,555,244
General merchandise stores' sales ($000)	$9,230,884	$3,448,368	$182,310,557

To construct a customized BPI for evaluating each state, the company made the following calculations:

Step 1. The ratio of each state's markets to those of the entire United States are:

Pennsylvania	**Kentucky**
% of households aged 25–45:	% of households aged 25–45:
1,805,780/41,231,931 = .043	590,118/41,231,931 = .014
% of households EBI > $35,000:	% of households EBI > $35,000:
2,046,065/42,555,244 = .048	483,254/42,555,244 = .011
% of general merchandise stores' sales:	% of general merchandise stores' sales:
$9,230,884/$182,310,557 = .051	$3,448,368/$182,310,557 = .019

Step 2. The company assigns importance weights as follows:

Households aged 25–45	(20%) or .20
Households EBI > $35,000	(50%) or .50
General merchandise stores' sales	(30%) or .30

Note: These weights sum to 1.0.

Step 3. The BPI is the weighted sum of the three components:

Pennsylvania

$(.20 \times .043) + (.50 \times .048) + (.30 \times .051) = .0479$

Kentucky

$(.20 \times .014) + (.50 \times .011) + (.30 \times .019) = .0140$

Price Determination

In this section of the appendix, we discuss the break-even formula, elasticities of demand, and methods for computing retail markups. First, we present break-even formulas for quantity (units) and revenue (dollars). Second, we look at examples of other forms of elasticity and discuss profit maximization. Third, we explain markups and markdowns.

Break-Even Analysis

The traditional break-even formula is based on the premise that the break-even point in units occurs when total revenues equal total costs. The break-even quantity in units is defined as:

$$Q(BE) = \frac{\text{Fixed costs}}{\text{Price} - \text{Variable cost per unit}}$$

The break-even point in dollars is computed as:

$$Q(BE\$) = \frac{\text{Fixed costs}}{1 - (\text{Variable cost} / \text{Price})}$$

The *BEP* in units is derived as follows. Remember that the *BEP* occurs where total costs equal total revenues:

$$TR = TC$$
$$P \times Q = FC + (VC \times Q)$$
$$\text{and } TC = FC + (VC \times Q)$$
$$P \times Q - VC \times Q = FC$$
$$Q(P - VC) = FC$$

Therefore, the *BEP* in units is $Q(BEP) = FC/(P - VC)$.

This analysis can be extended by considering the effects of different prices and quantity demanded. For example, the data presented in Exhibit B–3 show how the break-even quantity can vary as prices rise and demand declines. Notice the inverse relationship between price and demand. In this example, total fixed cost is $15,000 and variable cost per unit is $7.

This "sensitivity analysis" allows managers to consider alternative assumptions and conditions. It greatly enhances the managerial usefulness and realism of the break-even approach.

Elasticity

Price elasticity represents the change in quantity demanded from a change in price. Elasticities greater than 1 indicate elastic demand; that is, a 1 percent change in price causes a greater percentage change in demand. Inelastic demand occurs when a 1 percent price change results in less than a 1 percent change in demand. A commonly used computational approach for estimating elasticity is to compute the arc

Exhibit B–3							

Break-even points from different prices and quantities demanded

Price	Quantity Demanded (000s)	Total Revenue ($000)	Total Fixed Costs ($000)	Total Variable Costs ($000)	Total Costs ($000)	Break-Even Quantity (000s)	Profit ($000)
$10	5.0	$50.0	$15.0	$35.0	$50.0	5.00	$ 0.0
11	4.8	52.8	15.0	33.6	48.6	3.75	4.2
12	4.7	56.4	15.0	32.9	47.9	3.00	8.5
13	4.6	59.8	15.0	32.2	47.2	2.50	12.6
14	4.0	56.0	15.0	28.0	43.0	2.14	13.0
15	3.4	51.0	15.0	23.8	38.8	1.87	12.2

elasticity, where the price elasticity of demand is measured over a range using the average price and quantity as the base.

Arc elasticity of demand is computed as follows:

$$E_d = \frac{(Q_2 - Q_1)/[(Q_1 + Q_2)/2]}{(P_2 - P_1)/[(P_1 + P_2)/2]}$$

For example, at the price of $6 per ticket, the average moviegoer demands two tickets per month. At a price of $4 per ticket, the average moviegoer purchases six tickets per month. The price elasticity for this example is:

$$E_d = \frac{(6 - 2)/[(6 + 2)/2]}{(4 - 6)/[(4 + 6)/2]} = -2.5$$

Therefore, the price elasticity of demand over this price range is elastic. Remember that price elasticities are normally negative and that typically the negative sign, while shown here, is omitted.

Cross-price elasticity reflects quantity changes in one good or service caused by changing prices of other goods or services. This concept is useful for examining relationships among complementary goods (printers, personal computers) and substitutes (competitive brands, items in a product line, and pure substitutes such as videotape rental charges and movie prices). Conceptually, cross elasticity can be expressed as:

$$E_c = \frac{\text{Change in quantity demanded for product A}}{\text{Change in price for product B}}$$

If E_c is positive, products A and B are substitutes. If E_c is negative, the two products are complementary.

Assume the price of a Kodak 35-millimeter camera is $145 and a comparable Minolta is $149. Further, assume the quantities demanded for the Kodak and Minolta cameras at these prices are 50,000 and 100,000 units, respectively. When Kodak lowers its price to $142, the demand increases to 60,000. The Minolta demand, however, declines to 95,000 units. The cross-price elasticity for the Minolta camera is:

$$E_c = \frac{-5,000/100,000}{-\$3/\$145} = 2.42$$

In this example, the two cameras are substitutes; hence, decreasing the price of one brand decreases the demand for the other.

Profit Maximization

The traditional economic perspective on price setting is based on the premise that profits are maximized when marginal revenue equals marginal cost. Marginal revenue is the amount obtained from selling one additional unit of a product—this is usually the price paid for the unit. Marginal cost is the cost of producing and selling one additional unit of a product.

The cost and revenue data presented in Exhibit B–4 can be used to analyze these relationships for a hypothetical manufacturer of personalized T-shirts. The corresponding cost and revenue curves are depicted in Exhibit B–5. Note that in columns 4, Marginal Revenue, and 7, Marginal Cost, the manufacturer continues to expand output as long as marginal revenue exceeds marginal cost. Any expansion in output beyond this point would increase costs more than it would revenue. Therefore, the optimal output is four units priced at $6. Profits are maximized at that level:

$$\text{Profits} = TR - TC = \$24 - \$18 = \$6$$

Exhibit B–5 plots these findings. It shows that profits are maximized when price equals $6 and quantity equals 4. Notice that marginal costs initially decline as output increases. The shaded profit area is computed by multiplying unit profit times quantity of output:

$$\begin{aligned} \text{Profits} &= (AR - ATC) \times Q \\ &= (\$6 - \$4.50) \times 4 \\ &= \$6 \end{aligned}$$

Exhibit B-4							
(1)	**(2)**	**(3)**	**(4)**	**(5)**	**(6)**	**(7)**	**(8)**
			Marginal Revenue	**Total Cost**	**Average Total Cost**	**Marginal Cost**	**Profit**
Quantity **Q**	**Price** **P**	**Total Revenue** **TR = Q × P**	**MR**	**TC**	**ATC** $= \dfrac{TC}{Q}$	**MC**	$\pi =$ **TR − TC**
0	$10	$ 0		$ 2.00	—		$ −2.00
1	9	9	$ 9	9.00	$9.00	$ 7.00	0.00
2	8	16	7	14.00	7.00	5.00	2.00
3	7	21	5	15.00	5.00	1.00	6.00
4	6	24	3	18.00	4.50	3.00	6.00
5	5	25	1	22.50	4.50	4.50	2.50
6	4	24	−1	30.00	5.00	7.50	−6.00
7	3	21	−3	49.00	7.00	19.00	−28.00

Sales and cost information for personalized T-shirts

Exhibit B-5	

Intersection of marginal cost and marginal revenue curves

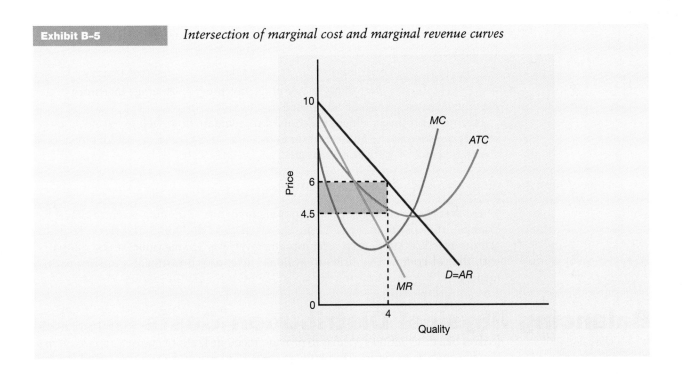

In this case, unit profit is the difference between average revenue and average total cost.

Markups and Markdowns

Retail markups can be computed on either cost or the selling price. Markup as a percentage of cost is calculated as:

$$\text{Markup} = \frac{\text{Selling price} - \text{Cost}}{\text{Cost}}$$

Assume, for example, that a new Wilson tennis racket costs a retailer $90 and the markup is $50. Therefore, the selling price is $140. The markups on cost and price are:

$$\text{Markup on cost} = \$50/\$90 = 56\%$$
$$\text{Markup on price} = \$50/\$140 = 36\%$$

Frequently, retailers desire to convert markup percentages on cost to markup percentages on price and vice versa. The computational procedures for making these conversions are:

$$\text{Markup on cost} = \frac{\text{Markup on selling price}}{100\% - \text{Markup on selling price}}$$

$$\text{Markup on price} = \frac{\text{Markup on cost}}{100\% + \text{Markup on cost}}$$

Price reductions are common practice in retailing. In these instances, the retailer may wish to know what the percentage markdown is:

$$\text{Markdown on initial selling price} = \frac{\text{Initial selling price} - \text{Reduced sale price}}{\text{Initial selling price}}$$

$$\text{Markdown on reduced sale price} = \frac{\text{Initial selling price} - \text{Reduced sale price}}{\text{Reduced sale price}}$$

Return on Inventory Investment

Retailers evaluate merchandising performance of departments using the *gross margin return on inventory investments (GMROI)*. The GMROI combines the effects of both profits and turnover. Since both are considered, the GMROI enables comparison between retail store areas that differ in turnover and gross margin. It is computed as:

$$GMROI = \frac{\text{Gross margin}}{\text{Net sales}} \times \frac{\text{Net sales}}{\text{Average inventory}} = \frac{\text{Gross margin}}{\text{Average inventory}}$$

Average inventory is usually expressed in terms of costs.

Inventory turnover, which is also used to evaluate how well investments in inventory are used, is the number of times inventory turns over or is sold, typically in a year. Inventory turnover is computed as:

$$\text{Inventory turnover} = \frac{\text{Costs of goods sold}}{\text{Average inventory cost}}$$

where average inventory equals (Beginning inventory + Ending inventory)/2. If for example, the cost of goods sold during a year was $600,000 and the average inventory was $200,000, then inventory turnover was 3. This value can be compared with that of competitive firms to evaluate inventory investment and firm performance.

Balancing Physical Distribution Costs

One of the objectives of a distribution system is to provide adequate levels of customer service at reasonable costs. Companies would like to carry high inventories so they can fill orders promptly and maintain high service levels. As inventories increase, however, costs to the firm rise as well. These relationships are depicted graphically in Exhibit B–6.

As Exhibit B–6 shows, total costs represent the sum of two offsetting costs. Order-processing costs, which decline as average inventory increases, include setup costs, manufacturing costs, and administrative costs. Inventory-carrying costs increase as average inventory increases. Carrying costs include storage, insurance, investment, and obsolescence costs. The *economic order quantity (EOQ)* model offers one approach for determining inventory order quantities that balance these costs. Specifically, the EOQ model can be derived from the total cost relationships presented in Exhibit B–6 as follows:

$$\text{Total costs} = \text{Carrying costs} + \text{Ordering costs} = \frac{QCI}{2} + \frac{RS}{Q}$$

where

Q = order quantity,
C = unit cost,
I = opportunity cost (%),
R = annual demand, and
S = ordering, setup cost.

Exhibit B–6   *Determining optimal order quantity*

Note that $(Q/2)$ is the average inventory and (R/S) is the number of orders required per year. The objective is to select the quantity that minimizes the total cost curve (see Exhibit B–6). Therefore, using basic calculus, the above equation can be differentiated with respect to Q:

$$TC'(Q) = \frac{CI}{2} + (-1)\frac{RS}{Q^2} = 0$$

By setting the above to zero and solving for Q, the EOQ model is derived:

$$EOQ = \sqrt{\frac{2RS}{CI}}$$

The model assumes that the pattern of demand is constant, that the lead time from order to delivery is constant, that all the order is received in a batch, and that stockouts do not occur. This approach can easily be modified to include the maintenance of safety stocks to further enhance service levels.

As an example, assume a manager wishes to determine the economic order quantity for a product that costs $3 and has annual sales of 600 units. The ordering cost is $80, and the opportunity cost of capital is 20 percent.

$$EOQ = \sqrt{\frac{2(600)(\$80)}{(\$3)(.2)}} = 400 \text{ units}$$

Total inventory costs for this product then would be:

$$TC = \frac{400}{2}(3)(.2) + \frac{600}{400}(80) = 120 + 120 = \$240$$

Income Statement and Performance Ratios   The

income statement summarizes the firm's revenues and expenses over an accounting period, usually 12 months beginning either July 1 or January 1. The income statement shown in Exhibit B–7 is for a manufacturer and marketer of aluminum components for compact disc manufacturers. (Income statements can also be developed for specific brands or projects.) Total and net sales are shown at the top of the statement. Net sales ($780,212) are determined by subtracting returns, allowances, and discounts from total sales. Gross profit is the amount remaining after costs of goods sold are subtracted from net sales. Operating income ($106,558) is the amount of funds available after operating expenses have been subtracted from gross profits. Net income is the final amount left after nonoperating items (interest expenses) and corporate income taxes have been paid.

Exhibit B-7	*Income statement for year ended December 31, 2000*		
Sales revenue			$839,490
	Less: Returns & allowances	$ 43,345	
	Discounts	15,933	
	Total		59,278
Net sales			780,212
	Less: Cost of goods sold		416,296
Gross profits on sales (gross margin)			363,916
Operating expenses			
	Salaries	$136,000	
	Rent	19,000	
	Miscellaneous office	2,046	
	Marketing	52,812	
	Depreciation	30,000	
	Insurance	2,320	
	Utilities	4,750	
	Payroll taxes	9,230	
	Bad debts	1,200	
	Total operating expenses		257,358
Operating income			106,558
Nonoperating items			
	Interest expense	$9,600	
	Purchase discounts lost	534	
	Total nonoperating items		10,134
Net income before corporate income taxes			96,424
	Less: Corporate income taxes		48,212
NET INCOME			$48,212
Net income per weighted share of common stock outstanding			5.3487

This statement is useful in evaluating the performance of the firm. From the income statement, a number of frequently used ratios can be determined. Performance ratios based on the income statement include gross margin ratio, net income ratio, cost-of-goods-sold ratio, operating expense ratio, sales efficiency ratio, and return on investment (ROI).

$$\text{Gross margin ratio} = \frac{\text{Gross margin}}{\text{Net sales}} = \frac{\$363,916}{\$780,212} = 47\%$$

This ratio represents the percentage of sales revenue available to cover operating expenses and profit objectives.

$$\text{Net income ratio} = \frac{\text{Net income}}{\text{Net sales}} = \frac{\$48,212}{\$780,212} = 6\%$$

The net income ratio reflects the percentage of each sales dollar that is profit before corporate income taxes.

$$\text{Cost-of-goods-sold ratio} = \frac{\text{COGS}}{\text{Net sales}} = \frac{\$416,296}{\$780,212} = 53\%$$

This ratio reflects the percentage of sales used to manufacture goods sold. If it is high, costs are either excessive or prices may be too low.

$$\text{Operating expense ratio} = \frac{\text{Total expenses}}{\text{Net sales}} = \frac{\$257,358}{\$780,212} = 33\%$$

This ratio reflects the company's operating efficiency and represents the percentage of each dollar needed to cover expenses.

$$\text{Sales efficiency ratio} = \frac{\text{Net sales}}{\text{Gross sales}} = \frac{\$780,212}{\$839,490} = 93\%$$

This ratio reflects adjustments to gross sales from returns, allowances, and discounts.

$$\text{Return on investment (ROI)} = \frac{\text{Net profit before taxes}}{\text{Total investment}}$$

Information regarding total investment from the firm's balance sheet is required to compute ROI. ROI figures can be compared with industry averages and opportunity costs of investing elsewhere to evaluate the firm's performance.

Glossary

ABILITY the consumer's knowledge about the product category sufficient to understand the advertised message

ACCEPTABLE PRICE RANGE the range of prices buyers are willing to pay for a product; prices above the range may be judged unfair, while prices below the range may generate concerns about quality

ACCESSIBILITY the degree to which a firm can reach intended target segments efficiently with its products and communications

ADAPTIVE SELLING a salesperson's adjustment of his or her behavior between and during sales calls to respond appropriately to the situation and address issues important to the customer

ADMINISTERED CHANNEL SYSTEM system designed to control a line or classification of merchandise; channel members agree on a comprehensive plan but no channel member owns another member

ADOPTION PROCESS the steps consumers follow in deciding whether to use a new product

ADVERTISING the element of the marketing communications mix that is nonpersonal, paid for by an identified sponsor, and disseminated through mass channels of communication to promote the adoption of goods, services, persons, or ideas

ADVERTISING AGENCY a company that develops advertising messages and provides media planning and scheduling for marketers

ADVERTISING ALLOWANCE money paid a reseller for including the manufacturer's product, along with other products, in the reseller's advertising efforts

ADVERTISING SPECIALTY an item of useful or interesting merchandise given away free and typically carrying an imprinted name or message; for example, a pen, calendar, or coffee mug

ADVERTORIAL a special advertising section with some editorial (nonadvertising) content included in magazines

AFFECT REFERRAL a choice heuristic in which consumers elicit from memory their overall evaluation of products and choose the alternative for which they have the most positive feelings

AIDED RECALL TESTS posttesting in which consumers are given lists of ads and asked which they remembered and read

AIO STATEMENTS survey responses concerning activities, interests, and opinions (AIO), used in psychographic research

ALL-YOU-CAN-AFFORD BUDGETING a method for determining the marketing communications budget that involves spending whatever's left over after other costs without considering the firm's objectives

AMERICANS WITH DISABILITIES ACT (ADA) a U.S. law passed in 1990 to prohibit discrimination against consumers with disabilities

ANCHOR POSITION retail stores, often department stores, that are strategically placed in malls, shopping centers, or downtown shopping areas to attract customers and stimulate traffic flow throughout the shopping area

ARBITRAGING see diverting

ATMOSPHERICS a retailer's combination of architecture, layout, color scheme, sound and temperature monitoring, special events, prices, displays, and other factors that attract and stimulate customers

ATTENTION the consumer's mental notice directed at a marketing communication (such as an ad), often stimulated by its physical characteristics; the second step in the information-processing model

ATTITUDES learned predispositions to respond favorably or unfavorably to a product or brand; based on beliefs about its attributes (price, service level, quality)

AUCTION HOUSE a company that sells merchandise at a given time and place to the highest bidder

AUTHENTICATION a way to verify the identity of users and hardware in order to secure Web sites

AUTOMATIC NUMBER IDENTIFICATION a system that identifies incoming phone numbers of respondents to an ad or promotion at the beginning of the call without the caller's knowledge

B2B EXCHANGES electronic marketplace exchanges

BACKWARD INTEGRATION a corporate marketing channel system in which the channel member owns one or more of its suppliers upstream (as opposed to forward integration, where it owns buyers downstream)

BAIT AND SWITCH advertising a product at an attractively low price to get customers into the store but not making it available, so customers must trade up to a more expensive version

BALANCED MATRIX ORGANIZATION an approach to new-product development in which a project manager oversees the project and shares responsibility and authority with functional managers

BANNER ADVERTISING ads on a Web site that are "clickable" should a viewer want more information about the product or service being advertised

BAR CODING a computer-coded bar pattern that identifies a product; see also **Universal Product Code**

BASES OF SEGMENTATION the distinguishing characteristics of market segments (such as demographics, benefits sought) within a firm's overall product or service market

BASIC PRICE MIX the basic components that define the size and means of payment exchanged for goods and services; less comprehensive than the price promotion mix

BATTLE OF THE BRANDS intense competition between manufacturer and distributor brands

BEHAVIOR-BASED PERSPECTIVE a way of evaluating salesperson performance that defines the sales behaviors expected, such as how many calls to make or which presentation tactics to use; see also **outcome-based perspective**

BENEFIT what a product feature can do for a particular customer; for example, a speakerphone built into a fax machine is a feature, but the fact that it allows hands-free conversation is a benefit

BENEFIT SEGMENTATION segmenting the market by the attributes or benefits consumers need or desire, such as quality, service, or unique features

BEST-VALUE STRATEGY purchasing the lowest-cost brand available with the desired level of quality

BIDS in government markets, written proposals from qualified suppliers in response to published governmental requirements or specifications

BRAND a name, term, sign, symbol, design, or combination that a firm uses to identify its products and differentiate them from those of competitors

BRAND AWARENESS when target consumers know about a brand and it comes to mind when thinking about the product category; for example, Kleenex comes to mind when thinking about tissues

BRAND COMPETITORS direct competitors that offer the same types of products (for example, Domino's Pizza and Pizza Hut)

BRAND EQUITY the value a brand has in the marketplace due to reputation and goodwill

BRAND EXPERIENCE consumer experience as a result of the received benefits offered by a brand promise

BRAND IDENTITY the brand concept from the brand owner's viewpoint; the specific aspects of the brand that the marketer wants to communicate to consumers

BRAND IMAGE consumers' impression about a brand

BRAND LOYALTY when consumers purchase a specific brand all or most of the time

BRAND MARK the element of a brand that cannot be vocalized (for example, the MGM lion or the Texaco star)

BRAND NAME the element of a brand that can be vocalized (for example, IBM, Tide, Coke)

BRAND PROMISE represents the benefits customers should expect from puchasing and using a brand

BRANDING identifying a firm's products to distinguish them from competitors' similar products

BREAK-EVEN ANALYSIS calculation of the number of units that must be sold at a certain price for the firm to cover costs (break even); revenues earned past the break-even point contribute to profits

BROADBAND INTERNET TECHNOLOGY a superfast connection to the Web via cable modem, digital subscriber lines, or satellites

BROKER an intermediary that brings buyers and sellers together and is paid a commission by whichever party it represents in a given transaction

BUILDING ON-LINE COMMUNITIES a step beyond personalization where customers who share interests can interact with other like-minded customers on a Web site

BUNDLING marketing two or more products in a single package at one price (for example, computer systems or ski weekends)

BUSINESS ANALYSIS the stage of new-product development where initial marketing plans are prepared, including a tentative marketing strategy and estimates of sales, costs, and profitability

BUSINESS FIRMS manufacturers of tangible goods and firms that provide services such as health care, entertainment, and transportation

BUSINESS LEVEL the smaller units within a complex organization that are managed as self-contained businesses

BUSINESS NETWORKS strategic alliances among suppliers, distributors, and the marketing firm

BUSINESS PRODUCTS goods and services purchased by a firm for its own use (as opposed to consumer products)

BUSINESS STRATEGIC PLAN a plan for how each business unit in the corporate family intends to compete in the marketplace, given the vision, objectives, and growth strategies of the corporate strategic plan

BUSINESS-TO-BUSINESS ADVERTISING promoting products or services directly to other firms, often through print ads in trade periodicals or direct-mail promotions to targeted potential buyers

BUSINESS-TO-BUSINESS BUYING BEHAVIOR the decision making and other activities of organizations as buyers

BUSINESS-TO-BUSINESS (B2B) E-COMMERCE businesses selling to other businesses or organizations over the Internet

BUSINESS-TO-CONSUMER (B2C) E-COMMERCE businesses selling to consumers over the Internet

BUYING ALLOWANCE payment of a specified amount of money to a reseller for purchasing a certain amount of a product during a particular period

BUYING CENTER business purchasing decision makers made up of people throughout all levels of the organization, not just the purchasing department; the buying center makeup may vary as purchasing decisions change

BUYING LOADER a dealer premium in the form of a gift, such as a free trip, for buying, displaying, and selling a certain amount of a product within a specified time

BUYING POWER INDEX (BPI) a measure of a particular market's relative ability to buy, based on population, effective buying income, and retail sales and expressed as a percentage of the total U.S. potential

CALLER ID INTRUSION see **automatic number identification**

CANNED SALES PRESENTATION a fully scripted presentation that the sales rep memorizes, or even an audiovisual presentation, that is not adaptable to individual customers

CANNIBALIZATION when a new product takes sales away from existing products, which leads merely to a shift in the company's sales instead of a gain

CAPITAL PRODUCTS expensive items that are used in business operations but do not become part of any finished product; examples include physical facilities (office buildings) and accessory equipment (copiers and forklifts)

CASH-AND-CARRY WHOLESALER a limited-function wholesaler that does not extend credit for or deliver the products it sells; its primary customers are small retailers

CATALOG WHOLESALER a limited-function wholesaler that offers a wide range of competitively priced products that customers order by phone or fax

CATEGORY an assortment of items seen by the customer as reasonable substitutes for each other

CATEGORY KILLERS discount retailers that offer a complete assortment and can thus dominate a product category, giving them the clout to negotiate excellent prices from suppliers and be assured of dependable sources of supply

CAUSAL RESEARCH experiments in which researchers manipulate independent variables and observe the dependent variable(s) of interest to identify cause-and-effect relationships

CAUSE-RELATED MARKETING companies aligning themselves with causes, such as drug-abuse prevention and environmental conservation

CELEBRITY ENDORSEMENT the use of a famous spokesperson, say a sports or movie star, to promote a product

CENTRAL BUSINESS DISTRICT a downtown area representing a city's greatest concentration of office buildings and retail stores

CENTS-OFF DEAL an offering of a brand at less than the regular price

CHANNEL CONFLICT conflict between members of a marketing channel, which may stem from poor communication, a power struggle, or incompatible objectives

CHANNEL COOPERATION a cooperative spirit among members of a marketing channel that helps reduce and resolve conflicts

CHANNEL LEADER a marketing channel member with enough power to control others in the channel

CHANNEL OBJECTIVES specific, measurable goals of a marketing channel that are consistent with the firm's

marketing objectives and are often stated in terms of sales volume, profitability, market share, cost, number of wholesale or retail outlets, or geographic expansion

CHANNEL OF DISTRIBUTION see **marketing channel**

CHANNEL POWER ways marketing channel members can gain control to enhance their position, including reward power, legitimate power, expert power, and referent power

CHANNEL STRATEGY an expression of a general action plan and guidelines for allocating resources to achieve the objective of a marketing channel

CHECKOUT DISPENSERS make coupons available to customers in supermarkets. Although they are more expensive than newspaper coupons, they tend to be redeemed at a higher rate

CHILD PROTECTION ACT a U.S. law passed in 1990 to regulate advertising on children's TV programs

CHILD SAFETY ACT a U.S. law passed in 1966 that prohibits the marketing of dangerous products to children

CHILDHOOD CONSUMER SOCIALIZATION the process by which young people acquire skills, knowledge, and attitudes to help them function as consumers in the marketplace

CLASSIFIED ADVERTISING advertising that typically promotes transactions for a single item or service and usually appears in newspapers

CLAYTON ACT a U.S. law passed in 1914 that prohibits anti-competitive activities

CLUSTER SAMPLING a probability sampling technique in which units are organized into similar clusters, such as neighborhoods; clusters are then selected randomly and each house in the selected clusters is included in the sample

COACHING the leadership function of providing guidance and feedback on a regular basis to direct salespeople's activities

CO-BRANDING when two brand names appear on the same product; for example, a VISA card with your university's name

COERCIVE POWER power a member of a marketing channel uses to pressure another member to do something; for example, a manufacturer threatens to

cut off a distributor's credit unless the distributor pays its bills more promptly

COGNITIVE DISSONANCE a consumer's postpurchase doubt about the appropriateness of a purchase decision; caused by an imbalance of information because each alternative has attractive features; most likely to occur when the purchase is important and visible, the perceived risk is high, and the decision involves a long-term commitment

COLLABORATIVE VENTURE an arrangement in which two or more firms share in the rights to market specified products; may take the form of a strategic partnership, strategic alliance, joint venture, or licensing agreement

CO-MARKETING ALLIANCES contractual arrangements between different companies offering complementary products in the marketplace or possessing complementary technology

COMBINATION STRATEGY aiming marketing communications at both resellers and ultimate consumers in a push–pull approach

COMMERCIAL ZAPPING changing the channels during TV commercials

COMMERCIALIZATION the stage of new-product development after the product tests successfully and the firm introduces it on a full-scale basis

COMMISSION MERCHANT a wholesaler that provides a wider range of services than do agents or brokers, often engaging in inventory management, physical distribution, and promotional activities and offering credit and market feedback to the companies it represents

COMMUNICATION the process of establishing shared meaning, exchanging ideas, or passing information between a source and a receiver

COMPARATIVE ADVERTISING advertising that compares a sponsored brand with a competitive brand on at least one product attribute (such as MCI versus AT&T services)

COMPETITIVE ADVANTAGE trying to get consumers to purchase one's products instead of competitors' products, through either lower prices or differentiation

COMPETITIVE ENVIRONMENT all the organizations that attempt to serve the same customers, including both brand competitors and product competitors

COMPETITIVE PARITY BUDGETING a budgeting method for marketing communications based on the percentage allocated by other companies in the industry

COMPETITIVE PRICING STRATEGIES pricing strategies based on a firm's position in relation to its competition; includes penetration pricing, limit pricing, and price signaling

COMPETITIVE STRATEGY-POSITIONING CONTINUUM competitive strategies are described as existing on a continuum anchored by "low cost leadership" on one end and "differentiation" on the other

COMPOSITE OF SALESFORCE ESTIMATES a means of forecasting sales in which sales reps give forecasts for their territories, which can then be combined

CONCENTRATED STRATEGY a strategy in which a firm seeks a large share of one or a few profitable segments of the total market, often concentrating on serving the selected segments innovatively and creatively

CONCEPT DEVELOPMENT the process of shaping and refining the idea for a new product into a complete description

CONCEPT TESTS having the concept for a new product evaluated by potential customers

CONSOLIDATED METROPOLITAN STATISTICAL AREA (CMSA) the largest designation of geographic areas based on census data; the 20 largest market areas in the United States that contain at least two PMSAs

CONSUMER ATTITUDES learned predispositions to respond favorably or unfavorably to a product or brand

CONSUMER BEHAVIOR the mental and emotional processes and the physical activities people engage in when they select, purchase, use, and dispose of products or services to satisfy particular needs and desires

CONSUMER CREDIT PROTECTION ACT a U.S. law passed in 1968 that requires full disclosure of financial charges for loans

CONSUMER DECISION PROCESS a four-step process: (1) recognizing a need or problem, (2) searching for information, (3) evaluating alternative products or brands, and (4) purchasing a product

CONSUMER INFORMATION PROCESSING represents the cognitive processes by which consumers interpret and integrate information from the environment

CONSUMER LEARNING a process that changes consumers' knowledge or behavior patterns through marketing communications or experience

CONSUMER PRODUCT SAFETY COMMISSION (CPSC) an agency of the U.S. government that protects consumers from unsafe products

CONSUMER PRODUCTS goods and services purchased by consumers for their own personal use (as opposed to business products)

CONSUMER PROTECTION LAWS laws that state what firms must do to give consumers the information they need to make sound purchasing decisions or to make sure the products they buy are safe

CONSUMER RIGHTS four inherent rights of consumers: (1) to safety, (2) to be informed, (3) to choose, and (4) to be heard

CONSUMER SALES PROMOTION sales promotion directed at ultimate users of the product or service (as opposed to trade sales promotion)

CONSUMERISM a social movement in which consumers demand better consumer information, quality, service, dependability, and fair prices

CONTENT PROVIDERS companies who send information through the Web

CONTEST a sales promotion that offers prizes based on the skill of contestants

CONTINUAL TRAINING ongoing sales training that helps firms stay current and competitive in an ever-changing environment

CONTRIBUTION MARGIN is the quantity P-VC where P1 unit price and Q (BEP) 5 break-even quantity

CONVENIENCE PRODUCTS consumer may prefer a specific brand but does not want to spend much time shopping for it; will buy another brand if preferred one is not available; normally low-priced, often-purchased goods

CONVENIENCE STORE retail store that carries a modest variety and shallow assortment of products and has

high prices but offers a convenient location and hours

CONVERSION RATES statistical measurement that is used to describe the percent of shoppers who are converted into buyers

COOKIES tiny computer files, stored on users' PCs, that Web sites use to track visitors to their sites

COOPERATIVE ADVERTISING advertising for a local dealer or retailer whose expense is contributed to by the manufacturer

CORE COMPETENCY the unique bundle of skills that are possessed by individuals across the organization and that provide the basis for competitive advantage

CORE PURPOSE the company's reason for being or its idealistic motivation for doing work

CORE VALUES the small set of guiding principles that represent the enduring tenets of the organization

CORPORATE ADVOCACY ADVERTISING advertising that announces a stand on some issue related to the firm's operation, often one threatening the company's well-being

CORPORATE IMAGE ADVERTISING advertising directed toward the general public or investors and stockholders promoting an organization's image and role in the community as a corporate citizen, independent of any product or service

CORPORATE LEVEL the highest level in any organization, at which managers address issues concerning the overall organization and their decisions and actions affect all other organizational levels

CORPORATE STRATEGIC PLAN a plan that determines what a company is and wants to become and that guides strategic planning at all organizational levels; it involves developing a corporate vision, formulating corporate objectives, allocating resources, determining how to achieve desired growth, and establishing business units

CORPORATE VISION the basic values of an organization, specifying what it stands for, where it wants to go, and how it plans to get there, and addressing the organization's markets, principal products or services, geographic domain, core technologies, objectives, basic philosophy, self-concept, and desired public image

CORRECTIVE ADVERTISING advertising the FTC mandates to remedy misleading impressions and information in an ad

COST PER THOUSAND (CPM) a factor in evaluating the cost effectiveness of a particular outlet for reaching desired market audiences

COUNTERSEGMENTATION combining market segments to appeal to a broad range of consumers and assuming an increasing consumer willingness to accept fewer product and service variations for lower prices

COUNTERTRADE trade between developed and less-developed countries that involves barter and exchanges instead of just currency

COUPON a printed certificate giving the bearer a stated price reduction or special value on a specific product, generally for a specific time period; especially useful in encouraging new-product trials; may be distributed in an ad, in a freestanding insert, or on the store shelf

CREATIVE STRATEGY combining what is said in an ad with how it is said; typically the marketer specifies the general theme of the message and the ad agency develops the presentation

CROSS ELASTICITY OF DEMAND the relation of the percentage change in quantity demanded for one product to percentage price changes for other products; a price increase for one brand of cola will increase demand for a substitute brand, but a price increase for computers will decrease demand for printers, a complementary product

CROSS-FUNCTIONAL TEAMWORK having employees from different functional areas of a firm work together to satisfy customer needs

CROSS-PROMOTION the collaboration of two or more firms in a sales promotion; also called a **tie-in**

CROSS-SECTIONAL STUDY a survey of customers administered at a given time to assess, for example, perceived satisfaction with service

CULTURAL ENVIRONMENT factors and trends related to how people live and behave, including the values, ideas, attitudes, beliefs, and activities of specific population subgroups; a component of the social environment

CULTURE the values, ideas, attitudes, and symbols people adopt to communicate, interpret, and interact as members of a society; a society's way of life, learned and transmitted from one generation to the next, that includes both abstract and material elements. Culture determines the most basic values that influence consumer behavior patterns and can be used to distinguish subcultures that represent substantial market segments and opportunities

CUSTOMARY PRICE pricing strategies that modify the quality, features, or service of a product without adjusting the price; customary price beliefs reflect consumers' strongly held expectations about what the price of a product should be

CUSTOMER EQUITY CONCEPT a focus beyond customer satisfaction toward customer retention as a way to generate sales and profit growth

CUSTOMER PRIVACY any way in which data is protected from unauthorized viewing on a Web site

CUSTOMER RELATIONSHIP MANAGEMENT (CRM) designed to achieve a continuing dialogue with customers, across all contact and access points, with personalized treatment of the most valuable customers designed to increase customer retention and the effectiveness of marketing strategies

CUSTOMER SERVICE the assistance a firm provides to help a customer with the purchase or use of a product or service; providing exceptional customer service can give a firm a marketing advantage

CUSTOMER VALUE what a customer gets (benefits from product use, related services) for what a customer gives (price paid, time to shop)

CUSTOMER VALUE PERSPECTIVE an emphasis on giving customers more of what they want for less than they have to give

CUSTOMIZED MARKETING STRATEGY implementing a different marketing mix for each target market country in international marketing

CYCLE TIME the total elapsed time to complete a business process

DATA INTEGRITY a condition required to ensure security, meaning that data cannot be corrupted by viruses, destroyed, or changed without authorization

DATA MINING the process by which market cells are derived from company databases by the use of sophisticated analytical and statistical procedures that discover interesting patterns within company data sets

DATABASE MARKETING the collection and use of individual customer-specific information stored on a computer to make marketing more efficient

DEALER LOADER a premium given to a reseller to encourage development of a special display or product offering

DECEPTIVE ADVERTISING communications intended to mislead consumers by making false claims or failing to disclose important information

DECLINE STAGE the fourth and final stage of the product life cycle, when falling sales and profits persist

DECODING the process in communications by which the receiver deciphers the meaning of the words, pictures, and other symbols used in the message

DECONGLOMERATION refers to the divestiture behavior of a conglomerate firm and the transformation of its business portfolio to one composed of relatively fewer and related businesses

DEMAND CURVE relationship that shows how many units a market will purchase at a given price in a given time period; generally, customers buy more units as prices drop and fewer units as prices rise

DEMOGRAPHIC ENVIRONMENT the size, distribution, and growth rate of groups of people with different traits that relate to buying behavior; a component of the social environment

DEPARTMENT STORE a retail store characterized by a wide variety of merchandise and extensive depth of assortment; typically organized around sales departments like apparel, cosmetics, and housewares

DEREGULATION promotes free competition, in some cases by means of legislation. It is one aspect of the legal environment

DERIVED DEMAND demand for business-to-business products that is dependent upon demand for other products in consumer markets, as when increased consumer demand for new automobiles causes the demand for products used to make them to also go up

DESCRIPTIVE RESEARCH research directed by one or more formal research questions or hypotheses, usually involving a survey or questionnaire

DIFFERENTIAL PRICING selling the same product to different buyers at a variety of prices; such price discrimination works because there are differences in reactions to price among consumers or consumer segments

DIFFERENTIAL RESPONSIVENESS the degree to which market segments exhibit varying responses to different marketing mix combinations

DIFFERENTIATED STRATEGY using different marketing strategies for different segments; either marketing a unique product and communications campaign to each segment, or marketing a common product to different segments with various communication strategies

DIFFERENTIATION offering consumers products or services that are better than the competition; one way to gain a competitive advantage

DIFFUSION PROCESS the adoption of an innovative product form over time

DIRECT CHANNEL the movement of the product from the producer to the user without intermediaries

DIRECT INVESTMENT investing in production, sales, distribution, and/or other operations in a foreign country; requires a large investment of resources but gives the marketer much control over operations

DIRECT MAIL any form of advertising addressed to prospects through public or private delivery services, including everything from a simple flyer to a package that contains a letter, multipage brochure, video, and response card

DIRECT MARKETING distributing goods, services, information, or promotional benefits to carefully targeted consumers through interactive (two-way) communication while tracking response, sales, interests, or desires through a computer database

DIRECT MARKETING CHANNEL a way to move the product from producer to user without intermediaries

DIRECT MARKETING COMMUNICATIONS a process of communications directly with target customers to encourage response by telephone, mail, electronic means, or personal visit; examples of DMC methods include direct mail, telemarketing, computer shopping services, TV shopping networks, and infomercials

DIRECT-RESPONSE ADVERTISING advertising intended to elicit immediate purchase; for example, TV commercials that show a toll-free phone number

DIRECT-RESPONSE RADIO ADVERTISING radio ads that provide a phone number or address to elicit immediate feedback from the consumer

DIRECT-RESPONSE TELEVISION ADVERTISING TV ads that include an 800 or 900 phone number and an address for placing orders in an attempt to get an immediate answer from the consumer

DIRECT RETAILING the portion of direct marketing in which ultimate consumers, not business consumers, do the buying (see also **direct marketing**)

DIRECT SELLING a method in which salespeople reach consumers directly or by telephone primarily at home or at work and sell through personal demonstration and explanation

DIRECT-TO-CONSUMER SALESPEOPLE sales reps who sell to individuals who personally use the products and services; they include retail salespeople, real estate agents, and financial securities agents

DISCOUNTS reductions from the market price; for example, cash discounts for prompt payment or quantity discounts for large orders. See also **trade sales promotion allowances**

DISPLAY ALLOWANCE money or a product provided to a retailer for featuring the manufacturer's brand in an agreed-on in-store display

DISPLAY LOADER a dealer premium that lets the reseller keep some or all of the display when the promotion ends

DISTRIBUTION CENTER an automated "superwarehouse" that serves a large geographic area and receives, processes, and ships customer orders in addition to storing products

DISTRIBUTOR BRAND a brand sponsored by a distributor such as a wholesaler or retailer; the distributor is responsible for the product's quality and marketing. Also called a **store brand, private brand,** or **private label**

DIVERSIFICATION STRATEGY expanding into new products and new markets; the riskiest growth strategy, since the company cannot build directly on its strengths in its current markets or products

DIVERTING secretly purchasing a product where it is less expensive, usually due to a trade promotion, and reselling it where prices are higher

DOWNWARD STRETCH STRATEGY adding products to the lower end of a product line; for example, IBM entered the market with high-priced microcomputers and later added lower-priced ones

DROP SHIPPER a limited-function wholesaler that arranges for shipments directly from the factory to the customer; it does not physically handle the product but does take title and all associated risks while the product is in transit, as well as provide sales support

DUMPING selling a product in a foreign country at a price lower than in the home country and lower than its marginal cost of production

DURABILITY the stability of market segments and whether distinctions between them will diminish or disappear as the product category or the markets mature

EARLY ADOPTERS the second group to adopt a new product (after innovators); they represent about 13.5 percent of a market

EARLY MAJORITY the third group to adopt a new product (after innovators and early adopters); they represent about 34 percent of a market

ECONOMIC ENVIRONMENT factors and trends that are related to the production of goods and services and population incomes and that affect the purchasing power of markets

EFFICIENT ASSORTMENT the practice of reducing the number of brands or sizes without affecting sales or consumers' perceptions of variety

ELABORATION LIKELIHOOD MODEL a theory of persuasion that includes individual motivation and the ability to elaborate information in advertisements as determinants of two different "routes" of persuasion

ELASTIC DEMAND demand for a product that changes substantially in response to small changes in price; when demand is elastic, a small decrease in price may substantially increase total revenues

ELECTRONIC BUSINESS (E-BUSINESS) use of the Internet to conduct business activities

ELECTRONIC COMMERCE (E-COMMERCE) use of the Internet for buying and selling products that are transported either physically or digitally from location to location

ELECTRONIC DATA INTERCHANGE (EDI) a computerized system that allows exchange of information between parties; part of a quick-response inventory control system

ELECTRONIC MARKETING (E-MARKETING) use of the Internet to perform marketing activities

EMBARGO prohibition against trade with a particular country, imposed by the UN or individual governments

EMOTIONAL APPEALS ad message strategies that attempt to evoke feelings, moods, and memories to sell a product

ENCODING the process in communications by which the source chooses the words, pictures, and other symbols used to transmit the intended message

ENCRYPTION in order to maximize site security, Web site operators use this to convert readable messages into an unreadable format unless the reader is authorized by the system

ENTREPRENEURIAL PERSPECTIVE an emphasis on innovation, risk taking, and proactiveness in all marketing activities

ENTRY STRATEGY the approach used to begin marketing products internationally; options run the gamut from exporting to joint ventures to direct investment

ENVIRONMENTAL PROTECTION AGENCY (EPA) agency of the U.S. government whose goal is to protect the environment

ENVIRONMENTAL SCANNING identifying relevant factors and trends and assessing their potential impact on the organization's markets and marketing activities

E-RETAILING retail sales over the Internet

ETHICS PERSPECTIVE addressing the morality of marketing decisions and practicing social responsibility

ETHNIC PATTERNS the norms and values of specific groups or subcultures, which may be formed around nationality, religion, race, or geographic factors

ETHNOGRAPHIC RESEARCH technique in which market researchers record how consumers actually use products, brands, and services from day to day by entering their homes, observing consumption behavior, and recording pantry and garbage content

EUROPEAN UNION (EU) the world's largest consumer market, consisting of 16 European nations: France, Germany, Italy, the Netherlands, Belgium, Luxembourg, Britain, Ireland, Denmark, Greece, Spain, Portugal, Sweden, Finland, Norway, and Austria

EVERYDAY-LOW-PRICING (EDLP) suppliers reduce discounts and promotions to retailers; and retailers demand low prices from suppliers and minimize advertising and sales promotions to keep prices consistently low

EXCHANGE the transfer of something tangible or intangible, actual or symbolic, between two or more social actors

EXCHANGE RATE the price of one country's currency in terms of another country's currency

EXCLUSIVE DEALING AGREEMENT a marketing channel arrangement between producer and reseller that restricts the reseller from carrying a competing product line

EXCLUSIVE DISTRIBUTION using only one outlet in a geographic marketplace

EXCLUSIVE TERRITORIES a marketing channel arrangement between a producer and a reseller that prohibits other resellers from selling a particular brand in a given geographic area

EXISTING-BUSINESS SALESPEOPLE sales reps who work with established customers, writing up fairly routine orders, to provide a steady stream of sales revenue

EXPANSION ADVERTISING advertising designed to increase usage by current customers with high awareness and high penetration

EXPERT OPINION a qualitative approach to forecasting sales in which analysts ask executives within the company or other experts to provide forecasts based on their own judgments

EXPERT POWER power a member of a marketing channel gains by accumulating expertise and knowledge; for example, large retailers have gained much expert power using point-of-sale

scanners to gauge product movements, price sensitivities, and trade promotion effectiveness

EXPLICIT COMMUNICATIONS a distinct, clearly stated message conveyed through personal selling, advertising, public relations, sales promotion, direct marketing, or some combination of these methods

EXPLORATORY RESEARCH research carried out to gain greater understanding or develop preliminary background and suggest hypotheses for a detailed follow-up study; may involve literature reviews, case analyses, interviews, and focus groups

EXPORT AGENT a wholesaler that locates and develops markets abroad for products manufactured in its home country, operating on commission

EXPORTING selling products to buyers in international markets, either directly or through intermediaries

EXTERNAL REFERENCE PRICES prices charged by other retailers or comparison prices a retailer provides to enhance perceptions of the advertised price

EXTERNAL SECONDARY DATA secondary data that are collected from outside the firm and may be proprietary (provided by commercial marketing research firms) or nonproprietary (available from public sources)

EXTERNAL SOURCING acquiring specific brands from another firm or purchasing the entire firm to obtain ownership of its products

FAD a subcategory of fashion that has a very short product life

FAIR CREDIT REPORT ACT a U.S. law passed in 1970 to regulate the reporting and use of credit information

FAIR DEBT COLLECTIONS PRACTICE ACT a U.S. law passed in 1970 to regulate methods for collecting on debts

FAIR PACKAGING & LABELING ACT a U.S. law passed in 1965 to regulate the packaging and labeling of products

FAMILY BRAND NAME STRATEGY branding all items in a product line or even the entire product mix with a family name or the company name

FAMILY LIFE CYCLE the sequence of steps a family goes through, from young single adults to the married couple whose children have left home; household consumption patterns vary greatly across the family life cycle

FASHION a component of style whose products reflect what is currently popular

FAX-ON-DEMAND SYSTEMS allow instant response to 800-number requests for information. In these systems, a fax machine receives the request for information and immediately faxes the information back to the requester

FEAR APPEAL a type of emotional appeal used in an ad message strategy; for example, Michelin's "baby in a tire" theme

FEATURE a statement of fact about some aspect of a product or service (as opposed to a benefit, which is what the feature can do for the customer)

FEDERAL COMMUNICATIONS COMMISSION (FCC) agency of the U.S. government that regulates the interstate communications industry

FEDERAL TRADE COMMISSION (FTC) agency of the U.S. government that regulates business practices; established by the Federal Trade Commission Act of 1914

FEEDBACK the part of the receiver's response that is communicated to the sender

FIELDWORK the process of contacting respondents, conducting interviews, and completing surveys in market research

FIVE CS OF PRICING five critical influences on pricing decisions—costs, customers, channels of distribution, competition, and compatibility

FIXED COSTS costs that cannot be changed in the short run and do not vary with the quantity produced; they include plant investments, interest, and the costs of production facilities. See also **variable costs**

FLYER a single-page piece of direct mail printed on one or both sides of 8 1/2 × 11-inch paper and folded

FOB ORIGIN PRICING a form of geographic pricing in which buyers are charged the unit cost of goods plus shipping costs, which vary with location; in FOB (free on board), the goods are placed on a carrier and shipped to the customer, who pays the transportation charges

FOCUS GROUP an exploratory research method in which a moderator leads 8 to 12 people in a focused, in-depth discussion on a specific topic; used most for examining new-product concepts and advertising themes, investigating the criteria underlying purchase decisions, and generating information for developing consumer questionnaires

FOOD AND DRUG ADMINISTRATION (FDA) an agency of the U.S. government that regulates the food, drug, and cosmetics industries; established by the Food, Drug & Cosmetic Act of 1938

FORWARD BUYING when distributors or consumers stock up on enough of a product at a deal price to carry them over to the next sale

FORWARD INTEGRATION a corporate marketing channel system in which a channel member owns one or more of its buyers downstream (as opposed to backward integration, where it owns suppliers upstream)

FRANCHISE SYSTEM a contractual marketing channel system where the franchisor grants a franchisee the right to distribute and sell specified goods and services and the franchisee agrees to operate according to marketing guidelines set forth by the franchisor under a recognized trademark or trade name

FRANCHISEE party that is granted rights (by the franchisor) to distribute and sell specified goods and services

FRANCHISOR parent company that grants rights to a franchisee to distribute and sell its goods and services

FREESTANDING INSERT (FSI) a preprinted ad, usually containing a coupon, placed in a separate publication, such as a newspaper

FREESTANDING SITES retail outlets that are not adjoined to other structures, but are often located adjacent to other retail locations

FREIGHT ABSORPTION PRICING a form of geographical pricing in which the seller absorbs freight costs

FREQUENCY the number of times a person or household is exposed to a communication vehicle such as an ad

FULL-SERVICE WHOLESALER a wholesaler that performs a wide range of services for its customers and the parties from which it purchases

FUNCTIONAL LEVEL the various functional areas within a business unit, where most of the unit's work is performed (for example, marketing and accounting are functional areas)

FUNCTIONAL MIDDLEMAN a wholesaler that does not take title to the products it sells

GAME a sales promotion that offers prizes like sweepstakes but covers a longer time period

GATEKEEPERS decision makers who control the flow of information and communication among buying-center participants

GENERAL AGREEMENT ON TARIFFS AND TRADE (GATT) an agreement under which countries meet periodically to negotiate matters related to trade and tariffs; in 1993, GATT was signed by 108 countries representing 80 percent of all global trade

GENERAL MERCHANDISE WHOLESALER a wholesaler that carries a wide variety of products and provides extensive services for its customers

GENERICS products that are not branded; they are labeled only by their generic name (tomato soup) and usually cost less and may be of lower quality than their branded competitors

GEODEMOGRAPHICS the combination of geographic information and demographic characteristics; used in segmenting and targeting specific segments

GLOBAL PERSPECTIVE a view of the marketplace that includes searching for marketing opportunities around the world, competing internationally, and working with multicultural suppliers, employees, channel participants, and customers

GLOBAL STRATEGY a corporate level strategy that views the whole world as a global market

GOING-RATE PRICING pricing at or near industry averages; strategy often when companies compete on the basis of attributes or benefits other than price

GOODS physical products such as cars, golf clubs, soft drinks, or other concrete entities (in contrast to services, which are nonphysical products)

GOVERNMENT MARKET federal, state, and local government organizations that purchase goods and services for use in many activities

GROSS DOMESTIC PRODUCT (GDP) the total size of a country's economy measured in the amount of goods and services produced

GROSS MARGIN sales revenue minus the retailer's cost of goods sold

GROWTH STAGE the second stage in the product life cycle, when sales and profits increase rapidly

HIERARCHY OF EFFECTS see information-processing model

HIGH-INVOLVEMENT DECISIONS purchasing decisions that involve high levels of importance or personal relevance, thorough information processing, and substantial differences between alternatives

HYBRID CAMPAIGNS ad campaigns that blend traditional media with the Web to make the consumer an active participant

HYPERMARKET market format that combines a discount store with an oversized supermarket

IDEA GENERATION the initial stage of the new-product development process, requiring creativity and innovation to generate ideas for potential new products

IDEA SCREENING evaluating the pool of new-product ideas to reduce it to a smaller, more attractive set, based on consistency with the company vision and strategic objectives, potential market acceptance, fit with the firm's capabilities, and possible long-term contribution to profit

IMPLICIT COMMUNICATIONS what the marketing message connotes about the product, its price, or the places it is sold

IMPORT AGENT a wholesaler that finds products in foreign countries to sell in its home country; in many countries, it is illegal to sell imported products without going through an import agent or similar intermediary

IMPULSE PURCHASES impulse purchases are decisions made with little or no cognitive effort; choices made on the spur of the moment without prior problem recognition, but possibly with strong positive feelings

INCENTIVE PAY commissions, bonuses, or both; about 75 percent of U.S.

firms use a combination pay plan, less than 15 percent pay a straight salary, and 10 percent pay straight commission

INCOME-BASED PRICING the determination of price based upon the income to be generated by the product under consideration

INDEPENDENT RETAILERS retailers that own and operate only one retail outlet; they account for more than three-fourths of all U.S. retail establishments

INDIRECT CHANNEL a way to move the product from producer to user with the help of intermediaries that perform functions related to buying or selling the product

INDIVIDUAL BRAND NAME STRATEGY establishing specific and different brand names for each individual product in a product line

INDIVIDUAL PRODUCT any brand or variant of a brand in a company's product line

INELASTIC DEMAND the demand that exists when price changes do not result in significant changes in the quantity of a product demanded

INFOMERCIAL a program-length TV ad that resembles a talk show or news program

INFORMATION-PROCESSING MODEL the sequence of advertising's effects: (1) exposure, (2) attention, (3) comprehension, (4) acceptance, and (5) retention; also called the **hierarchy-of-effects model**

INFORMATIONAL INFLUENCE an interpersonal process, based on consumers' desire to make informed choices and reduce uncertainty, in which they seek information and advice from people they trust

INITIAL TRAINING sales training that focuses on product knowledge and sales techniques

INNOVATORS consumers who are most willing to try new products (about the first 2.5 percent of product adopters)

INQUIRY EVALUATION posttesting of an ad based on the number of consumers responding to requests in it, such as using coupons or asking for samples or more product information

INSTITUTIONAL ENVIRONMENT all the organizations involved in marketing products and services, including marketing

research firms, ad agencies, wholesalers, retailers, suppliers, and customers

INSTITUTIONAL MARKET includes organizations such as profit or nonprofit hospitals, educational and religious institutions, and trade associations

INTEGRATED MARKETING COMMUNICATIONS the strategic integration of multiple means of communicating with target markets to form a comprehensive, consistent message; communications are integrated horizontally (across various methods of communications) and vertically (from the marketer down through the marketing channel)

INTENSIVE DISTRIBUTION distributing a product or service through every available outlet

INTERACTIVE COMPUTER KIOSK an electronic marketing medium, usually located in retail stores, that uses touch-screen technology to let the consumer access information of interest

INTERACTIVE COMPUTER SERVICES systems that allow consumers and marketers to communicate with each other through phone lines and a personal computer

INTERACTIVE MARKETING that portion of electronic business that is communicating directly with target customers to encourage response

INTERCEPTOR LOCATION a location between a residential area and the closest supermarket, where a convenience store does business

INTERMARKET SEGMENTS well-defined, similar clusters of customers across national boundaries that let firms standardize marketing programs and offerings for each segment globally

INTERMEDIARIES middlemen directly involved in the purchase or sale of products as they flow from originator to user; they include retailers and wholesalers

INTERMODAL SHIPPING using two or more modes of transportation to ship products; for example, loaded trailers may travel piggyback on railcars

INTERNAL DEVELOPMENT a way to generate new products in which a firm creates the products itself, possibly subcontracting product design, engineering, or test marketing or working in partnership with another firm

INTERNAL REFERENCE PRICES comparison price standards that consumers remember and use to judge the fairness of prices; they include the expected price, the price last paid, the average retail price, and the price the consumer would like to pay now

INTERNAL SECONDARY DATA secondary data collected within a firm, including accounting records, salesforce reports and customer feedback

INTERSTATE COMMERCE COMMISSION (ICC) agency of the U.S. government that regulates interstate transportation

INTERTYPE COMPETITION competition among retailers that use different business formats to sell the same products; for example, McDonald's intertype competitors include all food retailers, from vending machines to fine restaurants

INTRATYPE COMPETITION competition among retailers that use the same business format

INTRODUCTION STAGE the first stage in the product life cycle, when a new product is launched into the marketplace; it continues the commercialization stage of the new-product development process

INVENTORY TURNOVER the number of times a retailer sells its average inventory during the year, or how quickly merchandise is sold

INVOLVEMENT the level of importance, interest, or personal relevance generated by a product or a decision, which varies by the decision at hand and by the person's needs or motives

ISO 9000 the International Standards Organization's 25-page set of quality standards; certification shows that a company meets world standards

ISOLATED LOCATIONS freestanding retail sites where there are no adjoining buildings; best suited for large retailers that can attract a customer base on their own or for convenience businesses

JOINT VENTURE an arrangement between two or more organizations to market products internationally, through licensing agreements, contract manufacturing deals, or equity investments in strategic partnerships

JUST-IN-TIME (JIT) INVENTORY CONTROL SYSTEM a system that delivers raw materials, subassemblies, and component parts to manufacturers shortly before the scheduled manufacturing run that will consume the incoming shipment

LABEL a printed description of a product on a package

LAGGARDS the final group to adopt a new product; they represent about 16 percent of a market

LANHAM TRADEMARK ACT a U.S. law passed in 1946 that protects trademarks and brand names

LATE MAJORITY the fourth group to adopt a new product; they represent about 34 percent of a market

LEASED DEPARTMENTS sections in a retail store that the owner rents to another party; typically department stores rent their jewelry, shoe, hairstyling, and cosmetic departments

LEGITIMATE POWER power a member of a marketing channel gains through ownership or contractual agreements

LICENSING the right to use a trademark in exchange for paying royalties on the sale of the licensed product

LIFESTYLE RESEARCH a person's pattern of living, as expressed in activities, interests, and opinions; lifestyle traits are more concrete than personality traits and more directly linked to the acquisition, use, and disposition of goods and services. See also **psychographic research**

LIFETIME VALUE OF A LOYAL CUSTOMER the sales or profits generated from a customer who purchases a firm's product throughout their lifetime or some other extended time period

LIMIT PRICING a competitive pricing strategy that involves setting prices low to discourage new competition

LIMITED-FUNCTION WHOLESALER a truck jobber, drop shipper, cash-and-carry wholesaler, catalog wholesaler, or wholesale club that does not offer the comprehensive service of a full-service wholesaler

LIMITED-LINE WHOLESALER a full-service wholesaler that does not stock as many products as a general merchandise wholesaler but has more depth in its product offering

LINE-FILLING STRATEGY adding products in various places within a product line to fill gaps that may not be at either the high or the low end

LISTS databases of current or potential customers that include their names, addresses, telephone numbers, and perhaps data on demographics, lifestyles, brand and media preferences, and consumption patterns

LOGISTICS MANAGEMENT planning, implementing, and moving raw materials and products from point of origin to point of consumption

LONGITUDINAL RESEARCH research conducted over time, typically on a panel of consumers or stores

LOW-INVOLVEMENT DECISIONS purchase decisions that involve fairly little personal interest, relevance, or importance and simple decision processes

MAGNUSSON-MOSS ACT a U.S. law passed in 1975 to regulate warranties

MAIL SURVEYS marketing research method that involves sending questionnaires via mail, often to large, geographically diverse groups of people

MAJOR ACCOUNTS key, high-potential customers

MAJORITY FALLACY pursuing large "majority" market segments because they offer potential gains while overlooking the fact that they also may attract overwhelming competition

MALL INTERCEPT INTERVIEWS market research method in which consumers are interviewed one-on-one while shopping

MANUFACTURER BRAND a brand sponsored by the product's manufacturer, who is responsible for its quality and marketing. Also called a national brand or regional brand

MANUFACTURERS' AGENT a merchant wholesaler that sells related but noncompeting product lines for various manufacturers; also called **manufacturers' rep**

MANUFACTURER'S SALES BRANCH a manufacturer-owned wholesaler that maintains inventory and performs a wide range of functions for the parent company

MANUFACTURER'S SALES OFFICE a producer-owned wholesaler that differs from the manufacturer's sales branch in that it does not maintain inventory or perform as many functions for the parent company

MARGINAL COSTS costs that are incurred in producing one additional unit of output; they typically decline early due to economies of scale but increase as the firm approaches capacity

MARGINAL REVENUE the additional revenue a firm will receive if one more unit of product is sold (MR is usually the price of the product)

MARKET a group of people or organizations with needs to satisfy or problems to solve, the money to satisfy needs or solve problems, and the authority to make expenditure decisions

MARKET COVERAGE the number of outlets used to market a product; may involve intensive, selective, or exclusive distribution

MARKET EXPANSION STRATEGY a corporate growth strategy of marketing existing products to new markets (different market segments in the same geographic area or the same target market in different geographic areas)

MARKET FORECAST the amount of sales predicted based on the marketing effort (expenditures) put forth by all the companies competing to sell a particular product or service in a specific period

MARKET MAVENS people who share with other consumers their knowledge about kinds of products, places to shop, and other facets of the market

MARKET ORIENTATION used to describe firms implementing the marketing concept

MARKET PENETRATION STRATEGY achieving corporate growth objectives with existing products within existing markets, by persuading current customers to purchase more of the product or by capturing new customers

MARKET POTENTIAL the maximum amount of industry sales possible for a product or service for a specific period

MARKET SCOPE how broadly a business views its target market

MARKET SEGMENTATION dividing the market for a product into subsets of customers who behave in the same way, have similar needs, or have similar characteristics that relate to purchase behavior

MARKET SHARE a firm's percentage of the total market or total industry sales of a product

MARKET TESTS marketing a new product in test locations using the planned promotion, pricing, and distribution strategies

MARKETING the process of planning and executing the conception, pricing, promotion, and distribution of ideas, goods, and services to create exchanges that satisfy individual and organizational goals

MARKETING AS A SOCIETAL PROCESS a process that facilitates the flow of goods from producers to consumers in a society

MARKETING CHANNEL a combination of organizations and individuals (channel members) who perform the activities required to link producers to users to products to accomplish marketing objectives; also called **channel of distribution**

MARKETING COMMUNICATIONS marketer-initiated techniques directed to target audiences in an attempt to influence attitudes and behaviors; its three main objectives are to inform, persuade, and remind consumers; also called promotion

MARKETING COMMUNICATIONS ACTIVITIES activities that include advertising and public relations, sales promotion, personal selling, and direct marketing

MARKETING COMMUNICATIONS MESSAGE what the company is trying to convey about its products

MARKETING COMMUNICATIONS MIX the combination of advertising, public relations, sales promotion, personal selling, and direct marketing; also called the promotional mix

MARKETING COMMUNICATIONS PLANNING a seven-step process: (1) marketing plan review, (2) situation analysis, (3) communications process analysis, (4) budget development, (5) program development, (6) integration and implementation of the plan, and (7) monitoring, evaluating, and controlling the marketing communications program

MARKETING CONCEPT the interrelated principles that (1) an organization's basic purpose is to satisfy customer needs, (2) satisfying customer needs requires integrated, coordinated efforts throughout the organization, and (3) organizations should focus on long-term success

MARKETING DECISION SUPPORT SYSTEM (MDSS) a comprehensive entity that encompasses all data, activities, and computerized elements used to process information relevant to marketing decisions; designed to enhance managerial decision making and firm performance by providing timely, relevant internal and external information

MARKETING ENVIRONMENT the uncontrollable environment within which marketers must operate, encompassing social, economic, competitive, technological, legal/political, and institutional environments; all factors outside an organization that can affect its marketing activities

MARKETING MANAGEMENT specific strategic decisions for individual products and the day-to-day activities needed to execute these strategies successfully

MARKETING MIX the overall marketing effort to appeal to the target market, consisting of decisions in four basic areas: product, pricing, communications, and distribution

MARKETING PHILOSOPHY an organization's emphasis on satisfying customers' needs; a focus on the marketing concept

MARKETING RESEARCH activities linking marketer, customer, and public through information used to identify marketing opportunities; generate, refine, and evaluate marketing actions; monitor marketing performance; and improve understanding of marketing as a process. Marketing research specifies the information required to address these issues, designs the methods for collecting information, manages and implements the data collection process, analyzes the results, and communicates the findings and implications

MARKETING RESEARCH DESIGNS general strategies or plans of action for addressing research problems, data collection, and analysis

MARKETING RESEARCH PROCESS a six-step sequence: (1) problem definition, (2) determination of research design, (3) determination of data collection methods, (4) development of data collection forms, (5) sample design, and (6) analysis and interpretation

MARKETING STRATEGIC PLAN
a functional plan for how marketing managers will execute the business strategic plan, addressing the general target market and marketing mix

MARKETING STRATEGIES
selecting a target market and developing a marketing mix to satisfy that market's needs

MARKUP PRICING pricing where markup is the difference between the cost of an item and the retail price, expressed as a percentage

MASS CUSTOMIZATION the ability of complex manufactured products to be made to order; possible because of advances in manufacturing and information technology

MATURITY STAGE the third stage of the product life cycle, when competition intensifies and sales growth slows

MEASURABILITY the degree to which the size and purchasing power of market segments can be assessed

MEDIA CLASS one of seven classes of advertising media: TV, magazines, newspapers, radio, outdoor, transit, and direct mail

MEDIA SCHEDULE the frequency and timing of ads and commercials. See also **reach** and **frequency**

MEDIA VEHICLE a specific TV program, magazine, or the like in any of the seven media classes

MERCHANT WHOLESALER an independent distributor that takes title to the products it sells; may be either a full-service or a limited-function wholesaler

MESSAGE ACCEPTANCE the point where the consumer develops favorable attitudes about the advertised product and subsequent purchase; step 4 in the information-processing model

MESSAGE CHANNEL the means by which a company conveys its message about its products; for example, advertising vehicles like newspapers, TV, and billboards

MESSAGE COMPREHENSION
the point where the consumer understands an ad's meaning; step 3 in the information-processing model

MESSAGE EXPOSURE what a marketer achieves by placing ads in appropriate media, giving consumers the opportunity to process the message; step 1 in the information-processing or hierarchy of effects model

MESSAGE PRESENTER a person, perhaps a salesperson, actor, or TV personality who actually delivers the message

MESSAGE RETENTION the point where a consumer stores ad information in long-term memory, which is critical for affecting later purchase decisions and behavior; step 5 in the information-processing model

MESSAGE SPONSOR the organization that is attempting to market its goods, services, or ideas

METROPOLITAN STATISTICAL AREA (MSA) a geographic area identified by census data to contain a city with a population of at least 50,000 or be an urbanized area with 50,000 people that is part of a county of at least 100,000 residents

MICROMARKETING using computer analysis of census and demographic data to identify clusters of households that share similar consumption patterns (for example, the PRIZM market segmentation system)

MIDDLEMEN see **intermediaries**

MISSION STATEMENT an element in the strategic planning process that expresses the company's basic values and specifies the boundaries within which business units, marketing, and other functions must operate

MISSIONARY SALESPEOPLE
sales support personnel who work at the grassroots level to promote their company's products; especially important in the grocery and pharmaceutical markets

MODIFIED REBUY DECISIONS
business purchasing decisions that call for the evaluation of new alternatives; could involve considering new suppliers for current purchase needs or new products offered by current suppliers; an example is the purchase of complex component parts from a new supplier

MOTIVATION the desire to process ad information; a state or condition within a person that prompts goal-directed behavior; it generally occurs when some need or problem is recognized and it can affect information search, information processing, and purchase behavior

MULTINATIONAL STRATEGY
recognizes national differences and views the collection of other countries as a portfolio of markets

MULTIPLE-CHANNELS STRATEGY distributing a product through more than one channel to reach customers (for example, Prell shampoo is widely available at discount, drug, and grocery stores)

NATIONAL BRAND see **manufacturer brand**

NEGATIVE DISCONFIRMATION
an experience where a purchase does not turn out as well as the consumer expected

NEGOTIATED PRICING pricing in which negotiation between vendor and supplier replaces multiple bids; common for large investments. See also **sealed-bid pricing**

NETWORK ORGANIZATIONS
firms involved in many different types of organizational partnerships, including strategic alliances, joint ventures, and vendor partnering

NEURAL NETWORKS
sophisticated statistical techniques that can use a database to calculate weights for such traits as age, income, education, or time on the job

NEW-BUSINESS SALESPEOPLE
members of the salesforce who concentrate on selling new products or selling to new customers

NEW-TASK DECISIONS business purchasing decisions that occur when the buying problem is new and a great deal of information must be gathered; relatively infrequent decisions for a company, and the cost of making a wrong decision is high

NOISE any distraction or distortion during the communications process that prevents the message from being communicated effectively

NONPRICE COMPETITION
competition between brands for sales based on factors other than price, such as quality, service, or specific product features

NONPROBABILITY SAMPLING
market research in which selection of the sample is based on the researcher's or field worker's judgment

NONPROPRIETARY SECONDARY DATA secondary data that are available from libraries, computer databases, and other public sources

NONREPUDIATION a process that precludes the later denial of a valid transaction by either buyer or seller and is a key element in building Web site security

NONSTORE RETAILING the selling of products and services outside a physical structure through, for example, direct marketing, direct selling, or vending machine sales

NORMATIVE INFLUENCE a strategy in which marketers show consumers the favorable conditions that can occur when their brands are used or the unfavorable consequences that can occur when not used

NORMS the expectations, real or imagined, of other individuals or groups of people

NORTH AMERICAN FREE TRADE AGREEMENT (NAFTA) a treaty that eliminates many trade barriers among the United States, Mexico, and Canada

NORTH AMERICAN INDUSTRIAL CLASSIFICATION SYSTEM (NAICS) a numerical scheme developed by the federal government for categorizing businesses

OBJECTIONS buyer concerns about a product

OBJECTIVE CLAIMS advertising messages that describe product features or performance in measurable terms, often reflecting a quality/value perspective

OBJECTIVE PRICE see price

OBJECTIVE-TASK BUDGETING a budgeting method for marketing communications based on achieving stipulated objectives, identifying tasks to meet those objectives, and evaluating results

OBSERVATION RESEARCH market research technique where a researcher or a video camera monitors customer behavior, or anonymous shoppers evaluate the quality of services offered

ODD–EVEN PRICING setting prices at just below an even amount (for example, contact lenses for $199.95 instead of $200)

ON-LINE AUCTION COMPANY a firm that uses a computer network, typically the Internet, to bring buyers and sellers together

ON-LINE COUPONING refers to the distribution of coupons on the Internet

ON-SHELF COUPONING distributing coupons via a dispenser mounted near the manufacturer's product on a store shelf

OPERATIONAL PRODUCTS products that are used in a firm's activities but do not become part of any finished product; examples include lightbulbs, cleaning materials, and services (such as accounting or advertising)

OPINION LEADERS people who influence consumer behavior through word-of-mouth communications based on their interest or expertise in particular products

OPPORTUNITIES areas where a company's performance might be improved; typically ranked by managers so the most important can be addressed first in the next strategic planning stage

OPPORTUNITY the extent to which distractions or limited exposure time affect the buyer's attention to brand information in an ad

ORDER in order processing, either a customer's purchase order or an order transmitted by a sales rep

ORDER TAKERS see existing-business salespeople

ORGANIZATION OF PETROLEUM EXPORTING COUNTRIES (OPEC) a loose federation of many of the oil-producing countries, designed to influence market prices and short-term profits for crude oil

ORGANIZED SALES PRESENTATION a mental or written outline developed by the salesperson that is flexible enough to allow adaptive selling

OUTCOME-BASED PERSPECTIVE a way of evaluating salesperson performance that focuses on the results of sales behavior, such as total sales volume; see also **behavior-based perspective**

OUTSOURCING a firm's decision to purchase products and services from other companies rather than to make the products or perform the services internally; examples include components for computers, shipping, telecommunications, payroll administration

PACKAGE the container or wrapper for a product, including the label

PARTITIONED PRICING a pricing strategy in which a firm divides the price of a product or service into parts in lieu of charging a single price; the parts are often termed *base price* and *surcharge*

PAY-FOR-PERFORMANCE TRADE PROMOTION a sales promotion in which retailers are rewarded for making sales to consumers rather than purchases from manufacturers

PENETRATION PRICING setting a low initial price to encourage initial product trial, stimulate sales growth and lower unit production costs, increase total revenues, and enhance profits

PERCEIVED MONETARY PRICE the consumer's subjective perception of whether the price of a product is high or low, fair or unfair (in contrast to objective price)

PERCEIVED VALUE the buyer's overall assessment of a product's utility based on what is received and what is given; the quality per dollar

PERCENTAGE OF SALES BUDGETING a budgeting method for marketing communications based on the preceding year's or forecasted coming year's sales

PERCEPTUAL MAPS spatial representations of consumer perceptions of products or brands, used to evaluate brand positions in a market

PERIODIC DISCOUNTING offering occasional discounts to take advantage of consumer segments' differing price sensitivity; includes price skimming

PERMISSION MARKETING marketing that occurs when the customer grants the marketer permission to send regular updates of interest to the consumer via e-mail

PERSONAL INTERVIEWS one-on-one interactions—between a consumer, customer, or respondent and a market researcher—to gather data

PERSONAL SELLING the element of the marketing communications mix that involves face-to-face interactions between seller and buyer to satisfy buyer needs for their mutual benefit

PERSONALITY a person's consistent response to his or her environment, linked to susceptibility to persuasion and social influence and thereby to purchase behavior

PERSONALIZATION a way for marketers to build site stickiness by customizing the look and content of a portal's home page

PERSUASION KNOWLEDGE helps consumer understand why and how marketers are trying to persuade us and to adaptively respond to these attempts

PIPES the means used to get content from Web content providers into portals

PLUS-ONE DIALING method of telephone interview where a phone number is randomly selected from the local directory and a digit or digits added to it; allows inclusion of unlisted numbers in the sample

POINT-OF-PURCHASE DISPLAY a sales promotion, often provided free by the manufacturer to the retailer, to call customer attention to a featured product

POLITICAL/LEGAL ENVIRONMENT factors and trends related to governmental activities and specific laws and regulations that affect marketing practice

PORTALS search engines that offer general Internet functions and that direct visitors to additional sites

POSITIONING developing an overall image for a product or brand by designing a marketing program, including the product mix, that a market segment will perceive as desirable

POSITIVE DISCONFIRMATION an experience where a purchase turns out better than a consumer expected

POSTTESTING recall and attitude tests and inquiry evaluations marketers use to assess the effectiveness of an ad campaign

PRECALL PLANNING focusing on learning more about the customer's situation before making a sales call

PREDATORY DUMPING dumping intended to drive rivals out of business

PREDATORY PRICING charging very low prices to drive competition from the market and then raising prices once a monopoly has been established

PREDICTIVE DIALING SYSTEMS automated dialing machines that make telemarketing more productive by passing over answering machines, busy signals, and no answers and passing live calls on to a live telemarketer

PREDICTIVE MODELING manipulating a customer database to reach a desired target more effectively, using neural networks and other technologies

PRELAUNCH ACTIVITIES marketing research studies conducted before commercialization of a new product

PREMIUM an item given free or at a bargain price to encourage the consumer to buy

PREMIUM PRICING setting higher prices on one or more product versions; a popular strategy for beer, clothing, appliances, and cars

PRESTIGE PRICING keeping prices high to maintain an image of product quality and appeal to buyers who associate premium prices with high quality

PRETESTING evaluating consumer reactions to proposed ads through focus groups and direct questioning, based on overall likability, consumer recall of information, message communication, and effects on purchase intentions and brand attitudes

PRICE the amount of money a buyer pays a seller in exchange for products and services

PRICE-AVERSION STRATEGY buying the lowest-priced brand (in contrast to the best-value strategy, which takes quality into account)

PRICE COMPETITION competition between brands for sales based on price alone; most common for similar brands and for customers with limited budgets and weak brand loyalties; see also **nonprice competition**

PRICE DEAL a temporary reduction in the price of a product, in the form of a cents-off or price-pack deal, used to introduce a new brand, convince current users to purchase more, or encourage new users to try an established brand

PRICE DISCRIMINATION selling the same product to different customers at different prices; restricted in the United States by the Robinson-Patman Act; see also **differential pricing**

PRICE ELASTICITY OF DEMAND the responsiveness of customer demand to changes in a product's price

PRICE-PACK DEAL a product that offers consumers something extra through the packaging itself; for example, a box of cereal with 20 percent more cereal for the regular price

PRICE PROMOTION MIX the basic price plus such supplemental components as sale prices, temporary discounts, coupons, and favorable payment and credit terms; encourages purchase behavior by strengthening the basic price during relatively short periods of time

PRICE/QUALITY RELATIONSHIP the extent to which a consumer associates a higher product price with higher quality

PRICE-SEEKING STRATEGY purchasing the highest-priced brand to maximize expected quality

PRICE SIGNALING a competitive pricing strategy that puts high prices on low-quality products

PRICE SKIMMING setting prices high initially to appeal to consumers who are not price sensitive, then lowering prices sequentially to appeal to the next market segments

PRICE THRESHOLD the point at which buyers notice a price increase or decrease; the threshold level depends on a product's average price (for example, a 10¢ reduction on a 50¢ product is more meaningful than on a $10 product)

PRIMARY DATA data collected for a particular research problem—for example, survey information; typically more current and relevant than secondary data but more expensive to gather

PRIMARY DEMAND general demand for a new product form, which marketing tries to generate at the introduction stage of the product life cycle

PRIMARY METROPOLITAN STATISTICAL AREA (PMSA) a major urban area, often located within a CMSA, that has at least one million inhabitants

PRIVATE BRAND see **distributor brand**

PRIVATE EXCHANGES electronic marketplace that link invitation-only buyers and sellers

PRIVATE LABEL see **distributor brand**

PRIVATE RESPONSE a complaint in which a dissatisfied consumer bad-mouths a product to friends or family

PRIVATE WAREHOUSE a warehouse operated by the company that uses it

PRIZM potential rating index by ZIP markets, which divides every neighborhood in the United States into one of 40 distinct cluster types that reveal consumer data; PRIZM14 uses ZIP14 codes for even greater detail covering individual demographics, individual credit records, model-specific auto registration, and purchase behavior data from private sources

PROACTIVE PR a form of public relations that is positive and opportunity seeking, such as product release announcements, event sponsorship, and placement of articles in the business press

PROBABILITY SAMPLING
market research in which each person in the population has a known, nonzero chance of being selected by some objective procedure; such unbiased selection increases the sample's representativeness

PROBLEM DEFINITION the first step in the marketing research process; identifying the difference between the way things should be and the way they are or identifying the issues that need to be investigated

PRODUCT an idea, a physical entity (a good), a service, or any combination that is an element of exchange to satisfy individual or business objectives

PRODUCT COMPETITORS
companies that offer different kinds of products to satisfy the same basic need (for example, Domino's Pizza and Kentucky Fried Chicken both attempt to satisfy a consumer need for fast food but offer somewhat different products and services from each other)

PRODUCT DESIGN the styling, aesthetics, and function of a product, which affect how it works, how it feels, and how easy it is to assemble, fix, and recycle

PRODUCT DIFFERENTIATION
circumstance in which a firm's offerings differ or are perceived to differ from those of competing firms on any attribute, including price

PRODUCT EXPANSION STRATEGY marketing new products to the same customer base

PRODUCT LIFE CYCLE (PLC)
the advancement of a product through the stages of introduction, growth, maturity, and decline

PRODUCT LINE a group of individual products that are closely related in some way

PRODUCT-LINE CONTRACTION
deleting individual products from a product line

PRODUCT-LINE LENGTH the number of products in any one product line

PRODUCT-LINE PRICING
offering multiple versions of the same product, with those priced at the low end used to build traffic and those at the high end creating a quality image for the entire product line

PRODUCT MARKETING PLANS
plans within each business unit that focus on specific target markets and marketing

mixes for each product and include both strategic decisions (what to do) and execution decisions (how to do it)

PRODUCT MIX the total assortment of products and services marketed by a firm

PRODUCT-MIX CONSISTENCY
the relatedness of the different product lines in a product mix; for example, all of Schwab's product lines are investment-related, but J&J sells everything from contact lenses to baby powder

PRODUCT-MIX WIDTH the number of product lines in a company's product mix

PRODUCT PLACEMENT ADVERTISING the combined efforts of marketers with moviemakers, such that product exposure is obtained among moviegoers

PRODUCTION PHILOSOPHY an organization's emphasis on the production function, valuing activities related to improving production efficiency or producing sophisticated products and services

PRODUCTION PRODUCTS raw materials and components that become part of some finished product (for example, steel and paper)

PRODUCTIVITY PERSPECTIVE
getting the most output for each marketing dollar spent, by doing the same things better and/or doing different things

PROJECT MATRIX ORGANIZATION an approach to new-product development in which a project manager has primary responsibility and authority, and functional managers assign personnel as needed

PROJECT TEAM ORGANIZATION an approach to new-product development in which a project manager heads a core group of people selected from various functional areas; managers from the different functional areas are not formally involved

PROJECTIVE TECHNIQUES
market research methods, such as word association or sentence completion, that let researchers elicit feelings that normally go unexpressed

PROMOTIONAL INTERACTIVE COMPUTER DISKS a relatively new format for direct-mail campaigns in which the information is presented on disk and the consumer can respond

PROPRIETARY SECONDARY DATA data provided by commercial

marketing research firms that sell their services to other firms; examples are diary panels and scanner data

PROSPECTING the seller's search for and identification of qualified buyers, defined as buyers who are reasonably accessible to the seller, able to afford the purchase, and willing to consider making it

PROTOTYPE DEVELOPMENT
converting the concept for a new product into an actual product, using the information obtained from concept tests to design a tangible product that can be tested further

PSYCHOGRAPHIC RESEARCH
a concept for dividing a market into lifestyle segments on the basis of consumer interests, values, opinions, personality traits, attitudes, and demographics to develop marketing communications and product strategies

PSYCHOLOGICAL PRICING the recognition that buyers' perceptions and beliefs affect their evaluations of prices

PUBLIC RELATIONS (PR) the element of the marketing communications mix that identifies, establishes, and maintains mutually beneficial relations between an organization and the various publics on which its success or failure depends—for example, customers, employees, stockholders, community members, and the government

PUBLIC RELATIONS FUNCTIONS press relations; product promotions; internal and external corporate communications; lobbying to promote, defeat, or circumvent legislation and regulations; advising management about public issues and company positions and image; and overall responding to various occurrences in the marketplace, either reactively or proactively

PUBLIC SERVICE ADVERTISING (PSAS) advertising donated by the ad industry to promote activities for some social good

PUBLIC WAREHOUSE a for-hire facility available to any business that requires storage or handling of goods

PUBLICITY information about the company or product that appears, unpaid for, in the news media; primary publicity techniques are news releases, press conferences, and feature articles, often presented in the business press

PUFFERY advertising that contains claims including acceptable exaggeration

PULL STRATEGY concentrating marketing communications on consumers to stimulate demand in an attempt to get consumers to "pull" a product from the manufacturing company through the marketing channel

PUSH MONEY what a manufacturer pays retail salespeople to encourage them to promote its products over competitive brands or to sell specific products in the manufacturer's line

PUSH STRATEGY directing marketing communications toward intermediary channel members to "push" a product through the channel to the ultimate consumer

QUALITATIVE DATA open-ended responses obtained from in-depth interviews, focus groups, and some observation studies; characterized by depth of response and richness of description

QUALITY the totality of features and characteristics of a product or service that bear on its ability to satisfy stated or implied needs

QUALITY FUNCTION DEPLOYMENT (QFD) a procedure in the new-product development process that links specific consumer requirements with specific product characteristics

QUANTITATIVE DATA information collected using more structured response formats that can be more easily analyzed and projected to larger populations

QUICK-RESPONSE (QR) INVENTORY CONTROL SYSTEM a system for providing retailers with finished goods in which inventory is restocked according to what has just been sold, based on small but frequent orders

QUOTAS the quantitative outcomes (such as total sales volume, gross margin, market share, number of new accounts added, and accounts retained) used to assess sales reps' performance and effectiveness

RACK JOBBER a specialty-line wholesaler that sells to retail stores, setting up and maintaining attractive store displays and stocking them with goods sold on consignment

RANDOM-DIGIT DIALING a method of telephone interviewing where, for example, four random digits are added to three-digit telephone exchanges to reach consumers

REACH the number of different people or households exposed to an ad or campaign over a specified time period (usually four weeks)

REACTIVE PR a form of public relations that addresses negative events or changes in the marketplace that adversely affect the firm, such as negative publicity from product defects or employee behavior

READER-RESPONSE CARDS card inserts in magazines, used in conjunction with ads, that make it easy for readers to send for more information on a product

REBATE cash reimbursement for purchasing a product, in which the buyer must mail a rebate form, the receipt, and proof of purchase to the manufacturer within a certain time

RECEIVER the intended target for any basic communication; for example, a purchasing agent listening to a sales presentation or a consumer reading a magazine ad

RECIPROCITY when firm A purchases from supplier B who in turn buys A's own products and services

REFERENCE GROUPS interpersonal influences beyond the family, including friends and co-workers

REFERENT POWER power a member of a marketing channel gains through another member's desire to be associated with it

REGIONAL BRAND see **manufacturer brand**

RELATED DIVERSIFICATION branching out into new products and markets that have something in common with existing operations (for example, a video rental store diversifying into music retailing)

RELATIONSHIP MARKETING developing, maintaining, and enhancing long-term profitable relationships with customers

RELATIONSHIP PERSPECTIVE building partnerships with firms outside the organization and encouraging teamwork among different functions within the organization to develop long-term customer relationships

RELATIONSHIP SELLING see **relationship marketing**

RELATIONSHIP STRATEGY a framework for working with customers based on relationship selling; it includes

the counselor strategy, the supplier strategy, and the systems-designer strategy

RELIABILITY reflects the consistency of responses or the extent to which results are reproducible

REPOSITIONING developing new marketing programs to shift consumer beliefs and opinions about an existing brand; see also **positioning**

RESELLER MARKET firms that purchase goods and in turn sell them to others at a gain; includes wholesalers and retailers

RESERVATION PRICE the highest price a person is willing to pay for a product; one form of a consumer's internal reference price

RETAIL CHAIN a retailer that owns and operates multiple retail outlets; chains represent 20 percent of all retailers and account for 50 percent of all retail sales

RETAIL COOPERATIVE a group of stores that remain independently owned but adopt a common name and storefront and band together to increase their buying power

RETAIL FRANCHISING a form of chain ownership in which a franchisee pays the franchisor (parent company) fees or royalties and agrees to run the franchise by prescribed norms in exchange for use of the franchisor's name

RETAIL SALES sales to final consumers, as opposed to wholesale sales; a firm's retail sales must be at least half of its total revenues for it to be classified a retailer

RETAIL STRATEGY MIX the controllable variables of location, products and services, pricing, and marketing communications

RETAILER-OWNED COOPERATIVE GROUP a contractual marketing channel system in which the retailers own the wholesaler

RETAILING all of the activities involved in selling products and services to the final consumer; retailers include independents, chains, franchises, leased departments, cooperatives, and various forms of nonstore retailers

RETURN ON INVESTMENT (ROI) ratio of income before taxes to total operating assets associated with a product, such as plant and equipment and inventory

REVERSE AUCTIONS auctions in which sellers bid instead of buyers and prices fall instead of rise, enabling buyers to negotiate lower prices from multiple suppliers

REWARD POWER power a member of a marketing channel gains when it can offer another member widespread distribution, special credit terms, or some other reward

ROBINSON-PATMAN ACT a U.S. law passed in 1936 to prohibit price discrimination

ROLLOUT STUDIES marketing research studies performed on a new product after it has been introduced

SALES AUTOMATION SYSTEMS computerized systems sales managers use for routine supervisory chores such as processing sales reps' call reports, itineraries, and expense reports

SALES CHANNEL STRATEGY addresses how a company initiates and maintains contact with customer through the use of a company field salesforce, telemarketing, independent sales reps, distributors, or trade shows

SALES EFFECTIVENESS EVALUATIONS the most stringent tests of advertising efficiency, they assess whether the advertising resulted in increased sales

SALES MANAGEMENT managers who oversee the personal selling function, managing sales personnel and developing and implementing sales strategy

SALESFORCE EFFECTIVENESS how well the entire sales organization is performing, including an evaluation of individual salespeople's performance

SALESFORCE TURNOVER the proportion of salespeople who leave their jobs

SALES POTENTIAL the maximum amount of sales a specific firm can obtain for a specified time period

SALES PROCESS the process of initiating, developing, and enhancing long-term, mutually satisfying relationships with customers

SALES PROMOTION the element of the marketing communications mix that provides extra value or incentives to consumers, wholesalers, retailers, or other organizational customers to stimulate product interest, trial, or purchase; media and nonmedia marketing communications employed for a predetermined, limited time to stimulate

trial, increase consumer demand, or improve product availability

SALES RESISTANCE customer concerns about a product, both spoken (objections) and unspoken

SALES SUPPORT SALESPEOPLE employees who support the personal selling function by promoting a product or providing technical support, working in coordination with the salespeople who actually solicit customer purchases

SALES TERRITORY usually defined geographically, a territory consists of specific customers assigned to a specific salesperson

SALESPERSON PERFORMANCE how well individual salespeople meet job expectations, evaluated from a behavior-based perspective, an outcome-based perspective, or a combination of the two

SAMPLE a small size of a product made available to prospective purchasers, usually free, to demonstrate a product's value or use and encourage future purchase

SAMPLE SIZE the size of a sample in market research, based on the anticipated response rate, variability in the data, cost, and time considerations and desired level of precision

SAMPLING FRAME the outline or working description of the population used in sample selection for market research

SANCTIONS restrictions imposed by the UN or individual governments to limit trade with specific countries

SCANNER DATA a type of proprietary data derived from UPC bar codes

SCRAMBLED MERCHANDISING adding unrelated product categories to existing product lines

SEALED-BID PRICING pricing in which sellers submit sealed bids for providing their products or services and the buyer chooses among them. See also **negotiated pricing**

SEASONALITY product demand fluctuations related to the time of year, which may be affected by unpredictable changes in weather and in consumer preferences

SECOND-MARKET DISCOUNTING a form of differential pricing in which different prices are charged in different market segments (for example, foreign markets)

SECONDARY DATA proprietary and nonproprietary data already collected for some other purpose and available from various sources (such as library research); typically cheaper than collecting primary data but may be less current or relevant

SECONDARY DEMAND demand for a specific brand of new product form, which marketing tries to generate after competing brands are introduced

SELECTING choosing the candidates to be hired for a sales job

SELECTIVE DISTRIBUTION involves selling a product in only some of the available outlets and is commonly used when after-the-sale service is necessary, such as in the home appliance industry

SELECTIVE PERCEPTION information is only partially processed or is misinterpreted due to limited exposure, attention, or comprehension; caused most often by the consumer's limited ability and motivation to see and process everything

SELF-CONCEPT a person's overall perception and feelings about himself or herself; consumers buy products that are consistent with or that enhance their self-concept

SELLING PHILOSOPHY an organization's emphasis on the selling function to the exclusion of other marketing activities

SELLING STRATEGY an overall plan for a salesperson's course of action, developed at three levels: sales territory, customer, and individual sales call

SERVICE MERCHANDISER see rack jobber

SERVICE RETAILERS all retailers that sell services, from rental businesses to movie theaters, hotels, and car repair shops

SERVICES nonphysical products such as a haircut, a football game, or a doctor's diagnosis (in contrast to goods, which are physical products)

SHERMAN ACT a U.S. law passed in 1890 to prohibit monopolistic practices

SHIPPING CONTAINER MARKING (SCM) feeds information into a computerized tracking system to facilitate shipping of products

SHOPPING MALLS a concentration of retail stores enclosed under one roof and designed for more pedestrian flow

SHOPPING PRODUCTS categories of items within which consumers do not know exactly what they want and are willing to spend time shopping; usually expensive items such as cars, TVs

SIMPLE RANDOM SAMPLING a probability sampling approach in which each unit has an equal chance of being selected

SIMULATED TEST MARKETING evaluating a new-product prototype in situations set up to be similar to those where consumers would actually purchase or use the product (for example, intercepting shoppers at a high-traffic location in a mall)

SINGLE-CHANNEL STRATEGY using only one means to reach customers (for example, Nexxus shampoo is distributed exclusively through hair care professionals)

SINGLE-SOURCE DATA data produced by proprietary systems that combine information on product purchase behavior with TV viewing behavior

SITE STICKINESS a term used to describe a marketer's goal of boosting customer interactions and time spent on a site

SLOTTING ALLOWANCES fees manufacturers pay to retailers or wholesalers to obtain shelf or warehouse space for their products

SOCIAL CLASSES relatively homogenous divisions within a society that contain people with similar values, needs, lifestyles, and behavior. Usually divided into four classes: upper, middle, working, and lower

SOCIAL ENVIRONMENT all factors and trends related to groups of people, including their number, characteristics, behavior, and growth projections

SOCIAL RESPONSIBILITY minimizing social costs, such as environmental damage, and maximizing the positive impact of marketing decisions on society

SOCIALIZATION absorbing a culture, a process that continues throughout life and produces many specific preferences of products and services, shopping patterns, and interactions with others

SOURCE the message sender; in marketing communications, the marketer

SOURCE CREDIBILITY the state in which a customer perceives that its needs are satisfied by the combination of

the sales rep, the product or service, and the rep's company

SOURCES companies or individuals who sell products and services directly to buying organizations; also called **suppliers** or **vendors**

SPAM unsolicited e-mail

SPECIALTY-LINE WHOLESALER a wholesaler that sells only a single product line or part of a line but is an expert regarding those products

SPECIALTY PRODUCTS items for which consumers want a specific brand and are willing to hunt for it; they won't switch brands (as with convenience products) or shop to evaluate alternatives (as for shopping products)

SPIFF see **push money**

SPONSORSHIP investments in causes and events to support overall corporate and marketing objectives

STANDARD INDUSTRIAL CLASSIFICATION (SIC) SYSTEM a federal government numerical scheme for categorizing businesses from general industry groupings to specific product categories

STANDARD TEST MARKETING testing a new-product prototype and its marketing strategy in actual market situations

STANDARDIZED MARKETING STRATEGY implementing the same product, price, distribution, and communications programs in all international markets

STATEMENT STUFFERS promotional pieces that are included in other mail, such as bank or credit card statements

STATISTICAL DEMAND ANALYSIS forecasting sales from equations in which price, promotion, distribution, competitive, and economic factors are independent variables

STEALTH MARKETING involves a wide range of publicity generators, from product placement in movies and television to the naming of sports facilities, such as the United Center in Chicago

STORE BRAND see **distributor brand**

STORE IMAGE the picture shoppers have of a store's identity, composed of their perceptions of its location, goods and services sold, and atmospherics

STRAIGHT REBUY DECISIONS most common type of business purchasing decision in which products and services are simply repurchased; delivery, performance, and price are critical considerations

STRATEGIC BUSINESS UNIT (SBU) a unit of a company that focuses on a single product or brand, a line of products, or a mix of related products that meet a common market need and whose management oversees the basic business functions

STRATEGIC MARKETING marketing activities that encompass three functions: (1) helping to orient everyone in the organization toward markets and customers, (2) helping to gather and analyze information needed to examine the current situation, identify trends in the marketing environment, and assess their potential impact, and (3) helping to develop corporate, business, and marketing strategic plans

STRATEGY MIX one way by which retailers differentiate themselves from one another. This consists of the following (all controllable) elements: location, product and services, pricing, and marketing mixes

STRATIFIED SAMPLING a probability sampling technique in which the population is divided into mutually exclusive groups, such as consumers with different income levels, and random samples are taken from each group

STRIP CENTERS retail shopping districts that are not enclosed under one roof and usually feature parking in front of the stores

STYLE a unique form of expression that is defined by a product's characteristics and has a fluctuating life cycle

SUBJECTIVE CLAIMS advertising claims that are not measurable and often stress image enhancement

SUBLIMINAL ADVERTISING initially related to ad messages presented at a rate or level below thresholds of conscious awareness, this practice today most often involves the embedding of hidden symbols in advertisements

SUBSTANTIALNESS the degree to which identified target segments are large enough and have sufficient sales and profit potential to warrant separate marketing programs

SUPPLIERS see **sources**

SUPPLY-CHAIN MANAGEMENT the "effort involved in producing and delivering a final product from the supplier's supplier to the customer's customer," usually by cutting across organizational and company boundaries, in order to better serve the customer and gain a competitive advantage

SURROGATE SHOPPERS those who are a commercial enterprise, consciously engaged and paid, by a consumer or other interested partner on behalf of the consumer, to perform any or all of the activities involved in consumer decision making

SURVEY OF BUYERS' INTENTIONS sales forecast based on surveys of what either consumers or organizational buyers say they will do; such surveys are most reliable when the buyers have well-formed intentions and are willing to disclose them accurately

SWEEPSTAKES a sales promotion that offers prizes based on a chance drawing of participants' names

TARGET COSTING a pricing process that combines both cost and customer input into pricing decisions; determines what the manufacturing costs must be to achieve desired profits and customer features, as well as acceptable market prices

TARGET MARKET a defined group of consumers or organizations with whom a firm wants to create marketing exchanges

TARGET-RETURN PRICING a cost-oriented approach that sets prices to achieve a desired rate of return, with cost and profit estimates based on some expected volume or sales level

TARGETING selecting which segments in a market are appropriate to focus on and designing the means to reach them

TEAM SELLING a sales approach in which a company assigns accounts to sales teams of specialists according to the customers' purchase-information needs

TECHNICAL SUPPORT SALESPEOPLE the people in sales support who have expertise in areas such as design and installation of complex equipment and may provide specialized training to customer employees

TECHNOLOGICAL ENVIRONMENT factors and trends related to innovations that affect the development of new products or the marketing process

TECHNOLOGY PERSPECTIVE using new and emerging technologies as sources for new products and services and to improve marketing practice

TELEMARKETING an interactive direct marketing communications approach that uses the phone to initiate, develop, and enhance relationships with customers

TEST MARKETING testing the prototype of a new product and its marketing strategy in simulated or actual market situations

TESTIMONIALS third-party evidence, such as letters from satisfied customers, that enhance source credibility

THIRD-PARTY RESPONSE a complaint about a product in which the consumer takes legal action or files a complaint with a consumer-affairs agency instead of dealing just with the company

THREATS trends in the marketing environment that might adversely affect a company's situation; typically ranked by managers so the most important threats can be addressed first in the next strategic planning stage

TIE-IN see cross-promotion

TOTAL COSTS the sum of variable costs and fixed costs

TOTAL REVENUE total sales, or unit price multiplied by the quantity of the product sold; (before-tax) profits equal total revenue minus total costs

TRADE ALLOWANCE the amount a manufacturer contributes to a local dealer or retailer's advertising expense

TRADE CONTEST a sales promotion at the reseller level that associates prizes with sales of the sponsor's product

TRADE SALES PROMOTION sales promotion directed at retailers, wholesalers, or other business buyers to help push products through the marketing channel

TRADE SALES PROMOTION ALLOWANCES concessions a manufacturer allocates to wholesalers or retailers to promote its products (for example, supermarkets' cooperative advertising)

TRADE SHOW a periodic, semipublic event sponsored by a trade, professional, or industrial association at which suppliers rent booths to display products and provide information to potential buyers

TRADEMARK a brand or part of a brand that is registered with the U.S. Patent and Trademark Office, giving the owner exclusive rights to use the brand

TRANSACTION MARKETING producing sales in the short run at any cost

TRANSACTION VALUE the perceived merits of the deal itself; retailers provide comparison pricing in an effort to boost products' transaction value by raising shoppers' internal price standard

TREND ANALYSIS a quantitative forecasting approach that examines historical sales data for predictable patterns (also known as time-series analysis)

TRUCK JOBBER a limited-function wholesaler that delivers within a small geographic area to ensure freshness of goods (for example, bakery, meat, dairy)

TWO-WAY STRETCH STRATEGY adding products at both the low and the high end of a product line

TYING CONTRACT a marketing channel arrangement in which a manufacturer requires a reseller to buy products in addition to the one it really wants

UNAIDED RECALL TESTS posttesting in which consumers are questioned with no prompting about ads

UNDIFFERENTIATED STRATEGY marketing a single product using a single promotional mix for the entire market; most often used early in the life of a product category

UNIFORM DELIVERED PRICE a form of geographical pricing in which each customer, no matter where located, is charged the same average freight amount

UNIT PRICING price information presented on a per-unit weight or volume basis so shoppers can compare prices across brands and across package sizes within brands

UNIVERSAL PRODUCT CODE (UPC) bar code that is scanned at grocery checkouts and can provide secondary data for marketing research

UNPLANNED BUSINESS DISTRICT shopping area that evolved spontaneously and is made up of independently owned and managed retail operations; types include central business districts, secondary business districts, neighborhood business districts, and string locations

UNRELATED DIVERSIFICATION branching out into products or services that have nothing in common with existing operations

UPWARD STRETCH STRATEGY adding products at the higher end of a product line; for example, Japanese carmakers entered the U.S. market at the low end and gradually added higher-priced cars

U.S.–CANADA TRADE ACT a law passed in 1988 to allow free trade between the United States and Canada

UTILITARIAN INFLUENCE compliance with the expectations of others to achieve rewards or avoid punishments (for example, peer disapproval)

VALIDITY refers to the extent to which the measures or questions used in a study truly reflect the concepts being studied

VALUE-ADDED RESELLERS (VARS) intermediaries that add value to goods and services as they pass through the marketing channel

VALUE-EXPRESSIVE INFLUENCE a desire to enhance self-concept through identification with others (for example, by purchasing a product endorsed by a celebrity)

VALUE IN USE (VIU) an approach for determining the economic value that a product has relative to an existing competitive offering

VALUE-IN-USE PRICING basing pricing on customer estimates of the costs if the service could not be obtained (for example, downtime costs if a computer could not be repaired)

VALUES shared beliefs or cultural norms about what is important or right, which directly influence how consumers view and use products, brands, and services

VALUES AND LIFESTYLES PROGRAM (VALS) a lifestyle program from SRI International that segments consumers into eight groups: actualizers, fulfillers, believers, achievers, strivers, experiencers, makers, and strugglers

VARIABLE COSTS costs that change with the level of output, such as wages and raw materials; see also **fixed costs**

VENDORS see **sources**

VERTICAL MARKETING SYSTEMS centrally coordinated, highly integrated operations in which the product flows down the channel from producer to ultimate consumer; the basic vertical types are corporate, contractual, and administered channel systems

VIDEO CATALOG a direct-mail catalog in videocassette form

VOICE RESPONSE a complaint about a product in which the customer seeks satisfaction directly from the seller

WEBLINING the positive aspects of the Internet's ability to allow companies to identify high- and low-value customers so that deals and special services can be targeted only to the most profitable customers

WHOLESALE CLUB a club whose members pay an annual fee that entitles them to make tax-free purchases at lower-than-retail prices

WHOLESALE SALES sales to other businesses that resell the product or service or use it in running their own businesses (as opposed to retail sales)

WHOLESALER-SPONSORED VOLUNTARY GROUP a contractual marketing channel system consisting of independent retailers that operate under the name of a sponsoring wholesaler

WHOLESALERS firms that sell to manufacturers and industrial customers, retailers, government agencies, other wholesalers, and institutional customers such as schools and hospitals

WHOLESALING refers to the marketing activities associated with selling products to purchasers who resell the products, use them to make another product, or use them to conduct business activities

WRITTEN SALES PROPOSAL a detailed written presentation of a product's capabilities, benefits, and costs, often tailored to the individual customer

ZONE PRICING a form of geographical pricing in which customers within one area (say, the Northeast) are charged one freight price and more-distant zones are charged higher freight amounts

Notes

Prologue

[1]David Goetz, "New Name Reflects Tricon's Culture," *The Courier-Journal,* March 22, 2002, p. E3.

[2]Brian O'Keefe, "Global Brands," *Fortune,* November 26, 2001 (accessed from www.fortune.com).

[3]Stuart Elliott, "Pizza Hut Takes Aim at Sandwich Chains," *New York Times,* January 11, 2001, p. 6 (accessed from www.proquest.umi.com).

[4]Kate MacArthur, "Games People Play: Looking for Lift, Taco Bell Stakes $70 mil on Xbox," *Advertising Age,* October 1, 2001, pp. 3, 59 (accessed through www.proques.umi.com).

[5]Khanh T.L. Tran, "Microsoft Teams Up with SoBe, Taco Bell, Vans to Promote Xbox Video-Game System," *The Wall Street Journal,* September 5, 2001, p. B4 (accessed from www.proquest.umi.com).

[6]Susan Gosselin, "Pizza Wars," *The Lane Report,* September 1, 2001, p. 46 (accessed from www.proquest.umi.com).

[7]"Yum! Brands to Test Asian Restaurant Concept," *Business Finct of Louisville,* June 11, 2002, p. 1–2. (This was accessed through louisville.bizjournals.com/louisville.)

Chapter One

[1]Peter D. Bennett, ed., *Dictionary of Marketing Terms* (Chicago: American Marketing Association, 1988), p. 54.

[2]Steve Jarvis, "Theatre's Rebranding Efforts Take a Bow," *Marketing News,* June 10, 2002, pp. 6–8.

[3]Faith Keenan, "The Marines Learn New Tactics—from Wal-Mart," *Business Week,* December 24, 2001, p. 74.

[4]Steve Jarvis, "In Time of Need," *Marketing News,* April 15, 2002, p. 4.

[5]Mara Der Hovanesian, Heather Timmons, and Chris Palmeri, "For Small Banks, It's A Wonderful Life," *Business Week,* May 6, 2002, pp. 83–84.

[6]Eilene Zimmerman, "So, You Wanna Be a CEO," *Sales and Marketing Management,* January 2002, pp. 31–35.

[7]Dana James, "Marketing's a Good Place to Start That Next Career," *Marketing News,* June 10, 2002, pp. 4–5.

[8]Chad Rubel, "Managers Buy Into Quality When They See That It Works," *Marketing News,* March 25, 1996, p. 14.

[9]For different perspectives concerning the marketing concept, see Franklin S. Houston, "The Marketing Concept: What It Is and What It Is Not," *Journal of Marketing,* April 1986, pp. 81–87; Frederick E. Webster, Jr., "The Rediscovery of the Marketing Concept," *Business Horizons,* May–June 1988, pp. 29–39; Lynn W. McGee and Rosann L. Spiro, "The Marketing Concept in Perspective," *Business Horizons,* May–June 1988, pp. 40–45; and Ajay K. Kohli and Bernard J. Jaworski, "Market Orientation: The Construct, Research Propositions, and Managerial Implications," *Journal of Marketing,* April 1990, pp. 1–18.

[10]James L. Heskett, Thomas O. Jones, Gary W. Loveman, W. Earl Sasser, Jr., and Leonard A. Schlesinger, "Putting the Service-Profit Chain to Work," *Harvard Business Review,* March–April 1994, pp. 165–66.

[11]Robert C. Blattberg, Gary Getz, and Jacquelyn S. Thomas, *Customer Equity,* Boston, Massachusetts: Harvard Business School Press, 2001.

[12]Heskett et al., "Putting the Service-Profit Chain to Work," p. 164.

[13]Laura Struebling, "Customer Loyalty: Playing for Keeps," *Quality Progress,* February 1996, pp. 25–26.

[14]Thomas O. Jones and Earl Sasser, Jr., "Why Satisfied Customers Defect," *Harvard Business Review,* November–December 1995, pp. 91–93.

[15]Heskett et al., "Putting the Service-Profit Chain to Work," pp. 166–67.

[16]Neil King, Jr., "U.S. Decides to Grant Russia Status of 'Market Economy'," *The Wall Street Journal Online,* June 7, 2002, pp. 1–2.

[17]Paula Lyon Andruss, "Slow Boat to China," *Marketing News,* September 10, 2001, pp. 1, 11–12.

[18]Dexter Roberts, "A Tale of Two Families," *Business Week,* June 28, 1999, pp. 52–56.

[19]William L. Wilkie and Elizabeth S. Moore, "Marketing's Contribution to Society," *Journal of Marketing,* Special Issue 1999, pp. 198–218.

[20]Avraham Shama, "Management under Fire: The Transformation of Managers in the Soviet Union and Eastern Europe," *The Executive,* February 1993, pp. 22–35.

[21]See Franklin S. Houston and Jule B. Gassenheimer, "Marketing and Exchange," *Journal of Marketing,* October 1987, pp. 3–18, for a more complete discussion of exchange and marketing.

[22]Richard P. Bagozzi, "Toward a Formal Theory of Marketing Exchange," in *Conceptual and Theoretical Developments in Marketing,* eds. O. C. Ferrell, Stephen W. Brown, and Charles W. Lamb, Jr. (Chicago: American Marketing Association, 1979), p. 434.

Chapter Two

[1]Andrew Park and Spencer E. Ante, "Who Will Master the Server Biz," *Business Week,* June 24, 2002, pp. 92–93.

[2]Polly LaBarre, "How Skandia Generates Its Future Faster," *Fast Company,* December–January 1997, p. 58.

[3]Nafis Sadik, "World Population Continues to Rise." *The 1992 Information Please Almanac* (Boston: Houghton Mifflin, 1991), p. 131.

[4]John W. Wright, *The Universal Almanac 1993* (Kansas City, MO: Andrews and McMeel, 1992), p. 326.

[5]Ibid., p. 279.

[6]Dan Morse, "Follow the Demographics, Franchising Experts Agree," *The Wall Street Journal Interactive Edition,* December 21, 1999, pp. 1–4.

[7]Dom Del Prete, "Wall Street Bullish on Mature Adults," *Marketing News,* December 6, 1993, pp. 1–2.

[8]Michele Marchetti, "Talkin' 'bout My Generation," *Sales & Marketing Management,* December 1995, p. 66.

[9]"They Understand Your Kids," *Fortune,* Autumn–Winter 1993, pp. 29–30.

[10]Tom W. Smith, *The Emerging 21st Century American Family,* National Opinion Research Center, University of Chicago, GSS Social Change Report No. 42, November 24, 1999, p. 28.

[11]Laura Zinn, Heather Keets, and James B. Treece, "Home Alone—with $660 Billion," *Business Week,* July 29, 1990, pp. 76–77.

[12]Joseph Weber, "What's Not Cookin' at Campbell's," *Business Week,* September 23, 1996, p. 40.

[13]Amy Hilliard-Jones, "Consumers of Color Are Changing the American Marketplace," *Marketing News.* November, 18, 1996, p. 8.

[14]Ibrahim Sajid Malick, "New Americans: The Overlooked $400 Billion Market," *Marketing News,* July 15, 1996, p. 9.

[15]Hilliard-Jones, "Consumers of Color," p. 8.

[16]Malick, "New Americans," p. 9.

[17]Maria Puente and Martin Kasindorf, "Blended Races Make a True Melting Pot," *USA Today,* September 7, 1999, pp. 1A and 13A.

[18]Erika Rasmusson, "Marketing en Espanol," *Sales & Marketing Management,* September 1999, p. 16.

[19]Cyndee Miller, "She Succeeds Royally Even in a Bear Market," *Marketing News,* July 29, 1996, p. 2.

[20]Tim Triplett, "Increase in Women Golfers Sparks Marketing Interest," *Marketing News,* June 3, 1996, pp. 2, 14.

[21]"To Your Health," *Modern Maturity,* January–February 1999, p. 23.

[22]Susan Hansen, "Herbal-Tonic Bottler Has Healthy Start," *Inc.,* June 1999, pp. 21–22.

[23]Marvin Cetron and Owen Davies, *Crystal Globe* (New York: St. Martin's Press, 1991), pp. 353–54.

[24]"Edison Environmental Awards," *Marketing News,* May 6, 1996, p. E14.

[25]Ronald Grover, Joyce Barnathan, Dexter Roberts, and Stan Crock, "Go East, Media Moguls," *Business Week,* March 22, 1999, p. 40.

[26]"The Economy," *Business Week,* December 31, 2001, p. 68.

[27]Michael Mandell, ed., "The Recession Wasn't So Mild," *Business Week,* July 1, 2002, p. 30.

[28]John Ward Anderson, "Thundering Herd," *The Courier-Journal* (Louisville, KY), January 2, 1994, p. A8.

[29]Jay M. Tannon, "NAFTA is Good News for U.S. Trade," *Business First,* November 29, 1993, p. 7.

[30]Amy Borrus, Bill Javetski, John Parry, and Brian Bremner, "Change of Heart," *Business Week,* May 20, 1996, pp. 48–49.

[31]Margaret Popper, "The Payoff from Free Trade," *Business Week,* June 24, 2002, p. 26.

[32]Paul Magnusson, "Bush: What Price Fast Track?", *BusinessWeek,* June 3, 2002, p. 38.

[33]"Bush: Criminal CEOs Need Jail," *CNNMONEY,* accessed at www.cnn.com, June 30, 2002, pp. 1–3.

[34]John Rossant, Jack Ewing, and Brian Bremmer, "The Corporate Cleanup Goes Global," *Business Week,* May 6, 2002, pp. 80–81.

[35]Maxine S. Lans, "New Laws on Green Marketing Are Popping Up All the Time," *Marketing News,* February 15, 1993, pp. 22, 24.

[36]Elyse Tanouye, "Warner-Lambert Drug Is Approved for Epilepsy Cases," *The Wall Street Journal,* January 4, 1994, p. B12.

[37]Stephen Baker, "Did Smith kline Find the Smoking Gun?" *Business Week,* April 29, 1996, p. 44.

[38]Deborah Szynal, "Status Quo," *Marketing News,* March 4, 2002, pp. 1, 13–14.

[39]"The List: Adapt or Die," *Business Week,* July 26, 1999, p. 6.

[40]Michael Fitzgerald, "The Next Wave," *Business 2.0,* July 2002, pp. 53–58.

[41]Ian Wylie, "Green Giant," *Fast Company,* June 2002, p. 64.

[42]Catherine Yang, "The Pulse of the Future," *Business Week,* April 22, 2002, pp. 92–93.

[43]"Know Thy Enemy," *Success,* June 1996, p. 10.

Chapter Three

[1]Anil Menon, Sundar G. Bharadwaj, Phani Tej, and Steven W. Edison, "Antecedents and Consequences of Marketing Strategy Making: A Model and Test," *Journal of Marketing,* April 1999, p. 19.

[2]Rajdeep Grewal and Patriya Tansuhaj, "Building Organizational Capabilities for Managing Economic Crisis: The Role of Market Orientation and Strategic Flexibility," *Journal of Marketing,* April 2001, p. 67.

[3]Gary McWilliams, "Gateway Loss Will Be Larger than Expected," *The Wall Street Journal,* October 5, 2001, p. B6.

[4]Keith H. Hammonds, "Michael Porter's Big Ideas," *Fast Company,* March 2001, pp. 152–54, 156.

[5]Michael H. Morris and Leyland F. Pitts, "The Contemporary Use of Strategy, Strategic Planning, and Planning Tools by Marketers: A Cross-National Comparison," *European Journal of Marketing,* 1993, pp. 36–57.

[6]Michael Krauss, "Marketing Department Organization Is Destiny," *Marketing News,* February 18, 2002, p. 14.

[7]Ronald Grover and Eric Schine, "Can Hilton Draw a Full House?" *Business Week,* June 8, 1992, pp. 88–89.

[8]Emily Nelson, "Marketing & Media: Colgate Net Rose 12% in 1st Quarter on Toothpaste Sales," *The Wall Street Journal,* April 20, 2001, p. B8.

[9]Francy Blackwood, "Dissecting the Service," *Selling,* March 1996, pp. 26–28; *Hoover's Company Profile Database* (Austin, TX: The Reference Press, 1996); and Malcolm Fleschner, "Copy This, Copy This, Copy This," *Selling Power,* March 1996, pp. 22–26.

[10]Christine Bittar, "That's All, Folks," *Brandweek,* May 14, 2001, p. 4.

[11]Arjun Chaudhuri and Morris Holbrook, "The Chain of Effects from Brand Trust and Brand Affect to Brand Performance: The Role of Brand Loyalty," *Journal of Marketing,* April 2001, pp. 81–93.

[12]Katherine N. Lemon, Roland T. Rust, and Valarie A. Zeithaml, "What Drives Customer Equity," *Marketing Management,* Spring 2001, p. 21.

[13]Lee G. Cooper, "Strategic Marketing Planning for Radically New Products," *Journal of Marketing,* January 2000, p. 1.

[14]"Some Utilities Rake in Revenue Amid Crisis," *The Wall Street Journal,* January 23, 2001, www.djinteractive.com.

[15]Philip Kotler, *Marketing Management,* The Millennium Edition (Upper Saddle River, NJ: Prentice Hall); Anil Menon, Sundar G. Bharadwaj, Phani Tej Adidam, and Steve W. Edison, "Antecedents and Consequences of Marketing Strategy Making: A Model and a Test," *Journal of Marketing,* April 1999, pp. 18–40; and Charles H. Noble and Michael P. Mokwa, "Implementing Marketing Strategies: Developing and Testing a Managerial Theory," *Journal of Marketing,* October 1999, pp. 57–73.

[16]Charles H. Noble and Michael P. Mokwa, "Implementing Marketing Strategies: Developing and Testing a Managerial Strategy," *Journal of Marketing,* October 1999, pp. 57–73.

[17]Frederick E. Webster, Jr., "The Changing Role of Marketing in the Corporation," *Journal of Marketing,* October 1992, pp. 1–17.

[18]Ibid., p. 10.

[19]Ravi S. Achrol and Philip Kotler, "Marketing in the Network Economy," *Journal of Marketing,* Special Issue 1999, pp. 146–47.

[20]George S. Day and David B. Montgomery, "Charting New Directions for Marketing," *Journal of Marketing,* Special Issue 1999, pp. 3–13.

[21]Christine Moorman and Roland T. Rust, "The Role of Marketing," *Journal of Marketing*, Special Issue 1999, p. 180.

[22]Michael E. Porter, "Strategy and the Internet," *Harvard Business Review*, March 2001, 63–78.

[23]Tim Coltman, Timothy M. Devinney, Alopi Latukefu, and David F. Midgley, "E-business: Revolution, Evolution, or Hype," *California Management Review*, 44 (1), pp. 57–86; Sydney Finkelstein, "Internet Startups: So Why Can't They Win?", *Journal of Business Strategy*, July/August 2001, pp. 18–21; Michael E. Porter, "Strategy and the Internet," *Harvard Business Review*, March 2001, pp. 63–78.

[24]Adapted from John A. Pearce II and Fred David, "Corporate Mission Statements: The Bottom Line," *Academy of Management Executive*, May 1987, p. 109.

[25]James C. Collins and Jerry I. Porras, "Building Your Company's Vision," *Harvard Business Review*, September–October 1996, pp. 65–77.

[26]http://www.benjerry.co.uk/aboutbj/mission.htm.

[27]http://www.whirlpool.com/whr/ics/story/vision.html.

[28]Gilbert Fuchsberg, "'Visioning' Missions Becomes Its Own Mission," *The Wall Street Journal*, January 7, 1994, pp. B1, B4.

[29]http://www.boeing.com/companyoffices/aboutus/mission/index.html.

[30]Claes Fornell, "Customer Satisfaction, Capital Efficiency, and Shareholder Value," *Managing Customer Relationships*, Cambridge, MA: Marketing Science Institute, Report No. 00-107, 2000, pp. 9–12.

[31]George S. Day, "Capabilities for Forging Customer Relationships," Report No. 00-118, Cambridge, MA: Marketing Science Institute, 2000; George S. Day, "The Capabilities of Market-Driven Organizations, *Journal of Marketing*, October 1994, pp. 37–52.

[32]Linda Himelstein, "The Soul of a New Nike," *Business Week*, June 17, 1996, pp. 70–71.

[33]Ian P. Murphy, "Survey Finds Safe Growth Is Priority for New Products," *Marketing News*, July 15, 1996, p. 15.

[34]Terry Lefton, "Nike's New Golf Balls Aim Straight up Fairway," *Brandweek*, January 18, 1999, p. 5; and Chuck Stogel, "Nike Restages Golf Push for '00," *Brandweek*, June 28, 1999, p. 34.

[35]Rajesh K. Chandy and Gerard J. Tellis, "The Incumbent's Curse? Incumbency, Size, and Radical Product Innovation," *Journal of Marketing*, July 2000, pp. 1–17.

[36]Chad Holliday, "Sustainable Growth, the DuPont Way," *Harvard Business Review*, September 2001, pp. 129–134.

[37]David W. Cravens, *Strategic Marketing* (Homewood, IL: Richard D. Irwin, 1994), pp. 46–47.

[38]"The Genesis of a Giant's Stumble," *The New York Times*, January 21, 2001, pp. 1, 13.

[39]"Technology: Ricoh Tries to Put Multiple Brands Under One Roof," *The New York Times*, February 5, 2001, www.nytimes.com/archives.

[40]Webster, "The Changing Role of Marketing in the Corporation," p. 10.

[41]George S. Day, *Analysis for Strategic Marketing Decisions* (St. Paul, MN: West Publishing Company, 1995), pp. 202–5.

[42]Philip Kotler, *Marketing Management: Analysis, Planning, Implementation, and Control*, 8th ed. (Englewood Cliffs, NJ: Prentice Hall, 1994), p. 76.

[43]John A. Byrne, "Strategic Planning," *Business Week*, August 26, 1996, pp. 46–52; Peter Elstrom, "Did Motorola Make the Wrong Call?" *Business Week*, July 29, 1996, pp. 66–68; Gary Hamel and C. K. Prahalad, *Competing for the Future* (Boston: Harvard Business School Press, 1994); Webster, "The Changing Role of Marketing," pp. 1–17; and John O. Whitney, "Strategic Renewal for Business Units," *Harvard Business Review*, July–August 1996, pp. 84–98.

[44]Jay Barney, "Firm Resources and Sustained Competitive Advantage," *Journal of Management*, 17 (1), 1991, pp. 99–120.

[45]P. Rajan Varadarajan, Satish Jayachandran, and J. Chris White, "Strategic Interdependence in Organizations: Deconglomeration and Marketing Strategy," *Journal of Marketing*, January 2001, pp. 15–28.

[46]C. K. Prahalad and Richard A. Bettis, "The Dominant Logic: A New Linkage between Diversity and Performance," *Strategic Management Journal*, 7, 1986, pp. 485–501.

[47]Susan Carey, "Rough Climate on Airlines Takes Toll on Midwest Express—Extraordinary Service, Loyal Following Don't Shield Carrier from Industry Woes," *The Wall Street Journal*, July 9, 2001, B4; Amy Goldwasser, "Something Stylish, Something Blue," *Business 2.0*, February 2002, pp. 94–96; James Ott, "Cautionary Tale of Two Texas Airlines," *Aviation Week and Space Technology*, November 19, 2001, pp. 60–63; Pierre Sparaco, "British Carrier Expands Operation in France," *Aviation Week and Space Technology*, December 17, 2001, pp. 86–87; "The Pluck of the Irish; Low-Cost Airlines," *The Economist*, January 26, 2002, 58–59.

[48]"General Excellence: Southwest Airlines," *Sales & Marketing Management*, August 1993, p. 38.

[49]Kevin Kelly, Wendy Zellner, and Aaron Bernstein, "Suddenly Big Airlines Are Saying: 'Small Is Beautiful,'" *Business Week*, January 17, 1994, p. 37.

[50]Pierre Sparaco, "Swissair Expands Partnership Network," *Aviation Week and Space Technology*, August 23, 1999, p. 56.

[51]Jagdish Sheth and Rajendra Sisodia, *The Rule of Three: Surviving and Thriving in Competitive Markets* (New York, NY: The Free Press, 2002) p. 2.

[52]Christine Bittar, "Gillette's Edge: Male-Skewing Razor Backed By $60M," *Brandweek*, May 28, 2001, p. 5.

[53]Vijay Mahajan, Marcos V. Pratini De Moraes, and Jerry Wind, "The Invisible Global Market," *Marketing Management*, Winter 2000, pp. 31–35.

[54]Edmund Faltermayer, "Competitiveness: How U.S. Companies Stack Up Now," *Fortune*, April 18, 1994, pp. 52–64.

[55]Gary McWilliams, "Wang's Great Leap out of Limbo," *Business Week*, March 7, 1994, pp. 68–69.

[56]"Cadbury Buys Spanish Concern," *The Wall Street Journal*, April 22, 1994, p. A6.

[57]Kathy Rebello and Neil Gross, "A Juicy New Apple?" *Business Week*, March 7, 1994, pp. 88–90; "Ciba-Geigy Plans China Venture," *The Wall Street Journal*, April 22, 1994, p. A6; and Brian Coleman and Bridget O'Brian, "Delta Airlines, Virgin Atlantic Forge Alliance," *The Wall Street Journal*, April 13, 1994, p. A4.

[58]David M. Szymanski, Sundar G. Bharadwaj, and P. Rajan Varadarajan, "Standardization versus Adaptation of International Marketing Strategy: An Empirical Investigation," *Journal of Marketing*, October 1993, pp. 1–17; Subhash C. Jain, "Standardization of International Marketing Strategy: Some Research Hypotheses," *Journal of Marketing*, January 1989, pp. 70–79; and John A. Quelch and Edward J. Hoff, "Customizing Global Marketing," *Harvard Business Review*, May–June 1986, pp. 59–68.

[59]Quelch and Hoff, "Customizing," p. 59.

[60]James E. Ellis, "Why Overseas? 'Cause That's Where the Sales Are," *Business Week*, January 10, 1994, p. 63.

[61]John A. Quelch, "Does Globalization Have Staying Power?", *Marketing Management*, March/April, 2002, pp. 20–21.

[62]Richard A. Melcher and Stewart Toy, "On Guard, Europe," *Business Week*, December 14, 1992, pp. 54–55.

[63]Ellis, "Why Overseas?" p. 63.

[64]Sally Solo, "How to Listen to Consumers," *Fortune*, January 11, 1993, pp. 77–78.

65 Michael R. Czinkota and Ilka A. Ronkainen, *International Marketing,* 4th ed. (Fort Worth, TX: Dryden Press, 1995), pp. 263–65; and Jean-Pierre Jeannet and H. David Hennessey, *Global Marketing Strategies,* 3rd ed. (Boston: Houghton Mifflin Company, 1995), p. 336.

66 David A. Aaker and Erich Joachimsthaler, "The Lure of Global Branding," *Harvard Business Review,* November–December 1999, p. 138.

67 Carlos Ghosn, "Saving the Business Without Losing the Company," *Harvard Business Review,* January 2002, pp. 37–45.

68 Rajesh Sethi, Daniel C. Smith, and C. Whan Park, "Cross-Functional Product Development Teams, Creativity, and the Innovativeness of New Consumer Products," *Journal of Marketing Research,* February 2001, pp. 73–85.

69 Ginger Trumfio, "Kodak Adjusts Its Focus," *Sales & Marketing Management,* January 1994, p. 20.

70 Maricris G. Briones, "Strange Bedfellows," *Marketing News,* August 17, 1998, p. 2.

71 Louis Bucklin and Sanjit Sengupta, "Organizing Successful Co-Marketing Alliances," *Journal of Marketing,* April 1993, pp. 32–46; Manohar U. Kalwani and Narakesari Narayandas, "Long-Term Manufacturer-Supplier Relationships: Do They Pay Off for Supplier Firms?" *Journal of Marketing,* January 1995, pp. 1–16; and Robert M. Morgan and Shelby D. Hunt, "The Commitment-Trust Theory of Relationship Marketing," *Journal of Marketing,* July 1994, pp. 20–38.

72 "Making New Friends at Procter & Gamble; With Whirlpool, Trying to Change Consumer Habits," *New York Times,* March 16, 2001, pp. C1, C4.

73 Maricris G. Briones, "Strange Bedfellows," *Marketing News,* August 17, 1998, p. 2.

74 Bernard Simonin and Julie Ruth, "Is a Company Known by the Company It Keeps? Assessing the Spillover Effects of Brand Alliances on Consumer Brand Attitudes," *Journal of Marketing Research,* February 1998, pp. 30–42; "Credit Card Co-Branding on the Rise: Survey," *Supermarket News,* June 5, 1998, p. 21; Harriet Marsh, "P&G Enters the Age of Alliances," *Marketing,* February 11, 1999, p. 18; R. Venkatesh and Vijay Mahajan, "Products with Branded Components: An Approach for Premium Pricing and Partner Selection," *Marketing Science* 16, no. 2 (1997), pp. 146–65.

75 Aric Rindfleisch and Christine Moorman, "The Acquisition and Utilization of Information in New Product Alliances: A Strength-of-Ties Perspective," *Journal of Marketing,* April 2001, pp. 1–18.

Chapter Four

1 Sherrie E. Wehner, "10 Things to Know About Customers," *Marketing News,* December 4, 2000, pp. 20, 22.

2 David Whelan, "A Tale of Two Consumers," *American Demographics,* September 2001, pp. 54–55.

3 http://www.Ebea.doc.gov/bea/gdp401p.htm.

4 Annetta Miller, "The Millennial Mind-Set: It's Here, It's Clear, Get Used to It," *American Demographics,* January 1999, pp. 60–65; and Cheryl Russell, "The New Consumer Paradigm," *American Demographics,* April 1999, pp. 51–58.

5 Frank Solis, "The Next Big Market," *Success,* October 2000, pp. 36, 38.

6 "The Procter & Gamble Company: Global Opportunities and Growth," *1995 Annual Report,* Cincinnati, OH.

7 *What the Customer Wants: The Wall Street Journal's Guide to Marketing in the 1990s* (New York: Dow Jones, 1990), p. vi.

8 Sunil Gupta, Donald R. Lehmann, and Jennifer Ames Stuart, "Valuing Customers," MSI Report No. 01-119, Cambridge, MA: Marketing Science Institute, 2001.

9 Bernard J. Jaworski and Ajay K. Kohli, "Market Orientation: Antecedents and Consequences," *Journal of Marketing,* July 1993, p. 53.

10 Peter R. Dickson, "Toward a General Theory of Competitive Rationality," *Journal of Marketing,* January 1992, p. 70.

11 Jill Griffin and Michael Lowenstein, "Winning Back Lost Customers," Retailing Issues Letter, March 2001, Texas A&M University, College Station, TX: Center for Retailing Studies.

12 David J. Reibstein, "Who's Buying on the Internet and How Long Will They Be Loyal?", MSI Report 00-102, Cambridge, MA: Marketing Science Institute, December 1999, p. 33.

13 Subir Bandyopadhyay, Guangbo Lin, and Yan Zhong, "Smart Marketers Are Sold on Online Auctions," *Marketing Management,* November/December 2001, pp. 25–28; Michael J. Weiss, "Online America," *American Demographics,* March 2001, pp. 53–60.

14 Saul Hansell, "An Ambitious Internet Grocer Is Out of Both Cash and Ideas," *New York Times,* July 12, 2001, p. A1.

15 Merrie Brucks, "The Effects of Product Class Knowledge on Information Search Behavior," *Journal of Consumer Research,* June 1985, pp. 1–16; Patricia M. West, Christina L. Brown, and Stephen J. Hoch, "Consumption Vocabulary and Preference Formation," *Journal of Consumer Research,* September 1996, pp. 120–135.

16 Robert Hof, Heather Green, and Paul Judge, "Going, Going, Gone," *Business Week,* April 12, 1999, pp. 30–32; Sloane Lucas, "Lycos, mySimon Tout New User Guides," *Brandweek,* August 9, 1999, p. 31; Michael Schrage, "The Tangled Web of E-Deception," *Fortune,* September 27, 1999, p. 296; Erica Goode, "The On-Line Consumer? Tough, Impatient, and Gone in a Blink," *The New York Times,* September 22, 1999, p. 22; and Edward C. Baig, "The Biggest Used-Car Lot of All," *Business Week,* August 9, 1999, pp. 96–98.

17 J. Jeffrey Inman and Russell S. Winer, "Where the Rubber Meets the Road: A Model of In-Store Decision Making," *Report No. 98-122* (Cambridge, MA: Marketing Science Institute, October 1998), p. v.

18 Stanley C. Hollander and Kathleen M. Rassuli, "Shopping with Other People's Money: The Marketing Management Implications of Surrogate-Mediated Consumer Decision-Making," *Journal of Marketing 63* (April 1999), pp. 102–18; and Paco Underhill, "What Shoppers Want," *Inc.,* July 1999, pp. 72–82.

19 J. Paul Peter and Jerry C. Olson, *Consumer Behavior and Marketing Strategy,* 3rd ed. (Homewood, IL: Richard D. Irwin, Inc., 1993), p. 57.

20 James F. Engel, Roger D. Blackwell, and Paul W. Miniard, *Consumer Behavior,* 7th ed. (Ft. Worth, TX: Dryden Press, 1993), pp. 276–77.

21 Thomas S. Robertson, "Low-Commitment Consumer Behavior," *Journal of Advertising Research,* April 1976, pp. 19–24.

22 Jeffrey J. Stoltman, James W. Gentry, Kenneth A. Anglin, and Alvin C. Burns, "Situational Influences on the Consumer Decision Sequence," *Journal of Business Research,* November 1990, p. 196.

23 Emily Nelson, "Too Many Choices," *The Wall Street Journal,* April 20, 2001, p. B1.

24 Marcia Mogelonsky, "America's Hottest Markets," *American Demographics,* January 1996, p. 22.

25 John C. Mowen, *Consumer Behavior,* 2nd ed. (New York: Macmillan Publishing Company, 1990), pp. 332–33; and Dennis W. Rook, "The Buying Impulse," *Journal of Consumer Research,* September 1987, pp. 189–99.

26 Stephen J. Hoch and George F. Lowenstein, "Time-Inconsistent Preferences and Consumer Self-Control," *Journal of Consumer Research,* March 1991, pp. 492–502.

27 Geert Hofstede, "Culture and Organizations," *International Studies of Management and Organizations* 10, no. 4 (1981),

pp. 15–41; Martin S. Roth, "The Effects of Culture and Socioeconomics on the Performance of Global Brand Image Strategies," *Journal of Marketing Research,* May 1995, p. 172; and Mikael Sandergaard, "Hofstede's Consequences: A Study of Reviews, Citations, and Replications," *Organizational Studies* 15, no. 3 (1994), pp. 447–56.

[28]Jan-Benedict E. M. Steenkamp, Frenkel ter Hofstede, and Michael Wedel, "A Cross-National Investigation into the Individual and National Cultural Antecedents of Consumer Innovativeness," *Journal of Marketing,* April 1999, pp. 55–69.

[29]Lynn R. Kahle, Sharon E. Beatty, and Pamela Homer, "Alternative Measurement Approaches to Consumer Values: The List of Values (LOV) and Values and Life Style (VALS)," *Journal of Consumer Research,* December 1986, p. 406.

[30]Engel et al., *Consumer Behavior,* p. 87.

[31]Joel Garreau, *The Nine Nations of North America* (Boston: Houghton Mifflin, 1981).

[32]Mowen, *Consumer Behavior,* pp. 618–19.

[33]Michael M. Phillips, "Selling by Evoking What Defines a Generation," *The Wall Street Journal,* August 13, 1996, p. B1.

[34]Haidee E. Allerton, "Generation Why," *T + D,* November 2001, pp. 56–60; Pamela Paul, "Getting Inside Gen Y," *American Demographics,* September 2001; Joyce M. Wolburg and James Pokyrwczynski, "A Psychographic Analysis of Generation Y College Students," *Journal of Advertising Research,* September/October 2001, pp. 33–52.

[35]Richard P. Coleman, "The Continuing Significance of Social Class to Marketing," *Journal of Consumer Research,* December 1983, pp. 265–80.

[36]Jerry C. Olson, *Consumer Behavior and Marketing Strategy,* 3rd ed. (Homewood, IL: Richard D. Irwin, 1993), p. 490.

[37]Greg J. Duncan, Timothy M. Smeeding, and Willard Rogers, "The Incredible Shrinking Middle Class," *American Demographics,* May 1992, p. 38.

[38]Rebecca Piirto Heath, "The New Working Class," *American Demographics,* January 1998, p. 52.

[39]Mowen, *Consumer Behavior,* p. 527; and Scott Ward, "Consumer Socialization," *Journal of Consumer Research,* September 1974, pp. 1–14.

[40]Gregory M. Rose, "Consumer Socialization, Parental Style, and Developmental Timetables in the United States and Japan," *Journal of Marketing,* July 1999, p. 116.

[41]Sonia Reyes, "Into the Mouths of Babes," *Brandweek,* May 6, 2002, pp. 27–30.

[42]Robert Bontilier, "Pulling the Family's Strings," *American Demographics,* August 1993, p. 46.

[43]Chip Walker, "Can TV Save the Planet?" *American Demographics,* May 1996, pp. 42–48.

[44]William D. Danko and Charles M. Schaninger, "An Empirical Evaluation of the Gilly-Enis Updated Household Life Cycle Model," *Journal of Business Research,* August 1990, p. 39; Mary C. Gilly and Ben M. Enis, "Recycling the Family Life Cycle: A Proposal for Redefinition," in *Advances in Consumer Research,* vol. 9, ed. Andrew Mitchell (Ann Arbor, MI: Association for Consumer Research, 1982), pp. 271–76; Patrick Murphy and William Staples, "A Modernized Family Life Cycle," *Journal of Consumer Research,* June 1979, pp. 12–22; and Charles M. Schaninger and William D. Danko, "A Conceptual and Empirical Comparison of Alternative Household Life Cycle Models," *Journal of Consumer Research,* March 1993, pp. 580–94.

[45]Tom W. Smith, "The Emerging 21st Century American Family," *GSS Social Exchange Report No. 42,* (Chicago, IL: National Opinion Research Center, University of Chicago, November 24, 1999), p. 28.

[46]Diane Crispell, "Dual-Earner Diversity," *American Demographics,* July 1995, pp. 32–37, 55; and Marcia Mogelonsky, "The Rocky Road to Adulthood," *American Demographics,* May 1996, pp. 26–35, 56.

[47]Hal Espen, "Levi's Blues," *New York Times Magazine,* March 21, 1999, p. 54.

[48]Robert B. Cialdini, "Harnessing the Science of Persuasion," *Harvard Business Review,* October 2001, pp. 75–76.

[49]Hilary Cassidy, "College Guys Get Carded," *Brandweek,* November 12, 2001, p. 31.

[50]Lawrence F. Feick and Linda L. Price, "The Market Maven: A Diffuser of Marketplace Information," *Journal of Marketing,* January 1987, pp. 83–97.

[51]Chip Walker, "Word of Mouth," *American Demographics,* July 1995, p. 38.

[52]"Poor College Students Ain't What They Used to Be," *Marketing News,* August 16, 1999, p. 3.

[53]"Hey, Are You Listening to Me," *Business Week,* August 28, 2000, pp. 138–140; "How People Use Technology," *Business Week,* January 21, 2002, p. 10.

[54]Malcolm Gladwell, "The Coolhunt," *The New Yorker,* March 17, 1997, *www.gladwell.com.*

[55]M. Joseph Sirgy, "Self-Concept in Consumer Behavior: A Critical Review," *Journal of Consumer Research,* December 1982, pp. 287–88.

[56]Beth A. Walker and Jerry L. Olson, "Means-End Chains: Connecting Products with Self," *Journal of Business Research,* March 1991, p. 111.

[57]Stephen J. Hoch and George F. Lowenstein, "Time-Inconsistent Preferences and Consumer Self-Control," *Journal of Consumer Research,* March 1991, pp. 492–502; and Sirgy, "Self-Concept in Consumer Behavior," pp. 288–89.

[58]Harold H. Kassarjian and Mary Jane Sheffet, "Personality and Consumer Behavior: An Update," in *Perspectives in Consumer Behavior,* 4th ed., eds. H. H. Kassarjian and T. S. Robertson (Englewood Cliffs, NJ: Prentice Hall, 1990), pp. 281–363.

[59]John L. Lastovicka, "On the Validation of Lifestyle Traits: A Review and Illustration," *Journal of Marketing Research,* February 1982, p. 126.

[60]William L. Wilkie, *Consumer Behavior* (New York: John Wiley Sons, 1986), p. 307.

[61]Abraham H. Maslow, *Motivation and Personality,* 2nd ed. (New York: Harper and Row, 1970).

[62]Russell W. Belk, "An Exploratory Assessment of Situational Effects in Buyer Behavior," *Journal of Marketing Research,* May 1974, p. 156.

[63]Gordon C. Brunner, "Music, Mood, and Marketing," *Journal of Marketing,* October 1990, pp. 94–104; and Ronald E. Milman, "Using Background Music to Affect the Behavior of Supermarket Shoppers," *Journal of Marketing,* Summer 1982 pp. 86–91.

[64]Brian Wansink and Michael L. Ray, *How Expansion Advertising Affects Brand Usage Frequency: A Programmatic Evaluation,* MSI Report Summary, Report No. 93–126 (Cambridge, MA: Marketing Science Institute, 1993), p. 1.

[65]Stephen J. Hoch and John Deighton, "Managing What Consumers Learn from Experience," *Journal of Marketing,* April 1989, pp. 1–20.

[66]Walter R. Nord and J. Paul Peter, "A Behavior Modification Perspective on Marketing," *Journal of Marketing,* Spring 1980, p. 41; and Michael L. Rothschild and William C. Gaidis, "Behavioral Learning Theory: Its Relevance to Marketing and Promotions," *Journal of Marketing,* Spring 1981, pp. 70–78.

[67]Marian Friestad and Peter Wright, "The Persuasion Knowledge Model: How People Cope with Persuasion Attempts," *Journal of Consumer Research,* June 1994, 1–31.

[68]Susan Fournier and David Glen Mick, "Rediscovering Satisfaction," *Journal of Marketing* 63 (October 1999), pp. 5–23.

[69]Richard L. Oliver, "A Cognitive Model of the Antecedents and Consequences of Satisfaction Decisions," *Journal of Marketing Research,* November 1980, pp. 460–61.

[70]Jonathan Gutman and George Miaoulis, Jr., "Pat Experience Drives Future CS Behavior," *Marketing News,* October 22, 2001, p. 45.

[71]John A. Larson, "The Importance of Expectations," *Marketing Management,* Winter 2000, pp. 4–5.

[72]Richard L. Oliver, "Cognitive, Affective, and Attribute Bases of the Satisfaction Response," *Journal of Consumer Research,* December 1993, p. 419.

[73]Marsha L. Richins and Peter H. Bloch, "Post-Purchase Product Satisfaction: Incorporating the Effects of Involvement and Time," *Journal of Business Research,* September 1991, pp. 145–58.

[74]Kelly Shermach, "Don't Grow Complacent when Your Customers Are 'Satisfied,' " *Marketing News,* May 20, 1996, p. 7.

[75]Timothy L. Keiningham, Melinda K. M. Goddard, Terry G. Vavra, and Andrew J. Iaci, "Customer Delight and the Bottom Line," *Marketing Management,* Fall 1999, pp. 57–63; Steve Lewis, "All or Nothing: Customers Must Be 'Totally Satisfied,' " *Marketing News,* March 2, 1998, p. 11; and Don Peppers and Martha Rogers, "When Extreme Isn't Enough," *Sales & Marketing Management,* February 1999, p. 26.

[76]Fournier and Mick, "Rediscovering Satisfaction," pp. 5–23.

[77]Jagdip Singh, "Consumer Complaint Intentions and Behavior: Definitional and Taxonomical Issues," *Journal of Marketing,* January 1988, pp. 93–107.

[78]For a detailed discussion of managerial reactions to complaint behavior, see Alan J. Resnik and Robert R. Harmon, "Consumer Complaints and Managerial Response: A Holistic Approach," *Journal of Marketing,* Winter 1983, pp. 86–97; see also Howard Schlossberg, "Customer Satisfaction: Not a Fad, but a Way of Life," *Marketing News,* June 10, 1991, p. 18; and Judith Waldrop, "Educating the Customer," *American Demographics,* September 1991, p. 45.

[79]Waldrop, "Educating the Customer," p. 45.

[80]Stephanie Anderson Forest, "Customers 'Must Be Pleased, Not Just Satisfied,' " *Business Week,* August 3, 1992, p. 52.

[81]Waldrop, "Educating the Customer," p. 44.

[82]For additional explanation regarding the role of cognitive dissonance in marketing and consumer behavior, see William H. Cummings and M. Venkatesan, "Cognitive Dissonance and Consumer Behavior: A Review of the Evidence," *Journal of Marketing Research,* August 1976, pp. 303–8; and Pradeep K. Korgaonkar and George P. Moschis, "An Experimental Study of Cognitive Dissonance, Product Involvement, Expectations, Performance, and Consumer Judgments of Product Performance," *Journal of Advertising* 11, no. 3 (1982), pp. 32–44.

[83]Mowen, *Consumer Behavior,* p. 764.

[84]Carolyn Gatten, "Social Issues Guide Consumer Buying," *Marketing News,* December 9, 1991, p. 80.

[85]Kirk Davidson, "Like Marketers, Consumers Have Responsibilities," *Marketing News,* March 3, 1998, p. 24.

[86]John E. Richardson and David L. Ralph, "The Ethical Treatment of Consumers," *Annual Editions: Business Ethics 00/01,* Guilford, CT: Duskin/McGraw-Hill, p. 50.

Chapter Five

[1]Martha C. Cooper, Douglas M. Lambert, and Janus D. Pugh, "Supply Chain Management: More than a New Name for Logistics," *The International Journal of Logistics Management* 8, no. 1 (1997), p. 2.

[2]Roberta J. Duffy, "Defining Supply Management," *Inside Supply Management,* January 2002, pp. 30–32.

[3]Louis Lavelle, "First, Kill the Consultants," *Business Week,* January 14, 2002, p. 122.

[4]Steve Rosenbush, "Who's Answering AT&T's Phones?" *Business Week,* February 4, 2002, p. 8.

[5]From Michael F. Corbett & Associates Web site at www.corbettassociates.com/expertise/corbett_bio.asp, on May 31, 2002.

[6]"Supply Strategy in Tough Times," *Inside Supply Management,* March 2002, p. 6.

[7]Ben Elgin and Steve Hamm, "The New Teamwork," *Business Week e.biz,* February 18, 2002, pp. EB12–16.

[8]Michelle Kessler, "Lack of Customers Shuts Down Many B2B Internet Sites," *USA Today,* April 2, 2001, p. 2B.

[9]Timothy J. Mullaney, "Break Out the Black Ink," *Business Week,* May 13, 2002, pp. 74–76.

[10]Jeff Green, "As Suppliers Balk, Chrysler Blinks," *Business Week,* February 5, 2001, p. 14.

[11]Jeff Green, "The Tight Squeeze at Chrysler," *Business Week,* October 9, 2000, p. 54.

[12]John Yuva, "Collaborative Logistics: Building a Collaborative Network," *Inside Supply Management,* May 2002, pp. 42–53.

[13]Bill Millar, "The World's First Digital Hospital," *1 to 1 Magazine,* April 2002, p. 38.

[14]"Design for the Environment Program Advances Herman Miller's Sustainability Protocol," press release dated April 2, 2002, from Herman Miller's Web site, www.hermanmiller.com.

[15]For a revised and expanded version of this typology, see Michele D. Bunn, "Taxonomy of Buying Decision Approaches," *Journal of Marketing,* January 1993, pp. 38–56; see also Patrick J. Robinson, Charles W. Faris, and Yoram Wind, *Industrial Buying and Creative Marketing* (Boston: Allyn and Bacon, 1967).

[16]"Wal-Mart Stores, Inc. Supplier Proposal Guide," available at www.walmart.com.

[17]Elizabeth Wilson, Gary L. Lillien, and David T. Wilson, "Developing and Testing a Contingency Paradigm of Group Choice in Organizational Buying," *Journal of Marketing Research,* November 1991, pp. 452–53.

[18]Penny M. Simpson, Judy A. Siguaw, and Susan C. White, "Measuring the Performance of Suppliers: An Evaluation Process," *The Journal of Supply Chain Management,* Winter 2002, pp. 29–41.

[19]Kevin R. Fitzgerald, "What Makes a Superior Supplier?" *Velocity,* Spring 1999, pp. 22–24, 49.

[20]Joanne Lee-Young and Megan Barnett, "Furiously Fast Fashions," *The Industry Standard,* June 11, 2001, pp. 72–79.

[21]"Budget of the United States Government, Fiscal Year 2003," Office of Management and Budget, as presented at www.whitehouse.gov/omb/budget/fy2003/bud22.html.

[22]Information from online version of *Commerce Business Daily,* (Washington, DC: U.S. Department of Commerce), June 1, 2002, at www.cbdnet.access.gpo.gov.

[23]Gregory T. Gundlach and Patrick E. Murphy, "Ethical and Legal Foundations of Relational Marketing Exchanges," *Journal of Marketing,* October 1993, pp. 35–46; and Craig Smith and John A. Quelch, *Ethics in Marketing* (Homewood, IL: Richard D. Irwin, 1983), pp. 40–43.

Chapter Six

[1]Vincent P. Barabba, "The Market Research Encyclopedia," *Harvard Business Review,* January–February 1990, p. 105.

[2]"AMA Board Approves New Marketing Definition," *Marketing News,* March 1, 1985, pp. 1, 14.

[3]John Tarsa, "Ocean Spray Marketing Research: Delivering Insights in a Customer-Supplier Relationship," *Marketing Research: A Magazine of Management and Application,* September 1991, p. 8.

[4]Saul Hansell, "Some Hard Lessons for Online Grocers," *The New York Times,* February 19, 2001, pp. C1, C5; and David Miller, "McDonald's Is Missing the Mark," *Brandweek,* November 12, 2001, pp. 20, 23.

[5]Hilton Barrett, "Ultimate Goal Is to Anticipate the Needs of Market," *Marketing News,* October 7, 1996, p. 10; and Paul Gerhold, "Defining Marketing (or Is It Market?) Research," *Marketing Research: A Magazine of Management and Application* 5, no. 4, p. 67.

[6]Ty Albert, "Mindset Clearly Has Changed," *Marketing News,* December 6, 1999, p. 17.

[7]Sara Eckel, "Intelligence Agents," *American Demographics,* March 1999, p. 53; Ann M. Raider, "Programs Make Results out of Research," *Marketing News,* June 21, 1999, p. 14; and Jagdish Sheth and Rajendra S. Sisodia, "Feeling the Heat—Part 2," *Marketing Management* 3, no. 4 (Winter 1995), p. 22.

[8]Simon Chadwick, "The Research Industry Grows Up and Out," *Marketing News,* June 8, 1998, p. 9.

[9]Adapted from Gilbert A. Churchill, Jr., *Marketing Research: Methodological Foundations,* 5th ed. (Chicago: Dryden Press, 1991), p. 9.

[10]Nino DeNicola, "Casting Finer Net Not Necessary," *Marketing News,* March 4, 2002, p. 46.

[11]Earl Babbie, *The Practice of Social Research,* 5th ed. (Belmont, CA: Wadsworth, 1989), p. 80.

[12]See William R. Dillon, Thomas J. Madden, and Neil A. Firtle, *Marketing Research in a Marketing Environment,* 2nd ed. (Homewood, IL: Richard D. Irwin, 1990), p. 29; and Churchill, *Marketing Research,* pp. 130–43.

[13]Maria F. Flores Letelier, Charles Spinosa, and Bobby J. Calder, "Taking as Expanded View of Customers' Needs: Qualitative Research for Aiding Innovation," *Marketing Research,* Winter 2000, pp. 4–11.

[14]Jack Honomichl, "U.S. Total Spending and Segments," *Marketing News,* June 10, 2002, p. H3.

[15]See, for example, Johan K. Johansson and Ikujiro Nonaka, "Market Research the Japanese Way," *Harvard Business Review,* May–June 1987, pp. 16–18, 22; and Tim Powell, "Despite Myths, Secondary Research Is Valuable Tool," *Marketing News,* September 2, 1991, p. 28.

[16]Alvin C. Burns and Ronald F. Bush, *Marketing Research,* 2nd ed. (Upper Saddle River, NJ: Prentice Hall), p. 143.

[17]Ed Campbell, "CD-ROMs Bring Census Data In-House," *Marketing News,* January 1992, p. 15.

[18]Lawrence N. Gold, "The Coming of Age of Scanner Data," *Marketing Research: A Magazine of Management and Application,* Winter 1993, p. 23.

[19]For several recent descriptions, Joseph M. Winski, "Gentle Rain Turns to Torrent," *Advertising Age,* June 3, 1991, p. 34; Blair Peters, "The 'Brave New World' of Single Source Information," *Marketing Research: A Magazine of Management and Applications,* December 1990, pp. 13–21; and "Nielsen, NPD Start Single Source Service," *Marketing News,* August 28, 1987, p. 1.

[20]Thomas G. Exter, "The Next Step Is Called GIS," *American Demographics,* May 1992, p. 2.

[21]Jack Szergold, "Getting the GIS of Things," *Management Review,* July 1993, p. 6.

[22]David Churbuck, "Geographics," *Forbes,* January 6, 1992, pp. 262–67; and Eric Schine, "Computer Maps Pop Up All over the Map," *Business Week,* July 26, 1993, p. 75.

[23]See Bobby J. Calder, "Focus Groups and the Nature of Qualitative Marketing Research," *Journal of Marketing Research,* August 1977, pp. 353–64; and Edward F. Fern, "The Use of Focus Groups for Idea Generation: The Effects of Group Size, Acquaintanceship, and Moderator on Response Quantity and Quality," *Journal of Marketing Research,* February 1982, pp. 1–13.

[24]Judith Langer, "15 Myths of Qualitative Research: It's Conventional, But Is It Wisdom," *Marketing News,* March 1, 1999, pp. 13–14.

[25]Catherine Forrest, "Research with a Laugh Track," *Marketing News,* March 2, 2002, p. 48.

[26]Emily Nelson, "P&G Keeps Focus Groupies of Cincinnati Busy as Guinea Pigs in Product Studies," *The Wall Street Journal,* http://interactive.wsj.com/archieve/retrieve.cgi?id = SB10118218052849 38360.djm.

[27]Jack Honomichl, "Legislation Threatens Research by Phone," *Marketing News,* June 24, 1991, p. 4.

[28]Stephen W. McDaniel, Perry Verille, and Charles S. Madden, "The Threats to Marketing Research: An Empirical Reappraisal," *Journal of Marketing Research,* February 1985, pp. 74–80; and Howard Gershowitz, "Entering the 1990s—The State of Data Collection— Telephone Data Collection," *Applied Marketing Research,* Spring 1990, pp. 16–19.

[29]Michael P. Cronin, "On-the-Cheap Market Research," *Inc.,* June 1992, p. 108.

[30]Pamela Rogers, "One-on-Ones Don't Get the Credit They Deserve," *Marketing News,* January 2, 1991, p. 9.

[31]Susan Kraft, "Who Slams the Door on Research?" *American Demographics,* September 1991, p. 9.

[32]Alan J. Bush and Joseph F. Hair, Jr., "Mall Intercept versus Telephone Interviewing Environment," *Journal of Marketing Research,* May 1985, pp. 158–68.

[33]Howard Schlossberg, "Shoppers Virtually Stroll through Store Aisles to Examine Packages," *Marketing News,* June 6, 1993, p. 2.

[34]"Big Bytes," *Marketing News,* March 18, 2002, p. 3.

[35]Robert Hayes, "Internet-based Surveys Provide Fast Results," *Marketing News,* April 13, 1998, p. 13; Dana James, "Precision Decision," *Marketing News,* September 27, 1999, pp. 23–25; Phil Levine, Bill Ahlauser, Dale Kulp, and Rick Hunter, "Internet Interviewing," *Marketing Research: A Magazine of Management and Application,* Summer 1999, pp. 33–36; Seymour Sudman and Edward Blair, "Sampling in the Twenty-First Century," *Journal of the Academy of Marketing Science* 27, no. 2, p. 275.

[36]Sharon Hollander, "Projective Techniques Uncover Real Consumer Attitudes," *Marketing News,* January 4, 1988, p. 34.

[37]Stephen Groves and Raymond P. Fisk, "Observational Data Collection Methods for Services Marketing: An Overview," *Journal of the Academy of Marketing Science,* Summer 1992, pp. 217–24.

[38]William B. Helmreich, "Louder than Words: On-Site Observational Research," *Marketing News,* March 1, 1999, p. 16.

[39]Rebecca Piirto, "Socks, Ties, and Videotape," *American Demographics,* September 1991, p. 6.

[40]Sandra Yin, "Marketing Tools," *American Demographics,* November 2001, pp. 32–33.

[41]Debra Goldman, "Consumer Republic: Marketers Discover Surveillance Is Socially Acceptable," *Adweek,* June 4, 2001, p. 24; and Gerry Khermouch, "Consumers in the Mist," *Business Week,* February 26, 2001, pp. 92, 94.

[42]Shelby D. Hunt, Richard D. Sparkman, Jr., and James B. Wilcox, "The Pretest in Survey Research: Issues and Preliminary Findings," *Journal of Marketing Research,* May 1982, pp. 269–73.

[43]James D. Lenskold, "Marketing ROI: Playing to Win," *Marketing Management,* May/June, pp. 31–35.

[44]Diane Schmalensee, "One Researcher's Rules of Thumb for B-to-B Arena," *Marketing News,* November 19, 2001, pp. 17–18.

[45]Steve Jarvis, "CMOR Finds Survey Refusal Rate Still Rising," *Marketing News,* February 4, 2002, p. 4.

[46]Sudman and Blair, "Sampling in the Twenty-First Century," *Journal of the Academy of Marketing Science,* Vol. 27(2), p. 275.

[47]Gershowitz, "Entering the 1990s."

[48]Peter S. Tuckel and Harry W. O'Neil, "Call Waiting," *Marketing Research: A Magazine of Management and Application,* Spring 1995, p. 7.

[49]Thomas L. Greenbaum, "Focus Group by Video Next Trend of the 90s," *Marketing News,* July 29, 1996, p. 4; Leslie M. Harris, "Technology, Techniques Drive Focus Group Trends," *Marketing News,* February 27, 1995, p. 8; Beth Schneider, "Using Interactive Kiosks for Retail Research," *Marketing News,* January 2, 1995, p. 13; Barbara A. Schuldt and Jeff W. Totten, "Electronic Mail vs. Mail Response Rates," *Marketing Research: A Magazine of Management and Application* 6, no. 1, p. 36; and Gary S. Vazzana and Duane Bachmann, "Fax Attracts," *Marketing Research: A Magazine of Management and Application* 6, no. 2, p. 19.

[50]Daphre Chandler, "Eight Common Pitfalls of International Research," in *The Resurgence of Research in Decision Making: 1992 CASRO Annual Journal* (Port Jefferson, NY: The Council of American Survey Research Organizations, 1992), pp. 81–85.

[51]Elizabeth Loken, "Probing Japanese Buyers' Minds," *Business Marketing,* 1987, pp. 85–86.

[52]Neil Helgeson, "Research Isn't Linear When Done Globally," *Marketing News,* July 19, 1999, p. 13.

[53]Allyson L. Stewart-Allen, "EU's Future Consumers: 3 Groups to Watch," *Marketing News,* June 4, 2001, p. 9.

[54]William R. Dillon, Thomas J. Madden, and Neil Firtle, *Essentials of Marketing Research* (Homewood, IL: Richard D. Irwin, Inc., 1993), pp. 293–95.

[55]Howard N. Gundee, "Council Joins Industrial Effort to Support Research," *Marketing News,* January 4, 1993, p. 22.

[56]McDaniel, Verille, and Madden, "Threats to Marketing Research."

[57]Wade Lettwich, "How Researchers Can Win Friends and Influence Politicians," *American Demographics,* August 1993, p. 9.

[58]"The Persistence of Surveying," *Marketing News,* September 2, 1992, p. 4.

[59]Ishmael P. Akaah and Edward A. Riordan, "Judgments of Marketing Professionals about Ethical Issues in Marketing Research: Replication and Extension," *Journal of Marketing Research,* February 1989, p. 113.

[60]Patrick E. Murphy and Gene R. Laczniak, "Emerging Ethical Issues Facing Marketing Researchers," *Marketing Research,* June 1992, pp. 6–7.

[61]Mary B. W. Taylor, "Schools Profit from Offering Pupils for Market Research," *The New York Times,* April 5, 1999, pp. A1, A16.

[62]Tom Eisenhart, "After 10 Years of Marketing Decision Support Systems, Where's the Payoff?" *Business Marketing,* June 1990, pp. 46–48, 50.

[63]Alan J. Greco and Jack T. Hogue, "Developing Marketing Decision Support Systems," *Journal of Business and Industrial Marketing,* Summer–Fall 1990, p. 28; and Alan J. Greco and Jack T. Hogue, "Developing Marketing Decision Support Systems in Consumer Goods Firms," *Journal of Consumer Marketing,* Winter 1990, pp. 56–64.

[64]Rajerdra s. Sisodia, "Marketing Information and Decision Support Systems for Services," *Journal of Services Marketing,* Winter 1992, p. 53.

[65]Randolph E. Bucklin, Donald R. Lehmann, and John D. C. Little, *From Decision Support to Decision Automation: A 2020 Vision,* Marketing Science Institute, Report no. 98-119 (Cambridge, MA: June 1998).

[66]Doug Grisaffe, "See About Linking CRM and MR Systems," *Marketing News,* January 21, 2002, p. 13; Gordon A. Wyner, "Customer Relationship Management," *Marketing Research,* Summer 1999, pp. 39–41.

[67]James Heckman, "You Have Tools to Boost Your Budget," *Marketing News,* September 13, 1999, p. 4.

[68]Jagdish Sheth and Rajendra S. Sisodia, "Feeling the Heat—Part 2," p. 22.

[69]George R. Milne and Maria-Eugenia Boza, *A Business Perspective on Database Marketing and Consumer Privacy Practices,* Marketing Science Institute, Report no. 98-110 (Cambridge, MA: June 1998); and Joseph Phelps, Glen Nowak, and Elizabeth Ferrell, *Marketers' Information Practices and Privacy Concerns: How Willing Are Consumers to Provide Personal Information for Shopping Benefits?* Marketing Science Institute, Report no. 99-112, (Cambridge, MA: June 1999).

Chapter Seven

[1]Gordon A. Wyner, "Segmentation Architecture," *Marketing Management,* March/April 2000, pp. 6–7.

[2]For an in-depth review, see Gary L. Lilien and Philip Kotler, *Marketing Decision Making: A Model Building Approach* (New York: Harper and Row, 1983); and Peter R. Dickson and James L. Ginter, "Market Segmentation, Product Differentiation, and Marketing," *Journal of Marketing,* April 1987, pp. 1–10.

[3]Faye Brookman, "Companies Invest in Customer Loyalty," *Marketing News,* March 2, 1998, p. 12.

[4]Harper W. Boyd, Jr., and Orville C. Walker, Jr., *Marketing Management: A Strategic Approach* (Homewood, IL: Richard D. Irwin, 1990), p. 186.

[5]Cyndee Miller, "Researcher Says U.S. Is More of a Bowl than a Pot," *Marketing News,* May 10, 1993, p. 6; and Cynthia Webster, "The Effects of Hispanic Subcultural Identification on Information Search Behavior," *Journal of Advertising Research,* September–October 1992, pp. 54–62.

[6]Robert Sharoff, "Diversity in the Mainstream," *Marketing News,* May 21, 2001, pp. 1, 13.

[7]Daniel F. Hansler and Donald R. Riggin, "Geodemographics: Targeting the Market," *Fund Raising Management,* December 1989, pp. 35–43.

[8]Saeed Samiee, "A Conceptual Framework for International Marketing," in *International Business: Inquiry: An Emerging Vision,* eds. B. Toyne and Douglas Nigh (Columbia, SC: USC Press, 1994); see also Theodore Leavitt, "The Globalization of Markets," *Harvard Business Review,* May–June 1983, pp. 99–102; and Saeed Samiee and Kendall Roth, "The Influence of Global Marketing Standardization on Performance," *Journal of Marketing,* April 1992, pp. 1–17.

[9]Ugar Yavas, Bronislaw J. Verhage, and Robert T. Green, "Global Consumer Segmentation versus Local Market Orientation: Empirical Findings," *Marketing International Review,* 1992, pp. 266–68.

[10]Alpa Agarwal, "Profiting from India's Strong Middle Class," *Marketing News,* October 7, 1996, p. 6; and Cyndee Miller, "Teens Seen as the First Truly Global Consumers," *Marketing News,* March 27, 1995, p. 9.

[11]Peter D. Bennett, ed., *Dictionary of Marketing Terms* (Chicago: American Marketing Association, 1988), p. 199.

[12]James H. Gilmore and B. Joseph Pine, II, "The Four Faces of Mass Customization," *Harvard Business Review,* January–February 1997, pp. 91–101; and Suresh Kotha, "From Mass Production to Mass Customization: The Case of the National Industrial Bicycle Company of Japan," *European Management Journal,* October 1996, pp. 442–50.

[13]Jerry Wind and Arvind Rangaswamy, "Customerization: The Next Revolution in Mass Customization," Marketing Science Re-

port No. 00–108, Marketing Science Institute, Boston, MA, pp. 25–26.

[14]Gary L. Berman, "The Hispanic Market: Getting Down to Cases," *Sales & Marketing Management,* October 1991, p. 66.

[15]Shirley Young, Leland Ott, and Barbara Feign, "Some Practical Considerations in Market Segmentation," *Journal of Marketing Research,* August 1978, pp. 405–12.

[16]Jennifer Barron and Jim Hollingshead, "Making Segmentation Work," *Marketing Management,* January/February 2002, p. 25.

[17]"A Long Wait: Population Growth," *The Economist,* December 21, 2000, p. 69.

[18]Marcia Mogelonsky, "Watching in Tongues," *American Demographics,* April 1998, pp. 4–52.

[19]Ronald Grover, "Old Rockers Never Die—They Just Switch to CDs," *Business Week,* August 17, 1992, p. 54.

[20]Cyndi W. Greenglass, "It's All About People," *1 to 1,* September 2000, p. 44.

[21]"Multicultural Marketing Experts Give Their Two Cents on Census Data," *BrandWeek,* May 14, 2001, p. 25.

[22]Roger J. Calantone and Alan G. Sawyer, "The Stability of Benefit Segments," *Journal of Marketing Research,* August 1978, pp. 395–404.

[23]Howard Schlossberg, "Success with Seniors Depends on Dialogue and Long-Range Plans," *Marketing News,* January 4, 1993, p. 2.

[24]Henry Assael, "Segmenting Markets by Response Elasticity," *Journal of Advertising Research,* April 1976, pp. 27–35.

[25]Hartmarx, *Annual Report* (Chicago: Hartmarx Corporation, 1992).

[26]"The American Dream Is Alive and Well—In Mexico," *Business Week,* September 30, 1991, p. 102.

[27]Rebecca Gardyn, "Habla English," *American Demographics,* 2001, pp. 54–57.

[28]Paula Lyon Andruss, "Show Boat to China: Worth Eyeing Now More Than Ever—Carefully," *Marketing News,* September 10, 2001, pp. 1, 11.

[29]Philip Kotler, *Marketing Management: Analysis, Planning, Implementation, and Control,* 8th ed. (Englewood Cliffs, NJ: Prentice Hall, 1994), p. 265.

[30]See Yoram Wind and Richard Cardoza, "Industrial Market Segmentation," *Industrial Marketing Management,* March 1974, pp. 153–66, for a similar outline of business-to-business segmentation bases.

[31]Peter Francese, "America at Mid-Decade," *American Demographics,* February, 1995, pp. 23–31; and Peter Zollo, "Talking to Teens," *American Demographics,* November 1995, pp. 22–28.

[32]Susan Mitchell, *American Generations: Who They Are and How They Live,* 2nd ed. (Ithaca, NY: New Strategist Publications, 1998).

[33]Laura Koss-Feder, "Want to Catch Gen X? Try Looking on the Web," *Marketing News,* June 8, 1998, p. 20.

[34]Francese, "America at Mid-Decade"; Cyndee Miller, "Boomers Come of Age," *Marketing News,* January 15, 1996, pp. 1, 6; Karen Ritchie, "Marketing to Generation X," *American Demographics,* April 1995, pp. 34–39; and Zollo, "Talking to Teens."

[35]Wendy Bounds, "Rushing to Cash In on the New Baby Boom," *The Wall Street Journal,* pp. B1, B4; Pamela Paul, "Childless by Choice," *American Demographics,* November 2001, pp. 45–50.

[36]Lisa Modisette and Steve Huson, "Customer Knowledge Is Power," *Cellular Business,* September 1996, p. 98.

[37]Daniel F. Hansler and Don L. Riggen, "Geodemographics: Targeting the Market," *Fund Raising Management,* December 1989, p. 35.

[38]Eric A. Cohen, "Demos Alone Don't Sell Products," *Marketing News,* June 21, 1999, p. 16.

[39]Nick Fuller, "Finding Cable's Target," *Marketing,* February 18, 1992, p. 27.

[40]Susan Mitchell, "Birds of a Feather," *American Demographics,* February 1995, pp. 40–41.

[41]Geert Hofstede, *Culture's Consequences: Comparing Values, Behaviors, Institutions, and Organizations Across Nations,* 2nd ed. (Thousand Oaks, CA: Sage Publications); and V. Kumar and Anish Nagpal, "Segmenting Global Markets: Look Before You Leap," *Marketing Research,* Spring 2001, pp. 8–13.

[42]William D. Wells and Douglas J. Tigert, "Activities, Interests, and Opinions," *Journal of Advertising Research,* August 1971, pp. 27–35; and William D. Wells, "Psychographics: A Critical Review," *Journal of Marketing Research,* May 1975, pp. 196–213. See also Allen M. Clark, "'Trends' That Will Impact New Products," *Journal of Consumer Marketing,* Winter 1991, pp. 29–34; P. Valette-Florence and A. Jolibert, "Social Values, AIO, and Consumption Patterns: Exploratory Findings," *Journal of Business Research,* March 1990, pp. 109–22; and Steven Hoch, "Who Do We Know: Predicting the Interests and Opinions of the American Consumer," *Journal of Consumer Research,* December 1988, pp. 315–24.

[43]Joanna L. Krotz, "Divide and Conquer Your Customers with Psychographics," http://www.bcentral.com/articles/krotz/108.asp.

[44]Wells and Tigert, "Activities, Interests, and Opinions," p. 30.

[45]Brian Davis and Warren A. French, "Exploring Advertising Usage Segments among the Aged," *Journal of Advertising Research,* February–March 1989, pp. 22–29.

[46]Pamela Paul, "Getting Inside Gen Y," *American Demographics,* September 2001, pp. 43–49.

[47]Michael Gates, "VALS Changes with the Times," *Incentive,* June 1989, p. 27.

[48]Martha Farnsworth Riche, "Psychographics for the 1990s," *American Demographics,* July 1989, p. 30.

[49]Russell I. Haley, "Benefit Segmentation: A Decision-Oriented Tool," *Journal of Marketing,* July 1968, pp. 30–35.

[50]Ibid.; and Paul E. Green, Abba M. Krieger, and Catherine M. Schagger, "Quick and Simple Benefit Segmentation," *Journal of Advertising Research,* June–July 1985, pp. 9–17.

[51]William J. McDonald, "Internet Customer Segments: An International Perspective," *American Marketing Association Summer Educators' Proceedings,* Summer 1996, pp. 311–42.

[52]Michael Anthony, "More Customers or Right Customers: Your Choice," *Marketing News,* August 31, 1998, p. 13.

[53]Diane Brady, "Why Service Stinks," *Business Week,* October 23, 2000, pp. 118–28.

[54]Gerald E. Smith, "Segmenting B2B Markets with Economic Value Analysis," *Marketing Management,* March/April 2002, pp. 35–39.

[55]Kristaan Helson, Kamel Jedidi, and Wayne S. DeSarbo, "A New Approach to Country Segmentation Utilizing Multinational Diffusion Patterns," *Journal of Marketing,* October 1993, p. 61.

[56]Lisa Bertagnoli, "Continental Spendthrifts," *Marketing News,* October 22, 2001, pp. 1, 15.

[57]Karl Greenberg, "Nissan Clears 2002 Maxima for Takeoff," *BrandWeek,* November 12, 2001, p. 8.

[58]Robert H. Waterman, Jr., "Successful Small- and Medium-Sized Firms Stress Creativity, Employ Niche Strategy," *Marketing News,* March 15, 1984, p. 24.

[59]Boyd and Walker, Jr., *Marketing Management,* p. 294.

[60]John B. Mahaffie, "Why Forecasts Fail," *American Demographics,* March 1995, pp. 34–40.

[61]Raymond Serafin and Cleveland Horton, "Buick Ads Target Zip Codes," *Advertising Age,* April 1, 1991, pp. 1, 36.

[62]Lisa Napoli, "Staying with the Pitch," *New York Times,* February 23, 1998, p. 5; Joseph Pereira, "Sneaker Company Targets Out-of-

Breath Baby Boomers," *The Wall Street Journal,* January 16, 1998, p. B1; and B. G. Yovovich, "Scanners Reshape Grocery Business," *Marketing News,* March 16, 1998, pp. 1, 11.

[63]Martin R. Lautman, "The ABCs of Positioning," *Marketing Research: A Magazine of Management and Application,* Winter 1993, p. 12.

[64]Judann Pollack, "Snackwell's Rallies with New Focus," *Advertising Age,* January 25, 1999, p. 16.

[65]Mita Sujan and James R. Bettman, "The Effects of Brand Positioning Strategies on Consumers' Brand and Category Perceptions: Some Insights from Schema Research," *Journal of Marketing Research,* November 1989, p. 454.

[66]Jason M. Sherman, "Reducing the Risks of Target Marketing," *Marketing News,* November 11, 18, 1996, p. 12.

[67]Paula Munier Lee, "The Micromarketing Revolution," *Small Business Reports,* February 1990, pp. 73–82.

[68]James Heckman, "Today's Game Is Keep-Away," pp. 1, 7; and Allyson L. Stewart-Allen, "Rules for Reaching Euro Kids Are Changing," *Marketing News,* June 7, 1999, p. 10.

[69]Marcia Mogelonsky, "Product Overload?" *American Demographics,* August 1998, pp. 65–69; and "What's New," *Marketing News,* March 2, 1998, p. 2.

[70]Barbara Kahn and Leigh McAlister, *Grocery Revolution: The New Focus on the Consumer* (Reading, MA: Addison Wesley, 1997) pp. 66–67.

Chapter Eight

[1]Adapted from Peter D. Bennett, ed., *Dictionary of Marketing Terms* (Chicago: American Marketing Association, 1988), p. 153.

[2]"Business-to-Business Product: Hewlett-Packard," *Sales & Marketing Management,* August 1993, p. 42.

[3]Aixa M. Pascual, "Striking the Right Cord," *Business Week,* June 10, 2002, p. 98.

[4]Tricia Campbell, "A Card for the Future," *Sales & Marketing Management,* December 1999, p. 15.

[5]Tom Peters, *Liberation Management* (New York: Alfred A. Knopf, 1992), p. 295.

[6]Wendy Zellner, "Penney's Rediscovers Its Calling," *Business Week,* April 5, 1993, pp. 51–52.

[7]"Pen Wars," *Forbes,* January 6, 1992, pp. 88–89.

[8]Laura Johannes, "Smart Marketing Helps Biogen Match Schering," *The Wall Street Journal,* December 19, 1996, p. B8.

[9]Joann Muller and Katie Kerwin, "Cruising for Quality," *Business Week,* September 3, 2001, pp. 74–76.

[10]Brian Dumaine, "Design That Sells and Sells and . . . ," *Fortune,* March 11, 1991, pp. 86–94.

[11]Seanna Browder, "In This Dogfight, Boeing's Gutsy Maneuver Paid Off," *Business Week,* December 2, 1996, p. 46.

[12]Faith Keenan and Adam Aston, "Building 'Easy' Into Technology," *Business Week,* December 3, 2001, pp. 92B–92D.

[13]Bruce Nussbaum, "Winners: The Best Product Designs of the Year," *Business Week,* June 3, 1996, p. 73.

[14]Lisa Keefe, ed. "Panda, and Still Champion," *Marketing News,* April 1, 2002, p. 3.

[15]Cyndee Miller, "And Baby Gets Brands," *Marketing News,* March 11, 1996, p. 18.

[16]Erich Joachimsthaler and David A. Aaker, "Building Brands without Mass Media," *Harvard Business Review,* January–February 1997, pp. 39–50.

[17]Clint Willis, "Leaping Loyalty," *Business 2.0,* July 2002, p. 87.

[18]Meghan Henterly, "Retailers Hope Private Brands Will Boost Profits," *The Courier-Journal* (Louisville, KY), June 2, 1996, p. E2.

[19]Stephen E. Frank, "To More Bankers, 'Bank' Is a Bad Word," *The Wall Street Journal,* November 15, 1996, p. B9.

[20]Diana T. Kurylko, "Product Namer Attempts to Capture a Car's Feeling," *Business First,* April 5, 1993, pp. 30–31.

[21]Valerie Reitman, "P&G Uses Skills It Has Learned at Home to Introduce Its Brands to the Russians," *The Wall Street Journal,* April 14, 1993, pp. B1, B3.

[22]Steve Rivkin, "The Name Game Heats Up," *Marketing News,* April 22, 1996, p. 8.

[23]Nancy Armour, "Notre Dame Unique in Sports Marketing," *Marketing News,* May 20, 1996, p. 13.

[24]Kelly Shermach, "Proper Design Aids Sales of Do-It-Yourself Products," *Marketing News,* September 11, 1995, p. 12.

[25]Kathleen Deveny, "Toothpaste Makers Tout New Packaging," *The Wall Street Journal,* October 10, 1992, pp. B1, B10.

[26]Michael Connor, "Services Research Should Focus on Service Management," *Marketing News,* September 13, 1993, pp. 36, 41.

[27]"The List: Going the Distance," *Business Week,* August 12, 1996, p. 4.

[28]James B. Miller, "Bailing Out Customer," *Sales & Marketing Management,* January 1994, p. 29.

[29]John R. Graham, "Customer Service Redefined: It's What You Know, Not What You Sell," *Marketing News,* January 3, 1994, p. 25.

[30]Martin Everett, "Relate Is Good, Elate Is Better," *Sales & Marketing Management,* January 1994, pp. 31–32.

Chapter Nine

[1]Christopher Power, Kathleen Kerwin, Ronald Glover, Keith Alexander, and Robert D. Hof, "Flops," *Business Week,* August 16, 1993, p. 82.

[2]"Try It, They May Buy It," *The Wall Street Journal,* November 14, 1996, p. A1.

[3]Alan Farnham, "America's Most Admired Company," *Fortune,* February 7, 1994, pp. 50–54.

[4]Bruce Horovitz, "Fast-food Chains Hunger for New Hits," *The Courier-Journal,* July 5, 2002 pp. C1–C2.

[5]Power et al., "Flops," p. 77.

[6]Rahul Jacob, "Beyond Quality and Value," *Fortune,* Autumn–Winter 1993, pp. 8–11.

[7]"Shortening the Product Pipeline," *Sales and Marketing Management,* January 1999, p. 71.

[8]Cyndee Miller, "Little Relief Seen for New Product Failure," *Marketing News,* June 21, 1993, pp. 1, 10.

[9]Brenton R. Schlender, "How Sony Keeps the Magic Going," *Fortune,* February 24, 1993, pp. 76–84.

[10]www.newellco.com and www.rubbermaid.com, January 12, 2000.

[11]Suein Hwang, "Colgate-Palmolive Profit Rose 11% in Third Quarter," *The Wall Street Journal,* October 22, 1993, p. B5.

[12]Stephen D. Moore, "French Drug Maker Reaps Profits with Offbeat Strategy," *The Wall Street Journal,* November 14, 1996, p. B3.

[13]Thomas D. Kuczmarski, *Managing New Products: Competing through Excellence* (Englewood Cliffs, NJ: Prentice Hall, 1988), pp. 37–39.

[14]Power et al., p. 77.

[15]www.3M.com, January 14, 2000.

[16]Stephanie Clifford, "How to Get the Geeks and the Suits to Play Nice," *Business 2.0,* May 2002, pp. 92–93.

[17]Power et al., "Flops," p. 77.

[18]"Mercury's Mystique Tries No-Tuneup Tack," *The Courier-Journal,* February 3, 1994, p. D1.

[19]Kevin Kelly, "The New Soul of John Deere," *Business Week,* January 31, 1994, pp. 64–66.

[20]Quentin Hardy, "How a Wife's Question Led Motorola to Chase Global Cell-Phone Plan," *The Wall Street Journal,* December 16, 1996, pp. A1, A10.

[21]Amy Borrus, "Click Here to Pay Your Parking Ticket," *Business Week,* January 17, 2000, pp. 76, 78.

[22]Linda Rochford and Thomas R. Wotruba, "New Product Development under Changing Economic Conditions," *Journal of Business and Industrial Marketing* 8, no. 3 (1993), pp. 4–12.

[23]David Leonhardt, "It Was a Hit in Buenos Aires—So Why Not Boise?" *Business Week,* September 7, 1998, pp. 56–58.

[24]Kathleen Devery, "Failure of Its Oven Lovin' Cookie Dough Shows Pillsbury Pitfalls of New Products," *The Wall Street Journal,* July 17, 1993, pp. B1, B8.

[25]Jerry Flint, "The Car Chrysler Didn't Build," *Forbes,* August 12, 1996, pp. 89–91.

[26]Power et al., "Flops," p. 80.

[27]Christopher Power, "Will It Sell in Podunk? Hard to Say," *Business Week,* August 10, 1992, p. 46.

[28]William R. Dillon, Thomas J. Madden, and Neil H. Firtle, *Essentials of Marketing Research* (Homewood, IL: Richard D. Irwin, 1993), p. 732.

[29]Ian P. Murphy, "Ameritech Test Towns Market Innovation," *Marketing News,* November 18, 1996, pp. 2, 12.

[30]"Up Front," *Business Week,* April 19, 1999, p. 8.

[31]Warren B. Brown and Necmi Karagozoglu, "Leading the Way to Faster New Product Development," *The Executive,* February 1993, pp. 36–47.

[32]Kyle Pope, "Compaq Is Set to Introduce 'Subnotebook,'" *The Wall Street Journal,* February 2, 1994, p. 85.

[33]"Winning the New Product Launch," *On Target Research,* 1999, pp. 14–15.

[34]Wendy Bounds, "Camera System Is Developed but Not Delivered," *The Wall Street Journal,* August 7, 1996, p. B1.

[35]"Survey Reveals Better Planning Is Needed in New Product Development," *Quality Progress,* February 1996, pp. 16–17.

[36]This section draws heavily from Robert G. Cooper and Elko J. Kleinschmidt, "Stage Gate Systems for New Product Success," *Marketing Management* 1, no. 4, pp. 20–26.

[37]Richard Gibson, "A Cereal Maker's Quest for the Next Grape-Nuts," *The Wall Street Journal,* January 23, 1997, B1–2.

[38]Larry Armstrong, "The Best Products of 2001," *Business Week,* December 17, 2001, pp. 116–26.

Chapter Ten

[1]www.geappliances.com, August 15, 2002.

[2]Peter Bennett, *Dictionary of Marketing Terms* (Chicago: American Marketing Association, 1988), p. 156.

[3]Ibid.

[4]www.palm.com, January 17, 2000.

[5]Ibid.

[6]Louise Lee, "Why Levi's Still Looks Faded, *Business Week,* July 22, 2002, pp. 54–55.

[7]Cyndee Miller, "Another Win for Retro: Designer Jeans Are Back," *Marketing News,* June 3, 1996, pp. 18–19.

[8]Robert Berner, "Why P & G's Smile Is So Bright," *Business Week,* August 12, 2002, pp. 58–60.

[9]Dana James, "Rejuvenating Mature Brands Can Be Stimulating Exercise," *Marketing News,* August 16, 1999, pp. 16–17.

[10]Laura Johannes, "Hasbro Unveils Toys It Says Will Remain 99.9% Germ-Free," *The Wall Street Journal,* January 28, 1997, p. B8.

[11]Scott McCartney, "Airlines Face Implications of Dusseldorf Experiment," *The Wall Street Journal Online,* July 31, 2002, pp. 1–3.

[12]Christy Fisher, "Line Extension No Recipe for Success in Candy," *Advertising Age,* January 31, 1994, pp. 3, 38.

[13]Ian P. Murphy, "Yoo-Hoo Adds Flavors to Its Marketing Mix," *Marketing News,* February 3, 1997, p. 2.

[14]Gabriella Stern, "Makers of Frozen Diet Entrees Start Some Diets of Their Own," *The Wall Street Journal,* January 4, 1994, pp. B1, B7.

[15]Elizabeth A. Lesly, "Borden Faces Facts: It's Time to Shed the Flab," *Business Week,* November 9, 1992, p. 44.

[16]Geoffrey Smith and Nathans Spiro, "Fidelity Jumps Feet First into the Fray," *Business Week,* May 25, 1992, pp. 104–6.

[17]"Circuit City Stores Plans to Try Its Hand at Peddling a New Product—Used Cars," *The Wall Street Journal,* April 7, 1993, p. B6.

[18]Kathleen Kerwin, "Fixing the Engine Trouble at Ford Credit," *Business Week,* July 15, 2002, p. 116.

[19]Dean Foust, "Whipping A Behemoth Into Shape," *Business Week,* January 21, 2002, p. 84.

[20]Kyle Pope, "Texas Instruments Sees Path on Information Highway," *The Wall Street Journal,* March 9, 1994, p. B4.

[21]Allen D. Shocker, Rajendra K. Srivastava, and Robert W. Ruekert, "Challenges and Opportunities Facing Brand Management: An Introduction to the Special Issue," *Journal of Marketing Research,* May 1994, pp. 149–58.

[22]Srinivas K. Reddy, Susan L. Holak, and Subodh Bhat, "To Extend or Not to Extend: Success Determinants of Line Extensions," *Journal of Marketing Research,* May 1994, pp. 243–62.

[23]Gene R. Laczniak and Patrick E. Murphy, *Ethical Marketing Decisions: The Higher Road* (Boston, MA: Allyn and Bacon, 1993), p. 81.

[24]Fred W. Morgan, "Incorporating a Consumer Product Safety Perspective into the Product Development Process," in N. Craig Smith and John A. Quelch, eds., *Ethics in Marketing* (Homewood, IL: Richard D. Irwin, 1993), pp. 351–59.

[25]Douglas Lavin, "Chrysler Corp. Discloses a Third Recall of Its Neon Model for Brake Problem," *The Wall Street Journal,* April 8, 1994, p. A3; and "Some Crayon Brands Are Recalled by U.S., Citing Lead Levels," *The Wall Street Journal,* April 7, 1994, p. A8.

[26]Mary Agnes Carey, "Popcorn at Movies Gets Thumbs Down for Being Full of Fat," *The Wall Street Journal,* April 26, 1994, p. A5.

[27]Laczniak and Murphy, *Ethical Marketing Decisions,* p. 89.

[28]Marcus W. Brauchli, "Chinese Flagrantly Copy Trademarks of Foreigners," *The Wall Street Journal,* June 20, 1994, pp. B1, B5.

[29]Dexder Roberts, "Clear Sailing for Pirates," *Business Week,* July 15, 2002, p. 53.

[30]Laczniak and Murphy, *Ethical Marketing Decisions,* p. 103.

Chapter Eleven

[1]"That Falling Feeling," *The Economist,* March 17, 2001, p. 60.

[2]Stuart Sinclair, "A Guide to Global Pricing," *Journal of Business Strategy,* May–June 1993, p. 16.

[3]Rick Brooks, "Package Carriers Deliver Bad News to Shippers: Heap of Higher Prices," *The Wall Street Journal,* http://interactive.wsj.com/archive/retrie. . .00754067404440.djm.

[4]Walter van Waterschoot and Christophe Van den Butle, "The 4P Classification of the Marketing Mix Revisited," *Journal of Marketing,* October 1992, p. 90.

[5]Michael V. Marn and Robert Rosiello, "Managing Price, Gaining Profit," *Harvard Business Review,* September–October 1992, p. 86.

[6]David R. Bell and James M. Lattin, "Shopping Behavior and Consumer Preference for Store Price Format: Why 'Large Basket' Shoppers Prefer EDLP," Marketing Science Institute, Report no. 98–114 (Cambridge, MA: 1998); and Susan Keane, "Beyond EDLP/HiLo: A New Look at Retailer Pricing," *Insights from MSI,* Marketing Science Institute (Cambridge, MA: 1999), pp. 7–8.

[7]Marn and Rosiello, "Managing Price, Gaining Profit," p. 84.

[8]Hermann Simon, "Pricing Opportunities and How to Exploit Them," *Sloan Management Review,* Winter 1992, p. 56; and Gerard J. Tellis, "The Price Elasticity of Selective Demand: A Meta-Analysis of Econometric Models of Sales," *Journal of Marketing Research,* November 1988, p. 331–41.

[9]Kent B. Monroe, *Pricing: Making Profitable Decisions* (New York: McGraw-Hill, 1990), pp. 8–10; and Paul W. Farris and John A. Quelch, "In Defense of Price Promotion," *Sloan Management Review,* Fall 1987, p. 63.

[10]Nick Wreden, "How to Think about Pricing Strategies in a Downturn," *Harvard Business Update,* March 2002, pp. 9–10.

[11]John G. Lynch and Dan Ariely, "Electronic Shopping for Wine: How Search Costs Affect Consumer Price Sensitivity, Satisfaction with Merchandise, and Retention," Marketing Science Institute, Report no. 99–104 (Cambridge, MA: 1999).

[12]Pam Black, "All the World's an Auction," *Business Week,* February 8, 1999, pp. 120–21; and Gene Koretz, "Inflation's New Adversary," *Business Week,* October 4, 1999, p. 30.

[13]Walter Baker, Mike Marn, and Craig Zawada, "Price Smarter on the Net," *Harvard Business Review,* February 2001, pp. 122–27; Scott McNealy, "Welcome to the Bazaar," *Harvard Business Review,* March 2001, pp. 18–19; Peter Coy and Pamela L. Moore, "A Revolution in Pricing? Not Quite," *Business Week,* November 20, 200, pp. 48–49; and Kimberly Weisul, "Sucker Prices—but Who's the Sucker," *Business Week,* March 18, 2002, p. 16.

[14]Tommy Hanrahan, "Price Isn't Everything," *The Wall Street Journal,* July 12, 1999, p. R20; Gene Koretz, "Inflation's New Adversary," *Business Week,* October 4, 1999, p. 30; and Gary McWilliams, "Dealer Loses?" *The Wall Street Journal,* July 12, 1999, p. R20.

[15]Anne-Marie Crawford, "'Our Money Message for Euro's Ad Campaign," *Ad Age Global,* September 2001, p. 8; Christopher Rhoads, "Euro Launch Reaches Its Final Crucial Phase," *The Wall Street Journal,* December 17, 2001, p. A8; and Michael R. Sesit, "Euro's Launch Helps Consumers Easily Compare Cost of Goods," *The Wall Street Journal,* January 18, 2002, p. C11.

[16]Maricris G. Briones, "The Euro Starts Here," *Marketing News,* July 20, 1998, pp. 1, 39.

[17]Michael D. Mondello, "Naming Your Price," *Inc.,* July 1992, p. 80.

[18]Thomas T. Nagle, *The Strategy and Tactics of Pricing: A Guide to Profitable Decision Making* (Englewood Cliffs, NJ: Prentice Hall, 1989), p. 8.

[19]"Cruise Lines Deep in Discounts," *Advertising Age,* February 3, 1992, p. 16.

[20]Zachary Schiller, "Procter & Gamble Hits Back," *Business Week,* July 19, 1993, p. 20.

[21]Alison Rea, "Why Rising Bank Fees Are Backfiring," *Business Week,* August 19, 1996, p. 66.

[22]Reed K. Holden and Thomas T. Nagle, "Kamikaze Pricing," *Marketing Management,* Summer 1998, pp. 30–39.

[23]Peter R. Dickson, *Marketing Management* (Fort Worth, TX: Dryden Press, 1994), p. 476.

[24]Robert Jacobson and David A. Aaker, "Is Market Share All That It's Cracked Up to Be?" *Journal of Marketing,* Fall 1985, pp. 11–22.

[25]Greg Bowers, "Wiping the Mess from Gerber's Chin," *Business Week,* February 1, 1993, p. 32.

[26]Richard Gibson, "Kellogg's Cutting Prices on Some Cereals in Bid to Check Loss of Market Share," *The Wall Street Journal,* June 10, 1996, p. A3.

[27]Monroe, *Pricing,* p. 8.

[28]Marn and Rosiello, "Managing Price, Gaining Profit," pp. 84–85.

[29]Nagle, *Strategy and Tactics of Pricing,* pp. 114–15.

[30]Simon, "Pricing Opportunities," p. 64.

[31]"Sheraton's New Pricing Makes Rivals Cry Foul," *Advertising Age,* May 11, 1992, p. 6.

[32]Michael Porter, *Competitive Strategy* (New York, NY: Free Press, 1980); Joel E. Urbany, "Pricing Strategies and Determination," *Marketing: Best Practices* (Fort Worth, TX: The Dryden Press, 2000), p. 510.

[33]Bob Francis, "Luxury for the Masses," *BrandWeek,* June 25, 2001, pp. 16–20.

[34]Mondello, "Naming Your Price," p. 80.

[35]Doug Carroll, "Price Wars Make Airlines Shrink," *USA Today,* November 24, 1993, p. 18B.

[36]Allan J. McGrath, "Ten Timeless Truths about Pricing," *Journal of Business and Industrial Marketing,* Summer–Fall 1991, p. 17.

[37]Ralph G. Kauffman, "The Future of Purchasing and Supply: Strategic Cost Management," *Purchasing,* September 1999, pp. 33–35; Leslie Kaufman, "Downscale Moves Up," *Newsweek,* July 27, 1998, pp. 32–33; and Zachary Schiller, Greg Burns, and Karen Lowry Miller, "Make It Simple," *Business Week,* September 9, 1996, pp. 96–104.

[38]Raymond Serafin, "U.S. Cars Build Share with Value Pricing," *Advertising Age,* July 12, 1993, p. 4; and Wendy Zeller, "Penney's Rediscovers Its Calling," *Business Week,* April 5, 1993, p. 51.

[39]Donald F. Blurnberg, "What Is Your Service Really Worth?" *Success,* July–August 1992, p. 13.

[40]Robert Hales and David Staley, "Mix Target Costing, QFD for Successful New Products," *Marketing News,* January 2, 1995, p. 18.

[41]David Wessel, "How Technology Tailors Price Tags," *The Wall Street Journal,* http://interactive.wjs,/com/archive/retrie. . . 81676486297602.djm.

[42]Stephen J. Hoch, Byung-Do Kim, Alan L. Montgomery, and Peter E. Rossi, "Determinants of Store-Level Price Elasticity," *Journal of Marketing Research* 32 (February 1995), pp. 17–29; and Barbara E. Kahn and Leigh McAlister, *Grocery Revolution: The Focus on the Consumer* (Reading, MA: Addison-Wesley, 1997), pp. 185–92.

[43]Monroe, *Pricing,* p. 204.

[44]Gerard P. Cachon and Martin A. Lariviere, "Turning the Supply Chain into a Revenue Chain," *Harvard Business Review,* March 2001, pp. 20–21.

[45]Peggy Simpson, "Poles Shop Till Prices Drop," *Business Week,* August 19, 1996, p. 4.

[46]Gene Koretz, "Inflation's New Adversary," *Business Week,* October 4, 1999, p. 30.

[47]Makoto Abe, "Behavioral Explanations for Asymmetric Price Competition," Marketing Science Institute, Report no. 98–123 (Cambridge, MA: 1998); George Cressman, Jr., "Utility Pricing: It's All in the Packaging," *Marketing News,* May 24, 1999, p. 12; and Nikhilm Deogun, "Coke and Pepsi Call Off Pricing Battle," *The Wall Street Journal,* June 12, 1997, p. A3.

[48]Susan M. Broniarczyk and Joseph W. Alba, "The Importance of the Brand in Brand Extension," *Journal of Marketing Research,* May 1994, pp. 214–25. For recent reviews, see David A. Aaker and Kevin Lane Keller, "Consumer Evaluations of Brand Extensions," *Journal of Marketing,* January 1990, pp. 27–41; and C. Whan Park, Sandra Milberg, and Robert Lawson, "Evaluation of Brand Extensions: The Role of Product Feature Similarity and Brand Concept Consistency," *Journal of Consumer Research,* September 1991, pp. 185–93.

[49]Joseph Weber, "Drug Prices: So Much for Restraint," *Business Week,* March 4, 1996, p. 40.

[50]Greg Wright, "Net Music a Factor in Falling CD Prices," *Fort Collins Coloradan,* January 21, 2002, p. D8.

[51]Kent B. Monroe and Susan M. Petroshius, "Buyers' Perceptions of Price: An Update of the Evidence," in *Perspectives in Consumer Behavior,* 3rd ed., ed. H. H. Kassarjian and T. S. Robertson (Glenview, IL: Scott, Foresman, 1991), p. 44.

[52]Valarie Zeithaml, "Consumer Perceptions of Price, Quality, and Value: A Means-End Model and Synthesis of Evidence," *Journal of Marketing*, July 1988, p. 10; and Peter R. Dickson and Alan G. Sawyer, "The Price Knowledge and Search of Supermarket Shoppers," *Journal of Marketing*, July 1990, pp. 42–53.

[53]Zeithaml, "Consumer Perceptions," p. 14.

[54]Kent B. Monroe and R. Krishnan, "The Effect of Price on Subjective Product Evaluations," *Perceived Quality: How Consumers View Stores and Merchandise,* ed. Jacob Jacoby and Jerry Olson (Lexington, MA: Lexington Books, 1985), pp. 209–32.

[55]Gary Levin, "Price Rises as Factor for Consumers," *Advertising Age*, November 8, 1993, p. 37.

[56]Leonard Berry, "Strengthening the Service Brand," *Marketing Science Institute Review* (Cambridge, MA: Marketing Science Institute, Spring 1998), p. 4.

[57]Robert A. Peterson and William R. Wilson, "Perceived Risk and Price-Reliance Schema and Price–Perceived-Quality Mediators," in *Perceived Quality: How Consumers View Stores and Merchandise,* ed. Jacob Jacoby and Jerry Olson (Lexington, MA: Lexington Books, 1985), pp. 247–68. Studies of firm behavior reveal that pursuit of product-quality strategies can improve profitability and that price and quality are related at the firm level. See Robert Jacobson and David A. Aaker, "The Strategic Role of Product Quality," *Journal of Marketing*, October 1987, pp. 31–44.

[58]Donald R. Lichtenstein and Scot Burton, "The Relationship between Perceived and Objective Price Quality," *Journal of Marketing Research*, November 1989, pp. 429–43.

[59]Gerard J. Tellis and Gary J. Gaeth, "Best Value, Price Seeking, and Price Aversion: The Impact of Information and Learning on Consumer Choices," *Journal of Marketing*, April 1990, pp. 34–45.

[60]Niraj Dawar, "The Signaling Impact of Low Introductory Price on Perceived Quality and Trial," *Marketing Letters* 8, no. 3, p. 252.

[61]Robert Jacobson and Carl Obermiller, "The Formation of Expected Future Price: A Reference Price for Forward-Looking Consumers," *Journal of Consumer Research*, March 1990, p. 421.

[62]Noreen M. Klein and Janet E. Oglethorpe, "Cognitive Reference Points in Consumer Decision Making," in *Advances in Consumer Research*, vol. 14, ed. M. Wallendorf and J. Anderson (Provo, UT: Association for Consumer Research, 1987), pp. 183–97.

[63]Margaret C. Campbell, "Perceptions of Price Unfairness: Antecedents and Consequences," *Journal of Marketing Research* 36 (May 1999), pp. 187–99.

[64]Joel E. Urbany and Peter R. Dickson, *Consumer Knowledge of Consumer Prices: An Exploratory Study and Framework,* Marketing Science Institute, Report no. 90–112 (Cambridge, MA: 1990), p. 18.

[65]Dickson and Sawyer, "Price Knowledge and Search," p. 42–53.

[66]Aradha Krishna, "Effect of Dealing Patterns on Consumer Perceptions of Deal Frequency and Willingness to Pay," *Journal of Marketing Research*, November 1991, pp. 441–51.

[67]Abhijit Biswas and Edward A. Blair, "Contextual Effects of Reference Prices in Retail Advertisements," *Journal of Marketing*, July 1991, p. 4.

[68]Richard Thaler, "Mental Accounting and Consumer Choice," *Marketing Science*, Summer 1985, pp. 199–214.

[69]Dhruv Grewal, Kent B. Monroe, and R. Krishnan, "The Effects of Price-Comparison Advertising on Buyers' Perceptions of Acquisition Value, Transaction Value, and Behavioral Intentions," *Journal of Marketing* 62 (April 1998), pp. 46–59.

Chapter Twelve

[1]Shantanu Dutta, Mark Bergen, and Mark Zbaracki, "Pricing Process as a Capability," MSI Report No. 01–117, Cambridge, MA: Marketing Science Institute.

[2]Harper W. Boyd, Jr., Orville C. Walker, Jr., John Mulling, and Jean-Clarde Larreche, *Marketing Management: A Strategic Decision-Making Approach*, 4th ed., (New York: McGraw-Hill/Irwin, 2002), p. 283.

[3]Allan B. Krueger, "Seven Lesson about Super Bowl Tickets," *New York Times*, February 1, 2001, p. C2.

[4]Scott C. Friend and Patricia H. Walker, "Welcome to the New World of Merchandising," *Harvard Business Review,* November 2001, p. 134.

[5]Michael Parkin, *Microeconomics*, 2nd ed. (Reading, MA: Addison-Wesley, 1992), p. 109.

[6]Philip Kotler, *Marketing Management: Analysis, Planning, Implementation, and Control*, 8th ed. (Englewood Cliffs, NJ: Prentice Hall, 1994), p. 495.

[7]Rockney G. Walters, "Assessing the Impact of Retail Price Promotions on Product Substitution, Complementary Purchase, and Interstore Sales Displacement," *Journal of Marketing*, April 1991, p. 17.

[8]Paul A. Samuelson and William D. Nordhaus, *Economics*, 14th ed. (New York: McGraw-Hill, 1992), p. 210.

[9]Ford S. Worthy, "Japan's Smart Secret Weapon," *Fortune*, August 12, 1991, pp. 72–73.

[10]Stephan A. Butscher and Michael Laker, "Market-Driven Product Development," *Marketing Management,* Summer 2000, pp. 48–52.

[11]Allen L. Appell, "Income-Based Pricing: An Additional Approach to Teaching the Subject of Pricing in Marketing Courses," *Marketing Education Review* 7 (Summer), pp. 61–64.

[12]Klaus Wertenbroch and Bernd Skiera, "Measuring Consumer Willingness to Pay at the Point of Purchase," *Journal of Marketing Research*, May 2002, p. 230.

[13]Timothy Matanovich, Gary L. Lilien, and Arvind Rangaswamy, "Engineering the Price-Value Relationship," *Marketing Management,* Spring 1999, pp. 48–53.

[14]The organization and content of this section are based on the typology and discussion of Gerard J. Tellis, "Beyond the Many Faces of Price: An Integration of Pricing Strategies," *Journal of Marketing,* October 1986, pp. 146–60.

[15]Kent B. Monroe, *Pricing: Making Profitable Decisions*, 2nd ed. (New York: McGraw-Hill, 1990), p. 490.

[16]Evan I. Schwartz, *Digital Darwinism: 7 Breakthrough Business Strategies for Surviving in the Cutthroat Web Economy* (New York, NY: Broadway Books, 1999).

[17]Kotler, *Marketing Management*, p. 512.

[18]Gerard J. Tellis and Gary J. Gaeth, "Best Value, Price-Seeking, and Price Aversion: The Impact of Information and Learning on Consumer Choices," *Journal of Marketing,* April 1990, p. 36.

[19]Tellis, "Beyond the Many Faces of Price," p. 153.

[20]Teresa Andreoli, "Value Retailers Take the Low-Income Road to New Heights," *Discount Store News*, February 19, 1996, pp. 1, 19.

[21]Monroe, *Pricing*, p. 304.

[22]Stefan Stemersch and Gerald J. Tellis, "Strategic Bundling of Products and Prices: A New Synthesis for Marketing," *Journal of Marketing*, January 2002, p. 57.

[23]David Barboza, "A Weed Killer Is a Block for Monsanto to Build On," *New York Times*, August 2, 2001, p. C1.

[24]Tim Clark, "Four H-P Success Story Strategies," *Business Marketing*, July 1993, pp. 18, 20.

[25]Vicki Morwitz, Eric A. Greenleaf, and Eric J. Johnson, "Divide and Prosper: Consumers' Reactions to Partitioned Prices," *Journal of Marketing Research* 35 (November 1998), pp. 453–63.

[26]Robert Schindler, "How to Advertise Price," in *Attention, Attitude, and Affect in Response to Advertising,* ed. E. M. Clark, T. C. Brock, and D. W. Stewart (Hillsdale, NJ: Lawrence Erlbaum Associates, 1994), pp. 251–69.

[27]"Package Ploy Not Fair Play," *Advertising Age,* May 28, 2001, p. 20; and Sonia Reyes, "Honey, They Shrunk the Bag," *BrandWeek,* October 23, 2000, pp. 1, 60.

[28]Cornelia Pechmann, "Do Consumers Overgeneralize One-Sided Comparative Price Claims, and Are More Stringent Regulations Needed?" *Journal of Marketing Research* 33 (May 1996), pp. 150–62.

[29]Peter M. Noble and Thomas S. Cruca, "Industrial Pricing: Theory and Managerial Practice," *Marketing Science,* 18, no. 3, (1999), pp. 435–54.

[30]Donald V. Potter, "Discovering Hidden Pricing Power," *Business Horizons,* November/December 2000, p. 41.

[31]Dean Forest, Michael Ardnt, Robert Berner, and Amy Barrett, "Raising Price Won't Fly," *Business Week,* June 3, 2002, pp. 34–36.

[32]Kotler, *Marketing Management,* p. 514.

[33]Barbara E. Kahn and Leigh McAlister, *Grocery Revolution: New Focus on the Consumer* (Reading, MA: Addison-Wesley, 1997), pp. 69–72.

[34]For research regarding acceptable price limits, see Peter R. Dickson and Alan G. Sawyer, "The Price Knowledge and Search of Supermarket Shoppers," *Journal of Marketing,* July 1990, pp. 42–53; Rustan Kosenko and Don Rahtz, "Buyer Market Price Knowledge on Acceptable Price Range and Price Limits," in *Advances in Consumer Research,* vol. 15, ed. Michael J. Houston (Provo, UT: Association for Consumer Research, 1987), pp. 328–33; and Patricia Sorce and Stanley M. Widrick, "Individual Differences in Latitude of Acceptable Prices," in *Advances in Consumer Research,* vol. 18, ed. Rebecca H. Holman and Michael R. Soloman (Provo, UT: Association for Consumer Research, 1991), pp. 802–5.

[35]Margaret C. Campbell, "Perceptions of Price Unfairness: Antecedents and Consequences," *Journal of Marketing Research* 36 (May 1999); pp. 187–99; Daniel Kahneman, Jack L. Knetrch, and Richard Thaler, "Fairness and the Assumptions of Economics," *Journal of Business* 59, no. 4 (1986), pp. S285–S300; and Wendy Zeller, "Straightened Up and Flying Right," *Business Week,* April 5, 1999, p. 42.

[36]Kate Fitzgerald, "Target Accuses Wal-Mart in Ads," *Advertising Age,* March 29, 1993, pp. 1, 50.

[37]"A Merger's Bitter Harvest," *Business Week,* February 5, 2001, p. 112.

[38]Alan Radding, "Big Blue Takes Aim at Toshiba, Compaq," *Advertising Age,* March 25, 1991, pp. 1, 48; Kathy Rebello and Stephanie Anderson, "They're Slashing as Fast as They Can," *Business Week,* February 17, 1992, p. 40; and Hal Lancaster and Michael Allen, "Compaq Computer Finds Itself Where It Once Put IBM," *The Wall Street Journal,* January 13, 1992, p. B4.

[39]Kathleen Madigan, Joseph Weber, and Geoffrey Smith, "The Latest Mad Plunge of the Price Slashers," *Business Week,* May 11, 1992, p. 36.

[40]Akshay R. Rao, Mark E. Bergen, and Scott Davis, "How to Fight a Price War," *Harvard Business Review,* March–April 2000, p. 109; and Mike Troy, "Kmart: Drop EDLP and Continue Promoting the Value Message," *Dsn Retailing Today,* March 11, 2002, p. 33.

[41]Robert C. Blattberg, Richard Briesch, and Edward J. Fox, "How Promotions Work," *Marketing Science* 14, no. 3, pp. G123–4.

[42]Michael J. Zenor, Bart J. Bronnenberg, and Leigh McAlister, *The Impact of Marketing Policy on Promotional Price Elasticities and Baseline Sales,* Marketing Science Institute, Report no. 98–101 (Cambridge, MA: 1998).

[43]Hugh M. Cannon and Fred W. Morgan, "A Strategic Pricing Framework," *Journal of Business and Industrial Marketing,* Summer–Fall 1991, p. 62.

[44]Monroe, *Pricing,* p. 427.

[45]Michael L. Mellot, "Systematic Approach to Pricing Increases Profits," *Marketing News,* May 24, 1993, p. 3.

[46]"Going, Going, Gone! The B2B Tool That Really Is Changing the World," *Fortune,* March 20, 2000, pp. 132–45.

[47]Jim Hansen, "Fees for Loans: Just Part of the Marketing Equation," *Credit Union Executive,* November–December 1992, pp. 42–45; Clifford L. Ratza, "A Client-Driven Model for Service Pricing," *Journal of Professional Services Marketing* 8, no. 2 (1993), pp. 55–64; and Madhav N. Segal, "An Empirical Investigation of the Pricing of Professional Services," *Journal of Professional Services Marketing,* 1991, pp. 169–81.

[48]Kristen Young, "When Morris Took Flight, Fares Fell," *USA Today,* August 30, 1993, pp. 1B–2B.

[49]Guiltinan, "The Price Bundling of Services," p. 74.

[50]Zachary Schiller, Susan Garland, and Julia Flynn Siler, "The Humana Flap Could Make All Hospitals Feel Sick," *Business Week,* November 4, 1991, p. 34.

[51]Gwendolyn K. Ortmeyer, "Ethical Issues in Pricing," in *Ethics in Marketing,* ed. N. Craig Smith and John A. Quelch (Homewood, IL: Richard D. Irwin, 1993), p. 401; and Andrea Rothman, "The Airlines Get Out the Good China," *Business Week,* February 3, 1992, p. 66.

[52]Marc Rice, "Profiteering Claimed as Wood Prices Rise," *The Commercial Appeal,* August 28, 1992, pp. B4–B5; and "Home Depot Offers Storm Victims Break," *The Commercial Appeal,* August 29, 1992, p. B4.

[53]*Code of Federal Regulations,* 16, 233.0 FTC, Office of the Federal Register, National Archives and Records Administration, Washington, DC, pp. 26–30.

[54]"News Release," Colorado Department of Law, Attorney General, June 21, 1989, pp. 2–3.

[55]Dan Morse, "Breakthrough Product Visits Funeral Homes," *The Wall Street Journal,* January 7, 2000, p. A1.

[56]Nagle, *Strategy and Tactics of Pricing,* p. 324.

[57]Adam Bryant, "Aisle Seat Bully," *Newsweek,* May 24, 1999, p. 56; Anna Wilde Mathews and Scott McCartney, "U.S. Sues American Air in Antitrust Case," *The Wall Street Journal,* May 15, 1999, pp. A3, A6; and Wendy Zeller, "Straightened Up and Flying Right," *Business Week,* April 5, 1999, p. 42.

[58]Ortmeyer, "Ethical Issues in Pricing," pp. 396–97.

Chapter Thirteen

[1]Adapted from Peter D. Bennett, ed., *Dictionary of Marketing Terms,* 2nd ed. (Chicago: American Marketing Association, 1995), p. 167.

[2]Information furnished by Agco National Presto Industries via e-mail to the author on June 4, 2002.

[3]"Marketing: Selling the Superstores," from *Inc.* magazine's Web site at www.inc.com, February 12, 2002.

[4]Information from Building Materials Distributors' Web site at www.bmdusa.com, April 24, 2002.

[5]Emily Nelson, "Colgate Net Rises 3% as Company Books Charges Linked to Kmart," *The Wall Street Journal,* February 6, 2002, p. B8.

[6]Information from *PR Newswire* site at www.prnewswire.com, June 4, 2002.

[7]Bennett, *Dictionary of Marketing Terms,* p. 300.

[8]Information furnished by Episode Stores, March 28, 1997.

[9]Information from Agco Corporation corporate relations department via phone interview June 6, 2002, and from Agco's Web site at www.agcocorp.com on June 5, 2002.

[10]Steven Wheeler and Evan Hirsh, *Channel Champions* (San Francisco: Jossey-Bass Publishers, 1999), pp. 30–33.

[11]Marcia Savage, "McAffee Gives Channel a Lift," *Crn,* February 4, 2002, p. 8.

[12]Mike Duff, "Stride Rite Steps into Target with Exclusive Kids Line," *Retailing Today,* January 21, 2002, pp. 2, 25.

[13]Martha Brannigan and Nicole Harris, "Travel Agents Prepare Response to Move by Delta to Eliminate Most Commissions," *The Wall Street Journal,* March 18, 2002, p. B2; and Kortney Stringer, "More Car Renters Cut Commissions to Travel Agents," *The Wall Street Journal,* April 10, 2002, p. D5.

[14]Betsy McKay, "Coke Reaches Pact with Danone for U.S. Distribution of Evian," *The Wall Street Journal,* April 26, 2002, p. B4.

[15]Information from Amazon.com Web site at www.amazon.com, June 6, 2002.

[16]Pamela Sebastian, "Business Bulletin," *The Wall Street Journal,* October 31, 1996, p. A1.

[17]Shizuo KambaYashi, "Fans, Artists and Industry: Nobody's Rockin'," *USA Today,* June 5, 2002, pp. 1A–2A.

[18]James R. Healey, "Circuit City Plans to Push CarMax out of the Nest," *USA Today,* February 25, 2002, p. 3B.

[19]Joel Hoekstra, "Bif G's Big Boss," *World Traveler,* March 2002, pp. 40–43.

[20]Melinda Ligos, "Clicks & Misses," *Sales & Marketing Management,* June 2000, pp. 69–76.

[21]Mike Graen, "Technology in Manufacturer/Retailer Integration: Wal-Mart and Procter & Gamble," *Velocity,* Spring, 1999, pp. 12–17.

[22]"NFC-FTC Alternative Rule Enforcement Program from the Web site of the National Franchise Council at www.nationalfranchise-council.org on June 6, 2002; and Dan Morse, "First Firms Undergo Franchise Council's Reform School," *The Wall Street Journal,* August 10, 1999, p. B2.

[23]The types of power discussed in this section can be traced back to John French, Jr., and Bertram Raven, "The Bases of Social Power," in *Studies in Social Power,* D. Cartwright, ed. (Ann Arbor, MI: University of Michigan Press, 1959), pp. 150–67.

[24]Betsy McKay and Luhnow, "Mexico Finds Coke and Its Bottlers Guilty of Abusing Dominant Position in Market," *The Wall Street Journal,* March 8, 2002, p. B3.

[25]Aravind Adiga, Adrienne Carter, Amy Feldman, Pablo Galarza, Jeff Nash, Ilana Polyak, and Stephanie D. Smith, "2002 Best Investments," *Money,* January 2002, pp. 68–69.

[26]Kristen Kennedy, "Channel Poaching," *Crn,* February 4, 2002, pp. 3, 10.

[27]Shelly Branch, "Hershey Turns to Convenience Stores to Sweeten Revenue," *The Wall Street Journal,* March 29, 2002, p. B4.

Chapter Fourteen

[1]*Statistical Abstract of the United States* (Washington, D.C.: U.S. Department of Commerce, 2001), p. 480.

[2]Anne D'Innocenzio, "Cheap Chic," *Fort Collins Colorodoan,* March 17, 2002, pp. E1, E4; Amy Merrick, "New Game at Kohl's: Dressing Up," *The Wall Street Journal,* March 12, 2002, p. B1; and Lorrie Grant, "Drooping Department Stores Strategize," *USA Today,* January 15, 2002, p. 3B.

[3]Earle Eldridge, "Five Wal-Marts Test Out Used Car Sales for 6 Months," *USA Today,* April 23, 2002, p. B1.

[4]Nanette Byrnes and Christopher Palmeri, "A Showstopper on Broadway," *Business Week,* December 24, 2001, p. 54.

[5]Information from Mail of America's Web site at www.mallofamerica.com, June 10, 2002.

[6]Information from www.franchiseinfomall.com, June 10, 2002.

[7]Laura Tiffany, "The Wild Frontier," *Entrepreneur International,* March 1999, as it appeared in *Entrepreneur International* magazine online at www.entrepreneurmag.com, January 9, 2000.

[8]Information from www.franchiseinfomall.com, June 10, 2002.

[9]Tiffany, "The Wild Frontier."

[10]Information from www.franchiseinfomall.com, June 10, 2002.

[11]Stephanie Anderson Forest, "A Speedy Makeover for Penney's," *Business Week,* April 29, 2002, pp. 92–94.

[12]Amy Merrick, Jeffrey A. Trachtenberg, and Ann Zimmerman, "Department Stores Fight an Uphill Battle Just to Stay Relevant," *The Wall Street Journal,* pp. A1, A17.

[13]Information from Carrefour's Web site at www.carrefour.com, June 12, 2002.

[14]Roger O. Crockett, Heather Green, Andy Reinhardt, and Jay Greene, "All Net, All the Time," *Business Week,* April 29, 2002, pp. 100–104; and Heather Green, "You Say You Want a Wireless Revolution?" *Business Week,* April 29, 2002, p. 108.

[15]Lorrie Grant, "Container Store's Worker's Huddle to Help You Out," *USA Today,* April 30, 2002, pp. 1B–2B.

[16]Stan Rapp, "Getting the Words Right," *Direct,* July 1993, p. 98.

[17]Information from the Direct Marketing Association Web site at www.the-dma.org, June 13, 2002.

[18]Nick Wingfield, "Online Retailing Still Growing Despite Some Losses Last Year," *The Wall Street Journal,* June 12, 2002, p. B4.

[19]"The Multi-Channel Retail Report," from www.shop.org/research/tmcrr2.html, June 13, 2002.

[20]Ibid.

[21]Wingfield, "Online Retailing."

[22]Ibid.

[23]Information from Yahoo! Web site at www.yahoo.com, June 14, 2002.

[24]Information from the Direct Selling Association Web site at www.dsa.org, June 12, 2002

[25]Ibid.

[26]Information from the National Automatic Merchandising Association Web site at www.vending.org, June 12, 2002.

[27]Pamela Sebastian Ridge, "Tool Sellers Tap Their Feminine Side," *The Wall Street Journal,* March 29, 2002, p. B1.

[28]Monica Roman, "No Fun and Games at Toys "R" Us, *Business Week,* February 11, 2002, p. 46; "Staples Reports Fourth-Quarter Profit on Store Revamping and Closing Outlets," *The Wall Street Journal,"* March 6, 2002, p. B9; and Anne Marie Chaker, "Pep Boys Curbs Its Enthusiasm, and Wall Street Applauds," *The Wall Street Journal,* February 25, 2002, p. B13.

[29]Dillard's Profit Jumps 55%, Kohl's 31%, Encouraging Struggling Retail Industry," *The Wall Street Journal,* March 6, 2002, p. B4.

[30]Information from Radio Shack's Web site at www.radioshackcorporation.com, on June 13, 2002.

[31]Earle Eldridge, "Glut of New Cars Could Mean Price War Later," *USA Today,* June 14, 2002, p. B1.

[32]Elliot Spagat, "Best Buy Inc. Slims Down to Continue Expansion," *The Wall Street Journal,* March 12, 2002, P. B4.

[33]Anne D'Innocenzio, "Kohl's Poses a Threat to Big Rivals as It Expands Its Reach," *Fort Collins Coloradoan,* June 2, 2002, p. E1.

[34]Information from Amazon.com's Web site at www.amazon.com, June 14, 2002.

[35]Information from the National Association of Convenience Stores Web site at www.csstorecentral.com, June 14, 2002.

[36]Ibid.

[37]Jane Spencer, "The Point of No Return," *The Wall Street Journal,* May 14, 2002, pp. D1–D2; and Ron Leiber, "I Take Thee . . . Back to the Store," *The Wall Street Journal,* May 30, 2002, p. D1.

[38]"2001 Retail Theft Report," as presented at www.retailindustry.about.com/library, June 14, 2002.

[39]Tara Parker-Pope, "Consortium to Develop Security Tags for Items Sold in Groceries, Drug Stores," *The Wall Street Journal,* March 10, 1999, p. B3.

[40]Stephen Bitsoli, "The Practice and Money behind Displaying Goods," *The Macomb Daily,* December 12, 1999, p. 1C; and Paul N. Bloom, Gregory T. Gundlach, and Joseph P. Cannon, *Slotting Allowances and Fees: Schools of Thought and the Views of Practicing Managers,* Marketing Science Institute working paper no. 99–106, (1999).

[41]Julie Forster, "The Hidden Cost of Shelf Space," *Business Week,* April 15, 2002, p. 103.

[42]Information from Wal-Mart's Web site at www.walmart.com, June 15, 2002.

[43]Information from Home Depot's Web site at www.homedepot.com, June 15, 2002.

Chapter Fifteen

[1]*1997 Economic Census of Wholesale Trade (summary section),* Washington, D.C.: U.S. Census Bureau, June 24, 2002, pp. 7–24.

[2]Molly Prior, "eBay Connects with Accenture to Move Excess Inventory Online," *Retailing Today,* May 20, 2002, p. 6, 65.

[3]Alexandra Peers and Nick Wingfield, "Sotheby's, eBay Team Up to Sell Fine Art Online," *The Wall Street Journal,* January 31, 2002, p. B8.

[4]Information from DoveBid's Web site at www.dovebid.com, April 30, 2002.

[5]"Office Depot Expands Its Successful European Services Division into Germany," *Business Wire,* June 24, 2002, as presented at Hoover's Online at www.hoovers.com; and information from Office Depot's Web site at www.officedepot.com, June 25, 2002.

[6]Information from Ingram Micro's Web site at www.ingrammicro.com, April 29, 2002.

[7]Michele Marchetti, "Peace Offering," *Sales & Marketing Management,* September 1999, pp. 59–67.

[8]Robert D. Hof and Heather Green, "How Amazon Cleared That Hurdle," *Business Week,* February 4, 2002, pp. 60–61.

[9]Peter, D. Bennett, ed., *Dictionary of Marketing Terms* (Chicago: American Marketing Association, 1998), p. 213.

[10]"Integrating Warehouses: A Game Like No Other," *Inbound Logistics,* January 2002, pp. 194–98.

[11]"Logistics Planner 2002: Big Dog Logistics," from *Inbound Logistics* Web site at www.inboundlogistics.com, June 26, 2002.

[12]Mark Roberti, "Your Inventory Wants to Talk to You," *Business 2.0,* May 2002, pp. 84–87.

[13]"Xicor Enables Centralized Worldwide Sales and Order-Tracking Process with Acom's Solution: EZConnect for EDI-XML," from Acom Solutions' Web site at www.acom.com, June 11, 2001.

[14]Amy Tsao, "Where Retailers Shop for Savings," *Business Week Online,* at www.businessweek.com/technology/, April 15, 2002.

[15]James Cooke, "EDI-Electronic Data Interchange, What Lies Ahead . . ." *Modern Materials Handling,* March 2002, pp. 59–61; and James Cooke, "Is XML the Next Big Thing?" *Logistics Management & Distribution Report,* May 2002, p. 53.

[16]James R. Healey, "Snarled Parts Shipments Squeeze Automakers," *USA Today,* September 18, 2001, p. 6B.

[17]Information from the American Association of Railroads' Web site at www.aaa.org. June 26, 2002; and "Another High for U.S. Class I Traffic," from www.railwayage.com, June 26, 2002.

[18]Helen L. Richardson, "Rail Service on the Right Track—Finally," *Transportation and Distribution,* May 2002, pp. 50–54.

[19]"America Needs More Drivers," from the Professional Truck Driver Institute, Inc., at www.ptdi.org, June 26, 2002.

[20]Rick Brooks, "Air Shippers Hurt by Penny-Pinchers, Better Ground Service," *The Wall Street Journal,* June 18, 2002, pp. B1, B6.

[21]J. Douglass Coates, "What Lies Ahead for Intermodal?" *World Trade,* April 2002, pp. 32–34.

[22]Merrill Douglas, "A Strong Sense of Security," *Inbound Logistics,* January 2002, pp. 164–72.

[23]Ibid.

Chapter Sixteen

[1]Bill Britt and Dagmar Mussey, "VW's Big Bet," from the global section of the *Adverting Age* Web site at www.adageglobal.com, June 28, 2002.

[2]Dana James, "Cricket Plans Nationally, Acts Locally," *Marketing News,* May 13, 2002, pp. 5–6.

[3]Lawrence J. Speer, "Half a Million Worried Consumers Call Hotline after Anti-Smoking Ad Stunt," from the global section of the *Advertising Age* Web site at www.adageglobal.com, June 28, 2002.

[4]Stuart Elliott, "JetBlue's Confidence Game, *The New York Times Direct,* at www.nytimes.com, March 12, 2002.

[5]Examples of ads from the Partnership for a Drug-Free America as presented at www.mediacampaign.org/mg/print/ad_friend_home_html and www.mediacampaign.org/images/ad_4915a.jpeg, April 28, 2002.

[6]Information from *Advertising Age* Web sites at www.adage.com and www.adageglobal.com, June 29, 2002.

[7]Alessandra Galloni, "Ad Recovery Is Delayed to Late 2002," *The Wall Street Journal,* April 16, 2002, p. B5.

[8]George E. Belch and Michael A. Belch, *Introduction to Advertising and Promotion: An Integrated Marketing Communications Perspective,* 5th ed. (Homewood, IL: Richard D. Irwin, 2001), p. 21.

[9]Tom Duncan, *IMC: Using Advertising and Promotion to Build Brands* (Burr Ridge, IL: McGraw-Hill/Irwin, 2002), p. 570.

[10]Don E. Schultz, "New Media, Old Problem: Keeping Marcom Integrated," *Marketing News,* March 25, 1999, p. 12.

[11]"Questions and Answers with Stuart Elliott," *The New York Times Direct,* at www.nytimes.com, May 14, 2002.

[12]Karen J. Bannan, "Companies Look to Video Games for Product Placement," *The New York Times Direct,* at www.nytimes.com, March 5, 2002.

[13]Maureen Tkacik, "Puma Uses Sushi to Move its Cleats," *The Wall Street Journal,* May 9, 2002, p. B8; Allison Fass, "GQ Steps out of its Past and Opens a Lounge," *The New York Times Direct,* at www.nytimes.com, February 15, 2002; Bruce Horowitz, "Ahh, the Sun, the Surf. . . and Tons of Ads," *USA Today,* May 24, 2001, p. 3B; and Stuart Elliott, "The Power of the Flower," *The New York Times Direct,* at www.nytimes.com, January 22, 2002.

[14]T. Bettina Cornwell, "Sponsorship-Linked Marketing Development," *Sport Marketing Quarterly* 4, no. 4 (1995), pp. 13–24.

[15]Lesa Ukman, "Naming Rights: Not Just for Stadiums Anymore," from the IEG, Inc. Web site at www.sponsorship.com, June 28, 2002.

[16]"How Sponsorship's Growth Compares to Advertising and Sales Promotion," from the IEG Inc. Web site at www.sponsorship.com, June 28, 2002.

[17]"Why Companies Sponsor," from *IEG's Complete Guide to Sponsorship* at the IEG, Inc. Web site at www.sponsorship.com, June 28, 2002.

[18]Rich Thomaselli, "Coke Ponies Up $500 Million for NCAA," from the *Advertising Age* Web site at www.adage.com, June 28, 2002.

[19]Rance Crain, "AT&T's Ads' Confused Message Boosts Met Life," from the *Advertising Age* Web site at www.adage.com, February 25, 2002; and Michael McCarthy, "What's an mLife? Who Cares?" *USA Today,* June 3, 2002, p. 4B.

[20]Theresa Howard, "1-800-Collect Relies on Big Guy to Sell Big Savings," from the *USA Today* Web site at www.usatoday.com/money, on March 20, 2002.

21 Geoffrey A. Fowler, "Shoppers Choose Convenience over Ecological Benefits; Landfills Piled with Plastic," *The Wall Street Journal,* March 6, 2002, pp. B1, B4.

22 Kipp Cheng, "Mixed Messages: How Ethnic Ads Succeed With, Then Transcend, Niche Markets," from Diversity, Inc. Web site at www.diversityinc.com, May 8, 2002.

23 Kipp Cheng, "Does Diversity-Conscious Advertising Prove a Diversity Commitment?" from Diversity, Inc. Web site at www.diversityinc.com, May 14, 2002.

24 Cheng, "Mixed Messages."

25 George S. Low and Jakki J. Mohr, *Brand Managers' Perceptions of the Marketing Communications Budget Allocation Process,* Marketing Science Institute, (Cambridge, MA: 1998), pp. 35–38.

26 Dagmar Mussey, "Mars Goes Local," from the global section of the *Advertising Age* Web site at www.adageglobal.com, June 28, 2002.

27 Vanessa O'Connell, "Drug Czar Says Ad Campaign Has Flopped," *The Wall Street Journal,* May 11, 2002, pp. B1, B10.

28 Stephanie Clifford, "Most Bang for the Buck," *Business 2.0,* May 2002, p. 102.

29 Information from Target's Web site at www.target.com, July 1, 2002.

30 Joe Flint and Shelly Branch, "In Face of Widening Backlash, NBC Gives Up Plan to Run Liquor Ads," *The Wall Street Journal,* March 1, 2002, pp. B1, B3; and Theresa Howard, "Liquor Ad TV Outlets Sought," *USA Today,* April 8, 2002, p. 2B.

31 Ann Zimmerman and David Armstrong, "FTC Asked to Study Promotion of More-Costly Brands of Drugs," *The Wall Street Journal,* May 6, 2002, p. B6.

32 Information from the American Advertising Federation Web site at www.aaf.org/government/position_bans.html, July 1, 2002.

33 Edward Iwata, "Officials Say Deceptive Tech Advertising on Rise," *USA Today,* May 29, 2001, p. B1.

34 "Internet Wholesale Operator Settles FTC Charges," from the Federal Trade Commission Web site at www.ftc.gov/opa/2002/06/bargains.htm, June 28, 2002.

35 For more on deceptive advertising, see the Better Business Bureau site at www.bbb.org, and the Federal Trade Commission site at www.ftc.gov.

36 "Appeals Court Upholds FTC Ruling: Doan's Must Include Corrective Message in Future Advertising and Labeling," from the Federal Trade Commission Web site at www.ftc.gov/opa/2000/08/doans.htm, June 28, 2002.

37 "Kellogg's Agrees to Modify Ad Claims," from the Web site of the Council of Better Business Bureau's National Advertising Division at www.caru.org/nad99, January 27, 2000.

Chapter Seventeen

1 Charles H. Patti and Charles F. Frazer, *Advertising: A Decision-Making Approach* (Chicago: Dryden Press, 1988), p. 4.

2 Laurie Petersen, "A Short-Sighted View of Advertising," *Adweek's Marketing Week,* November 11, 1991, p. 9.

3 John Kenneth Galbraith, "Economics and Advertising: Exercise in Denial," *Advertising Age,* November 9, 1988, p. 81.

4 John Deighton, Caroline M. Henderson, and Scott A. Nelson, "The Effects of Advertising on Brand Switching and Repeat Purchasing," *Journal of Marketing Research,* February 1994, p. 28.

5 Dana L. Alden, Jan-Benedict E. M. Steenkamp, and Rajeev Batra, "Brand Positioning Through Advertising in Asia, North America, and Europe: The Role of Global Consumer Culture," *Journal of Marketing,* January 1999, pp. 75–87.

6 "Top 200 Brands," *Advertising Age,* May 6, 1996, p. 34.

7 Dean M. Krugman and Roland T. Rust, "The Impact of Cable and VCR Penetration on Network Viewing: Assessing the Decade," *Journal of Advertising Research,* January–February 1993, pp. 67–73; and Joe Mandese, "Nets Get Less for More," *Advertising Age,* March 2, 1992, p. 1.

8 Mel Mandell, "Getting the Word Out," *World Trade,* November 1993, p. 30.

9 Iris Cohen Selinger, "Big Profits, Risks with Incentive Fees," *Advertising Age,* May 15, 1995, p. 3; and Mark Gleason, "Driver's Mart Pacing Agency Pay to Sales," *Advertising Age,* May 6, 1996, p. 3.

10 Paul Allen, "New Ad Agency Model Needed to Cope with Info Overload," *Marketing News,* August 31, 1998, p. 4; Sarah Lorge, "Paying Ad Agencies their Due," *Sales & Marketing Management,* November 1999, p. 13; and Daniel McGinn, "Pour on the Pitch," *Newsweek,* May 31, 1999, pp. 5–51.

11 Marin Bihl, "Who's the Boss?," *AdWeek,* February 4, 2002, p. 10; Alan Gottsman, "No Pain, No Gain," *AdWeek,* February 18, 2002, p. 9; and Tom Lowry, "Advertisers Are Still Hiding Out," *Business Week,* January 14, 2002, p. 100.

12 Allan J. Magrath, "The Death of Advertising Has Been Greatly Exaggerated," *Sales & Marketing Management,* February 1992, p. 23.

13 Sergey Frank, "Avoiding the Pitfalls of Business Abroad," *Sales & Marketing Management,* March 1992, p. 57.

14 James M. Kolts, "Adaptive Marketing," *Journal of Consumer Marketing,* Summer 1990, pp. 39–40.

15 C. Anthony Di Benedetto, Marik Tamate, and Rajan Chandran, "Developing Creative Advertising Strategy for the Japanese Marketplace," *Journal of Advertising Research,* January–February 1992, pp. 39–48.

16 Fred S. Zufryden, James H. Pendrick, and Avu Sankaralingam, "Zapping and Its Impact on Brand Purchase Behavior," *Journal of Advertising Research,* January–February 1993, p. 58.

17 Joanne Lipman, "TV Ad Deals to Set Big Price Increases," *The Wall Street Journal,* June 25, 1992, p. B8.

18 Judith Waldrap, "And Now a Break from Our Sponsor," *American Demographics,* August 1993, pp. 16–18.

19 Amy Harmon, "Skip-the-Ads TV Has Madison Ave. Upset," *The New York Times,* May 23, 2002, pp. A1, C3.

20 Dana Wechsler Linden and Vicki Contavespi, "Media Wars," *Forbes,* August 19, 1991, p. 38.

21 John Gaffney, "The Online Advertising Comeback," *Business 2.0,* June 2002, pp. 118–19; Sandeep Krishnamurthy, "Deciphering the Internet Advertising Puzzle," *Marketing Management,* Fall 2000, pp. 35–39; "Looking Beyond Banner Ads to Revive Web Advertising," *The Wall Street Journal,* February 26, 2001, www.djinteractive.com; Lynda Richardson, "Window Seat," *AdWeek,* July 23, 2001, p. 15; Hillary Rosner, "Reality Check," *AdWeek,* February 4, 2002, pp. IQ9–IQ11; Deborah Szynal, "Next Step in Taming Net Frontier," *Marketing News,* March 4, 2002, p. 4; and Deborah L. Venice, "B-to-C Advertisers Learn Online Tricks from Biz Colleagues," *Marketing News,* June 24, 2002, p. 4.

22 William F. Arens and Courtland L. Bovée, *Contemporary Advertising,* 5th ed. (Burr Ridge, IL: Richard D. Irwin, 1994), p. 8.

23 Peggy Conlon, "Letter from the President," *AdWeek,* June 10, 2002, p. 24.

24 Jim Garner, "Sneakers, Soap, and Semiconductors," *Marketing News,* March 1, 1999, p. 55; and Bob Lamons, "Resolve to Promote Your Firm's Brand Image in the New Millennium," *Marketing News,* January 17, 2000, p. 4.

25 Richard Brunelli, "B2B and Beyond," *Trade Media,* May 7, 2001, pp. SR14–SR15; Bob Lamons, "Tips for Distinguishing Your Ads from Bad Ads," *Marketing News,* November 19, 2001, p. 10; and

Mark McMaster, "Advertising B-to-B Brands on TV," *Sales and Marketing Management,* November 2001, p. 11.

[26]Scott B. MacKenzie, "The Role of Attention in Mediating the Effect of Advertising on Attribute Importance," *Journal of Consumer Research,* September 1986, pp. 174–95.

[27]Demetrios Vakratsas and Tim Ambler, "How Advertising Works: What Do We Really Know," *Journal of Marketing,* January 1999, pp. 26–43.

[28]Ibid.

[29]Deborah J. MacInnis, Christine Moorman, and Bernard J. Jaworski, "Enhancing and Measuring Consumers' Motivation, Opportunity, and Ability to Process Brand Information from Ads," *Journal of Marketing,* October 1991, pp. 32–53.

[30]Robert J. Kent, "Competitive Interference Effects in Consumer Memory for Advertising: The Role of Brand Familiarity," *Journal of Marketing,* July 1994, pp. 97–105.

[31]James F. Engel, Roger D. Blackwell, and Paul W. Miniard, *Consumer Behavior,* 7th ed. (Fort Worth, TX: Dryden Press, 1993), p. 277.

[32]Richard E. Petty, John T. Cacioppo, and David Schumann, "Central and Peripheral Routes to Advertising Effectiveness: The Moderating Role of Involvement," *Journal of Consumer Research* 10 (September 1983), pp. 135–46.

[33]Seema Nayyar and Jennifer Lach, "We're Being Watched," *American Demographics,* October 1998, pp. 53–58; and Bill Stoneman, "Beyond Rocking the Ages," *American Demographics,* May 1998, pp. 45–49.

[34]Don E. Schultz, "Make Communications Worth the Profits," *Marketing News,* January 15, 2001, p. 13.

[35]Joann Lublin, "As VCRs Advance, Agencies Fear TV Viewers Will Zap More Ads," *The Wall Street Journal,* January 4, 1991, p. B3.

[36]Tom Dougherty, "Create Great Advertising for the Millennuim," *Marketing News,* March 15, 1999, p. 2; Jean Halliday, "Chrysler Officials Admit to Flubbing the Intrepid Relaunch," *Advertising Age,* June 18, 1998, p. 10; and George F. Will, "The Perils of Brushing," *Newsweek,* May 10, 1999, p. 92.

[37]Sandra Dolbow, "Levi's Leaning on Past Tactics to Design Jean Maker's Future," *BrandWeek,* June 24, 2002, p. 9.

[38]Gary T. Ford, Darlene B. Smith, and John L. Swasy, "Consumer Skepticism of Advertising Claims: Testing Hypotheses from Economics of Information," *Journal of Consumer Research,* March 1990, pp. 433–41.

[39]Brian Wansik and Michael L. Ray, "Advertising Strategies to Increase Usage Frequencies," *Journal of Marketing,* January 1996, pp. 31–46.

[40]Ajay Karla and Ronald C. Goodstein, "The Impact of Advertising Positioning Strategies on Consumer Price Sensitivity," *Journal of Marketing Research,* May 1998, pp. 210–24.

[41]Thomas E. Barry, "Comparative Advertising: What Have We Learned in Two Decades?" *Journal of Advertising Research,* March–April 1993, p. 20.

[42]Daniel Golden and Suzanne Vranica, "Duracell's Duck Ad Will Carry Disclaimer," *The Wall Street Journal,* February 7, 2002, p. B7.

[43]"Ad-Vantage: The Williams Sisters," *Business Week,* February 5, 2001, p. 71.

[44]"Humor Remains Top Tool for Ad Campaign," *USA Today,* September 30, 1996, p. 3B.

[45]Bruce Horowitz, "Most Dot-Coms Don't Have Super Night," *USA Today,* January 31, 2000, p. 1.

[46]Scott Hume, "Best Ads Don't Rely on Celebrities," *Advertising Age,* May 25, 1992, p.20; and Kevin Goldman, "Candice Bergen Leads the List of Top Celebrity Endorsers," *The Wall Street Journal,* September 17, 1993, pp. B1, B6.

[47]Timothy E, Moore, "Subliminal Advertising: What You See Is What You Get," *Journal of Marketing,* Spring 1982, pp. 27–47; and Terence A. Shimp, *Advertising, Promotion, and Supplemental Aspects of Integrated Marketing Communications,* 4th ed. (Fort Worth, TX: Dryden Press, 1997), pp. 310–12.

[48]Scott Donaten, "Advertorials Are Like a Drug," *Advertising Age,* March 9, 1992, p. S16.

[49]Ronald Grover and Gerry Khermouch, "The Trouble with Tie-Ends," *Business Week,* June 3, 2002, p. 63.

[50]David Leonhardt, Peter Burrows, and Bill Vlasic, "Cue the Soda Can," *Business Week,* June 24, 1996, pp. 64–65.

[51]Alison Stein Wellner, "The Female Persuasion," *American Demographics,* February 2002, pp. 24–29.

[52]Brad Edmondson, "In the Driver's Seat," *American Demographics,* March 1998, pp. 46–52.

[53]Giles D'Souza and Ram C. Rao, "Can Repeating an Advertisement More Frequently than the Competition Affect Brand Preference in a Mature Market?" *Journal of Marketing,* April 1995, p. 39.

[54]Vicki R. Lane, "The Impact of Ad Repetition and Ad Content on Consumer Perceptions of Incongruent Extensions," *Journal of Marketing,* April 2000, pp. 80–91.

[55]Joe Mandese, "Revisiting Ad Reach, Frequency," *Advertising Age,* November 27, 1995, p. 46.

[56]Gerard J. Tellis, "Effective Frequency: One Exposure or Three Factors," *Journal of Advertising Research,* July–August 1997, pp. 75–80.

[57]Leonard M. Lodish et al., "How TV Advertising Works: A Meta-Analysis of 389 Real World Split Cable TV Advertising Experiments," *Journal of Marketing Research,* May 1995, p. 138.

[58]Dwight R. Riskey, "How TV Advertising Works: An Industry Response," *Journal of Marketing Research,* May 1997, pp. 202–3.

[59]Chris Grindem, "The Whole Truth," *AdWeek,* June 24, 2002, p. 16.

[60]Cyndee Miller, "Study Says 'Likability' Surfaces as Measure of TV Ad Success," *Marketing News,* January 7, 1991, p. 14.

[61]Laurence N. Gold, "Advertising Tracking: New Tricks of the Trade," *Marketing Research: A Magazine of Practice and Application 5,* p. 42.

[62]Faye Rice, "A Cure for What Ails Advertising?" *Fortune,* December 16, 1991, p. 121.

[63]Lorraine Calvacca, "Making a Case for the Glossies," *American Demographics,* July 1999, p. 36; Juliana Koranteng, "A. C. Nielsen to Offer Data on Net Ad Effectiveness," *Advertising Age International,* October 1999, p. 4; "Net Ads on Pace for $4 Billion Year," *Content Factory,* November 4, 1999, http://www.comtexnews.com; and "Net Newbie @ Plan: Still Undiscovered," *Business Week,* January 17, 2000, p. 115.

[64]Gerard J. Tellis, Rajesh K. Chandy, and Pattana Thaivanich, *Decomposing the Effects of Direct TV Advertising: Which Ad Works, When, Where, and How Often?* Marketing Science Institute, MSI Working Paper No. 99–118 (Cambridge, MA: 1999).

[65]D. Kirk Davidson, "Marketing This 'Hope' Sells Our Profession Short," *Marketing News,* July 20, 1998, p. 6.

[66]Raymond Serafin and Gary Levin, "An Industry Suffers Crushing Blow," *Advertising Age,* November 12, 1990, pp. 1, 76, 77.

[67]"Misleading Advertising," *The New York Times,* February 18, 2001, p. C1.

[68]Jim Edwards, "The Book," *BrandWeek,* April 15, 2002, pp. 19–20.

[69]David A. Aaker, Rajeev Batra, and John G. Myers, *Advertising Management,* 4th ed. (Englewood Cliffs, NJ: Prentice Hall, 1992), p. 557.

[70]Michel Arndt, Wendy Zellner, and Peter Coy, "Too Much Corporate Power," *Business Week,* September 11, 2000, p. 154.

71"Anything for a Ratings Boost," *Marketing News,* September 13, 1999, p. 2; and Kathryn C. Montgomery, "Gov't Must Take the Lead in Protecting Children," *Advertising Age,* June 22, 1998, p. 40.

72Wendy Melillo, "Paper Chase," *AdWeek,* April 13, 2001, p. 12.

73Maxine Lans Retsky, "Junk Faxes Subject to Telemarketing Laws," *Marketing News,* April 26, 1999, p. 7.

74Minette E. Drumwright, "Company Advertising with a Social Dimension," Report #96-110, Marketing Science Institute (Cambridge, MA: 1996), p. i; and Bob Garfield, "This Heavy-Handed Ad Exploits Someone New," *Advertising Age,* May 10, 1993, p. 50.

75Allyson L. Stewart-Allen, "Europe Ready for Cause-Related Campaigns," *Marketing News,* July 6, 1998, p. 9; and "Why P&G Is Linking Brands to Good Causes," *Marketing,* August 26, 1999, p. 11.

76Kirk Davidson, "Look for Abundance of Opposition to TV Liquor Ads," *Marketing News,* January 6, 1997, pp. 4, 30; Ian P. Murphy, "Competitive Spirits: Liquor Industry Turns to TV Ads," *Marketing News,* December 12, 1996, pp. 1, 17; and Tar Parker-Pope, "Tough Tobacco-Ad Rules Light Creative Fires," *The Wall Street Journal,* October 9, 1996, p. B1.

77Tim Johnson, "Audits Aren't Just for the Accountants," *Marketing News,* March 18, 2002, p. 13.

78Donald P. Robin and R. Eric Reidenbach, "Social Responsibility, Ethics, and Marketing Strategy: Closing the Gap between Concept and Application," *Journal of Marketing,* January 1987, pp. 44–58.

79Steve Jarvis, "In Time of Need," *Marketing News,* April 2002, p. 4.

80Patricia Winters, "Drugmakers Portrayed as Villains, Worry about Image," *Advertising Age,* February 22, 1993, p. 1; Kate Fitzgerald, "Health Concerns Don't Slow Down Cellular Phones," *Advertising Age,* February 8, 1993, p. 4; Annetta Miller, "Do Boycotts Work?" *Newsweek,* July 6, 1992, p. 56; and Howard Schlossberg, "Members Only to Introduce Homeless in Cause Marketing," *Marketing News,* July 20, 1992, p. 6.

81Caleb Solomon, "Exxon Attacks Scientific Views of *Valdez* Oil Spill," *The Wall Street Journal,* April 15, 1993, p. B1.

82Philip Kotler, *Marketing Management: Analysis, Planning, Implementation, and Control,* 8th ed. (Englewood Cliffs, NJ: Prentice Hall, 1994), pp. 676–77.

83Adriana Cento, "7 Habits for Highly Effective Public Relations," *Marketing News,* March 16, 1999, p. 8; Dana James, "Dot-Coms Demand New Kind of Publicity," *Marketing News,* November 22, 1999, p 6; and Kathleen V. Schmidt, "Public Relations," *Marketing News,* January 17, 2000, p. 13.

84Dana James, "Code Blue: How Crisis Management Has Changed," *Marketing News,* November 6, 2000, pp. 1, 15.

85Bob Lamons, "Taco Bell Rings in the New Age of Publicity Stunts," *Marketing News,* May 20, 1996, p. 15.

86Joseph B. Cahill, "Net Chats: Big Business Is Listening," *Crain's Chicago Business,* April 8, 1996, pp. 1, 53; and Helen Roper, "Letters from Cyberhell," *Inc. Technology,* September 1995, pp. 67–70.

87Joan McGrath and Myrna Pedersen, "Don't Wait for Disaster; Have a Crisis Plan Ready," *Marketing News,* December 2, 1996, p. 6.

Chapter Eighteen

1Adapted from Peter D. Bennett, ed., *Dictionary of Marketing Terms* (Chicago: American Marketing Association, 1988), p. 179.

2Pierre Chandon, Brian Wansink, and Gilles Laurent, "A Benefit Congruency Framework of Sales Promotion Effectiveness," *Journal of Marketing,* October 2000, pp. 65–81.

3Information from Overstock.com Web site at www.overstock.com, July 10, 2002.

4Chandon et al., "A Benefit Congruency Framework."

5Matthew Kinsman, "Coupons: Recession Poof!" *PROMO Magazine,* April 1, 2002, as appearing at www.promomagazine.com, July 2, 2002.

6Ibid.

7Lorrie Grant, "Stores Expand Use of Coupons," *Fort Collins Coloradoan,* December 9, 2001, p. E1.

8Information from RebateCatcher.com Web site at www.rebate-catcher.com, July 8, 2002.

9Peter Edmondson, "Free-With-Rebate Costs Web Buyers Some Big Bucks," *The Wall Street Journal,* May 18, 2001, pp. B1, B4.

10"Loews Pops for Summer Campaign," from *PROMO Magazine's Online Exclusive,* June 20, 2002 at www.promomagazine.com.

11Information from the Promotions Web site at www.promotions.com, July 2, 2002.

12Information from Kraft Foods Web site at www.kraft.promotions.com/balancebar, July 2, 2002.

13Information from the Promotions Web site at www.promotions.com, July 2, 2002.

14Information from the Jeep Web site at www.jeep.com, July 9, 2002.

15Alfred Branch Jr., "Premium Incentives: Holding On," *PROMO Magazine,* April 1, 2002, as presented at www.promomazine.com.

16Shirley Leung, "Happy Meals Angle for Little Girls' Loyalty with Well-Dressed Dolls," *The Wall Street Journal,* April 5, 2002, pp. B1, B4.

17David Vaczek, "Hard, Cold Merchandise," *PROMO Magazine,* May 1999, pp. S3–S5.

18"Sampling: A Softer Sell," *PROMO Magazine,* June 1, 2002, as presented at www.promomagazine.com.

19Miriam Jordan, "Fuel and Freebies," *The Wall Street Journal,* June 10, 2002, pp. B1, B6.

20Information from the Promotional Products Association International Web site at www.ppa.org, July 2, 2002.

21Adapted from Robert C. Blattberg and Scott A. Neslin, *Sales Promotion, Concepts, Methods, and Strategies* (Englewood Cliffs, NJ: Prentice Hall, 1990), p. 314.

22Information from the Promotional Products Association International Web site at www.ppa.org, July 9, 2002.

23Ibid.

24Tara J. Radin and Carolyn E. Predmore, "The Myth of the Salesperson: Intended and Unintended Consequences of Product-Specific Sales Incentives," *Journal of Business Ethics,* March 2002, pp. 79–92.

25Anna Wilde Mathews and Jennifer Ordonez, "Music Labels say It Costs Too Much to Get Songs on the Radio," *The Wall Street Journal,* June 10, 2002, pp. B1, B6; and Daniel Pearl and Steve Stecklow, "Drug Firms' Incentives to Pharmacists in India Fuel Mounting Abuse," *The Wall Street Journal,* August 16, 2001, pp. A1, A5;

26"Games, Contests, Sweeps: Front and Center," *PROMO Magazine,* June 1, 2002, as presented at www.promomagazine.com.

Chapter Nineteen

1Derrick C. Schnebelt, "Turning the Tables," *Sales & Marketing Management,* January 1993, pp. 22–23.

2David Topus, "Keep It Short . . . and Smart," *Selling,* August 1993, p. 30.

3Tom Murray, "Team Selling: What's the Incentive?" *Sales & Marketing Management,* June 1991, pp. 89–92.

4Jon M. Hawes, Kenneth E. Mast, and John E. Swan, "Trust Earning Perceptions of Sellers and Buyers," *Journal of Personal Selling and Sales Management,* Spring 1989, pp. 1–8.

5Ingrid Abramowitz, "The Trust Factor," *Success,* March 1993, p. 18.

6Stuart Miller, "Beating the Clock—and Records," *Sales & Marketing Management,* February 1997, pp. 20–21.

[7]Mark McNaster, "Connecting with Customers," *Sales and Marketing Management,* May 2002, pp. 59–60.

[8]Rosann L. Spiro and Barton A. Weitz, "Adaptive Selling: Conceptualization, Measurement, and Nomological Validity," *Journal of Marketing Research,* February 1990, pp. 61–69.

[9]"Pipe Down," *Sales & Marketing Management,* January 1994, p. 22.

[10]David W. Cravens, Thomas N. Ingram, and Raymond W. LaForge, "Evaluating Multiple Sales Channel Strategies," *Journal of Business and Industrial Marketing,* Summer–Fall 1991, pp. 37–48.

[11]Ibid.

[12]Chad Kaydo, "You've Got Sales," *Sales & Marketing Management,* October 1999, pp. 30–34.

[13]Ibid., pp. 36–38.

[14]Erin Stout, "Planning to Profit from National Accounts," *Sales & Marketing Management,* October 1999, p. 107.

[15]Bob Attanasio, "How PC-Based Sales Quotas Boost Productivity and Morale," *Sales & Marketing Management,* September 1991, pp. 148–50.

[16]"Microsoft Boosts Salesforce by 450," *USA Today,* June 25, 2002, p. 1B

[17]Sheree Curry, "Coping With the Ever-Enlarging Sales Territory," *Sales and Marketing Management,* March 2002, p. 11

[18]"Taking Aim at Tomorrow's Challenges," *Sales & Marketing Management,* September 1991, pp. 66–67.

[19]Francy Blackwood, "A Prescription for Change," *Selling,* August 1993, pp. 22–25.

[20]William Keenan, Jr., "Time Is Everything," *Sales & Marketing Management,* August 1993, pp. 60–62.

[21]"Sales Training Points the Way toward Successful Total Quality Management," *Sales and Marketing* (newsletter of the American Society of Training and Development), Winter 1993, pp. 1, 6.

[22]Christine Galea, "2002 Sales Training Survey," *Sales & Marketing Management,* July 2002, pp. 34–37.

[23]Lawrence B. Chonko, John F. Tanner, Jr., William A. Weeks, and Melissa R. Schmitt, *Reward Preferences of Salespeople,* Center for Professional Selling, Baylor University, Research Report no. 91-3 (Waco, TX: 1991).

[24]"Compensation and Expenses," *Sales & Marketing Management,* June 28, 1993, p. 65.

[25]Christine Galea, "2002 Salary Survey," *Sales & Marketing Management,* May 2002, pp. 32–36.

[26]"Bonuses for Breaking New Ground," *Inc.,* March 1993, p. 27.

[27]Kathleen Cholewka, "Motivating Mentors," *Sales and Marketing Management,* June 2002, p. 61.

[28]"Compensation and Expenses," p. 65.

[29]Karl A. Boedecker, Fred W. Morgan, and Jeffrey J. Stoltman, "Legal Dimensions of Salespersons' Statements: A Review and Managerial Suggestions," *Journal of Marketing,* January 1991, pp. 70–80.

[30]I. Frederick Trawick, John E. Swan, Gail McGee, and David R. Rink, "Influence of Buyer Ethics and Salesperson Behavior on Intention to Choose a Supplier," *Journal of the Academy of Marketing Science,* Winter 1991, pp. 17–23.

[31]Reported in Bernard L. Rosenbaum, "What You Need for Success in the 21st Century," *Selling,* November 1999, pp. 8–9.

Chapter Twenty

[1]"Economic Impact: U.S. Direct Marketing Today Executive Summary," from the Direct Marketing Association's Web site at www.the-dma.org. July 23, 2002.

[2]Ibid.

[3]Ibid.

[4]"Case Study: GMC Suburban, Yukon, and Yukon Denali," from the Script to Screen Web site at www.scriptoscreen.com, July 24, 2002.

[5]Peter D. Bennett, ed., *Dictionary of Marketing Terms,* 2nd ed. (Chicago: American Marketing Association, 1995), p. 75.

[6]"Focus USA Debuts Small Business Database," presented at www.dmnews.com, July 23, 2002.

[7]"MasterFiles National New Users," presented at www.dmnews.com, July 23, 2002.

[8]Jane E. Zarem, "From the Store to the Web . . . and Back Again," *1 to 1 magazine,* January/February, 2002, pp. 22–26.

[9]Patricia Odell, "Reader's Digest Backs Off Sweeps," from www.directmag.com, July 1, 2002.

[10]"Economic Impact: U.S. Direct Marketing Today Executive Summary."

[11]Ibid.

[12]Melissa Campanelli, "British Tourist Authority Targets U.S. Seniors," from www.dmnews.com, July 8, 2002.

[13]"Economic Impact: U.S. Direct Marketing Today Executive Summary."

[14]Ibid.

[15]Steve Jarvis, "U.S., EU Still Don't Agree on Data Handling," *Marketing News,* August 13, 2001, p. 5.

[16]Allison McCoy, "Advancing CRM Around the World," *1 to 1 magazine,* April 2002, pp. 41–45.

[17]"Economic Impact: U.S. Direct Marketing Today Executive Summary."

[18]"2001 Reggie Award Winners: BMW Films," from www.pmalink.org, July 2, 2002.

[19]Mickey Alam Khan, "Persistence Pays Off in BTB Mail Campaign," from www.dmnews.com, July 23, 2002.

[20]"Experts Saddened by Medication Infomercial," *Marketing News,* June 7, 1999, p. H33.

[21]Jean Halliday, "Mercury Pumps Muscle Car with Infomercials," from www.adage.com, July 8, 2002; Patricia Odell, "Pennzoil Starts First DRTV Campaign," *Direct,* June 2002, p. 9; and Peter Blacklow, "First Person: Monster Marketing," *Sales and Marketing Management,* January 2002, p. 55.

[22]Richard H. Levey, "Chicago Tribune Returns to DRTV," *Direct,* February 2002, p. 12.

[23]"Economic Impact: U.S. Direct Marketing Today Executive Summary."

[24]"USA Today Snapshots," *USA Today,* June 13, 2002, p. D1.

[25]"JunkBusters Anti-Telemarketing Script," from the JunkBusters Web site at www.junkbusters.com, July 25, 2002.

[26]Michael McCarthy and Jayne O'Donnell, "FTC Idea Could Get Telemarketers to Stop Calling," *USA Today,* June 5, 2002, pp. B1–B2; and Patricia Odell, "FTC Plans National Do-Not-Call List," *Direct,* March 1, 2002, p. 14.

[27]"Client Solutions," from the FaxBack Web site at www.faxback.com, July 25, 2002.

[28]"Random Sampling," *Marketing News,* April 29, 2002, p. 7.

[29]For more on the privacy of teens and younger consumers, see the National Consumers League Web site at www.natlconsumersleague.org.

[30]Jarvis, "U.S., EU Still Don't Agree on Data Handling."

[31]From the National Consumers League Web site at www.natlconsumersleague.org, July 25, 2002.

[32]"A Little Restraint, Please," *Marketing News,* May 27, 2002, p. 3.

[33]Deborah Szynal, "Spam Opponents Try to Act Locally," *Marketing News,* April 1, 2002, p. 5; and Mylene Mangalindan, "Spam Multiplies, Spurring New Efforts to Curb It," *The Wall Street Journal,* June 19, 2002, pp. B1, B5.

Source Notes

Chapter 1

Page 2: *www.amazon.com*; Heather Green, "How Hard Should Amazon Swing?" *Business Week,* January 14, 2002, p. 38; Robert D. Hof, "Amazon: 'We've Never Said We Had to Do It All,' " *Business Week,* October 15, 2001, p. 53; Leslie Kaufman, "Amazon II: Will This Smile Last?" *New York Times On the Web,* May 19, 2002, pp. 1–5.

Exhibit 1–1: Adapted from James L. Heskett, Thomas O. Jones, Gary W. Loveman, W. Earl Sasser, Jr., and Leonard A. Schlesinger, "Putting the Service-Profit Chain to Work," *Harvard Business Review,* March–April 1994, pp. 164–74; and Frederick F. Reichheld, *The Loyalty Effect: The Hidden Force behind Growth, Profits, and Lasting Value* (Boston: Harvard Business School Press, 1996).

Exhibit 1–2: Frederick F. Reichheld, *The Loyalty Effect: The Hidden Force behind Growth, Profits, and Lasting Value* (Boston: Harvard Business School Press, 1996), pp. 39–50.

Exhibit 1–3: Frederick E. Webster, Jr., "Executing the New Marketing Concept," *Marketing Management 3,* no. 1, p. 10.

Exhibit 1–8: Rolph Anderson, *Professional Personal Selling.* © 1991, p. 105. Reprinted by permission of Prentice-Hall. Englewood Cliffs, New Jersey.

Case 1–1: Dean Foust, Geri Smith, and David Rocks, "Man on the Spot," *Business Week,* May 3, 1999, pp. 142–51; Dean Foust, David Rocks, and Mark L. Clifford, "Is Douglas Daft the Real Thing?" *Business Week,* December 20, 1999, pp. 44–45; Patricia Sellers, "Who's in Charge Here," *Fortune,* December 24, 2001 (accessed from www.fortune.com); Lee Clifford, "Winning in the Water Fight," *Fortune,* March 4, 2002 (accessed from www.fortune.com).

Case 1–2: Hugh Filman, "Happy Meals for a McDonald's Rival," *Business Week,* July 29, 1996, p. 77; "King of Fast Food at Home, Jollibee Plans Six More Stores in the U.S.," *Fox Market Wire,* March 12, 1999, pp. 1–3; *www.jollibee.com.ph,* June 6, 2002.

Chapter 2

Page 22: www.dell.com, June 20, 2002; Andrew Park and Spencer E. Ande, "Who Will Master the Server Biz?" *Business Week,* June 24, 2002, pp. 92–93.

Using Technology, p. 24: Jim Kerstetter, "Information is Power," *Business Week,* June 24, 2002, pp. 94–96.

Exhibit 2–3: Excerpt from *The World Almanac and Book of Facts 2000* (World Almanac Books, 1999), pp. 878–79. Used with permission of the publisher. All rights reserved.

Exhibit 2–4: *The World Almanac and Book of Facts 2000* (World Almanac Books, 1999), p. 878.

Exhibit 2–5: Data from United Nations Population Division.

Exhibit 2–6: Data from *The World Almanac and Book of Facts 2000* (World Almanac Books, 1999), p. 391. Used with permission of the publisher. All rights reserved.

Being Entrepreneurial, p. 34: Marcus Green, "Wired for Success," *The Courier-Journal* (Louisville, KY), June 24, 2002, pp. C1–C2.

Case 2–1: Margaret Littman, "Sponsors Take to the Court with New Women's NBA," *Marketing News,* March 3, 1997, pp. 1 and 6; Gigi Barnett and Skip Rozin, "A Lot of Leagues of Their Own," *Business Week,* March 3, 1997, pp. 54–56; www.wnba.com, July 1, 2002.

Case 2–2: Geoffrey Smith and Faith Keenan, "Kodak is the Picture of Digital Success," *Business Week,* January 14, 2002, p. 39.

Chapter 3

Page 46: http://disney.go.com/park/homepage/today/flash/index.html; "Business: Disney or Doesn't He?", *The Economist,* January 12, 2002, p. 61; Marc Gunther, "Has Eisner Lost the Disney Magic?", *Fortune,* January 7, 2002, pp. 64–69; Richard Linnett and Wayne Friedman, "Disney Picks Starcom Strategy," *Advertising Age,* December 31, 2001, pp. 3, 28; Bruce Orwall, "Disney CEO Acknowledges Woes, Stresses Confidences in a Rebound," *The Wall Street Journal,* January 4, 2002, p. A.

Exhibit 3–5: James C. Collins and Jerry I. Porras, "Building Your Company's Vision," *Harvard Business Review,* September–October, 1996, p. 69.

Exhibit 3–6: Gary Hamel and C. K. Prahalad, *Competing for the Future* (Boston: Harvard Business School Press, 1994), p. 18.

Exhibit 3–7: Shelby D. Hunt and Robert M. Morgan, "The Comparative Advantage Theory of Competition," *Journal of Marketing,* April 1995, pp. 1–15; and Gary Hamel and C. K. Prahalad, *Competing for the Future* (Boston: Harvard Business School Press, 1994), p. 223.

Exhibit 3–9: B. Heldey, "Strategy and the Business Portfolio," *Long Range Planning,* February 1977, p. 12; and George S. Day, "Organizing the Product Portfolio," *Journal of Marketing,* April 1977, p. 34.

Building Customer Equity, p. 61: Robert C. Blattberg and John Deighton, "Manage Marketing by the Customer Equity," *Harvard Business Review,* July–August 1996, pp. 136–44; Frederick F. Reichheld, *The Loyalty Effect: The Hidden Force behind Growth, Profits, and Lasting Value* (Chicago: Bain and Company, 1996); "Mail-Order Legend Masters E-Commerce," *Computer Shopper,* May 1999, p. 280; Cara Beardi, "Lands' End Cuts, Grows," *Advertising Age,* August 13, 2001, p. 26; Tischelle George and Sanfra Swanson, "Not Just Kid Stuff," *Informationweek,* September 3, 2001, pp. 37–39; Ted Kemp, "Virtual Models Equal Real Buyers," *Internetweek,* October 8, 2001, pp. 16–17; Amy Merrick, "The People behind the Sites: Land's End: Keep It Fresh," *The Wall Street Journal,* December 10, 2001, p. R6.

Being Entrepreneurial, p. 63: Ross Snel, "Small-Cap Fund Seeks Postattack Bargains," *The Wall Street Journal,* October 23, 2001, p. C21; Chantal Tode, "Evolution of Tweens Tastes Keeps Retailers on their Toes," *Advertising Age,* February 12, 2001, p. 56; Erik Torkells, "Abercrombie & Fitch," *Fortune,* June 25, 2001, p. 198; Erin White, "Abercrombie Seeks to Send Teeny-Boppers Packing—to Keep Juveniles from Marring Its Image, A&F Lures Them to Its New 'Surferish' Chain," *The Wall Street Journal,* August 30, 2001, p. B1.

Case 3–1: John Bissell, "A Sad End for the Saturn Experiment," *Brandweek,* November 20, 2000, p. 26; Irene Cherkassky, "A Show of Diversity," *Beverage World,* May 15, 2001, pp. 59–62; Kenneth Hein, "Pepsi's Mr. Green Leads Charge against Coke for 2002 Launches," *Brandweek,* October 22, 2001, p. 16; Jeffrey A. Tannenbaum, "Beverage Marketers See Refreshing Distribution Possibilities—PepsiCo's Acquisition of South Beach Leaves Greater Room for Lesser-Known Brands," *The Wall Street Journal,* May 29, 2001, p. B2; "Turning the Tides," *Beverage Industry,* June, 2001, pp. 16–20.

Case 3–2: "Advantages of the Versatile Voucher," *Marketing: Incentive 95 Preview,* April 27, 1995, pp. 5–6; Edmond Lawler, "How Underdogs Outmarket Leaders," *Advertising Age,* November 13, 1995, p. 24; Becky Ebenkamp, "JB, Virgin Unite Again for U.K. Trip," *Brandweek,* March 8, 1999, p. 14; Julia Flynn, Wendy Zeller, Larry Light, and Joseph Weber, "Then Came Branson," *Business Week,* October 26, 1998, pp. 116–20; "Virgin Atlantic Ads Take Aim at United, American," *Brandweek,* October 11, 1999, p. 8; "Virgin Aims to 'Shag' Greater Awareness in U.S.," *Adweek,* June 7, 1999, p. 5; Matthew Arnold, "Airlines Fight to Survive Crisis," *Marketing,* September 27, 2001, p. 15; Rafer Guzman, "Takeoffs and Landings," *The Wall Street Journal,* November 23, 2001, p. W.11C; and Stephen Power, "British Air-AMR Plan Is Dealt a Setback—U.S. Antitrust Officials Say Tie-Up Should Be Pared to Protect Competition," *The Wall Street Journal,* December, 18, 2001, p. A3.

Chapter 4

Page 74: Hilary Cassidy, "Cards Seek More 'You' in Usage," *BrandWeek,* June 4, 2001, p. S44; Kevin Higgins, "Marketing Visa Everywhere It Wants to Be," *Marketing Management,* November/December, 2001, pp. 14–17; www.usa.visa.com/personal/about_visa/who/index.html.

Exhibit 4–1: Allan Magrath, "Emerging and Burgeoning," *Across the Board,* January 2000, pp. 38–41.

Building Customer Equity, p. 77: Shirley Leung, "Subway Goes Express, Passing McDonald's in the Number of U.S. Restaurant Outlets," *The Wall Street Journal,* February 1, 2002, p. B2; Bob Sperber, "In Search of Fresh Ideas," *Brandweek,* October 15, 2001, pp. 55–57.

Exhibit 4–3: J. Paul Peter and Jerry C. Olson, *Understanding Consumer Behavior,* 5th ed. (Burr Ridge, IL: Irwin/McGraw-Hill, 1999) p. 250.

Exhibit 4–4: Adapted from Kenneth Lubich, "Class in America, © *Fortune,* February 7, 1994, p. 116. 1994 Time Inc. All rights reserved.

Exhibit 4–5: Adapted from Robert Boutilier, "Pulling the Family Strings," *American Demographics,* August 1993, p. 46. © American Demographics, Inc., Ithaca, NY.

Exhibit 4–6: 2002 www.census.gov.

Using Technology, p. 91: Ann M. Mack, "Volvo S60," *Adweek,* November 2001, p. 4; Karen Lundegaard, "Volvo's Web-Only Vehicle Launch Ends Amid Ford Unit's Questioning of Tactic," *The Wall Street Journal,* January 11, 2001, p. B13; Suzanne Vranica, "Volvo Campaign Tests New Media Waters," *The Wall Street Journal,* March 16, 2001, p. B5.

Case 4–1: Jeffrey Ball, "DaimlerChrysler Turnaround Seems to Be Going in Reverse," *The Wall Street Journal,* October 11, 2002, B.4; Karl Greenberg, "Overdrive," *Brandweek,* January 14, 2002, pp. 19–24; Scott Miller and Karen Lundegaard," *The Wall Street Journal,* February 4, 2002, B.1; Alex Taylor, III, "A Mercedes for the Masses," *Fortune Small Business,* December 2001/January 2002, p. 98.

Case 4–2: Alice C. Cuneo, "Gap's Ad Guru Departs," *Advertising Age,* May 6, 1996, pp. 1, 56; "Marketing Briefs," *Marketing News,*

July 1, 1996, p. 2; Cyndee Miller, "Another Win for Retro: Designer Jeans Are Back," *Marketing News,* June 3, 1996, pp. 18–19; Kelly Barron, "Gaplash," *Forbes,* June 14, 1999, pp. 110–12; Alice Cuneo, "Gap's First Global Ads Confront Dockers on a Khaki Battlefield," *Advertising Age,* April 20, 1998, pp. 3, 49; "Daddy Gap," *Business Week,* January 11, 1999, p. 63; Hal Espen, "Levi's Blues," *New York Times Magazine,* March 21, 1999, p. 54; Bob Garfield, "Gap Secretes Sweet Smell of Ad Success," *Advertising Age,* August 16, 1999, p. 55; Alan Treadgold, "The Outlook for Asian Retailing," *Discount Merchandiser,* May 1999, pp. 45–46; Louise Lee and Nanette Byrnes, "More Than Just a Bad Patch at Gap," *Business Week,* February 11, 2002; Amy Merrick, "Gap Posts Losses, Reshuffles Executives," *The Wall Street Journal,* February 27, 2002, p. B7; "The Goods on the Gap," *Advertising Age,* December 17, 2001, p. 10; and "U.S., International Units Separated at the Gap Inc.," *The Wall Street Journal,* January 17, 2002, p. B4.

Chapter 5

Page 102: "Heinz Outlines Strategy for Profitable Growth at CAGNY Conference," from the H.J. Heinz Web site at www.heinz.com/jsp/ news_f.jsp, June 2, 2002; "H.J. Heinz Corporation: e-Sourcing Adoption Ramp," available as a e-Sourcing seminar Webcast at www.FreeMarkets.com, February 8, 2002; and "The H.J. Heinz Company (case study), available at www.FreeMarkets.com, April 26, 2002.

Exhibit 5–2: United States Census Bureau, www.ntis.gov/naics, May 30, 2002.

Exhibit 5–3: Phillip L. Carter, Joseph R. Carter, Robert M. Monczka, Thomas H. Slaight, and Andrew J. Swan. *The Future of Purchasing and Supply: A Five- and Ten-Year Forecast.* Arizona State University: The Center for Advanced Purchasing Studies, 1998, pp. 27–36; and Roberta J. Duffy, "18 Initiatives: Following the Trends, Combining Elements, and Progressing Forward," *Purchasing Today,* November 2000, pp. 1–2.

Exhibit 5–4: Alex Brown, Kristopher K. Andrew, Connie R. Mullins, and Kenneth D. Litton, "What Are the Key Factors You Use to Determine If Outsourcing Is Appropriate?" *Inside Supply Management,* May 2002, p. 60.

Exhibit 5–5: Terri Tracey, "The State of Electronic Commerce," *Purchasing Today,* August 1999, pp. 21–24; and Bruce Temkin, "Taking Advantage of the Report on eBusiness," *Purchasing Today,* November 2001, pp. 32–35.

Using Technology, p. 108: Nicole Harris, "Private Exchanges May Allow B-to-B Commerce to Thrive After All," *The Wall Street Journal,* March 16, 2001, p. B 1, 4.

Exhibit 5–6: A. T. Kearney, as reported in Phillip P. Carter, Joseph R. Carter, Richard M. Monczka, Thomas H. Slaight, and Andrew J. Swan, "The Future of Purchasing and Supply: A Five- and Ten-Year Forecast," p. 23. Copyright the Center for Advanced Purchasing Studies, Arizona State University, 1998.

Building Customer Equity, p. 110: Elizabeth Crowley, "Down the Line," *The Wall Street Journal,* March 27, 2002, p. R16.

Exhibit 5–7: Erin Anderson, Wujin Shu, and Barton Weitz, "Industrial Purchasing: An Empirical Examination of the Buyclass Framework," *Journal of Marketing,* July 1987, p. 72. © 1987 by the American Marketing Association. Reprinted with permission.

Case 5–1: Joel L. Smith, "All Hail, Harley Davidson," *Detroit News,* February 22, 2002, p. B1; Lara Lee, "Hogging the Market. (Best Practices)," *Sales and Marketing Management,* April 2002, p. 70; Martha Richards, "High on the Hog," *Supply Chain Management Review,* November 2001, p. S86; Brian Milligan, "Harley Davidson Wins by Getting Suppliers on Board," *Purchasing,* September 21, 2000, pp. 52–65; and Missy Sullivan, "High-Octane Hog," *Best of the Web,* September 10, 2001 as presented on Forbes.com at www.forbes.com/best/2001/0910/008.

Case 5–2: Christopher Koch, "Motorcity Shakeup," *Darwin,* January 2002, pp. 46–51; "Auto Suppliers Will Be Pressured to Be e-Quipped," *Solutions,* February 2002, p. 12; Jeff Green, "Can Chrysler Get Blood From a Supplier? *Business Week,* December 25, 2000, p. 56; Ed Kean, "Auto Parts Suppliers Dwindle in Number," *Kiplinger Business Forecasts,* December 19, 2001, p. 12; Doug Bartholomew, "The Big Squeeze," *Industry Week,* p. 68; and "Top 250 Purchasing Departments," *Supply Chain Management Review,* March 30, 2002, p. 88.

Chapter 6

Page 122: http://www.nfow.com/default2.asp; Jack Homomichl, "Homomichl Top 50," *Marketing News,* June 10, 2002, pp. H15–H16; "Interpublic Deal Keys on Web Snynergies," *Mergers and Acquisitions,* March 2000, pp. 13–14; "Interpublic Group to Acquire NFO Worldwide Inc. for 1.29 Times Revenue," *Weekly Corporate Growth Report,* April 10, 2000, p. 10691.

Using Technology, p. 130: Gilbert A. Churchill, Jr., and Dawn Iacobucci, *Marketing Research: Methodological Foundations,* 8th ed. (Fort Worth, TX: Harcourt College Publishers, 2002), pp. 748–62; David J. Lipke, "Product by Design," *American Demographics,* February 2001, pp. 38–41.

Being Entrepreneurial, p. 132: Steve Jarvis and DeBorah Szynal, "Show and Tell: Spreading the Word About Online Qualitative Research," *Marketing News,* November 19, 2001, pp. 1, 13; Dana James, "New Tricks for Old Dogs," *Marketing News,* January 15, 2001, p. 19; David Jamieson, "Online Research Gets Fewer Online Cheers," *Marketing News,* January 21, 2002, p. 15.

Case 6–1: Aaron Barr, "Aleve Gets in the Fighting Spirit," *Adweek,* March 25, 2002, p. 6; Sara Eckel, "Road to Recovery," *American Demographics,* March 2001, p. S8.

Pat Sloan, "Rapid Gains Set Table for Jung Move at Avon," *Advertising Age,* February 3, 1997, p. S12; "Avon Names Asian-American Woman as CEO," *USA Today,* November 5, 1999, p. B1; Andrew Edgecliffe-Johnson, "Avon Lady Promoted to Chief Post," *The Financial Times Limited,* November 5, 1999, p. 32; Rachel Beck, "Avon Calls on Woman to Be Chief Executive," *The Coloradoan,* November 5, 1999, p. B4; Dana Canedy, "Opportunity Re-Knocks at Avon," *The New York Times,* November 5, 1999, p. C1; Christine Bittar, "Avon Refreshes 'Let's Talk' Campaign; Goes Global for Skincare Line Debut," *Brandweek,* February 18, 2002, p. 4; Don Davis, "Course Change for Avon," *Global Cosmetic Industry,* November 2000, p. 16; and Marianne Kolbasuk McGee, "Innovators and Influencers 2001: A New-Generation Avon Lady," *Informationweek,* January 1, 2001, p. 56.

Chapter 7

Page 148: Rebecca Piirto Heath, "The Frontier of Psychographics," *American Demographics,* July 1996, pp. 38–43; Rebecca Piirto Heath, "Psychographics," *Marketing Tools,* November/December 1995, pp. 75–79; Anne Marie Chaker, "Lifestyles: They Know What They Like," *The Wall Street Journal,* September 15, 1999, p. F4; and Anne Marie Chaker, "Lifestyles: No Life of Leisure," *The Wall Street Journal,* May 19, 1999, p. S3. Written comments by Carrie Hollenberg, the VALS Program; http://www.sirc-bi.com/VALS/.

Being Entrepreneurial, p. 157: Janet Guyon, "Nokia Rocks Its Rivals," *Fortune,* March 4, 2002, pp. 115–18; Almar Latour, "Nokia Unit Targets Wealthy Customers with a Line of Luxury Mobile Phones," *http://interactive. wsj.com/archive/retrie. . .35280242240840.djm;* "New Nokia Unit Will Make Phones of Fancy Materials," *The Wall Street Journal,* January 11, 2002, p. B6.

Exhibit 7–4: SRI International.

Exhibit 7–6: Elissa Moses, *The $100 Billion Allowance: Accessing the Global Teen Market,* New York: John Wiley & Sons, 2000.

Exhibit 7–9: Joseph P. Guiltinan, Gordon W. Paul, and Thomas J. Madden, *Marketing Management: Strategies and Programs,* 6th ed. (New York, NY: The McGraw-Hill Companies, 1997), p. 111.

Building Customer Equity, p. 169: http://www.mastercardintl.com/about/press/factsheet.html downloaded June 20, 2002; Lisa Bertagnoli, "'Priceless' a Hit with Hispanic Audiences," *Marketing News,* January 15, 2001, p. 5; Cris Prystay, "MasterCard Hopes to Score in Asia With Prepaid Plastic," *The Wall Street Journal,* May 21, 2002, p. D2; Mary Shacklett, "MasterCard Positions Itself for m-Commerce," *Credit Union Magazine,* March 2002, pp. 70–73.

Exhibit 7–10: James H. Meyers, *Segmentation and Positioning for Strategic Marketing Decisions,* Chicago: American Marketing Association, 1996, p. 209.

Case 7–1: "A Higher Profile for Audience Measurement," *Broadcasting & Cable,* December 1, 1997, p. S20; "The PRIZM Advantage," *The Frame* (Fairfield, CT: Survey Sampling, Inc.), August 1999, p. 1; http://yawl.claritas.com/about.asp, December 12, 1999; Deborah D. McAdams, "Micro-Marketing," *Broadcasting & Cable,* July 17, 2000, p. 50; Amy Merrick, "The 2000 Count: Counting on the Census," *The Wall Street Journal,* February 14, 2001, p. B1; and Evan St. Lifer, "Tapping into the Zen of Marketing," *Library Journal,* May 1, 2001, pp. 44–46.

Case 7–2: Christina Brinkley, "Marriott Outfits an Old Chain for a Brand-New Market," *The Wall Street Journal,* October 13, 1998, http://interactive.wsj.com/articles/; "Marriott's New View of Downtown," *Business Week,* July 26, 1999, p. 78; Marty Whitford, "Marriott International Restructures Management," *Hotel & Management,* October 18, 1999, p. 23; Marty Whitford, "Old and New Flags Vanish with Rebranding Strategy," *Hotel & Management,* October 4, 1999, p. 30; and http://www.Marriott.com/corporate-info. Downloaded June 20, 2002.

Chapter 8

Page 178: The Frito-Lay Web site, http://www.fritolay.com, July 7, 2002.

Using Technology, p. 180: Robert D. Hof, "Turning Rust into Gold," *Business Week,* June 10, 2002, p. 102.

Exhibit 8–7: Data: Interbrand Corp., J.P. Morgan Chase & Co.

Building Customer Equity, p. 194: Thomas Mucha, "The Payoff for Trying Harder," *Business 2.0,* July 2002, pp. 84–86.

Case 8–1: Michael Behar, "Computer, Heal Thyself," *Business 2.0,* July 2002, pp. 100–01.

Case 8–2: Stanley Holmes, "Gert Gets the Last Laugh," *Business Week,* June 10, 2002, p. 100.

Chapter 9

Page 200: www.3m.com, July 15, 2002, and Michael Arndt, "3M: A Lab for Growth?" *Business Week,* January 21, 2002, pp. 50–51.

Exhibit 9–1: Adapted from C. Merle Crawford, *New Products Management,* 4th ed. (Burr Ridge, IL: Richard D. Irwin, 1994), p. 11.

Being Entrepreneurial, p. 204: George Anders, "The Innovator's Solution," *Fast Company,* June 2002, pp. 132–38.

Exhibit 9–4: James J. McKeown, "New Products from New Techologies," *Journal of Business and Industrial Marketing,* Winter–Spring 1990, p. 70.

Using Technology, p. 210: Irene Kunii, "This Cute Little Pet Is a Robot," *Business Week,* May 24, 1999, pp. 56–57; www.us.aibo.com, July 15, 2002.

Exhibit 9–8: Adapted from Robert G. Cooper and Elko J. Kleinschmidt, "Stage Gate Systems for New-Product Success," *Marketing Management* 1, no. 4, pp. 20–29. Reprinted by permission of the American Marketing Association.

Exhibit 9–9: William R. Dillon, Thomas J. Madden, and Neil H. Firtle, *Essentials of Marketing Research* (Homewood, IL: Richard D. Irwin, 1993), p. 50.

Case 9–1: J. Lynn Lunsford, "New Jet Promises to Be Cheaper to Buy, Fly; Unveiling 'Air Taxi'," *The Wall Street Journal Online*, July 12, 2002, pp. 1–2; www.eclipseaviation.com.

Case 9–2: Kathleen Kerwin, "Where are the Hot Cars?," *Business Week*, June 24, 2002, pp. 66–68.

Page 203: Rogier Van bakel, "The Art of Brand Revival," *Business 2.0*, September 2002, pp. 45–48.

Page 207: Lisa Bannon, "Mattel's project Platypus Aims To Inspire Creative Thinking," *The Wall Street Journal Online*, June 6, 2002, pp. 1–3.

Chapter 10

Page 220: www.starbucks.com, July 16, 2002; and Jeff Schlegel, "Something Brewin'," *Individual Investor*, February 2000, pp. 60–61; "How Much Starbucks Is Too Much," *Business 2.0*, July 2002, p. 35.

Being Entrepreneurial, p. 223: Leslie Earnest, "Skechers Strides Away from the Competition," *The Courier-Journal*, June 30, 2002, p. E4.

Exhibit 10–4: Adapted from Eric N. Berkowitz, Roger A. Kerin, Steven W. Hartley, and William Redslius, *Marketing*, 4th ed. (Burr Ridge IL: Richard D. Irwin, 1994), p. 327.

Building Customer Equity, p. 231: David Goetz, "Pumps Plus," *The Courier-Journal*, July 14, 2002, pp. E1–E2.

Case 10–1: Mike McNamee, "Don't Leave Home without a Free-bie," *Business Week*, November 8, 1999, pp. 150, 152; www.americanexpress. com, July 16, 2002.

Case 10–2: Peter Burrows, "What's in Store for This Happy Couple?", *Business Week*, May 20, 2002, p. 45; and Cliff Edwards and Andrew Park, "HP and Compaq: It's Showtime," *Business Week*, June 17, 2002, pp. 76–77.

Chapter 11

Page 242: *http://www.edmunds.com/edweb/about*; Jeff Green, "Auto Info Source Edmunds.com Revs Ad Plans after Getting Holiday Lift," *Brandweek*, February 7, 2000, p. 55; David Welch, "Car Dealers Say: Follow that Mouse," *Business Week*, April 10, 2000, pp. 106, 100; Joseph B. White and Fara Warner, "Car Makers Try to Alter Pricing Practices," *The Wall Street Journal*, January 24, 2000, p. A4; Karl Greenberg, "Korilko Clicks on Consumers for Edmunds.com," *Brandweek*, May 21, 2001, p. 38; Jean Halliday, "Overhaul Near End for Edmunds.com," *Advertising Age*, April 9, 2001, p. 28; and Weston Pugh, "Internet Research Becoming Key to Automobile Purchases," *San Antonio Business Journal*, March 23, 2001, p. 34.

Exhibit 11–2: Adapted from John A. Farris and John A. Quelch, "In Defense of Price Promotion," *Sloan Management Review*, Fall 1989, p. 64; and Rockney G. Walters, "Assessing the Impact of Retail Price Promotions on Product Substitution, Complementary Purchase, and Interstore Displacement," *Journal of Marketing*, April 1991, p. 17.

Exhibit 11–4: Hermann Simon, "Pricing Opportunities and How to Exploit Them," *Sloan Management Review*, Winter 1992, p. 59. Copyright by Sloan Management Review Association. All rights reserved.

Using Technology, p. 251: "Getting the Bugs Out," *Progressive Grocer*, March 1996, p. 56; Ronald Goodstein, "UPC Scanner Pricing Systems: Are They Accurate?" *Journal of Marketing*, April 1994, pp. 20–30; 6; Bill Commun, "Don't Just Scan, Analyze," *Journal of Petroleum Marketing*, May 1999, p. 19; Amanda Loudin, "'Been There, Done That' with Scanner Technology," *Warehousing Management*, June 1999, pp. 38–41; Julie Clark, "Life in the Fast-Lane: Self-Checkouts Are the Remedy for the 'Drop and Walk' Customer," *Display & Design Ideas*, March 2002, p. 74; "L. A. Laws Aimed at Price Accuracy," *Progressive Grocer*, March 1, 2002, p. 14; and "Transcendental Transactions," *Chain Store Age*, February 2002, pp. 5C–6C.

Building Customer Equity p. 257: Christine Bittar, "High Anxiety: Patents Expire, Successes Wane," *Brandweek*, June 17, 2002, p. S64; "Profit Warnings," *Scrip Magazine*, February 2002, p. 50; and Venkatesh Shankar, "New Product Introduction and Incumbent Response Strategies: Their Interrelationship and the Role of Multi-market Contact," *Journal of Marketing Research*, August 1999, p. 327.

Exhibit 11–8: Adapted from Kent B. Monroe, *Pricing: Making Profitable Decisions*, 2nd ed. (New York: McGraw-Hill, 1990), p. 46; and William B. Dodds, Kent B. Monroe, and Druv Grewal, "Effects of Price, Brand, and Store Information on Buyers' Product Evaluations," *Journal of Marketing Research*, August 1991, p. 308.

Exhibit 11–9: Adapted from Joel E. Urbany and Peter R. Dickson, *Consumer Knowledge of Normal Prices: An Exploratory Study and Framework*, Marketing Science Institute, report no. 90-112 (Cambridge, MA: 1990), p. 18.

Exhibit 11–10: Adapted from Abhijit Biswas and Edward A. Blair, "Contextual Effects of Reference Prices in Retail Advertisement," *Journal of Marketing*, July 1991, p. 4. © 1991 by the American Marketing Association. Reprinted with permission.

Case 11–1: Winifred Capowski, "A Grinch in Your Future," *Super-market Business*, September 15, 2001; Doug Desjardins, "DVD Prices Continue to Drop as Market Keeps Maturing," *Dsn Retailing Today*, February 19, 2001, pp. 19–22; Brandon Mitchener, "Probes into Online Music Services, DVD Pricing Are Launched by EU," *The Wall Street Journal*, June 12, 2001, p. A17; Bruce Orwall, Martin Peers, and Ann Zimmerman, "DVD Gains on Tape, but Economics Have Hollywood in a Tizzy," *The Wall Street Journal*, February 5, 2002, p. A1.

Case 11–2: Robert D. Hof, Heather Green, and Paul Judge, "Going, Going, Gone," *Business Week*, April 12, 1999, pp. 30–32; Nick Wingfield, "Priceline Adds Three Airlines to System, Resulting in a Charge of $1.1 Billion," *The Wall Street Journal*, November 17, 1999, p. B2; Nick Wingfield, "Priceline.com Names Microsoft in Suit, Alleging Violation of One of Its Patents," *The Wall Street Journal*, October 14, 1999, p. B18; http://www.priceline.com/PriceLineASOPourCompany? asp/ company.asp; Dan Selicaro, "Curtain Call for Priceline.com," *Upside*, February 2001, pp. 36–37; Mark Veverka, "Plugged In: Can Jay Walker Pull a New Rabbit Out of His Hat," *Barrons*, January 8, 2001, p. 41; and Suh-kyung Yoon, "Priceline.com, Hutchinson Launch an Online Travel Service for Asia," *The Wall Street Journal*, April 17, 2002, D3.

Chapter 12

Page 268: Sally B. Donnelly and Mitch Frank, "Auction Nation: Town Square Community Center, Social Scene—eBay Turned into Much More than Auction," *Time*, December 27, 1999, p. 82; Michael Krantz, "The Attic of e:>>From Yesteryear's Treasures to Yesterday's Garbage, There's a Price and a Place for Everything; What Are You Collecting?" *Time*, December 27, 1999, p. 74; Kathleen Melymuka, "Internet Intuition," *Computer World*, January 10, 2000, p. 48; Jerry Adler "The eBay Way of Life," *Newsweek*, June 17, 2002, pp. 51–60; "eBay to Buy France's iBazar for $66 Million to $112 Million," *Futures World News*, May 7, 2001, p.1008053r0738; "eBay Revenue Increases 81% As Net Surges," *The Wall Street Journal*, January 19, 2001, www.djinteractive.com; and Collin Keefe, "Where Haves Meet Wants," *Dealerscope*, January 2002, pp. 50–54.

Exhibit 12–1: Harper W. Boyd, Jr., Orville C. Walker, Jr., John Mulling, and Jean-Clarde Larreche, *Marketing Management: A*

Strategic Decision-Making Approach, 4th ed., 2002, New York, NY: McGraw-Hill/ Irwin, p. 283.

Being Entrepreneurial, p. 271: Diane Brady, "Insurers Step Gingerly into Cyberspace," *Business Week,* November 22, 1999, pp. 160–161; http://www.quotesmith. com/ir/corporate profile.html, July 2, 2002.

Using Technology, p. 273: Neal Templin, "Hotels Adopt System Used by Airlines That Helps to Maximize Revenue," *The Wall Street Journal,* http://interactive. wsj.com, May 5, 1999; Scott Woolly, "I Got It Cheaper than You," *Forbes,* November 2, 1998, pp. 82, 84; and Scott McCartney, "Absurd Airfare-Pricing System Leads to Confusion, Irritation for Travelers," *The Wall Street Journal,* April 17, 2002, http:// online.wsj. com/article/0,,SB1018960058246050560.djm,00.html.

Exhibit 12–5: Adapted from Ford S. Worthy, "Japan's Smart Secret Weapon," *Fortune,* August 12, 1991, p. 73. © 1991 Time Inc. All rights reserved.

Exhibit 12–6: Klaus Wertenbroch and Bernd Skiera, "Measuring Consumer Willingness to Pay at the Point of Purchase," *Journal of Marketing Research,* May 2002, p. 230.

Exhibit 12–7: Timothy Matanovich, Gary L. Lilien, and Arvind Rangaswamy, "Engineering the Price-Value Relationship," *Marketing Management,* Spring 1999. p. 49.

Exhibit 12–9: Peter M. Noble and Thomas S. Cruca, "Industrial Pricing: Theory and Managerial Practice," *Marketing Science,* 18, no. 3 (1999), p. 438.

Case 12–1: Barbara E. Kahn and Leigh McAlister, *Grocery Revolution: The New Focus on the Consumer* (Reading, MA: Addison-Wesley, 1997); Dagmar Mussey and Amy Barone, "Heat's on Value Pricing: Sales Drop Only a Blip Say EDLP Backers," *Advertising Age* 68, no. 2 (January 13, 1997), p. 121; Raju Narisetti, "P&G Bets on Low Prices 'Every Day' to Cut Out Need for Company Coupons," *The Wall Street Journal,* January 8, 1996, p. 15B; "Procter's Gamble," *The Economist* 351 (June 12, 1999), p. 10; Kusum L. Ailawadi, Donald R. Lehmann, and Scott A. Neslin, "Market Response to a Major Change in the Marketing Mix: Learning from Procter & Gamble's Value Pricing," *Journal of Marketing,* January 2001, pp. 44–61; Tim Ambler, "P&G Learnt the Hard Way from Dropping Its Price Promotions," *Marketing,* June 7, 2001, p. 22; Katrina Brooker, "A Game of Inches," *Fortune,* February 5, 2001, pp. 98–100; and Mike Troy, "Drop EDLP—Continue Promoting the Value Message," *Dsn Retailing Today,* March 11, 2002, p. 33.

Case 12–2: Shirley Leung, "Fast-Food Chains Vie to Carve Out Empire in Pricey Sandwiches," *The Wall Street Journal,* April 5, 2002, p. A1, A10; James Peters, "Starbucks' Growth Still Hot; Gift Cared Jolts Chain's Sales," *Nation's Restaurant News,* February 11, 2002, pp. 1, 47; Greg W. Prince, "Doubleshot of Starbucks' Love," *Beverage World,* March 15, 2002, p. 76; Terry Pristin, "Starbucks Strikes Deep in Wary Land of Pushcarts and Delis," *New York Times,* April 29, 2002, p. B1; and Howard Schultz, "Starbucks," *Business Week,* January 14, 2002, p. 55.

Chapter 13

Page 296: Pui-Wing Tam, "Apple Sees Outlays of $200 Million For This Fiscal Year," *The Wall Street Journal,* December 27, 2001, p. B4; Janet Kornblum, "Mac Sales Coming to a Mall Near You," *USA Today,* May 16, 2001, p. 3D; and information from Apple's Web site at www.apple.com.

Building Customer Equity, p. 306: Elizabeth Montalbano, "Channel Champions 2002: IBM Serves its Channel," *Crn,* March 18, 2002, p. 78.

Using Technology, p. 311: Jane E. Zarem, "From the Store to the Web and Back Again," *1 to 1 Magazine,* January/February 2002, pp. 22–26.

Case 13–1: James R. Healey, "Circuit City Plans to Push CarMax Out of the Nest," *USA Today,* February 25, 2002, p. 3B; Elliot Spagat, "Circuit City Cuts Estimates, Citing Inventory Shortages,"

The Wall Street Journal, February 25, 2002, p. B13; and information from the CarMax Web site at www.carmax.com.

Case 13–2: "Best Sales Forces 1999: Caterpillar," *Sales & Marketing Management,* July 1999, p. 64; Sandra Ward, "The Cat Is Back," *Barron's,* February 25, 2002, pp. 21–24; Lee Copeland, "Caterpillar Digs Into Agile Development," *Computerworld,* January 7, 2002, p. 14; Donald V. Fites, "Make Your Dealers Your Partners," *Harvard Business Review,* March–April, 1996, pp. 84–95; and information from Caterpillar's home page at http://www.caterpillar.com.

Chapter 14

Page 322: Louise Lee, "Williams-Sonoma Tries a New Recipe," *Business Week,* May 6, 2002, p. 36; Amy Merrick, "The Rivalry Behind Retro Chic," *The Wall Street Journal,* November 23, 2001, pp. B1, B4; and information from the Williams-Sonoma Web site at www.williams-sonomainc.com, on June 10, 2002.

Exhibit 14–1: "Fortune One Thousand Ranked within Industries," *Fortune,* April 15, 2002, pp. 51–62. Copyright 2002 Time Inc. Reprinted with permission.

Building Customer Equity, p. 326: Maureen Tracik, "Hey Dude, This Sure Isn't the Gap," *The Wall Street Journal,* February 12, 2002, pp. B1, B4.

Exhibit 14–2: Selected from "*Entrepreneur* magazine's Top 200 International Franchises," www.franchiseinfomall.com, June 11, 2002.

Using Technology, p. 329: Kevin Maney, "New Chips Could Make Everyday Items Talk," *USA Today,* April 12, 2002, pp. B1–B2.

Exhibit 14–3: Adapted from Michael Levy and Barton A. Weitz, *Retailing Management,* 4th ed. (Burr Ridge, IL: Richard D. Irwin, 2001), p. 586. © 2001 Irwin/McGraw-Hill. Reprinted with permission of the publisher.

Exhibit 14–5: Michael Levy and Barton A. Weitz, *Retailing Management,* 4th ed. (Burr Ridge, Illinois: McGraw-Hill Irwin, 2001) p. 250.

Exhibit 14–7: Adapted from Barry Berman and Joel R. Evans, *Retail Management: A Strategic Approach,* 5th ed. (New York: Macmillan, 1992), pp. 98–99. Copyright © 1992 by Macmillan College Publishing Company, Inc. Reprinted with permission of the publisher.

Exhibit 14–8: ADT Security Systems and "The Peter Berlin Report on Shrinkage Control—Store Manager's Edition," The Peter Berlin Retail Consulting Group, Jericho, New York, as presented at www. retailindustry. about.com, June 14, 2002.

Case 14–1: Lauren Lipton, "Too Trendy for You?" *The Wall Street Journal,* May 17, 2002, pp. W1, W14; Olivia Barker, "Shoppers Have a Fit About Sizes," *USA Today,* May 15, 2002, pp. 1D–2D; Lorrie Grant, "Customers Take Comfort in Chico's," *USA Today,* May 3, 2001; "Chico's FAS, Inc., Company Capsule," from Hoover's Online at www.hoovers.com, June 15, 2002; and "Catalog and Internet Sales Boom for Chico's FAS," *Direct Newsline,* March 5, 2002, www.industryclick.com.

Case 14–2: Lorrie Grant, "Home Depot Chief Builds on Big Dreams," *USA Today,* June 14, 2002, pp. 1B–2B; Aixa M. Pascual, "Lowe's Is Sprucing Up its House," *Business Week,* June 3, 2002, PP. 56, 58; Thomas A. Fogarty and Lorrie Grant, "Home Improvement Raises the Roof on Growth," *USA Today,* May 22, 2002, p. 3B; Chad Terhune, "Home Depot Chief Expects Slower Growth," *The Wall Street Journal,* December 3, 2001, p. B12; and Pamela Sebastian Ridge, "Tool Sellers Tap their Feminine Side, *The Wall Street Journal,* March 29, 2002, p. B1.

Chapter 15

Page 350: "The 75-Year-Old Supply Chain," *Inbound Logistics,* January 2002, pp. 96–104; and information from Grainger's Web site at www.grainger.com, June 17, 2002.

Exhibit 15–3: Adapted with permission of the International Hardware Distributors Association.

Exhibit 15–4: "Trade Relations," *Progressive Grocer Annual Report*, April 2001, pp. 20–21.

Exhibit 15–5: Mushtaq Luqmani, Donna Goehle, Zahir A. Quraeshi, and Ugur Yavas, "Tracing the Development of Wholesaling Thought and Practice," *Journal of Marketing Channels*, April 1991, p. 95. Reprinted with permission of The Hawworth Press, Inc.

Exhibit 15–6: Deborah Catalano, "Measuring Carrier Performance," *Inbound Logistics*, April 2002, p. 88.

Using Technology, p. 361: "TaylorMade-adidas Golf Taps into the Power of i2," from i2 Technologies, Inc., Web site at www.i2.com, June 24, 2002.

Exhibit 15–7: Adapted from "Quick Response: What It Is; What It's Not," *Chain Store Age Executive*, March 1991, pp. B4, B5. Used by permission from *Chain Store Age Executive*, March 1991. Copyright Lebhar-Friedman, Inc., 425 Park Avenue, New York, NY 10022.

Being Entrepreneurial; p. 365: Jeff Bailey, "For One Trucking Entrepreneur, Success is in the Details," *The Wall Street Journal*, November 27, 2001, p. B4; "Sears Awards Heartland as Quality Vendor of the Year," from Heartland Express Web site at www.heartlandexpress.com, April 10, 2002; and "Georgia Pacific Awards Heartland Carrier of the Year Award," from Heartland Express Web site at www.heartlandexpress.com, February 28, 2002.

Case 15–1: Jo Bennett, "Gallo Connects with Customers," *1 to 1 magazine*, May/June 2002, pp. 16–17; and information from E & J Gallo Winery Web site at www.gallo.com, June 27, 2002.

Case 15–2: Jeff Manning, "Columbia Shifts into High Gear," *The Oregonian*, April 9, 1999, as printed at www.oregonianlive.com; Stanley Holmes, "Gert Gets the Last Laugh," *Business Week*, June 10, 2002, p. 100; and "Columbia Sportswear Company Reports Record First Quarter 2002 Results," April 25, 2002, from Columbia's Web site at www.columbia.com.

Chapter 16

Page 374: John Gaffney, "First Annual Sweet Spots Awards: Most Innovative Campaign," *Business 2.0*, May 2002, pp. 98–99; and information from the Mini Cooper Web site at www.miniusa.com, June 29, 2002.

Being Entrepreneurial, p. 379: Bob Garfield, "The Magnificence of Nike's Grand Prix Winner," from *Advertising Age's Ad Review* Web site at www.adreview.com, June 28, 2002; and Michael McCarthy, "Advertisers Compete to Become Pride of Lions," *USA Today*, June 18, 2002, pp. 1B–2B.

Building Customer Equity, p. 391: Andrew Zippern, "Effort to Measure Online Ad Campaigns," from *The New York Times on the Web* at www.nytimes.com, January 15, 2002; and Karen J. Bannan, "Helping Businesses Evaluate Their Internet Presence," *The New York Times on the Web* at www.nytimes.com, June 12, 2002.

Case 16–1: Joe Flint and Shelly Branch, "In Face of Widening Backlash, NBC Gives Up Plan to Run Liquor Ads," *The Wall Street Journal*, March 21, 2002, pp. B1, B3; Theresa Howard, "Liquor Ad Outlets Sought," *USA Today*, April 8, 2002, p. 2B; Vanessa O'Connell, "Landmark TV Liquor Ad Created by D.C. Insiders," *The Wall Street Journal*, January 3, 2002, pp. B1, B3.

Case 16–2: Maureen Tkacik, "As Extreme Goes Mass, Nike Nips at Skate-Shoe Icon," *The Wall Street Journal*, April 24, 2002, pp. A1, A6; information from Savier, Inc. Web site at www.savier.com, July 2, 2002, and the Vans Web site at www.vans.com, July 2, 2002.

Chapter 17

Page 400: Matt Carmichael, "British Airways Pops Up in Most Unobtrusive Way," *Advertising Age*, October 11, 1999, p. 64; Ian Darby, "Joshua Fights for the Battle of BA Long-Haul," *Marketing*, September 2, 1999, p. 11; Janet Guyon, "British Airways Takes," *Fortune*, September 27, 1999, pp. 214–17; Danny Rogers, "Will BA Take Off Again?" *Marketing*, August 26, 1999, pp. 18–19; "BA Opts for PR to Retain Full-Service 'Premium' Image," *Marketing*, May 23, 2002, p. 6; "Business: AA = No-No; BA Thwarted," *The Economist*, February 2, 2002, pp. 58–59; Daniel Michaels, "British Airways Posts Loss, Says Cost Cuts Help," *The Wall Street Journal*, May 21, 2002, p. D5; and Daniel Rogers and Matthew Arnold, "BA to Challenge 'Expensive' Tag with Tactical Ads," *Marketing*, February 14, 2002, p. 3.

Exhibit 17–1: *Ad Age*, http://www.adage.com/page.cms?pageId= 681, May 21, 2002.

Exhibit 17–2: "9th Annual Agency Report Cards," *AdWeek*, April 15, 2002, p. 49.

Building Customer Equity, p. 412: Nikhil Deogun, "Media and Marketing: Coca-Cola Rethinks Its Ad Strategy," *The Wall Street Journal*, July 13, 1999, p. B2; Stuart Elliott, "Another Revamping at Leo Burnett," *The New York Times*, October 25, 1999, p. C22; Stuart Elliott, "2 Big Advertisers Consolidate Work," *The New York Times*, March 29, 1999, p. C11; Daniel McGinn, "Pour on the Pitch," *Newsweek*, May 31, 1999, p. 50; Terence A. Shimp, *Advertising, Promotion, and Supplemental Aspects of Integrated Marketing Communications*, 5th ed. (Fort Worth, TX: Dryden Press, 2000). Scott Donaton, "Bcom3's Haupt Proves It's the Quiet Ones You Have to Watch," *Advertising Age*, April 22, 2002, p. 26; "National 2001 Agency Report Cards," *AdWeek*, April 15, 2002, pp. 20–30; Wendy Melillo, "Burnett Enlist Legal Aid on Army," *AdWeek*, April 15, 2002, p. 8.

Using Technology, p. 418: Louis Chunovic, "Satellite TV Hits Stores," *Electronic Media*, May 6, 2002, p. 8; Sandra Dolbow, "Wal-Mart Networking Consumers with PRN," *BrandWeek*, July 2, 2001, p. 19; Victoria Murphy, "Attention, Wal-Mart Shopper," *Forbes*, April 16, 2001.

Case 17–1: Hillary Chura and Wayne Friedman, "TV Toasts NBC Drive to Drink," *Advertising Age*, December 17, 2001, pp. 1, 24; Joe Flint, Shelly Branch, and Vanessa O'Connell, "Breaking Longtime Taboo, NBC Network Plans to Accept Liquor Ads," *The Wall Street Journal*, December 14, 2001, p. B1; Matthew Grimm, "A Spirited Debate," *American Demographics*, April 2002, pp. 48–50; Jeremy Murphy and Megan Larson, "The Booze Will Still Flow," *MediaWeek*, March 25, 2002, p. 8; Ira Teinowitz, "Booze Hounded," *Advertising Age*, March 25, 2002, pp. 1, 27.

Case 17–2: "Bates Saatchi to Open Kosovo Agency," *Advertising Age*, August 2, 1999, p. 41; David Kiley, "A New Set of Wheels," *American Demographics*, August 1999, pp. 38–39; Diana T. Kurylko, "Toyota to Consolidate Its Dealers in Europe," *Automotive News*, December 6, 1999, p. 55; Jo-Anne Walker, "Toyota Poaches Director of Marketing from Ford," *Marketing Week*, March 29, 1996, p. 9; Matthew Arnold, "Toyota Backs U.K. Style Show to Boost Corolla," *Marketing*, May 30, 2002, p. 6; Chester Dawson, Larry Armstrong, Joann Muller, and Kathleen Kerwin, "The Americanization of Toyota," *Business Week*, April 15, 2002, pp. 52–54; Ken Gofton, "Toyota Uses Humor to Change Perceptions," *Marketing*, June 6, 2002, p. 25; Jules Grant, "Toyota to Blitz Commuter Railway Sites," *Marketing*, February 28, 2002, p. 8; Jean Halliday, "Young Buyers Increasingly Critical to Toyota Efforts," *Advertising Age*, April 1, 2002, p. S10.

Chapter 18

Page 429: Val-Pak Web site, http://www.valpak.com.

Exhibit 18–1: Adapted with permission from William F. Arens, *Contemporary Advertising*, 8th ed. (Burr Ridge, IL: McGraw-Hill/Irwin, 2002), p. 323. © 2002, McGraw-Hill/Irwin. Reproduced with permission from McGraw-Hill Companies.

Building Customer Equity, p. 438: "2002 Reggie Award Winners, Silver Local, Target, or Ethnic Consumer Promotion Budget Over

$1 Million," from the Promotion Marketing Association Web site at www.pmalink.org/ html/2002reggiewinners2.html, July 2, 2002.

Being Entrepreneurial, p. 441: "Book Promo Uses Truly Valuable Local Goods," from the PromoMart Web site at www.promo-mart.com, July 9, 2002.

Exhibit 18–6: Yumiko Ono, "Wobblers and Sidekicks Clutter Stores, Irk Retailers," *The Wall Street Journal,* September 8, 1998, pp. B1, B3.

Exhibit 18–7: Cristopher Power, "Coupon Scams Are Clipping Companies," *Business Week,* June 15, 1992, pp. 110–11. Reprinted by special permission, copyright © 1992 by McGraw-Hill, Inc. Permission conveyed through the Copyright Clearance Center, Inc.

Case 18–1: Information from Wyndham's Women on Their Way Web site at www.womenbusinesstravelers.com, July 10, 2002; and Sonia Reyes, "Tapping Girl Power," *Brandweek,* April 22, 2002, pp. 26–30.

Case 18–2: Daniel Pearl and Steve Stecklow, "Drug Firms' Incentives to Pharmacists in India Fuel Mounting Abuse," *The Wall Street Journal,* August 16, 2001, pp. A1, A5; P. T. Jyothi Datta, "Patents for Pharma Companies Must be Dealt With Cautiously," *Global News Wire—Asia Africa Intelligence Wire,* February 15, 2002, Copyright 2002 Kasturi & Sons Ltd, *Business Line;* Ravi Dyal, "Doctors Turn Their Backs on Hippocratic Oath," February 1, 2002, *Global News Wire,* Copyright 2002, *The Times of India,* Bennett, Coleman & Co., Ltd; information from the GlaxoSmith-Kline Web site at www.gsk.com/about/about.htm, July 10, 2002; and information from the Pharmaceutical Research and Manufacturers of America at www.phrma.org., July 10, 2002.

Chapter 19

Page 454: www.pfizer.com, July 17, 2002; Malcolm Campbell, "Fantastic Pfizer," *Selling Power,* May 1999, pp. 50–56; Amy Barrett and Michael Arudt, "Can Pfizer Stay This Robust?", *Business Week,* March 18, 2002, pp. 68–69.

Exhibit 19–1: Linda Corman, "The World's Toughest Customers," *Selling,* September 1993, p. 53.

Exhibit 19–3: Thomas N. Ingram, Raymond W. LaForge, and Charles H. Schwepker, Jr., *Sales Management: Analysis and Decision Making,* 3rd ed. (Fort Worth, TX: The Dryden Press/Harcourt Brace Jovanovich, 1997), p. 57. Copyright © 1997 by The Dryden Press, reproduced by permission of the publisher.

Exhibit 19–4: Thomas N. Ingram, Michael D. Hartline, and Charles A. Schwepker, "Gatekeeper Perceptions: Implications for Improving Sales Ethics and Professionalism," *Proceedings of the Academy of Marketing Science,* 1992, pp. 328–32.

Exhibit 19–5: Phillip Schembra, "Often Overlooked Listening Habits," *The Selling Advantage,* January 1991, p. 3; and Phillip Schembra, "A Checklist on Asking Questions," *The Selling Advantage,* July 1991, p. 3.

Exhibit 19–6: Adapted from: *Making . . . Serving . . . Keeping Customers* (Chicago: The Dartnell Corporation, 1990).

Building Customer Equity p. 463: John Schultenover, "Selling Five-Star in a Budget Economy," *Sales & Marketing Management,* March 2002, p. 60.

Exhibit 19–7: Adapted from Thomas N. Ingram, Raymond W. LaForge, and Charles H. Schwepker, Jr., *Sales Management and Decision Making,* 3rd ed. (Fort Worth, TX: The Dryden Press, 1997), p. 3. Copyright © 1997 by The Dryden Press, reproduced by permission of the publisher.

Exhibit 19–8: Thomas N. Ingram, Raymond W. LaForge, and Charles H. Schwepker, Jr., *Sales Management: Analysis and Decision Making,* 3rd ed. (Fort Worth. TX: The Dryden Press, 1997), p. 140.

Using Technology, p. 469: Mark McMaster, "Express Train," *Sales & Marketing Management,* May 2002, p. 46–54.

Exhibit 19–9: Adapted from Thomas N. Ingram and Raymond W. LaForge, *Sales Management: Analysis and Decision Making,* 2nd ed. (Fort Worth, TX: The Dryden Press/Harcourt Brace Jovanovich, 1992), p. 533. Copyright © 1992 by The Dryden Press, reproduced by permission of the publisher.

Exhibit 19–10: Excerpted from *Sales and Marketing Executives International Certified Professional Salesperson Code of Ethics* (Cleveland: Sales and Marketing Executives International, 1994).

Exhibit 19–11: Rosemary R. Lagace, Thomas N. Ingram, and Michael Borom, "An Exploratory Study of Salesperson Unethical Behavior: Scale Development and Validation," forthcoming in the *Proceedings,* American Marketing Association Summer Educators' Conference, 1994.

Case 19–1: "STEP . . . Training to Integrate the Saturn Difference," *Marketing Journal,* Winter 1993, pp. 1–2; Dorothy Cottrell, Larry Davis, Pat Detrick, and Marty Raymond, "Sales Training and the Saturn Difference," *Training and Development,* December 1992, pp. 38–43; Andrea Sawyers, "No-Haggle Pricing Hits Full Throttle," *Advertising Age,* March 22, 1992, p. S10, and Saturn Web site (http://www.saturncars.com) July 17, 2002.

Case 19–2: John A. Byrne, "Main Street Trumps Wall Street," *Business Week,* June 10, 2002, pp. 134–38.

Chapter 20

Page 480: Coldwater Creek Web site at http://www.coldwater-creek.com; "Coldwater Creek Named #1 for Customer Service Centers in U.S.," as reported at www.prnewswire.com, June 19, 2001; and "Coldwater Creek Boosts Earnings in Midst of Channel Shift," as reported at www.directmag.com, June 26, 2002.

Exhibit 20–1: First appeared in *Success,* February 1993. Written by Jody Hewgill. Reprinted with permission of *Success* magazine. Copyright © 1993 by Hal Holdings Corporation.

Using Technology, p. 483: Ann Therese Palmer, "Online Savings are in Bloom," *Business Week,* July 22, 2002, p. 10.

Being Entrepreneurial, p. 487: Kris Oser, "Soaring High," *Direct,* January 2002, pp. 51–53.

Exhibit 20–4: Adapted from Bill Furlong, "Reach All Levels of the Decision-Making Process," from www.DMNews.com. June 27, 2002.

Exhibit 20–5: The National Consumers League's National Fraud Information Center at www.natlconsumersleague.org, July 25, 2002.

Exhibit 20–6: Laura Hansen, "Dialing for Dollars," *Marketing Tools,* January–February 1997, pp. 47–51.

Case 20–1: Larry Riggs, "Cisco Scuttles Postal Mail," *Direct,* June 2002, p. 16; Larry Riggs, "Cisco Starts Major DM Effort," *Direct,* February 2002, p. 18; and information from Cisco's Web site at www.cisco.com, July 25, 2002.

Case 20–2: Jim Emerson, "Turnaround: Sam Goody Revives and Expands Sagging Loyalty Program," *Direct,* November 1999, pp. 1, 11; information from Group 3 Marketing's Web site at www.group3marketing.com, July 25, 2002, and information from Musicland's Web site at www.musicland.com., July 25, 2002.

Photo Credits

Chapter 15

Michael J. Hruby, p. 350

© 2002 Ingram Micro. Ingram Micro and the Ingram Micro logo are registered trademarks of Ingram Micro Inc., p. 351

Courtesy Don Becker, p. 352

© 2002 W.W. Grainger, Inc., p. 353

Courtesy Sam's Club, p. 354

This image is printed with permission of United Parcel Service of America, Inc. © 2002 United Parcel Service of America, Inc. All rights reserved, p. 360

Courtesy Knight-Ridder, Inc., p. 360

Courtesy Unilever P.L.C., p. 362

Jeff Zaruba/The Stock Market, p. 364

Courtesy Seaboard Marine, p. 364

Lester Lefkowitz/The Stock Market, p. 366

Chapter 16

Michael J. Hruby, p. 374

© The Procter & Gamble Company, p. 376

Courtesy Orbitz.com, p. 376

Courtesy Dorothy Brazil, p. 377

Courtesy The Gillette Company, p. 378

Flip Chalfant, p. 380

Courtesy National Fluid Milk Processor Promotion Board; agency: Bozell Worldwide, p. 382

Courtesy Bailey's Nursery; art director: Tim Ward; creative director/copywriter, photographer: Michael La Monica, p. 385

Courtesy Timex Corporation, p. 389

Courtesy Shell Oil Company, p. 391

© 2002 Wyeth Consumer Healthcare, p. 393

Chapter 17

Courtesy British Airways, p. 400

Courtesy Saatchi & Saatchi, p. 404

Courtesy Jim Ensign, p. 405

Courtesy Courtroom TV Network, p. 405

Courtesy IBM, p. 406

Courtesy Penn Racquet Sports, p. 410

Courtesy of the Iams Company, p. 413

Courtesy Cramer-Krasselt, p. 413

Michael J. Hruby, p. 413

Courtesy Plano Molding Co., p. 413

Courtesy Nike, Inc., p. 416

Wide World Photo, p. 423

Chapter 18

Michael J. Hruby, p. 430

Courtesy Samsung, p. 431

Courtesy SportPharma USA Inc., p. 433

Courtesy Duraflame, p. 434

Courtesy Kevin Marie Nuss, p. 434

Courtesy Catalina Marketing, p. 436

Courtesy Fiskars, p. 437

Courtesy CNN/Sports Illustrated, p. 438

Courtesy Lamb Weston, Inc.: agency: Strahan Advertising, Inc., p. 442

Michael J. Hruby, p. 443

© Einzig Photographers, Inc., p. 444

Keith Dannemiller/SABA, p. 445

Chapter 19

Courtesy Pfizer, p. 454

Marc Bolster/ImageState, p. 455

Courtesy Gerald J. Bauer, p. 456

Courtesy Hunt Wesson, Inc., p. 456

Courtesy Colgate-Palmolive Company, p. 458

Mark Tuschman/The Stock Market/Corbis, p. 459

Melanie Carr/Custom Medical Stock, p. 460

Images Colour Library/ImageState, p. 465

Courtesy TerrAlign, p. 467

Image Bank, p. 468

Courtesy companydna, p. 469

Chapter 20

Courtesy Coldwater Creek, Inc., p. 480

Courtesy Avon, p. 481

Courtesy Info USA, p. 482

Courtesy Don Condit, p. 484

Courtesy Johnson & Hayward, Inc., p. 485

Michael J. Hruby, p. 486

Courtesy Office Depot, Inc., p. 487

Michael J. Hruby, p. 488

Courtesy Busy Body, Inc., p. 490

Name Index

Organization Index

Subject Index